MATHEMATICS OF DIGITAL IMAGES
Creation, Compression, Restoration, Recognition

Compression, restoration and recognition are three of the key components of digital imaging. The mathematics needed to understand and carry out all these components is here explained in a textbook that is at once rigorous and practical with many worked examples, exercises with solutions, pseudocode, and sample calculations on images. The introduction lists fast tracks to special topics such as Principal Component Analysis, and ways into and through the book, which abounds with illustrations. The first part describes plane geometry and pattern-generating symmetries, along with some text on 3D rotation and reflection matrices. Subsequent chapters cover vectors, matrices and probability. These are applied to simulation, Bayesian methods, Shannon's Information Theory, compression, filtering and tomography. The book will be suited for course use or for self-study. It will appeal to all those working in biomedical imaging and diagnosis, computer graphics, machine vision, remote sensing, image processing, and information theory and its applications.

DR S. G. HOGGAR is a research fellow and formerly a senior lecturer in mathematics at the University of Glasgow.

MATHEMATICS OF DIGITAL IMAGES
Creation, Compression, Restoration, Recognition

S. G. HOGGAR
University of Glasgow

CAMBRIDGE
UNIVERSITY PRESS

CAMBRIDGE UNIVERSITY PRESS
Cambridge, New York, Melbourne, Madrid, Cape Town, Singapore, São Paulo

Cambridge University Press
The Edinburgh Building, Cambridge CB2 2RU, UK

www.cambridge.org
Information on this title: www.cambridge.org/9780521780292

© Cambridge University Press 2006

First published 2006

Printed in the United Kingdom at the University Press, Cambridge

A catalogue record for this book is available from the British Library

ISBN-13   978-0-521-78029-2 hardback
ISBN-10   0-521-78029-2 hardback

To my wife, Elisabeth

Contents

Preface

This text is a successor to the 1992 *Mathematics for Computer Graphics*. It retains the original Part I on plane geometry and pattern-generating symmetries, along with much on 3D rotation and reflection matrices. On the other hand, the completely new pages exceed in number the total pages of the older book.

In more detail, topology becomes a reference and is replaced by probability, leading to simulation, priors and Bayesian methods, and the Shannon Information Theory. Also, notably, the Fourier Transform appears in various incarnations, along with Artificial Neural Networks. As the book's title implies, all this is applied to digital images, their processing, compresssion, restoration and recognition.

Wavelets are used too, in compression (as are fractals), and in conjuction with B-splines and subdivision to achieve multiresolution and curve editing at varying scales. We conclude with the Fourier approach to tomography, the medically important reconstruction of an image from lower-dimensional projections.

As before, a high priority is given to examples and illustrations, and there are exercises, which the reader can use if desired, at strategic points in the text; these sometimes form part of the exercises placed at the end of each chapter. Exercises marked with a tick are partly, or more likely fully, solved on the website. Especially after Chapter 6, solutions are the rule, except for implementation exercises. In the latter regard there are a considerable number of pseudocode versions throughout the text, for example ALGO 11.9 of Chapter 11, simulating the d-dimensional Gaussian distribution, or ALGO 16.1, wavelet compression with limited percentage error.

A further priority is to help the reader know, as the story unfolds, where to turn back for justification of present assumptions, and to point judiciously forward for coming applications. For example, the mentioned Gaussian of Chapter 11 needs the theory of positive definite matrices in Chapter 8. In the introduction we suggest some easy ways in, including journeys by picture alone, or by light reading.

Much of the material of this book began as a graduate course in the summer of 1988, for Ph.D. students in computer graphics at the Ohio State University. My thanks are due to Rick Parent for encouraging the idea of such a course. A further part of the book was developed from a course for final year mathematics students at the University of Glasgow.

I thank my department for three months' leave at the Cambridge Newton Institute, and Chris Bishop for organising the special period on Neural Nets, at which I learned so much and imbibed the Bayesian philosophy.

I am indebted to Paul Cockshott for kindly agreeing to be chief checker, and provoking many corrections and clarifications. My thanks too to Jean-Christoph Nebel, Elisabeth Guest and Joy Goodman, for valuable comments on various chapters. For inducting me into Computer Vision I remain grateful to Paul Siebert and the Computer Vision & Graphics Lab. of Glasgow University. Many people at Vision conferences have added to my knowledge and the determination to produce this book. For other valuable discussions at Glasgow I thank Adrian Bowman, Nick Bailey, Rob Irvine, Jim Kay, John Patterson and Mike Titterington.

Mathematica 4 was used for implementations and calculations, supplemented by the downloadable *Image* from the US National Institutes of Health. Additional images were kindly supplied by Lu, Healy & Weaver (Figures 16.35 and 16.36), by Martin Bertram (Figure 17.52), by David Salesin *et al.* (Figures 17.42 and 17.50), by Hughes Hoppe *et al.* (Figures 17.44 and 17.51), and by 'Meow' Porncharoensin (Figure 10.18). I thank the following relatives for allowing me to apply algorithms to their faces: Aukje, Elleke, Tom, Sebastiaan, Joanna and Tante Tini.

On the production side I thank Frances Nex for awesome text editing, and Carol Miller and Wendy Phillips for expertly seeing the book through to publication.

Finally, thanks are due to David Tranah, Science Editor at Cambridge University Press, for his unfailing patience, tact and encouragement till this book was finished.

Introduction

Beauty is in the eye of the beholder ...

Why the quote? Here beauty is a decoded message, a character recognised, a discovered medical condition, a sought-for face. It depends on the desire of the beholder. Given a computer image, beauty is to learn from it or convert it, perhaps to a more accurate original. But we consider creation too.

It is expected that, rather than work through the whole book, readers may wish to browse or to look up particular topics. To this end we give a fairly extended introduction, list of symbols and index. The book is in six interconnected parts (the connections are outlined at the end of the Introduction):

I	*The plane*	Chapters 1–6;
II	*Matrix structures*	Chapters 7–8;
III	*Here's to probability*	Chapters 9–11;
IV	*Information, error and belief*	Chapters 12–13;
V	*Transforming the image*	Chapters 14–16;
VI	*See, edit, reconstruct*	Chapters 17–18.

Easy ways in   One aid to taking in information is first to go through following a sub-structure and let the rest take care of itself (a surprising amount of the rest gets tacked on). To facilitate this, each description of a part is followed by a quick trip through that part, which the reader may care to follow. If it is true that one picture is worth a thousand words then an easy but fruitful way into this book is to browse through selected pictures, and overleaf is a table of possibilities. One might take every second or third entry, for example.

Chapters 1–6 (Part I) The mathematics is geared towards producing patterns automatically by computer, allocating some design decisions to a user. We begin with *isometries* – those transformations of the plane which preserve distance and hence shape, but which may switch left handed objects into right handed ones (such isometries are called *indirect*). In this part of the book we work geometrically, without recourse to matrices. In Chapter 1 we show that isometries fall into two classes: the direct ones are rotations

Context	Figure (etc.)	Context	Figure (etc.)
Symmetry operations	2.16, 2.19	Daubechies wavelets	16.30
Net types	Example 4.20	Fingerprints	16.33
The global scheme	page 75	Wavelets & X-rays	16.35
Face under PCA & K–L	10.15	B-spline designs	17.15, 17.29
Adding noise	11.21	B-spline filter bank	17.32
MAP reconstruction	11.48	Wavelet-edited face	17.39
Martial cats and LZW	12.20	Progressive Venus face	17.52
The DFT	15.2, 15.4	Perceptron	18.15
Edge-detection	15.6, 15.23	Backpropagation	18.20
Removing blur	15.24, 15.27	Kohonen training	18.42
Progressive transmission	15.40	Vector quantisers	18.54
The DCT	15.42, 15.43	Tomography	18.66
Fractals	16.1, 16.17		

or translation, and the indirect ones reflections or glides. In Chapter 2 we derive the rules for combining isometries, and introduce groups, and the dihedral group in particular. In a short Chapter 3 we apply the theory so far to classifying all 1-dimensional or 'braid' patterns into seven types (Table 3.1).

From Chapter 4 especially we consider symmetries or 'symmetry operations' on a plane pattern. That is, those isometries which send a pattern onto itself, each part going to another with the same size and shape (see Figure 1.3 ff). A plane pattern is one having translation symmetries in two non-parallel directions. Thus examples are wallpaper patterns, floor tilings, carpets, patterned textiles, and the Escher interlocking patterns such as Figure 1.2. We prove the crystallographic restriction, that rotational symmetries of a plane pattern must be multiples of a 1/2, 1/3, 1/4 or 1/6 turn (1/5 is not allowed). We show that plane patterns are made up of parallelogram shaped cells, falling into five types (Figure 4.14).

In Chapter 5 we deduce the existence of 17 pattern types, each with its own set of interacting symmetry operations. In Section 5.8 we include a flow chart for deciding into which type any given pattern fits, plus a fund of test examples. In Chapter 6 we draw some threads together by proving that the 17 proposed categories really are distinct according to a rigorous definition of 'equivalent' patterns (Section 6.1), and that every pattern must fall into one of the categories provided it is 'discrete' (there is a *lower* limit on how far any of its symmetries can move the pattern).

By this stage we use increasingly the idea that, because the composition of two symmetries is a third, the set of all symmetries of a pattern form a group (the definition is recalled in Section 2.5). In Section 6.3 we consider various kinds of regularity upon which a pattern may be based, via techniques of Coxeter graphs and Wythoff's construction (they apply in higher dimensions to give polyhedra). Finally, in Section 6.4 we concentrate the theory towards building an algorithm to construct (e.g. by computer) a pattern of any type from a modest user input, based on a smallest replicating unit called a fundamental region.

Chapters 1–6: a quick trip Read the introduction to Chapter 1 then note Theorem 1.18 on what isometries of the plane turn out to be. Note from Theorem 2.1 how they can all be expressed in terms of reflections, and the application of this in Example 2.6 to composing rotations about distinct points. Look through Table 2.2 for anything that surprises you. Theorem 2.12 is vital information and this will become apparent later. Do the exercise before Figure 2.19. Omit Chapter 3 for now.

Read the first four pages of Chapter 4, then pause for the crystallographic restriction (Theorem 4.15). Proceed to Figure 4.14, genesis of the five net types, note Examples 4.20, and try Exercise 4.6 at the end of the chapter yourself. Get the main message of Chapter 5 by using the scheme of Section 5.8 to identify pattern types in Exercises 5 at the end of the chapter (examples with answers are given in Section 5.7). Finish in Chapter 6 by looking through Section 6.4 on 'Creating plane patterns' and recreate the one in Exercise 6.13 (end of the chapter) by finding one fundamental region.

Chapters 7–8 (Part II) After reviewing vectors and geometry in 3-space we introduce *n*-space and its vector subspaces, with the idea of independence and bases. Now come matrices, representing linear equations and transformations such as rotation. Matrix partition into *blocks* is a powerful tool for calculation in later chapters (8, 10, 15–17). Determinants test row/equation independence and enable *n*-dimensional integration for probability (Chapter 10).

In Chapter 8 we review complex numbers and eigenvalues/vectors, hence classify distance-preserving transformations (*isometries*) of 3-space, and show how to determine from the matrix of a rotation its axis and angle (Theorem 8.10), and to obtain a normal vector from a reflection matrix (Theorem 8.12). We note that the matrix M of an isometry in any dimension is *orthogonal*, that is $MM^T = I$, or equivalently the rows (or columns) are mutually orthogonal unit vectors. We investigate the *rank* of a matrix – its number of independent rows, or of independent equations represented. Also, importantly, the technique of *elementary row operations*, whereby a matrix is reduced to a special form, or yields its inverse if one exists.

Next comes the theory of quadratic forms $\sum a_{ij}x_ix_j$ defined by a matrix $A = [a_{ij}]$, tying in with eigenvalues and undergirding the later multivariate normal/Gaussian distribution. Properties we derive for matrix norms lead to the *Singular Value Decomposition*: a general $m \times n$ matrix is reducible by orthogonal matrices to a general diagonal form, yielding approximation properties (Theorem 8.53). We include the Moore–Penrose *pseudoinverse* A^+ such that $AX = b$ has best solution $X = A^+b$ if A^{-1} does not exist.

Chapters 7–8: a quick trip Go to Definition 7.1 for the meaning of orthonormal vectors and see how they define an orthogonal matrix in Section 7.2.4. Follow the determinant evaluation in Examples 7.29 then 'Russian' block matrix multiplication in Examples 7.38. For vectors in coordinate geometry, see Example 7.51.

In Section 7.4.1 check that the matrices of rotation and reflection are orthogonal. Following this theme, see how to get the geometry from the matrix in 3D, Example 8.14.

Next see how the matrix row operations introduced in Theorem 8.17 are used for solving equations (Example 8.22) and for inverting a matrix (Example 8.27).

Now look at quadratic forms, their meaning in (8.14), the positive definite case in Table 8.1, and applying the minor test in Example 8.38. Finally, look up the pseudoinverse of Remarks 8.57 for least deviant solutions, and use it for Exercise 24 (end of chapter).

Chapters 9–11 (Part III) We review the basics of probability, defining an *event E* to be a subset of the sample space *S* of outcomes, and using axioms due to Kolmogorov for probability $P(E)$. After conditional probability, independence and Bayes' Theorem we introduce random variables $X: S \to R_X$, meaning that X allocates to each outcome s some value x in its range R_X (e.g. score x in archery depends on hit position s). An event B is now a subset of the range and X has a pdf (probability distribution function), say $f(x)$, so that the probability of B is given by the integral

$$P(B) = \int_B f(x)\, dx,$$

or a sum if the range consists of discrete values rather than interval(s). From the idea of average, we define the *expected value* $\mu = E(X) = \int x f(x)\, dx$ and *variance* $V(X) = E(X - \mu)^2$. We derive properties and applications of distributions entitled binomial, Poisson and others, especially the ubiquitous normal/Gaussian (see Tables 9.9 and 9.10 of Section 9.4.4).

In Chapter 10 we move to random vectors $X = (X_1, \ldots, X_n)$, having in mind message symbols of Part IV, and pixel values. A joint pdf $f(x_1, \ldots, x_n)$ gives probability as an n-dimensional integral, for example

$$P(X < Y) = \int_B f(x, y)\, dx\, dy, \quad \text{where } B = \{(x, y): x < y\}.$$

We investigate the pdf of a function of a random vector. In particular $X + Y$, whose pdf is the *convolution product* f^*g of the pdfs f of X and g of Y, given by

$$(f^*g)(z) = \int_R f(t)g(z - t)\, dt.$$

This gives for example the pdf of a sum of squares of Gaussians via convolution properties of the gamma distribution. Now we use *moments* $E(X_i^r)$ to generate new pdfs from old, to relate known ones, and to prove the *Central Limit Theorem* that $X_1 + \cdots + X_n$ (whatever the pdfs of individual X_i) approaches a Gaussian as n increases, a pointer to the important ubiquity of this distribution.

We proceed to the *correlation* $\text{Cov}(X, Y)$ between random variables X, Y, then the covariance matrix $\text{Cov}(X) = [\text{Cov}(X_i, X_j)]$ of a random *vector* $X = (X_i)$, which yields a pdf for X if X is multivariate normal, i.e. if the X_i are normal but not necessarily independent (Theorem 10.61). Chapter 10 concludes with *Principal Component Analysis*, or PCA, in which we reduce the dimension of a data set, by transforming to new uncorrelated coordinates ordered by decreasing variance, and dropping as many of the last few variables as have total variance negligible. We exemplify by compressing face image data.

Given a sample, i.e. a sequence of measurements $X_1, \ldots, X_n$ of a random variable X, we seek a statistic $f(X_1, \ldots, X_n)$ to test the hypothesis that X has a certain distribution or, assuming it has, to estimate any parameters (Section 11.1). Next comes a short introduction to the Bayesian approach to squeezing useful information from data by means of an initially vague prior belief, firmed up with successive observations. An important special case is *classification*: is it a tumour, a tank, a certain character, ... ?

For testing purposes we need *simulation*, producing a sequence of variates whose frequencies mimic a given distribution (Section 11.3). We see how essentially any distribution may be achieved starting from the usual computer-generated uniform distribution on an interval [0, 1]. Example: as suggested by the Central Limit Theorem, the sum of uniform variables $U_1, \ldots, U_{12}$ on [0, 1] is normal to a good approximation.

We introduce Monte Carlo methods, in which a sequence of variates from a suitably chosen distribution yields an approximate n-dimensional integral (typically probability). The method is improved by generating the variates as a *Markov chain* $X_1, X_2, \ldots$, where X_i depends on the preceding variable but on none earlier. This is called Markov Chain Monte Carlo, or MCMC. It involves finding joint pdfs from a list of conditional ones, for which a powerful tool is a *Bayesian graph,* or *net*.

We proceed to Markov Random Fields, a generalisation of a Markov chain useful for conditioning colour values at a pixel only on values at nearest neighbours. *Simulated annealing* fits here, in which we change a parameter ('heat') following a schedule designed to avoid local minima of an 'energy function' we must minimise. Based on this, we perform Bayesian Image Restoration (Example 11.105).

Chapters 9–11: a quick trip Note the idea of *sample space* by reading Chapter 9 up to Example 9.2(i), then *random variable* in Definition 9.32 and Example 9.35. Take in the binomial case in Section 9.4.1 up to Example 9.63(ii). Now look up the *cdf* at (9.29) and Figure 9.11.

Review *expected value* at Definition 9.50 and the prudent gambler, then *variance* at Section 9.3.6 up to (9.39) and the gambler's return. Now it's time for normal/Gaussian random variables. Read Section 9.4.3 up to Figure 9.20, then follow half each of Examples 9.75 and 9.76. Glance at Example 9.77.

Check out the idea of a joint pdf $f(x, y)$ in Figure 10.1, Equation (10.4) and Example 10.2. Then read up the pdf of $X + Y$ as a convolution product in Section 10.2.2 up to Example 10.18. For the widespread appearance of the normal distribution see the introduction to Section 10.3.3, then the Central Limit Theorem 10.45, exemplified in Figure 10.7. See how the covariance matrix, (10.44), (10.47), gives the n-dimensional normal distribution in Theorem 10.61.

Read the introduction to Chapter 11, then Example 11.6, for a quick view of the hypothesis testing idea. Now the Bayesian approach, Section 11.2.1. Note the meaning of 'prior' and how it's made more accurate by increasing data, in Figure 11.11.

The Central Limit Theorem gives a quick way to simulate the Gaussian/normal: read from Figure 11.21 to 11.22. Then, note how the Choleski matrix decomposition from Chapter 8 enables an easy simulation of the n-dimensional Gaussian.

On to Markov chains, the beginning of Section 11.4 up to Definition 11.52, and their generalisation to Markov random fields, modelling an image, Examples 11.79 and preceding text. Take in Bayesian Image Restoration, Section 11.4.6 above Table 11.13, then straight on to Figure 11.48 at the end.

Chapters 12–13   (Part IV) We present Shannon's solution to the problem of measuring information. In more detail, how can we usefully quantify the information in a message understood as a sequence of symbols X (random variable) from an alphabet $\mathcal{A} = \{s_1, \ldots, s_n\}$, having a pdf $\{p_1, \ldots, p_n\}$. Shannon argued that the mean information per symbol of a message should be defined as the *entropy*

$$H(X) = H(p_1, \ldots, p_n) = \sum -p_i \log p_i$$

for some fixed basis of logarithms, usually taken as 2 so that entropy is measured in bits per symbol. An early vindication is that, if each s_i is encoded as a binary word c_i, the mean bits per symbol in any message cannot be less than H (Theorem 12.8). Is there an encoding scheme that realises H? Using a graphical method Huffman produced the most economical coding that was *prefix-free* (no codeword a continuation of another). This comes close to H, but perhaps the nearest to a perfect solution is an *arithmetic code*, in which the bits per symbol tend to H as message length increases (Theorem 12.35). The idea here extends the method of converting a string of symbols from $\{0, 1, \ldots, 9\}$ to a number between 0 and 1.

In the widely used LZW scheme by Lempel, Ziv and Welch, subsequences of the text are replaced by pointers to them in a dictionary. An ingenious method recreates the dictionary from scratch as decoding proceeds. LZW is used in GIF image encoding, where each pixel value is representable as a byte, hence a symbol.

A non-entropy approach to information was pioneered by Kolmogorov: the information in a structure should be measured as its Minimum Description Length, or MDL, this being more intrinsic than a probabilistic approach. We discuss examples in which the MDL principle is used to build prior knowledge into the description language and to determine the best model for a situation.

Returning to Shannon entropy, we consider protection of information during its transmission, by encoding symbols in a redundant way. Suppose k message symbols average n codeword symbols X, which are received as codeword symbols Y. The *rate* of transmission is then $R = k/n$. We prove Shannon's famous *Channel Coding Theorem*, which says that the transition probabilities $\{p(y|x)\}$ of the channel determine a quantity called the *channel capacity* C, and that, for any rate $R < C$ and probability $\varepsilon > 0$, there is a code with rate R and

$$P(\text{symbol error } Y \neq X) < \varepsilon.$$

The codes exist, but how hard are they to describe, and are they usable? Until recent years the search was for codes with plenty of structure, so that convenient algorithms could be produced for encoding and decoding. The codewords usually had alphabet $\{0, 1\}$, fixed length, and formed a vector space at the least. Good examples are the Reed–Solomon codes of Section 13.2.4 used for the first CD players, which in consequence could be surprisingly much abused before sound quality was affected.

A new breakthrough in closeness to the Shannon capacity came with the turbocodes of Berrou *et al.* (Section 13.3.4), probabilistic unlike earlier codes, but with effective encoding and decoding. They depend on belief propagation in Bayesian nets (Section 13.3.1), where $\text{Belief}(x) = p(x|e)$ quantifies our belief about internal node variables x in the light of evidence e, the end node variables. Propagation refers to the algorithmic updating of $\text{Belief}(x)$ on receipt of new information. We finish with a review of belief propagation in computer vision.

Chapters 12–13: a quick trip Look up Shannon's *entropy* at (12.7) giving least bits per symbol, Theorem 12.8. Below this, read 'codetrees', then Huffman's optimal codes in Construction 12.12 and Example 12.13. Proceed to LZW compression in Section 12.7 up to Example 12.38, then Table 12.7 and Figure 12.20.

For Kolmogorov's alternative to entropy and why, read Section 12.8.1 up to (12.34) and their ultimate convergence, Theorem 12.54. For applications see Section 12.8.3 up to 'some MDL features' and Figure 12.26 to 'Further examples'.

Get the idea of a *channel* from Section 13.1 up to *mutual entropy*, (13.3), then Figure 13.2 up to 'Exercise'. Look up *capacity* at (13.23) (don't worry about $C(\beta)$ for now). Next, channel coding in Section 13.1.6 to Example 13.33, the *Hamming code*, and we are ready for the Channel Coding Theorem at Corollary 13.36.

Read the discussion that starts Section 13.2.5. Get some idea of convolution codes at Section 13.3.2 to Figure 13.33, and turbocodes at Figures 13.39 and 13.40. For the belief network basis of their probabilistic handling, look back at Section 13.3.1 to Figure 13.24, then the Markov chain case in Figure 13.25 and above. More generally Figure 13.26. Finally, read the postscript on belief networks in Computer Vision.

Chapters 14–16 (Part V) With suitable transforms we can carry out a huge variety of useful processes on a computer image, for example edge-detection, noise removal, compression, reconstruction, and supplying features for a Bayesian classifier.

Our story begins with the Fourier Transform, which converts a function $f(t)$ to a new function $F(s)$, and its relative the N-point Discrete Fourier Transform or DFT, in which f and F are N-vectors:

$$F(s) = \int_{-\infty}^{\infty} f(t) e^{-2\pi i s t}\, dt, \quad \text{and} \quad F_k = \sum_{n=0}^{N-1} e^{-2\pi i k n/N} f_n.$$

We provide the background for calculus on complex numbers. Significantly, the relations between numbers of the form $e^{-2\pi i k/N}$ result in various forms of *Fast* Fourier Transform, in which the number of arithmetic operations for the DFT is reduced from order N^2 to order $N \log_2 N$, an important saving in practice. We often need a *convolution* f^*g (see Part III), and the Fourier Transform sends

$$f^*g \to F \circ G \text{ (Convolution Theorem)},$$

the easily computed *elementwise* product, whose value at x is $F(x)G(x)$; similarly for the DFT. We discuss the DFT as approximation to the continuous version, and the significance of frequencies arising from the implied sines and cosines. In general a 1D transform yields an n-dimensional one by transforming with respect to one variable/dimension at a time. If the transform is, like the DFT, given by a matrix M, sending vector $f \to Mf$, then the 2D version acts on a matrix array g by

$$g \to MgM^{\mathrm{T}} \ (= G),$$

which means we transform each column of g then each row of the result, or vice versa, the order being unimportant by associativity of matrix products. Notice $g = M^{-1}G(M^{\mathrm{T}})^{-1}$ inverts the transform. The DFT has matrix $M = [w^{kn}]$, where $w = \mathrm{e}^{-2\pi \mathrm{i}/N}$, from which there follow important connections with rotation (Figure 15.4) and with statistical properties of an image. The Convolution Theorem extends naturally to higher dimensions.

We investigate *highpass filters* on images, convolution operations which have the effect of reducing the size of Fourier coefficients F_{jk} for *low* frequencies j, k, and so preserving details such as edges but not shading (lowpass filters do the opposite). We compare edge-detection by the Sobel, Laplacian, and Marr–Hildreth filters. We introduce the technique of *deconvolution* to remove the effect of image noise such as blur, whether by motion, lens inadequacy or atmosphere, given the reasonable assumption that this effect may be expressed as convolution of the original image g by a small array h. Thus we consider

$$\text{blurred image} = g^*h \to G \circ H.$$

We give ways to find H, hence G by division, then g by inversion of the transform (see Section 15.3). For the case when noise other than blur is present too, we use probability considerations to derive the *Wiener filter*. Finally in Chapter 15 we investigate compression by the Burt–Adelson pyramid approach, and by the Discrete Cosine Transform, or DCT. We see why the DCT is often a good approximation to the statistically based K–L Transform.

In Chapter 16 we first indicate the many applications of fractal dimension as a parameter, from the classical coastline measurement problem through astronomy to medicine, music, science and engineering. Then we see how the 'fractal nature of Nature' lends itself to fractal compression.

Generally the term *wavelets* applies to a collection of functions $\Psi_i^j(x)$ obtained from a *mother wavelet* $\Psi(x)$ by repeated translation, and scaling in the ratio $1/2$. Thus

$$\Psi_i^j(x) = \Psi(2x^j x - i), \quad 0 \leq i < 2^j.$$

We start with *Haar* wavelets, modelled on the split box $\Psi(x)$ equal to 1 on $[0, 1/2)$, to -1 on $[1/2, 1]$ and zero elsewhere. With respect to the inner product $\langle f, g \rangle = \int f(x)g(x)\,\mathrm{d}x$

for functions on [0, 1] the wavelets are mutually orthogonal. For fixed resolution J, the *wavelet transform* is

$$f \to \text{its components with respect to } \phi_0(x) \text{ and } \Psi_i{}^j(x), 0 \le j \le J, 0 \le i < 2^j,$$

where $\phi_0(x)$ is the box function with value 1 on [0, 1]. Converted to 2D form in the usual way, this gives multiresolution and compression for computer images. We pass from resolution level j to $j + 1$ by adding the appropriate extra components. For performing the same without necessarily having orthogonality, we show how to construct the *filter bank*, comprising matrices which convert between components at different resolutions. At this stage, though, we introduce the orthogonal wavelets of Daubechies of which Haar is a special case. These are applied to multiresolution of a face, then we note the use for fingerprint compression.

Lastly in Part V, we see how the Gabor Transform and the edge-detectors of Canny and of Marr and Hildreth may be expressed as wavelets, and outline the results of Lu, Healy and Weaver in applying a wavelet transform to enhance constrast more effectively than other methods, for X-ray and NMR images.

Chapters 14–16: a quick trip Look at Equations (14.1) to (14.4) for the DFT, or Discrete Fourier Transform. Include Notation 14.3 for complex number foundations, then Figure 14.3 for the important frequency viewpoint, and Figure 14.6 for the related filtering schema.

For an introduction to convolution see Example 14.11, then follow the polynomial proof of Theorem 14.12. Read Remarks 14.14 about the Fast Transform (more details in Section 14.1.4). Read up the continuous Fourier Transform in Section 14.2.1 up to Figure 14.13, noting Theorem 14.22. For the continuous–discrete connection, see points 1, 2, 3 at the end of Chapter 14, referring back when more is required.

In Chapter 15, note the easy conversion of the DFT and its continuous counterpart to two dimensions, in (15.6) and (15.10). Observe the effect of having periodicity in the image to be transformed, Figure 15.3, and of rotation, Figure 15.4.

Notice the case of 2D convolution in Example 15.14 and the convolution Theorems 15.16 and 15.17. Look through the high-versus lowpass material in Sections 15.2.2 and 15.2.3, noting Figures 15.15, 15.18, and 15.20. Compare edge-detection filters with each other in Figure 15.23. Read up recovery from motion blur in Section 15.3.1, omitting proofs.

For the pyramid compression of Burt and Adelson read Section 15.4 up to Figure 15.37 and look at Figures 15.39 and 15.40. For the DCT (Discrete Cosine Transform) read Section 15.4.2 up to Theorem 15.49 (statement only). Note the standard conversion to 2D in Table 15.8, then see Figures 15.42 and 15.43. Now read the short Section 15.4.3 on JPEG. Note for future reference that the n-dimensional Fourier Transform is covered, with proofs, in Section 15.5.2.

For fractal dimension read Sections 16.1.1 and 16.1.2, noting at a minimum the key formula (16.9) and graph below. For fractal compression take in Section 16.1.4 up to

(16.19), then Example 16.6. A quick introduction to wavelets is given at the start of Section 16.2, then Figure 16.23. Moving to two dimensions, see Figure 16.25 and its introduction, and for image compression, Figure 16.27.

A pointer to filter banks for the discrete Wavelet Transform is given by Figure 16.28 with its introduction, and (16.41). Now check out compression by Daubechies wavelets, Example 16.24. Take a look at wavelets for fingerprints, Section 16.3.4. Considering wavelet relatives, look at Canny edge-detection in Section 16.4.3, then scan quickly through Section 16.4.4, slowing down at the medical application in Example 16.28.

Chapters 17–18 (Part VI) B-splines are famous for their curve design properties, which we explore, along with the connection to convolution, Fourier Transform, and wavelets.

The ith basis function $N_{i,m}(t)$ for a B-spline of order m, degree m-1, may be obtained as a translated convolution product $b*b* \cdots *b$ of m unit boxes $b(t)$. Consequently, the function changes to a different polynomial at unit intervals of t, though smoothly, then becomes zero. Convolution supplies a polynomial-free definition, its simple Fourier Transform verifying the usually used Cox–de Boor defining relations. Unlike a Bézier spline, which for a large control polygon $P_0 \ldots P_n$ requires many spliced component curves, the B-spline is simply

$$B_m(t) = \sum_{i=0}^{n} N_{i,m}(t)P_i.$$

We elucidate useful features of $B_m(t)$, then design a car profile, standardising on cubic splines, $m = 4$. Next we obtain B-splines by recursive subdivision starting from the control polygon. That is, by repetitions of

$$\text{subdivision} = \text{split} + \text{average},$$

where *split* inserts midpoints of each edge and *average* replaces each point by a linear combination of neighbours. We derive the coefficients as binomials, six subdivisions usually sufficing for accuracy. We recover basis functions, now denoted by $\phi_1^j(x)$, starting from hat functions. In the previous wavelet notation we may write

$$\Phi^{j-1} = \Phi^j P^j \text{ (basis)}, \quad \text{where } f^j = P^j f^{j-1},$$

the latter expressing level $j - 1$ vectors in terms of level j via a matrix P^j. Now we aim for a filter bank so as to edit cubic-spline-based images. It is (almost) true that for our splines (a) for fixed j the basis functions are translates, (b) those at level $j + 1$ are scaled from level j. As before, we take $V^j = \text{span } \Phi^j$ and choose wavelet space $W^{j-1} \subseteq V^j$ to consist of the functions in V^j orthogonal to all those in V^{j-1}. It follows that any f in V^j equals $g + h$ for unique g in V^{j-1} and h in W^{j-1}, this fact being expressed by

$$V^{j-1} \oplus W^{j-1} = V^j.$$

A basis of W^{j-1} (the wavelets) consists of linear combinations from V^j, say the vector of functions $\Psi^{j-1} = \Phi^j Q^j$ for some matrix Q^j. Orthogonality leaves many possible Q^j, and we may choose it to be antipodal (half-turn symmetry), so that one half determines the rest. This yields matrices P, Q, A, B for a filter bank, with which we perform editing at different scales based on (for example) a library of B-spline curves for components of a human face.

In the first appendix we see how to determine simple formulae for filter bank matrices, using connections with polynomials. The second appendix introduces surfaces wavelets as a natural generalisation from curves, and we indicate how a filter bank may be obtained once more.

(Chapter 18) An artificial neural network, or just net, may be thought of firstly in pattern recognition terms, converting an input vector of pixel values to a character they represent. More generally, a permissible input vector is mapped to the correct output by a process in some way analogous to the neural operation of the brain (Figure 18.1). We work our way up from Rosenblatt's Perceptron, with its rigorously proven limitations, to multilayer nets which in principle can mimic any input–output function. The idea is that a net will generalise from suitable input–output examples by setting free parameters called *weights*. We derive the Backpropagation Algorithm for this, from simple gradient principles. Examples are included from medical diagnosis and from remote sensing.

Now we consider nets that are mainly *self-organising*, in that they construct their own categories of classification. We include the topologically based Kohonen method (and his Learning Vector Quantisation). Related nets give an alternative view of Principal Component Analysis. At this point Shannon's extension of entropy to the continuous case opens up the criterion of Linsker that neural network weights should be chosen to maximise mutual information between input and output. We include a 3D image processing example due to Becker and Hinton. Then the further Shannon theory of rate distortion is applied to vector quantisation and the LBG quantiser.

Now enters the Hough Transform and its widening possibilities for finding arbitray shapes in an image. We end with the related idea of *tomography*, rebuilding an image from projections. This proves a fascinating application of the Fourier Transform in two and even in three dimensions, for which the way was prepared in Chapter 15.

Chapters 17–18: a quick trip Go straight to the convolution definition, (17.7), and result in Figure 17.7, of the ϕ_k whose translates, (17.15) and Figure 17.10, are the basis functions for B-splines. (Note the Fourier calculation below Table 17.1.) See the B-spline Definition 17.13, Theorem 17.14, Figure 17.12, and car body Example 17.18. Observe B-splines generated by recursive subdivision at Examples 17.33 and 17.34.

We arrive at filter banks and curve editing by Figure 17.32 of Section 17.3.3. Sample results at Figure 17.37 and Example 17.46. For an idea of surface wavelets, see Figures 17.51 and 17.52 of the second appendix.

Moving to artificial neural networks, read *Perceptron* in Section 18.1.2 up to Figure 18.5, note the training ALGO 18.1, then go to Figure 18.15 and Remarks following. Proceed to the multilayer net schema, Figure 18.17, read 'Discovering Backpropagation' as far as desired, then on to Example 18.11. For more, see the remote sensing Example 18.16.

Now for self-organising nets. Read the introduction to Section 18.2, then PCA by Oja's method at (18.28) with discussion following, then the k-means method at Equation (18.30) and Remarks 18.20. Consider Kohonen's topologically based nets via Example 18.21 (note the use of 'neighbourhoods') and remarks following.

Revisit information theory with *differential entropy* in Table 18.3, and the Gaussian case in Theorem 18.29. Now observe the application of mutual entropy to nets, in Example 18.34 down to Equation (18.47). Pick up rate distortion from (18.60) and the 'compression interpretation' below, then look at Theorem 18.48 (without proof) and Example 18.49. With notation from (18.67) and (18.68), note Theorem 18.50. Read Section 18.3.6 to find steps A, B then see the LBG quantization in Example 18.59 and the discussion following.

The last topic is *tomography*. Read through Section 18.4.2 then note the key projection property, (18.79), and the paragraph below it. Observe Figure 18.63, representing the interpolation step, then see the final result in Examples 18.65 and 66. Finally, note 'higher dimensions'.

Which chapters depend on which

1–6	Each chapter depends on the previous ones.
7	Depends generally on Chapter 1.
8	Depends strongly on Chapter 7.
9	Little reliance on previous chapters. Uses some calculus.
10	Depends strongly on Chapters 8 and 9.
11	Builds on Chapter 10.
12	Basic probability from Chapter 9; last section uses random vectors from Chapter 10.
13	Section 13.1 develops entropy from Section 12.1, whilst Section 13.2 uses vector space bases from Section 7.1.5. Belief networks in Section 13.3 recapitulates Section 11.4.4 first.
14	Uses matrices from Section 7.2, complex vectors and matrices from Section 8.1.1, convolution from Section 10.2.2; evaluating the FFT uses big O notation of Section 10.3.3.
15	Builds on Chapter 14. The Rotation Theorem of Section 15.1.3 uses the Jacobian from Section 10.2.1, rotation from Section 7.4.1. Filter symmetry in Section 15.2.3 uses Example 8.21(iii). The Wiener filter, Section 15.3.4, needs functions of a random vector, Section 10.2, and covariance, Section 10.4.2. Compression, Section 15.4, uses entropy from Chapter 12.
16	Fractals, Section 16.1, uses the regression line from Section 11.1.4. Sections 16.2 and 16.3 use vector spaces from Section 7.1.5, with inner product as in (7.8), and the block matrices of Section 7.2.5. Also the general construction of 2D transforms in Section 15.1.1, and the DCT in Section 15.4.2. Section 16.4 makes wide use of the Fourier Transform from Chapters 14 and 15.

17   Depending strongly on Section 16.2 and Section 16.3, this chapter also requires knowledge of the 1D Fourier Transform of Chapter 14, whilst Section 17.3.2 uses dependent vectors from Section 7.1.5 and symmetry from Example 8.21(iii).

18   The first three sections need probabililty, usually not beyond Chapter 10 except for Bayes at Section 11.2. Section 18.3 builds on the mutual entropy of Chapter 13, whilst Section 18.4.1 uses the Sobel edge-detectors of Section 15.2.4, the rest (Hough and tomography) requiring the Fourier Transform(s) and Projection Theorem of Section 15.1.

Table of crude chapter dependencies.

A chapter depends on those it can 'reach' by going down the graph.

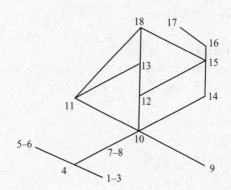

Some paths to special places

Numbers refer to chapters. Fourier Transform means the continuous one and DFT the discrete. ONB is orthonormal basis, PCA is Principal Component Analysis, Gaussian equals normal.

n-dim Gaussian or PCA (a choice)
ONB → eigenvalues/vectors → similarity → covariance → PCA or n-dim Gaussian
7   8   8   10   10

Simulating Gaussians
Independent vectors → moments → Central Limit Theorem → Cholesky factors → simulation
10   10   10   8   11

Huffman codes
Entropy → noiseless encoding → codetrees → Huffman
12   12   12   12

Channel Coding Theorem
Random variables → joint pdf → entropy → mutual entropy → capacity → Shannon Theorem
9   10   12   13   13   13

JPEG
ONBs & orthogonal matrices → complex numbers → Discrete Cosine Transform → JPEG
7   8   15   15

Wiener filter
Complex nos. → Fourier Transform → Convolution Thm → pdfs & Fourier → Wiener filter
8   14,15   15   15   15

Haar Wavelet Transform (images)
Inner product & ONBs $\rightarrow$ 1D Haar $\rightarrow$ 2D Haar$\rightarrow$ Haar Image Transform
   7   16   16   16

B-splines & Fourier
Fourier Transform (1D) $\rightarrow$ Convolution Thm. $\rightarrow$ ϕ_k as convolution $\rightarrow$ Fourier Transform
   14   14   17   17

Perceptron
Dot product $\rightarrow$ perceptron $\rightarrow$ edge-detector $\rightarrow$ learning algorithm
 7   18   18   18

Vector quantisation
Entropy $\rightarrow$ mutual entropy $\rightarrow$ rate distortion $\rightarrow$ LBG versus k-means
 12   13   18   18

Tomography
Complex numbers $\rightarrow$ DFT $\rightarrow$ Fourier Transform $\rightarrow$ Rotation & Projection Thms $\rightarrow$ Tomography
 8   15   15   15   18

A word on notation

(1) (*Vectors*) We write vectors typically as $x = (x_1, \ldots, x_n)$, with the option $x = (x_i)$ if n is known from the context. Bold x emphasises the vector nature of such x.

(2) (*Rows versus columns*) For vector–matrix multiplication we may take vector x as a row, indicated by writing xA, or as a column, indicated by Ax. The row notation is used through Chapters 1–6 in harmony with the image of a point P under a transformation g being denoted by P^g, so that successive operations appear on the right, thus:

$$xABC\ldots \quad \text{and} \quad P^{fgh\ldots}.$$

Any matrix equation with vectors as rows may be converted to its equivalent in terms of columns, by transposition: e.g. $xA = b$ becomes $A^{\mathrm{T}}x^{\mathrm{T}} = b^{\mathrm{T}}$. Finally, to keep matrices on one line we may write $\mathrm{Rows}[R_1, \ldots, R_m]$, or just $\mathrm{Rows}[R_i]$, for the matrix with rows R_i, and similarly for columns, $\mathrm{Cols}[C_1, \ldots, C_n]$.

(3) (*Block matrices*) Every so often it is expedient to perform multiplication with matrices which have been divided (partitioned) into submatrices called blocks. This is described in Section 7.2.5, where special attention should be paid to 'Russian multiplication'.

(4) (*Distributions*) Provided there is no ambiguity we may use the letter p generically for probability distributions, for example $p(x)$, $p(y)$ and $p(x, y)$ may denote the respective pdfs of random variables X, Y and (X, Y). In a similar spirit, the symbol list following concentrates on those symbols which are used more widely than their first context of definition.

Here too we should mention that the normal and Gaussian distributions are the same thing, the word Gaussian being perhaps preferred by those with a background in engineering.

Symbols

$\lvert\lambda\rvert$	Absolute value of real number λ, modulus if complex	*page* 8, 166, 167
$\lvert AB\rvert$, $\lvert \mathbf{a}\rvert$	Length of line segment AB, length of vector $\mathbf{a}$	7
$\underline{AB}$	Line segment directed from point A to B	7
$A(a_1, a_2)$	Point A with Cartesian coordinates (a_1, a_2)	7
$\mathbf{a} = (a_1, a_2)$	General vector a or *position vector* of point A	7
$\mathbf{a} \cdot \mathbf{b}$	Dot/scalar product $\sum a_i b_i$	127
$\mathbf{a} \times \mathbf{b}$	Vector product of vectors $\mathbf{a}, \mathbf{b}$	141
$g \colon X \to Y$	Function (mapping) from X to Y	
P^g and $g(P)$	Image of P under mapping g	11
T_{AB}	The translation that sends point A to point B	17
T_a	The translation given by $x \to x + a$	11
$R_A(\phi)$	Rotation in the plane about point A, through signed angle ϕ	11, 12
$R_A(m/n)$	Rotation as above, through the fraction m/n of a turn	12
R_m, R_{AB}	(In the plane) reflection in mirror line m, in line through A, B	12
I	The identity mapping, identity element of a group	39, 40
g^{-1}	The inverse of a function or group element g	32
h^g	The product $g^{-1}hg$, for transformations or group elements g, h	29
D_{2n}	The dihedral group of order $2n$	38
$\mathbf{R}, \mathbf{Q}, \mathbf{Z}, \mathbf{N}$	The real numbers, rationals, integers, and naturals $1, 2, 3, \ldots$	23, 24
$[a, b], (a, b)$	Closed interval $a \le x \le b$, open interval $a < x < b$	230

$\mathbf{R}^n$	Euclidean n-space	120, 121
$\boldsymbol{i}, \boldsymbol{j}, \boldsymbol{k}$	Unit vectors defining coordinate axes in 3-space	116
δ_{ik}	The Kronecker delta, equal to 1 if $i = k$, otherwise 0	119
$\delta(x)$	The Dirac delta function	544
$I = I_n$	The identity $n \times n$ matrix	127
$A_{m \times n}$	Matrix A with m rows and n columns	127
a_{ik} or $(A)_{ik}$	The entry in row i, column k, of the matrix A	126, 127
diag $\{d_1, \ldots, d_n\}$	The square matrix whose diagonal elements are d_i, the rest 0	128
A^{T}, A^{-1}	The transpose of matrix A, its inverse if square	128, 129
$|A|$ or det A	The determinant of a square matrix A	131
Tr A	The trace (sum of the diagonal elements a_{ii}) of a matrix A	164, 165
E_{ik}	Matrix whose i, k entry is 1, and the rest 0	140
$\langle A, B \rangle$	Inner product of matrices (as long vectors)	203
$\|A\|_{\mathrm{F}}, \|A\|_{\mathrm{R}}$	Frobenius and ratio norms of matrix A (subscript F may be omitted)	193
$R(A), N(A)$	Row space, null space, of matrix A	172, 177
$\mathbf{C}$	The complex numbers $z = x + y\mathrm{i}$, where $\mathrm{i}^2 = -1$	162, 163
Re z, Im z, $\bar{z}$, $|z|$	Real part, imaginary part, conjugate, modulus of z	163
$\mathrm{e}^{\mathrm{i}\theta}$	The complex number $\cos\theta + \mathrm{i}\sin\theta$	163
$\{x_n\}_{n \geq 1}$	Sequence $x_1, x_2, x_3, \ldots$	276
$\mathbf{Z}_2$	The field of size 2	469
$\mathcal{A} = \mathcal{A}_X$	Alphabet for a channel random variable X	445
$\mathcal{A}$	Attractor of an Iterated Function system	653
$\log x, \log_2 x, \ln x$	Logarithm to given base, to base 2, to base e (natural)	398
S	Sample space in probability theory	210
$A^c, A \cup B, A \cap B$	Complement, union, intersection, of sets or events	210, 211
$P(A)$	Probability that event A occurs	212
$_nC_r$ or $\binom{n}{r}$	Number of ways to choose r things from n. Equals $n!/(r!(n-r)!)$	215
$|A|$	Size of set or event A	
$P(A \mid B)$	Conditional probability of A given B	219
$P(X = x)$	Probability that random variable X takes value x	227
$E(X)$ and $V(X)$	Expected value and variance of random variable X	235, 237

$X \sim N(\mu, \sigma^2)$	X is normal (Gaussian) with $E(X) = \mu$, $V(X) = \sigma^2$	245
$\Gamma(x)$	Gamma function	238
$\Gamma_{\alpha,u}(x)$	Gamma distribution with parameters α, u	249
$\overline{X}$	Sample mean	305
$\hat{\theta}$	Estimate of distribution parameter θ	309
f^*g	Convolution product: functions ('continuous'), arrays ('discrete')	271, 531
$h = f \circ g$	Elementwise product $h(x) = f(x)g(x)$	533
$U[a, b]$	Uniform distribution on interval $[a, b]$	230
$\mathrm{Cov}(X, Y)$	Covariance/correlation between random variables X, Y	285
$\mathrm{Cov}(X)$	Covariance matrix of random vector $X = (X_i)$	287
$H(X) = $ $\mathrm{H}(p_1, \ldots, p_n)$	Entropy of random variable X with pdf $\{p_1, \ldots, p_n\}$	397
$H(x)$	Same as $H(x, 1 - x), 0 \le x \le 1$	399
$d(p\|q)$	Kullback–Liebler distance between probability distributions $p(x), q(x)$	432
$H(X, Y), H(X|Y)$	Joint entropy, conditional entropy	446
$I(X; Y)$	Mutual entropy	446
$f \to F$	Fourier Transform. F is also written $\hat{f}$ or $\mathcal{F}[f]$	523, 524, 542
R_{fg}	Cross-correlation of functions f, g	544
$\mathrm{sinc}(x)$	$(\sin \pi x)/\pi x$ (sometimes $(\sin x)/x$, as in Section 14.3)	542
$\nabla^2 f$	Laplacian of f	573
LoG, DoG	Laplacian of Gaussian, Difference of Gaussians	594
$\psi(x), \psi_i^j(x)$	Mother wavelet, derived wavelets	659
$W^j, \Psi^j(x)$	Wavelet space, basis	665
$V^j, \Phi^j(x)$	Scaling space, basis	665
$V \bigoplus W$	Sum of vector spaces	662
P, Q, A, B	Filter bank matrices	666, 667
$P_0 \ldots P_n$	Control polygon	668
$b(t), \phi_k(x)$	Box function, spline function	693
$N_{i,m}(x)$	B-spline basis function of order m, degree m-1,	698
$(\ldots, r_{-1}, r_0, r_1, \ldots)$	Averaging mask for subdivision	711
$e_i^j(x)$	Hat function	711
$\langle f, h \rangle$	Inner product of functions f and h	660, 748
G	Gram matrix of inner products: $g_{ik} = \langle f_i, h_k \rangle$ (allows $h = f$)	721

Part I
The plane

1
Isometries

1.1 Introduction

One practical aim in Part I is to equip the reader to build a pattern-generating computer engine. The patterns we have in mind come from two main streams. Firstly the *geometrical tradition*, represented for example in the fine Moslem art in the Alhambra at Granada in Spain, but found very widely. (See Figure 1.1.)

Less abundant but still noteworthy are the patterns left by the ancient Romans (Field, 1988). The second type is that for which the Dutch artist M. C. Escher is famous, exemplified in Figure 1.2, in which (stylised) motifs of living forms are dovetailed together in remarkable ways. Useful references are Coxeter (1987), MacGillavry (1976), and especially Escher (1989). In Figure 1.2 we imitate a classic Escher-type pattern.

The magic is due partly to the designers' skill and partly to their discovery of certain rules and techniques. We describe the underlying mathematical theory and how it may be applied in practice by someone claiming no particular artistic skills.

The patterns to which we refer are true *plane* patterns, that is, there are translations in two non-parallel directions (opposite directions count as parallel) which move every submotif of the pattern onto a copy of itself elsewhere in the pattern. A *translation* is a movement of everything, in the same direction, by the same amount. Thus in Figure 1.2 piece A can be moved to piece B by the translation represented by arrow **a**, but no translation will transform it to piece C. A reflection would have to be incorporated.

Exercise The reader may like to verify that, in Figure 1.1, two smallest such translations are represented in their length and direction by the arrows shown, and determine corresponding arrows for Figure 1.2. These should be horizontal and vertical.

But there may be much more to it.

More generally, we lay a basis for understanding *isometries* – those transformations of the plane which preserve distance – and look for the easiest ways to see how they combine or can be decomposed. Examples are translations, rotations and reflections. Our approach is essentially geometrical. An important tool is the idea of a *symmetry* of a plane figure; that is, an isometry which sends every submotif of the pattern onto another of the

Figure 1.1 Variation on an Islamic theme. For the original, see Critchlow (1976), page 112. The arrows indicate symmetry in two independent directions, and the pattern is considered to continue indefinitely, filling the plane.

%%%

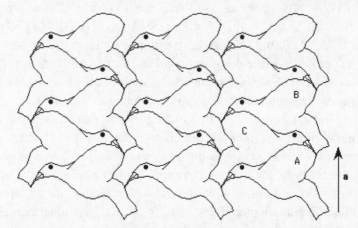

%%%

Figure 1.2 Plane pattern of interlocking birds, after M. C. Escher.

same size and shape. (The translations we cited for Figure 1.2 are thus symmetries, but we reiterate the idea here.) For example, the head in Figure 1.3(a) is symmetrical about the line AB and, corresponding to this fact, the isometry obtained by reflecting the plane in line AB is called a *symmetry* of the head. Of course we call AB a *line of symmetry*. In Figure 1.3(b) the isometry consisting of a one third turn about O is a symmetry, and O is called a 3-fold centre of symmetry. In general, if the $1/n$ turn about a point A (n maximal) is a symmetry of a pattern we say A is an *n-fold centre of symmetry* of the pattern.

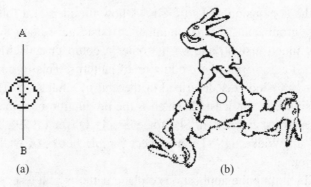

Figure 1.3

The key idea is that the collection of all symmetries, or *symmetry operations,* of a figure form a *group G* (see Section 2.5). Here this means simply that the composition of any two symmetries is another, which is sometimes expressed by saying that the set of symmetries is closed under composition. Thus, for Figure 1.3(a) the symmetry group *G* consists of the *identity I* (do nothing) and reflection in line AB. For Figure 1.3(b), *G* consists of *I*, a 1/3 turn τ about the central point, and a 2/3 turn which may be written τ^2 since it is the composition of two 1/3 turns τ. In fact, every plane pattern falls into one of 17 classes determined by its symmetry group, as we shall see in Chapter 5. That is, provided one insists, as we do, that the patterns be *discrete,* in the sense that no pattern can be transformed onto itself by arbitrarily small movements. This rules out for example a pattern consisting of copies of an infinite bar $\cdots$ ■■■■ $\cdots$.

Exercise What symmetries of the pattern represented in Figure 1.1 leave the central point unmoved?

Section 6.3 on tilings or tessellations of the plane is obviously relevant to pattern generation and surface filling. However, I am indebted to Alan Fournier for the comment that it touches another issue: how in future will we wish to divide up a screen into pixels, and what should be their shape? The answer is not obvious, but we introduce some of the options. See Ulichney (1987), Chapter 2.

A remarkable survey of tilings and patterns is given in Grünbaum and Shephard (1987), in which also the origins of many familiar and not-so-familiar patterns are recorded. For a study of isometries and symmetry, including the 'non-discrete' case, see Lockwood and Macmillan (1978), and for a connection with manifolds Montesinos (1987).

Now, a plane pattern has a smallest replicating unit known as a *fundamental region F* of its symmetry group: the copies of *F* obtained by applying each symmetry operation of the group in turn form a *tiling* of the plane. That is, they cover the plane without area overlap. In Figure 1.2 we may take any one of A, B, C as the fundamental region. Usually several copies of this region form together a *cell,* or smallest replicating unit which can be made to tile the plane using *translations only*. Referring again to Figure 1.2, the combination of A and C is such a cell.

Section 6.4, the conclusion of Part I, shows how the idea of a fundamental region of the symmetry group, plus a small number of basic generating symmetries, gives on the one hand much insight, and on the other a compact and effective method of both analysing and automating the production of patterns. This forms the basis of the downloadable program polynet described at the end of Chapter 6. This text contains commercial possibilities, not least of which is the production of books of patterns and teach-yourself pattern construction. See for example Oliver (1979), Devaney (1989), Schattschneider and Walker (1982), or inspect sample books of wallpaper, linoleum, carpeting and so on.

We conclude by noting the application of plane patterns as a test bed for techniques and research in the area of texture mapping. See Heckbert (1989), Chapter 3.

1.2 Isometries and their sense

We start by reviewing some basic things needed which the reader may have once known but not used for a long time.

1.2.1 The plane and vectors

Coordinates Points in the plane will be denoted by capital letters A, B, C, ... It is often convenient to specify the position of points by means of a *Cartesian coordinate system*. This consists of (i) a fixed reference point normally labelled O and called the *origin*, (ii) a pair of perpendicular lines through O, called the *x-axis* and *y-axis*, and (iii) a chosen direction along each axis in which movements are measured as positive.

Thus in Figure 1.4 the point A has coordinates $(3, 2)$, meaning that A is reached from O by a movement of 3 units in the positive direction along the x-axis, then 2 units in the positive y direction. Compare B $(-2, 1)$, reached by a movement of 2 units in the negative (opposite to positive) x-direction and 1 unit in the y-direction. Of course the two component movements could be made in either order.

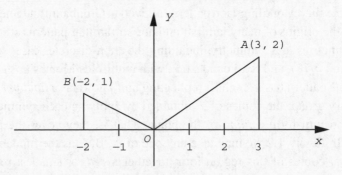

Figure 1.4 Coordinate axes. The x-axis and y-axis are labelled by lower case x, y and often called Ox, Oy. Positive directions are arrowed.

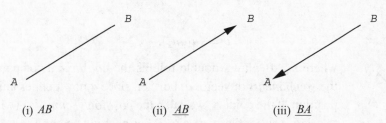

(i) *AB*   (ii) <u>*AB*</u>   (iii) <u>*BA*</u>

Figure 1.5(a) Directed and undirected line segments.

Lines The straight line joining two points A, B is called the *line segment AB*. As in the case of coordinates, we need the technique of assigning to AB one of the two possible directions, giving us the *directed line segments AB or BA*, according as the direction is towards B or towards A. This is illustrated in Figure 1.5(a).

Length $|AB|$ denotes the length of the line segment AB, which equals of course the distance between A and B. Sometimes it is useful to have a formula for this in terms of the coordinates $A\,(a_1, a_2)$ and $B\,(b_1, b_2)$:

$$|AB| = \sqrt{(b_1 - a_1)^2 + (b_2 - a_2)^2}. \tag{1.1}$$

Exercise Prove Formula (1.1) by using the theorem of Pythagoras.

Vectors A vital concept as soon as we come to translation (Section 1.2.2(a)), a *vector* is any combination of a distance, or magnitude, and a direction in space. (For now, the plane.) Thus every directed line segment represents some vector by its direction and length, but the same vector is represented by *any* line segment with this length and direction, as depicted in Figure 1.5(b).

$$\boldsymbol{a} = \underline{AB} = \underline{CD}$$

Figure 1.5(b) Directed line segments representing the same vector $\boldsymbol{a}$.

A letter representing a vector will normally be printed in bold lower case thus: $\boldsymbol{a}$, and although the directed line segment $\underline{AB}$ of Figure 1.5(b), for example, has the additional property of an *initial point A* and *end point B* we will sometimes allow ourselves to write for example $\boldsymbol{a} = \underline{AB} = \underline{CD} = \boldsymbol{b}$, to mean that all four have the same magnitude and direction. With the length (magnitude) of a vector $\boldsymbol{x}$ denoted by $|\boldsymbol{x}|$, the statement then includes $|\boldsymbol{a}| = |\underline{AB}| = |\underline{CD}| = |\boldsymbol{b}|$. Also it is often convenient to drop the letters, in a diagram, leaving an arrow of the correct length and direction thus: $\longrightarrow$. The *angle between two vectors* means the angle between representative directed line segments $\underline{AB}$, $\underline{AC}$ with the same inital point.

Components and position vectors By contrast with the previous paragraph, we may standardise on the origin as initial point, representing a vector $\boldsymbol{a}$ by segment $\underline{OA}$. Then

we write

$$a = (a_1, a_2),$$

Figure 1.6

where a_1, a_2 play a double role as the *coordinates* of point A, and the *components* of vector a. Further, since a now defines uniquely the position of the point A, we call a the *position vector* of A (with respect to origin O). Similarly a point B has position vector $b = (b_1, b_2)$, and so on (Figure 1.6). Alternatively we may write r_A for the position vector of A.

Of course x, y will remain alternative notation for the coordinates, especially if we consider a variable point, or an equation in Cartesian coordinates, such as $x = m$ for the line perpendicular to the x-axis, crossing it at the point $(m, 0)$.

Scalar times vector In the context of vectors we often refer to numbers as *scalars*, to emphasise that they are not vectors. We recall that the *magnitude* or *absolute value* of a scalar λ is obtained by dropping its minus sign if there is one. Thus $|\lambda| = -\lambda$ if $\lambda < 0$, otherwise $|\lambda| = \lambda$. If a is a vector and λ a scalar then we define λa as the vector whose magnitude equals the product $|\lambda| \, |a|$, and whose direction is that of a if $\lambda > 0$ and opposite to a if $\lambda < 0$. If $\lambda = 0$ then we define the result to be the anomalous vector $\mathbf{0}$, with zero magnitude and direction undefined. As in the illustration below, we usually abbreviate $(-1)a$ to $-a$, $(-2)a$ to $-2a$, and so on. Also $(1/c)a$ may be shortened to a/c ($c \neq 0$).

Examples

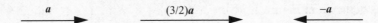

a $(3/2)a$ $-a$

Adding vectors To add two vectors we represent them by directed line segments placed nose to tail as in Figure 1.7(a). Subtraction is conveniently defined by the scalar times vector schema: $a - b = a + (-b)$, as in Figure 1.7(b). Diagrams are easily drawn to confirm that the order in which we add the vectors does not matter: $a + b = b + a$ (a parallelogram shows this), and $a + (b + c) = (a + b) + c$.

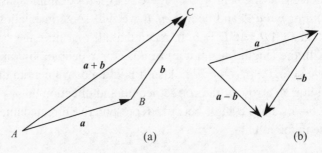

(a)   (b)

Figure 1.7 Finding (a) the sum and (b) the difference of two vectors by placing them nose to tail.

Rules Let a, b be the position vectors of A, B. Then

$$a + b = (a_1 + b_1, a_2 + b_2), \tag{1.2a}$$

$$\lambda a = (\lambda a_1, \lambda a_2), \tag{1.2b}$$

$$\underline{AB} = b - a. \tag{1.2c}$$

Proof For (1.2a) we refer to Figure 1.7(a), and imagine coordinate axes with point A as origin, taking the x-direction as due East. Then $a_1 + b_1 = $ (amount B is East of A) + (amount C is East of B) = amount C is East of A = first component of C. The second components may be handled similarly. Equation (1.2b) is left to the reader. To establish (1.2c), we note that the journey from A to B in Figure 1.6 may be made via the origin: $\underline{AB} = \underline{AO} + \underline{OB} = (-a) + b$.

The section formula The point P on AB with $AP : PB = m : n$ (illustrated below) has position vector p given by

$$p = \frac{1}{m+n}(mb + na). \tag{1.3}$$

Often called the *section formula*, this is extremely useful, and has the virtue of covering cases such as (i), (ii) shown below in which P does not lie between A and B.

(i) This means that $\underline{AP}$ and $\underline{PB}$ are in opposite directions and so m, n have opposite signs. Thus in Case (i) $\underline{AP} = -3\underline{PB}$ and we may write $\underline{AP} : \underline{PB} = 3 : -1$ (or, equally, $-3 : 1$), whilst Case (ii) entails

(ii) $\underline{AP} = -(3/5)\underline{PB}$, or $\underline{AP} : \underline{PB} = -3 : 5$.

This said, (1.3) is easily proved, for $n\underline{AP} = m\underline{PB}$, so by (1.2) $n(p - a) = m(b - p)$, which rearranges as $(m + n)p = mb + na$.

Exercise Draw the diagram for proving (1.2a), marking in the components of a and b.

Application 1.1 This is a handy illustration of the use of vectors to prove a well-known fact we will need in Chapter 6: the medians of a triangle ABC all pass through the point G (centre of gravity), whose position vector is

$$g = \tfrac{1}{3}(a + b + c).$$

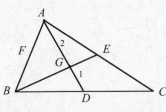

To prove this, label the midpoints of the sides by D, E, F as shown. By (1.3), D has position vector $d = (1/2)(b + c)$. So, again by (1.3), the point that divides median AD in the ratio $2 : 1$ has position vector $(1/3)(2d + 1a)$, which equals $(1/3)(a + b + c)$ on substituting for d. But this expression is symmetrical in a, b, c, and so lies on all three medians, dividing each in the ratio $2 : 1$.

Note The use of components gives an important way to calculate with vectors, which will come into its own in Chapter 7. Before then, our arguments will be mostly geometrical, with components as a tool in some exercises. However, we give both a geometrical and a coordinate proof of (1.14) a little further on, which the reader may find interesting for comparison purposes at that point.

Exercise Use position vectors and (1.3), which applies equally in 3-space (indeed, in any dimension), to prove the following facts about any tetrahedron *ABCD*. (i) The four lines joining a vertex to the centroid of its opposite face are concurrent at a point *G* which divides each such line in the ratio 3 : 1, (ii) the three lines joining midpoints of pairs of opposite edges all meet in *G*.

1.2.2 Isometries

Definition 1.2 A *transformation g* of the plane is a rule which assigns to each point *P* a unique point P^g, or P', called the *image of P under g*. (Note that P^g does not mean *P* 'to the power of' *g*.) We think of *g* as moving points around in the plane. We also call *g* a *map* or *mapping* of the plane onto itself, and say *g maps P to P'*. An *isometry* of the plane is a transformation *g* of the plane which preserves distances. That is, for any two points *P*, *Q*:

$$|P'Q'| = |PQ|. \tag{1.4}$$

The reader is advised not to think first of the formula (1.4) but to start from the idea of isometries preserving distance. Of course the same definition is applicable to 3-space or even higher dimensions, and we pursue this in Part II (Chapters 7–8). An important first consequence of the definition is as follows.

> *An isometry g transforms straight lines into straight*
> *lines, and preserves the (unsigned) size of angles.* (1.5)

Proof of (1.5). We refer to Figure 1.8. It suffices to show that if points *A*, *B*, *C* lie on a straight line, then so do their images A', B', C'. Suppose *B* lies between *A* and *C*. Then elementary geometry tells us that

$$|AC| = |AB| + |BC|,$$

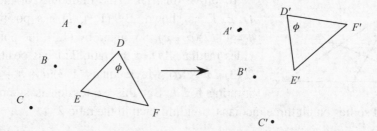

Figure 1.8 Points *A*, *B*, *C* on a straight line, a triangle *DEF*, and their images under an isometry. The magnitude of angle ϕ is preserved.

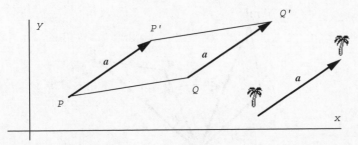

Figure 1.9 The translation T_a is an isometry as $|P'Q'| = |PQ|$ always.

and therefore, from condition (1.4) of an isometry, the same holds with A, B, C replaced by A', B', C'. Consequently, A', B', C' also lie on a straight line, and the first assertion of (1.5) is established: straight lines are transformed to straight lines. Now, given this, let us view the angle ϕ between two lines as the vertex angle of some triangle *DEF*, transformed by g into another triangle, $D'E'F'$ – which must be congruent to *DEF* because the lengths of the sides are unchanged by g. Thus the vertex angle is unchanged, laying aside considerations of sign. This completes the proof.

Notation 1.3 The following are convenient at different times for referring to the image of P under a transformation g:

$$(i)\ P', \qquad (ii)\ P^g, \qquad (iii)\ g(P).$$

We shall explain in Section 1.3.1 the significance of our choosing (ii) rather than (iii). In each case the notation allows us to replace P by any figure or subset F in the plane. Thus figure F^g consists of the images of the points of F, or $F^g = \{x^g : x \in F\}$. For example, if F is the lower palm tree in Figure 1.9, with $g = T_a$ (see previous page) then F^g is the upper. The heads of Figure 1.11 provide a further example.

Three types of isometry At this juncture it is appropriate to discuss the three most familiar types of isometry in the plane. The remaining type is introduced in Section 1.3.2.

(a) Translation For any vector a the translation T_a of the plane is the transformation in which every point is moved in the direction of a, through a distance equal to its magnitude $|a|$.

Thus $PP' = a$ (in magnitude and direction). To show that T_a is an isometry, suppose it sends another point Q to Q'. Then $a = QQ'$, so that PP' and QQ' are parallel and equal, making a parallelogram $PP'Q'Q$. Hence, by an elementary theorem in geometry, $|P'Q'| = |PQ|$, and T_a has indeed preserved distances.

Notation 1.4 P' is also called the *translate* of P (by T_a). Notice that T_a sends x to $x + a$, when we identify a point X with its position vector x. More geometrically, if $a = \underline{PQ}$ we may write unambiguously $T_a = T_{PQ}$, the translation which takes P to Q.

(b) Rotation As illustrated in Figure 1.10, let the transformation $R_A(\phi)$ be
$$R_A(\phi) = \text{rotation about the point } A \text{ through the angle } \phi.$$

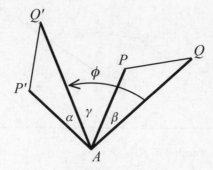

Figure 1.10 Rotation about the point A through positive angle ϕ.

Notice that ϕ is a *signed* angle; it is positive if the rotation is anticlockwise (counterclockwise), negative in the clockwise case. In Figure 1.10 we see why rotation is an isometry: by definition, $|AP'| = |AP|$, $|AQ'| = |AQ|$ and, signs excluded, $\beta + \gamma = \phi = \alpha + \gamma$, hence $\alpha = \beta$. This establishes congruence of triangles PAQ, $P'AQ'$ (two sides and the included angle), which includes the equality $|P'Q'| = |PQ|$. Thus $R_A(\phi)$ preserves distance and so is an isometry.

Remarks 1.5

1. We will often use the special notation $R_A(1/n)$ for a $1/n$ turn about point A and $R_A(m/n)$ for m $n$ths of a turn, negative m denoting a clockwise direction. Thus $R_A(2/3)$ is a $2/3$ turn about A. Note that $R_A(\phi)$ is distinguished from reflection notation below by the '(ϕ)' part.

2. A rotation through any number of complete turns leaves every point where it began, and so is the *identity isometry I* of Section 1.1 One whole turn is the angle 2π, measured in radians. Thus rotation through $\phi + 2\pi$ is the same isometry as rotation through ϕ. We only count the final position of each point, not its route to get there.

3. A $1/2$ turn $R_A(\pi)$, or $R_A(1/2)$, reverses the direction of every line segment AB starting at A. In particular the $1/2$ turn about the origin sends the point (x, y) to $(-x, -y)$.

4. The effect of a rotation through the angle ϕ may be obtained by rotation in the opposite direction, for example through the angle $-(2\pi - \phi)$. So $R_A(2/3)$ is equivalent to $R_A(-1/3)$, a clockwise $1/3$ turn.

(c) Reflection Let R_m denote the transformation of the plane obtained by reflecting every point P in the line m. That is, as we indicate in Figure 1.11, PP' is perpendicular to m, and P, P' are at equal distances from m but on opposite sides.

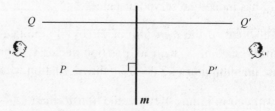

Figure 1.11 Reflection in a line m.

Notation 1.6 We may call m the *mirror*, or *mirror line*, for the reflection. It is often useful to let R_{AB} denote reflection in a line m which contains points A, B, and let $R_{ax+by=c}$ denote reflection in the line $ax + by = c$.

Example 1.7 The following simple formula will be especially useful in Section 6.4.4, and meanwhile for alternative ways to establish many results in the text (cf. the second part of Theorem 1.18) and Exercises. It states that, in coordinates, *reflection in the line* $x = m$ is given by

$$(x, y) \to (2m - x, y), \tag{1.6}$$

meaning that the isometry $R_{x=m}$ sends the point (x, y) to $(2m - x, y)$.

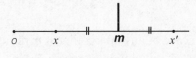

Proof From the definition of reflection, the y coordinate is unchanged since the mirror is parallel to the y-axis, but x becomes $m + (m - x)$, which equals $2m - x$.

Example 1.8 We use coordinates to show that reflection is an isometry. We may choose the coordinate system so that the mirror is the y-axis, giving $m = 0$ in the reflection formula (1.6). Referring to Figure 1.11, suppose the coordinates are $P(p_1, p_2)$, and so on. Then the distance formula (1.1) gives

$$\begin{aligned}
|P'Q'|^2 &= (q_1' - p_1')^2 + (q_2' - p_2')^2 \\
&= (-q_1 + p_1)^2 + (q_2 - p_2)^2 \\
&= |PQ|^2, \text{ as required.}
\end{aligned}$$

Exercise Give a geometrical proof that, in Figure 1.11, we have $|P'Q'| = |PQ|$ and hence that R_m is an isometry, considering also the case where P, Q are on opposite sides of the mirror.

1.2.3 The sense of an isometry

In Figure 1.11 the reflection transforms the right looking face into one that looks to the left (and vice versa). We will see in Theorem 1.10 that an isometry which reverses one face will consistently reverse all. In more directly geometrical terms, it reverses the direction of an arrow round a circle as in Figure 1.12, so we proceed as follows.

Sense Any three non-collinear points A, B, C lie on a unique circle, and the *sense* of an ordered triple ABC means the corresponding direction round the circle, as in Figure 1.12. This is also the direction of rotation of BC (about B) towards BA. We give angle ABC (letters in that order) a positive sign if triple ABC is anticlockwise; then CBA is clockwise and angle CBA is negative.

Notice that the cyclically related triples ABC, BCA, CAB all specify the same direction round a circle (anticlockwise in Figure 1.12) and that their reverses CBA, ACB, BAC

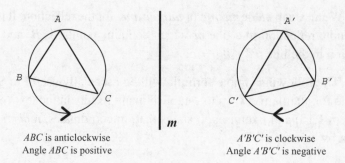

ABC is anticlockwise   *A'B'C'* is clockwise
Angle *ABC* is positive   Angle *A'B'C'* is negative

Figure 1.12 Reflection R_m reverses the sense of ordered triple *ABC*.

correspond to the opposite direction. Now we are ready for a definition which, happily, accounts for all isometries.

Definition 1.9 An isometry is *direct* if it preserves the sense of any non-collinear triple and *indirect* if it reverses every such sense. We note that the reflection isometry R_m in Figure 1.12 is indirect, since it reverses the sense of ABC (it must be one or the other by Theorem 1.10 below).

Theorem 1.10 *(a) Every isometry is either direct or indirect. (b) An isometry is determined by its effect on any two points and whether it is direct or indirect, or alternatively by its effect on three non-collinear points.*

Proof (a) Let g be an isometry and let A, B, P, Q be points with P and Q on the same side of the line AB, as in Figure 1.13(a).

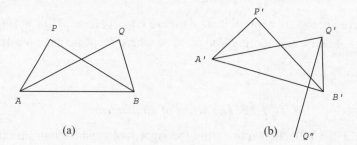

(a)   (b)

Figure 1.13

Then the images P' and Q' must be on the same side of $A'B'$ as shown in Figure 1.13(b) since, given A', B' and P', there are exactly two possible positions Q', Q'' for the image of Q, and by elementary geometry $|P'Q''| \neq |PQ|$, which rules out Q''. Since, therefore, points on the same side of a line are transformed to points on the same side of its image, we have that, for any two points A, B:

> *if the isometry g preserves (reverses) the sense of one triple*
> *containing A, B then it preserves (reverses) the sense of every*
> *such triple,*   (1.7)

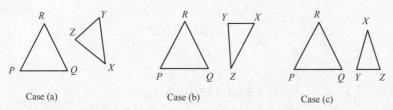

Figure 1.14 Diagram for the proof that if g preserves the sense of triple PQR then it preserves the sense of XYZ: (a) is the general case and (b), (c) are sample special cases.

where the parentheses mean that the statement holds with 'reverses' in place of 'preserves', and all triples referred to are non-collinear. Let g preserve the sense of PQR. We must deduce that g preserves the sense of an arbitrary triple XYZ, and we shall do this with (1.7) by changing one point at a time:

g preserves the sense of PQR

$\Rightarrow$ g preserves the sense of PQZ (unless P, Q, Z are collinear – see Figure 1.14(b))

$\Rightarrow$ g preserves the sense of PYZ (unless P, Y, Z are collinear – see Figure 1.14(c))

$\Rightarrow$ g preserves the sense of XYZ (since X, Y, Z are not collinear).

Special cases can be handled by judicious use of (1.7). For example, in Figure 1.14(b) we may proceed in the order $PQR \to XQR \to XQZ \to XYZ$. This completes the proof of part (a), reversal cases being handled similarly.

Proof (b) We refer to Figure 1.13. Suppose the images A', B' of A, B under the isometry g are given. Let Q be any point. If Q happens to lie on AB then Q' lies on $A'B'$, by (1.5), and the equalities $|Q'A'| = |QA|$, $|Q'B'| = |QB|$ determine its exact position. Otherwise these equalities leave two possibilites, represented by Q', Q'' in Figure 1.13(b). Since triples $A'B'Q'$ and $A'B'Q''$ have opposite senses, the image of Q is now determined by whether g is direct or indirect. Alternatively, if we specify the image C' of a third point C (C not collinear with A, B), then the distances of Q' from the other three images determine its position. This completes the proof of (b).

Example 1.11 By considering when the sense of a triple is preserved we have the following categorisation from Theorem 1.10.

Rotation, translation	Direct.
Reflection	Indirect.

We shall determine the result of performing first a half turn about the point A shown in Figure 1.15, then a half turn about B. Since both operations preserve distance and the senses of all triples, the result must be a direct isometry g. But which one? According to Theorem 1.10 we will have it when we find an isometry which is direct and which has the right effect on two points. Now, the result of g is that A moves to A', and B to B'' via

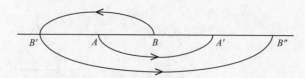

Figure 1.15 Half turns.

B'. But $A \to A'$, $B \to B''$ is achieved by the direct isometry T_{2AB}, which is therefore (by Theorem 1.10) the one we seek.

Exercise Find the result of a half turn about the point A (Figure 1.15), followed by a reflection in a mirror through B at right angles to AB; or give the argument in the proof of Theorem 1.10 for special case (c) (cf. the argument for Case (b)).

1.3 The classification of isometries

1.3.1 Composing isometries

We wish to prove Theorem 1.15, a simple and useful result which will assist us in classifying all possible isometries of the plane. First some notation is required. If g, h are two isometries, then their *composition*, or *product*, gh, is the transformation obtained by performing *first g, then h*. Since g and h both preserve distances, so does their composition, which is therefore also an isometry. In denoting this composition by gh (or $g \cdot h$), we are deliberately writing the transformations in the order in which they are performed, by contrast with the other standard system defined by $(gh)(A) = g(h(A))$ where gh means 'perform h, then g'. Occasionally, the latter will be convenient. Normally in Part 1 we will use our present definition, which is equivalent to

$$A^{gh} = (A^g)^h. \tag{1.8}$$

In words this says: 'to apply the isometry gh to an arbitrary point A, apply g, then h'. In the sense of (1.8), A^g behaves like A to the power of g. It follows that, for a composition of three isometries f, g, h, we have the *associative law*

$$f(gh) = (fg)h. \tag{1.9}$$

Power notation g^m denotes m successive repetitions $g \cdot g \cdots g$ of an isometry g, where $m \geq 1$. Consequently we have the power law (1.10) below for $m, n = 0, 1, 2, \ldots$ in which we write write $g^0 = I$, the identity (do nothing) isometry.

$$g^m g^n = g^{m+n} = g^n g^m, \qquad (g^m)^n = g^{mn}. \tag{1.10}$$

Example 1.12 The composition of a $1/7$ turn, a $2/7$ turn, and a $4/7$ turn about a given point A is a complete turn. Thus all points are returned to their original positions and the resulting isometry is the identity. We may write $R_A(1/7)\, R_A(2/7) R_A(4/7) = I$, without bracketing any pair together. On the other hand, two successive reflections $R_m R_m$ in the

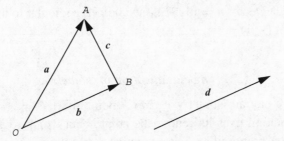

Figure 1.16 Resolving vector a along and perpendicular to d: $a = b + c$.

same mirror, or n successive $1/n$ turns about a point A, also give the identity, so we may write

$$R_m^2 = I = [R_A(1/n)]^n. \tag{1.11}$$

Composition of translations The rule is

$$T_a T_b = T_{a+b} = T_b T_a, \tag{1.12}$$

where the vector sum $a + b$ is obtained by placing representatives of a and b nose to tail in the manner of Figure 1.7. The first equality is a definition and the second is a consequence, conveniently placed here, which the reader is asked to prove below.

Exercise Use a parallelogram to show that $T_a T_b = T_b T_a$, where T_a is translation by the vector a. Express $(T_a)^n$ as a single translation; **or** let g denote a 3/10 turn about some point. Show that $(g^5)^3$ has the effect of a $1/2$ turn.

Resolving a translation into components This means re-expressing the corresponding vector as a sum of two others. See below.

Referring to Figure 1.16, suppose we are given a fixed direction, say that of a vector d. Then we may express any vector a as the sum of a vector b in the direction of d plus a vector c perpendicular to d:

$$a = b + c.$$

This is called *resolving* a into components along and perpendicular to d. To achieve this, we represent a by a directed line segment $\underline{OA}$, and then position a point B so that $\underline{OB}$ has the direction of d and $\underline{BA}$ is perpendicular to d. Then the required components are $b = \underline{OB}$ and $c = \underline{BA}$. Note that we do not require $\underline{OB} = d$.

At the same time we have *resolved* the translation T_a into *components* along and perpendicular to d in the sense that

$$T_a = T_c T_b = T_b T_c. \tag{1.13}$$

Remarks 1.13 (1) Resolving a with respect to the positive x-direction gives the (Cartesian) components of a. (2) T_{AB} is the unique translation which sends point A to point B. In particular, we interpret T_{AA} as the identity isometry I (do nothing).

Exercise Resolve the vector $a = (4, 0)$ along and perpendicular to the direction of OA, where A is the point $(1, 1)$.

1.3.2 The classification of isometries

Definition 1.14 We say an isometry g *fixes* a point A if $A^g = A$. This is especially pertinent since a rotation fixes its centre (the point about which rotation is made), and a reflection fixes the points of its mirror, whilst a translation moves everything. For this culminating section of Chapter 1 we first reduce (Theorem 1.15) the classification problem to that of isometries that fix some point (Theorem 1.16), plus the question of what happens when one of these is combined with a translation (see (1.14), (1.15)).

Theorem 1.15 *Let A be any point in the plane. Then every isometry g is the composition of an isometry that fixes A and a translation. Either order may be assumed.*

Proof Let the isometry g send A to A'. Then $T = T_{A'A}$ is a translation that sends A' back to A. We have

$$A \xrightarrow{g} A' \xrightarrow{T} A$$

so the isometry $h = g \cdot T$ fixes A. The argument then runs:

$$h = gT_{A'A},$$
$$\text{therefore} \qquad hT_{AA'} = gT_{A'A}T_{AA'} = g,$$

the last equality being because the combined effect of translation $T_{A'A}$ followed by $T_{AA'}$ is to do nothing (i.e. their composition is the identity isometry). In conclusion, we have $g = hT_1$, where, as required, h fixes A and T_1 is a translation (here $T_{AA'}$). A slight variation of the argument gives g in the form $T_2 h$, for different h fixing A, and translation T_2.

Exercise Adapt the proof above to obtain the isometry g as a composition $g = Th$.

Theorem 1.16 *An isometry that fixes a point O is either*
(a) a rotation about O (direct case), or
(b) reflection in a line through O (indirect case).

Proof Let an isometry g fix O and send A to A', B to B'.

Case g direct Here angles AOB, $A'OB'$ are equal in sign as well as magnitude and so, as in Figure 1.17(a), angles AOA', BOB' enjoy the same property. Hence g is rotation about O.

Case g indirect Now angles AOB, $A'OB'$ are equal in magnitude but opposite in sign, as in Figure 1.17(b), so in the case $B = C$, for any point C on the bisector m of angle AOA', we see that g fixes C. Since g preserves length and angles (in magnitude) g reflects points B not on m to their mirror image in m.

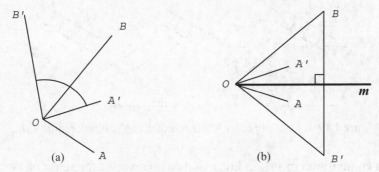

Figure 1.17 Diagrams for the proof of Theorem 1.16.

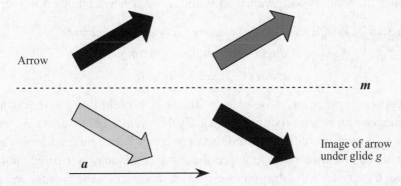

Figure 1.18 Black arrow, and its image under glide reflection *g*, composed of reflection R_m and translation T_a, in either order. The lightest arrow is an intermediate image, after reflection first. The darker shows translation done first.

Notice that we have incidentally shown that a rotation is direct and a reflection is indirect. Theorem 1.16 classifies isomorphisms that fix one or more points. What about those that fix none? We know from Theorem 1.15 that, given any point *A* we care to choose, we can represent any such isometry *g* as a composition $h \cdot T$, where *T* is a translation and *h* is an isometry that fixes *A*. Thus such isometries are obtainable from the point-fixing ones, rotation and reflection, by composing them with translations. The result includes a fourth type of isometry called a glide, which we shall now introduce.

Glides A *glide reflection*, or *glide*, with (mirror) line *m* is the composition of the reflection R_m in *m* with a translation T_a parallel to *m*. Obviously it does not matter in what order these two operations are done. The result is the same, as we can see in Figure 1.18. By *convention,* the mirror of a glide is drawn as a line of dashes. Notice that the composition of a glide $R_m T_a$ with itself is the translation T_{2a}, as illustrated in Figure 1.19, in which the first ladder yields the rest by repeated application of the glide. This illustrates the easy to see, but very useful, Remark 1.17.

Remark 1.17 The composition of two indirect isometries is direct. The composition of a direct and an indirect isometry is an indirect isometry.

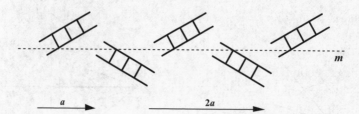

Figure 1.19 Images of ladder under repeated application of glide $T_a R_m$.

Proof The composition of two indirect isometries reverses the sense of every ordered triple twice, and therefore leaves their sense unchanged. If just one of the isometries is indirect, then the result is one reversal only, and so we obtain an indirect isometry.

Theorem 1.18 *(Classification) Every isometry is one of the four types:*

$$direct - translation\ or\ rotation;$$
$$indirect - reflection\ or\ glide.$$

Proof Suppose we are given an isometry g. Then by Theorem 1.15 g is the composition of a translation with a point-fixing isometry. By Theorem 1.16, the latter isometry is a rotation or reflection, according as it is direct or indirect. Therefore it suffices to establish the following composition rules, in which the composition may be carried out in either order (though the order will affect precisely *which* rotation or glide results). We give the proofs for only one order, the other being proved similarly.

$$\text{rotation} \cdot \text{translation} = \text{rotation}; \tag{1.14}$$
$$\text{reflection} \cdot \text{translation} = \text{glide}. \tag{1.15}$$

To prove (1.14), suppose that the rotation is τ and the translation is T_a. Referring to Figure 1.20(a), a line parallel to a, suitably placed relative to the centre of rotation O, contains a point A and its image A' under τ such that the vector $A'A$ equals a. Then $\tau \cdot T_a$ fixes A and is direct, so by Theorem 1.16 it is a rotation.

To establish (1.15), let the reflection be R_m, followed by translation T_a. Since this translation resolves into components T_v parallel to m and T_w perpendicular to m, we

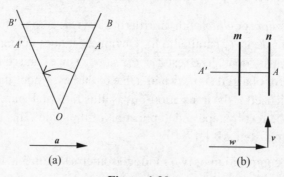

Figure 1.20

only need to show that $R_m T_w$ is reflection in a mirror n parallel to m and at a distance $(1/2)|w|$ from m, as indicated in Figure 1.20(b). But Theorem 1.10 tells us that an isometry is determined by its effect on any two points and whether it is direct or indirect. Now, $R_m T_w$, like the reflection R_n, is indirect (Remark 1.17), being the composition of an indirect and a direct isometry. Like R_n, it fixes every point A on n, and so by Theorem 1.10 it is indeed the reflection R_n. Finally, we have

$$R_m T_a = R_m(T_w T_v) = (R_m T_w)T_v = R_n T_v,$$

which is a glide, as asserted.

Proof of (1.15) using coordinates We may (and do) choose the coordinate system so that the mirror of the glide is the y-axis $x = 0$. Let the translation part be $T_{(t, u)}$. Then the reflection followed by translation has the effect $(x, y) \to (-x, y) \to (-x + t, y + u)$. But by the reflection formula (1.6) this is also the result of reflection in the line $x = t/2$ followed by translation $T_{(0, u)}$, thus it is a glide, since $T_{(0, u)}$ is parallel to the y-axis. If the translation is performed first, the corresponding reflection is in the line $x = -t/2$, with the same translation part as before.

Exercises 1

1   Verify that, in Figure 1.1, two smallest translations are represented in their length and direction by the arrows shown, and determine corresponding arrows for Figure 1.2. These should be horizontal and vertical.

2$\sqrt{}$ (i) What symmetries of the pattern represented in Figure 1.1 leave the central point unmoved? (ii) Prove Formula (1.1) by using the Theorem of Pythagoras. (iii) Draw the diagram for proving (1.2a), marking in the components of a and b.

3   Use position vectors and (1.3), which applies equally in 3-space (indeed, in any dimension), to prove the following facts about any tetrahedron $ABCD$. (i) The four lines joining a vertex to the centroid of its opposite face are concurrent at a point G which divides each such line in the ratio $3 : 1$ (ii) The three lines joining midpoints of pairs of opposite edges all meet in G.

4   Give a geometrical proof that, in Figure 1.11, we have $|P'Q'| = |PQ|$ and hence that R_m is an isometry, considering also the case where P, Q are on opposite sides of the mirror.

5$\sqrt{}$ Find the result of a half turn about the point A in the diagram of Example 1.11, followed by a reflection in a mirror through B at right angles to AB; **or** give the argument in the proof of Theorem 1.10 for the special case in Figure 1.14 (c) (see the argument for Case (b)).

6$\sqrt{}$ Use a parallelogram to show that $T_a T_b = T_b T_a$, where T_a is translation by the vector a. Express $(T_a)^n$ as a single translation. **Or** if g denotes a 3/10 turn about some point, what fraction of a turn is $(g^5)^3$?

7$\sqrt{}$ Resolve the vector $a = (4, 0)$ along and perpendicular to the direction of OB, where B is the point $(1,1)$.

8$\sqrt{}$ (i) Use coordinates to prove that the composition of reflections in parallel mirrors at distance d apart is translation through a distance $2d$ perpendicular to the mirrors. (ii) What is the result of reflection in the x-axis followed by reflection in the y-axis?

9√ For distinct points A, B determine the composition of a half turn about A followed by the translation T_{AB}, by considering the net effect upon A, B.

10 Mirror lines m, n intersect in a point A at angle ϕ. Determine the composition $R_m R_n R_m$, using Theorem 1.16, and following the motion of a point on one of the mirrors.

11√ The vertices A, B, C of an equilateral triangle are ordered in the positive sense. (i) Prove that $R_C(1/3)R_B(1/3) = R_A(2/3)$, by considering the images of A and C, or otherwise (see Theorem 1.10). (ii) Determine the composition $R_A(-1/3)R_B(1/3)$ [Hint: let D be the midpoint of BC].

12 The vertices A, B, C, D of a square are counterclockwise and E, F are the respective midpoints of AD, DC. Show that $R_E(1/2)R_{BD}$ is a glide with translation vector EF.

13√ Find a formula for reflection in the line with equation $ax + by = 1$. [Hint for gradients: recall that $\tan(\theta + \pi/2) = -\cot\theta$. In Section 7.4 we develop a more streamlined method for the occasions when it is expedient to work with isometries in terms of coordinates.]

2

How isometries combine

In Chapter 1 we combined two isometries g, h to produce a third by taking their compositions gh (do g, then h) and hg. There is another way to combine two isometries, of great practical use in the context of plane patterns, and which we will introduce in Section 2.3. We begin by highlighting two geometrical ways to find the composition (or product) of isometries. The first was already used in the proof of Theorem 1.18.

Method 1

(A) Determine the sense of the composition from those of its parts (Remark 1.17).

(B) Determine the effect of the composition on two convenient points P, Q.

(C) Find an isometry with the right sense and effect on P, Q. This must be the one required by Theorem 1.10.

Notice that (C) is now made easier by our knowledge of the four isometry types (Theorem 1.18). This method can be beautifully simple and effective for otherwise tricky compositions, but the second approach, given by Theorem 2.1 and Corollary 2.2, is perhaps more powerful for getting general results and insights. With Theorems 1.15 and 1.16 it says that every isometry can be decomposed into reflections, *and* it tells us how to combine reflections.

Method 2 Decompose the given isometries into reflections, using the available freedom of choice, so that certain reflections in the composition cancel each other out. See Examples 2.3 to 2.7. We note for later:

Method 3 Use Cartesian coordinates (See Chapter 7).

Notation We take this opportunity to recall some standard abbreviations from the list of symbols before Chapter 1 that will be useful from time to time. Each one is a subset of the next.

N   The set of *natural numbers* 1, 2, 3, . . .

Z   The *integers* . . . , −2, −1, 0, 1, 2, . . .

Q   The *rationals,* or rational numbers $\{m/n: m, n$ are integers and $n \neq 0\}$

23

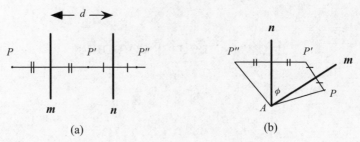

(a)   (b)

Figure 2.1 The proof of Theorem 2.1.

R   The *reals*, or *real numbers*, corresponding to the points of a line extending indefinitely
in both direction (the *real line*). Certain postulates are involved, which we do not need
to touch on until Definition 13.22.

2.1 Reflections are the key

Theorem 2.1 *Composing isometries (see Figure 2.1)*

(a) *If lines m, n are parallel at distance d then the composition of reflections $R_m R_n$ is a translation
of magnitude 2d perpendicular to these lines,*

(b) *If lines m, n intersect in the point A at angle ϕ then $R_m R_n$ is a rotation through an angle 2ϕ
about A: $R_m R_n = R_A(2\phi)$.*

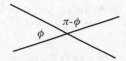

Figure 2.2

The proof (omitted) is by elementary geometry in Figure 2.1.
Notice in Figure 2.2 that crossing lines offer us two angles to
choose from. Signs apart, these angles add up to π, so, unless the
lines are perpendicular, one angle is acute and is taken as *the* angle
between the lines. Also, by mentioning m first, we imply a *signed*
turn of ϕ from m to n (if no order is implied then the angle may be taken as unsigned).

Corollary 2.2 *Decomposing isometries*

(i) *A rotation about a point A may be expressed as the product $R_m R_n$ of reflections in lines
through A at half the rotation angle.*

(ii) *A translation may be expressed as the product $R_m R_n$ of reflections in lines perpendicular to
the translation direction, at one half the translation distance.*

(iii) *In case (i) the direction and in (ii) the position of one line may be chosen arbitrarily. The
other line is then determined (see Figure 2.3).*

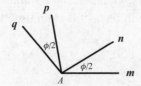

Figure 2.3 Two alternatives: $R_A(\phi) = R_m R_n = R_p R_q$.

Table 2.1. *Notation for the four isometry types in the plane.*

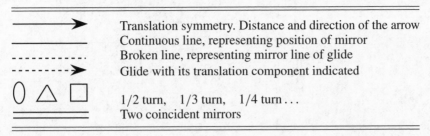

⟶	Translation symmetry. Distance and direction of the arrow
——	Continuous line, representing position of mirror
- - - - -	Broken line, representing mirror line of glide
- - - - ⟶	Glide with its translation component indicated
◯ △ ▢	1/2 turn, 1/3 turn, 1/4 turn...
═══	Two coincident mirrors

Remark 2.2a For a rotation of $1/n$ of a turn, i.e. an angle of $2\pi/n$, the mirrors should be at an angle π/n. Examples of using this second method are given in Section 2.2.

2.2 Some useful compositions

At the end of this section we give Table 2.2, showing the result of all types of products of isometries. First, we gain practice with special cases which are foundational to the study of isometries and plane patterns, and whose first use will be in the classification of braid patterns in Chapter 3. The notation of Table 2.1 will help to visualise what is going on.

First we try a composition problem already solved in the proof of Theorem 1.18 (the four isometry types). For clarity, a small '×' denotes composition.

Example 2.3

> *reflection R_m × translation T_a perpendicular to mirror*
> *= reflection in a mirror n parallel to the original one,*
>   *at one half translation distance, $|a|/2$, from it.* (2.1)

Thus, by repeatedly composing the latest mirror reflection with the translation T_a, we get a whole string of mirror positions:

$$ |\quad\quad|\quad\quad|\quad\quad|\quad\quad\quad|\ldots $$

at intervals of half the translation distance.

Proof of (2.1) By Corollary 2.2 we can express the translation T_a as the product of reflections in two parallel mirrors, one of which we may choose to be m itself. If the second mirror is n then we can compute as shown in Figure 2.4, with successive diagrams below each other to show relative horizontal positions. The argument is expressed geometrically on the left, and algebraically on the right.

Example 2.4

> *reflection R_m × rotation with centre on the mirror*
> *= reflection R_n in mirror at one half rotation angle to m.* (2.2)

We include this example before any further illustration, because it is exactly analogous to Example 2.3, with translation regarded as a special case of rotation in the manner of

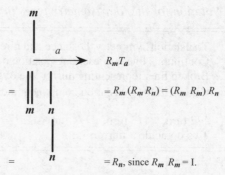

$$R_m T_a$$

$$= R_m (R_m R_n) = (R_m \, R_m) \, R_n$$

$$= R_n, \text{ since } R_m \, R_m = \text{I}.$$

Figure 2.4 Computing the result of reflection followed by translation. The argument is represented geometrically on the left and algebraically on the right.

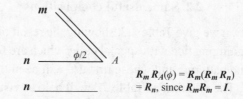

$$R_m \, R_A(\phi) = R_m(R_m \, R_n)$$
$$= R_n, \text{ since } R_m R_m = \boldsymbol{I}.$$

Figure 2.5 Rotation plus reflection computed (geometry on the left, algebra on the right).

Theorem 2.1(b). It will be used soon to investigate the group of all symmetries of the regular *n*-gon, in Section 2.4, the dihedral group. Now, if the rotation is $R_A(\phi)$ then the argument for Example 2.4 can be put simply in terms of geometry (Figure 2.5, left) or in terms of algebra (Figure 2.5, right), after the pattern of Example 2.3.

Example 2.5 *Rotation × translation = rotation (same angle). This adds to the composition statement (1.14) the fact that the result of composing translation with a rotation is a rotation through the* same *angle. In Exercise 3 the reader is asked to establish this by the methods of Examples 2.3 to 2.7. The argument will of course be a slight generalisation of what we give below for an important special case.*

> *1/2 turn × translation*
> *= 1/2 turn at half translation distance away from the original.*   (2.3)

Proof of (2.3) As before, the left side of Figure 2.6 is both a geometric proof and an illustration of the result, using results (2.1) and (2.2).

Note Analogously to Example 2.3, by repeatedly following the latest 1/2 turn with the translation we get a line of 1/2 turns at intervals of one half the translation distance, thus:

$$0 \quad 0 \quad 0 \quad 0 \dots$$

We emphasise that the composition of translation with *any* rotation is a rotation about some point, through the same angle, as the reader is invited to prove below.

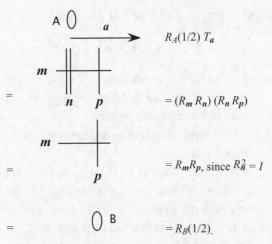

Figure 2.6 Calculating 1/2 turn × translation.

Exercise Use the methods above: (a) to establish the general case of Example 2.5, (b) to show that the product of two 1/2 turns is a translation through twice the distance between them.

Application *Symmetries of a braid pattern* We recall from Section 1.1 that a *symmetry* of a figure F is an isometry which sends every subfigure of F into a congruent subfigure (i.e. one of the same size and shape). It is important to appreciate that

$$\textit{any composition of symmetries of a figure}$$
$$\textit{is also a symmetry of the figure.} \tag{2.4}$$

The reason is simply that such a composition, being the result of performing one symmetry, then the other, also satisfies the above criteria for being itself a symmetry. Figure 2.7(a) is *a braid pattern*. That is, a pattern F with a translation symmetry T_a

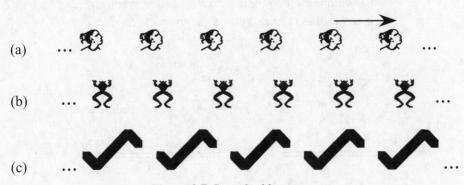

Figure 2.7 Some braid patterns.

such that the translation symmetries of F are all the repetitions, i.e. powers,

$$T_a^n = T_{na},\tag{2.5}$$

where n is a positive or negative integer. Indeed, F actually consists of the translates $T_{na}(M)\,(n = 0, \pm1, \pm2, \ldots)$ of a basic motif M, for example the woman's head in Figure 2.7(a). There we have also indicated the translation vector $\boldsymbol{a}$ (it could equally well be taken as $-\boldsymbol{a}$) (see (3.1)). By implication, F extends infinitely to the left and right of the representative part we have drawn.

The above remarks hold true for Figure 2.7(b), but with basic motif 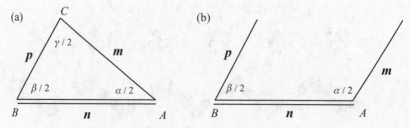, which has a reflection symmetry R_m. Clearly, whichever copy of the frog we choose as basic motif, R_m is a symmetry of the whole pattern. Since any composition of symmetries is a symmetry, Example 2.3 tells us that there are also reflection symmetries R_n with $\boldsymbol{n}$ midway between every two successive copies of the frog. Here, this conclusion is also easily reached by inspection, but some of its 2-dimensional relatives are rather less obvious. Theorem 2.12 expresses such symmetries in terms of a small number of 'basic' ones.

In Figure 2.7(c) the basic motif has a 1/2 turn symmetry and so, by the note below (2.3), there are 1/2 turn symmetries with centres spaced at a half the repetition distance of the basic motif. Thus the symmetries include 1/2 turns halfway between successive copies of the motif. In more complicated examples these 'extra' 1/2 turns are harder to spot visually, especially if we don't know that they must be there (see Figure 2.11 later in the chapter). It was convenient to introduce braid patterns here because they give rise to some nice but not too hard applications of our theory and techniques so far. Their classification is completed in Chapter 3, the shortest chapter of the book.

Example 2.6 Composing rotations: Euler's construction *Since a rotation is a direct isometry, the product of two rotations is also direct, so, of the four types, it must be a translation or rotation (Theorem 1.18). Euler's construction is to draw the lines $\boldsymbol{m}$, $\boldsymbol{n}$, $\boldsymbol{p}$ as in Figure 2.8 (a) or (b) and so determine the new rotation centre and angle, or direction and distance of the translation. Here is the result.*

> *The plane is turned through the sum of the component rotation angles, and we have a translation precisely when this sum is a multiple of the complete turn 2π.* (2.6)

Figure 2.8 Euler's construction for the composition of two rotations.

Proof in Case (a)

$$
\begin{aligned}
R_A(\alpha)R_B(\beta) &= (R_m R_n)(R_n R_p) \\
&= R_m R_p, && \text{since } R_n^2 = I \\
&= R_C(-\gamma) \\
&= R_C(\alpha + \beta), && \text{since } \alpha + \beta = 2\pi - \gamma.
\end{aligned}
$$

Exercise Use Euler's construction in the triangle of Figure 2.8 made equilateral to show the following, and find such implied 3-fold centres in Figure 1.1.

> *The existence of 1/3 turn symmetries of a figure, at two vertices of an*
> *equilateral triangle, implies the same symmetry at the third vertex.* (2.7)

Example 2.7 The product of glides and reflections

> *The product of two glides, or of reflection and glide,*
> *is a rotation through twice the angle between their lines*
> *– **unless** the lines are parallel, when the result is a translation.* (2.8)

Proof of (2.8) A reflection is a glide with zero translation part, so we need only consider the product of two glides. Suppose first that the mirrors are not parallel, but intersect at angle ϕ. Then since we may switch the translation and reflection parts of a glide, and combine reflection with rotations (Theorem 2.1), the two glides may be combined as

$$
(T_a R_m)(T_b R_n) = T_a(R_m R_n)T_b = T_a R_A(2\phi)T_b.
$$

But, by Example 2.5, rotation combined with translation is a rotation through the same angle, so the result follows. In the parallel case $R_A(2\phi)$ is replaced by a translation (Theorem 2.1), so the result is a translation. Figure 2.9 shows the specifics when the mirror lines cross at right angles, in the notation of Table 2.1. Case (i) is part of Theorem 2.1.

Proof of (iii) We compute the product of glides $h = T_a R_m$, $g = T_b R_p$, as indicated in Figure 2.10. This can also be established as $R_A(1/2)$ by verifying that hg fixes the point A and sends the intersection of mirrors p and n to the same point as does $R_A(1/2)$. This is sufficient, by Theorem 1.10, since the product of two glides must be direct.

Example 2.8 *The symmetries of the plane pattern in Figure 2.11 include horizontal glides in the positions indicated by dotted lines thus '......', and vertical glide lines*

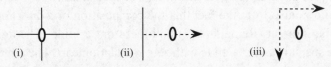

Figure 2.9 The right angle crossing of symmetry and glide lines of a pattern implies the presence of 2-fold centres as shown (cf. Table 2.1). We may think of each glide as pulling the 2-fold centre a 1/2 translation distance from the crossing.

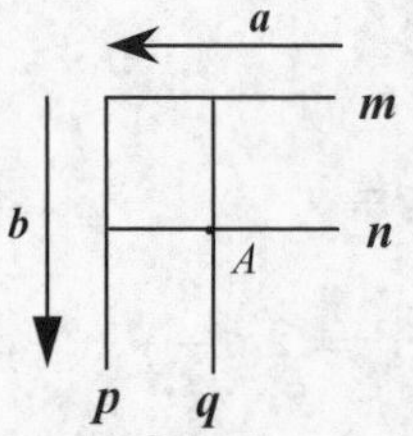

$$
\begin{aligned}
& (T_a R_m)\,(T_b R_p) \\
= \quad & (R_q R_p R_m)\,(R_m R_n R_p) && \text{(Theorem 2.1)} \\
= \quad & R_q R_p\ R_n R_p && \text{since } R_m^2 = I \\
= \quad & R_q R_p\ R_p R_n && \text{since } p \perp n \\
= \quad & R_q R_n && \text{since } R_p^2 = I \\
= \quad & R_A(1/2) && \text{(Theorem 2.1).}
\end{aligned}
$$

Figure 2.10 Proof of the assertion in Figure 2.9 (iii); $p \perp n$ means 'p, n perpendicular'.

Figure 2.11 A plane pattern with perpendicular glide lines. Finding the vertical ones is part of the next exercise.

too. The three emphasised points show successive images of one such glide (which?), illustrating that a glide performed twice gives a translation.

Exercise (a) Follow the successive images of a white subfigure under repetitions of a glide, noting that a horizontal glide must map horizontal lines to horizontal lines (suitable observations of this kind can greatly facilitate analysis of a pattern). (b) Find the *vertical* glide symmetries of the pattern represented, and verify that each small 'box' bounded by horizontal and vertical glide lines has a 2-fold centre of symmetry at its centre, as predicted in Figure 2.9(iii).

We conclude this section with Table 2.2, showing all possible compositions of isometry types, derived from Theorem 2.1 (and Corollary 2.2), the composition and decomposition theorems. Examples 2.5 to 2.7 contain derivations or special cases for the rows indicated. The last row follows also from the fact that the composition of a direct and an indirect isometry must be indirect (Remark 1.17) and therefore a glide (Theorem 1.18), with reflection as the special case of a glide with zero translation part. The table is unaffected by changing orders of composition.

Exercise Verify line (c) of Table 2.2.

Table 2.2. *How isometry types combine.*

Every line is a consequence of Theorem 2.1. Rows (a) and (b) come from Examples 2.5 to 2.7, whilst Examples 2.3 and 2.4 supply important special cases in row (c). The table is unaffected by changing orders of composition. It justifies the idea of the *point group* in Chapter 6, a key step in the classification of plane patterns into 17 types.

Isometries combined		Type of the product	
(a) Direct	Direct	Rotation[a]	
Rotation ϕ	Translation	Rotation ϕ	(Example 2.5)
Rotation α	Rotation β	Rotation $\alpha + \beta$	(Example 2.6)
(b) Indirect	Indirect	Rotation[a]	
Reflection/glide	Reflection/glide at angle ϕ	Rotation 2ϕ	(Example 2.7)
(c) Indirect	Direct	Glide[b]	
Reflection/glide	Translation	line parallel to original	
Reflection/glide	Rotation α	line at $\alpha/2$ to original	

[a] *Translation*, if this angle is a whole number of turns.
[b] *Pure reflection* in Examples 2.3 and 2.4.

2.3 The image of a line of symmetry

Notation 2.9 Let F be some figure in the plane. By definition, a line $\boldsymbol{m}$ is *a line of symmetry* of F if R_m is a symmetry of F, that is if R_m maps F onto itself; a point A is an *n-fold centre* (of symmetry) if $R_A(1/n)$ is a symmetry of F. We normally take n to be the largest possible. For example, the centre of a regular square is thought of as a 4-fold centre and only in a secondary sense as 2-fold. Sometimes 2-, 3-, ... 6-fold centres are called *dyad, triad, tetrad, pentad, hexad* respectively.

A typical consequence of the main result of this section, Theorem 2.12, is that if A is an *n*-fold centre then so is the image of A under any translation symmetry T_v of F. Thus we get at least a whole line of *n*-fold centres $\{T_{mv}(A): m = 1, 2, 3, \ldots\}$ at a translation distance $|a|$ apart. (A stronger result holds for lines of symmetry perpendicular to the translations, one gets them at $|a|/2$ apart: see Example 2.3.) All four parts of Theorem 2.12 follow from one basic fact which implies that an isometry sends lines of symmetry to lines of symmetry, proved as Lemma 2.10. For this, we need the idea of an inverse isometry.

Inverse isometries The list of isometry types in Theorem 1.18 shows that every isometry g is a *bijection*. That is, g transforms distinct points to distinct points and every point is the transform of *some* point. Thus every isometry g has a unique *inverse transformation* g^{-1}, sending P^g back to the point P. See Figure 2.12.

The inverse mapping g^{-1} obviously preserves distances because g does, and so is also an isometry. Also, if g reverses the sense of a triple then g^{-1} undoes the effect, so directness and indirectness are preserved by taking inverses. Further, if g is a symmetry of a figure F then so is g^{-1}. If g fixes a point P then g^{-1} fixes P too because g is bijective. More

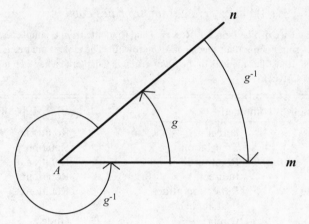

Figure 2.12 A rotation g and its inverse isometry. Here $g = R_A(1/6)$ maps a line $\boldsymbol{m}$ to line $\boldsymbol{n}$, and $g^{-1} = R_A(-1/6) = R_A(5/6)$ maps $\boldsymbol{n}$ back to $\boldsymbol{m}$.

formally, $P = P^{(gg^{-1})} = (P^g)^{g^{-1}} = P^{g^{-1}}$. We observe too that either property, $gf = I$ or $fg = I$, implies that $f = g^{-1}$. It follows from the associative property (1.8) that

$$(gh)^{-1} = h^{-1}g^{-1} \quad (g, \ h \text{ isometries}), \tag{2.9}$$

the argument being: $(h^{-1}g^{-1})(gh) = h^{-1}(g^{-1}g)h = h^{-1}Ih = h^{-1}h = I$. We therefore have the following table of inverse isometries, which may also be deduced directly.

g	R_m	T_a	$R_A(\phi)$	$R_A(1/n)$	$R_m T_a$	
g^{-1}	R_m	T_{-a}	$R_A(-\phi)$	$R_A(1/n)^{n-1}$	$R_m T_{-a}$	(2.10)

Proof of (2.10) We will verify the last two columns of the table. Firstly, $R_A(1/n) \cdot R_A(1/n)^{n-1} = R_A(1/n)^n = I$ (see (1.11)), hence the inverse of $R_A(1/n)$ is $R_A(1/n)^{n-1}$. For the glide we have $(R_m T_a)(T_{-a} R_m) = R_m(T_a T_{-a})R_m = R_m I R_m = R_m R_m = I$.

Conjugates Here is a widely used piece of notation which we shall immediately require for Lemma 2.11. It will appear at intervals throughout the whole book. We recall that $\boldsymbol{m}^g$ denotes the image of a line $\boldsymbol{m}$ under an isometry g. A suggestively similar notation R^g is used for the *conjugate of an isometry* R by an isometry g, defined as the composition

$$R^g \equiv g^{-1}Rg. \tag{2.11}$$

As we recall from (2.4), the composition of two (hence any number of) symmetries of a figure is also a symmetry, so if R, g are symmetries then so is R^g. We now show that, if S is a third isometry, then

$$(RS)^g = R^g \cdot S^g. \tag{2.12}$$

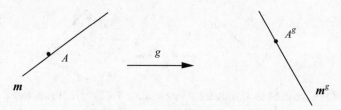

Figure 2.13 The image of a mirror is a mirror.

Proof of (2.12) Starting from the right of (2.12), we have

$$
\begin{aligned}
R^g \cdot S^g &= g^{-1}Rg \cdot g^{-1}Sg && \text{by (2.11)} \\
&= g^{-1}R(g \cdot g^{-1})Sg && \text{by associativity (1.9),} \\
&= g^{-1}RISg \\
&= g^{-1}(RS)g \\
&= (RS)^g, && \text{by (2.11).}
\end{aligned}
$$

Lemma 2.10 *Let g be an isometry, m a line. If R is reflection in m then R^g is reflection in m^g (Figure 2.13).*

Proof Clearly $R^g \equiv g^{-1}Rg$ is an indirect isometry, R being indirect, so it suffices to show that R^g has the same effect as reflection in m^g, on any two points (Theorem 1.10). In fact R^g fixes the point A^g for every point A in m, for

$$
\begin{aligned}
(A^g)^{g^{-1}Rg} &= A^{gg^{-1}Rg} && \text{by (1.8)} \\
&= A^{Rg} && \text{since } gg^{-1} = I \\
&= (A^R)^g && \text{by (1.8)} \\
&= A^g && \text{since } R \text{ fixes } A \text{ (} A \text{ being in } m \text{).}
\end{aligned}
$$

This proves Lemma 2.10.

Definition 2.11 Let $a = \underline{AB}$ and g be an isometry. Then $a^g = (\underline{AB})^g$.

This means that the new vector a^g is represented in magnitude and direction by the image under g of any directed line segment which represents a. The significance of this appears in the proof of Theorem 2.12(c) below, where it is shown that, in terms of the expression (2.11) for a conjugate,

$$
(T_a)^g = T_b, \quad \text{where} \quad b = a^g. \tag{2.13}
$$

Theorem 2.12 *Any symmetry g of a figure F maps as follows:*
(a) lines of symmetry to lines of symmetry,
(b) n-fold centres to n-fold centres,
(c) the direction of one translation symmetry to the direction of another of the same magnitude (Figure 2.15),
(d) glidelines to glidelines with same translation magnitude.
In each case, if R is the old symmetry then the conjugate $R^g (= g^{-1}Rg)$ is the new.

Figure 2.14 An isometry g maps one n-fold centre to another.

Proof Let g be a symmetry of the figure F. To prove (a), suppose that $\boldsymbol{m}$ in Figure 2.14 is a line of symmetry of F. Then $R = R_{\boldsymbol{m}}$ is a symmetry, hence so is $R^g \equiv g^{-1}Rg$. But by Lemma 2.10 this symmetry is the operation of reflection in the image $\boldsymbol{m}^g$ of $\boldsymbol{m}$ under g, i.e. $\boldsymbol{m}^g$ is a line of symmetry of F.

(b) Let A be an n-fold centre of symmetry of F. We wish to prove that A^g is an n-fold centre. That is, $R_{A^g}(1/n)$ is a symmetry of F. The key observation is that, by Corollary 2.2, we can decompose the symmetry $R_A(1/n)$ as $R_{\boldsymbol{m}}R_{\boldsymbol{n}}$, where m, n are lines intersecting in A at angle π/n. This is illustrated in Figure 2.14. Since g and $R_A(1/n)$ are symmetries of F, so is the composition

$$
\begin{aligned}
g^{-1}R_A(1/n)g &= g^{-1}(R_{\boldsymbol{m}}R_{\boldsymbol{n}})g \\
&= (R_{\boldsymbol{m}}R_{\boldsymbol{n}})^g && \text{by (2.11)} \\
&= (R_{\boldsymbol{m}})^g(R_{\boldsymbol{n}})^g && \text{by (2.12)} \\
&= R_{\boldsymbol{m}^g}R_{\boldsymbol{n}^g} && \text{by Lemma 2.10,}
\end{aligned}
$$

where the last expression equals $R_{A^g}(1/n)$ or $R_{A^g}(-1/n)$, according as g is direct or not, since the angle between $\boldsymbol{m}^g$ and $\boldsymbol{n}^g$ is the same in magnitude as that between $\boldsymbol{m}$ and $\boldsymbol{n}$ (see (1.5)). In the indirect case of g it still follows that $R_{A^g}(1/n)$ is a symmetry, being the inverse of $R_{A^g}(-1/n)$.

(c) This time we use Corollary 2.2 to write any translation $T_{\boldsymbol{a}}$ as a product of reflections $R_{\boldsymbol{m}}R_{\boldsymbol{n}}$ in parallel mirrors, as in Figure 2.15.

Then, arguing as in (b), we obtain $g^{-1}T_{\boldsymbol{a}}g = R_{\boldsymbol{m}^g}R_{\boldsymbol{n}^g}$. Since $\boldsymbol{m}$ and $\boldsymbol{n}$ are parallel and at a distance $|\boldsymbol{a}|/2$, the same holds for $\boldsymbol{m}^g$ and $\boldsymbol{n}^g$. Therefore the new isometry is a translation through distance $|\boldsymbol{a}|$ at right angles to $\boldsymbol{m}^g$ and $\boldsymbol{n}^g$, as indicated in Figure 2.15. The change in direction is found by applying g to a representative directed line segment AB for $\boldsymbol{a}$. With Figure 2.15, this justifies (2.13): $(T_{\boldsymbol{a}})^g = T_{\boldsymbol{b}}$, where $\boldsymbol{b} = \boldsymbol{a}^g$.

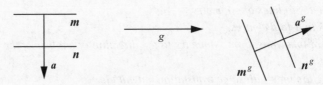

Figure 2.15 An isometry g maps translation vector $\boldsymbol{a}$ to $\boldsymbol{a}^g$.

Figure 2.16 A plane pattern and, side by side with it, a representation of where its 1/2 and 1/4 turn symmetries are located. The points A correspond. The notation is found in Table 2.1.

(d) Let m be a glide line and $R_m T_a$ the corresponding glide symmetry. Since g is an isometry, so is

$$(R_m T_a)^g = (R_m)^g (T_a)^g \qquad \text{by (2.12)},$$
$$= (R_m)^g T_b, \qquad \text{where } b = a^g, \qquad \text{by Part (c)}.$$

Here the new translation vector a^g is parallel to m^g, and of the same magnitude as a, so m^g is indeed a glide line, as claimed. The proof is complete.

Example 2.13 *The first part of Figure 2.16 represents a finite portion of a plane pattern, whose translation symmetries include two of equal length but at right angles. We see also points of 4-fold rotational symmetry, such as the one marked 'A'. By its side we represent the same area but this time we indicate (in the notation of Table 2.1) all the centres of rotational symmetry. They are either 2-fold or 4-fold.*

It is useful to know, and a nice application of results so far, to show that

> the presence of all the rotational symmetries in Figure 2.16 is implied by the
> translations, together with a single 1/4 turn at the point A. (2.14)

We consider three stages.

(i) The images of A under translation must be 4-fold centres, by the key Theorem 2.12, accounting for about a half of those shown, and forming the vertices of a division of the plane into squares.

(ii) By Euler's construction (Example 2.6) 1/4 turns at the vertices of a square imply 1/4 turns at the centre (see Exercise 2.2 at the chapter's end), and hence the presence of a second lattice of 4-fold centres.

(iii) There are points which are *not* 4-fold centres but *are* 2-fold centres, and this may be seen as follows. The 1/2 turn about A is a symmetry, since it equals the square of a 1/4 turn, and by (2.3) it combines with a translation to form a 1/2 turn about a further point which is not a 4-fold centre. This accounts for the 2-fold centres.

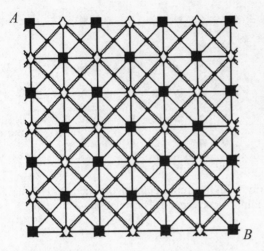

Figure 2.17 All the symmetries of the pattern of Figure 2.16. Here the glidelines are shown thickened for emphasis (cf. Table 2.1).

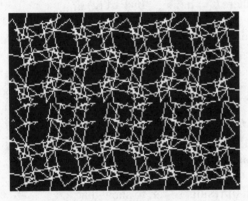

Figure 2.18 (by Mary Small)

The remaining symmetries There are many more symmetries of Figure 2.16, both reflections and glides, and the presence of all of them may be predicted once we observe that *AB* is a line of symmetry. They are shown in Figure 2.17. Many lines of symmetry are obvious, but finding them all *by inspection of the pattern* is harder in this case. The theory does aid our intuition.

The (thickened) glidelines divide the plane into squares, and the side of a square gives the magnitude of every glide's translation part.

Exercise Satisfy yourself that each symmetry portrayed in Figure 2.17 maps symmetry elements like to like. That is, *n*-fold centres to *n*-fold centres, and so on.

Exercise Find examples of mirrors, glidelines, and $1/n$ turn symmetries in the (plane-filling) pattern of Figure 2.18 (made, incidentally, from repetitions of the letter 'M').

Exercise Draw a diagram showing all the symmetries of the pattern in Figure 2.19, with translation symmetries T_u, T_v in two independent directions. Verify that these translations map lines of symmetry to other lines of symmetry, dyad centres to dyad centres, and glidelines to glidelines.

2.4 The dihedral group

This section leads to a more general look at groups in the next one. For now, we simply observe that the collection G of all symmetries of a figure F, with the usual law of composition (*gh* means 'do *g* then *h*'), satisfies

(i) the composition of any two symmetries of F is a third;

(ii) if f, g, h are symmetries of F then $f(gh) = (fg)h$;

(iii) there is a symmetry I (do nothing) of F such that $gI = g = Ig$ for every symmetry g of F;

(iv) for every symmetry g of F there is a unique symmetry g^{-1} (the *inverse* of g) with $gg^{-1} = I = g^{-1}g$.

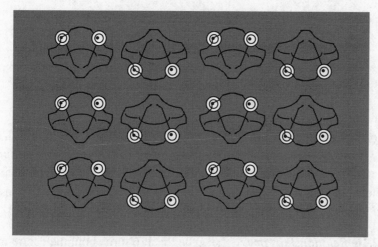

Figure 2.19 Imitation Escher. The symmetries include reflection, glides and 1/2 turns.

This means that G satisfies the requirements to be a *group* (see Section 2.5) and so is called the *symmetry group*, or *group of symmetries*, of F. Much that is useful flows from this, not least that we can now classify patterns by their symmetry groups. We begin not with plane or even 1-dimensional patterns, but with the regular n-gon, since its symmetry group provides building blocks for classifying more general patterns (as we shall see especially in Section 6.2).

Definition 2.14 The *dihedral group* D_{2n} $(n \geq 2)$ is the symmetry group of a regular n-gon. The regular 2-gon is thought of as a special case, with 'curved' sides:

Example 2.15 It is easy to see from Figure 2.20 that D_{10}, the symmetry group of a regular pentagon, consists of:

five reflection – one in each line of symmetry,
five rotations – the identity I, 1/5 turn, . . . , 4/5 turn about the centre,
total = 10.

There is a slight difference for polygons with an even number of edges, exemplified above by the square, whose lines of symmetry join *either* opposite vertices *or* mid-points

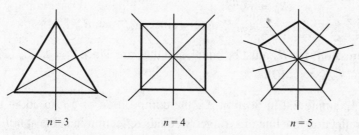

$n = 3$ $n = 4$ $n = 5$

Figure 2.20 Lines of symmetry of some regular n-gons.

of opposite edges. However, we can see that in all cases

> D_{2n} *consists of reflections in n equally spaced lines*
> *of symmetry through the centre C, and n rotations*
> $I, \tau, \tau^2, \ldots, \tau^{n-1}$, *where* $\tau = R_C(1/n)$, *and* $\tau^n = I$.
> *In particular,* D_{2n} *has exactly 2n elements.*   (2.15)

The rotation subgroup   Since the product of two rotations about C is a third, the collection $C_n = I, \tau, \tau^2, \ldots, \tau^{n-1}$ of all rotations forms itself a group, the *rotation subgroup* of D_{2n}. It is *cyclic of order n*, meaning that the elements of C_n consist of the powers of a single element, and the size of the group is n. The name C_n is given to groups with this structure in widely varying contexts. See e.g. Birkhoff and MacLane (1963).

Example 2.16 *Relationships in* D_{12} Let τ be the $1/6$ turn about the centre of a regular hexagon, as in Figure 2.21, with symmetry lines $s, m, n, \ldots, r$. We give two points of view, each useful for its insights.

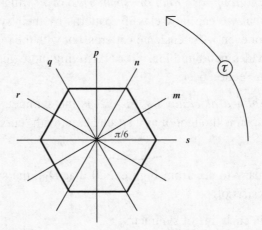

Figure 2.21 Symmetries of a regular hexagon (6-gon).

View 1 τ maps s to n, so $R_n = R_s^\tau (= \tau^{-1} R_s \tau)$, by Theorem 2.12. But R_m also maps s to n, so

$$R_n = R_s{}^{R_m},$$
$$= R_m R_s R_m, \quad \text{since } R_m{}^{-1} = R_m.$$

The two expressions for R_n must be equal, and they are, since $\tau = R_s R_m$ (Theorem 2.1) and $\tau^{-1} = R_m R_s$ (see (2.9)).

View 2   By Example 2.4 in Section 2.2 the composition of a turn about the hexagon centre with reflection in a line of symmetry equals reflection in a line at *half the rotation angle* to the original line. So taking the various powers of τ we obtain, with reference to Figure 2.21:

$$R_s \tau = R_m,$$
$$R_s \tau^2 = R_n,$$
$$\ldots$$
$$R_s \tau^5 = R_r.$$

Definition 2.17 We say a symmetry group G is *generated by* a subset $g_1, g_2, \ldots, g_s$ if every element g of G is expressible as a product of certain g_i (with or without repetition or powers greater than one). That is, g is a *word* in the g_i. We express this by writing $G = \text{Gp}\{g_1, g_2, \ldots, g_s\}$. An *odd* (*even*) word will mean one whose length is odd (even). Correspondingly, we say a word has even or odd *parity*. (The definitions of odd and even are the same for any group.)

Theorem 2.18 *Let R, S be reflections in any two adjacent lines of symmetry of an* n*-gon, and τ the $1/n$ turn about the centre. Then*

(a) *D_{2n} consists of n rotations: $I, \tau, \tau^2, \ldots, \tau^{n-1}$, and n reflections, which may be written $R, R\tau, R\tau^2, \ldots, R\tau^{n-1}$,*
(b) *We have $D_{2n} = \langle R, S: R^2 = S^2 = (RS)^n = I \rangle$, the notation $\langle \ldots \rangle$ meaning that D_{2n} is generated by R, S subject only to the given relations and their consequences. Moreover, however they are expressed, a reflection symmetry is an odd word and a rotation is an even word in R, S.*

Proof Part (a) is (2.15) with View 2 applied to general D_{2n}. For (b) we first substitute $\tau = RS$. Then clearly $R^2 = S^2 = I$ and $(RS)^n = \tau^n = I$ (see (1.11)), so the given relations do hold. But any relation *independent of these* would imply equalites amongst the $2n$ distinct elements we have enumerated, a contradiction. Concerning parity, any expression for a rotation (reflection) as a word in R, S must be even (odd) by Remark 1.17, because a rotation isometry is direct and a reflection indirect.

Exercises for Section 2.4 The symmetry groups of Figure 2.22 are all cyclic or dihedral. Name them. Answers are given near the end of the following section.

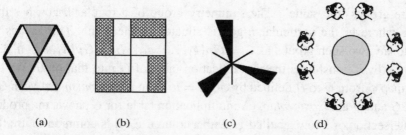

(a)   (b)   (c)   (d)

Figure 2.22 Figures with cyclic or dihedral symmetry groups.

2.5 Appendix on groups

Definition 2.19 A set G is a group with respect to a composition rule $g, h \to gh$ if the following axioms hold.

(A) [Associativity] $f(gh) = (fg)h$ for all f, g, h in G.
(B) [Identity] G contains an *identity element*, that is, an element I, such that for every g in G we have $Ig = g = gI$.
(C) [Inverses] every element g in G has an *inverse*. That is, a corresponding element g^{-1} exists in G such that $gg^{-1} = I = g^{-1}g$.

Theorem 2.20 *The set of all symmetries of a figure F forms a group under composition.*

For a proof, see the beginning of Section 2.4. The following theorem is often useful for finding an identity or inverse.

Theorem 2.21 *Let J be an element of a group G.*

(i) The identity of G is unique, and if $\mathbf{g}J = \mathbf{g}$ or $J\mathbf{g} = \mathbf{g}$ for some g in G, then J is that identity.
(ii) The inverse of an element is unique, and if $\mathbf{gh} = \mathbf{I}$ for some pair g, h in G, then g and h are inverses of each other.

Proof (i) Let J, K be identities in G. Then J equals JK as K is an identity, which equals K because J is an identity. Thus the identity is unique, and now we have the following chain of implications for any inverse g^{-1} of $g : gJ = J \Rightarrow g^{-1}gJ = g^{-1}g \Rightarrow J = I$. The other proofs are in the same spirit but require more work. They may be found in Birkhoff and MacLane (1963).

Definition 2.22 The order of an element g of a group is the least positive integer r such that $g^r = I$; if no such r exists we say g has *infinite order*.

Examples 2.23 A reflection has order 2, a $1/n$ turn has order n, but a translation has infinite order. In D_{12}, with $t = 1/6$ turn, the element t has order 6, and τ^3 has order 2, whilst

$$\text{order of } \tau^4 = \text{least } r \text{ such that } \tau^{4r} \text{ is a whole number of turns}$$
$$= \text{least } r \text{ such that } 6|4r \text{ ('6 is a factor of } 4r\text{')}$$
$$= 3.$$

When are groups 'the same'? The symmetry group of a regular n-gon has the same structure wherever the particular n-gon is situated in the plane. This means that we can write any two such groups as $G = Gp\{g_1, \ldots, g_m\}$, $H = Gp\{h_1, \ldots, h_m\}$, so that replacing g by h transforms the multiplication table of G into that of H. We then say that the map ϕ from G to H defined by $\phi(g_i) = h_i$ is an *isomorphism* between G and H, and that G and H are *isomorphic*. (A multiplication table for G shows the product $g_r g_s$ at the intersection of a row labelled g_r with a column g_s. It is common to use the word 'multiplication' where, as here, we write a composition in the notation associated with

	I	R		I	τ
I	I	R	I	I	τ
R	R	I	τ	τ	I

Figure 2.23 Multiplication tables of isomorphic but not equivalent symmetry groups $G = \{I, R\}$ and $H = \{I, \tau\}$, where $R^2 = I = \tau^2$.

multiplication and call it also a product.) But an isomorphism alone does not satisfy us in the present context of symmetries. For example, if R is a reflection and τ is a 1/2 turn, then the groups $G = \{I, R\}$ and $H = \{I, \tau\}$ are isomorphic, with $\phi(I) = I, \phi(R) = \tau$. Their multiplication tables are shown in Figure 2.23.

But we don't want to regard these two as essentially the same. A satisfactory tactic is to impose the additional restriction that ϕ must pair like with like: reflections with reflections, m/n turns with m/n turns, glides with glides, and translations with translations (not necessarily with the same direction or distance). If ϕ satisfies this, we call ϕ an *equivalence*, and say G and H are *equivalent* or 'the same'. In particular, the isometry groups of all regular n-gons, for a fixed n, are not only isomorphic but equivalent, and we call any one (an instance of) the dihedral group D_{2n}. Equivalence will be the basis of our classification of plane patterns into 17 types. (See Chapter 5 and Sections 6.1 to 6.2 for more details.)

Answers for Section 2.4: D_6, C_4, C_3, D_8.

Exercise In D_{14}, what are the orders of each of $\tau, \tau^2, \ldots, \tau^7$?

Exercise Write out the multiplication tables of C_4 and D_4.

Exercises 2

1 Use Euler's construction to show that some combination of 1/4 turns at the vertices of a square is a 1/4 turn about the centre, or show that this result can be obtained from a 1/4 turn at a vertex and a vertex to vertex translation.

2√ Show that the existence of 1/3 turn symmetries at two vertices of an equilateral triangle implies the existence of 1/3 turn symmetries about the third vertex and that a further symmetry translating one vertex to another implies a 1/3 turn symmetry about the triangle centre.

3 Show that the composition of a rotation through angle ϕ, with a translation, is rotation about some point, through the same angle ϕ (use decomposition into reflections).

4 Verify that the product of a reflection in line m, followed by a glide at right angles to m, is that given in Figure 2.9(ii). (Express the glide as a product of reflections.)

5√ What kind of isometry can be the result of three reflections? Of four?

6 (a) For the pattern of Figure 2.18, draw a diagram showing all 2- and 4-fold centres of symmetry.

(b) Find a glideline, and verify that the corresponding glide g sends n-fold centres to n-fold centres for $n = 2, 4$.

(c) Choose a 1/4 turn symmetry and verify that successive applications of it map the above glideline into successive glidelines.

7   Indicate in a diagram the reflection, glide and $1/n$ turn symmetries of Figure 2.19. Choose a symmetry and satisfy yourself that it sends mirrors to mirrors, glidelines to glidelines, and n-fold centres to n-fold centres.

8 ✓ Let A be a point and g be the isometry $R_A(2/7)$. Express in the form g^n (for smallest positive integer n) the isometries $g^2, g^{-1}g^5$.

9 ✓ Show that, if $(R_m R_n)^2 = I$, for lines m, n, then $(R_n R_m)^2 = I$. Do this first by algebra, using the fact that a reflection has order 2, then by geometry, considering turns. How do you know that m and n are not parallel?

10 ✓ What is the inverse of an isometry of the form $R_m R_n R_p$, where m, n, p are mirror lines?

11   Indicate in suitable diagrams the lines of symmetry of (a) a regular pentagon, (b) a regular octagon. What is the rotation subgroup C_n of the symmetry group in each case?

12   Let R, S be the reflections in successive lines of symmetry round a regular hexagon. Write each element of the dihedral group as a word in R, S. Determine the order of each element.

13   Construct multiplication tables for the dihedral groups D_4 and D_6.

14 ✓ What are the symmetry groups of (a) to (c) in Figure 2.24?

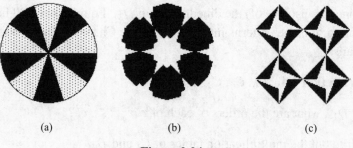

(a)   (b)   (c)

Figure 2.24

15 ✓ Prove that, in any group, the order of an element g equals the order of its inverse, g^{-1}. Verify this for the group D_{14}. Show that the groups C_{14} and D_{14} cannot be isomorphic.

3

The seven braid patterns

In Chapters 1 and 2 we have classified plane isometries, discovered some important principles of how they combine, and made a first application to patterns whose symmetry group is either the dihedral group D_{2n} or its rotation subgroup C_n. Before investigating plane patterns it is a logical and useful step to classify the 1-dimensional, or braid, patterns, be aware of their symmetries, and get a little practice in both recognizing and creating them.

Definition 3.1 We say v is a *translation vector* of pattern F if T_v is a translation symmetry. Then a *braid (band, frieze)* pattern is a pattern in the plane, all of whose translation vectors are parallel. In particular, a and $-a$ are parallel. We will usually call this parallel direction *horizontal*, and the perpendicular direction *vertical*. Other names used are *longitudinal* and *transverse*, respectively. A symmetry group of a braid is sometimes called a *line group*.

As noted in Section 1.1, we are investigating patterns which are *discrete*: they do not have translation or other symmetries which move the pattern by arbitrarily small amounts. Thus, amongst the collection of all translation symmetries of the pattern there is a translation T_a of least but not zero magnitude. Of course it is not unique, for example T_{-a} has the same magnitude $|a|$ as T_a. We rephrase an observation from the preliminary discussion of braids preceding Figure 2.7. It may be derived more formally from Theorem 3.3.

> *A braid pattern F consists of a finite motif M repeated
> along a line at regular intervals $|u|$, where u is a
> translation vector of F of least magnitude.* (3.1)

Note on glides If a figure F has translation vectors a parallel to lines of symmetry m, then every composition $g = R_m T_a$ is both a glide and a symmetry of F. However, we do not wish to emphasise this. In fact it is customary to restrict mention of 'glide-lines' and 'glide symmetries' to the case in which neither R_m nor T_a alone is a symmetry of F even though their composition *is* a symmetry of this figure. We note that $g^2 = T_{2a}$, and therefore *twice* the translation part of a glide symmetry *must* be a translation vector of the figure. Hence the following convention.

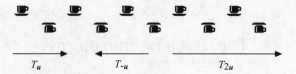

$$T_u \qquad\qquad T_{-u} \qquad\qquad T_{2u}$$

Figure 3.1 Braid pattern with least translations T_u, T_{-u}.

Convention 3.2 A *glide symmetry* or *glideline* of a figure F will normally refer to a composition $R_m T_{a/2}$, where a is a translation vector of F parallel to m, of *minimum possible length*.

Theorem 3.3 *The symmetries of a braid pattern F*

(a) The translation symmetries of F are the iterates T_{nu} of a translation symmetry T_u of least possible magnitude $|u|$, where $n = 0, \pm1, \pm2, \dots$

(b) The only possible $1/n$ rotation symmetries of F are the identity ($n = 1$), and $1/2$ turns ($n = 2$).

(c) Any line of symmetry of F is either horizontal or vertical.

(d) A glideline of F must be horizontal.

Proof (a) Let T_u have least possible magnitude among the translation symmetries of F. Suppose v is a translation vector. Then by repeated subtraction or addition of u we obtain $v = nu + w$ for some positive or negative integer n, where the vector w satisfies $0 \le |w| < |u|$. Hence another translation vector is $v - nu = w$. Since $|u|$ is least possible and $0 \le |w| < |u|$, we must have $w = 0$, so v has the form nu as asserted.

(b) Let v be a translation vector. If some $1/n$ turn is a symmetry then (by Theorem 2.12(c)) so is the translation of magnitude $|v|$ in the direction of a $1/n$ turn of v. But the only translations of magnitude $|v|$ are $\pm v$, so n equals 1 or 2.

(c) A reflection symmetry in a line which is not parallel or perpendicular to a translation vector v conjugates T_v to give a translation not parallel to v (by Theorem 2.12(c)). But this is impossible, since F is a braid pattern.

(d) If g is a non-horizontal glide symmetry then g^2 is a translation not parallel to the translation vectors of F. As in (c) above, this is not possible.

The classification of braids In fact, everything which is not explicitly forbidden by Theorem 3.1 is possible *except* that the presence of certain combinations of symmetries implies other symmetries. The following observations enable us to complete the classification.

> *A horizontal and a vertical line of symmetry intersect in a 2-fold centre of symmetry.* (3.2)

> *Vertical mirrors are separated by $1/2$ the minimum translation distance.* (3.3)

> *The presence of reflection and glide as in Figure 3.2 (a) implies 2-fold centres of symmetry A at points $1/4$ the minimum translation distance from the mirror, as in Figure 3.2(b).* (3.4)

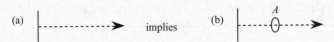

Figure 3.2 How half turn symmetries of a braid pattern arise from reflections and glides.

Exercise Verify assertions (3.2) to (3.4).

Notation 3.4 Each braid pattern type is specified by four symbol $\boxed{r}\,\boxed{n}\,\boxed{x}\,\boxed{y}$ with the following meaning.

$\boxed{r}$ Initial symbol denoting a braid as distinct from plane pattern.

$\boxed{n}$ The highest degree of rotational symmetry in the pattern. That is, n is the largest integer for which the pattern has a $1/n$ turn symmetry.

$\boxed{x}$ m if F has a vertical line of symmetry,
       g if F has a vertical glide line,
       1 if F has neither.

$\boxed{y}$ The same as above, but for horizontal lines. In both cases, the '1' is omitted if it would be the last symbol.

Remark 3.5 The case $x = g$ is ruled out for braids by Theorem 3.3, but the x, y symbols will be used later with similar meanings for plane patterns. Our preparatory work in Theorem 3.3 and (3.1) to (3.4) shows not only that there are seven braid types, but that each has a fixed configuration of symmetries. In Table 3.1 we give a simple example of each type with the symmetries indicated. The notation is that of Table 2.1 (a continuous line is a mirror and a broken one a glide, and so on). To prevent a glut of symbols, the basic translation symmetry is the same for each example, and is given only in the first one.

Note The symmetry configuration is useful for pattern identification.

Constructing braid patterns

The idea is to construct a motif M for translation in accordance with (3.1). To achieve the necessary symmetries in M we can start with a submotif, say ⌐, and append its images under suitable isometries. For example, in the pattern for $r2mm$ in Table 3.1 we reflect in a vertical mirror corresponding to the first 'm', to get ⌐⌐, then reflect in a horizontal mirror, obtaining ✕ as translation motif M. Inspection will show how each example in Table 3.1 was created in this way from the same submotif. For more refined braids, a subtler choice of submotif is required.

Identifying braid patterns We ask

(1) Are there vertical mirrors?
(2) Is there a horizontal mirror or glide line?

Table 3.1. *The seven braid pattern types and their symmetries*

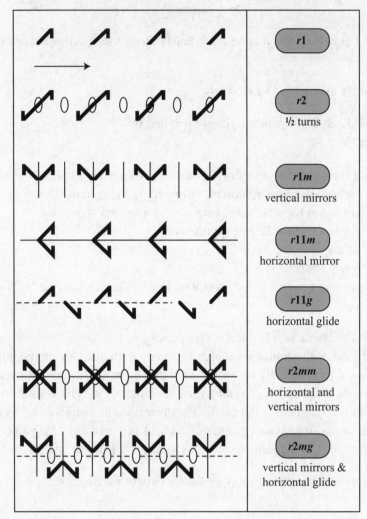

Note that there are 1/2 turn symmetries *if and only if* the answers to both (1) and (2) are affirmative.

Exercises 3

1√ Determine the braid types in Figure 2.7, the first row of Figure 2.19, and Figure 3.1.
2√ Determine the braid types in Figure 3.3. Suggest a motif and submotif in each case.
3 Verify your answers to Exercise 3.2 by predicting the total pattern of symmetries and checking with Table 3.1.
4 Prove statements (3.2) to (3.4).
5 Construct a flow chart for identifying braid types, building on the two suggested questions.

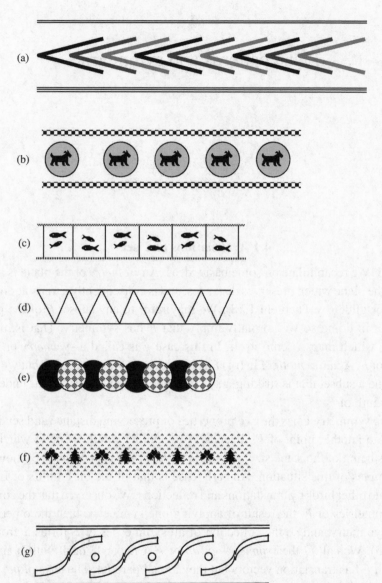

Figure 3.3 Braid patterns (a) to (g) for Exercise 3.2.

6   Write a computer program to produce a braid pattern for which the user specifies the type and a submotif. You may wish to extend this to optional printing of the symmetry pattern in the background.

4

Plane patterns and symmetries

4.1 Translations and nets

Review 4.1 We recapitulate on some basic ideas. An *isometry* of the plane is a transformation of the plane which preserves distances, and is consequently a translation, rotation, reflection or glide (by Theorem 1.18). We may refer to any subset F of the plane as a *pattern*, but in doing so we normally imply that F has symmetry. That is, there is an isometry g which maps F onto itself. In this case g is called a *symmetry* or *symmetry operation* of F. Again, a *motif M* in (of) F is in principle any subset of F, but we generally have in mind a subset that is striking, attractive, and/or significant for our understanding of the structure of F.

Since the symmetry g has the two properties of preserving distance and sending every point of F to another point of F, it sends M to another motif M' of F, which we may describe as being of the same size and shape as M, or *congruent to M*. By now we have many examples of this situation. An early case is that of the bird motifs of Figure 1.2, mapped onto other birds by translations and reflections. We observed that the composition of two symmetries of F, the result of applying one symmetry, then the other, qualifies also as a symmetry, and so the collection of all symmetries of F forms a group G (see Section 2.5). We call G the *symmetry group* of F. Chapter 3 dealt with braid patterns F, in which F has translation vectors but they are all parallel. The term *plane pattern* is reserved for F if there are translation vectors of F (vectors v for which T_v is a symmetry) in two non-parallel directions, and F may be assumed to denote such a pattern from now on.

The discreteness hypothesis As noted from time to time, we are restricting attention to patterns F whose symmetries do not move F continuously, that is by arbitrarily small amounts. Thus there is some least nonzero distance achieved by the translations, and if F has rotation symmetries then they too have a least nonzero magnitude. The same applies to the translation part of any glides, since a glide followed by itself is a translation. By the end of Chapter 6 we will have met at least two patterns corresponding to each possible discrete symmetry group, therefore we note a pattern-independent characterisation of

(a)   (b)

Figure 4.1 (a) Part of a plane pattern, whose translations include T_{ru} for all r, however small. The G-images of a point O centring a circle of any radius include, for example, a diameter of the circle as shown in (b), hence infinitely many points. This infringes (4.1), so the pattern is not discrete.

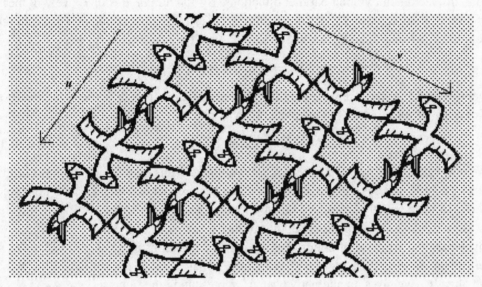

Figure 4.2 Escher-type birds (the pattern extends indefinitely over the plane).

such groups G:

> *for any point O in the plane, a circle of finite size around O*
> *contains only a finite number of G-images of O.*   (4.1)

By *G-images* of the point O we mean the images O^g for all isometries g belonging to G. By Criterion (4.1), a non-discrete example is Figure 4.1(a).

By contrast, we easily see that the plane pattern of Figure 4.2 has the property:

> *The translation vectors of the plane pattern F have a BASIS, that is,*
> *a pair u, v such that any translation vector of F can be uniquely*
> *expressed as $mu + nv$ ($m, n = 0, \pm1, \pm2, \dots$).*   (4.2)

In Theorem 4.6 we give a formal proof that (4.2) holds for all (discrete) plane patterns. Consequently here, as for braid patterns, the whole of F consists of the translations of one part, which we have called the *basic motif M*. A simple choice of M in Figure 4.2 is a square containing exactly four birds (can you suggest a suitable selection?). Later we discuss the options for M.

Definition 4.2 *The translation subgroup* Let T denote the set of all translation symmetries of a plane pattern F, including the identity $I = T_0$. It is easy to verify that T is a group (see Section 2.5), from a relation recalled from (1.12):

$$T_v T_w = T_{v+w}. \tag{4.3}$$

We call T the *translation subgroup* of G and say T is 2-*dimensional* or *plane,* since it contains vectors in two non-parallel directions. By '*the vector v is in T*' we will mean 'the translation T_v is in T', or equivalently 'v is a translation vector of F'. From the definition of scalar times vector in Section 1.2.1 we have for vectors v, w:

$$v, w \text{ are parallel} \Leftrightarrow v = \alpha w \text{ for some nonzero } \alpha. \tag{4.4}$$

Definition 4.3 A *net* N representing the plane translation group T is the *orbit,* or set of T-images, of some point O in the plane. In symbols:

$$N = \{O^g : g \text{ is in } T\} = O^T. \tag{4.5}$$

We may call O the *basepoint or initial point* of the net (this point need not be the origin of x, y coordinates). For Figure 4.2 we obtain a 'square' net of which a part is portrayed below (rotated slightly and scaled down for convenience).

We note that changing the basepoint to any other point of the net gives back the same set of points. Yet the net of translations of a pattern is not unique: choosing a new basepoint A that is not in the net we already have gives an alternative net A^T representing the same set of translations. This freedom facilitates our classifying plane patterns by allowing Convention 4.4 below. We divide them into five classes by net type, then investigate what symmetries are allowed by each type.

Convention 4.4 We choose the basepoint of the net to lie on both

(i) a point of highest rotational symmetry of the pattern, and
(ii) a line of symmetry of the pattern,

where condition (i) takes precedence over (ii) if they are incompatible, and refers to an n-fold centre with n as large as possible.

Exercise Find suitable net basepoints for Figures 4.2 and 1.1.

4.2 Cells

Construction 4.5 The vertices of a net may be joined up to form congruent parallelograms called **cells**. A cell for a plane translation group T or its net N is by definition a parallelogram whose adjacent sides, when directed, represent some basis u, v for T. If we locate this cell so that one of its vertices is the basepoint of the net we call it a *base*

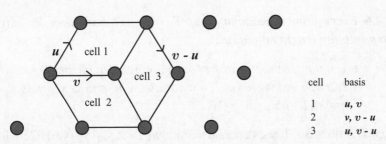

Figure 4.3 Three rows of a 'hexagonal' net portrayed. The cells of the three bases together form a regular hexagon.

Figure 4.4 Plane pattern with hexagonal net. Convention 4.4 allows the basepoint at the centre of any white star, a six-fold centre of symmetry which also lies on a line of symmetry. We indicate four net points giving cell 2 of Figure 4.3. The points where three dark 'lozenges' meet are points of only 3-fold rotational symmetry, not the highest in the figure.

cell or *unit cell*, and its translates occupy the net points as vertices and *tile* or *tessellate* the plane. That is, they fill the plane, with no area overlap. We say *N admits* this unit cell. In Figure 4.3 we show three choices of unit cell admitted by what is called a *hexagonal net* (see Section 4.3.3). These *diamond-shaped* cells are congruent but produce different tessellations (remember all cells in the tiling were to be translates of one cell). Figure 4.4 exhibits a pattern with the hexagonal net, whilst Figure 4.8 shows some non-congruent cells and their tilings for a different net.

Exercise Find net points in Figure 4.4 giving cell 1 and cell 3 of Figure 4.3. Locate a cell which violates Convention 4.4 for basepoints.

Surprisingly, not only does each choice of cell type have the same area, namely the least possible area of a parallelogram made by joining up points of the net, but also ... there are *infinitely many* possible cells of different shape. Our starting point, Theorem 4.6, tells us how to make the most useful choice (for the one exception see Section 4.3.3, Type (iii)).

Theorem 4.6 *Every plane translation group **T** contains a basis **u**, **v**. We may take **u**, **v** to satisfy a **minimum length condition**:*

> ***u** is a nonzero vector in T of least possible length, and*
> ***v** is a nonzero vector in T, not parallel to **u**, and as short as*
> *possible (note: $|\boldsymbol{u}| \leq |\boldsymbol{v}|$).* (4.6)

Proof Since ***T*** is discrete, ***T*** does contain vectors ***u***, ***v*** satisfying (4.6). Certainly the set $U = \{m\boldsymbol{u} + n\boldsymbol{v}: m, n = 0, \pm 1, \pm 2, \ldots\}$ is a subgroup of ***T***, since the composition of two translation symmetries is another. We require to prove that every vector ***w*** of ***T*** is in U. To this end we apply the subgroup U to some basepoint O, to obtain a net N. Then $U = \{\underline{OR}: R \in N\}$. Let $\boldsymbol{w} = \underline{OP}$. We must prove that (i) the point P is in N, and will do so by obtaining a contradiction in the contrary cases (ii) and (iii) of Figure 4.5 for the position of P relative to a cell $ABCD$ of the net N.

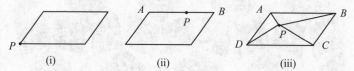

(i)   (ii)   (iii)

Figure 4.5 Diagrams for the proof of Theorem 4.6.

  (i) *P is a point of the net N.*

 (ii) *P is in the interior of an edge AB of a cell. Thus $|AP| < |AB|$.*

       The vector $\underline{AP} = \underline{OP} - \underline{OA}$ is in ***T*** (since $\underline{OP} \in$ T and $\underline{OA} \in U$, a subgroup of ***T***) and furthermore AB, being a cell edge, has length $|\boldsymbol{u}|$ or $|\boldsymbol{v}|$. Therefore $|AP| < |AB|$ contradicts the fact that ***u*** and ***v*** satisfy the minimum length condition (4.6) for ***T***.

(iii) *P is in the interior of a cell $ABCD$.*

Since the four (unsigned) angles which P subtends at the cell edges sum to $360°$, at least one, say angle APB, is at least $90°$. Therefore in triangle APB we have APB as the greatest angle and hence AB as greatest side. Thus $|AP| < |AB|$. Similarly to Case (ii), this contradicts the fact that ***u***, ***v*** satisfy the minimum length condition (4.6) (note that AP cannot be parallel to ***u*** since P is in the interior of the cell).

     It remains to prove the uniqueness of an expression for a vector ***w*** in ***T***. Suppose that $\boldsymbol{w} = m\boldsymbol{u} + n\boldsymbol{v} = r\boldsymbol{u} + s\boldsymbol{v}$ for integers m, n, r, s. Subtracting, we obtain $(m - r)\boldsymbol{u} = (s - n)\boldsymbol{v}$. Since ***u***, ***v*** are independent it follows that $m - r = 0 = n - s$ (see (4.4)), hence $m = r, n = s$, and the expression is unique.

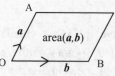

Figure 4.6 Diagram for Notation 4.7.

Notation 4.7 For vectors ***a***, ***b*** we define area $(\boldsymbol{a}, \boldsymbol{b})$ to be the area of a parallelogram with adjacent sides representing ***a***, ***b*** if these vectors are non-parallel, and otherwise zero. (See Figure 4.6). Let ***u***, ***v*** be a basis of the plane translation group ***T***. Then area$(\boldsymbol{u}, \boldsymbol{v})$ is the area of a *cell* defined by ***u***, ***v***.

Suppose a, b are related to u, v by (i) below.

(i) $\begin{aligned} a &= au + bv, \\ b &= cu + dv, \end{aligned}$ (ii) $A = \begin{bmatrix} a & b \\ c & d \end{bmatrix}$, $\det A = ad - bc$. (4.7)

The equations (i) may be specified by their *matrix of coefficients A*, an array of numbers in two rows and two columns called a 2 *by* 2 *matrix*. Thus we may define A by its *column vectors*, writing $A = [x \, y]$, where $x = (a, c)$, $y = (b, d)$. Here A is called an *integral* matrix because its *entries a, b, c, d* happen to be integers. The *determinant* of A, denoted by $\det(A)$ or simply $\det A$, is the number ad-bc. The following lemma suggests its importance.

Lemma 4.8 *(Determinant formulae for areas) We have*

(a) $\mathrm{area}(a, b) = |\det M|$, *where* $M = [ab]$ *(a, b arbitrary vectors)*,
(b) $\mathrm{area}(a, b) = |\det A| \, \mathrm{area}(u, v)$, *if a, b are related to u, v by (4.7)*.

Proof (a) We begin with a, b non-parallel in the manner of Figure 4.7. Thus the coordinates satisfy $0 < b_1 < a_1$ and $0 < a_2 < b_2$, and we have

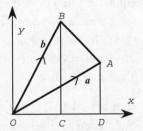

$$\begin{aligned} &\mathrm{area}(\mathbf{a}, \mathbf{b}) \\ &= 2(\text{area of } OAB) \\ &= 2(\text{area } OBC + \text{area } ABCD - \text{area } OAD) \\ &= b_1 b_2 + (a_1 - b_1)(a_2 + b_2) - a_1 a_2 \\ &= a_1 b_2 - a_2 b_1 \\ &= |\det M|, \text{ as required.} \end{aligned}$$

Figure 4.7 Diagram for proof of Lemma 4.8.

If we interchange the positions of A, B the area becomes $-(\det M)$, hence the need to take the absolute value (areas are unsigned in this context).

Considering variants of Figure 4.7, we find that the determinant formula (a) holds in all cases of a, b non-parallel. In the case $a = \alpha b$ for some scalar α we have $\det M = \alpha b_1 b_2 - \alpha b_2 b_1 = 0 = \mathrm{area}(a, b)$, so the formula remains true. Cases $a = 0$ and $b = 0$ are trivial.

Proof (b) Applying Part (a) to both $\mathrm{area}(a, b)$ and $\mathrm{area}(u, v)$, we obtain

$$\begin{aligned} \mathrm{area}(a, b) &= |a_1 b_2 - a_2 b_1| \\ &= |(au_1 + bv_1)(cu_2 + dv_2) - (au_2 + bv_2)(cu_1 + dv_1)| \quad \text{by (4.7)} \\ &= |(ad - bc)(u_1 v_2 - u_2 v_1)| \\ &= |\det A| \mathrm{area}(u, v), \text{ as required.} \end{aligned}$$

Exercise Prove that $\mathrm{area}(a, b) = |\det[a \, b]|$ for A, B on opposite sides of the y-axis.

Theorem 4.9 *Let u, v be a basis of T and a, b a pair of non-parallel vectors in T. Then*

$$\mathrm{area}(a, b) \geq \mathrm{area}(u, v),$$

with equality (i.e. $|\det A| = 1$) if and only if a, b is also a basis.

Proof The vital fact that u, v is a basis allows a, b to be expressed in terms of u, v by a relation (4.7)(i), giving area$(a, b) = |\det A|$ area(u, v), by Lemma 4.8. We require that $|\det A| \geq 1$, and it is true for reasons so simple they are easily missed. By definition of *basis* in (4.2) the entries in matrix A are integers, so $\det A$ itself is an integer from its definition. It cannot be zero because area(a, b) is nonzero, hence $|\det A| \geq 1$, and the first assertion follows.

For the equality assertion, suppose a, b as well as u, v is a basis. Then, by the first part, area$(u, v) \geq$ area$(a, b) \geq$ area(u, v), so the areas are equal. For the converse assume that u,v is a basis and the two areas are equal, implying that $\det A = \pm 1$ by Lemma 4.8. Then equations (4.7)(i) have a unique solution

$$u = (da - bb)/\det A, \qquad v = (-ca + ab)/\det A \qquad (4.8)$$

for u, v in terms of a, b. Furthermore the coefficients of a, b are integers, since $\det A$ equals ± 1 and a, b, c, d are integers. Thus any vector w in T may be expressed in the form $w = ma + nb$ by, for example, expressing w in terms of the basis u, v, then applying (4.8). The expression is unique as required, because $w = ma + nb = ra + sb$ implies $(m - r)a = (s - n)b$, and hence $m = r, n = s$, since a, b are not parallel (see (4.4)). Thus a, b is a basis.

Remarks 4.10 (1) We develop matrices in Chapter 7, so we have here a nice flier or motivation for later. In effect we have proved for the occasion some basic results such as Lemma 4.8. With Chapter 7 behind us it would be natural to invoke 'matrix inverses' in the proof of Theorem 4.9.

(2) We recall for the next corollary that a cell for a plane translation group T is a parallelogram whose adjacent sides, directed, represent basis vectors for T.

Corollary 4.11

(a) A pair u, v in T is a basis if and only if area(u, v) *is least possible for non-parallel vectors in T.*

(b) All cells have this least area.

(c) There are infinitely many cell shapes.

(d) All cells satisfying the minimum length condition (4.6) are congruent.

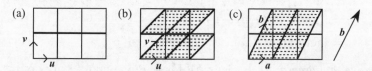

Figure 4.8 Three candidates for cell of a square net (one that admits a square cell). (a) A cell (square) which satisfies the minimum length condition (4.6), and (b) one which does not. By Corollary 4.11(d), every cell satisfying (4.6) is square, for this net. By Corollary 4.11(c), infinitely many parallelograms have the right area for a cell, but by Corollary 4.11(b) the long parallelograms (c) above do not. So a, b is not a basis of T.

Proof Parts (a) and (b) follow from the observation that by Theorem 4.9, if x, y is a basis and area(a, b) is least possible, then area$(a, b) \geq$ area$(x, y) \geq$ area(a, b), so the areas are equal. In (c) we start with, say, the basis u, v given by Theorem 4.6. Then for every 2 by 2 matrix A with integer entries and determinant 1 there is (Theorem 4.9, last part) a new basis a, b given by (4.7). Also, unless two matrices have identical entries they cannot yield the same pair a, b, because of the uniqueness of their expression in terms of the basis u, v.

To produce an infinitude of matrices establishing (c) we shall use two facts from elementary number theory (Niven & Zuckerman, 1980, Theorems 1.3 and 1.17): (i) there are infinitely many choices for a pair of distinct prime numbers p, q, and (ii) for any such pair of integers with no common factor there are integers x, y such that $px + qy = 1$. Then the matrix $A = \begin{bmatrix} p & -q \\ y & x \end{bmatrix}$ has determinant $px - (-q)y = 1$, and (c) is proved. (Other matrices will do: see Example 4.12.)

For (d), we note that if a cell satisfies (4.6) then the *lengths* of u, v are determined, though not necessarily their directions. But, by Part (b), the cell's area is determined. It equals $|u||v| \sin \phi$, where ϕ is the (unsigned) angle between u and v, with $0 < \phi < \pi$, and $|u| \sin \phi$ is

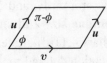

Figure 4.9

the 'height' of the cell. Thus $\sin \phi$ is determined and hence, although there is an apparent ambiguity in that $\sin \phi = \sin(\pi - \phi)$, the two possible parallelograms are congruent. See Figure 4.9.

Example 4.12 Some integral matrices with determinant ± 1.

$$\begin{bmatrix} 2 & 1 \\ 1 & 1 \end{bmatrix} \begin{bmatrix} 1 & -1 \\ 0 & 1 \end{bmatrix} \begin{bmatrix} 2 & 3 \\ 1 & 2 \end{bmatrix} \begin{bmatrix} 3 & 2 \\ 4 & 3 \end{bmatrix} \begin{bmatrix} 2 & 3 \\ 5 & 7 \end{bmatrix}$$

The second part of Figure 4.10 is a scaled down version of the first, and indicates how a tiling would proceed. The tiles are in alternate black and white layers.

What the eye sees The cell designs which the eye sees first are usually those with shortest edge length, our choice of cell in Theorem 4.6. As we take more complicated matrices to make new cells from this original, the new cells become rather thin and elongated.

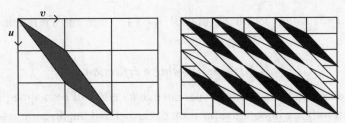

Figure 4.10 New cells from old by the first matrix of Example 4.12.

However, if we are looking for a tiling from which to begin a design, we can always use a matrix of determinant, say, 4, and/or scale the earlier net, to suit our purposes.

Exercise Do as in Figure 4.8 with your own matrix.

4.3 The five net types

We are moving towards a classification of plane patterns by symmetries, which will aid both their recognition and their creation. This section motivates the first step, of dividing them into five classes by net type.

Review 4.13 Soon (in Chapter 5) we will make extensive use of the notation in Table 2.1, of a continuous line for a mirror, broken line for glide, arrow for translation, and regular n-gon for n-fold centre of symmetry. Where construction lines or cell edges are required in addition, the mirror lines will usually be thickened. We choose a basepoint, at first arbitrarily, and join up the points of the resulting net so as to obtain cells of the **unique size and shape which satisfy the minimum length condition** (4.6) (see Corollary 4.11(d)). Later we will need to reposition the basepoint, for example to satisfy Convention 4.4 and to take advantage of the powerful Net Invariance Theorem 4.14 to come. To recapitulate, we let

$F = $ a given plane pattern;
$G = $ the group of all symmetries of F;
$T = $ the subgroup comprising all translation symmetries;
$N = $ net: all translates of some basepoint by the elements of T;
$M = $ motif: a part of pattern F whose translates form the whole.

Theorem 4.14 *(Net invariance) Let g be a symmetry of a pattern. If g fixes a point of some net for T then the net is invariant under g. That is, g maps net points to net points.*

Proof Let g fix the net point A. Then so does g^{-1} (see Notation 2.9 ff). In symbols, the double equality $A^g = A = A^{g^{-1}}$ holds. Noting too that any other net point P is the image A^T of a translation symmetry T, we have:

$$P^g = (A^T)^g = A^{Tg} = (A^{g^{-1}})^{Tg} = A^{g^{-1}Tg}$$

But, by Theorem 2.12(c), $g^{-1}Tg$ is a translation symmetry of the pattern, and therefore $P^g = A^{g^{-1}Tg}$ is a point of the net, as required.

Exercise Verify Theorem 4.14 in Figure 4.4, for a 1/6 turn and a reflection.

4.3.1 Nets allowing a reflection

In spite of Theorem 4.14, we cannot guarantee that cells will be mapped into cells, no matter how carefully we choose the position of the net and the division into cells. What we do find is that the alternative properties a net may have in order to allow a mirror

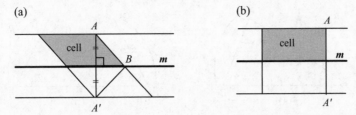

Figure 4.11 (a) One edge AB equals a diagonal BA' in length. (b) Adjacent cell edges are perpendicular.

symmetry already suggest the five net types required for a full classification of plane isometries. Naturally enough, since a study of reflections reveals so much about plane isometries.

Suppose the pattern F has at least one mirror line m. It will have others too because of translation symmetries, and perhaps glides and rotations, but we focus attention on the effect of m alone. Since there either is or is not a cell edge parallel to m, we may divide considerations into these two cases. For simplicity we will consider m as horizontal in Case 1, and other convenient directions in Case 2. We will not go into full detail, since we are using these cases simply to highlight the likely relevance of three criteria for a potential cell: are its edges at right angles, are they equal, does one edge have the same length as one diagonal?

Case 1 *The mirror m is parallel to a cell edge* We position the net so that m lies *along* a cell edge. Let A be a vertex (net point) as close to m as possible but not actually on it. Then the mirror m reflects A into another vertex A' (Theorem 4.14), and the minimum length condition, it may be verified, allows no *more* than the two possibilites shown in Figure 4.11. Note that the three horizontal lines in each diagram are successive lines composed of cell edges.

Case 2 The mirror m is parallel to no cell edge. Place the net so that m contains a vertex A. Let AB be an edge. In particular, B is not on m. Then again there are two subcases (see Figure 4.12).

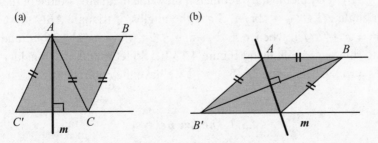

Figure 4.12 (a) m is at right angles to AB. One edge equals a diagonal in length. (b) m is not at right angles to AB. Adjacent cell edges are equal.

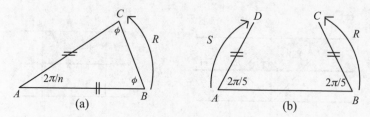

Figure 4.13 Diagram for proof of the crystallographic restriction.

4.3.2 Rotations – the crystallographic restriction

We begin with some consequences of our discreteness hypothesis which don't depend on the presence of translation symmetries of the pattern F. Let F have rotation symmetries about a point A and let α be the smallest positive angle for which $R = R_A(\alpha)$ is a symmetry. We claim that α is $1/n$ of a turn for some integer n. Firstly, α must be some fraction of a turn, for if not then R, R^2, R^3, ... are all different. Imagine their angles marked on a circle. Since there are infinitely many the marks must come arbitrarily close, contradicting the minimality of α. So now we have $\alpha = 2\pi r/n$ for some integers r, n with no common factor.

Appealing (again) to elementary number theory (Niven & Zuckerman, 1980), there is some integer multiple k of r/n which differs from $1/n$ by an integer. Thus $R^k = R_A(2\pi/n)$ is a symmetry. Since the least rotation is $2\pi r/n$ we must have $r = 1$, and $\alpha = 2\pi/n$ as asserted. Now we are ready to prove the famous crystallographic restriction for plane patterns, so named for its relation to the early work of crystallographers in classifying crystals by their symmetry groups. See e.g. Phillips (1971).

Theorem 4.15 *The crystallographic restriction If a plane pattern has an n-fold centre of symmetry, then $n = 2, 3, 4$ or 6.*

Proof Let A, B be n-fold centres of symmetry as close together as possible and R, S the corresponding $1/n$ turns, $R = R_A(1/n)$, $S = R_B(-1/n)$. Our proof refers to Figure 4.13. There are two cases to consider: (a) general n, (b) $n = 5$.

We first establish that $n \leq 6$, using Figure 4.13(a). The image $C = B^R$ of B under R is by Theorem 2.12(b) an n-fold centre, so from the hypothesis that $|AB|$ is least possible we have $|AB| \leq |BC|$. By elementary geometry, the same inequality holds for their opposite angles in triangle ABC: $\phi \leq 2\pi/n$. Since the angles of triangle ABC must sum to π, we have $2\phi = \pi - 2\pi/n$, whence $\pi/2 - \pi/n \leq 2\pi/n$, or $\pi/2 \leq 3\pi/n$, and so $n \leq 6$. It remains to rule out $n = 5$, using Figure 4.13(b). So let $n = 5$ and consider the points $C = B^R$, $D = A^S$. Then, since $2\pi/5 < \pi/2$ we have the contradiction $|CD| < |AB|$.

4.3.3 The five net types

We are now in a good position to motivate the classification of nets. Consider the Venn diagram in Figure 4.14, in which an enclosed subregion represents the set of all cells $ABCD$ with a certain property and the intersection of two such regions represents cells having

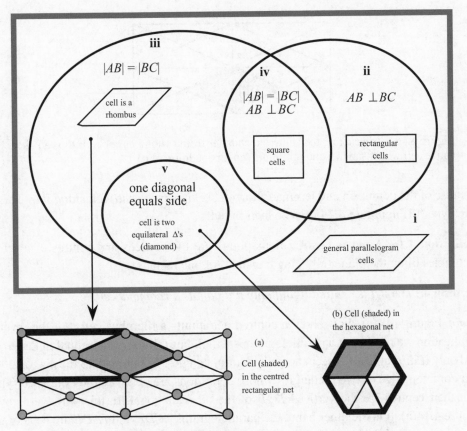

Figure 4.14 Genesis of the five net types.

both respective properties. The universal set, represented by an enclosing rectangle, is all possible cells (parallelograms). Section 4.3.1 on reflections suggests highlighting properties $AB = BC$ and $AB \perp BC$. These define the two large regions, and hence *four* possible net types, labelled (i) to (iv) in Figure 4.14.

The third property appearing in Section 4.3.1, that one side of a cell has the same length as one of the diagonals (the diamond shape), is put in as subcase (v) of (iii). According to the Net Invariance Theorem 4.14 this is the only net type to allow the 1/6 and 1/3 turns of the crystallographic restriction, since such a turn about any net point must send every net point into another. The net is called *hexagonal* because its points form the vertices and centres of a tiling of the plane by hexagons (see Figure 6.13). Again, it is not hard to see from Theorem 4.14 that (iv), the *square net*, is the only type to allow 1/4 turn symmetries.

Thus far we have divided nets into five types by their uniquely shaped cells which satisfy the minimum length condition (4.6) (Corollary 4.11(d)): rectangular, square, diamond, rhombus (other than square or diamond), and general parallelogram (none of those preceding). To complete the classification we extend the rhombus class to include all nets which admit a rhombus cell, even if it does not satisfy (4.6). Thus nets such as that of Figure 4.15 are reallocated from the general parallelogram to this type which,

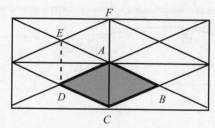

Figure 4.15 Constructing the centred rectangles from a rhombus cell. *FADE* is an alternative cell which satisfies the minimum length condition (4.6).

because of the definition and lemma following, is known as *centred rectangular*. This is how type (iii) in Figure 4.14 is to be interpreted.

Definition 4.16 A net is *centred* if its points are the vertices and centres of a set of rectangles tiling the plane (all being translates of one rectangle).

Lemma 4.17 *A net is centred if and only if it admits a rhombus cell.*

Proof Figure 4.14(a) shows how a centred net admits a rhombus cell. For the reverse implication we recall that a parallelogram is a rhombus (all four sides equal in length) if and only if its diagonals bisect each other at right angles. In Figure 4.15 the diagonal *AC* is a common edge of two rectangles whose definitions are completed by our specifying that their centres are the vertices *D*, *B* of the other diagonal. In this way we recover Figure 4.14(a). (On the other hand, the parallelograms *ACDE* and *FADE* are cells of the net which do satisfy the minimum length condition (4.6).)

Remark 4.18 In view of Lemma 4.17, the square and hexagonal nets are centred, since the square and diamond are special cases of a rhombus. To avoid confusion we do not emphasise this, but we show in Figure 4.16 the centred rectangles superimposed in dotted outline on these two types.

Résumé 4.19 The net types (numbered i to v in Figure 4.14).

(i) *The general parallelogram net* with no special properties nevertheless has 1/2 turn symmetries about the vertex of each cell, the midpoint of each cell edge, and the cell centre. See Section 5.2.

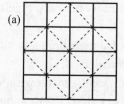 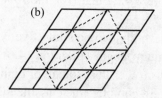

Figure 4.16 How (a) the square net and (b) the hexagonal net with its diamond cells may be exhibited as centred. In the first case the centred rectangle is square.

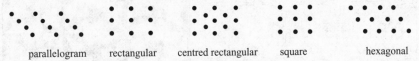

parallelogram   rectangular   centred rectangular   square   hexagonal

Figure 4.17 Dot patterns representing the five net types.

(ii) *The rectangular net* gives the option of mirrors in either one or two directions, and 1/2 turn symmetries.

(iii) *The centred rectangular net* Because the diagonals of a rhombus bisect each other at right angles, the points of this net can be grouped as the vertices of *centred rectangles*, as indicated in Figure 4.14(a). This insight not only gives the net its name, but is important in practice, for it is usually easier to see that copies of a motif mark the vertices and centre of a rectangle than to be sure that they are equidistant from their neighbours, especially if the motif has a very irregular shape. Mirror and rotation properties are as for (ii).

Note that a rhombus, though it will have least possible area (Corollary 4.11), may violate the minimum length condition (4.6). (This unavoidable exception causes no harm in the sequel.) It can nevertheless occur as Case 2b in Section 4.3.1.

(iv) *The square net* This is the first in our list which Theorem 4.14 (net invariance) allows to have 4-fold rotational symmetry. As a result it can support mirrors at 45° as well as 90°. On the other hand, Theorem 4.14 forbids 1/3 or 1/6 turns for this net.

(v) *The hexagonal net* The cell is a diamond, formed from two equilateral triangles, whose internal angles are of course 60°, or $\pi/3$. Consequently, each point of the net is in six equilateral triangles, tiling a regular hexagon. The hexagons in turn tile the plane. Thus it makes sense to call this net *hexagonal*. Later we see the various possibilities for reflections and glides. Here we note that 1/3 and 1/6 turns are permitted (for the first time), whilst 1/4 turns are not, by Theorem 4.14.

Example 4.20 One pattern of each net type.

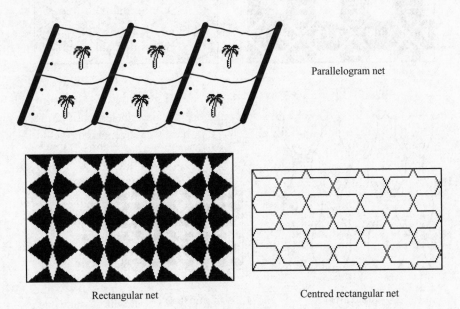

Parallelogram net

Rectangular net   Centred rectangular net

Figure 4.18

Square net

Hexagonal net

Figure 4.18 (*continued*)

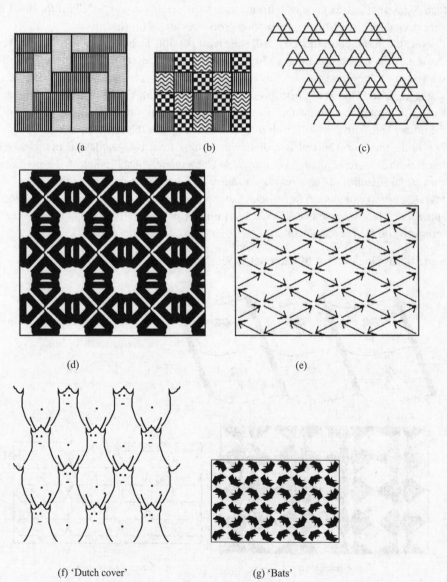

(a)

(b)

(c)

(d)

(e)

(f) 'Dutch cover'

(g) 'Bats'

Figure 4.19 Patterns for Exercise 4.6.

Exercises 4

1√ What is the highest rotational symmetry in Figure 4.2, and where?

2√ Find suitable net basepoints for Figures 4.2 and 1.1.

3   Find net points in Figure 4.4 giving cell 1 and cell 3 of Figure 4.3. Locate a cell which violates Convention 4.4 for basepoints.

4   Write down a matrix A with integer entries and determinant ±1. Starting with a tiling of the plane by rectangles, use matrix A to derive a tiling by parallelograms of the same area, as in Figure 4.4. Repeat for other such matrices A.

5   Prove that the diagonals of a rhombus (parallelogram with all four sides equal) bisect each other at right angles. Draw a tiling of the plane by rhombi and convert it into the corresponding tiling by (centred) rectangles.

6√ Identify the nets of the plane patterns (a) to (g) represented in Figure 4.19.

7   Prove that area$(a, b) = |\det[a\,b]|$ for a case in which A, B are on opposite sides of the y-axis.

8   Verify Theorem 4.14 for the indicated net, in Figure 4.4, using a 1/6 turn, a 1/3 turn, a 1/2 turn, and a reflection.

5

The 17 plane patterns

In this chapter we introduce and exemplify the division of plane patterns into 17 types by symmetry group. This begins with the broad division into net type. The chapter concludes with a scheme for identifying pattern types, plus examples and exercises. It then remains to show that all the types are distinct and that there are no more; this will be done in Chapter 6.

5.1 Preliminaries

Here we recapitulate on some important ideas and results, then introduce the signature system which will label each type of plane pattern according to its symmetry group. For the basics of a plane pattern F and its group of symmetries G, see Review 4.1. We have introduced the subgroup T of G, consisting of all translation symmetries of F (Definition 4.2), and the representation of those translations by a net N of points relative to a chosen basepoint O (Definition 4.3). The points of N are the vertices of a tiling of the plane by parallelogram cells (Construction 4.5 – see especially Figure 4.3).

The division of patterns into five classes according to net type (determined by T) is motivated by reflection issues in Section 4.3.1. In Section 4.3.3 we described the five types, indicating case by case which of the feasible rotational symmetries for a plane pattern (Section 4.3.2) are permitted by net invariance, Theorem 4.14. The result is a very natural fit, for example the last type, the hexagonal net, allows 3-fold and 6-fold centres but not 4-fold. Indeed, we might have led up to the net types by starting with rotations rather than reflections.

Translations $\boldsymbol{u}$, $\boldsymbol{v}$, represented by adjacent sides of a cell, will denote a basis for the translation symmetries, except in the case of a centred net when it is convenient to use a 3-vector approach to integrate the rhombus and centred rectangle viewpoints (see Section 5.4).

Glide symmetries, we recall, are appropriately limited to the kind $R_m T_{w/2}$ whose translation component has one half the length of the shortest translation vector $\boldsymbol{w}$ parallel to it, and $R_m T_{w/2} = T_{w/2} R_m$ (see Convention 3.2 and preceding discussion).

New symmetries from old We remind the reader of two main ways of deducing the presence of further symmetries of a figure from those already identified. (a) Any symmetry maps mirrors to mirrors, glidelines to glidelines, n-fold centres to n-fold centres, and translation directions to translation directions, in accordance with Theorem 2.12. (b) The composition of two symmetries is another, details being given in Table 2.2. This said, the following observations as to what symmetries can exist or coexist for a given pattern are important ingredients in classifying plane patterns. The first results from (a), because a rotation moves any mirror to the position of another, non-parallel mirror.

> *The presence of both rotation and reflection symmetries implies at*
> *least two mirror directions. Similarly for glides.* $\hspace{2cm}$ (5.1)
> *The presence of non-parallel mirrors, glides, or a combination,*
> *implies rotations. (Table 2.2(b).)* $\hspace{2cm}$ (5.2)
> *The **least** angle between the lines of two mirrors, glides, or a*
> *combination, is π/n for $n = 2, 3, 4,$ or 6.* $\hspace{2cm}$ (5.3)

Observation (5.3) holds because the product of reflections in mirrors at angle θ is rotation through angle 2θ, which the crystallographic restriction Theorem 4.15 lays down to be a multiple of $2\pi/n$, $n = 2, 3, 4, 6$. We will append $n = 1$ as representing the case of no rotational symmetry. A special case of (5.2), the *mirror–glide combination*, was considered in Chapter 3 on braids, for lines at right angles (see (3.4)). For convenience we reproduce as Figure 5.1 the three situations portrayed in Figure 2.9: the position of one of the $1/2$ turns produced by right angle crossing of glide/reflection lines with each other. In summary, the translation component w of a crossing glide ensures that the implied 2-fold centre is a translation by $(1/2)w$ from the intersection. This happens in two directions for the glide/glide crossing, as seen in Figure 5.1(iii).

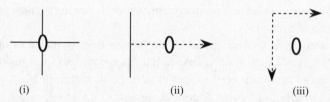

Figure 5.1 The crossing at right angles of the line of a mirror/glide symmetry with another in either category implies 2-fold centres in the positions shown. This notation was given in Table 2.1.

Notation 5.1 Each plane pattern type is specified by four symbols $\boxed{z \mid n \mid x \mid y}$, a development of the braid notation 3.4, interpreted as follows.

z	Initial symbol c if net is centred rectangular, otherwise p for 'primitive'.
n	The highest degree of rotational symmetry in the pattern. That is, n is the largest integer for which the pattern has an n-fold centre.
x	m if F has a line of symmetry, g if, failing the above, F has a glideline, 1 if F has neither.
y	The same as for x, but for lines in a 'second direction'.
	In both cases the 1 is omitted if it would be the last symbol.

Interpreting x, y As with the braid patterns of Chapter 3 it is convenient to consider one mirror direction as horizontal for the purpose of illustration, but we do not wish to consider patterns to be of different type simply because of our choice of which mirror is 'horizontal'. Again, we don't want a pattern to change its type by being rotated through 90 degrees or any other angle. Thus the formulation above allows $xy = mg$ but not $xy = gm$, because the distinction is not required. In the hexagonal net the distinction for mirror directions is between perpendicular and parallel to the sides of a triangle. This will be explained in its own place, Section 5.6, but see below.

Convention 5.2 We have just noted that it makes sense for certain patterns to be considered as of the same type (or 'equivalent'). Since we are about to draw representative cases of patterns we will anticipate the formal definition of equivalence in Chapter 6 by agreeing that a pattern remains the same type if we (a) transform the plane by an isometry – reflect, rotate, translate or glide, (b) change scale uniformly – i.e. we simply enlarge or contract, (c) change scale in one direction so as not to change the net type.

Presenting the cases In Sections 5.2 and 5.3, the order of cases for each net is guided by (5.1) to (5.3). We proceed from low to high rotational symmetry, with increasing number of mirrors or glides. In each case, after the symbol $znxy$, with its usual shortening highlighted, we give the following.

1. The outline of a representative cell, normally with vertices following the Basepoint Convention, 4.4, near the end of Section 4.1.
2. An example motif M, whose images under all the translation symmetries in a group of the given type $znxy$ form a pattern of that type. M in turn consists of images of a very simple submotif ⇁ placed at the cell vertices, and at other positions and in other ways required by the symmetries in $znxy$. Notice that M does not include the cell itself.
3. Below the cell, a representation of the rotation centres, mirrors and glide lines which intersect it. Cf. Figure 2.17, in which this is continued over nine cells.
4. A small list of symmetries (*generators*) which generate (Definition 2.17) the whole group.
5. Any outstanding explanation of the symmetry configuration.

5.2 The general parallelogram net

Possible $1/n$ turns: $n = 1, 2$. No mirrors, by Section 4.3.1.

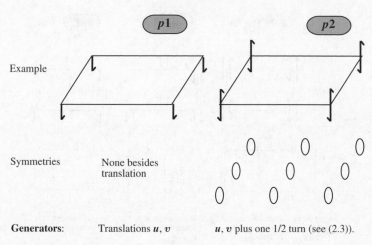

Figure 5.2

5.3 The rectangular net

Possible $1/n$ turns: $n = 1, 2$. The case of no m/g is covered under $p1, p2$.
Case $n = 1$ One reflection or glide.

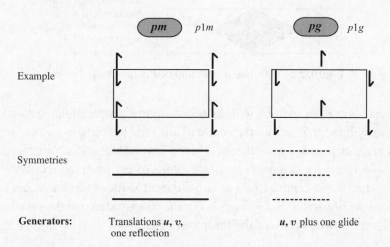

Figure 5.3

Case $n = 2$ Two reflection or glide directions (note: neither need be horizontal).

Basepoint position For convenience in drawing the motif in cases *pmg* and *pgg* we have (only) here set the net basepoint at an intersection of mirror lines which is not a centre of symmetry, giving priority to the second rather than the first criterion of Convention 4.4.

Exercise Redraw the diagrams for *pmg*, *pgg* so as to follow basepoint Convention 4.4; **or** satisfy yourself that the given generators do result in the configurations of symmetries shown in Cases 1 and 2 for the rectangular net.

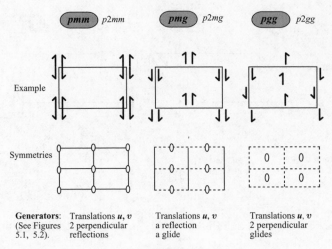

Figure 5.4

5.4 The centred rectangular net

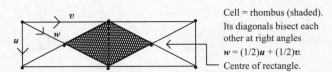

Cell = rhombus (shaded).
Its diagonals bisect each
other at right angles
$w = (1/2)u + (1/2)v$.
Centre of rectangle.

Figure 5.5 Translations, net and cell in the centred case.

'Centred' entails that, in addition to translations along the sides of the rectangle, there is a translation symmetry T_{-w} from the centre to one (and hence to every) corner. In some patterns it is easier to spot a rhombus, in others a centred rectangle. Note that *a rhombus is a parallelogram with diagonals perpendicular*. To get from the rectangle model to a rhombus, start at the centre. Lines to two adjacent vertices form adjacent edges of a rhombus cell, as illustrated in Figure 5.5. For the reverse step, see the proof of Lemma 4.17. In Figure 5.6 we get two of the seventeen types.

Explanation for symmetries The 1/2 turns in *cmm* arise from mirror–mirror and mirror–glide crossings; see Figure 5.1. For the glides, suppose we have a horizontal mirror line *m*, along a cell wall, and translations *u*, *v*, *w* as in Figure 5.5. Then the symmetries of the pattern include the composition $R_m T_w$, which is shown in Figure 5.7 to be one of the horizontal glides indicated, whose line cuts off 1/4 of a cell. Combining it with a vertical translation *u* gives the other glides of *cm*. A second mirror direction explains the glides of *cmm*.

This completes the net types with highest rotational symmetry $n = 2$.

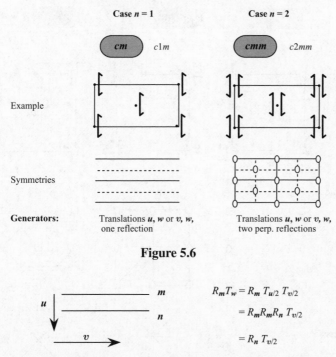

Figure 5.6

$$R_m T_w = R_m\, T_{u/2}\, T_{v/2}$$

$$= R_m R_m R_n\, T_{v/2}$$

$$= R_n\, T_{v/2}$$

Figure 5.7 How reflection and then diagonal translation produces a glide.

5.5 The *square net*

The square net is the only one to allow 1/4 turn symmetries. See Figure 5.8. With only 1/2 turns or none it counts as a special case of the rectangular net, so we consider only the square net with 1/4 turns: $n = 4$. There are three associated pattern types. The last two are distinguished by having *either* a mirror diagonally across the cell, *or* a glide (not both), and we choose generators accordingly.

Explanation for symmetries

Rotations in all three types The translations u, v map a 4-fold centre at one vertex of the cell to 4-fold centres at the other vertices (Theorem 2.12). A 1/4 turn at the centre can be obtained as the product of a translation with a 1/4 turn at a vertex (see Exercise 2.1). A 1/2 turn at the midpoint of an edge is the product of a translation with a 1/2 turn (= two 1/4 turns) at a vertex (Example 2.5).

Mirrors and glides in p4m It is an easy exercise to show that translations u, v plus the known rotations produce the mirrors of *p4m* from any one mirror, in particular from the diagonal one we take as generator. Assuming these, consider Figure 5.9(a). The combination of the 1/2 turn and reflection indicated in boldface is $R_A(1/2)R_n = (R_l R_m)R_n = R_l(R_m R_n) = R_l T_{AB}$, which is a glide since $AB = u/2 + v/2$. The 1/4 turn symmetry about the cell centre rotates the glideline AB successively into three others, forming the 'box' of glidelines as indicated.

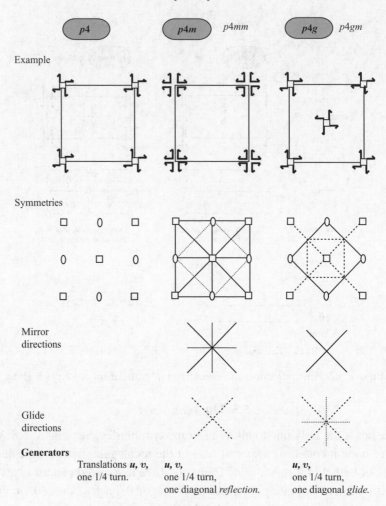

Figure 5.8

Mirrors of p4g We are given one diagonal glide, so rotation about the centre gives the other. In Figure 5.9(b), the combination of glide and 1/2 turn shown boldface equals $(T_{AB}R_l)(R_lR_m) = T_{AB}R_m = (R_nR_m)R_m = R_n$. Then by rotation we have the 'box' of mirrors shown, included in the symmetries of $p4g$.

Glides of p4g In Figure 5.9(c) let g be the diagonal glide in bold (a generator for $p4g$ by assumption), and h the horizontal glide backwards along mirror n, both through the distances indicated. Then $gh = (R_mT_{AC/2})(T_{DA/2}R_n) = R_mT_{DC/2}R_n$. This isometry is direct, being the product of one direct and two indirect isometries, so is determined by its effect on any two points (Theorem 1.10). Since gh fixes A and sends B to D, as does $R_A(1/4)$, we have $gh = R_A(1/4)$, whence $h = g^{-1}R_A(1/4)$. Now since the glide h is the product of two symmetries in the group, h is itself a symmetry, and rotation gives the 'box' of glidelines appertaining to $p4g$.

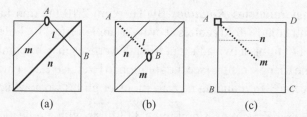

Figure 5.9 (a) Origin of side *AB* of the box bounded by glidelines in *p4m*, (b) origin of one side of the box, now formed from mirrors, in case *p4g*, (c) start of the glide box for *p4g*.

5.6 The *hexagonal net*

Cell = 60° rhombus = 2 equilateral triangles, called a *diamond*.

Rotation symmetries of the net

6-fold at triangle vertices
3-fold at triangle centres
2-fold at midpoints of triangle edges

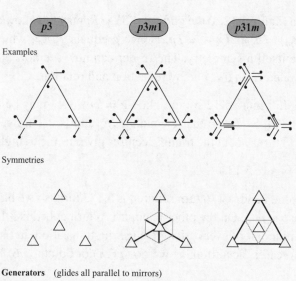

Figure 5.10

Case *n* = 3 (See Figure 5.11.) Here we suppose that the symmetries include a 1/3 turn (at one triangle vertex), but no 1/6 turn. For the illustrations we take a change of motif.

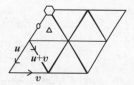

Examples

Symmetries

Generators   (glides all parallel to mirrors)

Translations *u, v,*
1/3 vertex turn.

u, v,
1/3 vertex turn,
reflection in a
triangle altitude.

u, v,
1/3 vertex turn,
reflection in a
triangle edge.

Figure 5.11

Explanation for symmetries *Rotations* By Theorem 2.10 the translation symmetries map the 3-fold centre onto 3-fold centres at every triangle vertex. By Euler's construction, Example 2.6, the 1/3 turns at two adjacent triangle vertices may be combined to produce a 1/3 turn about the triangle centre (see the solution to Exercise 2.2), which now translates to every triangle centre. Introducing no reflections or glides we now have case *p3*.

The two sets of mirror directions Combining 1/3 turns with a reflection produces mirrors at angles of 60°, the angle in a triangle of the net. Hence, starting with a mirror perpendicular to the *u*-direction, along the altitude of one triangle, we obtain mirrors along the altitudes of all triangles. This is case *p3m*1. It is notationally convenient to consider this as a case of one mirror direction only, counting all the altitude directions as one, via 1/3 turns. On the other hand, a mirror in the *u*-direction, along a triangle edge, yields mirrors along the sides of all triangles, via the 1/3 turns, giving case *p31m*.

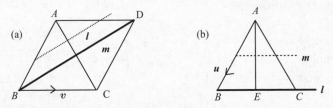

Figure 5.12 Source of the glides in (a) *p3m*1, (b) *p31m*. To achieve a more readable picture the dotted glide lines represent position only. A glide *distance* is, as always, one half the shortest translation in a parallel direction.

*Glides of p3m*1 In Figure 5.12(a) the glide $g = T_{BD/2}R_l$ may be followed by R_m to satisfy $gR_m = T_{BD/2}(R_lR_m) = T_{BD/2}T_{AC/2} = T_v$. Hence g equals T_vR_m, which is a product of symmetries, hence itself a symmetry. The reader can now see how all other glide lines of *p3m*1 are generated from this one by reflection and rotation.

Glides of p31m In Figure 5.12(b), the glide $g = T_{CB/2}R_m$ may be followed by R_l to satisfy $gR_l = T_{CB/2}T_{AE} = T_u$, so that g equals T_uR_l and is itself a symmetry. Rotating the glide line by 1/3 turns about the triangle centres gives us the triangle of glides shown.

Case $n = 6$ (See Figure 5.13.)

Rotations On the one hand, a 1/6 turn squared is a 1/3 turn, so we have all the 1/3 turn symmetries of Case $n = 3$. On the other hand, a 1/6 turn cubed is a 1/2 turn, giving us a 1/2 turn at the midpoint of every triangle edge via translation, in the manner of (2.3). There are thus two cases, according as we do (*p6m*) or do not (*p6*) have reflections at all (see below).

Reflections and glides In case *p6m* we may compose a 1/6 turn about a triangle vertex with reflection in a mirror along the side of a triangle. The result is reflection in an altitude. Therefore we have the mirror directions of both *p3m*1 and *p31m*.

This concludes the 17 plane patterns and their symmetries, and one choice for the generators of those symmetries. There follow a set of examples, a scheme for identifying

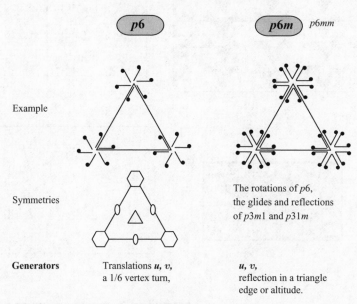

	p6	p6m p6mm
Example		
Symmetries		The rotations of *p6*, the glides and reflections of *p3m1* and *p31m*
Generators	Translations *u, v,* a 1/6 vertex turn,	*u, v,* reflection in a triangle edge or altitude.

Figure 5.13

the type, and a series of identification exercises for the reader. In the next chapter we see how to generate examples of any type to order.

5.7 Examples of the 17 plane pattern types

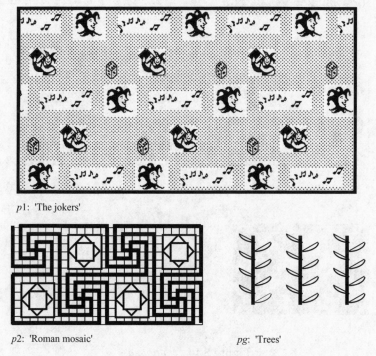

*p*1: 'The jokers'

*p*2: 'Roman mosaic'

pg: 'Trees'

Figure 5.14

pm

pmm

pgg

*p*4: 'Jigsaw 1'

pmg

cmm: 'Carpet 1'

cm: 'In clover'

*p*4*m:* 'Windows'

*p*4*g*

*p*3

Figure 5.14 (*continued*)

Figure 5.14 (continued)

5.8 Scheme for identifying pattern types

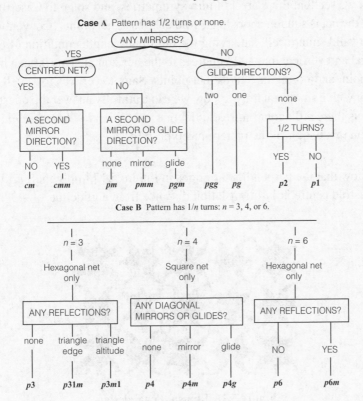

Case A Pattern has 1/2 turns or none.

Case B Pattern has 1/n turns: n = 3, 4, or 6.

Figure 5.15

Exercise Use the scheme in Figure 5.15 to check the type of one pattern from each net, in Section 5.7.

Notes

(i) *Nets versus rotation* The first question in our identification algorithm concerns rotations rather than nets, because of possible ambiguity. For example, the square is a special case of a rectangle, which is in turn a parallelogram. Indeed, the net of a $p1$ or $p2$ pattern can coincidentally be any one of the five net types, though counted as a parallelogram for classification purposes. On the other hand, $n = 3$ or 6 *requires* the hexagonal net and $n = 4$ the square, giving an important check as we proceed.

(ii) *1/2 turns* can be hard to spot, and therefore we use them (in the first instance) only to distinguish between $p1$ and $p2$. Notice that (i) does not require us to identify 1/2 turns, but simply to decide whether 1/3, 1/4 or 1/6 turn symmetries are present.

(iii) *Glides* As remarked earlier, for glide spotting it may help to think of a fish gliding left–right as it proceeds forwards.

(iv) *Confirming the decision* Having decided the type of a pattern from the scheme above, we can test this not only by the net but by the presence of any symmetries we choose which are predicted for this type (see Sections 5.2 to 5.6).

Example 5.3 (*Roman 'Pelta' design, Figure 5.16*). Following the scheme to find the pattern type, we see that there are 1/4 turn symmetries, and so go to Case B: $n = 4$. We confirm that the net is square, choosing 4-fold centres as net points (Convention 4.4). But notice that a valid square cell, satisfying the minimum length condition (4.6) has edges not horizontal and vertical, but at 45 degrees to the horizontal. This is seen by focussing on one net point and noting its nearest net points. Sample vertices for a cell are marked in the pattern with a small square: $\square$. Now we can truthfully answer the question relative to this cell: 'is there a diagonal mirror, glideline, or neither?' *There is a diagonal glide* (horizontal on this page), so the pattern has type $p4g$.

Exercise Show that the perpendicular glides in Figure 5.17 imply the 1/2 turns. Note: each 2-fold centre is 1/4 translation distance from a glideline.

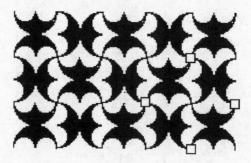

Figure 5.16 Roman 'Pelta' design.

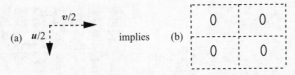

Figure 5.17 Some half turns that must be present in a symmetry group having translations
u, **v** and glidelines as in (a).

Exercises 5

1 √ Identify the type of each of the patterns in Figure 5.18.

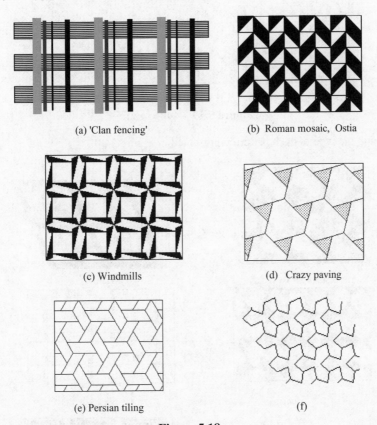

(a) 'Clan fencing'

(b) Roman mosaic, Ostia

(c) Windmills

(d) Crazy paving

(e) Persian tiling

(f)

Figure 5.18

2 √ Identify the type of each pattern in Figure 5.19.

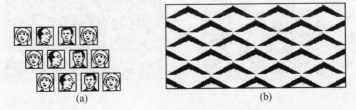

(a)

(b)

Figure 5.19

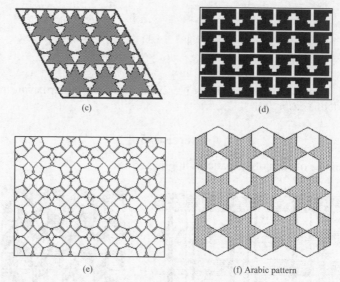

(c)

(d)

(e)

(f) Arabic pattern

Figure 5.19 (*continued*)

3 √ Determine the type of each pattern represented in Figure 5.20.

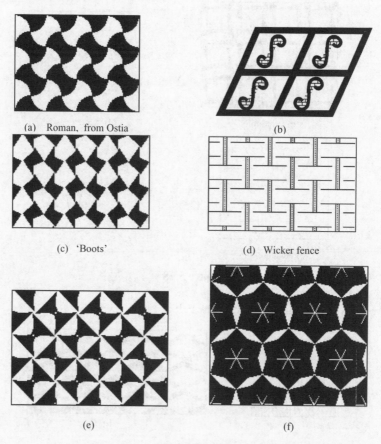

(a)   Roman, from Ostia

(b)

(c)   'Boots'

(d)   Wicker fence

(e)

(f)

Figure 5.20

6

More plane truth

We have indicated how nets fall naturally into five types for the purpose of classifying plane patterns, and found 17 possible configurations or groups of symmetries. But should they all be considered different, and are there more? After dealing with these questions via Sections 6.1 and 6.2, we look at some techniques for producing plane patterns to order. The most important for our purposes will be the use of a fundamental region, developed in Section 6.4.3, and concluded with the algorithm of Figure 6.32, by which most plane pattern examples in this book were produced.

6.1 Equivalent symmetry groups

Here we recapitulate and enlarge upon some material of Section 2.5 on groups in general. For two symmetry groups G, H to be considered 'the same', or equivalent, there must be a pairing between their elements so that their multiplication tables are the same apart from names of elements (cf. Figure 2.23). So far, this says that G and H are abstractly isomorphic. But we impose the additional requirement that like symmetries must pair with like.

Example 6.1 $G = \{I, R_m\}$, $H = \{I, R_p\}$, where m, p are different lines. (We permit ourselves to use the same symbol for the identity in either group.) Here G and H are equivalent according to the definitions that follow.

Definition 6.2 Groups G, H are *isomorphic* if there is a *bijection*, or pairing, $\phi: G \to H$ such that

$$\phi(fg) = \phi(f)\phi(g), \quad \text{for all } f, g \text{ in } G, \qquad (6.1)$$

where $\phi(f)$ means the image of element f under map ϕ. Then ϕ is called an *isomorphism* from G to H. Informally, (6.1) is described as saying that ϕ *preserves multiplication*. It follows that, for all g in G,

$$\phi(I) = I, \qquad (6.2)$$
$$\phi(g^{-1}) = \phi(g)^{-1}, \qquad (6.3)$$
$$g \text{ and } \phi(g) \text{ have the same order}, \qquad (6.4)$$

79

where the Is in (6.2) denote in order the identity elements in G and H. If necessary we may distinguish them by subscripts thus: I_G, I_H.

Proof of (6.2) We have

$$\phi(I) = \phi(I^2) \qquad \text{since } I = I^2$$
$$= \phi(I)\,\phi(I) \quad \text{by (6.1), } \phi \text{ being an isomorphism.}$$

By Theorem 2.21(i) on uniqueness of identities this is sufficient to prove that $\phi(I) = I$.

Proof of (6.3) Here we argue that

$$\phi(g^{-1})\phi(g) = \phi(g^{-1}g), \qquad \phi \text{ being an isomorphism,}$$
$$= \phi(I), \qquad \text{which equals } I \text{ by (6.2).}$$

This time we apply Theorem 2.21(ii), and Statement (6.3) follows.

Proof of (6.4) We observe, firstly, that $\phi(g^r) = \phi(g \cdot g \cdot \ldots \cdot g) = \phi(g)\phi(g)\cdots$ $\phi(g) = \phi(g)^r$. Hence if $\phi(g)^r = I$ we may write $\phi(g^r) = I = \phi(I)$, which implies that $g^r = I$, since ϕ is bijective (part of the definition of isomorphism). Now, this argument reverses: if $g^r = I$ then $\phi(g)^r = I$, so the least power which equals the identity is the same for both g and $\phi(g)$. That is, they have the same order.

Example 6.3 The cyclic group C_4 and dihedral group D_4 both have size 4 (see Section 2.4). Are they isomorphic? Let us first try a sledgehammer approach and use Theorem 2.18 to write out the multiplication tables of these groups (an exercise at the end of Chapter 2). Let C_4 have a 1/4 turn T as generator, and let D_4 contain a reflection R and 1/2 turn τ. Then with elements listed as the first row of their table we have Table 6.1.

Table 6.1. *The multiplication tables of C_4 and D_4.*

C_4	I	T	T^2	T^3	D_4	I	τ	R	$R\tau$
I	I	T	T^2	T^3	I	I	τ	R	$R\tau$
T	T	T^2	T^3	I	τ	τ	I	$R\tau$	R
T^2	T^2	T^3	I	T	R	R	$R\tau$	I	τ
T^3	T^3	I	T	T^2	$R\tau$	$R\tau$	R	τ	I

We observe that in the C_4 table row 2 is a cyclic shift of row 1, and so on down the rows, whilst the entries for D_4 partition into four quarters. It follows that the elements of D_4, say, cannot be reordered so as to give the same table as C_4 apart from the names. We will not give a more detailed argument because there is a very simple reason, based on (6.4) above, why the two groups are not isomorphic. That is, that C_4 has an element of order 4, whilst D_4 has not. However, the tables are instructive.

Example 6.4 The symmetry group of a cube is isomorphic to the group S_4 of all permutations of four objects. In fact, the symmetries of a cube permute its four main diagonals (see e.g. Coxeter, 1973).

Definition 6.5 Symmetry groups G, H are *equivalent* if there is an isomorphism $\phi :$ $G \to H$ that sends like to like (then ϕ is called an *equivalence*), that is

$$\begin{aligned} &\text{reflections to reflections, translations to translations,} \\ &\text{glides to glides, and } 1/n \text{ turns to } 1/n \text{ turns.} \end{aligned} \qquad (6.5)$$

Example 6.6 In the notation of Definition 2.17, let $T_1 = Gp\{T_u, T_v\}$, $T_2 = Gp\{T_w, T_x\}$, where vectors u, v are at right angles and w, x are at $60°$. A typical element of T_1 is T_{mu+nv} with m, n integers. Then

$$\phi(T_{mu+nv}) = T_{mw+nx} \qquad (6.6)$$

is an isomorphism satisfying (6.5). Thus T_1 and T_2 are equivalent, as are all plane translation subgroups, by an isomorphism ϕ which pairs the elements of a basis of the one group with a basis (see (4.2)) of the other. See Figure 6.1.

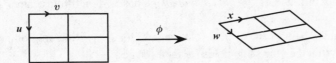

Figure 6.1 Equivalence ϕ between translation groups with bases u, v and w, x.

Example 6.7 The groups $G = \{I, R\}$ and $H = \{I, \tau\}$ are isomorphic, where R is a reflection and τ a $1/2$ turn, both therefore of order 2. But they are not equivalent, since the only possible isomorphism from G to H maps a reflection to a $1/2$ turn, infringing (6.5). In fact the conclusion follows without considering isomorphisms: we may simply note that G has a reflection whilst H does not.

Example 6.8 Pattern 6.2(a) is stretched to form pattern 6.2(b). This destroys the vertical symmetry, and so the symmetry groups of the two are not equivalent.

According to the scheme described in Section 5.8, the first pattern has type *cm*, whilst the second is designated $p1$. Of course, if we had instead stretched (a) equally in all directions we would still have had the 'same' symmetry group for (b).

Exercise Why cannot the groups C_6 and D_6 be isormorphic?

Remarks 6.9

(1) An *isometry* g of the plane sends every pattern F to one of the same type. That is, their symmetry groups are equivalent. For, by Theorem 2.12, the isometry g maps like to like, satisfying (6.5), and this theorem gives us the equivalence $\phi(R) = g^{-1}Rg$. For example, if m is a mirror line of F then $g^{-1}R_m g$ is the operation of reflection in the mirror line m^g of

(a)   (b)

Figure 6.2 Two patterns (a), (b) whose symmetry groups are not equivalent.

F^g. As required, ϕ satisfies the definition of an isomorphism; in detail $\phi(RS) = g^{-1}(RS)g = (g^{-1}Rg)(g^{-1}Sg) = \phi(R)\phi(S)$.

(2) *Uniform scaling* of the plane with respect to some origin, namely enlargement or scaling down, fortunately does not change the type of a pattern (if it did, the inconvenience would prompt a change of definition of equivalence). If $g(x) = rx$ $(r > 0)$ defines such a transformation then the formal equivalence required is given by $\phi(R) = g^{-1}Rg$. Note in particular that g preserves angles, shapes and the ratios between distances.

(3) Let g be a stretch (or contraction) in one direction, say $g(x, y) = (rx, y)$ $(r > 0)$.

   (a) The groups of F and F^g *are not equivalent* if F has 3-, 4- or 6-fold centres, since g *changes angles*.

   (b) g does map 2-fold centres to 2-fold centres, for if A, B, C are collinear points with $|AB| = |BC|$ then the same holds for their images.

   (c) A stretch parallel to an edge sends a rectangular cell to a rectangular cell.

Table 6.2. *Tests for equivalence. If any property in the list is possessed by symmetry group G but not H then they are inequivalent, by Definition 6.5.*

1. G has an n-fold centre	4. G has both reflections and glides
2. G has reflections	5. G has reflections in at least two directions
3. G has glides	6. G has glides in at least two directions

6.2 Plane patterns classified

We have in Chapter 5 a description of 17 types of plane group, each with a distinct *signature* or *symbol*, of the form *znxy*. To establish that this list does classify plane patterns up to equivalence, we must prove assertions A, B, C below.

A. Plane groups with different signatures are not equivalent,
B. Plane groups with the same signature *are* equivalent,
C. All plane groups are included in the signature system.

Besides their nets, which concentrate on translation, a further powerful tool we shall use for distinguishing between symmetry groups is their *point group* $\mathcal{P}$ which, in a complementary way, ignores translation and uses only reflection and rotation.

6.2.1 Patterns with different signatures – the point group

Definition 6.10 Let A be any given point of the plane. Then the *point group* $\mathcal{P}$ of a plane group G consists of the identity and:

(1) all those $R_A(m/n)$ for which there is an m/n turn in G,
(2) for every mirror or glideline of G, the reflection in the parallel mirror through A.

If A needs to be specified, we refer to '*the point group at A*'. That $\mathcal{P}$ **is indeed a group** may be seen as follows (see Section 2.5). From Table 2.2, the product of every two elements of $\mathcal{P}$ is also in $\mathcal{P}$. For example if $\mathcal{P}$ contains $R_A(\alpha)$, $R_A(\beta)$ then G contains $R_P(\alpha)$, $R_Q(\beta)$ for some points P, Q and hence their product $R_S(\alpha + \beta)$, say. Thus, by definition of $\mathcal{P}$, we have $R_A(\alpha + \beta)$ in $\mathcal{P}$. Multiplication in $\mathcal{P}$ is *associative* simply because its elements are transformations, $\mathcal{P}$ contains an *identity* by definition. The *inverse* of an element of $\mathcal{P}$ is in $\mathcal{P}$ because (i) a reflection is its own inverse, and (ii) if $R_A(\phi)$ is in $\mathcal{P}$ then $R_D(\phi)$ is in G for some point D, so is the inverse $R_D(-\phi)$, and hence $R_A(-\phi)$ is in $\mathcal{P}$.

Example 6.11 Figure 6.3 is an example, with glidelines thickened and lightened.

All the mirrors of $\mathcal{P}$ are shown in Figure 6.3(c), understood to intersect at the basepoint A, and we see that they are the lines of symmetry of a square, the regular 4-gon. The rest of $\mathcal{P}$ consists of I, R, R^2, R^3, where R is a 1/4 turn about A. Hence $\mathcal{P}$ is the dihedral group D_8, discussed in Section 2.4. Now we prove a key result for the usefulness of the point group.

(a) plane pattern.

(b) symmetries near a cell.

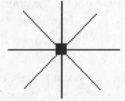

(c) the symmetries in the point group $\mathcal{P}$, except the 1/2 turn.

Figure 6.3 From pattern to point group $\mathcal{P} = D_8$.

Theorem 6.12 *The net is invariant under the point group.*

(a) *For any plane pattern group G, the net at a given point A is mapped onto itself by the point group $\mathcal{P}$ at A, and, consequently,*
(b) *$\mathcal{P}$ is contained in the point group of the net.*

Proof Let B be a net point. Then $B = A^T$ for some translation T. Suppose that g is an element of $\mathcal{P}$. Then we have $B^g = (A^T)^g = A^{Tg} = A^{g^{-1}Tg}$. But $g^{-1}Tg$ is a translation of the net, by Theorem 2.12, so B^g is indeed a point of the net.

Table 6.3. *The plane pattern types by net and point group*

Net	Plane group G	Point group of G	
Parallelogram	$p1$	1	$\{I\}$
(2)	$p2$	2	C_2
Rectangular	pm, pg	$1M$	
($2MM$)	pmm, pmg, pgg	$2MM$	D_4
Centred rectangular	cm	$1M$	
($2MM$)	cmm	$2MM$	D_4
Square	$p4$	4	C_4
($4MM$)	$p4m, p4g$	$4MM$	D_8
Hexagonal	$p3$	3	C_3
($6MM$)	$p3m1, p31m$	$3M$	D_6
	$p6$	6	C_6
	$p6m$	$6MM$	D_{12}

The basis for using the point group $\mathcal{P}$ is that if plane groups G, H are equivalent then so are their point groups, and hence:

$$\textit{if the point groups of H and H are not}$$
$$\textit{equivalent, then neither are G and H.} \tag{6.7}$$

It is customary to denote the point group by nxy analogously to the plane groups, except that now both 'm' and 'g' are replaced by M. We recall that n corresponds to the smallest $1/n$ turn in G. In Table 6.3 we list the point group of each net and of each of the 17 plane pattern types. These may be inferred in each case from the rotation, glide and mirror symmetries given in Sections 5.2 to 5.6 (cf. Figure 6.3). The cyclic and dihedral notation is given also. Note that it does not cover the group $1M$, consisting of the identity and a single reflection, $\{I, R_m\}$. The point group of each *net* (itself a plane pattern) is given in parenthesis beneath its name, and must contain the point group of each corresponding plane group, by Theorem 6.12. Dihedral groups D_{2m} and rotation groups C_m are reviewed in Section 2.4. We are now ready to prove assertion A as the next theorem.

Theorem 6.13 *Plane groups with distinct signatures are inequivalent.*

Proof We must prove inequivalence of all pairs chosen from the 17 types listed in Sections 5.2 to 5.6. The number of such pairs is $17 \cdot 16/2 = 136$. Since patterns with different point groups are inequivalent by (6.7), Table 6.3 shows that all pairs are distinguished by the point group except for the 11 pairs dealt with under four cases, next.

Now we continue the proof of Theorem 6.13.

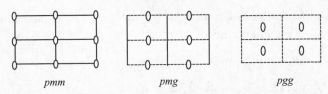

Figure 6.4 Recapitulation of some symmetry configurations.

Case 1 *M*: *three pairs from pm, pg, cm* These are handled easily by Table 6.2, since *pm* has one mirror direction but no glides, *pg* one glide direction but no reflections, whilst *cm* has both.

Case D_4: *six pairs from pmm, pmg, pgg, cmm* None of the first three groups are equivalent by an argument similar to Case 1*M* (see Figure 6.4). Further, *cmm* differs from both *pmm* and *pgg* by having both glides and reflections, and from *pmg* by having two mirror directions (see Section 5.4 for the symmetries in *cmm*).

Case D_6: *the pair p3m1, p31m* In the first group, reflection may be composed with translation of minimum length to obtain a reflection, but not in the second.

Case D_8: *the pair p4m, p4g* The first has more mirror directions than the second.

Exercise Verify some of the point groups given in Table 6.3.

6.2.2 The classification is complete

Starting from a series of 17 hypotheses which are easily seen to cover all possible discrete plane pattern groups G, we arrive each time at one of the types listed in Chapter 5. We exhibit equivalence by having the correct net type, and symmetries in the correct positions relative to a basis u, v for the translation vectors (5.2) of G. The equivalence map ϕ is a natural extension of (6.6) in Example 6.6. Let us temporarily denote a group listed in Chapter 5 by H, with basis x, y. If a point A has position vector $a = ru + sv$ let A' be the point with position vector $a' = rx + sy$. Then $\phi: G \to H$ is given by $T_a \to T_a'$, $R_{AB} \to R_{A'B'}$, $R_A(m/n) \to R_{A'}(m/n)$. We will incidentally confirm that there are no more symmetries than stated in each case of H. Much use will be made of discreteness: as examples, u and v will always be shortest translation vectors in their respective directions, and we can always choose a mirror and glideline to be as close as possible without coinciding. At the finish we will have established assertions A, B, C at the head of this section and so shown that discrete plane patterns may be classified into the 17 types of Chapter 5, distinguished by their labels *znxy*.

Case 1 Discrete plane groups with no reflections or glides

Case 1.1 (*Only translation symmetries*) All such groups are equivalent by Example 6.6, and form type *p*1.

Case 1.2 ($n = 2$) We assume G has a $1/2$ turn at the basepoint O, and deduce that G has all the symmetries of $p2$ and no more. We recall for here and future use

$$R_O(1/2)R_A(1/2) = T_{2OA}, \tag{6.8}$$

$$R_A(1/2) = R_O(1/2)T_{2OA}. \tag{6.9}$$

In fact (6.9) is proved in Figure 2.6 and implies (6.8) (multiply both sides by $R_O(1/2)$). We now have $2\underline{OA} \in \boldsymbol{T} \Rightarrow R_A(1/2) \in G$ (by (6.9)) $\Rightarrow 2\underline{OA} \in \boldsymbol{T}$ (by (6.8)). Thus the $1/2$ turns of G are at the same points as for $p2$, namely those A for which $2\underline{OA}$ is a translation vector, geometrically the cell vertices, midpoints of edges, and centres (see Section 5.2). The position vectors of these points are all $(1/2)(r\boldsymbol{u} + s\boldsymbol{v})$, for r, s in $\boldsymbol{Z}$, the set of integers, including zero and the negatives. Thus G is of type $p2$.

Case 1.3 ($n = 4$) We assume G contains $R_O(1/4)$. Then the net is square and there are no $1/3$ turns (Résumé 4.19). By the argument of Section 5.5, G contains the rotational symmetries listed for $p4$, namely $1/4$ turns at the cell vertices and centres, and $1/2$ turns at the midpoints of the edges. We record the position vectors $r\boldsymbol{u} + s\boldsymbol{v}$ or $(r + 1/2)\boldsymbol{u} + (s + 1/2)\boldsymbol{v}$ for the $1/4$ turns, and $r\boldsymbol{u} + (s + 1/2)\boldsymbol{v}$ or $(r + 1/2)\boldsymbol{u} + s\boldsymbol{v}$ for the $1/2$ turns (r, s in $\boldsymbol{Z}$). There are no more $1/2$ turns $R_A(1/2)$ (so no $1/4$ turns) because (6.8) implies $2\underline{OA} = r\boldsymbol{u} + s\boldsymbol{v}$ (r, s in $\boldsymbol{Z}$); and we have accounted for all such points, since the 4-fold centres also supply $1/2$ turns. Thus G is of type $p4$.

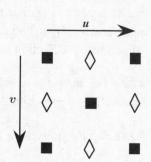

Figure 6.5 Case 1.3.

Case 1.4 ($n = 3$) We suppose G contains $R_O(1/3)$, and set the basepoint as usual at O. The net is necessarily hexagonal (Résumé 4.19), with basis $\boldsymbol{u}$, $\boldsymbol{v}$ along the sides of one of the equilateral triangles making up the unit cell. There are the 3-fold centres at the vertices and centres of every equilateral triangles in the net (see Section 5.6), the position vectors being $(1/3)(r\boldsymbol{u} + s\boldsymbol{v})$, for r, s in $\boldsymbol{Z}$. However, there are no $1/2$ turns, for such would imply a $1/6$ turn, say $R_A(1/2)R_O(-1/3) = R_B(1/6)$. It remains to show that there are no more $1/3$ turns $R_A(1/3)$, for which we make use of Figure 6.6.

Suppose $R_A(1/3)$ is a symmetry but A is not a vertex. We need only deduce it must be a triangle centre. We have $R_A(2/3)R_O(1/3) = T_{AC}$, shown enlarged in Figure 6.6(b). By relocating the basepoint if necessary we may assume $|OA| < |OP|$, and then AC is shorter than the long diagonal of a cell $OPQR$. Since $\underline{AC}$ is a translation vector of G

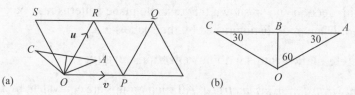

Figure 6.6 There is no $1/3$ turn at a point A which is not a triangle vertex or centre.

we have $\underline{AC} = \underline{QR}$ for a triangle edge QR. By elementary geometry A is the centre of triangle OPQ. Thus there are no more $1/3$ turns and G is of type $p3$.

Case 1.5 ($n = 6$) Our hypothesis is that G contains $R_O(1/6)$ (but still no reflections or glides). As in Case 1.4, this implies that the net is hexagonal and that there are no $1/4$ turns. But this time there are $1/2$ turns. By taking the square and cube of the $1/6$ turn we obtain the rotation symmetries deduced for $p6$ in Section 5.6: $1/6$ turns at the triangle vertices, $1/3$ turns at their centres and $1/2$ turns at the midpoints of edges. Our task is to explain why there can be no more symmetries. This was done for $1/3$ turns in Case 1.4. We will rule out new $1/6$ turns by ruling out new $1/2$ turns (their cubes). Suppose $R_A(1/2)$ is a symmetry. We may suppose $|OA| < |OP|$ as illustrated in Figure 6.6. Then there is a translation symmetry $R_O(1/2)R_A(1/2) = T_{2OA}$, by (6.8). Therefore A is the midpoint of an edge, so is already accounted for. Hence G is of type $p6$.

Case 2 **Discrete plane groups with reflections/glides all parallel**

Case 2.1 (*Mirrors only*) Let G have reflection in a mirror $\boldsymbol{m}$. Since all mirrors of G are parallel there is no rotation symmetry, for it would rotate the mirrors to new directions. We find a basis $\boldsymbol{u}, \boldsymbol{v}$ of T as shortest translation vectors respectively parallel and perpendicular to $\boldsymbol{m}$. To prove this is so we note that in T every vector parallel to some vector $\boldsymbol{x}$ of T equals $\alpha\boldsymbol{x}$ for some constant α, and so the set of all such vectors forms a line group (Definition 3.1). Then Theorem 3.3(a) gives the first assertion below. The second is an elementary observation, illustrated in Figure 6.7(b).

> *In T, all vectors parallel to a given line $\boldsymbol{n}$ are integer multiples $r\boldsymbol{u}$,*
> *where $\boldsymbol{u}$ is a shortest vector parallel to $\boldsymbol{n}$.* (6.10)

> *If $\boldsymbol{x}$ is parallel to $\boldsymbol{u}$ then subtracting a suitable multiple $t\boldsymbol{u}$ leaves $\boldsymbol{w}_1$*
> $= \boldsymbol{x} - t\boldsymbol{u}$, *with* $|\boldsymbol{w}_1| \le (1/2)|\boldsymbol{u}|$. (6.11)

Suppose $\boldsymbol{u}, \boldsymbol{v}$ is not a basis and that $\boldsymbol{w}$ is a shortest translation vector they do not express ($\boldsymbol{w}$ need not be unique). We obtain a contradiction. Resolve $\boldsymbol{w}$ parallel to $\boldsymbol{u}$ and $\boldsymbol{v}$, say $\boldsymbol{w} = \boldsymbol{w}_1 + \boldsymbol{w}_2$, as in Figure 6.7(b). By (6.11) we may suppose that $|\boldsymbol{w}_1| \le (1/2)|\boldsymbol{u}|$, for otherwise we could subtract multiples of $\boldsymbol{u}$ to ensure this, and $\boldsymbol{w}$ would still not be expressible in terms of $\boldsymbol{u}, \boldsymbol{v}$, but would be shorter. This is illustrated in Figure 6.7(b) by the

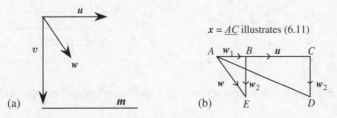

Figure 6.7 (a) Vector $\boldsymbol{w}$ is not expressible in the basis $\boldsymbol{u}, \boldsymbol{v}$. (b) How the $\boldsymbol{u}$ component of $\boldsymbol{w}$ can be shortened until $|\boldsymbol{w}| \le (1/2)\,|\boldsymbol{u}|$.

replacing of $\underline{AD}$ by $\underline{AE}$ for w. But now $R_m T_w = (R_m T_{w_2}) T_{w_1}$, which is a (non-allowed) glide since $R_m T_{w_2}$ is a reflection (see (2.1)), and its translation part w_1 is shorter than u. This contradiction shows that, after all, u, v is a basis of T. Finally, combining R_m with multiples tv (t in $\mathbf{Z}$) gives precisely the reflections of *pm*.

Case 2.2 (*Glides only*) As in the previous case there can be no rotations. Let $g = R_m T_x$ be a glide in G with shortest translation part. Let u, v be shortest translation vectors respectively parallel and perpendicular to the mirror m. Then since x is as short as possible we have $|x| \leq (1/2)|u|$ by (6.11). But $g^2 = T_{2x}$, so $|2x| \geq |u|$ by minimality of $|u|$. Hence $|x| = (1/2)|u|$ and we may take $g = R_m T_{u/2}$. We have derived a useful ancillary result for other cases:

> *if G has glides parallel to translation vector u, shortest in its own*
> *direction, then G has a glide with translation part $u/2$, and this is*
> *least for glides parallel to u.* (6.12)

If u, v is not a basis for the translation symmetries, let w be a shortest vector not expressible in terms of them. Decompose w parallel to u and v as in Figure 6.7(b): $w = w_1 + w_2$. As before, we have $|w_2| \leq (1/2)|u|$ by (6.11). Now, gT_w or gT_{-w} is a glide with translation part (parallel to u) strictly shorter than $u/2$. The only way this can be true is for g to be a reflection, but these are not allowed in this case, so we have a contradiction and u, v do indeed form a basis (in the next case reflections are allowed, and we infer a centred net). Combining g with translations rv, perpendicular to m, we obtain all the glides of *pg*. The presence of further glides in G would imply translations which are not integral multiples of v, contradicting (6.10). Hence G is of type *pg*.

Case 2.3 (*Mirrors and glides*) There are still no rotations because all mirrors and glide-lines are in one direction. Let u be a shortest vector in that direction. We shall construct a centred rectangular cell for G. As in Case 2.2, we may assume by (6.12) that G contains a glide $g = R_m T_{u/2}$. Let n be a mirror of G as close as possible to the mirror line m of this glide. Represent u by AB with n lying along AB. We have $R_n g = R_n R_m T_{u/2} = T_w$, say. Now let $\underline{AE}$ represent w and $\underline{AD}$, $\underline{BC}$ both represent $v = 2w - u$. Then we have the rectangle $ABCD$ with centre E of Figure 6.8.

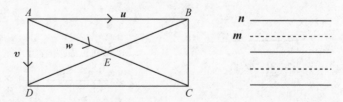

Figure 6.8 The centred rectangular cell, found from parallel mirrors and glides.

Notice that w is a shortest translation vector in its own direction, otherwise it would combine with R_n to give a glide too close to n. We prove that u, w (hence also v, w) is a basis for the translation vectors in the group. Let x be such a vector. Then since u, w are not parallel we have $x = \lambda u + \mu w$ for some constants λ, μ which must be shown to be integers to establish the basis assertion. By (6.11) we may subtract integer multiples of u, w from x so as to leave $|\lambda|$, $|\mu| < 1$. But then $\mu = 0$, otherwise $R_n T_x$ would be a glide with line closer to n than that of g. Thus $x = \lambda u$. Now, by the minimality of $|u|$ we may infer that $\lambda = 0$, which means that the original λ, μ were integers. Thus we have shown that u, w is a basis. Finally, T_v generates all the reflections and glides of cm by composition with R_n and g. Further glides or reflections cannot be present, for they would generate translations which cannot belong to the group. We have established that G has type cm.

Case 3 **Discrete groups with reflections/glides in exactly two directions**

Case 3.1 (Mirrors only) Here $n = 2$. The two directions must be at right angles, or mirrors would reflect each other into new directions. The shortest translation vectors u, v in the respective directions form a basis by the argument of Case 2.1. But now we obtain the mirrors and 2-fold centres of pmm, reproduced in Figure 6.4. The existence of further mirrors or 1/2 turn symmetries would contradict the minimality of $|u|$, $|v|$. Thus G has type pmm.

Case 3.2 (Glides only) Again $n = 2$; the glides are in two perpendicular directions or they would generate more glide directions. The argument of Case 2.2 (glides only, one direction) applies here also to show that shortest vectors u, v in the respective directions form a basis. By (6.12) there are glides $R_m T_{u/2}$ and $R_n T_{v/2}$ with least translation parts. They generate the symmetry configuration of pgg, shown in Figure 6.4. Further glides or 1/2 turns would contradict the minimality of $|u|$, $|v|$. In short, G is of type pgg.

Case 3.3 (Glides and mirrors, no glide and mirror parallel) As before, $n = 2$ is implied. The mirrors are all in one direction and the glides in another, perpendicular to the first. The usual arguments show that shortest vectors u, v in the respective directions form a basis. A glide with shortest translation part has the form $R_n T_{v/2}$, by (6.12). One mirror and this glide, together with translations, generate the symmetry configuration of pmg (see Figure 6.4) and no more. We have G of type pmg.

Case 3.4 (Glides and mirrors: some mirror and glide parallel) As before, we have $n = 2$ and two perpendicular directions for mirrors and/or glides. However, things work out a little differently because glides and mirrors are allowed to be parallel.

Let mirror n have glidelines parallel to it and let the glide $g = R_m T_{u/2}$ be as close as possible, where u is a shortest translation vector parallel to m (cf. (6.12)). We perform the construction of Case 2.3 (cm) to obtain the centred rectangle $ABCD$, with u, w and v, w equally valid as bases, and u, v, w shortest translation vectors in their respective directions (see Figure 6.8). Now consider the mirror/glides in our second direction. We choose the basepoint as A, lying at the right angle intersection with n of a mirror $\mathcal{p}$ along AD. Then $g = R_n T_{u/2}$ is a glide parallel to u with least possible translation part. Now $R_\mathcal{P}$ and g, together with translations T_{ru} (r in Z) generate the remaining mirrors and glides of *cmm*, combining with those in the first direction to give the $1/2$ turns. We have exactly the symmetry configuration of *cmm* (and no more), as reproduced in Figure 6.9, and so G falls into type *cmm*.

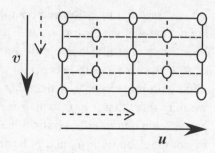

Figure 6.9 The *cmm* symmetries.

Case 4 Discrete plane groups with mirrors and 1/4 turns

Case 4.1 (Some mirror contains a 4-fold centre) We recall from Case 1.3 that as a consequence of $1/4$ turns being present, the net is square, no $1/3$ or $1/6$ turns are possible, and the rotational symmetries are those of $p4$ and no more, as depicted in Figure 6.10. It remains to decide what configurations of mirrors and glides are possible. Now, every mirror must reflect r-fold centres to r-fold centres (Theorem 2.12), and this restricts its position to one of those shown in $p4m$ or $p4g$. It may or may not pass through a 4-fold centre, and in this present case we suppose that one mirror does so. Whichever mirror we choose for this role, its presence implies (by combination with rotations and translations) that of all mirrors in $p4m$. Also, combining $1/2$ turns and diagonal reflections gives the box of glides in $p4m$ (see Section 5.5). Any further reflections or glides imply the presence of disallowed translations or rotations, and so are ruled out. Hence the present choice of first mirror considered leads to G being of type $p4m$.

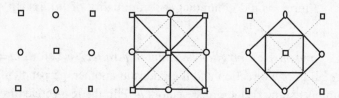

Figure 6.10 Possible symmetry configurations over a cell for a discrete plane pattern with $1/4$ turn symmetries; cf. Figure 6.3.

Case 4.2 (No mirror contains a 4-fold centre) From the discussion of Case 4.1 up to choice of mirror, the remaining choice is to have a mirror containing a 2-fold but not a 4-fold centre. This generates the mirrors and glides of $p4g$ (Section 5.5). Again, the configuration is complete, or contradictions arise, and so G has type $p4g$.

Case 5 Discrete plane groups with mirrors and 1/3 turns

Case 5.1 (Mirrors along triangle edges, no 1/6 turn) In Case 1.4 we dealt with the consequences of allowing a $1/3$ turn. The net is hexagonal, meaning that a cell is diamond-shaped, consisting of two equilateral triangles back to back. Quarter turns are ruled out,

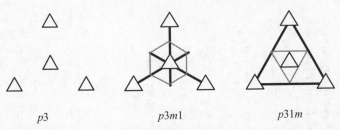

Figure 6.11 Possible symmetry configurations over a half cell for a discrete plane pattern with 1/3 turn symmetries.

but there are 1/3 turns at every vertex and centre, as depicted for *p*3 in Figure 6.11. What are the options for a mirror? It must reflect 3-fold centres to 3-fold centres (Theorem 2.12), and consequently lies along a triangle edge or altitude. The two cases cannot arise at once, for then we would have a 1/6 turn (this situation is dealt with as Case 5.3). (*) So let us suppose that there is a mirror along some triangle altitude. Invoking translations and rotations we generate the reflections and glides of *p*3*m*1, recalled in Figure 6.11 (see also Figure 6.6 for the argument). As usual, a check shows that no more are possible without contradiction. We conclude that *G* is of type *p*3*m*1.

Case 5.2 (Mirrors in triangle edges, no 1/6 turn) Here we follow Case 5.1 up to the choice of mirror direction (*). Then we specify that some mirror lies along a triangle edge. Again referring to Figures 6.11 and 6.6 we obtain precisely the symmetries of *p*31*m*, and so *G* is of this type.

Case 5.3 (Mirrors and 1/6 turns) The 1/6 turn combines with an altitude reflection to give an edge reflection, and therefore we have the glide/mirror symmetries of both *p*3*m*1 and *p*31*m*. A 1/6 turn at one vertex is translated to all (Theorem 2.12). Its square is a 1/3 turn, ensuring that the rotational symmetries of *p*3 are included, and its cube is a 1/2 turn which combines with translations to produce a 1/2 turn at the midpoint of every triangle edge. A little checking shows that further symmetries would violate the hypotheses of this case. Thus *G* is of type *p*6*m*.

This completes a fairly rigorous justification of the standard classification of discrete plane groups of symmetries, and hence of plane patterns. A concise 'pure mathematical' derivation may be found in Schwarzenberger (1980), and a more geometrical approach in Lockwood and Macmillan (1978).

Exercise Verify some of the point groups given in Table 6.4.

6.3 Tilings and Coxeter graphs

Definition 6.14 A plane *tiling* or *tessellation* is a countable set of regions $F_1, F_2, \ldots$ called *tiles or faces*, which cover the plane without area overlap. To say the faces are *countable* means that we can index them by integers 1, 2, 3, ... as we have just done. Two tiles may have a common boundary, say a line segment, but this contributes no area.

Table 6.4. *Categories of discrete plane group to be identified with the 17 types of Chapter 5. In each case n is the largest integer for which there is a 1/n turn symmetry. Parentheses denote an inference from what is given. For each row of the table it is shown there are no more possibilities.*

mirrors/glidelines	All possible situations that can arise			
None	$n = 1, 2, 3, 4$ or 6 — (p1, p2, p3, p4, p6)			
One direction only ($n = 1$)	Mirrors only (pm)	glides only (pg)	mirrors and glides (cm)	
Two directions only ($n = 2$)	mirrors only (pmm)	glides only (pgg)	mirrors and glides — no m/g parallel (pmg)	some m/g parallel (cmm)
Mirrors, $n = 4$ (square net, no 1/3, 1/6 turns)	some 4-fold (but no 2-fold) centre on a mirror (p4m)	some 2-fold (but no 4-fold) centre on a mirror (p4g)		
Mirrors, $n = 3, 6$ (hexagonal net, no 1/4 turns)	$n = 3$ mirror = triangle edge (p31m)	$n = 3$ mirror = triangle altitude (p3m1)	$n = 6$ mirror = edge / altitude (p6m)	

For our purposes we may assume each face is continuously deformable to a closed disk $D = \{(a, b): a, b \text{ real}, a^2 + b^2 \leq 1\}$. Thus a tile is not allowed to have 'holes'. A tiling is *polygonal* if every tile is a (not necessarily regular) polygon.

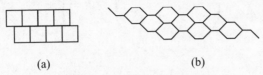

(a)   (b)

Figure 6.12 General tilings.

6.3.1 Archimedean tilings

We consider tilings by polygons which fit *edge to edge*, that is, each edge of a polygon is an edge of exactly one other. This rules out (a) of Figure 6.12, even though the tiles are polygons. Nevertheless it will prove a very convenient starting point. A simple but important special case is that of the *regular tilings* $\{m, n\}$ by regular m-gons, n at a point. It is easy to prove directly by the approach of (6.13) shortly below that the three well-known tilings of Figure 6.13 are the only possibilities. Note that we exhibit $\{3, 6\}$ as the *dual* of $\{6, 3\}$, *dual* being defined after Figure 6.13.

$\{4, 4\}$

$\{3, 6\}$ light,
$\{6, 3\}$ in bold

Figure 6.13 The regular tilings, with $\{3, 6\}$ as dual of $\{6, 3\}$.

Definition 6.15 The *dual* of a polygonal tiling is the division into polygonal regions obtained by joining the centre of each polygon to that of every polygon with which it has a common edge. Of course the dual of $\{4, 4\}$ is a translated copy of itself, and taking the dual of $\{3, 6\}$ in Figure 6.13 gives us back $\{6, 3\}$. We require some notation introduced by Ludwig Schläfli (see Coxeter, 1973).

Notation 6.16 (See Figure 6.14.) A vertex around which we have in cyclic order an n_1-gon, an n_2-gon, ..., an n_r-gon, is said to have *type* $(n_1, n_2, \ldots, n_r)$. We abbreviate repeated numbers by an index. Thus (4, 6, 12), (6, 12, 4) and (12, 6, 4) are the same vertex type, as are (4, 8, 8) and $(4, 8^2)$.

Definition 6.17 A tiling by regular polygons is *Archimedean* of type $(a, b, \ldots)$ if each vertex has the same type, $(a, b, \ldots)$. This of course includes the regular tilings, of types (4^4), (6^3), (3^6). We now investigate what other Archimedean tilings exist. Firstly, consider the situation at an individual vertex. We may anticipate that some possibilities for

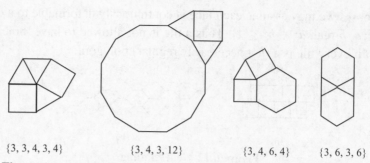

$$\{3, 3, 4, 3, 4\} \qquad \{3, 4, 3, 12\} \qquad \{3, 4, 6, 4\} \quad \{3, 6, 3, 6\}$$

Figure 6.14 New vertex types by rearrangement of entries in Table 6.5.

arranging polygons around this point will not extend to a tiling, but we will not miss any that do by starting this way. (Archimedes' name is given to these tilings because he studied polyhedra with faces obeying similar rules to this plane case. See Coxeter, 1973.)

Since the interior angle of a regular n-gon ($n \geq 3$) has angle $\pi - 2\pi/n$ and the angles at a point sum to 2π, we have for a vertex of type $(n_1, n_2, \ldots, n_r)$ that r is at least 3 and $(\pi - 2\pi/n_1) + (\pi - 2\pi/n_2) + \cdots + (\pi - 2\pi/n_r) = 2\pi$, or

$$(1 - 2/n_1) + (1 - 2/n_2) + \cdots + (1 - 2/n_r) = 2. \tag{6.13}$$

We show that this equation can have, fortunately, only a finite number of solutions, and enumerate them. Since Equation (6.13) is unaffected by the order of the integers n_i we may assume they are arranged in non-decreasing order. Further, $n \geq 3$ implies $1 - 2/n \geq 1/3$, so there cannot be more than six terms on the left hand side of (6.13), thus

$$3 \leq n_1 \leq n_2 \leq \cdots \leq n_r, \quad \text{and} \quad 3 \leq r \leq 6. \tag{6.14}$$

And now, since $1 - 2/n$ ($n \geq 3$) is increasing with n, the number of solutions is finite. They are found as follows. For each of $r = 3, 4, 5, 6$ we test the r-tuples $(n_1, \ldots, n_r)$, in lexicographical order, to see if they satisfy (6.13), until $r(1 - 2/n_1) \geq 2.4$ The last condition means of course that the left hand side of (6.13) must now be at least 2. The solutions are given in Table 6.5, lexicographically for each r.

Table 6.5. *Solution sets for r regular n-gons*
surrounding a point.

$r = 3$	$r = 3$	$r = 4$	$r = 5$	$r = 6$
3, 7, 42	4, 5, 20	$3^2, 4, 12$	$3^4, 6$	3^6
3, 8, 24	4, 6, 12	$3^2, 6^2$	$3^3, 4^2$	
3, 9, 18	$4, 8^2$	$3, 4^2, 6$		
3, 10, 15	$5^2, 10$	4^4		
$3, 12^2$	6^3			

We may pick out the regular tilings as special cases. Four of the solutions as given can be rearranged to produce, up to cyclic permutations and reverse ordering, exactly one further point type each, as shown in Figure 6.14.

We now have 21 point types that are guaranteed to exist as the surroundings of a single point, but how many extend to a tiling? We will shortly give a list (Figure 6.23) but, as noted in Grünbaum & Shephard (1987), a finite diagram does not automatically prove the existence of a tiling. We have to give, in effect, an algorithm for constructing the constructible to an arbitrary number of tiles. We take the opportunity to do so in terms of isometries, applying and reinforcing ideas already built up. There are far-reaching extensions to three and higher dimensions (Coxeter, 1973, 1974).

Exercise Verify that the solutions of Equation (6.13) for $r = 3$ are as given in Table 6.5.

6.3.2 Coxeter graphs and Wythoff's construction

This construction applies to a configuration of mirrors whose mutual angles are all of the form π/p, $p \geq 2$. It can be used in three dimensions, and more generally in n dimensions, but our concern here will be the 2-dimensional plane. The *Coxeter graph* of a group generated by reflections $R, S, \ldots$ has *nodes* labelled $R, S, \ldots$ We join typical nodes R, S by an *edge* marked p if their mirrors are at angle π/p, $p \geq 3$. But we do not join these nodes if $p = 2$. Corresponding mirror lines are likewise labelled $R, S, \ldots$ as illustrated in Figure 6.15.

Key Example 6.18 Mirrors forming a right-angled triangle thus:

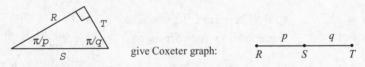

give Coxeter graph:

Figure 6.15

Note 6.19 The Coxeter graph here depicted denotes the dihedral group $D_{2p} = Gp\{R, S\}$, the symmetry group of a regular p-gon, generated by reflections R, S in two mirrors at angle π/p. (See Section 2.4 and especially Theorem 2.18.)

Wythoff's construction The 3-node graph in Figure 6.15 gives in principle up to seven distinct tilings of the plane for each allowable pair $p, q \geq 3$, corresponding to our assigning a special significance to one or more nodes by placing a small circle round each. This works as follows. The vertices of the tiling are the images under the group of one fixed *initial point*. The construction allocates these points to edges, and edges to polygonal faces, based on their belonging to *initial edges*, which belong in turn to *initial faces*. This works consistently because, for example, if A is a vertex of an edge e then A^g is a vertex of edge e^g for any isometry g. We begin with the simplest case.

One node ringed

The instructions are: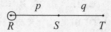

(a) Choose an initial point A on the intersection of all mirrors with unringed nodes, S and T in Figure 6.16(a).

(b) Form an initial edge AB, symbolised as $\underset{R}{\ominus}$, where $B = A^R$.

(c) Form an *initial polygon* (tile) t_0, symbolised as

$$\underset{R}{\ominus}\!\!\overset{p}{-\!-\!-\!-}\!\!\underset{S}{\bullet}$$

whose edges are the images of AB under $Gp\{R, S\}$, namely the rotated copies of AB through successive $1/p$ turns SR: $AB, BC, CD, \ldots$ It is shown in Figure 6.16(b) as a regular hexagon.

(d) Our tiling is defined to consist of the images of the initial polygonal tile t_0 under $Gp\{R, S, T\}$. The **inductive step** as applied to A is given below.

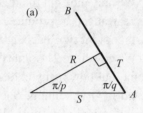

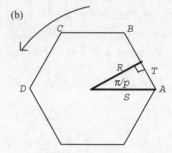

Figure 6.16(a),(b)

> Form the q images of t_0 under successive $1/q$ turns TS about A.

In Figure 6.16(c), $p = 6$ and $q = 3$. At every stage, a vertex P of the tiling formed so far has $1/q$ turns in terms of R, S, T and we use them to surround P with q copies of t_0 as was done the first time for A. For example:

$R_A(1/q) = TS$, so by Theorem 2.12 we have
$R_B(1/q) = TS^{SR}$, since the $1/p$ turn SR maps A to B, and
$R_C(1/q) = TS^{(SR)^2}$, since $(SR)^2$ maps A to C, and so on.

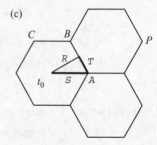

It remains to observe that all the isometries we have, such as the above, for t_0, go over into any adjacent p-gon via a reflection $T^{(SR)^r}$ in their common edge.

Figure 6.16(c)

Exercise Find a basis for the translation symmetries of $\{6, 3\}$ in terms of R, S, T above.

Exercise $\underset{R}{\ominus}\!\!\overset{3}{-\!-}\!\!\underset{S}{\bullet}\!\!\overset{6}{-\!-}\!\!\underset{T}{\bullet}$ has dual $\overset{3}{-\!-}\!\!\underset{R}{\bullet}\!\!\overset{6}{-\!-}\!\!\underset{S}{\bullet}\underset{T}{\ominus}$. Verify this by constructing both from the same mirrors R, S, T as shown in Figure 6.13.

It is very useful to understand this basic procedure first before going beyond what we have just constructed, namely a regular tiling $\{p, q\}$ for each allowable p, q that gives a right-angled triangle: $(4, 4)$, $(3, 6)$ or $(6, 3)$.

Initial polygons The general rule is: for each node, if deleting it and the adjacent edges leaves a 2-node subgraph with at least one node ringed, then this subgraph defines an initial polygon (unless the corresponding mirrors are at angle $\pi/2$). More details below.

A non-regular tiling Now let us obtain something new, still with only one node ringed, by interpreting Wythoff instructions (a) to (d) for this graph.

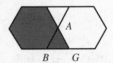

To show the relationship of this to $\{p, q\}$ and $\{q, p\}$ we put our right-angled *RST* triangle as before within a regular p-gon ($p = 6$ in Figure 6.17(a)). The initial point A is on the intersection of mirrors R and T (by Wythoff rule (a) above).

The initial edge $\overset{\odot}{S} = AB$ is common to two initial faces: the p-gon $\overset{p}{\underset{R}{\bullet\!\!-\!\!-\!\!-\!\!}}\overset{\odot}{S} = ABCDEF$, and q-gon

$\overset{\odot}{\underset{S}{\circ}}\overset{q}{\underset{T}{-\!\!-\!\!-\!\!\bullet}} = ABG.$

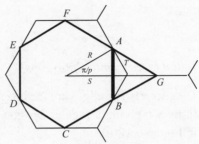

Figure 6.17(a)

We note that *FAG* is a straight line because $\pi/p + \pi/q = \pi/2$. Thus, in the tiling, A is surrounded by the initial pair of tiles plus their images under the $1/2$ turn *RT*, as shown here. Furthermore, it is clear from the construction, by a discussion similar to that for the preceding cases, that every point of the tiling is surrounded in the same way. Thus we have an Archimedean tiling of type (p, q, p, q). The *one new case* is $(3, 6, 3, 6)$. In three and higher dimensions we get rather more (see remarks at the end of this chapter).

Figure 6.17(b)

Cases with two rings

Case 1: Initial vertices and edges The only unringed vertex is T. On mirror T we place initial vertex A at the intersection with the angle bisector of mirrors R, S, as in Figure 6.18(a). This is the unique position which ensures that the initial edges $\overset{\odot}{R} = AB$ and $\overset{\odot}{S} = AL$ have the same length. Further, this is half the side length of the regular p-gon in which we place the *RST* triangle. See Figure 6.18(b).

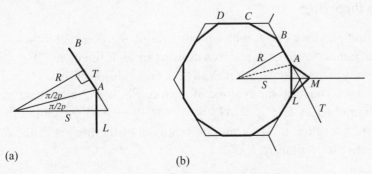

(a)   (b)

Figure 6.18

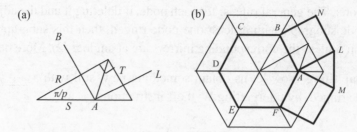

Figure 6.19

Initial faces (= tiles, polygons)

Diagram (i) The edges are the images of both AB and AL under $1/p$ turns SR, giving a regular $2p$-gon $ABC\ldots L$, inscribed as shown in Figure 6.18(b).

(i)

Diagram (ii) A regular q-gon $AL\ldots M$ formed from the images of AL under $1/q$ turns TS.

(ii)

Conclusion Polygons (i) and (ii) with their images under the $1/2$ turn RT surround vertex A, giving it type $(q, 2p, 2p)$. Hence we have a tiling of this type. Altogether the p, q pairs 4, 4; 3, 6; 6, 3 yield two new tilings, of types $(3, 12^2)$ and $(4, 8^2)$.

Case 2 The initial point A is the intersection of mirror S with the bisector of the angle between mirrors R and T, hence the initial edges $\overset{\odot}{R} = AB$, and $\overset{\odot}{T} = AL$ have the same length, as shown in Figure 6.19 (a).

Initial faces (tiles): (i) $\overset{p}{R\quad S}$ and (ii) $\overset{q}{S\quad T}$

Diagram (i) is a p-gon $ABC\ldots F$ whose edges are the images of AB under $1/p$ turns SR and are parallel to corresponding edges of the background polygon. Diagram (ii) is the q-gon $AL\ldots M$ bounded by q images of AL ($q = 3$ in Figure 6.19(b)). Now we apply the $1/2$ turn RT to (i) and (ii). They, with their copies, each provide one edge of a square $ABNL$. We see that A has type $(p, 4, q, 4)$. This gives one new tiling, of type $(3, 4, 6, 4)$.

Cases with three rings

Case 1 In the previous cases, with just two rings, the potential ambiguity of *initial vertex* A was resolved by using an angle bisector. Now we specify that A lie on two (hence all three) angle bisectors of the RST triangle. Thus A is the centroid of the triangle, and is equidistant from all three sides. The initial edges are: $\overset{\odot}{R} = AL,$ $\overset{\odot}{S} = AM,$ $\overset{\odot}{T} = AN$, shown in Figure 6.20(a), and have equal lengths. L, M, N are the centroids of the images of the RST triangle under respective reflections R, S, T.

Initial faces: (i) $\overset{p}{R\quad S}$ and (ii) $\overset{q}{S\quad T}$

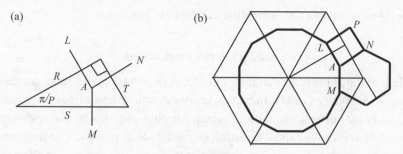

Figure 6.20

Here (i) is a $2p$-gon $AL\ldots M$ inscribed within the background p-gon as in Figure 6.20 (b), whilst (ii) is a $2q$-gon $AN\ldots M$ ($q = 3$). These, together with their images under the $1/2$ turn RT, contribute one edge each to bounding a square $ANPL$, also with A as a vertex. The type is $(4, 2q, 2p)$, giving us (besides some old ones) a new tiling type, $(4, 6, 12)$. The point types we have not covered are $(3^4, 6)$, $(3^3, 4^2)$, $(3^2, 4, 3, 4)$. They are not difficult, but we refer to Grünbaum and Shephard (1987) and give next a finite sample of all Archimedean tilings and their types. There appear 10 of the 21 types we identified as possible around a single point. One, $(3^4, 6)$, has a right handed and a left handed form obtained from it by an indirect isometry.

6.4 Creating plane patterns

6.4.1 Using nets and cells

Given a net type and a cell, we can do a little design work focussed on any or all of the vertices, edges, or cell interior, whilst keeping the same translation symmetries. A simple example is Figure 6.21(a). From a viewpoint which may intersect this, we can redraw the left edge with a meaningful cavity provided we put a corresponding bulge on the right edge. Similarly for horizontal edges, as in Figure 6.21(b). See also the excellent discussion in McGregor and Watt (1984), p. 237.

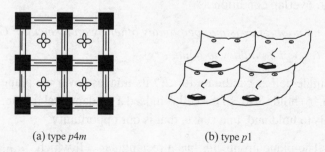

(a) type $p4m$ (b) type $p1$

Figure 6.21 Patterns formed by modifying aspects of a cell which is (a) a square, (b) a general parallelogram type.

Figure 6.21 shows two examples, followed by an exercise for the reader. Creative experimentation can reveal a great diversity of possibilities.

Exercise Design a pattern by embellishing the hexagonal net.

6.4.2 Patterns from tilings

Every tiling of the plane has a symmetry group. A great variety of tilings are described in Grünbaum & Shephard (1987). In particular, our Archimedean tilings have independent translations in two directions, their symmetry groups are clearly discrete (see Review 4.1 ff.), and therefore they must be some of the 17 plane groups. The first three tilings in Figure 6.23 are already nets, but the last nine give new examples in their own right. However, we can modify them in many ways, such as those shown in Figure 6.22.

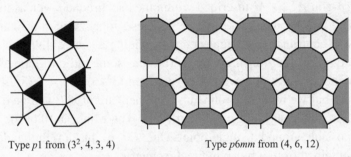

Type $p1$ from $(3^2, 4, 3, 4)$ Type $p6mm$ from $(4, 6, 12)$

Figure 6.22 Two plane patterns from simple additions to Archimedean tilings.

Exercise Design a sweater pattern by embellishing Archimedean tiling $(3^3, 4^2)$.

6.4.3 Using the fundamental region

Definition 6.20 A *fundamental region* $\mathcal{F}$ for a discrete group G of isometries of the plane is a closed region satisfying (see Definition 6.14)

$$\textit{the images of } \mathcal{F} \textit{ under } G \textit{ tile the plane.} \tag{6.15}$$

That is, the images cover the plane with no area overlap. It will be useful in the sequel to restate this no-overlap condition as

$$\textit{no point of } \mathcal{F} \textit{ is mapped to any other by an element of } G$$
$$\textit{(except boundary to boundary).} \tag{6.16}$$

What about a single cell as candidate for $\mathcal{F}$? Its images cover the plane, and for group $p1$ condition (6.16) holds also, so the cell is indeed a fundamental region. But in all other cases (6.16) fails to hold and, in a sense, that is our opportunity.

Example 6.21 The plane group pm has a rectangular cell which, with basepoint on one of the parallel mirrors, is bisected by another of these mirrors, as illustrated to the right with vertical mirror m. Because m reflects each half of the cell into the other, condition

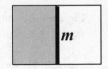

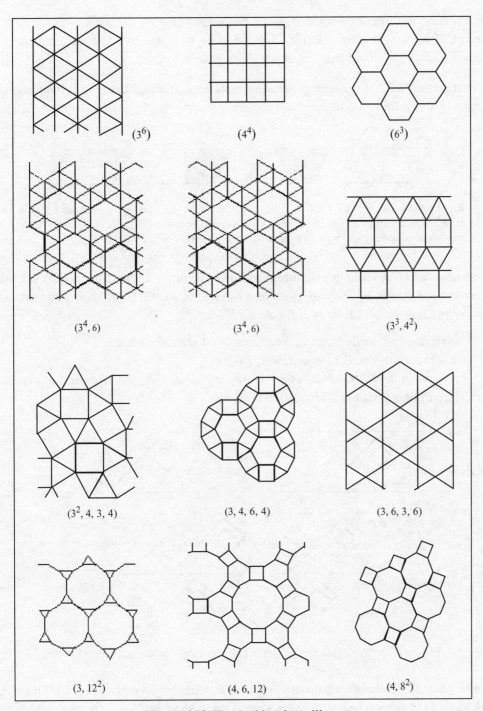

(3^6) (4^4) (6^3)

$(3^4, 6)$ $(3^4, 6)$ $(3^3, 4^2)$

$(3^2, 4, 3, 4)$ $(3, 4, 6, 4)$ $(3, 6, 3, 6)$

$(3, 12^2)$ $(4, 6, 12)$ $(4, 8^2)$

Figure 6.23 The Archimedean tilings.

(6.16) fails. But either the shaded or the unshaded half may be taken as fundamental region. Two step-by-step examples will illustrate how we may use the fundamental region as a tool to obtain patterns of any given type 'to order'.

Construction 6.22 *A pattern generation method* *Cut a cell down to a fundamental region, insert a submotif, then rebuild the cell.*

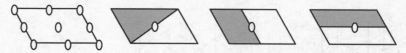

Figure 6.24 The *pg* cell with its 1/2 turns, and three choices of fundamental region (shaded). Condition (6.16) is satisfied (no overlap) because the central 1/2 turn sends the fundamental region onto an unshaded area. There are no mirrors here.

Example 6.23 We make a *p*2 pattern by Construction 6.22; first we need a suitable fundamental region, and we can get it as a subarea of a cell. Three ways to do this are shown in Figure 6.24. Then, as in Figure 6.25, we

1. draw an asymmetric motif in the chosen fundamental region;
2. add in its image under the central 1/2 turn;
3. now put in the *p*2 translates of this combined motif. The guidelines may or may not be part of the pattern. They are *not* mirrors.

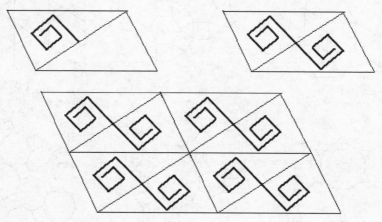

Figure 6.25 Stages in constructing a pattern of type *p*2 from an initial motif.

Example 6.24 We create a pattern of type *cmm*, again by Construction 6.22. This time finding a fundamental region $\mathcal{F}$ takes several steps, shown in Figure 6.26, in which we start with a cell and repeatedly discard an area because it is the image of another part of the cell under a symmetry in *cmm*, and so is not required for $\mathcal{F}$, by (6.16). Unlike in the previous example, we may take the cell edges as mirrors. There are glides too, as well as 1/2 turns (Section 5.4).

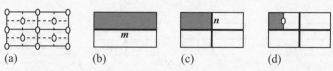

Figure 6.26 (a) The symmetries of *cmm*. In cutting down the cell to a fundamental region we discard (b) the lower (white) half of the cell since it is the image of the shaded half under the mirror *m*, (c) the right half of the cell because of mirror *n*, (d) another 1/8th because of the 1/2 turn shown.

The shaded area (d) of Figure 6.26 is a fundamental region $\mathcal{F}$, since it cannot be further subdivided by symmetries of *cmm* (Condition (6.16)), and its images fill the cell (without overlap) and hence the whole plane after translations are applied (Condition (6.15)). Now we put a simple motif $M = \ \rule[0.4ex]{0.8em}{0.4pt}\!\!\rule[-0.4ex]{0.4pt}{1em}\,\rule[0.4ex]{0.8em}{0.4pt}$ in $\mathcal{F}$ and rebuild the cell, working back the way we came, and including the motif in each image of $\mathcal{F}$. See Figure 6.27.

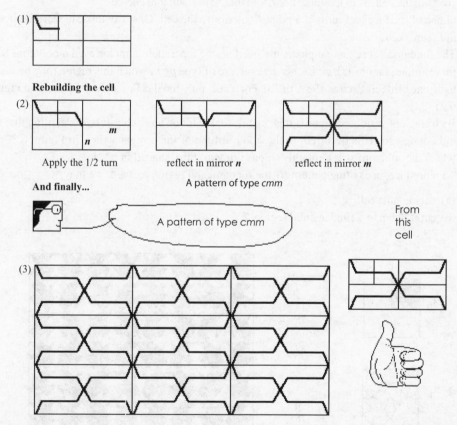

Figure 6.27 Building a *cmm* type pattern: (1) draw motif in fundamental region, (2) fill the cell, (3) tile the plane.

Remarks 6.25

(i) As in Examples 6.23 and 6.24 above, it often helps to create a pleasing result if the motif is in contact with the boundary of the fundamental region.

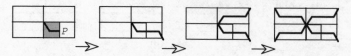

Figure 6.29 Reconstruction of cell contents from fundamental region 7.

(ii) There are many possible choices of fundamental region and, in choosing a succession of symmetries in G to reduce the cell to a fundamental region, we have in fact found a set of generators for G. A diagram of the configuration of symmetries around a cell, as in Sections 5.2 to 5.6, enables us to assess the choices (Figure 6.28). For a given effect, some may be more convenient than others.

1	2	3	4
5	6	7	8

Figure 6.28 Eight congruent choices of $\mathcal{F}$ in Example 6.24.

Convenient generators are the horizontal and vertical mirrors crossing the cell, as in Example 6.24, together with a suitable choice of one of the four half turns at a point P interior to the cell. One way this can work is shown in Figure 6.29.

(iii) The fundamental region emphatically need not be a parallelogram, or even a polygon. See, for example, Figure 1.2, an Escher-like picture of type pg in which this region may be taken to be one bird (cf. Escher, 1989, p. 30). For a non-polygonal cell, see the $p1$ pattern in Figure 6.21.

(iv) By trying out various submotifs it is not unusual to hit on an Escher-type dovetailing that we did not design. This occurred, to the good fortune of the present writer, in Figure 6.30, in which the submotif was a roughly 'mouse-drawn' bird, shaded in black.

(v) To reproduce an existing pattern by the fundamental region method, we may

(a) decide on a cell,

(b) cut it down to a fundamental region $\mathcal{F}$,

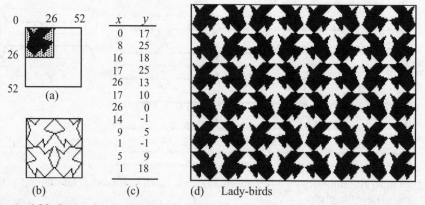

x	y
0	17
8	25
16	18
17	25
26	13
17	10
26	0
14	-1
9	5
1	-1
5	9
1	18

(a)   (b)   (c)   (d)   Lady-birds

Figure 6.30 Stages in computer generation of a *cm* pattern with square cell. (a) Bird motif in fundamental region. The scale is in pixels. (b) Copies of unshaded motif filling the cell, corresponding to generators of *cm*. (c) Local pixel coordinates of 'moused-in' submotif. (d) The *cm* pattern obtained by tiling the plane with cells. Note the Chinese ladies outlined in white.

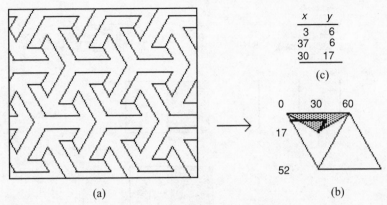

Figure 6.31 Converting a plane pattern to a generating submotif. (a) A common Islamic pattern, (b) a suitable submotif, (c) its calculated coordinates.

(c) note the portion of the picture contained in $\mathcal{F}$,

(d) recreate this submotif and apply to it the group of symmetries, building up to a cell, then to the plane area it is desired to cover. See Figure 6.31.

Exercise Notice that in Figure 6.31 the submotif does not quite lie within the fundamental region. What is gained by this? Redraw diagram (b) to produce the same pattern (a), but this time starting from a submotif lying entirely within the fundamental region. Use your diagram to reconstruct the pattern by hand.

6.4.4 Algorithm for the 17 plane patterns

Nomenclature Coordinates are rectangular, measured in pixels or otherwise, from an origin at O, the top left hand corner of the given cell. G is the centroid of the cell, with coordinates (xg, yg). For the hexagonal net only, G_1 and G_2 are the centroids of the two equilateral triangles shown forming a cell. Their coordinates are (xg_1, yg_1), (xg_2, yg_2). On the other hand, the subscripted g_1 and g_2 are glides, with mirror position and translation component together represented by a dashed directed line segment $---\rightarrow$. Without the arrowhead thus: $------$, only the position of the glideline is being specified, but its translation component may be taken to be one half the shortest translation symmetry along its line (see (6.12)).

How to read the list Figure 6.32 describes the algorithm by listing isometries to be applied in succession to a cell, starting with a submotif in the fundamental region, so that tiling the plane with the drawn-in cell will produce a pattern of prescribed type. This was the procedure followed in Examples 6.23 and 6.24. Thus for example 'Do: R_m, R_n' in *pmm* means: 'In addition to the pixels already illuminated in the cell, turn on all their images under R_m (but don't turn any off). Then repeat this for R_n.'

Exercise Reposition the *pmg* cell so that the vertices are 2-fold centres, and obtain a new fundamental region and generator system.

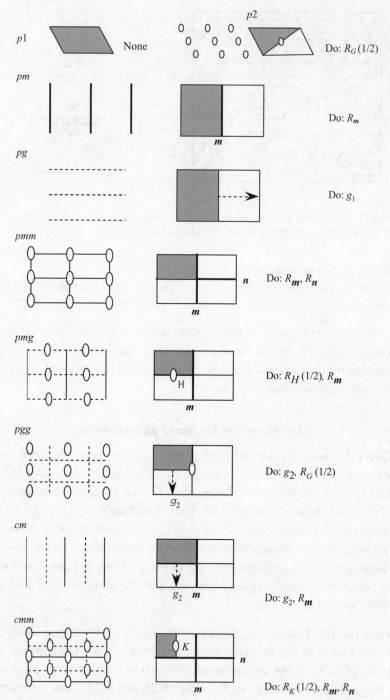

Figure 6.32 (*Algorithm for the 17 plane patterns*) Isometry sequence to fill a cell, centre G, starting with a submotif in the fundamental region.

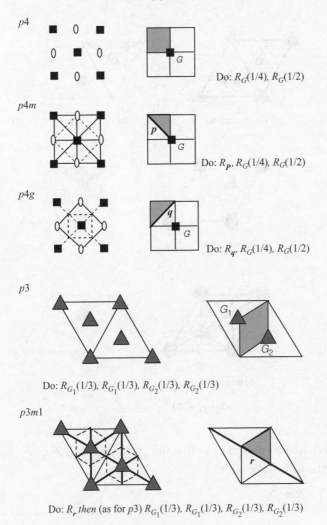

p4

Do: $R_G(1/4)$, $R_G(1/2)$

p4m

Do: R_P, $R_G(1/4)$, $R_G(1/2)$

p4g

Do: R_q, $R_G(1/4)$, $R_G(1/2)$

p3

Do: $R_{G_1}(1/3)$, $R_{G_1}(1/3)$, $R_{G_2}(1/3)$, $R_{G_2}(1/3)$

p3m1

Do: R_r then (as for p3) $R_{G_1}(1/3)$, $R_{G_1}(1/3)$, $R_{G_2}(1/3)$, $R_{G_2}(1/3)$

Figure 6.32 *(Continued)*

Exercise Follow through the steps by which the fundamental region is made to tile the cell in case *pgg*.

Exercise Verify that the cell of *p4g* is rebuilt from the fundamental region as implied. Can you suggest a way to do it using a glide?

Exercise Explain why no 1/6 turn is required as generator in case *p6m*.

Other approaches Having followed Figure 6.32, the reader will be able to find other formulations of fundamental region $\mathcal{F}$ and associated isometries $f, g, h, \ldots$ If it is desirable or necessary to fill the cell by straight copies of $\mathcal{F}$ rather than the procedure above,

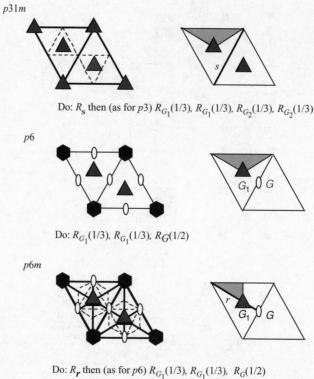

p31m

Do: R_s then (as for *p3*) $R_{G_1}(1/3)$, $R_{G_1}(1/3)$, $R_{G_2}(1/3)$, $R_{G_2}(1/3)$

p6

Do: $R_{G_1}(1/3)$, $R_{G_1}(1/3)$, $R_G(1/2)$

p6m

Do: R_r then (as for *p6*) $R_{G_1}(1/3)$, $R_{G_1}(1/3)$, $R_G(1/2)$

Figure 6.32 (*Continued*)

the way to do this may be inferred by noting that, for example: $(\mathcal{F} \cup \mathcal{F}^f)^g = \mathcal{F}^g \cup \mathcal{F}^{fg}$, so that we have the following table.

Done so far	Result
f	$\mathcal{F} \cup \mathcal{F}^f$
f, g	$\mathcal{F} \cup \mathcal{F}^f \cup \mathcal{F}^g \cup \mathcal{F}^{fg}$
f, g, h	$\mathcal{F} \cup \mathcal{F}^f \cup \mathcal{F}^g \cup \mathcal{F}^{fg} \cup \mathcal{F}^h \cup \mathcal{F}^{fh} \cup \mathcal{F}^{gh} \cup \mathcal{F}^{fgh}$

There may well now be redundancies, enabling us to delete some of the terms above in the unions.

Exercise Suppose the above method is applied. Can any terms in the union be dropped in the case of *p4g* or *p3*?

Exercise Derive the formulae for R_m and $R_G(1/4)$ in Table 6.6 (hint: use Corollary 2.2).

Remarks

1. There is a useful method of tiling the plane or higher dimensions starting from a collections of points. This is the Voronoi triangulation. It has been found useful in computer graphics and in our Sections 11.2 and 18.3.6. (Dobkin, 1988).

Table 6.6. *Coordinate form for generators of the 17 plane groups. $G(xg, yg)$ is the centre of gravity of a cell. In hexagonal net, $yg = xg/\sqrt{3}$, G_1 and G_2 have respective coordinates $(2/3)(xg, yg)$ and $(4/3)(xg, yg)$.*

Generating	First isometry appearance	Result $(x, y) \to x'$	$(x', y'), y'$
R_m	pm	$2xg - x$	y
R_n	pmm	x	$2yg - y$
R_p	$p4m$	y	x
R_q	$p4g$	$xg - y$	$xg - x$
R_r	$p3m1$	$(x + y\sqrt{3})/2$	$(x\sqrt{3} - y)/2$
R_s	$p31m$	$(4xg - x - y\sqrt{3})/2$	$(4yg - x\sqrt{3} + y)/2$
$R_G(1/2)$	$p2$	$2xg - x$	$2yg - y$
$R_H(1/2)$	pmg	$xg - x$	$2yg - y$
$R_K(1/2)$	cmm	$2xg - x$	$yg - y$
$R_G(1/4)$	$p4$	y	$2xg - x$
g_1	pg	$x + xg$	$2yg - y$
g_2	pgg	$xg - x$	$y + yg$
$R_O(1/3)$		$-(x + y\sqrt{3})/2$	$(x\sqrt{3} - y)/2$
$R_{G_1}(1/3)$	$p3$	$4xg/3 - (x + y\sqrt{3})/2$	$(x\sqrt{3} - y)/2$
$R_{G_2}(1/3)$	$p3$	$8xg/3 - (x + y\sqrt{3})/2$	$(x\sqrt{3} - y)/2$

Note: Some of the formulae above are conveniently derived by techniques found in Section 7.4. The matrix of a transformation, though they could be done by a judicious combination of Theorem 2.1 and brute force. Many are straightforward, and are set as exercises.

2. In Wythoff's construction for 3-space, mirror lines become firstly the intersection of planes with the surface of a sphere (great circles). We get a fundamental region bounded by such curves and a unifying approach to the polyhedra with some degree of regularity such as the Platonic solids (cube, icosahedron, ...) and many others. The techniques cover tilings of 3-space and beyond (Coxeter, 1973, 1974).
3. All this is intimately connected with the construction of 'error-correcting codes' for communications. See Section 13.2 and e.g. Conway & Sloane (1988).

Exercises 6

1 $\checkmark$ Why cannot the groups C_{12} and D_{12} be isomorphic? Give an example of two symmetry groups which are isomorphic but not equivalent (not from amongst the 17 types). See Section 2.4 and Table 6.2.

2 Write out the ten elements of D_{10} in terms of reflections R, S in mirrors at the least possible angle (see Section 2.4).

3 In a pattern of type pgg pick out symmetries which yield the elements of the point group. (Cf. Example 6.11. See Section 5.7 and Exercise 5.1.) Do the same for one of type p3m1.

4 $\checkmark$ Prove that there are only three regular tilings of the plane.

5   Write a computer program to produce the solutions of Table 6.5 for Archimedean plane tilings.

6   Find a basis for the translation symmetries of the plane tiling by squares, in terms of three generating reflections R, S, T for the symmetry group.

7   This Coxeter diagram, with $p = 3$, $q = 6$, produces an Archimedean plane tiling of type (3, 6, 3, 6) by Wythoff's construction. Apply this construction by hand up to at least six hexagons.

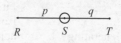

8   Obtain a tiling of type (3, 4, 6, 4) from the Coxeter diagram shown, with $p = 3$, $q = 6$.

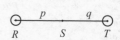

9   Obtain a plane pattern by suitable shading of one of the Archimedean tilings of Figure 6.23. Which of the 17 types results? Find the plane pattern type of each example in the table.

10. Starting with the hexagonal net, design plane patterns of type (i) $p6m$, (ii) $p3m1$.

11   For each plane pattern in Examples 4.20, find a fundamental region and submotif, then regenerate the pattern. State the type. Record what you do at each stage.

12   Repeat Exercise 6.11 for patterns (a) to (g) in Exercise 4.6.

13 ✓ Identify the pattern type in Figure 6.33. Find fundamental regions of two distinct shapes and their associated submotifs and generators. Illustrate by regenerating (enough of) each pattern by hand.

14 ✓ Referring to Figure 6.32, type pmg, reposition the basepoint at a 2-fold centre. Can you find a fundamental region $\mathcal{F}$ within the cell? If so, give at least one possible list of symmetries with their images of $\mathcal{F}$ which tile the cell. Does this work for pgg with basepoint at the intersection of two glidelines?

15   For one pattern type in each net type, use Figure 6.32 to design a plane pattern, using the same submotif in the fundamental region for each case.

16   Extend Exercise 15 to all 17 types.

17   Write a computer program implementing the method of Figure 6.32 for pattern type cmm, in which the user specifies what lies inside the fundamental region.

18   Extend Exercise 17 to all patterns with rectangular cell.

19   Derive at least four lines of Table 6.6.

20   Project: implement all procedures of Figure 6.32.

Figure 6.33 Pattern for Exercise 13.

Program polynet

This software is an implementation of the plane pattern algorithm of Figure 6.32, and may be down loaded, with manual, from www.maths.gla.ac.uk/~sgh.

Operation	Choose the pattern type–this determines the net type
	Draw motif in an enlarged fundamental region
	Save and/or print the resulting pattern
Features	Works (so far) on any Macintosh computer
	Adjusts to screen size
	Works in colour, black and white, or greyscale
	User may vary size and shape of cell within its net type
	Motif specified via mouse or exact typed coordinates

Notes The majority of plane patterns in this book were produced by polynet, for example Figure 6.30, in case of design *plus* accident, and Figure 6.31, in which motif coordinates were precisely calculated.

Indeed, many users have obtained surprising and striking results by complete 'accident', by drawing partly ouside the fundamental region and thereby creating overlap which can be very hard to predict.

Part II
Matrix structures

7

Vectors and matrices

In this chapter we ease the transition from vectors in the plane to three dimensions and n-space. The angle between two vectors is often replaced by their scalar product, which is in many ways easier to work with and has special properties. Other kinds of vector product are useful too in geometry. An important issue for a set of vectors is whether it is dependent (i.e. whether one vector is a linear combination of the others). This apparently simple idea will have many ramifications in practical application.

We introduce the first properties of matrices, an invaluable handle on transformations in 2-, 3- and n-space. At this stage, besides identifying isometries with orthogonal matrices, we characterise the matrices of projection mappings, preparatory to the Singular Value Decomposition of Chapter 8 (itself leading to an optimal transform in Chapter 10.)

7.1 Vectors and handedness

This section is something like an appendix. The reader may wish to scan quickly through or refer back to it later for various formulae and notations. We reviewed vectors in the plane in Section 1.2.1. Soon we will see how the vector properties of having direction and length are even more useful in 3-space. The results of Section 1.2.1 still hold, but vectors now have three components rather than two.

7.1.1 Recapitulation – vectors

A *vector* v consists of a magnitude $|v|$, also called the *length* of v, and a direction. Thus, as illustrated in Figure 7.1, v is representable by any directed line segment AB with the same length and direction. Note that $|v| = |AB|$. Vectors may be *added* 'nose to tail', also illustrated in Figure 7.1. Further, if α is a real number, often called in this context a *scalar*, we can form the *product* αv: scale the length of v by a factor $|\alpha|$, and reverse its direction if α is negative. This is a very convenient system, allowing us to write $-\alpha a$ for $(-\alpha)a$, $-a$ for $(-1)a$, and a/α for $(1/\alpha)a$, and to define subtraction by $a - b = a + (-b)$ (see Figure 1.7).

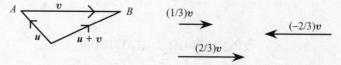

Figure 7.1 Vector addition, and multiplying a vector by a scalar.

We use **0** for the anomalous vector with length 0 and direction undefined, and refer to vector **a** as being nonzero if **a** $\neq$ **0**. Two vectors are (by definition) equal if they have the same magnitude and direction. We follow the custom of writing **a** $= PQ = RS$ to mean that the length and direction of all three are the same, although PQ and RS have the additional property of a position in space (not necessarily the same position). Now we give a simple definition and remark with far-reaching usefulness in the sequel. Note that in forming **a**$/|$**a**$|$ we are scaling the length $|$**a**$|$ of **a** by a factor $1/|$**a**$|$, so the new length is 1.

Definition 7.1 A *unit vector* is a vector of length 1. A set of mutually orthogonal, i.e. perpendicular, unit vectors is said to be *orthonormal*.

$$\textit{If } \textbf{a} \textit{ is any nonzero vector then } \textbf{a}/|\textbf{a}| \textit{ is a unit vector.} \tag{7.1}$$

7.1.2 Recapitulation – coordinate axes

In ordinary Euclidean 3-space, three mutually orthogonal unit vectors $\textbf{i}, \textbf{j}, \textbf{k}$, starting from a chosen origin O, define coordinate axes as in Figure 7.2. A directional convention we will normally use is that vectors arrowed down and to the left point out of the paper towards the reader. This means that any point P has unique *coordinates* x, y, z (with respect to $\textbf{i}, \textbf{j}, \textbf{k}$), defined by

$$OP = x\textbf{i} + y\textbf{j} + z\textbf{k}. \tag{7.2}$$

We use (x, y, z) to mean, according to context,

1. The point P,
2. The *position vector OP* of P,
3. Any vector with the same magnitude and direction as OP.

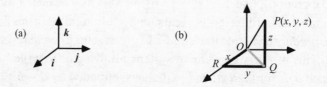

Figure 7.2 How coordinates (x, y, z) define the position of a point P, starting from the origin. Vector $\textbf{i}$ points towards the reader, with $\textbf{j}, \textbf{k}$ in the plane of the paper.

In 2 and 3 we call x, y, z the *components* of the vector with respect to i, j, k, which itself is an *orthonormal set*, since i, j, k are *orthogonal*, of length 1. They are also called a *basis* for 3-space because any vector is a unique linear combination (7.2) of them. To add vectors, we add corresponding components. To multiply by a scalar, we multiply each component by that scalar.

Notation 7.2 The point A will have position vector a, with components (a_1, a_2, a_3). Similarly for other letters, except $P(x, y, z)$. For the distance $|OP|$ we have

$$|OP|^2 = x^2 + y^2 + z^2, \quad \text{by Pythagoras,}$$

hence

$$|AB| = \sqrt{(b_1 - a_1)^2 + (b_2 - a_2)^2 + (b_3 - a_3)^2}. \tag{7.3}$$

Proof In Figure 7.2(b) we have $|OP|^2 = |OQ|^2 + |QP|^2$ by Pythagoras in triangle $OPQ, = (x^2 + y^2) + z^2$, by Pythagoras in triangle OQR. For (7.3) we may imagine the line segment AB translated so that A becomes the origin and B plays the part of P. Then P has coordinates $x = b_1 - a_1$, and so on, and $|AB|^2 = |OP|^2$.

Direction cosines For general OP these are the cosines of the angles α, β, γ between OP and the positive directions on the x-, y- and z-axes. The angle γ is shown in Figure 7.3. Thus with $|OP| = r$ we have $x = r \cos \alpha, y = r \cos \beta, z = r \cos \gamma$.

Exercise Prove that $\cos^2 \alpha + \cos^2 \beta + \cos^2 \gamma = 1$.

7.1.3 Right handed versus left handed triples

In Section 1.2.3 we used the idea of the sense (clockwise or anti-clockwise) of a non-collinear triple of points in the plane. Here we investigate its analogue in 3-space. By convention i, j, k is always a *right handed* system or triple, as in the definition below.

Definition 7.3 Vectors a, b, c are *coplanar* if the points O, A, B, C are coplanar. An ordered triple a, b, c of non-coplanar vectors is *right handed* if:

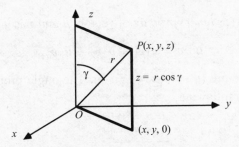

Figure 7.3 The direction cosine of OP with respect to the z-axis is $\cos \gamma$.

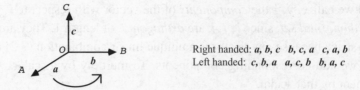

Figure 7.4 Right handed versus left handed triples, with a towards the reader.

> *in plane OAB viewed from C, the rotation about O that moves A to B by the shorter route is anti-clockwise (i.e. the sense of OAB is anti-clockwise),*

otherwise a, b, c is a *left handed triple* (NB: a, b, c need not be orthogonal in this definition).

We see that if a, b, c is right handed then so are the cyclic shifts of this ordering, namely b, c, a and c, a, b. The other possible orderings, the reverses of the above, are then the left handed ones.

Right Hand Corkscrew Rule The righthandedness condition is equivalent to the statement: c points to the same side of plane *OAB* as the direction of motion of a right handed screw placed at O perpendicular to this plane, and turning *OA* towards *OB*. An alternative description of right-handedness in the case a, b, c are mutually perpendicular is: if the first finger of the right hand points along *OA* and the second along *OB*, then the thumb, when at right angles to the first two, points along *OC*.

 With a computer screen in mind it is quite usual to take our b, c as defining respectively x-, y-axes, in the plane of the page/screen. Then the z-axis points towards the reader in a right handed system and into the page/screen in the left handed case.

Exercise Is the triple a, b, c right or left handed, where $a = (0, 0, -1)$, $b = (-1, 1, 0)$, and $c = (1, 0, 2)$? What if the order of a, b is interchanged? See Theorems 7.41, 7.42.

7.1.4 The scalar product

Given a pair of vectors we may calculate, as below, a scalar product. From this flows a systematic and short way to determine for example (i) the angle between vectors and (ii) whether a triple is right handed.

Definition 7.4 The *dot* (or *inner*) *product* of vectors u and v is

$$u \cdot v = u_1 v_1 + u_2 v_2 + u_3 v_3. \tag{7.4}$$

Angles Other notations are (u, v), $\langle u, v \rangle$, $(u|v)$. The angle properties of this product stem from (7.5) to (7.7) following.

$$\boxed{u \cdot u = |u|^2.} \tag{7.5}$$

If ϕ is the angle between nonzero vectors $\boldsymbol{u}$, $\boldsymbol{v}$
(that is, the one satisfying $0 \leq \phi \leq \pi$) then

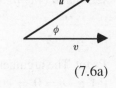

$$\cos\phi = \frac{\boldsymbol{u}\cdot\boldsymbol{v}}{|\boldsymbol{u}||\boldsymbol{v}|}. \tag{7.6a}$$

(*Component formula*) A vector $\boldsymbol{u}$ has components $\boldsymbol{u}\cdot\boldsymbol{i}, \boldsymbol{u}\cdot\boldsymbol{j}, \boldsymbol{u}\cdot\boldsymbol{k}$. (7.6b)

These are its *direction cosines* if $\boldsymbol{u}$ is a unit vector. Thirdly, expressing the inner product in terms of distances (see also (7.8)).

$$2\boldsymbol{u}\cdot\boldsymbol{v} = |\boldsymbol{u}|^2 + |\boldsymbol{v}|^2 - |\boldsymbol{u}-\boldsymbol{v}|^2. \tag{7.7}$$

Proof Formula (7.5) is the trivial but useful observation that $\boldsymbol{u}\cdot\boldsymbol{u} = u_1^2 + u_2^2 + u_3^2$, whilst (7.6) comes from the Cosine Rule in triangle OUV (Figure 7.5) and (7.7) is by direct calculation:

$$\begin{aligned}
2|\boldsymbol{u}||\boldsymbol{v}|\cos\phi &= |\boldsymbol{u}|^2 + |\boldsymbol{v}|^2 - |\boldsymbol{u}-\boldsymbol{v}|^2 \quad \text{(Cosine Rule)}\\
&= (u_1^2 + u_2^2 + u_3^2) + (v_1^2 + v_2^2 + v_3^2)\\
&\quad - (u_1-v_1)^2 - (u_2-v_2)^2 - (u_3-v_3)^2\\
&= 2u_1v_1 + 2u_2v_2 + 2u_3v_3 = 2\boldsymbol{u}\cdot\boldsymbol{v}.
\end{aligned}$$

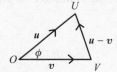

Figure 7.5 The cosine rule.

So $\cos\phi = \boldsymbol{u}\cdot\boldsymbol{v}/|\boldsymbol{u}||\boldsymbol{v}|$. The deduction (7.6b) about components is typified by $u_1 = |\boldsymbol{u}|\cos\alpha$ (where α is the angle between $\boldsymbol{u}$ and the x-axis) $= |\boldsymbol{i}||\boldsymbol{u}|\cos\alpha$ (as $|\boldsymbol{i}| = 1$) $= \boldsymbol{u}\cdot\boldsymbol{i}$ (by (7.6a)). Thus, if $|\boldsymbol{u}| = 1$ then $u_1 = \boldsymbol{u}\cdot\boldsymbol{i} = \cos\alpha$.

Basic properties Definition 7.4 of scalar product $\boldsymbol{u}\cdot\boldsymbol{v}$ was given in coordinates, but by (7.7) it is independent of the choice of $\boldsymbol{i}, \boldsymbol{j}, \boldsymbol{k}$, even if we should choose a left handed system. The basic commutative and distributive laws stated below are a consequence of (7.4).

$$\begin{aligned}
\boldsymbol{v}\cdot\boldsymbol{u} &= \boldsymbol{u}\cdot\boldsymbol{v},\\
\boldsymbol{u}\cdot(\boldsymbol{v}+\boldsymbol{w}) &= \boldsymbol{u}\cdot\boldsymbol{v} + \boldsymbol{u}\cdot\boldsymbol{w},\\
\boldsymbol{u}\cdot(\alpha\boldsymbol{v}) &= \alpha(\boldsymbol{u}\cdot\boldsymbol{v}) = (\alpha\boldsymbol{u})\cdot\boldsymbol{v}.
\end{aligned} \tag{7.8}$$

Notice that (7.7) now follows from (7.8) without the Cosine Rule, for $|\boldsymbol{u}-\boldsymbol{v}|^2 = (\boldsymbol{u}-\boldsymbol{v})\cdot(\boldsymbol{u}-\boldsymbol{v}) = \boldsymbol{u}\cdot\boldsymbol{u} + \boldsymbol{v}\cdot\boldsymbol{v} - \boldsymbol{u}\cdot\boldsymbol{v} - \boldsymbol{v}\cdot\boldsymbol{u} = |\boldsymbol{u}|^2 + |\boldsymbol{v}|^2 - 2\boldsymbol{u}\cdot\boldsymbol{v}$. Any scalar product of two vectors that satisfies (7.8) is called an *inner product*, with the dot product as *standard inner product*. We need the compact notation of the *Kronecker delta* δ_{ik}, defined as 1 if $i = k$ and 0 otherwise.

Theorem 7.5 *(a) Two nonzero vectors $\boldsymbol{u}$, $\boldsymbol{v}$ are perpendicular if and only if $\boldsymbol{u}\cdot\boldsymbol{v} = 0$.*
(b) Three vectors $\boldsymbol{e}_1, \boldsymbol{e}_2, \boldsymbol{e}_3$ are mutually orthogonal unit vectors (form an orthonormal

set) if and only if

$$e_i \cdot e_k = \delta_{ik}. \tag{7.9}$$

Proof The argument is simple but important. We use the notation of (7.6).

(a) $u \cdot v = 0 \Leftrightarrow \cos \phi = 0 \Leftrightarrow \phi = \pi/2$ (i.e. u and v are perpendicular).

(b) (7.9) combines two statements: (i) $e_i \cdot e_i = 1 \Leftrightarrow |e_i|^2 = 1 \Leftrightarrow e_i$ is a unit vector, and (ii) $e_i \cdot e_k = 0$ if $i \neq k$. That is, the three vectors are mutually perpendicular.

Notice that e_1, e_2, e_3 play the same role as the orthonormal i, j, k. This often helps notationally, as in Chapter 8. Further results about vector products must be postponed until we have reviewed matrices in Section 7.2.

Exercise Show that the vectors $a = (1, 2, 3)$ and $b = (6, 3, -4)$ are perpendicular (Theorem 7.5). Find the angle between a diagonal OA of a cube and an adjacent face diagonal by using suitable coordinates for A. (Use (7.6).)

7.1.5 A trip through n-space

Though 3-space is an important concern, it is essential for the sequel that we consider vectors with more than three components. The current Section, 7.1.5, will be more abstract than most in Chapter 7, but it serves as an introduction to general abstract vector spaces, as well as providing a necessary foundation for our particular cases.

We define $\mathbf{R}^n$ to be the set of all n-tuples $x = (x_1, x_2, \ldots, x_n)$, where we call x both a *vector with components* x_i and a *point with coordinates* x_i, as in the case $n = 3$. We perform the same calculations with coordinates as before, for example adding vectors and multiplying by a scalar. The dot product extends simply to

$$u \cdot v = u_1 v_1 + u_2 v_2 + \cdots + u_n v_n,$$

for which (7.1) to (7.9) continue to hold, with the proviso that the angle between vectors u, v is now *defined* by (7.6a): $\cos \phi = u \cdot v / |u||v|$, where $|u| = \sqrt{\sum u_i^2} = u \cdot u$, and the component formula (7.6b) requires a separate proof (Theorem 7.14). The *unit sphere* in n-space is $S^{n-1} = \{x \in \mathbf{R}^n \colon |x| = 1\}$.

Setting $n = 3$, we obtain the usual model of our three-dimensional world. Thus S^1 is a circle in the plane and S^2 the usual sphere in 3-space.

Definition 7.6 Vectors $u_1, u_2, \ldots, u_k$ in $\mathbf{R}^n$ are called *linearly dependent*, or LD, if some *linear combination* $\lambda_1 u_1 + \lambda_2 u_2 + \cdots + \lambda_k u_k$ equals $\mathbf{0}$ (i.e. the *zero vector* $(0, 0, \ldots, 0)$), where not all the coefficients λ_i are zero. In this case any vector with nonzero coefficient, say $\lambda_1 \neq 0$, equals a linear combination of the rest, $u_1 = (-\lambda_2/\lambda_1)u_2 + \cdots + (-\lambda_k/\lambda_1)u_k$. The u_i are called *(linearly) independent*, or LI, if they are not dependent.

An often useful test is:

> $u_1, u_2, \ldots, u_k$ are independent (LI) if, for any scalars c_i,
> $c_1u_1 + c_2u_2 + \cdots + c_ku_k = 0 \Rightarrow$ all c_i are zero.

Theorem 7.7 *Any $n + 1$ vectors in $\mathbf{R}^n$ are linearly dependent.*

Proof We use the Principle of Mathematical Induction. That is, if the result holds for $n = 1$, and its truth for $n = k$ implies its truth for $n = k + 1$ for $k = 1, 2, 3, \ldots$, then the result holds for all $n \in \mathbf{N}$. Proceeding with the proof we check the case $n = 1$: if a, b are two numbers then there are coefficients λ, μ, not both zero, such that $\lambda_a + \mu b = 0$. This is almost trivial, for if $a = b = 0$ we may take $\lambda = \mu = 1$, whilst if $a \neq 0$ then $\lambda = -b/a, \mu = 1$ will do; the remaining case $a = 0, b \neq 0$ is covered by $\lambda = 1, \mu = -a/b$. So suppose that Theorem 7.7 is true for some positive integer $n = k$. We are to deduce the truth for $n = k + 1$.

Thus let $u_1, \ldots, u_{k+2}$ be $k + 2$ arbitrary vectors in R^{k+1}. To deduce they are dependent, suppose, reordering if necessary, that $c_{k+2} \neq 0$, and consider the $k + 1$ vectors

$$v_i = u_i - (c_i/c_{k+2})u_{k+2} \qquad (1 \leq i \leq k + 1).$$

Since the last coordinate of each is 0 by construction, these amount to $k + 1$ vectors in $\mathbf{R}^k$, so by the inductive hypothesis there are scalars λ_i ($1 \leq i \leq k + 1$), not all zero, such that $\sum \lambda_i v_i = 0$. But from the definition of the v_i this gives a linear relation on $u_1, \ldots, u_{k+2}$ with not all coefficients zero. Hence these vectors are LD and the theorem follows by induction.

Theorem 7.8 *If $u_1, u_2, \ldots, u_n$ are linearly independent vectors of $\mathbf{R}^n$ then they form a basis of $\mathbf{R}^n$, that is, any a in $\mathbf{R}^n$ is a unique linear combination of $u_1, u_2, \ldots, u_n$.*

Proof The $n + 1$ vectors $a, u_1, u_2, \ldots, u_n$ are dependent by Theorem 7.7, so we have that $\lambda_0 a + \lambda_1 u_1 + \lambda_2 u_2 + \cdots + \lambda_n u_n = \mathbf{0}$ with not all coefficients zero. In fact λ_0 is nonzero, otherwise the u_i would be dependent. Thus a is some combination of the vectors u_i. Furthermore, the combination is unique, because $a = \sum \lambda_i u_i = \sum \lambda_i' u_i$ implies $\sum (\lambda_i - \lambda_i')u_i = \mathbf{0}$ and hence, since the u_i are independent, each coefficient $\lambda_i - \lambda_i'$ is zero, or $\lambda_i = \lambda_i'$.

Definition 7.9 We have considered n-space, $\mathbf{R}^n$, consisting of n-vectors, but we need something broader because, for example, a plane through the origin in $\mathbf{R}^3$ is effectively a copy of $\mathbf{R}^2$. We define more generally a **vector space** V to be either $\mathbf{R}^n$ for some n, or a subset thereof closed under vector addition and multiplication by scalars. If U, V are vector spaces with $U, \subseteq V$ we say U is a *subspace* of V (or V is a *superspace* of U). As before, a **basis** of V is a subset $B = \{v_1, \ldots, v_n\}$ such that every element of V is a unique linear combination of the v_i (this idea was first introduced at (4.2)). To find B we may

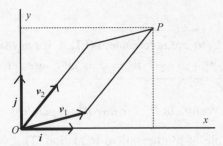

Figure 7.6 Exemplifying Part (ii) of Theorem 7.10. With respect to the basis $\{i, j\}$ we have $OP = 3i + 2j$, but taking $\{v_1, v_2\}$ as basis gives $OP = v_1 + 2v_2$.

use its property (see below) of being a *maximal linearly independent subset* (MLI) of V. That is, B itself is LI but the set $v_1, \ldots, v_n, a$ is dependent for any a in V.

Theorem 7.10 (a) $B = \{v_1, \ldots, v_n\}$ *is a basis of a vector space V if and only if B is a maximal linearly independent subset.* (b) *Every basis of V has the same size. See Figure 7.6.*

Proof (a) If B is a basis it is clearly MLI, for any further element a of V is by definition a linear combination of the v_i. Conversely, suppose B is MLI and let a be in V. Then the $n + 1$ vectors $v_1, \ldots, v_n, a$ are dependent so a is a linear combination $\sum \lambda_i v_i$. To show this combination is unique, as required for a basis, suppose that also $a = \sum \mu_i v_i$. Then, by subtraction, $0 = \sum (\lambda_i - \mu_i) v_i$, implying by the independence of the v_i that $\lambda_i = \mu_i$ for each i. Thus our arbitrarily chosen vector a is a unique linear combination of $v_1, \ldots, v_n$, which therefore form a basis.

(b) Suppose $u_1, \ldots, u_m$ and $v_1, \ldots, v_n$ are bases of V, with $m > n$, and express each u_i in terms of the v-basis, say

$$u_1 = a_{11}v_1 + \cdots + a_{1n}v_n,$$
$$u_2 = a_{21}v_1 + \cdots + a_{2n}v_n,$$
$$\cdots$$
$$u_m = a_{m1}v_1 + \cdots + a_{mn}v_n.$$

Then we have m vectors of coefficients $(a_{i1}, \ldots, a_{in})$, $1 \leq i \leq m$. Since these vectors lie in R^n, and $m > n$, they are dependent by Theorem 7.7. But this implies that $u_1, \ldots, u_m$ are dependent, a contradiction since they form a basis. Hence $m > n$ is impossible, and by symmetry so is $n > m$. Thus $m = n$ as asserted.

Definition 7.11 The *dimension* of a vector space is the number of linearly independent vectors required for a basis. This is well-defined, by Theorem 7.10, and shown by Theorem 7.8 to be n for $\mathbf{R}^n$, as we would hope. The zero vector is by definition in V, and if it is the only member then V is allocated dimension 0 since no basis elements are required. Agreeably, lines and planes have respective dimensions 1 and 2.

We may abbreviate a list $e_1, e_2, \ldots, e_n$ to $\{e_i\}_{1 \leq i \leq n}$, or simply to $\{e_i\}$ if the range of i is known from the context. Then $\{e_i\}$ is called an *orthonormal set* if its members are mutually orthogonal unit vectors or, more briefly, $e_i \cdot e_k = \delta_{ik} (1 \leq i, k \leq n)$ as used earlier for the case $n = 3$ in (7.9). If in addition $\{e_i\}$ is a basis, it is called an *orthonormal basis*, or ONB.

Finding a basis Let $u_1, \ldots, u_m$ lie in vector space V. Their *span*, defined as

$$\text{span}\{u_1, \ldots, u_m\} = \{\text{all linear combinations of the } u_i\},$$

is a subspace of V. If it is the whole of V we say the u_i *span* V. Theorem 7.10 shows that the u_i form a basis of V if and only if two of the following hold (they imply the remaining one):

    1. $\{u_1, \ldots, u_m\}$ *spans* V,

    2. $m = \text{Dim} V$ (the dimension of V),

    3. $\{u_1, \ldots, u_m\}$ *is linearly independent.*   (7.10)

Example 7.12 (i) Extend the sequence of vectors u_1, u_2, u_3 below to a basis of $\mathbf{R}^4$, (ii) find a basis for the space spanned by v_1, v_2, v_3 below.

$$u_1 = (1, 2, 3, 4), \qquad v_1 = (1, 2, 1),$$
$$u_2 = (0, 1, 5, 1), \qquad v_2 = (0, 1, 2),$$
$$u_3 = (0, 0, 2, 3), \qquad v_3 = (1, 3, 3).$$

Solution (i) We are given the dimension is 4, and the vectors u_i are LI because of the 'triangle' of zeros. Formally, $\lambda u + \mu v + \nu w = 0 \Rightarrow (\lambda, 2\lambda + \mu, 3\lambda + 5\mu + 2\nu) = 0 \Rightarrow \lambda, \mu, \nu = 0$, so Definition 7.6 applies. Thus by criteria 2, 3 of (7.10) we only have to find a vector that is not a linear combination of them. An easy solution is $u_4 = (0, 0, 0, 1)$.

(ii) Since $v_3 = v_1 + v_2$ this vector is not required. Also v_1, v_2 are LI, for one is not a multiple of the other. Hence $\{v_1, v_2\}$ is a basis by satisfying criteria 1, 3 above. The space they span thus has dimension 2.

Remarks 7.13 (1) *Extending to a basis* As exemplified in (i) above, every LI subset of V may be extended to a basis: we repeatedly append any vector not dependent on those already chosen. Since we are working within some $\mathbf{R}^n$ of finite dimension, we must finish with an MLI set, hence a basis.

(2) *A dimension argument* If $X = \{x_1, \ldots, x_s\}$ and $Y = \{y_1, \ldots, y_t\}$ are sets of linearly independent vectors in a space V, with $s + t > \dim V$, then span(X) and span(Y) have a nonzero vector z in common.

Proof of (2) The set $X \cup Y$ has more than $\text{Dim} V$ vectors, so it is LD. Hence one vector, say x_1, is a linear combination of the rest. That is, it is a linear combination of vectors of which some are in X, some in Y, some possibly in both, and we may write $x_1 = x + y$, where x is in span(X) and y in span(Y). Then $z = x_1 - x = y$ is common to span(X) and span(Y).

(3) | *Orthogonal vectors are independent.* |

Proof of (3) Let $u_1, \ldots, u_m$ be nonzero orthogonal vectors in a space V, and suppose there is a linear relation $\sum \lambda_i u_i = 0$. Then for any k with $1 \le k \le m$ we have

$$0 = u_k \cdot \sum_i \lambda_i u_i = \sum_i \lambda_i (u_k \cdot u_i) = \lambda_k (u_k \cdot u_k) \quad \text{(the } us \text{ being orthogonal)}$$
$$= \lambda_k |u_k|^2.$$

Since $u_k \ne 0$, this implies that $\lambda_k = 0 \, (1 \le k \le m)$, and so $u_1, \ldots, u_m$ are independent.

Theorem 7.14 *(The Component Formula) Suppose that the n vectors $e_1, e_2, \ldots, e_n$ in $\mathbf{R}^n$ are an orthonormal set, that is, $e_i \cdot e_k = \delta_{ik} (= 1$ if $i = k$, otherwise 0). Then $\{e_i\}$ is an orthonormal basis of $\mathbf{R}^n$, and any vector a in $\mathbf{R}^n$ has components $a_i = a \cdot e_i$ with respect to this basis. That is, $a = a_1 e_1 + \cdots + a_n e_n$ (and $|a|^2 = \sum a_i^2$).*

Proof Firstly, the e_i are independent as shown above and, since there are n of them, they form a basis by Theorem 7.8. (They are given to be an orthonormal set, so this basis is orthonormal.) Thus $a = a_1 e_1 + \cdots + a_n e_n$ for unique coefficients a_i. Take the scalar product of each side with e_1, say. We obtain $a \cdot e_1 = (a_1 e_1 + \cdots + a_n e_n) \cdot e_1$ which (again since $e_1 \cdot e_i = 0$ if $i \ne 1$) gives $a \cdot e_1 = a_1 e_1 \cdot e_1 = a_1$ as required. Similarly for the other coefficients a_i.

Definition 7.15 The coordinates x_i of the point $x = (x_1, x_2, \ldots, x_n)$ are the components of x w.r.t. the *standard basis* $e_1, e_2, \ldots, e_n$, where e_i has a 1 in the ith place and zeros everywhere else. That is, $x = x_1 e_1 + x_2 e_2 + \cdots + x_n e_n$ with $e_1 = (1, 0, \ldots, 0), e_2 = (0, 1, 0, \ldots, 0), \ldots, e_n = (0, 0, \ldots, 0, 1)$. Note that the e_i are used to refer to basis vectors generally, so cannot be assumed to be the standard basis unless explicitly defined to be, as in this paragraph. In ordinary 3-space, whichever orthonormal basis i, j, k we choose becomes the standard basis by definition, for in coordinate terms $i = (1, 0, 0), j = (0, 1, 0), k = (0, 0, 1)$.

Example 7.16 One orthonormal basis of $\mathbf{R}^4$ is $e_1 = (1/2)(1, 1, 1, 1), e_2 = (1/2)(1, 1, -1, -1), e_3 = (1/2)(1, -1, 1, -1), e_4 = (1/2)(1, -1, -1, 1)$. The components of $a = (1, 2, 3, 4)$ with respect to this basis are $a \cdot e_1 = (1/2) \times (1 + 2 + 3 + 4) = 5, a \cdot e_2 = (1/2)(1 + 2 - 3 - 4) = -2, a \cdot e_3 = (1/2)(1 - 2 + 3 - 4) = -1, a \cdot e_4 = (1/2)(1 - 2 - 3 + 4) = 0$. So in fact a is a linear combination of just the first three basis vectors.

Exercise Express the vector $(2, 1, 0, 1)$ as a linear combination of the basis vectors in Example 7.16. Check your answer.

Definition 7.17 *(Extending to an ONB)* An orthonormal subset $e_1, e_2, \ldots, e_m$ of V, with $m < \text{Dim} V$, may be extended to an ONB by repetitions of the following steps for $m, m + 1, \ldots, (\text{Dim} V) - 1$; that is, until the extended set has size dim V.

1. Find a vector w independent of $e_1, e_2, \ldots, e_m$,
2. Subtract from w its components w.r.t. the e_i, to obtain, say, u,
3. Divide u by its own length to obtain e_{m+1}, where $e_1, e_2, \ldots, e_{m+1}$ is orthonormal.

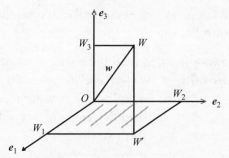

Figure 7.7 Illustration of projection and the Gram–Schmidt process.

This is called the *Gram–Schmidt process*. To verify its efficacy we note first that $u \neq 0$ since we obtained it by subtracting from w only a linear combination of $e_1, e_2, \ldots, e_m$, of which w is independent by construction. It remains to show $e_i \cdot u = 0$ for $1 \leq i \leq m$. But

$$e_i \cdot u = e_i \cdot [w - \sum_{k=1}^{m}(w \cdot e_k)e_k] = e_i \cdot w - \sum_{k=1}^{m}(w \cdot e_k)e_i \cdot e_k$$
$$= e_i \cdot w - w \cdot e_i \quad (\text{since } e_i \cdot e_k = \delta_{ik}) = 0.$$

If no orthonormal subset is specified we start with $\{e_1\}$, where e_1 is as any nonzero vector in V, divided by its own length.

Example 7.18 (i) Considering Figure 7.7, the vectors e_1, e_2 form an ONB for the plane $\mathbf{R}^2$ (shaded). An equally valid ONB results if we rotate the pair in its own plane, or change the sign and hence sense of either.

(ii) If in the Gram–Schmidt process we have a basis e_1, e_2, w of $\mathbf{R}^3$, as depicted in Figure 7.7, the next step is to subtract from w the sum of its components with respect to e_1 and e_2. This sum is represented in the figure by $OW_1 + OW_2 = OW'$. It is called the *projection* of w ($= OW$) onto the subspace spanned by e_1, e_2. Subtracting it from OW gives OW_3 which, scaled to unit length, gives e_3.

Exercise Find an orthonormal basis for span$\{u_2, u_3\}$ of Example 7.12.

Definition 7.19 Following Example 7.18 we state more generally that if $e_1, \ldots, e_k$ is an ONB for a subspace V of U that extends to an ONB $e_1, \ldots, e_n$ for U then $e_{k+1}, \ldots, e_n$ spans a subspace called the *orthogonal complement* $V^\perp$ of V in U and

(a) any w in U is a unique sum $w' + w^\perp$, with $w' \in V, w^\perp \in V^\perp$,
(b) w' is called the *orthogonal projection* of w onto V.

In Figure 7.7, OW' is the projection of OW onto the plane span$\{e_1, e_2\}$, and span$\{e_3\}$ is the orthogonal complement of span$\{e_1, e_2\}$ in $\mathbf{R}^3$. Because of the unique expression of a vector in terms of basis elements, $V^\perp$ is the subspace consisting of the vectors of U that are *orthogonal to every vector in V*. This in turn shows that $V^\perp$ is independent of which

ONB is chosen. The definition via some basis makes it clear that taking the orthogonal complement twice brings us back to V.

Remark 7.20 The following result is used in various forms throughout the book: *for vectors x, y in $\mathbf{R}^n$ we have* (a) $x \cdot y \leq |x||y|$, *and therefore* (b) $|x + y| \leq |x| + |y|$, *and* (c) $|x - y| \leq |x - z| + |z - y|$, the last called the *triangle inequality* because it states that (not only in the plane but in n-space) the length of one side of a triangle does not exceed the sum of the lengths of the other two sides.

$$\boxed{(a)\, x \cdot y \leq |x||y|}$$

Proof For all values of a real number t we have the inequality $0 \leq (tx + y) \cdot (tx + y) = |x|^2 t^2 + 2(x \cdot y)t + |y|^2$, by the formula $c \cdot c = |c|^2$ and (7.8). Since this quadratic in t can never be negative, it cannot have two distinct roots

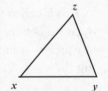

$$-x \cdot y \pm \sqrt{(x \cdot y)^2 - |x|^2 |y|^2},$$

and so $(x \cdot y)^2 \leq |x|^2 |y|^2$. Because $|x|^2 |y|^2 \geq 0$, we may infer assertion (a). Furthermore, (b) is equivalent to $|x + y|^2 \leq |x|^2 + |y|^2 + 2|x||y|$, or, by the formula $|c|^2 = c \cdot c$, to (a). Finally, $|x - y| = |(x - z) + (z - y)| \leq |x - z| + |z - y|$, by (b).

7.2 Matrices and determinants

Matrices are used in linear equation solving (Example 7.35) and linear transformations, each of which covers a great deal of ground. Our first major use will be in the probability chapters 9 to 11, and then generally throughout the text. Determinants play a supporting role in all this, for example detecting whether transformations are invertible, vectors dependent, or coordinate systems right handed.

This section is a reminder of the most basic theory and an introduction to what might not appear in a first course. Possible examples of the latter are matrix multiplication tips, Linear Dependence Rule 7.28(5), Vandermonde determinants, and especially Section 7.2.5 on block matrix multiplication.

7.2.1 Matrices

$$\text{Let } A = \begin{bmatrix} a_{11} & a_{12} & \dots & a_{1n} \\ a_{21} & a_{22} & \dots & a_{2n} \\ \dots & \dots & \dots & \dots \\ a_{m1} & a_{m2} & \dots & a_{mn} \end{bmatrix}, \qquad \begin{array}{l} \text{an array of } m \text{ rows of numbers} \\ \text{arranged in } n \text{ columns.} \end{array}$$

Then we say A is the $m \times n$ matrix $[a_{ik}]$, and call a_{ik} the ikth *entry*, or *element*. Thus the rows of A are indexed by the first subscript, i, and the columns by the second, k. Especially in proving results, it is sometimes useful to write $(A)_{ik}$ for a_{ik}. We may write

$A_{m \times n}$ to emphasise that matrix A is $m \times n$; the set of such matrices, with real entries, is $R_{m \times n}$. Equality of matrices, say $A = B$, means that A and B have the same *type* $m \times n$ (i.e., the same number of rows and columns) and that $a_{ik} = b_{ik}$ for each pair i, k.

Definition 7.21 (*Two special matrices*) The sequence of all elements of type a_{ii} (the *diagonal elements*) is called the *main diagonal*. The *identity* $m \times n$ matrix I (written I_n if ambiguity might arise) has diagonal elements 1 and the rest 0. The *zero* $m \times n$ *matrix* has all its entries zero, and is usually denoted by 'O' (or often just '0' if not displayed), the context making clear that this is the intended meaning. If necessary we write $O_{m \times n}$, or simply O_n if $m = n$. Thus for example:

$$O_3 = \begin{bmatrix} 0 & 0 & 0 \\ 0 & 0 & 0 \\ 0 & 0 & 0 \end{bmatrix}, \quad I_3 = \begin{bmatrix} 1 & 0 & 0 \\ 0 & 1 & 0 \\ 0 & 0 & 1 \end{bmatrix}.$$

Row vectors Any row $[a_{i1} \ \ldots \ a_{in}]$ forms a $1 \times n$ matrix or *row vector*, which may be identified with a vector in Euclidean n-space, $\boldsymbol{a}_i = (a_{i1}, \ldots, a_{in})$. Also we write $A = \text{Rows}(\boldsymbol{a}_i) = \text{Rows}(\boldsymbol{a}_1, \ldots, \boldsymbol{a}_m)$, possibly with [ ] instead of ( ), to mean that matrix A has rows $\boldsymbol{a}_1, \ldots, \boldsymbol{a}_m$. Thus $I_2 = \text{Rows}[(1, 0), (0, 1)]$. Similarly for columns.

By analogy with the matrix notation $A = [a_{ik}]$ we may specify a row (or column) vector by its ith element, writing $[x_i]$ for $[x_1 \ \ldots \ x_n]$ and (x_i) for $(x_1, \ldots, x_n)$. Thus for example $[2i + 1]_{1 \le i \le 3} = [3\,5\,7]$.

Matrix sums and products Matrices may be added, and multiplied by scalars, in the same way as vectors. Multiplication is different. If (and only if) the rows of matrix A have the same length n as the columns of matrix B, then the *product AB* exists, defined by

$$(AB)_{ik} = (\text{row } i \text{ of } A) \cdot (\text{column } k \text{ of } B) = \sum_{s=1}^{n} a_{is} b_{sk}, \tag{7.11}$$

which is the inner product of row i of A and column k of B, regarded as vectors. Thus if A is $m \times n$ and B is $n \times p$ then AB exists and is $m \times p$. We emphasise that n is the row length of A and column length of B. In forming AB we say B is *pre-multiplied by A*, or A is *post-multiplied by B*.

Examples 7.22 Sometimes we subscript a matrix by its dimensions $m \times n$, distinguished by the '$\times$'. For example it may be helpful to write $A_{m \times n} B_{n \times p} = C_{m \times p}$.

(1) $[a_1 \, a_2 \, a_3] \begin{bmatrix} b_1 \\ b_2 \\ b_3 \end{bmatrix} = a_1 a_1 + a_2 b_2 + a_3 b_3 = \boldsymbol{a} \cdot \boldsymbol{b},$

(2) $\underset{2 \times 3}{\begin{bmatrix} 1 & 2 & 1 \\ 2 & 3 & 5 \end{bmatrix}} \underset{3 \times 2}{\begin{bmatrix} 2 & 1 \\ 0 & 3 \\ 0 & 1 \end{bmatrix}} = \underset{2 \times 2}{\begin{bmatrix} 2 & 8 \\ 4 & 16 \end{bmatrix}},$

(3)	row i of AB = (row i of A)B,
(4)	col j of AB = A(col j of B).

Cases (3) and (4) provide a useful insight to bear in mind: the *rows* of a product correspond to those of the first matrix, whilst the *columns* correspond to those of the second.

Exercise Write down the products AB and BA for several pairs of 2×2 matrices A, B until you obtain AB different from BA. Can you get this using only the numbers 0 and 1?

Definition 7.23 A *diagonal* matrix D is one which is square and has all its off-diagonal entries zero: $d_{ij} = 0$ whenever $i \neq j$. Thus D may be defined by its diagonal entries, $D = \text{diag}(d_{11}, d_{22}, \ldots, d_{nn})$. The identity matrix $D = I$ is an important special case, as we begin to see soon in (7.14).

Example 7.24 The case $n = 3$.

$$\begin{bmatrix} \lambda_1 & 0 & 0 \\ 0 & \lambda_2 & 0 \\ 0 & 0 & \lambda_3 \end{bmatrix} \begin{bmatrix} 1 & 2 & 5 \\ 6 & 5 & 9 \\ 1 & 0 & 7 \end{bmatrix} = \begin{bmatrix} \lambda_1 & 2\lambda_1 & 5\lambda_1 \\ 6\lambda_2 & 5\lambda_2 & 9\lambda_2 \\ \lambda_3 & 0 & 7\lambda_3 \end{bmatrix}.$$

This leads us to see that, D being an $n \times n$ diagonal matrix,

$$\begin{aligned} \text{diag}(\lambda_i)\text{Rows}(R_i) &= \text{Rows}(\lambda_i R_i), \\ \text{Cols}(C_i)\text{diag}(\lambda_i) &= \text{Cols}(\lambda_i C_i). \end{aligned} \tag{7.12}$$

In particular,

$$\text{diag}(a_1, \ldots, a_n) \, \text{diag}(b_1, \ldots, b_n) = \text{diag}(a_1 b_1, \ldots, a_n b_n), \tag{7.13}$$

a matrix multiplied by the identity is unchanged,

$$AI = A \text{ and } IB = B. \tag{7.14}$$

Example 7.25 The product of n copies of A is written A^n, with A^0 defined to be I. The usual index laws hold: $A^m A^n = A^{m+n}$, $(A^m)^n = A^{mn}$.

Exercise (i) Find the product A of the 2×2 and 2×3 matrices of Examples 7.22(2) above. Can they be multiplied in either order? (ii) Write down a diagonal matrix D such that DA is matrix A with the first row unchanged and the second row multiplied by -2.

Transposes The *transpose* A^T of a matrix A is obtained by rewriting the successive rows as columns. In symbols, $(A^T)_{ik} = (A)_{ki} = a_{ki}$. Thus for example

$$A = \begin{bmatrix} 1 & 2 & 3 \\ 4 & 5 & 6 \end{bmatrix}, \quad A^T = \begin{bmatrix} 1 & 4 \\ 2 & 5 \\ 3 & 6 \end{bmatrix}.$$

Notice that we now have the option of writing a column vector as the transpose of a row vector thus: $[x_1 \, x_2 \, \ldots \, x_n]^T$. We have the following three calculation rules of which the second, $(AB)^{\mathrm{T}} = B^{\mathrm{T}}A^{\mathrm{T}}$, is often called the *reversal rule for matrix transposes*.

$$(A + B)^{\mathrm{T}} = A^{\mathrm{T}} + B^{\mathrm{T}}, (AB)^{\mathrm{T}} = B^{\mathrm{T}}A^{\mathrm{T}}, (A^{\mathrm{T}})^{\mathrm{T}} = A. \qquad (7.15)$$

Proof We prove the reversal rule by showing that $(AB)^{\mathrm{T}}$ and $B^{\mathrm{T}}A^{\mathrm{T}}$ have the same ik entry for each pair i, k. We have

$$
\begin{aligned}
((AB)^{\mathrm{T}})_{ik} &= (AB)_{ki} & &\text{by definition of transpose} \\
&= \textstyle\sum_s a_{ks}b_{si} & &\text{by definition of } AB \\
&= \textstyle\sum_s (B^{\mathrm{T}})_{is}(A^{\mathrm{T}})_{sk} & &\text{by definition of transpose} \\
&= (B^{\mathrm{T}}A^{\mathrm{T}})_{ik} & &\text{by definition of } B^{\mathrm{T}}A^{\mathrm{T}}.
\end{aligned}
$$

The third line used implicitly the commutativity of multiplication amongst numbers. In the context of transposition, two useful concepts are the following. A square matrix A is *symmetric* if $A^{\mathrm{T}} = A$, and *skew-symmetric* (*anti-symmetric*) if $A^{\mathrm{T}} = -A$. Notice that in the skew case every diagonal element a_{ii} satisfies $a_{ii} = -a_{ii}$, hence the main diagonal consists of zeros.

$$
\text{Symmetric:} \begin{bmatrix} 1 & 3 & 7 \\ 3 & -2 & 5 \\ 7 & 5 & 6 \end{bmatrix} \quad \text{Skew-symmetric:} \begin{bmatrix} 0 & 5 & -6 \\ -5 & 0 & 2 \\ 6 & -2 & 0 \end{bmatrix}.
$$

In particular, a symmetric matrix is determined by its elements on and above the main diagonal, whilst a skew-symmetric matrix requires only those above. As we see above, a 3×3 skew-symmetric matrix requires only three elements to specify it.

Remarks 7.26 (a) AA^{T} is symmetric for any matrix A, whilst for square A we have (b) $A + A^{\mathrm{T}}$ is symmetric but $A - A^{\mathrm{T}}$ is skew, and (c) *A can be expressed uniquely as the sum of a symmetric and a skew-symmetric matrix, namely*

$$A = (1/2)(A + A^{\mathrm{T}}) + (1/2)(A - A^{\mathrm{T}}), \qquad (7.16)$$

called respectively the *symmetric* and *skew-symmetric* parts of A.

Proof $(AA^{\mathrm{T}})^{\mathrm{T}} = (A^{\mathrm{T}})^{\mathrm{T}}A^{\mathrm{T}} = AA^{\mathrm{T}}$, by (7.15), whereas $(A + A^{\mathrm{T}})^{\mathrm{T}} = A^{\mathrm{T}} + (A^{\mathrm{T}})^{\mathrm{T}} = A^{\mathrm{T}} + A = A + A^{\mathrm{T}}$, again by (7.15). The skew case is an exercise below. (c) The equality holds trivially. To prove uniqueness, suppose that A has two expressions $A_1 + B_1 = A_2 + B_2$ (i), where A_1, A_2 are symmetric and B_1, B_2 skew-symmetric. Then taking the transpose of each side yields a second equation $A_1 - B_1 = A_2 - B_2$ (ii). Adding (i) and (ii) we obtain $2A_1 = 2A_2$, and subtracting, $2B_1 = 2B_2$. Thus the symmetric and skew-symmetric matrices in (7.16) are unique.

Exercise Prove that if matrix A is square then $A - A^{\mathrm{T}}$ is skew-symmetric.

Example 7.27 The matrix A below splits into symmetric and skew-symmetric parts as shown.

$$A = \begin{bmatrix} 1 & 5 & 7 \\ 3 & 2 & 1 \\ 2 & 6 & 0 \end{bmatrix} = \begin{bmatrix} 1 & 4 & 4.5 \\ 4 & 2 & 3.5 \\ 4.5 & 3.5 & 0 \end{bmatrix} + \begin{bmatrix} 0 & 1 & 2.5 \\ -1 & 0 & -2.5 \\ -2.5 & 2.5 & 0 \end{bmatrix}.$$

This technique will be useful in (8.6) of the next chapter for determining the axis of a rotation in 3-space from its matrix.

Exercise Find the symmetric and skew-symmetric parts of the transpose of A above.

Finally in this section we note that fortunately matrix multiplication is associative, that is, if all the implied products exist then

$$(AB)C = A(BC). \tag{7.17a}$$

As a result, we may bracket the product of any number of matrices in any way we wish, or omit the brackets altogether when writing such a product. The proof involves writing out the ikth element of $(AB)C$ as a double summation and reversing the order of summation, which gives the ikth element of $A(BC)$; indeed both may be written

$$(ABC)_{ik} = \sum_{r,s} a_{ir} b_{rs} c_{sk} \tag{7.17b}$$

and similarly (by induction) for any size of product. Another useful expression, from straightforward application of Examples 7.22(3), (4), is

$$(ABC)i_k = (\text{row } i \text{ of } A)(\text{col } k \text{ of } BC)$$
$$= (\text{row } i \text{ of } A) \times B \times (\text{col } k \text{ of } C). \tag{7.17c}$$

Lastly, a most ubiquitous formula which we require first in Section 7.2.4, and often in Chapter 8. Let A be an $m \times n$ matrix and $X = [x_1 \, x_2 \, \ldots \, x_m]$, $Y = [y_1 \, y_2 \, \ldots \, y_n]$. Then

$$XAY^{\mathrm{T}} = \sum_{r,s} a_{rs} x_r y_s. \tag{7.17d}$$

Exercise Deduce Formula (7.17d) from (7.17b).

7.2.2 Determinants

Determinants (first introduced at (4.7)) are important for computing with vectors and transformations, and for distinguishing between direct and indirect isometries in the plane (see Section 1.2.3), and in 3-space and higher dimensions. Their role in integration will be exploited in later chapters on probability.

First results

We have already introduced 2×2 determinants, proving certain results and making constructions for cells of plane patterns (see Notation 4.7 ff.):

$$\begin{vmatrix} a & b \\ c & d \end{vmatrix} = ad - bc.$$

(In case $n = 1$, the determinant of $A = [a_{11}]$ is defined to be a_{11}.) This enables us to define the determinant of an $n \times n$ matrix A, denoted by det A or more briefly $|A|$, by specifying how it is to be computed from determinants of $(n - 1) \times (n - 1)$ matrices. We first define the *minor* of an element a_{ik} to be the determinant of the submatrix of A obtained by deleting row i and column k. The *cofactor* A_{ik} of a_{ik} is the corresponding minor prefixed by $+$ or $-$ according to the sign of $(-1)^{i+k}$. Then the determinant of A is given by

$$|A| = a_{11}A_{11} + a_{12}A_{12} + \cdots + a_{1n}A_{1n}. \tag{7.18a}$$

For example,

$$n = 3: \begin{vmatrix} a_1 & a_2 & a_3 \\ b_1 & b_2 & b_3 \\ c_1 & c_2 & c_3 \end{vmatrix} = a_1 \begin{vmatrix} b_2 & b_3 \\ c_2 & c_3 \end{vmatrix} - a_2 \begin{vmatrix} b_1 & b_3 \\ c_1 & c_3 \end{vmatrix} + a_3 \begin{vmatrix} b_1 & b_2 \\ c_1 & c_2 \end{vmatrix}.$$

Notice the cofactor signs alternate as we proceed along the row; indeed they must do so, from their definition $(-1)^{i+k}$, as we proceed along *any* row or column. Moreover, since a row or column may contain a proportion of zeros, it is useful to be aware of the following possibilities.

$$\text{Expansion by row } i: \quad |A| = \sum_{r=1}^{n} a_{ir}A_{ir}. \tag{7.18b}$$

$$\text{Expansion by column } k: \quad |A| = \sum_{s=1}^{n} a_{sk}A_{sk}. \tag{7.18c}$$

The determinant below is most simply expanded by its third column, which contains two zeros

$$\begin{vmatrix} 1 & 2 & 3 & 4 \\ 2 & 1 & 0 & 9 \\ 5 & -2 & 0 & 6 \\ 2 & 4 & 8 & 1 \end{vmatrix} = 3 \begin{vmatrix} 2 & 1 & 9 \\ 5 & -2 & 6 \\ 2 & 4 & 1 \end{vmatrix} - 8 \begin{vmatrix} 1 & 2 & 4 \\ 2 & 1 & 9 \\ 5 & -2 & 6 \end{vmatrix}.$$

There follow some rules that will be very useful in the sequel; they are proved in the last section, 7.5. The first rule will be used to justify the expansion of $|A|$ by any row, given the expansion by row 1, whilst $|A^{\mathrm{T}}| = |A|$ extends this to expansion by any column. (For machine computation, see Golub & van Loan, 1996.)

Rules 7.28 (*Evaluating determinants*)

1. Switching two rows or columns changes the sign of a determinant. Hence a deter-minant with two identical rows or columns must equal zero.
2. Multiplying each element of a row (or each element of a column) by the same scalar α multiplies the determinant by α.
3. The value of a determinant is unaffected by the addition of a multiple of one row to another. Similarly for columns.
4. $|AB| = |A||B|$ and $|A^{\mathrm{T}}| = |A|$.
5. $|A| = 0$ if and only if some linear combination $a_1 C_1 + a_2 C_2 + \cdots + a_n C_n$ of the columns (or of the rows) of A is zero. Of course, not all the coefficients a_i are allowed to be zero. Thus the condition amounts to *linear dependence* of the columns (or of the rows). (For the case $n = 3$ see also Theorems 7.41(c) and 7.42).

Example 7.29 In evaluating the determinant below we have first simplified by subtracting $2\times$ column 1 from column 2, then $5\times$ column 1 from column 3 (Rule 3).

$$
\begin{vmatrix} 1 & 2 & 5 \\ 2 & 5 & 2 \\ 1 & 6 & 3 \end{vmatrix} = \begin{vmatrix} 1 & 0 & 0 \\ 2 & 1 & -8 \\ 1 & 4 & -2 \end{vmatrix} = 1 \cdot \begin{vmatrix} 1 & -8 \\ 4 & -2 \end{vmatrix} = -2 + 32 = 30.
$$

Exercise Use some of Rules 1–5 to evaluate the above determinant in a different way (the answer should of course be the same).

Three special cases

(1) (*Diagonal matrices*) $\begin{vmatrix} d & 0 & 0 \\ 0 & e & 0 \\ 0 & 0 & f \end{vmatrix} = d \begin{vmatrix} e & 0 \\ 0 & f \end{vmatrix}$ (plus two zero terms) $= def$

More generally, the determinant of diag $(d_1, \ldots, d_n)$ equals $d_1 d_2 \ldots d_n$, the product of the diagonal elements.

(2) (*Triangular matrices*) An upper triangular matrix is one with its nonzero elements confined to the diagonal and above. That is, it looks like the example following, with a triangle of zeros below the diagonal.

$$
\begin{vmatrix} d_1 & 1 & 2 & 3 \\ & d_2 & 4 & 5 \\ & & d_3 & 6 \\ & & & d_4 \end{vmatrix} = d_1 \begin{vmatrix} d_2 & 4 & 5 \\ & d_3 & 6 \\ & & d_4 \end{vmatrix} = d_1 d_2 \begin{vmatrix} d_3 & 6 \\ & d_4 \end{vmatrix} = d_1 d_2 d_3 d_4.
$$

Expanding each determinant above by its first column, we see that, for this larger class than (1), the determinant is still the product of the diagonal elements. The same holds for a *lower* triangular matrix, with zeros above the diagonal, because the upper and lower types are transposes of each other, and $|A^{\mathrm{T}}| = |A|$. In fact, converting a matrix to triangular form by row operations can be the easiest way to evaluate a determinant. Notice too that the rows of a triangular matrix with nonzero diagonal elements are independent, by Rule 5.

Triangular matrices are developed further in Section 8.3.3, where they provide an important matrix factorisation algorithm which is used for simulation with the normal distribution in Section 11.3.5 and later.

Exercise Find $|A|$, where $A = \text{Rows}\,[(1, 2, 3, 4), (0, 0, 2, 9), (0, 0, 0, 4), (0, 5, 6, 0)]$.

Notation We use det A rather than $|A|$ if the vertical lines $|\ |$ might be construed as the modulus or absolute value of a number, or as the norm of a vector. Thus the absolute value of the determinant is written $|\det A|$. Notice that when we evaluate the determinant of a matrix the result is a *polynomial* in the matrix elements, since we use multiplication, addition and subtraction, but not division. Here is a result which may give this polynomial in a factorised form, bypassing a potentially tedious calculation; then we are ready for Vandermonde.

Theorem 7.30 *(Factor Theorem) Let α be a real number, $f(x)$ a polynomial. Then $x - \alpha$ is a factor of $f(x)$ if and only if $f(\alpha) = 0$.*

Proof Suppose we divide $x - \alpha$ into $f(x)$, obtaining quotient $q(x)$ and remainder R. That is, $f(x) = q(x)(x - \alpha) + R$. Setting $x = \alpha$, we obtain $R = f(\alpha)$. Hence the result.

Example 7.31 (i) Let $f(x) = x^5 - x^4 + x^2 + 9x - 10$. It is not obvious that this polynomial has a factor $x - 1$, but $f(1) = 1 - 1 + 1 + 9 - 10 = 0$ so, by the Factor Theorem, $x - 1$ *is* a factor.

(ii) Let $f(x) = x^3 - (a + b + c)x^2 + (ab + bc + ca)x - abc$. This looks pretty symmetrical; in fact we find that $f(a) = 0$, and the same for $f(b), f(c)$. By the Factor Theorem $(x - a), (x - b), (x - c)$ are all factors of the third degree polynomial $f(x)$, which is therefore a constant multiple K of their product: $f(x) = K(x - a)(x - b)(x - c)$. Finally, the coefficient of x^3 in $f(x)$ is 1, so $K = 1$.

(iii) The Factor Theorem is particularly powerful for certain polynomials defined as determinants. Let $f(x)$ be the quadratic polynomial:

$$f(x) = \begin{vmatrix} 1 & 1 & 1 \\ x & b & c \\ x^2 & b^2 & c^2 \end{vmatrix}, \quad \text{so that} \quad f(b) = \begin{vmatrix} 1 & 1 & 1 \\ b & b & c \\ b^2 & b^2 & c^2 \end{vmatrix},$$

which equals zero since two columns are identical (Rule 1). By the Factor Theorem $x - b$ is a factor of the quadratic polynomial $f(x)$. Similarly, so is $x - c$, and hence $f(x) = K(x - b)(x - c)$, where the constant K is given by (expanding $f(x)$ by its first column)

$$K = [\text{coefficient of } x^2 \text{ in } f(x)] = \begin{vmatrix} 1 & 1 \\ b & c \end{vmatrix} = c - b.$$

Exercise Repeat (iii) for the 4×4 matrix with ith row $[x^i \ b^i \ c^i \ d^i]$, $0 \le i \le 3$.

(3) (*Vandermonde determinants*) An inductive step based on the arguments above (NB the exercise) gives a formula for the general Vandermonde determinant,

$$\Delta = \begin{vmatrix} 1 & 1 & \cdots & \cdots & 1 \\ a_1 & a_2 & \cdots & \cdots & a_n \\ a_1^2 & a_2^2 & \cdots & \cdots & a_n^2 \\ \cdots & \cdots & \cdots & \cdots & \cdots \\ a_1^{n-1} & a_2^{n-1} & \cdots & \cdots & a_n^{n-1} \end{vmatrix} = \prod_{i>j} (a_i - a_j),$$

in which the requirement $i > j$ causes exactly one of the differences $a_p - a_q$ and $a_q - a_p$ for each pair $p \neq q$ to appear in the product. In particular Δ is nonzero if and only if the a_i are distinct (that is, no two are equal). Sometimes it is more convenient to change $>$ to $<$ in the formula and prefix $(-1)^N$, where N is the number of factors. Let us verify the formula in the case $n = 3$, which asserts that $\Delta = (a_3 - a_2)(a_3 - a_1)(a_2 - a_1)$. We have already computed this case as $f(x)$ with $(a_1, a_2, a_3) = (x, b, c)$, and the results agree (check).

> A Vandermonde determinant is nonzero if and only if the a_i are distinct.

The property in the box above is used in, for example, the moment-generating functions of probability (Section 10.3.2) and in the theory of error-correcting codes (Section 13.2.4).

Exercise Use some of Rules 1 to 5 to evaluate the determinant of Example 7.29 differently. The answer of course should be the same. Give the argument of Example 7.31(iii) in the case $n = 4$.

7.2.3 The inverse of a matrix

Let A be an $n \times n$ matrix. Then there is an *inverse matrix* of A, i.e. an $n \times n$ matrix A^{-1} such that

$$AA^{-1} = I = A^{-1}A, \tag{7.19}$$

provided the necessary and sufficient condition $\det A \neq 0$ holds. This follows from Cramer's Rule below. Inverses are unique, for if A^{-1} exists and $AP = I$ then left multiplication by A^{-1} gives $P = A^{-1}$. Calculations are reduced by the fact that, *for an $n \times n$ matrix P,*

$$\boxed{AP = I \Leftrightarrow PA = I \Leftrightarrow P \text{ is the inverse of } A,} \tag{7.20}$$

and furthermore

$$\boxed{(AB)^{-1} = B^{-1}A^{-1}, \quad (A^{\mathrm{T}})^{-1} = (A^{-1})^{\mathrm{T}}, \quad and \quad |A^{-1}| = |A|^{-1}.} \tag{7.21}$$

The first formula of (7.21) is called the *Reversal Rule for matrix inverses*, and includes the assertion that if A and B are invertible then so is AB. The second asserts that if A is invertible then so is A^T, with inverse the transpose of A^{-1}. Compare the similar rule for transposes in (7.15). A single application of each rule shows that if *A, B commute*, that is $AB = BA$, then so do their transposes, and so do their inverses if they exist. Finally, if an inverse exists then Cramer's Rule below will find it, for $AB = I$ implies no linear combination of rows of A is zero, thus $|A| \neq 0$ (see Example 7.22(3) and Rule 7.28(5)).

Exercise Deduce the Reversal Rule for inverses from (7.19). Does (7.20) help?

Theorem 7.32 *(Cramer's Rule) The inverse of a matrix $A = [a_{ik}]$ with nonzero determinant is $|A|^{-1}[b_{ik}]$, where b_{ik} is the cofactor of a_{ki} (see (7.18)).*

Proof With $B = [b_{ik}]$ we have $(BA)_{ij} = \sum_k b_{ik}a_{kj} = \sum_k a_{kj}A_{ki}$. If $i = j$ this is the expansion of $|A|$ by column i of A. Otherwise it is the same as the expansion $\sum_k a_{ki}A_{ki}$ of $|A|$ by column i, but with a_{kj} in place of a_{ki} (for all k). The result is the determinant of a matrix with ith and jth columns identical (note: A_{ki} does not involve column i of A), and hence is zero by Rule 7.28(1). Thus $BA = |A|I$, or $(|A|^{-1}B)A = I$, as required.

Case $n = 2$ Let $A = \begin{bmatrix} a & b \\ c & d \end{bmatrix}$. Then $A^{-1} = \dfrac{1}{|A|}\begin{bmatrix} d & -b \\ -c & a \end{bmatrix}$, if $|A| \neq 0$. $\qquad$ (7.22)

For example $\begin{bmatrix} 3 & 2 \\ 6 & 5 \end{bmatrix}^{-1} = \dfrac{1}{3}\begin{bmatrix} 5 & -2 \\ -6 & 3 \end{bmatrix}$.

Inverses in practice Though convenient to state, Cramer's formula involves much arithmetic if $n > 2$, and we give it only for completeness, since most inverses we require will be evident by shortcuts. As a simple example the matrix corresponding to a rotation through an angle θ has inverse corresponding to rotation by $-\theta$ (see Examples 7.35 below). Also, any polynomial equation in a matrix yields a formula for the inverse. For example $A^2 - 3A - I = 0$ rearranges to $A(A - 3I) = I$, showing that $A^{-1} = A - 3I$. For an important method based on row operations and involving less calculation than Cramer's Rule, see ALGO 8.2 in the next chapter. Here we note the following.

A diagonal matrix $D = \mathrm{diag}(d_1, \ldots, d_n)$ is invertible if and only if its diagonal elements are nonzero, and then $D^{-1} = \mathrm{diag}(d_1^{-1}, \ldots, d_n^{-1})$.

Matrix inverses, and bases Let $\{u_i\}$ and $\{v_i\}$ $(1 \leq i \leq n)$ be bases for the same vector space. Expand each basis element in terms of the other basis, say

$$u_i = \sum_{j=1}^{n} p_{ij}v_j; \qquad v_j = \sum_{k=1}^{n} q_{jk}u_k.$$

Then $P = [p_{ij}]$ and $Q = [q_{jk}]$ are mutual inverses, or $PQ = I$. $\qquad$ (7.23)

Proof Substitute for v_j in the expression for u_i to obtain

$$u_i = \sum_j p_{ij} \sum_k q_{jk} u_k = \sum_k \left(\sum_j p_{ij} q_{jk} \right) u_k = \sum_k (PQ)_{ik} u_k.$$

This expresses u_i in terms of the basis $\{u_k\}$ and since (by definition of *basis*) such an expression is unique, it must reduce to $u_i = u_i$. Thus $(PQ)_{ik} = 1$ if $i = k$, otherwise 0. In other words, $PQ = I$.

Example 7.33 Let $E = \text{Rows}(e_1, \ldots, e_k)$ and $A = \text{Rows}(u_1, \ldots, u_k)$, where the e_i are orthonormal and the u_i only independent, both lying in $\mathbf{R}^n$ with $n > k$. Prove that (i) $EE^T = I_k$ and (ii) the matrix AA^T is invertible.

Solution (i) $(EE^T)_{ij} = e_i \cdot e_j = \delta_{ij}$, since the e_i are given to be orthonormal. That is, $EE^T = I_k$. For (ii) we apply Part (i) to an ONB $\{e_i\}$ for $\text{span}(u_1, \ldots, u_k)$, which may be found by the Gram–Schmidt process of Definition 7.17. Then each u_i is a unique linear combination, say $\sum_j p_{ij} e_j$, or, equivalently, row i of $A = (\text{row } i \text{ of } P)E$, where $P = [p_{ij}]$. Thus $A = PE$ (if in doubt, see Example 7.22 (3)). But $\{u_i\}$ are independent and so themselves form a basis of $\text{span}\{u_1, \ldots, u_k\}$. Hence P is invertible by (7.23) and we may argue that $AA^T = PEE^T P^T = PP^T$, which is invertible by (7.21).

Exercise Let the square matrix A satisfy $(I - A)^3 = 0$. Deduce that A^{-1} exists, and find an expression for it.

7.2.4 Orthogonal matrices

Definition 7.34 An $n \times n$ matrix A is called *orthogonal* if $AA^T = I$. Such matrices will turn out to be exactly those that describe point-fixing isometries in n-space. The orthogonality condition is equivalent to each of

(a) $A^T A = I$,
(b) A has an inverse, and $A^{-1} = A^T$,

> (c) the rows (or columns) of A form a set of *n orthonormal vectors*, that is, mutually orthogonal unit vectors.

Proof

$$A^T A = I \Leftrightarrow A^T \text{ is the inverse of } A \quad \text{by (7.20)}$$
$$\Leftrightarrow AA^T = I \quad \text{by (7.20)}$$
$$\Leftrightarrow (AA^T)_{ik} = \delta_{ik} \text{ (1 if } i = k, \text{ otherwise 0)}$$
$$\Leftrightarrow (\text{row } i \text{ of } A) \cdot (\text{column } k \text{ of } A^T) = \delta_{ik}$$
$$\Leftrightarrow (\text{row } i \text{ of } A) \cdot (\text{row } k \text{ of } A) = \delta_{ik}$$
$$\Leftrightarrow \text{the rows of } A \text{ form an orthonormal set of vectors.}$$

A slight addition to the argument justifies the assertion about columns of A, and is left as an exercise. A nice consequence of (c) is that orthogonality is preserved under permutation of the rows or of the columns, and sign changes of whole rows or columns. Notice that orthogonality in the form (c) may be the simplest way to check by inspection, as in the following example.

Examples 7.35 (i) (*Prime example*) In Section 7.4.1 we will show how the matrix given below describes rotations:

$$A = \begin{bmatrix} \cos\phi & \sin\phi \\ -\sin\phi & \cos\phi \end{bmatrix}.$$

It is orthogonal for any angle ϕ because (i) its rows have length $\sqrt{(\cos^2\phi + \sin^2\phi)} = 1$, and (ii) they are orthogonal, since their inner product is $(\cos\phi)(-\sin\phi) + (\sin\phi)(\cos\phi) = 0$.

(ii) A classical use of matrices is to write equations in compact form, exemplified as follows. The system of three equations

$$\left.\begin{array}{r} x + 2y - 2z = 6 \\ 2x + y + 2z = 9 \\ 2x - 2y - z = -3 \end{array}\right\} \quad \text{becomes} \quad \frac{1}{3}\begin{bmatrix} 1 & 2 & -2 \\ 2 & 1 & 2 \\ 2 & -2 & -1 \end{bmatrix}\begin{bmatrix} x \\ y \\ z \end{bmatrix} = \begin{bmatrix} 2 \\ 3 \\ -1 \end{bmatrix},$$

which we write as $AX = H$, where $X = [x\ y\ z]^T$. It happens here that A is orthogonal, so the inverse of A is immediately known to be A^T. Multiplying both sides of the equation by A^{-1} we have a standard argument: $AX = H \Rightarrow A^TAX = A^TH \Rightarrow X = A^TH$, whence $x = 2$, $y = 3$, $z = 1$. Notice that $AX = H$ is equivalent to the transposed equation $X^TA^T = H^T$, that is to say $[x\ y\ z]A^T = [2\ 3\ -1]$. This way round is used in Section 7.4.

Exercise Verify that the matrix A of (ii) is orthogonal by inspecting the rows, as in Definition 7.34(c). Make a new orthogonal matrix based on A.

Remarks 7.36 (1) *The determinant of an orthogonal matrix* If A is orthogonal then $|A|^2 = |A||A^T| = |AA^T| = |I| = 1$, hence A has determinant ±1 (which of Rules 7.20 were used?)

(2) *Creating orthogonal matrices* For a matrix S which is *skew* (i.e. $S^T = -S$), the product $A = (I - S)(I + S)^{-1}$ is orthogonal. First we establish the non-obvious fact that $(I + S)^{-1}$ actually exists: if it does not, then by Rule 7.28(5) some linear combination $\sum_i x_i C_i$ of the columns of $I + S$ is zero. That is, $(I + S)X = 0$, where $X = [x_1\ x_2\ \ldots]^T \neq 0$. But this gives a contradiction by $0 = X^T(I + S)X = \sum_{ij}(I + S)_{ij}x_ix_j$ (by (7.17d)) $= \sum_i x_i^2 + \sum_{i\neq j} s_{ij}x_ix_j = \sum_i x_i^2$ (since $s_{ji} = -s_{ij}$) > 0. For orthogonality,

$$\begin{aligned} AA^T &= (I - S)(I + S)^{-1}((I + S)^{-1})^T(I - S)^T \\ &= (I - S)(I + S)^{-1}((I + S)^T)^{-1}(I + S) \quad \text{by (7.21) and } S^T = -S \\ &= (I - S)(I + S)^{-1}(I - S)^{-1}(I + S) \\ &= I \quad\quad\quad\quad\quad\quad\quad\quad\quad\quad \text{since } I + S \text{ and } I - S \text{ commute.} \end{aligned}$$

It can be shown that *every* orthogonal matrix can be obtained from such a product, by changing the sign of certain whole rows or columns of A.

Example $S = \begin{bmatrix} 0 & \frac{1}{2} \\ -\frac{1}{2} & 0 \end{bmatrix}$, $I + S = \begin{bmatrix} 1 & \frac{1}{2} \\ -\frac{1}{2} & 1 \end{bmatrix}$, $(I + S)^{-1} = \frac{4}{5} \begin{bmatrix} 1 & -\frac{1}{2} \\ \frac{1}{2} & 1 \end{bmatrix}$,

by (7.22), and so $(I - S)(I + S)^{-1} = \begin{bmatrix} 1 & -\frac{1}{2} \\ \frac{1}{2} & 1 \end{bmatrix} \frac{4}{5} \begin{bmatrix} 1 & -\frac{1}{2} \\ \frac{1}{2} & 1 \end{bmatrix} = \frac{1}{5} \begin{bmatrix} 3 & -4 \\ 4 & 3 \end{bmatrix}$.

Definition 7.37 The set of all $n \times n$ orthogonal matrices, with multiplication as its law of composition, is called the *orthogonal group* $O(n)$ (it *is* a group, see Definition 2.19).

Exercises Show that the product of two orthogonal matrices is another orthogonal matrix and hence that the orthogonal group is indeed a group. (Hint: see (7.15).)

7.2.5 Block matrices

An idea which aids proofs and calculations surprisingly often is that of a *block matrix*, one partitioned into submatrices called *blocks* by dividing lines (drawn or imaginary) between columns and/or rows. Some notable applications are the Singular Value Decomposition in Section 8.4, Principal Component Analysis in Section 10.4, the Discrete Fourier Transform in Chapter 15, wavelets in Chapter 16, and B-splines in Chapter 17.

By convention a block of all zero elements may be designated by a single zero. Apart from simply drawing attention to features of a matrix, the convenience of block structure is that matrices can be multiplied 'blockwise', *as if the blocks were single elements*, provided the column divisions of the first are identical to the row divisions of the second. For example, if A, B, P, Q are matrices, I is the $p \times p$ identity matrix, and p, q, r indicate numbers of rows or columns in a block, then we may write

$$
\begin{matrix} \\ p \\ q \end{matrix}
\begin{bmatrix} I & 0 \\ A & B \end{bmatrix}
\begin{matrix} \\ p \\ r \end{matrix}
\begin{bmatrix} I & P \\ 0 & Q \end{bmatrix}
=
\begin{matrix} \\ p \\ q \end{matrix}
\begin{bmatrix} I & P \\ A & AP + BQ \end{bmatrix}. \tag{7.24}
$$

There is no restriction other than matrix size on the number of divisions. More generally, we may specify a block matrix by its (i, j) blocks; thus $A = [A_{ij}]_{m \times n}$, $B = [B_{ij}]_{n \times p}$ imply $AB = [C_{ij}]_{m \times p}$, where $C_{ij} = \sum_k A_{ik} B_{kj}$. The actual matrices may be represented as

$$
\begin{bmatrix} A_{11} & \ldots & A_{1n} \\ \ldots & \ldots & \ldots \\ A_{m1} & \ldots & A_{mn} \end{bmatrix}
\begin{bmatrix} B_{11} & \ldots & B_{1p} \\ \ldots & \ldots & \ldots \\ B_{n1} & \ldots & B_{np} \end{bmatrix}
=
\begin{bmatrix} C_{11} & \ldots & C_{1p} \\ \ldots & \ldots & \ldots \\ C_{m1} & \ldots & C_{mp} \end{bmatrix}. \tag{7.25}
$$

Of course we were already using the idea of blocks in the notation $\text{Rows}(R_1, \ldots, R_m)$ and $\text{Cols}(C_1, \ldots, C_n) = [C_1 \ldots C_n]$. Several other types we encounter deserve special names by analogy with ordinary matrix/vector multiplication, and we offer these to aid the memory.

1 Block 'scalar times vector'

$$B[C_1 \ldots C_n] = [BC_1 \ldots BC_n], \qquad (7.26)$$

$$\mathrm{Rows}(R_1, \ldots, R_m)B = \mathrm{Rows}(R_1 B, \ldots, R_m B). \qquad (7.27)$$

2 Block 'inner product'

$$[A_1 \ldots A_n] \begin{bmatrix} B_1 \\ \ldots \\ B_n \end{bmatrix} = A_1 B_1 + \cdots + A_n B_n \text{ (no. of columns of } A_i = \text{no. of rows of } B_i).$$

$$\qquad (7.28)$$

Three constantly recurring cases of this have A_i as a *single column*, hence B_i as a *single row*. The second case was already used to prove invertibility of $I + S$ in Remarks 7.36.

$$[x_1 \ldots x_n] \begin{bmatrix} R_1 \\ \ldots \\ R_n \end{bmatrix} = x_1 R_1 + \cdots + x_n R_n \quad (A_i = x_i, B_i = R_i), \qquad (7.29)$$

$$[C_1 \ldots C_n] \begin{bmatrix} y_1 \\ \ldots \\ y_n \end{bmatrix} = y_1 C_1 + \cdots + y_n C_n \quad (A_i = C_i, B_i = y_i), \qquad (7.30)$$

$$(\textit{Russian multiplication}) \; [C_1 \ldots C_n] \begin{bmatrix} R_1 \\ \ldots \\ R_n \end{bmatrix} = C_1 R_1 + \cdots + C_n R_n. \qquad (7.31)$$

3 Block 'weighted inner product'

$$[C_1 \ldots C_n] \begin{bmatrix} d_1 & & \\ & \ddots & \\ & & d_n \end{bmatrix} \begin{bmatrix} R_1 \\ \ldots \\ R_n \end{bmatrix} = d_1 C_1 R_1 + \cdots + d_n C_n R_n. \qquad (7.32a)$$

This is a formula prominent in the Singular Value Decomposition of Chapter 8 (see Theorem 8.53). It follows from (7.31) with $d_i R_i$ in place of R_i.

Examples 7.38 (i) Case (7.31) above is at first sight a strange one. After all, we have defined matrix multiplication to be done by rows times columns, not, as here, by columns times rows. Nevertheless it fulfils the requirements for block multiplication, and here is an example.

$$\textit{Standard multiplication:} \begin{bmatrix} 1 & -1 \\ 2 & 0 \\ 3 & 2 \end{bmatrix} \begin{bmatrix} 2 & 3 & 0 \\ -1 & 4 & 1 \end{bmatrix} = \begin{bmatrix} 3 & -1 & -1 \\ 4 & 6 & 0 \\ 4 & 17 & 2 \end{bmatrix},$$

$$\quad\; 3 \times 2 \qquad\quad 2 \times 3 \qquad\quad 3 \times 3$$

$$\textit{Russian (7.31):} \quad \begin{bmatrix} 1 \\ 2 \\ 3 \end{bmatrix} \begin{bmatrix} 2 & 3 & 0 \end{bmatrix} + \begin{bmatrix} -1 \\ 0 \\ 2 \end{bmatrix} \begin{bmatrix} -1 & 4 & 1 \end{bmatrix} = \begin{bmatrix} 2 & 3 & 0 \\ 4 & 6 & 0 \\ 6 & 9 & 0 \end{bmatrix} + \begin{bmatrix} 1 & -4 & -1 \\ 0 & 0 & 0 \\ -2 & 8 & 2 \end{bmatrix},$$

and the two answers are identical.

(ii) Let E_{ij} be the $m \times n$ matrix of zeros except for 1 in position (i, j). Let $C_1 \ldots C_n$ be column m-vectors and $R_1 \ldots R_m$ be row n-vectors. Then

$$[C_1 \ldots C_n] E_{ij} \begin{bmatrix} R_1 \\ \ldots \\ R_m \end{bmatrix} = C_i R_j. \tag{7.32b}$$

Proof Let e_i be a column m-vector of zeros except for 1 in position i, and let f_j be a row n-vector of zeros except for 1 in position j. Then $E_{ij} = e_i f_j$ and the left hand side of (7.32b) becomes

$$[C_1 \ldots C_n] e_i f_j \, \mathrm{Rows}(R_1, \ldots, R_m) = C_i R_j \text{ by (7.30) and (7.29).}$$

Special case (especially useful in Chapter 15) Let $M = [C_1 \ldots C_n]$. Then

$$\boxed{M E_{ij} M^{\mathrm{T}} = C_i C_j{}^{\mathrm{T}}.} \tag{7.32c}$$

Corollary *Let A be any $m \times n$ matrix. Then in the present notation $A = \sum_{ij} a_{ij} E_{ij}$, hence*

$$[C_1 \ldots C_n] A \, \mathrm{Rows}(R_1, \ldots, R_m) = \sum_{ij} a_{ij} C_i R_j. \tag{7.32d}$$

Exercise Let $A = \mathrm{Cols}[(1, 0, -2), (2, 3, 5)]$ and $B = \mathrm{Rows}[(6, 1), (0, 7)]$. Express AB as the sum of two matrices using (7.31). Now check your answer by standard matrix multiplication.

7.3 Further products of vectors in 3-space

Note that, in the vector context, the word *scalar* is used for an object to emphasise its identity as a number rather than a vector. Besides the scalar product of two vectors, there are three other ways of forming new vectors or scalars from vectors which, amongst other uses, provide effective means of calculation in terms of coordinates.

7.3.1 The standard vector product

Definition 7.39 Let non-parallel nonzero vectors a, b be at angle ϕ. Thus $0 < \phi < \pi$ (by definition of angle between vectors, and 'parallel'). The *vector product* $c = a \times b$ of the ordered pair a, b is defined by (see Figure 7.8):

(a) $|a \times b| = |a||b| \sin \phi$. Note that this is the area of the parallelogram with a, b as adjacent edges, since this area equals base length, $|a|$, times height, $|b| \sin \phi$.

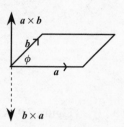

(b) $a \times b$ is perpendicular to a and b, and is such that $a, b, c = a \times b$, is a right handed triple. We define $a \times b$ to be the zero vector if a, b are parallel or either vector is zero.

Figure 7.8 Diagram for Definition 7.39.

Properties

$$a \times a = 0, \tag{7.33}$$

$$b \times a = -a \times b, \tag{7.34}$$

$$\alpha a \times b = a \times \alpha b = \alpha(a \times b), \text{ if } \alpha \text{ is a scalar}, \tag{7.35}$$

$$a \times (b + c) = (a \times b) + (a \times c). \tag{7.36}$$

The hardest to prove is (7.36), which may be done (Hoggar, 1992) using the scalar triple product defined below. Once available, it gives the connection to an exceedingly important and useful determinant formula (Theorem 7.42) for the vector product, starting with the immediately deducible products from the right handed system i, j, k of Section 7.1.3:

$$i \times j = k = -j \times i, \qquad i \times i = 0,$$
$$j \times k = i = -k \times j, \qquad j \times j = 0,$$
$$k \times i = j = -i \times k, \qquad k \times k = 0. \tag{7.37}$$

Notice that the cyclic permutation $i \to j \to k \to i$ applied to each line above yields another. As a consequence we have the practical determinant formula

$$a \times b = \begin{vmatrix} i & j & k \\ a_1 & a_2 & a_3 \\ b_1 & b_2 & b_3 \end{vmatrix}. \tag{7.38}$$

Exercise Use (7.38) to compute the product $(1, 2, 3) \times (2, 0, -5)$, then check that it is orthogonal to both vectors.

7.3.2 Triple products of vectors

Definition 7.40 The *scalar triple product* of vectors a, b, c is the scalar $[a, b, c] = a \cdot (b \times c)$.

Theorem 7.41 *Let a, b, c be nonzero vectors. Then*

(a) *$[a, b, c]$ equals $\pm$ the volume of the figure (parallelepiped) with opposite faces parallel and a, b, c represented by adjacent edges, as shown in Figure 7.9,*

(b) *$[a, b, c]$ is constant under cyclic shifts of a, b, c and reverses sign under interchanges,*

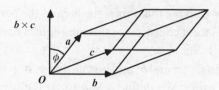

Figure 7.9 A solid bounded by parallelograms whose volume is $\pm a \cdot (b \times c)$.

(c) $[a, b, c] = 0$ *if and only if* a, b, c *are coplanar; in particular* $[a, b, c] = 0$ *if any two of* a, b, c *are equal or parallel,*

(d) *the triple* a, b, c *is right handed if* $[a, b, c] > 0$ *and left handed if* $[a, b, c] < 0$,

(e) *let* a, b, c *be unit vectors. Then* a, b, c *is a right handed or left handed* **orthonormal** *set according as* $[a, b, c] = 1$ *or* -1 *(it may be neither).*

Proof We think of the volume as $V = $ (area of base) times (height) $= |b \times c| \times |a| |\cos \phi| = \pm[a, b, c]$. If a, b, c is right handed then $b \times c$ points to the same side of the base as does a and so $0 \leq \phi < \pi/2, \cos \phi > 0$. Consequently we have $V = |a| |b \times c| \cos \phi = [a, b, c]$. In the left handed case $-\pi \leq \phi < -\pi/2$, and $\cos \phi < 0$, therefore $V = |a| |b \times c| (-\cos \phi) = -[a, b, c]$. This is sufficient to establish (a) to (d). Extending the argument gives (e) (see e.g. Hoggar, 1992).

Theorem 7.42 *Scalar triple products are given by the following determinant.*

$$[a, b, c] = \begin{vmatrix} a_1 & a_2 & a_3 \\ b_1 & b_2 & b_3 \\ c_1 & c_2 & c_3 \end{vmatrix}.$$

Proof We have $[a, b, c] = a \cdot (b \times c) = a_1 (b \times c)_1 + a_2 (b \times c)_2 + a_3 (b \times c)_3$, which equals the above determinant, by (7.38).

Remarks 7.43 (1) For a left handed coordinate system we must switch the last two rows in the determinant formula of (7.38) and Theorem 7.42 above. (2) The latter has a nice spinoff in two dimensions; by considering the various cases we obtain Corollary 7.44 below.

Exercise Determine whether the following ordered triple of vectors forms a right handed triple, a left handed triple, or is coplanar: $(1, 1, 1), (1, -1, 1), (0, 1, 0)$.

Corollary 7.44 *Let* $A(a_1, a_2, 0), B(b_1, b_2, 0)$ *be points in the xy-plane, distinct from the origin. Then* $a \times b = (0, 0, D)$, *where*

$$D = \begin{vmatrix} a_1 & a_2 \\ b_1 & b_2 \end{vmatrix}.$$

If $D = 0$ *then the points* O, A, B *are collinear (or* $A = B$). *If* $D \neq 0$ *then rotation of* OA *about* O *towards* OB *is anti-clockwise if* $D > 0$, *and clockwise if* $D < 0$. *In any case, the triangle with adjacent sides* OA, OB *has area half the absolute value* $|D|$.

Corollary 7.45 *The area of a triangle in the xy-plane with vertices A, B, C is*

$$1/2 \text{ the absolute value of } \begin{vmatrix} 1 & 1 & 1 \\ a_1 & b_1 & c_1 \\ a_2 & b_2 & c_2 \end{vmatrix}.$$

Proof From Definition 7.39, twice the area is $|AB \times AC|$.

Theorem 7.46 *(Evaluating vector and scalar triple products) The following equalities hold:*

$$a \times (b \times c) = (a \cdot c)b - (a \cdot b)c,$$
$$[\alpha a + \beta b, c, d] = \alpha[a, c, d] + \beta[b, c, d].$$

Proof Since $b \times c$ is perpendicular to the plane of b, c (as vectors starting from the origin, say), $a \times (b \times c)$ lies in that plane, and so equals $\lambda b + \mu c$ for some scalars λ, μ. We check the first coordinates in the equality, then the corresponding results for the other coordinates are obtained by cyclically permuting the subscripts $1 \to 2 \to 3 \to 1$. The second formula follows from (7.8) and the definition $[u, v, w] = u \cdot (v \times w)$.

Example 7.47 $[a, b, a + c] = [a, b, a] + [a, b, c]$ (by Theorem 7.46) $= [a, b, c]$, since $[a, b, a]$ has two entries equal and so is zero by Theorem 7.41(c). See also Exercise 7.17 at the end of the chapter.

Exercise Express $[a + 2b - 3c, a - c, b]$ as a multiple of $[a, b, c]$ or prove more generally that

$$[x_1 a + x_2 b + x_3 c, y_1 a + y_2 b + y_3 c, z_1 a + z_2 b + z_3 c] = \begin{vmatrix} x_1 & x_2 & x_3 \\ y_1 & y_2 & y_3 \\ z_1 & z_2 & z_3 \end{vmatrix} [a, b, c].$$

7.3.3 Vectors and coordinate geometry

We include this short section to give at least a sample of how the use of vectors can simplify calculations and proofs in 3-dimensional coordinate geometry (cf. Application 1.1 in the plane). We will concentrate on lines and planes, starting with their equations. As before, an arbitrary point A has coordinates (a_1, a_2, a_3), which are the components of its position vector a.

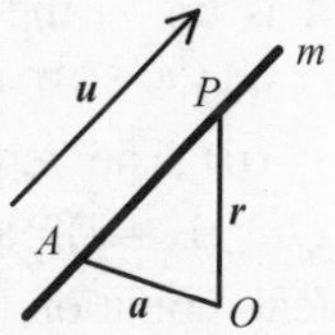

Example 7.48 (See Figure 7.10.) The line m through the point A, parallel to the vector u, has a parametric equation

$$r = a + tu, \quad \text{i.e. } \begin{cases} x = a_1 + tu_1 \\ y = a_2 + tu_2 \\ z = a_3 + tu_3 \end{cases}$$

Figure 7.10
Diagram for
Example 7.48.

That is to say, all points of this form, with $t \in \mathbf{R}$, are on the line, and every point of the line may be so expressed. We call $\mathbf{u}$ a *direction vector* for m.

Proof Let the point P have position vector $\mathbf{r}$. Then: P is on $m \Leftrightarrow AP$ is parallel to $\mathbf{u} \Leftrightarrow AP = t\mathbf{u}$ (some $t \in \mathbf{R}$) $\Leftrightarrow \mathbf{r} - \mathbf{a} = t\mathbf{u}$, i.e. $\mathbf{r} = \mathbf{a} + t\mathbf{u}$ $(t \in \mathbf{R})$. Alternatively we could invoke the section formula (1.3).

Example 7.49 Determine where the line through points $A(1, 2, 1)$ and $B(2, 8, 4)$ cuts the sphere $x^2 + y^2 + z^2 = 2$. See Figure 7.11 (not to scale).

Figure 7.11 Diagram for Example 7.49.

Solution A direction vector for the line, m say, is $AB = (1, 6, 3)$. The point on m with parameter t is then $\mathbf{r} = \mathbf{a} + tAB$, or in coordinates $(1 + t, 2 + 6t, 1 + 3t)$, which is on the sphere when t satisfies $(1 + t)^2 + (2 + 6t)^2 + (1 + 3t)^2 = 2$. The solutions are approximately $t = -0.16$ and $t = -0.53$, giving intersection points $P(0.84, 1.04, 0.52)$ and $Q(0.47, -1.18, -0.59)$.

Example 7.50 Any vector perpendicular to plane π is called a *normal vector* to π (see Figure 7.12). The plane π through a point A, having a normal vector $\mathbf{n} = (l, m, n)$, has equation

$$lx + my + nz = la_1 + ma_2 + na_3.$$

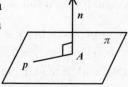

Figure 7.12 Diagram for Example 7.50.

Proof Let the point P have position vector $\mathbf{r}$. Then $\mathbf{P}$ is on $\pi \Leftrightarrow AP$ is perpendicular to $\mathbf{n} \Leftrightarrow (\mathbf{r} - \mathbf{a}) \cdot \mathbf{n} = 0$ (by Theorem 7.5) $\Leftrightarrow \mathbf{r} \cdot \mathbf{n} = \mathbf{a} \cdot \mathbf{n}$.

One reason why the vector product is so useful is that it gives us a simple way to compute the coordinates of a *vector at right angles to two given vectors*. Here are some applications of this.

Example 7.51 Find (i) the equation of the plane π through points $A(1, 0, 1)$, $B(2, -1, 3)$, $C(2, 3, -2)$, (ii) the foot of the perpendicular from $Q(1, 1, -2)$ to π. See Figure 7.13.

Solution (i) One vector normal to π is $AB \times AC = (1, -1, 2) \times (1, 3, -3) = (-3, 5, 4)$ by (7.38). Since A is on π, the latter has equation $-3x + 5y + 4z = -3(1) + 5(0) + 4(1) = 1$.

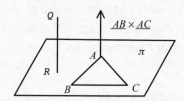

Figure 7.13 Diagram for Example 7.51.

(ii) The required point R is on the line through $Q(1, 1, -2)$ parallel to the normal $(-3, 5, 4)$. A typical point on this line is $(1 - 3t, 1 + 5t, -2 + 4t)$. At R, on the plane, t satisfies $-3(1 - 3t) + 5(1 + 5t) + 4(-2 + 4t) = 1$, giving $t = 7/50$. Hence R is $(29/50, 17/10, -36/25)$.

Exercise Use the ideas of Examples 7.48 to 7.51 to find an equation for the plane through points $A(1, 2, 3)$, $B(-1, 0, 1)$ and at right angles to the plane $x - y + 2z = 5$. ($4x - y - 3z = -7$.)

A 'real life' application This cropped up in work on 'inverse displacement mapping' (see Patterson, Hoggar and Logie, 1991). We have a sample ray (line) for which the parametric equation of Example 7.48 is $r = p + tq$, as illustrated in Figure 7.14. The radius vector OR from the origin to the ray meets a unit sphere, centre O, at the point with angular coordinates u, v (think of latitude and longitude). Finding an equation $v = f(u)$ for the ray is rather hard work until we observe that, since $p \times q$ is perpendicular to OE and ER, it is perpendicular to the plane of triangle OER, and in particular to OR. Hence $(p \times q) \cdot r = 0$, leading after some simplification to the ray equation $v = (2/\pi)\tan^{-1}(k \cdot \cos(\pi u + a))$, where k, a are given by the coordinates of constant vectors p, q. Details are found in the cited paper.

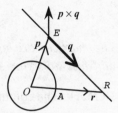

Figure 7.14 Real life application.

7.4 The matrix of a transformation

We explore the relationship between transformations, especially the length-preserving *isometries* (see Chapter 1), their defining matrices, and the orthonormal basis being used. After deriving the matrices corresponding to plane rotations and reflections, we see why a transformation is linear if and only if it may be defined by a matrix with respect to some basis of the space transformed. We establish important consequences of changing that basis, and the constancy of the determinant and of the orthogonality property.

Most vectors will be written in row form in this chapter and the next; however, to convert an equality into the same statement for vectors in column form, we simply transpose both sides of an equation. This applies firstly to (7.39) below.

7.4.1 Rotations and reflections

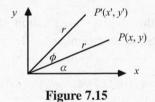

Figure 7.15

Theorem 7.52 *Rotation through angle ϕ about the origin in the xy-plane is given by* $(x, y) \to (x', y')$, *where in matrix notation*

$$[x' \quad y'] = [x \quad y] \begin{bmatrix} \cos\phi & \sin\phi \\ -\sin\phi & \cos\phi \end{bmatrix}. \tag{7.39}$$

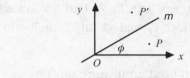

Figure 7.16

The matrices arising in this way form the special orthogonal group $SO(2)$ of 2×2 matrices satisfying $MM^{\mathrm{T}} = I, |M| = 1$.

Remark The column version is obtained by transposing:

$$\begin{bmatrix} x' \\ y' \end{bmatrix} = \begin{bmatrix} \cos\phi & -\sin\phi \\ \sin\phi & \cos\phi \end{bmatrix} \begin{bmatrix} x \\ y \end{bmatrix}.$$

Proof of (7.39) In polar coordinates, with $|OP| = r = |OQ|$ in Figure 7.15, we have $x = r\cos\alpha, y = r\sin\alpha$, and so

$$x' = r\cos(\alpha + \phi) = r\cos\alpha\cos\phi - r\sin\alpha\sin\phi = x\cos\phi - y\sin\phi,$$
$$y' = r\sin(\alpha + \phi) = r\cos\alpha\sin\phi + r\sin\alpha\cos\phi = x\sin\phi + y\cos\phi,$$

which together form matrix equation (7.39). For the last part we note first that the matrix of rotation in (7.39) is indeed in $SO(2)$, so it remains to show that every 2×2 matrix

$$M = \begin{bmatrix} a & b \\ c & d \end{bmatrix}, \quad \text{with } MM^{\mathrm{T}} = I, \quad |M| = 1,$$

arises from a rotation. Now, these conditions on M imply that $M^{\mathrm{T}} = M^{-1}, |M| = 1$, or by the matrix inverse formula (7.22) for the 2×2 case,

$$\begin{bmatrix} a & c \\ b & d \end{bmatrix} = \begin{bmatrix} d & -b \\ -c & a \end{bmatrix}, \quad \text{hence } c = -b, d = a, \text{ and } \quad M = \begin{bmatrix} a & b \\ -b & a \end{bmatrix}.$$

Thus, from $|M| = 1$, we have $a^2 + b^2 = 1$ and so may write $a = \cos\phi, b = \sin\phi$ for some angle ϕ, giving M the rotation form (7.39).

Remarks 7.53 (1) If M is the matrix for rotation through ϕ then M^{-1} is that for $-\phi$. (2) An orthogonal matrix has determinant ± 1.

Theorem 7.54 *Reflection in a mirror m through the origin in the plane, at angle ϕ to the x-axis, is given by $[x\ y] \to [x'\ y']$, where*

$$[x'\ y'] = [x\ y] \begin{bmatrix} \cos 2\phi & \sin 2\phi \\ \sin 2\phi & -\cos 2\phi \end{bmatrix}. \tag{7.40}$$

Such matrices are those in the orthogonal group $O(2)$ which have determinant -1.

Proof We use the previous theorem to calculate this matrix as a composition. As in Part I, let R_m be the reflection in any mirror m. Then

$$R_m = R_{Ox} R_{Ox} R_m \qquad (R_{OX} \text{ is reflection in the } x\text{-axis})$$
$$= R_{Ox} R_O(2\phi), \qquad \text{by Theorem 2.1,}$$

where the last isometry is rotation about the origin through angle 2ϕ. Since these maps are written in their order of application, R_m has matrix

$$\begin{bmatrix} 1 & 0 \\ 0 & -1 \end{bmatrix} \begin{bmatrix} \cos 2\phi & \sin 2\phi \\ -\sin 2\phi & \cos 2\phi \end{bmatrix} = \begin{bmatrix} \cos 2\phi & \sin 2\phi \\ \sin 2\phi & -\cos 2\phi \end{bmatrix}$$

as stated. Now, this matrix is orthogonal, of determinant -1, and the theorem asserts that every 2×2 matrix M with $MM^T = I$, of determinant -1, has the form (7.40) for some angle, written as 2ϕ. This follows in the same way as the last part of Theorem 7.52. Alternatively, with $D = \text{diag}(1, -1)$ and so $D^2 = I$, the matrix $N = DM$ satisfies $NN^T = I, |N| = |D||M| = 1$ so, by Theorem 7.52,

$$N = \begin{bmatrix} \cos \alpha & \sin \alpha \\ -\sin \alpha & \cos \alpha \end{bmatrix}, \qquad \text{for some angle } \alpha.$$

Now $D^2 = I$ converts $N = DM$ to $M = DN$, which has the stated form (7.40) when we replace α by 2ϕ.

Exercise Compute the product AB, where A is the matrix of rotation about O through 90 degrees and B gives reflection in the line $y = x\sqrt{3}$. Does your answer agree with geometrical predictions?

3D Rotations What we can readily say at this stage is that, in three dimensions, rotation through ϕ about the z-axis does not change the z-coordinate, and so is given by

$$[x'\, y'\, z'] = [x\ y\ z] \begin{bmatrix} \cos \phi & \sin \phi & 0 \\ -\sin \phi & \cos \phi & 0 \\ 0 & 0 & 1 \end{bmatrix}.$$

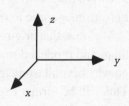

(7.41)

For the case of rotation about an arbitrary axis in three dimensions see Hoggar (1992), where we classify isometries in 3-space. Meanwhile, here is a short recapitulation.

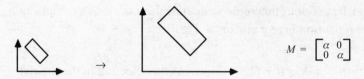

Figure 7.17 Dilation $x \to \alpha x, \alpha > 0$.

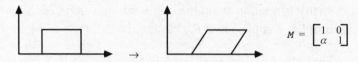

Figure 7.18 Shear $(x, y) \to (x + \alpha y, y), \alpha > 0$.

How to

Determine the angle between vectors	(7.6)
Multiply by a diagonal matrix	(7.12)
Evaluate a determinant	Rules 7.28
Detect left handed vs right handed system	Theorems 7.41, 7.42
Detect clockwise vs anti-clockwise rotation	Corollary 7.44
Evaluate $a \times b$, $[a, b, c]$, and $a \times (b \times c)$	(7.38), Theorem 7.42,
	and Theorem 7.46.

7.4.2 Linearity

Definition 7.55 A transformation T of n-space is linear if, for all vectors x and real numbers α,

$$T(x + y) = T(x) + T(y), \qquad T(\alpha x) = \alpha T(x). \tag{7.42}$$

This certainly holds if T is given by a matrix, $T(x) = xM$, for $T(x + y) = (x + y)M = xM + yM = T(x) + T(y)$, and $T(\alpha x) = (\alpha x)M = \alpha(xM) = \alpha T(x)$. The converse is proved in Theorem 7.56. Note though that a linear map must fix the origin, since $T(0) = T(0x) = 0T(x) = 0$, for any x. The definition of *linear* applies to any map (function) from n-space to m-space, though we do not yet require this degree of generality.

We know that origin-fixing isometries of the plane are linear because we have classified them and produced matrices for each case. Let us note here, however, that linear maps go way beyond isometries, for example in dilation and shear (see Figures 7.17 and 7.18). This will be further explored under *Fractal Compression* in Chapter 16.

In fact, it is very useful to define certain transformations to be of the same type if one can be obtained from the other by composition with an isometry. We note though that, as is fitting, a linear transformation T maps lines to lines, for the line L joining points a, b consists of the points $x = a + t(b - a)$ for all real numbers t, and by linearity $Tx = Ta + t(Tb - Ta)$. Hence T maps L to the line joining points Ta and Tb.

We will often need the coordinate formula (Theorem 7.14) which is requoted here for convenience.

> *The ith coordinate of a vector **u** in an orthonormal basis $\{e_k\}$ is $u \cdot e_i$.* (7.43)

Theorem 7.56 *If T is a linear transformation of n-space, then it is given by a matrix M as follows.*

$$T(x) = xM, \quad M = [m_{ij}], \quad m_{ij} = T(e_i) \cdot e_j \qquad (7.44a)$$

*where the coordinates of **x** are taken with respect to any orthonormal basis $\{e_i\}$. In particular, the ith row of M consists of the coordinates $m_{i1}, m_{i2}, \ldots, m_{in}$ of $T(e_i)$. Taking $e_i = (0 \ldots 0 \ 1 \ 0 \ldots 0)$ with ith entry 1,*

> $\{i, j, k\} \to \{u, v, w\}$ *under matrix* $M = \text{Rows}[u, v, w]$. (7.44b)

Proof Let T be linear. Statement (7.44) simply asserts that the jth coordinate of $T(x)$ is $\sum_i x_i m_{ij}$, with m_{ij} as defined. This is true because by Formula (7.43) the component is $T(x) \cdot e_j = (T(\sum_i x_i e_i)) \cdot e_j = \sum_i x_i T(e_i) \cdot e_j$, by linearity, (7.42).

Remarks 7.57 (1) The proof above holds if any n linearly independent (i.e. non-coplanar, in the case $n = 3$) vectors are taken as basis, except that we no longer have the explicit formula $m_{ij} = T(e_i) \cdot e_j$.

(2) We may express a linear map in the form $T(y) = Ny$, where y is a column vector, by the abovementioned technique of transposing each side of a matrix equation. Thus xM in Equation (7.44) becomes $M^T x^T$ and we may write $T(y) = Ny$, where $N = [n_{ij}]$ and $n_{ij} = T(e_j) \cdot e_i$ (note: $n_{ij} = m_{ji}$). That is, the components of $T(e_j)$ form column j of N.

Example 7.58 Find the matrices of the linear transformations of $\mathbf{R}^3$ given by (i) $T(i) = j + k, T(j) = i - j + k, T(k) = 2i - j$, and (ii) $T(x, y, z) = (2x + y, x + z, x + y - 3z)$.

Solution (i) Theorem 7.56, case (7.44b) applies. For instance, $T(i) = j + k$, so the first row of M consists of the components $(0, 1, 1)$. Thus M is the second matrix below.

(ii) The matrix of the transformation is defined by $T(x, y, z) = [x \ y \ z]M$, so by definition of matrix multiplication the coefficients of x, y, z in successive coordinates form the *columns* of the first matrix below.

$$\begin{bmatrix} 2 & 1 & 1 \\ 1 & 0 & 1 \\ 0 & 1 & -3 \end{bmatrix}, \begin{bmatrix} 0 & 1 & 1 \\ 1 & -1 & 1 \\ 2 & -1 & 0 \end{bmatrix}.$$

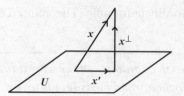

Figure 7.19 Projection x' of x onto a subspace U, and consequent expression as $x' + x^\perp$.

Exercise Find the matrix M when basis i, j, k is transformed to j, $(i + k)/\sqrt{2}$, $(i - k)/\sqrt{2}$. Verify that M is orthogonal and state its determinant.

7.4.3 Projection mappings

We have introduced (Definition 7.19) the *orthogonal projection* x' of an element x of the vector space V onto a subspace U of V. This splits x into its component x' in U and a component $x^\perp$ orthogonal to U; that is, $x^\perp$ is orthogonal to every vector in U. This is briefly recalled in Figure 7.19, following which we give some key results useful in the sequel (e.g. the optimisation properties of Singular Value Decomposition in Section 8.4.3 and application to compression in Chapter 10).

Theorem 7.59 *Let the subspace U of V have as ONB the rows $u_1, \dots, u_k$ of a matrix E. Then (a) the orthogonal projection $p : V \to U$ has matrix $P = E^T E$ (see also (7.45)),*

(b)
$$\boxed{P^2 = P = P^T \text{ and } p(V) = U,}$$

(c) the unique decomposition of any x in V as $x = x' + x^\perp$ ($x' \in U, x^\perp \in U^\perp$) is given by $x' = xP, x^\perp = x(I - P)$.

Proof (a) We have $p: x \to \sum_i (x \cdot u_i)u_i = \sum_i x u_i^T u_i = x \sum_i u_i^T u_i = x E^T E$ (by Russian matrix multiplication, (7.31)). For (b) notice that $E E^T$ has i, j entry $u_i \cdot u_j = \delta_{ij}$, hence $E E^T = I$ and $P^2 = E^T (E E^T)E = E^T E = P$. Clearly $P^T = P$. Also $p(V) \subseteq U$ by construction, and if x is in U then $x = \sum x_i u_i$ ($1 \le i \le k$) has components $x_j = x \cdot u_j$, so the formula of (a) for $p(x)$ gives $p(x) = \sum(x \cdot u_j)u_j = \sum x_j u_j = x$. Thus $U \subseteq p(V)$ and hence $U = p(V)$. (c) For uniqueness we refer to the discussion in Definition 7.19. It remains to show that $x(I - P)$ is orthogonal to every vector u in U. Let $u = p(v)$ for some v in the larger space V. Then

$$\begin{aligned} x(I - P) \cdot u &= x(I - P)(vP)^T & \text{since } u = vP \\ &= x(I - P)P^T v^T & \text{by the reversal rule for transposes} \\ &= x(P - P^2)v^T & \text{since } P = P^T \\ &= 0 & \text{since } P^2 = P. \end{aligned}$$

Example 7.60 Let $u = (1, 2, -2)$, $v = (2, 1, 2)$. Find the respective matrices P, Q of the orthogonal projections onto span$\{u\}$ and span$\{u, v\}$.

Solution We have $|u| = 3 = |v|$ and $u \cdot v = 0$, so the rows of $U = (1/3)$ Rows (u, v) are orthonormal and the matrices P, Q are given by Theorem 7.59 (a) as

$$P = \frac{1}{9} \begin{bmatrix} 1 \\ 2 \\ -2 \end{bmatrix} \begin{bmatrix} 1 & 2 & -2 \end{bmatrix} = \frac{1}{9} \begin{bmatrix} 1 & 2 & -2 \\ 2 & 4 & -4 \\ -2 & -4 & 4 \end{bmatrix},$$

$$Q = U^{\mathrm{T}}U = \frac{1}{9} \begin{bmatrix} 1 & 2 \\ 2 & 1 \\ -2 & 2 \end{bmatrix} \begin{bmatrix} 1 & 2 & -2 \\ 2 & 1 & 2 \end{bmatrix} = \frac{1}{9} \begin{bmatrix} 5 & 4 & 2 \\ 4 & 5 & -2 \\ 2 & -2 & 8 \end{bmatrix}.$$

Notice that by (7.31) the matrix Q is the sum of the matrices of projections onto span$\{u\}$ and span$\{v\}$, as it should be.

Exercise Why is the last sentence true?

Remarks 7.61 (1) The properties of P as a matrix are enough to ensure that P gives a projection. Let P be the matrix of a plane transformation $p: x \to xP$, where $P^2 = P = P^{\mathrm{T}}$. Then p is the orthogonal projection mapping onto its image U. For it suffices to show that $x - xP$ lies in the orthogonal complement of U, and this is performed in the proof of Theorem 7.59 (c).

$$\boxed{P \text{ is a projection matrix if and only if } P^2 = P = P^{\mathrm{T}}.}$$

(2) *Projection onto a column space* $p: V \to \text{span}\{u_1^{\mathrm{T}}, \ldots, u_k^{\mathrm{T}}\}$. By the usual transposition argument, $x \to xP$ if and only if $x^{\mathrm{T}} \to P^{\mathrm{T}}x^{\mathrm{T}}$. Since $P^{\mathrm{T}} = P$, the matrix is unchanged.

To project onto a k-space with given ONB:

$$\boxed{\begin{aligned} E &= \text{ matrix of ONB as ROWS (so } EE^{\mathrm{T}} = I_k), \\ P &= E^{\mathrm{T}}E, \text{ projection matrix, symmetric,} \\ &\text{as rows: } x \to xP, \text{ as columns } x^{\mathrm{T}} \to Px^{\mathrm{T}}. \end{aligned}} \quad (7.45)$$

7.4.4 Changing bases

Theorem 7.62 *Given ONBs $\{e_i\}$, $\{f_i\}$ of an n-dimensional vector space V, there is a unique linear mapping that sends e_i to f_i ($1 \leq i \leq n$). Its matrix w.r.t. $\{e_i\}$ is $[f_i \cdot e_j]$, and is orthogonal.*

Proof A transformation T of V with $Te_i = f_i$ is linear if and only if $T(\sum x_i e_i) = \sum x_i T(e_i)$. But this defines T uniquely. The matrix M of T, given by Theorem 7.56, satisfies

$$(MM^{\mathrm{T}})_{ij} = \sum_k m_{ik}m_{jk}$$

$$= \sum_k (T(e_i) \cdot (e_k)(T(e_j) \cdot ek)$$

$$= \sum_k (f_i \cdot e_k)(f_j \cdot e_k)$$

$$= f_i \cdot f_j \text{ calculated in coordinates w.r.t. } \{e_i\} \text{ (see Theorem 7.14)}$$

$$= \delta_{ij} \text{ as required for orthogonality.}$$

Example 7.63 *Find the matrix M of any isometry which will map the axes i, j, k so as to send i into $u = (1, 1, 1)/\sqrt{3}$.*

Solution For this, we complete u in any way to a set of three mutually orthogonal unit vectors u, v, w. First we satisfy the orthogonality condition, then we divide each vector by its own length. One possibility is $v = (1, -1, 0)/\sqrt{2}, w = (1, 1, -2)/\sqrt{6}$, as illustrated below.

$$\begin{array}{cccc} & i & j & k \\ u & \begin{bmatrix} 1/\sqrt{3} & 1/\sqrt{3} & 1/\sqrt{3} \\ v & 1/\sqrt{2} & -1/\sqrt{2} & 0 \\ w & 1/\sqrt{6} & 1/\sqrt{6} & -2/\sqrt{6} \end{bmatrix} \end{array}$$

The matrix M: an entry is the scalar product of corresponding vectors on the borders. Thus the w, j entry is $w \cdot j$.

Now we take $i, j, k \to u, v, w$ respectively. With the formula $m_{ij} = T(e_i) \cdot e_j$ of Theorem 7.56, the matrix is now particularly simple to write down, the rows being the coordinates of u, v, w with respect to i, j, k, as indicated by the bordering (same matrix as above).

Remark 7.64 (*From single vector to a basis*) The example above suggests a simple scheme for extending a unit vector $u = (a, b, c)$ with $a, b, c \neq 0$, to an orthonormal basis, by appending $(-b, a, 0), (a, b, c - 1/c)$, then dividing each vector by its length. Now for the non-ONB case.

Theorem 7.65 *If a basis $\{e_i\}$ of n-space is transformed to $\{e_i A\}$ by an invertible matrix A then*

(a) *the coordinates undergo $x \to xA^{-1}$,*

(b) *the matrix M of a linear transformation becomes AMA^{-1}.*

Proof (a) The short argument is that moving the axes (i.e. the ONB) one way is equivalent to moving points the opposite way. Thus coordinates should change by $x \to xA^{-1}$. (b) To map a point y in the new coordinate system we may convert it to old coordinates, apply the old matrix, then convert back to new coordinates. That is, $y \rightarrow yA \rightarrow yAM \rightarrow yAMA^{-1}$. Thus the new matrix is AMA^{-1}.

Example 7.66 *What are the new coordinates of point* $(1, 6, 4)$ *if the basis* i, j, k *is cycled round to* j, k, i? We have $i, j, k \rightarrow j, k, i$ under the matrix $A = \text{Rows}[j, k, i]$ by (7.44b), so the corresponding transformation of coordinates is $x \rightarrow xA^{-1}$, which equals xA^{T} since A happens to be orthogonal.

$$
\begin{array}{c}
\begin{array}{ccc} i & j & k \end{array} \\
\begin{array}{c} j \\ k \\ i \end{array}
\begin{bmatrix} 0 & 1 & 0 \\ 0 & 0 & 1 \\ 1 & 0 & 0 \end{bmatrix}
\end{array}
\qquad
[1 \quad 6 \quad 4]
\begin{bmatrix} 0 & 0 & 1 \\ 1 & 0 & 0 \\ 0 & 1 & 0 \end{bmatrix}
= [6 \quad 4 \quad 1]
$$

$$\qquad\qquad A \qquad\qquad\qquad\qquad A^{\text{T}} \qquad\qquad \text{result}$$

Exercise Verify that the rows of matrix A^{T} with A as above are the coordinates of the old basis in terms of the new. Is this true for any change of orthonormal basis?

Example 7.67 *What becomes of the matrix of half turn about the z-axis after the basis* i, j, k *is changed to* $(j + k)/\sqrt{2}, (k + i)/\sqrt{2}, (i + j)/\sqrt{2}$? For the matrix M of the $1/2$ turn about the z-axis we don't need to recall the sine and cosine of $\pi/2$, for geometry shows us immediately the images of i, j, k are respectively $j, -i, k$, enabling us to write M straight down. The new matrix is

$$
AMA^{-1} = \frac{1}{\sqrt{2}}\begin{bmatrix} 0 & 1 & 1 \\ 1 & 0 & 1 \\ 1 & 1 & 0 \end{bmatrix}
\begin{bmatrix} 0 & 1 & 0 \\ -1 & 0 & 0 \\ 0 & 0 & 1 \end{bmatrix}
\frac{1}{\sqrt{2}}\begin{bmatrix} -1 & 1 & 1 \\ 1 & -1 & 1 \\ 1 & 1 & -1 \end{bmatrix}
= \begin{bmatrix} 1 & 0 & -1 \\ 1 & 0 & 0 \\ 1 & -1 & 0 \end{bmatrix}.
$$

Exercise Calculate the 3×3 matrix for a rotation of $\pi/6$ about the z-axis. Determine the new matrix N when the axes are changed by $i \rightarrow j \rightarrow k \rightarrow i$. Verify your answer geometrically.

Remark 7.68 *The determinant of the matrix of a linear transformation T is the same, with respect to any ONB.* For, if M is the matrix with respect to one ONB, the determinant after changing ONB by a matrix A is, by Theorem 7.65, $|AMA^{-1}| = |A||M||A^{-1}| = |AA^{-1}||M| = |M|$. Thus we may speak of the *determinant of T* independently of a choice of basis.

Isometries and orthogonal matrices

Definition 7.69 A transformation T of n-space is an *isometry* if T preserves distances:

$$|Tx - Ty| = |x - y| \qquad \text{for all } x, y \text{ in } R^n, \tag{7.46}$$

and hence T preserves angles (up to sign), areas and volumes. Especially important for us is: *if T fixes the origin, TO = O, then*

$$Tx \cdot Ty = x \cdot y \qquad \text{for all } x, y \text{ in } \mathbf{R}^n, \tag{7.47}$$

and hence

$$\boxed{\begin{array}{c} \textit{if } \{\mathbf{e}_i\} \textit{ is an orthonormal basis of n-space} \\ \textit{then so is } \{T\mathbf{e}_i\}. \end{array}} \tag{7.48}$$

Proof Equation (7.47) follows from (7.46) because an inner product is completely expressible in terms of distances, by (7.7) (see also above Theorem 7.5). The argument begins with $|T\mathbf{x}| = |T\mathbf{x} - T\mathbf{O}| = |\mathbf{x} - \mathbf{O}| = |\mathbf{x}|$, and then

$$\begin{aligned} 2\,T\mathbf{x} \cdot T\mathbf{y} &= |T\mathbf{x}|^2 + |T\mathbf{y}|^2 - |T\mathbf{x} - T\mathbf{y}|^2 \qquad \text{by (7.7) for } n\text{-space} \\ &= |\mathbf{x}|^2 + |\mathbf{y}|^2 - |\mathbf{x} - \mathbf{y}|^2 \qquad \text{by (7.46)} \\ &= 2\mathbf{x} \cdot \mathbf{y} \qquad \text{by (7.7).} \end{aligned}$$

For (7.48) we now have $T\mathbf{e}_i \cdot T\mathbf{e}_j = \mathbf{e}_i \cdot \mathbf{e}_j = \delta_{ij}$, by (7.47). This completes the proof.

The following theorem was stated in Chapter 1 for the plane, but the proof given there is clearly valid for general $\mathbf{R}^n$. It is simple and useful, and we shall need to keep it in mind.

Theorem 7.70 *If A is any point of n-space then any isometry T is composed of a translation and an isometry that fixes A.*

Shortly we concentrate on the isometries that fix the origin O, and prove the important facts that they are linear, that their matrices form the orthogonal group, and that the determinant distinguishes between direct and indirect isometries (for the last, see Theorem 8.10).

Theorem 7.71 *(Isometries and the orthogonal group) An isometry T of n-space which fixes the origin is linear. With respect to any orthonormal basis the matrix of T is orthogonal.*

Proof Let $\{\mathbf{e}_i\}$ be an orthonormal basis. Then by (7.48) so is $\{\mathbf{f}_i\}$, where $\mathbf{f}_i = T\mathbf{e}_i$. Let $\mathbf{x} = \sum x_i \mathbf{e}_i$ and $T\mathbf{x} = \sum z_i \mathbf{f}_i$. Then

$$\begin{aligned} z_i &= (T\mathbf{x}) \cdot \mathbf{f}_i \qquad \text{by the component formula (7.43)} \\ &= (T\mathbf{x}) \cdot T\mathbf{e}_i \qquad \text{by definition of } \mathbf{f}_i \\ &= \mathbf{x} \cdot \mathbf{e}_i \qquad \text{by (7.47), since } T \text{ is an isometry} \\ &= x_i \qquad \text{by the component formula (7.43).} \end{aligned}$$

Thus $T(\sum x_i \mathbf{e}_i) = \sum x_i \mathbf{f}_i$ for any vector $\sum x_i \mathbf{e}_i$. Now let $\mathbf{y} = \sum y_i \mathbf{e}_i$ and α be a scalar. Then $T(\alpha \mathbf{x} + \mathbf{y}) = T \sum (\alpha x_i + y_i)\mathbf{e}_i = \sum (\alpha x_i + y_i)\mathbf{f}_i = \alpha \sum x_i \mathbf{f}_i + \sum y_i \mathbf{f}_i = \alpha T(\mathbf{x}) + T(\mathbf{y})$. Thus T is linear. Finally, its matrix is orthogonal by Theorem 7.62.

Remarks 7.72 (1) It is easy to see that every orthogonal matrix N produces an isometry by $\mathbf{x} \to \mathbf{x}N$, in fact $|\mathbf{x}N|^2 = \mathbf{x}(N)(\mathbf{x}N)^{\mathrm{T}} = \mathbf{x}(NN^{\mathrm{T}})\mathbf{x}^{\mathrm{T}} = \mathbf{x}\,I\,\mathbf{x}^{\mathrm{T}} = |\mathbf{x}|^2$. The converse is the hard part, and we included it in Theorem 7.71. Thus, using any fixed coordinate system,

> *the orthogonal group $O(n)$ corresponds to the group of all isometries that fix the origin.*

(2) We have the expression $m_{ij} = T(e_i) \cdot e_j$ for the elements of the matrix M of T, assuming only that T is linear, not necessarily an isometry, and that the e_i are orthonormal. If in addition T is an isometry then the $T e_i$ are also orthonormal, (7.48), in particular they are unit vectors, and as a result m_{ij} is the cosine of the angle between $T e_i$ and e_j. In this situation we call M *the matrix of cosines;* every orthogonal matrix can be so represented.

7.5 Permutations and the proof of determinant rules

This section may be omitted on a first reading, its main purpose being to justify the important Rules 7.28 for evaluating determinants. It is numbered from Definition 1 through to Theorem 10.

Definition 1 A *permutation* σ of n objects is a reordering of them. If σ reorders the objects $a_1 a_2 \ldots a_n$ as $b_1 b_2 \ldots b_n$ we may write $\sigma: a_1 a_2 \ldots a_n \to b_1 b_2 \ldots b_n$. Usually the objects are integers or represented by integers.

Now we introduce tools for analysing and combining permutations. The permutation $c_1 c_2 \ldots c_k \to c_k c_1 \ldots c_{k-1}$ of all or part of a list of objects is called a *cycle of period k*, or simply a *k-cycle*. It may be written out as $c_1 \to c_2 \to \cdots \to c_k \to c_1$, or abbreviated to $(c_1 c_2 \ldots c_k)$. Thus (1234) is the same 4-cycle as (2341). In the special case of a 2-cycle $(c_1 c_2)$, exchanging c_1 and c_2 is called a *transposition*. As an interchange of elements in a larger list it is called *simple* if c_1 and c_2 are adjacent. Thus in the list 24613 the transposition (46) is simple but (41) is not.

Example 2 *Find the permutation* of $12 \ldots 6$ *given by the composition* (124)(2316). We simply find the final position of each integer. By convention the cycles are processed starting with the leftmost.

$1 \to 2 \to 3$	The cycle (124) sends 1 to 2 then (2316) sends the 2 to 3.
$2 \to 4$	The cycle (124) sends 2 to 4, which is left unchanged by (2316).
$3 \to 1$	The cycle (124) leaves 3 unchanged but (2316) sends it to 1.
$4 \to 1 \to 6$	The cycle (124) sends 4 to 1 then (2316) sends 1 to 6.

Also 5 is unmoved and $6 \to 2$, so the resulting combined permutation is $123456 \to 341652$.

Example 3 We express the permutation of Example 2 as a composition of cycles which are disjoint (i.e they cycle disjoint sets), as compared with the non-disjoint cycles (124) and (2316). The method is to choose one integer, and to follow its progress. This gives a cycle. Now repeat until all of 12 ... 6 lie in one of the cycles which, by construction, are disjoint.

$1 \rightarrow 3 \rightarrow 1$ cycle (13), a non-simple transposition (1, 3 not adjacent)
$2 \rightarrow 4 \rightarrow 6 \rightarrow 2$ cycle (246).

The result (13)(246)(5) is called a *cycle decomposition*, and may be similarly obtained for any permutation. It is by construction unique (up to the order in which the cycles are written, which is immaterial).

Definition 4 Let the cycle decomposition of a permutation σ have exactly N cycles of even period. Then the *parity* of σ is even/odd according as N is even/odd. The *sign* of σ is $\text{sgn}(\sigma) = (-1)^N$, namely 1 if the parity is even and -1 if it is odd. Example 3 has just one cycle of even period, hence $\text{sgn}(\sigma) = -1$.

Proposition 5 *When a permutation is multiplied by a transposition, its parity is reversed.*

Proof We suppose the permutation σ is written in cycle form and that $(a_1 b_1)$ is a transposition. The respective possible cases, that a_1 and b_1 are in the same cycle or in different ones, are covered in the following two lines, in which we represent only the affected cycles of σ.

$$(a_1 \ldots a_r b_1 \ldots b_s)(a_1 b_1) = (a_1 \ldots a_r)(b_1 \ldots b_s),$$
$$(a_1 \ldots a_r)(b_1 \ldots b_s)(a_1 b_1) = (a_1 \ldots a_r b_1 \ldots b_s).$$

This suffices because either one or all three of $r, s, r + s$ must be even. For example if r, s are even then in the first case displayed one even cycle is converted to two, and therefore the total number of even cycles changes parity, as asserted.

Corollary 6 | *A product of N transpositions has the parity of N.*

Remarks 7 *Any permutation may be expressed as a product of transpositions* since transpositions can convey an element to its desired position in the sequence without disturbing the ordering of the rest. For example, to move x to fourth position in $xabcd$, we move it in succession past a, b, c using the sequence of simple transpostions $(xa)(xb)(xc)$, to achieve $abcxd$. More generally, the first object in a sequence may be moved to the ith position, keeping other objects in the same ordering, by a sequence of $i - 1$ simple transpositions which thus constitutes a permutation of sgn $(-1)^{i-1}$.

Remarks 8 (*Inverses*) We first observe that a transposition (ab) satisfies $(ab)(ab) = 1$, here denoting the *identity permutation*, which leaves the order of objects unchanged. Moreover, if $\sigma = (a_1 b_1)(a_2 b_2) \ldots (a_r b_r)$ for some positive integer r, and τ is this product in reverse order, then $\sigma\tau = \tau\sigma = 1$. Thus every permutation σ has an inverse τ, usually written σ^{-1}. Importantly, σ^{-1} has the same parity as σ. A simple and useful exercise is to state why this is so.

In particular, a transposition is its own inverse and, for a general cycle, $(a_1a_2 \ldots a_n)^{-1} = (a_n \ldots a_2a_1)$. Applying this to Example 2: $[(124)(2316)]^{-1} = (2316)^{-1}$ $(124)^{-1} = (6132)(421)$.

Remarks 9 (*Determining the parity by inspection*) Given a permutation σ of $12 \ldots n$, let λ_i be the number of integers k less than i that are placed after i in the new order. Each such wrongly reordered pair is called an *inversion*. We claim that the parity of σ is that of the *total number of inversions*. To see this, observe that we can restore the greatest integer n to its original position by λ_n simple transpositions. Then $n - 1$ is greatest amongst those that precede n, so we can restore it by λ_{n-1} transpositions, and so on down to 2, leaving 1 in first position.

For example, $\sigma \colon 12 \ldots 6 \to 261453$ has $(\lambda_1 \ldots \lambda_6) = (0, 1, 0, 1, 1, 4)$. The parity is therefore that of $1 + 1 + 1 + 4 = 7$, which is odd. The actual restorative steps are $261453 \to 214536 \to 214356 \to 213456 \to 123456$. In preparation for the application to determinants we compute a table of parities for all permutations abc of 123. For this, a further shortcut is to note that, by Proposition 5, permutations differing by a transposition have opposite parity and sign.

abc	123	132	213	231	312	321
$\text{sgn}(\sigma)$	1	-1	-1	1	1	-1

Theorem 10 (*Determinant formula*) *Let the $n \times n$ matrix A be written*

$$A = \begin{bmatrix} a_1 & a_2 & \ldots & a_n \\ b_1 & b_2 & \ldots & b_n \\ \ldots & \ldots & \ldots & \ldots \\ z_1 & z_2 & \ldots & z_n \end{bmatrix}.$$

Then $|A| = \sum_{\sigma} \pm a_r b_s \ldots z_t$, *where the sum is taken over all permutations* $\sigma \colon 12 \ldots n \to rs \ldots t$, *and the sign is that of* σ. *In particular, the diagonal term* $a_1 b_2 \ldots z_n$ *has positive sign.*

Proof For $n = 1$ the result is trivial, whilst for $n = 2$ it states (21 being a transposition of 12), that $|A| = a_1 b_2 - a_2 b_1$, which accords with the original definition preceding (7.18). Now, though not necessary for the proof (for which indeed $n = 1$ would suffice to start the induction), we illustrate further with the case $n = 3$, using the parity table of Remarks 9. The assertion becomes

$$|A| = a_1 b_2 c_3 - a_1 b_3 c_2 - a_2 b_1 c_3 + a_2 b_3 c_1 + a_3 b_1 c_2 - a_3 b_2 c_1$$
$$= a_1(b_2 c_3 - b_3 c_2) - a_2(b_1 c_3 - b_3 c_1) + a_3(b_1 c_2 - b_2 c_1),$$

in agreement with the example following (7.18). Now assume inductively that the theorem holds for determinants of size $n - 1$ (some $n \geq 2$) and that A is an $n \times n$ matrix as displayed above. Translating the definition $|A| = \sum a_{1i} A_{1i}$ ($1 \leq i \leq n$) from (7.18) into the present notation we see that, for given i, any term involving a_i has the form

$\pm a_i b_r c_s \dots z_t$, with sign given by the inductive hypothesis on the A_{1k} to be

$$(-1)^{i+1} \operatorname{sgn}(12 \dots \hat{i} \dots n \to rs \dots t) \qquad (\hat{i} \text{ means ``omit } i\text{''})$$
$$= (-1)^{i-1} \operatorname{sgn}(i\,12 \dots \hat{i} \dots n \to irs \dots t) \qquad (\text{noting } (-1)^2 = 1)$$
$$= \operatorname{sgn}(12 \dots i \dots n \to irs \dots t), \qquad (\text{see below}),$$

since i is moved from first to ith position by $i - 1$ simple transpositions. Thus the formula is implied for determinants of size n and hence for all positive integer sizes by induction.

The proofs of Rules 7.28 Let A be an $n \times n$ matrix. We first establish that $|A^{\mathrm{T}}| = |A|$ (part of Rule 4), so that rules which apply both to rows and to columns will only require to be proved for rows *or* for columns. Now, if we transpose matrix A, interchanging the roles of rows and columns, then the same terms result as before in Theorem 10, but with σ replaced by its inverse. However, since σ^{-1} has the same sign as σ (by Remarks 8), the value of the determinant is unchanged.

Rule 1 Switching two rows of the matrix A changes each σ in Theorem 10 by a single transposition, reversing the sign of each term and hence of $|A|$. But if two rows are identical then switching them has no effect, implying $-|A| = |A|$, or $|A| = 0$.

Expansion of $|A|$ *by row i* To obtain this formula, (7.18b), we cycle the rows of A so that i becomes the top row, expand by row 1 (the definition of $|A|$), then perform the reverse cycle. Since a cycle and its inverse have the same parity, Rule 1 shows we have achieved $+|A|$.

Rule 2 If each element of a given row is multiplied by the same scalar α then so is each term in the formula of Theorem 10, and hence $|A|$ becomes $\alpha|A|$. Alternatively, we can expand by row i if this is the one multiplied by α, and the same result follows.

Rule 3 We write $A = \operatorname{Rows}[R_1 \dots R_n]$ to mean that R_i is the ith row of $A (1 \le i \le n)$, and form a new matrix B by adding $\alpha \times$ row 2 to row 1. Then, expanding $|B|$ by row 1:

$$|B| = |A| + |\operatorname{Rows}[\alpha R_2, R_2 \dots R_n]|$$
$$= |A| + \alpha|\operatorname{Rows}[R_2, R_2 \dots R_n]| \qquad \text{by Rule 2}$$
$$= |A| \text{ by Rule 1, since the second matrix has two rows identical.}$$

More generally, if a multiple of row j is added to row i, we may see the determinant is unchanged by first expanding by row i.

Rule 4 We have established the second part. The first is proved, in the case $|A| \ne 0$, by writing A as the product of special matrices $M_1, \dots, M_n$ for which $|M_i B| = |M_i||B|$ for any $n \times n$ matrix B. Details await a discussion on elementary row operations in Chapter 8. The relevant results are at Example 8.27(ii). The case $|A| = 0$ is left as an exercise, with the hint that a linear relation between rows of A implies the same relation between the rows of AB.

Rule 5 (i) Suppose that there is a linear relation $\sum a_i C_i = 0$ with some $a_k \neq 0$. For simplicity let $k = 1$. Then $C_1 = \sum (-a_i/a_1)C_i$, summing over just $2 \leq i \leq n$. Subtracting this linear combination from column C_1 we obtain a matrix with a zero column, and hence zero determinant. It follows from Rule 3 that $|A| = 0$.

(ii) We show conversely that $|A| = 0$ implies the columns of A are linearly dependent. For $n = 1$ we have the trivial linear dependence relation $1 \cdot a_{11} = 0$, so assume inductively that the result holds for matrices of size $n - 1$, and that A is $n \times n$. We may assume $C_1 \neq 0$, otherwise there is the trivial relation $1 \cdot C_1 + 0 \cdot C_2 = 0$. Clearly, permuting and scaling the rows of A does not affect the *existence* of linear relations amongst the columns, so we may reorder the rows so that the top element of C_1 is nonzero, in fact 1, without loss of generality. Write row 1 as $[1 \ d_2 \ldots d_n]$ and subtract $d_i \times$ column 1 from column i, for $i = 2, \ldots, n$, Then we have

$$A \rightarrow \begin{bmatrix} 1 & 0 \ldots 0 \\ ? & B \end{bmatrix},$$

where B is a matrix of size $n - 1$. Considering expansion by row 1 we see that $|A|$ is a nonzero multiple of $|B|$ and therefore $|B|$ is zero. The inductive hypothesis now implies a linear dependency between the columns $B_1, \ldots, B_{n-1}$ of B, say $\sum_i \lambda_i B_i = 0$, with not all coefficients λ_i being zero, and hence the relation $\sum_i \lambda_i (C_{i+1} - d_{i+1}C_1) = 0 \, (1 \leq i \leq n - 1)$ between the columns of A, in which not all the coefficients of columns are zero.

Exercises 7

1   (i) Find the distance between the points $(1, 4)$ and $(-3, 7)$. (ii) Give an example of a left handed orthonormal triple of vectors.

2√   By drawing a sketch, decide whether the triple of vectors $(1, 1, 0)$, $(1, -1, 0)$, $(0, 0, -1)$ is left or right handed. According to their inner products, should any two of them be at right angles?

3√   Find the angle between a main diagonal and an adjacent edge of a cube by using suitable coordinates for the endpoints of the diagonal (see (7.4) to (7.6)).

4√   Find two vectors $\boldsymbol{b}, \boldsymbol{c}$ such that $\{(1, 1, 1)/\sqrt{3}, \boldsymbol{b}, \boldsymbol{c}\}$ is an ONB for 3-space. What are the components of $(1, 2, 1)$ in this basis?

5   Find every possible product of two of the three matrices in Example 7.22 (2) (see Section 7.2.1).

6√   (a) Write down a 4×4 triangular matrix with diagonal $\{1, 2, 3, 5\}$. Deduce that the rows are independent. (b) What is the determinant of the 4×4 Vandermonde-type matrix with (i, j) element $a_i^j \, (0 \leq i, j \leq 3)$? Evaluate this in the case $a_n = n$.

7√   Prove that, when the implied products exist, (i) $(AB)^{\mathrm{T}} = B^{\mathrm{T}} A^{\mathrm{T}}$, (ii) $A^{\mathrm{T}} B + B^{\mathrm{T}} A$ is symmetric, (iii) $A^{\mathrm{T}} B - B^{\mathrm{T}} A$ is skew-symmetric.

8√   What is the inverse of the matrix $\mathrm{diag}(2, -1, 3)$? A square matrix A satisfies $A^4 = I$. What can we say about (i) the determinant of A, (ii) the inverse of A? Can you find such an example?

9√ (a) Solve the simultaneous equations $2x + 3y = 1, x - 5y = 7$ by first inverting a 2×2 matrix. (b) Show that, if the matrix A has an inverse, then so does its transpose, and $(A^{\mathrm{T}})^{-1} = (A^{-1})^{\mathrm{T}}$. (Use (7.20), (7.21).)

10√ Prove that (i) for a 2×2 matrix, if the rows are an orthonormal set then so are the columns, (ii) for a 3×3 matrix, the determinant of A^{T} equals the determinant of A. (This is Case 4 of Rules 7.28. Use (7.18).)

11√ Prove that the set of all orthogonal $n \times n$ matrices forms a group (see Section 2.5). Prove that the product of two upper (lower) triangular matrices is upper (lower) triangular.

12√ After checking that the vectors $(1/2)(1, 1, 1, 1), (1/2)(1, 1, -1, -1)$, and $(1/2)(1, -1, 1, -1)$ form an orthonormal set, find a fourth vector which, with them, forms the rows of an orthogonal matrix. Is the determinant $+1$ or -1?

13√ Let $P = \mathrm{Cols}[(1, 0, -3), (2, 0, 4)]$ and $Q = \mathrm{Rows}[(1, 1, 2),(0, -1, 3)]$. Compute the matrix product PQ by Russian multiplication and check your result.

14 Let $A = \mathrm{Cols}[(1, 0, -2), (2, 3, 5)]$ and $B = \mathrm{Rows}[(6, 1), (0, 7)]$. Express AB as the sum of two matrices using (7.31). Now check your answer by standard matrix multiplication.

15√ For each of the following triples of vectors, determine whether it is left handed, right handed, or coplanar. Check the first two by a rough sketch.
(a) $(1, 1, -3), (2, 1, 6), (3, -1, 4)$, (b) $(1, 1, 1), (-1, 0, 0), (0, 1, 0)$,
(c) $(1, 2, 3), (4, 5, 6), (5, 4, 3)$, (d) $(1, 1, 0), (0, 1, 1), (1, 0, 1)$.

16√ For the points $A(2, -5), B(-3, -40)$, determine by evaluating a determinant whether rotation of OA towards OB (O fixed) is clockwise or anticlockwise. Now check by a sketch.

17√ (a) Find the equation of the plane $\sum$ through the points $A(1, 2, 3), B(-1, 2, 3), C(2, 0, 1)$, and the foot Q of the perpendicular from $P(1, 4, 2)$ to this plane. (b) Prove the second formula of Theorem 7.46. (c) Simplify $[a + b, b + c, c + a]$ by cyclic symmetry and Theorem 7.46. (You should get $2[a, b, c]$.)

18√ (a) Use the parametric form of a straight line to find a formula for reflection in $L: ax + by + c = 0$. (Hint: $(p, q) \to (p, q) - 2t(a, b)$ for a certain t.) (b) Using this formula where necessary, find the images of an arbitrary point (x, y) after reflection in (i) $m: x = a$, (ii) $p: y = x$, (iii) $q: x + y = c$.

19 Determine the matrix for plane rotation about the origin through an angle $\pi/6$. What should its sixth power equal? Does it?

20 Write down the matrix R_n for rotation of π/n about the origin in the cases $n = 1, 2, 3, 4$. Verify that $R_4^2 = R_2, R_4^4 = R_1$ and $R_1^2 = I$.

21√ Find the matrix M of the transformation $T(u) = uM$ in the cases (a) $T(x, y, z) = (3x - y, 2x + z, x - y + z)$, (b) T maps i, j, k to $(i + k), (j + k), (i - j)$, (c) $T(i + j) = \sqrt{2}k, T(i - j) = \sqrt{2}i, T(k) = j$. Are any of these transformations isometries? (Note. $|M| = \pm 1$ is not sufficient to prove that a matrix M is orthogonal.)

22√ Check that the following are orthonormal triples, then find the matrix M that sends the first triple to the second. (a) $(1/3)(1, 2, 2), (1/3)(2, -2, 1), (1/3)(2, 1, -2)$, (b) $j, (i + k)/\sqrt{2}, (i - k)/\sqrt{2}$. (Hint: take i, j, k as go-between and use (7.44b).) Check your answer.

23√ Find the matrix of any isometry that maps i, j, k so as to send k into $w = (1/\sqrt{6})(1, 2, -1)$.

24√ Find the matrix of projection in 3-space onto the subspace spanned by $(-2, 1, 2)$, $(2, 2, 1)$. Express the images of i, j, k as linear combinations of the two basis vectors. (Hint: Russian multiplication gives the coefficients free.)

25√ Calculate the matrix M for a rotation $T(u) = uM$ of $\pi/4$ about the z-axis. What does this become if the axes are changed from i, j, k to $(j - k)/\sqrt{2}$, $(k - i)/\sqrt{2}$, k? (Hint: see Theorem 7.65.)

8
Matrix algebra

We begin this chapter with the characterisation of a matrix by its eigenvalues and -vectors and, in the first of many applications, use them to classify isometries in 3-space. In Section 8.2 appears the technique of row operations on a matrix, usually designed to convert them to a standard form. This leads naturally to the notion of the rank of a matrix, which determines for example how many are independent in a set of linear equations, as well as to a method of matrix inversion.

In Section 8.3 we see how the matrix A of a quadratic form $q = \sum a_{ij}x_ix_j$ is equivalent in some sense to the diagonal matrix of its eigenvalues λ_i, and consequently we can tell which forms may be re-expressed as a sum of squares $\sum \lambda_i y_i^2$. The signs of the λ_i show how q 'behaves', important for studying the normal/Gaussian distribution in n-space (see Section 10.4.3). Section 8.4 builds up to the remarkable Singular Value Decomposition (SVD), the representation of an arbitrary $m \times n$ matrix A by a diagonal one: $A = U^{\mathrm{T}}DV$, where U and V are orthogonal and $D_{m \times n}$ is generalised diagonal. Matrix norms both provide a tool of proof and express some striking optimisation properties of the SVD which we shall use for Principal Component Analysis and data compression in Chapter 10.

8.1 Introduction to eigenvalues

Eigenvalues and their corresponding eigenvectors are fundamental tools for the sequel. They will reappear time and again to good effect, and one must make friends with them. This section provides the minimal requirement of complex numbers, gives a grounding in the main topic, and applies it in this first instance to the classification of isometries in 3-space.

8.1.1 Complex numbers

For a fuller revision of complex numbers, see Section 9.1 of Hoggar (1992), but here is a quick 'fix'. The set **C** of complex numbers is an extension of the real numbers for which *every* quadratic equation has a solution because of the presence of the symbol i (not to be confused with a basis vector, though there are connections) which acts as a square root of -1. We may express the complex numbers as $\mathbf{C} = \{x + yi\colon x, y \in \mathbf{R}\}$, with multiplication requiring the extra definition $i^2 = -1$.

Thus, for example, $(1 - 2i)(3 + i) = 3 - 2i^2 - 5i = 5 - 5i = 5(1 - i)$. And $z^2 + 2z + 5 = 0 \Leftrightarrow (z + 1)^2 = -4 = 4i^2 \Leftrightarrow z = -1 \pm 2i$. The complex number $z = x + yi$ is said to have *real part* $x = \operatorname{Re} z$, *imaginary part* $y = \operatorname{Im} z$, *conjugate* $\bar{z} = x - yi$, and *modulus* $|z| \geq 0$, where $|z|^2 = x^2 + y^2 = (x + yi)(x - yi) = z\bar{z}$, the squared length of the vector (x, y) in the plane. The complex number $\cos\phi + i\sin\phi$ of modulus 1 is denoted by $e^{i\phi}$, because it behaves like this power for any angle ϕ. For example (see (14.24))

$$e^{i\phi} \cdot e^{i\theta} = e^{i(\phi+\theta)}, \quad (d/dt)e^{\alpha t} = \alpha e^{\alpha t} \ (\alpha = a + bi).$$

More on unit complex numbers and their derivatives is brought out at their place of application to the Discrete Fourier Transform, in Sections 14.1.1 and 14.2.1 (and Hoggar, 1992). We will occasionally need to allow such numbers as matrix entries, when the following definitions are useful. The *conjugate of a matrix A* is obtained in the obvious way, by conjugating its entries. In symbols, $\bar{A} = [\bar{a}_{ij}]$. This operation is usually combined with transposition to give the *conjugate transpose*

$$A^* = (\bar{A})^{\mathrm{T}} = \overline{A^{\mathrm{T}}}.$$

Indeed, A^* plays a similar role for complex matrices to that of A^{T} for the real case. In particular the equality $(AB)^* = B^*A^*$ holds, as shown by

$$(AB)^* = (\overline{AB})^{\mathrm{T}} = (\bar{A}\,\bar{B})^{\mathrm{T}} = \bar{B}^{\mathrm{T}}\bar{A}^{\mathrm{T}} = B^*A^*,$$

the same reversal rule as is satisfied by the transpose. A simplification occurs if one matrix in the product is a scalar, λ, when, because multiplication of complex numbers is commutative, $ab = ba$, we have $(\lambda A)^* = \bar{\lambda}A^*$. Moreover, a complex vector $x = (x_k)$ satisfies

$$x x^* = x\bar{x}^{\mathrm{T}} = \Sigma x_k \bar{x}_k = \Sigma |x_k|^2 = |x|^2,$$

where the last equality may be taken as definition of vector length in the complex case. Notice that for real numbers this becomes the usual definition of length and the operation $*$ becomes the same as transpose. The definition of dot product extends to complex vectors as

$$x \cdot y = x\bar{y}^{\mathrm{T}} = \Sigma x_k \bar{y}_k.$$

Example If $x = (4 + i, 3)$, then $|x|^2 = |4 + i|^2 + 3^2 = 4^2 + 1^2 + 3^2 = 26$.

The collection of all complex n-vectors is called *complex n-space*, $\mathbf{C}^n$. Correspondingly, we have linear combinations with complex coefficients, bases, and orthogonality. Right now we need the fact, not true in the real case, that EVERY polynomial with complex coefficients (which includes real ones) is a product of linear factors. This is one version of the *Fundamental Theorem of Algebra* (see Hoggar, 1992). We note, too, that a polynomial equation of degree n cannot have more than n distinct solutions, for each solution α implies a factor $x - \alpha$ of the polynomial, by the argument of Theorem 7.30 applied unchanged to complex numbers.

8.1.2 Eigenvalues and eigenvectors

Definition 8.1 The real or complex number λ is an *eigenvalue* of the $n \times n$ matrix M, with *eigenvector* $x = (x_1, \ldots, x_n)$, if

$$xM = \lambda x \quad \text{and} \quad x \neq 0. \tag{8.1}$$

Notice that

(i) $x \neq 0$ means not *all* entries of x are zero,
(ii) if x satisfies (8.1) then so does βx for every nonzero complex number β,
(iii) if M and λ are real and (8.1) is satisfied by some complex x then by taking either the real parts or the imaginary parts of x, which cannot *all* be zero, we obtain a *real* nonzero solution for x.

The context For most of this section our examples will show how eigenvalues and -vectors arise naturally with rotations and reflections. The context will widen from Section 8.3 on.

Examples 8.2 (a) *Rotation* For M as the matrix of rotation about axis vector a, we have $aM = 1a$. Thus M has an eigenvalue 1 with eigenvector a.

(b) *Reflection* If M is the matrix of reflection in a mirror through O with normal vector n, then $nM = -n$. That is, -1 is an eigenvalue, with n as an eigenvector. From observation (ii), any multiple of n is also an eigenvector corresponding to -1, as we know it should be.

> (A) *The axis vectors of a rotation with matrix M are the eigenvectors of M with eigenvalue 1.*
> (B) *The normal vectors to the plane, for a reflection with matrix M, are the eigenvectors of M with eigenvalue -1.*
> (C) *The eigenvalues of a reflection matrix M are ± 1.*
> (8.2)

Proof of (C) $xM = \lambda x \Rightarrow xM^2 = \lambda x M \Rightarrow x = \lambda^2 x$ (since $M^2 = I$) $\Rightarrow \lambda^2 = 1$, as we assume $x \neq 0$. Notice that the equation $\lambda^2 = 1$ cannot have more than two solutions, even if we admit complex numbers (again, by Theorem 7.30). Next we will see how one may compute eigenvalues in general.

Calculating eigenvalues *We derive an equation whose roots are precisely the eigenvalues of a given $n \times n$ matrix M.* Let λ be any real or complex number, then

$$xM = \lambda x, \text{ for some } x \neq 0,$$

$\Leftrightarrow \quad x(M - \lambda I) = 0, \text{ for some } x \neq 0 \text{ (the } eigenvector \text{ equation)}, \tag{8.3}$

$\Leftrightarrow \quad$ some linear combination $\sum_i x_i C_i$ of the rows of $M - \lambda I$ is zero (not all x_i zero)

$\Leftrightarrow \quad |M - \lambda I| = 0 \text{ (the } eigenvalue \text{ equation)}, \tag{8.4}$

by Rule 7.28(5). Thus for each solution $\lambda = \alpha$ of the *eigenvalue equation* (8.4) we have a nonzero vector x satisfying (8.1). It's very useful to highlight the three simplest terms of (8.4), by taking a look at the matrix $M - \lambda I$. We may write

$$
M - \lambda I = \begin{bmatrix} m_{11} - \lambda & m_{12} & \dots & m_{1n} \\ m_{21} & m_{22} - \lambda & \dots & m_{2n} \\ \dots & \dots & \dots & \dots \\ m_{n1} & m_{n2} & \dots & m_{nn} - \lambda \end{bmatrix}.
$$

(i) $|M - \lambda I|$ is a polynomial in λ whose constant term, obtained by setting $\lambda = 0$, is just $|M|$. (ii) All positive powers of λ come from diagonal elements $m_{kk} - \lambda$. In particular λ^n appears in the expansion of $|M - \lambda I|$ only in the diagonal term $D(\lambda) = (m_{11} - \lambda)(m_{22} - \lambda) \dots (m_{nn} - \lambda)$, which has leading power $(-\lambda)^n$. (iii) every other term contains at most $n - 2$ of the diagonal elements, *because* in forming the sub-determinant which multiplies an element M_{1k} of the first row ($k \geq 2$) we omit row 1 and column k, and hence both $(m_{11} - \lambda)$ and $(m_{kk} - \lambda)$. We conclude therefore that the coefficient of λ^{n-1} in the determinant $|M - \lambda I|$ equals the coefficient of λ^{n-1} in $D(\lambda)$, namely $(-1)^{n-1}(m_{11} + m_{22} + \dots + m_{nn})$. Dividing out a factor $(-1)^n$ we may write the eigenvalue equation as

$$
\lambda^n - c_1 \lambda^{n-1} + c_2 \lambda^{n-2} - \dots + (-1)^n |M| = 0 \ \textit{(eigenvalue equation)}, \tag{8.5}
$$

where $c_1 = m_{11} + m_{22} + \dots + m_{nn}$, written Trace (M), or Tr M.

We'll return more formally to the important Tr M after some examples on 2×2 matrices, in which (8.5) can be written down by inspection. We note that, by the Fundamental Theorem of Algebra, the left hand side of the eigenvalue equation (8.5) is the product of n linear factors $\lambda - \alpha_i$, possibly with repetitions, in which some α_i may be complex. We view the equation as having n roots, counted according to their multiplicities.

Example 8.3 Calculate the eigenvalues of the following matrices, and find eigenvectors for the third matrix.

$$
\text{(i)} \begin{bmatrix} 2 & 3 \\ 3 & 4 \end{bmatrix}, \quad \text{(ii)} \begin{bmatrix} 1 & 0 \\ 0 & 2 \end{bmatrix}, \quad \text{(iii)} \begin{bmatrix} 0 & -1 \\ 1 & 0 \end{bmatrix}, \quad \text{(iv)} \begin{bmatrix} 1 & 1 \\ 1 & 1 \end{bmatrix}.
$$

Solution In the 2×2 case we can read off the eigenvalue equation directly from (8.5):

(i) $\lambda^2 - (2 + 4)\lambda + (8 - 9) = 0$, or $\lambda^2 - 6\lambda - 1 = 0$; solution $\lambda = 3 \pm \sqrt{(10)}$;
(ii) $\lambda^2 - 3\lambda + 2 = 0$ and $\lambda = 1, 2$;
(iii) $\lambda^2 + 1 = 0$, with classic solution $\lambda = \pm i$;
(iv) $\lambda^2 - 2\lambda = 0$, $\lambda = 0, 2$.

For an eigenvector $x = [x \ y]$ of (iii) corresponding to eigenvalue $\lambda = i$ we have the standard equation of (8.3): $x(M - \lambda I) = \mathbf{0}$. Written out, this is

$$
[x \ y] \begin{bmatrix} -i & -1 \\ 1 & -i \end{bmatrix} = \mathbf{0}, \quad \text{or} \quad \begin{cases} -ix + y = 0, \\ -x - iy = 0. \end{cases}
$$

Now the matrix $(M - \lambda I)$ has determinant 0 so by Rule 7.28 (5), each column of the matrix, and hence each equation, must be a multiple of the other. And, indeed, on inspection we find that the first equation is i times the second, using $i^2 = -1$. Thus the only condition x, y must satisfy is $x = -iy$ and we may take $x = [-i \, 1]$. Starting again with eigenvalue $\lambda = -i$ we find a corresponding eigenvector $[i \, 1]$.

Exercise Derive the second eigenvector in part (iii) above.

Definition 8.4 The *trace* of an $n \times n$ matrix M is (we recall) the sum of its diagonal elements, $\mathrm{Tr}\, M = m_{11} + m_{22} + \cdots + m_{nn}$. Notice that if A is $r \times s$ and B is $s \times r$ then $\mathrm{Tr}(AB) = \mathrm{Tr}(BA)$ because $\Sigma_{i,j} a_{ij} b_{ji} = \Sigma_{i,j} b_{ji} a_{ij}$. By Lemma 8.5(b) below, the trace and determinant of the matrix of an isometry T depend not on the choice of basis, but only on T itself. Hence they are described as *invariants* of T and referred to as *the trace and determinant of T*. The trace will be useful for, amongst other things, identifying the angle of rotation of T when rotation is present (see Theorem 8.10).

Lemma 8.5 *Let M be an $n \times n$ matrix. Then*
(a) $\mathrm{Tr}\, M$ equals the sum of the eigenvalues of M, and $|M|$ equals their product;
(b) the eigenvalue equation of M is unchanged if we replace M by AMA^{-1}, where A is an invertible $n \times n$ matrix. In particular, if M is the matrix of an isometry, then the new matrix under a change of orthonormal basis has the same trace and determinant as M.

Proof (a) Let the eigenvalues be $\lambda_1, \ldots, \lambda_n$, of which some may be equal. Then the left hand side of the eigenvalue equation (8.5) is identical to $(\lambda - \lambda_1) \times (\lambda - \lambda_2) \cdots (\lambda - \lambda_n)$. The coefficient of λ^{n-1} is $-\sum \lambda_i$, which must therefore equal the coefficient $-\sum m_{ii}$ of λ^{n-1} in (8.5). This gives the first assertion of (i). For the second we observe that the two equal constant terms are $(-1)^n \lambda_1 \lambda_2 \cdots \lambda_n$ and $(-1)^n |M|$.

(b) We recall Rule 7.28(4), that $|BC| = |B||C|$ for the determinant of the product of two matrices B, C. Thus, since $|A||A^{-1}| = |AA^{-1}| = 1$, we have $|M - \lambda I| = |A||M - \lambda I||A^{-1}| = |A(M - \lambda I)A^{-1}| = |AMA^{-1} - A\lambda I A^{-1}| = |AMA^{-1} - \lambda I|$. Thus, replacing M by AMA^{-1} leaves the eigenvalue equation (8.5) and hence the trace and determinant unchanged. This proves (b), since the change of basis by a matrix A changes M to AMA^{-1} (Theorem 7.65), and A is an orthogonal matrix (Theorem 7.71), for which $A^T = A^{-1}$ (Definition 7.34(b)).

> *Let M be an $n \times n$ matrix.   Then*
> *$\mathrm{Tr}\, M$ equals the sum of the eigenvalues of M,*
> *and $|M|$ equals their product.*

Theorem 8.6 *(a) The eigenvalues of an orthogonal matrix M have modulus 1. (b) A linear isometry T of 3-space fixing the origin satisfies $Tv = \pm v$ for some nonzero vector v.*

Proof (a) We denote the complex conjugate of a number or matrix by an overbar. Equating the transposed complex conjugates of both sides of (8.1), we obtain $M^T \overline{x}^T = \overline{\lambda} \overline{x}^T$, which we combine with the original (8.1) to get $xMM^\mathrm{T}\bar{x}^\mathrm{T} = \lambda x \bar{\lambda}\bar{x}^\mathrm{T}$. This simplifies to $x\bar{x}^\mathrm{T} = |\lambda|^2 x\bar{x}^\mathrm{T}$, and hence to $|\lambda|^2 = 1$, for the reasons that $MM^\mathrm{T} = I$ and $x\bar{x}^\mathrm{T} = \sum_i x_i \bar{x}_i = \sum_i |x_i|^2$, which is nonzero since $x \neq 0$.

(b) Let M be the matrix of T. Since M is 3×3 the eigenvalue equation (8.5) is cubic and so has at least one real root α. On the other hand, we know that M is orthogonal and therefore, by part (a), $|\alpha| = 1$, implying $\alpha = \pm 1$. Then $xM = \lambda x$ becomes $xM = \pm x$. Finally, by remark (iii) of Definition 8.1, we may choose x to be real and so take $v = x$.

Exercise Prove that square matrices A and A^T have the same eigenvalues.

Example 8.7 *Find eigenvalues and -vectors for the rotation matrix M (shown) of θ about the z-axis.*

$$M = \begin{bmatrix} \cos\phi & \sin\phi & 0 \\ -\sin\phi & \cos\phi & 0 \\ 0 & 0 & 1 \end{bmatrix}$$

We already know 1 is an eigenvalue with eigenvector $[0\ 0\ 1]$. Write $c = \cos\phi$, $s = \sin\phi$, so that $c^2 + s^2 = 1$. Then the eigenvalue equation is $|M - \lambda I| = 0$ (8.4), with $M - \lambda I$ as shown.

$$M - \lambda I = \begin{bmatrix} c - \lambda & s & 0 \\ -s & c - \lambda & 0 \\ 0 & 0 & 1 - \lambda \end{bmatrix}$$

Thus $(\lambda - 1)(\lambda^2 - 2c\lambda + 1) = 0$, with $\lambda = 1$ a solution as predicted. For the others, $\lambda = \cos\phi \pm i\sin\phi = e^{\pm i\phi}$. These two complex conjugate numbers have modulus $c^2 + s^2 = 1$ in agreement with Theorem 8.6.

Eigenvectors With $\lambda = e^{i\phi}$ the leading entry of $M - \lambda I$ is $c - \lambda = -is$, whence the eigenvalue equation $[x\ y\ z](M - \lambda I) = 0$ gives, after taking out common factors s, the three equations $ix + y = 0$, $x - iy = 0$, $(1 - c - is)z = 0$. Thus we have only two independent equations, in agreement with $|M - \lambda I| = 0$ (see Rule 7.28 (5)). An eigenvector is $(1, -i, 0)$. Corresponding to $\lambda = e^{-i\phi}$ we may take $(1, i, 0)$ as eigenvector.

Example 8.8 The matrices M in (i) and (ii) below are for, respectively, a rotation and a reflection that fix the origin. Find the axis of (i) and plane of (ii) via eigenvectors.

$$\text{(i)} \quad \frac{1}{9}\begin{bmatrix} -7 & 4 & 4 \\ 4 & -1 & 8 \\ 4 & 8 & -1 \end{bmatrix}, \qquad \text{(ii)} \quad \frac{1}{7}\begin{bmatrix} -2 & 3 & -6 \\ 3 & 6 & 2 \\ -6 & 2 & 3 \end{bmatrix}.$$

Solution (i) An axis vector is any eigenvector with eigenvalue 1, by (8.3). The eigenvector equation is $x(M - \lambda I) = 0$, here $x(M - I) = 0$. With x written $[x\ y\ z]$ as usual, the first two equations are $-16x + 4y + 4z = 0$, $4x - 10y + 8z = 0$, with solution $z = y = 2x$. An axis vector is $(1, 2, 2)$.

(ii) Here a normal to the plane is any eigenvector with eigenvalue -1, by (8.2) (B). The eigenvector equation is $x(M + I) = 0$. Any two independent equations will do, and it is convenient to take the last two: $3x + 13y + 2z = 0$, $-6x + 2y + 10z = 0$, with solution $z = -2y$, $x = -3y$. A normal to the plane is $(-3, 1, -2)$; an equation for it is $3x - y + 2z = 0$.

Remarks 8.9 Let A be an $n \times n$ matrix.

(1) We have seen how eigenvalues and -vectors can be used to identify rotation axes and reflection normals. However, other methods may be faster for practical calculation: see Theorem 8.12 for reflection and Theorem 8.13 for rotation.

(2) Let $f(t)$ be a polynomial. *If λ is an eigenvector of A with eigenvalue x then $f(\lambda)$ is an eigenvalue of $f(A)$ with the same eigenvector.* An inductive proof can be given (Exercise 8.3) but an example makes the process clear. Let $xA = \lambda x$. Then $xAA = \lambda xA = \lambda^2 x$. This takes care of $f(t) = t^2$. Thus if A has eigenvalues $\{1, i, -i\}$ then A^2 has eigenvalues $\{1, -1, -1\}$.

(3) A satisfies its own eigenvalue equation, essentially because if $f(\lambda) = 0$ then $xf(A) = f(\lambda)x = 0$, for all eigenvectors x.

(4) (Inverses) If A^{-1} exists, its eigenvalues are $\{1/\lambda: \lambda$ is an eigenvalue of $A\}$. Of course, all eigenvalues of an invertible matrix are nonzero because, for example, $|A|$ is their product (Lemma 8.5), and is nonzero by (7.19).

Exercise Verify that the matrix for reflection in plane $x + 2z = 0$ has determinant -1 and that all its eigenvalues have modulus 1.

8.1.3 Linear isometries in 3-space

We have shown (Theorem 8.6) that a linear isometry T satisfies $Tv = \pm v$ for some nonzero vector v, and noted that we may replace v by any multiple of itself. Thus we may choose a coordinate system i, j, k with $k = v$, $Tk = \pm k$.

Since T preserves angles it maps the xy-plane onto itself and, by Theorem 1.16, it must do so either by a rotation of some angle ϕ about the origin O, or by reflection in a line m through O with polar angle, say, ϕ. We consider these two cases in turn.

Case 1 T rotates the xy-plane.
(a) Suppose $Tk = k$. Then by (7.41) T has matrix M as given on the right. Hence $|M| = 1$ and T is the rotation $R_k(\phi)$.

$$M = \begin{bmatrix} \cos\phi & \sin\phi & 0 \\ -\sin\phi & \cos\phi & 0 \\ 0 & 0 & 1 \end{bmatrix}$$

(b) Suppose $Tk = -k$. Then the matrix of T equals that of part (a) times the matrix that sends $[x\ y\ z]$ to $[x\ y\ -z]$, namely diag $(1, 1, -1)$. So we have matrix M as shown, $|M| = -1$, and T is the product of a reflection $z \to -z$ in the xy-plane and the rotation $R_k(\phi)$. Thus T is a rotary reflection, as defined below.

$$M = \begin{bmatrix} \cos\phi & \sin\phi & 0 \\ -\sin\phi & \cos\phi & 0 \\ 0 & 0 & -1 \end{bmatrix}$$

Definition A *rotary reflection* is any composition of a rotation and a reflection (note: it can be expressed so that axis and normal coincide).

Case 2 T acts on the xy-plane as a reflection R_m. See Figure 8.1.

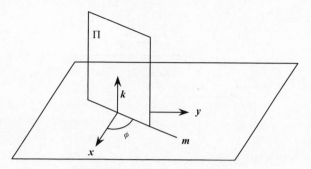

Figure 8.1 Diagram for Case 2.

(a) Suppose $T\boldsymbol{k} = \boldsymbol{k}$. Then the matrix of T is by (7.40)

$$M = \begin{bmatrix} \cos 2\phi & \sin 2\phi & 0 \\ \sin 2\phi & -\cos 2\phi & 0 \\ 0 & 0 & 1 \end{bmatrix}.$$
Here $|M| = -1$ and T is reflection in the plane Π which contains m and $\boldsymbol{k}$.

(b) Suppose $T\boldsymbol{k} = -\boldsymbol{k}$. Then M is as above, but with bottom diagonal entry -1 instead of 1. We have, for the first time in this situation, the diagonal entry -1 along with $|M| = +1$. Referring to Figure 8.1, we see that T is the product of reflection $z \to -z$ in the xy-plane with reflection in the plane Π. Since these planes are at right angles the result is a 1/2 turn about their intersection, the line m.

We now have our classification. Note that a rotation angle ϕ, $-\pi \le \phi \le \pi$, is determined only up to sign by its cosine alone. We must in addition know the sign, and, in both parts of the theorem below, *the rotation angle ϕ has the sign of $[\boldsymbol{a}, \boldsymbol{v}, T\boldsymbol{v}]$ for any non-axial vector $\boldsymbol{v}$*. However, we can avoid this determinant calculation by the later Theorem 8.13, which supplies the unique axis corresponding to a *positive* angle of rotation.

Theorem 8.10 *(Classification) Let T be a linear isometry of 3-space. Then there are the following possibilites.*

(i) *$|T| = 1$. Unless T is the identity it is a rotation, with axis vector $\boldsymbol{a}$ given by $T\boldsymbol{a} = \boldsymbol{a}$ (eigenvalue 1). The rotation angle ϕ satisfies $2\cos\phi + 1 = \operatorname{Tr} T$.*

(ii) *$|T| = -1$. T is a rotary reflection. If $T\boldsymbol{x} = -\boldsymbol{x}$ for all vectors $\boldsymbol{x}$ (matrix $-I$) then T is an inversion. Otherwise T has an axis vector $\boldsymbol{a}$ given by $T\boldsymbol{a} = -\boldsymbol{a}$ (eigenvalue -1). The rotation angle ϕ satisfies $2\cos\phi - 1 = \operatorname{Tr} T$. It is pure reflection if $\operatorname{Tr} T = 1$.*

Corollary 8.11 *(Euler's Theorem) The composition of rotations about two axes through a point A is rotation about a third axis through A.*

Proof Take A as origin for right handed coordinates. Let the rotations be T_1, T_2. Then $|T_1| = |T_2| = 1$ and so $|T_1 T_2| = |T_1||T_2|$ (Rule 7.28) $= 1$. By the Classification Theorem, 8.10, we know that $T_1 T_2$ must be a rotation.

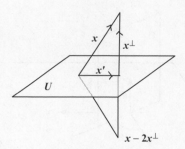

Figure 8.2 The relation between the projection x' and reflection $x - 2x^\perp$ of x.

Calculating axes and normals in practice

Theorem 8.12 *The matrix of reflection in a plane through the origin with UNIT normal n is the symmetric matrix $M = I - 2n^{\mathrm{T}}n$. Hence a normal is any nonzero row of $M - I$. See Figure 8.2.*

Proof Under reflection, $x \to x - 2x^\perp = x - 2$ (projection of x onto span$\{n\}$) $= x - 2x(n^{\mathrm{T}}n)$ (Theorem 7.59 with $u_1 = n$) $= x(I - 2n^{\mathrm{T}}n)$.

Exercise Use the result above to find a reflection normal for Example 8.8(ii).

Theorem 8.13 *The matrix for rotation θ about an axis along unit vector a (or $-\theta$ with $-a$) is*

$$M = A_\theta = (\cos\theta)I + (1 - \cos\theta)a^{\mathrm{T}}a + \sin\theta \begin{bmatrix} 0 & a_3 & -a_2 \\ -a_3 & 0 & a_1 \\ a_2 & -a_1 & 0 \end{bmatrix}, \qquad (8.6)$$

where the third term equals $(1/2)(M - M^{\mathrm{T}})$. Hence, given the matrix M of a rotation, either

(i) M is symmetric, giving a $1/2$ turn about any nonzero row of $M + I$ as axis, or

(ii) we may take axis $(\sin\theta)\,a$ given as above and angle $\theta > 0$ defined by $\cos\theta = (\mathrm{Tr}M - 1)/2$.

Proof Formula (8.6) is obtained as PBP^{-1} by mapping a to k by an orthogonal matrix P (see Example 7.63), rotating about k by the known matrix A of (7.41), then applying P^{-1}. More details are found in Hoggar (1992), Theorem 8.49.

(i) If M is symmetric the third term is absent since by (7.16) every matrix is uniquely the sum of a symmetric and a skew matrix. Hence $\sin\theta = 0$, implying $\theta = 0$ or $\theta = \pi$. If $\theta = 0$ then $M = I$, otherwise $M = -I + 2a^{\mathrm{T}}a$, so $M + I = 2a^{\mathrm{T}}a$, in which every row is a multiple of a.

(ii) If M is not symmetric then by (7.16) the skew third term is present and gives $(\sin\theta)a$. Since reversing the sign of a reverses that of θ this product is constant under such reversals and we may simply take $\theta > 0$ and divide the vector by its own length to get a corresponding unit axis vector.

> Rotation angle: $\cos\theta = (\mathrm{Tr}M - 1)/2, \ \theta > 0$.
> Axis given by $M - M^{\mathrm{T}}, \quad$ in (8.6).
> M symmetric: $\theta = \pi, \quad$ axis = row of $(M + I)$.

Example 8.14 Find the result of reflection in the plane $\Pi : x = y$, followed by reflection in the plane $\Sigma : x + y + 2z = 0$.

Solution A normal for Π is $\boldsymbol{a} = (1, -1, 0)$, with reflection matrix $M_1 = I - 2\boldsymbol{a}^{\mathrm{T}}\boldsymbol{a}/2$. The extra 2 normalises both copies of $\boldsymbol{a}$ to unit length as required, that is, we take $2(\boldsymbol{a}^{\mathrm{T}}/\sqrt{2})(\boldsymbol{a}/\sqrt{2})$. A normal for Σ is $\boldsymbol{b} = (1, 1, 2)$, yielding matrix $M_2 = I - 2\boldsymbol{b}^{\mathrm{T}}\boldsymbol{b}/6$. Thus

$$M_1 = I - \begin{bmatrix} 1 & -1 & 0 \\ -1 & 1 & 0 \\ 0 & 0 & 0 \end{bmatrix} = \begin{bmatrix} 0 & 1 & 0 \\ 1 & 0 & 0 \\ 0 & 0 & 1 \end{bmatrix},$$

$$M_2 = I - \frac{1}{3}\begin{bmatrix} 1 & 1 & 2 \\ 1 & 1 & 2 \\ 2 & 2 & 4 \end{bmatrix} = \frac{1}{3}\begin{bmatrix} 2 & -1 & -2 \\ -1 & 2 & -2 \\ -2 & -2 & -1 \end{bmatrix}.$$

Hence
$$M_1 M_2 = \frac{1}{3}\begin{bmatrix} -1 & 2 & -2 \\ 2 & -1 & -2 \\ -2 & -2 & -1 \end{bmatrix} = M, \text{ say.}$$

Notice that pre-multiplication by M_1 simply reassembles the rows of M_2 in the order 213. Let us see what our theorems reveal before any geometrical considerations. Firstly, M is orthogonal since the rows are mutually orthogonal, and of unit length after the scaling by 1/3. Secondly, the determinant, after column operations $C_2 \to C_2 + 2C_1, C_3 \to C_3 - 2C_1$, comes out as $(36 - 9)/3^3 = 1$. By Theorem 8.10, M is a rotation. Moreover, M is symmetric, and so we have by Theorem 8.13 a 1/2 about an axis from any nonzero row of $M + I$. The first row is $(2, 2, -2)/3$ so we may take $(1, 1, -1)$ as axis.

Geometry – why the 1/2 turn? The normals and hence the planes are at right angles, so we expect a rotation through π (a 1/2 turn) about their line of intersection. We need not solve equations to find this, for since it contains the origin (because Σ and Π do), any vector at right angles to both will do. One such is the vector product $(1, -1, 0) \times (1, 1, 2)$, which equals $(-2, -2, 2)$ by the determinant formula (7.38), in agreement with our previous conclusion.

Example 8.15 Find the composition of 1/4 turn about the z-axis followed by 1/2 turn about the axis $(0, 1, 1)$ (taken from the symmetry group of the regular cube centred at the origin).

Solution A 1/4 turn means angle $\pi/2$, with cosine 0 and sine 1. The axis is $(0, 0, 1)$. In fact the respective rotation matrices are

$$M_1 = \begin{bmatrix} 0 & 0 & 0 \\ 0 & 0 & 0 \\ 0 & 0 & 1 \end{bmatrix} + \begin{bmatrix} 0 & 1 & 0 \\ -1 & 0 & 0 \\ 0 & 0 & 0 \end{bmatrix} = \begin{bmatrix} 0 & 1 & 0 \\ -1 & 0 & 0 \\ 0 & 0 & 1 \end{bmatrix},$$

$$M_2 = -I + \frac{2}{2}\begin{bmatrix} 0 & 0 & 0 \\ 0 & 1 & 1 \\ 0 & 1 & 1 \end{bmatrix} = \begin{bmatrix} -1 & 0 & 0 \\ 0 & 0 & 1 \\ 0 & 1 & 0 \end{bmatrix}$$

Hence $M = M_1 M_2 = \begin{bmatrix} 0 & 0 & 1 \\ 1 & 0 & 0 \\ 0 & 1 & 0 \end{bmatrix}$ and $\frac{1}{2}(M - M^T) = \frac{1}{2}\begin{bmatrix} 0 & -1 & 1 \\ 1 & 0 & -1 \\ -1 & 1 & 0 \end{bmatrix}.$

The last matrix is computed because M is not symmetric and so is not simply a 1/2 turn. By Theorem 8.13, an axis vector is $(-1, -1, -1)$, with $\theta > 0$ given by $\cos\theta = (\text{Tr}M - 1)/2 = -1/2$, hence $\theta = 2\pi/3$. Thus the result is a 1/3 turn. (Equivalently, it is a $-1/3$ turn about the axis $(1, 1, 1)$.)

Exercise Find the composition of a 1/3 turn about $(1, 1, 1)$ followed by 1/3 turn about $(1, 1, -1)$.

Remark There is a nice way to achieve 3D rotations by the use of quaternions, Hoggar (1992), Chapter 9.

8.2 Rank, and some ramifications

The *rank* of a matrix is its number of independent rows, or equivalently the dimension of its row space (space spanned by the rows). Like the trace and determinant, it represents some significant features of the whole array by a single number with many applications.

8.2.1 Rank and row operations

For an arbitrary $m \times n$ matrix A with rows $R_1, \ldots, R_m$, the *range* or *row space* $R(A)$ and *rank* $r(A)$ are defined by

$$R(A) = \text{span}\{R_1, \ldots, R_m\},$$
$$r(A) = \text{Dim}\, R(A). \tag{8.7}$$

For a convenient way to determine and make use of these constructs, suppose M is a $p \times m$ matrix for some p. Then, as observed in Examples 7.22,

$$\text{row } i \text{ of } MA = [\text{row } i \text{ of } M]A = [x_1 \ldots x_m]A, \text{ say}$$
$$= x_1 R_1 + \cdots + x_m R_m, \quad \text{by (7.29)}. \tag{8.8}$$

Thus each row of the product MA is a linear combination of rows of A, and therefore contained in $R(A)$. This gives the first part of:

Theorem 8.16 *If the matrix product MA exists then $R(MA)$ is a subspace of $R(A)$ and hence $r(MA) \leq r(A)$, with equality in both cases if M is invertible.*

Proof It remains to consider the case of M an $m \times m$ invertible matrix. Using the first part twice gives $R(A) = R(M^{-1}MA) \subseteq R(MA) \subseteq R(A)$. Since the first and last expressions are equal, so are they all, and in particular $R(MA) = R(A)$ as required.

Theorem 8.17 *Rank and row space are invariant under (elementary) row operations, namely, with $i \neq j$ and $a \neq 0$,*

(a) *interchange rows i, j $(R_i \leftrightarrow R_j)$,*
(b) *multiply row i by the nonzero constant a $(R_i \rightarrow aR_i)$,*
(c) *add b times row j to row i $(R_i \rightarrow R_i + bR_j)$,*
(d) *do (b) then (c) $(R_i \rightarrow aR_i + bR_j)$.*

> *An operation f converts an $m \times n$ matrix A into the product MA, where $M = f(I_m)$ and is invertible.*

$$(|MA| = |M||A| \text{ if } A \text{ is square.})$$

Proof We begin by showing that M performs as stated. Let A have rows $R_1, \ldots, R_m$. Case (d) covers all except (a), which is similar. So consider $f: R_i \rightarrow aR_i + bR_j$ with $a \neq 0$ and $j \neq i$. Now, when $M = f(I)$ is formed the only change to I is that row $i = [x_1 \ldots x_n] = [0 \ldots a \ldots b \ldots 0]$ is all zeros except for $x_i = a, x_j = b$. Hence MA is the same as A except for

$$\text{row } i \text{ of } MA = [0 \ldots a \ldots b \ldots 0]A$$
$$= aR_i + bR_j \text{ by } (8.8)$$
$$= \text{row } i \text{ of } f(A) \text{ as required.}$$

Now we observe that f has inverse $R_i \rightarrow (R_i - bR_j)/a$, which therefore gives an inverse for M. Since M is invertible, the rank and row space are invariant by Theorem 8.16. Finally, the determinant equality holds by a case by case check. In Case (a), $|M| = -|I| = -1$, and so we may write $|MA| = -|A| = |M||A|$, whilst in Case (d) we have $|M| = a|I| = a$, giving $|MA| = a|A| = |M||A|$.

Example Let $\begin{bmatrix} 1 & 2 \\ 3 & 4 \end{bmatrix} \rightarrow \begin{bmatrix} 1 & 2 \\ 0 & -2 \end{bmatrix}$ under the operation $R_2 \rightarrow R_2 - 3R_1$. Find M.

Solution $\begin{bmatrix} 1 & 0 \\ 0 & 1 \end{bmatrix} \rightarrow \begin{bmatrix} 1 & 0 \\ -3 & 1 \end{bmatrix} (= M)$.

Check: $MA = \begin{bmatrix} 1 & 0 \\ -3 & 1 \end{bmatrix} \begin{bmatrix} 1 & 2 \\ 3 & 4 \end{bmatrix} = \begin{bmatrix} 1 & 2 \\ 0 & -2 \end{bmatrix}$.

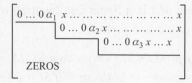

Figure 8.3 Echelon form of a matrix, with three nonzero rows. A sequence $x \ldots x$ denotes entries which are not necessarily zero. Entries below the staircase shape are all zero. The α_i are *leading entries*.

Now we can use row operations to reduce A to *echelon form*, as depicted in Figure 8.3.

ALGO 8.1 Reducing a matrix to echelon form

1. Permute the rows by operations of type (a) so that a leftmost nonzero entry α_1 of the matrix is in row 1.
2. Use type (c) operations to get zeros in each entry directly below α_1. By construction, all columns to the left of the *leading entry* α_1 consist of zeros.

We proceed iteratively: repeat 1, 2 for the submatrix obtained by deleting the α_i row and all columns up to and including that of α_i.

Call the new leading entry α_{i+1}. The process terminates when either α_i is in the last row, or the remaining rows are all zero.

Here *directly below* means 'in the same column, one or more places down'. Notice that entries to the right of α_i in the same row need not be zero (see $x \ldots x$ in Figure 8.3). Also, it may be worth arranging that $\alpha_i = 1$, especially if computing by hand (this becomes more important in Section 8.2.3).

Echelon properties We may characterise an echelon form by (a) each leading entry $\alpha_i + 1$ is below and to the right of its predecessor, (b) all entries but α_i are zero in the submatrix with top right entry α_i. This guarantees that the nonzero rows in the echelon form are independent. Since the row space remains the same under row operations (Theorem 8.17) we have the following result.

Theorem 8.18 *(a) The rank of a matrix A equals the number of nonzero rows in any echelon form of A. These rows provide a basis for the row space. (b) Any echelon form of A may be written PA for some invertible matrix P. (c) We may instead choose P so that the first $r(A)$ rows of PA are an ONB for $R(A)$, and the rest are zero.*

Proof (a) Let an echelon form E of A have d nonzero rows. Since these rows are independent and span $R(E)$ they consitute a basis thereof. This gives the first equality in: $d = \text{Dim } R(E) = \text{Dim } R(A) = r(A)$, as required.

(b) By Theorem 8.17 the sequence of row operations which convert A to an echelon form E may be achieved by pre-multiplication by a sequence of invertible matrices thus:

$E = M_r \cdots M_2 M_1 A$. Now we may take $P = M_r \cdots M_2 M_1$, which is invertible because the M_i are invertible.

(c) By Theorem 8.17 it suffices to note that the following steps produce the desired effect on A, and may be achieved by a sequence of row operations.

(1) Reorder the rows of A so that the first $r = r(A)$ rows form a basis of $R(A)$. This is possible because every spanning set of a vector space contains a basis (see Remark 7.13(1)).

(2) Use the Gram–Schmidt process (Definition 7.17) to convert the basis to an orthonormal one.

(3) For $i = r + 1$ to m the current ith row R_i is a unique linear combintion of the first r, say $R_i = a_{i1} R_1 + \cdots + a_{ir} R_r$. Perform $R_i \to R_i - a_{i1} R_1 - \cdots - a_{ir} R_r$.

Example 8.19 We find range, rank, and the matrix P that converts A to echelon form.

$$
A = \begin{bmatrix} 1 & 5 & 9 \\ 2 & 6 & 10 \\ 3 & 7 & 11 \\ 4 & 8 & 12 \end{bmatrix}
\begin{matrix} R_2 \to R_2 - 2R_1 \\ R_3 \to R_3 - 3R_1 \\ R_4 \to R_4 - 4R_1 \end{matrix}
\begin{bmatrix} 1 & 5 & 9 \\ 0 & -4 & -8 \\ 0 & -8 & -16 \\ 0 & -12 & -24 \end{bmatrix}
\begin{matrix} R_3 \to R_3 - 2R_2 \\ R_4 \to R_4 - 3R_2 \\ R_2 \to (-1/4)R_2 \end{matrix}
\begin{bmatrix} 1 & 5 & 9 \\ 0 & 1 & 2 \\ 0 & 0 & 0 \\ 0 & 0 & 0 \end{bmatrix}
\text{ (echelon form).}
$$

The operations we used are shown between each matrix and their result. The last operation, scaling row 2, was not essential, but performed for aesthetic purposes. By Theorem 8.17 we have found two things: $R(A) = \mathrm{span}\{(1, 5, 9), (0, 1, 2)\}$, and so A has rank 2. Now we find P by applying to I_4 the row operations we applied to A. Scaling row 2 is given a separate stage (can you see why?). Lastly we verify that PA is the echelon form as Theorem 8.17 predicts.

$$
I = \begin{bmatrix} 1 & 0 & 0 & 0 \\ 0 & 1 & 0 & 0 \\ 0 & 0 & 1 & 0 \\ 0 & 0 & 0 & 1 \end{bmatrix}
\to
\begin{bmatrix} 1 & 0 & 0 & 0 \\ -2 & 1 & 0 & 0 \\ -3 & 0 & 1 & 0 \\ -4 & 0 & 0 & 1 \end{bmatrix}
\to
\begin{bmatrix} 1 & 0 & 0 & 0 \\ -2 & 1 & 0 & 0 \\ 1 & -2 & 1 & 0 \\ 2 & -3 & 0 & 1 \end{bmatrix}
$$

$$
\to
\begin{bmatrix} 1 & 0 & 0 & 0 \\ 1/2 & -1/4 & 0 & 0 \\ 0 & -2 & 1 & 0 \\ 2 & -3 & 0 & 1 \end{bmatrix} = P.
$$

$$
\text{Check: } PA =
\begin{bmatrix} 1 & 0 & 0 & 0 \\ 1/2 & -1/4 & 0 & 0 \\ 1 & -2 & 1 & 0 \\ 2 & -3 & 0 & 1 \end{bmatrix}
\begin{bmatrix} 1 & 5 & 9 \\ 2 & 6 & 10 \\ 3 & 7 & 11 \\ 4 & 8 & 12 \end{bmatrix}
=
\begin{bmatrix} 1 & 5 & 9 \\ 0 & 1 & 2 \\ 0 & 0 & 0 \\ 0 & 0 & 0 \end{bmatrix}, \text{ the echelon form.}
$$

Column operations For every row operation there is a corresponding operation on columns, equivalent to transposing (columns become rows), performing the desired operation on rows instead, then transposing back again: $A \to A^T \to MA^T \to AM^T$.

Thus, if forming PB performs a set of row operations on a matrix B then forming CP^{T} performs these operations on the columns of a matrix C.

Theorem 8.20 *The rank of a matrix is invariant under the following operations:*

(a) transposition: $r(A^{\mathrm{T}}) = r(A)$,
(b) both row and column operations,
(c) left and right multiplication by invertible matrices.

Proof (a) Observe that column operations do not affect linear relationships between the rows of A. For a column operation changes A to AP, with P invertible, so $\sum x_i$ (row i of A) $= 0 \Leftrightarrow xA = 0 \, (x = (x_i)) \Leftrightarrow xAP = 0$. Hence we need only consider A in echelon form, as in Figure 8.3. But column operations easily eliminate all nonzero elements except the α_i, so both $r(A^{\mathrm{T}})$ and $r(A)$ equal the number of α_i.

Part (b) now follows since, as remarked, column operations may be achieved by a combination of row operations and transpositions. For (c), invariance under *left* multiplication by an invertible matrix was established in Theorem 8.16. Invariance under right multiplication follows by (a), since we only need to combine left multiplication with suitable transpositions to achieve right multiplication.

Examples 8.21 (i) *(Rank)* Notice that Theorem 8.20(a) implies $r(A) \le \mathrm{Min}(m,n)$. Here are some matrices whose ranks can be stated by inspection.

$$A = \begin{bmatrix} 2 & 3 \\ 4 & 5 \\ 6 & 7 \end{bmatrix}, \quad B = \begin{bmatrix} 1 \\ 3 \\ 2 \end{bmatrix} [2\ 1\ 5] = \begin{bmatrix} 2 & 1 & 5 \\ 6 & 3 & 15 \\ 4 & 2 & 10 \end{bmatrix}, \quad C = \begin{bmatrix} 6 & 2 & 27 \\ 0 & 5 & 18 \\ 0 & 0 & 4 \end{bmatrix}.$$

Firstly, $r(A) = r(A^{\mathrm{T}}) = 2$, since the two columns are LI (one is not a multiple of the other). The construction of B shows each row is a multiple of the first, so the rank is 1. The same applies to any matrix of form ab^{T}. The matrix C is already in echelon form, so $r(C) = 3$.

Exercise Find invertible P such that PB is an echelon form of matrix B above.

(ii) *(Operations)* Consider the equality $M(AB) = (MA)B$ in the case where M is the row operation matrix of Theorem 8.17. This shows that a row operation on any matrix product AB can be achieved by performing the operations on the rows of A, then forming the matrix product. Using the connection with column operations observed above, we conclude that

> any row operation on an extended matrix product $A_1 A_2 \cdots A_n \, (n \ge 2)$ may be achieved by performing that operation on the *rows of A_1* and any column operation by performing it on the *columns of A_n*.

(iii) *(The permutation case)* If P performs only permutations of rows then P is orthogonal.

Proof P is obtained by permuting the rows of the orthogonal matrix I and is therefore itself orthogonal (see Definition 7.34(c)). This remark is used in Section 15.2.3, the Fourier Transform, and in Section 17.3.2, cubic B-splines.

8.2.2 Rank, nullity and linear equations

We define the *null space* $N(A)$ and *nullity* $n(A)$, of an $m \times n$ matrix A, as follows:

$$N(A) = \{x \in \mathbf{R}^m : xA = \mathbf{0}\},$$
$$n(A) = \dim N(A). \tag{8.9}$$

It is a simple exercise to show that the null space is a subspace of $\mathbf{R}^m$. It is associated with solving a set of linear equations (see below), for which we sometimes require the *reduced echelon form* of a matrix, in which each leading term α_i is 1, and all other entries in the same column as α_i are zero. An example follows.

Example 8.22 (*Solving equations*) We find the null space and nullity of the matrix A of Example 8.19. Notice that $xA = 0 \Leftrightarrow A^T x^T = 0$, and since row operations on A^T give an equivalent equation set the argument may be handled thus:

$$\begin{bmatrix} 1 & 2 & 3 & 4 \\ 5 & 6 & 7 & 8 \\ 9 & 10 & 11 & 12 \end{bmatrix} \begin{bmatrix} x_1 \\ \cdots \\ x_4 \end{bmatrix} = 0 \Leftrightarrow \begin{bmatrix} 1 & 2 & 3 & 4 \\ 0 & -4 & -8 & -12 \\ 0 & -8 & -16 & -24 \end{bmatrix} \begin{bmatrix} x_1 \\ \cdots \\ x_4 \end{bmatrix} = 0$$

$$\Leftrightarrow \begin{bmatrix} 1 & 2 & 3 & 4 \\ 0 & 1 & 2 & 3 \\ 0 & 0 & 0 & 0 \end{bmatrix} \begin{bmatrix} x_1 \\ \cdots \\ x_4 \end{bmatrix} = 0$$

$$\Leftrightarrow \begin{bmatrix} 1 & 0 & -1 & -2 \\ 0 & 1 & 2 & 3 \\ 0 & 0 & 0 & 0 \end{bmatrix} \begin{bmatrix} x_1 \\ \cdots \\ x_4 \end{bmatrix} = 0$$

$$\Leftrightarrow \begin{cases} x_1 = x_3 + 2x_4, \\ x_2 = -2x_3 - 3x_4 \end{cases}$$

$$\Leftrightarrow \begin{cases} x = (x_3 + 2x_4, -2x_3 - 3x_4, x_3, x_4) \\ \quad = x_3(1, -2, 1, 0) + x_4(2, -3, 0, 1). \end{cases}$$

Here, the *reduced* echelon form was convenient for solving the equations, enabling us to conclude that $N(A) = \text{span}\{(1, -2, 1, 0), (2, -3, 0, 1)\}$, and the nullity is 2.

To bring out a relation between rank and nullity we return briefly to linear maps. We define the *kernel*, $\ker f$, and *image*, $\text{im} f$, of a linear map $f : \mathbf{R}^m \to \mathbf{R}^n$ by

$$\ker f = \{x \in \mathbf{R}^m : f(x) = 0\}, \tag{8.10}$$
$$\text{im} f = \{y \in \mathbf{R}^n : y = f(x) \text{ for some } x \in \mathbf{R}^m\}. \tag{8.11}$$

Theorem 8.23 *If the matrix A defines the linear map* $f: \mathbf{R}^m \to \mathbf{R}^n$, $x \to xA$, *then*
(a) $N(A) = \ker f$,
(b) $R(A) = \operatorname{im} f$, *and*
(c) rank $r(A)$ + *nullity* $n(A) = m$.

Proof (a) and (b) are immediate from the definitions. For (c), let $e_1, \ldots, e_s$ be a basis of
$\ker f$ and extend it to a basis $e_1, \ldots, e_m$ of $\mathbf{R}^m$. We claim that $\{f(e_i)\}$ spans $\operatorname{im} f$. For let
y be in $\operatorname{im} f$ with $y = f(x)$. Then $x = \sum \lambda_i e_i$ for m constants λ_i, so $y = f(\sum \lambda_i e_i) = \sum \lambda_i f(e_i)$. But $f(e_1), \ldots, f(e_s) = 0$ by definition of $\ker f$ and hence $f(e_{s+1}), \ldots, f(e_m)$
alone span $\operatorname{im} f$: we must show they are independent. Let $\sum \lambda_i f(e_i) = 0$ ($s + 1 \leq i \leq m$). This may be re-expressed as $f(\sum \lambda_i e_i) = 0$. Thus the vector sum in parenthesis is
in $\ker f$ but is not a nonzero linear combination of $e_1, \ldots, e_s$. Hence it is zero, implying
$\lambda_{s+1} = \cdots = \lambda_m = 0$. But this shows in turn that $f(e_{s+1}), \ldots, f(e_m)$ are independent
(Definition 7.6). Finally, we are entitled to conclude that $\dim \ker f + \dim \operatorname{im} f = s + (m - s) = m$, as asserted.

$$\operatorname{rank} r(A) + \operatorname{nullity} n(A) = m \ (A = A_{m \times n}).$$

Corollary 8.24 *The solutions of a set* $Ax^{\mathrm{T}} = 0$, *of m linear equations in n unknowns*
form a subspace of $\mathbf{R}^n$ *of dimension* $n - r(A)$. *We distinguish three cases.*

(a) $r(A) = n$. *The zero solution is the only one.*
(b) $m < n$. *There is always a nonzero solution.*
(c) $m = n$. *There is a nonzero solution if and only if* $|A| = 0$.

Proof The equations may be written $x A^{\mathrm{T}} = 0$, so the solutions are by definition the
null space of the $n \times m$ matrix A^{T}. But $\operatorname{Dim} N(A^{\mathrm{T}}) = n - r(A^{\mathrm{T}})$ (by Theorem 8.23) $= n - r(A)$ by Theorem 8.20. Thus in (a) the solution space has dimension 0, hence contains
only the zero solution. In case (b), $r(A) \leq m < n$, so the solution space dimension
$n - r(A)$ is positive. Finally, in (c) with $m = n$, there is a nonzero solution $\Leftrightarrow$ the
columns of A are dependent $\Leftrightarrow |A| = 0$ (Rules 7.28).

Examples 8.25

(i) In $\mathbf{R}^n$, the vectors x perpendicular to independent vectors a, b are defined by $a \cdot x = 0$, $b \cdot x = 0$, and so form a subspace of dimension $n - 2$.
Reason: the vectors x form the null space of $A = \operatorname{Rows}(a, b)$, which has rank 2 since a, b
are independent. We apply Theorem 8.23(c).

(ii) (Rank 1 matrices) The special $n \times n$ matrix $B = a^{\mathrm{T}}a$, where a is an n-vector, has rank 1
because every row is by definition a multiple of a (the ith row is $a_i a$). Hence the solutions of
$Bx^{\mathrm{T}} = 0$ form a subspace of dimension $n - 1$ (the null space of B), by Theorem 8.23(c).

(iii) Each further independent linear relation placed on the entries of vectors in an n-space reduces
the dimension of the resulting subspace by 1.

(iv) Sometimes it is useful to consider the *column* null space of A, defined as the (row) null space of A^T. Such a situation occurs in Section 17.3.1, spline wavelets. It's the same as the

> space of solutions of $Ax^T = 0$, with dimensions $n - r(A)$,
> which equals $n - m$ if $m < n$ and the rows are LI.

Exercise Find a basis for the 4-vectors at right angles to $(1, 1, 0, 1)$ and $(1, 0, -2, 3)$.

8.2.3 Inverting a matrix by row operations

Theorem 8.26 *The following are equivalent for an $n \times n$ matrix A:*
(a) A is invertible, (b) $|A| \neq 0$, (c) A has rank n, (d) A has reduced echelon form I_n.

Proof The equivalence of (a) and (b) was established with Cramer's Rule, Theorem 7.32. To incorporate (c) and (d), let E be the reduced echelon form of A, with $PA = E$ and P invertible (Theorem 8.18). Then $r(A) = n \Leftrightarrow E$ has n nonzero rows $\Leftrightarrow E$ is I_n (since A is square) $\Leftrightarrow |E| \neq 0 \Leftrightarrow |A| \neq 0$ (since P is invertible and Theorem 8.20 (c) applies).

> *ALGO 8.2 To invert an $n \times n$ matrix A*
>
> Form the block matrix $[AI_n]$ (see Section 7.2.5);
> perform row operations on $[AI_n]$ that reduce A to I;
> then $[AI_n]$ becomes $[IA^{-1}]$.

Validity The operations convert $[AI]$ to $[PA\ PI]$, where $PA = I$ and hence $P = A^{-1}$. By Theorem 8.26, the algorithm will produce a result if and only if an inverse exists.

Examples 8.27(i) Convert $[A\ I]$ below to $[I\ P]$, and verify that $A^{-1} = P$, (ii) show that every invertible matrix is a product of row operation matrices.

Solution (i) $\begin{bmatrix} 1 & 2 & 3 & 1 & 0 & 0 \\ 1 & 2 & 4 & 0 & 1 & 0 \\ 2 & 3 & 4 & 0 & 0 & 1 \end{bmatrix} \rightarrow \begin{bmatrix} 1 & 2 & 3 & 1 & 0 & 0 \\ 0 & 0 & 1 & -1 & 1 & 0 \\ 0 & -1 & -2 & -2 & 0 & 1 \end{bmatrix}$

$\rightarrow \begin{bmatrix} 1 & 2 & 3 & 1 & 0 & 0 \\ 0 & -1 & -2 & -2 & 0 & 1 \\ 0 & 0 & 1 & -1 & 1 & 0 \end{bmatrix} \rightarrow \begin{bmatrix} 1 & 2 & 3 & 1 & 0 & 0 \\ 0 & 1 & 2 & 2 & 0 & -1 \\ 0 & 0 & 1 & -1 & 1 & 0 \end{bmatrix}$

$\rightarrow \begin{bmatrix} 1 & 0 & -1 & -3 & 0 & 2 \\ 0 & 1 & 2 & 2 & 0 & -1 \\ 0 & 0 & 1 & -1 & 1 & 0 \end{bmatrix} \rightarrow \begin{bmatrix} 1 & 0 & 0 & -4 & 1 & 2 \\ 0 & 1 & 0 & 4 & -2 & -1 \\ 0 & 0 & 1 & -1 & 1 & 0 \end{bmatrix}.$

$$\text{Hence } A^{-1} = \begin{bmatrix} -4 & 1 & 2 \\ 4 & -2 & -1 \\ -1 & 1 & 0 \end{bmatrix}.$$

$$\text{Check: } \begin{bmatrix} -4 & 1 & 2 \\ 4 & -2 & -1 \\ -1 & 1 & 0 \end{bmatrix} \begin{bmatrix} 1 & 2 & 3 \\ 1 & 2 & 4 \\ 2 & 3 & 4 \end{bmatrix} = \begin{bmatrix} 1 & 0 & 0 \\ 0 & 1 & 0 \\ 0 & 0 & 1 \end{bmatrix}.$$

(ii) Let A be invertible. Then some sequence of row operation matrices M_i converts A to its reduced echelon form I_n (Theorem 8.26(d)), say $(M_r \cdots M_2 M_1)A = I$. But this implies that $A = M_1^{-1} M_2^{-1} \cdots M_r^{-1}$, another product of row operation matrices.

> Every invertible matrix is a product of row operation matrices.

Exercise Use row operations to invert the matrix with rows $[1\ 2\ -2]$, $[2\ -2\ -1]$, $[2\ 1\ 2]$.

8.3 Similarity to a diagonal matrix

The results of this section are important for many purposes, including the study of normal distributions and Gaussian noise. We shall require some background on complex numbers, which was given at Section 8.1.1. However, our first task in the present section will be to use this background to show that, in the important special case of a symmetric matrix S, certain potentially complex numbers are actually real, and S may have behaviour very close to that of a diagonal matrix.

8.3.1 Diagonalisation

Definition 8.28 Let A, B be $n \times n$ matrices. We say A is *similar to B (by P)* if $A = PBP^{-1}$ for some invertible matrix P. Then $B = QAQ^{-1}$ with $Q = P^{-1}$, so B is similar to A and the relation is symmetric. If P may be chosen orthogonal we say A is *orthogonally similar* to B; in this case we may and often do substitute P^{T} for P^{-1}. Our main focus is the case of B diagonal, when P is said to *diagonalise A*.

Theorem 8.29 *(a) If A is similar to $D = \mathrm{diag}(\alpha_1, \ldots, \alpha_n)$ by an invertible matrix P then row i of P is an eigenvector of A with eigenvalue α_i $(1 \leq i \leq n)$, (b) If A is symmetric then its eigenvalues are real, and the eigenvectors may be chosen to be real.*

Proof (a) We have $PAP^{-1} = D$, hence $PA = DP$, and equating ith rows of either side gives (row i of P)$A = \alpha_i$(row i of P), as required.

(b) Let A be symmetric, with an eigenvalue λ and corresponding eigenvector $\boldsymbol{x}$. Then $\boldsymbol{x}A = \lambda\boldsymbol{x}$ $(\boldsymbol{x} \neq 0)$, and, on taking the conjugate transpose of both sides, $A\boldsymbol{x}^* = \bar{\lambda}\boldsymbol{x}^*$ (A being both real and symmetric). Since matrix multiplication is associative we may write $x(Ax^*) = (xA)x^*$ and by substitution $x \cdot \bar{\lambda}x^* = \lambda x \cdot x^*$, or $(\lambda - \bar{\lambda})xx^* = 0$. But $xx^* = |x|^2$, which is positive because x is by definition nonzero, and we may infer $\lambda - \bar{\lambda} = 0$, which implies λ is real as required. Since the corresponding eigenvector equation is real linear and has solutions, it has a real solution.

What matrices can be diagonalised? The most useful answer by far can be given for symmetric matrices, in which case we have the strong result below, with full orthogonal diagonalisation.

Theorem 8.30 *A square matrix A is orthogonally similar to a diagonal matrix if and only if A is symmetric.*

Proof (i) Let A be orthogonally similar to a diagonal matrix D, say $PAP^{\mathrm{T}} = D$. Then $A = P^{\mathrm{T}}DP$ and is symmetric since $A^{\mathrm{T}} = P^{\mathrm{T}}D^{\mathrm{T}}(P^{\mathrm{T}})^{\mathrm{T}} = P^{\mathrm{T}}DP$.

(ii) The converse, the harder part, is performed by induction on n. The result is true for $n = 1$, because $\lambda = 1 \cdot \lambda \cdot 1^{-1}$ for any scalar λ. Assume it holds for matrices of size $n - 1$, let $A_{n \times n}$ be symmetric, and let λ_1 be a real eigenvalue of A with real eigenvector u_1 (Theorem 8.29). Extend to an ONB $u_1, \ldots, u_n$ of $\mathbf{R}^n$ and take these as rows of an $n \times n$ orthogonal matrix Q. Then, for $1 \le i \le n$,

$$(1, i) \text{ entry of } QAQ^{\mathrm{T}} = (\text{row 1 of } Q)A(\text{row } i \text{ of } Q)^{\mathrm{T}} \quad \text{by formula (7.17c.)}$$
$$= u_1 A u_i^{\mathrm{T}} = \lambda_1 u_1 u_i^{\mathrm{T}} = \lambda_1 \delta_{1i}.$$

Thus the first row of QAQ^{T} is $[\lambda_1 \, 0 \ldots 0]$ and, since QAQ^{T} is symmetric, we have in terms of block matrices (see Section 7.2.5)

$$QAQ^{\mathrm{T}} = \left[\begin{array}{c|c} \lambda_1 & 0 \\ \hline 0 & B \end{array}\right] \text{ (where } B \text{ is symmetric, of size } n - 1).$$

By the inductive hypothesis there is an orthogonal matrix P with $PBP^{\mathrm{T}} = \mathrm{diag}(\lambda_2, \ldots, \lambda_n) = D$, say. Define

$$R = \left[\begin{array}{c|c} 1 & 0 \\ \hline 0 & P \end{array}\right].$$

Then R is orthogonal, hence so is RQ, and $(RQ)A(RQ)^{\mathrm{T}} = R \cdot QAQ^{\mathrm{T}} \cdot R^{\mathrm{T}}$

$$= \left[\begin{array}{c|c} 1 & 0 \\ \hline 0 & P \end{array}\right]\left[\begin{array}{c|c} \lambda_1 & 0 \\ \hline 0 & B \end{array}\right]\left[\begin{array}{c|c} 1 & 0 \\ \hline 0 & P^{\mathrm{T}} \end{array}\right] = \left[\begin{array}{c|c} \lambda_1 & 0 \\ \hline 0 & PBP^{\mathrm{T}} \end{array}\right] = \mathrm{diag}(\lambda_1, \ldots, \lambda_n). \quad (8.12)$$

Hence the result, by induction; it is displayed below.

> A square matrix A is orthogonally similar to a diagonal matrix if and only if A is symmetric.

Remark 8.31 Let A be a symmetric matrix. The two preceding results not only show that if A is symmetric it may be diagonalised by an orthogonal matrix P (sometimes called the *modal matrix* of A), but yield the following practical consequences for calculation:

(i) the diagonal elements are the eigenvalues of A with the correct multiplicities,
(ii) the rows of P are eigenvectors corresponding to the eigenvalues of A in their diagonal order, and provide an ONB for $\mathbf{R}^n$,
(iii) rows corresponding to an eigenvalue λ of multiplicity k provide an ONB for the eigenspace V_λ, the k-dimensional space of all eigenvectors of λ,
(iv) eigenvectors corresponding to distinct eigenvalues are orthogonal (Exercise 8.15).

Example 8.32 We use the remark above to assist in finding an orthogonal matrix P to diagonalise the matrix A shown below. In first finding the eigenvalues (here by hand) it is worth using a row operation $R_1 \to R_1 - R_2$ to obtain a zero. Having taken out a factor $t + 1$ from row 1, it is worth doing $C_2 \to C_2 + C_1$ to reduce to a simple 2×2 determinant.

$$A = \begin{bmatrix} 3 & 4 & -2 \\ 4 & 3 & -2 \\ -2 & -2 & 0 \end{bmatrix}, \quad |A - tI| = \begin{vmatrix} 3 - t & 4 & -2 \\ 4 & 3 - t & -2 \\ -2 & -2 & -t \end{vmatrix}$$

$$= \begin{vmatrix} -1 - t & 1 + t & 0 \\ 4 & 3 - t & -2 \\ -2 & -2 & -t \end{vmatrix} = (t + 1) \begin{vmatrix} -1 & 1 & 0 \\ 4 & 3 - t & -2 \\ -2 & -2 & -t \end{vmatrix}$$

$$= (t + 1) \begin{vmatrix} -1 & 0 & 0 \\ 4 & 7 - t & -2 \\ -2 & -4 & -t \end{vmatrix} = -(t + 1)[-t(7 - t) - 8] = -(t + 1)^2(t - 8).$$

Eigenvalue $\lambda = 8$ (We list the eigenvalues in order: $8, -1, -1$.) An eigenvector x with eigenvalue 8 is by definition any solution of $x(A - 8I) = 0$. However, it is convenient to use the symmetry of A to rewrite this as $(A - 8I)x^T = 0$ so that we may solve by finding the reduced echelon form. But $\lambda = 8$ has multiplicity 1 so the matrix $A - 8I$ has nullity 1, hence rank 2 (Corollary 8.24). Thus any two LI rows determine x (up to the usual multiplication by a scalar). We select rows 1, 2 and compute the reduced echelon form.

$$\begin{bmatrix} -5 & 4 & -2 \\ 4 & -5 & -2 \end{bmatrix} \to \begin{bmatrix} -1 & -1 & -4 \\ 4 & -5 & -2 \end{bmatrix} \to \begin{bmatrix} 1 & 1 & 4 \\ 0 & -9 & -18 \end{bmatrix} \to \begin{bmatrix} 1 & 0 & 2 \\ 0 & 1 & 2 \end{bmatrix}. \quad \text{Solution: } (2, 2, -1).$$

Eigenvalue $\lambda = -1$ Now λ has multiplicity 2 and $A - \lambda I$ has rank 1 (Corollary 8.24), so any nonzero row will do. The first gives, after a scaling by $1/2$,

$$2x_1 + 2x_2 - x_3 = 0. \tag{8.13}$$

We need a pair of orthogonal solutions. Method: choose one easy solution $x = (1, -1, 0)$, then determine another from the two conditions (8.13) and orthogonality to x. These combine to give in matrix terms

$$\begin{bmatrix} 1 & -1 & 0 \\ 2 & 2 & -1 \end{bmatrix} \to \begin{bmatrix} 1 & -1 & 0 \\ 0 & 4 & -1 \end{bmatrix}. \quad \text{Solution: } (1, 1, 4).$$

After normalising the eigenvectors to unit length we may take the diagonalising matrix P to have rows $(2, 2, -1)/3, (1, -1, 0)/\sqrt{2}, (1, 1, 4)/\sqrt{18}$. The reader may wish to check that P is indeed orthogonal and fulfils its role as diagonaliser of A. First see the comment below!

Checking $PAP^T = D$. We can avoid the square roots caused by normalising the eigenvectors as follows. Let $P = \mathrm{Rows}(R_i)$, where $R_i = u_i/|u_i|$. Then $PAP^T = \mathrm{diag}(\lambda_i) \Leftrightarrow R_i A R_j^T = \lambda_i \delta_{ij} \Leftrightarrow u_i A u_j^T = \lambda_i |u_i|^2 \delta_{ij}$. Thus the condition to check may be written

$$QAQ^T = \mathrm{diag}(\lambda_i)\mathrm{diag}(|u_i|^2), \quad \text{where } Q = \mathrm{Rows}(u_i).$$

Our check for the present example becomes

$$\begin{bmatrix} 2 & 2 & -1 \\ 1 & -1 & 0 \\ 1 & 1 & 4 \end{bmatrix} \begin{bmatrix} 3 & 4 & -2 \\ 4 & 3 & -2 \\ -2 & -2 & 0 \end{bmatrix} \begin{bmatrix} 2 & 1 & 1 \\ 2 & -1 & 1 \\ -1 & 0 & 4 \end{bmatrix} = \begin{bmatrix} 72 & 0 & 0 \\ 0 & -2 & 0 \\ 0 & 0 & -18 \end{bmatrix}$$

$$= \mathrm{diag}\,(9, 2, 18) \times \mathrm{diag}\,(8, -1, -1), \text{ as required.}$$

P as rotation matrix The orthogonality of P means it is either a rotation matrix, case $|P| = 1$, or rotation combined with reflection, case $|P| = -1$ (Theorem 8.10). Our present P has negative determinant, but may be converted into a rotation and still diagonalise A, as follows: *choose any row of P and change its sign*, say $R_1 \to -R_1$. Then (i) the determinant is multiplied by (-1) (Rules 7.28), becoming $+1$, but the rows of P remain orthonormal and so P is now rotation, and (ii) since we have performed $R_1 \to -R_1$ on the rows of P and $C_1 \to -C_1$ on the columns of P^T, the product $D = PAP^T$ has sign change of both first row and column, by Remark 8.3. However, D is diagonal, so the net effect is no change.

Exercise Diagonalise the matrix Rows ([1 2], [2 1]).

8.3.2 Quadratic forms

The *quadratic form* associated with a symmetric matrix Q is the function (see 7.17d)

$$q(x) = x Q x^T = \sum_{ij} q_{ij} x_i x_j. \tag{8.14}$$

Such forms are important for higher-dimensional normal distributions, as well as many other areas of applied mathematics, science and engineering. Their behaviour is illuminated by re-expression as a sum of squares $a_1 z_1^2 + \cdots + a_n z_n^2$ via an invertible linear transformation $x = zP$. The first observation is that on substituting for x we obtain $q(x) = z(PQP^T)z^T$, whence $PQP^T = \mathrm{diag}\,(a_1, \ldots, a_n)$. This can be regarded as a method of diagonalising by a matrix P which is *not necessarily orthogonal*. First an example.

Example 8.33 (*The completion of squares method*) We express the quadratic form

$$q(x) = 2x_1^2 + 13x_2^2 + x_3^2 - 2x_1x_2 - 2x_1x_3 - 4x_2x_3 \tag{8.15}$$

as a sum of squares; then, as described above, find an invertible matrix P for which PQP^T is diagonal. To obtain such a sum of squares we repeatedly choose a variable x_i for which the form has both a cross-term $x_i x_j$ (for some j) and a square x_i^2, gather all the terms involving x_i, and 'complete the square' with them. We shall discuss termination shortly. Here we can most easily begin with x_3 because x_3^2 has the simplest coefficient, namely 1. Thus

$$\begin{aligned} q(x) &= \left[x_3^2 - 2x_1x_3 - 4x_2x_3\right] + 2x_1^2 + 13x_2^2 - 2x_1x_2 \\ &= \left[(x_3 - x_1 - 2x_2)^2 - x_1^2 - 4x_2^2 - 4x_1x_2\right] + 2x_1^2 + 13x_2^2 - 2x_1x_2 \\ &= (x_3 - x_1 - 2x_2)^2 + x_1^2 + 9x_2^2 - 6x_1x_2 \\ &= (x_3 - x_1 - 2x_2)^2 + (x_1 - 3x_2)^2 \\ &= z_1^2 + z_2^2 + 0z_3^2, \end{aligned}$$

where

$$\begin{cases} z_1 = -x_1 - 2x_2 + x_3, \\ z_2 = x_1 - 3x_2, \\ z_3 = x_1, \end{cases} \quad \text{whence} \quad \begin{cases} x_1 = z_3, \\ x_2 = \frac{1}{3}(x_1 - z_2) = \frac{1}{3}(z_3 - z_2), \\ x_3 = x_1 + 2x_2 + z_1 = z_1 - \frac{2}{3}z_2 + \frac{5}{3}z_3. \end{cases}$$

Thus $PQP^T = \operatorname{diag}(1, 1, 0)$ under the transformation $x = zP$, where

$$P = \begin{bmatrix} 0 & 0 & 1 \\ 0 & -1/3 & -2/3 \\ 1 & 1/3 & 5/3 \end{bmatrix}, \quad Q = \begin{bmatrix} 2 & -1 & -1 \\ -1 & 13 & -2 \\ -1 & -2 & 1 \end{bmatrix}.$$

If we run out of terms x_k^2 but some cross-term $x_i x_j$ remains we may transform this to the difference of two squares by setting $x_i = y_i - y_j$ and $x_j = y_i + y_j$, so that $x_i x_j = y_i^2 - y_j^2$. The off-diagonal terms of Q are *well-defined*, by (8.15), because Q is specified to be symmetric. For example, the term $-2x_1x_2$ in $q(x)$ yields $q_{12} + q_{21} = -2$ and hence $q_{12} = -1 = q_{21}$.

The possibility of orthogonal P and consequent appearance of eigenvalues is important to keep in mind, as evidenced by the following conclusion from Theorem 8.30.

Corollary 8.34 *Let Q be a symmetric matrix with eigenvalues $\lambda_1, \ldots, \lambda_n$. Then the form $q(x)$ may be expressed as a sum of squares in $z = xP$ for some orthogonal P:*

$$q(x) = \lambda_1 z_1^2 + \cdots + \lambda_n z_n^2. \tag{8.16}$$

Rank of a form Since, by Theorem 8.20, left or right multiplication by an invertible matrix preserves rank, we have

$$\operatorname{rank} Q = \operatorname{rank} PQP^T = \text{number of nonzeros in sum of squares form,}$$

which applies for every P for which PQP^T is diagonal, so we may consistently define the *rank of a form q* as the rank of its matrix Q, or the number of nonzeros in any sum of squares form of q. Thus, in the example above, the rank of q and Q is 2. The eigenvalue

Table 8.1. *Main types of quadratic form $q(x)$. Note that the third column applies in particular when the a_i are the eigenvalues of Q.*

Q and q said to be:	Condition on q	Coefficients a_i
Positive definite (pd)	$x \neq 0 \Rightarrow xQx^{\mathrm{T}} > 0$	all $a_i > 0$
Positive semi-definite (psd)	$x \neq 0 \Rightarrow xQx^{\mathrm{T}} \geq 0$	all $a_i \geq 0$
Indefinite (see e.g. Figure 8.4)	$xQx^{\mathrm{T}} > 0,\, yQy^{\mathrm{T}} < 0$ for some x, y	$a_i > 0,\, a_j < 0$ for some i, j

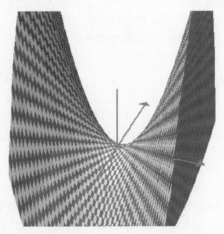

Figure 8.4 Saddle shape resulting from the indefinite form $z = x^2 - y^2$.

option (8.16) shows that for general symmetric Q *the rank of Q is its number of nonzero eigenvalues*, and its nullity the number that *are* zero. Applying this to our particular case of Q, the eigenvalues are $8 \pm \sqrt{29}, 0$ implying again rank 2.

Type of a form We consider the values that may be taken by a form $q(x) = xQx^{\mathrm{T}}$ as x varies. Since $x = zP$ is an invertible transformation, these values are exactly the same when q is expressed in squares, $a_1 z_1^2 + \cdots + a_n z_n^2$. Notice firstly that xQx^{T} is automatically zero if x is zero. If the form is otherwise always positive we say it is *positive definite*. If never negative, it is positive semi-definite, and if both signs occur, indefinite. These three main cases are reviewed in Table 8.1.

We say further that Q, q are *negative (semi-)definite* if their negatives are positive (semi-)definite. Notice that Example 8.33 is positive semi-definite, and that by inverting a matrix we invert the eigenvalues (Remarks 8.9). We have proved the following.

Corollary 8.35 *(a) A symmetric matrix Q is positive definite, positive semi-definite, or indefinite, according as its eigenvalues are positive, or non-negative, or include both signs, (b) a positive definite matrix has a positive definite inverse.*

> A quadratic form is positive definite if all its eigenvalues are positive, positive
> semi-definite if none are negative, and indefinite if both signs occur.

Example 8.36 (i) Is the origin a maximum, minimum or saddle for

$$q(x) = x_1x_3 + x_2x_3 + x_2x_4 + x_3x_4?$$

This is (by definition) the same as asking if the form is negative definite, positive definite
or indefinite. On inspection we guess it can take both signs, so let us first set some
variables zero to simplify things, say $x_2 = x_4 = 0$. This leaves only the first term x_1x_3
and we are done. For example, $q(1, 0, 1, 0) = 1$ but $q(1, 0, -1, 0) = -1$. Thus the form
is indefinite and the origin is a saddle point.

(ii) *Use eigenvalues to determine the type of the form (8.15).* The eigenvalue equation
is

$$|tI - Q| = \begin{vmatrix} t-2 & 1 & 1 \\ 1 & t-13 & 2 \\ 1 & 2 & t-1 \end{vmatrix} = \begin{vmatrix} t-2 & 0 & 1 \\ 1 & t-15 & 2 \\ 1 & 3-t & t-1 \end{vmatrix}$$

$$= (t-2)[(t-15)(t-1) - 6 + 2t] + [3 - t - t + 15]$$

$$= t^3 - 16t^2 + 35t.$$

Fortunately, we only have to solve a quadratic, and the eigenvalues are $0, 8 \pm \sqrt{29}$. These
are non-negative so the form is positive semi-definite by Corollary 8.35, in agreement
with our earlier expression as a sum of squares, $z_1^2 + z_2^2 + 0z_3^2$ (Example 8.33).

(iii) *Show that the form below is positive definite:*

$$q(x) = x_1^2 + 2x_2^2 + 6x_3^2 + 15x_4^2 - 2x_1x_2 - 2x_1x_3 - 2x_1x_4 - 4x_2x_4. \tag{8.17}$$

The easiest way available at present is to 'complete the squares' as used for (8.15). But
since $n = 4$ one has to solve an equation of degree 4 for the eigenvalues. Resorting to
machine computation yields the approximate values 0.017, 2.432, 6.200, 15.351. Given
the three significant decimal places, we are entitled to conclude these values really are
positive and hence that the form is positive definite. However, we are about to introduce
a method which involves no polynomial equation-solving.

Exercise Find the rank and type of the quadratic form $x^2 - 4xy + 4y^2$ in the quickest
way.

Positive definite needs symmetric We could say a matrix Q is positive definite simply if
$xQx^T = \sum q_{ij}x_ix_j$ is positive except when all x_i are zero, and similarly for the other
types, without requiring Q to be symmetric. However, in practice it is a huge advantage
to have Q symmetric, not least because it can be diagonalised and has real eigenvalues,
as we have begun to see.

Exercise Show that a positive definite matrix has positive diagonal. (Hint: fix i, and set
$x_j = 0$ for $j \neq i$.)

8.3.3 Positive definite forms

The most important question is whether a form/matrix is positive definite (a special case of positive *semi*-definite), and this may be determined without the equation-solving process of computing eigenvalues, or even finding a sum of squares form. Consider linear transformations $x = yP$ of the form

$$x_k = y_k + (\text{terms in } y_{k+1}, \dots, y_n) \quad \text{for} \quad 1 \le k \le n, \text{ hence}$$
$$y_k = x_k + (\text{terms in } x_{k+1}, \dots, x_n) \quad \text{for} \quad 1 \le k \le n. \tag{8.18}$$

To derive the second line from the first we observe that $x_n = y_n$ implies $y_n = x_n$ and work downwards, and similarly for the first line from the second. The first statement is equivalent to saying that P is a *lower triangular* matrix, one in which the above-diagonal entries are zero (see after Example 7.29). Indeed, P is called *unit triangular* because the diagonal consists of ones. In particular $|P| = 1$. Considering $y = P^{-1}x$ in the second line of (8.18), we see without further calculation that P^{-1} is also unit triangular. Thus it is appropriate to call transformations of type (8.18) *triangular*. The case $n = 3$ looks like

$$[x_1 \ x_2 \ x_3] = [y_1 \ y_2 \ y_3] \begin{bmatrix} 1 & 0 & 0 \\ \times & 1 & 0 \\ \times & \times & 1 \end{bmatrix}, \tag{8.19}$$

where each '$\times$' represents some real number. Now observe that under a transformation (8.18) the *discriminant* of a form (the determinant of its matrix) is unchanged, since $|PQP^{\mathrm{T}}| = |P|^2|Q| = |Q|$. The result we want is a criterion on the *leading principal minor* Δ_k of Q, namely the determinant of the submatrix obtained by deleting all but the first k rows and columns. Thus, for example,

$$\Delta_1 = q_{11}, \quad \Delta_2 = \begin{vmatrix} q_{11} & q_{12} \\ q_{21} & q_{22} \end{vmatrix}, \quad \Delta_3 = \begin{vmatrix} q_{11} & q_{12} & q_{13} \\ q_{21} & q_{22} & q_{23} \\ q_{31} & q_{32} & q_{33} \end{vmatrix}.$$

Theorem 8.37 *A form is positive definite if and only if its leading principal minors Δ_k are positive.*

Proof (i) Suppose the form q is positive definite. Then so is the form in $x_1, \dots, x_k$ obtained by setting the remaining variables to zero. Its matrix is

$$Q_k = \begin{bmatrix} q_{11} & \cdots & q_{1k} \\ \cdots & \cdots & \cdots \\ q_{k1} & \cdots & q_{kk} \end{bmatrix}, \quad |Q_k| = \Delta_k. \tag{8.20}$$

But by Corollary 8.35 the eigenvalues of Q_k are all positive and by Lemma 8.5 the determinant $|Q_k| = \Delta_k$ is their product. Therefore Δ_k is positive.

(ii) For the converse suppose $\Delta_i > 0$ for $1 \le i \le n$. Assume inductively that, for some k with $2 \le k \le n$, the terms of $q(x)$ with some subscript less than k can be expressed as a sum of squares whose coefficients are positive and have product Δ_{k-1}. Say

$$q(\mathbf{x}) = t_{11}y_1^2 + \cdots + t_{k-1,k-1}\, y_{k-1}^2 + \sum_{i,j\geq k} t_{ij}y_iy_j, \tag{8.21}$$

where $t_{11}\cdot t_{22}\cdots t_{k-1,k-1} = \Delta_{k-1}$. Perform the following transformation of type (8.18), based on the square completing technique of Example 8.33, where z_k^2 will incorporate all terms that involve y_k:

$$\begin{cases} z_k = y_k + (t_{k,k+1}/t_{kk})y_{k+1} + \cdots + (t_{kn}/t_{kk})y_n, \\ z_i = y_i \text{ for } 1 \leq i \leq n, i \neq k. \end{cases}$$

Then $q(\mathbf{x}) = t_{11}z_1^2 + \cdots + t_{kk}z_k^2 +$ (a quadratic form in $z_{k+1}, \ldots, z_n$). Now consider the form $q(\mathbf{x})$ and its expression in terms of z. Set $z_{k+1}, \ldots, z_n = 0$ and hence $x_{k+1}, \ldots x_n = 0$. The resulting forms in k variables are related by a triangular transformation (8.18) and so have the same discriminant, that is $t_{11}\cdots t_{kk} = \Delta_k$. But the inductive hypothesis includes $t_{11}\cdot t_{22}\cdots t_{k-1,k-1} = \Delta_{k-1}$, hence we may write $t_{kk} = \Delta_k/\Delta_{k-1} > 0$. Since trivially $t_{11} > 0$, we have by induction up to n that q is a sum of squares with positive coefficients t_{ii} and so is positive definite.

> A form is positive definite if and only if
> all its leading principal minors are positive.

Exercise Can the matrix Rows $([1\ -2\ 3], [-2\ 5\ 0], [3\ 0\ t])$ be positive definite (Theorem 8.37)? An example is worked out below.

Example 8.38 We use Theorem 8.37 show that the form (8.17) is positive definite.

$$Q = \begin{bmatrix} 1 & -1 & -1 & -1 \\ -1 & 2 & 0 & -2 \\ -1 & 0 & 6 & 0 \\ -1 & -2 & 0 & 15 \end{bmatrix}, \text{ hence } \Delta_4 = \begin{bmatrix} 1 & 0 & 0 & 0 \\ -1 & 1 & -1 & -3 \\ -1 & -1 & 5 & -1 \\ -1 & -3 & -1 & 14 \end{bmatrix} = \begin{bmatrix} 1 & 0 & 0 & 0 \\ 1 & 1 & 0 & 0 \\ -1 & -1 & 4 & -4 \\ -1 & -3 & -4 & 5 \end{bmatrix}$$
$$= 1\cdot 1\cdot(20-16) = 4 > 0,$$

where the zeros in the last two matrices were obtained by column operations designed to reduce the original near enough to triangular form to make the determinant evaluation very simple. Next

$$\Delta_3 = \begin{bmatrix} 1 & -1 & -1 \\ -1 & 2 & 0 \\ -1 & 0 & 6 \end{bmatrix} = \begin{bmatrix} 1 & 0 & 0 \\ -1 & 1 & -1 \\ -1 & -1 & 5 \end{bmatrix} = 4 > 0,\ \Delta_2 = \begin{bmatrix} 1 & -1 \\ -1 & 2 \end{bmatrix} = 1 > 0,\ \Delta_1 = 1 > 0.$$

Every leading principal minor is positive, and so q is positive definite by Theorem 8.37.

Remark Whatever the dimensions of a matrix A, it holds good that AA^{T} and $A^{\mathrm{T}}A$ are not only square but symmetric, albeit of different sizes if A is non-square. These products play a central role in developing the Singular Value Decomposition (Section 8.4.2) of a matrix, the basis of Principal Component Analysis; the following theorem is basic and important for this. For the mention of multiplicity see Remark 8.31 and, for positive semi-definite, Table 8.1.

Theorem 8.39 *Let $A_{m \times n}$ be a real matrix. Then (a) AA^T and A^TA are positive semi-definite (psd). They have the same nonzero eigenvalues with the same multiplicities, and both have the same rank, k, as A. (b) If AA^T has eigenvectors $\boldsymbol{w}_1, \ldots, \boldsymbol{w}_t$ ($t \leq k$) for positive eigenvalues $\lambda_1, \ldots, \lambda_t$, then $\{\lambda_i^{-1/2}\boldsymbol{w}_iA\}$ play the same role for A^TA and are orthonormal if $\{\boldsymbol{w}_i\}$ are orthonormal. (c) If a matrix Q is positive semi-definite, then it factorises as $Q = A^TA$ for some matrix A whose nonzero rows are orthogonal.*

Proof (a) *The psd property* Let $\boldsymbol{x}$ be an arbitrary nonzero m-vector. Then $\boldsymbol{x}(AA^T)\boldsymbol{x}^T = \boldsymbol{y}\boldsymbol{y}^T (\boldsymbol{y} = \boldsymbol{x}A) = |\boldsymbol{y}|^2 = 0$. Thus AA^T is by definition psd. Replacing A by A^T shows A^TA is also psd. *Equal eigenvalues* Now we need only prove the equal eigenvalue property and the rest is immediate from part (b). Let $A_{m \times n}$ have rank k. Then there is an invertible matrix P such that the first k rows of PA form a matrix U with orthonormal rows, and the remaining rows are zero (Theorem 8.18). Thus AA^T has (Theorem 8.20) the same rank as the product

$$PAA^TP^T = \begin{bmatrix} U \\ 0 \end{bmatrix} \begin{bmatrix} U^T | 0 \end{bmatrix} = \begin{bmatrix} UU^T & 0 \\ \hline 0 & 0 \end{bmatrix} = \begin{bmatrix} I_k & 0 \\ \hline 0 & 0 \end{bmatrix}. \tag{8.22}$$

Hence $r(AA^T) = k$. The same argument with A replaced by A^T, of equal rank k (Theorem 8.20), shows that A^TA also has rank k. For (b) we suppose that, for $1 \leq i \leq t$,

$$\boldsymbol{w}_i(AA^T) = \lambda_i\boldsymbol{w}_i \quad (\boldsymbol{w}_i \neq 0, \lambda_i \neq 0). \tag{8.23}$$

Then $\boldsymbol{w}_iA \neq 0$, and is an eigenvector of A^TA because $(\boldsymbol{w}_iA)(A^TA) = \boldsymbol{w}_i(AA^T)A = \lambda_i(\boldsymbol{w}_iA)$. Now let $\{\boldsymbol{w}_i\}$ be orthonormal. Then the vectors $\{\boldsymbol{w}_iA\}$ are orthogonal, for if $i \neq j$ then $(\boldsymbol{w}_iA)(\boldsymbol{w}_jA)^T = \boldsymbol{w}_i(AA^T)\boldsymbol{w}_j^T = \lambda_i\boldsymbol{w}_i\boldsymbol{w}_j^T = 0$. Note that this still holds if $\lambda_i = \lambda_j$. Finally $|\boldsymbol{w}_iA|^2 = (\boldsymbol{w}_iAA^T)\boldsymbol{w}_i^T = \lambda_i\boldsymbol{w}_i\boldsymbol{w}_i^T = \lambda_i$ (since $|\boldsymbol{w}_i|^2 = 1$), so that $(1/\sqrt{\lambda_i})\boldsymbol{w}_iA$ is a unit vector. This completes the proof of (b).

(c) A positive semi-definite matrix Q has real eigenvalues $\lambda_1, \ldots, \lambda_n \geq 0$, and $Q = P^T \cdot \text{diag}(\lambda_i) \cdot P$ for some orthogonal P (Theorems 8.29 and 8.30), so let $A = \text{diag}(\lambda_i^{1/2})P$.

Example 8.40 We check the ranks and eigenvalues predicted in Theorem 8.39.

$$A = \begin{bmatrix} 1 & 0 & -1 \\ 2 & 3 & 1 \end{bmatrix}, \quad AA^T = \begin{bmatrix} 2 & 1 \\ 1 & 14 \end{bmatrix}, \quad A^TA = \begin{bmatrix} 5 & 6 & 1 \\ 6 & 9 & 3 \\ 1 & 3 & 2 \end{bmatrix}.$$

Ranks The three ranks equal 2 by inspection, for the rows of A are independent, as are those of AA^T, and the third row of A^TA equals the second minus the first (and these two are LI).

Eigenvalues We have $|tI - AA^T| = t^2 - t\,\text{Tr}(AA^T) + |AA^T| = t^2 - 16t + 27$, with positive eigenvalue roots $8 \pm \sqrt{37}$. Thus the eigenvalues of A^TA should be $8 \pm \sqrt{37}$ and 0.

Table 8.2. *The effect of matrix operations on the type of a triangular matrix T*
and its main diagonal. The matrix M performs row operations
$R_i = R_i + aR_j$ *so as to convert A to B.*

Operation	Triangle type (upper/lower)	Diagonal type (unit/zero/positive)	Reference
Transpose	switched	preserved	Reader's inspection
Multiplication $T_1 T_2$	preserved	preserved	Above & Exercise 7.11
Inversion	preserved	preserved	Exercise 8.14
Row ops. $MA = T$	M, T opposite	P has unit diagonal	Proof of Theorem 8.41

We obtain

$$|A^{\mathrm{T}}A - tI| = \begin{vmatrix} 5-t & 6 & 1 \\ 6 & 9-t & 3 \\ 1 & 3 & 2-t \end{vmatrix} = \begin{vmatrix} 5-t & 0 & 1 \\ 6 & -9-t & 3 \\ 1 & -9+6t & 2-t \end{vmatrix}$$

$= -t(t^2 - 16t + 27)$, yielding the predicted eigenvalues.

Remarks (1) The second part of Theorem 8.39 is very useful for reducing eigenvector calculations when AA^{T} and $A^{\mathrm{T}}A$ have significantly different sizes (we may choose the smaller), and is exemplified at the end of Chapter 10. Meanwhile we offer Exercise 8.20.

(2) Though we stressed orthogonality in Theorem 8.39, the lesser property of *independence* of eigenvectors w_i of AA^{T} implies independence of the corresponding eigenvectors $w_i A$ of $A^{\mathrm{T}}A$ (Exercise 8.4).

Factorising positive definite matrices We have established that a positive *semi*-definite matrix Q may be factorised in the form $A^{\mathrm{T}}A$. However, if Q is positive definite more follows, leading for example to a method for generating multivariate normal samples (Section 11.3.5) for the purpose of simulation (another use relates to deblurring an image, Section 15.3).

For this factorisation we turn once more to the *triangular matrices* introduced in Example 7.29 and most recently discussed at (8.18). Suppose U is upper triangular, its nonzero entries lying on and above the main diagonal. Then so is U^{-1} if it exists (Exercise 8.14), whilst U^{T} is *lower* triangular, with a triangle of zeros above the main diagonal.

The main diagonal plays an important role. As previewed in (8.18), the *type* of a matrix diagonal is defined to be unit/zero/positive if every diagonal element is respectively one/zero/positive. Table 8.2 records how such properties are affected by the matrix operations we use, in preparation for the factorisation result.

Exercise Upper triangular matrix products UV preserve diagonal type. (Hint: $(UV)_{kk} = u_{kk}v_{kk}$).

Theorem 8.41 *(Choleski factorisation) If a matrix S is positive definite it may be factorised uniquely as $U^{\mathrm{T}}U$ for some U upper triangular with positive diagonal. Indeed, U is determined by ALGO 8.3 below.*

ALGO 8.3 The Choleski decomposition

To express a positive definite matrix $S = \mathrm{Rows}(S_1, \ldots, S_n)$ in the form $U^{\mathrm{T}}U$, where U is upper triangular with positive diagonal and $U = \mathrm{Rows}\,(R_1, \ldots, R_n)$, we perform in succession for $k = 1, 2, \ldots, n$:

1. Compute $u_{kk} = \sqrt{[s_{kk} - \sum_{i=1}^{k-1} u_{ik}^2]}$,
2. Set $R_k = (1/u_{kk})[S_k - \sum_{i=1}^{k-1} u_{ik} R_i]$.

Proof We first derive steps 1 and 2 of ALGO 8.3. The case $n = 3$ of $U^{\mathrm{T}}U = S$ is represented below to help visualise general n.

$$\begin{bmatrix} u_{11} & 0 & 0 \\ u_{12} & u_{22} & 0 \\ u_{13} & u_{23} & u_{33} \end{bmatrix} \begin{bmatrix} u_{11} & u_{12} & u_{13} \\ 0 & u_{22} & u_{23} \\ 0 & 0 & u_{33} \end{bmatrix} = \begin{bmatrix} s_{11} & s_{12} & s_{13} \\ s_{21} & s_{22} & s_{23} \\ s_{31} & s_{32} & s_{33} \end{bmatrix}. \tag{8.24}$$

Equating the (k, k) element of $U^{\mathrm{T}}U$ to that of S in the general case of n, we obtain $\sum_{i \leq k} u_{ik}^2 = s_{kk}$, or, after rearranging,

$$u_{kk}^2 = s_{kk} - u_{1k}^2 - \cdots - u_{k-1,k}^2. \tag{8.25}$$

Equating the kth row of $U^{\mathrm{T}}U$ to that of S yields, on similar rearrangement,

$$u_{kk} R_k = S_k - u_{1k} R_1 - \cdots - u_{k-1,k} R_{k-1}. \tag{8.26}$$

The existence of U is equivalent to the existence of a solution to Equations (8.25) and (8.26) with $1 \leq k \leq n$. In such a solution, we have $0 \neq |S| = |U|^2 = u_{11}^2 \cdots u_{nn}^2$, hence all $u_{kk} \neq 0$. The equations determine each R_k in terms of the previous ones, and uniquely so if we insist on the positive square root for u_{kk} in (8.25). This gives ALGO 8.3. On the other hand, replacing u_{kk} by $-u_{kk}$ replaces R_k by $-R_k$ but leaves the rest unchanged, because only squared elements of U appear in (8.25). It remains to prove that U exists.

Stage 1 Let A_k be the the submatrix in the first k rows and first k columns of S. Suppose row operations involving no interchange or scaling are performed on the first k rows of S, to eliminate, column by column, all nonzero elements below the diagonal in A_k. Let M_k be the result of the operations being performed on a $k \times k$ identity matrix I_k, so the result of the operations on A_k is $M_k S$ (Theorem 8.17), and M_k is lower triangular with unit diagonal. Now, for the elimination to succeed, the diagonal element in each successive column must be nonzero. Then the following matrix product holds:

$$
\left[\begin{array}{c|c} M_k & 0 \\ \hline 0 & I_{d-k} \end{array}\right]
\left[\begin{array}{c|c} A_k & \times\times \\ \hline \times\times & \times\times \end{array}\right]
=
\left[\begin{array}{ccc|c} b_{11} & & & \\ 0 & \ddots & & \times\times \\ 0 & 0 & b_{kk} & \\ \hline & \times\times & & \times\times \end{array}\right],
\qquad (8.27)
$$

where the pairs $\times\times$ denote unknown submatrices. By block multiplication (7.25) and taking determinants, we have $b_{11}b_{22}\cdots b_{kk} = |M_k| \cdot |A_k| = |A_k|$, the leading principal $k \times k$ minor of S, which is positive because S is positive definite (Theorem 8.37). Thus $b_{11}b_{22}\cdots b_{kk} > 0$, and if the first $k-1$ factors are positive so is the kth; this provides an inductive demonstration that the process may be continued to obtain $MS = B$ upper triangular with positive diagonal, where $M = M_n$ is lower triangular with unit diagonal.

Stage 2 Write $MS = DU_1$, where $D = \mathrm{diag}(b_{kk})$ and so U_1 is *unit* upper triangular. Denoting an inverse tranpose by $-\mathrm{T}$, we have the following symmetric matrices: $U_1^{-\mathrm{T}}SU_1^{-1} = U_1^{-\mathrm{T}}(M^{-1}DU_1)U_1^{-1} = U_1^{-\mathrm{T}}M^{-1}D$. Since $U_1^{-\mathrm{T}}M^{-1}$ is therefore both symmetric and triangular (Table 8.2), it is diagonal. But U_1 and M both have unit diagonal so (Table 8.2) $U_1^{-\mathrm{T}}M^{-1} = I$, whence $M^{-1} = U_1^{\mathrm{T}}$. Substituting, $S = M^{-1}DU_1 = U_1^{\mathrm{T}}DU_1 = U^{\mathrm{T}}U$, where $U = D^{1/2}U_1$ is upper triangular and exists because D has positive diagonal. Thus U exists and the proof is complete.

Example 8.42 We show the calculation of U from the matrix S below, by ALGO 8.3.

$$
S = \begin{bmatrix} 1 & 0 & 1 \\ 0 & 4 & -2 \\ 1 & -2 & 11 \end{bmatrix}, \qquad
U = \begin{bmatrix} 1 & 0 & 1 \\ 0 & 2 & -1 \\ 0 & 0 & 3 \end{bmatrix}.
$$

$k = 1.\, u_{11} = \sqrt{s_{11}} = 1,\ R_1 = (1/u_{11})S_1 = [1\ 0\ 1]$.
$k = 2.\, u_{22} = \sqrt{[s_{22} - u_{12}^2]} = \sqrt{[4-0]} = 2,\ R_2 = (1/2)[S_2 - u_{12}R_1] = [0\ 2\ -1]$.
$k = 3.\, u_{33} = \sqrt{[s_{33} - u_{13}^2 - u_{23}^2]} = 3,\ R_3 = (1/3)[S_3 - u_{13}R_1 - u_{23}R_2] = [0\ 0\ 3]$.

8.4 The Singular Value Decomposition (SVD)

In the previous section we saw that a symmetric matrix A could be diagonalised by an orthogonal matrix P. Here we tackle the case of a general (real) $m \times n$ matrix A, and derive the powerful *Singular Value Decomposition* of A. This provides a more numerically stable foundation than diagonalising when we introduce the K–L Transform of Principal Component Analysis in Chapter 10. Some preliminary results are required.

8.4.1 Matrix norms

Classically, many results depend on a matrix having greatest possible rank, but have little to say if, for example, small errors happen to lower the rank. Matrix norms are a way to approach this problem. We must extend the definition of *length*, or *norm*, from vectors to matrices. We recall that the norm for *n*-vectors is a function $n(x) = \sqrt{(x_1^2 + \cdots + x_n^2)}$, or in the complex case $\sqrt{(|x_1|^2 + \cdots + |x_n|^2)}$, which satisfies for all x, y:

(1) $n(x) \geq 0$, with equality if and only if $x = 0$,
(2) $n(x + y) \leq n(x) + n(y)$,
(3) $n(ax) = |a|n(x)$, for a scalar a,

where property (2) is Remark 7.20. Each property has proved its worth, but the one without which the others are rendered ineffective is the 'bottom line' that if $n(x) = 0$ then x itself is zero (the zero vector). Any function on $m \times n$ matrices that satisfies (1), (2), (3) above will be called a *matrix norm*. There are two distinct matrix norms we shall need, both now and later. Firstly, we may take the view that, with elements listed row by row, our matrix is an element of *mn*-space, giving the *Frobenius sum of squares norm, or F-norm*,

$$\|A\|_F = \sqrt{\Big(\sum_{i,j} a_{ij}^2\Big)} \quad \text{(F-norm)}. \tag{8.28}$$

Another possibility is to measure the size of A by the way it magnifies lengths, yielding the *ratio norm*, or *R-norm*

$$\|A\|_R = \sup_{x \neq 0} \frac{|xA|}{|x|} \quad \text{(R-norm)}. \tag{8.29}$$

Notation 8.43 (i) We see later that replacing xA by $A^T x^T$ in (8.29) leaves $\|A\|$ unchanged, giving what to some will be the more familiar way round, multiplying a vector variable by a matrix on the *left*.

(ii) *Matrices blocked into rows* Write $U = \text{Rows}(u_1, u_2, \ldots, u_k)$ for the matrix U with rows as listed, or $U = \text{Rows}(u_1, U_1)$, where $U_1 = \text{Rows}(u_2, \ldots, u_k)$.

(iii) A nonzero vector x may be expressed as sy, where $|y| = 1$ (set $s = |x|$).

(iv) We continue to use single lines for the norm $|x|$ of a vector regarded as such, and to reserve the double line symbolism $\|A\|$ for a matrix. As indicated, we will sometimes drop the subscript R or F when the current choice of matrix norm is otherwise known.

Theorem 8.44 *We have in the usual row/column notation*
$(a)\|A\|_R = \text{Max}\{|xA|: |x| = 1\}$,
$(b)\ \|A\|_F = \sqrt{\Sigma|R_i|^2} = \sqrt{\Sigma|C_j|^2} = \sqrt{\text{Tr}(AA^T)}$.

Proof (a) In Notation 8.43(iii) above we may write $|xA|/|x| = |syA|/|sy|$ (with $|y| = 1$) $= |yA|$, so $\|A\|_R = \sup\{|yA| : |y| = 1\}$. But the continuous function $y \rightarrow yA$ on the compact space $\{y: |y| = 1\}$ must achieve a greatest value (see e.g. Hoggar, 1992), hence the simplification to both unit vectors and strict maximum. Part (b) is immediate from the definitions of trace and norm.

Exercise Deduce Theorem 8.44(b) from the definitions.

Remark 8.45 The three norms, vector norm, F-norm and R-norm (or just norm) all apply to a row or column matrix, but we shall show that, happily, the definitions agree.

Proof Let A be a row vector $\boldsymbol{a}$. Then $\|\boldsymbol{a}\|_R = \text{Max}\{|\boldsymbol{xa}|\colon |\boldsymbol{x}| = 1\}$, where $\boldsymbol{x}$ is by definition a *row* vector such that the matrix product $\boldsymbol{xa}$ exists. Hence $\boldsymbol{x}$ is 1×1, or a scalar, and therefore $\|\boldsymbol{a}\|_R = 1 \cdot |\boldsymbol{a}|$ as asserted. On the other hand, $\|\boldsymbol{a}\|_F = |\boldsymbol{a}|$ immediately from the Frobenius definition, and similarly if A is a column vector.

It remains to prove that $\|A\|_R = |A|$ when A is a column vector $\boldsymbol{a}^T$. Here $\|\boldsymbol{a}^T\|_R = \text{Max}\{|\boldsymbol{xa}^T|\colon |\boldsymbol{x}| = 1\} = \text{Max}\{|\boldsymbol{x} \cdot \boldsymbol{a}|\colon |\boldsymbol{x}| = 1\} \leq 1 \cdot |\boldsymbol{a}|$ (by Remark 7.20). But this upper bound is achieved with $\boldsymbol{x} = \boldsymbol{a}/|\boldsymbol{a}|$, so the proof is complete.

> The three norms agree on vectors.   (8.30)

Theorem 8.46 *The three norms (vector and two matrix) are invariant under multiplication by an orthogonal matrix.*

Proof Let P, Q be orthogonal matrices of appropriate dimensions. (a) The *vector norm* case is covered by results on isometries (Remarks 7.72 for $\boldsymbol{x}P$; also $|Q\boldsymbol{x}^T| = |\boldsymbol{x}Q^T| = |\boldsymbol{x}|$ since Q^T is also orthogonal, see Definition 7.34).

(b) *Ratio norm* $\|PAQ\|_R = \|A\|_R$, because the former equals:

$$\text{Max}\{|\boldsymbol{x}PAQ|\colon |\boldsymbol{x}| = 1\}$$
$$= \text{Max}\{|\boldsymbol{y}AQ|\colon |\boldsymbol{y}| = 1\}, \quad \text{since } \boldsymbol{y} = \boldsymbol{x}P \text{ runs through all unit vectors as } \boldsymbol{x} \text{ does}$$
$$= \text{Max}\{|\boldsymbol{y}A|\colon |\boldsymbol{y}| = 1\}, \quad \text{since } |(\boldsymbol{y}A)Q| = |\boldsymbol{y}A|, \ Q \text{ being orthogonal.}$$

(c) *Frobenius norm* We handle the pre- and post-multiplication situations separately. $\|PA\|_F = \sqrt{\sum|\text{column } j \text{ of } PA|^2}$ (by Theorem 8.44) $= \sqrt{\sum|PC_j|^2}$ (Examples 7.22) $= \sqrt{\sum|C_j|^2}$ (because P is orthogonal) $= \|A\|_F$. Similarly, $\|AQ\| = \sqrt{\Sigma|R_iQ|^2} = \sqrt{\sum|R_i|^2} = \|A\|$.

> The three norms are invariant under multiplication by an orthogonal matrix.

(8.31)

Example 8.47 (i) Show that the norms of a symmetric matrix A with eigenvalues $\lambda_1, \ldots, \lambda n$ are $\|A\|_R = \text{Max}|\lambda_i|$, and $\|A\|_F = \sqrt{\sum\lambda_i^2}$; (ii) deduce that if P is a projection matrix onto a k-dimensional subspace then P has R-norm 1 but F-norm $k^{1/2}$. (See more generally (8.5).)

Solution (i) Because A is symmetric it may be diagonalised by an orthogonal matrix (Theorem 8.30), which does not change the norms (Theorem 8.46), so we need only consider the case $A = D = \text{diag}(\lambda_1, \ldots, \lambda_n)$, where the diagonal elements must be the eigenvalues by Theorem 8.29. The expression for Frobenius norm is now immediate. To obtain an expression for the ratio norm we may assume for simplicity that $|\lambda_1| \geq |\lambda_i|$ for $2 \leq i \leq n$. Then

$$
\begin{aligned}
\|D\|_{\mathrm{R}}^2 &= \mathrm{Max}\{|xD|^2 : |\boldsymbol{x}| = 1\} = \mathrm{Max}\{x_1^2\lambda_1^2 + \cdots + x_n^2\lambda_n^2 : |\boldsymbol{x}| = 1\} \\
&= \mathrm{Max}\{(1 - y_2 - \cdots - y_n)\lambda_1^2 + y_2\lambda_2^2 + \cdots + y_n\lambda_n^2 : 0 \leq y_i \leq 1\}
\end{aligned}
$$
(setting $y_i = x_i^2$).

The function $f(y_2, \ldots, y_n)$ to be maximised has partial derivatives $\partial f/\partial y_i = -\lambda_1^2 + \lambda_i^2 \leq 0$, where $2 \leq i \leq n$, so the greatest value occurs when each y_i takes its least value 0, giving $\|A\|_{\mathrm{R}}^2 = \|D\|_{\mathrm{R}}^2 = \lambda_1^2$ and $\|A\|_{\mathrm{R}} = |\lambda_1|$ as required.

(ii) Since P satisfies $P^{\mathrm{T}} = P = P^2$ (Theorem 7.59), its eigenvalues λ satisfy $\lambda^2 = \lambda$ (Remarks 8.9), hence $\lambda = 0$ or 1. Its rank is given to be k, so there are k ones. Thus, by (i), P has R-norm 1 but F-norm $k^{1/2}$.

Theorem 8.48 *Let A, B be matrices and* $\boldsymbol{x}$ *a vector. Then both R-norm and F-norm satisfy*

$$
\begin{aligned}
&(a) \ \ |\boldsymbol{x}A| \leq |\boldsymbol{x}|\|A\|, && \textit{if the product } \boldsymbol{x}A \textit{ exists,} \\
&(b) \ \ \|AB\| \leq \|A\|\|B\|, && \textit{if the product } AB \textit{ exists.}
\end{aligned}
$$

Proof (a) follows from (b) as the special case $A = \boldsymbol{x}$, since vector and matrix norms agree. We prove (b). For the *ratio* norm, $\|AB\| = \mathrm{Max}|\boldsymbol{x}AB|$ ($|\boldsymbol{x}| = 1$) $\leq \max|\boldsymbol{x}A|\|B\|$ (why?) $\leq \|A\|\|B\|$. For the F-norm, write $A = \mathrm{Rows}(R_1, \ldots, R_m)$, $B = [C_1, \ldots, C_n]$, so that the ij element of AB is $R_i \cdot C_j$, a dot product. By definition $\|AB\|_{\mathrm{F}}^2 = \sum_{i,j} |R_i \cdot C_j|^2 \leq \sum_{i,j} |R_i|^2|C_j|^2$ (Remark 7.20) $= (\sum_i |R_i|^2)(\sum_j |C_j|^2) = \|A\|_{\mathrm{F}}^2\|B\|_{\mathrm{F}}^2$.

An approximation result We note that matrix norms can be used to investigate quantitatively the effects of ill-conditioning in a set of linear equations (Golub & van Loan, 1996) though we do not pursue this here.

The result below is a generalisation of the idea of regression, or representing a set of data points by a straight line $y = mx + c$. We shall use it to establish optimising properties of the 'SVD' at the end of this chapter, later to be applied in Chapter 10. See Remarks 8.57 for the relation to the pseudoinverse, and the generalisation to complex matrices.

Theorem 8.49 *(a) The best F-norm approximation to matrix* $Y_{m \times n}$ *by a product MX, where* $M_{m \times k}$ *has its* $k < n$ *columns independent, is given by* $X = (M^{\mathrm{T}}M)^{-1}M^{\mathrm{T}}Y$. *(b) The best approximation to matrix* $Y_{n \times m}$ *by a product XM, where* $M_{k \times m}$ *has its* $k < n$ *rows independent, is given by* $X = YM^{\mathrm{T}}(MM^{\mathrm{T}})^{-1}$.

Proof Notice that (a) and (b) are equivalent via the operation of transpose. To show that (b) implies (a), for example, apply (b) to $Y^{\mathrm{T}}, M^{\mathrm{T}}, X^{\mathrm{T}}$, then transpose the resulting formula for X^{T}. We prove (b). It suffices to establish the special case $n = 1$, which gives the general case row by row. Thus we consider

$$Y_{1 \times m} - X_{1 \times k} M_{k \times m} \quad (M \text{ has linearly independent rows}).$$

With $Y = (y_s)$ and $M = \text{Cols}(C_s)$, we minimise $S(X) = \|Y - XM\|^2 = \sum_s (y_s - XC_s)^2$. Since X lies in $\mathbf{R}^m$, a space with no boundary, any maximum or minimum occurs at a turning point (see e.g. Hoggar, 1992), that is, where, for $1 \le r, m$,

$$\begin{aligned}
0 = \frac{\partial S}{\partial x_r} &= \Sigma_s 2(y_s - XC_s)\frac{\partial}{\partial x_r}(-XC_s) \\
&= -\Sigma_s 2(y_s - XC_s)(C_s)_r, \quad \text{since } \partial/\partial x_r(x_1 a_1 + \cdots + x_k a_k) = a_r.
\end{aligned}$$

This says that $\Sigma_s(y_s - XC_s)C_s^{\mathrm{T}} = 0$ as row vector, or $\Sigma_s y_s C_s^{\mathrm{T}} = X\Sigma_s C_s C_s^{\mathrm{T}}$. We recognize the left hand side as YM^{T} (see e.g. (7.29)), and the right hand side as XMM^{T}, an example of 'Russian multiplication', (7.31). Noting that MM^{T} is invertible because the rows of M are independent (see Example 7.33(ii)), we may write $X = YM^{\mathrm{T}}(MM^{\mathrm{T}})^{-1}$. Since $S(X)$ can be arbitrarily large, this unique turning point gives the least value of $S(X)$, and the proof is complete. The case $n = 1$ is important in its own right, as we discuss in Remarks 8.57.

Exercise Find the two norms of Rows([1 2], [2 1]).

8.4.2 The SVD – existence and basics

We have seen that a symmetric matrix A can be diagonalised as PAP^{T} by a single orthogonal matrix P. Remarkably, an arbitrary $m \times n$ matrix can be converted by two orthogonal matrices to a *generalised diagonal matrix* $\text{diag}(s_1, \ldots, s_p)_{m \times n}$, which is $\text{diag}(s_1, \ldots, s_p)$ extended to size $m \times n$ by rows and columns of zeros. Below we illustrate the two cases of $m \ne n$, with $p = \text{Min}(m, n)$.

$$\text{diag}(s_1, \ldots, s_p)_{m \times n} = \begin{bmatrix} s_1 & & \\ & \ddots & \\ & & s_p \end{bmatrix} (m < n), \text{ or } \begin{bmatrix} s_1 & & \\ & \ddots & \\ & & s_p \end{bmatrix} (m > n).$$

The process is the *singular value decomposition*, or SVD. The continued presence of orthogonality in spite of matrix A not being symmetric or even square is a powerful factor in deriving results.

Theorem 8.50 (*The Singular Value Decomposition, or SVD*) *Let A be a real $m \times n$ matrix. Then there are orthogonal matrices $U = \text{Rows}(u_1, \ldots, u_m)$ and $V = \text{Rows}(v_1 \ldots, v_n)$, and non-negatives $s_1 \ge s_2 \ge \cdots \ge s_p \ge 0$, such that*

$$UAV^{\mathrm{T}} = \text{diag}(s_1, \ldots, s_p)_{m \times n} = D, \text{ say,}$$

$$\text{or equivalently } A = U^{\mathrm{T}}DV, \tag{8.32}$$

Proof We establish the result for the case when A is a row vector, the case of a column vector being similar, then provide the inductive step from an $(m-1) \times (n-1)$ matrix to an $m \times n$ matrix. Let A be a row vector $\boldsymbol{a}$ and define the orthogonal 1×1 matrix $U = [1]$. Extend the unit vector $\boldsymbol{v}_1 = \boldsymbol{a}/|\boldsymbol{a}|$ to an ONB $\{\boldsymbol{v}_1, \boldsymbol{v}_2, \ldots, \boldsymbol{v}_n\}$ forming the rows of an orthogonal matrix V. Then $UAV^T = [\boldsymbol{a}\boldsymbol{v}_1^T \boldsymbol{a}\boldsymbol{v}_2^T \ldots \boldsymbol{a}\boldsymbol{v}_n^T] = [|\boldsymbol{a}|0 \ldots 0]$, which has the required form.

Now let A be a general $m \times n$ matrix; we shall use the ratio norm. By Theorem 8.44 there are unit vectors $\boldsymbol{x}$ in $\mathbf{R}^m$ and $\boldsymbol{y}$ in $\mathbf{R}^n$ such that $\|A\| = |\boldsymbol{x}A| = \sigma$, say, and $\boldsymbol{x}A = \sigma\boldsymbol{y}$. Extend $\boldsymbol{x}, \boldsymbol{y}$ to ONBs forming the rows of respective orthogonal matrices U, V, so that we may write $U = \text{Rows}(\boldsymbol{x}, U_1)$, $V = \text{Rows}(\boldsymbol{y}, V_1)$, where U_1 consists of $m - 1$ orthonormal rows and V_1 of $n - 1$. We calculate $B = UAV^T$ in terms of block matrices:

$$B = \begin{bmatrix} \boldsymbol{x} \\ U_1 \end{bmatrix} A \begin{bmatrix} \boldsymbol{y}^T & V_1^T \end{bmatrix} = \begin{bmatrix} \boldsymbol{x} \\ U_1 \end{bmatrix} \begin{bmatrix} A\boldsymbol{y}^T & AV_1^T \end{bmatrix} = \begin{bmatrix} \boldsymbol{x}A\boldsymbol{y}^T & \boldsymbol{x}AV_1^T \\ U_1 A\boldsymbol{y}^T & U_1 AV_1^T \end{bmatrix} = \begin{bmatrix} \sigma & 0 \\ \boldsymbol{w}^T & B_1 \end{bmatrix},$$

where we defined $B_1 = U_1 AV_1^T$ as $(m-1) \times (n-1)$, also $\boldsymbol{w}^T$ represents the column vector $U_1 A\boldsymbol{y}^T$, and two verifications are required:

(1) $\boldsymbol{x}A\boldsymbol{y}^T = \sigma\boldsymbol{y}\boldsymbol{y}^T = \sigma|\boldsymbol{y}|^2 = \sigma$;
(2) $\boldsymbol{x}AV_1^T = \sigma\boldsymbol{y}V_1^T$, which is the zero vector since $\text{Rows}(\boldsymbol{y}, V_1)$ is orthonormal.

The inductive step We must first show that $\boldsymbol{w} = \boldsymbol{0}$, an excellent use of matrix norms. Considering the block matrix product $[\sigma|\boldsymbol{w}]B = [\sigma^2 + \boldsymbol{w}\boldsymbol{w}^T|B_1]$ we have, with 'norm' denoting vector norm,

$$\|B\| \geq \text{norm}[\sigma^2 + \boldsymbol{w}\boldsymbol{w}^T|\boldsymbol{w}B_1]/\text{norm}[\sigma|\boldsymbol{w}], \quad \text{by Theorem 8.48, hence}$$
$$\|B\|^2 \geq (\sigma^2 + \boldsymbol{w}\boldsymbol{w}^T)^2/(\sigma^2 + \boldsymbol{w}\boldsymbol{w}^T) \,(\text{neglecting } \boldsymbol{w}B_1)$$
$$= \sigma^2 + \boldsymbol{w}\boldsymbol{w}^T.$$

But $\sigma^2 = \|A\|^2$ (by definition) $= \|UAV^T\|^2$ (by Theorem 8.46) $= \|B\|^2 \geq \sigma^2 + \boldsymbol{w}\boldsymbol{w}^T$ by the argument above. Hence $\boldsymbol{w}\boldsymbol{w}^T = 0$, implying $\boldsymbol{w} = 0$. Now we assume inductively that, B_1 being $(m-1) \times (n-1)$, there are orthogonal U_0, V_0 for which $U_0 B_1 V_0^T$ equals a generalised diagonal matrix D. Then B, and hence A, can be transformed to diagonal form, completing the induction, for

$$\begin{bmatrix} 1 & 0 \\ 0 & U_0 \end{bmatrix} \begin{bmatrix} \sigma & 0 \\ 0 & B_1 \end{bmatrix} \begin{bmatrix} 1 & 0 \\ 0 & V_0^T \end{bmatrix} = \begin{bmatrix} 1 & 0 \\ 0 & U_0 B_1 V_0^T \end{bmatrix} = \begin{bmatrix} 1 & 0 \\ 0 & D \end{bmatrix}. \tag{8.33}$$

First properties of the SVD

The s_i are called the *singular values* of A and are unique (though U, V are not – see later). To see this, and for later use, let $s_1, \ldots, s_r$ be the positive numbers amongst the s_i, that is

$$s_1 \geq \cdots \geq s_r > s_{r+1} = \cdots = s_p = 0. \tag{8.34}$$

From (8.32), denoting the diagonal matrix by D, we have the $m \times m$ matrix $AA^T = U^T DV \cdot V^T D^T U = U^T(DD^T)U$. Thus AA^T is diagonalised by U^T and so has eigenvalues the diagonal elements of $DD^T = \text{diag}(s_1^2, \ldots, s_r^2, 0, \ldots, 0)$. The nonzero s_i are the *positive square roots* of these eigenvalues, determined by A via AA^T, and hence are unique. Their number, r, is the common rank of A, AA^T, and $A^T A$ (Theorem 8.39).

The SVD gives an immediate result for the norm of an $m \times n$ matrix. Since our two versions of matrix norm are invariant under both orthogonal transformations in (8.32), we need only determine these norms for a diagonal matrix, writing $\|A\| = \|\text{diag}(s_1, \ldots, s_r)\|$. The work was done in Example 8.47; the result is Theorem 8.51 below.

Theorem 8.51 *For an arbitrary $m \times n$ matrix with nonzero singular values $s_1 \geq \cdots \geq s_r$, the norms are invariant under matrix transpose, and are given by*

$$
\boxed{
\begin{aligned}
&(a) \ \|A\|_R^2 = s_1 = \sqrt{(\text{greatest eigenvalue of } AA^T)}, \\
&(b) \ \|A\|_F^2 = \sqrt{(s_1^2 + \cdots + s_r^2)}.
\end{aligned}
} \tag{8.35}
$$

If A is symmetric the s_i^2 are the eigenvalues of $AA^T = A^2$, so A has eigenvalues $\pm s_i$ (by Remark 8.9). Thus

$$\boxed{\text{if } A \text{ has eigenvalues } \lambda_i \text{ then its singular values are } |\lambda_i|.}$$

Formula 8.35(a) is used for Iterated Function Systems in Fractal Compression, Section 16.1.3. Its advantage is that, though the eigenvalues of A may not be real, those of AA^T are.

But what is the SVD? For a concrete example let $A = U^T DV$ be 2×2 with $D = \text{diag}(3, 0.8)$. Consider the transformation $x \to xA$ in stages: $x \to xU^T \to xU^T D \to xU^T DV$, applied to the unit circle centred at the origin. The first stage rotates/ reflects the circle but leaves it intact, the second scales the minor and major axes by respectively 3 and 0.8, and the third rotates/reflects the result. This is depicted in Figure 8.5. More generally, the s_i are the lengths of the semi-axes of the hyperellipsoid $\{y = xA : |x| = 1\}$.

Theorem 8.52 *Let $A_{m \times n}$ have nonzero singular values $s_1 \geq \cdots \geq s_r$ and Singular Value Decomposition $A = U^T DV$. Then*

(a) $UA = DV = \text{Rows}(s_1 v_1, \ldots, s_r v_r, 0, \ldots 0)_{m \times n}$, *or* $u_i A = s_i v_i$ ($1 \leq i \leq m$),

(b) $R(A) = \text{span}\{v_1, \ldots, v_r\}$, *and* $N(A) = \text{span}\{u_{r+1}, \ldots, v_m\}$,

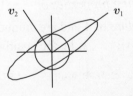

Figure 8.5 Circle and its image under $x \to xA$, where A has singular values 3.0, 0.8 and $V = \text{Rows}\{v_1, v_2\}$.

Proof For (a) we post-multiply both sides of (8.32) by the inverse V of V^T, then make a row-by-row restatement. For (b) we have, since $\{u_i\}_{1 \le i \le m}$ is an ONB,

$$R(A) = \{yA : y \in \mathbf{R}^m\} = \left\{ \left(\sum x_i u_i \right) A : x = (x_i) \in \mathbf{R}^m \right\},$$

$$= \left\{ \left(\sum x_i s_i v_i \right) A : x \in \mathbf{R}^m \right\}, \text{ by (b)}$$

$$= \text{span}\{v_1, \ldots, v_r\} \text{ since } s_i = 0 \text{ for } i > r.$$

$$N(A) = \left\{ \left(\sum x_i u_i \right) : x \in \mathbf{R}^m, \left(\sum x_i u_i \right) A = 0 \right\}$$

$$= \left\{ \left(\sum x_i u_i \right) : x \in \mathbf{R}^m, \sum x_i s_i v_i = 0 \right\}$$

$$= \left\{ \sum x_i u_i : x_1 = \cdots = x_r = 0 \right\} = \text{span}\{u_{r+1}, \ldots, u_m\}.$$

Exercise Why do the singular values of the matrix [1 3] consist of just $\sqrt{10}$?

8.4.3 Optimisation properties of the SVD

Theorem 8.53 *Let $A_{m \times n}$ have nonzero singular values $s_1 \ge \cdots \ge s_r$ and SV decomposition $A = U^T D V$. Let D_k be the result of setting $s_i = 0$ for $i > k$ in D, where $k \le r$. Then, in the usual notation (8.32), A is the sum of r matrices of rank 1,*

(a)
$$A = \sum_{i=1}^{r} s_i u_i^T v_i \quad (= U^T D V). \tag{8.36}$$

The projection A_k of A onto the first k columns of U^T has rank k and is given by

$$A_k = \sum_{i=1}^{k} s_i u_i^T v_i \quad (= U^T D k V). \tag{8.37}$$

(b) Amongst $m \times n$ matrices of rank k this, the sum of the first k matrices of (8.36), is closest possible to A in both norms. The actual distances are (see Figure 8.6)

$$\|A - A_k\|_R = s_{k+1} \text{ and } \|A - A_k\|_F = \sqrt{(s_{k+1}^2 + \cdots + s_r^2)}. \tag{8.38}$$

(c) $\|p(A)\|_F$ is maximised over projections p onto k-dimensional subspaces of m-space.

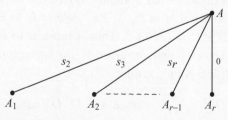

Figure 8.6 Distances in the R-norm between a matrix A of rank r and its SVD-derived approximations A_k of rank k (Theorem 5.53(b)). The singular values are $\{s_i\}$. For F-norm distances, replace s_{k+1} by $\sqrt{(s_{k+1}^2 + \cdots + s_r^2)}$.

Proof (a) Formula (8.36) is the block 'weighted inner product' (7.32a) applied to $U^{\mathrm{T}}DV$. The first k columns of U^{T} form a matrix $E^{\mathrm{T}} = U^{\mathrm{T}}[I_k|0]^{\mathrm{T}}$ so, by Theorem 7.59 for columns (Remark 7.61(2)), the projection of A onto them is $E^{\mathrm{T}}EA = U^{\mathrm{T}}[I_k|0]^{\mathrm{T}}[I_k|0]UU^{\mathrm{T}}DV = U^{\mathrm{T}}(I_k)_{m \times n}DV = U^{\mathrm{T}}D_kV$, since U is orthogonal. Block formula (7.32a) converts this to the required form in (8.37). Its rank, unchanged by U,V, equals $r(D_k)$, namely k.

(b) *Formula (8.38) and optimality in the R-norm* In either norm, $\|A - A_k\| = \|U^{\mathrm{T}}(A - A_k)V\| = \|D - D_k\| = \|\mathrm{diag}(s_{k+1}, \ldots, s_r)\|$, yielding the given expressions (8.38), as a consequence of (8.35). Now we must show that A_k is as close to A as possible for an $m \times n$ matrix of rank k. Suppose $B_{m \times n}$ has rank k and let $\{x_1, \ldots, x_{m-k}\}$ be an ONB for the null space $N(B)$ (see Theorem 8.23(c)). Considering dimensions (Remark 7.13(2)), there must be a nonzero vector and hence a unit vector z, common to $\mathrm{span}\{x_1, \ldots, x_{m-k}\}$ and $\mathrm{span}\{u_1, \ldots, u_{k+1}\}$, since they total $m + 1$ vectors in m-space. This enables us to argue that

$$zA = z\sum_{i=1}^{r} s_i u_i^{\mathrm{T}}v_i = \sum_{i=1}^{k+1} s_i z u_i^{\mathrm{T}}v_i \quad \text{since} \quad z u_i^{\mathrm{T}} = 0 \quad \text{for} \quad i > k + 1,$$

and hence

$$
\begin{aligned}
\|A - B\|^2 &\geq \|z(A - B)\|^2 && \text{since } |z| = 1 \text{ (see Theorem 8.48)}\\
&= \|zA\|^2 && \text{since } zB = 0\\
&= \textstyle\sum_{i=1}^{k+1} s_i^2 (z u_i^{\mathrm{T}})^2, && \text{since } z u_i^{\mathrm{T}} \text{ is a scalar and } \{v_i\} \text{ is orthonormal}\\
&\geq s_{k+1}^2 \text{ (see below)}
\end{aligned}
$$

since z is in $\mathrm{span}\{u_1, \ldots, u_{k+1}\}$, and $z u_i^{\mathrm{T}}$ is the component of z with respect to u_i, implying $\sum_{i=1}^{k+1}(z u_i^{\mathrm{T}})^2 = |z|^2 = 1$; the argument is that $s_1 \geq s_2 \geq \cdots \geq s_{k+1}$, so the sum $\sum_{i=1}^{k+1} s_i^2 (z u_i^{\mathrm{T}})^2$ is least when $(z u_i^{\mathrm{T}})^2 = 0$ except for $(z u_{k+1})^2 = 1$.

(b) *Optimality in the F-norm, and* (c) Let $M_{m \times k}$ be given, with k independent columns. We consider approximations to A of the form $Z = M_{m \times k}C_{k \times n}$, as C varies. Then MC runs through all $m \times n$ matrices with at most k independent columns, because the columns of MC are linear combinations of those of M (see (7.30)). By Theorem 8.49, the best approximation satisfies $C = (M^{\mathrm{T}}M)^{-1}M^{\mathrm{T}}A$. Thus $Z = M(M^{\mathrm{T}}M)^{-1}M^{\mathrm{T}}A$. We show this is a projection onto the column space of M.

By Theorem 8.18(c) in column form there is an invertible matrix P such that $MP = E$, a matrix with orthonormal columns. By Remarks 7.61 the matrix of projection onto the column space of M is $P_M = EE^{\mathrm{T}}$, where $I_k = E^{\mathrm{T}}E = P^{\mathrm{T}}M^{\mathrm{T}}MP$, and therefore $M^{\mathrm{T}}M = (P^{\mathrm{T}})^{-1}P^{-1} = (PP^{\mathrm{T}})^{-1}$. Thus A projects to $EE^{\mathrm{T}}A = MPP^{\mathrm{T}}M^{\mathrm{T}}A = M(M^{\mathrm{T}}M)^{-1}M^{\mathrm{T}}A = Z$, showing that, *for given M, the best approximation is the projection $A \to P_M A$ onto $CS(M)$*. Now consider

$$
\begin{aligned}
\|P_M A\|^2 &= \|P_M U^{\mathrm{T}}D\|^2 && \text{since } A = U^{\mathrm{T}}DV \text{ and } V \text{ is orthogonal}\\
&= \textstyle\sum_{i=1}^{n} \|P_M(s_i u_i^{\mathrm{T}})\|^2 && \text{by Theorem 8.44, since } U^{\mathrm{T}}D = \mathrm{Cols}(s_i u_i^{\mathrm{T}})\\
&= \textstyle\sum_{i=1}^{n} s_i^2 p_i^2 \text{ (see below)}, && (8.39)
\end{aligned}
$$

where $p_i \leq 1$ is the length of projection of a unit vector $\boldsymbol{u}_i$, and so

$$\sum_{i=1}^{n} p_i^2 = \sum_i \left| P_M \boldsymbol{u}_i^{\mathrm{T}} \right|^2 = \| P_M U^{\mathrm{T}} \|^2 = \| P_M \|^2 = k \text{ (Example 8.47).}$$

Since $s_1 \geq s_2 \geq \cdots$, the greatest value of (8.39) occurs when the first k s_is are 1 and the rest zero, therefore

$$\| P_M A \|^2 \leq s_1^2 + \cdots + s_k^2. \tag{8.40}$$

Now let M be chosen so as to minimise $\| A - P_M A \|^2$. Then

$$
\begin{aligned}
s_{k+1}^2 + \cdots + s_n^2 &= \| A - A_k \|^2 && \text{by (8.38)} \\
&\geq \| A - P_M A \|^2 && \text{by optimality of } M \\
&= \| A \|^2 - \| P_M A \|^2 && \text{(see below)} \\
&\geq s_{k+1}^2 + \cdots + s_n^2 && \text{by (8.40),}
\end{aligned}
$$

the last *equality* holding because P_M projects vectors orthogonally and the F-norm is used. Since the first and last lines are equal in the chain of equality/inequality, all terms are equal, implying that A_k is closest possible to A and that $\| P_M A \|^2$ is maximised by this choice. This completes the proof of Theorem 8.53.

Example 8.54 Below is shown the SV decomposition $A = U^{\mathrm{T}} D V$ of a rank 3 matrix A with singular values $s_1, s_2, s_3 = 5, 3, 1$. Determine the best approximations of ranks 1 and 2. Verify the predicted error in the Frobenius norm for A_1.

$$
A = \frac{1}{21} \begin{bmatrix} 12 & -48 & -15 \\ 80 & -47 & -16 \\ -13 & -32 & -52 \end{bmatrix} = \frac{1}{7} \begin{bmatrix} 3 & -2 & -6 \\ 6 & 3 & 2 \\ 2 & -6 & 3 \end{bmatrix} \begin{bmatrix} 5 & & \\ & 3 & \\ & & 1 \end{bmatrix} \begin{bmatrix} 2 & -2 & -1 \\ 2 & 1 & 2 \\ 1 & 2 & -2 \end{bmatrix} \frac{1}{3}.
$$

Solution We first write down the terms of the 'Russian Sum' $\sum s_i \boldsymbol{u}_i^{\mathrm{T}} \boldsymbol{v}_i$ of (8.36):

$$
A = \frac{5}{21} \cdot \begin{bmatrix} 3 \\ 6 \\ 2 \end{bmatrix} \begin{bmatrix} 2 & -2 & -1 \end{bmatrix} + \frac{3}{21} \cdot \begin{bmatrix} -2 \\ 3 \\ -6 \end{bmatrix} \begin{bmatrix} 2 & 1 & 2 \end{bmatrix} + \frac{1}{21} \cdot \begin{bmatrix} -6 \\ 2 \\ 3 \end{bmatrix} \begin{bmatrix} 1 & 2 & -2 \end{bmatrix}
$$

$$
= \frac{5}{21} \cdot \begin{bmatrix} 6 & -6 & -3 \\ 12 & -12 & -6 \\ 4 & -4 & -2 \end{bmatrix} + \frac{3}{21} \cdot \begin{bmatrix} -4 & -2 & -4 \\ 6 & 3 & 6 \\ -12 & -6 & -12 \end{bmatrix} + \frac{1}{21} \cdot \begin{bmatrix} -6 & -12 & 12 \\ 2 & 4 & -4 \\ 3 & 6 & -6 \end{bmatrix}.
$$

Hence, by (8.37), $A_1 = \dfrac{5}{21} \cdot \begin{bmatrix} 6 & -6 & -3 \\ 12 & -12 & -6 \\ 4 & -4 & -2 \end{bmatrix}$ and $A_2 = \dfrac{1}{21} \cdot \begin{bmatrix} 18 & -36 & -27 \\ 78 & -51 & -12 \\ -16 & -38 & -46 \end{bmatrix}$.

Check: Predicted $\|A - A_1\|^2 = s_2^2 + s_3^2 = 9 + 1 = 10.$ But $A - A_1 = \dfrac{1}{21} \cdot$

$\begin{bmatrix} -18 & -18 & 0 \\ 20 & 13 & 14 \\ -33 & -12 & -42 \end{bmatrix}$,   so $\|A - A_1\|^2 = (18^2 + 18^2 + 20^2 + 13^2 + 14^2 + 33^2 + 12^2 + 42^2)/21^2 = 10$, which agrees.

Exercise Find the best rank 1 approximation to Rows([1 2], [2 1]).

Remark 8.55 (*Duality*) The projection (8.37) A_k of A onto the first k columns of U^T is identical to the projection of A onto the first k rows of V.

Proof The SVD for A transposes to $A^T = V^T D^T U$, an SVD for A^T, so (Theorem 8.53) the projection B_k of A^T onto the first k *columns* of V^T is given by

$$B_k = \sum_{i=1}^{k} s_i v_i^T u_i. \tag{8.41}$$

Hence the projection of A onto the first k rows of V is $B_k^T = \Sigma s_i u_i^T v_i$ by (8.41) $= A_k$ by (8.37).

Remark 8.56 (*Choices in the SVD*) We recall that an orthogonal matrix P is a rotation if $|P| = 1$, otherwise $|P| = -1$ (Theorem 8.10). Now, a row operation on U has the effect of performing the same operation on D (Example 8.21(ii)). Hence, if the last k rows of D are zero we can change the sign of any of the last k rows of U without affecting D (more generally we could replace the last k rows of U by an ONB for their span). Thus U with $|U| = -1$ can be converted into a rotation matrix if desired by changing the sign of a single row of U (hence the sign of $|U|$). Similarly for the last k columns of D and of V^T.

In all cases we can change the signs of $|U|$ and $|V|$ simultaneously by changing the sign of, say, the first row of U and the first row of V, for, as in diagonalisation (Example 8.32), the net effect on the diagonal matrix D is no change.

Remarks 8.57 (1) (*The Moore–Penrose pseudoinverse*) The matrix equation $MX = Y$ has unique solution $X = M^{-1}Y$ provided M^{-1} exists. If not, then Theorem 8.49 shows that the closest we can get to a solution is, by minimising $\|Y - MX\|$,

$$X = M^+ Y, \text{ with } M^+ = (M^T M)^{-1} M^T,$$

where M^+ is the *Moore–Penrose pseudoinverse* of M, and exists provided the columns of M are independent, so that $M^T M$ is invertible. (Exercise 8.28 derives M^+ from the SVD.)

(2) In the complex case, the result above holds with transpose 'T' replaced by conjugate transpose '$*$' (we appeal to this in Chapter 15, Theorem 15.24). This is easily deduced from the real case via the correspondence

$$\rho = A + iB \leftrightarrow \begin{bmatrix} A & B \\ -B & A \end{bmatrix} = R$$

between complex matrices, and real ones of twice the dimensions; for if also $\sigma \leftrightarrow S$ then the following properties hold (see Exercise 8.27):

(a) $\rho\sigma \leftrightarrow RS$ (if $\rho\sigma$ exists), (b) $I_n \leftrightarrow I_{2n}$, (c) $\rho^* \leftrightarrow R^{\mathrm{T}}$, and (d) $\|\rho\|^2 = (1/2)\|R\|^2$.

> The pseudoinverse of M is $M^+ = (M^{\mathrm{T}}M)^{-1}M^{\mathrm{T}}$.
> The best solution of $Y = MX$ is $X = M^+Y$.

(3) Sometimes it is useful to have an explicit expression for a vector of derivatives $\partial f/\partial y = [\partial f/\partial y_i]$. The following gives an alternative approach to Theorem 8.49; a generalisation is used in the Wiener filter of Section 15.3.4.

$$\text{(a) } \partial/\partial y(a \cdot y) = a, \text{ (b) } \partial/\partial y \, \|By\|^2 = 2B^{\mathrm{T}}By \text{ (Frobenius norm).}$$

Proof (a) $\partial/\partial y_i(a_1y_1 + \cdots + a_ny_n) = a_i$, and $[a_i] = a$.

$$\begin{aligned}
\text{(b) } \partial/\partial y_p \|By\|^2 &= \partial/\partial y_p \mathrm{Tr}[(By)(By)^{\mathrm{T}}](\text{put A} = By \text{ in Theorem 8.44}) \\
&= \partial/\partial y_p \sum_i (\sum_r b_{ir}y_r)^2 = \sum_i 2(\sum_r b_{ir}y_r)b_{ip} \\
&= 2\sum_{i,r} b_{pi}^{\mathrm{T}}b_{ir}y_r \\
&= 2(B^{\mathrm{T}}By)_p, \text{ as required.}
\end{aligned}$$

(4) We record the product rule for differentiating matrices, and some consequences. Let $\dot{B}$ denote $\partial B/\partial t = [\partial b_{ij}/\partial t]$. Then for matrices A (symmetric, constant), P, Q and row vectors x, y,

$$\text{(a) } \partial/\partial t \, PQ = \dot{P}Q + P\dot{Q}, \text{ (b)} \partial/\partial t \, xAy^{\mathrm{T}} = \dot{x}Ay^{\mathrm{T}} + xA\dot{y}^{\mathrm{T}}, \text{(c)} \partial/\partial x \, xAx^{\mathrm{T}} = 2xA.$$

Proof (a) is an exercise, (b) follows. For (c) $\partial/\partial t \, xAx^{\mathrm{T}} = \dot{x}Ax^{\mathrm{T}} + xA\dot{x}^{\mathrm{T}} = 2xA\dot{x}^{\mathrm{T}}$, and hence $\partial/\partial x \, xAx^{\mathrm{T}} = [\partial/\partial x_i x Ax^{\mathrm{T}}] = 2xA[\delta_{ki}] = 2xAI = 2xA$.

(5) The Frobenius norm may be obtained from an *inner product* of matrices

$$\langle A, B \rangle = \mathrm{Tr}(AB^{\mathrm{T}}) = \sum_{ij} a_{ij}b_{ij}$$

in the form $\|A\|_{\mathrm{F}}^2 = \langle A, A \rangle$, because $\langle A, B \rangle$ is the usual dot product when the rows are concatenated into vectors of length mn. This fits with Theorem 8.44(ii).

Exercise Verify that $\|A\|_{\mathrm{F}}^2 = \langle A, A \rangle$ for the matrix Rows$[(1, -1, 2), (2, 3, 0)]$.

Exercises 8

1√ Plot the complex number $\alpha = (1 + i)/\sqrt{2}$ and hence state its modulus and argument. Now plot the distinct powers $\alpha, \alpha^2, \ldots$, and express them in the standard form $a + ib$.

2√ (i) Find the modulus of the complex vector $(1 - 2i, 3 + i, -2 + 5i)$. (ii) Let $w = e^{2\pi i/N}$, where $N = 2M$ is even. Show $w^N = 1$ and $w^M = -1$. Deduce that $1 + w + w^2 + \cdots + w^{N-1} = 0$ and verify this for Exercise 8.1.

3√ Show that one of A, B below is a rotation matrix. Find a rotation axis and corresponding angle. Check the axis by an eigenvector method. Verify the angle by choosing a simple vector u perpendicular to the axis and calculating the cosine of the angle between u and its rotated image.

$$A = \frac{1}{9} \begin{bmatrix} 4 & -1 & 8 \\ -7 & 4 & 4 \\ 4 & 8 & -1 \end{bmatrix}, \ B = \frac{1}{7} \begin{bmatrix} -2 & 3 & -6 \\ -6 & 2 & 3 \\ 3 & 6 & 2 \end{bmatrix}.$$

4√ (i) Show that if x is an eigenvector of matrix M with eigenvalue λ then x is also an eigen-value of M^{-1}, with eigenvector λ^{-1}. Verify this for $M = \text{Rows}((2, -1), (1, 4))$. (ii) Let $w_1, \ldots, w_t$ be independent eigenvectors of AA^{T} with nonzero eigenvalues λ_i. Prove that $\{w_i A\}$ are independent.

5√ Why is $z = x + iy$ purely imaginary if and only if $z + \bar{z} = 0$? (i) Show that an eigenvalue λ of a skew matrix S is a pure imaginary number ic (c real) (Hint: set $A^{\mathrm{T}} = -A$ instead of $A^{\mathrm{T}} = A$ in the proof of Theorem 8.29(b), to obtain $\lambda + \bar{\lambda} = 0$). (ii) Deduce that if S is skew then $I + S$ is necessarily invertible.

6√ Use Formula (8.6) to find the matrix for a $1/3$ turn about the axis $(1, 1, 1)$. Compute the result of this followed by a $1/4$ turn about the z-axis.

7√ Find the result of reflection in the plane Π: $x = z$, followed by reflection in the plane Σ: $x + 2y + z = 0$.

8√ (i) Show that matrix A or matrix B of Exercise 8.3 is rotary reflection but not pure reflection, (ii) if this isometry is preceded by reflection in the plane $x = 0$, what is the resulting isometry?

9√ Show that if $M = I - 2n^{\mathrm{T}}n$, a reflection matrix, then $M^2 = I$ (Hint: $nn^{\mathrm{T}} = n \cdot n$).

10√ Perform elementary row operations to convert the matrix $A = \text{Rows}[(1, 2, 3, 4), (5, 6, 7, 8), (9, 10, 11, 12)]$ to echelon form E, hence find a matrix P such that $PA = E$. Check your answer. What are the rank and range of A?

11√ Use elementary COLUMN operations to reduce the matrix $B = \text{Rows}((1, 2, 3, 4), (5, 6, 7, 8))$ to a number of columns equal to its rank. What column operation matrix Q achieves the same effect?

12√ Determine by inspection the rank and nullity of each matrix below.

$$(\text{i}) \begin{bmatrix} 2 & 4 \\ 7 & 14 \\ 6 & 12 \end{bmatrix}, (\text{ii}) \begin{bmatrix} 1 & 2 & 3 \\ 2 & 4 & 6 \\ 5 & 6 & 7 \end{bmatrix}, (\text{iii}) \begin{bmatrix} 1 & 5 & 5 \\ 0 & 2 & 7 \\ 0 & 0 & 3 \end{bmatrix}, (\text{iv}) \begin{bmatrix} 1 \\ 4 \\ 6 \end{bmatrix} \begin{bmatrix} 5 & 6 & 8 \end{bmatrix}.$$

13√ What is the dimension of the space V of vectors in 4-space that are perpendicular to all of the following: $(1, -1, 0, 7)$, $(2, -4, 3, 0)$, $(3, -5, 3, 7)$ (see Corollary 8.24). Find a basis for this space.

14√ Use row operations to invert $A = \text{Rows}((1, 4, 3), (0, 1, 5), (0, 0, 1))$ and $B = \text{Rows}((1, a, b), (0, 1, c), (0, 0, 1))$. Do your answers agree? Why is the inverse of an upper triangular matrix upper triangular? Why is the diagonal type (positive/unit) preserved under inversion?

15√ Show that eigenvectors x, y corresponding to distinct eigenvectors λ, μ of a symmetric matrix A are orthogonal (Hint: $x(Ay^{\mathrm{T}}) = (xA)y^{\mathrm{T}}$).

16.✓ Determine the eigenvalues of the matrix A below and hence find an orthogonal matrix P which diagonalises A. Check your answer (see below Example 8.32).

$$A = \begin{bmatrix} 5 & 2 & 4 \\ 2 & 8 & -2 \\ 4 & -2 & 5 \end{bmatrix}.$$

17.✓ Express as a sum of squares the quadratic function $q(x)$ below. Write down its matrix Q and rank r. Use your conversion to sum of squares to find an invertible matrix P such that PQP^T is diagonal. Must the diagonal elements be the eigenvalues of Q (see Theorem 8.29)?

$$q(x) = x_1^2 + 2x_2^2 + 13x_3^2 - 2x_2x_3 - 2x_1x_2 - 4x_1x_3.$$

18.✓ What type is the form $q(x)$ of Exercise 8.17? Verify this by computing the eigenvalues of Q.

19.✓ Determine whether the form below gives a maximum or minimum at the origin, without completing squares or computing eigenvalues from a fourth degree polynomial equation:

$$q(x) = x_1^2 + 5x_2^2 + 3x_3^2 + 5x_4^2 + 4x_1x_2 + 2x_1x_3 + 4x_2x_3 + 4x_2x_4.$$

20.✓ Let $A = \text{Rows}[(1, 0, 3, 2), (2, 3, 0, 1)]$. Find eigenvalues and vectors for the 4×4 matrix A^TA by finding them first for the 2×2 matrix AA^T (Theorem 8.39). Check your answers on A^TA.

21.✓ Let $S = \text{Rows}[(1, 2, 1), (2, 5, 4), (1, 4, 7)]$. Verify that S is positive definite and find its Choleski factorization by ALGO 8.3. This may be done by hand or by computer.

22.✓ Let $x = (1, 2, -1)$, $A = \text{Rows}[(1, -1, 2), (2, 3, 4), 0, 1, 2)]$, and $B = \text{Rows}[(1, 1, 0), (0, 1, 1), (1, 0, 1)]$. By computing the various quantities, verify that $|xA| \leq |x|\|A\|$ and $\|AB\| \leq \|A\|\|B\|$, in the F-norm.

23.✓ Calculate the R-norms (ratio norms) of the matrices $A = \text{Rows}[(1, 2), (2, 1)]$ and $B = \text{Rows}[(1, 2), (3, 1)]$. Obtain a formula for the R-norm of an arbitrary 2×2 matrix A in terms of $\|A\|_F$ and $\text{Det}(A)$.

24.✓ What is wrong with the following system of equations: $x + 2y = 5$, $3x + 4y = 11$, $x + y = 4$? Find the best compromise solution (Remarks 8.57).

25.✓ Express the matrix A, with its given Singular Value Decomposition, as a 'Russian' sum of matrices of rank 1, and write down its best approximation A_1 of rank 1.

$$\frac{1}{6} \begin{bmatrix} 7 & -5 & 7 & -5 \\ 5 & -1 & 5 & -1 \\ -4 & 8 & -4 & 8 \end{bmatrix} = \frac{1}{3} \begin{bmatrix} 1 & 2 & 2 \\ 2 & 1 & -2 \\ 2 & -2 & 1 \end{bmatrix} \begin{bmatrix} 1 & 0 & 0 & 0 \\ 0 & 3 & 0 & 0 \\ 0 & 0 & 0 & 0 \end{bmatrix} \frac{1}{2} \begin{bmatrix} 1 & 1 & 1 & 1 \\ 1 & -1 & 1 & -1 \\ 1 & -1 & -1 & 1 \\ -1 & -1 & 1 & 1 \end{bmatrix}.$$

26.✓ Find the singular values, an SVD, and the best rank 1 approximation of the symmetric matrix $(1/9)\text{Rows}[(-7, 10, -2), (10, -4, 8), (-2, 8, 2)]$.

27.✓ Show that, if $f(A + iB) = \text{Rows}[(A, B), (-B, A)]$ in block matrix form, then $f(\rho\sigma) = f(\rho)f(\sigma)$, $f(I_n) = I_{2n}$, $f(\rho^*) = f(\rho)^T$, and $\|\rho\|_F^2 = (1/2)\|f(\rho)\|_F^2$.

28.✓ Use the SVD to derive the pseudoinverse without differentiating.

Part III

Here's to probability

9

Probability

In this chapter we recapitulate the beginnings of probability theory. The reader to whom this subject is completely new may wish first to consult a more leisurely introduction, such as McColl (1997).

9.1 Sample spaces

There are different schools on the meaning of probability. For example, it is argued that a statement such as 'The Scottish National Party has a probability of 1/5 of winning the election' is meaningless because the experiment 'have an election' cannot be repeated to order. The way out has proved to be an axiomatic approach, originated by Kolmogorov (see Figure 9.1) in 1933, in which all participants, though begging to differ on some matters of interpretation, can nevertheless agree on the consequences of the rules (see e.g. Kolmogorov, 1956b). His work included a rigorous definition of conditional expectation, a crucial and fruitful concept in current work in many areas and applications of probability.

Figure 9.1 A. N. Kolmogorov, 1903–1987, sketch by Ward Somerville.

9.1.1 Sample spaces and events

Model 9.1 We begin with the idea that, corresponding to an *experiment E*, there is a set S, the *sample space*, consisting of all possible outcomes. In the present context an *event A* is a set of outcomes, that is $A \subseteq S$. Then it is a matter of definition that, if E is performed with outcome *a, the event A occurs* if and only if $a \in A$.

Often, but not always, the outcomes are conveniently represented by numbers, as illustrated in examples below.

Examples 9.2

(i) E: Toss a coin twice,

   $S = \{HH, HT, TH, TT\}$, where H signifies the outcome *Heads* and T is *Tails*,

   $A = \{$Both tosses have the same result$\} = \{HH, TT\}$.

(ii) E: Throw a die,

   $S = \{1, 2, 3, 4, 5, 6\}$,

   $A = \{$Even throw$\} = \{2, 4, 6\}$.

(iii) E: A sequence of letters from the English alphabet $\mathcal{A} = \{a, \ldots, z\}$ is transmitted, and the first three are recorded,

   $S = \{x_1 x_2 x_3$: each x_i is in $\mathcal{A}\}$,

   $A = \{$Letter b appears exactly twice$\} = \{bbx, bxb, xbb$: x is in $\mathcal{A}\backslash\{b\}\}$.

(iv) E: $\{$Record the lifetime of a memory chip$\}$,

   $S = \{x \in \mathbf{R}: x \geq 0\}$,

   $A = \{$Lifetime is between 5 and 10 units$\} = \{x$: $5 \leq x \leq 10\} = [5, 10]$.

Thus, in (iii) above, if E is performed with outcome abc the event A does not occur, but it does, should the outcome be bbc. Notice that sample spaces and events may be specified in a variety of ways. Also, whilst it may be convenient to model the sample space by a continuous range of real numbers, the times will be recorded in practice up to some minimum unit of measurement, so not all real numbers in such an interval are attained in practice. A set such as S, of which every set to be considered is a subset, is called a *universal set*. Some standard notation and rules for subsets are given in Table 9.1.

New events from old Here are some nice consequences of the definition of an event as a subset of S. If E is performed with outcome a, then the 'universal event' S necesarily occurs, because $a \in S$, but the empty event ø does not, since by definition $a \notin$ ø. Further, if A and B are events then so are their complements, union and intersection, and

   event A^c occurs $\Leftrightarrow$ A does not,
   event $A \cup B$ occurs $\Leftrightarrow$ A, B or both occur,
   event $A \cap B$ occurs $\Leftrightarrow$ both A and B occur.

For illustration take Example 9.2(iv) and let B be the event: lifetime is between 8 and 17 units, in symbols the interval $[8, 17]$. Then $A \cup B = [5, 10] \cup [8, 17] = [5, 17]$, a lifetime between 5 and 17 units. On the other hand, if two events A, B are disjoint ($A \cap B = $ ø) then they cannot occur together, and so are also called *mutually exclusive*. However, we shall normally use the shorter term *disjoint*.

Table 9.1. *Rules for operations on subsets A, B, C of a set X (the 'universal set').*

DEFINITIONS $x \in A$ means 'x is a member of A', $A \subseteq B$ means 'A is a subset of B'. See Figure 9.2.

$A \cup B = \{x \in X: x \in A \text{ or } x \in B \text{ (or both)}\}$,   the *union* of A and B,

$A \cap B = \{x \in X: x \in A \text{ and } x \in B\}$,   the *intersection* of A and B,

$A\backslash B = \{x \in A: x \notin B\}$,   the *complement* of B in A, also written $A - B$,

$A^c = X\backslash A = \{x \in X: x \notin A\}$,   the *complement* of A.

A, B are called *disjoint* or *non-overlapping* if $A \cap B = \emptyset$, the empty set.
A is a *proper* subset of B if $A \subseteq B$ and A is neither empty nor the whole of B.
A is a *superset* of B if $A \supseteq B$.

BASIC RULES

(a) $A \cup B = B \cup A$, $A \cap B = B \cap A$ (symmetry laws)
(b) $(A \cup B) \cup C = A \cup (B \cup C)$, $(A \cap B) \cap C = A \cap (B \cap C)$ (associative laws)
(c) $A \cap (B \cup C) = (A \cap B) \cup (A \cap C)$, $A \cup (B \cap C) = (A \cup B) \cap (A \cup C)$ (distributive laws)

(d)   *De Morgan's laws* $(A \cup B)^c = A^c \cap B^c$,
                               $(A \cap B)^c = A^c \cup B^c$.

SOME OBVIOUS LAWS

$A \cup \emptyset = A$, $A \cap X = A$, $(A^c)^c = A$,
$A \cap \emptyset = \emptyset$. $A \cup X = X$, $A \cup A = A = A \cap A$.

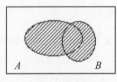   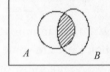

$A \cup B$ shaded $A \cap B$ shaded A^c shaded

Figure 9.2 Basic set operations: union, intersection and complement.

But is every subset an event? The answer is YES if S is finite or countably infinite (see e.g. Hoggar, 1992). Otherwise some sets cannot be considered as events, for technical reasons beyond the scope of our discussion. This will not affect the present text, and it suffices in all cases to rule that the complement of an event is an event, as is every finite or countable union or intersection of events.

Exercise Use one of De Morgan's Laws (see Table 9.1) to express $A \cap B \cap C$ as a the complement of a union.

9.1.2 First rules of probability

We include here the agreed axioms which ensure consistency, and some simple but important consequences. Historically, the motivation for these axioms is as follows. If an event A occurs n_A times in N trials of an experiment, its *relative frequency* is defined to be

$$f_A = \frac{n_A}{N}, \tag{9.1}$$

representing intuitively the likelihood, or probability, of event A occurring. Hence we look at the rules governing frequency to suggest suitable probability axioms. For example, $f_S = N/N = 1$, and more generally $0 \le f_A \le 1$. Further, for *disjoint* events $A,\ B$

$$f_{A \cup B} = \frac{n_{A \cup B}}{N} = \frac{n_A + n_B}{N} = \frac{n_A}{N} + \frac{n_B}{N} = f_A + f_B. \tag{9.2}$$

Definition 9.3 A *probability function* (on the sample space S) is a function P which associates with each event A a real number $P(A)$, called the *probability of A*, and satisfying the following axioms:

P1: $0 \le P(A) \le 1$,
P2: $P(S) = 1$,
P3: If events $A,\ B$ are disjoint then $P(A \cup B) = P(A) + P(B)$,
P4: If $A_1, A_2, \ldots$ are pairwise disjoint events then $P(A_1 \cup A_2 \cup \ldots) = P(A_1) + P(A_2) + \cdots$.

A sample space S endowed with the function P is called a *probability space*, though we shall not normally emphasise the distinction. Notice that, by applying P3 repeatedly, we may obtain for pairwise disjoint events $A_1, \ldots, A_n$ the result

$$P\left(\bigcup_{i=1}^{n} A_i\right) = \sum_{i=1}^{n} P(A_i) \tag{9.3}$$

for every finite n. This does not imply P4, the infinite case, which may be written as (9.3) with n replaced by the infinity symbol. Here are some first consequences of the axioms, tailored to calculating probabilities we do not know on the basis of those we do.

Rule 9.4 (*Complements*) Any event A satisfies $P(A^c) = 1 - P(A)$.

Rule 9.5 (*Subsets*) (i) $P(\emptyset) = 0$, (ii) if $A \subseteq B$ then $P(A) \le P(B)$.

Rule 9.6 (*Unions*) If $A,\ B$ are any events, $P(A \cup B) = P(A) + P(B) - P(A \cap B)$.

Proof In Rule 9.4 the union of disjoint sets A and A^c is S so by Axiom P3 we have $P(A) + P(A^c) = P(S)$, which equals 1 by Axiom P2. Rearranging terms gives the rule. For Rule 9.5(i) we have by definition $\emptyset = S^c$, so Rule 9.4 gives $P(\emptyset) = 1 - P(S) = 1 - 1 = 0$. For (ii), decompose B into disjoint events $A, B \backslash A$. Then $P(A) \le P(A) + P(B \backslash A)$, which equals $P(B)$ by Axiom P3. To establish Rule 9.6 we decompose $A \cup B$ into the union of three disjoint sets as shown in Figure 9.3, namely $X = A \backslash B, Y = A \cap B, Z = B \backslash A$. The following argument yields the result.

$$
\begin{aligned}
P(A \cup B) &= P(X) + P(Y) + P(Z) &&\text{by (9.3) or P3} \\
&= [P(X) + P(Y)] + [P(Y) + P(Z)] - P(Y) &&\text{on rearranging} \\
&= P(A) + P(B) - P(A \cap B) &&\text{by P3}
\end{aligned}
$$

Figure 9.3 Decomposing $A \cup B$ into disjoint sets X, Y, Z.

This result generalises to three sets by writing $A \cup B \cup C = (A \cup B) \cup C$, applying Rule 9.6 twice, and using the Set Theory Laws of Table 9.1. (A formula for n sets exists but will not be displayed here.) We obtain

$$P(A \cup B \cup C)$$
$$= P(A) + P(B) + P(C) - P(A \cap B) - P(B \cap C) - P(C \cap A) + P(A \cap B \cap C).$$
$$(9.4)$$

Example 9.7 Suppose that events A, B, C each have probability 1/4, that neither A, B nor A, C can occur together, and that $P(B \cap C) = 1/8$. Determine the probability that at least one of A, B, C occurs.

Solution We require $P(A \cup B \cup C)$ and so wish to use formula (9.4). Since A, B cannot occur together we have $A \cap B = \emptyset$, $P(A \cap B) = 0$, and similarly for A, C. The probability of $A \cap B \cap C$ seems to be missing, but the rules come to our aid: $A \cap B \cap C$ is a subset of $A \cap B$, so is also empty, with zero probability (by Rule 9.5). We are ready to calculate:

$$P(A \cup B \cup C) = 1/4 + 1/4 + 1/4 - 0 - 0 - 1/8 + 0 = 5/8.$$

Exercise Derive Equation (9.4) from Rule 9.6.

9.1.3 Finite sample spaces

For a finite sample space $S = \{a_1, a_2, \ldots, a_n\}$, Axiom P4 is redundant, and any probability function assigns to each outcome a_i a probability p_i in such a way that, corresponding to respective Axioms P1 to P3 there hold:

F1: $0 \le p_i \le 1$,
F2: $p_1 + p_2 + \cdots + p_n = 1$,
F3: An event A has probability $P(A) = \sum p_i \ (a_i \in A)$.

Before proceeding to the first major application of finiteness in the next section, we exemplify the use of Rules 9.4 to 9.6.

Example 9.8 Three companies denoted by H, I, M compete to get their new computer model to the market. Assuming H is twice as likely to win as I, which is twice as likely to win as M, determine (i) their respective probabilites of being first, (ii) the probability that I is not first.

Solution (i) Let X be the event: company X is first, and let $P(M) = p$. Since I is twice as likely as M to win, $P(I) = 2p$. Similarly $P(H) = 4p$. But by F2 the sum of the probabilities is 1, and so $p + 2p + 4p = 1$, or $p = 1/7$. Thus $P(M) = 1/7$, $P(I) = 2/7$, $P(H) = 4/7$. Finally, (ii), by the Complement Rule 9.4 the probability that I does not win is $1 - P(I) = 5/7$.

Exercise What is the probability that H is not first, in Example 9.8?

9.1.4 Finite equiprobable spaces

Frequently we wish to assume all outcomes in a finite sample space S are equally likely. That is, we may assign equal probability p to each outcome. S is then said to be *equiprobable*. In the notation of the previous section we have $1 = p_1 + p_2 + \cdots + p_n = np$, whence $p = 1/n$, and if $|A| = r$ then $P(A) = \sum p_i \, (a_i \in A) = r/n$, or

$$P(A) = \frac{|A|}{|S|} = \frac{\text{number of elements in } A}{\text{number of elements in } S}. \tag{9.5}$$

Example 9.9 (*Traditional*) Suppose a playing card is chosen at random from a standard deck of 52 cards. Define the events A: the card is a spade, B: the card is a Jack, King or Queen (the face cards). Determine the probabilities of A, B, $A \cap B$, $A \cup B$.

Solution The phrase *at random* in this context means that we may assume all cards are equally likely. Then according to (9.5) and, for the last part, Rule 9.6,

$$P(A) = \frac{\text{number of spades}}{\text{number of cards}} = \frac{13}{52} = \frac{1}{4}, \quad \text{whilst } P(B) = \frac{|B|}{|S|} = \frac{12}{52} = \frac{3}{13}.$$

$P(A \cap B) = (\text{number of face spade cards})/(\text{number of cards}) = 3/52.$

$P(A \cup B) = P(A) + P(B) - P(A \cap B) = 1/4 + 3/13 - 3/52 = 11/26.$

Methods of counting We review some techiques that will be extremely useful for equiprobable spaces. The key is the *Multiplication Principle* (MP): suppose an operation is performed in r steps, or stages, and that there are n_i ways to perform stage i, independently of what went before. Then

$$\text{number of ways to complete the operation} = n_1 \times n_2 \times \cdots \times n_r. \tag{9.6}$$

The operation with its choice may be thought of as working through a decision tree, as indicated in Figure 9.4 with $r = 2$. These are especially useful for keeping track of the structure in complicated cases.

Example 9.10 (i) How many 3-letter words can be formed from an 8-letter alphabet? (ii) In how many of these are the letters distinct?

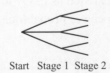

Start Stage 1 Stage 2

Figure 9.4 Decision tree illustrating the Multiplication Principle. There are three choices at the first stage and two at the second, hence a total of $3 \times 2 = 6$ possibilities.

Solution We may choose a word in three steps, letter by letter. In case (i) there are exactly eight choices at each stage, so the total is $8 \times 8 \times 8 = 512$. Case (ii) is different: the first letter has eight choices, the second seven, and the third six, hence by MP a total of $8 \cdot 7 \cdot 6 = 336$.

Notation 9.11 (*Permutations and combinations*) (i) A *combination of r objects from n* is a choice of r of the objects without regard to order. The number of such choices is denoted by $\binom{n}{r}$ or $_nC_r$, and is often read as '*n* choose *r*'.

(ii) A *permutation of r objects from n* is a choice of r of the objects in a particular order. The number of such permutations is denoted by $_nP_r$. In the case $r = n$ they are called simply *permutations of the n objects*.

(iii) For a positive integer n, we make the abbreviation $n! = n(n-1) \cdots 1$, read as '*n* factorial', and extend the notation by defining $0! = 1$.

Theorem 9.12 *The following formulae hold for $1 \leq r \leq n$ (and for $r = 0$ in (iii)):*

(i) *the number of permutations of n objects is n!,*

(ii) $_nP_r = n(n-1)\cdots(n-r+1) = n!/(n-r)!,$

(iii) $\binom{n}{r} = \dfrac{n!}{r!(n-r)!} = \binom{n}{n-r},$

(iv) $\binom{n}{r} = \dfrac{n(n-1)\cdots(n-r+1)}{r!},$

(v) (*Binomial Formula*) $(x+y)^n = \sum_{r=0}^{n} \binom{n}{r} x^{n-r} y^r$

$$= x^n + nx^{n-1}y + \binom{n}{2} x^{n-2}y^2 + \cdots + y^n.$$

(vi) $\binom{n}{r-1} + \binom{n}{r} = \binom{n+1}{r}$ (see *Pascal's Triangle* below proof).

Proof (i) is the special case $r = n$ of (ii). In the latter case imagine we build up a permutation object by object.

> Choose the first – there are n ways.
> Choose the second – there are now $n-1$ ways ...
> Choose the rth – there are $n-r+1$ ways.

By the Multiplication Principle the total number of choices is $n(n-1)\cdots(n-r+1)$ as stated. The expression $n!/(n-r)!$ equals this after cancelling factors $1, 2, \ldots, n-r$ in top and bottom.

(iii) In the case $r = 0$, all three expressions equal 1 trivially. Now suppose $1 \leq r \leq n$ as before, but this time choose a permutation in two stages:

> Choose the r objects – there are $_nC_r$ ways.
> Put them in order, i.e. permute them. By (i) there are $r!$ ways.

By the MP the number of ways to do the combined process is $_nC_r \times r!$. But this by definition equals $_nP_r$, so $_nC_r = {_nP_r}/r!$, and invoking the two formulae of (ii) we obtain (iii) and (iv). Note that replacing r by $n - r$ in the first equality of (iii) gives the second (equivalently, we choose $n - r$ to reject!).

(v) We are expanding the *binomial*, or two-term expresssion, $x + y$, to the power n. Writing this out as $(x + y)(x + y) \cdots (x + y)$ we see it is by definition the sum of products of an x or y from each binomial $x + y$. All products with exactly r factors y and $n - r$ factors x are equal, with one such product for each choice of r binomials from which to select y. Thus the term $x^{n-r}y^r$ appears in the sum with coefficient $_nC_r$, for $r = 0, 1, \ldots, n$, as given in (v).

(vi) The right hand side of (vi) is the number of ways to choose r objects from $n + 1$. But any given object X can be chosen or rejected. If it is rejected there remain r choices from n; if accepted, there are $r - 1$ choices from n. This yields the two terms in the left hand side of (vi).

Pascal's Triangle It is often convenient to construct the *Pascal's Triangle* below, in which the nth level lists the coefficients in the expansion (v) of $(x + y)^n$. Formula (vi) says that a coefficient in level $n + 1$ is the sum of its two neighbours above to left and right, giving an easy way to build up to, say, the coefficients in $(x + y)^5$. We show this carried out below.

$$
\begin{array}{ccccccccccc}
 & & & & 1 & & 1 & & & & \\
 & & & 1 & & 2 & & 1 & & & \\
 & & 1 & & 3 & & 3 & & 1 & & \\
 & 1 & & 4 & & 6 & & 4 & & 1 & \\
1 & & 5 & & 10 & & 10 & & 5 & & 1
\end{array}
$$

Exercise Use the Binomial Theorem and/or Pascal's Triangle to expand $(x + 1)^6$.

Example 9.13 (i) Calculate the number of ways to choose a team of 18 people from 20, (ii) A committee of five is chosen by lot from a pool of eight women and five men. Find the probability that three women and two men are chosen.

Solution (i) Number of ways $= \dbinom{20}{18} = \dbinom{20}{2} = \dfrac{20.19}{1.2} = 190$, by Theorem 9.12 parts (iii), (iv).

(ii) We write $S = \{$choices of 5 from 13$\}$, and seek the probability of event $A = \{$3 women and 2 men$\}$. We have by Theorem 9.12: $|S| = \dbinom{13}{5} = \dfrac{13 \cdot 12 \cdot 11 \cdot 10 \cdot 9}{1 \cdot 2 \cdot 3 \cdot 4 \cdot 5} = 1287$, and by the Multiplication Principle $|A| = \dbinom{8}{3}\dbinom{5}{2} = \dfrac{8 \cdot 7 \cdot 6}{1 \cdot 2 \cdot 3} \cdot \dfrac{5 \cdot 4}{1 \cdot 2} = 560$. By (9.5), $P(A) = |A|/|S| = 0.44$ approx.

Exercise Solve (ii) above for a pool of five women and five men.

9.2 Bayes' Theorem

This section covers the basics of conditional probability and independence, leading to Bayes' Theorem. We emphasise the latter because it has come to increasing prominence as a practical method, almost a philosophy, in recent times (see e.g. Leonard and Hsu, 1999). Of special interest in this volume is the application to object recognition in digital images.

9.2.1 Conditional probability

Intuitively, some events are not 'independent' and it should be possible to update probabilites in the light of new relevant information. For example, the proportion of the UK population with defective vision is 0.1% so a natural model for a person chosen at random would be P(defective vision) $= 1/1000$. However, the proportion is much greater for men, namely 0.4%, so we should like to say P(defective vision, given the subject is male) $= 4/1000$. The way to a formal definition is through relative frequency, (9.1). In this notation the relative frequency of an event A among those outcomes in which an event M occurred is $n_{A \cap M}/n_M$. We may also think of this as the conditional relative frequency of A, given that M occurred. If the total number of outcomes is n, our expression connects to previously defined frequencies:

$$\frac{n_{A \cap M}}{n_M} = \frac{n_{A \cap M}/n}{n_M/n} = \frac{f_{A \cap M}}{f_M}. \tag{9.7}$$

This suggests the formal definition below (for arbitrary sample spaces), in which we continue to use M as a convenient marker for the given event.

Definition 9.14 Let A, M be events with $P(M) > 0$. The *conditional probability of A given M* is defined to be

$$P(A|M) = \frac{P(A \cap M)}{P(M)}. \tag{9.8}$$

The reduced sample space view As suggested by the Venn diagram of Figure 9.5, conditional probability given M is in some sense measuring probability with respect to a reduced sample space M (and the diagram can help one to remember that it is M that appears in the denominator of the definition above).

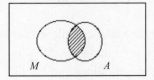

Figure 9.5 Illustration of Equation (9.8), suggesting $P(A|M) = P(A \cap M)/P(M)$ is a probability with respect to M as reduced sample space.

Table 9.2. *Number of office computers in various*
categories for Example 9.16.

	Old	New (N)	Total
Connected (C)	40	25	65
Not connected	30	5	35
Total	70	30	100

Conditional probability axioms So far so good, but to be a genuine probability, one to which we can apply probability results, $P(A|M)$ (for fixed M) must satisfy axioms P1 to P4, which in this case look like:

C1: $0 \leq P(A|M) = 1$,
C2: $P(S|M) = 1$,
C3: $P(A \cup B|M) = P(A|M) + P(B|M)$, if $A \cap B = \emptyset$,
C4: $P\left(\bigcup_{i=1}^{\infty} A_i\right) |M) = \sum_{i=1}^{\infty} P(A_i|M)$, where $\{A_i\}$ is a countable union of pairwise disjoint events.

Proof C1, C2 are a useful short exercise and C3, which we now prove, points to a proof of C4. We consider $(A \cup B) \cap M$, which is a union of two disjoint events $A \cap M$ and $B \cap M$, because A, B are given to be disjoint. Axiom P3 applies to give $P((A \cup B) \cap M) = P(A \cap M) + P(B \cap M)$. Dividing both sides of this equation by $P(M)$, we obtain C3.

Theorem 9.15 *Let A, M be events in a finite equiprobable sample space. Then*

$$P(A|M) = \frac{|A \cap M|}{|M|} = \frac{number\ of\ ways\ A,\ M\ can\ occur\ together}{number\ of\ ways\ M\ can\ occur}. \tag{9.9}$$

Proof $\begin{aligned} P(A|M) &= P(A \cap M)/P(M) &&\text{by Definition (9.8)}\\ &= (|A \cap M|/|S|) \div (|M|/|S|) &&\text{by (9.5)}\\ &= |A \cap M|/|M|) &&\text{upon cancelling } |S|. \end{aligned}$

Example 9.16 An office contains 100 computers. Some have internet connection (C), and some are new (N). Table 9.2 shows the numbers in each category. A new employee arrives first thing, chooses a computer at random, and finds it has a connection. Find the probability that it is (i) new (ii) old.

Solution (i) In the notation implied, we are asked for $P(N|C)$, and by (9.9) it is given by $|N \cap C|/|C| = 25/65 = 5/13$.

(ii) Here we require the probability of a complementary event. If the probability were not conditional we would use the formula $P(A^c) = 1 - P(A)$ (Rule 9.4). Can we do so here? The answer is YES, for conditional probability satisfies the standard axioms P1 to P4, and hence obeys the consequent rules, such as Rule 9.4. Thus $P(N^c|C) = 1 - P(N|C) = 8/13$.

Table 9.3. *Numbers of defective and good items chips after various selections.*

	Defective	Good	Total
At start	4	11	15
After first defective	3	11	14
After second defective	2	11	13

Theorem 9.17 *(Chain Rule for conditional probabilities)*

(i) $P(A)P(B|A) = P(A \cap B) = P(B)P(A|B)$,

(ii) $P(A \cap B \cap C) = P(A)P(B|A)P(C|A \cap B)$,

(iii) $P(A_1 \cap A_2 \cap \cdots \cap A_n) = P(A_1)P(A_2|A_1) \cdots P(A_n|A_1 \cap A_2 \cap \cdots \cap A_{n-1})$.

Proof (i) In (9.8) multiply both sides by $P(M)$, then set $M = B$ to get $P(A \cap B) = P(B)P(A|B)$; the latter equals $P(A)P(B|A)$ because $A \cap B = B \cap A$. Equality (ii) is a special case of (iii), which is in turn a consequence of the first equality of (i) and the inductive step given by setting $A = A_1 \cap A_2 \cap \cdots \cap A_{n-1}$ and $B = A_n$ therein.

Example 9.18 A box contains 15 memory chips, of which four are defective. Three are chosen at random. Find the probabilities that (i) all three are defective, (ii) exactly one is defective.

Solution (i) Let event $A_i = \{i$th item chosen is defective$\}$. According to (9.5) the probability $P(A_1)$, that the first item taken is defective, is 4/15. Given A_1 occurred, there remain three defectives out of a total of 14, and taking a second defective leaves two defectives out of 13. Displaying the figures in Table 9.3 helps to make, and to confirm the correctness of, the argument.

The Chain Rule, Theorem 9.17, gives

$$P(A_1 \cap A_2 \cap A_3) = P(A_1)P(A_2|A_1) \, P(A_3|A_1 \cap A_2) \qquad (9.10)$$
$$= \frac{4}{15} \times \frac{3}{14} \times \frac{2}{13} \quad \text{(by (9.9))} = 0.01 \text{ approx.}$$

(ii) Let $D =$ defective and $G =$ good. Then, in an obvious notation, our calculation is

$$P(\{DGG, GDG, GGD\}) = P(DGG) + P(GDG) + P(GGD) \quad \text{(by (9.3))}$$
$$= \frac{4}{15} \times \frac{11}{14} \times \frac{10}{13} + \frac{11}{15} \times \frac{4}{14} \times \frac{10}{13} + \frac{11}{15} \times \frac{10}{14} \times \frac{4}{13}$$
$$= 0.48 \text{ approx.}$$

In more detail the sample space is a set of ordered triples

$$S = \{x_1 x_2 x_3 : x_i = i\text{th item chosen}\}.$$

Thus, for example, there is no outcome for which *DGG* and *GDG* both occur, since the first item cannot be simultaneously defective and good. Indeed *DGG*, *GDG* and *GGD* are pairwise disjoint, as required for our application of (9.3). Keeping *S* in mind, there is another way to proceed, using (9.5):

$$P(DGG) = \frac{\text{number of ways to choose one defective, then two good, items}}{\text{number of ways to choose a sequence of three items}}$$
$$= \frac{4 \cdot 11 \cdot 10}{15 \cdot 14 \cdot 13}, \quad \text{as obtained above.}$$

Exercise In Example 9.18, calculate *P(DGD)*.

9.2.2 Independence

In the previous section we introduced the idea that the occurrence of one event *M* might affect the probability of another event *A*, writing the modified probability as $P(A|M)$. Here we focus on the equally important opposite, that *A, M* are independent – the occurrence of one event has no bearing on that of the other. Intuitively this says that $P(A|M) = P(A)$ and $P(M|A) = P(M)$, both equivalent to $P(A \cap M) = P(A)P(M)$ by (9.8). Here are the formal definitions.

Definitions 9.19 Events *A, B* are *independent* if

$$P(A \cap B) = P(A)P(B). \tag{9.11}$$

More generally, a finite collection of events $A_1, A_2, \ldots, A_n$ are *pairwise* independent if every pair is independent, i.e. satisfies (9.11). They are *mutually independent* (or just *independent*) if *every* sub-collection *A, B, C, . . .* satisfies

$$P(A \cap B \cap C \cap \cdots) = P(A)P(B)P(C)\ldots \tag{9.12}$$

In particular, *A, B, C, . . .* are pairwise independent. Most often, independence is an assumption in our model of a situation, as in the next example. However, sometimes (9.11) and (9.12) can be tested on the basis of other assumptions, and this we do in Example 9.21 to show that, in the case of three or more events, independence does not follow from pairwise independence. The value of the extra conditions involved is to ensure that the operations of union, intersection and taking complements yield many new independent events from old. Theorems 9.22 and 9.23 cover a useful range of such cases, with an application to circuits in Example 9.24.

Example 9.20 Diseases *A, B* are caught independently, with respective probabilites 0.1 and 0.2. What is the probability of catching at least one of them?

Solution Define events X: disease X is caught. We calculate as follows.

$$\begin{aligned}
P(A \cup B) &= P(A) + P(B) - P(A \cap B) & \text{by Rule 9.6} \\
&= P(A) + P(B) - P(A)P(B) & \text{by (9.11)} \\
&= 0.1 + 0.2 - (0.1)(0.2) \\
&= 0.28.
\end{aligned}$$

Example 9.21 A fair coin is tossed twice. Define events A: first throw is heads, B: second throw is heads, and C: exactly one throw is heads. Show that the events A, B, C are pairwise independent but not (mutually) independent.

Solution In the usual notation, we have an equipotential sample space $S = \{HH, HT, TH, TT\}$ with $A = \{HH, HT\}$, $B = \{HH, TH\}$, $C = \{TH, HT\}$. By Formula (9.5), $P(A) = 2/4 = 1/2 = P(B) = P(C)$. Similarly, $P(A \cap B) = P(\{HH\}) = 1/4 = P(A \cap C) = P(B \cap C)$. Thus A, B, C are pairwise independent. However, they are not independent, for

$$P(A \cap B \cap C) = P(\emptyset) = 0 \neq P(A)P(B)P(C).$$

Theorem 9.22 *(i) If events A, B are independent then $P(A \cap B) = P(A) + P(B) - P(A)P(B)$.*
(ii) If events A, B, C are independent, so are $A \cup B$ and C.

Proof Part (i) is a simple observation covered in Example 9.20. For (ii) the argument is

$$\begin{aligned}
P((A \cup B) \cap C) &= P((A \cap C) \cup (B \cap C)) \\
&= P(A \cap C) + P(B \cap C) - P(A \cap B \cap C) & \text{by Rule 9.6} \\
&= P(A)P(C) + P(B)P(C) - P(A)P(B)P(C) & \text{by (9.12)} \\
&= [P(A) + P(B) - P(A)P(B)]P(C) \\
&= P(A \cup B)P(C) & \text{by (i).}
\end{aligned}$$

Theorem 9.23 *Let events $A_1, \ldots, A_n$ be independent. Then (i) so are their complements, (ii) if the sequence is split, say as $A_1, \ldots, A_r, A_{r+1}, \ldots, A_s, A_{s+1}, \ldots, A_t \ldots$, then the unions*

$$B = \bigcup_{i=1}^{r} A_i, \quad C = \bigcup_{i=r+1}^{s} A_i, \quad D = \bigcup_{i=s+1}^{t} A_i, \ldots$$

are independent. And similarly for intersections.

Proof For the purpose of this proof it is convenient to begin with (ii). Note that the last part, concerning intersections, is an immediate consequence of (9.12) because, for example, $P(B) = \prod P(A_i)(1 \leq i \leq r)$. In particular, the three events $A_1, A_2, A_3 \cap \cdots \cap A_n$ are independent. Then, denoting the third set by E, we have by Theorem 9.22(ii) the independence of $A_1 \cup A_2$ and E. That is, $P((A_1 \cup A_2) \cap E) = P(A_1 \cup A_2)P(E)$, whence, by the independence of $A_3, \ldots, A_n$,

$$P((A_1 \cup A_2) \cap A_3 \cap \cdots \cap A_n) = P(A_1 \cup A_2) \prod_{i=3}^{n} P(A_i),$$

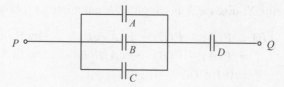

Figure 9.6 On–off circuit. Current flows between terminals P, Q if and only if relay D and at least one of A, B, C is closed. Each relay is closed with probability p.

which says that that the $n - 1$ events $A_1 \cup A_2, A_3, \ldots, A_n$ are independent. Applying this result repeatedly, with suitable relabelling of subscripts, yields (ii) of the present theorem. For (i) we must show that $P(\cap A_i^c) = \Pi P(A_i^c)$, or equivalently by De Morgan's Laws,

$$1 - P(A_1 \cup \cdots \cup A_n) = \prod_{i=1}^{n}(1 - P(A_i)). \tag{9.13}$$

Case $n = 1$ is $1 - P(A_1) = 1 - P(A_1)$, manifestly true, so let us assume inductively that (9.13) holds with $n - 1$ in place of n. We may write Theorem 9.22(i) in the form

$$1 - P(A \cup B) = (1 - P(A))(1 - P(B)) \text{ (given } A, B \text{ independent).} \tag{9.14}$$

By Part (ii) the events $A = A_1 \cup \cdots \cup A_{n-1}$ and $B = A_n$ are independent, and so (9.14) supplies the inductive step:

$$1 - P(A_1 \cup \cdots \cup A_n) = (1 - P(A_1 \cup \cdots \cup A_{n-1}))(1 - P(A_n))$$
$$= \prod_{i=1}^{n}(1 - P(A_i)), \quad \text{by the inductive hypothesis,}$$

completing the proof of (i) by induction.

Example 9.24 In the on–off circuit shown in Figure 9.6, relays A, B, C, D work independently, each with probability p of being closed. Find the probability of the event E, that current flows between terminals P, Q.

Solution Let X be the event: relay X is closed. From the circuit's definition we may write $E = (A \cup B \cup C) \cap D$. Now, since A, B, C are independent, so are their complements by Theorem 9.23 (i), and so we have

$$\begin{aligned} P(A \cup B \cup C) &= P[(A^c \cap B^c \cap C^c)^c] & &\text{by De Morgan's Laws} \\ &= 1 - P(A^c \cap B^c \cap C^c) & &\text{by Rule 9.4} \\ &= 1 - P(A^c)P(B^c)P(C^c) & &\text{by independence} \\ &= 1 - (1 - p)^3 & &\text{by Rule 9.4.} \end{aligned}$$

Also, the events $A \cup B \cup C$ and D are independent by Theorem 9.23(ii), and so

$$P(E) = P(A \cup B \cup C)P(D) = [1 - (1 - p)^3]p.$$

Exercise Repeat Example 9.24 with C in series with D.

Independent trials In Example 9.21 we wrote down a sample space for repeated tossing of a coin, basing it on the sample space for a single toss. More generally, suppose experiment E has finite sample space S and probability function P. Then the experiment consisting of n independent trials of E has by definition the sample space and probability function

$$T = S \times S \times \cdots \times S = \{(x_1, x_2, \ldots, x_n): x_i \text{ is in } S\}, \tag{9.15}$$

$$P(x_1, x_2, \ldots, x_n) = P(x_1)P(x_2) \cdots P(x_n), \tag{9.16}$$

where we have used P as a general symbol for probability. The formal verification that (9.16) satisfies the axioms for a probability function is routine except for $P(T) = 1$. The latter is included in the following result, which will be much used in the information theory sequel, as well as providing simplifications in the examples below.

Theorem 9.25 *If $A, B, \ldots, T$ is a finite collection of finite sets of numbers, then*

$$\left(\sum_{a \in A} a\right)\left(\sum_{b \in B} b\right) \cdots \left(\sum_{t \in T} t\right) = \sum ab \cdots t \ (a \in A, b \in B, \ldots, t \in T). \tag{9.17}$$

Hence if $X, Y, \ldots, Z$ is a finite collection of finite probability spaces then

$$\sum P(x)P(y) \cdots P(z) \ (x \in X, y \in Y, \ldots, z \in Z) = 1. \tag{9.18}$$

Proof Because multiplication of numbers is distributive over addition, $a(b + b') = ab + ab'$, the left hand side of (9.17) is the sum over all products of factors taken one at a time from each bracketed expression. This is easily seen in Example 9.26. To deduce (9.18) we let the set A have elements $P(x) \ (x \in X)$, and so on, and start from the right hand side of (9.17) to obtain $\sum P(x)P(y) \cdots P(z) = (\sum P(x))(\sum P(y)) \cdots (\sum P(z)) = 1 \cdot 1 \cdots 1 = 1$.

Example 9.26 The conclusion of (9.17) for a simple but representative special case:

$$(a_1 + a_2)(b_1 + b_2 + b_3) = a_1(b_1 + b_2 + b_3) + a_2(b_1 + b_2 + b_3)$$
$$= a_1b_1 + a_1b_2 + a_1b_3 + a_2b_1 + a_2b_2 + a_2b_3.$$

Example 9.27 A die is thrown five times. Find the probabilites of the events A: the third throw is a four, B: 1, 2, 3 are thrown in succession.

Solution The sample spaces are $S = \{1, 2, \ldots, 6\}$ for a single trial, and for the five throws $T = \{(x_1, \ldots, x_5): 1 \le x_i \le 6\}$. We have therefore

$$
\begin{aligned}
P(A) &= \sum P(x)P(y)P(4)P(z)P(t) && (x, y, z, t \in S) \\
&= (1/6)\sum P(x)P(y)P(z)P(t) && (x, y, z, t \in S) \quad \text{since } P(4) = 1/6 \\
&= 1/6 && \text{by (9.18)}.
\end{aligned}
$$

It is now clear, as we would hope, that in the repeated trials model the probability of a throw achieving a given score does not depend on where this throw comes in the sequence of trials. For the second probability we may write B as the union of sets

Table 9.4. *Statistics of hypothetical diseases A, B, C.*

	A	B	C
Comparative frequency of occurrence	20%	50%	30%
Probability of disease leading to symptom	0.4	0.1	0.5

$\{123xy\}$, $\{x123y\}$, $\{xy123\}$, where x, y in each set range over the elements of S, and these sets are disjoint because $123xy$ always has third symbol 3 whilst $x123y$ has third symbol 2 and $xy123$ has third symbol 1. Thus, since the three sets have equal probabilities,

$$P(B) = 3\sum_{x,y} P(1)P(2)P(3)P(x)P(y) \quad (x, y \in S)$$
$$= 3P(1)P(2)P(3) \quad \text{by (9.18)}$$
$$= 3(1/6)^3.$$

Example 9.28 A typist hits each key with probability 0.02 of error. Assuming errors occur randomly, find the probabilities of the events (i) a ten-letter word is mistyped, (ii) a ten-letter word has just two errors, and these are consecutive.

Solution (i) Since an incorrect word may have anything from one to ten errors it is probably simplest to use the complementary event, and to argue that the required probability is

$$1 - P(\text{no error in ten symbols}) = 1 - (0.98)^{10} = 0.18 \text{ approx.}$$

(ii) For each 'trial' symbol let G, B be respective outcomes correct, incorrect. Since there are nine starting places for the two errors, the probability is

$$9P(BBGG\ldots G) = 9\,(0.02)^2(0.98)^8 = 0.003 \text{ approx.}$$

Such trials as above, where each has exactly two outcomes, are called *Bernoulli trials*. Often they may be thought of as success or failure. They are the basis of the important Binomial Distribution, to be introduced in Section 9.4.1.

Exercise Find the probability that two out of four dice thrown show a 6.

9.2.3 Bayes' Theorem

How may we determine the probability of a 'cause'? A patient reports a certain vision problem. The specialist knows that only diseases A, B, C can cause the symptom experienced. Neglecting the possibility of two diseases at once, for which disease should a doctor test first?

Given information such as that depicted in Table 9.4, the solution comes by a result known as *Bayes' Theorem*, or *Rule*, which has applications in many areas besides medical diagnosis; in this text, for example, information theory, image processing, object recognition and tomography. The first step is the result below.

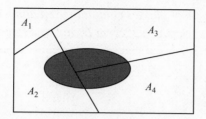

Figure 9.7 Events A_i form a partition of the sample space S. That is, $S = \cup A_i$ and the A_i are pairwise disjoint (mutually exclusive). Then an event B (shaded) is the union of its intersections with the A_i.

Theorem 9.29 *Let $A_1, \ldots, A_n$ be a partition of the sample space (see Figure 9.7) and let B be any event. Then for any i,*

$$P(A_i|B) = \frac{P(B|A_i)P(A_i)}{P(B)} \quad \text{(Bayes' Rule)}, \tag{9.19}$$

where $P(B)$ is given by the Total Probability Formula

$$P(B) = P(B|A_1)P(A_1) + \cdots + P(B|A_n)P(A_n). \tag{9.20}$$

Proof Bayes' Rule is named after its originator, the Rev. Thomas Bayes (shown in Figure 9.8), for its rich implications, explored more today than in his own time (in the field of object recognition to name but one). It may be regarded as arising from the simple observation: $P(B)P(A_i|B) = P(B \cap A_i)$ (by Theorem 9.17(i)) $= P(A_i \cap B) = P(A_i) \times P(B|A_i) = P(B|A_i)P(A_i)$. Dividing through by $P(B)$ gives the rule. Now let us derive the formula for $P(B)$ (not due to Bayes but frequently incorporated in his formula (9.19)). As illustrated in Figure 9.7, event B is the union of pairwise disjoint events

Figure 9.8 Rev. Thomas Bayes, 1702–1761, sketch by Ward Somerville.

$$B = (B \cap A_1) \cup \cdots \cup (B \cap A_n) \tag{9.21}$$

and because they are disjoint we have by (9.3) that $P(B) = \sum P(B \cap A_i)$. On substituting $P(B \cap A_i) = P(B|A_i)P(A_i)$ we complete the proof.

Example 9.30 At a party, tray 1 holds two glasses of red wine and three of white, whilst tray 2 holds six red and four white. A mischievous guest transfers a glass at random from tray 1 to tray 2. Shortly after, the hostess (who prefers red wine) closes her eyes and takes a glass from tray 2. Find (i) the probability it is red, (ii) given that it is red, the probability the transferred glass was white.

Table 9.5. *Numbers of glasses containing red and white wine. Event*
A: red was transferred, event B: red was later selected.

Tray 1	red	white	Tray 2	red	white
At start	2	3	At start	6	4
			After A	7	4
			After A^c	6	5

Solution (i) Here we are asked not for the probability of a cause A: 'the wine trans-ferred was red', but for that of a result B: 'the wine selected was red'. Hence we re-quire just the Total Probability Formula (9.20). Our partition can be of the simplest type: A and its complement A^c. The relevant probabilities can be picked out from Table 9.5.

(ii) Now for a cause: we require $P(A^c|B)$ which, according to Bayes' Rule, equals $P(B|A^c)P(A^c)/P(B)$. We happen to have computed the various factors already, and the answer is $(18/55)/(32/55) = 9/16 = 0.56$ approx. This is less than the uncondi-tional value of 0.60, and represents an adjustment to a probability in the light of further information, facilitated by Bayes' Rule.

We have

$$P(B) = P(B|A)P(A) + P(B|A^c)P(A^c) = \frac{7}{11} \cdot \frac{2}{5} + \frac{6}{11} \cdot \frac{3}{5} = \frac{32}{55} = 0.58 \text{ approx.}$$

Example 9.31 Given the data of Table 9.4, for which disease should the doctor test first? Let X be the event 'the disease is X', and let E be the occurrence of the symptom. We are to assume that exactly one disease must be present, and must calculate which is most likely. The assumption tells us that A, B, C partition the sample space, and by Bayes' Rule with numerator and denominator finally scaled by 100 we have

$$P(A|E) = \frac{P(E|A)P(A)}{P(E|A)P(A) + P(E|B)P(B) + P(E|C)P(C)} \qquad (9.22)$$

$$= \frac{(0.4)(0.2)}{(0.4)(0.2) + (0.1)(0.5) + (0.5)(0.3)} = \frac{8}{8 + 5 + 15} = \frac{2}{7}.$$

Given the form of Bayes' Rule, the numbers we need to complete the calculation are already displayed. Indeed, $P(B|E) = 5/28$ and $P(C|E) = 15/28$. Since the latter is the largest of the three disease probabilities given the symptom, one should test first for disease C.

Exercise Given the wine switch was white, what is the probability the hostess tasted red?

9.3 Random variables

Definition 9.32 A *random variable* X on a sample space S is a function assigning a real number $X(s)$ to every outcome s, as illustrated below. The *range space*, or *range*, R_X is the set of values taken by X. The assertion X *is concentrated on* T means that R_X is contained, perhaps strictly, in the set T. We say X is *discrete* if R_X is discrete, meaning R_X is finite or we may write it in the form $\{x_1, x_2, \ldots\}$ (the countably infinite case, see Example 9.36 below). We shall focus first on discrete X and later on the somewhat different, continuous, type of random variable, in which the range, is typically a continuous interval. In all cases a random variable will be denoted by a capital, and typical values by corresponding lower case letters, often subscripted.

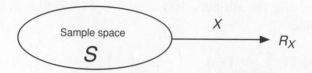

9.3.1 Discrete random variables

If the random variable X is discrete, each element of R_X is assigned a probability, that of its pre-image in S. That is,

$$P(X = a) = P(\{s \in S: X(s) = a\}). \tag{9.23}$$

Example 9.33 A sample space for the experiment 'throw two dice' is the set of pairs $S = \{(x, y): x, y = 1, 2, \ldots, 6\}$. Let the random variable X be the total score, $X(x, y) = x + y$. Then, for example, writing xy for a pair (x, y) in S,

$$P(X = 5) = P(\{xy: x + y = 5\}) = P(\{14, 23, 32, 41\}) = 4/36.$$

Definition 9.34 The *probability distribution function* (pdf) of a discrete random variable X is the function $p: R_X \to [0, 1]$ given by $p(x) = P(X = x)$. Equivalently, it is the set of pairs $(x, p(x))$, customarily displayed as a table or bar chart, as in the next example. The probability axioms along with (9.23) imply

$$p(x_i) \geq 0 \ (x_i \in R_X), \quad \text{and} \quad \sum p(x_i) = 1. \tag{9.24}$$

(Indeed, any function Z from a discrete set T into $[0, 1]$ is called a (discrete) *probability function* on T if it satisfies (9.24), for Z gives T the structure of a probability space as in Definition 9.3ff, with $S = T$.)

Example 9.35 Suppose the random variable X is the number of heads in two throws of a coin. Let us find the pdf of X. Here $S = \{HH, HT, TH, TT\}$ and $R_X = \{0, 1, 2\}$. Hence

$$p(0) = P(X = 0) = P(TT) = 1/4,$$
$$\text{whilst } p(1) = P(X = 1) = P(HT, TH) = 2/4,$$
$$\text{and } p(2) = P(X = 2) = P(HH) = 1/4.$$

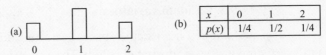

Figure 9.9 Probability distribution of Example 9.36 represented by (a) bar chart, (b) table.

Example 9.36 (i) A sequence of ultra-fast disk drives is tested until one is found that fails the test. Assuming a drive has probability $1/5$ of failure, find the pdf of the number X tested, and show it satisfies (9.24). See Figure 9.9.

Solution Clearly $R_X = \{1, 2, 3, \ldots\}$, an infinite set, and $X = n$ if and only if the first $n - 1$ drives pass and the nth fails. Hence $p(n) = P(X = n) = (4/5)^{n-1}(1/5)$. Our verification becomes

$$\sum_{n \geq 1} p(n) = \sum_{n \geq 1} \left(\frac{4}{5}\right)^{n-1} \left(\frac{1}{5}\right) = \left(\frac{1}{5}\right) \left(1 + \frac{4}{5} + \frac{4^2}{5^2} + \cdots \right) = 1,$$

according to the ubiquitous formula for the sum of a geometric progression:

$$1 + r + r^2 + \cdots = \frac{1}{1 - r} \qquad \text{if } |r| < 1. \tag{9.25}$$

(ii) Let X be a random variable and M an event with the same sample space. Show that

$$\sum_x P(X = x | M) = 1. \tag{9.26}$$

Solution The events $\{X = x\}$ partition the sample space, so

$$\sum_x P(X = x | M) = \sum_x P(\{X = x\} \cap M) / P(M)$$
$$= \left[\sum_x P(\{X = x\} \cap M)\right] / P(M) = P(M) / P(M).$$

Exercise Tabulate the pdf of X in Example 9.33.

9.3.2 Continuous random variables

If instead of discrete values X takes, say, all values in some interval, then a new type of pdf must be introduced in which sums are replaced by integrals.

Definition 9.37 A random variable X is *continuous* if there is a real function $f(x)(x \in \mathbf{R})$, called the *probability density function,* or pdf, of X, satisfying

$$P(a \leq X \leq b) = \int_a^b f(x)\,dx,$$

where $f(x) \geq 0$ for all x, and $\int_{-\infty}^{\infty} f(x)\,dx = 1. \tag{9.27}$

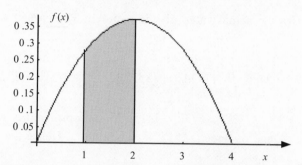

Figure 9.10 Graph of the pdf $f(x) = cx(4 - x), 0 \leq x \leq 4$. Only one value of the constant c is possible (calculated in Example 9.38), because the area beneath the curve must be 1. The shaded area represents $P(1 \leq X \leq 2)$, according to Equation (9.27).

Thus $P(a \leq X \leq b)$ is the area beneath the graph of $f(x)$ between $x = a$ and $x = b$ (see Figure 9.10), and the second equality in (9.27) arises from $P(S) = 1$. Now, the requirement is not that f be continuous, simply that it be integrable, and changing the value of $f(x)$ at isolated points does not affect the value of the integrals in (9.27). Thus, given one pdf there are many possible pdfs that yield the same probabilities. We take advantage of this to insist not only that $f(x)$ is never negative, but that

$$f(x) = 0 \quad \text{for } x \text{ outside } R_X. \tag{9.28}$$

With this understanding we need only specify $f(x)$ for x in the range R_X. A further simplification comes from observing that, according to (9.27), the probability that X equals any specific value is zero. This implies, for example, $P(a \leq X \leq b) = P(a < X \leq b) + P(X = a) = P(a < X \leq b) = P(a < X < b)$. Thus inequalities may be taken as strict or not, according to convenience. Now it is time for examples.

Example 9.38 The quality of a computer monitor is given by a continuous random variable X with pdf $f(x) = cx(4 - x), 0 \leq x \leq 4$. Find (i) the constant, c, (ii) the probability that X exceeds 1, given that it does not exceed 2, (iii) the size of the largest batch that can be tested before the probability of all being special (defined by $X > 3$) falls below 0.01.

Solution (i) The second property in (9.27) gives $c = 3/32$, because

$$1 = \int_{-\infty}^{\infty} f(x)dx = c \int_{0}^{4} x(4 - x)dx = c \left[2x^2 - x^3/3 \right]_{0}^{4} = 32c/3.$$

(ii) We are asked for the conditional probability $P(A|B)$ with A: $X > 1$ and B: $X \leq 2$. Notice that, since by implication the range is $[0, 4]$, event B is the same as $0 \leq X \leq 2$, whilst $A \cap B$ is $1 < X \leq 2$. We therefore have

$$P(A|B) = \frac{P(A \cap B)}{P(B)} = \frac{P(1 \leq X \leq 2)}{P(0 \leq X \leq 2)} = \frac{c[2x^2 - x^3/3]_1^2}{c[2x^2 - x^3/3]_0^2} = \frac{11/3}{16/3} = \frac{11}{16}.$$

(iii) Unlike Part (ii), the actual value of c is required. The easiest way to begin is to calculate

$$P(X \leq 3) = \int_0^3 f(x)\mathrm{d}x = (3/32)[2x^2 - x^3/3]_0^3 = 27/32.$$

Then $P(\text{special}) = 1 - 27/32 = 5/32 = 0.156\,25$. The probability of two specials is $(5/32)^2 = 0.024\ldots$, and of three is $(5/32)^3 = 0.0038\ldots$ Hence the largest batch size is just 2.

Remark 9.39 A linguistic point: the abbreviation 'pdf' refers to *distribution* in the discrete case and to *density* in the continuous case of a random variable to reflect their differing ways of determining probabilities. In this double capacity 'pdf' reflects the common task of yielding probabilities. Indeed, *distribution* is commonly used for either case.

Exercise Find $P(1 \leq X \leq 3)$ in Example 9.38.

9.3.3 The cdf of a random variable

A tool whose applications begin in the next section is the cdf, a function expressing the accumulation of probabilities from that of the least value in R_X to that of a specified value. Following Remark 9.39 we aim for unity between the discrete and continuous cases.

Definition 9.40 The *cumulative distribution/density function*, or *cdf*, of a random variable X is the function defined for all real numbers by $F(x) = P(X \leq x)$. That is,

$$F(x) = \begin{cases} \sum_j p(x_j)\,(x_j \leq x), & \text{if } X \text{ is discrete with pdf } p, \\ \int_{-\infty}^x f(s)\mathrm{d}s, & \text{if } X \text{ is continuous with pdf } f. \end{cases} \tag{9.29}$$

A first consequence of both definitions is that $P(a \leq X \leq b) = F(b) - F(a)$.

Example 9.41 (*Discrete case*) Suppose the random variable X takes values 1, 2, 3 with respective probabilities 1/6, 1/2, 1/3. Figure 9.11 shows the pdf and cdf superimposed.

Example 9.42 (*Uniform distribution*) The random variable X is called *uniform* if it is continuous, with range some finite interval $[a, b]$, and if the probability of a subinterval is proportional to its length. Since the area under the graph of the pdf $f(x)$ must equal 1 (see (9.27)), we must have $f(x) = 1/(b - a)$ on $[a, b]$ and hence,

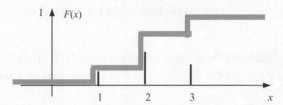

Figure 9.11 Graphs of a discrete pdf (black) and its cdf (grey).

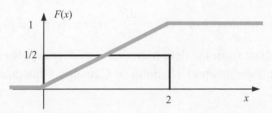

Figure 9.12 The pdf of a uniform random variable with values in interval [0, 2] (black), and its cdf (grey). As illustrated here, if $F(x)$ once attains height 1, it must remain there. In this case $F(x) = x/2$ for $0 \leq x \leq 2$.

as shown in Figure 9.12,

$$F(x) = \begin{cases} 0, & \text{if } x < a, \\ \dfrac{x - a}{b - a}, & a \leq x \leq b, \\ 1, & \text{if } x \geq b. \end{cases} \tag{9.30}$$

Example 9.43 (*Exponential distribution*) Let X be a continuous random variable with pdf $f(x) = \alpha e^{-\alpha x}$, $x > 0$, for some positive parameter α. (i) Determine the cdf, (ii) show X has the property that, for $s, t > 0$,

$$P(X > s + t \mid X > s) = P(X > t). \tag{9.31}$$

Solution We have $F(x) = 0$ for $x = 0$, and, for $x > 0$, $F(x) = \int_0^x \alpha e^{-\alpha s} ds = \left[-e^{-\alpha s}\right]_0^x = 1 - e^{-\alpha x}$. The respective functions are represented in Figure 9.13.
(ii) Observe that $P(X > x) = 1 - F(X) = e^{-\alpha x}$. Thus the conditional probability in (9.31) is $P(X > s + t \ \& \ X > s)/P(X > s) = P(X > s + t)/P(X > s) = e^{-\alpha(s+t)}/e^{-\alpha s} = e^{-\alpha t} = P(X > t)$, as required. We remark that this distribution occurs

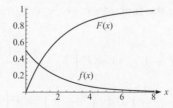

Figure 9.13 $f(x)$ and $F(x)$ for the exponential distribution.

widely in reliability theory, where Property (9.31) is viewed as stating that *X has no memory*.

Theorem 9.44 *The following hold for a random variable X. (i) F(x) is non-decreasing; that is, s < t implies F(s) ≤ F(t). Further, (ii) F(x) tends to 0 as x tends to −∞, and to 1 as x tends to +∞.*

$$(iii) \quad \begin{cases} \text{If } X \text{ is discrete then } \; p(x_j) = F(x_j) - F(x_{j-1}), \\ \text{if } X \text{ is continuous then } f(x) = \dfrac{\mathrm{d}F}{\mathrm{d}x}, \text{ wherever } F \text{ is differentiable.} \end{cases}$$

Proof This is immediate from the definition (9.29) of F except for the statement about $\mathrm{d}F/\mathrm{d}x$, which is the Fundamental Theorem of Calculus – integration is 'opposite' to differentiation.

Remark 9.45 The various parts of the result above are illustrated in Figures 9.11 to 9.13. In particular, $f(x) = \mathrm{d}F/\mathrm{d}x$ may be seen in Figure 9.13: as $f(x)$ decreases towards zero, so $F(x)$ increases less rapidly, approaching but never quite reaching the upper limit of 1. The relation between F and f will be first used in the next section, to determine new pdfs from old.

Exercise Derive the cdf of a uniform random variable, given in (9.30).

9.3.4 Functions of a random variable

We recall that a random variable is a function $X: S \to R$; thus if $y = u(x)$ represents a real function on real x then $Y = u(X)$ defines another random variable. For example $X =$ voltage, $Y =$ power in a system, or $Y =$ cost in terms of X. We give two methods for determining a pdf $g(y)$ for Y. Firstly, a general method illustrated in Example 9.46: we deduce the cdf $G(y)$ of Y in terms of that of X, then use $g(y) = \mathrm{d}G/\mathrm{d}y$ (Theorem 9.44). Secondly, with more restrictions, we may apply the direct formula of Theorem 9.47 below. As implied, we use lower case letters to denote a pdf and corresponding upper case for the cdf.

Example 9.46 (General method) Let the random variable X have pdf $f(x) = 2x, 0 < x < 1$. Find a pdf $g(y)$ for the random variable $Y = 3X + 1$.

Solution It is convenient to establish the range of Y at the start. This is the image of the interval $R_X = (0, 1)$ under the function $x \to 3x + 1$, namely $R_Y = (1, 4)$. On these intervals we have

$$G(y) = P(Y \le y) = P(3X + 1 \le y) = P\left(X \le \frac{y-1}{3}\right) = F\left(\frac{y-1}{3}\right), \text{ and so}$$

$$g(y) = \mathrm{d}G/\mathrm{d}y \;\; = F'\left(\frac{y-1}{3}\right)\mathrm{d}/\mathrm{d}y\left(\frac{y-1}{3}\right) = f\left(\frac{y-1}{3}\right) \times \frac{1}{3}$$

$$= (2/9)(y-1), \, 1 < y < 4.$$

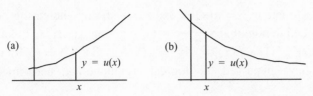

Figure 9.14 (a) $u(x)$ strictly increasing, (b) $u(x)$ strictly decreasing.

Theorem 9.47 *Let X be a continuous random variable with pdf $f(x)$, and let $Y = u(X)$, where u is strictly increasing or strictly decreasing on R_X. Then a pdf for the random variable Y is*

$$g(y) = f(x)\,|dx/dy| = f(x)/|u'(x)|,\ y \in R_Y \qquad (9.32)$$

(where we substitute for x to get an equation in terms of y), provided dx/dy exists for this range of y.

Proof We give the proof in both cases of u (see Figure 9.14) since their difference is instructive. Let x, y be a pair with $y = u(x)$.

(a) *u increasing* Here dy/dx is positive and hence so is dx/dy. We argue as follows.

$$\begin{aligned} G(y) &= P(Y \le y) && \text{since } G(y) \text{ is the cdf of } Y \\ &= P(X \le x) && \text{since } u \text{ is increasing} \\ &= F(x) && \text{since } F(x) \text{ is the cdf of } X. \end{aligned}$$

Hence

$$g(y) = \frac{dG}{dy} \text{ (Theorem 9.44)} = \frac{dF}{dx}\frac{dx}{dy} \quad \text{(Chain Rule)}$$
$$= f(x)|dx/dy|, \text{ since } dx/dy \text{ is positive and so equals its}$$
$$\text{absolute value.}$$

(b) *u decreasing* In this case dx/dy is negative, and so equals $-|dx/dy|$. However, this is compensated for by reversal of the inequality in the second line below, compared with the corresponding argument above.

$$\begin{aligned} G(y) &= P(Y \le y) && \text{since } G(y) \text{ is the cdf of } Y \\ &= P(X \ge x) && \text{since } u \text{ is decreasing} \\ &= 1 - P(X < x) && \text{by the Complement Rule 9.4} \\ &= 1 - F(x) && \text{since } F(x) \text{ is the cdf of } X. \end{aligned}$$

We now have $g(y) = \dfrac{dG}{dy} = -\dfrac{dF}{dx}\dfrac{dx}{dy} = +f(x)|dx/dy|$, completing the proof.

Example 9.48 (i) Re-solve the last example using Theorem 9.47, and compare. (ii) The mean time to failure of a certain electronic component is a continuous random variable T with pdf $f(t) = 2e^{-2t}, t > 0$. Find a pdf for the cost per unit time of use, $Y = 250/T$. (iii) Given that the continuous random variable X has a pdf $f(x)$, determine the pdf of $Y = X^2$. Apply this in the case that X is uniformly distributed on $[-1, 1]$.

Solution (i) The function $y = u(x) = 3x + 1$ is strictly increasing so Theorem 9.47 does apply. We need to note that $x = (y - 1)/3$, giving $dx/dy = 1/3$ and $f(x) = 2x = 2(y - 1)/3$. Hence $g(y) = f(x)|dx/dy| = 2(y - 1)/3 \times 1/3 = (2/9)(y - 1)$ as before. Essentially we have bypassed the logical argument and performed the necessary calculation.

(ii) Here the variable t takes the place of x. The function $y = u(t) = 250/t$ is strictly decreasing so once more we may automate the calculation by means of Theorem 9.47. We calculate that $t = 250/y$, $dt/dy = -250/y^2$, $f(t) = 2e^{-2t} = 2e^{-500/y}$. The new pdf is therefore $g(y) = f(t)|dt/dy| = 500y^{-2}e^{-500/y}$.

(iii) This time we cannot apply the formula, since $u(x) = x^2$ both increases and decreases (except on intervals of fixed sign). However, the general method does work, though in a slightly different way from Example 9.46. For y in R_Y we may argue that

$$G(y) = P(Y \leq y) = P(X^2 \leq y) = P(-\sqrt{y} \leq X \leq \sqrt{y})$$
$$= F(\sqrt{y}) - F(-\sqrt{y}) \quad \text{and, differentiating to obtain g:}$$
$$g(y) = F'(\sqrt{y})\frac{d}{dy}(\sqrt{y}) - F'(-\sqrt{y})\frac{d}{dy}(-\sqrt{y}), \quad \text{writing } F' \text{ for } dF/dx$$
$$= [f(\sqrt{y}) + f(-\sqrt{y})]/2\sqrt{y}, \quad \text{because } F' = f.$$

Since X is to be uniformly distributed on $[-1, 1]$, it has pdf $f(x) = 1/(\text{interval width}) = 1/2$, for x in $[-1, 1]$, and zero elsewhere. Hence $g(y) = (1/2 + 1/2)/2\sqrt{y} = 1/(2\sqrt{y})$ $(y \in [0, 1])$.

Theorem 9.49 *Let a, b be constants, with a positive. If the continuous variable X has pdf $f(x)$ then $Y = aX + b$ and $Z = X^2$ have respective pdfs given, over their ranges, by*

$$\frac{1}{|a|}f\left(\frac{y - b}{a}\right) \quad and \quad \frac{1}{2\sqrt{z}}(f(\sqrt{z}) + f(-\sqrt{z})). \tag{9.33}$$

Proof Suppose $a > 0$. Then $P(aX + b \leq y) = P(X \leq (y - b)/a) = F((y - b)/a)$. Differentiating this gives the pdf as stated (see Theorem 9.47), since $dF/dx = f$. The case $a < 0$ is left as an exercise. The second formula of the theorem is worked out similarly to Example 9.48(iii).

Exercise Find the pdf of $Y = e^{2x}$, when X has pdf $f(x) = 2x, 0 \leq x \leq 1$.

9.3.5 Expected value

We seek a function of a random variable to correspond to mean, or average. If in N trials the random variable X takes values $x_1, x_2, \ldots, x_n$ with relative frequencies $f_i = n_i/N$ (note that $N = \sum n_i$) then the mean value is $(1/N)\sum n_i x_i = \sum x_i f_i$. As in Section 9.1.2 we take the appearance of f_i as our cue for invoking $P(X = x_i)$, abbreviated to $p(x_i)$ or just p_i, and make the following definitions. If X is continuous then $f(x)$ denotes as usual its pdf.

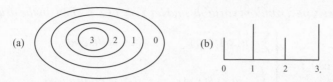

Figure 9.15 (a) Target for Example 9.52. (b) Score as a function $u(i)$ of ring number, i.

Definition 9.50 The *expected value $E(X)$* of a random variable X is given by

$$E(X) = \begin{cases} \sum x_i p(x_i), & \text{if } X \text{ is discrete,} \\ \int_{-\infty}^{\infty} x f(x) \mathrm{d}x, & \text{if } X \text{ is continuous.} \end{cases}$$

Example 9.51 (*The prudent gambler*) A gambler is invited to play a game in which he tosses two fair coins, winning x chips if x heads appear but losing five if no heads are seen. *Should he accept?* Let X be the amount won. Then $R_X = \{1, 2, -5\}$, and the respective probabilities are simply those of 1, 2, 0 heads, namely 1/2, 1/4, 1/4. Thus, by Definition 9.50,

$$E(X) = 1 \cdot \frac{1}{2} + 2 \cdot \frac{1}{4} - 5 \cdot \frac{1}{4} = -0.25.$$

With his expected score negative he would, no doubt, knowing this, reject the invitation.

Example 9.52 A marksman scores A points if he hits rings 0, 2 in the target shown in Figure 9.15, and B points for rings 1, 3. Find his expected score in terms of the probabilities p_i of ring i being hit, $0 \le i \le 3$.

Solution If Y denotes the score, then $R_Y = \{A, B\}$. The pdf of Y consists of two pairs $(A, P(Y = A)), (B, P(Y = B))$ so, provided we can evaluate the probabilities, we need not directly invoke the function u expressing score in terms of ring number, and shown as (b) in Figure 9.15. We have, by Definition 9.50,

$$\begin{aligned} E(Y) &= A P(Y = A) + B P(Y = B) \\ &= A(p_0 + p_2) + B(p_1 + p_3) \\ &= A p_0 + B p_1 + A p_2 + B p_3 \\ &= u(0) p_0 + u(1) p_1 + u(2) p_2 + u(3) p_3. \end{aligned}$$

The last but one line answers the question as set. However, the very last line shows how we may proceed more generally to arrive at the first assertion of the theorem below (the second is essentially similar). It removes the need for an additional calculation of the pdf of Y from that of X when we only wish to find the expected value $E(Y)$.

Theorem 9.53 *Let X be a random variable and let* $Y = u(X)$. *Then, in the usual notation,*

$$E(Y) = \begin{cases} \sum u(x_i)p(x_i), & \text{if } X \text{ is discrete,} \\ \int_{-\infty}^{\infty} u(x)f(x)\mathrm{d}x, & \text{if } X \text{ is continuous.} \end{cases} \qquad (9.34)$$

Example 9.54 Given that current X is uniform on the interval $[-1, 1]$ and power is $Y = u(x) = X^2$, compute the expected values of current and power.

Solution Since X is uniform it has pdf $f(x) = 1/(\text{interval width}) = 1/2$. Hence $E(X) = \int_{-1}^{1} x \cdot \frac{1}{2}\mathrm{d}x = [x^2/4]_{-1}^{1} = 0$, as we would intuitively expect. For the expectation $E(Y)$ we have a choice of methods. *Method 1* (usually harder) First calculate the pdf of Y then apply the definition of $E(Y)$. By (9.32) this pdf is $g(y) = 1/(2\sqrt{y}), 0 \le y \le 1$. *Method 2* Use Theorem 9.53. Let us compare the integrations.

Method 1. $$E(Y) = \int_{0}^{1} yg(y)\mathrm{d}y = \int_{0}^{1} \frac{1}{2}y^{1/2}\mathrm{d}y = 1/3.$$

Method 2. $$E(Y) = \int_{-1}^{1} u(x)f(x)\mathrm{d}x = \int_{-1}^{1} x^2 \frac{1}{2}\mathrm{d}x = 1/3.$$

Example 9.55 (*An application of Theorem 9.53*) Let X be a discrete random variable taking values $x_1, x_2, \ldots, x_n$. Shannon's entropy function H measures the amount of information provided by an observation of X as (see Chapter 12)

$$H(X) = E(u(X)), \quad \text{where } u(x_i) = \log(1/p_i). \qquad (9.35)$$

With logs to base 2 the information is measured in binary digits, or 'bits'. Here is an example. Suppose a coin is tossed until either a head appears, or four tails have landed. Let us find the number of information bits supplied by an observation of X, the number of coin tosses. The pdf of X is given by $p(1) = P(H) = 1/2$, $p(2) = P(TH) = 1/4$, $p(3) = P(TTH) = 1/8$, $p(4) = P(TTTH) + P(TTTT) = 1/16 + 1/16 = 1/8$. Hence

$$\begin{aligned} H(X) &= \sum u(x_i)p_i \quad \text{(by Theorem 9.53)} = \sum p_i \log(1/p_i) \\ &= \frac{1}{2}\log 2 + \frac{1}{4}\log 4 + \frac{1}{8}\log 8 + \frac{1}{8}\log 8 \\ &= \frac{1}{2} \cdot 1 + \frac{1}{4} \cdot 2 + 2 \cdot \frac{1}{8} \cdot 3 \\ &= 1.75 \text{ bits.} \end{aligned}$$

Remark 9.56 Finally in this section, we derive an elementary yet useful result, applying equally to both discrete and continuous random variables. Its proof presents a nice opportunity for parallel proofs in the two cases. Here, as is often the case, there is no difficulty in converting a proof in one case to a proof in the other simply by interchanging integration and summation. It leads in Section 9.5.2 to Jensen's Inequality (much used in Information Theory), another result that does not require us to specify whether a random variable is discrete or continuous.

Corollary 9.57 *For any random variable X, constants a, b and functions $u(x)$, $v(x)$, we have*

$$E(aX + b) = aE(X) + b,$$
$$E[u(X) + v(X)] = E[u(X)] + E[v(X)]. \tag{9.36}$$

Proof Two necessary equalities are provided by (9.24) and (9.27), namely, in the usual notation, $\sum f(x_i) = 1 = \int_{-\infty}^{\infty} f(x)dx$. Then by Theorem 9.53 we may re-express $E(aX + b)$ in the discrete and continuous cases as respectively (the rest is similar)

$$\sum (ax_i + b)p(x_i) = a \sum x_i p(x_i) + b \sum p(x_i) = aE(X) + b,$$
$$\int (ax + b)f(x)dx = a \int xf(x)dx + b \int f(x)dx = aE(X) + b.$$

Exercise Solve Example 9.54 with $u(x) = x^4$.

9.3.6 Variance

In the context of measured values one argues that the mean is a dubious guide to what we may expect in any given measurement in the absence of at least some idea of the typical divergence from the mean. For example, a mean annual income of 10 000 units in a population of 89 million earners could mean 9 million are rich on 90 000 units annually, whilst the rest are starving on 1000. The well-tried second statistic to the mean is the average squared divergence from it (or the square root of this, the standard deviation). Since, when we pass from measurements to a probability model, mean or average becomes expected value, the natural thing to use is the *variance* $E[(X - \mu)^2]$, where μ denotes the expected value of X.

Definition 9.58 *The variance $V(X)$ of a random variable X, discrete or continuous, is given by*

$$V(X) = E[(X - \mu)^2], \quad \text{where } \mu = E(X). \tag{9.37}$$

The positive square root, $\sigma = \sigma_x$, is called the *standard deviation* (thus $V(X) = \sigma^2$), and is widely used in practice. However, calculations are often phrased in terms of $V(X)$ because it has simpler mathematical properties. For this purpose the following theorem is very useful.

Theorem 9.59 *Let a, b be constants, and X a random variable with $E(X) = \mu$. Then*

$$V(X) = E(X^2) - \mu^2, \tag{9.38}$$
$$V(aX + b) = a^2 V(X). \tag{9.39}$$

Proof We have

$$V(X) = E(X^2 - 2\mu X + \mu^2) \qquad \text{by definition}$$
$$= E(X^2) - 2\mu E(X) + \mu^2 \qquad \text{by (9.36)}$$
$$= E(X^2) - 2\mu^2 + \mu^2,$$

hence the expression in (9.38). Continuing, we note that $E(X + b) = \mu + b$ and hence $V(X + b) = E[((X + b) - (\mu + b))^2] = E[(X - \mu)^2] = V(X)$. Finally, $E(aX) = a\mu$, giving $V(aX) = E[(aX - a\mu)^2] = E[a^2(x - \mu)^2] = a^2 E[(x - \mu)^2] = a^2 V(X)$. This completes the proof.

Example 9.60 (*Return of the prudent gambler*) Variance gives another slant on the decision making in Example 9.51. We recall the possible winnings $X = 1, 2, -5$ with respective probabilities $1/2, 1/4, 1/4$. The expected value μ was -0.25. For the variance we calculate:

$$E(X^2) = 1^2 \cdot \frac{1}{2} + 2^2 \cdot \frac{1}{4} + 5^2 \cdot \frac{1}{4} = 7.75,$$

hence, using Theorem 9.59, $V(X) = E(X^2) - \mu^2 = 7.6875$, with square root $\sigma = 2.8$ approx. Since this dwarfs the small expected loss, the gambler may figure he should try a couple of games in the hope of coming out on top.

Example 9.61 We find the variance of X, a continuous random variable with the exponential distribution $f(x) = \alpha e^{-\alpha x}$, $x > 0$, where α is a positive constant. From Table 9.6 there holds the formula

$$\int_0^\infty x^n e^{-x} dx = n! \quad (n \text{ any non-negative integer}). \tag{9.40}$$

Hence $\quad E(X) = \displaystyle\int_0^\infty x\alpha e^{-\alpha x} dx = (\text{with } z = \alpha x, dz = \alpha dx) \int_0^\infty (z/\alpha) e^{-z} dz = 1/\alpha.$

Secondly, $E(X^2) = \displaystyle\int_0^\infty x^2 \alpha e^{-\alpha x} dx = (\text{with } z = \alpha x) \int_0^\infty (z/\alpha)^2 e^{-z} dz = 2/\alpha^2.$ Thus $V(X) = 1/\alpha^2$.

Table 9.6. *The gamma function $\Gamma(x)$ and beta function $B(u, v)$. Playing an important role for the pdfs of the same names, in Section 9.4.4, they are introduced here for the useful integration formulae they provide.*

DEFINITIONS $\quad \Gamma(p) = \displaystyle\int_0^\infty x^{p-1} e^{-x} dx, \; p > 0. \quad B(u, v) = \Gamma(u)\Gamma(v)/\Gamma(u + v).$

PROPERTIES

(a) $\quad \Gamma(2) = 1 = \Gamma(1)$;

(b) $\quad \Gamma(p + 1) = p\Gamma(p)$;

(c) $\quad \Gamma(p)\Gamma(1 - p) = \pi/\sin p\pi$, hence $\Gamma(1/2) = \sqrt{\pi}$;

(d) $\quad \Gamma(n + 1) = n! = \displaystyle\int_0^\infty x^n e^{-x} dx$ for $n = 0, 1, 2, \ldots$ (thus Γ is a generalised

factorial);

(e) $\quad \displaystyle\int_0^1 x^{u-1}(1 - x)^{v-1} dx = B(u, v) = 2 \int_0^{\pi/2} \cos^{2u-1}\theta \sin^{2v-1}\theta \, d\theta \; (u, v > 0).$

Exercise Find the variance of a random variable X uniformly distributed on the interval $[a, b]$ (the answer is given in Table 9.9 of Section 9.4.4).

9.4 A census of distributions

9.4.1 The binomial distribution

We may think of this distribution as that of the number of heads obtained on n tosses of an unfair coin, or as that of the identically structured example in which we test n independent examples from a production line and count the number of perfect samples (or equally the number of imperfect ones). In terms of symbols we single out some event A in a trial of experiment E, often regarding it as 'success', and let X be the number of times event A occurs in n independent trials of E, where $P(A) = p$.

In this case we say X is a *binomial* random variable, or has the *binomial distribution*, with *parameters* n, p. Denoting the distribution by $\text{Bin}(n, p)$, we may write $X \sim \text{Bin}(n, p)$. The sample space is $T = \{(a_1, a_2, \dots, a_n): a_i = A \text{ or } A^c\}$. Here is a formula for the distribution.

Theorem 9.62 *If X is a binomial random variable with parameters n, p then*

$$P(X = r) = \binom{n}{r} p^r (1 - p)^{n-r}, \quad r = 0, 1, \dots, n. \tag{9.41}$$

Proof Since $P(A^c) = 1 - p$, the probability of the sequence $AA \dots AA^c \dots A^c$ (r symbols A followed by $n - r$ symbols A^c) is $p^r (1 - p)^{n-r}$. But this is unchanged if the sequence is permuted, since we multiply the same real numbers; and the quantity of sequences so obtained is the number of ways to choose r out of n positions for an 'A', namely $\binom{n}{r}$. Now the result follows by Axiom P3, since the sequences are individual outcomes, and thus disjoint.

Example 9.63 Suppose $1/3$ of a certain organisation are smokers. Of five chosen at random, find the probabilities that (i) exactly two smoke, (ii) at least two smoke, (iii) the last chosen is the third smoker to be found.

Solution Here we make five trials of the experiment 'check for a smoker'. The success event A is 'the person smokes'. Then the number X who smoke is a binomial random variable with parameters $n = 5$, $p = 1/3$. We calculate as follows.

(i) $P(X = 2) = \binom{5}{2} \left(\frac{1}{3}\right)^2 \left(\frac{2}{3}\right)^3 = \frac{80}{243}$ by (9.41).

(ii) $P(X \geq 2) = 1 - P(X = 0) - P(X = 1)$ by the complement rule

$= 1 - \left(\frac{2}{3}\right)^5 - \binom{5}{1}\left(\frac{1}{3}\right)\left(\frac{2}{3}\right)^4 = \frac{131}{243}$ by (9.41).

(iii) P(5th chosen is 3rd smoker) $= P$(2 smoke in the first 4 and the 5th smokes)

$$= P(2 \text{ smoke in the first 4})P(\text{the 5th smokes})$$

$$= \binom{4}{2}\left(\frac{1}{3}\right)^2\left(\frac{2}{3}\right)^2 \cdot \left(\frac{1}{3}\right) = \frac{8}{81}.$$

Remark 9.64 Notice that in (ii) we could have calculated $P(X \geq 2)$ as $P(X = 2) + P(X = 3) + P(X = 4) + P(X = 5)$ but were able to reduce the calculation from four to two terms using the Complement Rule to infer $P(X \geq 2) = 1 - P(X = 0) - P(X = 1)$. In (iii) we used independence between the first four samples and the fifth to simplify the problem, before applying the binomial formula (9.41).

Theorem 9.65 *Let X be a binomial random variable with parameters n, p. Then the expected value and variance are given by*

$$\boxed{E(X) = np \quad and \quad V(X) = np(1 - p).} \tag{9.42}$$

Proof Substituting for $P(X = r)$ from (9.41) we have

$$E(X) = \sum_{r=0}^{n} rP(X = r) = \sum_{r=0}^{n} r\binom{n}{r}p^r(1 - p)^{n-r}$$

$$= \sum_{r=1}^{n} r\binom{n}{r}p^r q^{n-r} \qquad \text{where } q = 1 - p, \text{ since the } r = 0 \text{ term is zero}$$

$$= \sum_{r=1}^{n} n\binom{n-1}{r-1}p^r q^{n-r} \qquad \text{by the formula for} \binom{n}{r}, \text{Theorem 9.12}$$

$$= np \sum_{s=0}^{n-1} \binom{n-1}{s}p^s q^{n-1-s} \qquad \text{on setting } s = r - 1$$

$$= np(p + q)^{n-1} \qquad \text{by the Binomial Formula, Theorem 9.12(v)}$$

$$= np \qquad \text{since } p + q = 1.$$

The variance can be derived similarly, with somewhat more effort; however, both $E(X)$ and $V(X)$ can be obtained after the theory of Section 10.2.3 by a much simpler calculation, so we will be content with the one direct derivation at this stage.

9.4.2 The Poisson distribution

We seek a distribution for a random variable X which counts for example

- phone calls in one minute at an exchange,
- misprints in one page of a large text,
- alpha particles emitted by a radioactive source per second,
- vehicles passing a busy intersection per hour,
- white blood corpuscles in a sample.

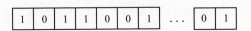

Figure 9.16 Time/space subdivided so that each box contains one or zero event.

Why should such a search be successful? One thing common to these examples is the counting of isolated arrivals in time or space. Let us tentatively assume the further features listed below.

(A) The events do not bunch together arbitrarily closely, so for a small enough portion of space or time we may neglect the possibility of more than one occurring,
(B) they occur at a fixed average rate λ per unit of time or space,
(C) events in one interval do not affect occurrence in any other (non-overlapping) interval.

Suppose time/space is divided into a sufficiently large number n of equal boxes, so that in accordance with (A), each box contains either one or zero event (Figure 9.16).

At this stage of modelling, X is a binomial random variable based on n trials. By hypothesis the probability of the event under consideration occurring in any one box is a constant, p. But we know that in the binomial case $E(X) = np$ (Theorem 9.65), and hence we may equate np and λ. For a model allowing arbitrarily large n, we let n tend to infinity whilst keeping $np = \lambda$ or $p = \lambda/n$. Then

$$P(X = r) = \binom{n}{r} p^r (1 - p)^{n-r}$$

$$= \frac{n(n - 1)(n - 2) \cdots (n - r + 1)}{r!} \left(\frac{\lambda}{n}\right)^r \left(1 - \frac{\lambda}{n}\right)^{n-r}$$

$$= \frac{\lambda^r}{r!} \left[\left(1 - \frac{1}{n}\right)\left(1 - \frac{2}{n}\right) \cdots \left(1 - \frac{r - 1}{n}\right)\right] \left(1 - \frac{\lambda}{n}\right)^{-r} \left(1 - \frac{\lambda}{n}\right)^{n}.$$

Since $(1 - x/n) \to 1$ as $n \to \infty$, for any fixed x, so does any finite product of such factors, and it remains to investigate $(1 + x/n)^n$. According to the Binomial Formula (Theorem 9.12), the coefficient of x^k in this expression is

$$\binom{n}{k} \cdot \frac{1}{n^k} = \frac{n(n - 1) \cdots (n - k + 1)}{n^k k!} = \left(1 - \frac{1}{n}\right) \cdots \left(1 - \frac{k - 1}{n}\right) \bigg/ k! \to 1/k!$$

Hence $(1 + x/n)^n \to \sum_{k=0}^{\infty} \frac{x^k}{k!}$, which is the series expansion of e^x (see Swokowski, 2000, or Moore, 2003). Setting $x = -\lambda$, we obtain $P(X = r) \to e^{-\lambda}\lambda^r/r!$. Notice that besides $E(X)$ constant at value λ, we have $V(X) = \lambda(1 - \lambda n)$ (by Theorem 9.65) which tends to λ as $n \to \infty$. All this both motivates the next definition (first given by Poisson in 1837, see Figure 9.17) and establishes the theorem following it.

Definition 9.66 A discrete random variable X has a *Poisson distribution* Po(λ) if

$$P(X = r) = \frac{e^{-\lambda}\lambda^r}{r!} \quad (r = 0,\, 1,\, 2, \ldots). \tag{9.43}$$

Theorem 9.67 *(a) If X has the Poisson distribution* Po(λ) *then $E(X) = \lambda = V(X)$, (b) the binomial distribution* Bin(n, p) *tends to the Poisson* Po(λ) *as $n \to \infty$ with $np = \lambda$.*

Remark 9.68 According to (b) above, the Poisson distribution is a candidate for approximating the binomial distribution Bin(n, p) for large n. When used as such we shall call it the *Poisson approximation* to the binomial. The discussion above Definition 9.66 shows the accuracy is better for r small relative to n. We will test this after a Poisson example.

Example 9.69 A book of 600 pages contains 40 typographical errors. If these occur randomly throughout the text, what is the probability that ten pages selected at random will (i) be error-free, (ii) contain not more than two errors.

Figure 9.17 Siméon Denis Poisson, 1781–1840, sketch by Ward Somerville.

Solution We assume that typing errors are a Poisson process. Let X be the number of errors on ten pages. The mean error rate over one page is $40/600 = 1/15$, and over ten pages is $E(X) = \lambda = 10/15 = 2/3$. For (i) we require $P(X = 0) = e^{-2/3}$ (by (9.43)) = 0.51 approx. For (ii) we calculate

$$P(X \leq 2) = p(0) + p(1) + p(2) \quad \text{where as usual } p(x) \text{ denotes } P(X = x)$$

$$= e^{-\lambda}(1 + \lambda + \lambda^2/2) \quad \text{with } \lambda = 2/3, \ \text{by (9.43)}$$

$$= 0.97 \text{ approx.}$$

Example 9.70 Compare results from the binomial distribution and Poisson approximation for the following problem. A certain connector is sold in boxes of 100. Given that the probability of an individual item being defective is 0.005, determine the probability that not more than one in a box is defective.

Solution Let X denote the number of defective items in a box. Then X is binomial with parameters $100, 0.005$, so the probability is (to four decimal places)

$$P(X \leq 1) = p(0) + p(1) = (0.995)^{100} + 100(0.005)(0.995)^{99} = 0.9102.$$

The Poisson approximation has $\lambda = np = 0.5$, giving

$$P(X \leq 1) = P(X = 0) + P(X = 1) = e^{-\lambda}(1 + \lambda) = e^{-0.5}(1.5) = 0.9098.$$

Example 9.71 A volume of fluid contains on average five bacteria per cc. Find the probability that (i) a sample of 1 cc contains no bacterium, (ii) a sample of 2 cc does not exceed four bacteria.

Solution (i) X = number of bacteria in a 1 cc sample is Poisson with parameter $\lambda = 5$. Hence $P(X = 0) = e^{-\lambda} = 0.0067$ approx. (ii) In a 2 cc sample the expected value is $\lambda = 10$, and, if Y is the number of bacteria found, then $P(Y \leq 4) = e^{-\lambda}(1 + 10 + 50 + 1000/6 + 10^4/24) = 0.029$.

9.4.3 The normal distribution

The *normal*, or *Gaussian*, distribution is in some sense the mother, or perhaps archetype, of all distributions; see Figure 9.18. Many processes are well-modelled by this distribution; some examples for which it is often valid are

- numerical features in manufacture, such as height, lifetime, ...,
- ditto for individuals in a population, human or otherwise,
- scores in an examination,
- errors in measurement,
- noise in a general sense, including visual distortions.

Moreover, the normal distribution, although itself continuous, may be used as an approximation even for some discrete discriptions such as the binomial and Poisson cases (see later). Probably the best explanation for this universal behaviour is to be found in the celebrated Central Limit Theorem (Theorem 10.45), which asserts that any random variable which is the sum of a large number N of others tends to be normally distributed as N tends to infinity.

Figure 9.18 Abraham de Moivre, 1667–1754, sketch by Ward Somerville. He and Laplace used the normal/Gaussian distribution before Gauss.

A further characteristic is mathematical simplicity, in ways which will appear as we proceed. The normal/Gaussian distribution $N(\mu, \sigma^2)$ has two parameters μ, σ^2 which are, as the notation suggests, the expected value and variance of any corresponding random variable. However, results for the general normal case flow from those for the simplest case $N(0, 1)$, which we define below.

The standard normal distribution

Definition 9.72 A continuous random variable Z has the *standard normal distribution* $N(0, 1)$ if its pdf has the form

$$\phi(z) = \frac{1}{\sqrt{(2\pi)}}e^{-z^2/2} \quad (z \in \mathbf{R}). \tag{9.44}$$

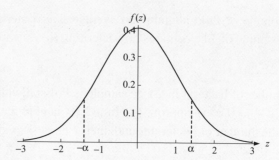

Figure 9.19 Graph of the standard normal distribution $\phi(z)$. By symmetry, $P(Z \geq \alpha) = P(Z \leq -\alpha)$.

This is illustrated in Figure 9.19. Notice first that it is a valid distribution, for (i) $\phi(z) \geq 0$ because every real power of e is positive, and (ii) the constant $\sqrt{(2\pi)}$ has been chosen so that $\int \phi(z)\mathrm{d}z = 1$, over the whole real line **R**; this equality, together with $E(Z) = 0$, $V(Z) = 1$, follows from the lemma below. Of course the symmetry of the graph about the y-axis suffices in itself to show that $E(Z) = 0$ (why?). Note the standard notation below: an integral over **R** is an integral from $-\infty$ to ∞.

Lemma 9.73

$$\int_{\mathbf{R}} x^n e^{-x^2/2}\mathrm{d}x = \begin{cases} \sqrt{2\pi}, & \text{if } n = 0, 2, \\ 0, & \text{if } n = 1. \end{cases}$$

Proof Denote the integral value by I. In the hardest case, $n = 0$, the difficulty of integrating $e^{-x^2/2}$ is circumvented by using properties of infinity! We first express the square of I as an integral over the whole plane. To evaluate this we change to polar coordinates (for more on this, see Remarks 10.13), integrate over a disk $D(R)$ of radius R centred at the origin, then let R tend to infinity to obtain the integral over the whole plane. Thus

$$I^2 = \int_{\mathbf{R}} e^{-x^2/2}\mathrm{d}x \int_{\mathbf{R}} e^{-y^2/2}\mathrm{d}y = \iint_{\mathbf{R}^2} e^{-(x^2+y^2)/2}\mathrm{d}x\,\mathrm{d}y$$

$$= \operatorname*{Lim}_{R \to \infty} \iint_{D(R)} e^{-r^2/2}\, r\,\mathrm{d}r\,\mathrm{d}\theta$$

$$= \operatorname*{Lim}_{R \to \infty} \int_0^{2\pi} \mathrm{d}\theta \int_0^R r e^{-r^2/2}\mathrm{d}r = \operatorname*{Lim}_{R \to \infty} 2\pi\big[-e^{-r^2/2}\big]_0^R$$

$$= \operatorname*{Lim}_{R \to \infty} 2\pi\big(1 - e^{-R^2/2}\big),$$

which equals 2π; hence $I = \sqrt{2\pi}$. (Hence $\int_{\mathbf{R}} \phi(z)\mathrm{d}z = (1/\sqrt{2\pi})(\sqrt{2\pi}) = 1$.) Given this, the calculation for $n = 2$ proceeds by parts:

$$\int_{\mathbf{R}} x^2 e^{-x^2/2}\mathrm{d}x = \big[x\big(-e^{-x^2/2}\big)\big]_{-\infty}^{\infty} + \int_{\mathbf{R}} e^{-x^2/2}\mathrm{d}x = \sqrt{2\pi}.$$

Finally we have for $n = 1$

$$\int_{\mathbf{R}} x e^{-x^2/2}\mathrm{d}x = \big[-e^{-x^2/2}\big]_{-\infty}^{\infty} = 0 - 0 = 0.$$

Table 9.7. *The cdf* $\Phi(z)$ *of the standard normal distribution to two decimal places. To four places the value is zero for* $z \leq -4$, *and for* $z = -3, -2, -1$ *it is respectively* 0.0013, 0.0228, *and* 0.1587.

z	0	0.1	0.2	0.3	0.4	0.5	0.6	0.7	0.8	0.9	1.0
$\Phi(z)$	0.50	0.54	0.58	0.62	0.66	0.69	0.73	0.76	0.79	0.82	0.84

Theorem 9.74 *The standard normal distribution with pdf* $\phi(z)$ *and cdf* $\Phi(z)$ *has expected value* 0 *and variance* 1. *It satisfies for any real number* a, *and for* $b \geq 0$,

$$(i)\Phi(-a) = 1 - \Phi(a), \quad and \quad (ii) \ P(|Z| \leq b) = 2\Phi(b) - 1. \qquad (9.45)$$

Proof We have $E(Z) = 0$ by Lemma 9.73 with $n = 1$, and then $V(Z) = E(Z^2) - E(Z)^2$ (by (9.38)) $= 1$ by Lemma 9.73. For (i) we observe that $\Phi(-a) = P(Z \leq -a) = P(Z \geq a)$ (by symmetry) $= 1 - P(Z \leq a) = 1 - \Phi(a)$. Finally, $P(|Z| \leq a) = P(-a \leq Z \leq a) = \Phi(a) - \Phi(-a) = 2\Phi(a) - 1$, by part (i).

The cumulative distribution function $\Phi(z)$ cannot be written usefully in terms of standard functions, so it is tabulated for the purpose of calculating probabilities. A sample is Table 9.7, with $\Phi(z)$ for negative z given by (i) of (9.45).

Example 9.75 With Z a standard normal random variable, $Z \sim N(0, 1)$, we have

(i) $P(Z \leq 0) = 0.5$,
(ii) $P(0.2 \leq Z \leq 0.4) = \Phi(0.4) - \Phi(0.2) = 0.66 - 0.58 = 0.08$,
(iii) $P(Z \leq -0.1) = 1 - \Phi(0.1)$ (by (9.45)) $= 1 - 0.54 = 0.46$,
(iv) $P(|X| \leq 0.3) = 2\Phi(0.3) - 1$ (by (9.45)) $= 2(0.62) - 1 = 0.24$.

The normal distribution in general

Starting with a standard normal variable Z, we may multiply by σ and add μ to create a new random variable $X = \sigma Z + \mu$, with mean μ and variance σ^2 according to (9.36) and (9.39). Furthermore, by (9.33) the pdf of X may be expressed as $f(x) = (1/\sigma)f((X - \mu)/\sigma)$, or

$$f(x) = \frac{1}{\sqrt{2\pi\sigma^2}} \, e^{-\frac{1}{2}\left(\frac{x-\mu}{\sigma}\right)^2} \quad (x \in \mathbf{R}). \qquad (9.46)$$

See Figure 9.20.

When X has this pdf, (9.46), we say X is *normal with mean/expected value* μ *and variance* σ^2; in symbols, $X \sim N(\mu, \sigma^2)$. Setting $\mu = 0$ and $\sigma = 1$, we recover the standard normal distribution as a special case. As suggested above, calculations with the normal distribution are often best done by reducing to this case and using tables: we simply observe that if $X \sim N(\mu, \sigma^2)$ then $(X - \mu)/\sigma \sim N(0, 1)$. The next example illustrates this.

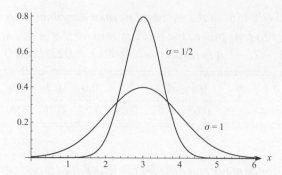

Figure 9.20 The normal distribution with two values of σ. Both have $\mu = 3$ and so are symmetrical about $x = 3$. The smaller value of σ causes variable values to be more closely clustered around the mean.

Example 9.76 The radius of a certain cable is normally distributed with mean 0.7 units and variance 0.0004. (i) Find the probability that the radius exceeds 0.71. (ii) The cable is considered defective if its radius differs from the mean by more than 0.008. How satisfactory is the manufacturing process?

Solution The radius X satisfies $X \sim N(0.7, 0.0004)$, hence the variable $Z = (X - 0.7)/0.02$ is standard normal. The solutions are therefore, with the help of (9.45),

(i) $P(X > 0.71) = P\left(\dfrac{X - 0.7}{0.02} > \dfrac{0.71 - 0.7}{0.02}\right) = P(Z > 1/2) = 1 - \Phi(1/2) = 0.31,$

(ii) $P(\text{good cable}) = P(|X - 0.7| \leq 0.008) = P(|Z| \leq 0.4) = 2\Phi(0.4) - 1$ (by (9.45)) $= 0.32$.
   This is too small! The process must be improved to increase the proportion of successful outputs.

Measuring in units of σ Let $X \sim N(\mu, \sigma^2)$. Then we have for any number k that

$$P(X \leq \mu + k\sigma) = P(Z \leq k) \quad \text{where } Z \sim N(0, 1)$$

$$= \Phi(k), \text{ independently of } \mu, \sigma.$$

See Table 9.8.

This independence has important practical consequences. Here are two viewpoints from which it may be applied. (i) The probability of being between j and k standard deviations from the mean depends only on j, k, and not on which particular normal distribution is involved. Specifically,

$$P(\mu + j\sigma \leq X \leq \mu + k\sigma) = \Phi(k) - \Phi(j). \tag{9.47}$$

Table 9.8. *The probability that a random variable X in*
$N(\mu, \sigma^2)$ *is within $k\sigma$ of the mean is by definition*
$P(|X - \mu| \leq k\sigma)$, *or equivalently*
$P(\mu - k\sigma \leq X \leq \mu + k\sigma)$. *Here are some key values.*

k	1	2	3
$P(\mu - k\sigma \leq X \leq \mu + k\sigma)$	0.6826	0.9544	0.9974

(ii) We can compare the likelihoods of outcomes from different normally distributed variables by reducing both to $N(0, 1)$. This is exemplified below.

Example 9.77 If maths scores are $N(40, 400)$ and biology $N(60, 100)$, which is more creditable: a score of 70 in maths or 80 in biology?

Solution A natural first thought is that, moving from maths to biology, the mean goes up by 20 whereas the score goes up by only 10, therefore the maths score is better. But now consider the more delicate approach of (ii) above.

Maths scores have $\mu = 40, \sigma = 20$, so the score of 70 reduces to 1.5 in $N(0, 1)$. In biology, however, $\mu = 60$ and $\sigma = 10$ so that 80 reduces to 2. This is higher than 1.5 and we conclude that *biology represents a better score*. The problem is solved, but to dispel any lingering doubt let X, Y be the maths and biology scores respectively. The biology score is the *less likely to be exceeded*, for, with $Z \sim N(0, 1)$,

$$P(X \geq 70) = P(Z \geq 1.5)$$
$$> P(Z \geq 2.0) \quad \text{(see Figure 9.19)} = P(Y \geq 80).$$

9.4.4 Other distributions

We introduce here, briefly, some distributions we shall occasionally require, and which are also useful for illustrating general results and providing exercises.

The discrete case The *binomial* distribution, the topic of Section 9.4.1, is that of the number of times an event A occurs in n Bernoulli trials. We recall that a trial is *Bernoulli* if it has exactly two outcomes – an event A does or does not occur. We sometimes need the natural generalisation to the *multinomial distribution*, in which the outcomes of each of n independent trials must be one of k events A_i ($1 \leq i \leq k$). If event A_i has probability p_i and occurs X_i times, then

$$P(X_i = n_i, 1 \leq i \leq k) = \frac{n!}{n_1! n_2! \cdots n_k!} p_1^{n_1} p_2^{n_2} \cdots p_k^{n_k}.$$

The *geometric* and *Pascal* distributions are often used in the context of testing a batch of manufactured articles for defects, whilst a random variable X with a *hypergeometric*

Table 9.9. *Some discrete distributions including binomial and Poisson.*
In Bernoulli trials $p = P(\text{success})$, *in the hypergeometric case*
$p = r/N$. *Always* $q = 1 - p$.

Name	$P(X = r)$	Context	$E(X)$	$V(X)$
Binomial, Bin(n, p)	$\binom{n}{r} p^r (1 - p)^{n-r}$ $r = 0, 1, \ldots, n.$	$X =$ number of successes in n Bernoulli trials (Section 9.4.1)	p	npq
Poisson, Po(λ)	$e^{-\lambda}\lambda^r / r!$ $r = 0, 1, 2, \ldots$	$X =$ number of occurrences of an isolated event in time or space, with mean rate λ (Section 9.4.2)	λ	λ
Pascal	$\binom{r-1}{k-1} p^k q^{r-k}$ $r \geq k \geq 1$ integers	$X =$ number of Bernoulli trials if last trial is kth success (Example 9.63)	k/p	kq/p^2
Geometric	pq^{r-1}	case $k = 1$ of Pascal	$1/p$	q/p^2
Hypergeometric	$\binom{s}{r}\binom{N-s}{N-r} / \binom{N}{n}$, $r = 0, 1, \ldots, n$	$X =$ number of special objects in random choice of n objects (without replacement) from N of which s are special (Example 9.13)	np	$npq \cdot \dfrac{N - n}{N - 1}$

distribution may be thought of as the number of men (or women) in a committee chosen from a pool of both sexes. Further information about these distributions is given in Table 9.9.

The continuous case

Arguably second only to the ubiquitous *normal* distribution, the *uniform* distribution is widely used in its capacity as a simple but effective starting point for simulating many others (Section 11.3), because it is especially easy to simulate on a computer (see Section 11.3.2). The *gamma* distribution is used in reliability theory (Meyer, 1970) in predicting the time to multiple failure, with the *exponential* distribution as the special case of a single failure. However, the gamma distribution is also useful in providing links between other distributions (Section 10.2.2), indeed another special case is the *chi-squared* distribution, that of a sum of squares of normal variables, and used in hypothesis testing (Section 11.1.6). We mention finally the *Cauchy* distribution, that of the ratio of two normal variables (Example 10.16). Below we give another instance of *Cauchy*, together with a summary table (9.10) of those noted here.

Example 9.78 Let Θ be uniformly distributed on the interval $[-\pi/2, \pi/2]$. We show that $X = a \tan \Theta$ has the Cauchy distribution of Table 9.10. This situation arises when, for example, X defines the spot illuminated by a narrow beam whose direction is measured by angle θ, as represented in Figure 9.21.

Proof X is well defined, strictly increasing, and takes all real values, for θ in the open interval $(-\pi/2, \pi/2)$. From Table 9.10, the random variable Θ has pdf $f(\theta) = 1/\pi$ on

Table 9.10. *Some continuous distributions.*

name	pdf	context	$E(X)$	$V(X)$
Normal, $N(\mu, \sigma^2)$	$\dfrac{1}{\sqrt{2\pi}\sigma^2}\mathrm{e}^{-\frac{1}{2}\left(\frac{x-\mu}{\sigma}\right)^2}$ $(x \in \mathbf{R})$	physical characteristics, measurement errors, noise, approximation to binomial, Poisson and others (Section 10.3.3).	μ	σ^2
Uniform on $[a, b]$, $U[a, b]$	$1/(b-a)$, $x \in [a, b]$	a default assumption (see Example 9.42). Used mostly for simulation (Section 11.3.2).	$\dfrac{a+b}{2}$	$\dfrac{(b-a)^2}{12}$
Gamma, $\Gamma_{\alpha, u}$ $(\alpha, u > 0)$	$\dfrac{\alpha^u}{\Gamma(u)}x^{u-1}\mathrm{e}^{-\alpha x}$ $(x > 0)$	1. Reliability theory (Meyer, 1970), 2. Generalises and links several other distributions (Section 10.2.2). See Table 9.6 for $\Gamma(z)$.	$\dfrac{u}{\alpha}$	$\dfrac{u}{\alpha^2}$
Gamma, $G(\alpha, \beta)$ $\alpha, \beta > 0$	$\dfrac{x^{\alpha-1}\mathrm{e}^{-x/\beta}}{\beta^\alpha \Gamma(\alpha)}$ $(x > 0)$	Alternative notation: $G(\alpha, \beta) = \Gamma_{1/\beta, \alpha}$, α = shape parameter (for skewness), β = scale parameter.	$\alpha\beta$	$\alpha\beta^2$
Exponential, $\exp(\alpha)$ $\alpha > 0$	$\alpha\mathrm{e}^{-\alpha t}$ $(t > 0)$	Time to failure if failure rate is constant α. (Case $u = 1$ of gamma, see Example 9.43)	$\dfrac{1}{\alpha}$ (Example 9.41)	$\dfrac{1}{\alpha^2}$

(cont.)

Table 9.10 (*cont.*)

name	pdf	context	E(X)	V(X)
Chi-squared, with n degrees of freedom χ^2_n	$\dfrac{z^{n/2-1}e^{-z/2}}{2^{n/2}\Gamma(n/2)}$ $(z > 0)$	1. Statistical inference (Section 11.1.6), 2. Sum of squares of n normal random variables (Section 10.2.2). (Case $\alpha = 1/2$, $u = n/2$ of gamma.)	n,	$2n$
Cauchy, $a > 0$	$\dfrac{a}{\pi(x^2 + a^2)}$ $x \in \mathbf{R}$	Ratio of two normal variables (Example 10.16; see also Example 9.78)	0	undefined
Beta, Be (α, β) $\alpha, \beta > 0$	$\dfrac{x^{\alpha-1}(1-x)^{\beta-1}}{\mathrm{B}(\alpha, \beta)}$ $0 < x < 1$	If U, V are independent and either chi-squared with $2k$, $2m$ degrees of freedom, or gamma with same scale parameter and shape parameters k, m, resp., then $U/(U+V)$ is Be(k, m)	$\dfrac{\alpha}{\alpha + \beta}$	$\dfrac{\alpha\beta}{(\alpha + \beta)^2(\alpha + \beta + 1)}$
Laplace, or doubly exponential, $\lambda > 0$	$\dfrac{\lambda}{2}e^{-\lambda|x|}$ $x \in \mathbf{R}$	$\lambda =$ dispersion parameter Additive image noise	0	2λ

Note: Be denotes the beta *distribution*, whose definition involves the beta *function* B.

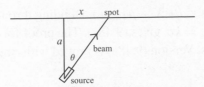

Figure 9.21 The position of the spot illuminated by a narrow beam is given by $x = a \tan \theta$. Hence if θ is uniformly distributed then x has the Cauchy distribution.

this interval. Hence, by Formula (9.32), the random variable X has pdf

$$g(x) = f(\theta)/|dx/d\theta| = 1/(\pi a \sec^2\theta) = 1/[\pi a(1 + \tan^2 \theta)] = a/[\pi(a^2 + x^2)],$$

which is indeed the Cauchy distribution.

Exercise Derive the Pascal pdf of Table 9.9.

9.5 Mean inequalities

Here we present two famous inequalites which we shall need in succeeding chapters, concerning the mean of a pdf; they are valid for both discrete and continuous random variables.

9.5.1 Chebychev's Inequality

How does σ measure variability about the mean $\mu = E(X)$? Given μ, σ we cannot reconstruct the actual pdf unless we already know something about its structure (if normal, it is given exactly by these parameters). Neverthelesss, we can in all cases give very useful bounds on the quantities $P(|X - \mu| \geq c)$ for any constant c. The result is known as *Chebychev's Inequality*, which we give in the variously convenient forms appearing below.

Theorem 9.79 *(Chebychev's Inequality) Let X be a random variable, discrete or continuous, with mean μ and variance σ^2 both finite. Then, for any positive numbers ε, k and real c,*

$$P(|X - c| \geq \varepsilon) \leq E[(X - c)^2]/\varepsilon^2, \tag{9.48a}$$

$$P(|X - \mu| \geq \varepsilon) \leq \sigma^2/\varepsilon^2, \tag{9.48b}$$

$$P(|X - \mu| \geq k\sigma) \leq 1/k^2. \tag{9.48c}$$

Proof Let X be continuous with pdf $f(x)$; then

$$\sigma^2 = E[(X - \mu)^2] = \int_{\mathbf{R}} (x - \mu)^2 f(x)dx.$$

But, since $(x - \mu)^2 f(x) \geq 0$ for all values of x, the integral cannot increase when the range of integration is reduced, hence

$$\sigma^2 \geq \int_{|x-\mu|\geq\varepsilon} (x - \mu)^2 f(x)dx \geq \int_{|x-\mu|\geq\varepsilon} \varepsilon^2 f(x)dx = \varepsilon^2 \int_{|x-\mu|\geq\varepsilon} f(x)dx,$$

which by definition equals $\varepsilon^2 P(|X - \mu| \geq \varepsilon)$. Dividing through by ε^2, we obtain Equation (9.48b), then setting $\varepsilon = k\sigma$ gives (9.48c). The proof for discrete X is similar, with integrals replaced by sums. Version (9.48a) is proved with c replacing μ, the steps being identical.

Example 9.80 Setting $k = 2$ in (9.48c) we obtain $P(|X - \mu| \geq 2\sigma) \leq 0.25$ for *all* pdfs, discrete and continuous. How does this compare with the exact value, say for $X \sim N(\mu, \sigma^2)$? In that case we have, using the complementary event,

$$P(|X - \mu| \geq 2\sigma) = 1 - P(|X - \mu| < 2\sigma) \quad = 1 - P(|(X - \mu)/\sigma| < 2)$$
$$= 2 - 2\Phi(2) \quad \text{(by (9.45))} = 0.0456,$$

about one fifth of the upper bound 0.25.

Remark 9.81 In practice Chebychev's Inequality is used to obtain estimates when it is impossible or inconvenient to compute exact values, or when we wish to prove a general result. Indeed, the inequality is most important for the derivation of the illuminating Law of Large Numbers, giving limits on how large a sample must be taken for relative frequency to be close to probability. We shall be ready to do this after random vectors are introduced in the next chapter.

Zero variance We close this section with an observation related to the next. According to the Chebychev form (9.48b), zero variance implies that $P(|X - \mu| \geq \varepsilon) = 0$ and hence $P(|X - \mu| \leq \varepsilon) = 1$, for all $\varepsilon > 0$. It follows that $P(X = \mu) = 1$, and in this case we say (see introduction to Section 9.3) that X is *concentrated at the single point* μ.

Exercise If discrete X is concentrated at a point, what does the pdf look like?

9.5.2 Jensen's Inequality

In this section we prove a result concerning expected value, known as *Jensen's Inequality*. It will be applied to good effect time and again in Chapter 13 on information theory. First some definitions and a little discussion are necessary.

Definitions 9.82 Let lower case p denote the position vector, or coordinate vector, of a point P, and x_P its x-coordinate. The point on a line segment AB dividing AB internally in the ratio $t : 1$, where $0 \leq t \leq 1$, has position vector $(1 - t)a + tb$, which we shall also write $sa + tb$ subject to $s + t = 1$ (see (1.2)). Thus AB consists precisely of such points. Let $u(x)$ be a real function defined on some real interval I. If A, B are points on the graph of u the segment AB is called a *chord* of u. Then we say that:

> $u(x)$ is a *convex function* if all its chords lie on or above the graph.   (9.49)

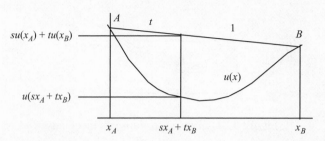

Figure 9.22 The graph of a convex function $u(x)$: every chord AB lies above the graph. The $t : 1$ ratio is indicated above the chord.

That is, if, for distinct points A, B on the graph, we have as depicted in Figure 9.22,

$$su(x_A) + tu(x_B) \geq u(sx_A + tx_B). \tag{9.50}$$

The function $u(x)$ is called *strictly* convex if the inequality in (9.50) is strict (for $0 < t < 1$). If it is reversed we have the definition of $u(x)$ as a *concave function*. Equivalently, $-u(x)$ is convex. Notice that, geometrically, the minus sign is equivalent to a reflection in the x-axis. Clearly, adding any constant to $u(x)$, or multiplying it by a positive constant, does not affect its being convex or being concave, whilst multiplying by a negative constant interchanges these properties. Thus, for $x \geq 1$, $\log x$ is concave but $2 - \log x$ is convex, as illustrated in Figure 9.23. This statement is independent of the base of logs because $\log_d x = (\log_d e) \log_e x$, so that we convert from one base to another by multiplying by a positive constant.

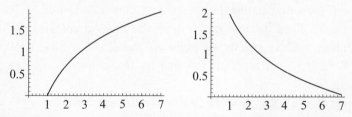

Figure 9.23 For $x \geq 1$ the function $\log x$ is concave and $2 - \log x$ is convex.

Suppose the derivatives $u'(x)$ and $u''(x)$ exist. For u to be strictly convex, as in Figure 9.22, it clearly suffices for the gradient $u'(x)$ to be an increasing function of x, and this will be so if its derivative in turn, $u''(x)$, is positive. Hence the following result from calculus.

Theorem 9.83 *If the real function $u(x)$ on interval I is twice differentiable, then we have the following, in which, if the left hand part is strict, then so is the right.*

$$u''(x) \geq 0 \text{ on } I \Rightarrow u(x) \text{ is convex,}$$
$$u''(x) \leq 0 \text{ on } I \Rightarrow u(x) \text{ is concave.}$$

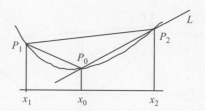

Figure 9.24 Diagram for Jensen's Inequality.

Note If $u(x) = \log x$ to base e then $u'(x) = 1/x$ and $u''(x) = -1/x^2 < 0$, confirming by Theorem 9.83 that the log function to any base is concave, indeed strictly so. Here is the result we are aiming at.

Theorem 9.84 *(Jensen's Inequality) (a) Let $u(x)$ be a concave or convex function on the open interval I in R_X. Then*

$$E[u(X)] \leq u(E[X]) \quad (u \text{ concave}), \tag{9.51a}$$
$$E[u(X)] \geq u(E[X]) \quad (u \text{ convex}). \tag{9.51b}$$

(b) Suppose concavity/convexity is strict, but equality holds in (9.51). If X is discrete it is concentrated at the mean, $X = E[X]$. If X is continuous then $u(X) = u(E[X])$ except at a set of isolated points of R_X.

Proof Let $u(x)$ be convex. It suffices to prove the results in this case, because if $v(x)$ is concave then $u(x)$ defined as $-v(x)$ is convex. (a) Let x_0 be an arbitrary point of $I = (a, b)$. Then because $a < x_0 < b$ the interval contains points x_1 strictly between a and x_0, and x_2 strictly between x_0 and b. Thus $x_1 < x_0 < x_2$. Consider the triangle $P_1 P_0 P_2$ of corresponding points on the graph of $u(x)$, as portrayed in Figure 9.24.

By convexity of $u(x)$, the point P_0 lies below (or on) the chord $P_1 P_2$ and so slope $P_1 P_0 \leq$ slope $P_0 P_2$. Hence P_1, and indeed any graph point to the left of P_0, lies above (or on) the line L through P_0 and P_2. Similarly any graph point to the right of P_2 lies above (or on) L. Now consider x_2 as a variable and let it tend to x_0.

The slope of $P_0 P_2$ decreases but is bounded below by that of $P_1 P_0$, and hence $P_0 P_2$ tends to a line L_0 through P_0 of slope λ, say, and such that any graph point lies on or above L_0. That is,

$$u(x) \geq u(x_0) + \lambda(x - x_0).$$

Substituting the random variable X for x in this inequality gives a relation between the values of two random variables at every point of a common sample space:

$$u(X) \geq u(x_0) + \lambda(X - x_0). \tag{9.52}$$

Therefore the same inequality holds for their expectations, so applying (9.36) to the right hand side and then setting $x_0 = E[X]$ we obtain, for both discrete and continuous X,

$$E[u(X)] \geq u(x_0) + \lambda(E[X] - x_0)$$
$$= u(E[X]) \tag{9.53}$$

(b) The case of equality Now we suppose further that convexity is strict and that $E[u(X)] = u(E[X])$. Consider firstly the case that X *is discrete*, $R_X = \{x_i\}$. We show by induction that, for $n = 2, 3, \ldots,$ if $\sum p_i = 1$ (all $p_i \geq 0$), then

$\sum_{i=1}^{n} p_i u(x_i) \geq u(\sum_{i=1}^{n} p_i x_i)$, where equality implies all but one p_i is zero.

Proof (This includes an alternative proof of (9.51) for X discrete.) In the starting case $n = 2$ we have $p_1 + p_2$; hence by strict convexity $p_1 u(x_1) + p_2 u(x_2) > u(p_1 x_1 + p_2 x_2)$, *unless* of course we are really considering only one point, when $p_1 = 1$ or $p_2 = 1$. Suppose inductively that the result holds for $n = k - 1 (\geq 2)$ and consider the case $n = k$. Assuming $p_k \neq 1$ (or there is nothing to prove), we obtain

$$\sum_{i=1}^{k} p_i u(x_i) = p_k u(x_k) + (1 - p_k) \sum_{i=1}^{k-1} q_i u(x_i) \quad q_i = p_i / (1 - p_k), \sum q_i = 1$$
$$\geq p_k u(x_k) + (1 - p_k) u \left(\sum_{i=1}^{k-1} q_i x_i \right) \quad \text{by the inductive hypothesis}$$
$$\geq u \left(p_k x_k + (1 - p_k) \sum_{i=1}^{k-1} q_i x_i \right) \quad \text{by case } n = 2$$
$$= u \left(\sum_{i=1}^{k} p_i x_i \right) \quad \text{since } (1 - p_k) q_i = p_i, 1 \leq i < k.$$

Overall equality implies (i) equality in case $n = 2$, whence $p_k = 0, q_i = pi$, and (ii) equality in case $n = k - 1$, whence exactly one p_i equals 1 and the rest are zero. This completes the proof by induction on n. If X is *continuous* the sums are replaced by integrals, which may be viewed as the limits of ever closer approximation by sums. This results in the slightly different conclusion given for this case. More information may be found in McEliece (1983).

Example 9.85 Given a concave function $u(x)$, all we need to make Jensen's Inequality work for us is a set of non-negative numbers p_i summing to 1, and an arbitrary set of corresponding real numbers x_i. Then we regard $\{x_i\}$ as the values taken by a random variable, with pdf given by $\{p_i\}$. With this framework the inequality translates to

$$\sum p_i u(x_i) \leq u \left(\sum p_i x_i \right). \tag{9.54a}$$

In particular, since the log function is concave,

$$\sum p_i \log(x_i) \leq \log \left(\sum p_i x_i \right). \tag{9.54b}$$

This gives an easy proof of hard-looking but necessary results we shall require later in information theory, such as (putting $x_i = 1/p_i$ above)

$$\sum_{i=1}^{n} p_i \log \frac{1}{p_i} \le \log \sum_{i=1}^{n} p_i \cdot \frac{1}{p_i} = \log n. \tag{9.55}$$

Exercise What does Jensen's Inequality state in the case $u(x) = e^x$?

Exercises 9

1 ✓ (i) Derive Formula (9.4) for $P(A \cup B \cup C)$. (ii) Suppose that events A, B, C each have probability $1/3$, that $A \cap B$ and $B \cap C$ have probability $1/4$, but that A, C cannot occur together. Find the probability that at least one of A, B, C occurs.

2 ✓ A random 3-letter word is formed using a 26-letter alphabet V. Write down an expression for the sample space and for the event A: the word has three distinct letters. Find the probability of A, and of the event that at least two letters are the same.

3 ✓ A sample of six components is taken from a box containing 15 good and five defective ones. Find the probability that exactly half the sample are good.

4 ✓ A ball is drawn at random from a bag containing four red balls, five white, and six blue. Find the probability it is (a) red, (b) white, (c) not red, (d) red or blue.

5 ✓ Write down the Chain Rule formula for $P(A \cap B \cap C \cap D)$. From the bag of Exercise 9.4, four balls are removed in succession. Find the probability that exactly two in succession are red.

6 ✓ Black box 1 consists of components A, B in parallel; it functions if A, B or both function. Black box 2 is similar with components C, D. The boxes are connected in series. If the components work independently with respective probabilities 0.8, 0.6, 0.5, 0.7, find the probability of functioning of each box separately, and of the series combination.

7 ✓ Prove that if events A and B are independent then so are A and B^c.

8 ✓ Four dice are thrown. Find the probabilities of (a) a total score of five, (b) at least one six.

9 ✓ A company has three factories A, B, C all producing computer X, the respective outputs forming 20%, 50% and 30% of the total. The respective proportions of defective machines are $1/20$, $1/15$ and $1/10$. Find the probability that a randomly chosen computer (a) is defective, (b) came from factory A, given that it was defective. Which factory is it most likely to have come from, if defective?

10 ✓ Compute the pdf of X in Example 9.33. Can you express $p(n)$ as a formula? Verify that $\sum p(n) = 1$.

11 ✓ The pdf of a continuous random variable X is $f(x) = cx^2(3 - x), 0 \le x \le 3$. Determine (a) the constant, c, (b) $P(X \le 1)$, (c) the conditional probability that X is less than $1/2$, given that it lies between 0 and 1.

12 ✓ Let the random variable X be uniform on the interval $[0, 2]$ and let $Y = e^x$. Find (a) the pdf of Y, (b) the expected value of Y by two methods, (c) the variance of Y. (Sections 9.3.4 to 9.3.6)

13 ✓ Suppose $1/4$ of a population have the Z phobia. Find the probabilities that, of four people chosen at random (a) exactly two have the phobia, (b) at least one has it, (c) the last chosen is the third found to have the phobia. (Section 9.4.1)

14 √ An average of 90 phone calls are received by a company during the working day of 8 am to 5 pm. Assuming a Poisson process, find the probability that not more than two calls are received during a 30 minute period. (Section 9.4.2)

15 √ If noise in certain pixels is normally distributed, with mean 5 and variance 4, what is the probability that noise exceeds level 6? (Section 9.4.4)

16 √ Let X be a Poisson random variable with parameter 5. Use a suitable form of Chebychev's Inequality to show that the probability that X lies in $\{3, 4, 5, 6, 7\}$ is at least 4/9. (Section 9.5.1)

17 √ Let X be binomial with $n = 5$, $p = 1/3$. Write down Jensen's Inequality in the case $u(x) = 1/(x + 1)$, and verify its truth numerically. (Section 9.5.2)

10

Random vectors

10.1 Random vectors

The pair (X, Y) is called a *2-dimensional random variable, or random vector*, if X and Y are random variables with the same sample space. See Figure 10.1.

We consider two cases: *discrete*, meaning that the ranges of X, Y are both discrete, and *continuous*, in which the pairs (X, Y) range over an uncountable plane subset (for example a rectangle or disk). The discrete case is often used as a stepping stone to the continuous (see Section 18.3 on information theory), but both are essential in their own right. We shall seek to draw out common properties as well as distinctions, and to present corresponding definitions in parallel. As a foretaste, we define the cdf in both cases as $F(x, y) = P(X \leq x, Y \leq y)$.

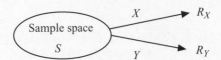

Figure 10.1 (X, Y) is a 2-D random variable when X, Y are random variables with the same sample space. If instead the respective sample spaces are S_X and S_Y we may maintain the structure of this figure by taking $S = S_X \times S_Y$.

10.1.1 Discrete versus continuous

The discrete case Here we make the discrete space of pairs $R = R_X \times R_Y$ into a probability space by associating with each (x, y) in R a number $p(x, y)$ representing $P(X = x, Y = y)$ such that, for $B \subseteq R$,

$$P(B) = \sum_{(x,y) \in B} p(x, y), \tag{10.1}$$

where $$p(x, y) \geq 0 \text{ for all } x, y, \text{ and } \sum_{(x,y) \in R} p(x, y) = 1. \tag{10.2}$$

We call the function p the *joint distribution*, or *joint pdf* of (X, Y). When numerical values are taken we may distinguish the variable, say V, by writing for example $p_V(a)$

Table 10.1. *General form of the joint pdf of a discrete random vector* (X, Y), *showing marginal distributions* $p(x)$, $p(y)$. *If necessary we write* $q(y)$ *in place of* $p(y)$, *for distinctiveness.*

$X \backslash Y$	y_1	y_2	$\ldots$	y_n	Sum
x_1	$p(x_1, y_1)$	$p(x_1, y_2)$	$\ldots$	$p(x_1, y_n)$	$p(x_1)$
x_2	$p(x_2, y_1)$	$p(x_2, y_2)$	$\ldots$	$p(x_2, y_n)$	$p(x_2)$
$\ldots$	$\ldots$	$\ldots$	$\ldots$	$\ldots$	$\ldots$
x_m	$p(x_m, y_1)$	$p(x_m, y_2)$	$\ldots$	$p(x_m, y_n)$	$p(x_m)$
Sum	$p(y_1)$	$p(y_2)$	$\ldots$	$p(y_n)$	

for $P(V = a)$. Or with the present X, Y one may use $q(b)$ for $P(Y = b)$ alongside $p(a)$ for $P(X = a)$. If R is finite, $p(x, y)$ may be represented in a table, of the general form of Table 10.1.

What about the distributions of X, Y individually, known as their respective *marginal distributions*? As suggested by Table 10.1, we write $R_X = \{x_1, x_2, \ldots\}$, $R_Y = \{y_1, y_2, \ldots\}$, terminating when finite with x_m, y_n. Now, since $X = x_i$ must occur with $Y = y_j$ for one and only one value of j at a time, we have

$$P(X = x_i) = P(X = x_i, Y = y_1 \text{ or } X = x_i, Y = y_2 \text{ or} \ldots)$$
$$= P(X = x_i, Y = y_1) + P(X = x_i, Y = y_2) + \cdots,$$

by the Total Probability Formula, (9.20), and similarly for $P(Y = y_j)$. Hence the marginal distribution formulae as indicated in Table 10.1,

$$p(x_i) = \sum_j p(x_i, y_j), \quad p(y_j) = \sum_i p(x_i, y_j). \tag{10.3}$$

Notice that, for simplicity of notation, we often use x, y for typical elements of R_X, R_Y, rather than x_i, y_j as above, provided this suffices for clarity. Thus the first part of (10.3) might be written $p(x) = \sum_y p(x, y)$.

Example 10.1 We calculate sample probabilities from the pdf shown in Table 10.2:

$$p(5, 2) = 1/20,$$
$$p(5) = 1/10 + 1/20 + 1/20 = 1/5,$$
$$q(3) = 1/5 + 1/20 = 1/4,$$
$$P(X < Y) = p(1, 2) + p(1, 3) = 2/5 + 1/5 = 3/5.$$

Table 10.2. *Example pdf for a discrete random vector*
(X, Y) *with* $R_X = \{1, 5\}$, $R_Y = \{1, 2, 3\}$.

$X \backslash Y$	1	2	3
1	1/5	2/5	1/5
5	1/10	1/20	1/20

The continuous case A random vector (X, Y) is by definition continuous if it takes values in some uncountable region R of the plane, and there is a real function $f(x, y)$ that assigns a probability to every event B in R by

$$P(B) = \iint\limits_{B} f(x, y)\mathrm{d}x\,\mathrm{d}y, \tag{10.4}$$

where $f(x, y) \geq 0$ for all x, y and $\iint\limits_{R} f(x, y)\,\mathrm{d}x\,\mathrm{d}y = 1.$ (10.5)

Similarly to the 1-dimensional case, $f(x, y)$ is called the (joint) *probability density function*, or *pdf*, of (X, Y), and we insist without loss of generality that $f(x, y) = 0$ for (x, y) outside R. Also, although the pdf of (X, Y) is actually induced from the original sample space S, we continue to focus on the range space of (X, Y). The *marginal distributions* are pdfs for X, Y individually, given by

$$g(x) = \int_{-\infty}^{\infty} f(x, y)\mathrm{d}y \quad \text{and} \quad h(y) = \int_{-\infty}^{\infty} f(x, y)\mathrm{d}x. \tag{10.6}$$

For example, $P(a \leq X \leq b) = P(a \leq X \leq b, Y \in \mathbf{R}) = \int_a^b \mathrm{d}x \int_{-\infty}^{\infty} f(x, y)\mathrm{d}y = \int_a^b g(x)\mathrm{d}x.$ Thus g is indeed a pdf for X.

Example 10.2 Calculate $P(B)$, where B is the event $\{X + Y \geq 1\}$, for the continuous random vector (X, Y) with joint pdf $f(x, y) = y^2 + xy/3,\ 0 \leq x \leq 2, 0 \leq y \leq 1$ (see Figure 10.2).

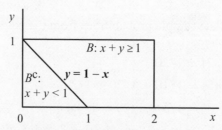

Figure 10.2 Region of integration for event B: $x + y \geq 1$. A rectangle bounds the region outside of which $f(x, y) = 0$.

The integration is slightly simpler if we calculate $P(B)$ as $1 - P(B^c)$ by the Complement Rule:

$$P(B^c) = \int_{x=0}^{1} dx \int_{0}^{1-x} (y^2 + xy/3)dy = \int_{0}^{1} [(1-x)^3/3 + x(1-x)^2/6]dx$$

$$= \int_{0}^{1} (u^3/3 + (1-u)u^2/6)du \quad \text{(putting } u = 1-x) = 7/72.$$

Hence, $P(B) = 65/72$.

Random n-vectors The definitions (10.1) to (10.6) for the case $n = 2$ extend naturally to general n and we shall comment on these as the occasion arises, perhaps most notably in Section 10.2.5.

10.1.2 Independence

Definition 10.3 Let (X, Y) be a random vector. We say X, Y are *independent* if their joint pdf is the product of the marginal pdfs. Equivalently, their joint pdf factorises into a function of x times a function of y (an exercise for the reader, shortly below). Thus, in the discrete case $P(X = x, Y = y) = P(X = x)P(Y = y)$ or in shorter notation $p(x, y) = p(x)p(y)$. More generally, random variables $X_1, \ldots, X_n$ are independent if they have a joint pdf which is the product of a pdf for each X_i separately.

We have the following result, expressing consistency with the 1-dimensional version of independence.

Theorem 10.4 *Let (X, Y) be a random vector and let A, B be events depending only on the individual random variables X, Y respectively (see Figure 10.3). Then, if X, Y are independent,*

$$P(A \cap B) = P(A)P(B). \tag{10.7}$$

Proof (Continuous case) We have $P(A \cap B)$ equal by definition to

$$\iint_{A \cap B} f(x, y)\, dx\, dy = \iint_{A \cap B} g(x)h(y)\, dx\, dy = \int_A g(x)\, dx \int_B h(y)\, dy = P(A)P(B).$$

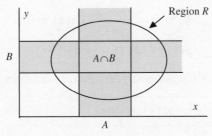

Figure 10.3 Here the random vector (X, Y) takes values in the elliptical region R, but event A depends only on X, and event B only on Y.

Example 10.5 (i) The discrete variables with joint pdf displayed in Table 10.2 are *not* independent because $P(X = 1, Y = 2) = 2/5 = 0.40$, whereas

$$P(X = 1)P(Y = 2) = \left(\frac{1}{5} + \frac{2}{5} + \frac{1}{5}\right)\left(\frac{2}{5} + \frac{1}{20}\right) = \frac{4}{5} \cdot \frac{9}{20} = 0.36.$$

(ii) Daily demand for coal is a continuous random variable X with a pdf $g(x) = \mathrm{e}^{-x}$ ($x > 0$), whilst, independently, supply is a continuous random variable Y with pdf $h(y) = y\mathrm{e}^{-y}$ ($y > 0$). Find the probability that demand exceeds supply.

Solution We require $P(X > Y)$. Since X and Y are given to be independent, (X, Y) has joint pdf $f(x, y) = \mathrm{e}^{-x}y\mathrm{e}^{-y} = y\mathrm{e}^{-x-y}$ ($x, y > 0$).

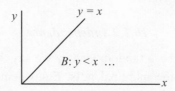

Figure 10.4 Region representing the event $\{X > Y\}$.

The event $X > Y$ corresponds to the region B in Figure 10.4, with probability

$$\iint_B y\mathrm{e}^{-x-y}\mathrm{d}x\,\mathrm{d}y = \int_0^\infty y\mathrm{e}^{-y}\mathrm{d}y \int_{x=y}^\infty \mathrm{e}^{-x}\mathrm{d}x = \int_0^\infty y\mathrm{e}^{-2y}\mathrm{d}y = 1/4 \text{ (by parts)}.$$

Exercise Show that a continuous pdf $f(x, y) = g(x)h(y)$ has marginal pdfs $g(x)$, $h(y)$.

10.1.3 Conditional probability

The discrete case Let (X, Y) be a discrete random vector and let x, y be arbitrary elements of the ranges R_X, R_Y. Continuing the spirit of previous abbreviated notation, we write $p(x|y)$ for $P(X = x|Y = y)$, which equals $P(X = x, Y = y)/P(Y = y)$ from the definition of conditional probability. Then we have the compact expressions

$$p(y|x) = \frac{p(x, y)}{p(x)} \quad (p(x) > 0), \tag{10.8}$$

$$p(x, y) = p(x)p(y|x), \tag{10.9}$$

whence the *Chain Rule for Conditionals* on random variables $X_1, \ldots, X_n$,

$$p(x_1, x_2, \ldots, x_n) = p(x_1)p(x_2 \mid x_1)p(x_3 \mid x_1, x_2)\cdots p(x_n \mid x_1, x_2, \ldots, x_{n-1}).$$

$$p(y) = \sum_x p(x)p(y|x) \quad (\textit{total probability}), \tag{10.10}$$

Table 10.3. *Transition matrix of values $p(y|x)$ for the channel of Example 10.6.*

$x \backslash y$	0	1	*
0	0.7	0.2	0.1
1	0.7	0.1	0.2

$$p(x|y) = p(y|x)p(x)/p(y) \quad \text{(Bayes' Theorem)}, \tag{10.11}$$

$$X, Y \text{ are independent} \Leftrightarrow p(y) = p(y|x) \Leftrightarrow p(x) = p(x|y). \tag{10.12}$$

Here (10.9) is a rearrangement of (10.8) and (10.10) is the Total Probability Formula (9.20) which gives the denominator in Bayes' Theorem. Notice that for fixed $a \in R_X$ the function $k(y)$ defined as $p(y|a)$ is indeed a distribution, because $\sum_y k(y) = p(a)^{-1} \sum_y p(a, y)$ (by (10.8)) $= p(a)^{-1} p(a) = 1$. It is called the *conditional distribution of Y given $X = a$*. Correspondingly, the *expected value of Y given $X = a$* is given by $\sum_y y k(y)$, or

$$E(Y \mid X = a) = \sum_y y p(y \mid a). \tag{10.13}$$

Example 10.6 Let the random variable X, taking values 0, 1, denote the input to a noisy channel, and Y its output, which is 0, 1, or a special symbol * if the input was unrecognisable. The channel is characterised by its *transition matrix*, a table of values of $p(y|x)$, shown as Table 10.3.

Given that symbols 0, 1 are input with equal probability 1/2, determine (i) the probability of output *, (ii) the probability that 0 was sent, given that it was unrecognisable, (iii) the conditional pdf of Y given $X = 1$, and (iv) the expected value of Y given $X = 1$, if we let * = 2.

Solution (i) Since numerical values are to be used here we shall adopt the notation $p(b|a) = P(Y = b|X = a)$ and $p(a) = P(X = a)$. Then $P(Y = *) = p(*|0)p(0) + p(*|1)p(1) = (0.1)\frac{1}{2} + (0.2)\frac{1}{2} = 0.15$.

(ii) Here we determine the probability of a 'cause', so Bayes' Theorem is appropriate. It gives $P(X = 0|Y = *) = p(*|0)p(0)/P(Y = *) = (0.1)(0.5)/0.15 = 1/3$.

(iii) The pdf of Y given $X = 1$ is by definition the second row of Table 10.3, and so (iv) the expected value is $0(0.7) + 1(0.1) + 2(0.2) = 0.5$.

The continuous case We want a continuous analogue of the conditional distribution as used in the discrete case. The problem is that the probability of a continuous random variable taking a specific value is zero, and only intervals, or areas in the 2D case, have nonzero probabilities. To solve this we start on safe ground by considering $P(Y \leq \eta | a \leq X \leq a + \varepsilon)$, which is a cdf for Y given that X lies in the interval $[a, a + \varepsilon]$. This interval may be arbitrarily small provided it remains an *interval* rather than a value.

The crucial question is, does the cdf collapse to zero as ε tends to zero? We shall see that the answer is NO; in fact subsequent differentiation to obtain a pdf gives an expression formally identical to that for the discrete case, a highly desirable state of affairs. We need an ancillary result.

Lemma 10.7 *Let a real function $\phi(x)$ have a continuous derivative on an open interval containing $a, a + \varepsilon$, where $\varepsilon > 0$. Then, for some function $\lambda(\varepsilon)$ with $\lambda(\varepsilon) \to 0$ as $\varepsilon \to 0$,*

$$\int_a^{a+\varepsilon} \phi(x)\mathrm{d}x = \varepsilon\phi(a) + \varepsilon\lambda(\varepsilon).$$

Proof Rearranging, we must show that $\mu(\varepsilon) \to 0$ as $\varepsilon \to 0$, where

$$\mu(\varepsilon) = \frac{1}{\varepsilon} \int_a^{a+\varepsilon} \phi(x)\mathrm{d}x - \phi(a)$$

$$= \frac{1}{\varepsilon} \int_a^{a+\varepsilon} (\phi(x) - \phi(a))\mathrm{d}x, \text{ since } \int_a^{a+\varepsilon} \phi(a)\mathrm{d}x = \varepsilon\phi(a).$$

But by Taylor's Theorem of Elementary Calculus (see e.g. Swokowski, 2000) we may write $\phi(x) = \phi(a) + R(x - a)$, where R is a function satisfying $|R(y)| \le K|y|$ for some constant, K. So

$$\mu(\varepsilon) = \frac{1}{\varepsilon} \int_a^{a+\varepsilon} R(x - a)\mathrm{d}x, \text{ and}$$

$$|\mu(\varepsilon)| \le \frac{1}{\varepsilon} \int_a^{a+\varepsilon} |R(x - a)|\mathrm{d}x = \frac{1}{\varepsilon} \int_0^\varepsilon |R(y)|\mathrm{d}y \le \frac{K}{\varepsilon} \int_0^\varepsilon y\mathrm{d}y = K\varepsilon/2,$$

where we substitute $y = x - a \ge 0$, and note that $|y| = y$ here. Thus $\mu(\varepsilon) \to 0$ as required.

Main result We suppose that (X, Y) has a continuous pdf $f(x, y)$ with marginal distribution $g(x)$ for X. Then

$$P(Y \le \eta \mid a \le X \le a + \varepsilon) = \frac{P(Y \le \eta, a \le X \le a + \varepsilon)}{P(a \le X \le a + \varepsilon)}$$

$$= \int_a^{a+\varepsilon} \mathrm{d}x \int_{-\infty}^\eta f(x, y)\mathrm{d}y \bigg/ \int_a^{a+\varepsilon} g(x)\mathrm{d}x \qquad (*)$$

$$= \left[\varepsilon \int_{-\infty}^\eta f(a, y)\mathrm{d}y + \varepsilon\lambda_1(\varepsilon) \right] \bigg/ [\varepsilon g(a) + \varepsilon\lambda_2(\varepsilon)],$$

where λ_1, λ_2 are the results of applying Lemma 10.7 to (*) with $\phi(x) = \int_{-\infty}^\eta f(x, y)\mathrm{d}y$ and $\phi(x) = g(x)$ for the numerator and denominator respectively. In this form we can divide top and bottom by $\varepsilon > 0$, then let $\varepsilon \to 0$, obtaining

$$P(Y \le \eta \mid a \le X \le a + \varepsilon) \longrightarrow \int_{-\infty}^\eta f(a, y)\mathrm{d}y/g(a).$$

Differentiating to convert the cdf to a pdf, we obtain $f(a, \eta)/g(a)$, so it is indeed appropriate to define the *conditional pdf* $p(y|x)$ *of Y given X* for the continuous case in a manner formally similar to the discrete case:

$$p(y|x) = f(x, y)/g(x) \tag{10.14}$$

and, further,

$$E(Y \mid X = a) = \int_{-\infty}^{\infty} y p(y|a) \mathrm{d}y. \tag{10.15}$$

Theorem 10.8 *If the continuous random variables X, Y have joint pdf $f(x, y)$ and marginals g, h then X, Y are independent if and only if $p(y|x) = h(y)$. There are the relations*

$$f(x, y) = g(x)p(y|x), \quad h(y) = \int g(x)p(y|x)\mathrm{d}x, \quad p(x|y) = p(y|x)g(x)/h(y),$$

and the general Chain Rule for Conditionals, on continuous random variables $X_1, \ldots, X_n$:

$$p(x_1, x_2, \ldots, x_n) = p(x_1)p(x_2 \mid x_1)p(x_3 \mid x_1, x_2) \cdots p(x_n \mid x_1, x_2, \ldots, x_{n-1}).$$

Proof This is a series of short applications of definitions, for example $h(y) = \int f(x, y)\mathrm{d}x$, which equals $\int g(x)p(y \mid x)\mathrm{d}x$ by (10.14).

10.2 Functions of a random vector

10.2.1 Product and quotient

Let variable $Z = u_1(X, Y)$, a function of the random vector (X, Y). Since X, Y are functions of s, the sample space variable, so is Z, and hence Z is itself a random variable.

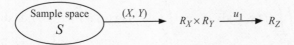

Figure 10.5 Here u_1 represents a function of a random vector.

We shall see how to find a pdf for Z in terms of the joint pdf of (X, Y), both in general and for important cases such as $X + Y$, XY, X/Y, $\mathrm{Min}(X, Y)$.

The discrete case First let us make the point that the discrete case is most easily disposed of because it requires enumeration rather than integration. The examples below illustrate what is involved.

Example 10.9 Suppose two production lines produce outputs which are random variables X, Y with respectively $R_X = \{0, 1, 2\}$, $R_Y = \{1, 2, 3, 4\}$. (i) Let $Z = X + Y$, the total items produced. Then $R_Z = \{1, 2, \ldots, 6\}$ and $P(Z = 3) = p(0, 3) + p(1, 2) + p(2, 1)$.

(ii) Let $W = X/Y$, the ratio of production scores. Then $R_W = \{0, 1/2, 1/3, 1/4, 1, 2, 2/3\}$ and, for example, $P(W = 1/2) = p(1, 2) + p(2, 4)$.

Exercise Determine $P(W = 1)$ above, given that all outcomes (x, y) are equally likely.

Back to continuous The easiest way to obtain a pdf for $Z = u_1(X, Y)$ is, paradoxically, to introduce a second function $W = u_2(X, Y)$, use the formula for change of variables in a 2-dimensional integral, Corollary 10.11, then extract the pdf for Z as a marginal. We begin with the n-dimensional version (see Sections 10.2.5 and 10.4.3).

Theorem 10.10 *Let ψ, ϕ be inverse transformations between n-dimensional subsets of real n-space $\mathbf{R}^n$, given by*

$$y = \phi(x) = (u_1(x), \ldots, u_n(x)),$$
$$x = \psi(y) = (v_1(y), \ldots, v_n(y)).$$

Suppose that the partial derivatives $\partial x_i / \partial y_j$ exist and are continuous. Denote the Jacobian J of ψ, namely the determinant of the $n \times n$ matrix with i, j element $\partial x_i / \partial y_j$, by either expression:

$$\partial x / \partial y \text{ or } \partial(x_1, \ldots, x_n)/\partial(y_1, \ldots, y_n).$$

Then, writing $dx = dx_1 \cdots dx_n$ and $dy = dy_1 \ldots dy_n$, the change of coordinates $x \to y$ in an n-dimensional integral is given by

$$\boxed{\int_A f(x)dx = \int_{\phi(A)} f(\psi(y))|\partial x / \partial y|dy.} \tag{10.16}$$

The derivatives $\partial y_j / \partial x_i$ exist continuously and $\partial x / \partial y = 1/(\partial y / \partial x)$. In the linear case $x = yA$, where A is a matrix, the Jacobian reduces to $\partial x / \partial y = \det(A)$, with absolute value 1 in the case of an isometry.

Corollary 10.11 *In the case $n = 2$ above, with $\phi(x, y) = (z, w)$, and $\phi(R) = T$, we have*

$$\iint\limits_R f(x, y)dx\, dy = \iint\limits_T |J| f(x(z, w), y(z, w))dz\, dw. \tag{10.17}$$

Hence, if (X, Y) has joint pdf $f(x, y)$ then (Z, W) has joint pdf $k(z, w) = |J| f(x(z, w), y(z, w))$.

Corollary 10.12 *Let (X, Y) be a continuous random vector with joint pdf $f(x, y)$. Define random variables $W = XY$ and $Z = X/Y$. Then pdfs for W and Z are given by*

$$p(w) = \int_{-\infty}^{\infty} \frac{1}{|u|} f(u, w/u)du \ (W = XY), \tag{10.18}$$

$$q(z) = \int_{-\infty}^{\infty} |v| f(vz, v)dv \ (Z = X/Y). \tag{10.19}$$

Proof Observe that, in theory, we could transform variables from x, y to w, z and get both p and q from the new joint pdf. However, more manageable formulae are obtained if w, z are treated separately, as outlined above Theorem 10.10. Let us change coordinates from (x, y) to (u, w). Thus, we let $w = xy$ and take as ancillary variable $u = x$. Then

$x = u$, $y = w/u$ and the Jacobian determinant is

$$J = \frac{\partial x}{\partial u}\frac{\partial y}{\partial w} - \frac{\partial x}{\partial w}\frac{\partial y}{\partial u} = 1 \cdot \frac{1}{u} - 0 = \frac{1}{u}.$$

So a joint pdf for U, W is given by Corollary 10.11 to be $f(u, w/u)/|u|$, whence (10.18) is obtained. For the rest we change coordinates from (x, y) to (v, z), taking $z = x/y$ with ancillary variable $v = y$. Then $y = v$, $x = vz$ and the Jacobian $\partial(x, y)/\partial(v, z)$ comes out to just $-v$. Hence the joint pdf is $|v| f(vz, v)$ for V, Z, by Corollary 10.11, and the marginal pdf is given by (10.19).

Remarks 10.13 (i) Notice that, in both cases above, we inverted the transformation to obtain expressions for x, y before computing J, because these were in any case required for substitution into $f(x, y)$. However, it is sometimes more convenient to perform the partial differentiations of J with respect to the new variables and use $1/J$ as noted at the end of Theorem 10.10.

(ii) A classic application of Corollary 10.11 is the change from plane Cartesian coordinates x, y to polars r, θ, given by $x = r\cos\theta$, $y = r\sin\theta$. For integration the change is from $dx\,dy$ to $r\,dr\,d\theta$ (cf. the proof of Lemma 9.73), because the Jacobian is

$$\frac{\partial(x, y)}{\partial(r, \theta)} = \begin{vmatrix} \cos\theta & -r\sin\theta \\ \sin\theta & r\cos\theta \end{vmatrix} = r\cos^2\theta + r\sin^2\theta = r.$$

As an example the annular region R: $4 \le x^2 + y^2 \le 9$, $x, y \ge 0$, is converted to a rectangle S: $2 \le r \le 3$, $0 \le \theta \le \pi/2$, portrayed in Figure 10.6.

Such a transformation may reduce a 2-dimensional integral to the product of two 1-dimensional integrals, such as (using Table 9.6 of Section 9.3.6 for the angle integration):

$$\iint_R \frac{x^4 y^4}{(x^2 + y^2)^{3/2}} dx\,dy = \iint_S \frac{r^8 \sin^4\theta \cos^4\theta}{r^3} r\,dr\,d\theta$$

$$= \int_0^{\pi/2} \sin^4\theta \cos^4\theta\,d\theta \int_2^3 r^6 dr = \frac{6177\pi}{512}.$$

Figure 10.6

Table 10.4. *The pdfs considered in Example 10.15.*

Variable	pdf
C	$g(c) = 1$ on $[1, 2]$
D	$k(d) = e^{-d}, d > 0$
$V = D^2$	$h(v) = e^{-\sqrt{v}}/2\sqrt{v}, v > 0$
$Z = C/V$	$q(z), z > 0$ (see solution)

(iii) So far we have not needed to compute a region of integration explicitly. However, to apply formulae (10.18) and (10.19) we must reduce their 1-dimensional ranges of integration to that implied by the range set of $f(x, y)$. This occurs in the next example.

Example 10.14 Suppose that, in a certain circuit, current I and resistance R are continuous random variables with respective pdfs $g(i) = i/2, 0 \le i \le 2$, and $h(r) = r^2/9$, $0 \le r \le 3$. Find the pdf of the voltage $W = IR$.

Solution With I, R assumed independent their joint pdf is $f(i, r) = g(i)h(r)$. Since the ranges of i, r are $[0, 2]$ and $[0, 3]$ the range of W is $[0, 6]$. Its pdf is therefore given by (10.18) as

$$p(w) = \int_{-\infty}^{\infty} g(u)h(w/u)\frac{1}{|u|}du \; (0 \le w \le 6).$$

Following Remark 10.13(iii), we note that $g(u) = 0$ unless $0 < u < 2$, and $h(w/u) = 0$ unless $0 \le w/u \le 3$, i.e. $u \ge w/3$. Thus for w in its range,

$$p(w) = \int_{w/3}^{2} \frac{u}{2}(w^2/9u^2)\frac{1}{u}du = (w^2/18)\int_{w/3}^{2} u^{-2}du = w(6 - w)/36.$$

Example 10.15 The light intensity Z at a point P is given by $Z = C/D^2$, where C is the source candlepower and D is the source distance from P. We assume that C, D are independent, that C is uniformly distributed on the interval $[1, 2]$, and that D has pdf $k(d) = e^{-d}, d > 0$. Find the pdf $q(z)$ of Z.

Solution We set $V = D^2$, find the corresponding pdf $h(v)$, then apply (10.19) to C/V. Clearly the range of Z is $z > 0$. Table 10.4 shows the various pdfs in the order in which we shall compute them.

(i) The uniform variable C has pdf $g(c) = 1$ for c in $[1, 2]$. The function $v(d) = d^2$ is increasing, so, by Formula (9.32), V has pdf $h(v) = k(d)/|v'(d)| = e^{-d}/2d = e^{-\sqrt{v}}/2\sqrt{v}, v > 0$.

(ii) *The pdf q(z) of Z.* Let $f(c, v)$ be the joint pdf for C, V. Then by (10.19)

$$q(z) = \int_{\mathbf{R}} |v| f(vz, v) \mathrm{d}v \qquad \text{the integral from } -\text{infinity to infinity}$$

$$= \int_{\mathbf{R}} |v| g(vz) h(v) \mathrm{d}v \qquad \text{since } C, V \text{ are independent}$$

$$= \int v \cdot 1 \cdot (\mathrm{e}^{-\sqrt{v}}/2\sqrt{v}) \mathrm{d}v \qquad \text{the range is to be determined}$$

$$= \int x^2 \mathrm{e}^{-x} \mathrm{d}x \qquad \text{on setting } x = \sqrt{v}$$

$$= [-\mathrm{e}^{-x}(x^2 + 2x + 2)] = [\lambda(x)], \text{ say.}$$

Now for the range of integration. The range of C is $[1, 2]$ so the factor $g(vz)$ is zero except when $1 \le vz \le 2$, that is, $1/z \le v \le 2/z$. Hence $q(z) = \lambda(\sqrt{2/z}) - \lambda(\sqrt{1/z})$, where $z > 0$.

Example 10.16 (*Ratio of normal variables*) We find the pdf of $Z = X/Y$, where $X \sim N(0, \sigma_1^2)$ and $Y \sim N(0, \sigma_2^2)$ are independent and so have a joint pdf $f(x, y)$ which is the product of their individual densities. By Formula (9.46) this product is

$$f(x, y) = (1/2\pi\sigma_1\sigma_2)\mathrm{e}^{-(x^2/2\sigma_1^2 + y^2/2\sigma_2^2)}. \tag{10.20}$$

Using (10.19) for the pdf $q(z)$ of Z, we obtain

$$q(z) = \int_{\mathbf{R}} |v| f(vz, v) \mathrm{d}v \qquad \text{(nonzero for all } z\text{)}$$

$$= \int_{\mathbf{R}} \frac{a|v|}{2\pi\sigma_1^2} \mathrm{e}^{-v^2(z^2 + a^2)/2\sigma_1^2} \mathrm{d}v \qquad \text{where } a = \sigma_1/\sigma_2$$

$$= 2\int_0^\infty \frac{av}{2\pi\sigma_1^2} \mathrm{e}^{-v^2(z^2 + a^2)/2\sigma_1^2} \mathrm{d}v \qquad \text{by symmetry in } v$$

$$= \int_0^\infty \frac{a}{\pi\sigma_1^2} \cdot \frac{\sigma_1^2}{z^2 + a^2} \cdot \mathrm{e}^{-t} \mathrm{d}t \qquad \text{where } t = v^2(z^2 + a^2)/2\sigma_1^2$$

$$= \frac{a}{\pi(z^2 + a^2)}, z \in \mathbf{R},$$

which is the *Cauchy distribution* listed in Table 9.10.

10.2.2 Convolution: from $X + Y$ to sum of squares

Theorem 10.17 *If the independent continuous random variables X, Y have pdfs g, h concentrated on $(0, \infty)$ then $X + Y$ has pdf the convolution $g*h$, given by*

$$(g * h)(s) = \int_0^s g(x)h(s - x)\mathrm{d}x = \int_0^s g(s - x)h(x)\mathrm{d}x. \tag{10.21}$$

Further, convolution is (i) commutative: $g*h = h*g$, (ii) associative: $g*(h*k) = (g*h) * k$, and (iii) distributive over addition: $g*(h + k) = g*h + g*k$.

Proof Since X, Y are independent they have a joint pdf $f(x, y) = g(x)h(y)$. We transform the variables to $u = x + y, v = y$, so that the pdf sought is that of the random variable U. Now $y = v$ and $x = u - v$ so the Jacobian is $\partial(x, y)/\partial(u, v) = 1 \cdot 1 - (-1)(0) = 1$. Hence, according to Corollary 10.11, the pair U, V has joint pdf $1 \cdot f(x(u, v), y(u, v)) = g(u - v)h(v)$, whence the marginal pdf for $U = X + Y$ is $\int g(u - v)h(v)dv$ with range of integration **R**. But $g(u - v)$ is zero unless $u - v > 0$, that is $v < u$, whilst $h(v)$ is zero unless $v > 0$, so the range reduces to $0 < v < u$. This gives the second integral in (10.21) on substitution of $u = s, v = x$.

For the first two convolution properties let g, h, k be pdfs of X, Y, Z respectively and observe that $X + Y = Y + X, (X + Y) + Z = X + (Y + Z)$. Alternatively they may be proved directly. In any case property (i) is the second equality in (10.21). For (iii) we observe that

$$\int g(u - v)(h(v) + k(v))dv = \int g(u - v)h(v)dv$$
$$+ \int g(u - v)k(v)dv, \text{ over any fixed range.}$$

Example 10.18 Given that X, Y are independent continuous random variables with the same pdf $f(t) = te^{-t}, t > 0$, we find the pdf of their sum. By the result above, $X + Y$ has pdf $(f^* f)(s)$ equal to

$$\int_0^s f(t)f(s - t)dt = \int_0^s te^{-t}(s - t)e^{-(s-t)}dt = e^{-s} \int_0^s t(s - t)dt = s^3 e^{-s}/6.$$

Convolution and the Γ distribution Besides its use in reliability theory, the gamma distribution, reviewed below, provides links between, and insights into, several other distributions of importance (see especially Example 10.20). As may be expected, it is related to the gamma function of calculus, whose most relevant properties for the present study are reviewed in Table 9.6. A continuous random variable X is said to have a *gamma probability distribution* if its pdf is

$$\Gamma_{\alpha,u}(x) = \frac{\alpha^u}{\Gamma(u)} x^{u-1} e^{-\alpha x}, \ x > 0, \tag{10.22}$$

for some parameters $\alpha, u > 0$ (Table 9.9). Notice that X is concentrated on $(0, \infty)$. The fact that $\Gamma_{\alpha,u}$ *is* a pdf, that is, it is non-negative and its integral over **R** is 1, follows from the definition of $\Gamma(u)$ in Table 9.6. This easily yields $E(X)$ and $V(X)$, as follows:

$$E(X) = \int_0^\infty x[\alpha^u/\Gamma(u)]x^{u-1}e^{-\alpha x}dx = (u/\alpha)\int_0^\infty [\alpha^{u+1}/\Gamma(u + 1)]x^u e^{-\alpha x} \, dx = u/\alpha.$$

Similarly $E(X^2) = (u(u + 1)/\alpha^2)\int_0^\infty [\alpha^{n+2}/\Gamma(u + 2)]x^{u+1}e^{-\alpha x}dx = u(u + 1)/\alpha^2$. And finally $V(X) = E(X^2) - E(X)^2 = [u(u + 1) - u^2]/\alpha^2 = u/\alpha^2$. We are ready to establish the *convolution property of* Γ, for later application.

Theorem 10.19 *The gamma distribution satisfies* $\Gamma_{\alpha,u}{}^*\Gamma_{\alpha,v} = \Gamma_{\alpha,u+v}$, *or in the G notation (Table 9.9)* $G(\alpha_1, \beta)^*G(\alpha_2, \beta) = G(\alpha_1 + \alpha_2, \beta)$.

Proof We have, for some constant K,

$$(\Gamma_{\alpha,u} * \Gamma_{\alpha,v})(s) = K \int_0^s x^{u-1} e^{-\alpha x} (s-x)^{v-1} e^{-\alpha(s-x)} dx \qquad \text{by definition}$$

$$= K \int_0^s x^{u-1} (s-x)^{v-1} e^{-\alpha s} dx \qquad \text{on simplifying}$$

$$= K \int_0^1 s^{u+v-1} t^{u-1} (1-t)^{v-1} e^{-\alpha s} dt \qquad \text{putting } x = st$$

$$= K s^{u+v-1} e^{-\alpha s} \int_0^1 t^{u-1} (1-t)^{v-1} dt,$$

which is a constant multiple of $\Gamma_{\alpha,u+v}(s)$ by (10.22). But this and the left hand side are both pdfs, so the multiple must be 1, and the proof is complete.

Example 10.20 Find the distribution of $Z = X_1^2 + \cdots + X_n^2$, a sum of squares of n independent normal random variables $X_i \sim N(0, \sigma^2)$.

Solution We know that each X_i has pdf $g(x) = (2\pi\sigma^2)^{-1/2} e^{-x^2/2\sigma^2}$, and according to (9.33) the variable $Y = X_i^2$ has pdf and scena of squares

$$h(y) = [g(\sqrt{y}) + g(-\sqrt{y})]/2\sqrt{y}$$
$$= (2\pi\sigma^2)^{-1/2} y^{-1/2} e^{-y/2\sigma^2}$$
$$= K \cdot \Gamma_{1/2\sigma^2, 1/2}(y), \qquad \text{for some constant, } K.$$

We could calculate K and find that it is 1, but such a calculation would be superfluous, since $K = 1$ is implied by the fact that h and g are both pdfs. Thus, by Theorems 10.17 and 10.19, the sum of squares Z has pdf

$$\left(\Gamma_{1/2\sigma^2, 1/2} * \Gamma_{1/2\sigma^2, 1/2} * \cdots * \Gamma_{1/2\sigma^2, 1/2} \right)(z) = \Gamma_{1/2\sigma^2,\, n/2}(z). \qquad (10.23)$$

Remarks (1) When $V(X) = 1$ the distribution above is called the χ^2 *distribution with n degrees of freedom* or χ_n^2 (see Table 9.9), and is extensively used to test the validity of probability models for the 'real world' (see Section 11.1.6). A particular concern for us will be the hypothesis of a normal distribution of errors.

(2) *The sum of normal random variables is normal* but the convolution method of showing this presents an impossible integral. Nevertheless, an explicit pdf is easily obtained by the method of moments in Section 10.3.1, Example 10.41.

Exercise What are $E(X)$ and $V(X)$ for the χ_n^2 distribution.

More on convolution

Notice that in (10.21) the integrand is zero outside the interval $[0, s]$, so we could equally well write

$$(f * g)(s) = \int_{-\infty}^{\infty} f(x)g(s-x)dx = \int_{\mathbf{R}} f(x)g(s-x)dx,$$

and indeed this is the definition of $f*g$ for functions which are not necessarily pdfs, but for which the integral does exist. Thus we conveniently obviate the need to write in finite limits, until we are ready to take them into account. We note here the effect on convolution, of scaling or translating the variables and of differentiating the functions. This will be useful in Chapter 16, for example, for wavelet edge-detection, and in Chapter 17 for B-splines by convolution.

Theorem 10.21 *Let $f*g = h$ and denote differentiation by f' etc. Then, for any translation α and scaling factor d, we have (i) $f(t + \alpha)*g(t) = h(s + \alpha)$, (ii) $f(t/d) * g(t/d) = d \times h(s/d)$, (iii) with $f(t)$, $f'(t)$, and $g(t)$ all continuous on the given integration intervals, we have following cases of dh/ds (the third under further conditions noted below).*

$g(t)$, $f(t)$ concentrated on	$h = f*g$ reduces to	dh/ds
$[a, b]$	$\int_a^b f(s - t)g(t)dt$	$f'*g$
$[0, \infty)$	$\int_0^s f(s - t)g(t)dt$	$f'*g + f(0)g(s)$
All of **R**	$\int_{-\infty}^{\infty} f(s - t)g(t)dt$	$f'*g$

Proof (i) $f(t + a)*g(t) = \int_R f(t + a)g(s - t)dt = \int_R f(z)g(s + a - z)dz$ (putting $z = t + a$) $= h(s + a)$.

(ii) $f(t/d)*g(t/d) = \int_R f(t/d)g((s - t)/d)dt = \int_R f(z)g(s/d - z)dz$ (putting $z = t/d$) $= d \times h(s/d)$.

(iii) This result requires the Leibnitz formula for *differentiating under the integral sign*:

$$\frac{d}{dx} \int_a^b \phi(s, t)dt = \int_a^b \frac{\partial \phi}{\partial s}(s, t)dt + b'(0)\phi(s, b) - a'(0)\phi(s, a),$$

allowing a, b to be functions of s. In our case, $\phi(s, t) = f(s)g(s - t)$. Provided a, b are finite, it suffices for ϕ and $\partial f/\partial s$ to be continuous, satisfied since f, f' and g are continuous. In the third case it suffices that $|\phi(s, t)| \leq M(t)$ for some function $M(t)$ whose integral over **R** exists. See e.g. Maxwell (1962) or Wrede and Spiegel (2002).

Example We verify Theorem 10.21(iii) for $f(t) = t^2$, $g(t) = e^{-t}$ both concentrated on $[0, \infty)$:

(i) $f(t) * g(t) = \int_0^s (s - t)^2 e^{-t}dt = s^2 - 2s + 2 - 2e^{-s}$, with derivative $2s - 2 + 2e^{-s}$,

(ii) $f'(t) * g(t) + f(0)g(s) = \int_0^s 2(s - t)e^{-t}dt + 0 = 2s - 2 + 2e^{-s}$, as required.

10.2.3 Expectation and variance

Let $Z = u(X, Y)$ be a 1-dimensional random variable, where X, Y are random variables on the same sample space. We consider only the cases that X, Y, Z are all continuous or all discrete. If discrete, we write in the usual way $R_Z = \{z_1, z_2, \ldots\}$, the sequence terminating if the range is finite.

In computing $E(Z)$ we can avoid determining the pdf of Z if it is not otherwise needed, by the following result, which is proved similarly to its counterpart in the 1-dimensional case. We recall that a random vector (X, Y) has by definition a joint pdf denoted by $p(x, y)$ in the discrete case, $f(x, y)$ in the continuous.

Theorem 10.22 *The following holds with the random vector (X, Y) replaced by $(X_1, \ldots, X_n)$. We cite $n = 2$ for simplicity: the expectation of $Z = u(X, Y)$ satisfies*

$$E(Z) = \begin{cases} \sum_{x,y} u(x, y) p(x, y) \, (Z \text{ discrete}), \\ \iint_{\mathbf{R}^2} u(x, y) f(x, y) \mathrm{d}x \, \mathrm{d}y \, (Z \text{ continuous}). \end{cases}$$

Proof For the second equality we will be content with the argument that it is the limit of the discrete case, obtained by dividing regions of integration into ever smaller discrete parts. A formal argument for the discrete case is that $E(Z)$ equals the first expression below by definition, and hence the rest:

$$\sum_z z P(Z = z) = \sum_z z \sum_{x,y:\, z=u(x,y)} p(x, y) = \sum_z \sum_{x,y:\, z=u(x,y)} u(x, y) p(x, y)$$

$$= \sum_{x,y} u(x, y) p(x, y).$$

Theorem 10.23 *The following holds with the random vector (X, Y) replaced by $(X_1, \ldots, X_n)$. Let $Z = u_1(X, Y)$ and $W = u_2(X, Y)$ for functions u_1, u_2. Then $E(Z + W) = E(Z) + E(W)$.*

Proof In the discrete case (the continuous case replaces sums by integrals)

$$E(Z + W) = \sum_{x,y} [u_1(x, y) + u_2(x, y)] p(x, y) \qquad \text{by Theorem 10.22},$$

$$= \sum_{x,y} u_1(x, y) p(x, y) + \sum_{x,y} u_2(x, y) p(x, y)$$

$$= E(Z) + E(W) \qquad \qquad \text{by Theorem 10.22}.$$

Exercise Repeat the proof steps of Theorem 10.23 with $n = 3$.

Corollary 10.24 *Let $X_1, \ldots, X_n$ be random variables (not necessarily independent). Then*

$$\boxed{E(X_1 + \cdots + X_n) = E(X_1) + \cdots + E(X_n).} \qquad (10.24)$$

Proof The result follows by induction on n, using Theorem 10.23. For the starting case $n = 2$ we set $Z = X_1$, $W = X_2$, and for the inductive step $Z = X_1 + \cdots + X_{n-1}$, $W = X_n$.

Remarks 10.25 (i) Let $c_1, \ldots, c_n$ be constants. Since $E[c_i X_i] = c_i E(X_i)$ by (9.36) we have full *linearity of E* in the sense that $E[\sum_i c_i X_i] = \sum_i c_i E(X_i)$.

(ii) So far we do not have a convenient way to prove that a sum of normal random variables is normal (this will come in Example 10.41), but Corollary 10.24 does enable us to calculate the expected value of the result, and Corollary 10.27 will give the variance.

Theorem 10.26 *The product of independent random variables* $X_1, \ldots, X_n$ *satisfies*

$$E(X_1 \cdots X_n) = E(X_1) \cdots E(X_n). \tag{10.25}$$

Proof We consider only the discrete case $n = 2$, since the extension to general n is similar, and the continuous case analogous. Let independent random variables X, Y have a joint pdf $p(x)q(y)$. Then $E(XY) = \sum_{x,y} xy \cdot p(x)q(y) = \sum_x xp(x) \cdot \sum_y yq(y) = E(X)E(Y)$.

Corollary 10.27 *Let* $X_1, \ldots, X_n$ *be independent random variables, with* $\mu_i = E(X_i)$, *then*

$$
\begin{aligned}
&\text{(a)} \ \ V(X_1 + \cdots + X_n) = V(X_1) + \cdots + V(X_n), \\
&\text{(b)} \ \ V(X_1 X_2) = V(X_1)V(X_2) + \mu_1^2 V(X_2) + \mu_2^2 V(X_1).
\end{aligned} \tag{10.26}
$$

Proof (a) We prove the result here in the case $n = 2$. Induction extends it to general n (this strictly requires the independence results of Theorem 10.36). With $(X_1, X_2) = (X, Y)$ the random variable $Z = X + Y$ satisfies

$$
\begin{aligned}
V(Z) &= E[Z^2] - (E(Z))^2 &&\text{by (9.38)} \\
&= E(X^2 + 2XY + Y^2) - (E(X) + E(Y))^2 &&\text{by Corollary 10.24} \\
&= E(X^2) + 2E(X)E(Y) + E(Y^2) - (E(X) + E(Y))^2 &&\text{by Theorem 10.26} \\
&= E(X^2) - (E(X))^2 + E(Y^2) - (E(Y))^2 &&\text{by cancelling} \\
&= V(X) + V(Y) &&\text{by (9.38).}
\end{aligned}
$$

(b) Consider the discrete case, the continuous being similar, and let X, Y have respective pdfs $p(x), q(y)$. Firstly, we observe that $E(X^2 Y^2) = \sum_{x,y} x^2 y^2 p(x)q(y) = \sum_x x^2 p(x) \sum_y y^2 q(y) = E(X^2)E(Y^2)$. Hence, if we write $W = XY$ the following equalities give Equation (10.26b).

$$
\begin{aligned}
V(W) &= E(W^2) - E(W)^2 = E(X^2)E(Y^2) - (\mu_1 \mu_2)^2 &&\text{by Theorem 10.26} \\
&= \left(V(X) + \mu_1^2\right)\left(V(Y) + \mu_2^2\right) - (\mu_1 \mu_2)^2.
\end{aligned}
$$

Example 10.28 The above results give a delightfully simple way to calculate $E(X), V(X)$ for a binomial random variable $X \sim \text{Bin}(n, p)$. We have $X = X_1 + \cdots + X_n$, where X_i is based on a single trial. Hence

$$
\begin{aligned}
E(X_i) &= 0 \cdot P(X_i = 0) + 1 \cdot P(X_i = 1) = p. \\
V(X_i) &= E(X_i^2) - (E(X_i))^2 \\
&= 0^2 \cdot P(X_i = 0) + 1^2 \cdot P(X_i = 1) - p^2 \\
&= p - p^2.
\end{aligned}
$$

By Corollary 10.24: $E(X) = np$.

By Corollary 10.27: $V(X) = np(1 - p)$ (this completes the alternative proof of (9.42)).

10.2.4 The Law of Large Numbers

The heading of this section is the classic answer to the question of how many trials must be made so that the relative frequency of an event A is close to its theoretical probability.

Theorem 10.29 *(The Law of Large Numbers, Bernoulli form) Let A be an event with $P(A) = p$. Suppose that in n independent trials the relative frequency of A is $f_A = n_A/n$. Then for any $\varepsilon > 0$, and δ with $0 < \delta < 1$,*

$$P(|f_A - p| < \varepsilon) \geq 1 - \delta \text{ provided } n \geq p(1 - p)/\varepsilon^2\delta. \tag{10.27}$$

Proof We use form (9.48) of Chebychev's inequality: $P(|X - \mu| \geq \varepsilon) \leq \sigma^2/\varepsilon^2$, or, taking the complementary event,

$$P(|X - \mu| < \varepsilon) \geq 1 - \sigma^2/\varepsilon^2. \tag{10.28}$$

Now take $X = n_A$, a binomial random variable with parameters n, p and hence with $\mu = np$ and $\sigma^2 = np(1 - p)$ (Example 10.28). Substituting in (10.28) gives $P(|n_A - np| < \varepsilon) \geq 1 - np(1 - p)/\varepsilon^2$, or, replacing ε by $n\varepsilon$,

$$P(|f_A - p| < \varepsilon) \geq 1 - p(1 - p)/n\varepsilon^2.$$

Finally, $1 - p(1 - p)/n\varepsilon^2 \geq 1 - \delta \Leftrightarrow p(1 - p)/n\varepsilon^2 \leq \delta \Leftrightarrow n \geq p(1 - p)/\varepsilon^2\delta$.

Example 10.30 Given that the proportion of smokers in a population is 5%, how large a sample must be taken to ensure a probability of at least 0.95 that the observed proportion lies between 4% and 6%.

Solution (i) For the purpose of applying the Law of Large Numbers, the probability of event A: a smoker, is $p = 5/100 = 1/20$,
(ii) a difference of 1% means we require $\varepsilon = 1/100$, (iii) we want probability ≥ 0.95, so we take $\delta = 0.05$. Then (10.27) states that we must have $n \geq p(1 - p)/\varepsilon^2\delta = (1/20)(19/20)/(1/100)^2(1/20) = 9500$.

Example 10.31 (i) How many times must an unbiased die be tossed to be at least 95% certain that the observed frequency of a 3 is within 0.01 of the theoretical probability. (ii) A coin, assumed to be unbiased, is tossed 300 times. Can we be 90% certain that the relative frequency of heads appearing is within 0.1 of its expected value?

Solution (i) We make three observations: (a) the theoretical probability of a 3 is of course $p = 1/6$, (b) the difference we tolerate is $\varepsilon = 0.01$, (c) 95% certain means probability 0.95 and hence $\delta = 0.05$. According to (10.27) this can be achieved with $n \geq p(1 - p)/\varepsilon^2\delta = (1/6)(5/6)/(0.01)^2(0.05) = 27\,777.77\ldots$ and, since n is an integer, the number of tosses is at least $27\,778$.

(ii) The model $p = 0.5$, $\varepsilon = 0.1 = \delta$ gives $p(1 - p)/\varepsilon^2\delta = 250$, so the answer is YES.

Notation 10.32 In the following result and often thereafter we will consider a sequence of random variables $X_1, X_2, \ldots$ which both are independent and have the same pdf. They will be described as *independent identically distributed*, or simply *iid*.

Theorem 10.33 *(The Weak Law of Large Numbers) Let the sequence of random variables $X_1, X_2, \ldots$ be iid with expected value μ. Then, for any $\varepsilon > 0$,*

$$P(|X_1 + X_2 + \cdots + X_n - n\mu| \geq \varepsilon) \to 0 \text{ as } n \to \infty. \tag{10.29}$$

Proof Let $V(X_i) = \sigma^2$. Then the random variable $X = (1/n)(X_1 + \cdots + X_n)$ has mean μ and variance σ^2/n (see (9.36), (9.39)). Furthermore,

$$
\begin{aligned}
P(|X_1 + \cdots + X_n - n\mu| \geq \varepsilon) &= P(|X - \mu| \geq \varepsilon/n) \\
&\leq P(|X - \mu| \geq \varepsilon) \\
&\leq V(X)/\varepsilon^2 \qquad \text{by Chebychev form (9.48)} \\
&= \sigma^2/(n\varepsilon^2) \to 0, \ \text{as } n \to \infty.
\end{aligned}
$$

10.2.5 Independence and n-vectors

Here we provide justification for certain assumptions which easily pass unnoticed but strictly require proof. We recall from Theorem 10.10 the formula for change of variables $\phi \colon \boldsymbol{x} \to \boldsymbol{y}$ with inverse ψ, in an n-dimensional integral,

$$\int_A f(\boldsymbol{x})\mathrm{d}\boldsymbol{x} = \int_{\phi(A)} f(\psi(\boldsymbol{y})) \, |\partial \boldsymbol{x}/\partial \boldsymbol{y}| \, \mathrm{d}\boldsymbol{y}, \tag{10.30}$$

observing that, in the linear case $\boldsymbol{x} = \boldsymbol{y}A$, the Jacobian $\partial \boldsymbol{x}/\partial \boldsymbol{y}$ equals $\det(A)$.

Theorem 10.34 *Let $X_1, \ldots, X_n$ be independent random variables and let $Y_i = u_i(X_i)$ where, on the range of X_i $(1 \leq i \leq n)$, the derivative of u_i exists, is continuous, and is either everywhere positive or everywhere negative. Then $Y_1, \ldots, Y_n$ are independent.*

Proof We consider the (harder) continuous case. In the notation of (10.30),

$$(Y_1, \ldots, Y_n) = \boldsymbol{y} \Leftrightarrow (X_1, \ldots, X_n) = \psi(\boldsymbol{y}).$$

Hence, if A is an event for the random vector $(Y_1, \ldots, Y_n)$, then, since $X_1, \ldots, X_n$ are independent,

$$P(A) = P(\psi(A)) = \int_{\psi(A)} f_1(x_1) \cdots f_n(x_n)\mathrm{d}\boldsymbol{x},$$

where f_i is the pdf of X_i. We change coordinates in this integral from $\boldsymbol{x}$ to $\boldsymbol{y}$. In the present case, because x_i is a function of y_i alone, the Jacobian matrix is nonzero only on its diagonal, so $\partial \boldsymbol{x}/\partial \boldsymbol{y} = \mathrm{d}x_1/\mathrm{d}y_1 \cdots \mathrm{d}x_n/\mathrm{d}y_n$. Thus, by (10.30),

$$
\begin{aligned}
P(A) &= \int_A f_1(v_1(y_1)) \ldots f_n(v_n(y_n)) \left| \frac{\mathrm{d}x_1}{\mathrm{d}y_1} \cdots \frac{\mathrm{d}x_n}{\mathrm{d}y_n} \right| \mathrm{d}\boldsymbol{y}, \qquad \text{where } v_i = u_i^{-1} \\
&= \int_A g_1(y_1) \cdots g_n(y_n) \, \mathrm{d}\boldsymbol{y}, \qquad \text{where } g_i(y_i) = f_i(v_i(y_i)) \, |\mathrm{d}x_i/\mathrm{d}y_i|.
\end{aligned}
$$

That is, $Y_1, \ldots, Y_n$ have a fully factorised joint pdf and so are independent. Notice that g_i is the pdf of Y_i, by (9.32).

Example 10.35 If random variables $X_1, \ldots, X_n$ are independent, then so are $e^{x_1}, \ldots, e^{x_n}$, since taking u_i to be the function $u(x) = e^x$ for each i satisfies the conditions of Theorem 10.34. So too are $a_1 X_1 + b_1, \ldots, a_n X_n + b_n$, where the a_i, b_i are constants with a_i nonzero.

Theorem 10.36 *If random variables* $X_1, \ldots, X_n$ *are independent, then so are sums of disjoint subsets of the* X_i. *In particular, the variables* $X_1 + X_2, X_3, \ldots, X_n$ *are independent.*

Proof It suffices to prove the result for an independent triple X, Y, Z of continuous random variables and then to apply this repeatedly (as usual the discrete case is easier). Let (X, Y, Z) have joint pdf $f(x)g(y)h(z)$ and write $W = X + Y$. Then we must find a joint pdf for (W, Z). Let A be an event in the (W, Z) plane and let $B = \{(x, y, z): (x + y, z) \in A\}$. Then

$$P(A) = \int_B f(x)g(y)h(z)\, dx\, dy\, dz.$$

We use (10.30) to change coordinates from (x, y, z) to (x, w, z) as follows: $x = x, w = x + y, z = z$ with inverse transformation $x = x, y = w - x, z = z$. Then $(x, y, z) \in B$ in the old coordinates if and only if $(w, z) \in A$ in the new (x unrestricted), the Jacobian is

$$\frac{\partial(x, y, z)}{\partial(x, w, z)} = \begin{vmatrix} 1 & 0 & 0 \\ -1 & 1 & 0 \\ 0 & 0 & 1 \end{vmatrix} = 1, \quad \text{and}$$

$$\begin{aligned} P(A) &= \int_{\substack{x \in \mathbf{R} \\ (w,z) \in A}} f(x)g(w - x)h(z)\, dx\, dw\, dz \\ &= \int_A h(z) dz \int_{\mathbf{R}} f(x)g(w - x) dx\, dw \\ &= \int_A (f^* g)(w) h(z) dz, \qquad \text{by definition (10.21) of } f^* g. \end{aligned}$$

Thus (W, Z) has joint pdf factorised as $(f^* g)(w) \times h(z)$, so W, Z are by definition independent.

Exercise If X, Y, Z are independent random variables, so are $X, -Y, Z$ and hence $(X - Y)^2, Z$.

10.3 The ubiquity of normal/Gaussian variables

10.3.1 Moments

We introduce *moments* of a random variable X, a generalisation of mean and variance, and the moment generating function $M_X(t)$ whose coefficients reveal these moments.

Their value is twofold: practical – for the derivation of certain pdfs and relations between them; and theoretical – for establishing the Central Limit Theorem which explains why the normal distribution crops up in so many places. A basic calculus result we sometimes use without comment is the series expansion (see e.g. Swokowski, 2000, or Moore, 2003):

$$\mathrm{e}^x = \sum_{n=0}^{\infty} \frac{x^n}{n!}.$$

Definition 10.37 The *moment generating function*, or *mgf*, of a random variable X is

$$M_X(t) = \begin{cases} \sum \mathrm{e}^{tx_i} p(x_i) \, (x_i \in R_X), & \text{if } X \text{ is discrete,} \\ \int_{\mathbf{R}} \mathrm{e}^{tx} f(x)\mathrm{d}x, & \text{if } X \text{ is continuous.} \end{cases} \tag{10.31}$$

$$\boxed{M_X(t) = E(\mathrm{e}^{tX}), \qquad \text{in both case.}} \tag{10.32}$$

The relation between (10.31) and (10.32) is that if $Y = \mathrm{e}^{tX}$ then, according to (9.34), $E(Y)$ can be obtained by applying the formulae of (10.31). The function $M_X(t)$ is indeed a *moment* generating function, where the nth *moment* is defined as $E(X^n)$, because

$$M_X(t) = E\left(1 + tX + \frac{t^2}{2!}X^2 + \frac{t^3}{3!}X^3 + \cdots\right)$$

$$= 1 + tE(X) + \frac{t^2}{2!}E(X^2) + \frac{t^3}{3!}E(X^3) + \cdots \tag{10.33}$$

Notice that, by elementary calculus, $E(X^n)$ equals the nth derivative $M_X^{(n)}(0)$.

Theorem 10.38 *Let α, β be real and X, Y independent random variables. Then*

$$\boxed{M_{\alpha X + \beta}(t) = \mathrm{e}^{\beta t} M_X(\alpha t),} \tag{10.34}$$

$$\boxed{M_{X+Y}(t) = M_X(t)M_Y(t).} \tag{10.35}$$

And similarly for the sum of three or more independent random variables.

Proof $M_{\alpha X+\beta}(t) = E(\mathrm{e}^{(\alpha X + \beta)t}) = E(\mathrm{e}^{\alpha X t} \cdot \mathrm{e}^{\beta t}) = \mathrm{e}^{\beta t} E(\mathrm{e}^{\alpha X t}) = \mathrm{e}^{\beta t} M_X(\alpha t)$, and $M_{X+Y}(t) = E(\mathrm{e}^{(X+Y)t}) = E(\mathrm{e}^{Xt} \cdot \mathrm{e}^{Yt})$. But $\mathrm{e}^{Xt}, \mathrm{e}^{Yt}$ are independent because X, Y are (Example 10.35) and so the expected value of their product equals $E(\mathrm{e}^{Xt})E(\mathrm{e}^{Yt})$ (by (10.25)), which is by definition $M_X(t)M_Y(t)$. A similar argument holds for the sum of three or more such variables.

Example 10.39 (*mgfs of some distributions*) See Table 10.5.

(1) *Poisson*, $X \sim \mathrm{Po}(\lambda)$. By definition, $M_X(t) = E(\mathrm{e}^{tX}) = \sum_{r=0}^{\infty} \mathrm{e}^{tr} p(r) = \sum_{r=0}^{\infty} \mathrm{e}^{tr} \mathrm{e}^{-\lambda} \lambda^r / r! = \mathrm{e}^{-\lambda} \sum_{r=0}^{\infty} (\lambda \mathrm{e}^t)^r / r! = \mathrm{e}^{-\lambda} \mathrm{e}^{\lambda \mathrm{e}^t} = \mathrm{e}^{\lambda(\mathrm{e}^t - 1)}$.

(2) *Binomial*, $X \sim \mathrm{Bin}(n, p)$. The calculation of expectation and variance was greatly simplified in the binomial case by viewing X as the sum of n independent random

Table 10.5. *Moment generating functions of some important pdfs.*

Distribution	Moment generating function
Uniform on $[a, b]$	$(e^{bt} - e^{at})/t(b - a)$
Bin(n, p)	$(pe^t + q)^n, q = 1 - p$
Po(λ)	$e^{\lambda(e^t - 1)}$
Gamma, $\Gamma_{\alpha,u}$	$(\frac{\alpha}{\alpha - t})^u, t < \alpha$
Exponential(α)	$\frac{\alpha}{\alpha - t}, t < \alpha$
Chi-squared, n degrees of freedom	$(1 - 2t)^{-n/2}, t < 1/2$
Cauchy	does not exist
Normal/Gaussian, $N(0, 1)$	$e^{t^2/2}$
$N(\mu, \sigma^2)$	$e^{\mu t + \sigma^2 t^2/2}$

variables, $X = X_1 + \cdots + X_n$, where each X_i is based on one Bernoulli trial with $P(X_i = 1) = p$. A similar simplification is afforded in the determination of $M_X(t)$ by the use of Property (10.35). We have, with $q = 1 - p$,

$$M_{X_i}(t) = E\left(e^{tX_i}\right) = p \cdot e^{t \cdot 1} + q \cdot e^{t \cdot 0} \text{ (by (9.34))} = pe^t + q.$$

Hence $\qquad M_X(t) = M_{X_1}(t) \cdots M_{X_n}(t) \text{ (by (10.35))} = (pe^t + q)^n.$

(3) *Gamma*, $X \sim \Gamma_{\alpha,u}$. Using the properties of the Γ function in Table 9.6:

$$M_X(t) = E(e^{tX}) = \int_0^\infty e^{tx}(\alpha^u / \Gamma(u))x^{u-1}e^{-\alpha x}dx = (\alpha^u / \Gamma(u)) \int_0^\infty x^{u-1}e^{-x(\alpha-t)}dx$$

$$= \frac{\alpha^u}{\Gamma(u)} \cdot \frac{1}{(\alpha - t)^u} \int_0^\infty y^{u-1}e^{-y}dy \qquad \text{on setting } y = x(\alpha - t)$$

$$= (\alpha/(\alpha - t))^u \qquad \text{by definition of } \Gamma(u).$$

(4) *Normal*, $X \sim N(0, 1)$.

$$M_X(t) = E(e^{tX}) = \tfrac{1}{\sqrt{2\pi}} \int_{\mathbf{R}} e^{tx}e^{-x^2/2}dx \qquad \text{(now put } u = x - t\text{)}$$

$$= \tfrac{1}{\sqrt{2\pi}}e^{t^2/2} \int_{\mathbf{R}} e^{-u^2/2}du \qquad \text{(check this!)}$$

$$= e^{t^2/2} \qquad \text{since the integral equals } \sqrt{(2\pi)} \text{ (Lemma 9.73)}.$$

Exercise Deduce the last line of Table 10.5 from the line before, using (10.34).

10.3.2 Transforms and uniqueness

We state the main result of this section, illustrate its importance by a 'reproductive property', then give a proof for the finite discrete case that offers insight into why the result should be true.

Theorem 10.40 (*Uniqueness property of the moment generating function*) *If X, Y are random variables with $M_X(t) = M_Y(t)$ then X, Y have the same pdf.*

Example 10.41 (1) (*Reproductive property*) Show that any finite sum of independent normal variables is also normal, hence so is a finite linear combination.

Solution First consider independent variables $X \sim N(\mu_1, \sigma_1^2)$ and $Y \sim N(\mu_2, \sigma_2^2)$. We already know $X + Y$ has mean $\mu_1 + \mu_2$ and variance $\sigma_1^2 + \sigma_2^2$ but so far have not shown that $X + Y$ is actually normal. Now, according to the Uniqueness Theorem 10.40 we have only to show that $M_{X+Y}(t)$ equals $M_Z(t)$, where Z is normal. But this is now easy thanks to Property (10.35). We have

$$
\begin{aligned}
M_{X+Y}(t) &= M_X(t) M_Y(t) && \text{by (10.35)} \\
&= e^{\mu_1 t} \cdot e^{(\sigma_1 t)^2 / 2} \cdot e^{\mu_2 t} \cdot e^{(\sigma_2 t)^2 / 2} && \text{by Table 10.5} \\
&= e^{(\mu_1 + \mu_2) t} \cdot e^{(\sigma_1^2 + \sigma_2^2) t^2 / 2} \\
&= M_Z(t), && \text{where } Z \sim N(\mu_1 + \mu_2, \sigma_1^2 + \sigma_2^2).
\end{aligned}
$$

Theorem 10.40 now implies that $X + Y = Z$. The argument follows the same steps for any finite number of independent normal variables.

(2) Even without knowing the actual pdfs we can infer from Table 10.5 of mgfs that the exponential distribution is case $u = 1$ of the gamma, and that chi-squared with n degrees of freedom is the case $\alpha = 1/2$, $u = n/2$. We can also prove that the reproductive property is possessed by the Poisson and exponential distributions.

Exercise Why is the *difference* between normal random variables normal?

Why uniqueness holds The phrase 'uniqueness property' for mgfs is used because Theorem 10.40 says equivalently that, given $M_X(t)$, there is a unique pdf that must be possessed by X. Let us see this for the case of discrete X with finite range $\{x_1, \ldots, x_n\}$. Writing $M_X(t)$ in the form $\sum m_r(t^r / r!)$, we have $E(X^r) = m_r$, or $x_1^r p_1 + x_2^r p_2 + \cdots + x_n^r p_n = m_r$, for $r = 0, 1, 2, \ldots$ Consider the first n equations in matrix form.

$$
\begin{bmatrix}
1 & 1 & \cdots & \cdots & 1 \\
x_1 & x_2 & \cdots & \cdots & x_n \\
x_1^2 & x_2^2 & \cdots & \cdots & x_n^2 \\
\cdots & \cdots & \cdots & \cdots & \cdots \\
x_1^{n-1} & x_2^{n-1} & \cdots & \cdots & x_n^{n-1}
\end{bmatrix}
\begin{bmatrix}
p_1 \\
p_2 \\
p_3 \\
\cdots \\
p_n
\end{bmatrix}
=
\begin{bmatrix}
1 \\
m_1 \\
m_2 \\
\cdots \\
m_{n-1}
\end{bmatrix}.
\tag{10.36}
$$

The determinant of the coefficient matrix is of Vandermonde type (Examples 7.31) and so equals the product $\Pi(x_i - x_j)$ $(i > j)$, which is nonzero because $x_1, \ldots, x_n$ are distinct. Thus the probabilities $p_1, \ldots, p_n$ are determined uniquely. The remaining equations can introduce no inconsistency since they are constructed from the same given pdf. The conclusion is that this is the *only* pdf that has this (infinite) set of moments.

Existence The mgf does not always exist. In particular $E(X^2)$ fails to exist for the Cauchy distribution because

$$
\int_{-N}^{N} \frac{x^2 \, \mathrm{d}x}{x^2 + a^2} = \int_{-N}^{N} \left(1 - \frac{a^2}{x^2 + a^2} \right) \mathrm{d}x = 2N - 2a \tan^{-1} \frac{N}{a} \to \infty \text{ as } N \to \infty.
$$

Instead we may use the *characteristic function* $C_X(t)$, defined for all X, and given by

$$C_X(t) = E(\mathrm{e}^{\mathrm{i}tX}) = M_X(\mathrm{i}t), \tag{10.37}$$

where i denotes the standard square root of -1. The first equality is the definition and the second is a consequence. We have defined

$$C_X(t) = \begin{cases} \sum_{j=1}^{\infty} \mathrm{e}^{\mathrm{i}tx_j} p(x_j), & \text{if } X \text{ is discrete}, \\ \int_{\mathbf{R}} \mathrm{e}^{\mathrm{i}tx} f(x)\mathrm{d}x, & \text{if } X \text{ is continuous}. \end{cases} \tag{10.38}$$

The discrete case is the Fourier series and the continuous is the Fourier Transform (with i replaced by $-$i), so we may appeal to the theory in each case for existence and inverse formulae. We have

$$p(x_j) = \frac{1}{2\pi} \int_0^{2\pi} \mathrm{e}^{-\mathrm{i}tx_j} C_X(t)\mathrm{d}t,$$

$$f(x) = \frac{1}{2\pi} \int_{\mathbf{R}} \mathrm{e}^{-\mathrm{i}tx} C_X(t)\mathrm{d}t. \tag{10.39}$$

This gives the uniqueness property of $C_X(t)$, and of $M_X(t) = C_X(-\mathrm{i}t)$ when it exists.

10.3.3 The Central Limit Theorem

We are ready to prove the celebrated Central Limit Theorem, that a large number of independent random variables, even though of varying distributions, sum to an approximately normal distribution. This supplies a reason why normal random variables are found so widely in practice – anything that is the sum of many small effects is a candidate.

It also points to the normal distribution as a useful approximation to others, and this too is borne out. We shall see it for binomial variables, a special case that pre-dated the discovery of our main theorem, and which was known as the De Moivre–Laplace Limit Theorem.

We begin with some calculus preliminaries, especially the idea that a function $f(x)$ may behave like a simpler function $g(x)$ when x is large.

Definition 10.42 (*Order of magnitude*) Let f, g be two real functions. We say $f(x) = O(g(x))$ (as $x \to \infty$) if, for some constants K, x_0,

> (i) $|f(x)| \leq K|g(x)|$ whenever $x \geq x_0$, or
> (ii) $|f(x)/g(x)| \to K$ as $x \to \infty$ (stronger).

(Alternatively, $x \to 0$ and $|X| \leq x_0$.)

Consequence If $g(x) \to 0$ as $x \to \infty$ then so does $f(x)$. Both tests fail if $|f(x)/g(x)| \to \infty$. The second is stronger because it implies $|f(x)/g(x)| \leq K + 1$, say, for sufficiently large x.

Example 10.43 (1) $f(x) = x^2 + \sin x$ gives $|f(x)| \leq x^2 + 1 \leq 2x^2$ for $x \geq 1$, so $f(x) = O(x^2)$

(2) Let $g(n) = 1/n^2 + 1/n^3$. Then $g(n) = O(1/n^2)$ as $n \to \infty$. But $g(n) \neq O(1/n^3)$, since $g(n)/(1/n^3) = n + 1$, unbounded. More generally and most importantly, we have the boxed observation below.

> If $f(n) = O(1/n^a)$ and $g(n) = O(1/n^b)$, with $a \leq b$,
> then $f(n) + g(n) = O(1/n^a)$. (10.40)

(3) We have by definition that $Kf(x) = O(f(x))$ for any constant K. Similarly, if $f(x) = O(x^s)$ then $f(x)^t = O(x^{st})$.

(4) According to the Taylor Theorem of Calculus (see Swokowski, 2000 or Moore, 2003), if $f(x)$ has continuous derivatives up to order n on an open interval I that includes 0, then, for some constant K and sufficiently *small x*,

$$f(x) = f(0) + xf'(0) + \cdots + \frac{x^{n-1}}{(n-1)!} f^{(n-1)}(0) + R(x), |R(x)| \leq K|x|^n. \quad (10.41)$$

Hence, setting respectively $n = 3$ and $n = 2$, we obtain for the exponential and the natural logarithm,

$$e^x = 1 + x + x^2/2 + R_1(x), |R_1(x)| \leq K_1|x|^3, \quad (10.42a)$$
$$\log(1 + x) = x + R_2(x), \qquad |R_2(x)| \leq K_2|x|^2. \quad (10.42b)$$

Lemma 10.44 *Let* $\lambda_i(n) = O(1/n^{1+d})$ $(1 \leq i \leq n)$ *as* $n \to \infty$, *where* $0 < d < 1$ *and* n *is a positive integer. Then* $\Pi_i(1 + w/n + \lambda_i(n)) \to e^w$ *as* $n \to \infty$.

Proof Denote the product by $g(n)$ and take logarithms to base e. Then

$$\log g(n) = \sum_i \log(1 + w/n + \lambda_i(n)) \text{ (now set } x = w/n + \lambda_i(n) \text{ in (10.24b))}$$
$$= \sum_i \{w/n + \lambda_i(n) + O[(w/n + \lambda_i(n))^2]\}$$
$$= \sum_i (w/n + \rho_i(n)), \text{ where } \rho_i(n) = O(1/n^{1+d}), \text{ by (10.40)}.$$

But $|\sum_i \rho_i(n)| \leq \sum_i |\rho_i(n)| \leq \sum_i K_i/n^{1+d}$ (some K_i) $\leq n \operatorname{Max}\{K_i\}/n^{1+d} = O(1/n^d)$, so $\log g(n) = w + O(1/n^d) \to w$ as $n \to \infty$. Hence finally $g(n) \to e^w$.

Theorem 10.45 *(Central Limit Theorem) Let* $X_1, X_2, \ldots$ *be independent random variables, with finite moments, and* $E(X_i) = \mu_i$, $V(X_i) = \sigma^2$ *(independent of* i). *If* $S_n = X_1 + \cdots + X_n$ *and* $\mu = (\mu_1 + \cdots + \mu_n)/n$. *Then* S_n *is asymptotically normal in the sense that*

$$\boxed{\operatorname*{Lim}_{n \to \infty} P \left(a \leq \frac{S_n - n\mu}{\sigma\sqrt{n}} \leq b \right) = \Phi(b) - \Phi(a).} \quad (10.43)$$

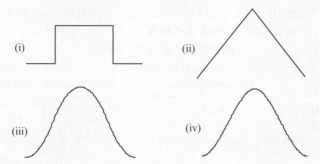

Figure 10.7 Let X_i be uniform on $[-1, 1]$, $i = 1, 2, \ldots$, and let $S_n = X_1 + \cdots + X_n$. Above are shown the pdfs of S_1, S_2, S_3, S_4. Even by the fourth, the shape is close to normal.

Figure 10.7 illustrates the Central Limit Theorem for sums of uniformly distributed random variables. The restriction that all X_i have the same variance may be replaced by technical restrictions on the pdfs involved (Feller, 1968, Vol. 2).

Proof of Theorem 10.45 Let $Y_i = (X_i - \mu_i)/\sigma$. Then $E(Y_i) = 0$, $E(Y_i{}^2) = V(Y_i) = 1$, and we investigate S_n via $(S_n - n\mu)/\sigma \sqrt{n} = \sum Y_i/\sqrt{n} = Z$, say. Since the X_i have finite moments, so do the Y_i (see (10.34)). Also, the independence of $X_1, \ldots, X_n$ implies that of the variables Y_i, that of the $Y_i/\sqrt{n}$, and of exponentials $e^{Y_i/\sqrt{n}}$ (with $1 \leq i \leq n$ in each case) by Example 10.35. We have $e^{tY_i/\sqrt{n}} = 1 + tY_i/\sqrt{n} + t^2 Y_i^2/2n + \mathrm{O}(tY_i/\sqrt{n})^3$, as $n \to \infty$, by (10.42a).
Hence, since $E(Y_i)$ and t are constant as n varies,

$$M_{Y_i/\sqrt{n}}(t) = E(1) + (t/\sqrt{n})E(Y_i) + (t^2/2n)E\big(Y_i^2\big) + \mathrm{O}(1/n^{1.5}).$$

Therefore

$$
\begin{aligned}
M_Z(t) &= \Pi_i M_{Y_i/\sqrt{n}}(t) \quad \text{by (10.35)} \\
&= \Pi_i(1 + t^2/2n + \lambda_i(n)), \ \text{where } \lambda_i(n) = \mathrm{O}(1/n^{1.5}) \\
&\to e^{t^2/2} \text{ by Lemma 10.44 with } d = 1/2. \text{ This completes the proof.}
\end{aligned}
$$

Exercise Derive Equation (10.40).

Corollary 10.46 *In the usual notation, let X be a binomial random variable with mean μ and variance σ^2. Then $Z = (X - \mu)/\sigma$ is approximately $N(0, 1)$.*

Example 10.47 An electronic device can function if at least 75 of its 100 components are in order. Each component has, independently, a probability of 0.05 of being defective. Find the probability that the device functions on being switched on.

Solution Let the random variable X be the number of components that are in order. Then, in the usual notation, X is binomial with parameters $n = 100$ and $p = P$ (a component is in order) $= 0.95$. Hence $\mu = np = 95$ and $\sigma = \sqrt{(npq)} = 2.18$. We require $P(75 \leq X \leq 100)$, however, the normal distribution provides a more accurate value if we take

Table 10.6. *Accuracy of the normal approximation to the*
binomial formula for $P(X = 3)$ with parameters
$n = 8$ and $p = 0.2$ or 0.5.

p	Binomial value	Normal approximation
0.2	0.147	0.164
0.5	0.219	0.220

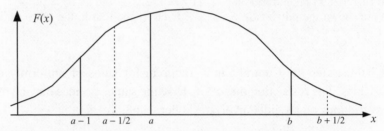

Figure 10.8 If we approximate a distribution which takes integer values by a continuous distribution $F(x)$, then a corresponding approximation is to take $P(a \leq X \leq b) = F(b + 1/2) - F(a - 1/2)$. Thus $P(X \leq a - 1) = F(a - 1/2)$, so no area is omitted overall in using the correction. Also we take $P(X = a) = F(a + 1/2) - F(a - 1/2)$.

account of the fact that we are approximating a discrete variable by a continuous one, and apply the following *continuity correction*, suggested by Figure 10.8.

$P(74.5 \leq X \leq 100.5) = P(\frac{74.5-95}{2.18} \leq Z \leq \frac{100.5-95}{2.18}) = \Phi(2.52) - \Phi(-9.4) = \Phi(2.52) = 0.994$, since $\Phi(-9.4) = 0$ to 4 dp by Table 9.7. This compares with a strict binomial calculation of

$$\sum_{k=75}^{100} \binom{100}{k}(0.95)^k(0.05)^{100-k} = 0.986.$$

The error amounts to less than 1 in the second decimal place (8 in the third). If we increase the requirement of the device to 90 correctly functioning components, the respective calculations give 0.988 and 0.989, an error of 1 in the third decimal place.

Remarks 10.48 (1) Accuracy of the normal approximation to the binomial distribution increases both with n, and as $p, 1 - p$ become closer to 0.5. Table 10.6 gives some comparative results.

(2) Other distributions which can conveniently be represented as a sum of independent variables, and so have a normal approximation, are the Poisson (for large parameter), Pascal and gamma distributions.

(3) We employ the Central Limit Theorem to generate samples for simulation of the normal distribution in Chapter 11. This is a very important simulation, and is used often in subsequent chapters.

(4) Some other sections where the idea of $O(f(x))$ is used are Sections 11.1.2, 11.2.1, 11.4.7, 12.5, 14.1.4 and 15.2.1.

10.4 Correlation and its elimination

We shall define *correlation* between random variables X, Y, and the *covariance matrix* of correlations that defines a multivariate normal distribution (Section 10.4.2). Correlation is a useful tool for investigating independence. Indeed, for normal random variables, zero correlation is equivalent to independence. In any case, zero correlation alone simplifies many situations – for example it implies $E(XY) = E(X)E(Y)$ and $V(X + Y) = V(X) + V(Y)$, so it need be no surprise that, having defined correlation, we look for ways to achieve zero correlation by a change of variables. This is especially profitable for normal variables because, as mentioned, it results in independence; but the story extends far beyond this, issuing firstly for us in the much-valued Principal Component Analysis.

10.4.1 Correlation

We write $\mu_Z = E(Z)$ for any random variable Z and make frequent use of the rules for expectation and variance established in Section 10.2.3. The idea of *variance* is generalised to that of the *covariance*, or *correlation*, $\mathrm{Cov}(X, Y)$ of a pair of random variables X, Y. Also denoted by σ_{XY}, it is defined by

$$\sigma_{XY} = \mathrm{Cov}(X, Y) = E[(X - \mu_X)(Y - \mu_Y)]. \tag{10.44}$$

Setting $Y = X$ we recover $V(X)$ as σ_{XX}, usually written σ_X^2 or just σ^2. The following theorem reflects the connection between covariance and independence. As implied, X, Y may be either discrete or continuous.

Theorem 10.49 *Let X, Y be random variables. Then*

> (a) $E(XY) = E(X)E(Y) + \sigma_{XY}$,
> (b) *if X, Y are independent then $\sigma_{XY} = 0$,*
> (c) $V(X + Y) = V(X) + V(Y) + 2\sigma_{XY}$.

Proof (a) $\quad \sigma_{XY} = E[XY - \mu_Y X - \mu_X Y + \mu_X \mu_Y]$ $\qquad$ by (10.44)

$\qquad\qquad = E(XY) - \mu_Y E(X) - \mu_X E(Y) + \mu_X \mu_Y$ $\quad$ by linearity, Remark 10.25

$\qquad\qquad = E(XY) - \mu_X \mu_Y$ $\qquad\qquad\qquad\qquad$ since $\mu_X = E(X)$, etc.

(b) X, Y independent $\Rightarrow E(XY) = \mu_X \mu_Y$ (by (10.25)) $\Rightarrow \sigma_{XY} = 0$ by part (a).

(c) $V(X + Y) = E[(X^2 + 2XY + Y)^2] - (\mu_X + \mu_Y)^2$ $\qquad\qquad$ by(9.38)

$\qquad\quad = \left(E(X^2) - \mu_X^2\right) + \left(E(Y^2) - \mu_Y^2\right) + 2(E(XY) - \mu_X \mu_Y)$

$\qquad\quad = V(X) + V(Y) + 2\sigma_{XY}$ $\qquad\qquad\qquad\qquad$ by part (a).

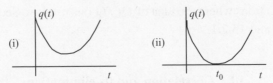

Figure 10.9 Case (i): the graph of the quadratic $q(t)$ lies above the t-axis for all t. Case (ii): the graph of $q(t)$ meets the axis in a single point t_0.

Remarks 10.50 If X, Y are independent then $\sigma_{xy} = 0$, indeed a nonzero value for σ_{XY} measures to some degree the extent of dependence, for in both (a), (c) above it measures the difference between quantities which would be equal in the independence case. We can obtain more information about the *type* of independence from the *correlation coefficient* ρ, given by

$$\rho = \rho_{XY} = \sigma_{XY}/\sigma_X\sigma_Y. \tag{10.45}$$

This normalised quantity is described as *dimensionless* because multiplying X, Y by constants leaves ρ unchanged. In the extremal case below, the form of dependency is linear.

Theorem 10.51 *Let ρ be the correlation coefficient of random variables X, Y. Then $\rho^2 \leq 1$, and in the case of equality there is, with probability 1, a linear relation $Y = aX + b$.*

Proof Write $Z = X - E(X)$ and $W = Y - E(Y)$. Then $0 = E(Z) = E(W) = E(Z + tW)$ for any scalar t, so that we have a function

$$q(t) = V(Z + tW) = E[(Z + tW)^2] \geq 0, \quad \text{for all } t.$$

On the other hand, we can use linearity of E to express $q(t)$ directly as a quadratic polynomial

$$q(t) = E(Z^2) + 2t E(ZW) + t^2 E(W^2)$$

and, since its graph is above or touches the t-axis at most once (as in Figure 10.9), the discriminant D of $q(t)$ cannot be strictly positive. That is, $D = [E(ZW)]^2 - E(Z^2)E(W^2) \leq 0$, and, since by definition ρ^2 is the quotient $[E(ZW)]^2/E(Z^2)E(W^2)$ of the two terms, we have $\rho^2 \leq 1$.

Furthermore, with $\rho^2 = 1$ the discriminant is zero, giving case (ii) in Figure 10.9: there is some t_0 for which $q(t_0) = 0$ (but $t_0 \neq 0$, why?). Thus $V(Z + t_0W) = 0 = E(Z + t_0W)$. Now we may apply Remark 9.81: $V(X) = 0 \Rightarrow P(X = \mu) = 1$, to our case, obtaining $P(Z + t_0W = 0) = 1$. But, after substituting for Z, W we may write this in the form $P(Y = aX + b) = 1$, as required.

Remarks 10.52 If $\rho = 0$ (or equivalently $\sigma_{XY} = 0$) we say X, Y are *uncorrelated*. This condition is equivalent to $E(XY) = E(X)E(Y)$, and to $V(X + Y) = V(X) + V(Y)$ (Theorem 10.49), but it is weaker than independence, as shown by the example in Table 10.7.

Table 10.7. *An example of the joint pdf $p(x, y)$ and marginal pdfs*
$p(x), q(y)$ for a discrete pair X, Y (format of Table 10.1), showing
that zero correlation need not imply independence.

$X\backslash Y$	-1	0	1	$p(x)$
0	1/4	0	1/4	1/2
1	0	1/2	0	1/2
$q(y)$	1/4	1/2	1/4	

However, in the crucial case of *normal* random vectors, it is equivalent to independence, as we shall see in the next section (Theorem 10.63).

$$\boxed{\begin{array}{c} X, Y \text{ uncorrelated is equivalent to each of} \\ \rho = 0, \sigma_{XY} = 0, \text{Cov}(X, Y) = 0, \\ E(XY) = E(X)E(Y), V(X + Y) = V(X) + V(Y). \end{array}} \qquad (10.46)$$

In the Table 10.7 example, *X and Y are uncorrelated*, for $E(Y) = -1(1/4) + 0(1/2) + 1(1/4) = 0$, and $E(XY) = \sum xyp(x, y) = 0 + \cdots + 0 = 0$. Hence $\sigma_{XY} = E(XY) - E(X)E(Y)$ (Theorem 10.49) $= 0$, and so $\rho = 0$.

However *X, Y are not independent*, because $p(0, 1) = 1/4$, but $p(0)q(1) = (1/2)(1/4) = 1/8$.

10.4.2 The covariance matrix

Notation 10.53 We recall that a random d-vector is a vector $X = (X_1, \ldots, X_d)$ whose components are themselves random variables. Case $d = 2$ is sometimes called the *bivariate* case, and the general case $d \geq 2$, the *multivariate*. By implication there is a joint distribution $p(\boldsymbol{x}) = p(x_1, \ldots, x_d)$, where $\boldsymbol{x} = (x_1, \ldots, x_d)$ is also abbreviated to (x_i), or alternatively to $[x_i]$ when we wish to emphasise its role as a row matrix.

The *expected value of a vector or matrix* is defined as the object of the same dimension obtained by replacing each entry with its expected value. Thus, in the present notation $E(X) = [E(X_i)] = [E(X_1), \ldots, E(X_d)]$, also denoted by $\boldsymbol{\mu}$, with components $\mu_i = E(X_i)$. The *covariance matrix* of X, denoted by $\text{Cov}(X)$, Σ_X, or just Σ, is given by

$$\boxed{\text{Cov}(X) = E[(X - \boldsymbol{\mu})^{\text{T}}(X - \boldsymbol{\mu})],} \qquad (10.47a)$$

with diagonal elements $E[(X_i - \mu_i)^2] = V(X_i),$ \qquad (10.47b)

and *ij* element $E[(X_i - \mu_i)(X_j - \mu_j)] = E(X_i X_j) - \mu_i \mu_j.$ \qquad (10.47c)

Hence

$$\mathrm{Cov}(X) = E[X^{\mathrm{T}}X] - \boldsymbol{\mu}^{\mathrm{T}}\boldsymbol{\mu}. \tag{10.47d}$$

Sometimes this is the formula we need. On the other hand it may be more useful to suppresss the appearance of $\boldsymbol{\mu}$, and this we can easily do by writing $Y = X - \boldsymbol{\mu}$, so that $E(Y) = 0$. Then

$$\mathrm{Cov}(X) = E(Y^{\mathrm{T}}Y),\ (Y = X - \boldsymbol{\mu},\ \text{and}\ E(Y) = 0). \tag{10.47e}$$

Notice that $X^{\mathrm{T}}X$ has ith row equal to X_i times the vector $[X_1, \ldots, X_d]$, and therefore has rank 1: every row is a multiple of a single nonzero row (Section 8.2.2), as seen below.

$$X^{\mathrm{T}}X = \begin{bmatrix} X_1 \\ X_2 \\ \ldots \\ X_d \end{bmatrix} \begin{bmatrix} X_1\ X_2 \ldots X_d \end{bmatrix} = \begin{bmatrix} X_1^2 & X_1X_2 & \ldots & X_1X_d \\ X_2X_1 & X_2^2 & \ldots & X_2X_d \\ \ldots & \ldots & \ldots & \ldots \\ X_dX_1 & X_dX_2 & \ldots & X_d^2 \end{bmatrix}.$$

Similarly $Y^{\mathrm{T}}Y$. It does not follow that $\mathrm{Cov}(X) = E(Y^{\mathrm{T}}Y)$ shares the rank 1 property – indeed $\mathrm{Cov}(X)$ is invertible in the multivariate normal case of Theorem 10.61 below, and so has full rank d. However, the properties of expected value do suffice to carry *positive semi-definiteness* (Section 8.3.3) over to $\mathrm{Cov}(X)$, as we now show.

Theorem 10.54 *A correlation/covariance matrix is positive semi-definite.*

Proof As in (10.47e) we write the correlation matrix as $\mathrm{Cov}(X) = E(Y^{\mathrm{T}}Y)$, where $E(Y) = 0$. Symmetry is immediate, for $E(Y_iY_j) = E(Y_jY_i)$. Now let $\boldsymbol{a}$ be an arbitrary d-vector. Then $\boldsymbol{a}E(Y^{\mathrm{T}}Y)\boldsymbol{a}^{\mathrm{T}} = \sum_{i,j} a_ia_j E(Y_iY_j) = \sum_{i,j} E(a_ia_jY_iY_j) = E(\sum_{i,j} a_ia_jY_iY_j) = E[(a_1Y_1 + \cdots + a_dY_d)^2]$, which cannot be negative. Thus $\mathrm{Cov}(X)$ is by definition positive semi-definite.

Example 10.55 Suppose the components of $X = (X_1, \ldots, X_d)$ are independent, with $X_i \sim N(\mu_i, \sigma_i^2)$. Then $\mathrm{Cov}(X)$ has diagonal elements $\sum_{ii} = E[(X_i - \mu_i)^2] = \sigma_i^2$, whereas if $i \neq j$ then $\sum_{ij} = E[(X_i - \mu_i)(X_j - \mu_j)] = E(X_i - \mu_i)E(X_j - \mu_j)$ (by independence) $= 0$. Thus

$$\mathrm{Cov}(X) = \mathrm{diag}\left(\sigma_i^2, \ldots, \sigma_d^2\right)\ (X_i\text{s independent}). \tag{10.48}$$

Theorem 10.56 *(a) We have $E(AMB) = AE(M)B$, where A, B are constant matrices and M is a matrix of random variables, (b) $\mathrm{Cov}(XB) = B^{\mathrm{T}}\mathrm{Cov}(X)B$, where X is a random vector for which the product XB exists, (c) $\mathrm{Cov}(X \pm Y) = \mathrm{Cov}(X) + \mathrm{Cov}(Y)$ if X, Y are independent random vectors (X_i and Y_j independent for all i, j).*

$$\begin{aligned} E(AMB) &= AE(M)B, \\ \mathrm{Cov}(XB) &= B^{\mathrm{T}}\mathrm{Cov}(X)B, \\ \mathrm{Cov}(X \pm Y) &= \mathrm{Cov}(X) + \mathrm{Cov}(Y)\ (X, Y\ \text{independent}). \end{aligned}$$

Proof (a) $E(AMB)_{ij} = E\left(\sum_{rs} a_{ir} m_{rs} b_{sj}\right)$ (see (7.17b)) $= \sum_{r,s} a_{ir} E(m_{rs}) b_{sj} = (AE(M)B)_{ij}$.

(b) Let $E(X) = \mu$. Then $E(XB) = \mu B$ by (a), whence $\text{Cov}(XB) = E[(XB - \mu B)^T (XB - \mu B)] = E[B^T (X - \mu)^T (X - \mu) B] = B^T E[(X - \mu)^T (X - \mu)] B$ (by (a)) $= B^T \text{Cov}(X) B$.

(c) We may without loss of generality assume X, Y have zero means and argue as follows. $\text{Cov}(X \pm Y) = E[(X \pm Y)^T (X \pm Y)] = E(X^T X) + E(Y^T Y) \pm E(X^T Y) \pm E(Y^T X)$. But X, Y are independent, so $E(X^T X) = E(Y^T Y) = 0$, and $\text{Cov}(X \pm Y) = \text{Cov}(X) + \text{Cov}(Y)$.

10.4.3 The d-dimensional normal/Gaussian distribution

Definition 10.57 Let Q be a symmetric $d \times d$ matrix. The associated quadratic form (Section 8.3.2) in the coordinate variables $x_1, \ldots, x_d$ is $q(x) = x Q x^T = \sum q_{ij} x_i x_j$. A continuous pdf ϕ in $\mathbf{R}^d$ is called *normal* and said to be *centred at the origin* if it has the form

$$\phi(x) = \gamma e^{-q(x)/2}, \tag{10.49}$$

where γ is a constant, and $q(x)$ is positive definite (strictly positive for $x \neq 0$). Then Q has positive diagonal because setting $x_i = 1$ and other variables zero gives $0 < q(x) = q_{ii}$. The constant γ, we recall, is determined from the pdf condition $\int \phi(x) dx = 1$, so $\gamma = 1/(\int e^{-q(x)/2} dx)$.

A normal density *centred at* $a = (a_1, \ldots, a_d)$ has the form $\phi(x - a)$. We see after the next result that ϕ is the joint pdf of d normal variables (not necessarily independent), by showing that *each marginal pdf is of normal type*. Meanwhile, the special case $d = 1$ may be written $\phi(x) = \gamma e^{-(x-\mu)^2/2}$, in agreement with the earlier definition (9.46).

Lemma 10.58 *In the above notation, ϕ factorises as*

$$\phi(x) = \gamma e^{-\bar{q}(x_1, \ldots, x_{d-1})/2} \cdot e^{-y_d^2/2 q_{dd}}, \tag{10.50}$$

where $\bar{q}$ is a quadratic form in only the variables $x_1, \ldots, x_{d-1}$ and $y_d = q_{1d} x_1 + \cdots + q_{dd} x_d$. Thus the variables in a normal pdf can be transformed by a matrix A with $|A| > 0$, so as to factor out a 1-dimensional normal pdf.

Proof Using the completion of squares technique (Example 8.33) we set $Y = XA$ as follows:

$$\begin{cases} y_1 = x_1, \\ \ldots \\ y_{d-1} = x_{d-1}, \\ y_d = \sum_{i=1}^d q_{id} x_i, \end{cases} \quad \text{i.e. } A = \begin{bmatrix} 1 & & & q_{1d} \\ & \ddots & & q_{2d} \\ & & 1 & \ldots \\ 0 & & & q_{dd} \end{bmatrix}. \tag{10.51}$$

Then $|A| = q_{dd} > 0$. Define the quadratic form $\bar{q}(y) = q(x) - y_d^2/q_{dd}$ which, after cancellation, involves only the $d - 1$ variables $y_1, \ldots, y_{d-1} (= x_1, \ldots, x_{d-1})$ because the terms of q involving x_d may be written in the form $q_{dd}x_d^2 + \sum_{i<d} 2q_{id}x_i x_d$, and similarly for y_d^2/q_{dd}. This gives the required factorisation (10.50).

Theorem 10.59 *For $n < d$, a marginal pdf $g(x_1, \ldots, x_n)$ of a normal d-dimensional pdf is normal.*

Proof It suffices to take $n = d - 1$, then the result may be applied repeatedly until the number of variables is reduced to those required. Thus we must show that the marginal distribution $g(x_1, \ldots, x_{d-1}) = \int_{\mathbf{R}} \phi(\mathbf{x}) \mathrm{d}x_d$ has the form (10.49). Now, a change of variables in Lemma 9.73 shows that for any constants a, λ with λ positive we have

$$\int_{\mathbf{R}} \mathrm{e}^{-(x+a)^2/\lambda} \mathrm{d}x = \int_{\mathbf{R}} \mathrm{e}^{-x^2/\lambda} \mathrm{d}x = \sqrt{\lambda\pi}. \tag{10.52}$$

Hence, in (10.50),

$$\int_{\mathbf{R}} \mathrm{e}^{-y_d^2/2q_{dd}} \mathrm{d}x_d = \int_{\mathbf{R}} \mathrm{e}^{-q_{dd}x_d^2/2} \mathrm{d}x_d = \sqrt{2\pi/q_{dd}}, \tag{10.53}$$

independently of the values of $x_1, \ldots, x_{d-1}$ fixed during the integration, and so g has the required form. Finally, $\int g(x_1, \ldots, x_{d-1}) \mathrm{d}x_1 \cdots \mathrm{d}x_{d-1} = 1$ because $\int \phi(\mathbf{x}) \mathrm{d}\mathbf{x} = 1$.

Corollary 10.60 *Given a normal random vector X with pdf $\phi(\mathbf{x})$ there is a matrix C with $|C| > 0$, such that $Z = XC$ is a row vector whose components Z_i are independent normal random variables.*

Proof We apply (10.50) $d - 1$ times to split off $d - 1$ squares and so express $q(\mathbf{x})$ as a sum of squares, $q(\mathbf{x}) = \lambda_1 z_1^2 + \cdots + \lambda_d z_d^2$, where $\lambda_i > 0$, $z_i = c_{1i}x_1 + \cdots + c_{di}x_d$, for $1 \le i \le d$. In matrix form $Z = XC$, where $C = [c_{ij}]$. Since C is the product of $d - 1$ linear transformations with positive determinant, $|C| > 0$ also. The Z_i are by definition *independent* normal because they have a joint pdf in factorised form: (constant) $\Pi_i \exp[-\lambda_i z_i^2]$.

Theorem 10.61 *Suppose the pdf $f(\mathbf{x})$ of a normal random vector X has matrix Q. Then $Q = \mathrm{Cov}(X)^{-1}$, and*

$$f(\mathbf{x}) = (2\pi)^{-d/2}|Q|^{1/2} \exp[-\tfrac{1}{2}(\mathbf{x} - \boldsymbol{\mu})Q(\mathbf{x} - \boldsymbol{\mu})^{\mathrm{T}}]. \tag{10.54}$$

Proof We suppose without loss of generality that $\boldsymbol{\mu} = \mathbf{0}$ and apply Corollary 10.60. Note that $X = ZP$, where $P = C^{-1}$, and that the pdf of the Gaussian Z_i is a constant times

$\exp[-z_i^2/2\sigma_i^2]$, where $\sigma_i^2 = V(Z_i)$. The form XQX^T transforms to $Z(PQP^T)Z^T$, with diagonal matrix

$$
\begin{aligned}
D = PQP^T &= \mathrm{diag}(\sigma_1^{-2}, \ldots, \sigma_d^{-2}), \sigma_i^2 = V(Z_i) \\
&= \mathrm{Cov}(Z)^{-1} && \text{by (10.48)} \\
&= [C^T\mathrm{Cov}(X)C]^{-1} && \text{by Theorem 10.56(b), since } Z = XC \\
&= P\,\mathrm{Cov}(X)^{-1}P^T && \text{since } P = C^{-1}.
\end{aligned}
$$

Equality of the first and last lines, $PQP^T = P\mathrm{Cov}(X)^{-1}P^T$, shows that $Q = \mathrm{Cov}(X)^{-1}$ as required. In the first integral below we apply the transformation $x = zP$, which requires an extra factor $|P|$ (see (10.30)). Let γ denote the constant factor in the pdf of X. Then

$$
\begin{aligned}
1 &= \int \gamma e^{-\frac{1}{2}q(x)}dx \\
&= \gamma \int |P| \exp\big[-\tfrac{1}{2}(z_1^2/\sigma_1^2 + \cdots + z_d^2/\sigma_d^2)\big]dz && \text{since } x = zP, \text{ as noted} \\
&= \gamma|P| \cdot \Pi_i(2\sigma_i^2\pi)^{1/2} && \text{by (10.53)} \\
&= \gamma|P|(2\pi)^{d/2}|D|^{-1/2} && \text{with } D \text{ as above} \\
&= \gamma|Q|^{-1/2}(2\pi)^{d/2} && \text{since}|D| = |Q| \cdot |P|^2 \quad \text{from } D = PQP^T.
\end{aligned}
$$

This rearranges to $\gamma = |Q|^{1/2}(2\pi)^{-d/2}$, and the proof is complete.

Example 10.62 Let the random 3-vector X have pdf $\gamma \exp[-q(x)/2]$, where

$$
q(x) = 6x_1^2 + 5x_2^2 + x_3^2 - 4x_1x_3 - 2x_2x_3.
$$

(a) Determine the covariance matrix of X and verify that it is positive definite, (b) find a matrix C with $|C| > 0$ such that the components of $Z = XC$ are independent, (c) find the constant, γ.

Solution (a) By definition $q(x) = \sum q_{ij}x_ix_j$, with $q_{ij} = q_{ji}$. This means that, for example, $-4x_1x_3$ is split as $-2x_1x_3 - 2x_1x_3$, and $q_{13} = q_{31} = -2$. Thus, inverting Q by ALGO 8.2 (Section 8.2.3) or by the method of Theorem 7.32 (Cramer's Rule), we obtain

$$
Q = \begin{bmatrix} 6 & 0 & -2 \\ 0 & 5 & -1 \\ -2 & -1 & 1 \end{bmatrix}, \quad \text{and } \mathrm{Cov}(X) = Q^{-1} = \frac{1}{2}\begin{bmatrix} 2 & 1 & 5 \\ 1 & 1 & 3 \\ 5 & 3 & 15 \end{bmatrix}.
$$

Positive definiteness holds because $\Delta_1, \Delta_2, \Delta_3 = 6, 30, 4$ are all positive (Theorem 8.37).

 (b) We begin with $q(x)$ and repeat the following. Select a square term, say x_i^2, group all terms involving x_i and complete the square for them. Lemma 10.58 (for example) guarantees there will always remain such a squared term until we are done. We calculate as follows.

$$
\begin{aligned}
q(x) &= 6x_1^2 + 5x_2^2 + \left(x_3^2 - 4x_1 x_3 - 2x_2 x_3\right) \\
&= 6x_1^2 + 5x_2^2 + (x_3 - 2x_1 - x_2)^2 - 4x_1 x_2 - 4x_1^2 - x_2^2 \\
&= 2x_1^2 + 4x_2^2 - 4x_1 x_2 + z_3^2, \quad \text{where } z_3 = x_3 - 2x_1 - x_2, \\
&= 2x_1^2 + 4\left(x_2^2 - x_1 x_2\right) + z_3^2 \\
&= 2x_1^2 + 4\left(x_2 - \tfrac{1}{2}x_1\right)^2 - x_1^2 + z_3^2 \\
&= 2z_1^2 + 4z_2^2 + z_3^2,
\end{aligned}
$$

where

$$
\begin{cases}
z_1 = x_1, \\
z_2 = -\tfrac{1}{2}x_1 + x_2, \\
z_3 = -2x_1 - x_2 + x_3,
\end{cases}
\quad \text{i.e.} \quad
C = \begin{bmatrix} 1 & -\tfrac{1}{2} & -2 \\ 0 & 1 & -1 \\ 0 & 0 & 1 \end{bmatrix}.
$$

(c) We have $|Q| = 4$, so by Theorem 10.61 the constant is $\gamma = (2\pi)^{-3/2}|Q|^{1/2} = 1/\pi\sqrt{2\pi}$.

Theorem 10.63 *If (X_1, X_2) is normally distributed then X_1, X_2 are independent if and only if they are uncorrelated, $\mathrm{Cov}(X_1, X_2) = 0$. More generally, if $(X_1, \ldots, X_d)$ has a normal density then $(X_1, \ldots, X_n)$ and $(X_{n+1}, \ldots, X_d)$ are independent if and only if $\mathrm{Cov}(X_i, X_j) = 0$ for $i \le n < j$.*

Proof Let $\mathrm{Cov}(X_i, X_j) = 0$ for $i \le n < j$. Then the covariance matrix $\Sigma = \mathrm{Cov}(X)$, and inverse Q, have the forms shown below, where Σ_k and its inverse Q_k ($k = 1, 2$) are $n \times n$:

$$
\Sigma = \begin{bmatrix} \Sigma_1 & | & 0 \\ -\,-\,- & | & -\,-\,- \\ 0 & | & \Sigma_2 \end{bmatrix}, \quad
Q = \begin{bmatrix} Q_1 & | & 0 \\ -\,-\,- & | & -\,-\,- \\ 0 & | & Q_2 \end{bmatrix}.
$$

Indeed, block matrix multiplication gives immediately $\Sigma Q = I$. Thus $q(x) = q_1(x_1, \ldots, x_n) + q_2(x_{n+1}, \ldots, x_d)$, for certain quadratic forms q_1, q_2. This implies that X has pdf of the form $\gamma e^{-q_1(x_1, \ldots, x_n)/2} \cdot e^{-q_2(x_{n+1}, \ldots, x_d)/2}$, i.e. $(X_1, \ldots, X_n)$ and $(X_{n+1}, \ldots, X_d)$ are independent. The argument may be reversed and so the result follows.

Theorem 10.64 *If $(X_1, \ldots, X_d)$ has a normal density then so does $(X_d | X_1, \ldots, X_{d-1})$.*

Proof We may suppose that $(X_1, \ldots, X_d)$ has the factorised pdf $\phi(x)$ of (10.50) and hence that $(X_1, \ldots, X_{d-1})$ has the marginal distribution $g(x_1, \ldots, x_{d-1})$ calculated from (10.53). The conditional distribution of $(X_d | X_1, \ldots, X_{d-1})$ is therefore

$$
f(x_d) = \phi/g = \sqrt{q_{dd}/2\pi}\, e^{-y_d^2/2q_{dd}}, \tag{10.55}
$$

where $y_d = q_{1d}x_1 + \cdots + q_{dd}x_d$. This has the required form, given that $x_1, \ldots, x_{d-1}$ are fixed parameters. Indeed $f \sim N(\mu, \sigma^2)$, with $\mu = -(q_{1d}x_1 + \cdots + q_{d-1, d}x_{d-1})$ $/q_{dd}, \sigma^2 = 1/q_{dd}$.

Theorem 10.65 *A symmetric matrix S is the covariance matrix of a normal distribution if and only if S is positive definite.*

Proof S is the covariance matrix of a multivariate normal random variable $\Leftrightarrow$ S has an inverse Q which is positive definite (Definition 10.57 and Theorem 10.61) $\Leftrightarrow$ S itself is positive definite (Corollary 8.35).

10.4.4 Principal Component Analysis

The title of the major section 10.4 referred not only to correlation but also to its elimination. We have seen in Section 10.4.3 how eliminating correlation in a multivariate normal distribution is equivalent to re-expressing the variables as normal ones which are actually independent. Here we discover the possibility and the benefits of eliminating correlation in the wider context of *Principal Component Analysis*, or PCA.

At the time of its introduction by Pearson (1901) (see Figure 10.10), and later independent development by Hotelling (1933), the required intensity of calculation for PCA limited its practical use. However, modern computers have opened the way for PCA into deservedly wide and effective application, as we hope to indicate. The key idea is to reduce the dimension of data whilst losing nothing of significance, by transforming coordinate variables to a new and uncorrelated set. Important applications to data compression (see e.g. Example 10.69) have resulted in PCA being referred to as the Karhunen–Loève transformation in that context. Useful references are Jollife (1986), Jackson (1991), Bishop (1995) and Schalkoff (1992).

Figure 10.10 Karl Pearson 1857–1936.

Returning from the Gaussian case to d-vectors of random variables in general, here are some of the cases we have in mind.

A Points (X, Y) in the plane, for example:
  (i) the outline of a car body (Example 10.69),
  (ii) the distribution of small entities on a microscope slide,
  (iii) adjacent pixels of a black and white image.

B General vectors $(X_1, \ldots, X_d)$, for example:
  (iv) successive pixel colour values in a computer image,
  (v) successive symbols sent out by a transmitter.

Principal components The principal components of $X = (X_1, \ldots, X_d)$ are its components with respect to an ONB (orthonormal basis) of d-space, this basis being chosen to take account of statistical properties of X in an especially useful way. One idea we use is ordering variables by variance, for which one motivation is that a variable with larger variance has greater uncertainty and so carries more information (Chapter 12). The implementation is ALGO 10.1, following a proof and discussion.

Definition 10.66 *(PCA)* Let $X = (X_1, \ldots, X_d)$ be a random vector with $E(X) = 0$. Let R be a unit d-vector. If the dot product $X \cdot R$ has greatest variance when $R = R_1$ we call R_1 the *first principal axis of X*. Restricting R to be orthogonal to R_1, we obtain the second principal axis R_2, with $X \cdot R_2$ of maximal variance. We continue this, so that R_{k+1} is orthogonal to $R_1, \ldots, R_k$ with $V(X \cdot R_{k+1})$ maximal for $1 \le k \le d - 1$. The *ith principal component* of X is then $Y_i = X \cdot R_i$.

Method of the modal matrix We now describe how the Y_i are obtained, show that the objectives, as so far described, are achieved, and give examples. For this it is not necessary to posit any normal distribution, or even a joint distribution for $X_1, \ldots, X_d$. We need only the lesser assumption that $\mathrm{Cov}(X)$ is well defined by a joint distribution for each pair X_i, X_j.

Since $\Sigma = \mathrm{Cov}(X)$ is symmetric and positive semi-definite (Theorem 10.54) it has only non-negative eigenvalues (Corollary 8.35), which we may put in descending order: $\lambda_1 \ge \lambda_2 \ge \cdots \ge \lambda_d$. There is (Remark 8.31) an orthonormal set of corresponding eigenvectors $R_1, \ldots R_d$, forming the rows of the *modal matrix* $M = \mathrm{Rows}(R_i)$ of Σ; these will be our principal axes, as we now show.

Theorem 10.67 *(PCA Theorem) Let $X = (X_1, \ldots, X_d)$ be a random vector with $E(X) = 0$ and let $\mathrm{Cov}(X)$ have eigenvalues $\lambda_1 \ge \cdots \ge \lambda_d$ with corresponding orthonormal eigenvectors $R_1, \ldots, R_d$. Then (a) $\{R_i\}$ is a set of principal axes for X, (b) the principal components Y_i of X are uncorrelated, with $V(Y_i) = \lambda_i$, (c) if projecting X onto $\mathrm{span}\{R_1, \ldots, R_k\}$ $(k < d)$ gives error ε then*

$$E(\varepsilon^2) = \lambda_{k+1} + \cdots + \lambda_d.$$

Proof (a), (b) We already know that $\{R_i\}$ is an ONB, so let X have components $\{Y_i\}$ and write $Y = (Y_i)$. Then for $1 \le i \le d$, see illustration in Figure 10.11,

$$Y_i = X \cdot R_i = X R_i^{\mathrm{T}}, \tag{10.56}$$

$$Y = X M^{\mathrm{T}}, \quad \text{where} \quad M = \mathrm{Rows}(R_i). \tag{10.57}$$

The modal matrix M diagonalises $\mathrm{Cov}(X)$ (Remark 8.31) and, because M is constant, we have the relation between covariance matrices (Theorem 10.56):

$$\mathrm{Cov}(Y) = \mathrm{Cov}(X M^{\mathrm{T}}) = M \mathrm{Cov}(X) M^{\mathrm{T}} = \mathrm{diag}(\lambda_1, \ldots, \lambda_d). \tag{10.58}$$

This says both that the Y_i are uncorrelated and that $V(Y_i) = \lambda_i$. The Y_i will be principal components if the R_i are principal axes, which fact remains to be proved. Consider an

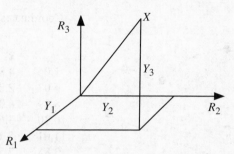

Figure 10.11 Component Y_i obtained by projecting X onto the ith eigenvector R_i of $\text{Cov}(X)$ as prescribed in Equation (10.56).

arbitrary d-vector R with components z_i with respect to basis $\{R_i\}$. We have

$$X \cdot R = X \cdot \sum z_i R_i = \sum z_i X R_i^{\mathrm{T}} = \sum z_i Y_i, \text{ by (10.56).}$$

But $E(Y) = E(X M^{\mathrm{T}}) = E(X) M^{\mathrm{T}} = 0$, and the Y_i are uncorrelated, so the variance of $X \cdot R$ is

$$V \left[\sum z_i Y_i \right] = \sum z_i^2 V(Y_i) = \sum z_i^2 \lambda_i,$$

which is greatest when $(z_i) = (1, 0, \ldots, 0)$, i.e. when $R = R_1$. Repeating this argument for $R = \sum z_i R_i$ with $i \geq 2$ we obtain $R = R_2$, and so on. Thus the R_i are principal axes, and we have proved (a) and (b). For (c), we observe that, more generally, the error ε in expanding X with respect to the orthonormal basis $\{R_i\}$, then dropping all components with subscripts in a set S, is given by $\varepsilon^2 = |\sum Y_i R_i|^2 \ (i \in S) = \sum Y_i^2 (i \in S)$, since $\{R_i\}$ is an ONB, and so

$$E[\varepsilon^2] = \sum E\left[Y_i^2\right] = \sum \lambda_i \ (i \in S).$$

Remark 10.68 If $E(X) \neq 0$ we subtract $E(X)$ from X to reduce the mean to zero, perform our calculation of the approximation, then add the mean back on again. We may use PCA for two complementary objectives:

1. *Principal Component Analysis* We focus on, say, the k most significant components $Y_1, \ldots, Y_k$.

2. *Data compression: the Karhunen–Loève (K–L) transform.* This is especially important for saving space in computer memory, or in reducing the time taken to transmit images or other information. We discard the least significant components, say Y_{k+1} to Y_d, aiming to retain an acceptably close version of the original. Thus a d-component vector X is transformed into a k-component one $(Y_1, \ldots, Y_k)$, with $k < d$.

Example 10.69 We first try a case of type (A), the fairly crude outline of a car body shown in Figure 10.12 with six points marking the notional corners. These points are to be thought of as instances of a random pair $X = (X_1, X_2)$. We are given no distributions, so expected values must be estimated via means. Let the points be (x_1^k, x_2^k), $1 \leq k \leq 6$,

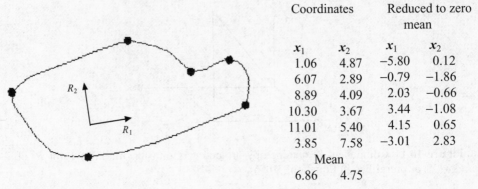

Coordinates		Reduced to zero mean	
x_1	x_2	x_1	x_2
1.06	4.87	−5.80	0.12
6.07	2.89	−0.79	−1.86
8.89	4.09	2.03	−0.66
10.30	3.67	3.44	−1.08
11.01	5.40	4.15	0.65
3.85	7.58	−3.01	2.83
Mean			
6.86	4.75		

Figure 10.12 Rough outline of car, with selected points and directions of the 'principal components' they generate.

and write $x_i = (x_i^1, \ldots, x_i^6)$. We use

$$E(X_i X_j) = \frac{1}{6} \sum_{k=1}^{6} x_i^k x_j^k = \alpha x_i \cdot x_j, \tag{10.59}$$

where we have taken the constant α to be $1/6$. A better value in general is $1/5$, as we shall see in Chapter 11, but here the value of α, given that it is fixed and nonzero, does not affect the result.

We obtain, after reducing x_1, x_2 to have zero means,

$$\mathrm{Cov}(X) = \frac{1}{6} \begin{bmatrix} x_1 \cdot x_1 & x_1 \cdot x_2 \\ x_2 \cdot x_1 & x_2 \cdot x_2 \end{bmatrix} = \begin{bmatrix} 12.75 & -1.68 \\ -1.68 & 2.25 \end{bmatrix}, \tag{10.60}$$

with eigenvalues $\lambda_1 = 13.01$, $\lambda_2 = 1.99$ whose unit eigenvectors R_1, R_2 form the rows of the modal matrix

$$M = \mathrm{Rows}(R_1, R_2) = \begin{bmatrix} 0.988 & -0.155 \\ 0.155 & 0.988 \end{bmatrix}. \tag{10.61}$$

It can be seen that the directions R_1, R_2 represent to some extent our intuitive view of the car and the six points, including an uphill inclination. The 'uphill' direction/axis R_1 corresponds to the higher variance $V(Y_1) = 13.01$, reflecting a more significant feature.

The K–L transform in practice Usually, even if we are given the covariance matrix Σ, it has been computed as an estimation from a suitably large number of instances of X, viewed as a *class* in which future cases are envisioned to lie. Determining the modal matrix $\mathrm{Rows}(R_1, \ldots, R_d)$ of Σ is *Principal Component Analysis*, and enables us to perform the K–L transform

$$X_1, \ldots, X_d \to Y_1, \ldots, Y_k \qquad (k < d)$$

for every new case, thereby compressing its data. *Image compression*, reducing the data that defines a computer image, is often performed on 8×8 blocks of pixels, with a colour property such as grey level or redness defined by a vector $X = (X_1, \ldots, X_{64})$, $0 \leq X_i \leq$

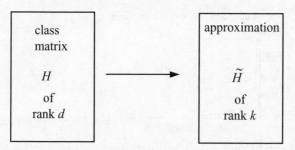

Figure 10.13 The $N \times d$ class matrix H is mapped to an $N \times d$ matrix $\tilde{H}$ of rank $k < d$.

255. For generality let us suppose we have a class of N vectors with zero mean (Remark 10.68), forming the rows of a *class matrix* $H_{N \times d}$. Then the *covariance matrix* is taken to be, similarly to (10.59),

$$\Sigma = \alpha H^{\mathrm{T}} H \ (\alpha \neq 0). \tag{10.62}$$

Suppose the rows of H are mapped to d-vectors which lie in a space of dimension $k < d$, forming row by row an $N \times d$ matrix $\tilde{H}$. See Figure 10.13.

With PCA on random variables we minimised the expected error in representing $X_1, \ldots, X_d$ by $Y_1, \ldots, Y_k$. Correspondingly, we choose $\tilde{H}$ so as to minimise the mean squared norm of the difference between a row of H and the corresponding row of $\tilde{H}$. Equivalently, we minimise the *sum* of these squared norms which, by Theorem 8.44, equals the Frobenius matrix norm of the difference:

$$\left\| H - \tilde{H} \right\|_{\mathrm{F}}^2 . \tag{10.63}$$

But Theorem 8.53 with Remark 8.55 tells us this quantity is least when $\tilde{H} = H_k$, the projection of H onto the first k rows of the orthogonal matrix V, in the Singular Value Decomposition of H:

$$H = U^{\mathrm{T}} D V, \tag{10.64}$$

and D is the $N \times d$ diagonal matrix with diagonal elements $s_1 \geq s_2 \geq \cdots \geq s_d$ (the singular values). But V *is the modal matrix of* $\alpha H^{\mathrm{T}} H$ (for any $\alpha \neq 0$), since firstly (10.64) implies $HV^{\mathrm{T}} = U^{\mathrm{T}} D$ and hence secondly $V(H^{\mathrm{T}} H)V^{\mathrm{T}} = D^{\mathrm{T}} D = \mathrm{diag}(s_1^2, \ldots, s_d^2)$.

Conclusion Let $V = \mathrm{Rows}(R_i)$. For each $k \leq d$ the K–L transform

$$X \to (X \cdot R_1, \ldots, X \cdot R_k) \tag{10.65}$$

minimises the mean squared error for mapping d-vectors in the given class into a space of dimension k. By the matrix norm formula (8.35), and the fact that the eigenvalues λ_i of $H^{\mathrm{T}} H$ are the squares of the singular values s_i of H, this mean error equals

$$\lambda_{k+1} + \cdots + \lambda_d, \tag{10.66}$$

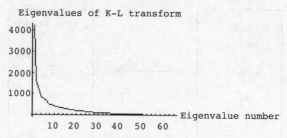

Figure 10.14 Successively smaller eigenvalues in Example 10.70.

where $\lambda_i = s_i^2$ is the ith eigenvalue, in descending order, of $H^T H$ (cf. Theorem 10.67). We have the algorithm:

ALGO 10.1 PCA for a matrix H of sample d-vectors, and the K–L transform to dimension $k < d$

1. Compute the SV decomposition $H = U^T D V$ (or calculate V directly as the modal matrix of $H^T H$).
2. Set $V = \text{Rows}(R_i)$ and $V_k = [R_1^T \ldots R_k^T]$, the first k columns of V^T.
3. Return the ith principal axis as R_i for $i = 1, 2, \ldots, d$.
4. Return the K–L transform as $X \to X V_k$.

Example 10.70 Here we apply ALGO 10.1 to a digital image. It seems appropriate to use our earlier greyscale image of the inventor of PCA, Karl Pearson. The original 82×109 pixels are trimmed to 80×104 and partitioned into 8×8 blocks, each yielding a sample 64-vector of values in the range 0 to 255. The total of 130 samples form the rows of our class matrix H after subtracting the mean (Remarks 10.68 and 10.71). We use a Singular Value Decomposition to obtain the modal matrix $V = \text{Rows}(R_i)$ of $H^T H$. A sample vector X has principal components $\{X \cdot R_i\}$, corresponding in order to the *decreasingly* significant eigenvalues $\lambda_1, \lambda_2, \ldots$ (see (10.66)) represented in Figure 10.14.

Figure 10.14 indicates that as many of 50% of the principal axes can be neglected in re-constituting the picture, and thus encouraged we try varying numbers of components, with approximated pictures as shown in Figure 10.15 (note: the mean has to be added back).

The picture can be reduced to 32 and perhaps down to 20 components without significant loss of quality. Such excellent results are a pointer to the value of Principal Component Analysis. As a postscript we show in Figure 10.16 the first five principal axis vectors, portrayed as 8×8 blocks of grey values.

Remark 10.71 (i) (*Zero mean*) In calculation we have reduced the set of sample vectors to zero mean before combining them as rows of a matrix H and estimating $\text{Cov}(X)$ by $\alpha H^T H$. An alternative is to use the matrix B of samples, with sample mean $\boldsymbol{m}$, and then the estimate may be written

$$\alpha[B^T B - N(\boldsymbol{m}^T \boldsymbol{m})] \quad \text{(for } N \text{ samples)}. \tag{10.67}$$

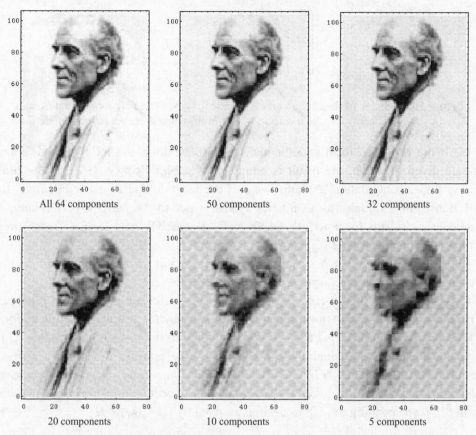

All 64 components   50 components   32 components

20 components   10 components   5 components

Figure 10.15 Greyscale picture of Example 10.70 with varying number of PCA principal components used for its reconstruction, out of a full complement of 64.

Figure 10.16 The first five (unit) principal axis vectors. Of length 64, they have their elements regrouped into 8 × 8 blocks for display purposes.

Proof Let $B = \mathrm{Rows}(B_1, \ldots, B_N)$. Then

$$H^{\mathrm{T}}H = \sum_i (B_i - m)^{\mathrm{T}}(B_i - m) \text{ by Russian multiplication (7.31)}$$

$$= \sum_i B_i{}^{\mathrm{T}}B_i - m^{\mathrm{T}}\sum_i B_i - \left(\sum_i B_i^{\mathrm{T}}\right)m + N(m^{\mathrm{T}}m)$$

$$= B^{\mathrm{T}}B - N(m^{\mathrm{T}}m) \quad \text{substituting } m = (1/N)\sum_i B_i.$$

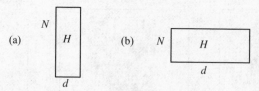

Figure 10.17 Shape of the class matrix H in case (a) when there are more samples than the number of dimensions (the usual case), and in (b) when there are fewer samples.

(ii) If the K–L transform is computed, as we have done, via the SVD rather than straight diagonalisation, the result is numerically stabler (Ripley, 1996) at the price of a lengthier computation. Although one of the most computationally intensive, the K–L transform is valuable as a yardstick against which to compare the performance of candidate transforms for practical use. In particular, the Discrete Cosine Transform is compared in Section 15.4.2.

(iii) Usually the number N of sample vectors is greater than their dimension d, and the class matrix H has the shape of (a) in Figure 10.17.

However, should this not be so, and H has the shape of (b), then we can perform PCA or the K–L transform much more quickly by the following considerations. (1) We only require principal axes R_i corresponding to the *nonzero* eigenvalues λ_i of the $d \times d$ matrix $H^T H$, which (Theorem 8.39) are the same as the nonzero eigenvalues of the *smaller* matrix HH^T. (2) If $\{R_i\}$ is an orthonormal set of eigenvectors of HH^T corresponding to $\{\lambda_i\}$, then by Theorem 8.39 an orthonormal set of eigenvectors for $H^T H$ corresponding to $\{\lambda_i\}$, as desired, is given by $\{(1/\sqrt{\lambda_i})R_i H\}$.

Example 10.72 (*Using the smaller matrix*) With 15 samples of dimension 30, we would perform SVD or diagonalisation on a 15×15 matrix rather than 30×30, with a single multiplication by H at the end. However, we illustrate the method with a toy case, where H has two samples of size 3 (not here reduced to zero mean).

$$H = \begin{bmatrix} 1 & 2 & 3 \\ 4 & 2 & 7 \end{bmatrix}, H^T H = \begin{bmatrix} 17 & 10 & 31 \\ 10 & 8 & 20 \\ 31 & 20 & 58 \end{bmatrix}, HH^T = \begin{bmatrix} 14 & 29 \\ 29 & 69 \end{bmatrix}, \text{ only } 2 \times 2.$$

We find eigenvectors for HH^T of $\lambda_1 = 81.466, \lambda_2 = 1.534$, with corresponding unit orthogonal eigenvectors $w_1 = [0.395 \ 0.919]$ and $w_2 = [0.919 \ -0.395]$ (apply the SVD to H^T). Thus the required principal axes are

$$\begin{bmatrix} R_1 \\ R_2 \end{bmatrix} = \begin{bmatrix} 1/\sqrt{\lambda_1} & 0 \\ 0 & 1/\sqrt{\lambda_2} \end{bmatrix} \begin{bmatrix} w_1 \\ w_2 \end{bmatrix} H$$

$$= \begin{bmatrix} 1/9.026 & 0 \\ 0 & 1/1.239 \end{bmatrix} \begin{bmatrix} 0.395 & 0.919 \\ 0.919 & -0.395 \end{bmatrix} \begin{bmatrix} 1 & 2 & 3 \\ 4 & 2 & 7 \end{bmatrix} = \begin{bmatrix} 0.451 & 0.291 & 0.844 \\ 0.534 & -0.846 & 0.007 \end{bmatrix}.$$

Example 10.73 Cootes *et al.* (1995) introduced *Active Shape Models* – using PCA to produce a variety of new but realistic faces from a set of samples.

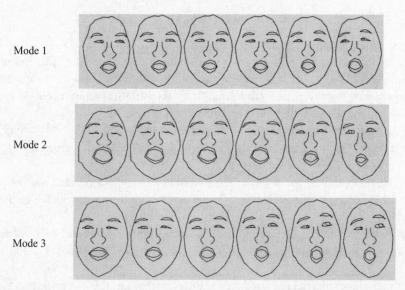

Mode 1

Mode 2

Mode 3

Figure 10.18 Face variants obtained by using only the first three principal components. In Mode *i* the *i*th component y_i is increased from left to right, the rest being fixed.

Figure 10.18 is an illustration due to Porncharoensin (2002). Recalling notation, the principal axes of the sample data are $R_1, R_2, \ldots$, with corresponding eigenvalues/variances $\lambda_1 \geq \lambda_2 \geq \cdots$. It was found in this case that 98% of the total variance $\sum \lambda_i$ was already present in the leading three components, so new faces were generated by

$$y_1 R_1 + y_2 R_2 + y_3 R_3 \qquad (-\sqrt{\lambda_i} \leq y_i \leq \sqrt{\lambda_i}), \qquad (10.68)$$

with y_i taking equally spaced values within one standard deviation $\sqrt{\lambda_i}$ of the mean.

Some further details The sample consisted of 30 faces, rotated and translated into a standard position, and characterised by 92 positions used as landmarks. In each mode, 29 component values were used; the results in Figure 10.18 are from the first six.

Remarks 10.74 (1) (*The invalid straight line problem*) Sometimes a dubious straight line is drawn through a set of experimental points (x_i, y_i). In such a case credibility may be regained by asserting only that the first principal component of the data is shown, and that a linear relationship between variables is not claimed to exist (see Example 10.69 and Remarks 11.22).

(2) (*PCA as feature organiser*) To extract information from a random vector $X = (X_1, \ldots, X_d)$ we may look for the most significant *features*, formally described as being any functions of $X_1, \ldots, X_d$. They may be recognisable to human intuition – such as mean colour value $(X_1 + \cdots + X_d)/d$, or functions evidencing the position of bounding edges (Chapter 15). General features are considered in Section 11.2.2, but in PCA we explore *linear features*, those which are linear combinations $\sum a_i X_i$.

Exercises 10

1 ✓ Suppose the random variables X, Y have a joint pdf $f(x, y) = x(x + y), 0 \leq x, y \leq 1$. Determine the marginal pdfs $g(x), h(y)$ and deduce that X, Y are not independent.

2 ✓ Daily demand for power is a random variable X with pdf $g(x) = xe^{-x}$ $(x > 0)$, whilst, independently, supply Y has a pdf $h(y) = 2e^{-2y}$ $(y > 0)$. Breakdown occurs if supply falls below half the demand; find the probability that this happens.

3 ✓ Let the dependent variables X, Y have a conditional pdf $p(y|x) = \gamma e^{-(1/2)(y-x)^2}$ $(x, y$ in $\mathbf{R})$, where $\gamma = (2\pi)^{-1/2}$. Determine the expectation $E(Y|X = a)$ of Y given $X = a$ (Lemma 9.73 may be useful).

4 ✓ Use (10.18) to find the pdf of $W = XY$, given that X, Y are independent random variables, that X has pdf $g(x) = 2x/9, 0 \leq x \leq 3$, and that Y is uniformly distributed on the interval $[0, 4]$.

5 ✓ Find the pdf of $S = T + U$, where T and U are independent random variables with respective pdfs $f(t) = \sin t$ and $g(u) = \cos u$, on $0 \leq t, u \leq 2\pi$. (Note: $2 \sin A \cos B = \sin(A + B) + \sin(A - B)$.)

6 ✓ How many times must an unbiased coin be tossed so that we are 99% certain that the relative frequency of heads is within 0.01 of a half (use the Law of Large Numbers).

7 ✓ (i) Let X be standard normal and let Y be $N(3, 4)$. Deduce the mgf of Y from that of X (see Table 10.5 and Equation (10.34)). (ii) Use mgfs to prove the reproductive property of Poisson random variables. That is, show that if $X \sim Po(\lambda)$ and $Y \sim Po(\mu)$ are independent then $X + Y \sim Po(\lambda + \mu)$.

8 ✓ (i) Show that $\sin(1/n) = 1/n + O(n^{-3})$ as n tends to ∞. (ii) A robust chip gives correct results if at least 80 of its 100 components are in order. Each component has, independently, a probability 0.05 of failure on test. Find to two decimal places the probability that the chip functions correctly when tested. (The required values of Φ are found in Example 10.47. Note that $\Phi(a)$ may be neglected for $a \leq -4$.)

9 ✓ $X = (X_1, X_2, X_3)$ is a random vector, where X_i takes values 0, 1 and the pair X_i, X_j has a joint pdf given by $P(X_i = \alpha, X_j = \beta)$ equal to the α, β element of the matrix M_{ij} below $(1 \leq i, j \leq 3)$. Thus, for example, $P(X_1 = 1, X_3 = 0) = 1/3$.

$$M_{12} = \begin{bmatrix} 0 & 1/2 \\ 1/2 & 0 \end{bmatrix}, M_{13} = \begin{bmatrix} 1/2 & 0 \\ 1/3 & 1/6 \end{bmatrix}, M_{23} = \begin{bmatrix} a & b \\ c & 0 \end{bmatrix}.$$

(i) Use M_{12} and M_{13} to determine the marginal pdfs $p_i(\alpha) = P(X_i = \alpha)$ and hence compute the values of a, b, c in M_{23}. (ii) Find the values of $E(X_i)$ and $E(X_i^2)$, $1 \leq i \leq 3$. (iii) Determine the covariance matrix $Cov(X)$ (see (10.47a)). Verify that $Cov(X)$ is positive semi-definite, of rank 2.

10 ✓ Let the random vector $X = (X_1, X_2, X_3)$ have pdf $\gamma \exp[-q(x)/2]$, where

$$q(x) = 8x_1^2 + 4x_2^2 + x_3^2 - 2x_1x_2 - 4x_1x_3 - 2x_2x_3.$$

(a) Determine the covariance matrix of X, (b) find a matrix A with positive determinant such that the components of $Z = XA$ are independent, (c) find the constant, γ. (Hint: see Example 10.62).

11 ✓ A matrix N of samples of a random d-vector has Singular Value Decomposition $N = A^T DB$. How may the principal axes of PCA be extracted from this information (give reasons)?

11

Sampling and inference

The purpose of this chapter is to provide a modest introduction to the huge and important topics of sampling and inference, which will serve our purpose in succeeding chapters. This is not a stand-alone chapter, indeed it provides many illustrations of the significance of early sections on probability, just as they in turn utilise the preceding linear algebra/matrix results. So what is the present chapter about? The short answer, which will be amplified section by section, is *the interpretation of data*, having in mind ultimately the interpretation of pixel values in computer images.

We begin with the idea of a *sample*, a sequence of determinations $X_1, \ldots, X_n$ of a random variable X. We seek *statistics*, i.e. functions $f(X_1, \ldots, X_n)$, to help answer questions such as (a) given that a distribution is of a certain type: Poisson, exponential, normal, $\ldots$, how can we estimate the distribution parameters and with what certainty, (b) given a sample, what is the underlying distribution, again with what certainty? Sections 11.2, 11.3 and 11.4 utilise the methods of Section 11.1.

In Section 11.2 we introduce the *Bayesian approach*, distinct from the Bayesian Theorem, but ultimately based upon it. The idea is to improve on an imprecise model of a situation or process by utilising every piece of data that can be gathered. The section concludes with the *Bayes pattern classsifer*, a first step in object/pattern recognition.

Section 11.3 tackles the problem of simulation, generating a sequence of samples from a specified distribution, as required for many applications. Most methods start with the built-in computer sampling from a uniform distribution and proceed to the desired case on the basis of relevant theoretical results. A nice method of sampling from multivariate normal distributions (ALGO 11.9) is enabled by the Choleski decomposition, for which the work is done in Chapter 8.

In the final section of this chapter we apply Bayesian methods to obtain a sample from a distribution when we have relevant if approximate information but not the explicit distribution. A key idea is to produce samples as a Markov chain whose stationary distribution is that sought (Metropolis *et al.*, 1953), an idea rendered very practicable by an improvement due to Hastings (1970). The general method, known as Markov Chain Monte Carlo, or MCMC, is becoming well established. Our first application will be to image restoration.

This all requires techniques such as Bayesian networks, for manipulating the host of conditional probabilities involved. The local connections between pixel values in an image are modelled naturally by a Markov Random Field, itself equivalent to a distribution given by a so-called Gibbsian energy function. We end with the promising combinatorial approach via network flows.

11.1 Statistical inference

Here are some kinds of questions the theory of statistics is designed to address.

1. The life length of a certain piece of equipment is given by an exponential distribution, but what is the value of the parameter?
2. Black and white noise on a computer image is governed by a Poisson distribution. But, again, the parameter is unknown.
3. It is claimed that those who smoke increase their risk of lung cancer. How can this be established or rebutted?
4. Errors in a certain measurement are believed to be normally distributed. How can we test the truth of this belief?

In all this we are replacing a question about the real world by one about an assumed probability distribution by which we aim to model certain aspects of that world. The standard approach is to start with a *sample*, meaning a sequence of values $x_1, \ldots, x_n$ taken by a random variable X. In effect we perform an underlying experiment n times: say testing n light bulbs to destruction, or examining n computer images.

Next, we compute the value of a *statistic*, a pre-determined function of the x_i such as their mean $\bar{x} = (x_1 + \cdots + x_n)/n$. Finally, perhaps the hardest part, we make an *inference* from the value of our statistic, concerning the situation under focus. Because a sample does not determine the whole, our conclusion will not be deterministic, but rather a statement about probabilities, such as 'the probability that smoking causes lung cancer in 80% of cases is 0.99', or 'the best estimate of λ according to a certain criterion is 2.57'. What such a criterion should be is an issue we shall address.

Values of the normal cdf $\Phi(z)$ sufficient for most examples of this chapter may be found in Table 9.7, whilst Tables 9.9 and 9.10 are résumés on standard distributions. At this stage we recapitulate some elementary results that will be used frequently in the sequel. Firstly, for constants a, b and random variable X we have from Section 9.3 that $E(aX + b) = aE(X) + b$ and $V(aX + b) = a^2 V(X)$. More generally (Section 10.2.3) for constants $c_1, \ldots, c_n$ and random variables $X_1, \ldots, X_n$, which need not be identically distributed,

$$E\Big[\sum c_i X_i\Big] = \sum c_i E[X_i] \quad \text{always,}$$
$$V\Big[\sum c_i X_i\Big] = \sum c_i^2 V[X_i] \quad \text{if the } X_i \text{ are independent, or just uncorrelated.} \quad (11.1)$$

11.1.1 Sampling

Definition 11.1 Let X be a random variable. Then a *random sample from X* is a random vector $(X_1, \ldots, X_n)$, where the X_i are independent and each has the same distribution as X. We say the X_i are *iid X*, standing for independent, identically distributed to X. The same meaning is intended when we say the X_i are (statistical) copies of X. A *statistic from the sample* is a function of $X_1, \ldots, X_n$. Thus it is a particular kind of random variable $Y = H(X_1, \ldots, X_n)$ with its own distribution, called the *sampling distribution*.

Example 11.2 (*Some principal statistics*)

(i) $\overline{X} = \dfrac{1}{n} \sum_{i=1}^{n} X_i$, the *sample mean*,

(ii) $S^2 = \dfrac{1}{n-1} \sum_{i=1}^{n} (X_i - \overline{X})^2$, the *sample variance*

(iii) $\mathrm{Min}_i(X_i)$ and $\mathrm{Max}_i(X_i)$, the *sample minimum* and *maximum*.

Notice that all four cases above are indeed functions of the sample $(X_1, \ldots, X_n)$. To use them for our ultimate aim of inference we need to know how their distributions depend on that of the X_i. The reaon for the factor $n-1$ when n might be expected, in (ii), will appear shortly when we consider what makes one statistic preferable to another for estimating or testing the same thing. We begin with a result holding for any random variable X.

Distribution of the sample mean

Theorem 11.3 *Let the random variable X, not necessarily normal, have expectation μ and variance σ^2. Then*

$$\boxed{(a)\ E(\overline{X}) = \mu, \qquad (b)\ V(\overline{X}) = \sigma^2/n,} \tag{11.2}$$

and for large n we have approximately $\dfrac{\overline{X} - \mu}{\sigma/\sqrt{n}} \sim N(0, 1)$.

Proof (a) The linearity (11.1) of E yields $E(\overline{X}) = E(\frac{1}{n} \sum_i X_i) = \frac{1}{n} \sum_i E(X_i) = \frac{1}{n}(n\mu) = \mu$. For (b) we argue that $V(\overline{X}) = V(\frac{1}{n} \sum_i X_i) = (1/n^2)V(\sum_i X_i) = (1/n^2) \sum_i V(X_i)$ (since the X_i are independent) $= (1/n^2)(n\sigma^2) = \sigma^2/n$. The last part follows from the Central Limit Theorem (Theorem 10.45) because $\overline{X}$ is the sum of a large number of random variables, and taking $(\overline{X} - \mu)/(\sigma/\sqrt{n})$ reduces it to mean 0, variance 1.

This general result gives the expectation and variance for $\overline{X}$ in all cases. The actual distribution is of course another matter; some commonly used cases are covered in Table 11.1. Here is an example in which the distribution of $\overline{X}$ is easily found from that of X.

Example 11.4 (*Normal sampling mean*) By the reproductive property of the normal distribution (Example 10.41), a sum of independent normal variables is normal, as is a scalar multiple $1/n$ thereof, by (9.33), so we only need to determine the expectation and variance. But these are supplied by (11.2), giving $\overline{X} \sim N(\mu, \sigma^2/n)$.

Example 11.5 (*Exponential sampling mean*) The exponential distribution has nearly a reproductive property, and we can easily find an exact formula using the mgf, or moment

Table 11.1. *The distribution $g(x)$ of $S_n = X_1 + \cdots + X_n$, where the X_i are iid X (independent, identically distributed to X). The sampling distribution of the mean, S_n/n, is given by $ng(nx)$ (normal case $N(\mu, \sigma^2/n)$, exponential $\Gamma_{na,n}$).*

Distribution of X	$g(x)$, the distribution of $S_n = X_1 + \cdots + X_n$
binomial(k, p)	binomial(nk, p)
Poisson(λ)	Poisson$(n\lambda)$
normal, $N(\mu, \sigma^2)$	$N(n\mu, n\sigma^2)$
gamma: $\Gamma_{\alpha,u}, G(\alpha, \beta)$	$\Gamma_{\alpha,nu}, G(n\alpha, \beta)$
exponential$(\alpha) = \Gamma_{\alpha,1}$	$\Gamma_{\alpha,n}$

generating function, of Section 10.3.1. The mgfs required are found in Table 10.5. The mgf of $\exp(\alpha)$ is $\alpha/(\alpha - t)$ and hence by (10.35) the mgf of $S_n = \sum_i X_i$ is $(\alpha/(\alpha - t))^n$. But this is the mgf of $\Gamma_{\alpha,n}$, hence $S_n \sim \Gamma_{\alpha,n}$, the second of three pdfs we are about to list. To proceed from this point to the pdf of $\overline{X}$ we recall from (9.33) that if X has pdf $f(x)$ then $Y = aX$ has pdf $(1/|a|)f(y/a)$; we set $a = 1/n$. Hence we have the following pdfs:

$$X : \Gamma_{\alpha,1}(x) = \alpha e^{-\alpha x}, \quad \text{the exponential distribution,}$$
$$S_n : \Gamma_{\alpha,n}(x) = (\alpha^n / \Gamma(n)) x^{n-1} e^{-\alpha x}, \quad \text{the gamma distribution,}$$
$$\overline{X} : n\Gamma_{\alpha,n}(nx) = (n\alpha^n / \Gamma(n))(nx)^{n-1} e^{-\alpha nx} = \Gamma_{n\alpha,n}(x).$$

Exercise Check the last equality.

Example 11.6 Assuming that the height H, in metres, of men in a certain population follows a normal distribution $N(1.8, 0.2)$, how likely is it that, in a sample of 20 men selected at random, the mean height is under 1.6 metres?

Solution The sample size is $n = 20$, so $\overline{H} \sim N(1.8, 0.2/n) = N(1.8, 0.01)$. Therefore

$$P(\overline{H} < 1.6) = P\left(\frac{H - 1.8}{0.1} < \frac{1.6 - 1.8}{0.1}\right) = \Phi\left(\frac{-0.2}{0.1}\right) = \Phi(-2) = 0.023,$$

from Table 9.7. This is a very small probability, suggesting the original hypothesis that H is $N(1.8, 0.2)$ was most likely inaccurate. The example itself points towards methods of hypothesis testing we shall develop shortly.

Distribution of the sample variance S^2

The following observations concerning a sample (X_i) from a random variable X are often useful for simplifying calculations here and later. The first holds for any i $(1 \le i \le n)$, the third for any constant, c.

$$E[(X_i - \mu)^2] = \sigma^2, \tag{11.3}$$
$$E[(\overline{X} - \mu)^2] = \sigma^2/n = V(\overline{X}), \tag{11.4}$$
$$\sum_{i=1}^{n}(X_i - \overline{X})^2 = \sum_{i=1}^{n}(X_i - c)^2 - n(\overline{X} - c)^2. \tag{11.5}$$

Proof (11.3) holds because X_i is a copy of X, whilst (11.4) is a recasting of (11.2). Thirdly,

$$\sum_{i=1}^{n}(X_i - \overline{X})^2 = \sum_{i=1}^{n}[(X_i - c) - (\overline{X} - c)]^2$$

$$= \sum_{i=1}^{n}(X_i - c)^2 - 2(\overline{X} - c)\sum_{i=1}^{n}(X_i - c) + \sum_{i=1}^{n}(\overline{X} - c)^2$$

$$= \sum_{i=1}^{n}(X_i - c)^2 - 2(\overline{X} - c)(n\overline{X} - nc) + n(\overline{X} - c)^2$$

$$= \sum_{i=1}^{n}(X_i - c)^2 - n(\overline{X} - c)^2.$$

A key role is played by the χ^2 distribution, that of a sum of squares of standard normal random variables. Later we'll see why the phrase 'degrees of freedom' is appropriate, in the more general context of hypothesis testing, Section 11.1.6. Conveniently, χ^2 is a special case of the gamma distribution (Example 10.20), as we now recall.

> If $Z = X_1^2 + \cdots + X_n^2$, and $X_i, \sim N(0, 1)$, then we say
> $Z \sim \chi_n^2$, the χ^2 *distribution with n degrees of freedom.* (11.6a)
> In fact $\chi_n^2 = \Gamma_{1/2, n/2}$,

where

$$\Gamma_{\alpha, u}(z) = [\alpha^u / \Gamma(u)]z^{u-1}e^{-\alpha z}, \ E(Z) = u/\alpha, \ V(Z) = u/\alpha^2.$$

Theorem 11.7 *Let* $U = (U_1, \ldots, U_n)$ *be a random vector of iid variables in* $N(0, 1)$ *and let the* $n \times n$ *real matrix A be psd (positive semi-definite). Then the psd form* UAU^T *has* χ^2 *distribution if and only if* $A^2 = A$. *In the affirmative case the number of degrees of freedom is* $r(A)$, *which equals* Tr(A).

Proof We recall two key facts about the normal distribution, from Chapter 10.

(1) A linear combination of independent normal random variables is normal (Section 10.3.2),
(2) If normal random variables are uncorrelated then they are independent (Section 10.4.3).

Because A is by implication symmetric, it may be diagonalised by an orthogonal matrix P (Theorem 8.30); then we may define inverse linear transformations $U = ZP$ and $Z = UP^T$, resulting in an expression of the original form as a sum of squares whose coefficients are the nonzero eigenvalues of A:

$$UAU^T = \lambda_1 z_1^2 + \cdots + \lambda_r z_r^2 \quad \text{(see (8.16) ff)}, \tag{11.6b}$$

where r is the rank of A. Now, since the U_i are independent normal random variables, each component Z_i of the vector Z is normal by (1). Further, Cov$(U) = I$ because the U_i are $N(0, 1)$, and so Cov$(Z) = P$Cov$(U)P^T = PP^T = I$. That is, the Z_i are uncorrelated and hence, in the light of (2), they are iid in $N(0, 1)$. Thus UAU^T is χ^2 if and only if $\lambda_1 = \cdots = \lambda_r = 1$.

Suppose $A^2 = A$. Then the eigenvalues λ of A satisfy $\lambda^2 = \lambda$ (see Remark 8.9), hence they are all 0 or 1. Thus $UAU^T = Z_1^2 + \cdots + Z_n^2$ is χ_r^2, where $r = r(A)$, which equals the sum of the eigenvalues in this case because each nonzero eigenvalue is a 1. But this sum equals $\text{Tr}(A)$ by Lemma 8.5. *Suppose conversely that all* $\lambda_i = 1$ *in* (11.6b). Then $PAP^T = \text{diag}(1 \ldots 1, 0 \ldots 0) = D$, say, where $D^2 = D$, and so $A^2 = P^T DP \cdot P^T DP = P^T D^2 P = P^T DP = A$, completing the proof.

Corollary 11.8 *If* $X \sim N(\mu, \sigma^2)$, *then the sampling sum of squares statistic* $T(X_1, \ldots, X_n) = \sum_i (X_i - \overline{X})^2$ *has distribution given by* $T/\sigma^2 \sim \chi_{n-1}^2$.

Proof Define new random variables $U_i = (X_i - \mu)/\sigma$, in $N(0, 1)$. Then by definition $\overline{X} = \Sigma X_i/n$ and $\overline{U} = \Sigma U_i/n$, giving $\overline{U} = (\overline{X} - \mu)/\sigma$ and $U_i - \overline{U} = (X_i - \overline{X})/\sigma$. But notice that, although $\{X_i\}$ are iid X and $\{U_i\}$ are iid $N(0, 1)$ we do not claim that $\{U_i - \overline{U}\}$ are independent. We know that T is a quadratic form in the U_i, and will see that Theorem 11.7 may be applied. To this end we define an n-vector j and an $n \times n$ matrix J, of 1s:

$$j = [1 \ldots 1]_{1 \times n}, \quad J = [1]_{n \times n}, \tag{11.7a}$$

for which, clearly, $\quad j^T j, = J, \quad \text{and} \quad J^2 = nJ. \tag{11.7b}$

Given this, we may argue as follows, where $U = [U_1 \ldots U_n]$,

$$
\begin{aligned}
T/\sigma^2 = \sum (U_i - \overline{U})^2 = \sum U_i^2 - n\overline{U}^2 \quad & \text{by (11.5) with } c = 0 \\
= UU^T - n(Uj^T/n)^2 \quad & \text{since } \sum U_i = Uj^T \\
= UU^T - Uj^T jU^T/n \quad & \text{since } Uj^T \text{ is a scalar} \\
= UU^T - UJU^T/n \quad & \text{by (11.7b)} \\
= UAU^T, \quad & \text{where } A = I - J/n \text{ is symmetric,}
\end{aligned}
$$

and $A^2 = I^2 - 2IJ/n + J^2/n^2 = I - 2J/n + J/n$ (by (11.7b)) $= A$. Thus Theorem 11.7 applies to give $T/\sigma^2 \sim \chi^2$, whose number of degrees of freedom equals $\text{Tr}(A) = \text{Tr}(I) - \text{Tr}(J)/n = n - n/n = n - 1$, as required.

Consequence for S^2 With this result we quickly obtain the distribution of S^2 (Exercise 11.1), which is simply a multiple of the sum of squares variable T above. We see that by choosing this multiple to be not the obvious $1/n$ but instead $1/(n - 1)$ we ensure that our estimator for σ^2 actually has σ^2 as expected value. In more detail, $[(n - 1)/\sigma^2]S^2 = T/\sigma^2 \sim \chi_{n-1}^2$ by Corollary 11.8, with expected value $n - 1$ by (11.6), and hence hence $E(S^2) = (\sigma^2/(n - 1)) \times (n - 1) = \sigma^2$.

Getting the desired expectation, and other ieues for an estimator, are discussed in the next section. Meanwhile, we have proved the following corollary.

Corollary 11.9 *For a normal distribution, the statistic* S^2 *satisfies* $E(S^2) = \sigma^2$.

Sampling distribution of the Min/Max It is useful to include this case, listed as Example 11.2(iii) at the start of the section, for it is in some sense extremal, and a source of counterexamples; see also Example 11.13.

Theorem 11.10 *Let the continuous random variable X have pdf $f(x)$ and cdf $F(x)$. Then the statistic $M = \text{Max}(X_i)$ of a sample has pdf $g(m) = nF(m)^{n-1} f(m)$. For $\text{Min}(X_i)$ the pdf is $h(m) = n[1 - F(m)]^{n-1} f(m)$.*

Proof Denoting the cdf of M by $G(m)$ we have, since the X_i are iid X: $G(m) = P(M \leq m) = P[X_i \leq m$ for all $i] = F(m)^n$. Differentiating: $g(m) = nF(m)^{n-1} dF/dm = nF(m)^{n-1} f(m)$. The case of $\text{Min}(X_i)$ is left as an exercise.

11.1.2 Estimating parameters

Let X be a random variable. Suppose we know the general type of the distribution of X (e.g. normal, Poisson, etc.). Can we find a statistic $g(X_1, \ldots, X_n)$ for estimating μ, σ^2 or more generally a parameter θ upon which the distribution depends? Given g, called an *estimator* for θ, the procedure may be summarised as follows.

1. Take a sample from X – that is: perform the underlying experiment, say n times. obtaining a value x_i for X_i ($1 \leq i \leq n$). Call X_i an *observation, realisation,* or *instance* of X_i.
2. Compute the *estimate* $\hat{\theta} = g(x_1, \ldots, x_n)$ of θ.

Definition 11.11 We need criteria for comparing candidate estimators, and the most basic criterion is that an estimator be *unbiased* in the sense that it has expected value equal to the parameter it estimates: $E(\hat{\theta}) = \theta$. Given this, we may ask how wildly the estimate can depart from the expected value – what is its variance? If the variance is least possible for an unbiased estimate, we say $\hat{\theta}$ is *efficient*. Thirdly, it is desirable that $\hat{\theta}$ get closer to θ as the sample becomes large, or more formally we say that $\hat{\theta}$ is a *consistent* estimator of θ if

$$P(|\hat{\theta} - \theta| \leq \varepsilon) \to 1 \quad \text{as} \quad n \to \infty \tag{11.8}$$

for arbitrarily small positive ε. A *linear* estimator is one of the form $\sum_i a_i X_i$, a *quadratic* estimator has the form $\sum_{i,j} q_{ij} X_i X_j$, where the a_i and q_{ij} are constants. For a summary see Table 11.3. The following result often enables consistency to be established.

Theorem 11.12 *If $E(\hat{\theta}) \to \theta$ and $V(\hat{\theta}) \to 0$ as $n \to \infty$, then $\hat{\theta}$ is a consistent estimator.*

Proof The Chebychev inequality in the form (9.48a): $P(|X - c| > \varepsilon) \leq \varepsilon^{-2} E[(X - c)^2]$, with $X = \hat{\theta}, c = \theta$, yields

$$\varepsilon^2 P(|\hat{\theta} - \theta > \varepsilon) \leq E[(\hat{\theta} - \theta)^2]$$
$$= E[(\hat{\theta} - E(\hat{\theta}) + E(\hat{\theta}) - \theta)^2]$$
$$= E[\{\hat{\theta} - E(\hat{\theta})\}^2 + \{E(\hat{\theta}) - \theta\}^2 + 2\{\hat{\theta} - E(\hat{\theta})\}\{E(\hat{\theta}) - \theta\}].$$

Letting $n \to \infty$ we have $E(\hat{\theta}) - \theta \to 0$ and $E[(\hat{\theta} - E(\hat{\theta}))^2] = V(\hat{\theta}) \to 0$. Hence the above right hand side tends to zero, implying $\varepsilon^2 P(|\hat{\theta} - \theta| > \varepsilon) \to 0$. But ε is fixed (though it may be very small), so $P(|\hat{\theta} - \theta| > \varepsilon) \to 0$, and hence $P(|\hat{\theta} - \theta| \le \varepsilon) \to 1$.

Exercise Show that the estimate $\overline{X}$ is unbiased and consistent (Theorem 11.12 and Equation (11.2)).

Example 11.13 (*Unbiased does not imply efficient*) A device has lifetime T with exponential pdf $f(t) = \alpha e^{-\alpha t}$. Determine the pdf $h(x)$ of $M = \text{Min}(T_i)$ for a sample of size n. Deduce that nM is unbiased but not efficient.

Solution We need $F(t) = \int \alpha e^{-\alpha x} dx \ (0 \le x \le t) = 1 - e^{-\alpha t}$, in order to compute the pdf from Theorem 11.10, which gives $h(t) = ne^{-\alpha t(n-1)}\alpha e^{-\alpha t} = n\alpha e^{-n\alpha t}$, the exponential distribution with parameter $n\alpha$. Now we consider the estimate nM for the mean $1/\alpha$. For the efficiency check we need the fact that $V(\overline{T}) = \sigma^2/n = 1/n\alpha^2$. Recalling that, from Table 9.6,

$$\int_0^\infty x^n e^{-x} dx = n! \quad \text{for} \quad n = 0, 1, 2, \ldots, \tag{11.9}$$

we calculate that $E(M) = 1/n\alpha$, hence $E(nM) = 1/\alpha$, which is unbiased. On the other hand, $V(M) = 1/n^2\alpha^2$, giving $V(nM) = 1/\alpha^2$, which is greater than $V(\overline{T}) \ (= 1/n\alpha^2)$ for $n \ge 2$, and hence not least possible. Thus nM is unbiased but not efficient.

Theorem 11.14 *If X is any random variable then $\overline{X}$ is the unique efficient linear estimator for μ, and S^2 is the unique efficient quadratic estimator for σ^2.*

Proof We have already seen that $\overline{X}$ is unbiased. Consider any unbiased estimator $\hat{\mu} = \sum_i a_i X_i$. We have $E(\hat{\mu}) = \sum_i a_i E(X_i) = \sum_i a_i \mu = \mu \sum_i a_i$, hence $\sum_i a_i = 1$. But $V(\hat{\mu}) = \sum_i a_i^2 V(X_i) = \sigma^2 \sum_i a_i^2$. Given the constraint on $\sum a_i$, this is least when $a_i = 1/n$ because we may write

$$\sum_i a_i^2 = \sum_i (a_i - 1/n)^2 + (2/n)\sum_i a_i - n/n^2. \tag{11.10}$$

And the estimate with $a_i = 1/n$ is $\sum(1/n)X_i$, in other words, $\overline{X}$. For consistency we may apply Theorem 11.12, because $E(\overline{X}) = \mu$, a special case of $E(\hat{\theta}) \to \theta$, and $V(\overline{X}) = \sigma^2/n \to 0$, as $n \to \infty$. Hence $\overline{X}$ is consistent. We omit the proof for S^2, but see Remark 11.15 below.

Remark 11.15 Notice that the estimators for μ, σ are symmetric in $X_1, \ldots, X_n$. This accords with the intuition that an estimate should not depend upon the order in which the sample observations of X_i are made. A theorem of Halmos asserts that efficiency implies this symmetry property. Assuming it can considerably shorten a proof. Thus a quadratic estimator for σ^2 has the form $\alpha \sum_i X_i^2 + \beta \sum_{i \ne j} X_i X_j$. For the rest, see e.g. Lloyd (1984b).

Table 11.2. *Some estimators, their expectation and variance. The last line holds approximately for non-normal distributions.*

parameter θ	estimator $\hat{\theta}$	$E(\hat{\theta})$	$V(\hat{\theta})$	reference
μ	$\overline{X}$	μ	σ^2/n	(11.2)
σ^2	S^2	σ^2	$O(1/n)$	Lloyd (1948b), p. 31
σ_{XY}	S_{XY}	σ_{XY}		(11.11)
ρ	r	$\rho + O(1/n)$	$O(1/n)$	Lloyd (1948b), p. 53–4
		(normal case)	(normal case)	

Theorem 11.16 *(Bivariate case) If (X, Y) is a random vector and $(x_1, y_1), \ldots, (x_n, y_n)$ a sample then the unique efficient bilinear estimator of σ_{XY} is*

$$S_{XY} = \frac{1}{n-1} \sum_{i=1}^{n} (x_i - \overline{x})(y_i - \overline{y}) = \frac{1}{n-1} \sum_{i=1}^{n} x_i y_i - \overline{x}\,\overline{y}. \qquad (11.11)$$

The corresponding estimate for the correlation coefficient $\rho = \sigma_{XY}/\sigma_X \sigma_Y$ is $r = S_{XY}/S_X S_Y$, where $S_X^2 = S_{XX}(= S^2)$.

The 'big O' notation of Table 11.2 was introduced in Section 10.3.3: $f(n) = O(g(n))$ means that $|f(n)| \le K|g(n)|$ for some constant K and all sufficiently large n. Notice that the last line of Table 11.2 implies that $E(r) \to \rho$ and $V(r) \to 0$, as $n \to \infty$, and so the estimator r is consistent by Theorem 11.12. We end this section with a résumé of some definitions, Table 11.3.

Table 11.3. *Some potential properties of an estimator based on a sample $X_1, \ldots, X_n$. In particular $\overline{X}$, S^2 and S_{XY} are the unique efficient estimators for X, σ^2 and σ_{XY} that are respectively linear, quadratic and bilinear.*

property	meaning
unbiased	$E(\hat{\theta}) = \theta$
efficient	unbiased AND has minimum variance
consistent	$P(|\hat{\theta} - \theta| \le \varepsilon) \to 1$ as $n \to \infty$ for all $\varepsilon > 0$
linear	of form $\sum_i a_i X_i$ (a_i constant)
quadratic	of form $\sum_{i,j} q_{ij} X_i X_j$ (q_{ij} constant)
bilinear	of form $\sum_{i,j} q_{ij} X_i Y_j$ (q_{ij} constant)
symmetric	unchanged by any reordering of $X_1, \ldots, X_n$

11.1.3 Maximum likelihood estimates

So far we have obtained estimates for distribution parameters θ in a distribution-free manner, that is, independently of which distribution applies. Now we introduce the *maximum likelihood estimate* (*MLE*), chosen to maximise the probability of our specific

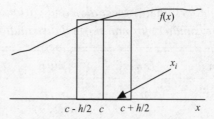

Figure 11.1 A point x_i is 'quantised' to the centre c of the small interval in which it falls.

sample values $(x_1, \ldots, x_n)$ being obtained. We proceed by means of a *likelihood function*, defined as follows. In the present notation, let

$$f(x; \theta) = \begin{cases} \text{the pdf of } X \text{ (at } x\text{)}, & \text{if } X \text{ is continuous,} \\ P(X = x), & \text{if } X \text{ is discrete.} \end{cases}$$

For example, $f(x; \theta) = \theta e^{-x\theta}$ if X follows an exponential distribution with parameter θ, as in Example 11.18 below. Then the likelihood function for a sample of size n is the product

$$L(x_1, \ldots, x_n; \theta) = f(x_1; \theta) \cdots f(x_n; \theta). \tag{11.12}$$

In the discrete case this is $P(X = X_1, \ldots, X_n = x_n)$, considered as a function of θ. On the other hand, if X is continuous, we may argue that the values of x_i actually *recorded* do not vary continuously but lie on a 1-dimensional mesh of some width h, as depicted in Figure 11.1. Then

$$P(X \text{ observed as } c) = P(c - h/2 \le X \le c + h/2)$$
$$= \int_{c-h/2}^{c+h/2} f(x)\mathrm{d}x = hf(x) \text{ approx.}$$

Thus $P(X = x_1, \ldots, X_n = x_n)$ is proportional to the likelihood function L, which is, therefore, in the continuous case as well as the discrete, a function whose maximisation results in the greatest probability of $x_1, \ldots, x_n$ being obtained.

Usually there is a unique value of θ to maximise L, conveniently found as the solution of the equation $\mathrm{d}L/\mathrm{d}\theta = 0$, or the simultaneous equations $\{\partial L/\partial \theta_i = 0\}$ if θ is a vector (θ_i). Also, because L already has the structure of a product, we normally differentiate instead the *log-likelihood function* $l(\theta) = \ln L$, which has the simplifying effect of turning products into sums. The solution for θ is unchanged, because ln is a strictly increasing function.

Example 11.17 It is known that a proportion θ of independently manufactured disk drives are defective, where $0 < \theta < 1$. A sample of size n is inspected, and k are found to be defective. Find the maximum likelihood estimate of θ.

Solution Let X_i be the random variable taking the value 1 if the ith article tested was defective, otherwise 0. Then $(X_1, \ldots, X_n)$ is a sample from the random variable X with

$$f(0; \theta) = P(X = 0) = 1 - \theta,$$
$$f(1; \theta) = P(X = 1) = \theta, \text{ and hence for } x = 0, 1:$$
$$f(x; \theta) = P(X = x) = \theta^x (1 - \theta)^{1-x}.$$

Table 11.4. *Signs of* dl/dθ *for* θ *everywhere to left and right of the turning point* k/n.

θ	→	k/n	→
dl/dθ	+	0	−

Thus the likelihood and log-likelihood functions are

$$L(x_1, \ldots, x_n; \theta) = \Pi_i \theta^{x_i}(1 - \theta)^{1-x_i} = \theta^k(1 - \theta)^{n-k}, \text{ where } k = \textstyle\sum_i x_i,$$

$$l(\theta) = \ln(L) = k \ln \theta + (n - k) \ln(1 - \theta).$$

Differentiating: $\dfrac{\partial l}{\partial \theta} = \dfrac{k}{\theta} - \dfrac{n - k}{1 - \theta} = \dfrac{k/n - \theta}{\theta(1 - \theta)/n}$,

which is zero if and only if $\theta = k/n$. But how do we know we have found a maximum in the desired sense of greatest value, and not, for example, a local maximum or minimum? One simple way to ascertain this is to note the sign of dl/dθ for θ everywhere to left and right of k/n, as indicated by the respective arrows in Table 11.4 of signs.

This sign pattern holds in spite of the denominator factors $\theta(1 - \theta)$, since $0 < \theta < 1$. Thus a unique maximum (greatest value) is achieved at $\theta = k/n$, which is therefore the maximum likelihood estimate.

Example 11.18 A type of electronic camera has lifetime following an exponential distribution. The lifetimes of n cameras are recorded, giving a sample $(T_1, \ldots, T_n)$. Find the distribution parameter α which maximises the likelihood function.

Solution The actual pdf for T may be written $f(t; \alpha) = \alpha e^{-\alpha t}$, and we calculate thus:

$$L(t_1, \ldots, t_n; \alpha) = \Pi_i \alpha e^{-\alpha t_i} = \alpha^n e^{-\alpha \Sigma t_i} \qquad \text{(likelihood function)},$$

$$l(\alpha) = \ln L = n \ln \alpha - \alpha \Sigma t_i \qquad \text{(log-likelihood function)},$$

$$\frac{dl}{d\alpha} = \frac{n}{\alpha} - \Sigma t_i = 0, \qquad \text{and} \quad \frac{d^2 l}{d\alpha^2} = -\frac{n}{\alpha^2} < 0.$$

Thus $\hat{\alpha} = n/\Sigma t_i$ gives the unique maximum of the likelihood function, and hence the required ML estimate. It is no coincidence that $\hat{\alpha} = 1/\overline{T}$, as the invariance result below shows.

Theorem 11.19 (*Invariance of the MLE*) *If the MLE for* θ *is* $\hat{\theta}$ *and* h *is any function, then the MLE for* $h(\theta)$ *is* $h(\hat{\theta})$.

Proof Suppose the pdf $f(x; \theta)$ becomes $g(x; \phi)$, where $\phi = h(\theta)$. If h is bijective then for given x the effect of replacing θ by ϕ is to move points in the graph of f horizontally but not vertically, moving the abscissa of the unique maximum from θ to $h(\theta)$.

Suppose h is many to one, for example $h(\theta) = \theta^2$, as illustrated in Figure 11.2. Then the pdf becomes $g(x; \phi) = f(x; h^{-1}(\phi))$, in the sense that for each x, ϕ, one of the perhaps many values of $h^{-1}(\phi)$ must be chosen. The choice should be the greatest value, and hence we are still left with a unique maximum (see Figure 11.2), occurring at $\phi = h(\theta)$.

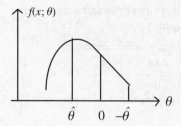 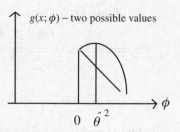

Figure 11.2 If $h(\theta) = \theta^2 = \phi$ there are possibly two values for $g(x; \phi) = f(x; h^{-1}(\theta))$. Nevertheless, a unique maximum of f implies a unique maximum for g.

Example 11.20 We find the ML estimate for $\theta = (\mu, \sigma)$ in the case X is normally distributed. Firstly, X has pdf $f(x) = (2\pi\sigma^2)^{-1/2} \exp[-(x - \mu)^2/2\sigma^2]$, so our calculation is as follows.

$$L(x_1, \ldots, x_n; \mu, \sigma) = (2\pi\sigma^2)^{-n/2} \exp \sum_i [-(x_i - \mu)^2/2\sigma^2],$$

$$l(\theta) = \ln L = -n \ln \sigma - (n/2) \ln(2\pi) - \sum_i (x_i - \mu)^2/2\sigma^2.$$

To determine the estimates of μ and σ we have $\partial l/\partial \mu = 0 = \partial l/\partial \sigma$. We shall see that, happily, it suffices to consider these two simultaneous equations individually.

(i) $\dfrac{\partial l}{\partial \mu} = \sum_i (x_i - \mu)/\sigma^2 = \dfrac{n}{\sigma^2}(\overline{x} - \mu)$, since $\overline{x} = \Sigma x_i/n$.

This shows that, for given nonzero σ, there is a unique maximum ($\neq$ greatest value) of l as μ varies, given by $\mu = \overline{x}$. It is because *this value of μ does not depend on σ* that the simultaneous equations for μ, σ are unlinked (may be solved separately and the results combined).

(ii) $\dfrac{\partial l}{\partial \sigma} = -\dfrac{n}{\sigma} + \sum_i (x_i - \mu)^2/\sigma^3 = \dfrac{n}{\sigma^3}\left[\frac{1}{n}\sum_i (x_i - \mu)^2 - \sigma^2\right].$

Hence as $\sigma(> 0)$ varies there is a unique maximum of l, which occurs when $\sigma^2 = \frac{1}{n}\sum_i (x_i - \mu)^2$. Thus the ML estimate for $\theta = (\mu, \sigma)$ is $\left(\overline{x}, \sqrt{\frac{1}{n}\sum_i (x_i - \mu)^2}\right)$.

Remarks 11.21 (1) The example above illustrates invariance of the MLE (Theorem 11.19): the same result for σ is obtained whether Equation (ii) is used to solve $\partial l/\partial \sigma = 0$ for σ directly, or to solve for σ^2 with square root extraction.

(2) The result we obtained by the MLE is not unbiased, for it equals $(n - 1)/n$ times the unbiased estimate S^2 (see Corollary 11.9); however, it therefore becomes unbiased if we multiply by $n/(n - 1)$ (this scaling method sometimes has disadvantages). Thus, as n increases, the MLE *approaches* an unbiased estimate, since $n/(n - 1) \to 1$.

(3) In the general case $\theta = (\theta_1, \ldots, \theta_k)$ a solution of $\{\partial l/\partial \theta_i = 0\}_{1 \le i \le k}$ is a maximum if and only if the matrix $(-H)$ is positive definite, where H is the *Hessian matrix* $[\partial^2 l/\partial \theta_i \partial \theta_j]$.

(4) For n large and θ real we have approximately (Lloyd, 1948b)

$$\hat{\theta} \sim N(\theta, 1/B), \text{ where } B = nE\left[\left(\frac{\partial}{\partial \theta} \ln f(x; \theta)\right)^2\right].$$

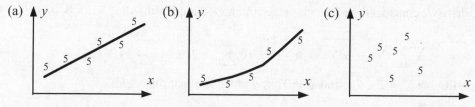

Figure 11.3 Fitting a 'best' curve of various types to data points. (a) Straight line, (b) parabola, (c) another approach is needed to structure this data (see Example 10.69).

11.1.4 Regression and least squares estimates

In its basic form, *regression* is the process of estimating an assumed relationship $y = f(x)$ between an independent variable x and a dependent variable y. We shall begin with no assumption concerning probability, and then see how probability enters in a natural way.

Suppose we are given a set of data points $(x_1, y_1), \ldots, (x_n, y_n)$. In finding suitable $f(x)$ there are two crucial questions:

Question 1 How wide is the class of functions $f(x)$ to be considered?
Question 2 How do we decide which permissible $f(x)$ is 'best'?

Answer 1 One common approach is to restrict the class to polynomial functions, such as the parabolas $y = ax^2 + bx + c$, or straight lines $y = a + bx$, of Figure 11.3. Our discussion will cover all these, but we shall focus for now on straight line approximations.

Later we shall have use for a piecewise linear function (the graph is a sequence of straight line segments) and will exploit the fact that a power relation $y = \alpha x^\beta$ is equivalent to $\ln y = \ln \alpha + \beta \ln x$, a linear relation between variables $u = \ln x$ and $v = \ln y$ (see fractal dimension, Section 16.1.2). In the same way, other relations may be explored through the linear approach by a change of variables.

Answer 2 The method of least squares The general method of minimising a sum of squares dates at least back to Gauss, whose remarkable work on many fronts was recently celebrated by a special stamp issue (see Figure 11.4). Here we take a permitted choice of $f(x)$ which minimises the sum of squared deviations of the curve $y = f(x)$ from the value y_i at x_i,

$$S = \sum_i [y_i - f(x_i)]^2. \qquad (11.13)$$

Such a curve is called the *best fitting* one for the data. It is also known as the *regression curve of y on x*, and $y = f(x)$ is the *regression equation of y on x*.

Figure 11.4 Gauss on a stamp.

In the linear case $y = a + bx$ we must minimise S as a function of a and b, where

$$S = \sum_i [y_i - a - bx_i]^2. \qquad (11.14)$$

To do so we consider the solutions of the simultaneous equations $\partial S/\partial a = 0$, $\partial S/\partial b = 0$, or:

$$\sum_{i=1}^{n} 2(y_i - a - bx_i)(-1) = 0, \quad \sum_{i=1}^{n} 2(y_i - a - bx_i)(-x_i) = 0.$$

Substituting $\bar{x} = \Sigma x_i/n$, and $\bar{y} = \Sigma y_i/n$ in these equations yields

$$\sum y_i = na + b \sum x_i, \quad \text{or} \quad \bar{y} = a + b\bar{x}, \tag{11.15}$$

$$\sum x_i y_i = a \sum x_i + b \sum x_i^2. \tag{11.16}$$

These are the *normal equations for* the parameters a, b. Using the first to eliminate a from the second, we obtain solutions $a = \hat{a}$, $b = \hat{b}$, then express them in terms of S_{XY} and S_X^2 by (11.11). The result is

$$\hat{b} = \frac{\sum x_i y_i - n\bar{x}\bar{y}}{\sum x_i^2 - n\bar{x}^2} = \frac{\sum(x_i - \bar{x})(y_i - \bar{y})}{\sum(x_i - \bar{x})^2} = \frac{S_{XY}}{S_X^2},$$

$$\hat{a} = \bar{y} - \hat{b}\bar{x}. \tag{11.17}$$

So far we have, strictly speaking, only established a unique turning point of the quantity S. To show this gives the least value of S it suffices now to observe that S becomes arbitrarily large as a and b vary in (11.14). Formulae (11.17) will be used in Chapter 16 both to compute fractal dimensions and in the service of fractal image compression.

Errors and probability Suppose we regard the deviations $e_i = f(x_i) - a - bx_i$ as random errors in observation/measurement, or random 'noise', letting e_i be a random variable with expected value zero. Then we have random variables Y_i, where

$$Y_i = a + bx_i + e_i, \quad E(Y_i) = a + bx_i, \tag{11.18}$$

the second equality holding since, by hypothesis, x_i, a and b, though unknown, have fixed values. We claim that the estimates for a, b are unbiased (the second assertion will be proven):

$$E(\hat{a}) = a, \quad E(\hat{b}) = b. \tag{11.19}$$

Firstly, $nE(\bar{y}) = \Sigma E(y_i) = \Sigma E(a + bx_i + e_i) = na + b\Sigma x_i = n(a + b\bar{x})$, hence $E(\bar{y}) = a + b\bar{x}$, and

$$\begin{aligned}
[\Sigma(x_i - \bar{x})^2]E(\hat{b}) &= E[\Sigma(x_i - \bar{x})(y_i - \bar{y})] && \text{from Formula (11.17)} \\
&= \Sigma(x_i - \bar{x})(E(y_i) - E(\bar{y})) && \text{since the } x\text{s are constants} \\
&= \Sigma(x_i - \bar{x})(a + bx_i - a - b\bar{x}) && \text{using (11.15)} \\
&= [\Sigma(x_i - \bar{x})^2]b, && \text{implying } E(\hat{b}) = b.
\end{aligned}$$

Remarks 11.22 (1) Notice that the regression equation may be written $y - \bar{y} = b(x - \bar{x})$, removing the need to estimate a. Further, if we assume $V(e_i) = \sigma^2$ then it can be shown that $\hat{b}$ has variance $\sigma^2/\Sigma(x_i - \bar{x}^2)$. (2) The direction of the regression line is that of the leading principal axis of PCA (Section 10.4.4), as applied to the data points.

(3) Next we see how the assumption of a specific but commonly arising distribution for the e_i brings the least squares and maximum likelihood estimates together.

Theorem 11.23 *If the deviations e_i are iid $N(0, \sigma^2)$ for some fixed σ, then the least squares and maximum likelihood estimates for the regression coefficients a, b coincide.*

Proof Since e_i is $N(0, \sigma^2)$, the random variable $Y_i = a + bx_i + e_i$ is $N(a + bx_i, \sigma^2)$ and so has pdf

$$f_i(y_i) = (2\pi\sigma^2)^{-1/2} \exp[-(y_i - a - bx_i)^2/2\sigma^2]. \tag{11.20}$$

Hence the required likelihood and log-likelihood functions for computing the MLE are

$$L(a, b) = (2\pi\sigma^2)^{-n/2} \Pi_i \exp[-(y_i - a - bx_i)^2/2\sigma^2],$$
$$l(a, b) = -\tfrac{n}{2}\ln(2\pi\sigma^2) - \Sigma_i(y_i - a - bx_i)^2/2\sigma^2.$$

Because of the minus sign before the Σ, this expression is greatest when $\Sigma_i(y_i - a - bx_i)^2$ is least. That is, we minimise the sum of squared deviations as in the least squares estimate.

Example 11.24 (*Weakness of LSE*) Here is an example in which the LSE and MLE differ. Suppose variables x, y are related by $y = \alpha + \beta x$ and that data points (x_i, y_i) contain an everywhere positive error in y_i, say the constant k. Then LSE regression minimises the sum of squared deviations to zero and produces a best fit exactly k units above the true one, as in Figure 11.5.

This is unfortunate, but does the MLE fare any better? Given a true relation $y = \alpha + \beta x$, we have

$$y_i = \alpha + \beta x + k, \quad \text{as measured, and}$$
$$Y_i = a + bx_i + e_i, \quad \text{the corresponding random variable,}$$

where the error random variable e_i may be considered discrete (its values lying on a fine mesh), with $P(e_i = r) = 1$ if $r = k$, otherwise zero. Then the pdf of Y_i and the likelihood function are

$$f(y_i) = P(Y_i = y_i) = P(a + bx_i + e_i = \alpha + \beta x_i + k),$$
$$L(a, b) = \Pi_i P[e_i = (\alpha - a) + (\beta - b)x_i + k)]$$
$$= 1, \text{ if } (\alpha - a) + (\beta - b)x_i = 0 \text{ for } 1 \le i \le n, \quad \text{otherwise zero.}$$

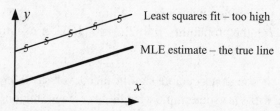

Figure 11.5 The result of regression by least squares under constant error k in the y-coordinates.

Hence there is a unique maximum of $L(a, b)$ and it occurs at $(a, b) = (\alpha, \beta)$, giving the true relation between x and y. The LSE gave a poor result because it fails to take into account the error *distribution*, and in this case the failure was costly.

Remark 11.25 In spite of its limitations, least squares has provided much service since its promulgation by Gauss. A fairly general context for the method is that of the 'black box' problem: given an input $x = (x_i)$, how do we achieve the correct process within the box to get the desired output $y = (y_j)$.

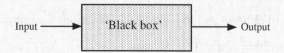

Some examples are medical image $\rightarrow$ probability of tumour, and scanned page $\rightarrow$ characters identified. If we possess a sufficiently representative set of input–output pairs we can sum the squares of deviations between (suitably measured) desired and actual output, and minimise over all permissible changes of parameters and other structures within the black box.

As exemplified above, a procedure that incorporates knowledge of pdfs may well give better results. But suppose we do know *something*, albeit vague, that we feel should somehow aid the process. How can we incorporate such information? A viable answer to this has been developed only in recent times, as an approach via Bayes' Theorem, and its introductory steps will be the topic of our next major section, 11.2. Before that we must cover the topic of hypothesis testing.

11.1.5 Hypothesis testing

In previous sections we saw how parameters of a distribution may be estimated, starting from a sample. This gives us a working hypothesis. Now we introduce *hypothesis testing* (applied in the next section to the wider question of a distribution's type – normal or otherwise). As before, we proceed via a sample and appropriate statistic, which we shall usually denote by Z. The method uses the following general components.

H_0:	the null hypothesis – e.g. fair coin, Poisson distribution,
H_1:	the alternative hypothesis, to be accepted if H_0 is rejected,
decision rule:	accept H_0 if z lies in a certain interval I, the *acceptance region,*
significance level:	the probability $p = P(z \notin I \mid H_0)$, of rejecting H_0 when it is true.

Remark 11.26 We choose an acceptable significance level, say 0.05 (also referred to as 5%), and use it along with H_0 to determine what the acceptance region should be. Suppose the hypothesis tells us that Z is $N(0, 1)$. From tables: $0.95 = P(-1.96 \leq Z \leq 1.96)$ and so, as illustrated in Figure 11.6,

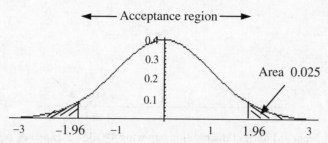

Figure 11.6 Normal distribution $N(0, 1)$ showing acceptance and rejection regions for significance level 0.05, the probability of rejection being represented by the hatched areas together.

significance level 0.05 $\Rightarrow$ acceptance region $-1.96 \leq Z \leq 1.96$,

significance level 0.01 $\Rightarrow$ acceptance region $-2.58 \leq Z \leq 2.58$.

Example 11.27 It is reputed that the weights of individuals in the province of Archangel follow a normal distribution with mean 140 units and variance 900. (a) In a sample of 60 people, the average weight was 160. Test the hypothesis at the 5% level of significance. (b) Does the conclusion change if a sample size 30 produces the same average as before? (c) What conclusions may we draw from a sample size 10 (same average) at the 5% and at the 1% significance levels?

Solution Formally, we take H_0: the weight W is $N(140, 900)$. For (a) the sample size is 60 so by (11.2) the sample mean $\overline{W}$ is in $N(\mu, \sigma^2/n) = N(140, 15)$. To benefit from the normality of these distributions, we may use the statistic

$$Z = \frac{\overline{W} - 140}{\sqrt{15}} \sim N(0, 1).$$

Then, by Remark 11.26, the significance level 0.05 has acceptance region $-1.96 \leq Z \leq 1.96$. The measured value of our statistic is

$$z = \frac{160 - 140}{\sqrt{15}} = 5.16 \text{ approx.},$$

which lies outside the acceptance region, and therefore we must reject the hypothesis H_0.

(b) With sample size $n = 30$, we have $\sigma^2/n = 30$, $\overline{W}$ is in $N(140, 30)$, and the statistic $Z = (\overline{W} - 140)/\sqrt{30}$ is in $N(0, 1)$. This time the statistic has value $z = (160 - 140)/\sqrt{30} = 3.65$ approx., so again we reject the hypothesis.

(c) With sample size $n = 10$ we obtain $\sigma^2/n = 90$, so $Z = (\overline{W} - 140)/\sqrt{90}$ is in $N(0, 1)$. The measured statistic now becomes $z = (160 - 140)/\sqrt{90} = 2.11$ approx., and at last the hypothesis is not rejected out of hand. At the 5% level it still lies outside the acceptance region, but if the level is chosen as 1%, with acceptance region $-2.58 \leq z \leq 2.58$, then $z = 2.1$ lies within, and we should accept the hypothesis (the evidence against is too slight with this small sample).

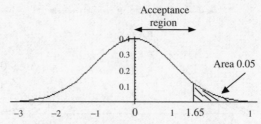

Figure 11.7 Standard normal distribution, showing 1-tailed acceptance region for significance level 0.05, the probability represented by the single hatched area.

Remark 11.28 (*Testing for differences/comparing populations*) Suppose (1) X_1, X_2 are random variables from different and not necessarily normal distributions, with $E(X_i) = \mu_i$ and $V(X_i) = \sigma_i^2$, and (2) large samples of sizes n_i (≥ 30) are taken so that X_1, X_2 may be treated as normal and the variances replaced by their estimates S_i^2. Then, using (11.1) and the reproducing property (Example 10.41), we have:

Conclusion The random variable $\overline{X}_1 - \overline{X}_2$ is $N\big(\mu_1 - \mu_2, S_1^2/n_1 + S_2^2/n_2\big)$.

Remark 11.29 (*The 1-tailed significance test*) This is used when $z \geq 0$ is enforced for the standard normal statistic z (or $z \leq 0$ with analogous conclusions to those below). The only way we can be wrong ($z \notin I$) is for z to be too large, hence only the positive 'tail' of the distribution applies. As illustrated in Figure 11.7, this means that for significance level 0.05 the acceptance region should be [0, 1.65] because $0.05 = 1 - \Phi(1.65)$. For level 0.01 the region is [0, 2.33].

Example 11.30 A new process is designed to manufacture a washing machine part to finer tolerance. To test this, a batch of 50 is tested from each process, old and new. Result: the mean error is reduced from 173.3 microns to 171.5 with respective variance estimates 6.4 and 7.1. Is there an improvement at the 0.05 significance level?

Solution Let X_1, X_2 be random variables for the old and the new error, with true means μ_1, μ_2. We are not asked to consider the possibility of the new system being actually worse, only whether it is better, so we shall need a 1-tailed approach (see Remark 11.29). We must decide between the hypotheses

H_0: $\mu_2 = \mu_1$, there is no difference in accuracy between the tow processes;

H_1: $\mu_2 > \mu_1$, the new process is better.

According to Remark 11.28, the random variable $\overline{X}_1 - \overline{X}_2$ is $N(\mu_1 - \mu_2, S_1^2/50 + S_2^2/50)$. Thus, under the hypothesis H_0, $\overline{X}_1 - \overline{X}_2$ is $N(0, 0.27)$ and the statistic

$$Z = \frac{\overline{X}_1 - \overline{X}_2}{\sqrt{0.27}} \quad \text{is standard normal, } N(0, 1).$$

Here its value is $z = \frac{173.3 - 171.5}{0.52} = 3.46$ approx., which is outside the 1-tailed acceptance region of $[0, 1.65]$ indicated in Figure 11.7. We conclude that the null hypothesis must be rejected and the claim of improvement accepted.

11.1.6 Hypothesis testing – distributions

Having applied the hypothesis testing method to parameters, we proceed to distribution types. But how do we make a good guess as to type? We listed in Section 9.4.3 some general scenarios that lead to the normal distribution, then in Section 10.3.3 we introduced the Central Limit Theorem, a theoretical basis for a wide range of situations in which normal is at least a good approximation. However, it is not necessary to appeal always to the normal distribution when others such as Poisson and exponential are more precise. The latter, for example, plays a key role in reliability theory, as can be predicted on theoretical grounds (Meyer, 1970). Indeed, we shall shortly exemplify the exponential case.

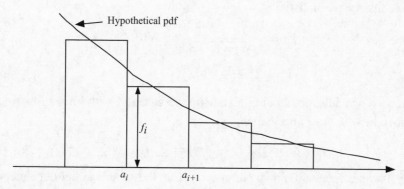

Figure 11.8 Histogram of observed frequencies of events A_i in N independent trials, compared with possible pdf governing this behaviour.

Both as a pointer to what the distribution might be, and for testing our conclusion (hypothesis), we need the idea of observed versus theoretical frequency. Referring to Figure 11.8, let the range of a random variable X be divided into k non-overlapping intervals by points $a_1, \ldots, a_{k+1}$, where the end points can represent $\pm\infty$. Let $X_1, \ldots, X_N$ be the result of a sample of N trials. We proceed with the following nomenclature.

N: the number of trials (sample size) of variable X,

A_i: the event that X falls into interval $[a_i, a_{i+1})$,

p_i: the probability $P(A_i)$ computed on the basis of our hypothesised distribution,

f_i: the *observed frequency*, or number of times A_i occurs in N independent trials.

Thus f_i is $\mathrm{Bin}(N, p_i)$, with N large, and so by the Central Limit Theorem (Theorem 10.45) f_i is approximately normal, whatever the distribution of X might be. Furthermore,

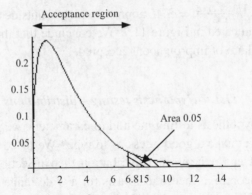

Figure 11.9 The graph of the pdf χ^2 with two degrees of freedom, showing (1-tailed) acceptance region for significance level 0.05, the probability represented by the hatched area.

$E(f_i) = Np_i$, the *theoretical frequency*, and $V(f_i) = Np_i(1 - p_i)$, by (9.42). Hence we are led to consider the statistics

$$Z_i = \frac{f_i - Np_i}{\sqrt{Np_i(1 - p_i)}} \sim N(0, 1), \tag{11.21}$$

$$Z = Z_1^2 + \cdots + Z_k^2. \tag{11.22}$$

There are two obstacles to Z being a statistic we can use, with known distribution χ_k^2 (see (11.6)). Firstly, *the Z_i are dependent*, for

$$\sum_i [Np_i(1 - p_i)]^{1/2} Z_i = \sum_i (f_i - Np_i) = \sum f_i - N \sum p_i = N - N = 0.$$

Secondly, if we estimate unknown parameters from the sample, other dependencies will be introduced. The problem was solved by Pearson (1900) in a remarkable result stated below (see also Lloyd, 1984b); notice the change to simpler denominators compared with (11.21).

Theorem 11.31 *(Pearson) With the notation above, the statistic*

$$Z = \sum_{i=1}^{k} \frac{(f_i - Np_i)^2}{Np_i} \tag{11.23}$$

has distribution converging to χ_{k-m-1}^2, where m is the number of parameters estimated by means of the sample. (Note: $v = k - m - 1$ is called the number of *degrees of freedom*, Remark 10.20).

The testing procedure As a sum of squares, the statistic Z cannot be negative, so the test is 1-tailed, as seen in Figure 11.9. We accept H_0, the hypothesised distribution, if z lies in $[0, C]$, with C taken from Table 11.5. Otherwise we reject H_0.

Example 11.32 *(Testing for completely specified distribution)* It is believed that the lifetime of the famous bulb tree follows an exponential distribution with mean 200 years.

Table 11.5. *Values C for which* $P(\chi_\nu^2 > C) = \alpha$, *the significance level.*

$\alpha \backslash \nu$	1	2	3	4	5	6
0.01	6.635	9.210	11.345	13.277	15.086	16.812
0.05	3.841	5.991	7.815	9.488	11.071	12.592

Table 11.6. *Theoretical and observed frequencies,* Np_i *and* f_i, *for events* A_1 *to* A_4 *(Example 11.32).*

i	a_i	$F(a_i)$	p_i	Np_i	f_i
1	0	0	0.39	58.5	48
2	100	$1-e^{-1/2}$	0.24	36.0	39
3	200	$1-e^{-1}$	0.15	22.5	34
4	300	$1-e^{-3/2}$	0.22	33.0	29
5	∞	1	—	—	—

Test this at the 5% significance level, given the following records of lifetimes of 150 trees.

0–100: 48 trees, 100–200: 39 trees, 200–300: 34 trees, over 300: 29 trees.

Solution Assuming the lifetime T is exponential (Table 9.10), the pdf is $f(t) = \beta e^{-\beta t}$ $(t \geq 0)$, where $\beta = 1/E(T) = 0.005$, and the cdf is $F(t) = \int_0^t f(x)dx = 1 - e^{-\beta t}$. We let A_i be the event: T falls in interval $[a_i, a_{i+1})$, where $(a_i) = (0, 100, 200, 300, \infty)$. The theoretical frequencies are Np_i, where $N = 150$ and $p_i = P(A_i) = F(a_{i+1}) - F(a_i)$. These are shown in Table 11.6, compared with the observed frequencies.

Since the *number of events* is $k = 4$ and there are no unknown parameters to estimate, the number of degrees of freedom given by Theorem 11.31 is $4 - 1 = 3$. From Table 11.5 the acceptance region for significance level 0.05 is $[0, C]$ with $C = 7.815$. Our statistic is

$$z = \frac{(48 - 58.5)^2}{58.5} + \frac{(39 - 36)^2}{36} + \frac{(34 - 22.5)^2}{22.5} + \frac{(29 - 33)^2}{33} = 8.49.$$

Since $z > 7.815$, the specified distribution must be rejected.

Example 11.33 (*Testing for a normal distribution, parameters unspecified*) It is believed that the pollution factor X of silicon produced by a certain process is normally distributed. A sample of 250 specimens led to the following figures for the various ranges of X. Test the normal hypothesis at the 5% significance level (assume estimates of 17.0 and 7.1 for mean and variance).

0 to 12: 7 cases, 12 to 15: 49 cases, 15 to 18: 109 cases, 18 to 21: 67 cases, over 21: 18 cases.

Solution With estimates of $E(X)$, $V(X)$ at $\mu = 17.0$ and $\sigma^2 = 7.1$ (omitting the 'hats'), and the normal hypothesis on X, the variable $Y = (X - \mu)/\sigma$ is $N(0, 1)$. We let A_i be

Table 11.7. *Theoretical and observed frequencies, NP_i and f_i,*
for events A_1 to A_5.

i	a_i	b_i	$\Phi(b_i)$	p_i	Np_i	f_i
1	0	−6.30	0	0.032	8	7
2	12	−1.85	0.032	0.198	49.6	49
3	15	−0.74	0.230	0.414	103.5	109
4	18	0.37	0.644	0.287	71.8	67
5	21	1.48	0.931	0.069	17.3	18
6	∞	∞	1	—	—	—

the event that X falls into the interval $[a_i, a_{i+1})$, where $(a_i) = (0, 12, 15, 18, 21, \infty)$. To use the standard normal tables it is convenient to set $b_i = (a_i - \mu)/\sigma$. Then the theoretical frequencies are Np_i, where $N = 250$ and $p_i = P(A_i) = P(a_i \leq X < a_{i+1}) = P(b_i \leq Y < b_{i+1}) = \Phi(b_{i+1}) - \Phi(b_i)$. These are shown in Table 11.7, compared with the observed frequencies.

Since the number of events is $k = 5$ and there are two unknown parameters estimated, the number of degrees of freedom given by Theorem 11.31 is $5 - 1 - 2 = 2$. From Table 11.5 the acceptance region for significance level 0.05 is $[0, C]$ with $C = 5.991$. Our statistic is

$$z = \frac{(7 - 8)^2}{8} + \frac{(49 - 49.6)^2}{49.6} + \frac{(109 - 103.5)^2}{103.5} + \frac{(67 - 71.8)^2}{71.8} + \frac{(18 - 17.3)^2}{17.3}$$
$$= 0.771.$$

Since $z < 5.991$, the claim of normality is to be accepted (cf. Sections 11.3 and 11.4.3).

Further examples For additional examples and solutions on the topics of this section see Spiegel *et al.* (2000).

11.2 The Bayesian approach

We are interested in the kind of input–output problems represented by Table 11.8. What calculation procedure, represented by the box of Remark 11.25, will convert input into desirable output?

Much depends on the type and quantity of data at our disposal, such as

1. scanned image,
2. training sets – examples of correct input–output pairs,
3. knowledge of relevant pdfs.

Historically, a tough problem has been how to build into the solution process *everything* we know about the problem, including ideas we are unable to express precisely. It is clearer now how to squeeze useful information from an initial vague yet reasonable belief,

Table 11.8. *Some desirable input–output pairs.*

input	output
image pixel values	list of edges
" "	list of objects
medical image	probability of tumour
digital image of eye	probability of various pathologies
scanned page	characters recognised
sequence of voice frequencies	boundaries of consonants

using techniques with Bayes' Theorem. That is our present topic, drawing strongly on the multivariate normal distribution of Section 10.4.3.

11.2.1 From prior to posterior

The vague belief is typically expressed in the form of a pdf. We don't have to worry (too much) about it being 'wrong' because it is to be progressively improved in the light of data. The choice involves (1) a functional form for the pdf; the fallback position is of course a normal pdf, but we may have reason to choose another, (2) one or more parameters, expressed in general as a vector $\theta = (\theta_1, \ldots, \theta_n)$ lying in some subset Θ of n-space. In the normal case we can express uncertainty by a large value of σ.

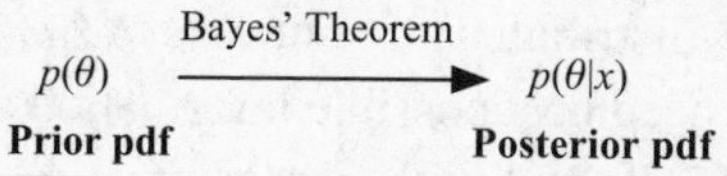

$$p(\theta) \xrightarrow{\text{Bayes' Theorem}} p(\theta|x)$$

Prior pdf   **Posterior pdf**

Figure 11.10 The basic structure of the Bayes method for estimating probabilities.

In what follows we shall make the common assumption that the problem is reduced to parameter estimation for the pdf of a random variable or vector X. The Bayesian method for the examples we have in mind, exemplified by those of Table 11.8, begins with Figure 11.10. Here a weak *prior* assumption about the distribution of θ is converted by Bayes' Theorem into a *posterior* version $p(\theta|x)$, meaning one computed in the light of an observation x of X:

$$p(\theta|x) = \frac{p(x|\theta)p(\theta)}{p(x)}. \tag{11.24}$$

Note that x could be replaced by a sequence of observations of X, and that, although we have used continuous notation, it is easy to represent the corresponding discrete calculation in a similar manner, with Σ in place of integration. It is useful to write (11.24) alternatively as

$$p(\theta|x) \propto p(x|\theta)p(\theta), \tag{11.25}$$

where $\propto$ means 'is proportional to' and, because $p(\theta|x)$ is a pdf and so has integral 1 over the range of θ, the proportionality or normalisation constant $1/p(x)$ is

Table 11.9. *Some examples of θ and its range Θ.*

Distribution	θ	Θ
$\text{Bin}(n, p)$	p	$[0, 1]$
$\text{Po}(\lambda)$	λ	$(0, \infty)$
$N(\mu, \sigma^2)$	(μ, σ)	$\mathbf{R} \times [0, \infty)$

determined by

$$p(x) = \int_{\Theta} p(x|\theta) p(\theta) d\theta. \qquad (11.26)$$

In general we may need to evaluate this integral by a numerical method, but, if, as in the next example, the integrand is a constant multiple of a standard pdf (see Table 9.10), then the value of $1/p(x)$ may be inferred and the integration bypassed. Moreover, in Section 11.4 we consider Markov Chain Monte Carlo methods, in which we do not need an explicit normalising constant because only a *ratio* of pdfs is required. Some standard cases of θ and Θ are noted in Table 11.9. The goal of the Bayesian method is to arrive at a narrowly peaked pdf for the unknown parameter (suitably generalised in higher dimensions of Θ).

Example 11.34 (*see Lloyd, 1984c*) Companies A, B propose to use a new technique of chip fabrication. A normally distributed amount $X \sim N(\mu, 4^2)$ of a noxious substance is involved, and the proposers need best possible information about μ. On general grounds μ is governed by a normal pdf, and both parties elect to start from their own choice of prior $N(\mu_0, \sigma_0^2)$ and update it in the light of data, using the Bayesian method. Their choices and the consequences are shown below.

Company A. They are very uncertain and express this by using a relatively large variance, choosing as prior $p_A(\mu) \sim N(40, 8^2)$.
Company B. Their wider experience leads them to choose prior $p_B(\mu) \sim N(50, 2^2)$.

The results are shown in Figure 11.11. Notice that, at first, the successive posterior updates of the vague prior p_A change the more rapidly, and approach those of p_B. By 40 samples the results are very close to each other and considerably narrowed in peak, but significant improvement is still possible, for by 100 samples the peak is narrower and has risen to a maximum of height 1. Thus the aim of the Bayesian method has been achieved.

Analysis To determine explicitly what has happened here, we recall a formula used earlier for the likelihood function. The independence of samples X_i of a random variable X, whose pdf depends on a parameter θ, means that

$$\boxed{p(x_1, \ldots, x_n \mid \theta) = \Pi_i p(x_i \mid \theta).} \qquad (11.27)$$

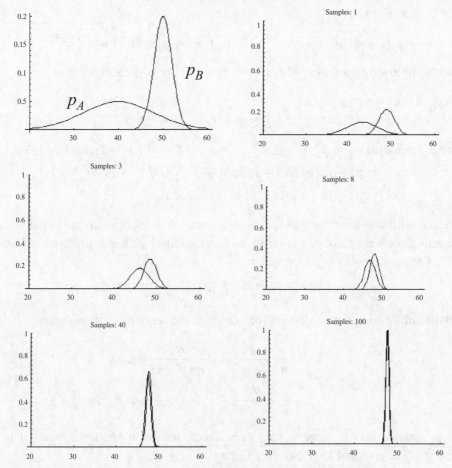

Figure 11.11 The priors of Companies *A* and *B* in Example 11.34, and their updates (corresponding posteriors) after 1, 3, 8, 40 and 100 samples. The p_A curve is left of the p_B until they coincide.

Note that previously the likelihood function $p(x_1, \ldots, x_n \mid \theta)$ was used to find a unique estimate for θ. Here with Bayes we do more: we find a pdf for θ by using prior knowledge.

Notation 11.35 (*Continuing Example 11.34*) The role of θ is played by μ: we assume X is $N(\mu, \sigma^2)$ with σ known and seek a pdf for μ. Denote the prior by $p_0(\mu)$, with posterior $p_n(\mu)$ after taking account of the n-sized sample $x = (x_1, \ldots, x_n)$. Our first step is to determine $p(x|\mu)$ from (11.27) using the hypothesis that x_i has pdf $p(x_i|\mu) = \phi((x_i - \mu)/\sigma)$, where ϕ is the standard normal distribution (9.44). Then we can apply (11.25). We begin with

$$
\begin{aligned}
p(x|\mu) &= \Pi_i p(x_i|\mu) = \Pi_i \phi((x_i - \mu)/\sigma) \\
&= \Pi_i (2\pi\sigma^2)^{-1/2} e^{-(x_i - \mu)/2\sigma^2} \\
&= (2\pi\sigma^2)^{-n/2} \exp\left[-\sum_i (x_i - \mu)^2/2\sigma^2\right].
\end{aligned}
$$

By the choice of prior,

$$p_0(\mu) = \phi((\mu - \mu_0)/\sigma_0) = \left(2\pi\sigma_0^2\right)^{-1/2} \exp\left[-(\mu - \mu_0)^2/2\sigma_0^2\right].$$

Hence the following posterior, where the k_j are 'constants', independent of μ:

$$
\begin{aligned}
p_n(\mu|x) &\propto k_1 p(x \mid \mu) p_0(\mu) &&\text{by (11.25)}\\
&= k_2 \exp\left[-\sum_i (x_i - \mu)^2/2\sigma^2 - (\mu - \mu_0)^2/2\sigma_0^2\right]\\
&= k_2 \exp\left[-\left(\sum_i x_i^2 - 2\mu \sum_i x + n\mu^2\right)/2\sigma^2 - \left(\mu^2 - 2\mu\mu_0 + \mu_0^2\right)/2\sigma_0^2\right]\\
&= k_2 \exp\left[-\mu^2 \left(n/2\sigma^2 + 1/2\sigma_0^2\right) + \mu \left(\sum x_i/\sigma^2 + \mu_0/\sigma_0^2\right) + k_3\right]\\
&= k_4 \exp\left[-(\mu - \mu_n)^2/2\sigma_n^2\right] \sim N\left(\mu_n, \sigma_n^2\right),
\end{aligned}
$$

where k_3 contributes a factor e^{k_3} to k_4, and μ_n, σ_n are 'constants' which can be determined by equating coefficients of μ and μ^2 in the last two lines (this is formalised in Lemma 11.37). The result (using $\sum_i x_i = n\bar{x}$), is

$$1/\sigma_n^2 = n/\sigma^2 + 1/\sigma_0^2, \quad \mu_n/\sigma_n^2 = n\bar{x}/\sigma^2 + \mu_0/\sigma_0^2,$$

which on substituting the expression for $1/\sigma_n^2$ into the second equation yields

$$
\begin{aligned}
\mu_n &= \frac{n\sigma_0^2}{n\sigma_0^2 + \sigma^2}\bar{x} + \frac{\sigma^2}{n\sigma_0^2 + \sigma^2}\mu_0,\\
\sigma_n^2 &= \frac{\sigma_0^2\sigma^2}{n\sigma_0^2 + \sigma^2}.
\end{aligned}
\tag{11.28}
$$

And, as implied above, since $p_n(\mu \mid x)$ is a pdf, the form obtained shows it to be $N(\mu_n, \sigma_0^2)$. The constant k_4 is therefore $(2\pi\sigma_n^2)^{-1/2}$.

Exercise Write down the constant k_2 as a multiple of k_1.

Remarks 11.36 (1) Equations (11.28) show that the effect of the specific choice of prior parameters μ_0, σ_0 fades away as n increases, because $\mu_n = \bar{x}/(1 + \sigma^2/n\sigma_0^2) + O(1/n)$, which tends to $\bar{x}$ as $n \to \infty$. Also, clearly $\sigma_0^2 \to$. (For $O(1/n)$, see Section 10.3.3.)

(2) Dependence on the samples x_i is via the symmetric expression $\bar{x}$, and so, for a given set $\{x_i\}$, the order of observation is unimportant. Also, Equation (11.27) shows that it does not matter whether we update sample by sample, or combine samples, taking $x = (x_i)$.

(3) After 100 samples the more flexible prior's successor, though indistinguishable in our Figure 11.11 illustration from that of prior B, has slightly outperformed it in having a mean 47.24, marginally closer to the underlying value of the 'true' mean 47 of X than B's mean of 47.36. The variances of both are indistinguishable from 0.40. The value of $\bar{x}$ was 47.26. Notice that the Bayesian process has converged to a complete pdf for the mean μ.

(4) Later, the methods of the above example will be extended for the purpose of assigning digital images into pre-defined classes with associated probabilities, in accordance with the agenda shown in Table 11.8, with which we began this section.

In order to produce Figure 11.11 we had to generate, to order, a sequence of samples whose frequencies followed a prescribed distribution, in this case the normal distribution. How to do this in general is the topic of the next major section, 11.3. We conclude the present section with a result useful for calculation, based upon the equating of coefficients technique which led to (11.28). Once stated, it can be used to considerably simplify such calculations.

Lemma 11.37 *(i) Let a, b, c be constants, with a > 0. Then*

$$\exp[-(ax^2 + bx + c)] = k \exp[-(x - m)^2/2s^2], \qquad (11.29\text{a})$$
$$\int_{\mathbb{R}} \exp[-(ax^2 + bx + c)]\, dx = k\sqrt{\pi/a}, \qquad (11.29\text{b})$$

where $a = 1/2s^2$, $m = -b/2a$ and $k = \exp[(b^2 - 4ac)/4a]$. (ii) Up to a constant multiple, a finite product of normal pdfs $\Pi_i\, \phi[(x - m_i)/s_i]$ is normal with mean M, variance $\sum^2$, where

$$\boxed{\frac{1}{\Sigma^2} = \sum_i \frac{1}{s_i^2}, \quad \frac{M}{\Sigma^2} = \sum_i \frac{m_i}{s_i^2}.} \qquad (11.30)$$

Proof (i) Completing the square,

$$ax^2 + bx + c = a\left(x + \frac{b}{2a}\right)^2 - \frac{b^2 - 4ac}{4a} = \frac{(x - m)^2}{2s^2} - \frac{b^2 - 4ac}{4a},$$

and equating coefficients of x^2 and x gives the expressions for a, m and k. The integral may be evaluated by a gamma function or by direct substitution in (10.52).

(ii) The point of this result is that it is not multivariate; only a single variable, x, is involved in the factors. Using the definition of ϕ and properties of the exponential function, we have $\Pi_i\phi[(x - m_i)/s_i] = \Pi_i \exp[-(x - m_i)^2/2s_i^2] = -\exp\sum_i[(x - m_i)^2/2s_i^2]$, and hence must show that

$$\sum_i \left[(x - m_i)^2/2s_i^2\right] = (x - M)^2/2\Sigma^2 + K$$

holds for some constant K, if and only if (11.30) holds. But (11.30) is the result of equating coefficients of x^2 and then of x in the equation above. This completes the proof.

Example 11.38 (i) We express the fourth power of $\phi[(x - a)/\sigma]$ as a normal pdf $f \sim N(M, \Sigma^2)$, up to a constant multiple. Relations (11.30) give $1/\Sigma^2 = 4/\sigma^2$ and $M/\Sigma^2 = 4a/\sigma^2$, whence $\Sigma = \sigma/2$ and $M = a$.

(ii) Let us see what difference the new formula makes to the derivation of (11.28). Using the proportionality symbol, we may write

$$P_n(\mu \mid x) \propto p(x \mid \mu)p_0(m) \propto \Pi_i\, p(x_i \mid \mu)p_0(\mu)$$
$$\propto \Pi_i\phi((x_i - \mu)/\sigma)\, \phi((\mu - \mu_0)/\sigma_0)$$
$$\propto \phi((\mu - M)/S), \text{ with } \mu \text{ as variable in place of } x \text{ in Lemma 11.37,}$$

whence $1/S^2 = n/\sigma^2 + 1/\sigma_0^2$ and $M/S^2 = (\sum x_i)/\sigma^2 + \mu_0/\sigma_0^2$. Substituting as before, we obtain (11.28), with M as μ_n and S as σ_n. For another 'real life' case, see Example 11.75.

Exercise Express the fifth power similarly, in Example 11.38(i).

11.2.2 Bayes pattern classifiers

In the previous section we discussed a Bayesian approach to squeezing as much information as possible out of a set of samples, having in mind, for example, the parameters of a distribution of some assumed type. Now we consider the problem of *object recognition*, interpreted as allocating an image (or part thereof) to one of a given list of classes. Some examples are (a) a digital image of a human retina $\rightarrow$ certain pathologies or none, (b) body scan image $\rightarrow$ tumour or benign growth, (c) scanned page area $\rightarrow$ font character, (d) remote sensing image $\rightarrow$ weather pattern, or which military hardware, or ...

The digital image may be improved for the purpose by some form of pre-processing, for example to bring out boundaries more sharply and to identify subregions. The input to our automatic classifier is a *pattern*, or *pattern vector*, $x = (x_1, \ldots, x_n)$, where each x_i is a number which is the value of a *feature*, or *descriptor*, of the image (features were briefly discussed in PCA, Remark 10.74(2)). Simple examples are perimeter, area, number of holes, but there are more detailed and sophisticated choices, some of which are indicated in Table 11.10. cf. Gonzalez and Woods (1993) and Vranic and Saupe (2001a,b).

Table 11.10. *Some features/descriptors x_i for a digital image.*

type	some details
geometrical	area, perimeter, diameter, curvature at special points (approximated)
topological	number of connected components, of holes
spatial moments	$m_{rs} = \sum x^r y^s$ over image pixels (x, y)
principal axis vectors	see Chapter 10
histogram moments	e.g. $m_r = \sum g^r f_g$, where g denotes a grey level and f_g its relative frequency amongst the pixel grey values
Fourier descriptors	certain coefficients in the Discrete Fourier Transform of a colour component (see Chapter 15)

A *pattern class* is a family of patterns with some common properties. We suppose an image is to be classified into one of an allowable set of M classes $w_1, \ldots, w_M$. This classification process is also known as *pattern recognition*, or PR for short, for our machine is to recognise to which class each offered pattern x belongs.

Decision-theoretic methods We consider a *decision theoretic* method, meaning we seek M *decision functions* $d_i(x)$ $(1 \leq i \leq M)$ such that

$$\text{if } x \in w_i \text{ then } d_i(x) > d_j(x) \quad \text{for } j \neq i. \tag{11.31}$$

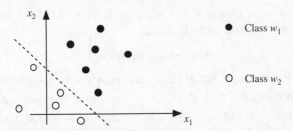

Figure 11.12 In the plane, with points $x = (x_1, x_2)$, the decision functions $d_1(x) = x_2$ and $d_2(x) = x_1 + 1$ define a decision boundary $d_{12}(x) = x_2 - x_1 - 1 = 0$, for separating two classes of vectors in the plane.

This implies that if x is in w_j then $d_i(x) < d_j(x)$ and, defining

$$d_{ij}(x) = d_i(x) - d_j(x) \quad (i \neq j), \tag{11.32}$$

we may say that the pattern vectors of distinct classes w_i, w_j lie on opposite sides of the *decision boundary* $d_{ij}(x) = 0$, with w_i on the positive side because by (11.31) $x \in w_i \Rightarrow d_{ij}(x) > 0$. The result is that the classes are partitioned off from each other by a set of $_MC_2$ decision boundaries (Notation 9.11), where $d_{ij}(x) = -d_{ji}(x)$, so that d_{ij} and d_{ji} specify the same boundary, and other coincidences may occur.

The Bayes minimum risk classifier We suppose that each mis-classification imposes a quantifiable penalty (e.g. a result of mis-diagnosis) and aim to minimise the average loss. Let L_{kj} be the loss incurred when a w_k pattern x is assigned to class w_j, and $p(w_k|x)$ the conditional probability that x is from w_k. Then the mean/expected loss $r_j(x)$ in assigning x to w_j is given by

$$r_j(x) = \sum_{k=1}^{M} p(x \text{ is from } w_k) \times (\text{loss in this case})$$

$$= \sum_{k=1}^{M} L_{kj} P(w_k|x)$$

$$= \frac{1}{p(x)} \sum_{k=1}^{M} L_{kj} p(x|w_k) p(w_k) \quad \text{by Bayes' Theorem, (10.11).}$$

The classifier should assign x to that w_j for which the loss r_j is least amongst $r_1(x), \ldots, r_M(x)$. For simplicity suppose the loss function is 0 for correct decisions and 1 for incorrect ones. That is, $L_{kj} = 1 - \delta_{kj}$, where δ_{kj}, called the Kronecker delta, equals 1 if $k = j$, and otherwise 0. Because we are only concerned with the *relative* magnitudes of the rs, which are unaffected by the value of $p(x)$, we may drop the factor $p(x)$ and take

$$r_j(x) = \sum_{k=1}^{M} (1 - \delta_{kj}) p(x|w_k) p(w_k)$$

$$= \sum_{k=1}^{M} p(x|w_k) p(w_k) - \sum_{k=1}^{M} \delta_{kj} p(x|w_k) p(w_k)$$

$$= p(x) - p(x|w_j) p(w_j) \quad \text{by Total Probability, (10.10),}$$

from the definition of δ_{kj}. Thus, once more dropping the $p(x)$, we should assign x to class

w_i if, for all $j \neq i$, $p(x|w_i)p(w_i) > p(x|w_j)p(w_j)$. This expresses the *Bayes classifier* as a decision theoretic method with functions

$$d_i(x) = p(x|w_i)p(w_i). \tag{11.33}$$

Implementation To operate a Bayes classifier we need the values of $p(w_i)$, which are usually not hard to estimate, and of $p(x|w_i)$. The latter is usually assumed to follow a multivariate normal distribution. Suppose for class $w = w_i$ we have a matrix S of N samples x, with mean m (x and m are n-vectors but we shall not bolden them here). Using the estimate of the covariance matrix Σ from (10.67) we may write

$$\Sigma = (1/N)S^T S - m^T m, \quad \text{and } Q = \Sigma^{-1}, \tag{11.34}$$

giving the required multivariate normal pdf from (10.54) as

$$p(x|w) = (2\pi)^{-n/2}|Q|^{1/2} \exp[-(1/2)(x-m)Q(x-m)^T], \tag{11.35}$$

where Q is thus the matrix of a quadratic form $(x-m)Q(x-m)^T$ in n variables. Because of the exponential part it is easier to work with the natural logarithm ln of the above, and it is valid to do so for the comparisons we propose because ln is a strictly increasing function. We take decision functions (11.33), restoring the subscripts: $d_i(x) = \ln[p(x|w_i)p(w_i)] = \ln p(x|w_i) + \ln p(w_i)$, or

$$d_i(x) = \ln p(w_i) + (1/2)\ln|Q_i| - (1/2)(x-m_i)Q_i(x-m_i)^T, \tag{11.36}$$

where the term $-(n/2)\ln(2\pi)$, common to all d_i, is omitted.

Example 11.39 (*The distance classifier*) Consider the very special case $p(w_i) = 1/M$ and all Σ_i (and hence all Q_i) equal to the identity matrix I. Then $\ln|Q_i| = \ln(1) = 0$ and $d_i(x) = -\ln M - (1/2)(x-m_i)(x-m_i)^T = -\ln M - (1/2)\|x-m_i\|^2$, resulting in the assignment $x \to w_i$ if x is closer to m_i than to any m_j ($j \neq i$). This method is the *distance classifier*, and is a form of n-dimensional quantisation (Section 18.3.4) in which the n-vector x is quantised to (i.e. replaced by) the nearest of a chosen set of representative vectors m_i. A decision boundary is necessarily a *hyperplane*, a subset defined by a single linear equation; in fact the boundary condition $d_i(x) = d_j(x)$ is converted by the relation $(x-m)(x-m)^T = xx^T - 2mx^T + mm^T$ into the linear equation

$$2(m_i - m_j)x^T = \|m_i\|^2 - \|m_j\|^2 \quad \text{(boundary)}. \tag{11.37}$$

Thus, given any regular or irregular distribution of points m_i, these boundaries partition n-space into n-dimensional polyhedra $P_i = \{x \in \mathbb{R}^n : \|x - m_i\| \leq \|x - m_j\| \text{ for all } j \neq i\}$. Such polyhedra are called *Voronoi regions* and are extensively and interestingly studied in Conway & Sloane (1988). A simple 2-dimensional example is Figure 11.13(a), the honeycomb of regular hexagons obtained by taking the m_i as hexagon centres. The edges are recovered by (11.37). In 3-space we can obtain the partition into cubes but also into more exotic possibilities (Coxeter, 1973).

Example 11.40 Generalising the previous example to the case $p(w_i) = 1/M$ and all Q_i equal to some fixed Q, not necessarily the identity, we obtain formally the same as before, but with distance defined by $\|u\|_1 = uQu^T$ (this is a true distance,

Figure 11.13 Partitions of the plane obtained by inserting decision boundary lines where the points m_i are (a) centres of a honeycomb partition (thereby recovering the hexagonal edges), (b) randomly scattered points. In either case, a boundary edge is the perpendicular bisector of the line joining the points m_i, m_j that define it.

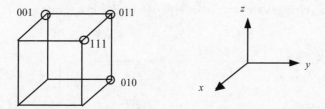

Figure 11.14 The ringed sample points have the same covariance matrix as the set of their antipodes, in this cube.

for $d(x, y) = \|x - y\|$ satisfies the axioms: (a) $d(x, y) \geq 0$, and $d(x, y) > 0$ if $x \neq y$, (b) $d(y, x) = d(x, y)$, (c) $d(x, z) \leq d(x, y) + d(y, z)$). Now $\|x - m_i\|_1 = \|x - m_j\|_2$ gives the hyperplane

$$2(m_i - m_j)Qx^{\mathrm{T}} = m_i Q m_i^{\mathrm{T}} - m_j Q m_j^{\mathrm{T}}. \tag{11.38}$$

For an example we observe that the covariance matrix of a set of sample points is unchanged under (a) translation $x \to x + a$, since the mean also changes by a, and (b) the reflection transformation $x \to -x$. Hence in the cube of Figure 11.14 Σ is the same for the four ringed sample vertices (class 1) and for their antipodes (class 2).

For computation we use the matrix S of ringed sample points, with mean $m_1 = (1/4)[1\,3\,3]$. Then, with the ordering 001, 011, 010, 111, we obtain, noting that $m_2 = (1/4)[3\,1\,1]$,

$$\Sigma = \frac{1}{4}S^{\mathrm{T}}S - m^{\mathrm{T}}m = \frac{1}{4}\begin{bmatrix} 0 & 0 & 0 & 1 \\ 0 & 1 & 1 & 1 \\ 1 & 1 & 0 & 1 \end{bmatrix}\begin{bmatrix} 0 & 0 & 1 \\ 0 & 1 & 1 \\ 0 & 1 & 0 \\ 1 & 1 & 1 \end{bmatrix} - \frac{1}{16}\begin{bmatrix} 1 \\ 3 \\ 3 \end{bmatrix}[1\,3\,3]$$

$$= \frac{1}{16}\begin{bmatrix} 3 & 1 & 1 \\ 1 & 3 & -1 \\ 1 & -1 & 3 \end{bmatrix},$$

$$Q = \Sigma^{-1} = 4\begin{bmatrix} 2 & -1 & -1 \\ -1 & 2 & 1 \\ -1 & 1 & 2 \end{bmatrix},$$

whence (11.38) gives decision boundary d_{12}: $-x_1 + x_2 + x_3 = 2$.

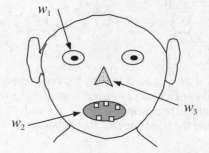

Figure 11.15 Average case of a certain type of face. The classes are w_1: eye, w_2: mouth, and w_3: nose.

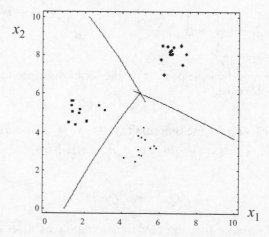

Figure 11.16 Three classes partitioned by Bayes decision boundaries. Notice the boundaries are curves rather than straight lines, reflecting the general case of unequal covariance matrices. See Example 11.41.

Exercise Locate the decision boundary in Figure 11.14 (hint: where does it cut cube edges?).

Example 11.41 (*A general Bayes classifier*) We suppose certain regions of a set of scanned faces have been identified and are to be automatically allocated by a Bayes classifier to classes w_1: eye, w_2: mouth, and w_3: nose. Just two features will be selected, so that the process can be portrayed in the plane:

$$x_1 = \text{aspect ratio (height over width) of a bounding box,}$$

$$x_2 = \text{most frequent grey level.}$$

Figure 11.15 represents the average of a (fictitious) sample set of faces, and the spread of pattern/feature vectors x is shown in Figure 11.16 with classes distinguished by point size; Bayesian decision boundaries are determined by (11.36). Assuming the points in each class to be governed by a bivariate normal distribution, the means and covariance matrices are estimated from class samples of equal size 12 (generated by ALGO 11.9 of Section 11.3), using (11.34).

It is not just a happy coincidence that the curved boundaries can be shortened so as to radiate out from a single point and still partition the classes from each other, for at the intersection of, say, boundary $d_1(x, y) = d_2(x, y)$ with boundary $d_1(x, y) = d_3(x, y)$ there holds $d_2(x, y) = d_3(x, y)$. Thus all three boundaries contain the point given by

$$d_1(x, y) = d_2(x, y) = d_3(x, y). \tag{11.39}$$

In the next section we introduce methods for simulation which will be required for the further development of the Bayes approach in Section 11.4.

References Useful references for the Bayesian approach are: Bishop (1995), Lloyd (1984c), Leonard & Hsu (1999) and Ripley (1996). A survey of priors for shape analysis in images is given by Dryden & Mardia (1998), Chapter 11.

11.3 Simulation

11.3.1 The idea of simulation

If a thing cannot, but must, be done, then simulation is a possible way forward. *Cannot* may refer for example to expense, danger, or inability to solve or even formulate necessary equations. Things simulated can be terrestrial or space flight, weather, explosion, a country's economy, the effect of noise. The last is a case of wide relevance to our topics of image processing and object recognition. Section 11.4 takes up the problem of simulation from a pdf we cannot precisely state. In the present context, simulation comes down to generating a random sample $\{X_i\}$ from a *given* distribution $f(x)$. In other words, we generate a sequence $X_1, \ldots, X_N$ in such a way that the frequencies of the various range values attained by the X_i are governed by $f(x)$, say. That is, as N increases

$$\frac{1}{N}|\{i : a \le X_i \le b\}| \to \int_a^b f(x)\mathrm{d}x, \quad \text{or} \quad \frac{1}{N}|\{i : X_i = a\}| \to p(a). \tag{11.40}$$

Each X_i is called a *random variate* and is said to be drawn from $f(x)$. A simple and immediate application is an estimate of $E(X)$ from the generated sample:

$$\hat{\mu} = \frac{1}{N}(X_i + \cdots + X_N). \tag{11.41}$$

With large N we expect something like Figure 11.17.

11.3.2 Basis: the uniform distribution

Let $U(a, b)$ denote a uniform distribution on the closed interval $[a, b]$. The pdf is thus $f(x) = 1/(b - a) \, (a \le x \le b)$. The most frequent use is that of $U(0, 1)$, on which almost all variate generation is based (the 10 we describe may be sourced in the text from

Table 11.11. *Summary: some main pdfs and their*
sample generation.

distribution	source of variate generation method
uniform	(11.42)
general pdf	ALGO 11.1
exponential	ALGO 11.2
beta	ALGO 11.5
gamma	ALGO 11.6
$N(\mu, \sigma^2)$	ALGO 11.7 and ALGO 11.8
multivariate normal	ALGO 11.9
general discrete	ALGO 11.10
binomial, large n	ALGO 11.11
Poisson	ALGO 11.12

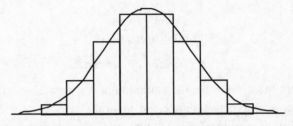

Figure 11.17 Simulation of the normal distribution. The area of a rectangle represents the number of generated variates X_i lying between its vertical edges (on the x-axis).

Table 11.11). A typical method of generating variates with this distribution is to generate a sequence of (pseudo)random integers $X_0, X_1, X_2, \ldots$ in the range $0, 1, \ldots, m$ where m, is large, typically the largest exact integer conveniently handled in the host computer. The *seed*, or *starting value*, X_0 is set, and the required sequence of variates $U_i \sim U(0, 1)$ defined by

$$X_{n+1} = (aX_n + c) \, \text{Mod} \, m, \quad U_i = X_i/m, \tag{11.42}$$

where a, c are positive integers and c is chosen to have no divisors in common with m, to ensure that the sequence $\{X_n\}$ has period m (Knuth, 1981). Thus, over m generations every integer from 0 to $m - 1$ appears exactly once, and so each number in $[0, 1]$ that does appear does so equally often. With 64-bit words the numbers are spaced at adequately small intervals of about 5×10^{-20}.

Starting from the uniform distribution there are three main methods to obtain random variates from the given, or *target*, pdf. These are: (1) the *inverse transform* method, using the target cdf, (2) the *accept–reject* method, in which a series of candidates is proposed and an acceptance criterion guarantees that it's correctly distributed, and (3) summing variates from a simpler distribution. We first consider these in turn for continuous distributions, leading to ALGO 11.1, ALGO 11.2, and so on. Useful references: Ripley (1987), Rubinstein (1981).

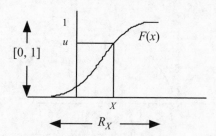

Figure 11.18 The cdf $F(x)$, over the range R_X, of a continuous random variable X.

11.3.3 The inverse transform method (IT)

We wish to generate a variate X with pdf $f(x)$. Whatever the shape of $f(x)$, its cdf $F(x)$ is certainly non-decreasing, and a failure to *increase* marks a dropping down of the pdf to zero (Theorem 9.44), so we may as well take $F(x)$ to be strictly increasing on the range R_X of X. There is thus a bijection $F: R_X \to [0, 1]$, and we have the following theoretical basis of the IT method.

Theorem 11.42 *Let $U \sim U[0, 1]$ and $X = F^{-1}(U)$. Then X has cdf $F(x)$, and hence pdf $f(x)$.*

Proof Considering Figure 11.18, we have

$$\begin{aligned} P(X \le x) &= P(U \le u) && \text{since } F \text{ is strictly increasing} \\ &= u && \text{since } U \text{ is uniform on } [0, 1] \\ &= F(x) && \text{by construction.} \end{aligned}$$

ALGO 11.1 To generate X with pdf $f(x)$

Generate $U \sim U[0, 1]$;
Return $X = F^{-1}(U)$.

Remarks 11.43 (1) We can allow for $F(x)$ to be constant on part of the range by setting $X = \text{Min}\{x: U = F(x)\}$, (2) if R_X has the form $(-\infty, b)$ we can replace $-\infty$ in computation by a value c for which $F(c)$ is suitably small. For example, $c = -2$ in the case $X \sim N(0, 1)$, (3) the IT method is most practicable when we have an explicit form for F^{-1} on $[0, 1]$.

Example 11.44 *Generate a variate with pdf $f(x) = 2x, 0 \le x \le 1$.* We have $R_X = [0, 1]$ and $u = F(x) = \int_0^x 2t\,\mathrm{d}t = x^2$. Thus we generate $U \sim U[0, 1]$ and return $X = \sqrt{U}$.

Example 11.45 *Generate a random variate from the exponential distribution* $\exp(\beta)$.

Here the pdf is $f(x) = \beta e^{-\beta t}$ (Table 9.10) and we take $u = F(x) = \int_0^x \beta e^{-\beta t}\,\mathrm{d}t = 1 - e^{-\beta x}$. But $u = 1 - e^{-\beta x} \Leftrightarrow e^{-\beta x} = 1 - u \Leftrightarrow -\beta x = \log(1 - u)$. Also, since U and $1 -$

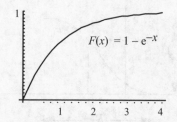

Figure 11.19 The cdf of the exponential distribution approaches $y = 1$ as x increases.

U have the same distribution we may replace $\log(1 - U)$ by $\log(U)$, as is done below. See Figure 11.19.

> *ALGO 11.2 To generate $X \sim \exp(\beta)$*
>
> Generate $U \sim U[0, 1]$
> Return $X = -(\log U)/\beta$.

Exercise Write down an IT algorithm for the Cauchy distribution.

11.3.4 The accept–reject method (AR)

(Due to von Neumann, see Rubinstein, 1981.) It is helpful to begin with the algorithm itself and then to introduce the theoretical underpinning, which here includes the expected number of trials required in order to achieve acceptance. Given the target pdf $f(x)$, we employ *another pdf $h(x)$* for which it is relatively easy to generate variates, and factorise $f(x)$ in the form

$$f(x) = C \cdot h(x)g(x), \tag{11.43}$$

where $C \geq 1$ is a constant, and $g(x)$ is a function satisfying $0 < g(x) \leq 1$ ($x \in \mathbf{R}$).

> *ALGO 11.3 To generate X, with pdf $f(x)$*
> *factored as in (11.43)*
>
> *Repeat*: Generate $U \sim U[0, 1]$ and $Y \sim h(Y)$
> *Until* $U \leq g(Y)$ (acceptance test)
> Return Y.

Theorem 11.46 *The conditional pdf f_Y of Y given $U \leq g(Y)$ is $f(x)$.*

Proof By Bayes' Theorem

$$f_Y(Y = x \mid U \leq g(Y)) = \frac{P(U \leq g(Y)|Y = x)\, h(x)}{P(U \leq g(Y))}. \tag{11.44}$$

We consider the numerator and denominator separately. For the acceptance test $U \leq g(Y)$, we note that U, Y are independent and so have a joint pdf equal to the product of their individual pdfs, namely $1 \cdot h(y)$. Evaluating the probability as an integral (10.4) in Figure 11.20,

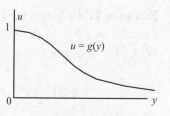

Figure 11.20

$$P(U \leq g(Y) = \underset{u \leq g(y)}{\int} 1 \cdot h(y) \, du \, dy$$

$$= \int_{\mathbf{R}} h(y) dy \int_0^{g(y)} 1 \cdot du = \int_{\mathbf{R}} g(y) h(y) dy$$

$$= \int_{\mathbf{R}} (1/C) f(y) dy = 1/C.$$

Thus

$$P(U \leq g(Y)) = 1/C. \tag{11.45}$$

On the other hand, setting $Y = x$, then noting that U is uniform on [0, 1], we have

$$P(U \leq g(Y) | Y = x) = P(U \leq g(x)) = g(x). \tag{11.46}$$

Substituting this and (11.45) into the Bayes expression (11.44) gives Theorem 11.46.

Corollary 11.47 *The expected number of trials before acceptance in ALGO 11.3 is the constant C of (11.43).*

Proof The trials are independent, each with probability $p = P(U \leq g(Y)) = 1/C$ of success. Hence the expected number of trials required for success is the expected value of the geometric distribution (Table 9.9), namely $1/p$, which here equals C.

AR2 – a remarkable special case Let $h(x)$ be uniform on the interval $[a, b] = R_X$, that is $h(x) = 1/(b - a), a \leq x \leq b$. In the following version of the factorisation (11.43), the expected number of trials is $M(b - a)$, and the constant M is chosen with quick acceptance in mind (the functions on the second row are the choices for those immediately above them):

$$f(x) = \begin{cases} C \cdot h(x) \cdot g(x), \\ M(b - a) \cdot \dfrac{1}{b - a} \cdot \dfrac{f(x)}{M}. \end{cases} \tag{11.47}$$

Referring to ALGO 11.3, we can obtain Y as $Y = a + (b - a)U_2$, where U_2 is uniform on $[a, b]$. The result follows:

ALGO 11.4 To generate $f(x)$ by method AR2

Repeat
    Generate $U_1, U_2 \sim U[a, b]$
    Set $Y = a + (b - a)U_2$
Until $U_1 \leq f(Y)/M$
Return Y.

Example 11.48 Generate a variate from $f(x) = 3x^2, 0 \le x \le 1$, using ALGO 11.4. In this case the range of X is $[a, b] = [0, 1]$, so that $Y = U_2$, effecting a further simplification. With $M = 3$ and hence $g(x) = f(x)/3$, the process is simply:

Repeat : generate $U_1, U_2 \sim U[0, 1]$ until $U_1 \le U_2^2$. Return U_2.

Example 11.49 We use ALGO 11.4 to generate from the beta distribution $\mathrm{Be}(\alpha, \beta), a, \beta > 0$, with density

$$f(x) = x^{\alpha-1}(1 - x)^{\beta-1}/B(\alpha, \beta), \quad 0 \le x \le 1, \tag{11.48}$$

where the normalising constant is the beta *function* $B(\alpha, \beta) = \Gamma(\alpha)\Gamma(\beta)/\Gamma(\alpha + \beta)$ (Table 9.10). The X range is again [0,1], giving $Y = U_2$. We take M to be the least value of $f(x)$, which occurs when $x = (\alpha - 1)/(\alpha + \beta - 2)$, with expected number of trials just $2/\pi$ in the case $\alpha = \beta = 1/2$.

ALGO 11.5 To generate from $\mathrm{Be}(\alpha, \beta)$ *with pdf* $f(x)$

Set $M = f((\alpha - 1)/(\alpha + \beta - 2))$
Repeat
    Generate $U_1, U_2 \sim U[0, 1]$
Until $U_1 \le f(U_2)/M$
Return U_2.

Example 11.50 We derive a method of generating from the gamma distribution using variates of the beta and exponential distributions. In this section we use the second notation for gamma $G(\alpha, \beta)$, with pdf in the form

$$f(x) = \frac{x^{\alpha-1}e^{-x/\beta}}{\beta^\alpha \Gamma(\alpha)} \, (\alpha, \beta > 0), x \ge 0. \tag{11.49}$$

Notice that $G(1, \beta) = \exp(\beta)$, the exponential distribution. We generate for $G(\alpha, \beta)$ in the case $\alpha = \delta$ with $0 < \delta < 1$, then extend to general $\alpha > 0$ by the reproductive property (Theorem 10.19) in the form

$$G(m + \delta, \beta) = G(1, \beta) * \cdots * G(1, \beta)^* G(\delta, \beta). \tag{11.50}$$

That is, if $Y_0 \sim G(\delta, \beta)$ and $Y_1, \ldots, Y_m \sim G(1, \beta)$ are independent, then $\sum Y_i \sim G(m + \delta, \beta)$. Returning to $G(\delta, \beta)$, we need the following theorem.

Theorem 11.51 *Let* δ, β *satisfy* $0 < \delta < 1, \beta > 0$. *If* $W \sim \mathrm{Be}(\delta, 1 - \delta)$ *and* $V \sim \exp(1)$ *then* $X = \beta V W$ *is a variate of* $G(\delta, \beta)$.

Proof We introduce an auxiliary variable u and transform coordinates in the plane from w, v to u, x as described in Theorem 10.10. We take

$$\begin{cases} u = v, \\ x = \beta wv, \end{cases} \quad \text{with inverse} \quad \begin{cases} w = x/\beta u, \\ v = u, \end{cases}$$

$$\text{and Jacobian } J = \frac{\partial(w, v)}{\partial(u, x)} = \begin{vmatrix} -x/\beta u^2 & 1/\beta u \\ 1 & 0 \end{vmatrix} = -1/\beta u.$$

The pair (W, V), being independent, have as joint distribution the product $w^{\delta-1}(1 - w)^{-\delta} \cdot e^{-v}/B(\delta, 1 - d)$, and, according to Theorem 10.10, substituting for w, v and multiplying by $|J|$ gives the pdf for (U, X). After some rearrangement this becomes

$$f_{U,X}(u, x) = x^{\delta-1}(u - x/\beta)^{-\delta}e^{-u} \cdot \beta^{-\delta}/B(\delta, 1 - \delta).$$

The marginal distribution for X is therefore

$$f_X(x) = \int_{x/\beta}^{\infty} f_{U,X}(u, x)\mathrm{d}u = \frac{x^{\delta-1}\beta^{-\delta}}{B(\delta, 1 - \delta)} \int_{x/\beta}^{\infty} \left(u - \frac{x}{\beta}\right)^{-\delta} e^{-u}\mathrm{d}u.$$

On substituting $y = u - x/\beta$ we may evaluate the integral as a gamma function (Table 9.6) because $1 - \delta > 0$, then, noting that $B(\delta, 1 - \delta) = \Gamma(\delta)\Gamma(1 - \delta)/\Gamma(1)$, we obtain the pdf (11.49) as required. Hence the following algorithm.

$$\boxed{\begin{array}{l} \qquad\qquad ALGO\ 11.6\ \textit{To generate from } G(\alpha, \beta) \\[4pt] \text{Set } m = \text{Floor}[\alpha],\ \delta = \alpha - m. \\ \text{Generate } W \sim \text{Be}(\delta, 1 - \delta) \text{ and } V, X_1, \ldots, X_m \sim \exp(1) \\ \text{Set } X_0 = \beta V W \\ \text{Return } \sum X_i\ (0 \le i \le m). \end{array}}$$

11.3.5 Generating for the normal/Gaussian

For this we return to the general AR method (11.43). Since the standard normal pdf $\phi(x)$ is symmetrical about the y-axis, it suffices to generate for $x \ge 0$ and assign a random sign to the variate obtained. Thus, we generate first from $f(x) = 2\phi(x)$, $x \ge 0$. A factorisation that leads to a nice method is

$$f(x) = \begin{cases} C \cdot h(x) \cdot g(x), \\ \sqrt{\frac{2e}{\pi}}e^{-x} \exp[-(x - 1)^2/2]. \end{cases}$$

The expected number of trials is $C = 1.3$ approx. The acceptance criterion simplifies, because $U \le g(Y) \Leftrightarrow -\log U \ge (y - 1)^2/2$, but $-\log U \sim \exp(1)$ (Example 11.45), so the condition may be written $V_2 \ge (V_1 - 1)^2/2$ with $V_1, V_2 \sim \exp(1)$, and the algorithm

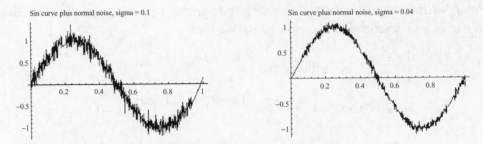

Figure 11.21 Sine curve with Gaussian/normal noise added by ALGO 11.7. The respective distributions are $N(0, 0.1)$ and $N(0, 0.04)$.

becomes:

ALGO 11.7 To generate from $N(0, 1)$

Repeat
$\quad$ Generate $V_1, V_2 \sim \exp(1)$
Until $V_2 \geq (V_1 - 1)^2 / 2$
Generate $U \sim U[0, 1]$
If $U < 1/2$ set $V_1 = -V_1$
Return V_1 {for $N(\mu, \sigma^2)$ return $\sigma V_1 + \mu$}.

In Figure 11.21, a sine graph is distorted by noise in two ways. For each point (x_i, y_i) used in plotting we apply ALGO 11.7 to generate a variate e_i, coming in the first case from $N(0, 0.1)$ and in the second case from $N(0, 0.04)$; we then plot $(x_i, y_i + e_i)$.

Another approach is given by the Central Limit Theorem 10.45, according to which the sum of a large number of independent random variables, of whatever distributions, is approximately normal $N(0, 1)$ after reducing to mean 0 and variance 1. It is most economical to generate uniformly distributed $U_i \sim U[0, 1]$. Each has mean $1/2$ and variance $1/12$, so it is convenient to sum exactly 12 of such variates, to give the simple algorithm below. It is illustrated in Figure 11.22.

ALGO 11.8 To generate from $N(0, 1)$

Generate $U_1, \ldots U_{12} \sim U[0, 1]$
Return $(\sum U_i) - 6$.

Multivariate normal generation Let $Z = (Z_1, \ldots, Z_d)$, a random vector with iid components in $N(0, 1)$. If a potential covariance matrix Σ satisfies $\Sigma = U^T U$ with U non-singular, and we set $X = ZU$, then $\text{Cov}(X) = U^T \text{Cov}(Z) U$ (Theorem 10.56) $= U^T I U = U^T U = \Sigma$. Thus we can obtain multivariate normal variates with any given covariance, by generating sufficient $N(0, 1)$ variates. A great simplification occurs in the calculation of suitable U, compared with the usual determination of eigenvalues and

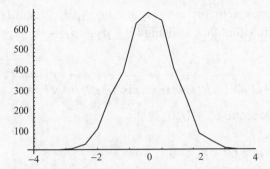

Figure 11.22 Frequency distribution based on 16 intervals and 3500 generated samples from ALGO 11.8 for the normal distribution.

vectors, if we specify that U be upper triangular with positive diagonal elements. This is the Choleski decomposition (see Theorem 8.41) in which, writing $U = \text{Rows}(R_1, \ldots, R_d)$ and $\Sigma = [s_{ij}] = \text{Rows}(S_1, \ldots, S_d)$, we perform for successive values $k = 1, 2, \ldots, d$:

$$u_{kk} = \sqrt{\left[s_{kk} - \sum_{i=1}^{k-1} u_{ik}^2\right]}, \text{ then } R_k = (1/u_{kk})\left[S_k - \sum_{i=1}^{k-1} u_{ik}R_i\right]. \quad (11.51)$$

The decomposition is guaranteed to work, by Theorem 8.41, because Σ is (by definition) positive definite for multivariate normal vectors. It results in the following algorithm, which we used for the Bayes classifier of Example 11.41.

ALGO 11.9 To generate from d-dimensional $N(\mu, \Sigma)$.

Compute U so that $\Sigma = U^T U$
Generate $Z_1, \ldots, Z_d$ from $N(0, 1)$
Set $Z = (Z_1, \ldots, Z_d)$ and return $X = ZU + \mu$.

11.3.6 Generating for discrete distributions

Discrete variates are generally easier to generate than continuous ones. Suppose the discrete variable X has range $\{x_0, x_1, \ldots\}$ and pdf $P(X = x_k) = p_k$. The cdf may be represented as a step function (Figure 9.11) with successive heights $g_k = p_0 + p_1 + \cdots + p_k$ and, having generated $U \sim U[0, 1]$, we wish to determine the unique k for which $g_{k-1} < U \leq g_k$ (take $g_{-1} = 0$). This process is illustrated on the horizontal line in Figure 11.23, showing how the Inverse Transform Method may be adapted for use in virtually all cases.

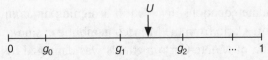

Figure 11.23 The cdf $\{g_k\}$ of a discrete distribution with $P(X = x_k) = p_k$. We determine the unique integer k such that $g_{k-1} < U = g_k$.

We can work up from p_0 by successively adding $p_1, p_2, \ldots$ until the condition on U is satisfied. The following does this, utilising $U \leq p_0 + p_1 + \cdots + p_k \Leftrightarrow U - p_0 - p_1 - \cdots - p_k \leq 0$.

ALGO 11.10 Generate discrete X from (p_i)

Generate $U \sim U[0, 1]$
Set $k = 0$
While $U - p_k > 0$:
    Set $U = U - p_k$; set $k = k + 1$.
Return x_k.

For large n the computation of the probabilities may be excessive, and the Central Limit Theorem provides an excellent alternative option. We shall give the formulation for the often-used binomial and Poisson cases. For $\text{Bin}(n, p)$ the approximate normal random variable is $Z = (X - np + 1/2)/\sqrt{(npq)}$, where as usual $q = 1 - p$ (Table 9.9). The following is suitable in the cases $np > 10$, $p \geq 1/2$ and $nq > 10$, $p < 1/2$ (Meyer, 1970). The result is rounded to the nearest integer, and taken to be zero if approximation causes a spill onto the negative x-axis.

ALGO 11.11 Generating $\text{Bin}(n, p)$ *from* $N(0, 1)$

Generate $Z \sim N(0, 1)$
Return $\text{Max}\{0, \text{Round}(Z\sqrt{(npq)} + np - 1/2)\}$

The Poisson distribution If X is Poisson with parameter $\lambda > 10$ the Central Limit Theorem gives the variable $Z = (X - \lambda + 1/2)/\sqrt{\lambda}$ as a reasonable approximation to $N(0, 1)$. Including as before the end correction of $1/2$, we have the following algorithm.

ALGO 11.12 Generating Poisson $\text{Po}(\lambda)$ *from* $N(0, 1)$

Generate $Z \sim N(0, 1)$
Return $\text{Max}\{0, \text{Round}(\lambda + Z\sqrt{\lambda} - 1/2)\}$

11.4 Markov Chain Monte Carlo

Monte Carlo methods go back a long way in their broad sense of simulation. In more recent times they have been used to verify the theory of the Student t-distribution, and by physicists to simulate equations involved in designing an atomic bomb (this group coined the name Monte Carlo from the Monaco gambling casino).

The early reputation of Monte Carlo methods was damaged by exaggerated claims of their efficacy. However, this was partly remedied by the idea of Metropolis *et al.* (1953) to realise a distribution via a Markov chain, as explained in Section 11.4.3, and by improvements due to Hastings (1970). Much is still not fully understood, especially on the issue of convergence, but the method has led to breakthroughs in many areas of statistical application, including image processing and object recognition (Gilks *et al.*, 1997).

11.4.1 Markov chains

Our topic in this section was first introduced by Andrei Markov (Figure 11.24) as a tool for analysing the works of the Russian poet Alexander Pushkin. Since then a huge variety of applications has emerged, including appropriately speech recognition (Levinson & Shepp, 1991) as well as our present topic of digital image analysis. In particular, it has proved a tool of choice for increasing the effectiveness of sample mean Monte Carlo for performing otherwise intractable integration of Bayes-related pdfs (see Section 11.4.3). An application to the Discrete Cosine Transform is found in Section 15.5.

A Markov chain may be regarded as the most natural extension of the idea of independence. Its definition follows.

Figure 11.24 A. A. Markov 1856–1922

Definition 11.52 Let $X_0, X_1, X_2, \ldots$ be random variables based on a sequence of trials, each variable having the same range $\{0, 1, \ldots, m\}$. The range values are called *states* of the X_r, and if $X_n = i$ we say the system $\{X_r\}$ is *in state i at time n (or at the nth step)*. The system is a *Markov chain* if its state at time n depends only on the previous state. That is, the *Markov Property* holds: for $r = 1, 2, 3 \ldots$

$$P(X_r = x_r | X_{r-1} = x_{r-1}, X_{r-2} = x_{r-2}, \ldots, X_0 = x_0)$$
$$= P(X_r = x_r | X_{r-1} = x_{r-1}). \tag{11.52a}$$

Thus the system's behaviour is governed by the *transitional probabilities*

$$p_{ij} = P(X_r = j | X_{r-1} = i) \, (r = 1, 2, \ldots), \tag{11.52b}$$

which we shall assume for now to be independent of r (the *homogeneous* case), together with the *initial probabilities* $p_i = P(X_0 = i)$ which constitute the pdf of X_0. The square matrix $Q = [p_{ij}]$ is called the *transition matrix* of the chain. A graphical diagram of transition probabilities may be composed from units of the type below, where a circled i represents the state i. It is also a memory aid for the meaning of p_{ij}.

$$\textcircled{i} \xrightarrow{p_{ij}} \textcircled{j} \qquad Q = [p_{ij}]$$

We note that $p = [p_i]$ is a *stochastic* (row) vector, one whose entries are non-negative and sum to 1; also Q is a *stochastic matrix*, where every row is a stochastic vector, because

$\sum_j p_{ij} = \sum_j P(X_{r+1} = j | X_r = i) = 1$ (conditional probability obeys the probability axioms, see (9.26)).

Example 11.53 (*The occupancy problem*) Consider the random equally likely placement of balls into N cells, in which each cell may contain up to N balls. Define the state of a corresponding system to be the number of occupied cells: $0, 1, 2, \ldots$, or N, and let X_r be the state after the rth ball is inserted. On the insertion of a ball the state remains the same or increases by 1. Thus $p_{i,i+1} = P(X_{r+1} = i + 1 | X_r = i) = P$(next ball placed in empty cell) = (number of empty cells)$/N = (N - i)/N$, whereas $p_{ii} = P$ (ball put in occupied cell) $= i/n$. The initial distribution is $\boldsymbol{p} = (1, 0 \ldots, 0)$ since the cells start unoccupied. The system is homogeneous, since $p_{i,i+1}$ and p_{ii} are independent of r. The case $N = 3$ is shown below.

$$Q = \begin{bmatrix} p_{00} & p_{01} & p_{02} & \cdots \\ p_{10} & p_{11} & p_{12} & \cdots \\ p_{20} & p_{21} & p_{22} & \cdots \\ \cdots & \cdots & \cdots & \cdots \end{bmatrix} = \begin{bmatrix} 0 & 1 & 0 & 0 \\ 0 & 1/3 & 2/3 & 0 \\ 0 & 0 & 2/3 & 1/3 \\ 0 & 0 & 0 & 1 \end{bmatrix}. \tag{11.53}$$

Exercise Verify the transition matrix (11.53). Why must it be upper triangular for all N?

The pdf of X_r The pdf vector $p^{(r)}$ of X_r is determined by any of those that come before, by means of the transition matrix. We have $p^{(0)} = \boldsymbol{p}$, and to pass from the pdf of one variable to that of the next we multiply on the right by Q. The example $p^{(1)} = p^{(0)}Q$ reveals the general case:

$$p_j^{(1)} = P(X_1 = j) = \sum_i P(X_0 = i)P(X_1 = j | X_0 = i) = \sum_i p_i^{(0)} p_{ij} = \left(p^{(0)}Q\right)_j,$$

$$p^{(r)} = p^{(r-1)}Q = p^{(0)}Q^r \ (r \geq 1). \tag{11.54}$$

Example 11.53 *continued* Given that the pdf of X_0 is $p^{(0)} = (1, 1, 1, 1)/4$, determine the pdf $p^{(r)}$ of X_r for $r = 1, 2, 3, 4$. We have by (11.54) that $p^{(1)} = (0, 1, 1, 1)/3$, $p^{(2)} = (0, 1, 4, 4)/9$, $p^{(3)} = (0, 1, 10, 16)/27$, $p(4) = (0, 1, 22, 58)/81$. This means, for example, that, after four balls are inserted, it is impossible that no cells are occupied, and the probability that exactly two cells are occupied is $22/81$.

Example 11.54 (*Random walk with absorbing barriers*) The walk takes place on non-negative integer coordinates on the x-axis, moving 1 unit at a time, forward with probability p, back with probability q. If barrier 0 or N is encountered, the walk stops. Interpreting this, the only transitions with nonzero probability are given by $p_{i,i+1} = p$, $p_{i,i-1} = q$ $(0 < i < N)$, and $p_{00} = p_{NN} = 1$. We exemplify below the transition matrix in the case $N = 3$.

$$Q = \begin{bmatrix} 1 & 0 & 0 & 0 \\ q & 0 & p & 0 \\ 0 & q & 0 & p \\ 0 & 0 & 0 & 1 \end{bmatrix}. \tag{11.55}$$

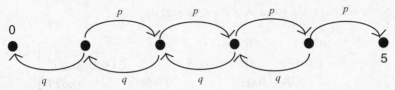

Figure 11.25 Allowable transitions and their probabilities in the random walk of Example 11.54.

Now consider Figure 11.25, showing the allowable transitions and their probabilities in the case $N = 5$. It is noteworthy that this example is equivalent to the 'gambler's ruin problem'. Their joint stake is N units, and at each throw of a coin the winner takes one unit from the loser. Gambler A wins a throw with probability p, and we equate the system's state to his current finance. The game ends when either is broke, that is when the state i is 0 or N.

***n*-step transitions** Now some theory to help the gambler and random walker on their way. If the state changes from, say, i to j in exactly n steps we say an *n-step transition* occurred from i to j. Denote the probability of this by $p_{ij}^{(n)} = P(X_{r+n} = j \mid X_r = i)$. Such a transition can occur by any path of length n (the number of arrows):

$$i \to a \to b \to \cdots \to d \to j.$$

The probability of this sequence is $p_i^{(r)} p_{ia} p_{ab} \cdots p_{dj}$, and hence its conditional probability given that it begins in state i is, on dividing by $p_i(r)$,

$$p_{ia} p_{ab} \cdots p_{dj} \tag{11.56}$$

and $p_{ij}^{(n)}$ is therefore the sum of the corresponding expressions for all such paths of length n:

$$p_{ij}^{(n)} = \sum_{1 \leq a,b,\ldots,d \leq m} p_{ia} p_{ab} \cdots p_{dj},$$

the states being labelled $0, 1, \ldots, m$. But this sum of n-fold products is, by the definition of matrix product (see (7.17b)), simply the ij element of Q^n. Writing $P^{(n)} = [p_{ij}^{(n)}]$, we state this important observation as a theorem.

Theorem 11.55 *The probability of n-step transitions in a Markov chain is given by the nth power of the transition matrix,*

$$P^{(n)} = Q^n. \tag{11.57}$$

Example 11.56 (*Continuation of Example 11.55*) Below we show the matrix Q^9 for the walk/gamble with $N = 5$ as depicted in Figure 11.25, taking $p = 2/3$ and $q = 1/3$. The matrix gives, by Theorem 11.56, the probability of every possible state of affairs and *indicates those that are not possible by a zero entry.*

$$Q^9 = \begin{bmatrix} 1 & 0 & 0 & 0 & 0 & 0 \\ 0.469 & 0 & 0.055 & 0 & 0.068 & 0.407 \\ 0.204 & 0.027 & 0 & 0.089 & 0 & 0.679 \\ 0.085 & 0 & 0.048 & 0 & 0.055 & 0.815 \\ 0.026 & 0.009 & 0 & 0.028 & 0 & 0.938 \\ 0 & 0 & 0 & 0 & 0 & 1 \end{bmatrix}$$

The zeros in the first and last rows are present in every power Q^n, as may be shown inductively. We have given Gambler A (and right steps) a $2:1$ advantage at each step. Suppose Gambler A starts with an unfairly small stake of 1 unit to his opponent's 4. The matrix entries show something decisive. He has by now lost with probability $p_{10} = 0.5$ approx., and won with probability 0.4. Other results are much less likely. And although he starts but one step from defeat he retains a realistic chance of victory.

With initial stake 2, his opponent having 3, Gambler A has $P(\text{lose}) = p_{20} = 0.2$, whilst $P(\text{win}) = p_{25} = 0.7$, so the tide is now overwhelmingly in his favour, and more so for a start still further to the right (in terms of the figure). What emerges too is that the chance of a result either way by step 9 is very high.

Markov and independence Let us compare a Markov chain with a sequence of iid random variables in which p_i is the probability of outcome i. For a sequence of oucomes $i, j, k, \ldots$ we have by (9.16) and Theorem 9.17 the two cases

$$p(i, j, k, \ldots) = \begin{cases} p_i p_j p_k \cdots & (\textit{independent trials}), \\ p_i p_{ij} p_{jk} \cdots & (\textit{Markov chain}). \end{cases} \tag{11.58}$$

Thus independence may be seen as the special case in which Q has constant columns, i.e. the rows are identical.

Example 11.57 We show that, in the independence case above, the Markov formulation results in $Q^n = Q$ $(n \geq 2)$. It suffices to prove $Q^2 = Q$, then the rest follows by repeated multiplication. Also, the 2×2 case shows how to proceed in general. Because the rows of Q are identical we may write $A = [1\ 1 \ldots 1]^T[\text{row 1 of } Q]$, according to the laws of matrix multiplication. Then, since the middle two matrices form a dot product $p + q = 1$,

$$Q^2 = \begin{bmatrix} 1 \\ 1 \end{bmatrix} \begin{bmatrix} p & q \end{bmatrix} \begin{bmatrix} 1 \\ 1 \end{bmatrix} \begin{bmatrix} p & q \end{bmatrix} = \begin{bmatrix} 1 \\ 1 \end{bmatrix} (p + q) \begin{bmatrix} p & q \end{bmatrix} = \begin{bmatrix} 1 \\ 1 \end{bmatrix} \begin{bmatrix} p & q \end{bmatrix} = Q.$$

The long term

Example 11.58 (*A 2-state Markov chain*) Due to glacial melting a certain river may flood, but only in the month of October. It is thought that, rather than being independent, the states of the river in consecutive Octobers (1 for *flood*, 0 for *no flood*) are better modelled by a Markov chain with transition matrix

$$Q = \begin{bmatrix} 1-\alpha & \alpha \\ \beta & 1-\beta \end{bmatrix} (0 < \alpha, \beta < 1). \tag{11.59}$$

Can we predict anything in the long term? It can be shown by induction on $n \geq 0$ that

$$Q^n = \frac{1}{\alpha+\beta} \left\{ \begin{bmatrix} \beta & \alpha \\ \beta & \alpha \end{bmatrix} + (1-\alpha-\beta)^n \begin{bmatrix} \alpha & -\alpha \\ -\beta & \beta \end{bmatrix} \right\}. \tag{11.60}$$

Now, the given condition $0 < \alpha, \beta < 1$ implies $1 - \alpha - \beta < 1$; also $\alpha + \beta < 2$ and so $1 - \alpha - \beta > -1$. In short, $|1 - \alpha - \beta| < 1$ and hence $(1 - \alpha - \beta)^n \to 0$ as $n \to \infty$. With (11.60) this shows that

$$Q^n \to \frac{1}{\alpha+\beta} \begin{bmatrix} \beta & \alpha \\ \beta & \alpha \end{bmatrix} \text{ as } n \to \infty,$$

and thus if $\boldsymbol{p}$ is an initial probability vector with components p, q we have

$$\boldsymbol{p}Q^n \to \frac{1}{\alpha+\beta} \begin{bmatrix} p & q \end{bmatrix} \begin{bmatrix} \beta & \alpha \\ \beta & \alpha \end{bmatrix} = \frac{p+q}{\alpha+\beta} \begin{bmatrix} \beta & \alpha \end{bmatrix} = \frac{1}{\alpha+\beta} \begin{bmatrix} \beta & \alpha \end{bmatrix}, \tag{11.61}$$

since $p + q = 1$. Of special note is that this long term effect is independent of the choice of $\boldsymbol{p}$. For now, we will be content with stating a general theorem of which this example is a particular case.

Theorem 11.59 *(Lipschutz, 1981) If some power of a transition matrix Q has all its elements positive then (i) Q has a unique fixed probability vector $\boldsymbol{t}$ (the chain's stationary distribution, given by $\boldsymbol{t}Q = \boldsymbol{t}$), and $\boldsymbol{t}$ has all its entries positive, (ii) $\boldsymbol{x}Q^n \to \boldsymbol{t}$ as $n \to \infty$, for any fixed probability vector $\boldsymbol{x}$.*

Sampling from a Markov chain Consider the pdf $p^{(n)}$ of X_n, converted into that of X_{n+1} by the transition matrix thus: $p^{(n+1)} = p(n)Q$. A *sample from the chain* is a sequence $X_0, X_1, \ldots$, possibly terminating, with X_i drawn from $p^{(i)}$. Thus, as $p^{(i)}$ approaches a stationary value $\boldsymbol{t}$, we are drawing, with increasing accuracy, samples from $\boldsymbol{t}$ itself. Here is a simple algorithm.

ALGO 11.13 A sample of length n from a Markov chain.

Initialise $p^{(0)}$
Repeat for $i = 1, 2, \ldots, n$
    Set $p^{(i)} = p^{(i-1)}Q$
    Generate X_i from $p^{(i)}$ (ALGO 11.10)
    Return X_i.

Exercise Perform the induction in (11.60) see Exercise 11.16.

Example 11.60 Let $\{0, 1\}$ denote the states in the chain of Example 11.58. Take $\alpha = 0.8, \beta = 0.4$ and $p^{(0)} = [1/2 \quad 1/2]$. Then we have transition matrix and stationary distribution

$$Q = \begin{bmatrix} 0.2 & 0.8 \\ 0.4 & 0.6 \end{bmatrix} \quad \text{and} \quad t = \begin{bmatrix} 1/3 & 2/3 \end{bmatrix}.$$

The first few $p^{(i)}$ are, transposed,

$$\begin{bmatrix} 0.5 \\ 0.5 \end{bmatrix} \rightarrow \begin{bmatrix} 0.3 \\ 0.7 \end{bmatrix} \rightarrow \begin{bmatrix} 0.332 \\ 0.668 \end{bmatrix} \rightarrow \begin{bmatrix} 0.3336 \\ 0.6664 \end{bmatrix} \rightarrow \begin{bmatrix} 0.3333 \\ 0.6667 \end{bmatrix} \rightarrow \cdots,$$

so even by $p^{(4)}$ we are close to the stationary distribution. The first 40 samples are 1110010110110110110001101111111111011100, and the relative frequency of a zero is shown below for various sample sizes.

Sample size	10	100	1000	10000
Relative frequency of zero	0.30	0.37	0.32	0.34

Remarks 11.61 (1) (*Sampling*) We will see in Section 11.4.3 that it is possible and very desirable to construct samples from an unknown density $\pi(x)$ by constructing a Markov chain which will have $\pi(x)$ as stationary distribution, and then sampling from this chain.

(2) (*Non-discrete case*) We can handle Markov chains with the discrete state space S replaced by a continuous space E. The pdfs become continuous ones and the transition rule $p^{(n)} = Qp^{(n-1)}$, or $p^{(n)}(y) = \sum_x p(y|x)p^{(n-1)}(x)$, becomes

$$p^{(n)}(y) = \int_E p(y|x)p^{(n-1)}(x)\mathrm{d}x \tag{11.61a}$$

The continuous conditional pdf $p(y|x)$ is now called the transition kernel of the chain. A pdf $\pi(x)$ is then stationary for the Markov chain if

$$\int_E \pi(x)p(y|x)\mathrm{d}x = \pi(y). \tag{11.61b}$$

(3) (*Non-homogeneous case*) So far our chains have been homogeneous, in that the transition probabilities have been stage-independent. If we remove this restriction then each contiguous pair X, Y has its own transition matrix $Q_{XY} = [p(y|x)]$, and the same notation is still utilised if X and Y are $n > 1$ steps apart. The previous n-step matrix Q^n of (11.57) is replaced by a product of 1-step matrices. Essentially the same argument as used for Q^n shows that in a chain $X, U, V, \ldots, W, Y$ we have, for any variable T between X and Y,

$$Q_{XY} = Q_{XU}Q_{UV} \cdots Q_{WY} = Q_{XT}Q_{TY}. \tag{11.62}$$

Joint pdfs The following form of a joint pdf, for the chain $X \ldots Y$ cited above, shows that *deleting X or Y leaves a Markov chain* with pdf as noted:

$$
\left.
\begin{array}{lll}
\text{(i)} & p(x, u, v, \ldots, w, y) & p(x)p(u|x)p(v|u) \cdots p(y|w), \\
\text{(ii)} & \text{pdf after deleting } X & p(u)p(v|u) \cdots p(y|w), \\
\text{(iii)} & \text{pdf after deleting } Y & p(x, u, v, \ldots, w, y)/p(y|w).
\end{array}
\right\}
\tag{11.63}
$$

Proof (i) $p(x, u, v, \ldots, w, y)$

$\qquad = p(x)p(u|x)p(v|x, u) \cdots p(y|x, u, v, \ldots, w)$ by Theorem 9.17

$\qquad = p(x)p(u|x)p(v|u) \cdots p(y|w)$ by the Markov Property (11.52).

(ii) $p(u, v, \ldots, w, y) = \sum_x p(x, u, v, \ldots, w, y) = \sum_x p(x, u)p(v|u) \ldots p(y|w) = p(u)p(v|u) \cdots p(y|w).$

(iii) Here the fact that $\sum_y p(y|w) = 1$, by (9.26), causes the factor $p(y|w)$ to disappear from (i).

References Lipschutz (1981), Lloyd (1984a) and Häggström (2002).

11.4.2 Monte Carlo methods

A Monte Carlo method is essentially one in which, instead of analysing a process, we somehow simulate it and are thereby able to study its properties. In perhaps the earliest known use, in 1876, de Forest picked cards randomly from a box as a way of simulating a Gaussian process (see Kotz & Johnson, 1985).

One application since the 1940s has been the computation of integrals for which other methods were unsuitable, often because of high dimensionality. For example, normal numerical methods are less suitable for dimensions greater than about 12 (for further details, see the end of this section). Such is the case for many integrals required in Bayesian (and other) applications. However, the essential idea of Monte Carlo may be conveyed through a 1-dimensional integral,

$$
I = \int_a^b g(x)\mathrm{d}x.
\tag{11.64}
$$

Method 1: hit or miss We begin with the earlier and more easily comprehended of two methods known as Monte Carlo. Suppose the graph of $y = g(x) \, (a \le x \le b)$ lies below the line $y = c$, and hence lies within the bounding box represented in Figure 11.26, of area $B = c(b - a)$. We expect intuitively that if the box is targeted at random points then the frequency of hits below the graph of $y = g(x)$ is proportional to this lower area, giving us an approximation to the integral I of (11.64).

More precisely, let X, Y be independent random variables uniformly distributed on respectively $[a, b]$ and $[0, c]$. Then the pair (X, Y) has joint pdf $1/c \times 1/(b - a) = 1/B$ for (x, y) in the bounding box $a \le x \le b, 0 \le y \le c$. A hit in formal terms is the event $H: Y \le g(X)$, with a probability p which, given n trials of (X, Y) in which H occurs n_H times, is estimated by its relative frequency:

$$
\hat{p} = n_H/n.
\tag{11.65}
$$

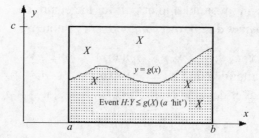

Figure 11.26 The Monte Carlo 'hit or miss' method. The area/integral shaded is estimated by the proportion of random points x targeted on a bounding box which 'hit' this
area.

But using the pdf of (X, Y), we have $I = Bp$ because

$$p = \iint_H (1/B)dx \, dy = (1/B)(\text{area under curve } y = g(x)) = I/B, \quad (11.66)$$

so we take our estimator θ of I to be

$$\theta_1 = B\hat{p} = Bn_H/n. \quad (11.67)$$

An unbiased estimate To vindicate our choice we should like θ_1 to be unbiased, that
is, having expected value $E(\theta_1) = I$. To check this we observe that n_H is based on
Bernoulli trials (two outcomes only) and so is a binomial random variable with parameters n, p. Hence $E(\theta_1) = (B/n)E(n_H)$ (by (11.67)) $= (B/n)np$ (by (9.42)) $=
Bp = I$, as required, where the last equality is from (11.66). The variance is an im-
portant consideration, affecting accuracy, and we now determine it.

Theorem 11.62 *In the above notation, $E(\theta_1) = I$ and $V(\theta_1) = I(B - I)/n$.*

Proof
$$\begin{aligned}
V(\theta_1) &= (B^2/n^2)V(n_H) && \text{since } Q_1 = (B/n)n_H, \quad (11.67) \\
&= (B^2/n^2)np(1-p) && \text{by (9.42), since } n_H \text{ is Bin}(n, p) \\
&= I(B-I)/n && \text{since } p = I/B, \quad (11.66).
\end{aligned}$$

We can use this straight away to estimate the number of trials required for a
given accuracy from the Chebychev result (9.48b): $P(|X - \mu) \geq \varepsilon) = V(X)/\varepsilon^2$. We
set $X = \theta_1, \mu = E(\theta_1) = I$, and $V(\theta_1) = I(B - I)/n$ to obtain $P(|\theta_1 - I| \geq \varepsilon) \leq
I(B - I)/n\varepsilon^2$ and, considering the complementary event,

$$P(|\theta_1 - I| < \varepsilon) \geq 1 - I(B-I)/n\varepsilon^2 \geq 1 - \delta \quad \text{if} \quad \delta \geq I(B-I)/n\varepsilon^2, \quad \text{or}$$
$$P(|\theta_1 - I| < \varepsilon) \geq 1 - \delta \qquad \text{if} \qquad n \geq I(B-I)/\varepsilon^2\delta. \quad (11.68)$$

Now let us try the method on an example which we can solve analytically, and so
produce a value of the integral for comparison.

Example 11.63 We use the Monte Carlo *hit or miss* method to determine $\int_0^2 xe^{-x^2/2}dx$.
See Figure 11.27.

Table 11.12. *Comparative results for the* hit and miss (θ_1) *and* sample mean (θ_2) *methods of Monte Carlo, for the integral I in Example 11.63. The correct value to three decimal places is 0.865.*

n	θ_1	θ_2
10	1.400	0.712
100	0.780	0.790
1000	0.882	0.860
10 000	0.885	0.865
20 000	0.864	0.865

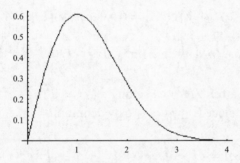

Figure 11.27 The graph of $y = xe^{-x^2/2}$.

We take $a = 0, b = 2$, and box height $c = 1$. The value of the integral I to three decimal places is 0.865, and (11.68) says that with $\delta = 1/10$ we may be 90% sure the estimate is within 0.02 of this if the number of trials is $n \geq (0.865)(1.135)/(0.02)^2(0.1)$ or approximately 24 500. In fact 20 000 trials estimated I as 0.864. More details are given in Table 11.12, comparing the present method with a second which we now describe.

Exercise In Example 11.63, how big a sample gives 90% certainty of obtaining an estimate within 0.01 of the true?

Method 2: a sample mean The idea is to represent the integral I of (11.64) as an expected value, generate variates $X_1, \ldots, X_n$ from the pdf (possibly a tall order) and then estimate I by a sample mean. More particularly, if $\pi(x)$ is any pdf which is positive when $g(x) \neq 0$ we may write

$$I = \int_a^b g(x)\mathrm{d}x = \int_a^b \frac{g(x)}{\pi(x)}\pi(x)\,\mathrm{d}x = E[g(x)/\pi(x)], \qquad (11.69)$$

where X has $g(x)$ as its pdf. The simplest choice for π is $\pi(x) = 1/(b-a)$, the pdf of a random variable X uniform on $[a, b]$. This gives $I = E[(b-a)g(x)] = (b-a)E[g(x)]$, to be estimated unbiasedly as $\theta_2 = (b - a)\overline{g(X)}$, or

$$\theta_2 = \frac{b - a}{n} \sum_{i=1}^{n} g(X_i).$$ (11.70)

It appears from Table 11.12 that the sample mean method is the more accurate. We investigate this via variances, starting with the result below.

Theorem 11.64 *In the above notation, the estimator θ_2 is unbiased, and*

$$V(\theta_2) = \frac{1}{n} \left((b - a) \int_a^b g(x)^2 \mathrm{d}x - I^2 \right) \leq V(\theta_1).$$ (11.71)

Proof It remains to see that, because the X_i are iid, we have from (11.70) that

$$V(\theta_2) = n[(b - a)/n]^2 V[g(X)] = ((b - a)^2/n)\{E[g(X)^2] - E[g(X)]^2\}$$

$$= ((b - a)^2/n) \left(\int_a^b g(x)^2 \pi(x) \mathrm{d}x - (I/(b - a))^2 \right),$$

which gives the formula for $V(\theta^2)$ on setting $\pi(x) = 1/(b - a)$ and simplifying. With $B = c(b - a)$ we have, since $0 \leq g(x) \leq c$ by definition,

$$\frac{n}{b - a}[V(\theta_1) - V(\theta_2)] = cI - \int_a^b g(x)^2 \mathrm{d}x \geq cI - \int_a^b cg(x)\mathrm{d}x = cI - cI = 0.$$

Remarks 11.65 The fact that $V(\theta^2)$ is upper-bounded by $V(\theta_1)$ explains the superior performance of θ_2 seen in Table 11.12. It can be shown that the inequality holds generally (Hammersley & Handscomb, 1964), indicating that the way ahead lies with improving the sampling technique. In the next section we introduce decisive improvements due to Metropolis, Hastings and others through the introduction of Markov chains. Meanwhile, here are the short comparative algorithms for the two methods.

ALGO 11.14 Estimate 1 *for $\int_a^b g(x)\mathrm{d}x$, $g(x) \leq c$*	*ALGO 11.15. Estimate 2* *for $\int_a^b g(x)\mathrm{d}x$*
Generate $U_1, V_1, \ldots, U_n, V_n$ in $U(0, 1)$ Set $X_i = a + (b - a)U_i$, $Y_i = cV_i$ Count n_H, the number of i for which $Y_i \leq g(X_i)$ Return $c(b - a)n_H/n$.	Generate $U_1, \ldots, U_n$ in $U(0, 1)$ Set $X_i = a + (b - a)U_i$ Set $S = g(X_1) + \cdots + g(X_n)$ Return $(b - a)S/n$.

Summary of advantages of Monte Carlo (see Kalos & Whitlock, 1986) Let NQ stand for numerical quadrature, or determining an integral by a standard numerical method. In one dimension, NQ is better than Monte Carlo, but NQ is dimension-dependent, and in higher dimensions things are different.

(i) Convergence of Monte Carlo integration is independent of dimension, hence there is always some dimension above which it converges faster than any NQ method.

(ii) A Monte Carlo method handles complicated regions much better than NQ.

(iii) Monte Carlo can always obtain greater accuracy by an increased number of sample points, whereas NQ will usually require higher-order approximation.

(iv) NQ may present great difficulties in error estimation, whereas in the Monte Carlo case we have a sample from which variance and more sophisticated error indications may be computed (further details may be found in Gilks *et al.*, 1997).

11.4.3 Markov Chain Monte Carlo

Our present objective is to improve the Monte Carlo sample mean method as a technique for evaluating integrals which are not otherwise amenable, especially, but not exclusively, those required for a Bayesian approach. This means finding a sampling method which minimises or at least reduces the variance of the estimate. We mention three standard methods before proceeding to the Markov chain approach of this section.

Reducing dimension – if possible, first integrate analytically with respect to a subset of the variables.

Importance sampling – we aim to identify subregions that contribute most to the integral and take a proportionately higher number of samples there.

Stratified sampling – we divide the domain of (usually) a single variable into subintervals and sample from each separately. A useful technique is to perform importance sampling, then stratify where the new formulation renders this convenient.

To establish notation, let $f(x)$ be a function and $\pi(x)$ a pdf, on the subspace S of real k-space $\mathbf{R}^k$, for some k. We seek the expected value of $f(x)$ with respect to $\pi(x)$,

$$E[f(x)] = \int_S f(x)\pi(x)\mathrm{d}x. \tag{11.72}$$

In the present context, $\pi(x)$ may be known only up to a constant γ, when the integral becomes $\gamma \int f(x)\pi(x)\mathrm{d}x$ with $\gamma = 1/\int \pi(x)\mathrm{d}x$; however, γ will not normally need to be determined, as we see shortly. We approximate $E[f(x)]$ as the mean of a sample $X_1 \ldots, X_n$ drawn from $\pi(x)$,

$$E[f(x)] \approx \frac{1}{n}\sum_{i=1}^n f(X_i), \quad (X_i \sim \pi). \tag{11.73}$$

A Markov chain If we could ensure the samples were independent and as many as we like, then the Weak Law of Large Numbers (10.29) would guarantee arbitrarily high accuracy with arbitrarily high probability. However, it suffices to get $\{X_t\}$ ranging over E in the correct proportions for our density $\pi(x)$ (cf. importance sampling), and the Metropolis–Hastings algorithm achieves this by drawing $X_1, X_2, \ldots$ from a cleverly constructed Markov chain with $\pi(x)$ as stationary distribution (cf. Theorem 11.59).

Part of the key to this lies in adapting the accept–reject concept of von Neumann, which we have already encountered in Section 11.3.4. Given the latest generated sample X_t, a proposal Y for X_{t+1} is generated from a *proposal distribution* $q(Y|X)$, with $X = X_t$. In principle the algorithm works for any choice of q (Theorem 11.66), though some choices result in better convergence. The proposal for X_{t+1} is accepted with probability $\alpha(X_t, X_{t+1})$, where

$$\alpha(X, Y) = \text{Min}\left(1, \frac{\pi(Y)q(X|Y)}{\pi(X)q(Y|X)}\right). \tag{11.74}$$

Here it is apparent that π and q need only be known up to constant multiples. The minimum condition avoids a probability greater than 1, but does much more than that (see the proof of Theorem 11.66). Leaving questions of convergence till later, the Metropolis–Hastings algorithm may be stated thus:

ALGO 11.16 Markov Chain Monte Carlo sampling

Initialise X_0
Repeat for $t = 0, 1, 2, \ldots$
    Generate $Y \sim q(Y|X_t)$
    Generate $U \sim U(0, 1)$
    If $U \leq \alpha(X_t, Y)$ set $X_{t+1} = Y$, else $X_{t+1} = X_t$
Until convergence occurs.

The next result ensures that a sequence of variates $\{X_i\}$ generated by ALGO 11.16 will, after a period of convergence, or 'burn-in time', follow the distribution $\pi(x)$. For the second, necessary part, and for further information, we refer to Roberts (1996) and Tierney (1994, 1996). For statement and proof we recall from Remarks 11.61 the notations of continuous state space E, transition kernel $p(X_{t+1}|X_t)$, and its n-step extension $p^{(n)}(X_n|X_0)$.

Theorem 11.66 *For the Metropolis–Hastings algorithm, the following hold, independently of the choice of X_0 and of the proposal distribution q: (i) $\pi(x)$ is a stationary distribution of the Markov chain, (ii) $p^{(n)}(X_n|X_0) \rightarrow \pi(x)$ as $n \rightarrow \infty$.*

Proof (i) We begin by establishing the equality

$$p(X_{t+1}|X_t) = q(X_{t+1}, X_t)\alpha(X_t, X_{t+1}) + \tau(X_{t+1} = X_t)(1 - A_t), \tag{11.75}$$

$$\text{where} \quad A_t = \int_E q(Y|X_t)\alpha(X_t, Y)dY \tag{11.76}$$

and τ is a function which equals 1 if its argument is TRUE, otherwise zero. Consider ALGO 11.16. For given X_t, we may think of $q(Y|X_t)$ as the probability that Y is proposed, and $\alpha(X_t, Y)$ as the probability that Y is then accepted. Then A_t is the probability that *some* Y is proposed and accepted. The two terms of (11.75) arise from the mutually exclusive possibilities that either some candidate is accepted, or none.

In the next required equality, to be applied to (11.75), each side is converted into the other by interchanging the expressions t and $t + 1$:

$$\pi(X_t)q(X_{t+1}|X_t)\alpha(X_t, X_{t+1}) = \pi(X_{t+1})q(X_t|X_{t+1})\alpha(X_{t+1}, X_t). \quad (11.77)$$

To prove this, we look directly at the definition (11.74) of α. There are two possibilities, Case 1 in which $\pi(X_{t+1})q(X_t|X_{t+1}) > \pi(X_t)q(X_{t+1}|X_t)$ and Case 2 with the inequality $\leq$. In Case 1 we have

$$\alpha(X_t, X_{t+1}) = 1, \alpha(X_{t+1}, X_t) = \frac{\pi(X_t)q(X_{t+1}|X_t)}{\pi(X_{t+1})q(X_t|X_{t+1})},$$

hence (11.77) holds, and similarly in Case 2 with X_t and X_{t+1} interchanged.

Now we are ready to use this with (11.75) to obtain what is known as the *detailed balance equation* of the chain, namely

$$\pi(X_t)p(X_{t+1}|X_t) = \pi(X_{t+1})p(X_t|X_{t+1}). \quad (11.78)$$

To see this we note that, according to (11.75), the left hand side minus the right of (11.78) is

$$\pi(X_t)q(X_{t+1}|X_t)\alpha(X_t, X_{t+1}) + \pi(X_t)\tau(X_{t+1} = X_t)$$

$$\times \left(1 - \int_E q(Y, X_t)\alpha(X_t, Y)dY\right) - \pi(X_{t+1})q(X_t|X_{t+1})\alpha(X_{t+1}, X_t)$$

$$-\pi(X_{t+1})\tau(X_{t+1} = X_t)\left(1 - \int_E q(Y, X_{t+1})\alpha(X_{t+1}, Y)dY\right)$$

$$= \tau(X_{t+1} = X_t)\{\pi(X_t)[\ldots] - \pi(X_{t+1})[\ldots]\}, \quad \text{by (11.7)}$$

where the expressions $[\ldots]$ are read respectively from the previous lines. Now, if $X_{t+1} = X_t$ then the second factor is zero, whereas $X_{t+1} = X_t$ implies by definition that $\tau = 0$. Thus (11.78) is proved. Finally, integrating both sides of this equation with respect to X_t, we obtain

$$\int_E \pi(X_t)p(X_{t+1}|X_t)dX_t = \int_E \pi(X_{t+1})p(X_t|X_{t+1})dX_t$$
$$= \pi(X_{t+1})\int_E p(X_t|X_{t+1})dX_t$$
$$= \pi(X_{t+1}), \quad \text{since} \quad p(X_t|X_{t+1}) \text{ is a pdf.}$$

This is a statement that $\pi(x)$ is stationary (see (11.61b)), which completes the proof of (i).

Choosing the proposal distribution q Although the Metropolis–Hastings algorithm converges ultimately for any q, the actual choice for a particular problem may affect considerably the number of iterations required for reasonable accuracy, and some experimentation may well be desirable. We illustrate two common types of proposal distribution.

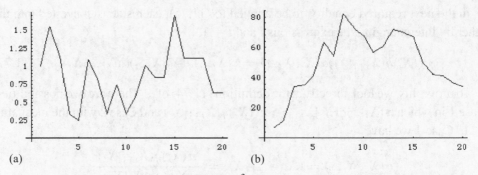

Figure 11.28 The case $\pi(x) = \gamma x \exp(-x^2/2)$ $(0 \le x \le 2)$, and $q(Y|X)$ uniform, independent of X. (a) The first 20 samples. Horizontal segments denote rejected proposals. (b) Frequencies out of 1000 for sample values from 0 to 2 in 20 intervals of width 0.1. The distribution so far is very roughly $\pi(x)$, the function shown in Figure 11.27.

Figure 11.29 Representation of some possible steps in a 2D random walk.

Example 11.67 *The independence sampler.* We take $q(Y|X) = q(Y)$, independently of the previous sample, X. The expression for $\alpha(x, y)$ simplifies to $\text{Min}[1, \lambda(y)/\lambda(x)]$, where $\lambda(y) = \pi(y)/q(y)$, a function of y alone. We show in Figure 11.28 some results with q uniform, independent of both X and Y.

Example 11.68 (*The random walk sampler*) Here the probability of Y being proposed depends only on its distance from X. Thus, all directions are equally likely, as in the best-known notion of a random walk (Kaye, 1989) but the *length* of the step from X to Y is governed by a probability distribution $q(y|x) = h(|y - x|)$. See Figure 11.29.

Since $|y - x| = |x - y|$, this form for q implies in particular that, as in the original Metropolis algorithm, q is *symmetric*, meaning that $q(y|x) = q(x|y)$, so that these expresssions cancel to give $\alpha(x, y) = \text{Min}[1, \pi(y)/\pi(x)]$. A widely used choice is to take q to be normal with mean X. Thus in the 1-dimensional case

$$
\begin{aligned}
&q(y|x) = \gamma e^{-(y-x)^2/2\sigma^2}, \\
&\alpha(x, y) = \text{Min}[1, \pi(y)/\pi(x)],
\end{aligned}
\tag{11.79}
$$

where $\gamma = (2\pi\sigma^2)^{-1/2}$. That is, $q = h(|y - x|)$ with $h(z) = \gamma e^{-z^2/2\sigma^2}$. We explore cases $\sigma^2 = 9$ and $\sigma^2 = 1/2$ in Figure 11.30.

Remarks 11.69 (1) As touched upon earlier, an important characteristic of the MCMC method is that a large sample is available for statistics. In particular, we may test the hypothesis that the samples do indeed follow the desired distribution $\pi(x)$, using the

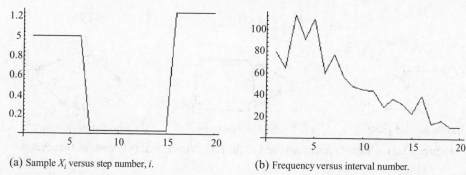

(a) Sample X_i versus step number, i. (b) Frequency versus interval number.

Figure 11.30 The case $\pi(x) = \gamma x \exp(-x^2/2)$ $(0 \leq x \leq 2)$, and $q(.|X) \sim N(X, \sigma^2)$. We consider (a) $\sigma^2 = 9$, the first 20 steps: too large a variance results in very slow mixing/convergence, (b) $\sigma^2 = 1/2$, the frequency distribution based on 1000 steps, divided into 20 intervals, shows superior convergence to the case of q uniform in Figure 11.28(b).

methods of Section 11.1.6. Thus we divide the interval [0, 2] into four equal subintervals, with $N = 1000$ samples, and compare the theoretical frequencies Np_i with sample frequencies f_i by the statistic

$$z = \sum_{i=1}^{4} (f_i - Np_i)^2 / Np_i = 8.74.$$

There are no parameters to be estimated, so there are $4 - 1 = 3$ degrees of freedom. According to Table 11.5 we should accept the $\pi(x)$ hypothesis at the 1% significance level if z lies in the interval [0, 11.3], which it does.

(2) Though we have worked with a 1-dimensional variable for illustration, the MCMC method deals also with general n-dimensional variables, whose pdfs may be hard to compute/handle. In the next few sections we seek to ameliorate this problem.

(3) For more information on issues of convergences, see Gelman (1996).

References *Texts*: Gilks *et al.* (1997), Robert and Casella (1999). *Pioneering papers*: Metropolis *et al.* (1953), Hastings (1970).

11.4.4 Bayesian networks

Here we approach the task of finding the distribution $\pi(x)$ for the application of MCMC methods and others. This in general can be difficult but is much facilitated by the Bayesian network approach, in which conditionals are combined into a full pdf by use of a Directed Acyclic Graph, or DAG (Frey, 1998). In the next section we use Bayesian networks for a second problem, that of determining the pdf of one variable given the rest (for Markov Random Fields). In Chapter 13 we apply belief propagation to such networks, for decoding convolution codes and the remarkable turbocodes; the first vision application in the present context is Bayesian Image Restoration, in Section 11.4.6. We need some graphical notation.

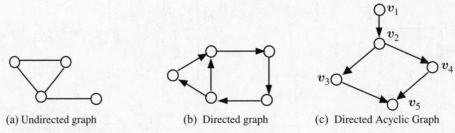

(a) Undirected graph　　　　(b) Directed graph　　　　(c) Directed Acyclic Graph

Figure 11.31 Graph types mentioned in the text. Notice that (b) contains two cycles.

Notation 11.70 A *(directed) graph* is abstractly a pair $G = (V, E)$, where V is a finite set of points $\{v_1, \ldots, v_n\}$, also called *nodes* or *vertices*, and E is a set of (ordered) pairs $(v_i, v_j) (i \neq j)$ called *edges*. A graph is represented in the plane by points or small circles for vertices, with a line segment between v_i and v_j to represent an edge (v_i, v_j). If (v_i, v_j) is ordered, the segment becomes an arrow $v_i \rightarrow v_j$, referred to as a *directed edge*. We then call v_i a *parent* of v_j, which is in turn a *child* of v_i. If there is a sequence of vertices $w_1 \rightarrow w_2 \rightarrow \cdots \rightarrow w_r$, where w_i is a parent of $w_{i+1}(1 \leq i \leq r - 1)$ we say w_1 is an *ancestor* of w_r, which is a *descendant* of w_1. If $w_r = w_1$ the sequence is a *cycle*.

We emphasise that in a directed graph every edge is directed. If also there are no cycles, we have a *Directed Acyclic Graph (DAG)*, as illustrated in Figure 11.31.

Ancestral orderings A *source* node/vertex is one with no parent. Thus Figure 11.31(b) has no source node whilst (c) has exactly one, namely v_1. An *ancestral ordering* is a relabelling of the vertices as, say, $y_1, \ldots, y_n$, so that the ancestors of a vertex precede it in the ordering. This is clearly equivalent simply to the parents of each vertex preceding it or, again, to the children of each vertex following it. In Figure 11.31(c) the ordering $v_1, \ldots, v_5$ is already ancestral. Here is the key lemma showing how such orderings may be constructed.

Lemma 11.71 *Every Directed Acyclic Graph has (i) a source node, and (ii) an ancestral ordering.*

Proof Suppose G is a Directed Acyclic Graph with n nodes. For (i), choose any vertex v, then any parent w of v, and so on. Since the number of vertices is finite and our construction cannot form a cycle, we must eventually encounter a node with no parent, i.e. a source node. For (ii), let y_1 be a source node, which exists by (i), and form a subgraph G_2 by removing y_1 and all edges starting at y_1. Then G_2 is acyclic and so contains a source node y_2. Repeating this we obtain subgraphs $G_2, \ldots, G_n$ and nodes $y_1, \ldots, y_n$, where the children of y_i follow y_i in the ordering $(1 \leq i \leq n - 1)$. Thus $y_1, \ldots, y_n$ is an ancestral ordering of G.

ALGO 11.17 Ancestral ordering for a directed acyclic graph

(i) To obtain a source node: choose any node y
    Repeat let y be any parent of y
    Until y is a source node.
(ii) To obtain an ancestral ordering of $G = G_1$
    Repeat for $i = 1, 2, 3, \ldots$
        Choose any source node y_i in G_i
        Construct G_{i+1} by removing y_i and all edges from y_i
    Until G_{i+1} is a single vertex y_n
Then $y_1, \ldots, y_n$ is an ancestral ordering.

Exercise Find a second ancestral ordering for the DAG of Figure 11.31.

Definition 11.72 (*Bayesian networks*) (i) Let G be a DAG with vertex set V. We need a notation for vertices relating to a given vertex v_k. Since p already stands for probability, let $\boldsymbol{u}_k$ be the set of all parents of v_k (u for 'upper'), $\boldsymbol{c}_k$ the children, $\boldsymbol{d}_k$ the descendants, and $\boldsymbol{n}_k = V \backslash \{v_k\} \backslash \boldsymbol{d}_k$ the non-descendants. (ii) A *Bayesian network* for a set of random variables $V = \{v_1, \ldots, v_n\}$ consists of a DAG with a vertex for each variable, and a set of *probability functions* $p(v_k | \boldsymbol{u}_k)$, $1 \le k \le n$, such that

$$p(v_k | \boldsymbol{u}_k \cup \boldsymbol{w}) = p(v_k | \boldsymbol{u}_k), \quad \text{if} \quad \boldsymbol{w} \subseteq \boldsymbol{n}_k. \tag{11.80}$$

Thus v_k is conditionally independent of any combination of its non-descendents, *given its parents*. The edges directed towards each vertex are of course implied by the sets $\boldsymbol{u}_k$ specified in (11.80). Notice that $\boldsymbol{u}_k$ contains neither ancestors of v_k (besides parents), nor children of v_k, variables which in general might give information about v_k itself; also, we do not assume the v_k already follow an ancestral ordering. In spite of this, we have the following result yielding the full joint distribution of $(v_1, \ldots, v_n)$ in terms of parental influence only.

Theorem 11.73 (*Joint pdf from a Bayesian network*) If $p(v_k | \boldsymbol{u}_k)$ are the probability functions of a Bayesian network for random variables $v_1, \ldots, v_n$ then a joint pdf is given by $\prod_k p(v_k | \boldsymbol{u}_k)$, or

$$p(v_1, \ldots, v_n) = \prod_{k=1}^{n} p(v_k | \text{the parents of } v_k). \tag{11.81}$$

Proof Since the right hand side of (11.81) is independent of the order of variables, and an ancestral ordering exists by Lemma 11.71, it suffices to prove (11.81) in the case that $v_1, \ldots, v_n$ are ancestrally ordered. Now, the Chain Rule for conditional probabilities (Section 10.1.3) gives

$$p(v_1, \ldots v_n) = \prod_k p(v_k | v_1, \ldots, v_{k-1}). \tag{11.82}$$

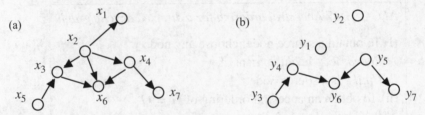

Figure 11.32 (a) Directed Acyclic Graph, (b) result of choosing and removing the first two vertices y_1, y_2 of an ancestral ordering. By now the rest of a possible ordering is obvious, and is indicated.

But, because $v_1, \ldots, v_n$ is an ancestral ordering, we have by definition of $\boldsymbol{u}_k$ and $\boldsymbol{n}_k$ that

$$\boldsymbol{u}_k \subseteq \{v_1, \ldots, v_{k-1}\} \subseteq \boldsymbol{n}_k, \tag{11.83}$$

and hence we may make the following partition into disjoint subsets:

$$\{v_1, \ldots, v_{k-1}\} = \boldsymbol{u}_k \cup \boldsymbol{w}, \quad \text{where } \boldsymbol{w} = \{v_1, \ldots, v_{k-1}\}\backslash \boldsymbol{u}_k \subseteq \boldsymbol{n}_k. \tag{11.84}$$

Finally, putting these facts together,

$$p(v_1, \ldots, v_n) = \prod_k p(v_k | \boldsymbol{u}_k \cup \boldsymbol{w}) \qquad \text{by (11.82) and (11.84)}$$

$$= \prod_k p(v_k | \boldsymbol{u}_k) \qquad \text{by (11.80), since } \boldsymbol{w} \subseteq \boldsymbol{n}_k.$$

Example 11.74 (*Markov chains*) A Markov chain is a special case of a Bayesian network. To prove this we consider a chain $X_1, \ldots, X_n, Y, Z$ and deduce (11.80) in the form

$$p(z|y, \boldsymbol{w}) = p(z|y), \qquad \text{for } \boldsymbol{w} \subseteq \{X_1, \ldots, X_n\}.$$

Proof $p(\boldsymbol{w}, y, z) = \displaystyle\sum_{x_i : X_i \notin \boldsymbol{w}} p(x_1, \ldots, x_n, y, z) = \sum_{x_i : X_i \notin \boldsymbol{w}} p(x_1, \ldots, x_n, y) p(z|y) =$
$p(\boldsymbol{w}, y) p(z|y)$, giving $p(z|y, \boldsymbol{w}) = p(\boldsymbol{w}, y, z)/p(\boldsymbol{w}, y) = p(z|y)$, as required.

(2) (*More general cases*) We show in Figure 11.32(a) a Bayesian network for the components of a random vector $X = (X_1, \ldots, X_7)$ with, as usual, the lower case lettering. Applying (11.81) we obtain the joint pdf $p(x_1, \ldots, x_7) =$
$p(x_1|x_2)p(x_2)p(x_3|x_2, x_5)p(x_4|x_2)p(x_5)p(x_6|x_2, x_3, x_4)p(x_7|x_4)$.

Example 11.75 Figure 11.33(a) depicts a Bayesian network connecting variables in an investigation of the effects and spread of Hepatitis B in West Africa (Spiegelhalter *et al.*, 1996). In part (b) the diagram is extended to show the existence of certain deterministic relations involved in the calculation, with shading on circles for observed variables (variables from which readings were to be taken).

Applying (11.81) to the Bayesian network (a), and considering the five source nodes first,

$$p(\alpha_0, \sigma_\alpha, \beta_0, \sigma_\beta, \sigma, \alpha_i, \beta_i, y_{ij}) =$$
$$p(\alpha_0)p(\sigma_\alpha)p(\beta_0)p(\sigma_\beta)p(\sigma)p(\alpha_i|\alpha_0, \sigma_\alpha)p(\beta_i|\beta_0, \sigma_\beta)p(y_{ij}|\alpha_i, \beta_i, \sigma). \tag{11.85}$$

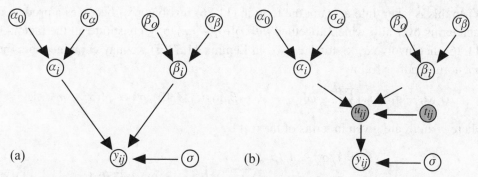

Figure 11.33 Bayesian network (a) and an expanded form (b), for Example 11.75.

To fill in these pdfs requires hypotheses gathered variously from evidence, experience, and tentative trial. For the time being we will keep expressions reasonably compact by using the standard normal pdf $\phi(x) = (2\pi\sigma^2)^{-1/2}e^{-x^2/2}$, so that $p(z) \sim N(a, b^2)$ means $p(z) = \phi[(z - a)/b)]$. The source nodes will be allocated priors which use the gamma distribution $g(z) \sim \Gamma_{a,b}$, that is $g(z) = (a^u/\Gamma(b))z^{b-1}e^{-ax}$ (see Table 9.10).

Priors $\alpha_0, \beta_0 \sim N(0, 10^4)$, $\sigma^{-2}, \sigma_\alpha^{-2}, \sigma_\beta^{-2} \sim \Gamma(^1/_{100}, ^1/_{100})$, writing $\Gamma(a, b)$ for $\Gamma_{a,b}$.

Conditional distributions $\alpha_i \sim N(\alpha_0, \sigma_\alpha^2)$, $\beta_i \sim N(\beta_0, \sigma_\beta^2)$, $y_{ij} \sim N(\mu_{ij}, \sigma^2)$.

Deterministic relation $\mu_{ij} = \alpha_i + \beta_i \log(t_{ij}/730)$.

It was convenient to specify the distributions $p(\sigma)$ via the distributions $g(\tau)$, with $\tau = \sigma^{-2}$. Then Formula (9.32) for the pdf of a function of a random variable gives $p(\sigma) = 2g(\sigma^{-2})/\sigma^3$, and similarly for σ_α and σ_β. Here $g(x) = \gamma x^{-0.99}e^{-0.01x}$, where $\gamma = (0.01)^{0.01}/\Gamma(0.01)$. After substitutions, the result is

$$p(\alpha_0, \sigma_\alpha, \beta_0, \sigma_\beta, \sigma, \alpha_i, \beta_i, y_{ij}) = \phi\left(\frac{\alpha_0}{10^4}\right)\phi\left(\frac{\beta_0}{10^4}\right)\frac{2g(\sigma^{-2})}{\sigma^3}\frac{2g(\sigma_\alpha^{-2})}{\sigma_\alpha^3}\frac{2g(\sigma_\beta^{-2})}{\sigma_\beta^3}$$
$$\times \phi[(\alpha_i - \alpha_0)/\sigma_\alpha]\phi[(\beta_i - \beta_0)/\sigma_\beta]$$
$$\times \phi[(y_{ij} - \alpha_i - \beta_i \log(t_{ij}/730))/\sigma]. \qquad (11.86)$$

Example 11.76 (*Expansion of Example* 11.75) We now give some more details of the current example, including the implications of subscripts i, j, and then simplify the resulting expanded version of (11.86).

(i) y measures, from a blood sample, a person's level of immunity to HB (Hepatitis B). Measurements were made for each of 106 infants, at fairly regular intervals.

(ii) y_{ij} denotes the jth sample from the ith infant, taken at time t_{ij}, and having expected value μ_{ij}. Let $j = 1, 2, \ldots, n_i$.

(iii) A deterministic straight line relationship was discovered between μ_{ij} and $\log t_{ij}$, with gradient β_i, namely that given above.

Thus, Figure 11.33 is to be regarded as a DAG 'layer' corresponding to infant i, and the figure implies a node y_{ij} (and its expanded version in (b)) for each of $j = 1, 2, \ldots, n_i$.

When this is taken into account the term in (11.86) involving y_{ij} becomes a product of such terms over all j which, together with $\phi[(\alpha_i - \alpha_0)/\sigma_\alpha]$, constitute all the factors in (11.86) that involve α_i. Setting $x = \alpha_i$ in Lemma 11.37(ii) we may combine them into *one* normal pdf as follows:

$$\phi[(\alpha_i - \alpha_0)/\sigma_\alpha] \prod_{j=1}^{n_i} \phi[(y_{ij} - \alpha_i - \beta_i \log(t_{ij}/730))/\sigma] \propto \phi[(\alpha_i - m)/s],$$

where m and s are given in terms of the rest by

$$1/s^2 = 1/\sigma_\alpha^2 + n_i/\sigma^2,$$
$$m/s^2 = \alpha_0/\sigma_\alpha^2 + (1/\sigma^2) \sum_{j=1}^{n_i} [y_{ij} - \beta_i \log(t_{ij}/730)]. \tag{11.87}$$

(iv) Though the purpose of this example is to illustrate the use of a Bayesian network, we remark that the investigators apply MCMC via a Gibbs sampler, the most widely used method (see Section 11.4.5). As a result they establish the simple model for change in immunity over time: (immunity at time t)/(immunity at time 0) $\propto 1/t$.

Exercise Verify (11.87) *or* write out explicit formulae for m and s.

11.4.5 Markov Random Fields and the Gibbs sampler

Definition 11.77 The *Gibbs sampler* for a random vector $X = (X_1, \ldots, X_n)$ is characterised as a special case of MCMC by the following.

(i) Only one component is changed at a time – in fixed or random order. For example $(X_1, X_2, X_3) \rightarrow (X_1, Y_2, X_3)$.
(ii) The proposal distribution, q, is the *full conditional* distribution of X_i, namely $P(X_i|$ all other components).
(iii) Every proposal is accepted.

Calculating q Along with all other conditionals, q is determined in principle by the joint pdf of $(X_1, \ldots, X_n)$, though the actual derivation may be impracticable. However, if we have a Bayesian network as in Section 11.4.4 we can read off the required full conditionals directly, according to the following argument. We take advantage of the fact that q need only be known up to a constant multiple; the proportionality symbol will be used as previously to express the fact that we are omitting such constants. Let v be any vertex, with children $c(v)$, and write V_{-v} for $V \backslash \{v\}$. Then q becomes, by (11.81),

$$p(v|V_{-v}) = p(v, V_{-v})/p(V_{-v}) = p(V)/p(V_{-v}) \tag{11.88}$$
$$\propto \Pi\{\text{terms in } p(V) \text{ that contain } v\} \text{ (see below)} \tag{11.89}$$
$$= p(v \,|\text{parents of } v) \prod_{w \in c(v)} p(w \,|\text{parents of } w). \tag{11.90}$$

In line (11.89) the proportionality symbol signifies that we *omit not only $p(V_{-v})$ but all other factors independent of v*. The remaining factors from the joint pdf (11.81) are formulated in the next line, (11.90). They may be read off from (11.81) or from the related graph. In particular they require no integration or summation to obtain.

$$p(v|V_{-v}) = \prod (\text{factors in (11.81) which refer to } v).$$ (11.90a)

Examples 11.78 We determine two of the full conditionals in Example 11.75 required for Gibbs sampling. (i) Consider α_i. According to (11.89), the required conditional is the product of $\phi[(\alpha_i - \alpha_0)/\sigma_\alpha]$ and all terms in (11.86) which contain α_i for any value of j from 1 to n_i (see Example 11.76(ii)). But this is precisely what we calculated at (11.87).

(ii) Consider σ_α. For simplicity we shall work with $\tau_\alpha = \sigma_\alpha^{-2}$. We calculate $p(\tau_\alpha|$ the rest) by applying the explicit formula (11.90). The children to be taken into account are by implication $\alpha_1, \ldots, \alpha_{106}$ (see Example 11.76(i)), and all have α_0 as a second parent. Let $c = 0.01$, which we take for both parameters in the gamma distribution, so that

$$p(\tau_\alpha|\text{ the rest}) \propto g(\tau_\alpha) \prod_{i=1}^{106} p(\alpha_i|\tau_\alpha, \alpha_0)$$

$$\propto \tau_\alpha^{c-1} e^{-c\tau_\alpha} \prod_{i=1}^{106} \tau_\alpha^{1/2} e^{-\frac{1}{2}(\alpha_i - \alpha_0)^2 \tau_\alpha}$$

$$= \tau_\alpha^{c-1+53} \exp\left[-\left(c + \frac{1}{2}\sum_i (\alpha_i - \alpha_0)^2\right)\tau_\alpha\right].$$

Thus $p(\tau_\alpha|$ the rest) $\sim \Gamma_{a,b}$, with parameters $a = 53.01$ and $b = 0.01 + \frac{1}{2}\sum_i (\alpha_i - \alpha_0)^2$.

Markov Random Fields For consistency the n full conditionals must satisfy restrictions, and a celebrated result of Hammersley and Clifford (Theorem 11.84) gives the consequences for the joint pdf $\pi(x)$. Consequences which, as we shall see, are welcome knowledge and useful in practice. The variables $X_1, \ldots, X_n$ are associated with graph points, now to be labelled $1, 2, \ldots, n$ respectively. These points are often called *sites*, especially when thought of as points in the plane.

Now, considering $p(x_i|x_1, \ldots, x_{i-1}, x_{i+1}, \ldots, x_n)$, it may be that some x_k may be omitted. Every j for which x_j may *not* be omitted is called a *neighbour* of i, the set of all such j being the *neighbourhood* Γ_i of i. We call $X_1, \ldots, X_n$ a *Markov Random Field* (MRF) *with neighbourhoods* $\Gamma_1, \ldots, \Gamma_n$. This notion lends itself naturally to modelling digital images. It is, as the name suggests, a generalisation of a Markov chain, in which case $\Gamma_i = \{i - 1, i + 1\}$ except for $\Gamma_1 = \{2\}$ and $\Gamma_n = \{n - 1\}$. The 2-elements Γ_i are explained by the Bayesian formula $p(x|y) = p(y|x)p(x)/p(y)$, which shows more generally that if j is a neighbour of i then i is a neighbour of j. Thus we may say simply that they are *neighbours*, and represent this by an undirected edge between graph points i, j.

In establishing the connection between MRFs and the Gibbs distribution, we follow the approach of Besag (1974) (though the argument in Lemma 11.82 differs slightly).

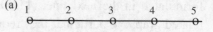

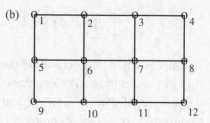

Figure 11.34 Graphs for Examples 11.79.

Example 11.79 (i) The graph of a Markov chain, with variables $X_1, \ldots, X_5$, exemplifying the simplest type of MRF, is shown in Figure 11.34(a).

(ii) Variables $X_1, \ldots, X_{12}$, with graph shown in Figure 11.34(b) as a *finite square lattice L of size* $a \times b$,

$$L = \{(r, s) : r = 1, 2, \ldots, a; \ s = 1, 2, \ldots, b\},$$

with *4-neighbour* system; that is, i and j are neighbours if and only if they are one unit apart in a horizontal or vertical direction.

(iii) Generalising (ii), we have an MRF whose variables are the grey values for images in which each pixel is statistically related to a small neighbourhood of surrounding pixels (see later in this section).

Assumptions 11.80 For present purposes we assume that (i) the variables are discrete, with finite joint sample space $\Omega = \{x: p(x) > 0\}$, (ii) a *positivity condition* holds: if $p(x_i) > 0$ for $1 \leq i \leq n$ then $p(x_1, \ldots, x_n) > 0$, and (iii) without loss of generality, each x_i can take the value 0 (by relabelling range spaces if necessary). Now we establish a formula holding for any x, y in Ω (Besag, 1974), which illustrates that many factorisations may be possible amongst the conditionals:

$$\frac{p(x)}{p(y)} = \prod_{i=1}^{n} \frac{p(x_i | x_1, \ldots, x_{i-1}, y_{i+1}, \ldots, y_n)}{p(y_i | x_1, \ldots, x_{i-1}, y_{i+1}, \ldots, y_n)}. \tag{11.91}$$

Proof We combine relations $p(x_n | x_1, \ldots, x_{n-1}) = p(x)/p(x_1, \ldots, x_{n-1})$ and $p(y_n | x_1, \ldots, x_{n-1}) = p(x_1, \ldots, x_{n-1}, y_n)/p(x_1, \ldots, x_{n-1})$ (cf. (11.88)) to introduce y_n beside the xs in a first step:

$$p(x) = \frac{p(x_n | x_1, \ldots, x_{n-1})}{p(y_n | x_1, \ldots, x_{n-1})} p(x_1, \ldots, x_{n-1}, y_n).$$

Now we perform a similar operation with x_{n-1} and y_{n-1} to obtain

$$p(x_1, \ldots, x_{n-1}, y_n) = \frac{p(x_{n-1} | x_1, \ldots, x_{n-2}, y_n)}{p(y_{n-1} | x_1, \ldots, x_{n-2}, y_n)} p(x_1, \ldots, x_{n-2}, y_{n-1}, y_n).$$

Continuing the process, we arrive at (11.91), the positivity condition ensuring the denominators involved are nonzero. This completes the proof.

Notation We display for reference two abbreviations it will be convenient to use. In the first, the *i*th value is absent, and in the (boldface) second it is set to zero.

$$x_{-i} = (x_1, \ldots, x_{i-1}, x_{i+1}, \ldots, x_n), \quad \text{and} \quad \mathbf{x}_i = (x_1, \ldots, x_{i-1}, 0, x_{i+1}, \ldots, x_n).$$
(11.92)

Corollary 11.81 *For any Markov Random Field* $X = (X_1, \ldots, X_n)$ *the conditional probability* $P(X_i = x_i, X_j = x_j, \ldots, X_k = x_k|$ the rest) *depends only on the values at sites* $i, j, \ldots, k$ *and their neighbours.*

Proof The case of $\{i, j, \ldots, k\} = \{1, 2\}$ shows how a proof is constructed in general. Considering the result for events A, B, C, that $P(A \cap B|C) = P(A|C)P(B|A \cap C)$ (easily verified from the definitions of (9.8)), we have as required

$$p(x_1, x_2|x_3, \ldots, x_n) = p(x_1|x_3, \ldots, x_n)p(x_2|x_1, x_3, \ldots, x_n) = p(x_1|\Gamma_1)p(x_2|\Gamma_2).$$

Exercise Prove the above formula for $P(A \cap B|C)$.

The Gibbs distribution Expressed positively, our goal is to establish the most general form of $p(x)$ for an MRF, given the neighbourhood structure. We shall do so by determining the most general form of a related function $Q(x)$ which, by the assumption $p(\mathbf{0}) > 0$, we may define as

$$Q(x) = \ln \frac{p(x)}{p(\mathbf{0})} \ (x \in \Omega).$$
(11.93)

To this end we consider the implications

$$e^{Q(x) - Q(\mathbf{x}_i)} = \frac{p(x)}{p(\mathbf{x}_i)} = \frac{p(x_i|x_{-i})p(x_{-i})}{p(0|x_{-i})p(x_{-i})} = \frac{p(x_i|x_{-i})}{p(0|x_{-i})}.$$
(11.94)

Lemma 11.82 *The function* $Q(x)$ *has the following unique expansion on* Ω, *where a function* $Q_{r \ldots s}$ *equals zero if any of its arguments are zero (the 'zero condition').*

$$Q(x) = \sum_{1 \leq i \leq n} Q_i(x_i) + \sum_{1 \leq i < j \leq n} Q_{ij}(x_i, x_j)$$

$$+ \sum_{1 \leq i < j < k \leq n} Q_{ijk}(x_i, x_j, x_k) + \cdots + Q_{12 \ldots n}(x).$$
(11.95)

Proof Notice first that, by definition, $Q(\mathbf{0}) = \ln(1) = 0$. There are two parts to the proof: (i) *uniqueness* – we show that if the $Q_{r \ldots s}$ exist satisfying (11.95) and the zero condition, then they are given by certain formulae in terms of $Q(x)$, and (ii) *existence* – we must show that these formulae actually do satisfy (11.95) and the zero condition. For *uniqueness*, then, we have, by the zero condition and (11.95), that for $1 \leq k \leq n$,

$$Q(x_1, \ldots, x_k, 0, \ldots, 0) = \text{all terms of (11.95) involving } x_1, \ldots, x_k \text{ only.}$$
(11.96)

Of course, a similar relation holds for any choice of k arguments from the n, and we are expressing this in terms of the first k only for easier reading. Now, the case $k = 1$ gives

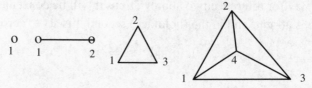

Figure 11.35 Cliques of sizes 1, 2, 3, 4. The first three are contained in the maximal clique of size 4.

$Q(x_1, 0, \ldots, 0) = Q_1(x_1)$, all other terms being zero. Also $Q_1(0) = Q(0, 0, \ldots, 0) = 0$. And similarly $Q_i(x_i)$ is uniquely $Q(0, \ldots, 0, x_i, 0, \ldots, 0)$, with $Q_i(0) = 0$. But now, the $Q_{r \ldots s}$ with k arguments are given by those with fewer than k arguments by (11.96) rearranged, as

$$Q_{12 \ldots k}(x_1, \ldots, x_k) = Q(x_1, \ldots, x_k, 0, \ldots, 0)$$
$$-(\text{all terms in } x_1, \ldots, x_k \text{ with fewer than } k \text{ arguments}). \qquad (11.97)$$

Further, if any of $x_1, \ldots, x_k$ are zero, the right hand side of (11.97) is zero, by general (11.96) with fewer than k arguments. This establishes uniqueness.

(ii) *Existence* We have already verified that the formulae for the $Q_{12 \ldots s}$ satisfy the zero condition. Now, the unique term $Q_{12 \ldots n}$ with n arguments is defined by (11.97) with $k = n$, but this is simply (11.95) itself rearranged. Thus, (11.95) holds with the $Q_{r \ldots s}$ given by the implicit formulae, and the proof is complete.

Example 11.83 In the case $n = 2$ of the lemma the right hand side $Q_1(x_1) + Q_2(x_2) + Q_{12}(x_1, x_2)$ equals $Q(x_1, 0) + Q(0, x_2) + [Q(x) - Q(x_1, 0) - Q(0, x_2)]$, which is $Q(x)$ as required.

Cliques To take full advantage of (11.95) we need another idea. A *clique* of graph points/sites is either a singleton $\{i\}$ or a subset in which every pair are neighbours, and is *maximal* if it is contained in no larger clique. The maximal cliques in Examples 11.79(i) and (ii) are all edges. We denote a typical clique by c and the set of all cliques by $\mathbf{C}$. The key result follows Figure 11.35, in which we give examples of cliques, each contained in the next.

Theorem 11.84 *(Hammersley & Clifford, 1974, unpublished) For any $1 \le i \le j < \cdots < s \le n$ the function $Q_{ij \ldots s}$ in the expansion (11.95) of $Q(x)$ is null (identically zero) unless the sites $i, j, \ldots, s$ form a clique. Subject to this restriction, the functions $Q_{r \ldots s}$ may be chosen arbitrarily.*

Proof Consider a pair of sites which are not neighbours, which, without loss of generality, we may take to be sites 1 and 2. Setting $x_1 = 0$ in (11.95) we see that $Q(x_1)$ is the sum of all terms in the expansion of $Q(x)$ which do not involve x_1 and therefore $Q(x) - Q(x_1)$ is the sum of all those that do. Hence, in the case $x_i = 0$ for $i > 2$ there holds

$$Q(x) - Q(x_1) = Q_1(x) + Q_{12}(x_1, x_2).$$

But (11.94) shows that $Q(x) - Q(x_1)$ does not vary with x_2 (2 is not a neighbour of 1), and so, for all x_1,

$$Q_1(x_1) + Q_{12}(x_1, x_2) = Q_1(x_1) + Q_{12}(x_1, 0) = Q_1(x_1),$$

whence Q_{12} is null. Similarly, using suitable values of x, we see in sucession that all 3-, 4-,..., n-variable Q-functions involving sites 1 and 2 must be null. Thus if $r \ldots s$ is not a clique, i.e. contains a pair of non-neighbours, then $Q_{r\ldots s}$ is null.

Conversely, any choice of Q-functions gives rise via (11.93) to a valid pdf $p(x)$ satisfying the positivity condition. Further, since $Q(x) - Q(x_i)$, as we have seen, depends upon x_k only if there is a non-null Q-function involving both x_i and x_k, it follows from (11.94) that the same holds for $p(x_i | x_{-i})$. This completes the proof.

Corollary 11.85 *(Equivalence of MRFs and Gibbs distribution) A random vector X is an MRF with respect to a neighbourhood system with cliques C if and only if its joint pdf has the form of a Gibbs distribution, namely*

$$\pi(x) = \gamma e^{-U(x)}, \quad with \quad U(x) = \sum_{c \in C} V_c(x), \tag{11.98}$$

where V_c is a function that depends only on the sites of clique c, and γ is a constant.

Remarks 11.86 (i) *The minus sign* of (11.98) is appended in agreement with the Gibbs distribution's origin in statistical physics; there V_c is typically interpreted as a potential energy and it is frequently helpful to maintain the analogy. Of course $V_c = -Q_{r\ldots s}$, where $c = \{r, \ldots, s\}$. We call $U(x)$ the *energy function*, and often work with this rather than $\pi(x)$.

(ii) *Maximal cliques* Since, for example, a general function of x_1 plus a general function of x_1, x_2 amounts to a general function of x_1, x_2, we may take the cliques in (11.98) to be maximal. This is usually done, even if only implicitly.

(iii) *Factorisation* Using the property $e^{a+b} = e^a \cdot e^b$, we may rewrite (11.98) as a useful factorisation into related clique potentials ψ_s, where $C = \{c_1, \ldots, c_m\}$, the set of cliques:

$$\pi(x) = \gamma \Pi_s \psi_s(c_s), \tag{11.99}$$

For example, the Markov chain $\overset{1}{\circ}\!\!-\!\!-\!\!-\!\!\overset{2}{\circ}\!\!-\!\!-\!\!-\!\!\overset{3}{\circ}$ has cliques $c_1 = \{1, 2\}$ and $c_2 = \{2, 3\}$, with a corresponding factorisation $p(x) = \gamma \psi_1(c_1) \psi_2(c_2) = [p(x_1)p(x_2|x_1)] \times p(x_3|x_2)$.

(iv) *Extension to general pdfs* As observed by Besag (1974), the Gibbs equivalence extends to a countably infinite sample space provided $\sum_x \exp Q(x)$ is finite, and to (absolutely) continuous $p(x)$ if $\exp Q(x)$ may be integrated over the whole of the sample space.

Simulated annealing A factor $1/T$ before the $\sum$ in (11.98) has the effect of introducing temperature T in the original physical situations, and in general if the temperature starts fairly 'high' and is judiciously lowered during Gibbs sampler iteration (see shortly) this avoids homing in on a premature conclusion. The original technique, a special feature of Gibbs distributions and MRFs, was named the 'heat bath' in physics, and called *simulated annealing* by Geman and Geman (1984) when they introduced it into the vision community.

The following result leads from the energy structure to this technique. Working with inverse temperature $\beta = 1/T$, consider the energy function $\beta U(x)$, with corresponding pdf $\pi^\beta(x) \propto e^{-\beta U(x)}$, or, inserting the constant,

$$\pi^\beta(x) = e^{-\beta U(x)} \Big/ \sum_z e^{-\beta U(z)}. \tag{11.100}$$

Theorem 11.87 *(See Winkler, 1991) Let π be a Gibbs distribution with energy function $U(x)$. Let m be the least value of $U(x)$ and write $M = \{z: U(z) = m\}$. Then*

$$\lim_{\beta \to \infty} \pi^\beta(x) = \begin{cases} 1/|M|, & \text{if } x \in M, \\ 0, & \text{otherwise.} \end{cases} \tag{11.101}$$

Further, for sufficiently large β, the function $\beta \to \pi^\beta(x)$ is increasing for $x \in M$ and decreasing for $x \notin M$.

Proof In the expression (11.100), we multiply top and bottom by $e^{\beta m}$ and split the sum into cases $U(z) = m$ and $U(z) > m$, obtaining

$$\pi^\beta(x) = \frac{e^{-\beta(U(x)-m)}}{\sum_{z:U(z)=m} e^{-\beta(U(z)-m)} + \sum_{z:U(z)>m} e^{-\beta(U(z)-m)}}. \tag{11.102}$$

Now consider the three exponential terms. If $U(z) = m$ then $\exp[-\beta(U(z) - m)] = \exp(0) = 1$, and the sum of such terms in the denominator equals $|M|$. Otherwise $U(z) > m$, implying $\exp[-\beta(U(z) - m)] \to 0$ as $\beta \to \infty$. As $\beta \to \infty$, therefore, if x is a minimum $\pi^\beta(x)$ increases monotonically to $1/|M|$, otherwise $\pi^\beta(x) \to 0$. For the rest, let $x \notin M$ and divide (11.102) through by its numerator to obtain in terms of $d(z) = U(z) - U(x)$:

$$\left(|\{z: d(z) = 0\}| + \sum_{d(z)<0} e^{-\beta d(z)} + \sum_{d(z)>0} e^{-\beta d(z)} \right)^{-1}.$$

It remains to show that this new denominator eventually increases with β. Differentiating it with respect to β gives

$$\sum_{d(z)<0} -d(z)e^{-\beta d(z)} + \sum_{d(z)>0} -d(z)e^{-\beta d(z)}.$$

As β increases without limit the first term tends to infinity and the second to zero. Therefore, for sufficiently large β, the derivative is positive, hence the denominator itself is increasing, and the function $\beta \to \pi^\beta(x)$ is decreasing, as required.

Conclusions (i) The limiting pdf of (11.101) as $\beta \to \infty$ is the uniform distribution on the set M of minimisers, (ii) sampling from this distribution yields minimisers of U,

(iii) sampling from π^β for high β gives approximate minima. Analysis concerning the implementation of (iii) leads to a *cooling schedule* for the temperature $T(k)$ at the kth sweep or update of the whole of x:

$$T(k) \propto 1/\ln k \quad (\beta = 1/T). \tag{11.103}$$

This is due to Geman and Geman (1984), who take the constant of proportionality to be 3 or 4, say $T(k) = 3/\ln k$. A geometrically decreasing temperature such as $T(k) \propto c^k$ $(0 < c < 1)$ may work well. For further information see their paper or Winkler (1991).

Applying Gibbs Finally, here is a formula that facilitates putting the Gibbs connection into practice, and assists in formulating priors for restoration problems and others (see next section). For the desired iteration we need the full conditionals $p(x_i | x_{-i})$ in terms of the potential functions.

Theorem 11.88 (*Full conditional formula*) *For a Markov random field* $X = (X_1, \dots, X_n)$, *with energy (11.98), we have*

$$p(x_i | x_{-i}) = \lambda \exp\left[-\sum_{c:i \in c} V_c(x) \right], \tag{11.104}$$

summed over the cliques which contain i, *and* $\lambda = 1/\sum p(x_i | x_{-i})$ *with summation over all* x_i *in the range space of* X_i.

Proof Dividing the cliques into those that contain i and those that do not, we define

$$S_i = \exp\left[-\sum_{c:i \in c} V_c(x) \right], \quad \text{and} \quad T_i = \exp\left[-\sum_{c:i \notin c} V_c(x) \right].$$

Then, recalling that $e^{a+b} = e^a \cdot e^b$, we have $p(x) = \gamma S_i T_i$ (i fixed), and hence

$$
\begin{aligned}
p(x_i | x_{-i}) &= p(x)/p(x_{-i}) & \text{since } p(x_i, x_{-i}) \text{ means } p(x) \\
&= S_i T_i / \sum (S_i T_i) & \text{over all } x_i \text{ in } R_{X_i} \\
&= S_i T_i / T_i \sum S_i & \text{since } T_i \text{ does } not \text{ depend on } x_i \\
&= S_i / \sum S_i, & \text{as asserted.}
\end{aligned}
$$

Example 11.89 (i) In this small but instructive example (our next is the image prior of Section 11.4.6), let the sites of $x_1, \dots, x_9$, with values in $\{1, 2, 3, 4, 5\}$, be arranged on a 3×3 lattice. The neighbours of a site are to be the nearest in a horizontal, vertical, or *diagonal* direction. Thus, in the representation in Figure 11.36, the central site 5 has eight neighbours, a corner has three, and an edge site other than a corner has five neighbours.

The clique functions For a clique $c = \{r, s\}$, define $V_c = 1$ if $x_r = x_s$, otherwise $V_c = 0$. Then $p(x_i | x_{-i})$ has by (11.104) an energy function $U_i = \sum V_c$ ($c: i \in c$) equal to the number of neighbours of site i with the same value as site i. This yields the following pdf for conditional probabilities at the central site $i = 5$, with normalisation constant λ given by $\lambda(3e^{-2} + 2e^{-1}) = 1$, or $\lambda = e^2/(3 + 2e)$. For example, if $x_5 = 1$ then site 5 has

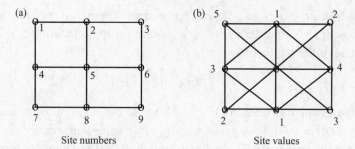

Figure 11.36 (a) The sites numbered and positioned on their lattice, (b) the graph showing *all* neighbour relations, and the site values except the central one, which we vary through its range in the present example.

two neighbours with the same value, and so $U_5 = 2$.

x_5	1	2	3	4	5
$U_5 =$ no. of equal neighbours	2	2	2	1	1
$p(x_5\|x_{-5})$	λe^{-2}	λe^{-2}	λe^{-2}	λe^{-1}	λe^{-1}

The normalisation constant λ is given by $\lambda = 1/(3e^{-2} + 2e^{-1})$, so we may conveniently express the finite pdf as a 5-vector, $p(x_5|x_{-5}) = (1, 1, 1, e, e)/(3 + 2e)$.

(ii) Mention should be made of the less interesting extreme cases (a) no neighbours, and (b) every point is a neighbour of every other, so that there is effectively no neighbourhood structure at all.

Exercise Find the conditional distribution $p(x_1|x_{-1})$ for Figure 11.36 with $x_5 = 5$ (see Exercise 11.22).

References *Texts*: Winkler (1991), Kinderman and Snell (1980). *Papers*: Geman & Geman (1984), Besag (1974).

11.4.6 Bayesian image restoration

It is natural to model a digital image as a Markov Random Field, or MRF, on the grounds that a pixel value is most influenced by its closest neighbours. Having done so, we find that, under quite broad assumptions concerning a degradation process, the consequent Bayesian posterior pdf for the original is also an MRF, and hence amenable to the Gibbs or more general MCMC sampling methods of the previous sections. We use sampling to estimate the *mode* of this pdf, that is, a hypothetical original image which maximises the pdf. This estimate of the original image is known therefore as the *maximum a posteriori*, or MAP, estimate.

Let x be a rectangular array of grey or colour values, at equally spaced points in an original 'true' image, and let y be the corresponding array of values recorded by some device such as a scanner, CCD camera, TV camera or remote sensing device. We may consider some sources of degradation under the four headings of Table 11.13.

Table 11.13. *Some principal sources of image degradation (see also Section 15.3).*

source	examples
optical	lens aberration or defocus
environmental	motion blur, atmospheric interference
electronic	1. thermal noise: electron fluctuations in components.
	2. shot noise: random arrival of photons (especially in emission tomography)
digitisation	1. limited bandwidth (see Fourier Transform, Chapters 14, 15).
	2. quantisation noise: errors due to rounding

Although we will not consider such full generality at this stage, the combined effect of these is generally modelled as a linear blur effect $x \to xB$ (x a row vector and B a matrix), followed by a nonlinear function Φ, and then by additive or multiplicative noise η. That is, in terms of random variables

$$Y = \Phi(XB) \circ \eta, \tag{11.105}$$

where $\circ$ denotes addition, multiplication, or possibly some other invertible operation on two arguments. We recall the Bayesian formulation for the posterior,

$$p(x|y) = p(x)p(y|x)/p(y) \propto p(x)p(y|x), \tag{11.106}$$

where proportionality $\propto$ means equality up to multiplication by a factor λ which is constant in the sense of being independent of x, and therefore recoverable as $\lambda = 1/\sum_x p(y|x)p(x) = 1/p(y)$ correctly. To evaluate the factors in (11.106) we must decide on a suitable prior for $p(x)$, and determine $p(y|x)$ from the details of the assumed noise model (11.105). Under the reasonable assumption that blur and noise at a given site i depend only on a set Γ_i of neighbours, the *product* $p(x)p(y|x)$ *is itself an MRF* (Geman & Geman, 1984), and therefore we may conveniently use Gibbs sampling to estimate it. We assume that blur and noise happen to sites independently, so that $p(y|x) = \Pi p(y_i|x)$. Now let $x_A = \{x_k : k \in A\}$ for a subset A of the sites. Then x_{Γ_i} denotes the set of all x_k that are neighbours of y_i and we may write

$$p(y|x) = \prod_{i=1}^{n} p(y_i|x_{\Gamma_i}). \tag{11.107}$$

Remark 11.90 The following relations not only are useful for our present purposes but provide an excellent exercise in handling conditionals.

$$p(x_i|x_{-1}) \propto p(x), \tag{11.108}$$

$$p(x_i|x_{-i}, y) \propto p(x|y). \tag{11.109}$$

It is important to notice that, in these results and their proofs, x_i for fixed i counts as the variable, with x_{-i} and y as parameters. Thus factors of $p(x_i|\ldots)$ that do not involve x_i may be taken as part of a normalisation constant, recoverable by a suitable summation over all values of x_i (see below). Alternatively, as here, their possible presence is indicated by a proportionality sign. We have, for (11.109),

$$p(x_i|x_{-i}, y) = p(x_i, x_{-i}, y)/p(x_{-i}, y) = p(x, y)/p(x_{-i}, y)$$
$$= p(x|y) \times [p(y)/p(x_{-i}, y)] \quad (*)$$
$$\propto p(x|y),$$

which may be written in terms of a proportionality or normalisation constant γ, as $p(x|y)/\gamma$, where γ is the sum of $p(x|y)$ over all values of x_i, namely

$$\gamma = \sum_{x_i} p(x|y) = \sum_{x_i} p(x_i, x_{-i}, y)/p(y) = p(x_{-i}, y)/p(y).$$

This correctly recovers the value apparent from (*). Equation (11.108) may be obtained by summing both sides of (11.109) over all values of y. The practical application of (11.109) is that, to obtain $p(x_i|x_{-i}, y)$ as required in Gibbs sampling, we may *start with* $p(x|y)$ *and simply pick out the factors that involve* x_i. These are given by (11.110) below. Indeed,

$$\begin{aligned} p(x_i|x_{-i}, y) &\propto p(x|y) && \text{by (11.109)} \\ &\propto p(x)p(y|x) && \text{by (11.106)} \\ &\propto p(x_i|x_{-i}) \prod_{k \in \Gamma_i} p(y_k|x_{\Gamma_k}) && \text{by (11.107), (11.108).} \end{aligned} \quad (11.110)$$

Exercise Prove (11.108) in the same manner as (11.109) (see Exercise 11.23).

Applications 11.91 (i) *The image prior* Let the *prior* for an original image be an MRF in which sites r, s are neighbours ($r \sim s$), if $\{r, s\}$ is a horizontal or vertical lattice edge. Then the (maximal) cliques are these edges. For energy potentials we use the Potts model (see e.g. Green, 1996) which means that, for a clique $c = \{r, s\}$, we let $V_c = 1_{x_r \neq x_s}$, the function which is 1 where the condition $x_r \neq x_s$ holds, and zero otherwise. By Theorem 11.88 the required conditional, which is $p(x_i|x_{-i})$, has energy function

$$\sum_{c:i \in c} V_c(x) = \sum_{r:r \sim i} V_{\{r,i\}}(x) = \sum_{r:r \sim i} 1_{x_r \neq x_i}. \quad (11.111)$$

(ii) *The noise model* Suppose the original image was degraded by Gaussian noise with zero mean and variance σ^2, *added independently to each pixel* (no neighbour dependency). That is, the Π part in (11.110) reduces to $k = i$, and

$$p(y_i|x_{\Gamma_i}) = p(y_i|x_i) \sim N(x_i, \sigma^2). \quad (11.112)$$

(iii) *The posterior conditional* The energy function $U_i(x)$ for the posterior $p(x_i|x_{-i}, y)$ of (11.110) is the sum of the energy (11.111) for $p(x_i|x_{-i})$ and the energy for $p(y_i|x_i)$ in (11.112). Since the normal pdf $\gamma \exp[-(y_i - x_i)^2/2\sigma^2]$ contributes energy $-(y_i - x_i)^2/2\sigma^2$, we have altogether

$$U_i(x_i) = \sum_{r:r \sim i} 1_{x_r \neq x_i} + (y_i - x_i)^2/2\sigma^2. \quad (11.113)$$

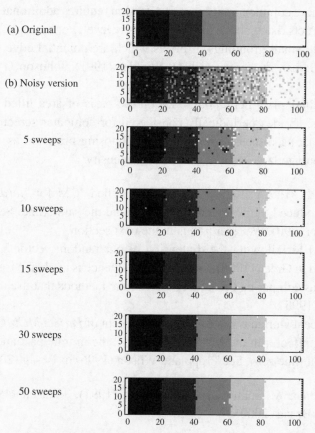

Figure 11.37 The Gibbs sampler applied to an original image (a) corrupted by noise with variance 1/4 into (b), with results shown after 5, 10, 15, 30, and 50 sweeps on temperature scedule $T(k) = 3/\log(1 + k)$.

Original image We start with the 20×100 rectangle of Figure 11.37(a), banded into five grey levels, with straight vertical boundaries, and use ALGO 11.8 to add noise with variance $\sigma^2 = 1/4$, to produce the corrupted version Figure 11.37(b). We perform a total of 50 Gibbs sweeps over the whole image, with *temperature schedule* $T(k) = 3/\log(1 + k)$; the results are shown after 5, 10, 15, 30 and 50 sweeps.

When Gibbs fails (*See Green, 1996*) In a similar manner to Bayesian restoration, one may perform Bayesian reconstruction for an emission tomography image. In this, the arrival of photons is modelled by a Poisson distribution and the energy function (11.111) has $1_{x_i \neq x_j}$ replaced by a more general function $\phi(x_i - x_j)$. The Gibbs sampler becomes impractical and we must resort to general MCMC which, though found to be 20 times more computationally expensive, is especially well-adapted to estimating accuracy of convergence. For further discussion, see Besag (2000).

Handling boundaries So far we have modelled only the pixel intensities, but the boundaries have been recovered reasonably well. However, with a greater number of pixel intensities and more complex images, edge detection requires additional modelling, a hierarchy of constructs rising above the pixel intensity level. For example, introducing and allocating pdfs to small groupings of pixels which are potential edge elements. Some references are Geman & Geman (1984), Winkler (1991), Johnson (1994) and Green (1996).

Johnson specifies pixel neighbourhoods on the basis of area filled not by squares, but by hexagons, an idea periodically considered for computer screens. His paper includes an iluminating discussion on the art of choosing priors so as, for example, to encourage/discourage large regions of constant intensity.

Related methods (i) An alternative to Gibbs, called ICM for *Iterated Conditional Modes*, was introduced by Besag, and others around the same time. See Besag (1986), (2000) or Green (1990). We refer to this in the next section.

(ii) A method for allowing the dimension of our random vector X to change with iteration is found in Green (1995). One nice consequence is a scheme for Bayesian curve fitting reported as comparing favourably with spline methods that use many more knots (Denison *et al.*, 1998).

(iii) Much recent work has focussed on the concept of *Perfect MCMC Simulation*, the aim being to, in effect, run the Markov chain from the infinite past and hence obtain a perfect sample at time zero. See Propp and Wilson (1996) or Besag (2000).

References Geman & Geman (1984), Winkler (1991), Johnson (1994), Kittle and Föglein (1984), Besag (2000).

11.4.7 The binary case – MAP by network flows

It turns out that in the special case of 2-colour, or binary, images, the MAP estimate can be derived exactly by viable combinatorial means. The qualification of *viable* is important, because it is well recognised that the MAP could in principle be determined by a brute force testing of all 2^n possible n-pixel images, the problem being that for, say, an 800×600 image the number of possibilities is too great, at 2^{480000}, or approximately 10^{144000}. Thus it was no mean achievement of Grieg *et al.* (1989) to find a combinatorial method, network flows, which reduces this to a manageable computation.

We set up the Bayesian formulation, then introduce the equivalent network flow problem and its solution, in the expectation that the flow method will be extended in due course to the case of more than two colours (a step in this direction was taken by Ferrari *et al.*, 1995). The present exact binary version has proved most useful as a check on the MAP estimates provided by both simulated annealing and the ICM technique of Besag (1986); see Grieg *et al.* (1989).

The energy function will be a quadratic expression in pixel variables $X = (X_1, \ldots, X_n)$, in which the observed values $Y = (Y_1, \ldots, Y_n)$ play the role of constants. Notice that 0 and 1 are the unique solutions of the equation $z^2 = z$.

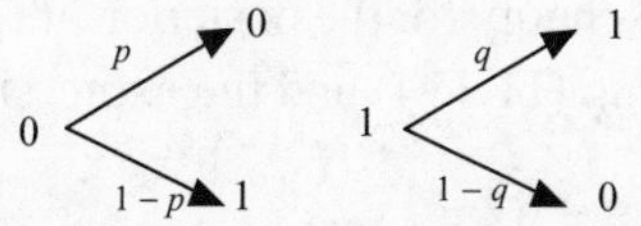

Figure 11.38 The probabilites in channel noise are given by parameters p, q, possibly equal. The transition matrix H has a, b element $p(y_i = b | x_i = a)$, where a, b are 0 or 1.

(i) The image prior The energy for the image prior given by Application 11.91 is $U(x) = \sum_c V_c(x)$, where c runs through all edges $c = \{i, j\}$ of the related graph, and $V_c = 1_{x_i \neq x_j}$, the function which equals 1 if $x_i \neq x_j$, and zero otherwise. But given the restriction to values $x_i, x_j \in \{0, 1\}$ we may write $V_c = (x_i - x_j)^2$, and then the following generality is convenient:

$$U(x) = \tfrac{1}{2} \sum_{1 \leq i, j \leq n} \beta_{ij}(x_i - x_j)^2, \tag{11.114}$$

with all $\beta_{ij} \geq 0$, but $\beta_{ii} = 0$ and $\beta_{ij} = \beta_{ji}$ (hence the factor 1/2). Now $\beta_{ij} > 0$ corresponds to i and j being neighbours. Also, if all nonzero β_{ij} equal a fixed number β, then $U(x) = \beta v$, where v is the number of unlike-coloured neighbour pairs.

(ii) The noise model Considering again the restriction to two colours, we concentrate on the model often referred to as *channel noise*, in which each pixel is changed with a probability depending on (at most) its present value. This is depicted in Figure 11.38, both by arrows and by a transition matrix.

We obtain an energy contribution which is linear in the x_i, by first observing that since x_i takes only the values 0, 1, and $p(y_i | x_i) = p(y_i | 0)$ if $x_i = 0$, but equals $p(y_i | 1)$ if $x_i = 1$, there holds

$$p(y_i | x_i) = p(y_i | 0)^{1 - x_i} p(y_i | 1)^{x_i}. \tag{11.115}$$

As before, we convert this to energy form by the property $p(y | x) = e^{\ln p(y | x)}$ and compute the *log-likelihood function*:

$$\begin{aligned}
\ln p(y | x) &= \ln \prod_i p(y_i | x_i) \\
&= \ln \prod_i p(y_i | 0)^{1 - x_i} p(y_i | 1)^{x_i} \\
&= \sum_i [x_i \{\ln p(y_i | 1) - x_i \ln p(y_i | 0)\} + \ln p(y_i | 0)] \\
&= \sum_i (\lambda_i x_i + \mu_i),
\end{aligned}$$

with constants $\lambda_i = \ln[p(y_i | 1)/p(y_i | 0)]$ and $\mu_i = \ln p(y_i | 0)$. The μ_i may be omitted since their values do not affect which vector x minimises our energy function below.

(iii) The posterior conditional Finally, the energy for the posterior $p(x|y) \propto p(y|x)p(x)$ is $U(x) = -\ln p(y|x) + \sum_c V_c(x)$ or, using (11.114) and the expression for $\ln p(y|x)$,

$$U(x) = -\sum_{i=1}^{n} \lambda_i x_i + \frac{1}{2} \sum_{1 \leq i,j \leq n} \beta_{ij}(x_i - x_j)^2. \tag{11.116}$$

The maximum a posteriori estimate, or MAP, is that $x = \hat{x}$ which minimises $U(x)$. We now reformulate this as a max/min problem in network flows, and derive the famous theorem of Ford and Fulkerson (1962) which leads to a solution algorithm.

Networks and flows

Definition 11.92 A *network N* consists of (i) a digraph (V, E) in which two vertices are distinguished, the source s and target (or sink) t, and (ii) a function c assigning to each edge e its capacity $c(e)$, a non-negative real number.

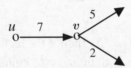

Figure 11.39 The total flow 7 into vertex v equals the flow out, $5 + 2$, in agreement with the conservation constraint of Definition 11.93.

Nomenclature for edges An edge $e = \{u, v\}$ is said to start from, or point out of, its *initial vertex* $\iota(e) = u$, and to end at, terminate at, or point into its *terminal* vertex $\tau(e) = v$ (see Figure 11.39). The *indegree* (*outdegree*) of u is the number of edges pointing into (out of) u. Sometimes a source is defined to have indegree 0 and a sink outdegree 0, but this is not essential in the present section. We define the notion of a *flow on N*, designed to accord with our intuition about the flow of any incompressible substance such as a liquid.

Definition 11.93 A *flow* on a network N is an assignment of a real number $f(e)$ to the edges satisfying (i) the capacity constraint: $0 \leq f(e) \leq c(e)$, and (ii) the *conservation constraint*: for each vertex v other than s or t, the flow into v equals the flow out of v, that is

$$\sum_{\tau(e)=v} f(e) = \sum_{\iota(e)=v} f(e). \tag{11.117}$$

The value of the flow, val(f), is the *net* flow out of s, that is

$$val(f) = \sum_{\iota(e)=s} f(e) - \sum_{\tau(e)=s} f(e). \tag{11.118}$$

Augmenting paths The objective is to maximise the flow, and an important tool for increasing the flow, if possible, is an $s - t$ path $s, u_1, \ldots, u_k, t$ which is *augmenting*, meaning that every *forward edge* $\{u_i, u_{i+1}\}$ has flow strictly below capacity and every

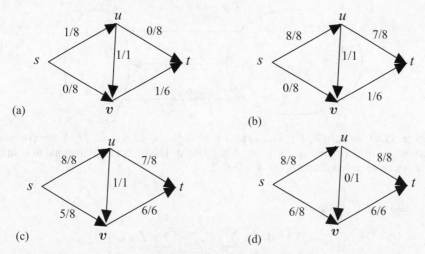

Figure 11.40 Increasing the flow in a network by use of augmenting paths.

edge directed the other way (backwards) has strictly positive flow. This means we can increase $val(f)$ by 1, still obeying the constraints, if we add 1 to the flow of each forward edge and subtract 1 from each backwards edge. Of course, we may be able to increase the flow by more than 1 unit, as we see in the next example.

An edge labelled f/c denotes flow f and capacity c. We call this edge *saturated* if $f = c$, since no increase in f is then possible.

Example 11.94 In the network of Figure 11.40(a), with $val(f) = 1$, the path s, u, t is an augmenting one. Indeed the *bottleneck* on this path (edge of least possible flow increase) is $1/8$ on the edge $\{s, u\}$, so we increase the flow by 7 on both edges of the path, to obtain (b), with $val(f) = 8$. The next easiest possibility is path s, v, t with bottleneck $1/6$. Increasing the flow on both edges by 5 we obtain (c), with $val(f) = 8 + 5 = 13$.

Considering (c), it looks at first as if there is no way to increase the flow further. However, we can proceed along edge $\{s, v\}$ because it is unsaturated. When we come to the *backwards* edge $\{u, v\}$ with positive *flow*, we *reduce* this flow, then go along $\{u, t\}$ increasing the flow of this forward edge to its capacity limit of 8. Thus we increase $val(f)$ by a further 1 and obtain network (d) with flow 14. It certainly seems obvious we can't do better here, but how would we prove this conviction in general? An answer is provided through the next idea, that of a *cut*.

Definition 11.95 A *cut* in a network N is a pair (A, B) of subsets which partition the vertex set V, with s in A and t in B. The set of edges *directed from A to B* (the edges $\{a, b\}$ with a in A and b in B) is denoted by A^+, whilst A^- is the set directed from B to A. The *capacity* $c(A, B)$ of the cut is the sum of the capacities of the A to B edges only. Thus the cut (A,B) depicted in Figure 11.41 has capacity $5 + 3 = 8$, where $A^+ = \{\{a, b\}, \{u, v\}\}$ The total *flow* $f(A, B)$ from A to B is the sum of the flows out of

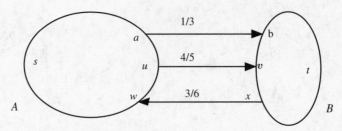

Figure 11.41 A cut (A, B) with capacity 8 (only the edges out of A are counted). Here $A^+ = \{ab, uv\}$ and $A^- = \{xw\}$. According to Theorem 11.96, the total flow in the network represented must be $1 + 4 - 3 = 2$.

A minus those into A, or

$$f(A, B) = \sum_{e \in A^+} f(e) - \sum_{e \in A^-} f(e). \tag{11.119}$$

Theorem 11.96 *Let (A, B) be a cut of the network N. Then the flow in N equals the flow from A to B. Indeed*

$$val(f) = f(A, B) = total\ flow\ into\ t. \tag{11.120}$$

Proof We interpret in two ways the sum

$$Z = \sum_{x \in A} \left(\sum_{\iota(e) = x} f(e) - \sum_{\tau(e) = x} f(e) \right).$$

Firstly, by the conservation constraint (Definition 11.93), the sum differences in parentheses are zero except for $x = s$, hence Z equals the total flow out of s or, by definition, $val(f)$. Secondly,

$$Z = \sum_{x \in A} \sum_{\iota(e) = x} f(e) - \sum_{x \in A} \sum_{\tau(e) = x} f(e)$$

$$= \sum_{\iota(e) \in A} f(e) - \sum_{\tau(e) \in A} f(e).$$

But an edge e with both ends in A makes a net contribution of $f(e) - f(e) = 0$, leaving only the terms of (11.119). Thus $val(f) = f(A, B)$, and the special case $A = V \setminus \{t\}$, $B = \{t\}$ shows that $val(f) =$ the total flow into t.

Corollary 11.97 *The value of any flow is bounded above by the capacity of any cut. Hence, in any case of equality the flow is greatest possible and the cut capacity least.*

Proof Let f be a flow and (A, B) a cut. Then

$$val(f) = f(A, B)\ (\text{Theorem 11.96}) \le \sum_{e \in A^+} f(e) \quad (\text{by (11.119)})$$

$$\le \sum_{e \in A^-} c(e) = c(A, B).$$

Exercise Deduce the second assertion of Corollary 11.97 from the first.

Theorem 11.98 *(Ford & Fulkerson, 1962) 'Max flow = Min cut': in a network, the greatest value of any flow equals the least capacity of any cut.*

Proof Let f be an arbitrary maximal flow on a network. Then, according to Corollary 11.97, we need only produce a cut whose capacity equals $val(f)$. Let A be the set of vertices reachable by an augmenting path from s (this includes s itself), and let B be the complement $V \backslash A$. Then t is in B, otherwise the flow could be increased by an augmenting path, contradicting the maximality of $val(f)$. Now, any edge $e = \{u, v\}$ in A^+ must be saturated, for otherwise an $s-u$ augmenting path could be extended to v, implying v was in A. Similarly, any edge in A^- must have zero flow, to avoid an extension. Hence

$$val(f) = f(A, B) \text{ (Theorem 11.96)} = c(A, B) \text{ (by Definition 11.95)}.$$

Remarks 11.99 (i) The proof of Theorem 11.98 shows that if (A, B) is a cut and f a flow then (A, B) has least possible capacity if and only if all edges pointing out of A are saturated and those pointing in have zero flow, (ii) taking $A = \{s\}$ we see that, if the source has only outward pointing edges and these are saturated by a flow, then $val(f)$ is greatest possible, (iii) the proof shows also that a flow is *maximum* – there *exists* no greater flow, if and only if it is *maximal* – no further augmented path can be added to what we already have. Thus, it does not matter by what route we have arrived at our non-increasable flow; it will be greatest possible.

> If there is no further augmenting path, we have maximum flow.

From energy to network

The energy function (11.116) is defined by nonzero constants λ_i depending on the observed image y, and by positive constants β_{ij} depending (partly) on the neighbourhood structure of our image model. These determine a network $N = (V, E, s, t, c)$ as follows. The vertex set V is $\{s, t, 1, 2, \ldots, n\}$, and there are two kinds of edges: (a) for each $\lambda_i > 0$, a directed edge $\{s, i\}$ of capacity $c_{si} = \lambda_i$, and for each $\lambda_i < 0$ a directed edge $\{i, t\}$ of capacity $-\lambda_i$, (b) for every neighbour pair i, j an undirected edge $\{i, j\}$ (see later), with capacity β_{ij}. The idea is to find a maximum flow, and then a minimum cut (B, W) specifies the pixels $i \in B$ which are black in the MAP estimate. We shall shortly justify all this, but first a simple example.

Example 11.100 Consider channel noise in which each pixel has a fixed probability p of being changed. We have

$$\lambda_i = \ln \frac{p(y_i|1)}{p(y_i|0)} = \begin{cases} \ln[(1-p)/p] = \lambda, \text{ say, if } y_i = 1, \\ \ln[p/(1-p)] = -\lambda, \text{ if } y_i = 0. \end{cases}$$

Also, $\lambda > 0 \Leftrightarrow 1 - p > p \Leftrightarrow p < 1/2$, so let us adopt the reasonable assumption that $p < 1/2$. Thus, letting black pixels correspond to $y_i = 1$, we have an edge $\{s, i\}$ of

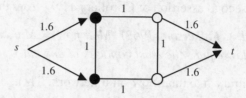

Figure 11.42 Network graph of Example 11.100 for 2 × 2 square of two black and two white pixels as indicated; the 4-neighbour lattice case with $\beta_{ij} = 1$ for neighbours i, j. We take $p = 1/6$, giving $\lambda_i = 1.6$ approx. for black pixels and $\lambda_i = -1.6$ for white (then $-\lambda_i = +1.6$).

capacity λ to each black pixel i, and an edge $\{j, t\}$ of capacity $-\lambda$ for each white pixel j. See Figure 11.42.

From MAP candidate to cut

A candidate x for the MAP defines a cut (B, W) by $B = \{s\} \cup \{\text{black pixels} : x_i = 1\}$ and $W = \{t\} \cup \{\text{white pixels} : x_i = 0\}$. The capacity of the cut, Σc_{bw} over all B–W edges $\{b, w\}$, has three types of contribution, where $1 \leq i, j \leq n$:

(a) *B–W edges of type* $\{s, i\}$. Given i, there is such an edge if and only if $x_i = 0$ and $\lambda_i > 0$, the capacity being λ_i. Hence we can represent its contribution by any expression which equals λ_i if $x_i = 0$, $\lambda_i > 0$, and otherwise zero. We use $(1 - x_i)\text{Max}(0, \lambda_i)$.

(b) *B–W edges of type* $\{i, t\}$ correspond to $x_i = 1$, $\lambda_i < 0$, and have capacity $-\lambda_i$, hence the contribution for given i may be represented by the expression $x_i\text{Max}(0, -\lambda_i)$.

(c) *B–W edges of type* $\{i, j\}$. Here we require an expression which equals β_{ij} if $x_i \neq x_j$ and otherwise zero. But this is precisely the condition of (11.114), so let us again use $\beta_{ij}(x_i - x_j)^2$. We have altogether $C(x)$, where

$$C(x) = \sum_{i=1}^{n} [(1 - x_i)\text{Max}(0, \lambda_i) + x_i\text{Max}(0, -\lambda_i)] + \tfrac{1}{2} \sum_{1 \leq i, j \leq n} \beta_{ij}(x_i - x_j)^2. \quad (11.121)$$

To demonstrate the equivalence of the max-flow, min-cut problem to finding the MAP we must show that x minimises $C(x)$ if and only if x minimises the energy $U(x)$ of (11.116). We shall prove this by showing that $C(x) - U(x)$ *is independent of* x. It remains to compare the λ_i terms of the two sums; we observe firstly that $\text{Max}(0, \lambda_i) - \text{Max}(0, -\lambda_i) = \lambda_i$ whether λ_i is positive or negative. The calculation is then, for each i,

$$x_i\lambda_i + (1 - x_i)\text{Max}(0, \lambda_i) + x_i\text{Max}(0, -\lambda_i)$$
$$= x_i[\lambda_i - \text{Max}(0, \lambda_i) + \text{Max}(0, -\lambda_i)] + \text{Max}(0, \lambda_i) \quad \text{(by rearranging)}$$
$$= \text{Max}(0, \lambda_i) = \text{constant}.$$

Example 11.101 For a simple but non-trivial illustration we suppose the 3 × 4 image of Figure 11.43 was observed, assume a 4-neighbour dependence amongst pixels, and take $\lambda = 2$, corresponding to a fixed error probability of 0.119 approx. at each pixel.

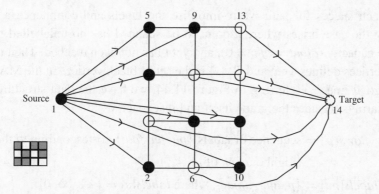

Figure 11.43 Graph (90 degrees rotated) corresponding to the observed 3×4 black and white pixel image, assuming $\lambda = 2$. Black pixels are represented by black graph points, and each pixel has four neighbours except on the corners. The flow is conveyed *outward* from the source along edges of capacity 2, along undirected edges (i, j) of capacity $\beta_{ij} = 1$, and *into* the target, or sink, along directed edges of capacity 2 (an undirected edge is simulated by a directed edge in each direction).

$$p \quad \xrightarrow{\textit{fin}} \quad pn$$
$$\xleftarrow{\textit{fout}}$$

Figure 11.44 The information recorded at position p of the array *flows*, namely a triple $\{p, \textit{fin}, \textit{fout}\}$, for each neighbour pn of p, with $\textit{fin} = \textit{fout} = 0$ initially. Point pn receives the label $\{p, \textit{afin}, \textit{afout}\}$ calculated from (11.122), and stored in *labels*[pn].

The cut-flow algorithm

In the graph we repeatedly construct an augmented s–t path, increasing the flow along it by the maximum possible. We reduce path construction to a series of 1-choice steps by first scanning the vertices, as follows. To scan a vertex p is to label its neighbours pn. Referring to Figure 11.44, the label is $\{p, \textit{afin}, \textit{afout}\}$, where *fin* stands for flow into pn from p, and *afin* is available flow, described shortly. Similarly for flow out. Denoting the capacity of the edge $\{p, pn\}$ by cp, we can increase total flow into pn according to the spare capacity $cp - \textit{fin}$, or by decreasing outward flow if *fout* is positive. Thus, we begin by labelling s as $\{-1, \infty, 0\}$ and proceed from the typical point p to its neighbour pn by defining

$$\begin{aligned} \textit{afin} &= \text{Min}[\textit{afin}(p), cp - \textit{fin}], \\ \textit{afout} &= \text{Min}[\textit{afout}(p), \textit{fout}]. \end{aligned} \tag{11.122}$$

Notice that each labelled point has a unique predecessor, so that if/when we reach t we may work back along a path to s, increasing inflow by $\textit{afin}(t)$, and decreasing outflow by $\textit{afout}(t)$. On the other hand, the fact that $\textit{afout} = 0$ at s ensures by (11.122) that $\textit{afout} = 0$ at all points on the path, including t, though we have allowed the possibility of a more general situation, should this be required.

After each successful path we re-initialise the labels and commence a new scan. Eventually the case arises where a point to be scanned has no unlabelled neighbours with spare capacity ($afout = afin = 0$), and yet t has not been reached. Then the set B of labelled vertices defines a cut and $B \backslash \{s\}$ is the set of black vertices in the MAP estimate of the original image. Referring to Figure 11.44, we have the data structured into the following arrays (besides the graph itself and its capacities):

$flows[p]$ = sequence of labels $\{pn, fin, fout\}$ corresponding to the neighbours pn of p;

$labels[pn]$ = $\{p, afin, afout\}$, where $labels[s] = \{-1, \infty, 0\}$;

$labelQ$ = queue of points labelled but not yet scanned, in order of appearance;

$scanned[p]$: set *True* when the scan of p is complete.

ALGO 11.18 Find the MAP estimate for an observed binary image

Procedure scan
Set $\{prevPt, afin(p), afout(p)\} = labels[p]$
Set $pNbrs = flows[p]$
For $i = 1, 2, \ldots$ (label the ith neighbour, pn)
    Get capacity p of edge (p, pn)
    Compute $afin, afout$ for pn, from (11.122)
    Abandon pn if already labelled or $afout = 0 = afin$
    Insert $\{p, afin, afout\}$ at $labels[pn]$
    Append pn to end of $labelQ$

Main algorithm
For $loopcount = 1, 2, 3, \ldots, Max$ do
    Initialise the arrays: *flows, scanned, labels, labelQ*
    While $labelQ$ is non-empty and $Last[labels] \neq t$
        Extract the first point, p, of $labelQ$
        Scan p then set $scanned[p] = True$
    If $labelQ$ is empty, exit the For loop (cut found)
    From t follow the unique labelled path back to s
    Increase the inflows by $afin(t)$ on path edges
    Decrease the outflows by $afout(t)$ on path edges
    (end of For loop)
Output list of labelled points as '1' positions in restored pic

---

Example 11.101 (*continued*) The algorithm applied to this example produced nine paths (i) and a labelling for an attempted tenth path (ii), as indicated in Figure 11.45. Failure

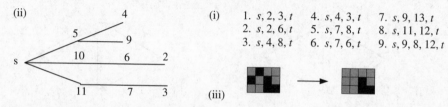

Figure 11.45 (i) List of successful augmentation paths for Example 11.101, (ii) points in the labelling for the failed tenth path to t, (iii) the change (arrowed) defined by these points.

occurred at vertex 3, from which there were no valid neighbours with which to proceed. Thus the black pixels in the MAP estimate of the original image are those numbered $\{2, 3, 4, 5, 6, 7, 9, 10, 11\}$.

The minimum value of $C(x)$ is 9, computed in under 1 second. For comparison, this flow was obtained by direct minimisation of $C(x)$ over all 2^{12} possible 3×4 binary images, the calculation taking 35 seconds.

Example 11.102 Figure 11.46 shows a simple 5×10 image, its noisy version with each pixel flipped with probability $p = 0.25$, and the MAP estimate with various values of β. The restoration is perfect for $0.8 \leq \beta \leq 2.4$, but all black thereafter. Notice the timing contrast between the flow method and a complete search. Since the number of points has increased from 12 (in Example 11.101) to a present 50, the computation time is increased in the approximate ratio 2^{38}, to about 2^{37} minutes, which is already unmanageable.

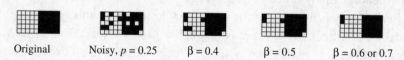

Original   Noisy, $p = 0.25$ $\beta = 0.4$ $\beta = 0.5$ $\beta = 0.6$ or 0.7

Figure 11.46 A simple binary image is corrupted by pixel noise with $p = 0.25$, and restored by the flow method with various values of β. For $\beta \geq 2.4$ the MAP estimate is black, but for $0.8 \leq \beta \leq 2.3$ the MAP restoration is perfect.

Termination So far we have been rather quiet about whether the flow algorithm must terminate, and, if so, how soon. Here is a point-by-point discussion.

(1) If the initial flows are all integral, say zero, and the capacities too, then an augmenting path increases flow by at least one unit, so the process terminates after finitely many steps (paths).

(2) Even if real numbers are involved, they are approximated by rationals for computer calculation, and we obtain an equivalent problem in integers by multiplying through by a common denominator M. However, M may be so large that the problem cannot be solved in acceptable time (cf. directly minimising $C(x)$ over all 2^n cases, $n \geq 50$). To fix ideas, suppose M is of the order of 10^9, and consider the network of Figure 11.47.

The order of augmenting paths chosen in Figure 11.47(b) involves the huge number $2M$ of paths, yet the same may be accomplished by just two paths s, a, t and s, b, t. The original algorithm of Ford and Fulkerson would have allowed this choice, but such

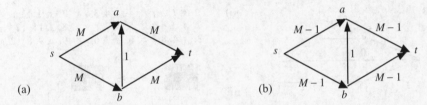

Figure 11.47 (a) A simple network, with edges labelled by capacity, illustrating how some choices of augmenting paths entail hugely more calculation than others, (b) the spare capacities after paths s, a, b, t and s, b, a, t each increase flow by 1. The vertical capacity 1 was lost then restored. Repeating this pair takes $2M$ paths to attain the maximum flow $2M$.

inefficiencies are eliminated by the simple additional feature due to Edmonds and Karp (1972) of 'first labelled, first scanned', here implemented via the queue of labelled but unscanned vertices, kept in array *labelQ*. Indeed, it results in a reasonable upper bound on the computation, as we shortly describe.

Exercise What paths result when ALGO 11.18 is applied to the network of Figure 11.47?

(3) As may be seen, *first labelled, first scanned* ensures that each successive augmenting path is shortest possible. Edmunds and Karp show that in this circumstance the number of paths satisfies, in the 'big O' notation (Definition 10.42),

$$\text{no. of paths} \leq |E|(|V| + 2)/2 = O(n^3), \tag{11.123}$$

where $|E|$ denotes the number of graph edges, not counting direction, and $n = |V|$; the equality holds because $|E| \leq n(n - 1)$. Now let us see if this can be significantly improved for the particular type of network graph with which we determine an MAP. One way to count edges is to notice that, since each edge is incident on exactly two vertices there holds $2E = \sum d_i$, where d_i is the number of edges incident on the ith vertex. This yields the equalities in the lemma below. The *inequalities* are obtained by maximising $k + m$ subject to $0 < k, m < n$ and $km = n$, the result being $2\sqrt{n}$.

Lemma 11.103 *For a $k \times m$ image with $n = km$ vertices we have*

$$|E| = \begin{cases} 3n - (k + m) \leq 3n - 2\sqrt{n} \ \text{(4-neighbour case)}, \\ 5n - 3(k + m) + 2 \leq 5n - 6\sqrt{n} + 4 \ \text{(8-neighbour case)}. \end{cases} \tag{11.124}$$

(4) It turns out that in our case the bound (11.123) may be reduced by a factor 2, as follows. We recall that a *bottleneck* in a path is an edge of least possible flow increase. The main step in the proof is to show that (given all augmenting paths are shortest possible), any given edge e may play the role of a bottleneck as a forward edge in at most $(|V| + 2)/4$ of these paths, and similarly as a backwards edge. Since there are $|E|$ edges altogether, the total number of paths cannot exceed $|E| \times (|V| + 2)/4 \times 2$, and we have (11.123). However, the factor 2 may be dropped in our case because, as observed below (11.122), all path edges are forward. Combining this fact with Lemma 11.103, we have the inequalities below.

Theorem 11.104 *For a $k \times m$ image with $n = km$, the number of augmenting paths is bounded above by*

$$\left\{ \begin{array}{l} \frac{1}{4}(3n - 2\sqrt{n})(n + 2) \text{ (4-neighbour case)}, \\ \frac{1}{4}(5n - 6\sqrt{n} + 4)(n + 2) \text{ (8-neighbour case)} \end{array} \right\} = O(n^2). \tag{11.125}$$

Example 11.105 Before commenting on timing and other issues, it is time to add a slightly larger example. We consider the letter 'A' in a 30×30 pixel matrix, as shown in Figure 11.48 followed by, as usual, a version with added noise in the form of a probability $p = 0.25$ for each pixel, of a change between black and white.

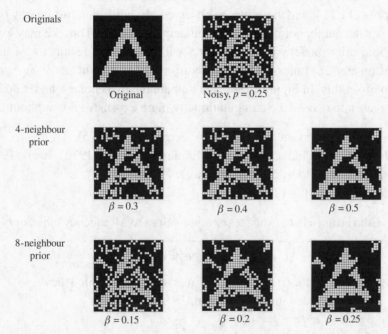

Figure 11.48 Original letter 'A', noisy version with probability $p = 0.25$ of corruption at pixels, followed by the exact maximum a priori estimates based on 4-neighbour 2β and 8-neighbour β priors, for various values of β.

Results and conjectures

1. *Complexity* Let us think of the number of paths as representing the complexity/time of the flow determination. By (11.125), the computation may be performed in polynomial time, indeed this polynomial has degree as little as 2. In Table 11.14, however, the bounds are roughly the squares of the actual values, suggesting that a closer analysis may reduce the bounds to O(n). This is borne out by experiments (Grieg *et al.*, 1989) in which, successively, the solution for each component of a fine partition of the image is the stepping stone for that of one with components twice the size. Such a technique typically reduces a factor n to $\log n$, which is worthwhile because $n \log n$ ultimately increases less rapidly than n^{1+e} for any positive e.

Table 11.14. *Upper bound and actual numbers of iterations for three*
examples. Varying B changed the number of paths by less than 2%,
and we give representative figures only.

Example	n	4-nbr bound	paths used	8-nbr bound	paths used
11.101	12	101	10	151	20
11.102	50	1766	34	2750	56
11.105	900	595 320	723	975 062	1385

2. *Neighbourhoods and the value of β* We are using a fixed value β for all nonzero β_{ij} in
the image prior (11.114) and therefore, as observed, the corresponding energy is $U(x) =$
βv, where v is the number of unlike-coloured neighbour pairs. Thus we may expect that
an 8-neighbour prior model with parameter β will give similar results to a 4-neighbour
one with parameter 2β, unless the 8-neighbour model is a sufficiently superior model
of reality to offset this. In Figure 11.48 we compare the two choices, and it does appear
there is no reason to choose the computationally more expensive 8-neighbour prior.

References *Exact MAP*: Grieg *et al.* (1989), Ferrari *et al.* (1995).
Flow algorithm: Ford & Fulkerson (1962), Edmonds & Karp (1972), Even (1973).
Algorithms, polynomial time, NP-completeness: Manber (1989).
ICM method: Besag (1986), (2000).

Appendix Converting a list of variates or other values to a frequency table, or *histogram*.

ALGO 11.19 Frequency table

Input: (1) vector *lst* of values, (2) interval $[a, b]$ in which they
lie, to be divided into n equal parts.
$dx = (b - a)/n; x_2 = a;$
vals = *lst* in increasing order;
$f = n$-vector with $f_n = $ Length[*lst*];
For $i = 1$ to $n - 1$ do
  $x_1 = x_2; x_2 = x_2 + d_x;$
  While *vals*$_k < x_2$ do $k = k + 1$
  $k = k - 1; f_i = k$
For $i = n$ down to 2 reduce f_i by f_{i-1}
Return f.

A Mathematica routine for drawing the frequency table

```
freqGraph[f_] := Module[{i, n = Length[f], pts, g};
  g = Table[0, {2n + 2}];
  Do[g[[{2i, 2i + 1}]] = f[[i]], { i, n }];
  pts=Table[{Ceiling[i/2], g[[i]]}, {i, 2n + 2}];
  Show[Graphics[Line[pts]], ImageSize − >72inches]; ];
```

Exercises 11

1 ✓ Let $X \sim \Gamma_{\alpha,u}$. (i) Show that for $c, d > 0$ there holds $d\Gamma_{\alpha,u}(dx) = \Gamma_{d\alpha,u}(x)$, and hence that $cX \sim \Gamma_{\alpha/c,u}$. (ii) Deduce that, for the normal distribution, $S^2 \sim \Gamma_{a,b}$, where $a = (n-1)/2\sigma^2$, $b = (n-1)/2$. (iii) Write down the mean and variance of S^2 and verify that $V(S^2) = O(1/n)$ (see Definition 10.42).

2 ✓ Which properties of Table 11.3 apply to the estimator $\overline{X}$?

3 ✓ A sample $(X_1, \ldots, X_n)$ is taken of a variable in $N(0, \sigma^2)$. Write down the likelihood function $L(x_1, \ldots, x_n; \sigma)$, and its logarithm $l(\sigma)$, and show that the most likely estimate of σ is given by $(1/n)\sum x_i^2$. Verify that the ratio of this to the usual estimate S^2 approaches 1 as $n \to \infty$.

4 ✓ The measured values $\{0.889, 1.6, 2, 1.78, 2.74, 2.9, 2.64, 2.71, 2.87, 3.51\}$ of y correspond respectively to $x = 1, 2, \ldots, 10$. Find the regression line of y on x given by (11.17).

5 ✓ With $S = \sum_i (y_i - a - bx_i)^2$, the sum of squares error given by (11.14), show that the Hessian matrix

$$H = \begin{bmatrix} \partial^2 S/\partial a^2 & \partial^2 S/\partial a\partial b \\ \partial^2 S/\partial b\partial a & \partial^2 S/\partial b^2 \end{bmatrix}$$

has determinant $4n \sum(x_i - \overline{x})^2$ and hence is positive definite (assuming not all x_i are equal).

6 ✓ Company A claims improved accuracy over Company B for a certain product. A batch of 40 items tested from each vendor shows a reduction of the mean error from 180.1 microns to 178.6. Does this imply a genuine improvement at the 5% significance level, given variance estimates 6.3, 7.4?

7 ✓ Is the *normal distribution* a reasonable model for the frequency distribution given below, at the 1% significance level? Let f_i denote the frequency of hits in interval $[a_i, a_{i+1})$, and assume a sample mean of 0.0244 and variance 0.234.

a_i	−1.309	−0.958	−0.607	−0.256	0.095	0.446	0.797	1.148	1.499
f_i	21	77	174	294	250	126	48	10	–

8 ✓ Let ϕ denote the standard normal pdf. (i) Express $[\phi((x - \mu)/\sigma)]^n$ in the form $\phi((x - M)/\Sigma)$. (ii) A posterior distribution calculation arrives at $\phi((x_1 - \mu)/\sigma) \cdots \times \phi((x_n - \mu)/\sigma)\phi((\mu - \mu_0)/\sigma)$; by viewing this as a product with a single variable, express it in the form $\phi((\mu - \mu_n)/\sigma_n)$. Show that $\mu_n = \overline{x}/(1 + 1/n) + O(1/n)$. Why may this be written more simply as $\overline{x} + O(1/n)$?

9 ✓ A Bayesian classifier has been arranged to correspond to plane decision functions $d_i(x) = \|x - m_i\|$, where $m_1 = (1, 5)$, $m_2 = (3, 2)$, $m_3 = (10, 7)$. Find equations for the decision boundaries d_{ij} and determine their common point C. Sketch the result, and classify the points $(5, 0)$, $(3, 7)$, $(7, 6)$, $(10, 9)$.

10 ✓ Specialise ALGO 11.1 to generate from the pdf $f(x) = 3x^2/8$ $(0 \le x \le 2)$. Construct a frequency diagram based on 100 generated variates and tenfold division of R_X (ALGO 11.19 at the chapter's end may be useful). Now get a more convincing result by using 1000 variates.

11 (i) Use ALGO 11.8 to generate 1000 variates in $N(0, 1)$ and hence draw a frequency diagram based on the interval $[-4, 4]$ divided into eight equal parts. (ii) Repeat for 2000 variates and a 16-fold division.

12   Test the variates in Exercise 11.11(i) for normality by the method of Example 11.33, estimating the parameters from the sample. Check both 1% and 5% levels of significance.

13 ✓ Use ALGO 11.9 to generate 10 variates from the 3D normal distribution with covariance matrix $\sum = $ Rows[(1, 2, 3), (2, 5, 10), (3, 10, 26)] and mean $(1, -1, 2)$.

14 ✓ A discrete random variable takes values 1, 2, 3, 4, 5 with probabilities $p = (1, 2, 4, 10, 3)/20$. Use ALGO 11.10 to generate 500 variates, then test for the correct distribution at the 1% level of significance.

15 ✓ The occupancy problem, Example 11.53. (i) With $N = 4$ cells, determine the probabilities of the various states 0, 1, 2, 3, 4 if the initial state is one cell occupied, and (a) four balls are inserted, (b) five are inserted. (ii) If the initial probabilities are $p^{(0)} = (1, 2, 0, 0, 2)/5$, find the probabilities after four insertions.

16 ✓ The stationary vector in Example 11.58 is by definition an eigenvector of Q with eigenvalue 1. (i) Find the other eigenvalue and an eigenvector. (ii) Provide the inductive step for formula (11.60) by showing that post-multiplying by Q just increases n by 1 in the formula. (Hint: brute force *or* note that the first matrix is unchanged by this multiplication, and write the second matrix as $[\alpha - \beta]^T[1 - 1]$; see (i).)

17 ✓ A Markov chain $\{X_r\}$ with states $\{0, 1, 2\}$ has the transition matrix shown below.

$$\begin{pmatrix} \frac{1}{3} & \frac{1}{3} & \frac{1}{3} \\ \frac{1}{2} & 0 & \frac{1}{2} \\ \frac{1}{4} & \frac{1}{2} & \frac{1}{4} \end{pmatrix}$$

(i) Show that for some N the matrix Q^N has only positive elements. Find the stationary distribution t approximately (Theorem 11.59), by considering $\{x Q^n\}$ for some x, and test t as an eigenvector. (ii) Use ALGO 11.13 to generate a sample of size 40 from the chain, with starting distribution $p^{(0)} = (1, 1, 1)/3$. How do the frequencies compare with those predicted by t?

18 ✓ Let $g(x) = (4 - x^2)^{-1/2}$. For Monte Carlo integration of $g(x)$ over the interval $[0, 1]$, estimate the number N of trials required to give 90% certainty of the result being within 0.004 of the true value (see (11.68)). Compare the calculated integral with the results of the two methods using N trials.

19 ✓ Use the random walk sampler given in (11.79) to generate a sample of size 10 000 from the distribution $\pi(x) = x \exp(-x^2/2)$, by the Markov Chain Monte Carlo method. Produce a frequency diagram for samples over the interval $[0, 2]$ divided into seven parts. Test for correctness of the results at the 1% level (see Section 11.1.6).

20 ✓ (i) Taking the Directed Acyclic Graph of Figure 11.31 to be that of a Bayesian network, write down the corresponding joint pdf $p(v_1, \ldots, v_5)$. (ii) A Bayesian network for variables $x_1, \ldots, x_9$ is labelled $1, \ldots, 9$ with edges (6, 7), (7, 8), (7, 9), (1, 9), (3, 9), (1, 2), (1, 5), (2, 5), (2, 3), (3, 4). Diagram the graph and write down the expression for $p(x_1, \ldots, x_9)$. Is the ordering ancestral?

21 ✓ For the Bayesian network (ii) of Exercise 11.20, write down the products for the full conditional $p(v|V_{-v})$ in the cases $v = x_1, \ldots, x_4$.

22 ✓ In Example 11.89 with $x_5 = 5$, determine the full conditionals $p(x_1|x_{-1})$ and $p(x_2|x_{-2})$.

23 ✓ (See Application 11.91 & preceding) (i) Derive (11.108) and verify the constant comes out correctly. (ii) Calculate $p(x_1|x_{-1})$ for the lattice of Figure 11.36 with $x_5 = 5$ and $V_{\{r,s\}} = 1$

if $x_r \neq x_s$, otherwise zero. (iii) Using (ii), write down the contribution $U_1(x_1)$ to the energy of the posterior conditional, as a function of $x_1 = 1, 2, 3, 4, 5$, by expressing it as the sum of two 5-vectors.

24 √ (i) Increase the flow in Figure 11.40(a) to its maximum, using fewer than four augmenting paths. (ii) Derive the second assertion of Corollary 11.97 from the first.

25 √ (i) Repeat Example 11.101 for the top left 2×3 section of the image. (ii) Implement ALGO 11.18 and repeat Example 11.102 with $p = 0.15$.

Part IV

Information, error and belief

12

Entropy and coding

In this chapter we introduce the basic idea of *entropy*, quantifying an amount of information, and in its light we consider some important methods of encoding a sequence of symbols. We shall be thinking of these as text, but they also apply to a byte sequence representing pixel values of a digital image. In the next chapter we shall develop information theory to take account of noise, both visual and otherwise. Here we focus on 'noiseless encoding' in preparation for that later step. However, before leaving this chapter we take time to examine an alternative approach to quantifying information, which has resulted in the important idea of Minimum Description Length as a new principle in choosing hypotheses and models.

12.1 The idea of entropy

Shannon (1948), the acknowledged inventor of information theory, considered that a basis for his theory already existed in papers of Niquist (1924) and Hartley (1928). The latter had argued that the logarithm function was the most natural function for measuring information. For example, as Shannon notes, adding one relay to a group doubles the number of possible states, but *adds* one to the base 2 log of this number. Thus information might be measured as the number of *bits*, or binary digits $b_i = 0, 1$, required to express an integer in binary form: $b_m \ldots b_1 b_0 = \sum_i b_i 2^i$. For example, $34 = 100010$ takes six bits. Shannon proposed a 5-component model of a communication system, reproduced in Figure 12.1.

He divided source types into the categories discrete, continuous and mixed. It is perhaps fortunate that Shannon had examples such as teletype and telegraphy to motivate the study

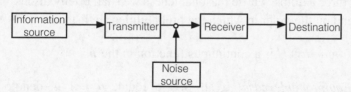

Figure 12.1 Shannon's model of a communication system.

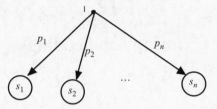

Figure 12.2 Tree with one root node '1', representing the choice of a symbol s_i with probability p_i from the source alphabet, where $i = 1, \ldots, n$.

of the discrete case, so that it was ready as the digital revolution drew near. For now we'll stick to a discrete source, emitting symbols from a fixed alphabet $S = \{s_1, \ldots, s_n\}$ of size n. The principal problems Shannon addressed first in laying out his theory may be stated thus.

1. (*Noiseless coding*) How can we encode the source symbols so as to minimise the message length on transmission?
2. (*Coding against noise*) In the presence of noise, how can we introduce redundancy in the coding so as to achieve an acceptably low error rate?

The idea is to invoke statistical properties of source symbols and transmission medium. Now, in some situations the likelihood of a particular symbol's appearance may be greater or less, depending on what went before. For example, in English T is more likely after an R than after a W. However, we begin by taking account only of the absolute probabilities $p_1, \ldots, p_n$ of our source alphabet, as represented in Figure 12.2.

When a symbol appears, how much information does that convey? To put it another way, how much uncertainty does its appearance remove? This information/uncertainty was named *entropy* by Shannon because of an analogous meaning in statistical physics; for more on this see Jaynes (1982) or Cover and Thomas (1991).

It seems reasonable to argue that the appearance of a *less* likely symbol tells us *more*, so a first thought might be that the information conveyed by a symbol of probability p is $1/p$ or, at any rate, an increasing function of $1/p$. If that function should be a logarithm, the information conveyed being $\log(1/p)$, then the mean information per symbol over the alphabet with probabilities $p_1, \ldots, p_n$ is the expected value $\sum_i p_i \log(1/p_i)$.

This proves remarkably prophetic, for in a more precise vein we arrive at the same function, denoted by $H(p_1, \ldots, p_n)$, which measures information in a deep mathematical sense, thoroughly vindicated in ensuing results. We derive H by requiring it to satisfy the following three axioms, whose reasonableness we shall briefly discuss. Implicitly, H does not depend on the order in which the probabilities are listed.

AXIOM 1 (*Continuity*) H is a continuous function in the p_i.

AXIOM 2 (*Equiprobable case*) If all p_i are equal, $p_i = 1/n$, denote the entropy $H(1/n, \ldots, 1/n)$ by $Q(n)$. Then $Q(n)$ increases monotonically with n.

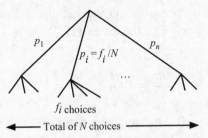

Figure 12.3 Choice from N equiprobable objects, split into choices from n subsets, weighted according their size f_i.

AXIOM 3 (*Equiprobable choice subdivided*) Let $N = f_1 + f_2 + \cdots + f_n$ and $p_i = f_i/N$. Then $Q(N) = H(p_1, p_2, \ldots, p_n) + \sum p_i Q(f_i)$.

Some explanations are as follows. *Axiom 1*: we expect a small change in probability to cause a correspondingly small change in uncertainty. *Axiom 2*: choosing from a bigger pool of equally likely objects suggests more uncertainty. *Axiom 3*: $Q(N)$ is the uncertainty in choosing one of N equally likely objects, but the choice may be subdivided thus. Partition the objects into n bags, the ith bag containing f_i of them. Now choose a bag. Weighting the bags according to their number of objects, we assign bag i the probability $p_i = f_i/N$: thus choosing which bag to use has entropy $H(p_1, \ldots, p_n)$. Finally, choose a single object from the selected bag. This choice has entropy $Q(f_i)$, according to Axiom 2. Now Axiom 3 states plausibly that the total entropy $Q(N)$ equals the sum of the entropy for each choice weighted by the probability of that choice occurring. (We suppose a base given for logarithms.)

Theorem 12.1 *A function H satisfying Axioms 1 to 3 has the form*

$$H = -K \sum_{i=1}^{n} p_i \log p_i \quad \text{(K any positive constant)}. \tag{12.1}$$

Proof Apply Axiom 3 with all f_i equal to f. Then $N = nf$ and $p_i = 1/n$, giving $Q(nf) = H(1/n, \ldots, 1/n) + \sum(1/n)Q(f)$ (the $\sum$ part sums n identical terms $1/n$) $= Q(n) + Q(f)$. Letting s, m be any positive integers (but $s \geq 2$) we have by repeated application of this relation that

$$Q(s^m) = mQ(s). \tag{12.2}$$

Now let t, n be positive integers with n arbitrarily large. Then there exists an integer m for which

$$s^m \leq t^n < s^{m+1}. \tag{12.3}$$

Since the log function to given base is monotonic increasing, we may take logs and divide by $n \log s$ in (12.3) to obtain

$$\frac{m}{n} \leq \frac{\log t}{\log s} < \frac{m}{n} + \frac{1}{n}. \tag{12.4}$$

In a similar manner we apply the monotonic increasing function Q of Axiom 2 to (12.3) to obtain $Q(s^m) \leq Q(t^n) < Q(s^{m+1})$, whence by (12.2) $m \, Q(s) \leq n Q(t) < (m+1)Q(s)$, or, on dividing by $n Q(s)$,

$$\frac{m}{n} \leq \frac{Q(t)}{Q(s)} < \frac{m}{n} + \frac{1}{n}. \tag{12.5}$$

Since $1/n$ is arbitrarily small we may infer from (12.4), (12.5) that $Q(t)/Q(s)$ and $(\log t)/(\log s)$ are *arbitrarily* close and hence equal. It follows that $Q(t)/(\log t) = Q(s)/(\log s) = $ constant, K, and hence, for any integer u,

$$Q(u) = K \log u \ (K > 0), \tag{12.6}$$

where K is positive because of Axiom 2. Making H the subject in Axiom 3 and substituting formula (12.6) for $Q(u)$ gives

$$\begin{aligned}
H(p_1, \ldots, p_n) &= Q(N) - \sum p_i Q(f_i) \ (i = 1, \ldots, n) \\
&= K \log N - \sum p_i \cdot K \log(f_i) \\
&= K \left\{ \sum p_i \log N - \sum p_i \log(f_i) \right\} \quad \text{since } \sum p_i = 1 \\
&= -K \cdot \sum p_i \log(f_i/N) \\
&= -K \cdot \sum p_i \log p_i.
\end{aligned}$$

This proves the theorem when the p_i are rational. However, any real number is the limit of a sequence of rationals (see e.g. Hoggar, 1992), so by continuity (Axiom 1), the result holds for real p_i also.

First consequences for H

Remark 12.2 (*Changing the base of logs*) The formula $\log_b x = \log_b a \cdot \log_a x$ from (12.8) below (think of the as as 'cancelling'), shows that choosing K is equivalent to setting $H = -\sum p_i \log p_i$ with a suitable choice of base for the logarithm. Any base gives the desired properties, and base 2 is the one appropriate when we are coding into binary form, since entropy is then expressed in binary bits. We will use base 2 except where otherwise stated, choosing K so that $H(p_1, \ldots, p_n)$ satisfies the first equality and hence the rest, in

$$H = -\sum p_i \log p_i = \sum p_i \log(1/p_i) = E[\log(1/p)]. \tag{12.7}$$

An occasional but important exception to the choice of base 2 is the *natural* logarithm, taken to base e, and denoted by ln or Ln. In particular, it fits in with the important properties below, where as usual the base is specified if necessary by a subscript.

$$\log_b a = 1/\log_a b, \quad \log_b x = \frac{\log_a x}{\log_a b}, \quad \frac{d}{dx} \log x = \frac{1}{x \ln 2}. \tag{12.8}$$

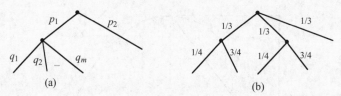

Figure 12.4 Decision paths involving more than one choice between alternatives.

Proof Set $\alpha = \log_a x$, whence $x = a^\alpha$, and take logs to base b to get $\log_b x = \alpha \log_b a = (\log_b a) \log_a x$ as noted above. This yields the first two equalities of (12.8) if we set $x = b$ to give $1 = \log_b b = \log_b a \cdot \log_a b$. The third now follows because $\log x = \log_2 x = \ln x / \ln 2$, and $\ln x$ has derivative $1/x$.

After a few preliminaries we shall be ready to prove a result, Shannon's Noiseless Encoding Theorem (Theorem 12.8) which, even by itself, justifies the entropy concept.

Example 12.3 Given the fomula (12.7) for H it is easy to see that Axiom 3 applies without choices needing to be equiprobable. The following calculation based on Figure 12.4 shows why this is so, and that, however many branchings there are, the total entropy is the sum of the entropy of probabilities at a branching node times the probability of arriving at that node. Figure 12.4(a) represents $m + 1$ symbols with associated probabilities the 2-fold products $p_1 q_1, \ldots, p_1 q_m$, and p_2 itself. Their entropy is by definition the negative of

$$\sum_{i=1}^{m} p_1 q_i \log(p_1 q_i) + p_2 \log p_2 = p_1 \Sigma (q_i \log p_1 + q_i \log q_i) + p_2 \log p_2$$
$$= (p_1 \log p_1) \Sigma q_i + p_1 \Sigma q_i \log q_i + p_2 \log p_2$$
$$= p_1 H(q_1, \ldots, q_m) + H(p_1, p_2), \quad \text{since } \Sigma q_i = 1.$$

Exercise Compute the entropy of the 5-symbol source represented in Figure 12.4(b).

Notation 12.4 (1) A sequence $p_1, p_2, \ldots, p_n$ of real numbers is called a *probability distribution* if $0 \le p_i \le 1$ for each i, and $\sum p_i = 1$. Then $H(p_1, \ldots, p_n)$ will be referred to as the *entropy* of this distribution, or of any source whose symbols are governed by this distribution, or of any random variable X whose probabilities are so governed. In the latter case we may write $H(X)$ instead of $H(p_1, \ldots, p_n)$.

(2) It is convenient and customary to make the abbreviation

$$H(p) = H(p, 1 - p) = -p \log p - (1 - p) \log(1 - p), \tag{12.9}$$

flagged by the appearance of H with only a single argument. This function on the unit interval $[0, 1]$ has its single maximum at $p = 1/2$, of value $\log 2$, which equals 1 for our *default base* 2 of logarithms. The graph is shown in Figure 12.5.

(3) There is an apparent difficulty with $H(x)$ at $x = 0$, since $\log 0$ is undefined. But the product $x \log x$ tends to 0 with x, for any base of logarithms, and so we may consistently

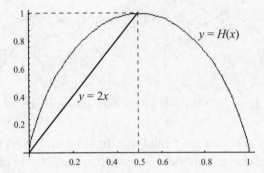

Figure 12.5 Graphs of $H(x) = -x \log x - (1 - x) \log(1 - x)$, and of $y = 2x$, meeting at $(1/2, 1)$.

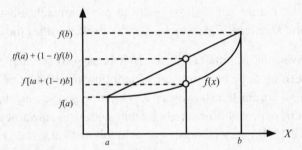

Figure 12.6 A convex function on the interval (a, b).

define $H(0) = 0$. Thus $0 \log 0$ as a summand of $H(p_1, \ldots, p_n)$ is always to be interpreted as 0.

(4) In the light of (3) we may write $H(x_1, \ldots, x_n, 0, \ldots, 0) = H(x_1, \ldots, x_n)$, and so in particular $H(p, q, 0) = H(p, q) = H(p)$, where of course $p + q = 1$.

We recall from Chapter 9 that a real-valued function f on an interval I of the real line is called *concave* if the graph of f lies above every chord. That is, for a, b in I and $0 \leq t \leq 1$,

$$f[ta + (1 - t)b] \geq tf(a) + (1 - t)f(b), \tag{12.10}$$

where we recall that $ta + (1 - t)\boldsymbol{b}$ divides in the ratio $1 - t : 1$ the segment AB whose endpoints have respective position vectors $\boldsymbol{a}, \boldsymbol{b}$. See Figure 12.6. The concavity is *strict* if the inequality in (12.10) is strict, and f is *convex* if it is reversed. The strict concavity property is visible for $H(x)$ in Figure 12.5. It holds for any f with a negative second derivative on the interior of I. In our case, up to a multiple of $\ln 2$ we have $H'(x) = -\log x + \log(1 - x)$, from (12.9), whilst $H''(x) = -1/x(1 - x) < 0$ on the interval $(0, 1)$. A useful elementary consequence is that $H(x)$ lies above the chord it cuts out from the line $y = 2x$ between $x = 0$ and $x = 1/2$ (Figure 12.5), a fact we include in part (iii) of the summary theorem now stated.

Theorem 12.5 *(i) $H(x)$ satisfies $0 \leq H(x) \leq 1$ on the interval $[0, 1]$. In particuar, $H(0) = 0 = H(1)$, with a maximum of 1 at $x = 1/2$. (ii) $H(x)$ is symmetrical about*

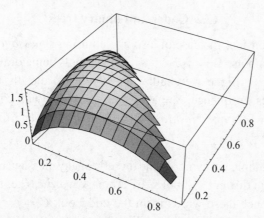

Figure 12.7 Illustration of the concavity property of $H(p_1, p_2, p_3)$, plotted as a function of p_1, p_2. Note that $p_3 = 1 - p_1 - p_2 \geq 0$ and so we are restricted to $p_1 + p \leq 1$.

the line $x = 1/2$, *that is* $H(1 - x) = H(x)$. *(iii)* $H(x)$ *is concave, with* $H(x) \leq 2x$ *for* $0 \leq x \leq 1/2$.

As we shall see in Chapter 13, the function $H(p_1, \ldots, p_n)$ satisfies a higher dimensional form of concavity, visible for $n = 3$ in Figure 12.7. However, a partial generalisation of Theorem 12.5 is given by the following result.

Theorem 12.6 *(Extremal values of entropy) The entropy H of* $(p_1, \ldots, p_n)$ *attains its greatest value,* $\log n$*, when all* p_i *take the same value* $1/n$*. Furthermore:*

(i) $H \geq 0$, *and* $H = 0$ *if and only if some* p_i *equals* 1,
(ii) *if* $0 < p_i < 1$ *for some* i, *then* $H \geq p_i \log(1/p_i) > 0$.

Proof First observe that $0 \leq p_i \leq 1$, $1/p_i \geq 1$, and so $p_i \log(1/p_i) \geq 0$, with equality if and only if $p_i = 0$ or $1/p_i = 1$. For (i) we have certainly $H \geq 0$. Further, the condition $H = 0$ means that each term $p_i \log(1/p_i)$ is zero; but we cannot have all $p_i = 0$ because $\sum p_i = 1$, and so at least one p_i is positive, implying $\log(1/p_i) = 0$, whence $p_i = 1$. Conversely, $p_i = 1$ implies that the term $p_i \log(1/p_i)$ is zero and (because $\sum p_i = 1$) that $p_k = 0$ for $k \neq i$. Thus $H = 0$. For (ii), suppose $0 < p_i < 1$ is given. Then $1/p_i > 1$ so $\log(1/p_i) > 0$, which establishes (ii). For the assertion $H \leq \log n$ we invoke Jensen's Inequality (9.51) for the single inequality sandwiched between the equalities below:

$$H = \sum p_i \log(1/p_i) = E[\log(1/p_i)] \leq \log E[1/p_i] \quad \text{since log is concave}$$

$$= \log \sum p_i(1/p_i) = \log n.$$

Since the logarithm function is in fact strictly concave, equality holds if and only if $1/p_i$, and hence p_i, is independent of i, implying that $p_i = 1/n$. The reverse implication is trivial.

12.2 Codes and binary trees

Notation 12.7 We consider the case of a source emitting a *message* which consists of a finite sequence of symbols, $D = d_1 d_2 \ldots d_N$, all symbols being drawn from an *alphabet* set $S = \{s_1, s_2, \ldots, s_n\}$. Since we shall wish to refer to the ith alphabet symbol we will usually write S as a sequence, $S = s_1 s_2 \ldots s_n$ (possibly with commas). An example is $S = abcd$ and $D = abbabccaaadadbd$, in which $n = 4$ and the message length is $N = 15$.

An *encoding* of the alphabet symbols and thereby of any message is a replacement $s_i \to c_i$ ($1 \le i \le n$) of each distinct symbol s_i by a binary *word* c_i (i.e. a sequence of binary bits). Taken in sequence these words form the codebook $C = c_1 c_2 \ldots c_n$. An example is $a \to 00, b \to 01, c \to 10, d \to 11$, with codebook 00, 01, 10, 11 (here commas are necessary to separate the words).

What we would like is to find an encoding by which messages use the least possible number of bits. Intuition suggests, rightly, that this means the most frequently used symbols should be allocated the shortest codewords. Thus we consider the frequency f_i with which symbol s_i appears in the message. We'll review and expand on the notation so far, then state and prove the ground-breaking result Shannon was able to achieve.

$S = s_1, s_2, \ldots, s_n$, the source symbols, or *alphabet*.

$D = d_1, d_2, \ldots, d_N$, the message sequence, of length N.

$F = f_1, f_2, \ldots, f_n$, where f_i is the *frequency* of s_i in message D. Thus f_i is the size of the set $\{k : 1 \le k \le N, d_k = s_i\}$.

$P = p_1, p_2, \ldots, p_n$, where $p_i = f_i/N$, the *relative frequency* of s_i in D. It is the probability that a symbol selected at random from D will be s_i (each symbol choice equally likely).

$C = c_1, c_2, \ldots, c_n$, the codebook, where $s_i \to c_i$. A set of such codewords, leaving open the actual pairing with symbols, is called simply a *code*. We denote the length of c_i by L_i or $|c_i|$.

$M = \sum\limits_{i=1}^{n} p_i L_i$, the mean number of bits per symbol on encoding D by the code C.

Theorem 12.8 *(Shannon's Noiseless Coding Theorem) The mean number of bits per symbol used in encoding a finite message cannot be less than the entropy. That is,*

$$M \ge H(p_1, p_2, \ldots, p_n).$$

Proof We use induction on n, the number of symbols in the alphabet. The result holds when $n = 1$, for the mean number of bits per symbol is the length of the unique codeword, whilst the entropy is $-1 \cdot \log_2 1 = 0$. Consider a general case $n \ge 2$ and define a code C_0 consisting of the codewords of C that start with '0'. Delete from D all symbols whose codewords are not in C_0, to obtain a message D_0.

Without loss of generality, C has least possible number of bits per symbol. Now, if C_0 were the whole of C, the code C_0' obtained by stripping off the initial 0s from the words of

C_0 would provide a codebook with fewer bits per symbol than C. Similarly for C_1. Thus neither C_0 nor C_1 exhausts the codewords of C and, since they have no codewords in common, each uses fewer than n symbols. Hence we may apply the theorem inductively to both.

Let $\sum_0$ denote summation over those integers i for which c_i is in C_0. Write $q_0 = \sum_0 p_i$. Similarly define $C_1, D_1, \sum_1, q_1$ from codewords starting with a '1'. Thus $q_0 + q_1 = 1$. In C_0 the new probability of symbol s_i is $f_i / \sum_0 f_i = (f_i/N)/(\sum_0 f_i/N) = p_i/q_0$, implying by the inductive hypothesis

$$\sum_0 \frac{p_i}{q_0}(L_i - 1) \geq -\sum_0 \frac{p_i}{q_0} \log_2 \frac{p_i}{q_0}.$$

After multiplying through by q_0 and expanding the log we obtain

$$\sum_0 p_i(L_i - 1) \geq -\sum_0 p_i \log_2 p_i + \left(\sum_0 p_i\right) \log_2 q_0.$$

Similarly,

$$\sum_1 p_i(L_i - 1) \geq -\sum_1 p_i \log_2 p_i + \left(\sum_1 p_i\right) \log_2 q_1.$$

Adding these inequalities and observing that $\sum_0 p_i + \sum_1 p_i = q_0 + q_1 = 1$, we find

$$\sum_{i=1}^n p_i L_i \geq 1 - \sum_{i=1}^n p_i \log_2 p_i + q_0 \log_2 q_0 + q_1 \log_2 q_1$$
$$= H(p_1, \ldots, p_n) + 1 - H(q_0)$$
$$\geq H(p_1, \ldots, p_n), \quad \text{since } H(x) \leq 1 \text{ by Theorem 12.5 (i).}$$

Example 12.9 Consider the message MERRY MEN MEET. We'll assume here that omitting the separating spaces between words presents no problem of interpretation (achieving this in general is the topic of our next section). Encoding the ith symbol s_i as the 3-bit binary form of integer i, we may write, in terms of Notation 12.7,

$$S = \text{MERYNT} \to C = (001, 010, 011, 100, 101, 110),$$
$$F = 3\,4\,2\,1\,1\,1,$$
$$P = \frac{1}{4}\frac{1}{3}\frac{1}{6}\frac{1}{12}\frac{1}{12}\frac{1}{12}.$$

Thus the encoding takes three bits per symbol, compared with the entropy of Theorem 12.8: $\sum p_i \log(1/p_i) = 2.34$ (to two decimal places). We have used 36 bits for the whole message against a theoretical minimum of $12 \times 2.34 = 28$. We shall shortly see a way to get closer. Meanwhile, Theorem 12.6 reassures us that the highest H can go depends only on the relative frequencies of the symbols used, and not on the message length.

Prefix-free codes Suppose we have a stream of codewords with no extra symbols or *separators* to mark the transitions from one codeword to another. A way to ensure we know where one codeword ends and another starts is to insist that the code be *prefix-free* (PF). That is, no codeword should form the first k digits, or *k-prefix*, of another, for any *k*. Prefix-free codes have an extremely useful graphical representation which we shall make use of. First some definitions.

Codetrees In the present context a *tree* is a set of vertices, some joined to each other by edges in such a way that

(1) every pair of vertices is joined by a path,
(2) there are no circuits.

Equivalently, every pair of vertices u, v is joined by a path which is unique. We can therefore define the *distance* between u and v to be the length of the path as measured by its number of edges. The tree is said to be *rooted* if one vertex is designated as root, and then the vertices are classified by their distance d from the root, called their *level* or *depth*. Vertices and edges of a tree are also known as respectively *nodes* and *branches*; we shall use the synonyms interchangeably. In diagrams, level d nodes will be positioned below those of level $d - 1$. This and the following are illustrated in Figure 12.8.

A vertex v is called the *parent* of any vertices to which it is joined in the next level. They in turn are *offspring* of the parent and *siblings* of each other. We shall consider only *binary* trees, in which a parent has exactly two offspring (and consequently there is an even number of nodes at each level below the root). Nodes with no offspring are called *leaves*, and play a key role. A PF code is *represented* by a rooted binary tree, called its **codetree**, in which

(1) the edges from parent to offspring are labelled 0, 1 in some order,
(2) each source symbol corresponds to a leaf, and the associated codeword is the sequence of labels from the root to that leaf.

Example 12.10 The code $C = 00, 01, 100, 101, 110, 111$ is prefix-free. We give its codetree in Figure 12.8, then describe how this may be arrived at.

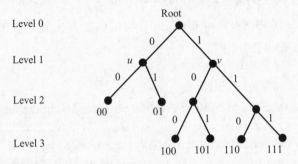

Figure 12.8 Code tree for the code of Example 12.10. There are two leaves at Level 2 and four at Level 3. Notice that, for example, v is the parent of sibling leaves labelled 00, 01.

From code to codetree We may proceed recursively from an initial root with offspring labelled u, v and joined to the root by edges labelled respectively 0, 1. The next thing is to construct a codetree with root u for the code C_0' obtained by collecting the codewords of C that start with '0' and deleting the 0 from each one (in our example 00, 01 becomes 0, 1, hence the level 2 leaves). Then similarly for those beginning with '1' and node v. Conversely, any binary rooted tree becomes the codetree for a PF code after its sibling pairs have been labelled with 0, 1 in some order. The fact that, by definition, no leaf is on the path to another ensures the prefix-free property.

Optimal codes Restricting ourselves to PF codes to solve the separator problem, we seek for each probability distribution P a code C which minimises the mean bit rate $M = \sum p_i L_i$, where L_i is the length of the ith symbol's codeword. Such a code will be called *optimal*. To find one it should help to know some of their characteristics. We claim firstly that after possibly reallocating codewords and relabelling, whilst keeping M constant, we may write

$$p_1 \leq p_2 \leq \cdots \leq p_n \quad \text{but} \quad L_1 = L_2 \geq \cdots \geq L_n. \tag{12.11}$$

We show that after we arrange $p_1 \leq p_2 \leq \cdots \leq p_n$ the codewords can be reallocated to achieve (12.11) as follows. (i) For every pair $i < j$ such that $L_i < L_j$ (out of order), we see that $p_i = \cdots = p_j$ so we can switch c_i and c_j to restore order. For if $p_i < p_j$ then switching c_i and c_j would reduce M by $p_i L_i + p_j L_j - p_i L_j - p_j L_i = (p_j - p_i)(L_j - L_i) > 0$, contradicting optimality. Thus $p_i \geq p_j$ and, along with $p_i \leq \cdots \leq p_j$, this implies $p_i = \cdots = p_j$.

(ii) It remains to deduce that $L_1 = L_2$. But if $L_1 > L_2$ then, since the unique codeword c_1 of greatest length L_1 cannot have another codeword as prefix, we may replace c_1 by its prefix of length L_2 without losing the PF property, and hence reduce M. But this contradicts optimality, so we are left with $L_1 = L_2$.

This establishes the form of (12.11). Notice that the least two probabilities are p_1, p_2, which may or may not be equal. If they are equal, we could switch the labels of symbols 1, 2 to obtain an equally valid list (12.11). For simplicity the p_i ordering of (12.11) will be described as *increasing* (rather than non-decreasing), and that of the L_i as *decreasing*. We are ready to prove the theorem below, which points to Huffman's solution.

Theorem 12.11 *(a) Any codetree with n leaves has $2n - 2$ non-root nodes, and $2n - 2$ edges, with an even number of both at each level. (b) An optimal code has two codewords of greatest length that differ only in their last digit. They may be taken as c_1, c_2 in (12.11).*

Proof (a) We can reduce a codetree to the root and two offspring leaves by repeatedly deleting two sibling leaves and their connecting edges. Such a deletion transforms the siblings' parent into a new leaf, so the total number of leaves is reduced by just 1. Thus $n - 2$ deletion operations are required to leave the node plus two leaves. Since each deletion reduces both edges and non-root nodes by 2, their original number was $2 + 2(n - 2) = 2n - 2$.

(b) By (12.11) an optimal code has two or more codewords of greatest length. If there aren't two of these that differ *only* in their last digit, we can delete the last digit of each and still have a PF code for the probabilities, contradicting the minimality of M.

12.3 Huffman text compression

We begin with a statement of Huffman's coding system for text compression, then explore the sense in which it achieves optimality. It is noteworthy that Huffman codes are routinely used as part of systems designed for the compression of digital images. See, for example, the JPEG system in Section 15.4.3.

Construction 12.12 (*Huffman, 1952*) Given a list L of nodes labelled with the probabilities, we progressively reduce it to a singleton R, which is the root of the codetree we construct in the process. We assume for convenience that all p_i are positive and that $n \geq 3$.

Repeat	
	Replace any two nodes in L of least probability by
	a parent labelled with the sum of their probabilities.
Until	L is a singleton, R.

For each parent, label the edges to its offspring 0, 1 in either order. Then c_i is the bit sequence in the unique path from the root to the leaf labelled p_i. Thus level d leaves are assigned d-bit codewords.

Example 12.13 Here is an example to clarify what Huffman's construction actually is, before we prove that it works. Starting again with the probabilities of Example 12.9, notice that at each stage there may be more than one valid choice. We aim to keep siblings at the same height in the diagram and to avoid crossing edges. Two decimal places of accuracy suffice for the following discussion; see Figure 12.9.

The original coding used 36 digits, an average of 3 per symbol, compared with the entropy bound of 2.34. Here the mean is $2(1/4 + 1/3) + 3(1/6 + 1/12 + 1/12 + 1/12) = 2.42$, not perfection but certainly an improvement. The improvement in general is such that Huffman codes are widely used in practice. Later we will see how to accomplish the apparently impossible, of actually meeting the entropy bound provided a longer calculation is acceptable. But our next task is to prove and then dramatically improve upon Huffman's original method. We recall that a code is called *optimal* if it encodes with bit rate $M = \sum p_i L_i$ least possible, *given that it is prefix-free*.

Theorem 12.14 *Huffman's construction gives an optimal code.*

Proof In the notation of (12.11) we are given probabilities $p_1 \leq p_2 \leq \cdots \leq p_n$. Suppose firstly that $n \geq 3$. Whether the special cases $p_1 < p_2$ and $p_2 = p_3$ occur it remains true that $p_1, p_2 \leq p_i$ for $i \geq 3$. We claim that there exists a (rooted binary) tree to minimise

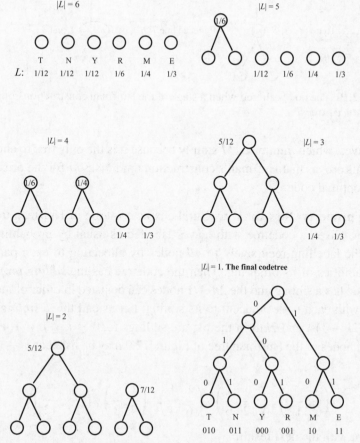

Figure 12.9 Stages in building a Hoffman codetree, starting from the probabilites of Example 12.9. We obtain a more efficient coding than before.

M for which the leaves p_1, p_2 are siblings (given this, it suffices to minimise over all such trees). To show this we begin by noting that by Theorem 12.11 the number of vertices and edges in a codetree with n leaves is finite, and so at least one tree T exists to minimise M. In this tree, let S be a parent furthest from the root. Switch the offspring labels with p_1, p_2. This cannot increase M, so M stays minimal.

In the Huffman manner, delete sibling nodes p_1, p_2, allocate probability $p_1 + p_2$ to the parent, and make it a leaf of new tree T'. The old and new situations are compared in Figure 12.10.

If the chosen parent is a distance d from the root, the change in M is $M(T) - M(T') = (d + 1)p_1 + (d + 1)p_2 - d(p_1 + p_2) = p_1 + p_2$, a quantity independent of the choice of how T is structured between the chosen parent and the root. It follows that T minimises M for probabilites p_1, p_2, ..., p_n if and only if T' minimises M for $p_1 + p_2, p_3 ..., p_n$. For example, if U is a variant on the structure as mentioned above and $M(U) < M(T)$, then $M(U') < M(T')$. However, by repeating the Huffman step we arrive at a tree with

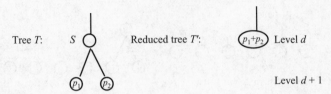

Figure 12.10 The nodes altered when a stage of the Huffman construction converts tree *T* into *reduced* tree *T′*.

only two leaves, which minimises *M* simply because it is the only tree to choose from in this case. This proves that Huffman's construction minimises *M* for the original tree and so gives an optimal code.

The sibling property Now for a structural characterisation of Huffman trees that will be used later. Given a codetree with leaves labelled as usual by probabilities (12.11), we extend the labelling recursively to *all* nodes by allocating to each parent the sum of the probabilities of its offspring. Then the codetree has the *sibling property* if each non-root node has a sibling and the $2n - 1$ nodes can be listed in order of increasing ($\leq$) probability with each node adjacent to its sibling. Let us call this a *sibling ordering*. It means the $(2k - 1)$st and $2k$th in the list are siblings for $1 \leq k \leq n - 1$. For example, the non-root nodes of the Huffman tree of Figure 12.9 may be listed as $n - 1 = 5$ sibling pairs:

$$\left(\frac{1}{2}, \frac{1}{12}\right), \left(\frac{1}{12}, \frac{1}{6}\right), \left(\frac{1}{6}, \frac{1}{4}\right), \left(\frac{1}{4}, \frac{1}{3}\right), \left(\frac{5}{12}, \frac{7}{12}\right),$$

in agreement with the next result.

Theorem 12.15 *A PF codetree is Huffman if and only if it has the sibling property.*

Proof If a codetree is generated by Huffman's construction then at each stage the sibling nodes with least probabilities provide the next pair in the ordered list required by the sibling property. Thus the codetree has the sibling property.

Starting, on the other hand, with a sibling property list for a codetree, we claim that *the first sibling pair p_1, p_2 must be leaves*, and so provide the first step of Huffman's construction. Working our way up the list, we complete the construction. It remains to justify our claim. Suppose that p_2 is not a leaf but is the parent of q, r as depicted in Figure 12.11. Then:

$$\begin{aligned} p_2 &\leq q, r && \text{being by hypothesis earlier in the sibling list} \\ &\leq q + r && \text{since } q, r \geq 0 \\ &= p_2 && \text{by construction, since } p_2 \text{ is the parent of } q, r, \end{aligned}$$

implying all three probabilities are equal to zero ($p_2 \leq q \leq q + r \leq p_2$), a condition we have ruled out. This completes the proof.

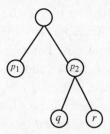

Figure 12.11 Figure for proof of Theorem 12.15.

Example 12.16 Figure 12.12 shows a Huffman codetree for probabilities (0.08, 0.12, 0.14, 0.16, 0.25, 0.25). The integer before each node shows its place in an ordering that exhibits the sibling property.

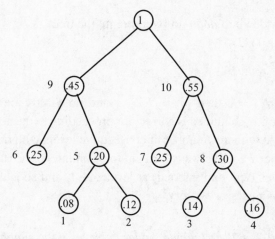

Figure 12.12 Illustration of the sibling property in a Huffman codetree.

Theorem 12.17 *In a sibling ordering on a codetree we have (i) every probability at level d is less than or equal to every probability at level $d - 1$ ($d \geq 1$), (ii) if p, q are probabilities on the same level, where p is a parent, then $p \leq 2q$.*

Proof (i) The result follows by induction on the number of sibling pairs, for clearly if it holds for the reduced tree T' of Figure 12.10 (with p_1, p_2 heading the list) then it holds for T. For (ii), if p has offspring p_1, p_2 then

$$p = p_1 + p_2 \quad \text{by definition of sibling ordering}$$
$$\leq q + q \qquad \text{by part (i)}$$
$$= 2q.$$

Canonical Huffman codes

If in Figure 12.12 we label the sibling edges 0, 1 in the usual way so as to obtain a coding of the original probabilities, say 1001100101 corresponding to the node order specified in the figure, we get the code 00, 10, 010, 011, 110, 111. A considerable time reduction in coding and decoding results if we can ensure that, unlike the present example, the codewords of a given length are consecutive binary integers. In this way much searching is reduced to short direct calculation. Such a code is called *canonical Huffman*, and we now describe how it may be obtained.

We begin with a Huffman tree to determine the number N_d of codewords of length d for $d = dmin, \ldots, dmax$. We then replace the d-bit codewords by the d-bit binary forms of a sequence of consecutive integers $F_d, \ldots, M_d$ in such a way that the PF property is retained. These integers are obtained by the construction given below (F is for 'first' and M is for 'maximum' integer).

> *(Converting to canonical Huffman)*
> $F_{dmax} = 0; M_{dmax+1} = -1$
> For $d = dmax$ down to $dmin$ do {working up the tree}
> $F_d = (M_{d+1} + 1)/2$
> $M_d = F_d + N_d - 1.$

Of course, if some $N_d = 0$ then $M_d = F_d - 1$ and no d-bit codewords are required. However, the value of M_d obtained is correct for proceeding to the next level, indeed, the construction can cope with any number of consecutive levels with no leaves/codewords. Moreover, the number F_d will always turn out to be an integer because $M_{d+1} + 1$ is the total number of nodes (leaf and internal) at level $d + 1$, and so is even. The following theorem provides the necessary theory.

Theorem 12.18 *(a) Let the Huffman nodes at level d be numbered 0 to M_d and the leaves F_d to M_d. Then $F_d = (M_{d+1} + 1)/2$ for $d = dmax - 1$ down to $dmin$. (b) The canonical Huffman code is prefix-free.*

Nodes at level d	$\bigcirc$	$\bigcirc$		$\bigcirc$		$\bigcirc$
Numbering	0	1	...	F_d	...	M_d

$\longleftarrow$ Leaves $\longrightarrow$

Proof (a) The key idea is that the nodes at a given level are partitioned into leaves and parents; no node can be both. Further, since in our notation the number of nodes at level $d + 1$ is $M_{d+1} + 1$, the number of parents at level d is $p = (M_{d+1} + 1)/2$. Therefore we can number parents 0 to $p - 1$ and leaves (corresponding to codewords) from p to M_d, as given in the construction.

(b) We must show that a d-bit codeword cannot be a prefix of any $(d + r)$-bit codeword, for any $r \geq 1$. For some fixed value of r, let the first d bits of M_{d+r} have integer value k, and the last r the value e. Then, because M_{d+r} is odd, $1 \leq e \leq 2^r$. We represent this division of M_{d+r} below:

d bits, value k	r bits, value e, $1 \leq e < 2^r$.

Then it suffices to show that $F_d \geq k + 1$. To do so we proceed step by step, showing that

$$F_{d+r-m} \geq 2^{r-m} \cdot k + 1 \quad \text{for} \quad 1 \leq m \leq r, \tag{*}$$

and then setting $m = r$. Firstly we observe that (*) holds for $m = 1$ because $M_{d+r} = 2^r \cdot k + e$, and by construction

$$F_{d+r-1} = (M_{d+r} + 1)/2 \geq 2^{r-1} \cdot k + 1, \quad \text{since } e \geq 1, e + 1 \geq 2.$$

It remains to show that the truth of (*) for any integer $1 \leq m \leq r - 1$ implies its truth for $m + 1$. We argue that

$$
\begin{aligned}
F_{d+r-m-1} &= (M_{d+r-m} + 1)/2 && \text{by construction} \\
&\geq (F_{d+r-m} + 1)/2 && (\text{given } N_{d+r-m} > 0) \\
&\geq (2^{r-m}k + 1 + 1)/2 && \text{by hypothesis} \\
&= 2^{r-m-1}k + 1.
\end{aligned}
$$

Thus (*) holds and we may set $m = r$ to obtain $F_d \geq k + 1$ as required. (The proof can be modified to take account of case $N_d = 0$.)

Notice that the step from M_{d+1} to F_d is equivalent to deleting the last bit from M_{d+1} and adding 1 to the resulting d-bit integer. This may be observed in Table 12.1.

Example 12.19 If a Huffman tree yields the numbers of codewords 2, 3, 3 for respective lengths $d = 5, 4, 3$ the canonical code is as shown in Table 12.1. A convenient exercise is to convert the code of Example 12.16 into canonical form, given the number of codewords of each length.

Table 12.1. *Canonical Huffman codewords with lengths from dmin = 3 to dmax = 5. The index i_d is the index of the first codeword of length d, and is used in encoding (see below).*

symbol	index	codeword	d	F_d	i_d
COMPUTER	1	00000	5	0	1
NAP	2	00001			
FOR	3	0001	4	1	3
THE	4	0010			
TAKE	5	0011			
E	6	010	3	2	6
A	7	011			
I	8	100			

A sample of the result for the text of the novel *Far from the madding crowd* is given in Witten *et al.* (1994). The codeword lengths run from 4 to 18.

Economical storage A canonical ordering is lexicographic with most significant bits to the left. That is to say, it follows the usual dictionary system: if x, y are symbols and T, U denote sequences of symbols, then $xT < yU$ if $x < y$, or if $x = y$ but $T < U$. This is because (a) the codewords of a given length are in numerical order and (b) a codeword of length d exceeds the d-prefix of any longer codeword ($F_d > k$ in the proof of Theorem 12.18). We store the corresponding symbols in this order in a 1-dimensional array with an index $i = 1, 2, \ldots, n$. For each length d, store as integers:

F_d: the first codeword of length d,
i_d: the index of the first codeword of length d.

To encode a symbol of index i:	To decode the next bit sequence
$d := dmax$;	$d := dmin$; $c :=$ the first $dmin$ bits;
while $i < i_d$ do $d := d - 1$;	while $c < F_d$ (lexicographic order) do
$codeword := F_d + i - i_d$.	append the next bit to c; $d := d + 1$;
(See Table 12.1)	$index := i_d + c - F_d$ (as integers).

Example 12.20 As arranged by the canonical ordering, we need only store information about the start and end of lists rather than the lists themselves. The storage requirements of Example 12.19 are simply $F_d = 0, 1, 2$ and $i_d = 1, 3, 6$ (corresponding to $d = 5, 4, 3$ in that order). The decoding algorithm applied to a received binary sequence 001101100001 interprets it as three successive codewords with indices $5, 7, 2$, by the 3-column calculation below. (Exercise: what is the message?) It is helpful to follow the progression from $<$ to $\geq$ in, say, the third column. The process is easily visualised in Table 12.1.

$$d = 3: c = 001 < F_3 \qquad d = 3: c = 011 \geq F_3 \qquad d = 3: c = 000 < F_3$$
$$d = 4: c = 0011 \geq F_4 \qquad index = i_3 + c - F_3 \qquad d = 4: c = 0000 < F_4$$
$$index = i_4 + c - F_4 \qquad\qquad = 6 + 3 - 2 = 7 \qquad d = 5: c = 00001 \geq F_5$$
$$= 3 + 3 - 1 = 5. \qquad\qquad\qquad\qquad\qquad index = i_5 + c - F_5 = 2$$

12.4 The redundancy of Huffman codes

Redundancy We proved Shannon's result (Theorem 12.8) that, if, in a finite message, the ith alphabet symbol is to appear with probability (relative frequency) p_i, then a lower bound on M, the mean bits per symbol used in encoding, is given by the entropy $H(p_1, \ldots, p_n)$. Thus the difference

$$r = M - H \tag{12.12}$$

is a measure of how well a chosen encoding performs, and is known as the *redundancy* of that code. For example, a redundancy of 0.1 suggests that for every 1 Mb of storage used,

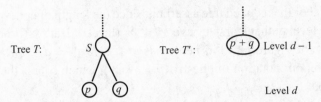

Figure 12.13 (Figure 12.10 with least probabilities p, q) Converting a Huffman tree into its reduced tree T'.

a theoretical 100 K might be pared off by an improved encoding method. Failing this degree of perfection, we would obviously like the redundancy to be as little as possible; for Huffman codes a very useful upper limit on redundancy is given by the following result, which we shall prove after some necessary groundwork.

Theorem 12.21 *(Gallager, 1978) Let p_n be the probability of the most likely symbol in a finite discrete source. Let $\sigma = 1 - \log_2 e + \log_2(\log_2 e) = 0.086$ (three decimal places). Then the redundancy of the Huffman code for that source satisfies*

$$r \leq p_n + \sigma \ \text{always}, \tag{12.13}$$

$$r \leq 2 - H(p_n) - p_n \leq p_n, \ \text{if } p_n \geq 1/2. \tag{12.14}$$

To prove this we shall progress through some interesting results on the structure of Huffman trees. Suppose we are given a Huffman codetree T. Then T has, by Theorem 12.15, a *sibling ordering* of the nodes: $1, 2, \ldots, 2n - 1$ in order of increasing probability $q_1, q_2, \ldots, q_{2n-1}$ ($q_{2n-1} = 1$), where the probability of a node is the sum of the probabilities of its two offspring and nodes $2k - 1$, $2k$ are siblings for $1 \leq k \leq n - 1$. Of course, node $2n - 1$ is the root. This leads to a simple and powerful method of obtaining results by comparing T with its derived tree T', the latter obtained by deleting leaves 1, 2 and redesignating their parent S as a leaf in the manner of Figure 12.13. Then T' has the sibling property with nodes $3, 4, \ldots, 2n - 1$, which may be relabelled $1, 2, \ldots, 2n - 3$.

Lemma 12.22 *For a sibling ordering of a Huffman tree, with $n \geq 2$ leaves, and probabilities $\{q_i\}$, we have*

$$M = \sum_{i=1}^{2n-2} q_i = \sum_{k=1}^{n-1} (q_{2k-1} + q_{2k}), \tag{12.15}$$

$$H = \sum_{k=1}^{n-1} (q_{2k-1} + q_{2k}) H\left(\frac{q_{2k-1}}{q_{2k-1} + q_{2k}}\right). \tag{12.16}$$

Proof The second equality in (12.15) is trivial; we consider only the first. For each of (12.15) and (12.16) it suffices to show that, when we pass to the reduced tree, *each side has the same net loss*, and that equality holds in the smallest case $n = 2$.

Equation (12.15) In the 2-leaf case, $n = 2$, the codewords are simply 0, 1 by construction, so there are automatically $M = 1$ bits per symbol. But $q_1 + q_2 = 1$, giving the desired equality. For the reduced tree assertion, since the length of codeword allocated to a leaf equals the level of that leaf, we have $M = \sum (\text{level of leaf}) \times (\text{probability of leaf})$, so in the notation of Figure 12.13 its net loss is $M_{\text{old}} - M_{\text{new}} = dp + dq - (d-1)(p+q) = p+q$ (note: our notation implies $p, q = q_1, q_2$), which equals the loss $q_1 + q_2$ in $\sum q_i$, as required.

Equation (12.16) In the case $n = 2$ the left hand side is $H(q_1)$, whilst the right hand side takes the form $(q_1 + q_2)H(q_1/(q_1 + q_2))$, which reduces correctly to $H(q_1)$ because $q_1 + q_2 = 1$. Considering the reduction part, the left hand side, H loses $(-p \log p - q \log q)$ corresponding to *leaves p, q*, but gains $-(p+q)\log(p+q)$ from *leaf p + q*, whilst the right hand side loses

$$(p+q)H\left(\frac{p}{p+q}\right) = (p+q)\left(-\frac{p}{p+q}\log\frac{p}{p+q} - \frac{q}{p+q}\log\frac{q}{p+q}\right)$$

$$\text{since } 1 - \frac{p}{p+q} = \frac{q}{p+q}$$

$$= -p\log\frac{p}{p+q} - q\log\frac{q}{p+q}$$

$$\text{on cancelling factors } p + q$$

$$= -p\log p + p\log(p+q) - q\log q + q\log(p+q)$$

$$\text{since } \log(a/b) = \log a - \log b$$

$$= -p\log p - q\log q + (p+q)\log(p+q),$$

and this equals the net loss in H in passing from T to T'. This completes the proof.

Definition 12.23 The following concept helps to show what is going on in a Huffman codetree T. We say T is *full down to level d* if every node of level less than d is a parent, or simply *full* if it is full down to its greatest level. The two cases are illustrated in Figure 12.14 and the first consequences appear in Lemma 12.24.

Lemma 12.24 *(a) If a Huffman tree T is full up to level d, then for any level $\lambda < d$ the number of nodes is 2^λ and their probabilities sum to 1 (thus, for a full subtree, the sum of probabilities at each level is the same), (b) a Huffman tree is full down to the level of leaf p_n, and no further, (c) if $p_n \geq 1/2$ then the leaf p_n has level 1.*

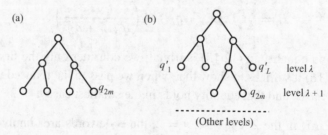

Figure 12.14 (a) A full tree, (b) a tree full down to level $\lambda = 2$, in the notation above.

Proof (a) At each succeeding level before d, the number of nodes doubles and each probability is split between siblings. But the root has assigned probability 1, so this remains the sum at the levels before d. (b) Each node is either a parent or a leaf, so a tree is full down to level d if and only if it has no leaf above level d. But by (12.11) no leaf can lie above p_n. (c) Since $p_n \geq 1/2$ and $\sum p_i = 1$, it follows that any p_i, or a sum thereof which excludes p_n, is less than $1/2$ and so less than p_n. Therefore, when Huffman's coding is performed, p_n will not be chosen until the last pair, and hence does not appear until level 1.

Remark 12.25 (*A formula for r*) Substituting (12.15), (12.16) into the definition $r = M - H$ of redundancy we obtain

$$r = \sum_{k=1}^{n-1} (q_{2k-1} + q_{2k})\left(1 - H\left(\frac{q_{2k-1}}{q_{2k-1} + q_{2k}}\right)\right). \tag{12.17}$$

Since there are $n \geq 3$ leaves, the root has two offspring and there is at least one other node, necessarily at a level at least 2. Hence there is a level λ less than the maximum, down to which the tree is full (after that it may or may not be full). At this level there are $L = 2^\lambda$ nodes (Lemma 12.24), whose probabilities may be written $q_1' \leq \cdots \leq q_L'$. Let m be the *greatest integer for which node $2m$ is at level $\lambda + 1$*; thus, for example, node $2m + 2$ is at level λ. The notation is illustrated in Figure 12.14.

Then the terms in (12.17) from $k = m + 1$ to $n - 1$ are those of $r = M - H$ for the full tree, and we determine the contributions of these terms separately for M and H. For M, we apply (12.15) and note that (by Lemma 12.24) the probabilities at each of the λ levels sum to 1, giving M's contributions as $\lambda \cdot 1 = \lambda$. The contribution of H is the entropy for a full tree with leaf probabilities (q_i'). Applying this fact to (12.17) we obtain

$$r = \lambda - H(q_1', \ldots, q_L') + \sum_{k=1}^{m} (q_{2k-1} + q_{2k})\left(1 - H\left(\frac{q_{2k-1}}{q_{2k-1} + q_{2k}}\right)\right). \tag{12.18}$$

Now, since $q_{2k-1} \leq q_{2k}$ we have $2q_{2k-1} \leq q_{2k-1} + q_{2k}$ and hence $q_{2k-1}/(q_{2k-1} + q_{2k}) \leq 1/2$. But $0 \leq x \leq 1/2$ implies $H(x) \geq 2x$ (Theorem 12.5), and so the second term in (12.18) is bounded above by

$$\sum_{k=1}^{m} (q_{2k-1} + q_{2k})\left(1 - \frac{2q_{2k-1}}{q_{2k-1} + q_{2k}}\right),$$

which after simplification may be bracketed as $-q_1 + (q_2 - q_3) + \cdots + (q_{2m-2} - q_{2m-1}) + q_{2m}$. This cannot exceed q_{2m} because $\{q_i\}$ is increasing, and hence by (12.18)

$$r \leq \lambda - H(q_1', \ldots, q_L') + q_{2m}. \tag{12.19}$$

Proof of the main result, Theorem 12.21 Firstly (12.14). With $p_n \geq 1/2$ the leaf p_n is at level 1 (Lemma 12.24) and taking $\lambda = 1$, $L = 2$ we have the situation depicted in Figure 12.15.

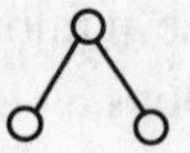

(Other levels exist below)

q_1' $q_2' = p_n$

Figure 12.15 If $p_n \geq 1/2$ then leaf p_n is at level 1.

Thus $r \leq 1 - H(1 - p_n, p_n) + q_{2m} = 1 - H(p_n) + q_{2m}$. By definition of m we have $q_{2m} \leq q_1' = 1 - p_n$, and so $r \leq 2 - H(p_n) - p_n$. This is the first and main inequality in (12.14). The second follows from Theorem 12.5 by $H(p_n) = H(1 - p_n) \geq 2(1 - p_n)$ (using $1 - p_n \leq 1/2$).

The rest of this main proof is devoted to (12.13). Referring to Figure 12.14, we choose λ so that the tree is full up to level λ but has a level $\lambda + 1$ in which q_{2m} lies. Hence $q_{2m} \leq p_n$ and, by (12.19) with Theorem 12.17,

$$r \leq \lambda + p_n - \text{Min}\{H(q_1', \ldots, q_L') : \ 0 \leq q_1' \leq \cdots \leq q_L' \leq 2q_1', \sum q_i' = 1\}.$$
(12.20)

Hence it remains to prove that the minimum in (12.20) is bounded below by $\lambda - \sigma$, where $\sigma = 1 - \log(e) + \log(\log e)$. Now, the equality and the $L + 1$ inequalities in (12.20), all linear, define a compact subset

$$Q = \{(x_1, \ldots, x_n) : \ 0 \leq x_1 \leq x_2 \leq \cdots \leq x_L \leq 2x_1, \text{ and } \sum x_i = 1\} \quad (12.21)$$

of real L-dimensional space, bounded by hyperplanes. Therefore the continuous function H on Q attains a minimum and this occurs at a vertex (see e.g. Hoggar, 1992). Each vertex satisfies the equations defining Q together with equality in $L - 1$ of the inequalities. That is, all but two of

(a) $x_1 = 0$,

(b) $x_1 = x_2, x_2 = x_3, \ldots, x_{L-1} = x_L$ ($L - 1$ equations),

(c) $x_L = 2x_1$.

We note firstly that (a) is ruled out in such a solution because, with the inequalities, it implies all x_i are zero, contradicting $\sum x_i = 1$. Further, not all of (b) can hold, for if they did we would have $x_i = 1$ for $1 \leq i \leq n$, which contradicts (c). Thus exactly one of (b) must be omitted and the equations for a vertex reduce to $\sum x_i = 1$ and $x_i = x_2 = \cdots = x_i, x_{i+1} = \cdots = x_L = 2x_1$ for some choice of $i = 1, 2, \ldots, L - 1$. Solving these: $ix_1 + (L - i)2x_1 = 1$, so $x_1 = 1/(2L - i)$, and

$$\begin{aligned}
H &= -ix_1 \log x_1 - (L - i)2x_1 \log(2x_1) \\
&= -x_1\{i \log x_1 + 2(L - i)(1 + \log x_1)\} \qquad \text{since } \log 2 = 1 \\
&= -x_1\{2(L - i) + (2L - i)\log x_1\} \qquad \text{now set } t = L - i \\
&= \log(L + t) + 2L/(L + t) - 2 \qquad \text{since } x_1 = 1/(L + t).
\end{aligned}$$

We obtain a lower bound by using elementary calculus to minimise H over $1 \le t \le L - 1$ with t varying continuously. From (12.8), $(d/dx) \log x = (1/x) \ln 2$, whence H has derivative and sign pattern thereof (the arrows indicate t-values to left and right of the zero):

$$\frac{dH}{dt} = \frac{t - L(2 \ln 2 - 1)}{(L + t)^2 \ln 2}, \qquad \begin{array}{ccc} t \to & L(2 \ln 2 - 1) & \to \\ dH/dt \quad - & 0 & + \end{array}$$

and hence the least value at the unique local minimum is given by $t = L(2 \ln 2 - 1)$, that is $L + t = 2L \ln 2$, and substituting this value gives

$$H = \log(2L \ln 2) + 2L/(2L \ln 2) - 2 = \log 2 + \log L + \log(\ln 2) + 1/\ln 2 - 2.$$

Finally this equals $\lambda - \sigma$ as required because of the relations $\log L = \lambda$, $\log 2 = 1$ and $1/\ln 2 = \ln e / \ln 2 = \log_2(e)$, where we have added the subscript 2 for emphasis. This completes the proof of Theorem 12.21, upper-bounding the redundancy of Huffman codes.

Example 12.26 If English text is encoded character by character, the most common character is the *space*, at about $p_n = 0.18$. Theorem 12.21 gives an upper limit on redundancy of approximately $0.18 + 0.086 = 0.266$ bits per symbol. Taking the entropy of English as 5 bits per character (see e.g. Cover & Thomas, 1991), the Huffman redundancy as a percentage is less than $0.266 \times 100/5$, or about 5%.

Remark 12.27 Slightly better bounds on Huffman redundancy can be obtained by subdividing further the range of p_n, and introducing p_1 as a second parameter. We have (Capocelli *et al.*, 1986):

$$r \le p_n - p_1 + 0.086, \qquad \text{if } 0 < p_n < 2/9,$$
$$r \le p_n - p_1 + 0.082, \qquad \text{if } 2/9 \le p_n < 1/3.$$

This does not improve the English language bound, but reduces the redundancy bound for 'making men merry', with $p_1 = 1/12$ and $p_n = 1/4$, down from 0.336 to 0.332.

12.5 Arithmetic codes

We have shown that no message code can average fewer bits per symbol than the value of entropy (Theorem 12.8), and we shall shortly show that arithmetic codes, to be described, come arbitrarily close to this bound as the message size increases. This is a property not enjoyed by Huffman codes, but is bought at a greater computational cost. However, if the cost is economic in our situation, we can have better compression. Like the Huffman case, these codes are an option in the image compression standard JPEG (see Chapter 15).

Arithmetic codes can seem hard to grasp, though the basic idea is simple (for their origin, see Witten *et al.*, 1994). The idea is an extension of the well-tried method of

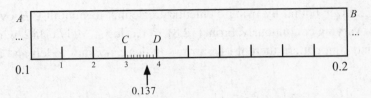

Figure 12.16 Representing 0.137 on a ruler.

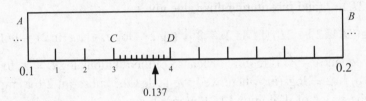

Figure 12.17 The ruler of Figure 12.16 as modified by an arithmetic code after the arrival of digit 1 then digit 3, just before taking account of the 7. The scale is *meant* to be distorted!

converting a string of symbols from the alphabet $\{0, 1, \ldots, 9\}$ to a number between 0 and 1. The connection may be expressed formally as $0.d_1 d_2 \ldots \leftrightarrow \sum d_i 10^{-i}$, but is more easily comprehended by the ruler representation recalled in Figure 12.16.

A first digit of 1 locates the number between A and B, a second digit of 3 locates it between C and D, and a third digit of 7 positions it still more precisely, as arrowed in the figure. The process is reversible: starting from our point on the ruler edge we read off the first digit as 1 because on the coarsest scale (tenths) the point lies between 1 and 2, then the second digit is 3 because the point lies between 3 and 4 (marked by C, D) on the next finest scale, and so on; we decode in the same order as encoding was performed, and recover the original 137.

The difference with arithmetic codes is that more-frequently occurring digits are allocated more space in the corresponding graduations. Indeed, the graduation widths at a given scale are altered so as to be proportional to the relative frequencies of the digits they represent. The frequencies are first set at 1 per digit, then updated after every time a new digit is processed.

Thus, in our example, we initialise the respective frequencies of $\{0, 1, \ldots, 9\}$ as $\{1, 1, \ldots, 1\}$. On receiving the first digit '1' we update this to $\{1, 2, 1, \ldots, 1\}$, and on the arrival of 3 update it to $\{1, 2, 1, 2, 1, \ldots, 1\}$. The ruler now looks something like Figure 12.17. Although the point generated from the digits 137 is not actually at distance 0.137 from the zero of the scale, it still decodes back to 137 provided we use the same ruler.

Using the same ruler in an algorithm means in practice that we compute the actual positions of the new gradations. Below is a pseudocode version. It computes, after each message symbol input, an interval $[lo, hi]$ in which the output number must lie, and

Table 12.2. *Case $n = 2$. How message string aba is encoded as*
$(1/3 + 5/12)/2 = 0.375$.

frequencies	successive intervals [*lo,hi*], shaded	*diff* $= hi - lo$
$\{1, 1\}$		$1/2$
$\{2, 1\}$		$1/6$
$\{2, 2\}$		$1/12$

outputs the midpoint. As usual, the alphabet is denoted by $S = s_1, \ldots, s_n$. The frequencies f_i are cumulative, referring to symbols processed so far.

ALGO 12.1 *Arithmetic encoding for a message string*

Set all $f_i = 1(1 \leq i \leq n)$ and $f_0 = 0, ftotal = n, lo = 0, hi = 1$;
For each new symbol, assumed to be sth in the alphabet, do:
$fmin = f_1 + \cdots + f_{s-1}$; $fmax = fmin + f_s$;
$diff = h_i - lo$;
$hi = lo + diff^* fmax/ftotal$;
$lo = lo + diff^* fmin/ftotal$;
$f_s = f_s + 1$; $ftotal = ftotal + 1$;
Output $(hi + lo)/2$.

Example 12.28 Arithmetic encoding of message strings *aba* (Table 12.2) and of *abc*. (Table 12.3).

We can express 0.375 exactly as a binary fraction: $0.375 = 3/8 = 1/4 + 1/8 = 0.011$. Thus arithmetic encoding sends *aba* to 011, which is neatly one bit per symbol. What is the entropy? This is defined, perhaps surprisingly, with probabilities based on *overall* rather than cumulative frequencies. Thus $H = H(2/3, 1/3) = (2/3) \times \log (3/2) + (1/3) \log 3 = 0.918$ approx. This, of course, implies the message cannot be reduced to two bits, but it also brings out the fact that even an arithmetic code may not reduce a message to entropy rate if the message is short. The strength of these codes emerges as more substantial bodies of text are introduced.

Finding the bits In the example above, the output number, which is exactly the decimal fraction 29/120, is not a finite binary fraction. However, all we need is a binary fraction strictly between *lo* and *hi* for it to be correctly decoded. To discover how this can be

Table 12.3. *Case $n = 3$. How message string abc is encoded as*
$(7/30 + 1/4)/2 = 0.2417$.

frequencies	successive intervals $[lo, hi]$, shaded	$diff = hi - lo$
$\{1, 1, 1\}$	$0 \quad\quad 1/3 \quad\quad\quad\quad\quad\quad\quad 1$	$1/3$
$\{2, 1, 1\}$	$0 \quad 1/6 \; 1/4 \; 1/3 \quad\quad\quad\quad\quad 1$	$1/12$
$\{2, 2, 1\}$	$0 \quad 7/30 \; 1/4 \quad\quad\quad\quad\quad\quad 1$	$1/60$

obtained with the least number of binary digits, we begin with a small but significant observation.

Theorem 12.29 *Suppose $\delta > 0$. Then (i) the number of bits required to express a real number z ($0 < z < 1$) so that the error is restricted to the interval $[-\delta/2, \delta/2)$, is at most* Ceil[Log$(1/\delta)$]. *Furthermore (ii) if* $\log(1/\delta) = d + e$, *where d is the integer part and e the fractional part, with $0 < e < 1$, then d digits suffice with probability 2^{-e}.*

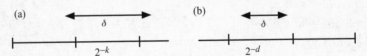

Figure 12.18 Intervals of width δ compared with binary fractions spaced at 2^{-k} and 2^{-d}.

Proof (i) As illustrated in Figure 12.18(a), z can be represented as prescribed by k bits if the interval $[z - \delta/2, z + \delta/2)$ of width δ contains a k-bit binary fraction, and this in turn holds if $2^{-k} \leq \delta$, a condition independent of the value of z. The least such k is

$$\text{Min}\{k : 2^{-k} \leq \delta\} = \text{Min}\{k : 2^k \geq 1/\delta\} = \text{Min}\{k : k \geq \log(1/\delta)\}$$
$$= \text{Ceil}[\log(1/\delta)].$$

(ii) Referring to Figure 12.18(b), the probability p that there is a d-bit binary fraction in an interval of width $\delta < 2^{-d}$ may be taken, on the basis of a uniform distribution of outcomes for z, to be the ratio $\delta/2^{-d}$. Then using the given notation, including that of (ii), we have $\log(p) = d + \log \delta$ (all to base 2) $= d - (d + e) = -e$, whence $p = 2^{-e}$.

Corollary 12.30 *Let the final interval width diff of an arithmetic encoding satisfy* $\log(1/diff) = d + e$, *where d is an integer and $0 < e < 1$. If the output is kept to d bits it will output correctly with probability 2^{-e}, but certainly correctly if $d + 1$ bits are used.*

Example 12.31 (1) The message string of Table 12.3 has $diff = 1/60$ and $d + e = \log 60 = 5.91$ approx. Hence five bits suffice with probability $2^{-0.91} = 0.53$, but six bits give correct decoding, with bits/symbol = 2. The entropy is $3(1/3)\log 3 = 1.58$, implying total bits of at least 4.7, hence of at least 5.

(2) Arithmetic encoding of the following text of 390 symbols was performed at a mean rate of 4.58 bits per symbol, compared with entropy of 4.33.

'Dear 4h graduand, I enclose some details of a PhD studentship whose closing date has been extended to allow our own graduates of this year, both single and combined, to apply. The amount of the grant is a little above the standard EPSRC award. A First or Upper second class degree is a prerequisite, but interviews can take place at any suitable time.

Yours sincerely   Stuart G. Hoggar'   (12.22)

Handling the small numbers The small example above coded to a bit sequence which, as a number, required accuracy of up to about 2^{-1700}. Thus it is unrealistic to handle the whole encoded version within a computer calculation. This problem is easily solved because of the linear nature of the calculation

$$diff = hi - lo,$$
$$hi = lo + a^*diff,$$
$$lo = lo + b^*diff,$$

where a, b are independent of hi, lo. When $diff$ is so small that hi and lo have the first one or more bits in common, say $lo = 0.011\,01\ldots$, $hi = 0.011\,10\ldots$, we can subtract the common start $c = 011$, output c, then continue encoding. The result is that $diff$ is unchanged but $hi = (lo - c) + a^*diff$, and $lo = (lo - c) + b^*diff$, which is what we want. The subtraction and output is repeated as appropriate.

ALGO 12.2 Arithmetic decoding

The decoder retraces (forwards) the path of the encoder. Similarly to the latter, it can be adapted to process the long binary fraction in steps.

Input: *code, symbolList, msgLength*;
Set all $f_i = 1$, *ftotal* = number of distinct symbols, $lo = 0$, $hi = 1$;
do *msgLength* times:
  $diff = hi - lo$; $s = 1$;
  While $code \geq lo + diff^* f_s/ftotal$ do : $lo = lo + diff^* f_s/ftotal$; $s = s + 1$;
  $hi = lo + diff^* f_s/ftotal$;
  Output symbol number s;
  $f_s = f_s + 1$; *ftotal* = *ftotal* + 1.

Example 12.32 *(Example 12.28 continued (decoding))* Table 12.3 concluded with the code 0.2417. Here are the three steps of ALGO 12.2 in which the original message is recovered as *abc*.

$f_1 f_2 f_3$	*ftotal*	*lo*	*hi*	Conclusion of the While loop		
111	3	0	1	$s = 1$	$lo = 0$	$hi = 1/3$
211	4	0	1/3	$s = 2$	$lo = 1/6$	$hi = 1/4$
221	5	1/6	1/4	$s = 3$	$lo = 7/30$	$hi = 1/4$

Arithmetic codes – best possible? We wish to show that arithmetic codes are best possible in the long run. That is, as N and the f_i increase, the expression (from Corollary 12.30)

$$\text{mean bits/symbol} = \tfrac{1}{N} \, \log(1/\textit{diff}) \tag{12.23}$$

comes arbitrarily close to the entropy bit rate. A quick, rough, but insightful, argument runs as follows. An encoder starts with *diff* = 1 and, for each new message symbol received, scales *diff* by the cumulative probability

$$p_i = f_i / \sum\nolimits_{s=1}^{n} f_s. \tag{12.24}$$

Thus *diff* is the product of the probabilities of the symbols encoded, and so log *diff* equals $\sum \log p_s$. Hence a symbol s of probability p_s contributes $-\log(p_s)$ to the output; but this is the symbol's entropy.

The argument of the last sentence *is* rough, indeed our small examples above do not have bit rate equal to entropy. To achieve a precise argument we must obtain a formula for *diff* in terms of the overall frequencies f_i (the number of times the ith symbol of the alphabet appears in the message). The following lemma provides this.

Lemma 12.33 *The width of the final interval in an arithmetic encoding of a message of length N from an alphabet of size n and frequencies f_i is*

$$\textit{diff} = \frac{(N + n)(n - 1)!(\Pi_i f_i!)}{(N + n)!} \tag{12.25}$$

Proof Suppose firstly that the message begins with all f_1 copies of symbol s_1, followed by the f_2 copies of s_2, and so on. Then *diff* is scaled from 1 down to

$$\left(\frac{1}{n} \cdot \frac{2}{n+1} \cdots \frac{f_1}{n+f_1-1} \right) \times \left(\frac{1}{n+f_1} \cdot \frac{2}{n+f_1+1} \cdots \frac{f_2}{n+f_1+f_2-1} \right) \times \cdots$$

$$\times \left(\frac{1}{n+f_1+f_2+\cdots+f_{n-1}} \cdot \frac{2}{n+f_1+f_2+\cdots+f_{n-1}+1} \cdots \frac{f_n}{n+N-1} \right),$$

where we have simplified the last factor using $\sum f_i = N$. It is easier to see in retrospect that, in whatever order the symbols arrive, we obtain a fraction with numerator the product of factors $f_i!$ for $i = 1, 2, \ldots, n$, and denominator $n(n + 1) \cdots (n + N - 1) = (n + N)!/[(n - 1)!(N + n)]$. Hence the result.

Notation 12.34 (1) To convert the expression for *diff* to one we can compare readily with entropy, it is helpful to use the following notations, meaning that functions $f(x)$ and $g(x)$ are 'the same' in some sense, as $x \to \infty$.

$$f(x) \sim g(x) \quad \text{if} \quad f(x)/g(x) \to 1 \text{ as } x \to \infty, \tag{12.26}$$
$$f(x) \approx g(x) \quad \text{if} \quad f(x) - g(x) \to 0 \text{ as } x \to \infty. \tag{12.27}$$

(2) The first need not entail closeness, for example $(x + 9)/x \to 1$ as $x \to \infty$, though the two functions always differ by 9. However, taking logs converts the $\sim$ relationship of (12.26) into actual closeness:

$$\text{if } f(x) \sim g(x) \quad \text{then} \quad \log f(x) \approx \log g(x). \tag{12.28}$$

This is easily verified by $\log f(x) - \log g(x) = \log[f(x)/g(x)] \to \log(1) = 0$. On the other hand, $(x + a)/x \to 1$ and $(1/x)\log x \to 0$, so we have the useful observations

$$\log(x + a) \approx \log x \text{ for any constant } a, \tag{12.29}$$
$$\frac{1}{x}\log x \approx 0. \tag{12.30}$$

(3) Finally, here is Stirling's classical formula for a positive integer k (see e.g. Ledermann and Vajda, 1982):

$$k! \sim \sqrt{2\pi}\,\mathrm{e}^{-k}k^{k+1/2}. \tag{12.31}$$

Theorem 12.35 *The bit rate of an arithmetic code tends to the message entropy as N and the frequencies f_i become arbitrarily large.*

Proof Applying Stirling's Formula to expression (12.25) for *diff*, we obtain

$$diff \sim (2\pi)^{(n-1)/2}\frac{(N + n)(n - 1)!\Pi_i \mathrm{e}^{-f_i} f_i^{f_i+1/2}}{\mathrm{e}^{-(N+n)}(N + n)^{N+n+1/2}}.$$

Since $\Pi_i \mathrm{e}^{-f_i} = \mathrm{e}^{-\Sigma f_i} = \mathrm{e}^{-N}$, we have after cancellations

$$diff \sim K_n \Pi_i f_i^{f_i+1/2}/(N + n)^{N+n-1/2} \qquad (K_n \text{ depends only on } n).$$

Now we invoke (12.28) to compute the long-term bit rate (12.23), with N and the f_i (but not n) tending to infinity, from

$$\frac{1}{N}\log(1/diff) \approx \frac{1}{N}\left[-\log K_n - \sum_i(f_i + \frac{1}{2})\log f_i + (N + n - \frac{1}{2})\log(N + n)\right]$$
$$\approx -\sum_i(f_i/N)\log f_i + \log N \text{ using (12.29), (12.30)}$$
$$\approx -\sum_i(f_i/N)\log f_i + \sum_i(f_i/N)\log N \qquad \text{since } \sum_i(f_i/N) = 1$$
$$= \sum_i(f_i/N)\log(N/f_i)$$
$$= \sum_i p_i \log(1/p_i) \qquad \text{on setting } p_i = f_i/N.$$

Table 12.4. *A small table of comparisons.*

Huffman codes	arithmetic codes
stores tree	no explicit tree stored
inefficient with high probabilites	OK with all probabilities
faster	slower but more compressed
OK for random access	less good for random access

That is, the mean rate of bits per symbol tends to the entropy of $p_1, \ldots, p_n$, as required. Now that we have described both the Huffman and arithmetic methods, some comparisons are in order. see Table 12.4.

12.6 Prediction by Partial Matching

Given that, as we have just shown, arithmetic codes approach the ideal entropy bit rate as the message size increases, we should like to know how they fare in practice. The answer is, very well, with long message compression better than Huffman, but they can still be improved. Here we are concerned with the fact that an arithmetic code takes no account of the frequency of *pairs* (or more generally k-tuples) of symbols. For example, in an English language text, letter g is more likely to be followed by an s than by a z, whilst *th* is a very common 2-letter combination, perhaps most often followed by e. We may take advantage of this form of redundancy as follows.

As an arithmetic code works through the text to be encoded, symbol by symbol, it predicts the probability of a symbol σ by its relative frequency of previous occurrence

$$P(\sigma) = \frac{\text{number of previous } \sigma\text{s}}{\text{total symbols occurring before } \sigma}. \tag{12.32}$$

Suppose the k symbols immediately before σ are $x_1 \ldots x_k$. We get a better prediction by comparing the number of previous occurences of $x_1 \ldots x_k$ with the number of times this sequence is followed by σ, which we may write as:

$$P(\sigma | x_1 \ldots x_k) = \frac{\text{number of times } x_1 \ldots x_k \, \sigma \text{ has occurred}}{\text{number of times } x_1 \ldots x_k \text{ has occurred}}. \tag{12.33}$$

This is called *Prediction by Partial Matching*, or PPM, and the symbol sequence $x_1 \ldots x_k$ is the *context* of σ. When PPM is combined with arithmetic encoding, the successive intervals (lo, hi) are computed as before, but are now based on the PPM probabilities. A simple example of the calculation is that for the last e in 'making merry men'. We have $P(e) = 1/14$, versus $P(e|m) = $ (no. of previous *mes*)/(no. of previous *ms*) $= 1/2$, reducing the corresponding number of bits to encode 'e' from $\log 14 = 3.8$ down to $\log 2 = 1$.

Example 12.36 We calculate the comparative probabilities and entropies for the last nine symbols of the text below. The results (which require discussion) are shown in Table 12.5.

In the beginning was the word, and the word was with God, and the word was God. He was in the beginning with God. All things were made by him, and without him was not anything made that was made.

Table 12.5. *Arithmetic versus PPM probabilities for last 'was made.' in the text above, using contexts x_1 of length 1. A space is denoted by []. Corresponding entropies are numbered 1, 2 and given to one decimal place.*

Symbol σ	w	a	s	[]	m	a	d	e	.
$P(\sigma)$	12/189	12/190	6/191	41/192	4/193	13/194	11/195	12/196	2/197
$P(\sigma \mid x_1)$	3/10	5/12	5/12	1	2/41	1/2	2/13	2/11	0
$P(\sigma)$ bits	4.0	4.0	5.0	2.2	5.6	3.9	4.1	4.0	6.6
$P(\sigma \mid x_1)$ bits	1.7	1.3	1.3	0	4.4	1.0	2.7	2.5	∞

Remark 12.37 The number of bits for 'was made.' is thus reduced from 33 to 13, but some questions about significance arise. (1) A probability of 1 in line 2 of the 'space' column corresponds to the fact that *s* has so far *always* been followed by [], as it is here. The decoder knows this, and zero bits are used. (2) The bottom right ∞ is caused by a zero probability, arising because the contex 'e' occurred previously but was *never* followed by a full stop sign '.'. Possible action for various situations of this kind is prescribed in Table 12.6.

Table 12.6. *Situations that may arise in using PPM with arithmetic codes, and how they are handled. A symbol σ is preceded by context $x_1 \ldots x_k$.*

situation	action	remarks
no previous occurrence of context $x_1 \ldots x_k$	try $x_2 \ldots x_k$	decoder has this information
no previous occurrence of x_k	take arith. code $P(\sigma)$	no context available
no previous occurrence of σ	take $P(\sigma) = 1/n$ (n = size of alphabet)	zero frequency situation

12.7 LZW compression

We come to an approach different from those of the previous sections, and characterised by the use of a dictionary (in other contexts this might be called a *codebook* or *look-up table*). That is, we replace a substring of the text, or phrase, by a pointer to that phrase. The idea is that a pointer will require fewer bits to specify than a string. Yet a dictionary that is good for one context will be inefficient in another, so a method is desirable which produces a new dictionary each time, specially adapted to the text proffered for encoding.

Ziv and Lempel (1977) introduced an ingenious implementation of this idea in which the dictionary has no separate existence but is spread throughout the text itself. One replaces the text, phrase by phrase, with reference to an earlier appearance, in the form of a triple $\langle offset, length, next \rangle$, where *offset* specifies how many characters back to refer, *length* is the number of successive symbols given, and *next* is the text symbol following these in the current position.

Example 12.38 The first few triples for the text below are $\langle 0, 0, t \rangle, \langle 0, 0, h \rangle, \cdots,$ $\langle 0, 0, \text{' '} \rangle$ because there is no earlier appearance of the corresponding text symbols, indeed a triple's third entry is present in order to handle that situation. However, after some way into the text this need rarely occurs, and quite long runs of symbols are repeated. This is illustrated even in the slightly artificial (to compensate for being short) example, in which repeated phrases of length 2 upwards may be shaded and the corresponding triples shown above.

$$\langle 11, 7, t \rangle \qquad \langle 8, 4, s \rangle \quad \langle 20, 3, a \rangle \langle 16, 3, i \rangle \quad \langle 20, 5, . \rangle$$

```
the sea is the seat of season, that is the reason.
1        8  11 12  15 18      23 25     31   34 37       45
```

If, as here, offset $< 2^5$ and length $< 2^3$, then the pair may be specified in eight bits, i.e. in one byte. With each character in the ASCII system (see www.cplusplus. com/doc/paper/ascii.html) normally allocated one byte, the encoding proceeds at two bytes per triple. Thus a triple, if compelled to specify one character, loses only one byte, but in representing, for example, 'is the' (which includes two spaces), it saves six.

The basic scheme is usually referred to as LZ77, but there are many variants, based principally on allocation of bits for the triples. A consideration is that a byte may be regarded as a symbol, and on that basis GZip introduces further compression by applying Huffman encoding to the offset parameters. A year later the authors (Ziv and Lempel, 1978) introduced the improvement LZ78, in which the triples are reduced to pairs (integer, symbol) via the allocation of a number to each dictionary phrase, and finally Welch (1984) contributed a dictionary system which removed the need for the symbol; thus the triples had been reduced to singletons and the code to a sequence of integers.

This apparent magic was performed at the essentially zero expense of building up a dictionary during both encoding and decoding which was initialised as the first 127 ASCII character codes. The result, which we now describe, is known as *LZW compression* (Lempel–Ziv–Welch). Amongst other direct applications it forms the basis of Unix's *compress*, and is a part of the Graphics file formats GIF and TIFF (see e.g. Murray and van Ryper, 1996).

LZW encoding The dictionary, *dict*, is an array of strings, initialised as ASCII characters 1 to 127 in order. The position of a string in *dict* will be called its *index*. We use also the following notation:

msg = the text string to be compressed, including spaces and punctuation marks;
code = the sequence of integers to which *msg* will be encoded;
max = greatest length of phrase allowed in *dict*;
i = position of current *msg* symbol;
str = a substring of *msg* beginning at the *i*th *msg* symbol;
next = the *msg* symbol following *str*.

ALGO 12.3 LZW encoding

Input the string *msg*

Set *code* = *empty*, $i = 1$, and repeat the following until *msg* is exhausted:

1. Locate in *dict* the message phrase *str* of greatest length $L \leq max$ that begins at the *i*th message symbol.
2. Append the index of *str* to *code*.
3. Extend *str* by its next symbol *next* in *msg*, and append the result to *dict* (omit if *dict* has reached a maximum allowable size).
4. Set $i = i + L$.

Output *code* and discard *dict*.

Example 12.39 The encoding of the short sequence *msg* = 'ABRACADABRA' shows how LZW compression works. To keep numbers simple we initialise the dictionary to the actual characters required, *dict* = {A, B, C, D, R}. Thus the first addition to *dict* has *index* 6. The table below shows, column by column, how encoding proceeds.

msg	A	B	R	A	C	A	D	A	B	R	A
code	1	2	5	1	3	1	4	6		8	
added to *dict*	AB	BR	RA	AC	CA	AD	DA	ABR			
index	6	7	8	9	10	11	12	13			

Notice that an infinite loop cannot arise in determining *str*. We start with *str* of length *max* and reduce to a minimum of a single symbol, at which stage it must be within *dict* because the latter was initialised to contain all such singleton strings.

In this example *str* reduces to a singleton each time, until we consider the eighth symbol of *msg*, an 'A', when *str* = AB with index 6. Therefore 6 is now appended to *code*, AB is extended to ABR before being appended to *dict* (index 13), and the current *msg* position is set at $i = 10$. But this leaves just RA, which is present in *dict* at index 8, so coding is complete. We output *code* = {1, 2, 5, 1, 3, 1, 4, 6, 8} and discard *dict*.

Decoding On receiving *code*, a decoder attempts to follow in the encoder's footsteps. This begins with the initialised *dict* = {A, B, C, D, R} (normally ASCII 1 to 127) and continues with repetition of the twin operations: looking up the dictionary phrase *str* corresponding to the latest codeword, and extending the dictionary itself. This means that *dict* must be far enough advanced for the necessary looking-up. In the present example, on reaching 6 the decoder finds this is the index of AB. For the dictionary insertion he (the decoder) needs one more symbol of *msg*, and he has it because the next codeword 8 is within *dict*, yielding RA; so ABR is inserted into *dict*, though by now decoding is complete.

Why decoding always works During encoding, the making of a dictionary entry always occurs before it is used. This means the next codeword is already an index unless it happens to be the entry we are in the process of making. But then we have the situation depicted in Figure 12.19.

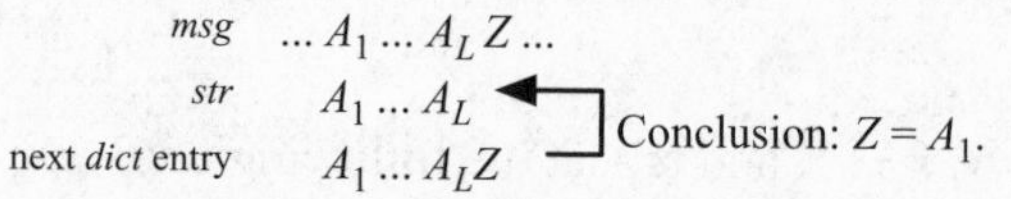

$$
\begin{array}{ll}
msg & \dots A_1 \dots A_L Z \dots \\
str & A_1 \dots A_L \\
\text{next } dict \text{ entry} & A_1 \dots A_L Z
\end{array}
\quad \text{Conclusion: } Z = A_1.
$$

Figure 12.19 If the current dictionary entry is the next *str*, then its first and last symbols are identical.

The equality shown in Figure 12.19 implies $Z = A_1$. That is, *str* is to be extended by repetition of its first symbol before insertion into the dictionary. Hence the *else* part in the decoding algorithm, which we are now ready to give.

ALGO 12.4 LZW decoding

Input *code*
dict = ASCII characters numbered 1 to 127;
for $i = 1$ to *codeLength* $- 1$ do
  ind = *code*[*i*];
  str = *dict*[*ind*];
  msg = *msg* + *str*;
  nx = *code*[*i* + 1];
  if *nx* $\leq$ *Length*[*dict*] then *next* = 1st character of *dict*[*nx*]
    else *next* = 1st character of *str*;
  Append *str* + *next* to *dict*; (* End for *)
Append *dict*[*codeLength*] to *msg*;
Return(*msg*);

Example 12.40 Here is a longer piece of text than in earlier examples.

Having spotted his prey in flight, Cat looked for a suitable path to the ceiling. Yes, the piano would make an excellent start. He leapt expertly onto the piano keys as he had done many times before, dislodging a small notebook and pencil, which he mildly regretted, for it was a point of honour and a demonstration of expertise to avoid disturbing those fragile things which the Owners seemed to find important. By now he was used to the sudden sound his first jump caused, and it disturbed him not a whit. Conserving momentum, because it felt good and seemed to work well, he continued in smooth flight upwards and gained the piano top. There to greet him was a vase of, what did they call it? He was unable to produce the sound even in imagination during those milliseconds in which he skidded with perfect judgement around it and turned towards the higher objective of the tall slim music cupboard. Gaining this superior top he regarded from close quarters, and with rapidly beating heart, the winged creature that cruised before him in blissful unawareness of the danger from its new companion. The moth took a new fancy and headed for the window with its flowers and scents. At this, Cat, quivering with desire, launched himself through space regardless of possible consequences, and narrowly escaped an impaling on peri-flower sticks by a last minute shift of paws in flight.

LZW encoding reduces this from 1456 characters to 760 integer codewords, a compression to about half size. See Table 12.7.

Table 12.7. *Some comparative compressions using the LZW method. Code size is given as a percentage of text size.*

text		length	code bytes	compression
abracadabra		11	9	82%
Sea	(Example 12.38)	50	36	72%
Letter	(Example 12.31)	390	269	69%
Word	(Example 12.36)	198	119	60%
Cat	(Example 12.40)	1456	760	52%

LZW in image compression Like other methods which encode a string of symbols, LZW can encode any data expressed as a stream of bytes. Indeed, it is widely used to encode image data, especially in standard GIF, where each pixel value is allocated up to one byte. In this case the pixel values may be specified as, say, 4-bit, generating only 16 distinct symbols, and the dictionary initialised to just those symbols. Other graphics formats such as TIFF make use of the byte-to-symbol idea in various ways, such as packing a whole number of pixel values into one byte, or vice versa, for example using two bytes for 16-bit colour. For encyclopaedic information on graphics formats, and some interesting history of LZW, see Murray and van Ruyper (1996). Figure 12.20 is a simple example in which LZW reduced an image to 61% of its size. As is to be expected, the reduction is less than for a true language message, but improves greatly with image size. The present case is already much better than a 1/4 sized version which reduced only as far as 77%.

12.8 Entropy and Minimum Description Length (MDL)

In this section we make a journey from what may seem a purely theoretical idea of complexity to the practical and useful Principle of Minimum Description Length.

Figure 12.20 '*Martial cats*' (adapted from Night mist Online). With bytes ordered row by row and treated as character symbols, this 206×170 greyscale image was reduced to 61% size by LZW compression.

12.8.1 Kolmogorov complexity

Kolmogorov, dissatisfied with entropy as a measure of information, strove for an approach which would be more intrinsic in the sense of dispensing with probabilities. Eventually (Kolmogorov, 1965, 1968) he hit upon the idea known as *Kolmogorov complexity*: the information carried by an object is the length of the shortest binary computer program that describes the object. We shall shortly give definitions that make this more precise, and show that it is computer-independent. To fix the meaning of *shortest program* we focus on the imaginary computing machine of Turing (1936).

The Turing machine In 1936 Turing (see Figure 12.21) grappled with the idea of encapsulating human thought in a machine. Whether he succeeded is perhaps still an open question, but most subsequent concepts of a universal computer proved equivalent to his original, in what they could and could not compute (Rojas, 1996, p. 5ff). Thus it remains a fundamental model. The Turing machine is a Finite State Machine: a machine able to vary between a finite number of states, the present state and input determining what happens next.

Figure 12.21 Alan Turing, 1912–1954.

In one version, a program tape feeds in from left to right the successive digits of a binary string $p = p_1 p_2 p_3 \dots$ (a computer program), as signalled by the machine. Represented in the simplified Figure 12.22, the machine has a working tape (part of Turing's human analogy), and outputs at intervals successive digits $x_1, x_2, x_3, \dots$ For the equivalence of Turing machines with varying tape arrangements, see Hennie and Stearns (1966). Turing machines and issues in geometry are discussed by Minsky and Papert (1988).

Any computer $\mathcal{U}$ equivalent to a Turing machine will be called a *universal computer*. An important question is: which binary strings x can be computed as the output $\mathcal{U}(p)$ of a program p (itself a string)? For x to be considered computable, the machine must

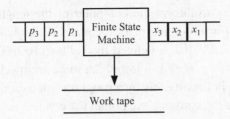

Figure 12.22 Simplified diagram of a Turing machine.

halt at some stage. Furthermore, since the tape always moves to the right in order to read successive characters of p, as in Figure 12.22, no program which halts can be the start of a larger one that halts, which is to say that the set of such programs is prefix-free, or PF (Section 12.2). We are ready to discuss Kolmogorov's key definition of complexity.

Definition 12.41 The *Kolmogorov complexity* $K = K_{\mathcal{U}}(x)$ of a string x, with respect to a universal computer $\mathcal{U}$ is the shortest length $l(p)$ of any computer program for $\mathcal{U}$ that outputs x. If we express the computation as $x = \mathcal{U}(p)$, we may write

$$K = \underset{p:\mathcal{U}(p)=x}{\text{Min}}\ l(p). \tag{12.34}$$

Example 12.42 The Mandelbrot set M is output by a very simple program, and therefore the Kolmogorov complexity of M is correspondingly small, in spite of the great and beautiful complications found in this set (see e.g. Hoggar, 1992).

Varying the computer We may be writing instructions for a universal computer $\mathcal{A}$ that possesses many functions and subroutines not present in our universal computer $\mathcal{U}$. Examples could range from the exponential function to an inbuilt LZW data compressor or even a Java compiler. But these can all be simulated in a pre-program fed into computer $\mathcal{U}$ ahead of the $\mathcal{A}$ program. Let this also include conversion of the instruction set of $\mathcal{A}$ into instructions for $\mathcal{U}$. Denoting the length of the pre-program by $c_{\mathcal{A}}$, we have:

Theorem 12.43 *(Universality of K) If $\mathcal{U}$ is a universal computer, then for any other such computer $\mathcal{A}$ we have*

$$K_{\mathcal{U}}(x) = K_{\mathcal{A}}(x) + c_{\mathcal{A}}, \tag{12.35}$$

for all strings x, where $c_{\mathcal{A}}$ is a constant.

We emphasise that $c_{\mathcal{A}}$ is independent of x and hence becomes negligible as the length of x increases. From now on we assume a fixed universal computer and simply write c for the length of whatever pre-program is required. Now, often the computer is given the length of x and may use this information to shorten a calculation. Thus we define the *conditional Kolmogorov complexity* $K(x|l(x))$ *of x, given $l(x)$,* to be the length of the shortest program that outputs x, given the length $l(x)$,

$$K(x|l(x)) = \text{Min}\{l(p): x = \mathcal{U}(p) \text{ and } l(x) \text{ is given}\}. \tag{12.36}$$

Example 12.44 One way to inform the computer of the length $n = l(x)$ is to repeat each digit of the binary form of n and mark the end unambiguously by the duo 01. For example, the length $53 = 110101$ is defined by 11110011001101. More generally, the binary form of n requires $\lceil \log n \rceil \leq 1 + \log n$ bits, so we are specifying n to the computer in up to $4 + 2 \log n$ bits. Following this by a program that uses the knowledge of n, and absorbing an extra 4 into the constant, we obtain the connection

$$K(x) \leq K(x|l(x)) + 2 \log l(x) + c. \tag{12.37}$$

Example 12.45 (*K and compression*) If LZW compresses scanned portraits down to at most 1/5 of their size, then for such an image of size n bytes we have, up to the addition of a constant, $K(\text{portrait}) \leq 8n/5 + 2 \log n$.

Is K of any use? We claim K is non-computable, meaning that there is no *general* algorithm to determine it for an arbitrary finite string. The reason is that at any time a candidate shortest program may not have halted, and there is no *general* way to tell whether it will and what it would print out. However, this emphatically does not render the concept useless; for example:

1. The idea seems intrinsically important, and provides a framework for thinking analogous to Occam's Razor: one should seek the simplest explanation (Vitanyi & Li, 2000).
2. It is close to entropy in the long run, as we make precise and prove in the next section.
3. It has provided a new principle, the *MDL Principle*, valuable in practice for choosing the 'best' model; this is the topic of Section 12.8.3.

12.8.2 Complexity and entropy

Our first task in connecting K and entropy is to prove what is known as a *source coding theorem* (Theorem 12.50). The nomenclature betokens a focus on coding the source symbols, by contrast with our earlier result, Theorem 12.8, which is known as a *channel coding* theorem because it makes a statement about the expected progress of a coded message. We require, first, two results which are important in their own right and useful later. The letter p now reverts to its more usual role as a pdf, with entropy $E \log(1/p(x))$. A form of relative entropy defines a distance between pdfs as follows.

Definition 12.46 Let $p(x)$ and $q(x)$ be two pdfs with the same finite range $\mathcal{A}$. The (*Kullback–Liebler* or *Mahalanobis*) *distance* $d(p\|q)$ from p to q is

$$d(p\|q) = \sum_{x \in \mathcal{A}} p(x) \log \frac{p(x)}{q(x)} = E_p \log \frac{p(x)}{q(x)}, \tag{12.38}$$

where the expected value E_p is taken, as indicated, with respect to $p(x)$. Because of the asymmetry in p and q, the relation $d(p\|q) = d(q\|p)$ demanded by the distance axioms fails, as does the triangle inequality $d(p\|r) \leq d(p\|q) + d(q\|r)$. Nevertheless, d is very useful because of the remaining (and most basic) distance axiom it does satisfy, as asserted in our next result.

Theorem 12.47 *In the notation above, $d(p\|q) \geq 0$, with equality if and only if $p = q$.*

Proof Let $\mathcal{B} = \{x\colon p(x) > 0\}$, a subset of the range $\mathcal{A}$ of p. We have

$$-d(p\|q) = -\sum_{x \in \mathcal{B}} p(x) \log \frac{p(x)}{q(x)} = \sum_{x \in \mathcal{B}} p(x) \log \frac{q(x)}{p(x)}$$

$$\leq \log \sum_{x \in \mathcal{B}} p(x) \frac{q(x)}{p(x)} \quad \text{by Jensen's Inequality, Theorem 9.84}$$

$$= \log \sum_{x \in \mathcal{B}} q(x) \leq \log \sum_{x \in \mathcal{A}} q(x) = \log(1) = 0.$$

Hence $d(p\|q) \geq 0$. If it is actually zero then both inequalities in the chain above become equalities. We need a little care here. Since log is strictly concave, Jensen's result (Theorem 9.84) implies $q(x) = p(x) = 1$ everywhere, on $\mathcal{B}$. But $\sum q(x)\,(x \in \mathcal{B}) = \sum q(x)\,(x \in \mathcal{A})$ shows $q(x) = 0 = p(x)$ for $x \in \mathcal{A} \backslash \mathcal{B}$, and the proof is complete.

Exercise Verify that $d(p\|p) = 0$.

Definition 12.48 We earlier discussed (Notation 12.7) an encoding $s_i \to c_i$ of message symbols from an alphabet $s_1, \ldots, s_n$, into binary words. There we began with a message and assigned s_i a probability p_i equal to its relative frequency of appearance in the message. Then the mean codeword length over the message is $M = \sum_i p_i L_i$, where c_i has length L_i.

Now we assign probabilities in advance, taking the symbols as the range of a random variable X. We call the rule $s_i \to c_i$ an *encoding of the source X*, or simply a *source code*. The expression $\sum_i p_i L_i$ becomes the *expected value L* of codeword length. For the following widely used ancillary result and its application we recall that an encoding is *prefix-free*, or *PF*, if no codeword consists of the initial bits of another (our codes are binary, but the result holds with k in place of 2 by a similar proof).

Theorem 12.49 *(Kraft Inequality) In the notation of Definition 12.48, the n codewords of a prefix-free source code satisfy*

$$\sum_{i=1}^{n} 2^{-L_i} \leq 1. \tag{12.39}$$

Given $L_1, \ldots, L_n$ satisfying (12.39), there is a prefix-free source code with word lengths $L_1, \ldots, L_n$

Proof Consider a rooted tree in which each node has two branches, labelled 0, 1 in some order. The successive symbols of a codeword define a path from the root to a node and, since root-to-node paths are unique in a tree, this node defines the codeword uniquely. This tree is to be *full*, all end-nodes being at a level D equal to the greatest length of any codeword. Thus $D = 3$ in Figure 12.23. The number of nodes at level D is 2^D, and a codeword node at level L_i has a set A_i of 2^{D-L_i} descendants at level D, as illustrated

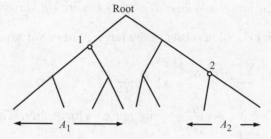

Figure 12.23 Binary tree for the proof of Theorem 12.49. It contains the codetree.

in Figure 12.23. By the prefix-free property, no codeword node is on the path from the root to any other, and so the sets A_i are disjoint, implying $\sum_i 2^{D-L_i} \leq 2^D$, and hence the result of the theorem on dividing through by 2^D.

Conversely, suppose we are given a set of desired codeword lengths satisfying (12.39). Consider a binary tree as before, and set the nodes at each level in some order, say lexicographic. Reorder the codewords by increasing length $L_1 \leq L_2 \leq \cdots$, and, for $i = 1, 2, \ldots, n$ in succession, label the first unlabelled node of level L_i as codeword i and delete its descendants (see Exercise 12.12 and solution). This gives the required PF code, and completes the proof.

Theorem 12.50 *Given a prefix-free source code for the random variable X, the expected codeword length, L, satisfies*

$$L \geq H(X). \tag{12.40}$$

Proof Recalling Definition 12.48, let X have range $\mathcal{A} = \{s_1, \ldots, s_n\}$ and pdf $p = \{p_1, \ldots, p_n\}$, the ith codeword having length L_i. Then with summations from $i = 1$ to n, we have

$$L - H(X) = \sum p_i L_i - \sum p_i \log(1/p_i)$$
$$= -\sum p_i \log 2^{-L_i} + \sum p_i \log p_i \quad \text{since } a = -\log 2^{-a}$$
$$= \sum p_i \big[\log p_i - \log 2^{-L_i} \big].$$

We define a second pdf $r = \{r_i\}$ on $\mathcal{A}$, where $r_i = 2^{-L_i}/\gamma$, and $\gamma = \sum 2^{-L_i}$ (we have just shown that $\gamma \leq 1$). This enables us to re-express $L - H(X)$ more simply. In fact we have $\log(p_i/r_i) = \log p_i - \log 2^{-L_i} + \log \gamma$, so that

$$L - H(X) = \sum p_i \log(p_i/r_i) - \Big(\sum p_i \Big) \log \gamma$$
$$= d(p\|r) - \log \gamma \quad \text{by Definition 12.46, and } \sum p_i = 1$$
$$\geq 0 \quad \text{by Theorem 12.47 for } d, \text{ and (12.39) for } \gamma.$$

Bounding K below To achieve the connection between complexity and entropy we now consider messages $x^m = x_1 \ldots x_m$ with symbols x_i in the alphabet $\{s_1, \ldots, s_n\}$

from which X takes its values. These x^m constitute the range of the random vector $X^m = (X_1, \ldots, X_m)$, where the X_k are independent identically distributed, or iid, copies of X. We consider the Kolmogorov complexity of X^m, given m, and relate it to $H(X)$ by the result below.

Corollary 12.51 *(Lower bound for complexity) Let $X^m = (X_1, \ldots, X_m)$, where the X_k are iid copies of the random variable X. The expected value of complexity satisfies*

$$E[K(X^m|m)] \geq mH(X). \tag{12.41}$$

Proof We apply Theorem 12.50 to the random variable X^m. Since the X_k are independent copies of X, the new pdf is $f(x^m) = \Pi p(x_i)\,(1 \leq i \leq m)$. We define a source code for X^m by $x^m \to$ a shortest program for x^m. This code is prefix-free because, as earlier observed, the halting property of a prefix program prevents a larger one being completed. We have thus

$$
\begin{aligned}
E[K(X^m|m)] \geq H(X^m) &= -\sum_{x^m} p(x_1)\cdots p(x_m)\log[p(x_1)\cdots p(x_m)] \\
&= -\sum_{x^m} p(x_1)\cdots p(x_m)[\log p(x_1)+\cdots+\log p(x_m)] \\
&= -\sum_{x^m} p(x_1)\cdots p(x_m)\log p(x_1)+\cdots \text{ terms for } p(x_2)\cdots p(x_m) \\
&= -\sum_{x_2,\ldots,x_m} p(x_2)\cdots p(x_m)\sum_{x_1} p(x_1)\log p(x_1)+\cdots \\
&= -\sum_{x_1} p(x_1)\log p(x_1)+\cdots \quad \text{since } \sum_{x_k} p(x_k)=1 \\
&= H(X_1)+\cdots+H(X_m) \\
&= mH(X) \quad \text{since the } X_k \text{ are iid copies of } X.
\end{aligned}
$$

An upper bound for K Our final task is to sandwich complexity between two bounds, of which we have just derived the lower. Then, letting m tend to infinity, we shall deduce a sense in which complexity is close to entropy in the long run. We start with a useful lemma.

Lemma 12.52 *For any base of logarithms, and integers $0 \leq k \leq m$ with $m > 0$, there holds*

$$\log\binom{m}{k} \leq mH(k/m) \tag{12.42}$$

Proof Writing the binomial coefficient as $_mC_k$ we have for $0 \leq p \leq 1$ that $1 = [p+(1-p)]^m \geq {}_mC_k p^k(1-p)^{m-k}$, the typical term of the binomial expansion. Taking logs with respect to any fixed base gives, on setting $p = k/m$:

$$0 \geq \log\binom{m}{k} + k\log p + (m-k)\log(1-p) = \log\binom{m}{k} - mH(k/m).$$

Exercise Check the last equality above.

Theorem 12.53 *Let $X^m = (X_1, \ldots, X_m)$, where the X_k are iid copies of the random variable X with range $\mathcal{A}$. The expected value of complexity satisfies*

$$E[K(X^m|m)] \leq mH(X) + |\mathcal{A}| \log m + c. \tag{12.43}$$

Proof in the case $\mathcal{A} = \{0, 1\}$ Suppose we seek a program to output a specific m-bit binary sequence $x^m = x_1 \ldots x_m$ with exactly k 1s. We shall input m, k and i, where our desired string comes ith in a lexicographic list of m-bit words with k ones. The length of this program, which includes the instructions for generating the list, will be an upper bound for $K(x^m|m)$. We bound from above the number of bits required to specify m, k and i, taken in order.

1. *Specify m* This is free because we are handling the conditional $K(X^m|m)$.
2. *Specify k* Since $0 \leq k \leq m$, Example 12.44 shows that $2 \log m + 4$ bits suffice.
3. *Specify i* The number of m-bit words with k 1s is the number of ways to choose k objects from m objects, namely the binomial coefficient of Lemma 12.52, whose $\log_2$ therefore does not exceed $mH(k/m)$. Hence we have, for some constant c,

$$K(X^m|m) \leq mH(k/m) + 2 \log m + c. \tag{12.44}$$

Since the range of X is $\{0, 1\}$, we have $k = x_1 + \cdots + x_m$ and $H(X) = H(p)$, where $p = E(X)$, whence

$$E[K(X^m|m)] \leq mE\left[H\left(1/m \sum X_i\right)\right] + 2 \log m + c$$

$$\leq mH\left[1/m \sum E(X_i)\right] + 2 \log m + c$$

by Jensen's Inequality (Theorem 9.84), since H is concave

$$= mH[1/m \times mE(X)] + 2 \log m + c$$

$$= mH(X) + 2 \log m + c, \text{ giving the required inequality (12.43).}$$

Now we are able to combine Corollary 12.51 and Theorem 12.53 into a 2-sided inquality in which the last term tends to 0 as m tends to infinity, giving the main result of this section, Theorem 12.54, on the connection between Kolmogorov complexity and entropy for sufficiently long sequences. We have:

$$H(X) \leq E\left[\frac{1}{m}K(X_m|m)\right] \leq H(X) + (|\mathcal{A}| \log m + c)/m. \tag{12.45}$$

Theorem 12.54 *Let $X_1, X_2, \ldots$ be iid copies of the random variable X. Then, as $m \to \infty$,*

$$E\left[\frac{1}{m}K(X_1, \cdots, X_m|m)\right] \to H(X). \tag{12.46}$$

Proof Let $m \to \infty$ in (12.45).

History and related ideas Several authors arrived at a similar definition to Kolmogorov at about the same time, particularly Solomonov (1964) and Chaitin (1996). Here are some further developments.

1. MML or *Minimum Message Length* was introduced by Wallace and Boulton (1968): a measure of the goodness of 'a classification based on information theory'. Unlike Kolmogorov complexity, it is not a probability-free approach.
2. Chaitin (1975), working with the idea of *program length* as entropy plus an error term, achieved some success in his search for definitions which would lead to at least close approximations to the powerful formal results of information theory (such as are explored in Chapter 13).
3. Rissanen (1978) expounded the use of *Minimum Description Length* (MDL), without pdfs, as a principle (see next section).
4. Vitanyi and Li (2000) defined *ideal MDL*, using Bayes' Rule plus more-recent deep results on a probability theory of individual objects.

12.8.3 The MDL Principle

Somewhat in the spirit of Kolmogorov complexity, Rissanen (1978) sugested that principles such as least squares, maximum likelihood and maximum a posteriori (MAP) estimates might be facets of a wider principle, namely one of Minimum Description Length (MDL). Let us consider this in the vision context. We are given certain data, say the colour values of a pixel array, and wish to determine the best model of the situation. This presupposes of course that we have certain allowable models in mind.

An example would be the segmentations of the image, that is, all divisions of the image into significant regions and their boundaries. This is illustrated in Figure 12.24. Choosing the 'best' segmentation is an important step toward higher level interpretation of an image, such as recognising a medical condition, a face, a tank, and so on.

An MDL approach might proceed thus. Let the allowable models be $M_1, \ldots, M_N$. Suppose we have a language in which model M_i receives a description $L_m(M_i)$, and a further language which describes the actual data D relative to the model, say as $L_c(D|M_i)$. If the bit length of a description is denoted by $| \ldots |$, then the model selected by the MDL

Figure 12.24 An image before and after segmentation.

Principle is that which minimises the total number of bits used,

$$|L_m(M_i)| + |L_c(D|M_i)|. \tag{12.47}$$

Notice that, whatever demands this evaluation makes upon us, it does not require the input of any probability density. Such a feature offers new options in problem-solving which we'll shortly illustrate. However, this is the place to bring out the connection with MAP. There is a shortcut if certain models *can* be allocated probabilities. Suppose, in a message or symbol sequence of length N, the symbol e occurs with frequency f_e. Shannon's Coding Theorem (Theorem 12.8) implies that in any encoding the number of bits corresponding to symbol e is at least $f_e \log(f_e/N)$, or $\log(f_e/N)$ for each occurrence.

We know this limit can be approached arbitrarily closely with, e.g., arithmetic codes, as messages lengthen (Theorem 12.35). On such grounds it is argued that when probabilities p_e are given in part of a problem we replace actual lengths in (12.47) by these theoretical minima, *even though* they may not be integral. This appears to be a small extension of Rissanen's original principle, but a reasonable one. For further discussion, see the survey of Barron, Rissanen and Yu (1998) and/or Rissanen (1983). In the extreme case that everything has an associated probability, we may write

$$|L_c(D|M_i)| = -\log P(D|M_i), \quad |L_m(M_i)| = -\log P(M_i), \tag{12.48}$$

so if such probabilities exist then we are by (12.47) minimising $-\log[P(D|M_i) \times P(M_i)]$, or equivalently maximising $P(D|M_i)P(M_i)$. But by Bayes' Theorem this is a constant multiple of $P(M_i|D)$, and we are back to the MAP estimate (see Chapter 11). For comments on least squares and other connections, see Bishop (1995). Here is a short list of MDL features.

Some MDL features

1. No probabilities or pdfs need be assumed or given.
2. Prior knowledge may be built into the descriptive language used.
3. Over-fitting is penalised, for extra parameters lengthen a description.
4. The MDL Principle may be used in part of a wider problem in which probabilities are invoked. See Examples 12.55, 12.56 and references thereafter.

Example 12.55 (*Segmentation*) See Figure 12.24. This example is due to Leclerc (1989), at the start of a wider investigation into MDL and image partitioning. Let N image pixels form an $m \times n$ array, with labels $i \in I = \{1, 2, \ldots, N\}$. Let u denote the underlying image intensity, with constant value $u(x_i, y_i) = u_i$ over the ith pixel area. We regard u as a vector (u_i). The measured image, the data, is a corresponding vector $z = (z_i)$, the result of a vector $r = (r_i)$ of white noise being added to the original. That is, $z = u + r$. The MDL approach is then: given z, together with a language L_u to describe u, and a language L_r to describe the noise according to its assumed type, we estimate u as that vector u^* which minimises

$$|L_u(u)| + |L_r(z - u)|. \tag{12.49}$$

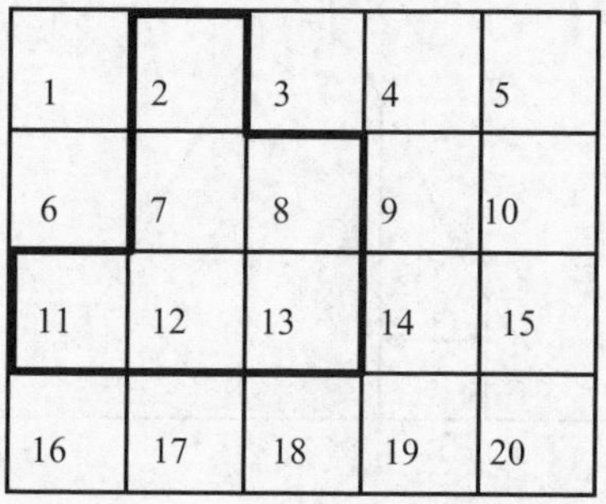

1	2	3	4	5
6	7	8	9	10
11	12	13	14	15
16	17	18	19	20

Figure 12.25 A 4×5 image u, with pixels numbered 1 to 20. One region is shown with its boundary line segments bold. Neighbour pixels of different intensity, such as those numbered 8 and 9, imply a bounding segment between them.

The language L_u By hypothesis u consists of *regions of constant intensity*, with bounding segments, necessarily horizontal or vertical, lying between neighbour pixels of differing intensity. In this 4-neighbour system, let N_i be the set of neighbours of pixel i. Then Figure 12.25 implies $N_8 = \{3, 9, 13, 7\}$ and the neighbours 3, 9 of 8 define respectively a horizontal and a vertical edge segment.

Thus the number of bits required to describe a region is proportional to the number of segments it contains, plus a constant for specifying the intensity. The bits for the whole image are proportional to the total length of boundaries plus the number of regions. To express this in terms of intensity values, consider the Kronecker delta, given by $\delta(u_i, u_j) = 1$ if $u_i = u_j$, otherwise $\delta = 0$. The number of boundary segments around pixel i may be written

$$\sum_{j \in N_i} [1 - \delta(u_i, u_j)]. \tag{12.50}$$

In Figure 12.25 with $i = 8$, this quantity equals 2. Since each bounding segment is contributed from two pixels (neglecting the image perimeter), the total bits required to describe u may be written approximately as

$$|L_u| = \frac{b}{2} \sum_{i \in I} \sum_{j \in N_i} [1 - \delta(u_i, u_j)], \tag{12.51}$$

where b equals (no. of bits required to encode each segment in a boundary sequence) plus (no. of bits to encode constant intensity)/(mean region boundary length).

The language L_r of noise Here we use estimated probabilities, and (12.48) allows us to assume a language L_r for which $|L_r(r)| = -\log P(r)$. We suppose intensity values are kept to precision q, so that k-bit accuracy means $q = 2^{-k}$. By assumption the noise occurs independently at each pixel, normally distributed, with common variance σ^2, quantised to the nearest q, as indicated in Figure 12.26. Thus, with the standard normal distribution,

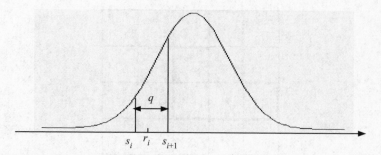

Figure 12.26 Quantising Gaussian noise r_i to the nearest q.

$\phi(z) = (2\pi)^{-1/2}e^{-z^2/2}$, we take

$$p(r_i) = \int_{s_i}^{s_{i+1}} (1/\sigma)\phi(x/\sigma)\mathrm{d}x = (q/\sigma)\phi(r_i/\sigma). \tag{12.52}$$

We shall need the log of this, for which the base change formula (12.8) gives, with ln denoting logarithm to base e, the relation $\log(e^y) = \ln(e^y)/\ln(2) = y/\ln(2)$. Hence $-\log p(r_i) = a(r_i/\sigma)^2 + c$, where $a = 1/\ln(2)$, and $c = \log(\sigma\sqrt{2\pi}/q)$. It follows that the least number of bits needed to describe the noise $r = (r_i)_{1 \le i \le N}$ is, by (12.48),

$$|L_r(r)| = -\log p(r) = -\log \Pi_i p(r_i) = -\sum_i \log p(r_i) = a \sum_i (r_i/\sigma)^2 + Nc.$$

Total bits Invoking also (12.51), and recalling that $r_i = z_i - u_i$, the total bits are $|L_u(u)| + |L_r(r)| = L(u) + Nc$, where the term Nc is constant and we are to minimise

$$L(u) = \frac{b}{2} \sum_{i \in I} \sum_{j \in N_i} [1 - \delta(u_i, u_j)] + a \sum_{i \in I} \left(\frac{z_i - u_i}{\sigma}\right)^2. \tag{12.53}$$

Now, the value of the second term, in which the pair u_i, u_j are always neighbouring intensities, depends only on the way in which u is characterised by regions $\{R_t\}$ of respective constant intensity u_t, with of course $\bigcup_t R_t = I$. Indeed, if $\partial(R_t)$ denotes boundary length, we may write

$$L(u) = a \sum_t \sum_{i \in R_t} \left(\frac{z_i - u_t}{\sigma}\right)^2 + b \sum_t \partial(R_t). \tag{12.54}$$

Thus, for a given set of regions, the second term is constant and the first is a sum of quadratics $f_t(u_t) = (1/s^2)\sum_i (z_i - u_t)^2$, which minimise independently at $0 = \mathrm{d}f_t/\mathrm{d}u_t$, and hence at $u_t = (\sum_i z_i)/(\sum_i 1)$, where i runs through R_t. This says that the intensity across a region is the mean of the measured intensity across that region, in agreement with the white noise model we adopted.

Finding the global minimum To complete the solution of this MDL problem we must minimise $L(u)$ over all 2^N possible images of size $m \times n = N$. Straightforward evaluation is not feasible; for example an 800×600 image has $2^{480\,000}$ such possibilities.

Descent based optimisation fails because $L(u)$ has many local minima arising from the Kronecker delta.

The complexity is even too great for simulated annealing (see Chapter 11). Leclerc proposes a continuation method, in which $L(u)$ is case $s = 0$ of a family $L(u, s)$ for which there exists a single computable minimum for sufficiently large s. Specifically, $\delta(u_i, u_j)$ is replaced by

$$e_{ij}(u, s) = \exp[-(u_i - u_j)^2/(s\sigma)^2], \tag{12.55}$$

so that $e_{ij}(u, s) \to \delta(u_i - u_j)$ and $L(u, s) \to L(u)$, as $s \to 0$. One can track back to the desired minimum of $L(u)$; for further details, see Leclerc (1989).

Example 12.56 (*Video tracking – Smith, Drummond & Cipolla, 2000*) The problem here is: given a digital video sequence, how may we automatically identify the moving objects and track them from frame to frame? A sample frame is shown in Figure 12.27.

Figure 12.27 Scene of a moving car and van. Initialisation of the tracking algorithm is best, according to the MDL Principle, if a 3-motion model is used (see Table 12.8).

A frame is segmented into regions of similar colour and intensity (likely to have the same motion). In the authors' approach the progress of region edges alone is observed from one frame to the next, and an iterative procedure is used to determine the most likely motions involved. The crucial *initialisation* step is decided via MDL. Given the first two frames, the bits are expended as follows.

1. *Motions* A motion is defined by the six constants of an affine transformation

$$\begin{bmatrix} x \\ y \end{bmatrix} \to \begin{bmatrix} a & b \\ c & d \end{bmatrix} \begin{bmatrix} x \\ y \end{bmatrix} + \begin{bmatrix} e \\ f \end{bmatrix}$$

   which includes rotation, reflection, translation, scaling and shear (see Chapter 16, Figure 16.10). With 10-bit accuracy and n_m distinct motions, this takes $60n_m$ bits.
2. *Edges* With n_e edges, each labelled by that one of the n_m motions to which it belongs, we require $n_e \log n_m$ bits.
3. *Edge residuals* The authors have a system of assigning a probability L_e to the observed movement of an edge e, given the assumed motion. The total bit cost here is $\sum_e \log L_e$, by (12.48).

The results are shown in Table 12.8. Since the 3-motion total uses the fewest bits, this is the correct choice according to the MDL principle. Indeed, the authors report that it worked well in practice.

Table 12.8. *Bit cost of initialisation for the car and van scene,*
allowing cases of 1, 2 or 3 motions.

n_m	1	2	3
motion	60	120	180
edges	0	322	510
residuals	3829	3362	2791
totals	3889	3804	3481

Further examples and applications of MDL

Denoising. Rissanen (2000).

Facet matching of automobiles. Maybank & Fraile (2000).

Feature extraction. Fua & Hansen (1991).

Generating segmentation break points. Lindeberg & Li (1997).

Motion tracking (differs from Example 12.56). Darrell & Pentland (1995).

Neural Networks. Zemel & Hinton (1995).

Object recognition. Pentland (1989).

Shape modelling. Davies *et al.* (2001), Thodberg & Olafsdottir (2003).

Survey. Barron, Risssanen and Yu (1998).

Wavelet thresholding. Hansen & Yu (2000).

Exercises 12

1√ (i) Calculate $H(1/2, 1/2)$ and $H(1/2, 1/4, 1/4)$ *exactly*. (ii) Calculate the entropy of the 5-symbol source represented by Figure 12.4(b), in the form $r + s\sqrt{3}$ (r, s rational). (iii) Show that $H(1/n, \ldots, 1/n) = \log n$. (iv) Prove that $\log_a b = 1/\log_b a$, from the definition of log.

2√ Construct a codetree for the PF code 11, 10, 011, 000, 010, 001. Does it agree with Theorem 12.11?

3√ Construct a Huffman codetree for the probabilities $(1, 10, 10, 10, 15, 16, 19, 19)/100$. List the codewords and verify they form a PF code. Write down a sibling ordering.

4√ A Huffman code has 2, 5, 1 codewords of respective lengths 4, 3, 2. Construct the corresponding canonical version.

5√ Taking relative frequencies for probabilities, Huffman encode COME TO THE CEILIDH HEIDI (don't ignore spaces).

6√ Calculate the redundancy in Exercise 12.5. Is it near the bounds of Theorem 12.21 or Remark 12.27?

7 Implement ALGOs 12.1 and 12.2 for arithmetic codes. Adapt them to deal with messages of arbitrary length. How close can you get to zero redundancy in an example?

8 Carry out the first line of the proof of Theorem 12.35 by using Stirling's Formula.

9✓ Determine $p(\sigma)$ and the contextual probability $p(\sigma|x_1)$ for each of the last four symbols of ABRACADABRA. Hence estimate the bits saved by using PPM in an arithmetic coding of these four.

10 Implement LZW compression via ALGOs 12.3 and 12.4. Test on ABRACADABRA, then on Example 12.40 or part thereof.

11✓ (i) Show that the distance $d(p\|q)$ between pdfs p, q with the same range satisfies $d(p\|p) = 0$. (ii) Let the discrete pdfs $p = \{a, 1 - a\}$ and $q = \{b, 1 - b\}$ have range $\{1, 2\}$. Find an expression for $d(p\|q)$. (iii) Show that $a = 1/2, b = 1/4$ give an example for which $d(p\|q) \neq d(q\|p)$, (a) by evaluating these approximately, (b) by showing that their equality implies $\log 3 = 8/5$.

12✓ For each n-tuple below, determine whether it can be the sequence of word lengths of a PF code. For those which can, construct such a code. (i) (1, 1), (ii) (1, 2, 2), (iii) (1, 2, 2, 3), (iv) (2, 2, 3, 3, 3, 3), (v) 2, 2, 3, 3, 3, 4), (vi) 2, 2, 3, 3, 4, 4, 4). Pick out by inspection (say how) one that cannot be optimal.

13

Information and error correction

In the previous chapter we introduced Shannon's concept of the amount of information (entropy) conveyed by an unknown symbol as being the degree of our uncertainty about it. This was applied to encoding a message, or sequence of symbols, in the minimum number of bits, including image compression. The theory was 'noiseless' in that no account was taken of loss through distortion as information is conveyed from one site to another. Now we consider some ways in which information theory handles the problem of distortion, and its solution. (For the historical development, see Slepian, 1974, Sloane and Wyner, 1993, or Verdú and McLaughlin, 2000.)

Physically, the journey can be anything from microns along a computer 'bus', to kilometres through our planet's atmosphere, to a link across the Universe reaching a space probe or distant galaxy. In Shannon's model of a communication system, Figure 12.1, we think of the symbols reaching their destination via a 'channel', which mathematically is a distribution of conditional probabilities for what is received, given what was sent.

The model incorporates our assumptions about 'noise', which could be due to equipment which is faulty or used outside its specifications, atmospheric conditions, interference from other messages, and so on. Some possibilities are shown in Table 13.1.

We prove Shannon's ('noisy') Channel Coding Theorem, then review progress in finding practical error-correcting codes that approach the possibilites predicted by that theorem for successful transmission in the face of corruption by a noisy channel. Besides algebraic methods we consider *probabilistic* decoding, which invokes as much evidence as possible concerning the original message, applied to convolutional codes and the new turbocodes. For this we derive the Forward–Backward message-passing algorithm for belief propagation in Bayesian networks.

13.1 Channel capacity

Shannon showed that every channel has a *capacity*, a maximum rate of reliable information transmission, given that we are willing to use sufficiently long codewords. Furthermore, the capacity exists as a function of the cost of using such codewords. Cost may be measured in, for example, bandwidth (see Chapter 14), power or finance.

Table 13.1. *Some channels and sources of error in traversing them.*

channel	some sources of distortion
cable	attenuation (power fall-off with distance)
telephone	thermal noise
fibre-optic	self-interference (between adjacent symbols)
shielded cable-TV wire	multi-user interference
radio (& TV)	atmospheric conditions
indoor	general electro-magnetic interference
terrestrial	interference from other transmissions
deep space	buildings, mountains, ...
	deliberate 'jamming'
optical disk	defect in medium
	scratching
	read/write head problems
RAM / ROM	shorted or broken bus lines
	arrival of atomic particles
	power surge

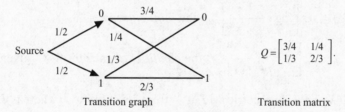

Transition graph   Transition matrix

Figure 13.1 Transition graph and matrix for Example 13.2.

13.1.1 The Discrete Memoryless Channel

Definitions 13.1 An (X, Y) *channel* is a pair of random variables X, Y possessing a conditional pdf $p(y|x) = P(Y = y \mid X = x)$. Then X, Y have a joint pdf given by $p(x, y) = p(x)p(y|x)$, and when $p(x) > 0$ a joint pdf determines the conditional by $p(y|x) = p(x, y)/p(x)$. In this channel context we call X the *input variable* and Y the *output*, and their ranges R_X, R_Y are the corresponding alphabet, sometimes denoted by $\mathcal{A}_X, \mathcal{A}_Y$. For now we assume the channel is *discrete*, meaning that the alphabets are actually finite, say $|R_X| = r, |R_Y| = s$, and *memoryless* – the values $p(y|x)$ do not depend on the outcomes of previous trials (see (13.10) later). The result is the *Discrete Memoryless Channel*, or DMC.

We may conveniently exhibit the *transition probabilities* $p(y|x)$ in an $r \times s$ *transition matrix* $Q = [p(y|x)]$, with rows indexed by R_X and columns by R_Y. This is exemplified in Figure 13.1 along with an equivalent *transition graph* defined by edges $x \to y$, each labelled with the corresponding value of $p(y|x)$. We will sometimes append edges

$S \to x$ (S for 'Source') labelled with the probability $P(X = x)$. All arrowheads are optional when the understood direction is from left to right.

Example 13.2 Let (X, Y) be a channel with alphabets $\{0, 1\}$, both symbols equally likely to be sent, and transition graph/matrix as shown in Figure 13.1. We determine the probability of a successful transmission, i.e. that the intended symbol is received:

$$P(X = 0, Y = 0) + P(X = 1, Y = 1)$$
$$= P(X = 0)P(Y = 0|X = 0) + P(X = 1)P(Y = 1|X = 1)$$
$$= (1/2)(3/4) + (1/2)(2/3) = 17/24.$$

Notice that we can simply read off the required probabilities from the graph, following the paths that together give us the required condition.

13.1.2 Entropies of a pair

Recalling from (12.7) that the entropy of X may be written $H(X) = E[\log 1/p(x)]$, we define related and exceedingly useful analogues for the random pair (X, Y).

$$H(X, Y) = E\left[\log \frac{1}{p(x, y)}\right], \quad \text{the *joint entropy* of } X, \ Y,$$

$$H(X|Y) = E\left[\log \frac{1}{p(x|y)}\right], \quad \text{the *conditional entropy* of } X, \text{ given } Y. \quad (13.1)$$

Notice that $H(X, Y)$ is symmetrical in X, Y from its definition, whereas $H(Y|X)$ is by implication defined via the values $p(y|x)$ and is not in general equal to $H(X|Y)$. At this point we should note for much future use the connections (see Section 10.1.3):

$$\frac{p(x|y)}{p(x)} = \frac{p(x, y)}{p(x)p(y)} = \frac{p(y|x)}{p(y)}. \quad (13.2)$$

This gives facility with our third and most important definition here, of a quantity upon which will be based the concept and properties of channel capacity:

$$I(X; Y) = E\left[\log \frac{p(x, y)}{p(x)p(y)}\right], \quad \text{the *mutual entropy* of } X, \ Y. \quad (13.3)$$

Again, symmetry in X, Y is clear from the definition which, like the previous two, may be re-expressed in several ways using (13.2). However, the following, less obvious, result points to an interpretation which suggests the relevance of mutual entropy.

Theorem 13.3 (i) *Mutual entropy satisfies* $I(X; Y) = H(X) - H(X|Y)$, (ii) *joint entropy satisfies* $H(X, Y) = H(X) + H(Y) - I(X; Y)$.

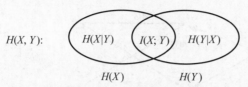

$H(X, Y)$:

Figure 13.2 Set theory analogue to relations between the various entropies.

Proof (i) Since $p(x) = \sum_y p(x, y)$ (marginal distribution) we have

$$H(X) - H(X|Y)$$

$$= \sum_x p(x) \log \frac{1}{p(x)} - \sum_{x,y} p(x, y) \log \frac{1}{p(x|y)} \qquad \text{by definition}$$

$$= \sum_{x,y} \left(p(x, y) \log \frac{1}{p(x)} - p(x, y) \log \frac{1}{p(x|y)} \right) \qquad p(x) = \sum_y p(x, y)$$

$$= \sum_{x,y} p(x, y) \log \frac{p(x|y)}{p(x)} \qquad \text{since } \log a - \log b = \log(a/b)$$

$$= I(X; Y) \qquad \text{by definition, using (13.2).}$$

For (ii),

$$H(X, Y) = E \left[\log \frac{1}{p(x, y)} \right] \qquad \text{by definition}$$

$$= E \left[\log \frac{1}{p(x)} + \log \frac{1}{p(y)} - \log \frac{p(x, y)}{p(x)p(y)} \right]$$

$$= H(X) + H(Y) - I(X; Y) \qquad \text{by linearity of } E.$$

Remarks 13.4 (1) Figure 13.2 portrays an analogue of parts (i) and (ii) with relations of set theory. It may be considered either as an insight or as an aidemémoire! Note the special case $H(X, X) = H(X) = I(X; X)$.

(2) Part (i) offers two viewpoints:

$$I(X; Y) = H(X) - H(X|Y)$$
$$= \text{amount of information sent minus uncertainty in what was sent}$$
$$(Y \text{ being received});$$
$$I(X; Y) = H(Y) - H(Y|X) \quad \text{by symmetry}$$
$$= \text{amount of information received minus the part due to noise.}$$

The conclusion is that $I(X; Y)$ *represents the 'reduction in uncertainty', or 'true' amount of information the channel carries* from X to Y. In the next section we consider sequences of transmissions and will be able to define the channel's capacity as the maximum mean rate at which information can possibly be transferred, given the channel characteristics defined by the transition matrix Q. But first we must know a little more about the behaviour of a single transmission, and develop some techniques for calculation.

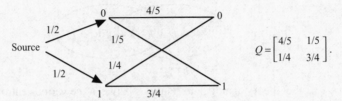

Figure 13.3 Transition matrix and graph for Example 13.5.

Exercise Prove that $H(X, X) = H(X) = I(X; X)$. (Hint: $P(X = x, X = x) = P(X = x)$.)

Example 13.5 Calculate $H(Y)$ and $I(X; Y)$ for the channel with probabilities given in Figure 13.3.

Solution Following the appropriate paths in Figure 13.3, we obtain for Y that $p(0) = (1/2)(4/5) + (1/2)(1/4) = 21/40$, and hence the distribution has entropy $H(Y) = H(21/40) = 0.998$. To two decimal places this equals 1, corresponding to choosing the output by the toss of a fair coin, so is information really carried? According to Remarks 13.4 the mutual information I gives an answer. It is easiest to compute as $H(Y) - H(Y|X)$ because the given probabilities are of the form $p(y|x)$. We obtain

$$
\begin{aligned}
H(Y|X) &= \sum_{x,y} p(x, y) \log \frac{1}{p(y|x)} && \text{by definition} \\
&= \sum_{x,y} p(x)p(y|x) \log \frac{1}{p(y|x)} && \text{substituting for } p(x, y) \\
&= \tfrac{1}{2} \sum_{x,y} p(y|x) \log \frac{1}{p(y|x)} && \text{since } p(x) = 1/2 \text{ always} \\
&= \tfrac{1}{2} \left(\tfrac{4}{5} \log \tfrac{5}{4} + \tfrac{1}{5} \log 5 + \tfrac{1}{4} \log 4 + \tfrac{3}{4} \log \tfrac{4}{3} \right) && \text{using } Q \\
&= \tfrac{1}{2} \left[H\left(\tfrac{1}{5}\right) + H\left(\tfrac{1}{4}\right) \right] && \text{by definition of H(x)} \\
&= 0.77, \text{ using Table 13.2.}
\end{aligned}
$$

Table 13.2. *Values of $H(x)$ (two decimal places).*

k	2	3	4	5	6	7	8	9	10
$H(1/k)$	1	0.92	0.81	0.72	0.65	0.59	0.54	0.50	0.47

Finally, the information passed, as measured by I, is $I(X; Y) = H(Y) - H(Y|X) = 0.23$ bits, which is more reassuring. Reviewing this calculation, we ask if such might be performed more automatically, without writing out definitions, and the answer is YES: we are led to the matrix formulation below.

Notation 13.6 (*Matrix method*) In the usual manner, write $Q = [q_{xy}] = \text{Rows}(R_x)$ $(x \in R_X)$, and let $[p(y)]$ denote the row vector with yth entry $p(y)$. Similarly for $[p(x)]$. Then

$$[p(y)] = [p(x)]Q, \tag{13.4}$$

$$H(Y|X) = \sum_x p(x)H(R_x). \tag{13.5}$$

To see this, notice that the first equality is another way of saying $p(y) = \sum_x p(x)p(y|x)$. In the second case, since $p(x)$ is constant as we sum over y, we obtain the second equality in

$$H(Y|X) = \sum_{xy} p(x, y) \log \frac{1}{p(y|x)} = \sum_x p(x) \sum_y p(y|x) \log \frac{1}{p(y|x)}, \tag{13.6}$$

and hence the result, since $H(R_x)$ has the form $\sum p \log(1/p)$, where p runs through the elements $p(y|x)$ of row R_x as y varies.

Example 13.7 We re-solve Example 13.5 using the new formula.

$$
\begin{aligned}
H(Y|X) &= \sum_x p(x)H(R_x) && \text{by (13.5)}\\
&= \tfrac{1}{2}H\left(\tfrac{4}{5}, \tfrac{1}{5}\right) + \tfrac{1}{2}H\left(\tfrac{1}{4}, \tfrac{3}{4}\right) && \text{from the expression for } Q\\
&= \tfrac{1}{2}\left[H\left(\tfrac{1}{5}\right) + H\left(\tfrac{1}{4}\right)\right] && \text{since } H(p, 1-p) = H(p).
\end{aligned}
$$

Example 13.8 (*The binary erasure channel*) In a situation where it is especially important not to get the wrong digit, there may be an arrangement for doubtful cases to be recorded as an erasure symbol, here represented by a question mark. We need a fixed order for the three output symbols, so let us take $R_Y = \{0, 1, ?\}$, along with $R_X = \{0, 1\}$. See Figure 13.4.

Problem Suppose digits 0, 1 are sent with probabilities $1/3$, $2/3$, each still decipherable with probability p when output. Draw a transition graph and matrix, and show that $H(Y|X) = H(p)$, $I(X;Y) = pH(1/3)$.

$$
\begin{aligned}
H(Y|X) &= \sum_x p(x)H(R_x) && \text{by (13.5)}\\
&= \tfrac{1}{3}H(p, 0, q) + \tfrac{2}{3}H(0, p, q) && \text{using } Q\\
&= \tfrac{1}{3}H(p) + \tfrac{2}{3}H(p) && \text{since } H(p, q, 0) = H(p, q) = H(p)\\
&= H(p).
\end{aligned}
$$

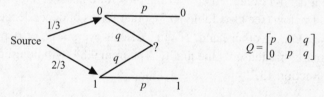

Figure 13.4 Transition graph and matrix for Example 13.8, where $q = 1 - p$.

We have by (13.4) that $[p(y)] = [p(x)]Q = [1/3 \; 2/3]Q = [p/3 \; 2p/3 \; q]$, whence

$$I(X;Y) = H(Y) - H(Y|X) = H(p/3, 2p/3, q) - H(p)$$

$$= -\frac{p}{3}\log\frac{p}{3} - \frac{2p}{3}\log\frac{2p}{3} - q\log q + p\log p + q\log q$$

$$= p\left[-\frac{1}{3}\log\frac{p}{3} - \frac{2}{3}\log\frac{2p}{3} + \log p\right] \quad (\log(ap) = \log a + \log p)$$

$$= p\left[-\frac{1}{3}\log p - \frac{1}{3}\log\frac{1}{3} - \frac{2}{3}\log p - \frac{2}{3}\log\frac{2}{3} + \log p\right]$$

$$= pH(1/3), \quad \text{after cancellations.}$$

Note: the above result holds with $1/3$ replaced by an arbitrary probability a.

Example 13.9 Suppose the input and output alphabets of an (X, Y) channel have size r, with $p(y|x) = \alpha$ if $x = y$, otherwise $p(y|x) = \beta$. Show that $H(R_x) = H(\alpha) + (1 - \alpha)\log(r - 1)$ for each row R_x of the transition matrix.

Solution Each row of Q has one entry α and $r - 1$ βs, with first row, say, $R_1 = [\alpha \; \beta \; \beta \; \cdots \; \beta]$, so

$$H(R_1) = -\alpha\log\alpha - (r-1)\beta\log\beta$$

$$= -\alpha\log\alpha - (1-\alpha)\log\frac{1-\alpha}{r-1} \quad \text{from } \alpha + (r-1)\beta = 1$$

$$= -\alpha\log\alpha - (1-\alpha)[\log(1-\alpha) - \log(r-1)]$$

$$= H(\alpha) + (1-\alpha)\log(r-1) \quad \text{by definition of } H(\alpha).$$

Exercise Deduce the value of $H(Y|X)$ for Example 13.9.

13.1.3 Three properties of mutual entropy

An independence test An important test for independence of random variables X, Y is whether their covariance is zero: we have the implications X, Y independent $\Rightarrow \text{Cov}(X, Y) = 0$ (Remarks 10.50). Some, but not all, instances of dependence result in $\text{Cov}(X, Y) \neq 0$. For example, if the correlation coefficient $\rho = \text{Cov}(X, Y)/\sigma_X\sigma_Y$ equals 1, which it cannot exceed, then $Y = aX + b$ for constants a, b. But, as exhibited in Example 13.11 below (see also Table 10.7), other forms of dependence may not result in $\text{Cov}(X, Y) \neq 0$. On the other hand, $I(X;Y)$ detects every kind of dependence, as we see next. We remark that Jensen's Inequality, Theorem 9.84, will be used routinely here and throughout Section 13.1.

Theorem 13.10 *If (X, Y) is a channel then $I(X, Y) \geq 0$, with equality if and only if X, Y are independent.*

Proof We have $-I(X;Y) = E\left[\log \dfrac{p(x)p(y)}{p(x,y)}\right]$ by (13.3) (note the minus sign)

$$\leq \log E\left[\frac{p(x)p(y)}{p(x,y)}\right] \qquad \text{by Jensen's Inequality (log is concave)}$$

$$= \log \sum_{x,y} p(x)p(y) \qquad \text{'cancelling' two factors } p(x,y)$$

$$= \log\left[\sum_x p(x) \sum_y p(y)\right]$$

$$= \log(1) = 0 \qquad \text{since } \sum p(x) = 1 = \sum p(y).$$

Hence $I \geq 0$. But Jensen tells us more: because the concavity of log is strict, equality in place of $\leq$ holds if and only if $p(x)p(y)/p(x,y)$ is a constant, say λ. But then we have $1 = \sum_{x,y} p(x)p(y) = \lambda \sum_{x,y} p(x,y) = \lambda$ (since $p(x,y)$ is a pdf). Thus $p(x,y) = p(x)(y)$; in other words equality holds if and only if X, Y are independent.

Example 13.11 (*Counterexample: I detecting dependency where covariance fails to do so*) Let an (X, Y) channel satisfy $Y = X^2$, where $R_X = \{0, 1, -1\}$, $R_Y = \{0, 1\}$ and $p(x) = 1/3$ for each x. We show that $\text{Cov}(X, Y) = 0$ but $I(X;Y) \neq 0$. See Figure 13.5.

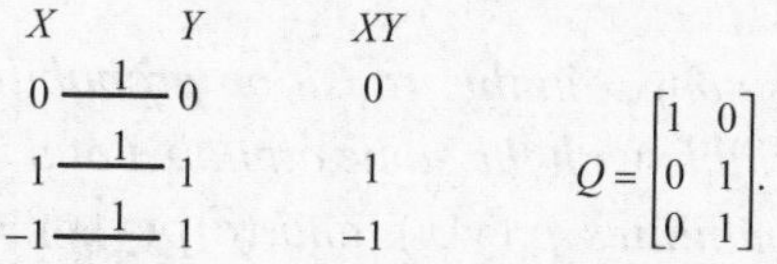

$$
\begin{array}{ccc}
X & Y & XY \\
0 \xrightarrow{\ 1\ } 0 & & 0 \\
1 \xrightarrow{\ 1\ } 1 & & 1 \\
-1 \xrightarrow{\ 1\ } 1 & & -1
\end{array}
\qquad
Q = \begin{bmatrix} 1 & 0 \\ 0 & 1 \\ 0 & 1 \end{bmatrix}.
$$

Figure 13.5 Transition graph and matrix for Example 13.11.

Covariance We have $E(X) = \sum xp(x) = (0 + 1 - 1)(1/3) = 0$, and $E(XY) = E(X^3) \sum_x x^3 p(x, y) = 0(1/3) + 1(1/3) + (-1)(1/3) = 0$. So $\text{Cov}(X, Y) = E(XY) - E(X)E(Y)$ (Theorem 10.49) $= 0$.

Entropy Using (13.4), $[p(y)] = [p(x)]Q = (1/3)[1\ 1\ 1]Q = (1/3)[1\ 2]$, so $H(Y) = H(1/3)$. By (13.5) we have $H(Y|X) = \sum_x p(x)H(R_x) = (1/3)[H(1) + H(1) + H(1)] = 0$. Finally, $I(X;Y) = H(Y) - H(Y|X) = H(1/3) \neq 0$. Hence, by Theorem 13.10, variables X, Y are not independent.

Concavity/convexity of I Reviewing its definition, the mutual entropy $I(X;Y)$ varies both with input probabilities $p(x)$ and with transition probabilities $p(y|x)$. It depends on each type in a special but different way, described by the concepts of concave and convex, as revealed in the next two results, where we spell out the meanings for $I(X;Y)$ explicitly.

Theorem 13.12 *$I(X;Y)$ is concave in the input probabilities: suppose that, for $i = 1, 2$, (a) $(X_i; Y_i)$ are random variables with the same alphabets and transition probabilities as (X, Y), (b) X_i has probability distribution $p_i(x)$, (c)$p(x) = \alpha p_1(x) + \beta p_2(x)$ for* *constants* $\alpha, \beta \geq 0$. *Then*

$$I(X;Y) \geq \alpha I(X_1;Y_1) + \beta I(X_2;Y_2). \tag{13.7}$$

Proof We observe firstly that, with $p_i(x, y)$ as joint distribution of $(X_i; Y_i)$, the distribution of Y_i is $p_i(y) = p_i(x, y)/p(x|y)$, and further we may by condition (c) write $p(x, y) = p(x)p(y|x) = \alpha p_1(x)p(y|x) + \beta p_2(x)p(y|x)$. Then the right side minus the left in (13.7), which we must show to be non-positive, is equal to

$$\sum_{x,y} \alpha p_1(x, y) \log \frac{p(y|x)}{p_1(y)} + \sum_{x,y} \beta p_2(x, y) \log \frac{p(y|x)}{p_2(y)}$$

$$- \sum_{x,y} [\alpha p_1(x, y) + \beta p_2(x, y)] \log \frac{p(y|x)}{p(y)} \text{ by (13.2)}$$

$$= \alpha \sum_{x,y} p_1(x, y) \log \frac{p(y)}{p_1(y)} + \beta \sum_{x,y} p_2(x, y) \log \frac{p(y)}{p_2(y)}, \text{after cancelling } p(y|x).$$

This has the form $\alpha L_1 + \beta L_2$, and is non-positive because by Jensen's Inequality

$$L_1 \leq \log \sum_{x,y} p_1(x, y) \frac{p(y)}{p_1(y)} = \log \sum_{x,y} p(x|y)p(y) = \log \sum_{x,y} p(x, y)$$

$$= \log 1 = 0,$$

and similarly for L_2.

Theorem 13.13 $I(X;Y)$ *is convex in the transition probabilities: suppose that, for* $i = 1, 2$, *(a)* Y_i *is a random variable with the same alphabet and input probabilities as* Y, *(b)* (X, Y_i) *has transition probabilities* $p_i(y|x)$, *and (c)* $p(y|x) = \alpha p_1(y|x) + \beta p_2(y|x)$ *for constants* $\alpha, \beta \geq 0$. *Then*

$$I(X;Y) \leq \alpha I(X;Y_1) + \beta I(X;Y_2). \tag{13.8}$$

Proof Analogously to above we let $p_i(x, y)$ denote the joint distribution of (X, Y_i), so that the corresponding distributions of X given Y_i may be written $p_i(x|y) = p_i(x, y)/p(y)$, and furthermore, by condition (c), $p(x, y) = p(x)p(y|x) = \alpha p(x)p_1(y|x) + \beta p(x)p_2(y|x) = \alpha p_1(x, y) + \beta p_2(x, y)$. Then the left side minus the right in (13.8), which we must prove non-positive, is equal to

$$\sum_{x,y} [\alpha p_1(x, y) + \beta p_2(x, y)] \log \frac{p(x|y)}{p(x)}$$

$$- \alpha \sum_{x,y} p_1(x, y) \log \frac{p_1(x|y)}{p(x)} - \beta \sum_{x,y} p_2(x, y) \log \frac{p_2(x|y)}{p(x)} \text{ by (13.2)}$$

$$= \alpha \sum_{x,y} p_1(x, y) \log \frac{p(x|y)}{p_1(x|y)} + \beta \sum_{x,y} p_2(x, y) \log \frac{p(x|y)}{p_2(x|y)}, \text{after cancelling } p(x).$$

This has the form $\alpha M_1 + \beta M_2$, and is non-positive because by Jensen's Inequality

$$M_1 \leq \log \sum_{x,y} p_1(x, y) \frac{p(x|y)}{p_1(x|y)} = \log \sum_{x,y} p(y)p(x|y)$$

$$= \log \sum_{x,y} p(x, y) = \log 1 = 0,$$

and similarly for M_2.

13.1.4 Random vectors

We have introduced the idea of a symbol transmitted across a potentially noisy channel being a random variable X and arriving at its destination as a random variable Y. Provided the effect of the channel may be modelled by an array of *transition* probabilities $p(y|x)$, these define a certain quantity $I(X;Y)$, which we put forward as a measure of the information that has been successfully carried across the channel. We also label X and Y as respectively *input* (or source) and *output*, and name $I(X;Y)$ the *mutual information* of X, Y.

The next step is to consider a sequence of input symbols $X_1, \ldots, X_d$ for some positive integer d, and their corresponding outputs $Y_1, \ldots, Y_d$. We take the viewpoint that our input is now a random vector $X = (X_1, \ldots, X_d)$, resulting in output random vector $Y = (Y_1, \ldots, Y_d)$, and we consider the random pair (X, Y). Because the earlier definitions of $I(X;Y)$, $H(X)$ and $H(X, Y)$ for $d = 1$ depend only on the pdfs $p(x)$, $p(y|x)$, and not on X, Y being scalars, these definitions and resulting theorems carry over immediately to the extended meaning of (X, Y). In particular,

$$I(X;Y) = E \, \log \frac{p(x, y)}{p(x)p(y)} = E \, \log \frac{p(y|x)}{p(y)} = E \, \log \frac{p(x|y)}{p(x)}, \qquad (13.9)$$

where expected values are given by $E[f(x, y)] = \sum_{x,y} p(x, y) f(x, y)$ with x and y ranging over all permitted d-vectors $x = (x_1, \ldots, x_d)$, $y = (y_1, \ldots, y_d)$. In this context $p(y|x)$ may be written as $p(y_1, \ldots, y_d | x_1, \ldots, x_d)$. An illustration is given in Figure 13.6.

Note 13.14 The following hold, both as stated and with the roles of x, y reversed.

(i) $\sum_x p(x_1)p(x_2) \cdots p(x_d) = \sum_{x_1} p(x_1) \cdots \sum_{x_d} p(x_d) = 1,$

(ii) $\sum_y p(y_1|x_1) \cdots p(y_d|x_d) = 1$, for any fixed $x = (x_1, \cdots, x_d)$.

Proof The first equality is a straightforward application of the laws of multiplication, with the observation that $\sum_{x_i} p(x_i) = 1$ for each i (cf. Theorem 9.25). The second is similar, with the latter equality replaced by $\sum_{y_i} p(y_i|x_i) = 1 (x_i \, fixed)$, which holds because $k(y_i)$ defined as $p(y_i|x_i)$ is a pdf. This is discussed in Section 10.1.3.

Examples 13.15 (*Frequently used properties*) Properties and arguments such as those following will be used often and to good effect. The reader is advised to follow throught the short examples below, in which we let $\{p_i\}$ be any probability distribution.

N1: log converts Π to $\sum$: $\log \Pi p_i = \sum \log p_i$.
N2: E commutes with $\sum$: $\sum E[\log p_i] = E[\sum \log p_i] \, (= E[\log \Pi p_i]$, by above) We may think of $\sum$ jumping over E, then log, being converted to Π by the latter.
N3: $\log A - \log B = \log A/B$. We shall typically argue that $E[\log \frac{A}{B}] - E[\log \frac{A}{C}] = E[\log \frac{A}{B} - \log \frac{A}{C}] = E[\log \frac{C}{B}]$ (A has vanished).

N4: log(1) = 0. This is highly valuable when taken with $\sum p_i = 1$, for example: $E[\log \sum p_i] = E[\log(1)] = E[0] = 0$.

Definition 13.16 An (X, Y) channel is *memoryless* if we may write

$$p(y|x) = \prod_{i=1}^{d} p(y_i|x_i), \tag{13.10}$$

where $p(y|x)$ stands for $p(y_1, \ldots, y_d|x_1, \ldots, x_d)$, or, in more detail, $P(Y_1 = y_1, \ldots, Y_d = x_d | X = x_1, \ldots, X_d = x_d)$. Of course, $p(x)$ denotes simply $p(x_1, \ldots, x_d)$. As a prelude to pairing two contrasting results on $I(X; Y)$, we recall that $X_1, \ldots, X_d$ are called *independent* if

$$p(x) = \prod_{i=1}^{d} p(x_i). \tag{13.11}$$

Example 13.17 Suppose a sequence X of three binary digits is transmitted, and received as the sequence Y. We compute the transition matrix $Q = [p(y|x)]$, assuming the (X, Y) channel to be memoryless. The matrix is 8×8, with rows indexed by the triples $x = x_1 x_2 x_3$, which run through the 3-bit binary words $000, 001, \ldots, 111$. The columns are indexed similarly by triples $y = (y_1, y_2, y_3)$. Thanks to the memoryless hypothesis we need the $p(y_j|x_i)$ only in the case $j = i$, to complete our task. We shall take this to be a simple matter of *bit error probabilities*, namely

$$p(y_j|x_i) = p, \text{ if } y_i \neq x_i \text{ (error)}, \tag{13.12}$$

implying that $p(y_i|x_i) = 1 - p$ if $y_i = x_i$. Thus, for example, if $x = 101$ and $y = 110$ then $p(y|x) = (1 - p)p^2$ because x and y differ in exactly two places. This is where the memoryless property (13.10) comes in. More generally, if triples x and y differ in exactly w places then

$$p(y|x) = p^w(1 - p)^{3-w}. \tag{13.13}$$

$x \backslash y$	000	001	010	$\cdots$	111
000	$(1-p)^3$	$p(1-p)^2$	$p(1-p)^2$	$\cdots$	p^3
$Q_1 = 001$	$p(1-p)^2$	$(1-p)^3$	$p^2(1-p)$	$\cdots$	$p^2(1-p)$
010	$p(1-p)^2$	$p^2(1-p)$	$(1-p)^3$	$\cdots$	$p^2(1-p)$
$\cdots$	$\cdots$	$\cdots$	$\cdots$	$\cdots$	$\cdots$

Figure 13.6 Transition matrix $[p(y|x)]$ restricted to the first few rows and columns, which are indexed by the eight binary triples $000, 001, 010, \ldots, 111$ in some fixed order, say as binary integers. The latter ordering is adopted in Example 13.20 for computing $I(X, Y)$.

Notice that w is the weight of the XOR (or Mod 2) combination $x + y$, where the weight of a binary vector is the number of 1s amongst its digits, a pointer to important things in the coding theorem to follow. In Figure 13.6 we illustrate the transition matrix Q_1

restricted to the first three rows and columns, corresponding to an ordering that begins 000, 001, 010.

Theorem 13.18 *For an* (X, Y) *channel we have*

$$I(X;Y) \leq \sum_i I(X_i;Y_i), \quad if (X, Y) \text{ is memoryless,} \tag{13.14}$$

with the reverse inequality if $X_1, \ldots, X_d$ *are independent. Hence equality, if the memoryless and independence conditions both hold.*

Proof Let (X, Y) satisfy the memoryless equality (13.10) for $p(y|x)$. Guided by this we choose from (13.9) the expression for I which involves $p(y|x)$, and argue as follows. The difference $I(X;Y) - \sum I(X_i;Y_i)$ is

$$E \log \frac{p(y|x)}{p(y)} - \sum_i E \log \frac{p(y_i|x_i)}{p(y_i)}$$

$$= E \log \frac{p(y|x)}{p(y)} - E \log \prod_i \frac{p(y_i|x_i)}{p(y_i)} \qquad \text{see N2 of Examples 13.15}$$

$$= E \log \left[\frac{p(y|x)}{p(y)} \Big/ \prod_i \frac{p(y_i|x_i)}{p(y_i)} \right] \qquad \text{see N3}$$

$$= E \log \frac{\prod_i p(y_i)}{p(y)} \qquad \text{(memoryless) by (13.10)}$$

$$\leq \log E \left[\frac{\prod_i p(y_i)}{p(y)} \right] \qquad \text{by Jensen's Inequality}$$

$$= \log \sum_y p(y) \frac{\prod_i p(y_i)}{p(y)} \qquad \text{by definition of } E$$

$$= \log(1) \text{ (by Note 13.14, since the } p(y)\text{s cancel)} = 0.$$

This proves the first part, the necessary $\leq$ sign reducing the result to inequality. Now suppose that $X_1, \ldots, X_d$ are independent. This time we choose the expression for I which involves $p(x)$. The difference $\sum_i I(X_i;Y_i) - I(X;Y)$ is

$$\sum_i E \log \frac{p(x_i|y_i)}{p(x_i)} - E \log \frac{p(x|y)}{p(x)} \qquad \text{by (13.9)}$$

$$= E \log \prod_{i=1}^d \frac{p(x_i|y_i)}{p(x_i)} - E \log \frac{p(x|y)}{p(x)} \qquad \text{see N2}$$

$$= E \log \frac{\prod_i p(x_i|y_i)}{p(x|y)} \qquad \text{since } p(x) = \prod_i p(x_i), \text{ see N3}$$

$$\leq \log E \frac{\prod_i p(x_i|y_i)}{p(x|y)} \qquad \text{by Jensen's Inequality.}$$

As before, since $\log(1) = 0$ the result will follow if the above expected value equals 1. It is

$$\sum_{x,y} p(x, y)\frac{\Pi_i p(x_i|y_i)}{p(x|y)} \qquad \text{by definition}$$

$$= \sum_y p(y) \sum_x \Pi_i p(x_i|y_i) \qquad \text{since } p(x, y) = p(y)p(x|y)$$

$$= \sum_y p(y) \text{ (by Note 13.14)} = 1, \text{ as required.}$$

Corollary 13.19 *A random vector X satisfies $H(X) \leq \sum_i H(X_i)$.*

Proof We apply Theorem 13.18 to the (X, Y) channel with $Y = X$, which is memoryless because $p(y|x) = 1 = p(y_i|x_i)$ for all permitted integers i. The conclusion is $I(X; X) \leq \sum_i I(X_i; X_i)$, in other words $H(X) \leq \sum_i H(X_i)$.

Example 13.20 Continuing Example 13.17, we calculate and compare $I(X; Y)$ with $\sum I(X_i; Y_i)$ for a sequence X of three binary digits sent down a noisy channel and recovered as a binary triple Y. We have already determined (Figure 13.6) the transition matrix $Q_1 = [p(y|x)]$, given that (X, Y) is memoryless and that each symbol has a probability p of being incorrectly conveyed (see (13.12)). To determine the various mutual entropies I we need to know how successive bits X_i depend upon each other. We shall suppose not that they are independent, but that the sequence X_1, X_2, X_3 is Markov. That is, X_2 depends on X_1, and X_3 depends only on X_2. We'll assume that 0, 1 are equally likely for X_1, with a subsequent 'sticky' bias towards repetition. Specifically, let $p(x_{i+1}|x_i) = 2/3$ if $x_{i+1} = x_i$, giving a Markovian transition matrix

$$Q_2 = \begin{bmatrix} 2/3 & 1/3 \\ 1/3 & 2/3 \end{bmatrix} = \frac{1}{3}\begin{bmatrix} 2 & 1 \\ 1 & 2 \end{bmatrix}. \tag{13.15}$$

Computing $\sum I(X_i; Y_i)$ In this part of the calculation the dependence on i seems to fade, in spite of the matrix Q_2 (results will be different for (X, Y)). We have in succession $[p(x_1)] = [\frac{1}{2} \ \frac{1}{2}]$, $[p(x_2)] = [p(x_1)]Q_2 = [\frac{1}{2} \ \frac{1}{2}]$, and similarly $[p(x_3)] = p(x_2)]Q_2 = [\frac{1}{2} \ \frac{1}{2}]$, a third time! It is given that the transition matrix Q_3 for each $x_i \rightarrow y_i$ has the form

$$Q_3 = \begin{bmatrix} 1-p & p \\ p & 1-p \end{bmatrix} = \text{Rows}\,(R_0, R_1), \text{ say.} \tag{13.16}$$

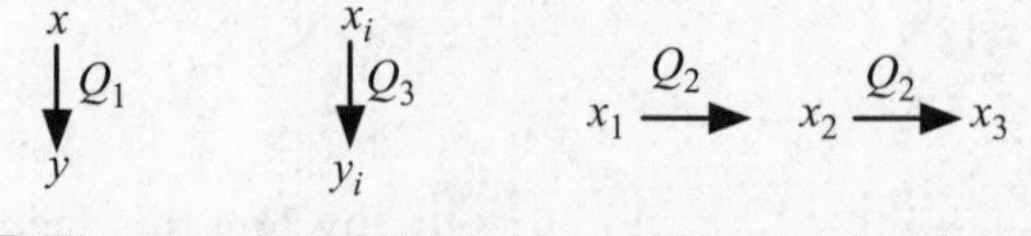

$$\begin{array}{ccc} x & x_i & \\ \downarrow Q_1 & \downarrow Q_3 & x_1 \xrightarrow{Q_2} x_2 \xrightarrow{Q_2} x_3 \\ y & y_i & \end{array}$$

Figure 13.7 The part played by each transition matrix of Example 13.20.

Thus $[p(y_i)] = [p(x_i)]Q_3 = [\frac{1}{2} \ \frac{1}{2}]$, for each of $i = 1, 2, 3$, whence $H(Y_i) = H(1/2) = 1$, and finally

$$H(Y_i|X_i) = \sum_{x_i=0,1} p(x_i)H(R_{x_i}) = \frac{1}{2}H(1-p, p) + \frac{1}{2}H(p, 1-p) = H(p),$$

$$\sum I(X_i; Y_i) = \sum [H(Y_i) - H(Y_i|X_i)] = 3(1 - H(p)).$$

Computing $I(X; Y)$ We calculate in succession $[p(x)]$, $[p(y)]$, $H(Y)$ and $H(Y|X)$. By the Markov property and (13.15) we may determine the vector $[p(x)]$ from $p(x) = p(x_1, x_2, x_3) = p(x_1)p(x_2|x_1)p(x_3|x_2)$. Here is the result, with triples ordered by the integer they represent (high bits to left).

$$
\begin{array}{c c c c c c c c c}
x & 000 & 001 & 010 & 011 & 100 & 101 & 110 & 111 \\
18p(x) & 4 & 2 & 1 & 2 & 2 & 1 & 2 & 4
\end{array}
\tag{13.17}
$$

Exercise Check the answers in (13.17).

Now we go from triples x to triples y, by applying the matrix Q_1. Notice that interchanging 0 and 1 leaves the same number of 11s plus 00s, each of probability 4/9, in any triple. We restrict this calculation to the case $p = 0.1$. We have exactly

$$[p(y)] = [p(x)]Q1 = (1/18) [3.37 \ 2.09 \ 1.45 \ 2.09 \ 2.09 \ 1.45 \ 2.09 \ 3.37],$$

whence $H(Y) = -\sum p(y) \log p(y) = 2.933$, and writing $Q_1 = \text{Rows}(R_x)$ yields $H(Y|X) = \sum_x p(x)H(R_x) = 1.407$. Finally, from the usual convenient formula $I = H(Y) - H(Y|X)$:

$$I(X; Y) = 1.526 < 1.593 = \sum I(X_i; Y_i).$$

This both verifies (13.14) for the memoryless case of (X, Y) and illustrates the difference in mutual entropy caused by dependence amongst the input symbols (independence of the X_i would force equality in (13.14)).

Exercise Compute $I(X; Y)$ for Example 13.20 with $p = 0.2$.

A further Markov connection A sequence X, Y, Z of random variables, which we take as usual to include the case of random *vectors*, is by definition a Markov chain if each variable depends only upon its immediate precursor, that is $p(z|x, y) = p(z|y)$ for all x, y, z for which $p(x, y, z) > 0$. Similarly for longer sequences. The pair (X, Y) is itself a random vector, and we have the following connection with mutual entropy.

Theorem 13.21 *Let X, Y, Z be a sequence of random variables. Then, with equality in case (13.18a) below if and only if X, Y, Z is a Markov chain, we have*

$$I(X, Y; Z) \geq I(Y; Z) \ (always), \tag{13.18a}$$

$$I(X; Z) \leq I(Y; Z) \ (if \ X, Y, Z \ is \ Markov). \tag{13.18b}$$

Proof (13.18a) The difference $I(Y; Z) - I(X, Y; Z)$ is by (13.9)

$$E \left[\log \frac{p(z|y)}{p(z)} - \log \frac{p(z|x, y)}{p(z)} \right]$$

$$= E \log \frac{p(z|y)}{p(z|x, y)} \qquad \text{see N3 of Examples 13.15}$$

$$\leq \log E \frac{p(z|y)}{p(z|x, y)} \qquad \text{by Jensen's Inequality}$$

$$= \log \sum_{x,y,z} p(x, y) p(z|y) \qquad \text{since } p(x, y, z) = p(x, y) p(z|x, y)$$

$$= \log \sum_{x,y} p(x, y) \sum_z p(z|y)$$

$$= \log \sum_{x,y} p(x, y) \text{ (by Note 13.14)} = \log(1) = 0.$$

This establishes the main inequality (13.18a). The single inequality in the argument is by Jensen's result an equality if and only if $p(z|y)/p(z|x, y)$ is a constant, say λ, as x, y and z vary. But Note 13.14 shows that in that case we have for any given x, y that $1 = \sum_z p(z|y) = \lambda \sum_z p(z|x, y) = \lambda$. Thus $\lambda = 1$, making X, Y, Z Markov, and the proof is complete. For (13.18b) see Exercise 13.5.

13.1.5 Channel capacity

We proceed in stages to define the *capacity* of a channel, which will be used to predict the rate at which information may be successfully transmitted to its destination, under various conditions. We consider henceforth a *discrete memoryless* channel (DMC), meaning that the input and output alphabets are finite as before, and that the *memoryless condition* (13.10) holds: $p(y|x) = \Pi p(y_i|x_i)$. Interpreting the subscripts in X_i, Y_i as time, we may say that output at discrete times $t = i$ depends only on input at time $t = i$.

Cost Following Shannon (1948), we take account of factors which may limit the optimisation of transmission, such as restrictions on power or bandwidth (see Chapter 14), under the blanket heading of a *cost function* κ for individual symbols x_i. This extends without ambiguity to d-vectors x by $\kappa(x) = \sum_i \kappa(x_i)$, with expected value

$$E[\kappa(X)] = \sum_x p(x) \kappa(x) = \sum_i E[\kappa(X_i)]. \tag{13.19}$$

Definition 13.22 We say the channel (X, Y) is a *d-channel* if X, Y are specifically d-vectors, and that X is *β-admissible* if $(1/d) E[\kappa(X)] \leq \beta$. The factor $1/d$ gives an average over the d variables X_i. In practice we shall usually write the condition as $E[\kappa(X)] \leq d\beta$. We are now ready to incorporate the measure $I(X; Y)$ of information successfully transmitted through the channel (X, Y), by defining the *dth capacity-cost function*

$$C_d(\beta) = \text{Max}_X \{ I(X; Y) : E[\kappa(X)] \leq d\beta \}, \tag{13.20}$$

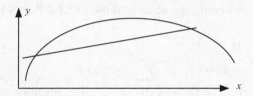

Figure 13.8 Graph of a concave function: characterised by lying above every chord.

the maximum being taken over all β-*admissible* X, with the transition probabilities $[p(y|x)]$ fixed (it is $[p(x)]$ that varies). That this maximum is actually achieved is (see Hoggar, 1992) a consequence of the fact that $I(X;Y)$ is a continuous function on the bounded and closed set

$$\{[p(x)]: p(x) \geq 0 \; \forall x, \sum_x p(x) = 1, \sum_x p(x)\kappa(x) \leq d\beta\}.$$

For the sequel we recall that *increasing*, for a function, will not be intended in the strict sense unless explicitly stated. Thus $f(t)$ is increasing if $s < t \Rightarrow f(s) \leq f(t)$.

Proposition 13.23 *The function $C_d(\beta)$ is increasing for $\beta \geq \beta_{\min}$, where $\beta_{\min}$ is the least value of β for which $C_d(\beta)$ is defined, namely the least cost of any symbol α:*

$$\beta_{\min} = \underset{\alpha}{\text{Min}} \, \kappa(\alpha). \tag{13.21}$$

Proof Firstly, $\beta < \beta_{\min}$ cannot occur, because $E[\kappa(X)] = \sum_i E[\kappa(X_i)] \geq \sum_i \beta_{\min} = d\beta_{\min}$. Secondly, the value $\beta_{\min}$ is actually attained for some X, as we now show. There is by definition of $\beta_{\min}$ some symbol α_0 for which $\beta_{\min} = \kappa(\alpha_0)$, and we may choose X so that each X_i satisfies $p(x_i) = 1$ if $x_i = \alpha_0$, otherwise $p(x_i) = 0$. With this choice there follows that $E[\kappa(X_i)] = \sum_\alpha p(X_i = \alpha)\kappa(\alpha) = \kappa(\alpha_0) = \beta_{\min}$, whence $E[\kappa(x)] = d\beta_{\min}$ as required.

C_d is increasing because $\beta_1 < \beta_2 \Rightarrow \{X: E[\kappa(X)] \leq d\beta_1\} \subseteq \{X: E[\kappa(X)] \leq d\beta_2\} \Rightarrow C_d(\beta_1) \leq C_d(\beta_2)$.

Theorem 13.24 *The function $C_d(\beta)$ is concave (see Figure 13.8).*

Proof We must show that given $s, t \geq 0$ with $s + t = 1$, and any costs $\beta, \gamma \geq \beta_{\min}$, there holds the concavity property $C_d(s\beta + t\gamma) \geq sC_d(\beta) + tC_d(\gamma)$. To show this we recast the various parts in terms of mutual entropy. Since C_d is a maximum that is actually attained, we may write, letting (X_i, Y_i) denote d-channels for the duration of this proof,

$C_d(\beta) = I(X_1; Y_1)$, where X_1 is β-admissible, with distribution $p_1(x)$, say,

$C_d(\gamma) = I(X_2; Y_2)$, where X_2 is γ-admissible, with distribution $p_2(x)$.

Now let the d-channel (X, Y) be defined by X having distribution $p(x) = sp_1(x) + tp_2(x)$, the transition probabilities being the same as those of $(X_1; Y_1)$ and $(X_2; Y_2)$. Then

$$
\begin{aligned}
E\kappa(X) &= \sum_x p(x)\kappa(x) \\
&= s\sum_x p_1(x)\kappa(x) + t\sum_x p_2(x)\kappa(x) \\
&= sE[\kappa(X_1)] + tE[\kappa(X_2)] && \text{by definition of } E \\
&\leq sd\beta + td\gamma = d(s\beta + t\gamma) && \text{by admissibilities of } X_1, X_2.
\end{aligned}
$$

Hence X is $(s\beta + t\gamma)$-admissible, and we may argue that

$$
\begin{aligned}
C_d(s\beta + t\gamma) &\geq I(X; Y) && \text{by the maximum property of } C_d \\
&\geq sI(X_1; Y_1) + tI(X_2; Y_2) && I \text{ being concave in } p(x) \\
&= sC_d(\beta) + tC_d(\gamma) && \text{by definition of } (X_1; Y_1), (X_2; Y_2).
\end{aligned}
$$

This completes the proof of concavity. We now come to a crucial and slightly surprising result, that enables us to formulate a definition of channel capacity which is independent of the parameter d.

Theorem 13.25 *We have $C_d(\beta) = dC_1(\beta)$ for any positive integer d.*

Proof We may write $E[\kappa(X_i)] = \beta_i$, and hence, with $X = (X_i)$, $Y = (Y_i)$,

$$
\begin{aligned}
C_d(\beta) &= I(X; Y) && \text{for some } X, Y \text{ with } E[\kappa(X)] \leq d\beta \\
&\leq \sum_i I(X_i; Y_i) && \text{by (13.14), the channel being memoryless} \\
&\leq \sum_i C_1(\beta_i) = d\sum_i \tfrac{1}{d}C_1(\beta_i) \\
&\leq dC_1\left(\tfrac{1}{d}\sum_i \beta_i\right) && \text{since } C_1 \text{ is concave by Theorem 13.24} \\
&= dC_1\left(\tfrac{1}{d}E[\kappa(X)]\right) && \text{since } \sum_i \beta_i = \sum_i E[\kappa(X_i)] = E[\kappa(X)] \\
&\leq dC_1(\beta) && \text{since } C_1 \text{ is increasing (Proposition 13.23)},
\end{aligned}
$$

and since $E[\kappa(X)] \leq d\beta$. Thus, if we can establish the reverse inequality, $C_d(\beta) \geq dC_1(\beta)$, the proof will be complete. Consider the case that $X_1, \ldots, X_d$ are independent and have the same distribution, with $E[\kappa(X_i)] \leq \beta$ and $I(X_i; Y_i) = C_1(\beta)$. Then

$$
\begin{aligned}
C_d(\beta) &\geq I(X; Y) && \text{since } E[\kappa(X)] = \sum_i E[\kappa(X_i)] \leq d\beta \\
&= \sum_i I(X_i; Y_i) && \text{by Theorem 13.18 (memoryless/independent)} \\
&= dC_1(\beta) && \text{since } I(X_i; Y_i) = C_1(\beta) \text{ is given.}
\end{aligned}
$$

The two equalities for $C_d(\beta)$ establish the desired equality. Hence the result for any d. $\qquad\blacksquare$

Definitions 13.26 We recall that, given the pdf of an input d-vector X, the channel transition probabilities determine the pdf of the output Y and the value of $I(X; Y)$. Thanks to Theorem 13.25, we are in a position to define formally the *capacity* $C(\beta)$ of the channel,

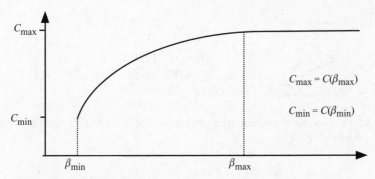

Figure 13.9 Typical graph of $C(\beta)$ as defined in Definitions 13.26.

independently of the size d of input sequence considered, by $C(\beta) = \mathrm{Sup}_d \; {}^1\!/_d C_d(\beta)$. See Figure 13.9. By Theorem 13.25 this limit exists; indeed, for any positive integer n,

$$C(\beta) = \tfrac{1}{n} C_n(\beta) = C_1(\beta). \tag{13.22}$$

The final two definitions below enable a convenient overview of the shape of the capacity function $C(\beta)$.

$$C_{\max} = \mathrm{Max}_\beta C(\beta) = \mathrm{Max}_X I(X;Y),$$
$$\beta_{\max} = \mathrm{Min}_X \{E[\kappa(X)] : I(X;Y) = C_{\max}\}. \tag{13.23}$$

Theorem 13.27 *The function $C(\beta)$ is (a) concave, (b) strictly increasing for $\beta_{\min} \leq \beta \leq \beta_{\max}$, and (c) constant for $\beta \geq \beta_{\max}$.*

Proof (a) The function $C(\beta)$ is concave because it equals $C_1(\beta)$, which we have shown to be concave. For (b), it remains to proves strictness. We note firstly that by Definitions (13.23), $C(\beta) < C_{\max}$ for all valid $\beta < \beta_{\max}$. Now let a, b be constants with $\beta_{\min} \leq a < b < \beta_{\max}$. Then $C(b) < C_{\max}$ by the above observations, and $C(a) \leq C(b)$ by Proposition 13.23. But if $C(a) = C(b)$ the concavity of $C(\beta)$ is contradicted (see Figure 13.10). Thus the increase in $C(\beta)$ is strict for $\beta_{\min} \leq \beta \leq \beta_{\max}$. Finally, it is immediate from (13.23) that $C(\beta) = C_{\max}$ for all $\beta \geq \beta_{\max}$.

Example 13.28 We determine the cost-capacity function for the channel data of Figure 13.11.

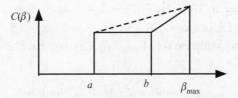

Figure 13.10 How $C(a) = C(b)$ contradicts concavity of $C(\beta)$.

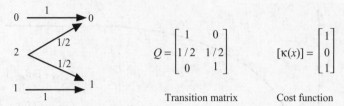

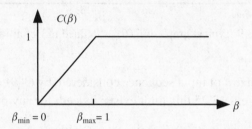

Transition matrix   Cost function

Figure 13.11 Transition probabilities and costs for an (X, Y) channel with $R_X = \{0, 2, 1\}$ and $R_Y = \{0, 1\}$.

Figure 13.12 $C(\beta)$ in the case of Example 13.28.

(1) We have $\beta_{\min} = \text{Min}_x \kappa(x)$ (by (13.21)) $= 0$, and consequently $C_{\min} = C(0)$

$$= \text{Max}_X\{I(X;Y): \sum p(x)\kappa(x) = 0\}$$
$$= \text{Max}_X\{I(X;Y): p(x) = 0 \text{ if } \kappa(x) > 0\}.$$

That is, $C_{\min}$ is the value of $I(X;Y)$ in the case $[p(x)] = [0\,1\,0]$, for which $H(X) = H(0, 1, 0) = H(1) = 0$ (see Notation 12.4). But then $0 \leq I(X;Y) \leq H(X) \leq 0$, implying that $I(X;Y)$, and hence $C_{\min}$, is 0.

(2) *General* $\beta \geq 0$ We determine $[p(x)]$, then $[p(y)]$ in terms of β. Let X be a 1-dimensional source/input which achieves $I(X;Y) = C(\beta)$, $E[\kappa(X)] = \beta$. Then $\beta = \sum p(x)\kappa(x) = p(0) + p(1)$ for the present cost function κ, whence by symmetry $p(0) = p(1) = \beta/2$ and $p(2) = 1 - \beta = \alpha$, say, where $0 \leq \alpha, \beta \leq 1$. So

$$[p(y)] = [p(x)]Q = [\beta/2 \ \alpha \ \beta/2]Q = \left[\frac{\alpha + \beta}{2} \ \frac{\alpha + \beta}{2}\right] = \left[\frac{1}{2} \ \frac{1}{2}\right].$$

Hence $H(X) = H(1/2) = 1$, and $H(Y|X) = \sum p(x)H(R_x)$ by (13.5)

$$= \frac{\beta}{2}H(1, 0) + \alpha H\left(\frac{1}{2}, \frac{1}{2}\right) + \frac{\beta}{2}H(0, 1) = \alpha.$$

Thus $C(\beta) = I(X;Y) = H(Y) - H(Y|X) = 1 - \alpha = \beta$ $(0 \leq \beta \leq 1)$, a simple linear relationship. Applying Definitions (13.23): $C_{\max} = \text{Max}_\beta C(\beta) = \text{Max}\{\beta\} = 1$, hence $\beta_{\max} = 1$ from the relationship established. We may summarise the results in the graph of Figure 13.12.

Remarks 13.29 (1) The example above shows that, though $C(\beta)$ is strictly increasing, its concavity need not be strict. (2) In calculating $C_{\min}$ we needed to restrict to the source symbols x for which $p(x) = \beta_{\min}$. A channel so restricted is called the *reduced channel*. (3) In retrospect, the definitions imply $C(\beta) = \text{Max}_X\{I(X;Y): E[\kappa(X)] = \beta\}$. (4) In general we need constrained optimisation to compute the capacity. For algorithms, see, e.g. Blahut (1972, 1987) or Cover & Thomas (1991) However, here is one type in which the answer is easy to compute.

Definition 13.30 A channel is *symmetric* if the transition matrix, not necessarily itself symmetric, has the property that each row is a permutation of every other, the same holding for columns also. An important special case is the Binary Symmetric Channel, or BSC, with two input and two output symbols and a matrix of the form

$$Q = \begin{bmatrix} a & b \\ b & a \end{bmatrix}, a, b \geq 0 \text{ and } a + b = 1. \tag{13.24}$$

Theorem 13.31 *The capacity $C_{\max}$ of a symmetric DMC is achieved with equiprobable inputs. If there are s output symbols and R_x is any row of the transition matrix, then*

$$C_{\max} = \log s - H(R_x). \tag{13.25}$$

Proof We invoke once more the formula $I(X;Y) = H(Y) - H(Y|X)$ (Theorem 13.3). According to Theorem 12.6, the first term $H(Y)$ has greatest value $\log s$ when $p(y)$ is constant. And this state of affairs is achievable by taking $p(x)$ constant, since the columns of Q differ only in the order of their elements and $[p(y)] = [p(x)]Q$. Further, the similar property for the rows R_x of Q implies that $H(R_x)$ is the same for each row, and hence

$$H(Y|X) = \sum_x p(x)H(R_x) \text{ (by (13.5))} = H(R_x)\sum_x p(x) = H(R_x).$$

Example 13.32 Determine the capacity of the channel with transition matrix

$$Q = \begin{bmatrix} 1/3 & 1/6 & 1/3 & 1/6 \\ 1/6 & 1/3 & 1/6 & 1/3 \end{bmatrix}.$$

Solution In Q, the rows are permutations of $\begin{bmatrix} 1/3 & 1/3 & 1/6 & 1/6 \end{bmatrix}$ and the columns are permutations of $\begin{bmatrix} 1/3 & 1/6 \end{bmatrix}$; so the channel is symmetric, and by Theorem 13.31 the capacity is $C_{\max} = \log 4 - H(1/3, 1/3, 1/6, 1/6) = 2 - (4/3 + \log 3) = 0.0817$ bits.

13.1.6 The Channel Coding Theorem

At this point we address the question of how we may convey information accurately through a noisy channel. The rough answer is to add redundancy, hoping that thereby the original message can be inferred in spite of errors. Both question and answer will shortly be made more precise.

Considering the message, it is convenient to regard this as consisting of d-bit binary words $u = (u_1, \ldots, u_d)$ ($u_i = 0$ or 1). For example, the ASCII code of 8-bit words, or bytes, is used to represent uniquely the lower and upper case versions of several language alphabets, together with numerals and special symbols; however, the d-tuples could equally well refer to pixel colour values, or to more general quantities such as the quantised values of an arbitrary input signal.

We have derived an upper limit C_{max}, the *channel capacity*, for the information per bit (or per unit time) at which information might be transferred across a given channel. We shall prove the *Channel Coding Theorem*, which asserts that there is *always* a way to get as close as we wish to this limit by suitably replacing our message d-vectors with members of some set $C = \{c_1, \ldots, c_M\}$ of n-tuples over a finite alphabet $\mathcal{A}$. We call C a *code* or *codebook* and its elements *codewords*. The theorem asserts further, and remarkably, that, no matter how much channel noise is present, the mean error rate per codeword can be brought down below any given level, by suitable choice of C and its *decoding method f*. The overall process is indicated in Figure 13.13.

Figure 13.13 Model of an encoding/decoding system, where X, Y is an input–output pair.

Of course, there must be enough codewords for a distinct encoding of each message d-tuple, and this will be so if $2^d \leq M$, or $d \leq \log_2 M$; we view $\log_2 M$ as representing the number of encodable bits, and the *rate R* of the code as the number of *bits per symbol*. Since there are n symbols, we have

$$\text{rate } R = \frac{\log_2 M}{n} \text{ bits/symbol,} \tag{13.26}$$

$$= k/n \text{ if } M = 2^k. \tag{13.27}$$

In any case, $$M = 2^{nR}. \tag{13.28}$$

That this definition of rate really corresponds to rate of infomation flow as measured by $I(X;Y)$ is borne out by the specifics of the Encoding Theorem. But first an example from perhaps the best known of 1-error-correcting-codes, invented by Hamming (1950), a contemporary of Shannon himself.

Example 13.33 (*Hamming codes*) Perhaps the most used alphabet is $\{0, 1\}$, the case of binary codewords. For many transmission situations, including binary storage devices, it may be realistically assumed that not more than one bit will be corrupted in any codeword. Here the codes of Hamming are the most efficient (Remarks 13.46 below), for they provide the largest possible 1-error-correcting codes of length $n = 2^m - 1$ ($m = 2, 3, \ldots$). In the case $m = 3$ the codewords may be taken as $00\ldots0, 11\ldots1, 1011000, 0100111$, and all cyclic permutations of these. As the reader may care to verify, any two codewords differ in at least three places, so if one is corrupted in a single bit position it is still closer to its original than to any other, and may thus be identified, or *decoded*. The encoding system is

$$[u_1 \ldots u_4] \rightarrow [u_1 \ldots u_4] \begin{bmatrix} 1 & 0 & 1 & 1 & 0 & 0 & 0 \\ 0 & 1 & 0 & 1 & 1 & 0 & 0 \\ 0 & 0 & 1 & 0 & 1 & 1 & 0 \\ 1 & 1 & 1 & 1 & 1 & 1 & 1 \end{bmatrix}. \tag{13.29}$$

The parameters are $M = 16 = 2^4$, $n = 7$, so from (13.27) the rate is $R = 4/7$.

Definition 13.34 Suppose the channel delivers c_i as vector y. A *decoding rule* is a function $f: Y \rightarrow C \cup \{?\}$, where '?' is a symbol denoting decoder failure (cf. Example 13.8). We need a notation for the probability of error, and will use

$$P_E^{(i)} = P\{f(y) \neq c_i\}. \tag{13.30}$$

Not forgetting the cost, given for each symbol of the code's alphabet, we say an n-tuple is *β-admissible* if its total cost, the sum of costs of its coordinates, does not exceed β. Shannon proved the following theorem (we follow the outline of McEliece (1987)); it says that we can get the rate close to capacity in spite of error.

Theorem 13.35 *Let $C(\beta)$ be the capacity-cost function for a DMC (discrete memoryless channel). If $\beta > \beta_0 \geq \beta_{\min}$, $R < C(\beta_0)$, $\varepsilon > 0$, there is a β-admissible code of size $M \geq 2^{nR}$, with a decoding rule for which the probability of error on a codeword is less than ε.*

Note the directions of the inequalities. We want many codewords but small errors. In the special case that cost need not be taken into account ('cost is no object') we set $\beta_0 = \beta_{\max}$ and obtain the result known as *Shannon's (noisy) Channel Coding Theorem*. (For a direct proof by a different approach, see Welsh, 1988.)

Corollary 13.36 (*'Noisy' Channel Coding Theorem*) *Suppose we are given a DMC, and real numbers $R < C_{\max}$, and $\varepsilon > 0$. Then there exist an n-code C of size M and a decoding rule such that (a) $M \geq 2^{nR}$, and (b) $P_E^{(i)} < \varepsilon$ for $i = 1, 2, \ldots, M$.*

Proof of Theorem 13.35 We shall think of this proof as being in three parts: (1) getting a handle on $P_E^{(i)}$, (2) bounding $P_E^{(i)}$, (3) completing the proof. For the duration of this proof, let $p(\alpha) (\alpha \in \mathcal{A})$ be a distribution that achieves $C(\beta_0)$ (see (13.20) ff).
(1) *A handle on $P_E^{(i)}$* We start to put into operation Shannon's ingenious idea of showing a desired encoding exists by considering expected values of a random code. We begin by structuring as a sample space the set of channel input–output pairs $\Omega = \{(x, y)\} = \mathcal{A}^n \times \mathcal{A}^n$, by defining its distribution to be $p(x, y) = p(x)p(y|x)$, where

$$\begin{aligned} p(x) &= p(x_1) \cdots p(x_n) & \text{(iid input symbols),} \\ p(y|x) &= \Pi_i p(y_i|x_i) & \text{(the memoryless hypothesis).} \end{aligned}$$

For the decoding rule we need a suitable definition of closeness so as to use 'spheres' round a point. With lower case x, y, write

$$I(x; y) = \log \frac{p(y|x)}{p(y)}, \tag{13.31}$$

representing a typical term in $I(X; Y) = \sum p(x, y) I(x; y)$, and let R' be a number strictly between R and $C(\beta_0)$. Based on this, we define two sets:

$$A = \{(x, y): I(x; y) \geq nR'\} \quad (x, y \text{ close in mutual information})$$
$$A^* = \{(x, y) \in A: \kappa(x) \leq n\beta\} \subseteq A.$$

Now we may define a decoding rule $y \to f(y)$ for an arbitrary code $\{c_1, \ldots, c_M\}$. This is done via a sphere $S(y)$ around y consisting of vectors which are both close to y and not too costly (see Figure 13.14).

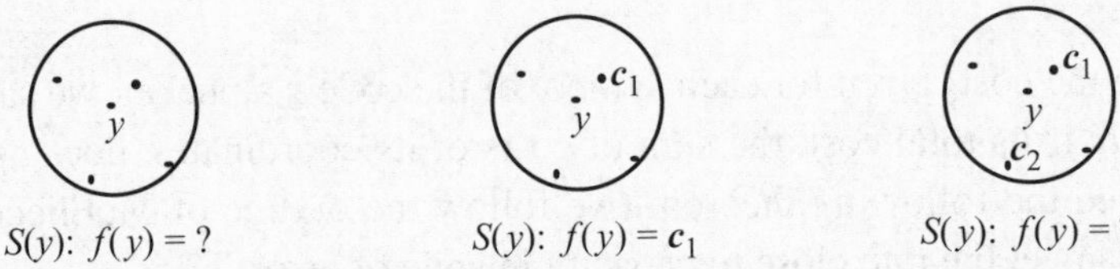

$S(y)$: $f(y) = ?$ $S(y)$: $f(y) = c_1$ $S(y)$: $f(y) = ?$

Figure 13.14 Three cases in the decoding rule of the Channel Coding Theorem. Each dot represents an n-tuple, which is a codeword if and only if so labelled.

$$S(y) = \{x: (x, y) \in A^*\}, \text{ and}$$
$$f(y) = \begin{cases} c_i, & \text{if } S(y) \text{ contains a single codeword } c_i, \\ ? & \text{otherwise.} \end{cases} \tag{13.32}$$

The argument is facilitated by use of an indicator function χ for A^*. That is, $\chi(x, y) = 1$ if (x, y) is in A^*, otherwise $\chi = 0$. In this notation, writing also $\overline{\chi} = 1 - \chi$, we have

$$x \in S(y) \Leftrightarrow \chi(x, y) = 1, \text{ and } x \notin S(y) \Leftrightarrow \overline{\chi}(x, y) = 1. \tag{13.33}$$

(2) *Bounding* $P_E^{(i)}$ Consider the case when a fixed codeword c_i is transmitted. From the definition of f, an error can occur on sending c_i and receiving y if and only if $c_i \notin S(y)$ and/or $c_j \in S(y)$ for some $j \neq i$. Therefore

$$P_E^{(i)} \leq \sum_y p(c_i \to y \& c_i \notin S(y)) + \sum_y p(c_i \to y \& c_j \in S(y), \text{ some } j \neq i)$$
$$= \sum_y \overline{\chi}(c_i, y) p(y|c_i) + \sum_{j \neq i} \sum_y \chi(c_j, y) p(y|c_i)$$
$$= T_i(c_1, \ldots, c_M), \text{ say.}$$

We would like to identify an n-code for which T_i is small for all i; what we can do within the scope of the present result is to show that one exists. A crucial idea here is to show that under certain conditions the *expected value* of T_i tends to zero as n tends to infinity. We view T_i as a random variable on the set of all possible n-codes of size M, with probability distribution given by choosing independently every entry c_{kj} of every codeword c_k. In symbols,

$$p(c_1, \ldots, c_M) = \Pi_k p(c_k) = \Pi_{k,j} p(c_{kj}), \tag{13.34}$$

where the distribution of individual entries $c_{kj} \in \mathcal{A}$ was chosen at the start of the proof to achieve $C(\beta_0)$. The required expected value is

$$E(T_i) = E[\sum_y \overline{\chi}(c_i, y) p(y|c_i)] + \sum_{j \neq i} E[\sum_y \chi(c_j, y) p(y|c_i)]$$

$$= E_1 + \sum_{j \neq i} E_{2,j}, \text{ say.} \tag{13.35}$$

We bound each term, noting that each c_k is an instance of x, and that i (but not c_i) is fixed:

$$E_1 = \sum_{c_1, \ldots, c_M} p(c_1) \cdots p(c_M) \sum_y \overline{\chi}(c_i, y) p(y|c_i) \quad \text{(by definition of } E\text{)}$$

$$= \sum_{c_i, y} p(c_i) \overline{\chi}(c_i, y) p(y|c_i) \qquad \text{since } \sum_{c_k} p(c_k) = 1 \text{ for each } k$$

$$= \sum_{x,y} p(x, y) \overline{\chi}(x, y) \qquad \text{since } p(x) p(y|x) = p(x, y)$$

$$= P[(x, y) \notin A^*] = P[I(x; y) < nR' \text{ or } \kappa(x) > n\beta]$$

$$\leq P[I(x; y) < nR'] + P[\kappa(x) > n\beta]. \tag{13.36}$$

Considering the first term above, we note that

$$I(x; y) = \log \frac{p(y|x)}{p(y)} = \log \prod_{i=1}^n \frac{p(y_i|x_i)}{p(y_i)} = \sum_i \log \frac{p(y_i|x_i)}{p(y_i)} = \sum_i I(x_i; y_i),$$

and since this is the sum of n iid random variables $Z_i = I(x_i; y_i)$, we may apply the Weak Law of Large Numbers (10.29):

$$P(|Z_1 + \cdots + Z_n - n\mu| \geq \varepsilon) \to 0, \text{ as } n \to \infty, \tag{13.37}$$

where, by construction, $\mu = E(Z_i) = C(\beta_0) > R'$, and hence, taking $\varepsilon = n\mu - nR'$, we may infer that

$$P[I(x; y) < nR'] = P[I - n\mu < -\varepsilon] \leq P[|I - n\mu| \geq \varepsilon] \to 0, \text{ as } n \to \infty,$$

which takes care of the first term of (13.36). For the second term we observe that $\kappa(x)$ equals $\sum_i \kappa(x_i)$, another sum of n iid random variables, each with mean $\mu \leq \beta_0 < \beta$. A second application of (13.37) gives $P[\kappa(x) > n\beta_0] \to 0$ as $n \to \infty$, and so E_1 is arbitrarily small for sufficiently large n.

Bounding $E_{2,j}$ The argument is shorter in this case. Note that i, j are unequal but fixed.

$$E_{2,j} = \sum_{c_1,\ldots,c_M} p(c_1) \cdots p(c_M) \sum_y \chi(c_j, y) p(y|c_i)$$

$$= \sum_{c_j,y} p(c_j) \chi(c_j, y) \sum_{c_i} p(c_i) p(y|c_i) \text{ since } \sum_{c_k} p(c_k) = 1 \text{ for each } k$$

$$= \sum_{c_j,y} p(c_j) \chi(c_j, y) p(y) \text{ by the Total Probability Formula (10.10)}$$

$$= \sum_{(x,y)\in A^*} p(x)p(y) \le \sum_{(x,y)\in A} p(x)p(y), \text{ since } A^* \subseteq A.$$

Now, when (x, y) is in A we have $p(x)p(y) \le 2^{-nR'} p(x, y)$, because $nR' \le I(x; y) = \log[p(y|x)/p(y)] = \log[p(x, y)/p(x)p(y)]$. Consequently, since $\sum_{x,y} p(x, y) = 1$,

$$E_{2,j} \le 2^{-nR'} \sum_{(x,y)\in A} p(x, y) \le 2^{-nR'}. \tag{13.38}$$

Completing the proof of Theorem 13.35 Considering the terms in (13.35), set $M = 2 \cdot 2^{\text{Ceil}(nR)}$, so that (13.38) gives

$$\sum_{j\ne i} E_{2,j} \le (M-1)2^{-nR'} \le (2^{2+nR} - 1) \le 4 \cdot 2^{-n(R'-R)}.$$

Since $R' - R$ is positive, we have that both E_1 and the sum above are arbitrarily small for sufficiently large n, and therefore, for any $\varepsilon > 0$,

$$E(T_i) < \varepsilon/2 \text{ (n sufficiently large)}. \tag{13.39}$$

With n such that (13.39) holds and M as specified above, define a random variable P_E on the space of all codes of size M by

$$P_E(c_1, \ldots, c_M) = (1/M) \sum_i P_E^{(i)}(c_1, \ldots, c_M). \tag{13.40}$$

Then $E(P_E) \le (1/M) \sum_i E(T_i) < \varepsilon/2$, by (13.39) and (13.40). It follows that there is a code with $P_E < \varepsilon/2$. It may contain codewords which are not β-admissible, or violate $P_E^{(i)} < \varepsilon$ for certain i, but if more than half of the codewords satisfy $P_E^{(i)} \ge \varepsilon$ the definition (13.40) gives $P_E \ge \varepsilon/2$, a contradiction. Thus, by deleting all codewords with $P_E \ge \varepsilon$ we obtain a code with at least $2^{\text{Ceil}(nR)}$ codewords, each satisfying $P_E < \varepsilon$. This establishes the first part of the theorem. If β-admissibility fails, say $\kappa(c_i) > n\beta$, consider the decoding $c_i \to y$. In fact, $S(y) = \{x: (x, y) \in A, \text{ and } \kappa(x) \le n\beta\}$ cannot contain c_i, and so $P_E^{(i)} = 1$, a contradiction. This completes the proof.

Remarks 13.37 Shannon's result says that, by suitable coding of the source symbols into codewords of some fixed length n, we can obtain information flow arbitrarily close to a quantity called *capacity*, defined by the transition probabilities of the channel, and which cannot be exceeded. There are three drawbacks:

(1) the goodness of the code may depend on its having extremely long codewords,
(2) determining a suitable code is left as a huge search problem, and
(3) even if we find such a code by searching, it may be of no practical use because there is no reasonably short decoding method.

Thus the search has focussed on *codes with extra structure* such as linearity, which give promise of concise description and/or decoding procedures. For this we proceed to the next section (recent success with a probabilistic approach is introduced in Section 13.3).

13.2 Error-correcting codes

In this section we take a brief look at some important milestones, following Shannon's Coding Theorem, in the attempts to find codes which are both close to his predictions of the possible and simultaneously practicable to use. They have performed an honourable role in communications. Some excellent general references are Sloane and MacWilliams (1977), Lin and Costello (1983), Pretzel (1992) and McEliece (1987). The background of linear algebra which we shall require is given in Chapters 7 and 8, especially Section 7.1.5. We restrict attention to a wide but restricted class of codes, shown by Elias (1955) to suffice for the conclusion of Shannon's Theorem to hold; namely binary codes with the following extra structure.

(A) The elements of the alphabet $\{0, 1\}$, now to be denoted by Z_2, may be added and multiplied as integers, subject to the extra rule $1 + 1 = 0$ (thus $+$ is the XOR operation).
(B) This enables *componentwise* addition of vectors, and multiplication by scalars λ in Z_2. That is, the ith components satisfy $(x + y)_i = x_i + y_i$ and $(\lambda x)_i = \lambda x_i$. For example $(1, 1, 0, 1) + (1, 0, 1, 1) = (0, 1, 1, 0)$. Thus we can form *linear combinations* $\sum_i \lambda_i x_i$, where we write $x_i = (x_{i1}, \dots, x_{in})$. Note that we normally resort to boldface for vectors only when notation is otherwise ambiguous.
(C) The code is *linear*, meaning here that the sum of any two codewords is another (and hence that the vector $\mathbf{0}$ is a codeword). Equivalently, any linear combination of codewords is another codeword.

Codes are subspaces For purposes of calculation we note that Z_2^n and a code C fit the definition of vector space and subspace in Chapter 7, with Z_2 in place of $\mathbf{R}$, and dimension k as the size of any maximal linearly independent subset. See further in Table 13.3.

Every basis $\{R_1, \dots, R_k\}$ of a code C has the same size, and the matrix $G = \text{Rows}(R_1, \dots, R_k)$ is called a *generator matrix* for C because the codewords may be generated by forming all linear combinations of the rows of G. Thus, specifying the 2^k codewords of C may be reduced to listing the k rows of G. We call C an (n, k) *code*. As a further shortening, in writing a binary codeword we will often omit the commas and/or parentheses.

Example 13.38 (*Proving the rows are independent*) We may rephrase independence as saying that *no linear combination of vectors equals the zero vector* (except the all-zeros

---

Table 13.3. *Vector space rules reviewed for the scalar field* Z_2.

Let V denote Z_2^n or a subspace C thereof (here a subset closed under addition). We say of vectors $u_1, \ldots, u_m$ in V that

(1) they are *linearly dependent* (LD) if one of the u_i equals a linear combination of the rest, otherwise they are linearly *independent* (LI),
(2) they *span* V, if every $v \in V$ is *some* linear combination $\sum \lambda_i u_i$,
(3) they form a *basis of* V if every $v \in V$ is a *unique* linear combination $\sum \lambda_i u_i$.

Finding a basis $u_1, \ldots, u_m$ is a *basis of* V if and only if any two of the following hold:

(4) $u_1, \ldots, u_m$ span V,
(5) $m = \dim V$,
(6) $u_1, \ldots, u_m$ are linearly independent.

---

combination). Let us apply this to the rows of G_1 below.

$$G_1 = \begin{bmatrix} R_1 \\ R_2 \\ R_3 \end{bmatrix} = \begin{bmatrix} 1 & 0 & 1 & 1 & 0 \\ 0 & 1 & 0 & 1 & 1 \\ 0 & 0 & 1 & 1 & 0 \end{bmatrix}.$$

$\sum \lambda_i R_i = \mathbf{0}$ says in detail that $\lambda_1 (1\ 0\ 1\ 1\ 0) + \lambda_2 (0\ 1\ 0\ 1\ 1) + \lambda_3 (0\ 0\ 1\ 1\ 0) = \mathbf{0}$, so equating the first three entries of the sum to zero we obtain

$$1\,\lambda_1 + 0\,\lambda_2 + 0\,\lambda_3 = 0, \text{ whence } \lambda_1 = 0,$$
$$0\,\lambda_1 + 1\,\lambda_2 + 0\,\lambda_3 = 0, \text{ whence } \lambda_2 = 0,$$
$$1\,\lambda_1 + 0\,\lambda_2 + 1\,\lambda_3 = 0, \text{ whence } \lambda_3 = 0, \text{ given that } \lambda_1 = 0.$$

We have shown formally that if a linear combination of the rows equals zero then all coefficients λ_i must be zero. Thus the rows are independent. We see in retrospect that such a method must work when, as here, the matrix possesses a diagonal of ones with all zeros below (or equally all zeros above), and in future we shall make such an inference of LI by inspection without further calculation.

Example 13.39 List the codewords of the code C generated by G_1 above, and show that the matrix G_2 below generates the same code.

$$G_2 = \begin{bmatrix} 1 & 1 & 1 & 0 & 1 \\ 0 & 1 & 1 & 0 & 1 \\ 1 & 1 & 0 & 1 & 1 \end{bmatrix}.$$

Solution The codewords are the sums of the rows R_i of G_1 taken 0, 1, 2 or 3 at a time. They are:

$$\mathbf{0} = 00000, \qquad R_1 = 10110, \qquad R_2 = 01011, \qquad R_3 = 00110$$
$$R_1 + R_2 = 11101,\ R_2 + R_3 = 01101,\ R_3 + R_1 = 10000,\ R_1 + R_2 + R_3 = 11011.$$

The three rows of G_1 have been shown to be LI, and since they do span the code we have by Table 13.3 (4), (6) that the code's dimension is 3 (number of elements in a basis). By inspection, the three rows of G_2 lie in the code. Using the criteria (5), (6) of Table 13.3, it suffices to show that these rows are LI. But in this simple case of just three vectors, LI holds because no two are equal and their sum is nonzero.

Definitions 13.40 We end this introduction with two important ideas to which we shall return. (1) A code C is said to be *cyclic* if, when $x = x_1 \ldots x_n$ is in C, so is its *cyclic shift*, $Sx = x_2 \ldots x_n x_1$. Thus the code of Example 13.39 is not cyclic. Neither is it equivalent to a cyclic code, where two codes C and C' are called *equivalent* if C' can be obtained from C by applying a fixed permutation to the entries of C. We shall discover that many codes can be made cyclic in this way and thus greatly simplified in their description and in calculations involving them.

13.2.1 Nearest neighbour decoding

We are using *nearest neighbour decoding* if, on receiving a codeword R, possibly corrupted, we assume the original was the closest actual codeword to R, where the (*Hamming*) *distance* $d(x, y)$ between codewords is defined to be the number of entries in which x, y differ. Thus $d(1010, 1101) = 3$. For both theory and practice it is expedient to relate this to the *weight* $w(x)$ of a codeword x, defined as the number of nonzero entries of x. Indeed, counting the places where x, y differ amounts to counting the nonzero elements of $x + y \ (= x - y)$. For example, $1010 + 1101 = 0111$, and it is an easy exercise to show that (as integers $0, 1, 2, 3, \ldots$)

$$d(x, y) = w(x + y), \text{ and } w(x) = d(x, 0) = x \cdot x. \tag{13.41}$$

The dot product equality depends on $1^2 = 1$ and implies that $d(x, y) = (x - y) \cdot (x - y)$, showing that $d(x, y)$ satisfies the usual axioms for a distance: (i) $d(x, y) \geq 0$, and $d(x, y) = 0 \Rightarrow x = y$, (ii) $d(x, y) = d(y, x)$, (iii) the *triangle inequality* $d(x, z) \leq d(x, y) + d(y, z)$. The following result gives the basic facts for nearest neighbour decoding, where the *minimum* distance δ of a code (also written $d_{\min}$) is the least distance between distinct codewords, and $w_{\min}$ is the least weight of any nonzero ($\neq \mathbf{0}$) codeword.

Theorem 13.41 *(i) The presence of error can be detected in a received codeword if there are fewer than δ errors, (ii) up to $(\delta - 1)/2$ errors can be corrected, (iii) $\delta = w_{\min}$.*

Proof Let c be sent and R received. (i) With fewer than δ errors c cannot have been transformed into another codeword; since R is therefore not in C, it is known that error has occured. (ii) If $e \leq (\delta - 1)/2$ then $2e + 1 \leq \delta$, hence R, being distance e from c, is still closer to c than to any other codeword c', as illustrated in Figure 13.15. Finally,

Figure 13.15 If the minimum distance is $2e + 1$ then after e errors the corrupted version R of codeword c is still nearer to c than to another codeword c'.

(iii) holds because by (13.41) every distance is a weight and every weight is a distance. Specifically, $\delta = d(x, y)$ (for some x, y) $= w(x + y) \geq w_{min} = w(z)$ (for some z) $= d(z, \mathbf{0}) \geq \delta$. Hence, equality of all terms in the chain.

Example 13.42 A code C has codewords $x = x_1, \ldots, x_7$, where $x_t = x_{t-1} + x_{t-2} + x_{t-4}$ ($t = 5, 6, 7$). (i) Express the defining relations in matrix form. (ii) Find a generator matrix and list the codewords. (iii) How many errors will C correct? Decode the received word 1011001, given that it has one error.

Solution (i) The relation given by $t = 5$ is $x_5 = x_4 + x_3 + x_1$, which, since $-1 = 1$, may be written $x_1 + 0x_2 + x_3 + x_4 + x_5 = 0$, or in matrix form $[1\,0\,1\,1\,1\,0\,0][x_1 \cdots x_7]^T = 0$.

The other two relations are similarly defined by matrices of their coefficients, and the three relations combine into a single matrix equation

$$\begin{bmatrix} 1 & 0 & 1 & 1 & 1 & 0 & 0 \\ 0 & 1 & 0 & 1 & 1 & 1 & 0 \\ 0 & 0 & 1 & 0 & 1 & 1 & 1 \end{bmatrix} \begin{bmatrix} x_1 \\ \cdots \\ x_7 \end{bmatrix} = 0, \tag{13.42}$$

where each row of the 3×7 *coefficient matrix H* defines one equation and the right hand zero stands for a column vector of three corresponding zeros. The form of H, with a *diagonal of ones above zeros*, show that its rows, and hence equivalently the three equations, are independent. They therefore reduce the code's dimension from a maximum possible of 7 down to $7 - 3 = 4$. By Table 13.3 the rows of a generator matrix can be any four LI codewords we can find, by whatever means we find them. It happens that each of the rows R of H satisfy $HR^T = 0$, and so does the all-ones vector $R = [11 \ldots 1]$, so these four will do. However, if inspection is not so easy, the next part provides a systematic approach.

(ii) *Listing the codewords* If we do happen to have a generator matrix then the code may be listed as the sums of its rows taken 1, 2, 3 or 4 at a time. However, this may be rather tedious, or computationally intensive, and we take the opportunity to illustrate a technique based on the row operations of Chapter 8, in which the equations are converted to an equivalent set expressing the last codeword entries x_5, x_6, x_7 in terms of the first four: x_1, x_2, x_3, x_4. With the latter going through all $2 \times 2 \times 2 \times 2 = 16$ possibilities we simply append x_5, x_6, x_7 in turn. Let us write $H \approx H_1$ if H_1 is obtained from H by a combination of the following two operations:

$$R_i \leftrightarrow R_j \text{ (interchange rows } i \text{ and } j),$$
$$R_i \rightarrow R_i - R_j \text{ (subtract row } j \text{ from row } i),$$

each of which changes the equations to an equivalent set (one with the same solutions). We have, by subtracting row 1 from the rest, then row 2 from row 3:

$$H = \begin{bmatrix} 1 & 0 & 1 & 1 & 1 & 0 & 0 \\ 0 & 1 & 0 & 1 & 1 & 1 & 0 \\ 0 & 0 & 1 & 0 & 1 & 1 & 1 \end{bmatrix} \approx \begin{bmatrix} 1 & 0 & 1 & 1 & 1 & 0 & 0 \\ 1 & 1 & 1 & 0 & 0 & 1 & 0 \\ 1 & 0 & 0 & 1 & 0 & 1 & 1 \end{bmatrix} \approx \begin{bmatrix} 1 & 0 & 1 & 1 & 1 & 0 & 0 \\ 1 & 1 & 1 & 0 & 0 & 1 & 0 \\ 0 & 1 & 1 & 1 & 0 & 0 & 1 \end{bmatrix}.$$

This gives the relations in the required form (which means the last three columns form an identity matrix). This new and equivalent set of relations is conveniently re-expressed from the third matrix in the form $x_5 = x_1 + x_3 + x_4$, $x_6 = x_1 + x_2 + x_3$, and $x_7 = x_2 + x_3 + x_4$. The codewords are therefore

$$
\begin{array}{cccc}
0000000 & 0100011 & 1000110 & 1100101 \\
0001101 & 0101110 & 1001011 & 1101000 \\
0010111 & 0110100 & 1010001 & 1110010 \\
0011010 & 0111001 & 1011100 & 1111111
\end{array}
$$

Any four independent codewords will do for the rows of a generator matrix G, in the present example. One simple choice consists of the words beginning 1000, 0100, 0010, 0001, giving G in the form $G = [I_4 | A]$, where I_4 is the 4×4 identity matrix and A is some 4×3 matrix. The I_4 means that, when we encode by $z \to zG$, the first four bits of a codeword are the four ('information') bits in z.

(iii) *Error-correction* Inspecting the codewords, we see that the nonzero ones have weights 3 or 4, so the minimum weight and hence minimum distance are 3, giving the capability to correct $(3 - 1)/2 = 1$ error (Theorem 13.41). Comparing our received word 1011001 with each codeword in turn, we find a unique codeword from which it differs in exactly one place, namely 1001001. Finally, notice that C is cyclic. A way to achieve this will appear in the next section.

Using the parity check matrix Notice that to determine δ directly the number of comparisons is $_{16}C_2 = 120$, whereas Theorem 13.41 reveals that $\delta = w_{min}$, so that we need only inspect the 15 nonzero codewords for their minimum weight. However, the example above points to an even quicker way which is often valid (as it is for Example 13.42), by inspecting only the matrix of relations. A matrix H with n-bit rows is called a *parity check matrix* for C if (as in the example above) C is the subspace of Z^n satisfying linear relations $Rx^T = 0$, where R runs through the rows of H. That is,

$$x \in C \Leftrightarrow Hx^T = 0. \tag{13.43}$$

If the row space of H has dimension m, then C may be defined by a set of m independent relations and so has dimension $k = n - m$ (Corollary 8.24 applies here). We will normally assume that the rows of H are LI, so that there are no 'redundant' rows, and H is $m \times n$.

Theorem 13.43 *Suppose the columns of a parity check matrix are nonzero and distinct. Then the corresponding code has $w_{min} \geq 3$ and so corrects one error.*

Proof Let e_i denote the n-vector with 1 in position i and 0 elsewhere. Suppose $w_{min} = 1$. Then C contains some e_i, and the definition of H implies $0 = He_i^T = $ column i of H, a contradiction. But if $w_{min} = 2$ then C contains a codeword $c = e_i + e_j$ ($i \neq j$), and so $0 = Hc^T = He_i^T + He_j^T = $ (column i of H) + (column j of H), implying equality of columns i and j of H. Since this is again a contradiction, we have $w_{min} \geq 3$.

$$H = \begin{bmatrix} A_1 \\ A_2 \\ A_3 \\ A_4 \end{bmatrix} = \begin{bmatrix} 1 & 0 & 0 & 0 & 1 & 1 & 1 & 1 & 0 & 1 & 0 & 1 & 1 & 0 & 0 \\ 0 & 0 & 0 & 1 & 1 & 1 & 1 & 0 & 1 & 0 & 1 & 1 & 0 & 0 & 1 \\ 0 & 0 & 1 & 1 & 1 & 1 & 0 & 1 & 0 & 1 & 1 & 0 & 0 & 1 & 0 \\ 0 & 1 & 1 & 1 & 1 & 0 & 1 & 0 & 1 & 1 & 0 & 0 & 1 & 0 & 0 \end{bmatrix}$$

Figure 13.16 Parity check matrix for a cyclic Hamming code in the case $m = 4$, with first row generated from initial values 1000 by the recurrence relation $a_n = a_{n-1} + a_{n-4}$.

13.2.2 Hamming single-error-correcting codes

Because the ability to correct a single error is enough in many hardware situations, it is worth describing the excellent codes of Hamming (1950) which do so. They are optimal in a sense to be described. They exploit Theorem 13.43 by specifying a parity check matrix H with maximum number of columns subject to their being nonzero and distinct, namely the binary integers 1 to $2^m - 1$ in some order. Thus a Hamming code has length $n = 2^m - 1$ for some $m \geq 2$, say, and all Hamming codes of a given length are equivalent by permuting the columns of H. The rows of H are independent because, for example, the columns include those of the identity matrix I_m (see Figure 13.16 and/or Theorem 8.20). It is natural to ask if the columns of H can be so ordered that the resulting code is cyclic, and the anwer is YES.

Construction 13.44a (*Cyclic Hamming codes*) The first row of H is a binary sequence $A_1 = a_1 a_2 \ldots$ of length $n = 2^m - 1$ which, if joined cyclically, *contains all nonzero m-bit words*. Such an A_1 can be obtained by a suitable linear recurrence $a_n = c_1 a_{n-1} + \cdots + c_m a_{n-m}$ with initial values, say, 1 followed by $m - 1$ zeros (see Remark 13.52(4) below). Let A_i denote the ith *shift* $a_i a_{i+1} \ldots a_{i+n-1}$; then the successive rows of H are to be $A_1, \ldots, A_m$. This produces a Hamming code because the m-bit words found in A_1 become the columns of H, as seen in Figure 13.16 in the case $m = 4$, where each digit is recycled one place down and to the left.

The code is cyclic because, the recurrence being linear, the sum of two distinct shifts $A_i + A_j$ is another, A_t, say (see Exercise 13.9); thus the set of all relations satisfied by the code is unchanged under cyclic permutations, and hence so is the code itself. The maximal property of Hamming codes is established from the following result for any binary code.

Example 13.44b (i) Show that the code of Example 13.42 is of Hamming type, (ii) construct a *cyclic* Hamming code of length 7, using the relations $x_t = x_{t-2} + x_{t-3} (t \geq 4)$.

Solution (i) The code has length 7 and a pcm (13.42) whose columns consist of the nonzero 3-bit words. Thus it satisfies the definition of a Hamming code with $n = 7$ and $m = 3$. (ii) For applying Construction 13.44a, the first row of the pcm must obey the recurrence, but its first three bits may be any nonzero 3-bit word. If one chooses 111, the resulting pcm is

$$H_1 = \begin{bmatrix} 1 & 1 & 1 & 0 & 0 & 1 & 0 \\ 1 & 1 & 0 & 0 & 1 & 0 & 1 \\ 1 & 0 & 0 & 1 & 0 & 1 & 1 \end{bmatrix}.$$

Exercise Determine the 16 codewords of the Hamming code defined above.

Theorem 13.45 *Let $_nC_i$ denote the number of ways of choosing i objects from n distinct objects (see Section 9.1.4). If a binary code C, not necessarily linear, has length n, and corrects e errors, then its size is bounded by $|C| \le 2^n/(1 + {}_nC_1 + {}_nC_2 + \cdots + {}_nC_e)$.*

Proof Since C corrects e errors, any word in the sphere $S_e(c_1)$ of radius e around a codeword c_1 is corrected to c_1, and is at distance at least $e + 1$ from any other codeword c_2. Hence this sphere is disjoint from the one of radius e around c_2, as depicted in Figure 13.17. On the other hand, a word at distance i from an arbitrary codeword c differs from c in i places, for which the number of possibilities is the number of ways to choose i objects from n, written $_nC_i$. Therefore the number N_e of words in $S_e(c_1)$ is $1 + {}_nC_1 + {}_nC_2 + \cdots + {}_nC_e$, independently of the choice of codeword. The disjoint spheres, one for each codeword, contain together $|C|N_e$ words, a subset of the 2^n words of Z_2^n. Hence the inequality.

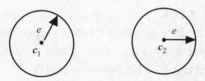

Figure 13.17 If a code corrects e errors then spheres of radius e around distinct codewords are disjoint.

Remarks 13.46 (1) The Hamming code satisfies $|C| = 2^k = 2^{n-m} = 2^n/2^m = 2^n/(n + 1)$, the bound of Theorem 13.45. Hence the code would be of greatest possible size (for its length and error-correcting), even were the linearity restriction to be removed.

(2) As a further application there is no $(17, 10)$ binary code C that corrects two errors, for the existence of C entails $2^{10} \le 2^{17}/(1 + 18 + 18 \cdot 17/2)$, or $1 \le 128/172$, a contradiction.

(3) There are, these days, good reasons for needing 2-error-correction. Reasons and solutions for this are given in Rao and Fujiwara (1989).

Linear feedback shift registers (LFSRs) The device represented in Figure 13.18, called a *linear feedback shift register*, or LFSR, extends initial values $a_0a_1 \ldots a_{r-1}$ to a binary sequence $\{a_n\}$ by the recurrence relation

$$a_n = c_1a_{n-1} + c_2a_{n-2} + \cdots + c_ra_{n-r}. \tag{13.44}$$

The upper cells, or stages, form a *shift register*, each cell representing a 2-state device which stores a digit 0 or 1, and connected to a successor cell. At equal intervals a master clock sends a 'tick' signal and the content of each cell is shifted to its successor, except for the last, whose content may be transmitted elsewhere. The first becomes zero if not replenished.

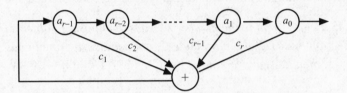

Figure 13.18 A linear feedback shift register, or LFSR.

Simultaneously, the content of cell i is multiplied by a binary digit c_i and sent to an adding device which sums the products and, in a feedback loop, sends the result $a_r = c_1 a_{r-1} + \cdots + c_r a_0$ to stage 1. Thus $n - r$ ticks later the device performs (13.44) and has so far output $a_0 a_1 \ldots a_{n-r}$. The diagram may be simplified, for since the multipliers c_i are 0 or 1 we obtain the desired result by omitting the ith connection (or *tap*) if c_i is 0, and making it if $c_i = 1$. Figure 13.19 shows an LFSR to generate the sequence of Construction 13.44a, with $a_n = a_{n-1} + a_{n-4}$.

Polynomial form of the LFSR This is required in recursive convolutional codes (see Section 13.3.2). Now, since the first r input values reappear unchanged, it will be convenient to denote them by $a_{-r}, \ldots, a_{-1}$, and to define a *generating function* $G(x) = \sum_{n \geq 0} a_n x^n$, which can then be shown to satisfy

$$G(x) = g(x)/f(x), \text{ with} \qquad (13.45)$$

$$f(x) = 1 + \sum_{i=1}^{r} c_i x^i,$$

$$\text{and } g(x) = \sum_{i=1}^{r} c_i x^i (a_{-i} x^{-i} + \cdots + a_{-1} x^{-1}), \qquad (13.46)$$

where $\deg(g) < \deg(f)$. Furthermore, $g(x) = 1$ under initial conditions $a_{-r} \ldots a_{-1} = 10 \ldots 0$.

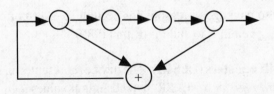

Figure 13.19 An LFSR to generate the sequence associated wih the polynomial $x^4 + x + 1$ and recurrence relation $a_n = a_{n-1} + a_{n-4}$ (it is an m-sequence; see Remarks 13.52(4)).

Proof Because we are working Mod 2, the following equalities establish the result.

$$G(x) = \sum_{n=0}^{\infty} \left(\sum_{i=1}^{r} c_i a_{n-i} \right) x^n \qquad \text{by (13.44)}$$

$$= \sum_{i=1}^{r} c_i x^i \sum_{n=0}^{\infty} a_{n-i} x^{n-i} \qquad \text{on reversing the order of summation}$$

$$= \sum_{i=1}^{r} c_i x^i [a_{-i} x^{-i} + \cdots + a_{-1} x^{-1} + G(x)] \qquad \text{by definition of } G(x), \text{ hence:}$$

$G(x) = g(x) + [f(x) - 1]G(x)$ by definition of f and g, which suffices, since $G = -G$.

Exercise Verify from formula (13.46) that $g = 1$ when $a_{-r} \ldots a_{-1} = 10 \ldots 0$ (see Exercise 13.15).

13.2.3 Finite fields and minimal polynomials

The structure of finite fields is extremely useful for constructing and proving results about error correcting codes. We begin with Mod 2 *polynomials*, or *polynomials over Z_2*, meaning polynomials $\sum_i f_i x^i$ whose coefficients lie in Z_2. The set of all such polynomials is denoted by $Z_2[x]$. We may abbreviate f to its sequence of coefficients $f_n \ldots f_1 f_0$ provided no zeros are omitted. Thus $x^4 + x + 1$ is 10011. Remembering that addition is performed Mod 2 (i.e. $1 + 1 = 0$) we may exhibit multiplication and division as in Figure 13.20. The addition has *no carry* from one digit to the next.

Because $1 + 1 = 0$, squaring a sum produces no cross-terms, for example $(x + y)^2 = x^2 + 2xy + y^2 = x^2 + y^2$, we have, for constants or polynomials $a, b, \ldots, z$ and polynomial $f(x)$:

$$(a + b + \cdots + z)^2 = a^2 + b^2 + \cdots + z^2 \tag{13.47}$$

$$f(x)^2 = \sum_i f_i^2 x^{2i} = \sum_i f_i x^{2i} = f(x^2), \tag{13.48}$$

and similar results hold with power 2 replaced by power $q = 2^t$, the result of squaring t times. For example, $(x^2 + x + 1)^2 = x^4 + x^2 + 1$, and $(x + y)^q = x^q + y^q$.

```
                                   1  1  1
            1  0  0  1  1    1 0 1 ) 1  1  0  0  1
                  1  1  1            1  0  1
            ─────────────            ─────────
            1  0  0  1  1            1  1  0
         1  0  0  1  1               1  0  1
      1  0  0  1  1                  ─────────
      ─────────────────             1  1  1
      1  1  1  1  0  0  1           1  0  1
                                    ─────────
                                    1  0
```

Figure 13.20 Multiplication and division in shorthand polynomial notation, representing $(x^4 + x + 1)(x^2 + x + 1) = x^6 + x^5 + x^4 + x^3 + 1$ and $(x^4 + x^3 + 1)/(x^2 + 1) = x^2 + x + 1$ with remainder x. Note: multiplication can alternatively be done with highest powers to the right.

Irreducible polynomials A polynomial $f(x)$ of degree n is *irreducible* if it is not divisible by a polynomial of positive lower degree. Equivalently, it does not factorise into a product of such polynomials. For example, $x^3 + 1$ is not irreducible because it factorises into $(x + 1)(x^2 + x + 1)$. A first observation is that to establish whether f is irreducible we need only test divisibility into f of polynomials which are themselves irreducible, and of degree $\leq n/2$ (why?). Further, if $n \geq 2$ then we can divide f by $x + c$ (c any constant) to obtain quotient $q(x)$ and remainder R, meaning $f(x) = q(x)(x + c) + R$. Setting $x = c$ yields $R = f(c)$, hence the *Factor Theorem*, in which '*is a factor of*' is abbreviated to '*divides*':

$$(x + c) \text{ divides } f(x) \text{ if and only if } f(c) = 0. \qquad (13.49)$$

To be irreducible f must be non-divisible by both x and $x + 1$, and so have both constant term 1 and odd number of nonzero coefficients. From these two observations and (13.47) we deduce:

Classification 13.47 The irreducible polynomials of degrees 1 to 4 are $x, x + 1$, then $x^2 + x + 1$, then $x^3 + x + 1, x^3 + x^2 + 1$, and, in degree 4, $x^4 + x + 1, x^4 + x^3 + 1, x^4 + x^3 + x^2 + x + 1$.

Finite fields A finite field F is essentially a set on which the usual laws of arithmetic apply, but which, unlike the real and complex number fields, is finite. To guarantee finiteness, F must have some extra laws governing the structure, otherwise, for example, if γ is in f then so are all its infinitely many powers. One way to construct such a field is as follows. Given an irreducible degree n polynomial of the form $p(x) = x^n + p_{n-1}x^{n-1} + \cdots + p_1x + 1$, we consider the set of all polynomials of degree $\leq n - 1$, subject to polynomial addition and multiplication, with a substitution rule for reducing polynomials to degree $\leq n - 1$:

$$x^n \to p_{n-1}x^{n-1} + \cdots + p_1x + 1. \qquad (13.50)$$

For example, with $n = 3$ and $p(x) = x^3 + x^2 + 1$ we substitute $x^3 \to x^2 + 1$, so that

$$\begin{aligned}
(x^2 + 1)^2 &= x^4 + 2x^2 + 1 = x^4 + 1 \qquad \text{since } 2 = 0 \\
&= x \cdot x^3 + 1 \\
&\to x(x^2 + 1) + 1 = x^3 + x + 1 \\
&\to x^2 + x.
\end{aligned}$$

Notice that replacing x^3 by $x^2 + 1$ changed $x \cdot x^3$ into $x(x^2 + 1)$, a difference of $x(x^3 - x^2 - 1)$, or simply $xp(x)$. This idea gives the key connection below.

Theorem 13.48 *Applying (13.50) results in subtraction of a multiple of $p(x)$. Hence polynomials f, g reduce to the same polynomial of degree $\leq n - 1$ if and only if f and g differ by a multiple of $p(x)$.*

Proof (i) Replacing a term $x^k \cdot x^n$ by $x^k(p_{n-1}x^{n-1} + \cdots + p_1x + 1)$ makes a difference of $x^k p(x)$. (ii) Suppose that f, g both reduce to h of degree $\leq n-1$. Then by (i) there are polynomials $a(x), b(x)$ such that

$$f(x) - a(x)p(x) = h(x) = g(x) - b(x)p(x),$$

impying that $f(x) - g(x) = (b(x) - a(x))p(x)$, a multiple of $p(x)$. (iii) Suppose conversely that f, g differ by a multiple of p, say $f(x) - g(x) = c(x)p(x)$, and that they reduce to polynomials h, k of degree $\leq n-1$, say $f(x) - a(x)p(x) = h(x)$ and $g(x) - b(x)p(x) = k(x)$. Then subtraction gives $h(x) - k(x) = (c(x) + b(x) - a(x))p(x)$, which, by considering degrees, is possible only if both sides are identically zero. Thus $h(x) = k(x)$ and the proof is complete.

Guided by Theorem 13.48, we group together as one object, denoted by $[f(x)]$, all mod 2 polynomials which can be converted to $f(x)$ by (13.50). These are the polynomials which differ from $f(x)$ by a multiple of $p(x)$, that is to say

$$[f(x)] = \{f(x) + g(x)p(x) \colon g \text{ in } Z_2[x]\}. \tag{13.51}$$

We call $[f(x)]$ a *class*, and all its elements *representives* of this class. Addition and multiplication of classes is performed via an arbitrary choice of representatives. That is, if $\beta = [f(x)]$ and $\gamma = [g(x)]$ then

$$\beta + \gamma = [f(x) + g(x)], \quad \text{and } \beta\gamma = [f(x)g(x)]. \tag{13.52}$$

It can be verified that these rules are independent of the choices of representative (an exercise), using the observation

$$\boxed{[f(x)] = [g(x)] \Leftrightarrow p(x) \text{ divides } f(x) - g(x).} \tag{13.53}$$

Notice that [0] acts as zero and [1] as 1, so we shall simply denote them by 0, 1 respectively. Also $[p(x)] = 0$, and more generally $[f(x)] = 0$ if and only if $p(x)$ divides $f(x)$.

Theorem 13.49 *Let F be the set whose elements are the classes* $[f(x)]$ *defined by an irreducible polynomial p, with addition and multiplication as given by (13.52). Then F is a finite field of order* 2^n, *with* [0] *acting as zero and* [1] *acting as identity.*

Proof The axioms for a field are given in Table 13.4. The only property not immediate from the construction of F is that any nonzero element α in F has an inverse δ in F. We establish this by first proving that if β, γ are in F then

$$\alpha\beta = \alpha\gamma \Rightarrow \beta = \gamma \quad \text{(Cancellation Law)}. \tag{13.54}$$

For this, let $\alpha = [f(x)]$, $\beta = [g(x)]$ and $\gamma = [h(x)]$. Then p does not divide f, since $\alpha \neq 0$, and

$$\alpha\beta = \alpha\gamma \Rightarrow p(x) \text{ divides } f(x)g(x) - f(x)h(x) \qquad \text{by (13.53)}$$
$$\Rightarrow p(x) \text{ divides } f(x)(g(x) - h(x))$$
$$\Rightarrow p(x) \text{ divides } g(x) - h(x),$$

Table 13.4. *Axioms for a field*

A field F is a set of elements together with operations $\alpha, \beta \to \alpha + \beta$ and $\alpha, \beta \to \alpha\beta$ satisfying, for all α, β, γ in F:

$$\begin{aligned}
\alpha + \beta &= \beta + \alpha, \quad \alpha\beta = \beta\alpha & \text{(Commutative Law)}, \\
\alpha + (\beta + \gamma) &= (\alpha + \beta) + \gamma, \quad \alpha(\beta\gamma) = (\alpha\beta)\gamma & \text{(Associative Law)}, \\
\alpha(\beta + \gamma) &= \alpha\beta + \alpha\gamma & \text{(Distributive Law)}.
\end{aligned}$$

Further, F must contain elements 0, 1, and for every element α an element $-\alpha$ and (if $\alpha \neq 0$) an element α^{-1}, such that

$$\begin{aligned}
0 + \alpha &= \alpha, \quad (-\alpha) + \alpha = 0, \quad 0\alpha = 0, \\
1\alpha &= \alpha, \quad (\alpha^{-1})\alpha = 1.
\end{aligned}$$

We normally refer to the respective operations as addition and multiplication, to 0 and 1 as the zero and identity, to $-\alpha$ and α^{-1} as the negative of α and its inverse, and to $\beta\alpha^{-1}$ as β divided by α. The *order* of F is the number of elements it contains. A *finite* field is one of finite order, in our case 2^n for some positive integer n.

---

since p is irreducible and does not divide $f(x)$. But this implies $\beta = \gamma$ by (13.53). Finally, consider the set of all elements $\alpha\delta$ as δ runs once through the nonzero elements of F. By the Cancellation Law, no two of these products are equal and none is zero. Hence exactly one equals 1, and we have unique δ with $\alpha\delta = 1$. This completes the proof, the number of elements of F being the number of ways to choose the n coefficients in a polynomial of degree $\leq n - 1$.

Working with finite fields The next example shows how we can calculate with finite fields in practice. Most of the time we can dispense with the class notation and denote an element of F by a single symbol, as previewed above. In particular we can often express all elements in terms of an element $\alpha = [x]$, the class of the single-term polynomial x.

Example 13.50 Let F be the finite field defined by $p(x)$. Taking $f(x) = 1 + x + x^3$ as an example, we express the element $[f(x)]$ in terms of $\alpha = [x]$. By the laws (13.52) for addition and multiplication in F, we have $[f(x)] = [1 + x + x^3] = [1] + [x] + [x]^3 = f(\alpha)$. This simple argument works for any $f(x)$, indeed we have the following (recall that $-1 = +1 \bmod 2$):

$$\begin{aligned}
[f(x)] &= f(\alpha), \text{ where } \alpha = [x], \text{ and} & (13.55) \\
p(\alpha) &= 0, \text{ hence } \alpha^n = p_{n-1}\alpha^{n-1} + \cdots + p_1\alpha + p_0. & (13.56)
\end{aligned}$$

Example 13.50 *continued* So far $p(x)$ could be any irreducible polynomial, but now take $p(x) = x^4 + x + 1$. Keeping $\alpha = [x]$, we may represent a polynomial in α by its sequence of coefficients, such as $a_3 a_2 a_1 a_0$ (shorthand notation). Thus we write $\alpha^3 = 1000, \alpha^2 = 0100, \alpha = 0010$, and $1 = \alpha^0 = 0001$. Notice how multiplication by α moves digits one place to the left, analogously to the decimal system. The key

Table 13.5. *Powers of* $\alpha = [x]$ *as polynomials of degree* ≤ 3 *in* α, *where* $\alpha^4 = \alpha + 1$.

i	α^i	i	α^i	i	α^i	i	α^i
1	0010	5	0110	9	1010	13	1101
2	0100	6	1100	10	0111	14	1001
3	1000	7	1011	11	1110	15	0000
4	0011	8	0101	12	1111		

observation is how, using (13.56) with this notation, we may write any power as such a polynomial. Thus $p(\alpha) = 0$ says $\alpha^4 = \alpha + 1$, or in shorthand notation $10000 = 0011$, whence $\alpha^5 = 0110, \alpha^6 = 1100$ and $\alpha^7 = 10000 + 1000 = 0011 + 1000 = 1011$. In this way we easily construct Table 13.5 of successive powers of α in terms of the 2^4 polynomials of degree ≤ 3.

$$\begin{array}{ll} \alpha^i & da_2a_1a_0 \qquad [\alpha^4 = b_3b_2b_1b_0] \\ \alpha^{i+1} & d(b_3b_2b_1b_0) + a_2a_1a_00. \end{array}$$

Thus (a) the $2^4 = 16$ elements of F may alternatively be written as $0, \alpha, \alpha^2, \alpha^3, \ldots, \alpha^{15} (= 1)$, and (b) we can express the sum of two or more powers as a single power by first converting them back to polynomials via the table. For example, $\alpha^2 + \alpha^{11} = 0100 + 1110 = 1010 = \alpha^9$. In this case α and $p(x)$ have the useful special properties defined below.

Definition 13.51 (i) (*Order*) In the notation of Table 13.4ff, let F be a finite field of order 2^n. The *order*, ord β, of an element β of F is the least positive integer e for which $\beta^e = 1$. It follows that $e|(2^n - 1)$ and that $\beta^t = 1$ if and only if (ord β)$|t$ (see Exercise 13.12 and its solution).

(ii) (*Primitivity*) We say β is *primitive* if it has order $2^n - 1$; equivalently, the nonzero elements of F may be listed as $\{\beta, \beta^2, \ldots, \beta^{2^n-1} (= 1)\}$. A *primitive polynomial* $p(x)$ is one for which $[x]$ is a primitive element in the field defined by $p(x)$.

Exercise What is the order of the element $\beta = \alpha^3$ in Table 13.5? Is α^2 primitive?

Remarks 13.52 (1) (*Example*) Table 13.5 shows that $x^4 + x + 1$ is primitive. Such polynomials exist in every degree and are extensively tabulated (see e.g. Lidl & Niederreiter, 1986). The first few degrees yield 111, 1011, 1101, 10011, 11001. See also Table 13.6.

(2) (*Why p must be irreducible*) If p were not irreducible the product of two nonzero elements could be zero, for $p(x) = f(x)g(x)$ implies $0 = [p(x)] = [f(x)][g(x)]$.

(3) (*Example*) We calculate the order of the element $\beta = \alpha^5$ in Example 13.50. In fact, $\beta^t = 1 \Leftrightarrow \alpha^{5t} = 1 \Leftrightarrow 15|5t$. The least possible t is 3, which is therefore the order of β. The ord column of our later Table 13.7 was obtained in this way.

Table 13.6. *Some primitive polynomials* Mod 2 *in degrees up to* 15.

$x + 1$	$x^6 + x + 1$	$x^{11} + x^2 + 1$
$x^2 + x + 1$	$x^7 + x + 1$	$x^{12} + x^6 + x^4 + x + 1$
$x^3 + x + 1$	$x^8 + x^4 + x^3 + x^2 + 1$	$x^{13} + x^4 + x^3 + x + 1$
$x^4 + x + 1$	$x^9 + x^4 + 1$	$x^{14} + x^5 + x^3 + x + 1$
$x^5 + x^2 + 1$	$x^{10} + x^3 + 1$	$x^{15} + x + 1$

(4) (*m-sequences and Hamming codes*) Relation (13.56) expresses a power of α in terms of the previous n powers. Since the rows of Table 13.5 are powers of α and $p(x) = x^4 + x + 1$, we have row $t = $ row $(t - 3) + $ row $(t - 4)$. This recurrence relation holds in particular for the end bits of each row, giving a sequence $0001001101011111\ldots$, which has period 15 because $\alpha^{15} = 1$. It is an alternative sequence in Construction 13.44a for a cyclic Hamming code, where $p(x) = x^4 + x^3 + 1$ is implied.

More generally, we can use a primitive polynomial of degree n to construct a sequence of period $2^n - 1$ containing all nonzero n-bit words. This sequence has longest possible period, for one generated by a recurrence of length n, and is called an *m-sequence*, or *maximal length linear recurring sequence*. The construction may be implemented by an LFSR as depicted in Figure 13.19, and provides the rows of a pcm for a Hamming code.

Exercise Repeat Example 13.50 with $p(x) = x^4 + x^3 + 1$. Is this $p(x)$ primitive?

Minimal polynomials

Definition 13.53 Let F be a field of order 2^n, and λ an element of F. A *minimal polynomial* of λ is a Mod 2 polynomial $M(x)$ of least possible degree such that λ is a root. Such a polynomial does *exist* because λ satisfies $x^{\text{ord}(\lambda)} = 1$. Furthermore, M *is unique*, for if f, g are minimal polynomials of λ, let $h = f - g$. Then $h(\lambda) = 0$, but the leading terms of f and g cancel, so $\deg(h) < \deg(f)$, contradicting the minimality of $\deg(f)$. Thus there is a unique minimal polynomial $M = M_\lambda$ of λ.

This polynomial is constructed via the *conjugates* of λ, namely λ itself together with successive squares $\lambda^2, \lambda^4, \lambda^8, \ldots$, and so on until a duplicate appears. In Table 13.7 we partition the elements of F into sets of mutual conjugates, one set per row.

Table 13.7. *Minimal polynomials of the sets of conjugates in field F defined by* $p(x) = x^4 + x + 1$. *We omit elements* 0, 1 *with respective minimal polynomials* x *and* $x + 1$. *For* ord λ *see Remarks 13.52 (3).*

λ	ord λ	M_λ	shorthand
$\alpha, \alpha^2, \alpha^4, \alpha^8$	15	$x^4 + x + 1$	10011
$\alpha^3, \alpha^6, \alpha^{12}, \alpha^9$	5	$1 + x + x^2 + x^3 + x^4$	11111
α^5, α^{10}	3	$1 + x + x^2$	111
$\alpha^7, \alpha^{14}, \alpha^{13}, \alpha^{11}$	15	$x^4 + x^3 + 1$	11001

A useful tool is the *reciprocal* f_* of a polynomial f, obtained by writing the coefficients in reverse order. For example, the reciprocal of 1011 is 1101. In formula terms, $f_*(x) = x^{\deg(f)} f(1/x)$.

Theorem 13.54 *Let F be a finite field containing an element λ, and let f, g be Mod 2 polynomials. Then (i) the minimal polynomial M_λ is irreducible, (ii) λ is a root of $f(x)$ if and only if M_λ divides f, (iii) if λ is a root of $f(x)$, then so are its conjugates, and λ^{-1} is a root of $f_*(x)$.*

Proof Write $M = M_\lambda$. (i) If $M(x) = f(x)g(x)$ with f, g of lower degree than M then we have $0 = M(\lambda) = f(\lambda)g(\lambda)$, whence $f(\lambda) = 0$ or $g(\lambda) = 0$, in either case contradicting the minimality of degree M. (ii) We take deg $M \leq$ deg f without loss of generality and divide M into f, to obtain quotient $q(x)$ and remainder $r(x)$, where $f(x) = q(x)M(x) + r(x)$. Setting $x = \lambda$ gives $f(\lambda) = r(\lambda)$, whence the result. (iii) The remark about conjugates holds because $f(\lambda^2) = f(\lambda)^2$ (see (13.48)). Regarding λ^{-1}, let $f(\lambda) = 0$. Then $f_*(\lambda^{-1}) = (\lambda^{-1})^{\deg(f)} f(\lambda) = 0$ as required.

Example 13.55 We determine minimal polynomials M_λ for elements of the field F of order $2^4 = 16$ defined by $p(x) = x^4 + x + 1$ (Example 13.50). By Theorem 13.54(iii) we have found M_λ if we produce a polynomial with λ as a root and having degree equal to the number of conjugates of λ. Further, M_λ is the minimal polynomial of each of these conjugates. We make use of these facts to construct Table 13.7, beginning with $p(x)$, which satisfies $p(\alpha) = 0$, (13.56), and has degree equal to 4, the number of conjugates of α. Notice that, in each list of conjugates, repeated squaring takes us through the list cyclically back to the start. This is true in general, though a proof is left as an exercise.

For the second line we observe that because $\beta = \alpha^3$ has order 5 (as do the other conjugates of β) we may write $0 = (\beta^5 - 1) = (\beta - 1)(1 + \beta + \beta^2 + \beta^3 + \beta^4)$. Since $\beta \neq 1$, this implies that $1 + \beta + \beta^2 + \beta^3 + \beta^4 = 0$, that is, β is a root of the fourth degree polynomial $1 + x + \cdots + x^4$. The third line follows similarly since α^5 has order 3. The last line follows from Theorem 13.54 (iii), since the conjugates are the inverses of those of the first line.

Product formula Sometimes we need the following elementary result, which is obtained by considering the $_mC_i$ ways a factor x^{m-i} arises in the expansion of $(x - a_1)(x - a_2) \cdots (x - a_m)$.

$$\prod_{i=1}^{m} (x - a_i) = x^m - \sigma_1 x^{m-1} + \sigma_2 x^{m-2} + \cdots + (-1)^m \sigma_m \qquad (13.57)$$

where σ_i is the sum of all products of $a_1, \ldots, a_m$ taken i at a time. For example, $\sigma_1(a_1, a_2, a_3) = a_1 + a_2 + a_3$ but $\sigma_2 = a_1 a_2 + a_1 a_3 + a_2 a_3$. This is especially useful when a minimal polynomial M_β must be computed directly, unlike the method of Table 13.7. Write $a_i = \beta^{2i}$, so that $a_i^2 = a_{i+1}$, and suppose the conjugates are cyclically $a_1, \ldots, a_m$. It follows that $[\sigma_i(a_1, \ldots, a_m)]^2 = \sigma_i(a_1^2, \ldots, a_m^2) = \sigma_i(a_2, \ldots, a_m, a_1) = \sigma_i(a_1, \ldots, a_m)$, the last being by symmetry, and hence σ_i is 0 or 1 (the only solutions of $z^2 = 1$). Thus (13.57) becomes a polynomial over Z_2 with least degree for which β is a root, and hence by definition equals M_β. As a check of M_α in Table 13.7, we have $\sigma_1 = \alpha + \alpha^2 + \alpha^4 + \alpha^8$ (by definition) $= 0$ (by Table 13.5). Similarly for σ_2, the sum of $_4C_2 = 6$ terms, whilst $\sigma_3 = 1 = \sigma_4$. Thus we recover the original $x^4 + x + 1$.

This completes some valuable groundwork for the celebrated codes of the next section and beyond.

13.2.4 BCH and Reed–Solomon codes

All codes in this section will be cyclic. BCH codes are named for their near simultaneous discovery by Hocquenghem (1959) and Bose and Ray-Chaudhuri (1960). They yield a *t*-error-correcting code for every positive integer *t*. At that time no satisfactory method was known for decoding in the presence of error, and improvements were made over the next 15 years by various authors, including notably Berlekamp (1974), and culminating in the method we shall present from Sugiyama *et al.* (1975). It uses the Euclidean Algorithm in a most ingenious way.

Reed–Solomon codes (1960) are especially suited for correcting errors which occur in a burst. They have been widely used in practice for error correction of CD players, for example. They can be approached as a generalisation of BCH codes, as we do here.

Generator polynomials for cyclic codes It turns out that cyclic codes of length n correspond to, and may be constructed from, *divisors of $x^n - 1$*. The story begins with our regarding a binary n-vector $a = (a_0, \ldots, a_{n-1})$ as a polynomial $a(x) = \sum_i a_i x^i$. Then $Z_2{}^n$ becomes the space V_{n-1} of Mod 2 polynomials of degree $\leq n - 1$, a code C being a subspace thereof. We arrange (similarly to using $p(x)$ in the previous section) that the product of two polynomials of V_{n-1} reduces to another, by taking $x^n - 1 = 0$.

The crucial observation is that, for any codeword $c(x)$, we may form the product $xc(x) = c_0x + c_1x^2 + \cdots + c_{n-2}x^{n-1} + c_{n-1}x^n = c_{n-1} + c_0x + \cdots + c_{n-2}x^{n-1}$, a cyclic shift. Thus if C is to be cyclic it must also contain $xc(x)$, whence it may be seen that C is cyclic if and only if

$$c(x) \in C, r(x) \in V_{n-1} \Rightarrow r(x)c(x) \in C. \tag{13.58}$$

Let $g(x)$ be a polynomial of least degree in a cyclic (n, k) code C. Then g is unique, for if h is in C and has the same degree then $g - h$ is a codeword of lower degree (leading terms cancel), a contradiction. An example is the Hamming $(7, 4)$ code of Example 13.42, whose codewords are the cyclic permutations of 0001101 and 1110010, together with the all-ones and all-zeros words. We cycle these round until the nonzero digits are as far to the left as possible and obtain as generator polynomial $g(x) = 1 + x + x^3$. The basic result that makes generator poynomials useful is proved below.

Exercise Find the generator polynomial for the Hamming code of Example 13.44b.

Theorem 13.56 *If the cyclic code C has generator polynomial g then the binary n-vector c is in C if and only if $g(x)|c(x)$.*

Proof If $g|c$ then c is in C by (13.58). Conversely, suppose that c is in C. Then $\deg g \leq \deg c$ by minimality of $\deg g$, and we can divide to obtain the identity between Mod 2 polynomials: $c(x) = q(x)g(x) + r(x)$, where $\deg r < \deg g$. From this, $q(x)g(x)$ has the same degree as c, and lies in C by (13.58). Therefore, by linearity of C, so does the polynomial $r(x) = c(x) - q(x)g(x)$. But r has lower degree than g, so, by the minimality of $\deg g$, we must have $r = 0$. Thus $g|c$ as required.

Theorem 13.56 shows that if g has degree m then C consists of all linear combinations of $1 \cdot g(x), xg(x), x^2g(x), \ldots, x^{k-1}g(x)$, where $k = n - m$. We can encode a k-vector $I = (I_0, I_1, \ldots, I_{k-1})$ of 'information bits' into codeword c by the simple formula $c(x) = I(x)g(x)$, or in more detail

$$c_0 + c_1 x + \cdots + c_{n-1}x^{n-1} = (I_{k-1}x^{k-1} + \cdots + I_1 x + I_0)(g_0 + g_1 x + \cdots + g_m x^m).$$

(13.59)

Equating coefficients of the x^i gives $c_i = \sum I_r g_{i-r}$ over certain integers r, or in matrix form

$$[c_0\, c_1 \ldots c_{n-1}] = [I_0\, I_1 \ldots I_{k-1}] \begin{bmatrix} g_0\, g_1\, \cdots\, g_m & & \\ & g_0\, g_1\, \cdots\, g_m & \\ & \cdots & \\ & & g_0\, g_1\, \cdots\, g_m \end{bmatrix}. \quad (13.60)$$

Thus G is a generator matrix, and *decoding in the absence of error* may be performed by $c(x) \to c(x)/g(x)$. In fact, with a little more work we can show that $g(x)|(x^n - 1)$, which gives both a classification of cyclic (n, k) codes in terms of divisors of $x^n - 1$ of degree $n - k$ and a way to obtain those codes. The new reader may be guessing that $h(x) = (x^n - 1)/g(x)$ leads to a pcm, and this is indeed so, after a reversal of coefficient order. That is, if $h(x) = h_0 + h_1 x + \cdots + h_k x^k$ then a pcm may be taken to have as rows $[h_k \ldots h_1 h_0\, 0 \ldots 0]$ and its next $k - 1$ cyclic shifts.

Example 13.57 A cyclic code of length 7 has a generator polynomial $1 + x^2 + x^3$. Encode the information bits 1100 (a) by polynomial multiplication, (b) by a generator matrix.

Solution (a) The coefficients in the generator polynomial may be written $g_0 g_1 \ldots g_m = 1011$, in particular $m = 3$, so the code has dimension $n - m = 7 - 3 = 4$ as implied by the information bits. Encoding by polynomials, $I(x)g(x) = (1 + x)(1 + x^2 + x^3) = 1 + x + x^2 + x^4$, giving a codeword 1110100. (b) The matrix equation $c = IG$ for encoding becomes

$$[c_0 \ldots c_6] = [1100] \begin{bmatrix} 1 & 0 & 1 & 1 & 0 & 0 & 0 \\ 0 & 1 & 0 & 1 & 1 & 0 & 0 \\ 0 & 0 & 1 & 0 & 1 & 1 & 0 \\ 0 & 0 & 0 & 1 & 0 & 1 & 1 \end{bmatrix} = [1110100], \text{ as before.}$$

The shift register as polynomial multiplier/encoder If what would be the successive feedback digits of an LFSR (Figure 13.18) are instead output from the adder as a new sequence $v_0, v_1, \ldots$, we have the Feed Forward Shift Register, or FFSR, as shown in Figure 13.21.

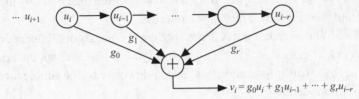

Figure 13.21 Feed Forward Shift Register to output successive coefficients v_i of x^i in a polynomial product $v(x) = g(x)u(x)$.

With the arrangement of Figure 13.21, the product $v(x) = g(x)u(x)$ is revealed by the succession of output digits $v_i = g_0 u_i + g_1 u_{i-1} + \cdots + g_r u_{i-r}$, this formula giving the coefficient of x^i in the product. On each tick, the sequence u is shifted one further stage and v_i is computed and output. Figure 13.22 shows steps in encoding the information digits $I_3 I_2 I_1 I_0$ for the Hamming code of Example 13.42, by multiplying $I(x)$ by the generator polynomial $g(x) = 1 + x + x^3$. It encodes $I_3 \ldots I_0 = 1110$ into $c_6 \ldots c_0 = 1100010$.

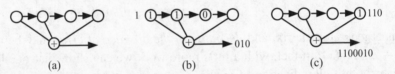

(a) (b) (c)

Figure 13.22 (a) LFSR for multiplying $u(x)$ by $1 + x + x^3$, (b) the result after three ticks in the case $u(x) = I(x)$ of degree 3, where $I_3 I_2 I_1 I_0 = 1110$, (c) the same, after seven ticks.

Exercise Check the output above, i.e. multiply the two polynomials by hand (see Figure 13.20).

BCH codes

Let n be a positive integer and $N = 2^n - 1$. We show how to construct, for every positive integer t with $2t + 1 < N$, a cyclic code of length N which corrects t errors. There are several equivalent possibilities, all said to be of type BCH(N, t). We construct the code by defining a generator polynomial and show by use of a pcm (13.43) that the minimum weight/distance is at least $2t + 1$, sufficient for correcting t errors (Theorem 13.41). Referring to Definition 13.51, let the primitive polynomial $p(x)$ define a field $F = \{0, \alpha, \ldots, \alpha^{N-1} (= 1)\}$ and, in a slightly extended version of a minimal polynomial, let $g(x)$ be the Mod 2 polynomial of least degree whose roots include all powers of α up to α^{2t}.

Now $g(x)$ is, by Theorem 13.54 (ii), the product of all M_{α^i} $(1 \le i \le 2t)$ after any repetitions are deleted (see Example 13.59 below). Thus, $g(x)$ need not be irreducible but there holds for any Mod 2 polynomial f, that $f(\alpha^i) = 0 \, (1 \le i \le 2t)$ if and only if $g \,|\, f$.

Theorem 13.58 *The cyclic code C with generator polynomial as above has a pcm the* $2t \times (n-1)$ *matrix* $H = [\alpha^{ij}]$, $1 \le i \le 2t$, $0 \le j \le n-1$, *and hence minimum weight* $2t + 1$.

Proof Note that row i of H is $[1 \; \alpha^i \; \alpha^{2i} \ldots \alpha^{(n-1)i}]$, whose elements are the ith powers of the similarly placed elements $[1 \; \alpha \; \alpha^2 \ldots \alpha^{(n-1)}]$ of row 1. We argue that H is a pcm, for if $c(x)$ is a binary n-vector then

$$c \text{ is in } C \Leftrightarrow g(x)|c(x) \qquad\qquad \text{by Theorem 13.56}$$
$$\Leftrightarrow c(\alpha^i) = 0 \, (1 \le i \le 2t) \qquad \text{by Theorem 13.54 (ii)}$$
$$\Leftrightarrow \textstyle\sum_j c_j(\alpha^i)^j = 0 \, (1 \le i \le 2t) \quad \text{by definition of } c(x)$$
$$\Leftrightarrow (\text{row } i \text{ of } H)c^{\mathrm{T}} = 0 \, (1 \le i \le 2t) \quad \text{by definition of } H$$
$$\Leftrightarrow Hc^{\mathrm{T}} = 0.$$

Thus H is a pcm of C as defined by $g(x)$. Now we must show that $w_{\min} \ge 2t + 1$. Let r be an integer satisfying $1 \le r \le 2t$. Then any $r \times r$ determinant from the first r rows of H is of Vandermonde type:

$$\begin{vmatrix} e_1 & e_2 & \ldots & e_r \\ e_1^2 & e_2^2 & \ldots & e_r^2 \\ \ldots & \ldots & \ldots & \ldots \\ e_1^r & e_2^r & \ldots & e_r^r \end{vmatrix} = e_1 e_2 \ldots e_r \prod_{i>j} (e_i - e_j) \qquad (13.61)$$

(see Examples 7.31), which is nonzero because the e_i are nonzero and distinct. Hence (Rules 7.28) the chosen r columns of H are linearly independent. Since this holds for each r, from 1 to $2t$, it follows that any set of *dependent* columns has size at least $2t + 1$. But $Hc^{\mathrm{T}} = 0$ is a linear relation between $w(c)$ columns, and so $w_{\min} \ge 2t + 1$ as required.

On the other hand, the generator polynomial, of degree $2t$, provides a codeword $1 \cdot g(x)$ of weight $w \le 2t + 1$, and so $2t + 1$ is the exact minimum weight.

Example 13.59 Find a generator polynomial/matrix for the BCH(15, 3) code obtained from the primitive polynomial $x^4 + x + 1$. Encode the message bits 10110.

Solution Since $t = 3$ the generator polynomial is the minimal polynomial of $\{\alpha, \alpha^2, \ldots, \alpha^6\}$, namely, by the comments above Theorem 13.58, $g(x) = M_\alpha M_{\alpha^3} M_{\alpha^5} = 10011 \times 11111 \times 111$ (Table 13.7) = 10100110111, of degree 10, whence $k = 15 - 10 = 5$. Note that in Formula (13.60) the order of coefficients is reversed to $g_0 g_1 \ldots$, giving in this case

$$G = \begin{bmatrix} 1 & 1 & 1 & 0 & 1 & 1 & 0 & 0 & 1 & 0 & 1 & & & & \\ & 1 & 1 & 1 & 0 & 1 & 1 & 0 & 0 & 1 & 0 & 1 & & & \\ & & 1 & 1 & 1 & 0 & 1 & 1 & 0 & 0 & 1 & 0 & 1 & & \\ & & & 1 & 1 & 1 & 0 & 1 & 1 & 0 & 0 & 1 & 0 & 1 & \\ & & & & 1 & 1 & 1 & 0 & 1 & 1 & 0 & 0 & 1 & 0 & 1 \end{bmatrix}, \qquad (13.62)$$

where empty spaces signify zeros. The encoding is $[10110]G = 110010100001110$.

Remark 13.60 BCH codes have minimum distance $\delta = w_{min}$ (see Theorem 13.41(iii)) $= 2t + 1 = \deg g(x) + 1$, hence the dimension is $k = n - \deg g(x) = n - \delta + 1$, or $\delta = n - k + 1$. This can be shown to be the greatest possible value of δ for a linear code with given values of n, k (hint: $Hc^T = 0$ is a linear relation amongst $w(c)$ columns of H, and $k = n - r(H)$). Codes such as those of BCH type satisfying $\delta = n - k + 1$ are therefore said to be *maximum distance separable*, or MDS.

Decoding BCH codes Suppose a codeword c is corrupted into the received word R. We calculate the *syndrome* $S(x) = S_1 + S_2 x + \cdots + S_{2t} x^{2t-1}$, noting that subscripts are shifted one from the usual numbering, where $S_i = [$row i of $H]R^T = \sum R_j \alpha^{ij}$ ($j = 0, \ldots, n - 1$). It follows that $S_{2i} = S_i^2$, a useful aid to calculation. Further, R is (by definition of pcm) a true codeword if and only if $S(x)$ is the zero polynomial, and we may hope that a nonzero $S(x)$ will contain useful information about the errors in R.

In fact, $S(x)$ determines all error positions after an application of the Euclidean Algorithm to $S(x)$ and x^{2t}. For notation, if a polynomial f_1 be divided into a polynomial f_2, we denote the quotient and remainder respectively by $\text{Quot}(f_1, f_2)$ and $\text{Rem}(f_1, f_2)$. Then a sequence of quotients $\{q_i\}$, remainders $\{r_i\}$, and an auxiliary sequence $\{t_i\}$ are constructed as follows.

> *Initial values* $r_{-1} = x^{2t}, r_0 = S(x), t_{-1} = 0, t_0 = 1$.
> *Repeat* for $i = 1, 2, 3, \ldots$
> $$q_i = \text{Quot}(r_{i-1}, r_{i-2})$$
> $$r_i = \text{Rem}(r_{i-1}, r_{i-2})$$
> $$t_i = q_i t_{i-1} + t_{i-2}$$
> *Until* $\deg(r_i) < t$. Set $L = i$. $\qquad$ (13.63)

The *Error Locator Polynomial* is $\sigma(x) = t_L$, and the error positions are those j for which α^{-j} is a root of $\sigma(x)$. A general algorithm for finding such roots in given in Pretzel (1992).

Example 13.61 A BCH(15, 2) code is defined by a primitive polynomial $x^4 + x + 1$. A codeword is transmitted and received with a maximum of two errors, as $R = 1001110\ldots0$. We decode completely the word R, using Table 13.5 to add the various powers of α. The syndrome coefficients are

$$
\begin{aligned}
S_1 &= [\text{row 1 of } H]R^T &&= 1 + \alpha^3 + \alpha^4 + \alpha^5 &&= \alpha^6, \\
S_2 &= S_1^2 &&= \cdots &&= \alpha^{12}, \\
S_3 &= (\text{cubes from row 1}) &&= 1 + \alpha^9 + \alpha^{12} + \alpha^{15} &&= \alpha^8, \\
S_4 &= S_2^2 &&= \alpha^{24} &&= \alpha^9.
\end{aligned}
$$

Enhanced shorthand It is convenient to use the enhanced notation $[d_n \ldots d_0]$ to denote the polynomial in which x^i has coefficient α^{d_i}, reserving the symbol $*$ for zero coefficients: an actual zero d_i signifies α^0, or unity. Note that $\alpha^{15} = 1$. The Euclidean Algorithm calculation proceeds as in Table 13.8.

Table 13.8. *Stages in the Euclidean algorithm calculation for* $\{q_i, r_i, t_i\}$.

i	q_i	r_i	t_i
1	[6 5]	[8 7 11]	q_1
2	[1 *]	[6]	$1 + q_1 q_2 = 1 + (\alpha^6 x + \alpha^5)\alpha x = [7 \quad 6 \quad 0]$

By the time the table extends to line $L = 2$ the remainder polynomial has degree less than 2, in fact degree 0, so we stop. The roots of the error locator polynomial $\sigma(x) = t_L = \alpha^7 x^2 + \alpha^6 x + 1$ can be found by trying each power of α until a root λ is found, then considering $\sigma(x)/(x - \lambda)$. Alternatively, we note that by (13.57) the roots λ, μ of $\sigma(x) = ax^2 + bx + c$ satisfy $\lambda + \mu = -b/a = \alpha^{14}$, $\lambda\mu = c/a = \alpha^8$, and then use Table 13.5 to find which of the allowed products $\alpha \cdot \alpha^7$, $\alpha^2 \cdot \alpha^6, \dots$ has sum α^{14}. In fact the roots are $\alpha \ (= \alpha^{-14})$ and $\alpha^7 \ (= \alpha^{-8})$, so the error positions are 8, 14 and the corrected codeword is $c = 100111001000001$. To complete the decoding we need the code's generator $g(x)$, the minimal polynomial of $\{\alpha, \alpha^2, \alpha^3, \alpha^4\}$, which by Table 13.7 is $10011 \times 11111 = 111010001$ (top bits to left). Then the information bits are given by $I(x) = c(x)/g(x) = x^6 + x^5 + x^3 + 1$, or in codeword notation 1001011.

Reed–Solomon codes

These codes are especially effective for correcting an error burst, or sequence of suspect bits. Like the BCH codes they have been well-used in practice. Starting with a finite field F of order 2^n with a primitive element α, we generalise from BCH(n, t) to *Reed–Solomon type* RS(n, t) by allowing coefficients of $g(x)$ and codeword entries to lie in F rather than be restricted to Z_2. The number of entries corrected is still t, but each entry takes in n successive bits which are corrected with that entry. We note two differences in calculation.

1. It is not now necessary for $g(x)$ to have all conjugates of a root as roots. Thus $g(x) = \Pi_i(x - \alpha^i)$ $(1 \le i \le 2t)$, of degree $2t$ only, but Formula (13.57) applies.
2. The *Error Evaluator Polynomial* $w(x) = r_L$ gives the required error E_i at position i, corresponding to a root $\beta = \alpha^{-i}$ of $S(x)$, by

$$E_i = w(\beta)/\sigma'(\beta), \tag{13.64}$$

where $\sigma'(x)$ is the formal derivative of $\sigma(x)$ with respect to x. That is, $d/dx(x^r) = rx^{r-1}$. For example, $d/dx\,(ax^2 + bx + c) = b$, since $2ax = 0$.

Example 13.62 A Reed–Solomon code of type RS(7, 2) is obtained over the field F of order 8, using the primitive polynomial $x^3 + x + 1$. In the usual notation: (i) encode the information word $[\alpha \ 0 \ 1]$ and express the result in binary form, (ii) a corrupted codeword is received as

$$R = [\alpha^3 \ \alpha \ 1 \ \alpha^2 \ 0 \ \alpha^3 \ 1]$$

after error bursts that affect at most two of the seven coordinate positions; determine the original codeword, (iii) what input word produced this codeword?

Solution The field is $F = \{0, \alpha, \alpha^2, \ldots, \alpha^7 = 1\}$, where $\alpha^3 = \alpha + 1$. Sums of powers of α, and hence also the binary form of codewords, may be read from the computed Table 13.9.

Table 13.9. *Powers of α as polynomials with coefficients abc,*
deduced from $\alpha^3 = \alpha + 1$.

i	1	2	3	4	5	6	7
α^i	010	100	011	110	111	101	001

(i) For encoding we determine the generator polynomial $g(x) = \Pi_i(x - \alpha^i) = x^4 + \sigma_1 x^3 + \sigma_2 x^2 + \sigma_3 x + \sigma_4$, where $\sigma_1 = \alpha + \alpha^2 + \alpha^3 + \alpha^4 = \alpha^3$, $\sigma_2 = \alpha^3 + \alpha^4 + \alpha^5 + \alpha^5 + \alpha^6 + \alpha^7 = 1$ (note $\alpha^5 + \alpha^5 = 0$), $\sigma_3 = \alpha^9 + \alpha^8 + \alpha^7 + \alpha^6 = \alpha$, and finally $\sigma_4 = \alpha^{10} = \alpha^3$. In enhanced shorthand $g(x) = [0 \ 3 \ 0 \ 1 \ 3]$. Then $c(x) = I(x)g(x)$, or in matrix form

$$c = [\alpha \ 0 \ 1] \begin{bmatrix} \alpha^3 & \alpha & 1 & \alpha^3 & 1 & & \\ & \alpha^3 & \alpha & 1 & \alpha^3 & 1 & \\ & & \alpha^3 & \alpha & 1 & \alpha^3 & 1 \end{bmatrix} = [\alpha^4 \ \alpha^2 \ 1 \ \alpha^2 \ \alpha^3 \ \alpha^3 \ 1].$$

The binary form of this codeword is, from Table 13.9, 110100001100011011001.

(ii) We first calculate the syndrome $S(x) = S_1 + S_2 x + S_3 x^2 + S_4 x^3$, where

$$S_1 = [\text{row 1 of } H]R^T = [1 \ \alpha \ldots \alpha^6]R^T = \alpha^3 + \alpha^2 + \alpha^2 + \alpha^5 + \alpha^8 + \alpha^6 = \alpha^3,$$
$$S_2 = [\text{row 2 of } H]R^T = [1 \ \alpha^2 \ldots \alpha^{12}]R^T = \alpha^4, \text{ similarly } S_3 = \alpha^4, S^4 = 0.$$

In the notation of (13.63), $r_0 = S(x) = [4 \ 4 \ 3]$, $r_{-1} = x^{2t} = x^4$. By stage $L = 1$, the remainder has degree less than $t (= 2)$, in fact q_1, r_1, t_1 equal respectively $[3 \ \ 3 \ \ 5]$, $[0 \ \ 1]$, $[3 \ \ 3 \ \ 5]$. Thus the error locator polynomial is $\sigma(x) = t_1 = \alpha^3(x^2 + x + \alpha^2)$, and the evaluator polynomial is $w(x) = r_1 = x + \alpha$. We shall find the roots of $\sigma(x)$ by trying all powers of α:

i	0	1	2	3	4	5	6
$\sigma(\alpha^i)$	α^5	α^4	1	α^4	0	0	1

The error positions are thus $7 - 4 = 3$ and $7 - 5 = 2$. To determine the actual coordinate errors E_i we apply (13.64), noting that $\alpha'(x) = \alpha^3$.

$$E_2 = w(\alpha^5)/\sigma'(\alpha^5) = (\alpha^5 + \alpha)/\alpha^3 = \alpha^6/\alpha^3 = \alpha^3,$$
$$E_3 = w(\alpha^4)/\sigma'(\alpha^4) = (\alpha^4 + \alpha)/\alpha^3 = \alpha^2/\alpha^3 = \alpha^6.$$

Adding these to positions 2, 3 of R we obtain the corrected codeword $c = [\alpha^3 \ \alpha \ \alpha \ 1 \ 0 \ \alpha^3 \ 1]$. The addition expressed in binary is

$$
\begin{array}{lllllllll}
R & = & 011 & 010 & 001 & 100 & 000 & 011 & 001 \\
E & = & 000 & 000 & 011 & 101 & 000 & 000 & 000 \\
& & & & \cdots & & & & \\
c & = & 011 & 010 & 010 & 001 & 000 & 011 & 001
\end{array}
$$

(iii) The input word corresponding to c is $c(x)/g(x)$. Noting that in shorthand notation the coefficients of higher powers go to the left, we obtain [0 3 * 0 1 1 3]/[0 3 0 1 3] = [0 * 0], or as a binary input word, 001000001.

Exercise How long a bit error burst can the RS code above be certain to correct?

13.2.5 *Aiming for the Shannon prediction*

We remarked at the end of Section 13.1 that the search for good codes has focussed on those with extra structure, especially linearity, with a view to an easily implemented description of the code and its decoding method. In particular, the structure of finite fields has given us the practical Hamming, BCH, and Reed–Solomon codes. These all have fixed length n (and are therefore called *block codes*), dimension k, and hence fixed rate $R = k/n$. Each will correct a certain fixed number of errors in a codeword with certainty. Beyond this, as channel noise increases so does the probability of decoding error. But Shannon's Coding Theorem says that the probability of decoding error can be made arbitrarily small (for any rate below capacity). This leads us to consider sequences $\{C^{(i)}\}$ ($i = 1, 2, 3, \ldots$) of linear codes with, say,

$$\text{length } n_i, \quad \text{dimension } k_i, \quad \text{minimum distance } d_i,$$

where n_i become arbitrarily large as i increases. We regard the behaviour of d_i/n_i as measuring the goodness of a code, and look for sequences of codes for which both this ratio and the rate $R_i = k_i/n_i$ approach positive constants as i tends to infinity. This proved elusive and was widely regarded as unattainable up to about 1972. For example the Hamming codes of Construction 13.44 form a sequence $\{C^{(m)}\}$, where $n = 2^m - 1$, $k = n - m$ and $d = 3$, whence $R_m := (2^m - m - 1)/(2^m - 1) \to 1$ as $m \to \infty$, which is very satisfactory; but unfortunately, because d remains constant, we have $d/n \to 0$. The BCH codes, with reduced rate, but better error-correction and practical decoding, nevertheless fall at the d/n hurdle, with $d/n \to 0$. Similarly for the Reed–Solomon case.

Construction 13.63 (*Justesen codes*) It was a considerable surprise when Justesen (1972) presented his sequence of codes derived in an ingenious yet simple way from a sequence of Reed–Solomon codes $\mathrm{RS}^{(m)}$ in which, for given m and limit rate $R < 1/2$ the code $\mathrm{RS}^{(m)}$ has

$$\text{length } N = N_m = 2^m - 1,$$
$$\text{dimension } K = K_m = \mathrm{Min}\{K \colon K/2N \geq R\},$$
$$\text{minimum distance } d = d_m = N - K + 1. \tag{13.65}$$

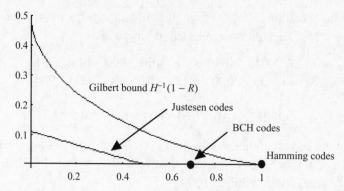

Figure 13.23 The presence of the curve known as the *Gilbert bound* implies that sequences of codes exist with the limit pairs above the curve, but the proof is non-constructive. The Justesen code graph points fall below but, unlike those for previous codes, they do rise above the horizontal axis.

The minimum distance formula above follows for RS codes in a similar manner to BCH codes (thus they, like the BCH codes, are maximum distance separable). The purpose of the dimension formula will appear shortly. Let α be the primitive element of the field F of order 2^m that defines $RS^{(m)}$. For each codeword $a = (a_0, \ldots, a_{N-1})$ of $RS^{(m)}$, we construct a codeword $c = (c_0, \ldots, c_{N-1})$ of a new code $C^{(m)}$ by replacing a_j by the pair $c_j = (a_j, \alpha^j a_j)$ $(j = 0, 1, \ldots, N - 1)$. A useful point to notice is that $c_i = c_j \neq 0 \Rightarrow \alpha^i = \alpha^j \Rightarrow i = j$. Thus all nonzero entries of c are distinct, and furthermore the code is linear over F because the multiple α_j appears precisely at the jth pair c_j. Expressing elements of F as m-bit binary words, we have the *Justesen code $C^{(m)}$*, of length $n = 2m(2^m - 1)$.

On the other hand the rate is $R_m = K/2N$ which, with K as defined in (13.65), implies that $R_m \to R$ as $m \to \infty$ since $k/2N$ becomes an ever closer rational approximation to R. Justesen proved the following result.

Theorem 13.64 *For any rate R with $0 < R < 1/2$ there is a sequence of Justesen codes $C^{(m)}$ with $R_m \to R$ as $m \to \infty$ and $\lim_{(m \to \infty)} d_m/n_m \geq (1 - 2R)H^{-1}(1/2)$.*

Remarks 13.65 (1) Justesen proved a similar result for $1/2 \leq R < 1$ by a modification for the construction we have outlined. (2) In Figure 13.23 we graph the pairs (Lim R_m, Lim (d/n)) for Hamming, BCH, and Justesen codes, along with the Gilbert bound (Sloane and MacWilliams, 1977).

Gallager codes As early as 1962 Gallager introduced his codes (Gallager, 1963), based on a probabilistic approach with sparse matrices. However, his decoding method was impractical in computing terms at the time and the codes lay largely forgotten for a further 35 years, to be rediscovered by MacKay and Neal (1997). The problem is to account theoretically for the excellent results these codes give in practice. Meanwhile, in investigating what turned out to be a special case of Gallager codes, Sourlas (1989) discovered a fruitful connection with statistical physics, currently exploited by various other workers also. See e.g. Kabashima and Saad (1998, 2004).

Turbocodes Whereas Justesen codes (Justesen, 1972) can be viewed as produced by a process of 'concatenation' of RS codes with a simple code, the turbocodes of Berrou, Glavieux and Thitimajshima (1993) are found by combining two or more codes of the type known as *convolutional*, in which instead of codewords of fixed length one uses a continuous bit stream. A useful further reference is Frey (1998). Turbocodes appear to be the best presently known, and are currently being implemented in the communications field. We introduce both types after preparing for their decoding with the necessary study of belief propagation, in the next section, 13.3.

13.3 Probabilistic decoding

The success of the codes and decoding methods we have described in detail so far is largely due to their inbuilt algebraic structure. Decoding, after the passage through a noisy channel, uses linear algebra over finite fields to operate nearest neighbour decoding. These are excellent methods, but an opportunity is lost when the received signal is quantised to, say, 0 or 1. Suppose, for example, that we are allowed to retain the actual signal value and it is 0.2; then, instead of simply interpreting this as 0, we can use it as evidence in a probabilistic analysis.

There are two main approaches, (i) the maximum likelihood, or ML, method for binary words (see e.g. Lin and Costello, 1983), and (ii) maximum a posteriori (MAP) determination for each bit variable z_k, given the vector e of all available data. The MAP method utilises knowledge of the pdf $p(z_k|e)$ for each k.

In proceeding with this approach our first task is to show how these pdfs may be obtained from a Bayesian network of the relevant probabilities by *belief propagation* (Pearl, 1997, Frey, 1998) as henceforth described. We remark that, though introduced here in time for its application to error-correcting codes, the method is of increasing importance in vision (see the Bayesian image restoration techniques of Section 11.4.6), and we shall have this in mind, though reserving further applications to their appropriate place.

13.3.1 Belief propagation in Bayesian networks

For a fuller introduction to Bayesian networks we refer to Section 11.4.4, especially Notation 11.70ff and Definition 11.72ff to which the reader may wish to refer, but here is a short recapitulation. A Bayesian network for random variables $v_1, \ldots, v_n$ consists of (i) a Directed Acyclic Graph, or DAG, with nodes labelled by the v_k, and (ii) a set of corresponding *probability functions* $p(v_k|u_k)$, with u_k as the set of all parents of v_k, satisfying what we may call the *separation property*

$$p(v_k|u_k \cup w) = p(v_k|u_k) \tag{13.66}$$

for any set w of non-descendants of v_k (this excludes v_k itself). Notice that if v_k is a *source* node, one without parents, then $p(v_k|u_k)$ reduces to $p(v_k)$. With this proviso, a

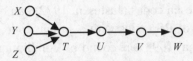

Figure 13.24 A simple Bayesian network. The end-nodes consist of source nodes X, Y, Z and a terminal node W. The belief network problem is to compute $p(u|x, y, z, w)$ for every internal node such as u. Notice that the subnetwork T, U, V, W is a Markov chain.

joint pdf is given by the product of the probability functions,

$$p(v_1, \ldots, v_k) = \prod_{k=1}^{n} p(v_k | \mathbf{u}_k). \tag{13.67}$$

Thus, all probabilistic questions about the v_k can in principle be answered from the network, and the local nature of the factors, each depending only on a small 'neighbourhood' of variables, may greatly reduce computation. Markov chains (Section 11.4) are a special case.

Now for belief propagation We use the following metaphor. The expressions Belief $(x) = p(x|e)$, to be determined, quantify our belief about internal nodes x in the light of evidence e, the vector of all end-node variables.

The source nodes are referred to as *causal* evidence; their pdfs are supplied from prior beliefs about, say, an image formation or bit encoding process, whilst the terminal nodes are called *diagnostic*, say bit or pixel values as actually measured (observed, instantiated). After some preliminaries we arrive at the *Forward–Backward Algorithm* for propagating information from the end nodes across the network via the probability functions; in other words, for *belief propagation*.

Examples 13.66 (i) *Conditioning on another variable* Given a Bayesian network, we can obtain for *any* two variables X, Y of the network, a matrix $Q = Q_{XY} = [p(y|x)]$, whose x, y entry is $p(y|x)$. To do so, we sum the joint pdf (13.67) over all other variables to obtain $p(x, y)$, sum $p(x, y)$ over y to get $p(x)$, then take $p(y|x) = p(x, y)/p(y)$. A standard formula is then

$$p(y) = \sum_x p(y|x)p(x), \qquad \text{or} \qquad [p(y)] = [p(x)]Q_{XY} \tag{13.68}$$

where, as usual, $[p(y)]$ is a row vector specifying the pdf of Y (see Notation 13.6). We refer to this as conditioning any variable, y, on any other variable, x.

(ii) *Using a subnetwork* Suppose we wish to determine $p(t|x)$ in Figure 13.24. In keeping with the comment below (13.67), this can be found by considering only the variables x, y, z, t because, with the probability functions relating them, they form a *subnetwork that is itself Bayesian* (more on this principle shortly). Thus $p(x, y, z, t) = p(x)p(y)p(z)p(t|x, y, z)$. As a check we may obtain this formally from the corresponding expression for the full $p(x, y, z, t, u, v, w)$ by summing over u, v, w (Exercise 13.16).

Then for $p(t|x)$ we have

$$p(t|x) = p(x,t)/p(x) = \sum_{y,z} p(x,y,z,t)/p(x) = \sum_{y,z} p(y)p(z)p(t|x,y,z).$$

(iii) *Markov chain reduction* We need two results for successive X, Y, Z in a Markov chain which hold even if there are other variables between them: $X \to \cdots \to Y \to \cdots \to Z$. The first says that we can *condition $p(z|x)$ on any variable Y between X and Z*, in a Markov chain.

$$p(z|x) = \sum_y p(z|y)p(y|x), \qquad (13.69a)$$

$$p(z|x,y) = p(z|y). \qquad (13.69b)$$

These are immediate because *removing any variable from a Markov chain leaves another Markov chain*. We have established this for first and last variables in (11.63) of Chapter 11. Now we'll prove it for an interior variable such as W in a chain $X_1 \ldots X_m W Y_1 \cdots Y_n$. If we write $\boldsymbol{x} = (x_1, \ldots, x_m)$ for brevity, it suffices to verify that $p(y_1|\boldsymbol{x}) = p(y_1|x_m)$. We have $p(y_1|\boldsymbol{x}) = p(\boldsymbol{x}, y_1)/p(\boldsymbol{x})$

$$= \sum_w p(\boldsymbol{x}, w, y_1)/p(\boldsymbol{x}) = \sum_w p(\boldsymbol{x})p(w|x_m)p(y_1|w)/p(\boldsymbol{x})$$

$$= \sum_w p(y_1|w)p(w|x_m),$$

which equals $p(y_1|x_m)$, as required, since the triple $X_m W Y_1$ is Markov.

Remarks 13.67 Continuing to use γ for a normalising constant determined by its context, we collect here some useful formulae for random variables $A, \ldots, Z$. The value of γ may be inferred in the first two cases by summing the right hand side over x and equating the result to 1. The third reduces to (13.69a) if X, Y, Z form a Markov chain, and this may be a useful way to remember it. We will use these formulae extensively in what follows.

$$p(x|a) = \gamma p(a|x)p(x) \quad \text{(Bayes)}, \quad \gamma = p(a)^{-1}, \qquad (13.70a)$$

$$p(x|a,b) = \gamma p(a|x,b)p(x|b), \qquad \gamma = p(a|b)^{-1}, \qquad (13.70b)$$

$$p(z|x) = \sum_y p(z|x,y)p(y|x), \qquad \text{('non-Markov')} \qquad (13.70c)$$

Proof (b) By definition of conditional probability we have $p(x|a,b) = p(x,a,b)/p(a,b) = p(x,a,b)/p(x,b) \times p(x,b)/p(b) \times p(b)/p(a,b) = p(a|x,b) \times p(x|b)/p(a|b)$.

Exercise Derive (13.70c) by noting that $p(x,z)$ is the sum of $p(x,y,z)$ over y (Exercise 13.17).

Assumption 13.68 For the duration of Section 13.3 we shall assume our Bayesian networks to be *singly connected*; that is, that there are no cycles even in the underlying undirected graph, where edge directions are discounted. This graph is therefore a tree, with a unique undirected path between any two points. With directions restored, the path might look like this: $A \to B \to C \leftarrow Z$. However, to establish some ideas, it is helpful

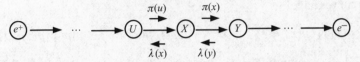

Figure 13.25 The Markov chain case of a Bayesian network.

to begin with the special case of a Markov chain. (For an approach to cycle inclusion, see e.g. Frey and MacKay, 1998.)

Markov chains and message passing

Let us assume the network is a Markov chain. Thus there are a single causal node e^+ and single diagnostic node e^-, as in Figure 13.25. Belief(x) is determined from a purely *causal part* $\pi(x) = p(x|e^+)$ and *diagnostic part* $\lambda(x) = p(e^-|x)$. These in turn are determined by the corresponding π, λ of the neighbours of x which, we say metaphorically, *pass them* to node x as messages. We imagine each node to have a memory and processor unit, and that a node's memory is always online to its neighbours.

Message passing essentially originates at the end-nodes, and an effective algorithm is one which does this in a coherent way, with each message sent exactly once. The following result handles the Markov case, with the implied message passing illustrated in Figure 13.25, where passing the π messages forward from the left, then the λ messages backwards from the right, enables Belief$(\cdots)$ to be computed for each internal node.

Theorem 13.69 *Let $U \to X \to Y$ be part of a Markov chain from e^+ to e^-. Then with the definitions $\pi(x) = p(x|e^+)$, $\lambda(x) = p(e^-|x)$, and Belief $(x) = p(x|e^+, e^-)$, we have*

$$\text{Belief}(x) = \gamma \lambda(x) \pi(x), \tag{13.71}$$

$$[\lambda(x)] = [\lambda(y)]Q_{XY}^{\mathrm{T}}, \text{ and } [\pi(x)] = [\pi(u)]Q_{UX}. \tag{13.72}$$

Proof Applying (13.70b) to the definition of Belief(x), with $a, b = e^-, e^+$ (note the order), we have

$$\begin{aligned}
\text{Belief}(x) &= \gamma p(e^-|x, e^+)p(x|e^+) &&\text{by (13.70b)} \\
&= \gamma p(e^-|x)p(x|e^+) &&\text{by (13.69b),} \\
&= \gamma \lambda(x)p(x) &&\text{by definition, whilst, by (13.69a):}
\end{aligned}$$

$$\lambda(x) = p(e^-|x) = \sum_y p(e^-|y)p(y|x) = \sum_y \lambda(y)p(y|x), \quad \text{as required,}$$

$$\pi(x) = p(x|e^+) = \sum_u p(x|u)p(u|e^+) = \sum_u \pi(u)p(x|u), \text{ completing the proof.}$$

Note 13.70 (i) (*Numerical answers*) Belief(x) has end-node variables as parameters. We may compare the normal distribution's $p(x|\mu) = \gamma \exp[-(x - \mu)^2/2]$ with the parameter μ allowed to be itself a random variable. By message passing from these end-nodes

Table 13.10. *Starting the message off from an end-node E.*

No.	situation	action
(i)	$E \rightarrow X$	$\pi(e) = p(e|e) = p(e)$, to be estimated
(ii)	$Z \rightarrow E$	observe $E = \acute{e}$, say. Estimate or use known $\lambda(z) = p(\acute{e}|z)$
(iii)	$Z \rightarrow E$, no observation	Assume all outcomes equally likely: $[\lambda(e)] = [p(e|e)] = \gamma[1 \ldots 1]$

we aim to reduce to zero the number of free (unfixed) parameters in Belief(x) for each node X. Table 13.10 show how passing begins.

(ii) (*Generic constants*) In worked examples we may encounter the product of several normalising constants named γ. We simply denote the unknown product also by γ, and calculate it at the appropriate time.

(iii) (*Independence*) In proofs we will often wish to infer independence of a pair of sets of random variables U, V from independence of a pair of super-sets $A \supseteq U, B \supseteq V$. The argument may be expressed as follows. Let x, y, u, v be variables, or sequences thereof, with $p(x, u, y, v) = p(x, u)p(y, v)$. We must deduce that $p(u, v) = p(u)p(v)$. We have $p(u, v) = \sum_{x,y} p(x, u, y, v) = \sum_{x,y} p(x, u)p(y, v) = \sum_x p(x, u) \sum_y p(y, v) = p(u)p(v)$, as required.

Example 13.71 (*Adapted from Pearl, 1997*) A murder weapon has been recovered from a crime scene and sent for fingerprint testing. It is certain one of three suspects is the guilty party. To analyse the likelihoods we use variables

$$X = \text{the killer,}$$
$$Y = \text{the last to hold the weapon,}$$
$$E = \text{possible fingerprint readings.}$$

Now, X generates expectations about the identity of Y, which generates expectations about E. However, X has no influence on E once Y is known. Thus we may model the probabilistic relationships by a Markov-type Bayesian network with message passing, as indicated below.

The killer is normally the last person to hold the murder weapon, say 80% of the time, and, assuming the other two suspects equally likely, this information is expressible by the transition matrix with, as usual, rows x and columns y:

$$Q_{XY} = [p(y|x)] = \begin{bmatrix} 0.8 & 0.1 & 0.1 \\ 0.1 & 0.8 & 0.1 \\ 0.1 & 0.1 & 0.8 \end{bmatrix},$$

which is independent of the order 1, 2, 3 in which the suspects are listed. In this case the fingerprint expert has identified a unique print *é* which is not submitted to the court. Rather, he passes on a list that says he is 80% sure it came from the first suspect, 60% sure it was from the second, and 50% sure it was from the third. These numbers do not add up to 100%, but, normalised by suitable γ, they provide probability estimates. We are in case (ii) of Table 13.10 (its *z* is our *y*), so we may take

$$[\lambda(y)] = [p(\acute{e}|y)] = \gamma [8\ \ 6\ \ 5], \gamma = 1/(8+6+5).$$

Our causal node happens to be labelled *X* rather than *E*, but, guided by Table 13.10, case (i), we produce, from the *non-fingerprint* trial evidence, estimates of the likelihood of guilt of the respective suspects as 80%, 10% and 10%, that is $[\pi(x)] = [0.8\ \ 0.1\ \ 0.1]\,(\gamma = 1)$.

Message passing Passing messages as depicted in the figure, we have by (13.72)

$$[\lambda(x)] = [\lambda(y)]Q_{XY}^{\mathrm{T}} = \gamma \begin{bmatrix} 8 & 6 & 5 \end{bmatrix} \begin{bmatrix} 0.8 & 0.1 & 0.1 \\ 0.1 & 0.8 & 0.1 \\ 0.1 & 0.1 & 0.8 \end{bmatrix} = \gamma \begin{bmatrix} 0.75 & 0.61 & 0.54 \end{bmatrix},$$

$$\text{and } [\pi(y)] = [\pi(x)]Q_{XY} = [0.8\ \ 0.1\ \ 0.1] \begin{bmatrix} 0.8 & 0.1 & 0.1 \\ 0.1 & 0.8 & 0.1 \\ 0.1 & 0.1 & 0.8 \end{bmatrix}$$

$$= [0.66\ \ 0.17\ \ 0.17].$$

Most likely suspect Using the elementwise multiplication notation $[a\ b] \circ [x\ y] = [ax\ by]$, we may represent $\text{Belief}(x) = \gamma\lambda(x)\pi(x)$ in matrix form as $[\text{Belief}(x)] = \gamma[\lambda(x)] \circ [\pi(x)] = \gamma[0.75\ 0.61\ 0.54] \circ [0.8\ 0.1\ 0.1]$, resulting in $[0.840\ 0.085\ 0.070]$, and pointing to suspect 1 as the most likely murderer by far.

The last gun handler Without jumping to conclusions, let us determine belief as to which suspect *Y* last touched the murder weapon. For this (see Note 13.70(ii)) we calculate $\text{Belief}\,(y) = \gamma\lambda(y)\pi(y)$, or in matrix form $[\text{Belief}(y)] = \gamma[8\ 6\ 5] \circ [0.66\ 0.17\ 0.17]$, which equals $[0.738\ 0.143\ 0.119]$, implicating the first suspect again.

Updating the evidence A new witness comes forward to say she saw the suspect elsewhere at the estimated time of death, reducing the odds on his guilt from 80% to 28% and causing a revision in $\pi(x)$ to $[0.28\ 0.36\ 0.36]$. Passing the new $\pi(x)$ message along to node *Y* causes the following re-computation:

$$[\pi(y)] = [\pi(x)]\,Q_{xy} = [0.30\ 0.35\ 0.35]$$
$$[\text{Belief}(x)] = \gamma[0.75\ 0.61\ 0.54] \circ [0.28\ 0.36\ 0.36] = [0.337\ 0.352\ 0.311],$$
$$[\text{Belief}(y)] = \gamma[8\ 6\ 5] \circ [0.30\ 0.35\ 0.35] = [0.384\ 0.336\ 0.280],$$

and now, although suspect 1 is most likely the last to handle the gun, suspect 2 is most likely to have committed the crime.

Belief networks in general

Suppose that, as in Figure 13.26, a Bayesian network G has a node X with parents $U_1, \ldots, U_r$ and children $Y_1, \ldots, Y_s$. We adopt the notation now descibed.

V^+: the set of vertices 'above' X, namely those joined to X via some parent. Then V^+ partitions into the sets V_i^+ of points joined to X by its parent U_i. The subset e^+ of end-nodes in V^+ partitions correspondingly into sets $e_i^+ \subseteq V_i^+$. In Figure 13.26 for example, V_1^+ includes T as well as U_1, and e_1^+ includes T.

V^-: the set of vertices 'below' X, those joined to X via some child. Corresponding divisions to the case of V^+ hold, with the plus sign replaced by minus. Thus e_1^- in Figure 13.26 includes the source node Z.

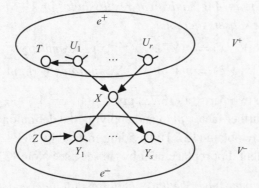

Figure 13.26 A node X whose parents are $U_1, \ldots, U_r$ and children $Y_1, \ldots, Y_s$. Because the network is singly connected, X divides the nodes into the set V^+ connected to X via a parent and the set V^- connected to X by a child. There is no edge joining V^+ and V^-.

Notes (i) These definitions of e^+ and e^- reduce in the Markov case to just one causal and one diagnostic node. Here e^+ and e^- may each contain both types. (ii) It is important that no two of the $r + s$ sets V_i^+ and V_j^- share a vertex/variable; indeed, such a vertex would create a cycle through X, contrary to Assumption 13.68. (iii) If A, B are sets of nodes/variables, we write A, B or (A, B) for their combination, e.g. (V^+, x) and (V^+, V^-).

Subnetworks

According to the notation for a Bayesian network described above, the parents of nodes of (V^+, x) all lie in (V^+, x), which is therefore itself a Bayesian net, and we have (13.73a) below. Further, the parents of V^- lie in (V^-, x), giving (13.73b), which says that (V^-, x) is a Bayesian net with X as a source node provided $p(x)$ is supplied.

$$p(V^+, x) = \Pi \text{ probability functions of nodes of } (V^+, x), \qquad (13.73a)$$

$$p(V^-, x) = p(x) \, \Pi \text{ probability functions of nodes of } (V^-). \qquad (13.73b)$$

Thus both (V^+, x) and (V^-, x) are Bayesian networks, creating a kind of symmetry.

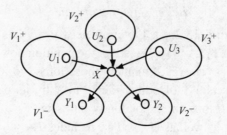

Figure 13.27 Expanded version of Figure 13.26, in the case $r = 3, s = 2$. The parents of V_i^+ nodes lie in V_i^+, and those of V_j^- lie in $\{V_j^-, x\}$.

Theorem 13.72 *The following equivalent results hold for V^- and V^+ and for these replaced by respective subsets thereof:*

$$p(V^+, V^-|x) = p(V^+|x)p(V^-|x) \quad (symmetry), \tag{13.74}$$

$$p(V^-|x, V^+) = p(V^-|x) \quad (X \text{ separates } V^- \text{ from } V^+). \tag{13.75}$$

Proof Combining the two parts of (13.73) gives $p(V^+, x, V^-) = p(V^+, x)\, p(V^-, x)/p(x)$. Dividing by a further factor $p(x)$ and applying the definition of conditional probability, we immediately obtain (13.74). Dividing instead by $p(V^+, x)$ gives (13.75), so the results are equivalent. For replacement by subsets, see Note 13.70(iii).

Theorem 13.73 *(Independence) We have the following independence results, in which the first two hold also if each set $V_i^{\pm}$ is replaced by a subset of itself. For the third we write $u = (u_i)$ and $e^+ = (e_i^+)$.*

$$p(V_1^+, \ldots, V_r^+) = \Pi_i\, p(V_i^+), \tag{13.76}$$

$$p(V_1^-, \ldots, V_s^-|x) = \Pi_j\, p(V_j^-|x), \tag{13.77}$$

$$p(u|e^+) = \Pi_i\, p(u_i|e_i^+). \tag{13.78}$$

Proof For the replacement by subsets, see Note 13.70(iii). As illustrated in Figure 13.27, the parents of V_i^+ lie in V_i^+, which gives (13.76). Also

$$
\begin{aligned}
p(V_1^-, \ldots, V_s^-|x) = p(V^-|x) &= \Pi(\text{probability functions of } V^-) \text{ by (13.73b)}\\
&= \Pi_j\, (\text{probability functions of } V_j^-) \quad \text{see Figure 13.27}\\
&= \Pi_j\, [p(V_j^-, x)/p(x)] \quad \text{see Figure 13.27}\\
&= \Pi_j\, p(V_j^-|x).
\end{aligned}
$$

This proves (13.77). We prove (13.78) in the case when no e_i^+ coincides with U_i; further work handles this special case. Now, since u_i, e_i^+ are in V_i^+, we have

$$
\begin{aligned}
p(u|e^+) &= p(u, e^+)/p(e^+)\\
&= p(u_1, e_1^+, \ldots, u_r, e_r^+)/p(e_1^+, \ldots, e_r^+)\\
&= \Pi_i\, p(u_i, e_i^+)/\Pi_i\, p(e_i^+) \quad \text{by (13.76)}\\
&= \Pi_i\, [p(u_i, e_i^+)/p(e_i^+)]\\
&= \Pi_i\, p(u_i|e_i^+).
\end{aligned}
$$

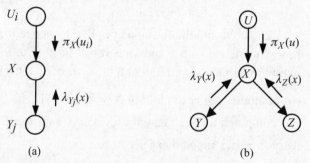

Figure 13.28 (a) A node X must receive a λ message from each child Y_i and a π message from each parent U_i, (b) the case of one parent, two children.

Computing Belief(x)

The key definitions in the Markov case hold good with the enlarged meaning of e^+ and e^-, namely $\lambda(x) = p(e^-|x)$, $\pi(x) = p(x|e^+)$, and $\text{Belief}(x) = p(x|e)$. To compute these, the node X is passed messages as depicted in Figure 13.28 and defined at (13.79) and (13.80). The results just obtained yield Theorem 13.74 below, enabling the calculation to be described concisely. We define

$$\pi_X(u_i) = p(u_i|e_i^+) \text{ for a parent } U_i \text{ of } X, \tag{13.79}$$

$$\lambda_{Yj}(x) = p(e_{Y_j}^-|x), \text{ for a child } Y \text{ of } X. \tag{13.80}$$

Theorem 13.74 *We have in the notation above that* $\text{Belief}(x) = \gamma\lambda(x)\pi(x)$, *where, with* $u = (u_1, \ldots, u_r)$,

$$\lambda(x) = \prod_{j=1}^{s} \lambda_{Yj}(x), \quad and \quad \pi(x) = \sum_u p(x|u) \prod_{i=1}^{r} \pi_X(u_i). \tag{13.81}$$

Proof The Markov case proof, that $\text{Belief}(x) = \gamma\lambda(x)\pi(x)$, holds formally for the enlarged meaning of $e^{\pm}$ because (13.75) says that X separates V^- from V^+. We have

$$\text{Belief}(x) = p(x|e) = p(x|e^-, e^+) = \gamma p(e^-|x, e^+) = p(x|e^+) \quad \text{by (13.70b)}$$
$$= \gamma p(e^-|x)p(x|e^+) \qquad \text{by (13.75), separation}$$
$$= \gamma\lambda(x)\pi(x) \qquad \text{by definition.}$$

$$\lambda(x) = p(e^-|x) = p(e_1^-, \ldots, e_s^-|x) \qquad \text{by definition}$$
$$= \Pi_j p(e_j^-|x) \quad \text{by (13.77),} \qquad \text{since } e_j^- \subseteq V_j^-$$
$$= \Pi_j \lambda_{Yj}(x) \quad \text{by (13.80), whereas}$$

$$\pi(x) = p(x|e^+)$$
$$= \sum_u p(x|u, e^+)p(u|e^+) \quad \text{by (13.70c)}$$
$$= \sum_u p(x|u)p(u|e^+) \qquad \text{by (13.66)}$$
$$= \sum_u p(x|u)\Pi_i p(u_i|e_i^+) \qquad \text{by (13.78)}$$
$$= \sum_u p(x|u)\Pi_i \pi_X(u_i) \qquad \text{by (13.79).}$$

The levels method

Referring to Figure 13.28 above and the formulae of (13.81), notice that the calculation of λs does not require knowledge of πs, and vice versa. Further, λ for X is computed from child λs and parent πs. An algorithm for computing them all must therefore satisfy:

$$\lambda \text{ is computed for each child of } X \text{ before } \lambda(x) \text{ itself,} \qquad (13.82a)$$

$$\pi \text{ is computed for each parent of } X \text{ before } \pi(x) \text{ itself,} \qquad (13.82b)$$

$$\text{every } \lambda, \pi \text{ is computed exactly once.} \qquad (13.82c)$$

Suppose for simplicity that our network allows only single parents. Then, starting from any node and proceeding against the arrows, we come to a unique source node S which we shall take as root, with all its arrows pointing downwards as in Figure 13.29(a). The *level* of each vertex V is its distance from S, the number of edges in the unique S–V path.

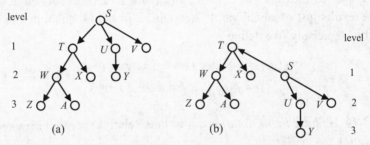

Figure 13.29 (a) A single parent network with root at source node S, showing the nodes level by level, (b) the same network with T selected as root. Notice how the subgraph S, U, V, Y is preserved one level down.

A method satisfying (13.82) Calculate the λs in one level at a time, from bottom to top, then the πs working from top to bottom. Does this work if *we replace S as root by another node T*, as depicted in Figure 13.29(b)? Certainly condition (13.82c) holds still. We must check that (13.82a, b) still hold in spite of any arrow reversals from down to up, such as that of $S \to T$. What happens in general is sufficiently illustrated in the case of Figure 13.30.

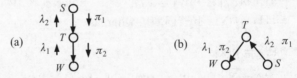

Figure 13.30 (a) Part of a Bayesian network, (b) the same with T as root node.

The order of computation in (a) is $\lambda_1, \lambda_2, \pi_1, \pi_2$ and in (b) it is λ_1 and π_1 in either order, followed by λ_2 and π_2 in either order. Thus (b) correctly maintains the order of λ_1

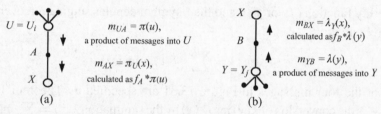

Figure 13.31 Achieving in two stages (a) the downward passing of π messages, or (b) the upward passing of λ messages. We see that (a) and (b) can be described in formally identical fashion. For the * notation see (13.83).

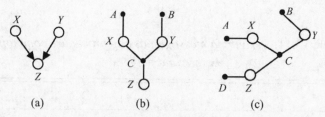

Figure 13.32 (a) Bayesian network, (b) its factor graph, (c) graph for Forward–Backward Algorithm, with Y chosen as root. The extra nodes A, B, D correspond to Remark 13.75.

before λ_2, and π_1 before π_2, and (13.82) remains true. Further, since a general Bayesian network may be split into single-parent ones (cf. Figure 13.27), the method is valid in this case too.

The factor graph

In search of an algorithm to implement Theorem 13.74 whilst keeping to the levels method, we convert the Bayesian network to its *factor graph* as follows. We add a node identified with each probability function. If node X has parents $U_1, \ldots, U_r$ we denote its probability function $p(x|u_1, \ldots, u_r)$ by f_A, say, add a node A (filled-in circle) and edge $A \to X$, and replace each edge $U_i \to X$ by an edge $U_i \to A$. The principle applies also to each child Y_j of X and its parents (which of course include X).

The result is indicated in the expansion of Figure 13.28(a) to the two diagrams of Figure 13.31; the conversion for a small but complete network is shown in Figure 13.32. The new node/function symbols are taken from early in the alphabet, whilst variables are denoted by later letters $U, \ldots, Z$. The name *factor graph* is appropriate because the new nodes specify the factorisation (13.67) of the network's joint pdf. Introducing it enables us to represent the two stages in message formation, implied by Theorem 13.74, by messages along its edges, and to handle both λ and π messages by a prescription which does not distinguish between them.

In Figure 13.31(a), the messages passed from U to A and from A to X are denoted by respectively m_{UA} and m_{AX}. Similarly for part (b). In both cases (see also below) we form a *product* $g(w)$ of messages, then change variables by forming a *sum* $f*g$, where f

is a probability function (f_A or f_B), and the $*$ symbol denotes summation over variables common to f and g:

$$(f^*g)(v) = \sum_w f(v, w)g(w). \tag{13.83}$$

Three out of the four messages in Figure 13.31 are specified by Theorem 13.74. The fourth, m_{BX}, is the conversion of $\lambda(y)$ into $\lambda(x)$ by the summation $\lambda(x) = \sum_y p(y|x)\lambda(y)$; where $p(y|x)$ plays the role of $f_B(x, y)$. And now, comparing the two halves of Figure 13.31, we discover the remarkable fact that *the same message-passing procedure can be carried out for both λ and π, albeit in opposite directions*. This single procedure is formulated in Table 13.11.

Table 13.11. *Deriving a message-passing procedure common to both λ and π types.*

	○——●		●——○	
λ	$m_{YB} = \prod_{C \neq B} m_{CY}$		$m_{BX} = f_B * \prod_{Z \neq X} m_{ZB}$	(Z is unique here)
π	$m_{UA} = \prod_{C \neq A} m_{CU}$	(C is unique here)	$m_{AX} = f_A * \prod_{Z \neq X} m_{ZA}$	
Both	$m_{XA} = \prod_{C \neq A} m_{CX}$	($XA = YB$ or UA)	$m_{AY} = f_A * \prod_{Z \neq Y} m_{ZA}$	($AY = AX$ or BX)

Remark 13.75 (i) *End-nodes* We can reduce the various end-node cases in Table 13.10 to one, in practice, by an extra function node A (see Figure 13.32, where $A = D$ for the terminal node Z). To formulate this, let $[\delta_{x,x'}]$ denote a pdf for X in which the probability of every value is zero except for $p(x') = 1$. The schema is:

Case ●——○
 A X

$$m_{AX} = f_A = \begin{cases} \text{estimated pdf for } X, & \text{if } X \text{ is a source node,} \\ [\delta_{x,x'}], & \text{if } X \text{ is observed as } x', \\ \gamma[1 1 \ldots 1] & \text{if } X \text{ is diagnostic but unobserved.} \end{cases}$$

(ii) *Nodes of degree 2* If node X is joined only to the function nodes A, B (see right), we have a shortcut

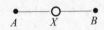

$$m_{XB} = m_{AX}.$$

Proof From Table 13.11 we have $m_{XB} = \Pi m_{DX}$ ($D \neq B$) $= m_{AX}$.

Belief(x) We note finally that the earlier formulation $\lambda(x)\pi(x)$ has become the product of all messages arriving at X, and so we have the algorithm below, with normalisation constant γ determined from $\sum_x \text{Belief}(x) = 1$.

> **ALGO 13.1** *The Forward–Backward Algorithm* for belief propagation in a Bayesian network (factor graph form)
>
> 1. Group the nodes in levels from a root, from right to left.
> 2. Perform message passing defined in Table 13.11, by levels, from extreme left forward, then back.
> 3. Return: for each internal network node X,
> $$\text{Belief}(x) = \gamma \prod_C m_{CX}(x).$$

Example 13.76 The dependent variables X, Y, Z take values 0, 1. The pdfs of X and Y are both given a prior estimation of [0.9 0.1]. Given that $f_C(x, y, 1) = p(z = 1|x, y)$ is the matrix $S = [s_{XY}]$ with rows [0.001 0.135] and [0.250 0.600], use the Forward–Backward Algorithm with root Y to determine Belief(x) and Belief(y) in the light of an observation $Z = 1$.

Solution Figure 13.32 shows steps (a), (b), (c) in forming the graph we are to use for the algorithm, with an extra node D catering for Z. Since Z is observed to take the *second* of the two range values, we give it the pdf $f_D = [0 \ 1]$. We are given $f_A = f_B = [0.9 \ 0.1]$ as initial estimates for the pdfs of X and Y. Notice that steps 1, 2 and 5 below use Remark 13.75(ii), and that we avoid unnecessary calculation in steps 5 and 6 (the steps are not level numbers).

Forwards
1. $m_{XC} = m_{AX} = f_A = [0.9 \ 0.1]$.
2. $m_{ZC} = m_{DZ} = f_D = [0 \ 1]$.
3. $m_{CY}(y) = \sum_{x,z} f_C(x, y, z) \, m_{ZC}(z) \, m_{XC}(x) = \sum_x p(z = 1|x, y) \, m_{XC}(x)$, using $m_{ZC}(0) = 0$. We can conveniently express this in matrix form because summation is over the first subscript in $S = [s_{xy}]$. In fact

$$m_{CY} = m_{XC}S = [0.9 \quad 0.1] \begin{bmatrix} 0.001 & 0.135 \\ 0.250 & 0.600 \end{bmatrix} = [0.026 \quad 0.182] \quad \text{(three decimal places)}.$$

4. $m_{BY} = f_B = [0.9 \quad 0.1]$.

Backwards
5. (m_{YB} is not needed) $m_{YC} = m_{BY} = [0.9 \quad 0.1]$.
6. (m_{CZ} is not needed) $m_{CX}(x) = \sum_{y,z} f_C(x, y, z)m_{YC}(y)m_{ZC}(z) = \sum_y f(x, y, 1)m_{YC}(y)$, whence $m_{CX} = m_{YC}S^T$ (summing over the *second* subscript in S)

$$= [0.9 \quad 0.1] \begin{bmatrix} 0.001 & 0.250 \\ 0.135 & 0.600 \end{bmatrix} = [0.014 \quad 0.285] \quad \text{(three decimal places)}.$$

Belief The messages have been propagated. Finally, $p(x|\text{data}) = \text{Belief}(x) = \gamma m_{AX}(x)m_{CX}(x)$, or, in vector form, $\gamma[0.9 \ 0.1] \circ [0.014 \ 0.285] = \gamma[0.013 \ 0.029] = [0.31 \ 0.69]$, whereas $p(y|\text{data}) = \gamma m_{BY}(y)m_{CY}(y)$, or, in vector form, $\gamma[0.9 \ 0.1] \circ$

$[0.026 \ 0.182] = \gamma[0.023 \ 0.018] = [0.56 \ 0.44]$.

	prior estimate	updated belief
$p(x)$	[0.9 0.1]	[0.31 0.69]
$p(y)$	[0.9 0.1]	[0.56 0.44]

This is a fairly radical updating of the prior estimate for both cases, in the light of an observed variable.

Exercise Repeat the forward step of Example 13.76 with X and Y having prior pdfs [0.8 0.2] (see Exercise 13.18).

The loopy case Although the Forward–Backwards Algorithm was established only for a network with no cycles, it is found to work in practice if some cycles are present. For progress in this case, see Frey and MacKay (1998) and McEliece and Yildirim (2003).

13.3.2 Convolutional codes

Rather than encoding binary data in blocks, a convolutional code takes an incoming data stream bit by bit and outputs in response two bits. These pairs are found by interleaving (taking alternate members of) two sequences $\{a_n\}$ and $\{b_n\}$, produced simultaneously from the original with the aid of a shift register. The code is called *systematic* if one sequence is in fact a duplicate of the input, and *non-recursive* if the shift register is used only in feed-forward mode (see Figures 13.21 and 13.22). Here is a non-recursive example.

Example 13.77 Encode the bit stream $u_6 \ldots u_1 u_0 = 1011010$ by the convolutional encoder shown in Figure 13.33.

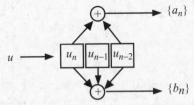

Figure 13.33 Convolutional encoding of an input sequence $u = u_0, u_1, \ldots$ The shift register is represented by three successive squares and is used in feed-forward mode for both sequences $\{a_n\}$ and $\{b_n\}$.

Solution In the convolutional code represented in Figure 13.33 we have, with $u_r = 0$ for $r < 0$ and $r > 6$,

$$c_{2n+1} = a_n = u_n + u_{n-2},$$
$$c_{2n} = b_n = u_n + u_{n-1} + u_{n-2}, \tag{13.84}$$

Table 13.12. *First few and last few steps in encoding the bit stream $u_6 \ldots u_1 u_0$.*

register $u_n\ u_{n-1}\ u_{n-2}$	Output a	Output b
$u_0\ \ 0\ \ 0$	$a_0 = u_0$	$b_0 = u_0$
$u_1\ u_0\ \ 0$	$a_1 = u_1$	$b_1 = u_1 + u_0$
$u_2\ u_1\ u_0$	$a_2 = u_2 + u_0$	$b_2 = u_2 + u_1 + u_0$
$\ldots$	$\ldots$	$\ldots$
$u_6\ u_5\ u_4$	$a_6 = u_6 + u_4$	$b_6 = u_6 + u_5 + u_4$
$0\ \ u_6\ u_5$	$a_7 = u_5$	$b_7 = u_6 + u_5$
$0\ \ 0\ \ u_6$	$a_8 = u_6$	$b_8 = u_6$

or in polynomial form $a(x) = (1 + x^2)u(x)$, $b(x) = (1 + x + x^2)u(x)$, $c(x) = xa(x^2) + b(x^2)$.

The easiest way 'by hand' is probably to perform polynomial multiplication for $a(x), b(x)$, then to interleave their coefficients directly. The calculation is shown to the right. The result is shown below, with a_n bold:

c = (**1101**)   00**1**0**1**0**0**0**0**1**1**1**00

(The bracketed bits are appended as u leaves the register, the first and last states being zero (see Table 13.12).

1011010	$u(x)$
101	$1+x^2$
1011010	
1011010	
100110010	$a(x)$
1011010	$xu(x)$
110000110	$b(x)$

The state diagram as encoder

A natural first thought is to equate the encoder state with the register bits, but instead it is more convenient to proceed as follows. When the shift register of a convolutional encoder contains $u_n \ldots u_{n-r}$, the *state* of the encoder is defined to be the binary word $u_{n-1} \ldots u_{n-r}$. The *input* bit is then u_n. The encoder is (by definition) a Finite State Machine, because it possesses a finite number of states, and the input and present state determine the output and next state. This connection, which we must explore, is conveniently seen in a state diagram, namely a directed graph with nodes $s_0, s_1, \ldots$ representing the possible states, and a directed edge $s_i \rightarrow s_j$ labelled $u_n/a_n b_n$ if input u_n and state s_i result in output $a_n b_n$ and next state s_j.

Example 13.78 In Figure 13.34 we give the state diagram for the encoder above, with the necessary information first calculated in table form to the left, from (13.84).

To encode our bit stream $u_6 \ldots u_1 u_0 = 1011010$ directly from the state diagram we simply follow successive edges whose labels have first digits $u_n = 0, 1, 0, 1, 1, 0, 1$ (then $0, 0$). The input starts with $u_0 = 0$ when the initial state is 00. We locate the edge outwards from this state whose label begins with $0 (= u_0)$. The complete label is $0/00$ so the output is 00. Further, this edge returns to state 00. However, the next input bit $u_1 = 1$ corresponds to an outward edge labelled $1/11$ so the output this time is 11. Now we have arrived at state

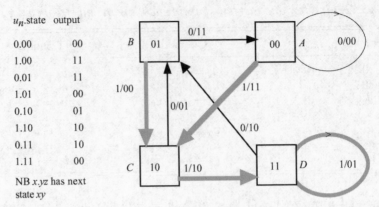

u_n.state	output
0.00	00
1.00	11
0.01	11
1.01	00
0.10	01
1.10	10
0.11	10
1.11	00

NB $x.yz$ has next state xy

Figure 13.34 State diagram for the convolutional encoder of Figure 13.33. The four states are represented by squares. A transition in response to input bit 0 is represented by a black arrow and response to input 1 by grey. An arrow labelled $u_n/a_n b_n$ denotes a transition in which bit u_n is input and bits a_n, b_n output. The given input stream is followed by zeros.

10, from which $u_2 = 0$ results in output 01. Continuing thus, and setting $u_7 = u_8 = 0$, we obtain as before the codeword $c_{17} \ldots c_0 = 11\ 01\ 00\ 10\ 10\ 00\ 01\ 11\ 00$.

Exercise Encode $u_6 \ldots u_1 u_0 = 0101001$.

Trellis diagrams for decoding

For illustration we have discussed the encoding of a bit stream of length only 7. By contrast, in practice, the stream may contain many thousands of bits. But although there is no theoretical limit on length, it will eventually terminate, and what is received after encoding and transmission is a finite word R which we can regard as a corruption (potentially) of an original finite codeword. We describe an ingenious technique for simultaneously decorrupting R and recovering the original bit stream (later we'll see how belief networks fit in).

A *trellis diagram* for a convolutional encoder is a graph whose nodes consist of a copy of those of the state diagram for each time/encoding step $t = 0, 1, 2, \ldots$, with a copy of each $s_i \rightarrow s_j$ edge, now running from s_i at time t to s_j at time $t + 1$. This has the great advantage that an encoding corresponds to a path in the trellis diagram from $t = 0$ to the greatest value t_{max}. Figure 13.35 shows the trellis diagram derived from the state diagram of Figure 13.34 for $t = 0$ to 7, the steps that handle an input stream of length 5. Above it is placed a sample received word R.

For the states we use the notation A, B, C, D of Figure 13.34. Let x_t be the node for state x at time t. Then the path for a complete encoding starts at A_0 and ends at A_7, because A is the all-zeros state. Notice that, by definition, each edge is part of a parallel set corresponding to a single edge of the state diagram, one copy for each time step; hence the name *trellis*. For decoding purposes we attach the output labels only to the

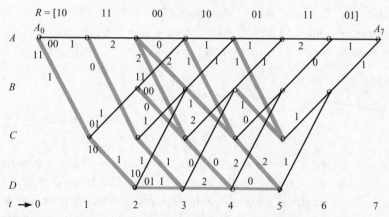

Figure 13.35 A received vector R, followed by the trellis diagram derived from Figure 13.34, for decoding R. Every edge is reproduced for each time step. See the text for details.

leftmost representatives. Thus the edge from A_t to C_{t+1} is labelled with a small 11 in the case $t = 0$.

The decoding of a sample received vector R proceeds as follows. We label each trellis edge with the Hamming distance 0, 1 or 2 between the 2-bit output obtained on traversing that edge and the corresponding bit pair of R. These distances may be verified for the vector R shown above the trellis diagram, in which they have been inserted. Summed for a path from A_0 to A_7, they give the Hamming distance of R from the codeword defined by that path. For example, the path $ACBACDBA$ gives distance 9 (the reader should check this). The following result says that we should minimise this total distance to determine the *maximum likelihood* original codeword.

Theorem 13.79 *Let each input bit to a convolutional encoder be 0 or 1 with equal probability $1/2$, and have a fixed probability of transmission error $p < 1/2$. Then the original codeword corresponds, with maximum likelihood, to a path through the trellis diagram whose length (in the sense specified above) is minimal.*

Proof We are assuming the discrete memoryless channel of Example 13.17 and so, if the original codeword was c, of length N, and its Hamming distance from R was w, then w bits were changed, in each case with probability p, and $N - w$ bits were unchanged, with probability $1 - p$. Therefore we have the likelihood, similarly to (13.13),

$$p(y|c) = p^w(1 - p)^{N-w} \text{ (N-bit words).} \tag{13.85}$$

On the other hand, $d/dw[\log p(y|c)] = d/dw[w \log p + (N - w) \log(1 - p)] = \log p - \log(1 - p) = \log[p/(1 - p)]$, which is negative because $0 < p < 1/2$ implies $p < 1 - p$. This proves the theorem.

Viterbi's decoder *Consider this observation.* If, in a trellis diagram, node x is on a minimal path from node v to node z, then the section of the path leading from v to x is minimal; otherwise we could shorten it and so reduce the v–z path.

In keeping with Viterbi's notation let the *metric* of a path (we have just been calling it simply distance) be the sum of the distance labels along it. A *survivor* of a set of v–z paths is one of least metric amongst them; by this definition there is always at least one survivor! Now we can state the algorithm which gives maximum likelihood decoding for a convolutional code, based on the preceding observation.

> *ALGO 13.2 (Viterbi) A path of least metric from $t = 0$ to greatest time t_{max} of a trellis.*
>
> For $t = 0$ to $t_{max} - 1$ do
> For each surviving path up to time t,
> determine the metrics of extensions to time $t + 1$,
> and keep only the survivors.

Example 13.80 We apply Viterbi's algorithm to decode the received vector R of Figure 13.35. The successive steps are charted in Figure 13.36. At each stage of the iteration we show possible path extensions, with surviving paths and their destination states indicated in bold.

For example, two paths survive to time $t = 1$, but only one to $t = 2$. By $t = 3$ there are two survivors, $a_0 a_1 c_2 b_3$ and $a_0 a_1 c_2 d_3$. By $t = 7$ there is a unique survivor $a_0 a_1 c_2 d_3 b_4 c_5 b_6 a_7$. Following this path in the trellis diagram gives 00 11 10 10 00 01 11 as the most likely correct codeword. The original input stream is easily obtained by following the same order $a_0 a_1 c_2 d_3 b_4 c_5 b_6 a_7$ in the state diagram, which gives $u_0 \ldots u_6 = 0110100$. Reversing the bit order, to compare with Figure 13.33, we have $u_6 \ldots u_0 = 0010110$. Since the encoder appends 00 to every codeword, the original bit stream was 10110. By

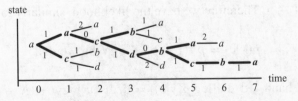

Figure 13.36 Possible 1-step paths starting at times $0, 1, \ldots, 6$, with surviving paths and their destination states shown bold.

implication it is one of $2^5 = 32$ possibilities and, inspecting the trellis diagram, we see, by way of confirmation, that there are exactly 2^5 distinct paths from left to right.

Exercise What was the distance from R of the most likely codeword in the example above?

13.3.3 Convolutional decoding by belief propagation

We outline the recent belief network approach to convolutional decoding. This time the state of the encoder is taken to be the whole contents of the register, for omitting the first bit as we did in the previous section results in (possibly undirected) cycles in the proposed network, which is then not singly connected (see Assumption 13.68). The variables are as follows. At time t we have input bit u_t, state s_t, output bits c_{2t}, c_{2t+1}, and their possibly corrupted versions y_{2t} and y_{2t+1} after transmission through a noisy channel. We consider firstly the case of a convolutional code that is systematic, that is $c_{2n} = u_n$. The result is Figure 13.37, with the probability functions to be defined below.

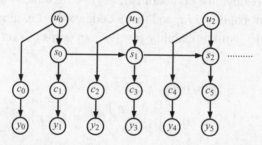

Figure 13.37 Bayesian network for a systematic convolutional code (after Frey, 1998). Removing the horizontal arrows reveals a sequence of connected units, each characterised by the unique s_t node it contains.

Deterministic relations Of course, some of our variables depend on others in a deterministic way, but we can nevertheless incorporate such relations in the structure by allocating probability 1 to outcomes which must be certain. This guarantees their occurrence, because ranges are finite. We can express the probability functions in a form suitable for computer implementation by using the Kronecker delta function: $\delta(v, w) = 1$ if $v = w$, and 0 otherwise. The result of this discusion is summarised in Table 13.13.

(i) *States* The encoder state at time t is by definition the sequence $s_t = u_t u_{t-1} \ldots u_{t-M}$, where the integer M is called the encoder's *memory*. Since $s_{t-1} = u_{t-1} \ldots u_{t-M-1}$ we may say that s_t is a function ρ of s_{t-1} and u_t, writing $s_t = \rho(s_{t-1}, u_t)$, where ρ returns the concatenation of u_t and the first M bits of s_{t-1}. We convert this to a probability function by the argument that, for $t \geq 1$,

$$
\begin{aligned}
p(s_t|s_{t-1}, u_t) &= p(S_t = s_t | S_{t-1} = s_{t-1}, U_t = u_t) && \text{by definition} \\
&= 1 \text{ if } s_t = \rho(s_{t-1}, u_t), \text{ otherwise } 0 && \text{by probability} \\
&= \delta(s_t, \rho(s_{t-1}, u_t)) && \text{by definition.}
\end{aligned}
$$

Table 13.13. *Deterministic relations converted to probability functions for a class of convolutional codes (systematic, non-recursive).*

original	probability function	remarks
$s_0 = [u_0 \ 0 \dots \ 0]$	$p(s_0\|u_0) = \delta(s_0, u_0)$	two values
$s_t = \rho(s_{t-1}, u_t),$	$p(s_t\|s_{t-1}, u_t) =$	ρ: prefix u_t to s_t, delete u_{t-M-1}
$\quad t \geq 1$	$\delta(s_t, \rho(s_{t-1}, u_t))$	
$c_{2t} = u_t$	$p(c_{2t}\|u_t) = \delta(c_{2t}, u_t)$	
$c_{2t+1} = \beta \cdot s_t$	$p(c_{2t+1}\|s_t) = \delta(c_{2t+1}, \beta \cdot s_t)$	$\beta = (\beta_i), s_t = [u_t \ u_{t-1} \ \dots \ u_{t-M}]$

(ii) *The sequences interleaved* The equality $c_{2t} = u_t$ becomes $p(c_{2t}|u_t) = \delta(c_{2t}, u_t)$, whilst c_{2t+1} is a linear combination of the bits of s_t, which we may write compactly as a dot product $\beta \cdot s_t$, where $\beta = (\beta_0, \dots, \beta_M)$. Then $p(c_{2t+1}|s_t) = \delta(c_{2t+1}, \beta \cdot s_t)$

Probabilistic relations Notice that, in the notation of Example 13.77, we have $b(x) = \beta(x)u(x)$. For the more obviously probabilistic part, we assume as usual that an input bit is 0 or 1 with equal probability $1/2$, and that a codeword bit is subject to channel error, flipped between 0 and 1, with probability $p < 1/2$. In terms of vectors and matrices this becomes

$$[p(u_t)] = [1/2 \ \ 1/2], \tag{13.86}$$

$$[p(y_t|c_t)] = \begin{bmatrix} q & p \\ p & q \end{bmatrix} \ (q = 1 - p). \tag{13.87}$$

Applying the Forward–Backward Algorithm The code's Bayesian/belief network shown in Figure 13.37 consists of units like those of Figure 13.38, each unit joined to the next by an edge $s_t \to s_{t+1}$, whilst our objective is to determine the 2-value pdf $p(u_t|$ the data) and hence the MAP estimate of u_t, for each t involved. For this we proceed as far as necessary with the Forward–Backward Algorithm. Notice that, in Figure 13.38, function nodes are introduced in accordance with Remarks 13.75 as follows. Nodes A, H incorporate the measured values of the received bits y_i, whilst B, G supply the assumed probability $1/2$ of error in those bits. The function identified with D is the assumed pdf $[1/2 \ 1/2]$ for each u_t.

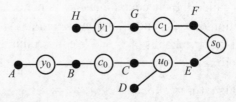

Figure 13.38 The first s_t unit in the belief network of Figure 13.37, shown in factor graph form. For more details, see the text.

One way to implement the Forward–Backward Algorithm is, referring also to Figure 13.37:

(a) for *each t*, propagate forward to E and F for the unit, and store the results at S_t,
(b) with the information from (a), propagate forwards along $s_0 \to s_1 \to \cdots$, then back to s_0,
(c) for each t, propagate from s_t to u_t (no more is needed).

Example 13.81 We perform step (a) in the case $t = 0$, supposing that the shift register part has $\beta_0 = 1$, and the transmitted bits are received as $y_0, y_1, \ldots = 1, 0, \ldots$ Considering Table 13.13, we have a complete list of the probability functions in matrix form after noting that, with I_2 as 2×2 identity matrix,

$$[p(c_0|u_0)] = I_2 = [p(s_0|u_0)] = [p(c_1|s_0)]. \tag{13.88}$$

The first two equalities are equivalent to the formulae $p(c_0|u_0) = \delta(c_0, u_0)$ and $p(s_0|u_0) = \delta(s_0, u_0)$ from Table 13.13. For the third we observe that the matrix $[p(c_1|s_0)] = [\delta(c_1, \beta \cdot s_0)]$ has rows indexed by s_0, whose two possible values are (i) $[00\ldots0]$, giving $c_1 = \beta \cdot s_0 = 0$, and (ii) $[10\ldots0]$, giving $c_1 = \beta \cdot s_0 = 1$.

The top layer of unit 0

(1) $m_{Y_1 G} = m_{HY_1}$ (Remark 13.75(ii)) = $[1\ 0]$ (Remark 13.75(i)), since the *observed* value of y_1 is the first value in its range (in this case, 0).
(2) $m_{C_1 F} = m_{GC_1} = m_{Y_1 G}[p(y_1|c_1)]^{\mathrm{T}}$ (the sum is over y_1 since the result is a function of c_1) =
$$[1\ 0]\begin{bmatrix} q & p \\ p & q \end{bmatrix} \text{(by (13.87))} = [q\ p].$$
(3) Similarly $m_{FS_0} = m_{C_1 F}[p(c_1|s_0)]^{\mathrm{T}} = [q\ \ p]I_2$ (by (13.88)) = $[q\ \ p]$.

The second layer of unit 0

(4) $m_{Y_0 B} = m_{AY_0} = [0\ 1]$, since the observed value of y_0 is the second in its range.
(5) $m_{C_0 C} = m_{BC_0} = m_{Y_0 B}[p(y_0|c_0)]^{\mathrm{T}} = [0\ \ 1]\begin{bmatrix} q & p \\ p & q \end{bmatrix}$ (by (13.87)) = $[p\ q]$.
(6) $m_{CU_0} = m_{C_0 C}[p(c_0|u_0)]^{\mathrm{T}} = [p\ q]I_2 = [p\ \ q]$.
(7) $m_{ES_0} = m_{U_0 E}[p(s_0|u_0)] = m_{U_0 E}I_2 = m_{U_0 E}$

$$= m_{CU_0} \circ m_{DU_0} = [p\ q] \circ [1/2\ \ 1/2] = (1/2)[p\ q].$$

(Further short cuts are possible, though we do not pursue them here.)

13.3.4 Turbocodes

To describe the turbocodes of Berrou, Glavieux and Thitimajshima (1993), the remarkable codes so close in performance to Shannon's predicted optimum, we need a little more on convolutional codes. Turbocodes are usually built by combining systematic convolutional codes which are *recursive*.

This means that, although as before we interleave two sequences $\{a_n\}$ and $\{b_n\}$, of which a_n is a copy of the incoming bit u_n, and b_n is produced by the register in feed-forward mode, there is a modification to the register input: it is now u_n plus a bit d_n obtained by linear feedback. The result is called an *RSC code*, for 'recursive systematic convolutional'. To illustrate this we have converted one feedforward part of the encoder shown in Figure 13.33 into feedback, giving Figure 13.39.

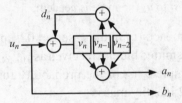

Figure 13.39 Recursive systematic convolutional code (adapted from Figure 13.33).

Polynomial description The register bits are no longer taken from the input, so let us denote them by $v_n, \ldots, v_{n-M}$. Then feedforward coefficients $g_0 \ldots g_M$ determine the output by $a_k = \sum g_i v_{k-i}$ $(0 \le i \le M)$ and the feedback coefficients $f_1 \ldots f_M$ invoke the input by $v_n = u_n + \sum f_i v_{n-i}$ $(1 \le i \le M)$, which may be rearranged (Mod 2) as $u_n = \sum f_i v_{n-i}$ $(0 \le i \le M, f_0 = 1)$. In polynomial terms $a(x) = g(x)v(x)$ and $u(x) = f(x)v(x)$, from which we eliminate $v(x)$ to obtain

$$f(x)a(x) = g(x)u(x). \tag{13.89}$$

Example 13.82 Consider the recursive systematic convolutional code represented in Figure 13.39. Equation (13.89) becomes $(1 + x^2)a(x) = (1 + x + x^2)u(x)$. Strictly speaking, this is a result for infinitely long input sequence $\{u_n\}$ and output $\{a_n\}$, because we cannot in general divide the right hand side by $1 + x^2$ but must resort to using $(1 + x^2)^{-1} = 1 + x^2 + x^4 + \cdots$.

Turbocodes Figure 13.40 represents a standard construction of turbocodes by using two RSC codes C_1, C_2 in parallel, with a second characteristic feature, that of scrambling the input before feeding it to the second RSC code C_2. The scrambling is always a form of interleaving, which means that we repeatedly buffer a fixed number of input bits and send them on in a different sequence. This is crucial for the superb performance of turbocodes.

A rough argument is as follows (see Berrou and Glavieux, 1996). We want to achieve maximum scattering of the data; a certain bit may be corrupted, but hopefully there will be bits at a safe distance which ensure correction. This, of course, goes with the long codewords associated with the Shannon limit (Remarks 13.37). An approach in the present context is that we want to create as many changes as possible in the (sequence-wise) distances between pairs of input bits before sending them to the second RSC code. Suppose we do this in sections of $N = m^2$ bits. That is, we have a function d sending $1, \ldots, N$ to the same set in a different order. Heegard and Wicker (1998) define a measure of the effectiveness of this function, the *dispersion* $\gamma(d)$, or proportion of pairs whose

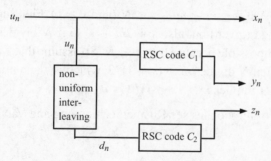

Figure 13.40 A typical turbocode, the parallel concatenation of two RSC codes with non-uniform interleaving. The variable x_n plays the role of the systematic parts of both RSC codes. The emerging output bits x_n, y_n, z_n are interleaved in threes. The rate of the turbocode is 1/3 since the output is three times as long as the input.

relative positions are changed. That is,

$$\gamma = |\{(\Delta_x, \Delta_y) : \Delta_x = b - a, \ \Delta_y = d(b) - d(a), \ 1 \le a < b \le N\}|/_N C_2, \quad (13.90)$$

where $|A|$ denotes the size of a set A (repeats are deleted, above) and $_N C_2 = N(N-1)/2$, the number of distinct pairs of integers lying from 1 to N.

Let us illustrate why non-uniformity is required. Uniform interleaving in this context amounts to writing the first $N = m^2$ integers row by row into an $m \times m$ matrix, then reading them column by column. This gives, in case $m = 3$,

$$\begin{bmatrix} 1 & 2 & 3 \\ 4 & 5 & 6 \\ 7 & 8 & 9 \end{bmatrix}, \text{ and so } 1, 2, \dots, 9 \text{ becomes } 1, 4, 7, 2, 5, 8, 3, 6, 9. \text{ The dispersion is}$$

$$|\{\{1, -5\}, \{1, 3\}, \{2, -2\}, \{2, 6\}, \{3, 1\}, \{4, -4\}, \{4, 4\}, \{5, -1\}, \{5, 7\}, \{6, 2\},$$
$$\{7, 5\}, \{8, 8\}\}|/36 = 1/3.$$

In fact, this innocent 1/3 disguises the fact that in the uniform case, dispersion tends to zero as N increases (Exercise 13.22). By contrast, a truly random procedure yields approximately $\gamma = 0.81$. Takeshita and Costello (2000) propose a non-uniform interleaving which satisfies the criteria of (a) reasonably high dispersion at approximately 0.72, and (b) simple to implement, of little computational cost. We give a partial proof.

Theorem 13.83 *Let k and r be positive integers, with k odd. Let $N = 2^r$ and define a non-uniform interleaving $d(m) = c_m$, where*

$$c_m = km(m+1)/2 \ (reduced \ \text{Mod} \ N), 0 \le m < N. \quad (13.91)$$

Then (i) c_m may be computed in linear fashion, $c_m = c_{m-1} + km \ (\text{Mod} \ N)$, and (ii) the sequence $\{c_m\}$ has greatest possible period, N.

Proof (i) We have $c_0 = 0$ and for $m \ge 1$ we calculate $c_m - c_{m-1} = (k/2)[m(m+1) - (m-1)m] = km$, as required. For (ii), observe that $c_{m+s} - c_m = (k/2)[(m+s)(m+s+1) - m(m+1)] = (k/2)s(s + 2m + 1)$. We must show that this cannot be 0 Mod N, that is, divisible by N, if $0 \le m < m + s < N$ (and $s \ge 1$). First suppose that s is even. Then not only k is odd (given) but also $s + 2m + 1$, so if N divides $c_{m+s} - c_m$ then N divides s, which is impossible because $0 < s < N$. So assume that s is odd. But now if N divides $c_{m+s} - c_m$ then N divides $m + (s + 1)/2$, which is again impossible on grounds of size, because $s \ge 1$ implies $m + (s + 1)/2 \le m + s$.

For further analysis of turbocodes see Rusmeviechientong and Van Roy (2001).

13.4 Postscript: Bayesian nets in computer vision

In Section 13.3 we developed belief propagation in Bayesian nets, for their application to codes for protecting transmitted data, including image data. But belief networks can be an important tool in a probabilistic approach to computer vision itself when Bayesian methods are to be used, typically in a high-level use under the heading of Image Understanding. Here are some examples.

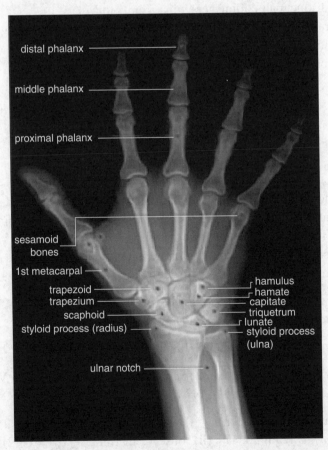

Figure 13.41 Radiograph of the human hand (Dartmouth College).

Example 13.84 (*Auto-detection of arthritic conditions in the hand, based on radiographs*) This proposed system by Levitt *et al.* (1993) points to the great potential of large belief networks.

Objective The input to the system consists of X-ray pictures of a human hand. The output consists of likelihoods of a variety of arthritic situations being present, or a statement that evidence so far is insufficient for a reliable conclusion (or is contradictory).

Method A Bayesian belief network, updated by successive pieces of evidence obtained by feature extraction (low-level image processing) from available radiographs. Included in the system is a mechanism for predicting the presence of further features and testing for them.

Model A 53-part 3-dimensional model is proposed, with pdfs for its parameters sourced from statistics of the population at large. Typical items are dimensions and relative sizes of the phalanges, the bones inside the digits (fingers and thumb), and metacarpals, the bones of the palm. See Figure 13.41. There is a 2-level hierarchy describing relations (a) between digits and their component metacarpals, and (b) between phalanges and their surrounding entities.

Priors Based on the general population we estimate prior probabilities of the kind *P*(phalanx information | evidence).

Further applications of belief networks

1. What kind of image? Jepson and Mann (1999).
2. 3D interpretation of images, Mann and Binford (1992).
3. Video surveillance. Park and Aggarval (2003).
4. Human motion analysis. Aggarval and Cai (1999).
5. Document analysis. Souafi-Bensafi *et al.* (2002).
6. Medical image segmentation. Levitt *et al.* (1993).
7. Analysis of aerial urban images. Jaynes *et al.* (2003).
8. Protein image analysis. Leherte *et al.* (1997).
9. Learning iris recognition. Freeman *et al.* (2002).

Further issues in channel coding

Zero-error capacity It is possible to find a channel capacity under the constraint that noise be eliminated, according to Shannon (1956). An important contribution was made with combinatorial techniques by Lovasz (1979).

Channels with memory As is common, we proved the Channel Coding Theorem for memoryless channels. A recent application of channels *with* memory is in wireless networking. For theory in this case see e.g. Rossi *et al.* (2004) and references therein.

Exercises 13

1 √ Let (X, Y) be a discrete memoryless channel with input and output symbols $\{0, 1\}$. Suppose that input 1 is twice as likely as input 0 and that, on the average, one in ten symbols 0 are changed to 1 and twice as many the other way. (i) Construct a transition graph and matrix. (ii) What is the likelihood of a successful transition? (iii) Use the formula $[p(y)] = [p(x)]Q$ of (13.4) to find whether more 0s or more 1s arrive over time.

2 √ Prove that an (X, Y) channel satisfies (i) $H(X, X) = H(X) = I(X; X)$, (ii) $H(Y) - H(Y|X) = I(X; Y)$.

3 √ A channel (X, Y) with input/output alphabet $\{0, 1\}$ satisfies $[p(x)] = [1/2 \ 1/2]$ and $P(Y = 0|X = 1) = P(Y = 1|X = 0) = 1/4$. Determine (i) $H(X)$ and $H(Y)$, (ii) $H(Y|X)$ and $I(X; Y)$.

4 √ The channel (X, Y) has $R_X = \{0, a, -a\}$ $(a \neq 0)$, with pdf $p = (1/2, 1/4, 1/4)$ and Y determined from X by $Y = X^2$. Show that $\text{Cov}(X, Y) = 0$ but I detects the dependence: $I(X; Y) \neq 0$.

5 √ (a) Compute $I(X; Y)$ for Example 13.20 with $p = 0.2$. (b) Prove (13.18b).

6 √ (i) Each matrix below is the transition matrix of a DMC. In any case that is symmetric, calculate the capacity C_{max}. (ii) Let $p_1 + \cdots + p_r = 1$ $(p_i \geq 0)$. Prove that $H(p_1/2, \ldots, p_r/2, p_1/2, \ldots, p_r/2) = H(p_1, \ldots, p_r) + \log 2$. Hence explain the coincidence of two answers in (i).

$$\begin{bmatrix} 1/3 & 2/3 \\ 2/3 & 1/3 \end{bmatrix}, \begin{bmatrix} 1/4 & 1/2 & 1/4 \\ 1/2 & 1/4 & 1/4 \end{bmatrix}, \begin{bmatrix} 1/6 & 1/12 & 1/6 & 1/12 & 1/6 & 1/12 & 1/6 & 1/12 \\ 1/12 & 1/6 & 1/12 & 1/6 & 1/12 & 1/6 & 1/12 & 1/6 \end{bmatrix}.$$

7 √ A code C has generator matrix $G = \text{Rows}[R_i] = \text{Rows}[01101, 11101, 11011]$. (i) List all the codewords as linear combinations of the R_i. (ii) Deduce using (i) that the rows of G are independent. (iii) Show that three nonzero codewords are independent if no two are equal and their sum is not zero. (iv) Find a generator matrix of C that involves no row of G. (v) Is the code C cyclic?

8 √ A code C has codewords $y = y_1 \ldots y_7$ defined by $y_r = y_{r+2} + y_{r+3} + y_{r+4}$ $(1 \leq r \leq 3)$. (i) Write down the parity check matrix H and use row operations to convert H so that the first three columns form an identity matrix (reduced echelon form). Write down the new form of the equations. (ii) List eight codewords using (i), check that the code includes 1111111, and hence list the other eight. (iii) Write down a generator matrix. (iv) State the minimum distance of C. How many errors can C correct? (v) Apply nearest neighbour decoding to 1001101, 0110001, 1110101, 0001111, 1011001.

9 √ (i) Sequences (x_i) and (y_i) satisfy a linear recurrence relation $z_n = c_1 z_{n-1} + c_2 z_{n-2} + \cdots + c_r z_{n-r}$ $(n \geq r)$. Show that their sum satisfies the same relation. (ii) Construct a pcm for a cyclic Hamming code of length 7 using the relation $x_t = x_{t-1} + x_{t-3}$. (iii) Show that there is no (18.10) binary code that corrects three errors. (iv) Verify from formula (13.46) that $g = 1$ when $a_{-r} \ldots a_{-1} = 10 \ldots 0$.

10 √ (i) Without performing division, show that $x + 1$ is not a factor of $x^3 + x + 1$ or of $x^3 + x^2 + 1$. (ii) Multiply the polynomials of (i) by longhand and by shorthand. Do you get the same answer? (iii) To factorise $x^5 + x + 1$, what single division is required? Perform it and draw the appropriate conclusion. Is $x^6 + x^4 + 1$ irreducible? (iv) Show the rules of (13.53) do not depend on choice of representatives.

11 √ Let F be the finite field defined by $p(x) = x^4 + x^3 + 1$. With $\alpha = [x]$ as usual, express α^4 as a polynomial $a_3a_2a_1a_0$ (abbreviated form). (i) Hence tabulate the powers of α in this form. (ii) What are the orders of α^i for $1 \le i \le 6$? (iii) How does the table show that α is primitive? (iv) Repeat the table for $p(x) = 1 + x + \cdots + x^4$. Is this polynomial primitive?

12 √ (i) Let β be an element of order e in a finite field. Show that $\beta^t = 1$ if and only if e divides t. (ii) Make a table of minimal polynomials (Table 13.7) for elements of the finite field defined by $p(x) = x^4 + x^3 + 1$.

13 √ A cyclic code of size 16 contains the words 1111111 and 0111001. Find a generator polynomial and hence a generator matrix and pcm. Is the code of Hamming type?

14 √ (This requires the solution to Exercise 13.12.) Construct a generator matrix for the BCH(15, 3) code defined by the primitive polynomial $x^4 + x^3 + 1$ and encode 11000.

15 (i) Construct a generator matrix for the Reed–Solomon code of type RS(7, 2) defined by the primitive polynomial $x^3 + x^2 + 1$. Encode $[1\ 0\ \alpha]$. (ii) For the RS code of Example 13.62, error-correct and decode the received word $R = [\alpha^5\ \alpha\ 1\ \alpha^2\ 0\ \alpha^3\ 1]$.

16 √ Perform the verification promised in Example 13.66(ii).

17 √ Prove (13.70c): $p(z|x) = \sum_y p(z|x, y)p(y|x)$ (Hint: $p(x, z) = \sum_y p(x, y, z)$).

18 Repeat the forward step of Example 13.76 with X and Y having prior pdfs [0.8 0.2].

19 Encode $u_6 \ldots u_0$ in the convolutional encoder of Example 13.78.

20 (i) Verify the distances for the received vector R in the trellis diagram of Figure 13.35. (ii) Check that the path *ACBACDBA* gives distance 9 from R. (iii) What is the distance from R of the most likely codeword in Example 13.80?

21 Check the details of Example 13.81.

22 Show that, in the uniform case, dispersion tends to zero as N increases (see (13.90)).

Part V

Transforming the image

14

The Fourier Transform

The Fourier Transform is a wonderful way of splitting a function into helpful parts, possibly modifying those parts and putting them back together again. One gains insight and/or the power to change things in a desired direction. Here we are particularly interested in its value for interpreting and restoring digital image data. Although the story of the Fourier Transform really begins with the so-called continuous case, where the definitions are integrals, our main concern is with the discrete version, which in any case is what is generally used when implementing even the continuous transform. We come to the continuous case second.

We begin in Section 14.1 with basic definitions and tools rooted in simple yet powerful properties of the complex numbers. We introduce filtering and the Convolution Theorem, two reasons for the wide use of the transform. Redundancy in the DFT is utilised to arrive at the Fast Fourier Transform (FFT), which reduces the complexity of calculation from $O(N^2)$ to $O(N \log_2 N)$, another reason for the DFT's ubiquity.

The short Section 14.2 introduces the Continuous Fourier Transform and its tool the Dirac delta function, concluding with the highly desirable properties listed in Table 14.2. In Section 14.3 we explore connections between the three types of Fourier Transform: Fourier series, the continuous transform, and the DFT; noting that for a finite interval appropriately sampled the DFT is a good approximation to the continuous version.

This chapter anticipates the next, in which we extend all things to two dimensions. By then we can model many effects, such as motion or focus blur, by the technique of convolution, which is handled especially simply by the Fourier Transform. This simplicity enables us to restore an image from many kinds of noise and other corruption.

14.1 The Discrete Fourier Transform

14.1.1 Basic definitions and properties

The Fourier Transform A wide and useful class of functions $f(x)$ can be reconstructed from their measured, or *sampled*, values f_i at N equally spaced points, for some N (see Section 14.3.3). The *N-point (discrete) Fourier Transform* $f \to F$ converts the N-vector

f of values $f_0, \ldots, f_{N-1}$ into an N-vector F of values $F_0, \ldots, F_{N-1}$, by

$$F_k = \sum_{n=0}^{N-1} e^{-2\pi i k n/N} f_n. \tag{14.1}$$

What does this mean? Firstly, the form of (14.1) means that, with f and F as columns (here preferred), the transform can be expressed in matrix form, $F = Tf$. Secondly, the F_k are complex numbers (see Section 8.1.1) so their introduction should be justified by their advantages (it is). Thirdly, a first hint of these benefits emerges when we denote $e^{-2\pi i/N}$ by a single variable w, and invoke the laws of complex numbers to write $e^{-2\pi i k n/N} = w^{kn}$. This enables us to write (14.1) in a simple form:

$$F = Tf, \quad \text{where}$$
$$T = [w^{kn}], \quad \text{and} \quad w = e^{-2\pi i/N}. \tag{14.2}$$

Here $[w^{kn}]$ is the $N \times N$ matrix with (k, n) entry w^{kn}, and is therefore symmetric. Note that the rows and columns are indexed from 0 to $N - 1$. To record the dependence on N we may write $T = T_N$ and $w = w_N$. Of course, (14.2) looks very compact, and often it's exactly what we need. But sometimes we want a more visible matrix form (N.B. Row $k = k$th powers of Row 1).

$$
\begin{bmatrix} F_0 \\ F_1 \\ \cdots \\ F_k \\ \cdots \\ F_{N-1} \end{bmatrix}
=
\begin{bmatrix}
1 & 1 & 1 & \cdots & 1 \\
1 & w & w^2 & \cdots & w^{N-1} \\
\cdots & & & & \\
1 & w^k & w^{2k} & \cdots & w^{(N-1)k} \\
\cdots & & & & \\
1 & w^{N-1} & w^{2(N-1)} & \cdots & w^{(N-1)^2}
\end{bmatrix}
\begin{bmatrix} f_0 \\ f_1 \\ \cdot \\ \cdot \\ \cdot \\ f_{N-1} \end{bmatrix}. \tag{14.3}
$$

Examples 14.1 In the case $N = 2$, we have $w = e^{-2\pi i/2} = e^{-\pi i} = -1$, whereas in the case $N = 4$ the result is $w = e^{-2\pi i/4} = e^{-\pi i/2} = -i$. The resulting matrices already illustrate simplifying features which we will soon state and prove for the general case (Theorem 14.5).

$$
\begin{bmatrix} F_0 \\ F_1 \end{bmatrix} = \begin{bmatrix} 1 & 1 \\ 1 & -1 \end{bmatrix} \begin{bmatrix} f_0 \\ f_1 \end{bmatrix}, \quad \text{and} \quad
\begin{bmatrix} F_0 \\ F_1 \\ F_2 \\ F_3 \end{bmatrix} = \begin{bmatrix} 1 & 1 & 1 & 1 \\ 1 & -i & -1 & i \\ 1 & -1 & 1 & -1 \\ 1 & i & -1 & -i \end{bmatrix} \begin{bmatrix} f_0 \\ f_1 \\ f_2 \\ f_3 \end{bmatrix}. \tag{14.4}
$$

Examples 14.2 The following example with $N = 4$, and using the matrix above, illustrates that the transform of a constant vector $[\alpha \; \alpha \ldots \alpha]$ is an *impulse* (a nonzero component followed by zeros). This fact is visible in (14.4) because our constant vector has the form $\alpha[1 \; 1 \; 1 \; 1]$, so F_k equals α times the sum of the elements of row k of T, which is 4 for $k = 0$ and otherwise zero. In this case the transform happens to be real, and so we can plot F_k on a graph in the manner of Figure 14.1.

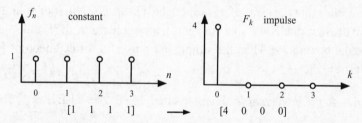

Figure 14.1 The Fourier Transform of a constant vector $[1 \; 1 \ldots 1]$ in the case $N = 4$. As will be shown in the general case, the result is an impulse (nonzero only at the zeroth position).

Notation 14.3 A transform component F_k is in general a complex number and so has both a real part $x = \mathrm{Re}(F_k)$ and an imaginary part $y = \mathrm{Im}(F_k)$, where $F_k = x + \mathrm{i}y$. This is illustrated in Figure 14.2(a), along with the second, and important viewpoint, that F_k is equivalently defined by its *amplitude* (or modulus) $r = |F_k| = \sqrt{(x^2 + y^2)}$, and *phase angle* (or argument) $\theta = \arctan(y/x)$.

We say F_k corresponds to *frequency* k (in what way will emerge later), and, in conformity with this, refer to the sequence $\{|F_k|\}$ as the *spectrum* of $[f_n]$, and to $\{|F_k|^2\}$ as the *power spectrum*.

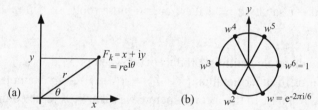

Figure 14.2 (a) Aspects of the complex number F_k, where $x = r\cos\theta$ and $y = r\sin\theta$, (b) the powers of the complex number $w_6 = \mathrm{e}^{-2\pi\mathrm{i}/6}$ are uniformly spaced round a circle, and comprise all sixth roots of 1.

Roots of unity We recall some key facts. The complex number $w = w_N = \mathrm{e}^{-2\pi\mathrm{i}/N} = \cos(2\pi/N) - \mathrm{i}\sin(2\pi/N)$ has argument $-2\pi/N$, which is $1/N$ of a full turn. Thus each time we multiply a number by w_N we increase its argument by $1/N$ of a turn, and after doing this precisely N times we are back to the original direction. Since also w_N has modulus $\sqrt{[\cos^2(2\pi/N) + \sin^2(2\pi/N)]} = 1$, the powers of w_N are spaced round a circle of radius 1, or *unit circle*, at intervals of $1/N$ turn, as illustrated for the case $N = 6$ in Figure 14.2(b). Such a figure, representing complex numbers in the plane, is called an *Argand diagram*. We highlight a fact about complex numbers that will shortly be useful (see e.g. Hoggar, 1992).

> A polynomial equation of degree n has no more than n distinct solutions, real or complex.

We call w_N an *Nth root of unity* because $w^N = 1$. It is not the only Nth root of 1, indeed all its powers are too, but w_N has the additional feature that no lesser power equals 1 (the circle spacing rules that out) and so it is said to be a *primitive* Nth root of unity. Since the N powers are distinct (the circle spacing again), they constitute all N solutions of $z^N = 1$ according to the box above. Then the simple but powerful result Theorem 14.4 enables us to exploit these facts.

Theorem 14.4 *Let α be a complex number satisfying $\alpha^N = 1$ but $\alpha \neq 1$. Then*

$$\alpha^{-1} = \overline{\alpha} = \alpha^{N-1}, \tag{14.5}$$

$$1 + \alpha + \cdots + \alpha^{N-1} = 0, \tag{14.6}$$

and, if $N = 2M$ with $\alpha^M \neq 1$, then $\alpha^M = -1$. $\tag{14.7}$

Proof Dividing both sides of the equation $\alpha^N = 1$ by α gives $\alpha^{N-1} = \alpha^{-1}$. On the other hand, α must have the form $e^{i\theta}$ for some angle θ, so that $\alpha \cdot \overline{\alpha} = e^{i\theta} \cdot e^{-i\theta} = e^0 = 1$, hence $\overline{\alpha} = \alpha^{-1}$ and (14.5) is established. Now observe that $0 = \alpha^N - 1 = (\alpha - 1)(1 + \alpha + \alpha^2 + \cdots + \alpha^{N-1})$. Since the first factor is not zero ($\alpha \neq 1$), the second *must* be, and we have the equality (14.6). For (14.7), note that the complex number $\beta = \alpha^M$ satisfies the equation $z^2 = 1$. But by the previous box this equation has at most two distinct roots. Since both 1 and -1 satisfy $z^2 = 1$ there are no more roots, so if $\beta \neq 1$ we must have $\beta = -1$.

Notation We recall the elementwise product of two vectors $(x_1, \ldots, x_k) \circ (y_1, \ldots, y_k) = (x_1 y_1, \ldots, x_k y_k)$, or in other notation $(X \circ Y)_i = (X)_i (Y)_i$. An example is $(1, w, w^2) \circ (1, w^2, w^4) = (1, w^3, w^6)$. In the theorem below we take X, Y to be columns or rows of the matrix T. The next use of this product is at (14.15).

Theorem 14.5 *The Discrete Fourier Transform is linear; that is, if $f \to F$ and $g \to G$, and λ is a constant, then $f + g \to F + G$ and $\lambda f \to \lambda F$. Furthermore, if R_k is the kth row of the N-point DFT matrix then (with (i) to (iii) holding similarly for columns),*

(i) $R_k \circ R_j = R_{k+j}$,
(ii) $R_{N-k} = \overline{R_k}$ *(the complex conjugate),*
(iii) $R_M = [1 \ -1 \ldots 1 \ -1]$ *if $N = 2M$ (N even),*
(iv) the transform of a constant vector is an impulse, and vice versa,
(v) if f is real then $F_{N-k} = \overline{F}_k$.

Proof The Fourier Transform is linear trivially, because it is given by a matrix. In (i) to (iii) it suffices to prove equality of nth elements for any n; the result for columns is immediate because T is symmetric. (i) According to the notation, $(R_k)_n = w^{kn}$, and so $(R_k \circ R_j)_n = (R_k)_n (R_j)_n = w^{kn} w^{jn} = w^{(k+j)n} = (R_{k+j})_n$. For (ii) we observe that $(R_{N-k})_n = w^{(N-k)n} = w^{Nn} w^{-kn} = w^{-kn}$ (since $w^N = 1$), which is the conjugate of w^{kn} and so equals $(\overline{R}_k)_n$ as required. For case (iii) we have $(R_M)_n = (w^M)^n$ which equals, correctly, $(-1)^n$ by (14.7). In case (iv) it suffices by linearity to consider only the transform of a vector with components 1. For $0 \leq k \leq N - 1$, there follows

$$F_k = R_k \cdot [11 \ldots 1] = \sum_{n=0}^{N-1} (R_k)_n = \sum_{n=0}^{N-1} w^{kn} = 1 + \alpha + \cdots + \alpha^{N-1},$$

where $\alpha = w^k$ satisfies $\alpha^N = (w^N)k = 1$. Hence, if $k = 0$ then $\alpha = 1$ and $F_k = N$, otherwise $\alpha \neq 1$ and (14.6) gives $F_k = 0$. It remains to remark that the transform of an impulse is a multiple of the first column of the DFT matrix T, which is all 1s. Part (v) is the exercise below.

Exercise Prove part (v) of Theorem 14.5 by giving the definition of each side of the equality.

Examples 14.6 (1) (*Evaluating $\sum w^k$*) Let $w = e^{2\pi i/6}$. Verify directly from the Binomial Theorem that, as predicted by Equation (14.6), there holds $1 + w + w^2 + w^3 + w^4 + w^5 = 0$. You may assume w^{6-n} is the conjugate of w^n.

Solution $w = \cos(2\pi/6) + i\sin(2\pi/6) = (1 + i\sqrt{3})/2$, whence
$w^2 = (1 + 2i\sqrt{3} + (i\sqrt{3})^2)/4 = (1 + 2i\sqrt{3} - 3)/4 = (-1 + i\sqrt{3})/2,$
$w^3 = (1 + 3i\sqrt{3} + 3(i\sqrt{3})^2 + (i\sqrt{3})^3)/8 = (1 + 3i\sqrt{3} - 9 - 3i\sqrt{3})/8 = -1,$
$w^4 = $ conjugate of $w^2 = (-1 - i\sqrt{3})/2,$
$w^5 = $ conjugate of $w = (1 - i\sqrt{3})/2.$
Adding: $\quad 1 + w + w^2 + w^3 + w^4 + w^5 = 1 - 1 + (1/2)(1 + i\sqrt{3} - 1 + i\sqrt{3} - 1 - i\sqrt{3} + 1 - i\sqrt{3} = 0.$
This does draw attention to the value of (14.6), bypassing a calculation such as that above yet predicting its result. We will repeatedly invoke this zero sum. For the reader: deduce that $w^3 = -1$ without using the Binomial Theorem.

(2) (*Reconstructing T*) In the case $N = 4$, given that row 1 of the DFT matrix is $[1 \ -i \ -1 \ i]$, can we use the various sections of Theorem 14.5 to reconstruct the rest? Of course, the first row (numbered zero) and column are all ones because $w^0 = 1$. Apart from this: by (iii) $R_2 = [1 \ -1 \ 1 \ -1]$,
by (i) $R_3 = R_2 \circ R_1 = [1 \ -1 \ 1 \ -1] \circ [1 \ -i \ -1 \ i] = [1 \ i \ -1 \ -i]$, in agreement with (14.4), and, as a further check, (ii) states that $R_3 = \overline{R}_{4-1} = \overline{R}_1 = [1 \ i \ -1 \ -i]$, correctly.

Exercise Recover the 4-point DFT matrix from its top left hand 2×2 submatrix.

Example 14.7 We sample the function $f(x) = (1/4)\sin 10x + (1/2)\sin 40x + \sin 50x$ at $N = 200$ equally spaced points over the interval $[0, 2\pi]$, to obtain a vector of values $[f_n]$ as graphed in Figure 14.3(a). The next graph, (b), shows the DFT amplitudes $|F_k|$ against k. The first thing to notice is symmetry about $k = 100$ as a result of $F_{N-k} = \overline{F}_k$ (Theorem 14.5(v)) implying $|F_{N-k}| = |F_k|$. Thus, as in the simpler previous example, we can infer the second half of the F_ks from the first half.

Now consider $0 \leq k \leq 100$. We find spikes at $k = 10, 40$ and 50 corresponding to the k in $\sin kx$ for each part of $f(x)$. This highlights the fact, to be established in Section 14.1.2, that F_k really does correspond to frequency within the limits of our 200-point approximation of $f(x)$. It also illustrates:

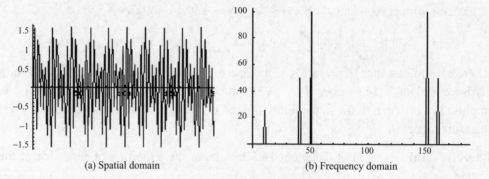

Figure 14.3 (a) Graph of 200 sample points of the function $f(x) = (1/4)\sin 10x + (1/2)\sin 40x + \sin 50x$, (b) the amplitudes of the DFT values, $|F_k|$, against k. Notice the occurrence in pairs predicted by Theorem 14.5(v). The labels of (a), (b) anticipate the discussion below.

linearity: each individual sine term transforms to a pair of spikes, and the sum of the three sines transforms to the sum of all the spikes, and

simplicity: though complicated to behold, the function is very simple after being transformed. This is part of a more general idea in which we seek a transform which brings out the essential nature of a function.

14.1.2 Inversion

We find that the DFT is invertible, with an inverse very similar to the original, enabling us to write down conveniently the *DFT pair* shown in the next theorem.

Theorem 14.8 *The inverse DFT, or IDFT, may be described in the following two ways:*

$$\boxed{T_N^{-1} = (1/N)\overline{T}_N \quad \textit{(matrix form)},}$$
(14.8a)

$$\left. \begin{array}{l} F_k = \sum_{n=0}^{N-1} w^{kn} f_n, \\[2mm] f_n = \frac{1}{N} \sum_{k=0}^{N-1} w^{-kn} F_k \end{array} \right\} \quad \textit{(DFT pair)}.$$
(14.8b)

Proof Formulas (14.8) are equivalent to $T_N \overline{T}_N = NI$, which we prove by considering the (k, m) element of $T_N \overline{T}_N$ with $0 \le k, m < N$, namely

$$(T\overline{T})_{km} = \sum_{r=0}^{N-1} w^{kr} w^{-rm} \qquad \text{by definition of } T \text{ and matrix multiplication}$$

$$= \sum_{r=0}^{N-1} \alpha^r \qquad \text{where } \alpha = w^{k-m}$$

$$= \begin{cases} 0, & \text{if } k \neq m, \text{ by}(14.6), \text{ since } \alpha \neq 1, \text{ but } \alpha^N = 1 \text{ (given } w^N = 1) \\ N, & \text{if } k = m, \text{ since } \alpha = w^0 = 1. \end{cases}$$

That is, $T\overline{T} = NI$, and so $T[(1/N)\overline{T}] = I$, implying that T has the stated inverse (see (7.20)). The first part of (14.8b) is a restatement of the definition (14.1) and the second states that $f_n = (\text{row } n \text{ of } T^{-1}) \cdot [F_0 \dots F_{N-1}]$, a consequence of $f = T^{-1}F$.

Bases, coefficients and frequencies Since T^{-1} exists, we may write $T^{-1} = [C_0 \, C_1 \dots C_{N-1}]$, with kth column C_k. Then the equation $F = Tf$ may be rewritten as $f = T^{-1}F$, or

$$\boxed{f = \Sigma_k F_k C_k,} \tag{14.9}$$

expressing f as a linear combination of the columns of T^{-1} as basis vectors (see (7.30)). Notice that $(^1\!/_N \overline{T})(^1\!/_N T) = ^1\!/_N I$, hence $C_j^T C_k = ^1\!/_N \delta_{jk}$ and so the C_j are orthogonal, each of length $1/\sqrt{N}$ (see Section 8.1.1).

Returning to $f = \Sigma_k F_k C_k$, we emphasise that F_k is called the *coefficient (or component) in frequency k*. This is appropriate because C_k is in an important sense a function with frequency k. Specifically, its nth column entry

$$C_k(n) = (1/N)\left(e^{-2\pi ik/N}\right)^n$$

varies with the discrete variable n, and if we make a complete cycle through the column, $n = 0, 1, \dots, N$, then the argument of the complex number $C_k(n)$ increases by $2\pi k$. That is, it undergoes k complete periods, or has frequency k.

In harmony with this, the transfer of a calculation from $\{f_n\}$ to $\{F_k\}$ is described as a transfer of the problem from the *spatial* domain (sometimes it is time), to the *frequency* domain. Sometimes we refer to *spatial/temporal* frequencies according as the variable refers to distance/time.

We develop the frequency idea under the next heading, but first a recapitulation applying equally to sine and cosine functions. The function $\sin x$ has period 2π; that is, the function values repeat after an increment of 2π in x, and 2π is the least interval with such a property; consequently (see Figure 14.4):

$$\begin{cases} \sin \omega x \text{ has period } 2\pi/\omega, \\ \sin 2\pi n x \text{ has frequency } n. \end{cases} \tag{14.10}$$

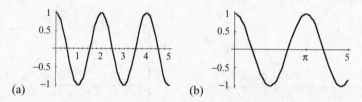

(a)   (b)

Figure 14.4 (a) $\cos \pi x = \cos 2\pi(1/2)x$; considering (14.10), this function has frequency $\omega = 1/2$ and period $1/\omega = 2$, (b) $\cos 2t$, with period $2\pi/2 = \pi$ and frequency $1/\pi$.

Lowpass filtering Often we want to modify or improve the original f in a way that can be described in terms of the frequency components F_k. For example, suppose we receive $f = g + h$, where h is an unknown 'noise' which we want to eliminate. Suppose further that, although h itself is unknown, we know it is restricted to higher frequencies $k > c$ than those occupied by the true signal g. Then we can recover g as follows.

ALGO 14.1 A lowpass filter with threshold c

1. Apply the DFT, $f \rightarrow F$.
2. Set all components with frequency $k > c$ to zero.
3. Apply the IDFT (inverse transform) to the result.

Why does this work? In step 1, since $f = g + h$, we get $F = G + H$, whose components with $k > c$ are precisely the components of H. That is, we may write $F = [G_0 \ldots G_c \, H_{c+1} \ldots H_{N-1}]$. Step 2 reduces this to $[G_0 \ldots G_c \, 0 \ldots 0]$, which is simply G, and is inverted by step 3 back to the desired g. See Figure 14.5.

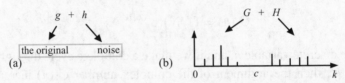

Figure 14.5 (a) Received signal consisting of an original g plus noise h, (b), transform of the result in which frequencies above $k > c$ are known to be those of the noise. Therefore the original signal g can be recovered by steps 1 to 3 in ALGO 14.1.

Example 14.9 In this example the function g, shown in Figure 14.6(a), was output with some noise distortions (see ALGO 11.8 and Figure 11.21). It is known that, to a good approximation, this noise can be considered restricted to frequencies above 32. After steps 1 to 3 are applied with $c = 32$, to remove this noise, we obtain the graph of Figure 14.6(b).

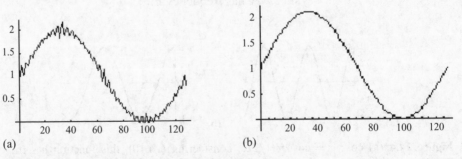

Figure 14.6 (a) Original noisy function, (b) result after removing all frequency components F_k with $k > 32$.

Filtering in general This means changing the components F_k in some way, then applying the inverse transform. By changing F_k to zero for $k > c$ we have applied a *lowpass
filter*, one in which we 'pass', or allow, only lower frequencies. Analogously, a *highpass
filter* preserves only frequency components F_k with k above some designated threshold.
Filters exist for many purposes, including the artistic, and we shall meet more of them
later. Figure 14.7 is a diagram of the general format. Example 14.9 is the special case
$g + f \to G + F \to G \to g$.

$$[f_n] \xrightarrow{\text{DFT}} [F_k] \xrightarrow{\text{FILTER}} [F'_k] \xrightarrow{\text{IDFT}} [f'_n]$$

Figure 14.7 The general schema for filtering (derivatives are not implied).

Such filters with a sharp threshold, or cutoff, are said to be *ideal*. Paradoxically so,
because, as we shall see in Section 15.2.2, this very sharpness causes a form of distortion
called *ringing*. However, this may be taken care of by more sophisticated filters.

14.1.3 Convolution

The Fourier transform has an important and useful relationship to the *convolution* of a
vector/sequence, in which the value f_n at a point is replaced by a fixed linear combination
of the values at that point and its neighbours.

Such replacement occurs in many situations, as we shall see, but a simple first example
is the 'smoothing' technique of averaging the immediate neighbours (Figure 14.8). In
every case, we can by suitable labelling regard the process as polynomial multiplication
if we wish; this is considered next.

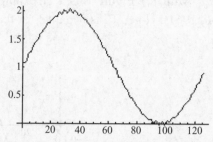

Figure 14.8 The noisy function of Figure 14.6(a) smoothed by the averaging effect of
convolution with [1/3 1/3 1/3].

Definition 14.10 Let $f(x) = \sum_i f_i x^i$ be the polynomial associated with a vector f. Then
the *convolution product* $h = f * g$ of two vectors f, g is given by

$$h(x) = f(x)g(x), \tag{14.11a}$$

That is, $h_n = \sum_{i+j=n} f_i g_j$, or equivalently $h_n = \sum_i f_i g_{n-i}$,   (14.11b) which simply expresses the way in which terms of $h(x)$ having given degree n are calculated when we multiply two polynomials. A simple example is: $(1-2x)(1-x+x^3) = 1 - 3x + 2x^2 + x^3 - 2x^4$, which gives $[1-2]*[1-1\ 0\ 1] = [1-3\ 2\ 1-2]$. (We discussed polynomial multiplication earlier, in Chapter 13, where we descibed a shift register method of carrying out the process.) Thus the properties of polynomial multiplication carry over to convolution, and in particular $*$ is associative, commutative and distributive over addition.

Exercise Determine the convolution product $[1\ 2\ 3]*[2-1]$.

Example 14.11 (Edge-detection) Replacing the function value at a point by a linear approximation to the second derivative leads to a method of edge-detection in a 2-dimensional image (see Section 15.2.4). The process will be carried out by 2D convolution in Chapter 15. Here we illustrate the 1D version. Suppose the function values f_n apply to points spaced at distance d. Then, by Taylor's Theorem (10.41),

$$f_{n+1} = f_n + df_n' + \frac{d^2}{2}f_n'' + \frac{d^3}{6}f_n''' + O(d^4),$$

$$f_{n-1} = f_n - df_n' + \frac{d^2}{2}f_n'' - \frac{d^3}{6}f_n''' + O(d^4),$$

where $O(d^4)$ means a function bounded in absolute value by a constant multiple of d^4, as $d \to 0$ (Section 10.3.3), and so

$$f_n'' = (f_{n-1} - 2f_n + f_{n+1})/d^2 + O(d^2).$$

Thus, on the basis of small d, the second derivative is proportional to $[1\ -2\ 1]*f$ (with a subscript shift to line up f_n'' with f_n). Figure 14.9 is an example in which f is a Bessel function (see e.g. Sneddon, 1961). Note, f'' is negative for the first peak of f, positive for the second, etc.

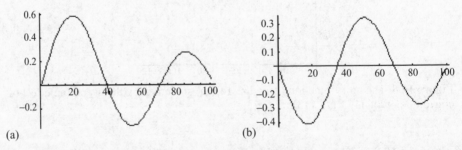

(a)   (b)

Figure 14.9 (a) Graph of the Bessel function J_1 on interval $[0, 10]$ with spacing $d = 0.1$, (b) graph of the *second derivative*, represented as the convolution $[1\ -2\ 1]*100J_1$.

Padding To bring out the connection with the DFT we extend ('pad') the vectors f, g with zeros before forming $f*g$ so that f, g, h all have the same length

$N = r + s + 1$, where f, g have respective degrees r, s. For example, $(1 + x)(1 + 2x - x^2) = 1 + 3x + x^2 - x^3$ tells us that

$$[1\ \ 1\ \ 0\ \ 0]^*[1\ \ 2\ \ -1\ \ 0] = [1,\ \ 3,\ \ 1\ -1].$$

Matrix view The equations (14.11) for $h = f^*g$ can be expressed by a matrix product:

$$[h_0 \ldots h_{N-1}] = [f_0 \ldots f_r] \begin{bmatrix} g_0 & g_1 & \cdots & g_s & & \\ & g_0 & g_1 & \cdots & g_s & \\ & & & \cdots & & \\ & & g_0 & g_1 & \cdots & g_s \end{bmatrix}, \tag{14.12}$$

where the blanks represent zeros. (This is how information bits were encoded in Chapter 13.) For example, $h_0 = f_0 g_0, h_1 = f_0 g_1 + f_1 g_0$, and so on. To exploit this in proving the theorem below, we describe (14.12) in terms of a shift operator S which, applied to a row or column vector, shifts its components backwards one place cyclically. Thus, $S[1\ \ 2\ \ 5] = [2\ \ 5\ \ 1]$, whereas $S^{-1}[1\ \ 2\ \ 5] = [5\ \ 1\ \ 2]$. Let u, v be vectors of the same length and write R_i for the ith row of the DFT matrix $T = [w^{kn}]$. Then

$$Su \cdot Sv = u \cdot v, \tag{14.13}$$

$$SR_i = \lambda R_i, \quad \text{where } \lambda = w^i. \tag{14.14}$$

This is because $S[u_0 \ldots u_{N-1}] \cdot S[v_0 \ldots v_{N-1}] = [u_1 \ldots u_{N-1}\ u_0] \cdot [v_1 \ldots v_{N-1}\ v_0] = \sum_i u_i v_i = u \cdot v$, and $SR_i = S[1\ \lambda\ \lambda^2 \ldots \lambda^{N-1}] = [\lambda\ \lambda^2 \ldots \lambda^{N-1} \lambda^N]$ (since $1 = \lambda^N$) = λR_i. Now we are ready for the relationship which helps to give the Fourier Transform its special place.

Theorem 14.12 *(Convolution Theorem for the DFT) The Discrete Fourier Transform converts convolution into the elementwise product. That is, $h = f^*g \Rightarrow H = F \circ G$, or simply*

$$\boxed{f^*g \to F \circ G.} \tag{14.15}$$

Matrix proof We let $h = f^*g$ and deduce $H = F \circ G$. Considering (14.12) we see that the rows of the $(r + 1) \times N$ matrix are successive shifts of the first (such a matrix is called a *circulant*). Hence its transpose C_g has ith column $S^{-i}g$, and, transposing both sides of (14.12), we obtain this equation in the form below, where, by implication, $g_0 \ldots g_s$ is padded with zeros on the right up to length N.

$$h = C_g f = [g\ \ S^{-1}g \ldots S^{-r}g]f,$$

with f, g, h written as column vectors. We must show that $H_i = F_i G_i$ for $0 \le i \le N - 1$.

We have

$$
\begin{aligned}
H_i &= (Th)_i = (\text{Row } i \text{ of } T)h & \text{Example 7.22(3)} \\
&= R_i C_g f = R_i[g \quad S^{-1}g \ldots S^{-r}g]f & \text{substituting for } h \\
&= [R_i g \quad R_i S^{-1}g \ldots R_i S^{-r}g]f & \text{Example 7.22(4)} \\
&= [R_i g \quad S R_i g \ldots S^r R_i g]f & \text{by (14.13)} \\
&= [R_i g \quad \lambda R_i g \ldots \lambda^r R_i g]f & \text{by (14.14)} \\
&= R_i g[1 \quad \lambda \ldots \lambda^r]f & R_i g \text{ is a scalar} \\
&= (R_i g)(R_i f) & \text{by definition of } R_i.
\end{aligned}
$$

Thus $H_i = F_i G_i$ for each i, in other words $H = F \circ G$ and the proof is complete. However, this is not the end of the story, as the next portion of text makes clear.

Polynomial proof It is important to bring out the Convolution Theorem in terms of matrices, but a proof directly in terms of polynomials is hard to beat for brevity, besides providing further insight as to why the result should be true at all. Let $h(x) = f(x)g(x)$ as before, and $w = e^{-2\pi i/N}$. A key observation is that

$$
F_k = \sum w^{kn} f_n = \sum f_n \cdot (w^k)^n = f(w^k),
$$

and similarly for g and h. For the polynomial identity $h(x) = f(x)g(x)$ implies $h(w^k) = f(w^k)g(w^k)$, giving the Convolution Theorem $H_k = F_k G_k$ ($0 \leq k \leq N - 1$). A similar argument will be applied later for higher dimensions.

Example 14.13 We verify the Convolution Theorem in the case $f = [1\ 2\ 0]$, $g = [1\ -1\ 0]$.
(i) Using polynomial multiplication, $(1 + 2x)(1 - x) = 1 + x - 2x^2$, so $f*g = [1\ \ 1\ -2]$
(ii) We must apply the 3-point DFT, with $w = e^{-2\pi i/3}$, and $w^3 = 1$:

$$
T(f*g) = \begin{bmatrix} 1 & 1 & 1 \\ 1 & w & w^2 \\ 1 & w^2 & w \end{bmatrix} \begin{bmatrix} 1 \\ 1 \\ -2 \end{bmatrix} = \begin{bmatrix} 0 \\ 1 + w - 2w^2 \\ 1 + w^2 - 2w \end{bmatrix} \ (T \text{ is simplified by } w^3{=}1),
$$

$$
(Tf) \circ (Tg) = \begin{bmatrix} 3 \\ 1 + 2w \\ 1 + 2w^2 \end{bmatrix} \circ \begin{bmatrix} 0 \\ 1 - w \\ 1 - w^2 \end{bmatrix}
$$

$$
= \begin{bmatrix} 0 \\ (1 + 2w)(1 - w) \\ (1 + 2w^2)(1 - w^2) \end{bmatrix} = \begin{bmatrix} 0 \\ 1 + w - 2w^2 \\ 1 + w^2 - 2w^4 \end{bmatrix},
$$

which equals $T(f*g)$ because $w^3 = 1$.

Remarks 14.14 (1) One of the great advantages of the Convolution Theorem is that it enables us to undo corruption to an image when, as often, this can be expressed as a convolution. Important examples are image blur from either camera or motion. (We come to this in Chapter 15, after the extension to two dimensions.) (2) A second, and famous, benefit is that it enables us to use the DFT to determine the result of convolution, leading to a huge speedup because of the Fast Fourier Transform, which we shall derive in Section 14.1.4. (3) We have $T^{-1} = (1/N)\overline{T}$ and, since the proof of the Convolution Theorem goes through equally well with w replaced by its conjugate, there is a convolution theorem for the IDFT with an extra factor N:

$$(1/N)T^{-1}(F^*G) = T^{-1}F \circ T^{-1}G, \quad \text{compared with } T(f^*g) = (Tf) \circ (Tf).$$

14.1.4 The Fast Fourier Transform (FFT)

By looking more closely at the DFT we find all manner of redundancies; the simplest is perhaps the symmetry $R_{N-k} = \overline{R}_k$, which reduces the calculation by one half. Let us create a baseline by assuming that addition, subtraction and multiplication take equal times, and call them simply *arithmetic operations*. In general the numbers involved will be complex, even though f is real. The dot product of two N-vectors involves N multiplications followed by $N-1$ additions, a total of $2N-1$ operations. Computing $F = Tf$ requires a dot product for each row, hence a total of $N(2N-1)$ operations, a function which increases as N^2.

The Fast Fourier Transform, or FFT, is really a class of algorithms which reduce the DFT arithmetic operations to $O(N \log_2 N)$, giving a roughly 100-fold reduction for 1024 points (see Section 10.3.3 for the 'O' notation). Since $\log N$ to any base increases ultimately less rapidly than any positive power of N, it is highly desirable to reduce an N to a $\log N$. We consider the most common case $N = 2^\gamma$ for a positive integer γ, to which others are frequently converted by a padding of zeros. For other cases, see the end of the present section.

The essential idea is to provide an economical way of reducing the calculation to one on vectors of half size, M, where $N = 2M$. Thus we shall refer to the M-point DFT with matrix $T_M = [w_M^{kn}]$, where by definition $w_M = e^{-2\pi i/M}$, compared with $w = e^{-2\pi i/N}$, hence both

$$\boxed{w^M = -1 \quad \text{and} \quad w_M = w^2.} \tag{14.16}$$

Notation We divide f into two M-vectors by even versus odd subscripts, but divide F by low versus high. More formally:

$$f_{ev} = [f_{2r}], \; f_{od} = [f_{2r+1}] \; (0 \le r \le M-1), \text{ and} \tag{14.17}$$

$$F_{lo} = [F_0 \dots F_{M-1}], \; F_{hi} = [F_M \dots F_{N-1}]. \tag{14.18}$$

We simplify diagrams by setting $D = D_M = \text{diag}(1, w, \dots, w^{M-1})$, the $M \times M$ matrix with the *first M powers* of w along its main diagonal and zeros elsewhere (recall w has $2M$ distinct powers). For example, corresponding to $N = 2, 4, 8$ respectively:

$$D_1 = [1], \; D_2 = \begin{bmatrix} 1 & 0 \\ 0 & -i \end{bmatrix}, \text{ and } \; D_4 = \begin{bmatrix} 1 & 0 & 0 & 0 \\ 0 & w & 0 & 0 \\ 0 & 0 & w^2 & 0 \\ 0 & 0 & 0 & w^3 \end{bmatrix} \left(w = e^{-2\pi i/8} \right).$$

Theorem 14.15 *Write $x = T_M f_{ev}$ and $y = T_M f_{od}$. Then the N-point DFT is given by*

$$F_{lo} = x + Dy, \quad F_{hi} = x - Dy. \tag{14.19}$$

Proof As n runs from 0 to $N - 1$ we describe the even values by $n = 2r$ and the odd by $n = 2r + 1$, where r runs from 0 to $M - 1$. This gives the second line below.

$$F_k = \sum_{n=0}^{N-1} w^{kn} f_n \qquad \text{by definition}$$

$$= \sum_{r=0}^{M-1} w^{2rk} f_{2r} + \sum_{r=0}^{M-1} w^{(2r+1)k} f_{2r+1}$$

$$= \sum_{r=0}^{M-1} w_M^{kr} f_{2r} + w^k \sum_{r=0}^{M-1} w_M^{kr} f_{2r+1} \qquad \text{by (14.16).}$$

Consider the last expression for F_k. With k running from 0 to $M - 1$, the F_{lo} range, we obtain the first equation of (14.19). For F_{hi} we replace k by $M + k$ (again, $0 \leq k \leq M - 1$), observing that $w_M{}^{M+k} = w_M^k$ because $w_M^M = 1$, whereas $w^{M+k} = -w^k$ because $w^M = -1$. This gives

$$F_{M+k} = \sum_{r=0}^{M-1} w_M^{kr} f_{2r} - w^k \sum_{r=0}^{M-1} w_M^{kr} f_{2r+1} = x_k - w^k y_k.$$

Thus, letting k run from 0 to $M - 1$, we obtain (F_{lo} is similar),

$$F_{hi} = \begin{bmatrix} x_0 - w^0 y_0 \\ x_1 - w^1 y_1 \\ \cdots \\ x_{M-1} - w^{M-1} y_{M-1} \end{bmatrix} = \begin{bmatrix} x_0 \\ x_1 \\ \cdots \\ x_{M-1} \end{bmatrix} - \begin{bmatrix} w^0 & & & \\ & w^1 & & \\ & & \ddots & \\ & & & w^{M-1} \end{bmatrix} \begin{bmatrix} y_0 \\ y_1 \\ \cdots \\ y_{M-1} \end{bmatrix}$$

$$= x - Dy.$$

Conclusion 14.16 Since Theorem 14.15 applies to x, y too, it gives a recursive method for the FFT when $N = 2\gamma$. Let us see if we have really shortened the calculation.

calculation	no. of arithmetic operations
Dy	M (D is diagonal)
$x \pm Dy$	M
Total	$3M$, or $(3/2)N$

In the next step, the vectors are half as long but there are twice as many, so we conclude that each step takes $(3/2)N$ operations. By γ steps, everything is expressed in terms of individual elements f_i, giving a final total of $(3/2)N_\gamma = (3/2)N \log_2 N$. Here are some comparative values of the speedup factor (old time)/(new time) =

$2(2N - 1)/3 \log_2 N$, to the nearest integer.

N	16	64	256	512	1024
speedup	5	14	43	76	136

ALGO 14.2 A recursive routine for the FFT of a vector f whose length is a power of 2

Function FFT(f)
Local variables $N = Length(f), w, f_{ev}, f_{od}, x, y, D, z$
If $N = 1$ then *Return* (f) else
    Construct f_{ev}, f_{od} from f
    $x = FFT(f_{ev})$
    $y = FFT(f_{od})$
    $w = \exp(-2\pi i/N)$
    $D = (1, w, \ldots, w^{N/2-1})$
    $z = D \circ y$ (elementwise product)
    Return $(Join [x + z, x - z])$
(*Join* makes F_{lo}, F_{hi} into the single vector F)

The butterfly notation We represent step (14.19) of the FFT by a diagram in which the expression on the right is the sum of those at the start of the arrows into it, possibly pre-multiplied by $\pm D$. The result is Figure 14.10, built in two stages, and suggestive of a butterfly. Our objective is to represent a complete FFT calculation in a single diagram.

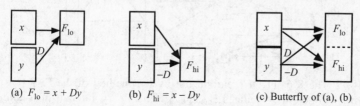

(a) $F_{lo} = x + Dy$ (b) $F_{hi} = x - Dy$ (c) Butterfly of (a), (b)

Figure 14.10 Building up the butterfly to incorporate both $F_{lo} = x + Dy$ and $F_{hi} = x - Dy$.

Case $N = 2$ At this, beginning stage, we have $M = 1$, $T_M = [1]$, whence $x = T_M f_{ev} = f_0$ and $y = T_M f_{od} = f_1$. The butterfly diagram simplifies to

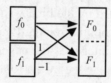

Thus F_0 and F_1 are given immediately in terms of the values of f_0 and f_1. Specifically, $F_0 = f_0 + f_1$ and $F_1 = f_0 - f_1$, in agreement with the earlier formula of (14.4).

Case N = 4 From this case on, everything depends on subscript order in the expressions for x, y, all of the form $T_M[f_a \ f_b \ \ldots \ f_c]$, Let us represent this expression by $ab\ldots c$ enclosed in a rectangle, the value of M being the number of subscripts. In the present case f_{ev}, f_{od}, F_{lo}, F_{hi} have respective subscript sequences [0 2], [1 3], [0 1], [2 3]. See Figure 14.11.

Figure 14.11 Case $N = 4$.

Case N = 8 Starting from the right in Figure 14.12, we express T_8 as two applications of T_4. Neither of the resulting 4-vectors has subscripts in order 0123, but (14.20) tells us what to do. We separate out even and odd subscript *positions*. This gives us the column preceding the rightmost in Figure 14.12. Similarly, we obtain the two preceding columns by considering the cases $N = 4$ and $N = 2$.

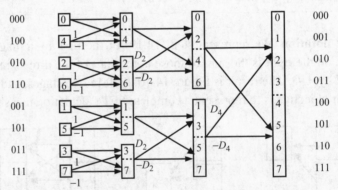

Figure 14.12 The 8-point DFT carried out by the method of the FFT (Fast Fourier Transform). A dotted line separates F_{hi} and F_{lo}. The binary numbers in columns are the binary forms of the integer subscripts nearest to them in the diagram. Observe that one column may be obtained from the other by reversing bit order.

Bit reversal ALGO 14.2 works from right to left in Figure 14.12. We may alternatively assemble the DFT parts by working rightwards from the individual function values, with no reordering, if they are listed in the appropriate order for this: 04261537. A strong clue to how the order changes is provided by the binary subscript values exhibited in Figure 14.12 (high bits to left). To pass from the standard ordering to that required we simply reverse bits and take the resulting integer as the new subscript. This may be seen level by level, but it *is* true in general, as we see by the following argument.

A quick proof of bit reversal Start with a list of the $(n + 1)$-bit binary words $b_n \ldots b_1 b_0$ in increasing order as integers. Then the words with $b_n = 0$ precede those with $b_n = 1$.

Similarly those with $b_n = 0$, $b_{n-1} = 0$ precede those with $b_n = 0$, $b_{n-1} = 1$, and so on, until we have successive bits b_1 as $0011\ldots$ and b_0 as $0101\ldots$ By selecting even numbers first at every stage in the FFT we reverse this situation, right back to b_n alternating $0101\ldots$

Exercise Find the DFT matrix T_4 from a 4-point FFT butterfly diagram (answer at (14.4), solution at Exercise 14.6).

Speeding up convolution by the FFT Since the FFT is such a fast way of doing the DFT, can we compute a convolution $f*g$ faster by transforming to the frequency domain, performing elementwise multiplication $F \circ G$, then transforming back? Notice first that the matrix of the inverse DFT is a factor $1/N$ times the conjugate of the DFT matrix itself, so inversion may also be performed (by the FFT) in $(3/2)N \log_2 N$ arithmetic operations. Here, then, are the steps in performing convolution of two N-point sequences using the FFT, and the number of operations required in each step:

$$f, g \to F, G \to F \circ G \to T^{-1}(F \circ G) = f*g,$$
$$\quad 3N \log_2 N \quad\quad N \quad\quad 1.5N \log_2 N$$

a total of order $O(N \log_2 N)$ operations compared with N^2 for a straight convolution calculation. Because $\log_2 N$ increases so slowly compared with N we obtain a great increase in speed overall.

Other FFTs Methods for the case when N is not a power of 2 naturally depend on the precise factorisation of N. Some good methods with similar speedup factor to the present case are surveyed in Chapter 10 of Briggs and Henson (1995). A wide range of FFTs are unified in the matrix framework of van Loan (1992).

14.1.5 Choices in defining the DFT

(1) *The initial constant* For the DFT, IDFT pair to work, the matrices $[w^{\pm kn}]$ used must be prefixed by constants whose product is $1/N$, because the product of these two matrices is N times the identity matrix (see the proof of (14.8)). We have followed the common convention used in signal processing. This and other possibilities are shown in Table 14.1.

Table 14.1. *Some choices for the DFT and IDFT.*

convention	DFT	IDFT	w
signal processing	$1 \cdot [w^{kn}]$	$(1/N)[w^{-kn}]$	$e^{-2\pi i/N}$
data analysis	$(1/N)[w^{kn}]$	$1 \cdot [w^{-kn}]$	$e^{2\pi i/N}$
also used	$(1/N)^{1/2}[w^{kn}]$	$(1/N)^{1/2}[w^{-kn}]$	$e^{\pm 2\pi i/N}$

(2) *The value of N* Most frequently, N is taken to be a power of 2 to facilitate fast calculation by the FFT method. However, there are fast methods for more general values of N, as mentioned above. We shall always assume that, at least, N is even.

(3) *The interval of n and k* For simplicity we have (mostly) opted for $n, k = 0, 1, \ldots, N-1$, but because of the periodicity of w^n, any N successive values of n will do to define the DFT. It may be convenient to have the interval centred on zero and this is easily achieved by shifting values by $N/2$ to the left, to obtain $n = -N/2, \ldots, 0, \ldots, N/2 - 1$. Similarly for k, with $F_{k \pm N} = F_k$.

(4) The *Hartley Transform* is an alternative to the DFT that has some advantages, including a restriction to real numbers, and moreover possesses a fast version. An introduction and comparison with the DFT are given in Briggs and Henson (1995).

(5) For further information on the FFT and its applications, see comments at the end of this chapter, and the standard text of Brigham (1988).

14.1.6 Converting a standard DFT/FFT routine

Cycle vector to required standard position
Apply standard routine
Cycle back

14.2 The Continuous Fourier Transform

Pre-dating the DFT was the *Fourier Transform*, identified more closely as being continuous rather than discrete, and defined by integration rather than summation. It is foundational, an important theoretical tool, and one that provides elegant proofs having counterparts for the DFT, the latter being the tool for practical calculation. Such results may be precise (the Convolution Theorem), or limited by an accuracy with which the DFT approximates the continuous version. An excellent example of the second case occurs in the extension to two dimensions: $f(x, y) \rightarrow F(u, v)$. Rotation of an image in the x–y plane causes the same rotation in the transformed image (Theorem 15.7), and this is easily visible in the DFT plane, though it cannot normally be expressed there with absolute precision (see Figure 15.4, Chapter 15).

14.2.1 The 1-dimensional case

Properties of the Continuous Fourier Transform are reflected in the DFT more and more clearly as its sample points are taken closer. An example is visibility of a spike at frequency k corresponding to a summand $\cos 2\pi kt$ in $f(t)$. We have already seen this in Example 14.7, and Section 14.2.2 will continue the theme (the delta function comes in here). But to define the Fourier Transform we must introduce integration and differentiation for a function of real variables that is allowed to take complex values.

Integration The Continuous Fourier Transform is defined as an integral of a complex function, but, because the variable is nevertheless real, everything works much as before if we define the derivative to *act on the real and imaginary parts separately*:

$$\frac{d}{dt}[f(t) + ig(t)] = \frac{df}{dt} + i\frac{dg}{dt}, \tag{14.20}$$

where the functions f and g are real (and differentiable), and similarly for integration. The exponential function works splendidly, as is most conveniently proved after we note the usual rules that still apply. We shall revert frequently to the compact notation f' or $f'(t)$ for df/dt.

Theorem 14.17 *Let ϕ and ψ be complex functions of a real variable t. Then*

$$(\phi\psi)' = \phi\psi' + \phi'\psi \qquad (Product\ Rule) \tag{14.21}$$

$$(\phi/\psi)' = (\psi\phi' - \phi\psi')/\psi^2 \quad (Quotient\ Rule) \tag{14.22}$$

$$\frac{d}{dt}\phi(\psi(t)) = \phi'(\psi(t))\psi'(t) \qquad (Chain\ Rule). \tag{14.23}$$

Proof The proofs are routine verifications. As a sample we consider the first. Write $\phi(t) = f(t) + ig(t)$ and $\psi(t) = u(t) + iv(t)$. Then

$$\begin{aligned}
[(f + ig)(u + iv)]' &= [fu - gv + i(gu + fv)]' \qquad \text{since } i^2 = -1 \\
&= (fu - gv)' + i(gu + fv)' \qquad \text{by (14.20)} \\
&= fu' + f'u - (gv' + g'v) + i(gu' + g'u + fv' + f'v) \\
&= (f + ig)(u + iv)' + (f + ig)'(u + iv) \qquad \text{by (14.20)}.
\end{aligned}$$

Theorem 14.18 *Let α be the complex number $a + ib$, where a, b are real. Then*

$$\frac{d}{dt}e^{\alpha t} = \alpha e^{\alpha t} \quad and, \quad if \quad \alpha \neq 0, \quad then \quad \int e^{\alpha t}dt = (1/\alpha)e^{\alpha t} + constant. \tag{14.24}$$

Proof We start with e^{ibt} and apply the Product Rule (14.21).

$$\begin{aligned}
\frac{d}{dt}e^{ibt} &= \frac{d}{dt}[\cos bt + i\sin bt] \\
&= -b\sin bt + ib\cos bt \quad \text{(by (14.20))} = ibe^{ibt}, \\
\frac{d}{dt}e^{\alpha t} &= \frac{d}{dt}e^{(a+ib)t} = \frac{d}{dt}[e^{at} \cdot e^{ibt}] \\
&= ae^{at} \cdot e^{ibt} + e^{at} \cdot ibe^{ibt} \quad \text{by the above, and the Product Rule (14.21)} \\
&= (a + ib)e^{at} \cdot e^{ibt} = (a + ib)e^{at+ibt} = \alpha e^{\alpha t}.
\end{aligned}$$

Now we are ready to define Fourier's original continuous transform $F(s)$ in which, compared with the discrete frequencies k of the DFT, the variable s is to be regarded as a continuously varying frequency. We often write $f \to F$ for the Fourier Transform, and sometimes $f \to \mathcal{F}[f]$.

Theorem 14.19 *(Fourier) With the first equality below defining the Fourier Transform, we have a (transform, inverse) pair.*

$$F(s) = \int_{-\infty}^{\infty} f(t)e^{-2\pi ist}\,dt,$$
$$f(t) = \int_{-\infty}^{\infty} F(s)e^{2\pi ist}\,ds.$$

(Fourier pair) (14.25)

Theorem 14.20 *Change of origin and scale have the following effect on the transforms:*

(i) $g(t) = f(t - a)$ transforms to $G(s) = e^{-2\pi ias}F(s)$ *(Shift Theorem),*
(ii) $f(t/a)$ transforms to $|a|F(sa)$ $(a \neq 0)$ *(Similarity Theorem).*

$$\text{Proof } f(t - a) \;\to\; \int_{-\infty}^{\infty} f(t-a)e^{-2\pi ist}\,dt$$

$$= \int_{-\infty}^{\infty} f(u)e^{-2\pi is(u+a)}\,du \qquad \text{where } u = t - a, \text{ hence}$$
$$\qquad\qquad\qquad\qquad\qquad\qquad\quad t = u + a, \, du = dt$$

$$= e^{-2\pi isa} \int_{-\infty}^{\infty} f(u)e^{-2\pi isu}\,du \qquad \text{since } e^{-2\pi isa} \text{ is constant}$$
$$\qquad\qquad\qquad\qquad\qquad\qquad\quad \text{as } t \text{ varies}$$

$$= e^{-2\pi isa} F(s) \qquad\qquad\qquad \text{as asserted.}$$

$$f(t/a) \;\to\; \int_{\infty}^{\infty} f(t/a)e^{-2\pi ist}\,dt \qquad \text{(now assume } a > 0)$$

$$= a \int_{-\infty}^{\infty} f(u)e^{-2\pi isau}\,du \qquad \text{where } u = t/a, \text{ hence } t = ua,$$
$$\qquad\qquad\qquad\qquad\qquad\qquad\quad dt = a\,du$$

$$= aF(as).$$

If $a < 0$, the limits of integation are reversed because, as t increase, u decreases. This introduces an extra minus sign, so both $a > 0$ and $a < 0$ are covered by the formula $|a|F(sa)$.

Example 14.21 *(Some transforms)* (i) A Gaussian type function $e^{-\pi t^2}$ transforms to $e^{-\pi s^2}$, (ii) A standard Gaussian $N(0, \sigma^2)$ transforms to $e^{-s^2/2\tau^2}$, with $\tau = 1/(2\pi\sigma)$. (iii) A centred unit box $\to$ sinc $(x) = \sin(\pi x)/(\pi x)$. See Figure 14.13.

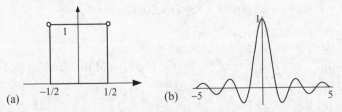

(a)   (b)

Figure 14.13 (a) Centred unit box, with height 1 for $|x| < 1/2$, otherwise zero (discontinuity is indicated by the small circles, (b) its Fourier Transform $\sin(\pi s)/\pi s$, known as the *sinc function*. Inverting back gives height 1/2 at the discontinuities (see Example 14.21 and Theorem 14.25).

Proof (i) $e^{-\pi t^2} \rightarrow \int_{-\infty}^{\infty} e^{-\pi t^2} e^{-2\pi i s t} dt = \int_{-\infty}^{\infty} e^{-\pi(t^2 + 2\pi i s t)} dt$

$$= e^{-\pi s^2} \int_{-\infty}^{\infty} e^{-\pi(t+is)^2} dt \qquad \text{since } e^{-\pi s^2} \text{ is constant as } t \text{ varies}$$

$$= e^{-\pi s^2} \int_{-\infty}^{\infty} e^{-\pi t^2} dt \quad \text{(Exercise 14.7)} = e^{-\pi s^2}, \text{ by (10.52)}.$$

(ii) The first part yielded $F(s) = e^{-\pi s^2}$ when $f(t) = e^{-\pi t^2}$. The second part is a nice application of the change-of-scale formula (Theorem 14.20) with $a = \sqrt{(2\pi\sigma^2)}$ written $(1/a)f(t/a) \rightarrow F(as)$.

(iii) Applying the definition (14.25), a centred unit box transforms to

$$\int_{-1/2}^{1/2} 1 \cdot e^{-2\pi i s t} dt = \left[e^{-2\pi i s t}/(-2\pi i s) \right]_{-1/2}^{1/2} = \frac{1}{\pi s} \frac{1}{2i} (e^{i\pi s} - e^{-i\pi s}) = (\sin \pi s)/\pi s.$$

Theorem 14.22 *(Convolution Theorem) Convolution becomes product under the Fourier transform:* $f(t)^*g(t) \rightarrow F(s)G(s)$. *That is,* $f * g \rightarrow F \circ G$.

Proof We have defined the convolution product in the context of pdfs (Section 10.2.2) and it applies here with

$$f(t)^*g(t) = \int_{-\infty}^{\infty} f(u)g(t-u)du \qquad \text{by definition}$$

$$\rightarrow \int_{-\infty}^{\infty} \left(\int_{-\infty}^{\infty} f(u)g(t-u)du \right) e^{-2\pi i s t} dt \qquad \text{by definition}$$

$$= \int_{-\infty}^{\infty} f(u) \left(\int_{-\infty}^{\infty} g(t-u)e^{-2\pi i s t} dt \right) du \qquad \text{after rearranging}$$

$$= \int_{-\infty}^{\infty} f(u)e^{-2\pi i u s} G(s)\, du \qquad \text{by the Shift Theorem}$$

$$= G(s) \int_{-\infty}^{\infty} f(u)e^{-2\pi i u s}\, du \qquad G(s) \text{ constant as } u \text{ varies}$$

$$= F(s)G(s) \qquad \text{by definition of } F(s).$$

The corresponding result for the DFT was proved as Theorem 14.12. The results of this and the next section are summarised in Table 14.2 of Section 14.2.2.

Example 14.23 (*Cross-correlation*) The cross-correlation of real functions f and g is

$$R_{fg}(s) = \int_{-\infty}^{\infty} f(t)g(t+s)\mathrm{d}t. \tag{14.26}$$

Show that (i) $f(-t) \to F(-s) = \overline{F}(s)$, and hence that (ii) $R_{fg} = f(-t)^*g(t) \to \overline{F}(s)G(s)$.

Solution (i) Theorem 14.20(ii) with $a = -1$ gives $f(-t) \to F(-s)$ as required. For the equality,

$$F(-s) = \int_{-\infty}^{\infty} f(t)\mathrm{e}^{-2\pi\mathrm{i}(-s)t}\mathrm{d}t = \int_{-\infty}^{\infty} \overline{f(t)\mathrm{e}^{-2\pi\mathrm{i}st}}\mathrm{d}t = \overline{F}(s).$$

(ii) To help get the definitions right, let us write $h(t) = f(-t)$. Then

$$f(-t)^*g(t) = h(t)^*g(t) = \int_{-\infty}^{\infty} h(t)g(s-t)\mathrm{d}t = \int_{-\infty}^{\infty} f(-t)g(s-t)\mathrm{d}t$$

$$= \int_{-\infty}^{\infty} f(u)g(u+s)\mathrm{d}u \quad (\text{putting } u = -t) = R_{fg}(s) \quad \text{by definition.}$$

By part (i) and the Convolution Theorem this implies $R_{fg} \to \overline{F}(s)G(s)$.

Exercise Deduce that $R_{ff} \to |F(s)|^2$.

Remark The Correlation Theorem provides another proof that * is commutative, associative and distributive over addition (cf. Section 10.2.2). For example, $(f*g)*h \to (F \circ G) \circ H = F \circ (G \circ H)$ gives associativity. Here, of course, $(F \circ G)(s) = F(s)G(s)$.

14.2.2 The Dirac delta function $\delta(x)$

This $\delta(x)$ is quite different from δ_{xy}, the Kronecker delta. The former, $\delta(x)$, is something slightly more general than a function, but to guide our intuition it is helpful to *think of it as a function* (see Penrose, 1999, Physics Section), and to describe it as the limit of well-defined functions $\{g_n(x)\}$ as $n \to \infty$, where the graph of $g_n(x)$ is a $(2/n) \times (n/2)$ rectangle of fixed area 1 but becoming arbitrarily thin and tall as n increases. Formally, $g_n(x) = n/2$ if $|x| \le 1/n$ and zero otherwise, as depicted in Figure 14.14. This is why $\delta(x)$ is often called a *spike*, and also an *impulse function*.

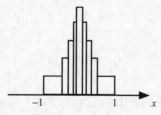

Figure 14.14 The graph of $g_n(x)$ for $n = 1, \dots, 5$. As n increases the area remains constant at 1, but the width tends to zero.

Strictly, $\delta(x)$ is a mapping from functions f to numbers, as defined below:

$$\int_{-\infty}^{\infty} f(x)\delta(x)\,dx = \lim_{n\to\infty} \int_{-\infty}^{\infty} f(x)g_n(x)\,dx. \qquad (14.27)$$

Remark The following is a simple but crucial consequence, and a characteristic feature of the delta function. It is known as the *sifting* or *testing* property:

$$\int_{-\infty}^{\infty} f(x)\delta(x - x_0)dx = f(x_0). \qquad (14.28)$$

Proof Following strictly the definition in (14.27), we start with (14.28) in the case $x_0 = 0$.

$$\int_{-\infty}^{\infty} f(x)g_n(x)dx = \int_{-1/n}^{1/n} f(x)(n/2)\,dx \qquad \text{by definition of } g_n(x)$$

$$= (2/n)[f(\alpha_n)n/2] \quad \text{for some } \alpha_n \text{ in } [-1/n, 1/n]$$

$$= f(\alpha_n),$$

by the Mean Value Theorem (Ledermann & Vajda, 1982), which states that, if f is continuous,

$$\int_a^b f(x)dx = (b - a)f(\alpha) \quad \text{for some } \alpha \text{ in } [a, b].$$

The integral thus simplifies to $f(\alpha_n)$, which tends to $f(0)$ as $n \to \infty$. Hence (14.28) is proved in the case $x_0 = 0$. For general x_0 we take $\delta(x - x_0)$ as the limit of $\{g_n(x)\}$ with the rectangles translated by x_0.

Exercise Write down the steps that give (14.28) for general x_0.

Example 14.24 (1) The Fourier transform of a spike at the origin has every frequency, at constant amplitude 1. This is because $\delta(x)$ transforms, by definition, to the integral

$$\int_{-\infty}^{\infty} f(x)\delta(x)\,dx \quad (\text{where } f(x) = e^{-i2\pi wx}) = f(0) \quad (\text{by } (14.28)) = e^0 = 1.$$

(2) The inverse transform of $\delta(w - w_0)$ is $\int_{-\infty}^{\infty} e^{i2\pi wx}\delta(w - w_0)\,dw = e^{i2\pi w_0 x}$, and similarly the inverse transform of $\delta(w + w_0)$ is $\int_{-\infty}^{\infty} e^{i2\pi wx}\delta(w + w_0)\,dw = e^{-i2\pi w_0 x}$, hence taking the averages we have by linearity that the inverse transform of $(1/2)[\delta(w - w_0) + \delta(w + w_0)]$ is $\cos 2\pi w_0 x$, a cosine function of frequency w_0 (see (14.10)). This verifies an entry in Table 14.2 to the effect that the Fourier Transform of a cosine of frequency k is a pair of spikes (impulses), at frequencies $\pm k$. This idealised description is easily visualised by the action of the Discrete Fourier Transform. For example, in Figure 14.3 the transform of the sum of three sines (similar effect to cosines) consists of three corresponding pairs of spikes, easily visible in their filled-out approximated form.

(3) More generally, a function expressible as a possibly infinite sum of sine and cosine functions of various frequencies (the Fourier series of the next section) transforms to a

Table 14.2. *The Continuous Fourier Transform in some useful cases. For the normal/ Gaussian distribution, see Chapter 9. If the normalisation constant γ is present we say* f *is* standardised Gaussian, *otherwise just of* Gaussian type.

$h(t)$	$H(s)$	remarks
centred unit square	$\sin(\pi s)/\pi s$	Figure 14.13
$e^{-\pi t^2}$	$e^{-\pi s^2}$	Example 14.21
$f \sim N(0, \sigma^2)$	Gaussian type $e^{-s^2/2\tau^2}$ $(\tau = 1/2\pi\sigma)$	Example 14.21
$f(t-a)$	$e^{-2\pi i a s F(s)}$	Shift Theorem
$f(t/a)$	$aF(as)$	Similarity Theorem
$f(t)^*g(t)$	$F(s)G(s)$	Convolution Theorem
$\delta(t)$ (impulse)	1 (constant)	Example 14.24 (1)
1 (constant)	$\delta(s)$ (impulse)	Example 14.24 (2)
$\cos(2\pi k t)$	impulse pair at frequencies $\pm k$	Example 14.24 (2)
$f(-t)$	$F(-s) = \overline{F}(s)$	Example 14.23
$f'(t)$	$2\pi i s F(s)$	Exercise 14.8
$t f(t)$	$(i/2\pi)F'(s)$	Example 14.24 (4)

corresponding sum of spikes, known variously as a *spike train*, *Shah function* or *comb function*.

(4) It is useful to include in Table 12.2 the transforms of the derivative $f'(t)$, and of $tf(t)$. The first is left as Exercise 14.8, and the second follows from

$$\frac{\mathrm{d}f}{\mathrm{d}s} = \frac{\mathrm{d}}{\mathrm{d}s} \int_{-\infty}^{\infty} f(t)e^{-2\pi i s t} \, \mathrm{d}t = \int_{-\infty}^{\infty} (-2\pi i t) f(t)e^{-2\pi i s t} \, \mathrm{d}t = -2\pi i \mathcal{F}[tf(t)].$$

Exercise Show $f'(t) \to 2\pi i F(s)$ (Use integration by parts and note that $|f(t)| \to 0$ as $t \to \infty$.)

Further information on the Fourier Transform and series may be found in Walker (1988) or Ledermann and Vajda (1982).

14.3 DFT connections

The DFT exists as a useful transform with an inverse, independently of whether it equals or approximates anything else, and can be used in its own right. We discussed the importance of relating the DFT and the Continuous Fourier Transform in the introduction to Section 14.2. In Figure 14.15 is an overview of the connections we shall explore. The journey begins with a small survey of Fourier series.

14.3.1 The background – Fourier series

We start here because it is an opportunity to state the widest class of functions we might possibly consider.

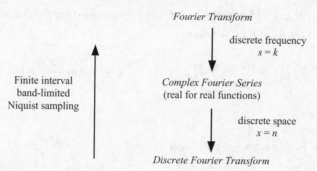

Fourier Transform

discrete frequency
$s = k$

Finite interval
band-limited
Niquist sampling

Complex Fourier Series
(real for real functions)

discrete space
$x = n$

Discrete Fourier Transform

Figure 14.15 Some relationships between the Fourier Transform, Fourier series, and DFT. Note that if time rather than space is a variable, then $x = n$ becomes $t = n$.

Real Fourier series

Suppose the real function $f(x)$ is defined *only on a finite interval I* of width L. We wish to represent $f(x)$ as a sum of *harmonics* (waves, modes) that is, of sines and cosines of various frequencies. This representation extends f by periodicity to the whole real line. Notice that, for every one unit increase in x, the wave $\sin(2\pi n)x$ goes through n complete periods of length 2π (similarly for cosines). We convert these periods from 2π to L by replacing x by x/L and hence using the forms

$$\sin \frac{2\pi n}{L}x, \qquad \cos \frac{2\pi n}{L}x,$$

and these appear in the Fourier expansion result stated as Theorem 14.25. It is only necessary that f be *piecewise continuous*, meaning that f has only a finite number of discontinuities, and that each such point c involves only a finite jump from the left hand limit $f(c^-)$ to the right hand limit $f(c^+)$, as defined respectively below.

$$f(c^-) = \operatorname*{Lim}_{\substack{x \to c \\ x < c}} f(x), \; f(c^+) = \operatorname*{Lim}_{\substack{x \to c \\ x > c}} f(x). \tag{14.29}$$

This is illustrated in Figure 14.16(a), where $f(0^-) = -1$ and $f(0^+) = 1$, a jump of height 2.

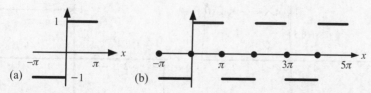

Figure 14.16 The graphs of (a) the step function $f(x)$ of Example 14.26, and (b) the sum of the Fourier series of $f(x)$ over $[-\pi, \; 5\pi]$. A solid dot indicates the mean value converged to at a discontinuity.

Theorem 14.25 *(Fourier) Let f(x) be piecewise continuous on the interval I of length L. Then the Fourier series of f(x), written*

$$f(x) \sim \frac{a_0}{2} + \sum_{n=1}^{\infty}\left(a_n \cos \frac{2\pi n}{L}x + b_n \sin \frac{2\pi n}{L}x\right), \qquad (14.30)$$

where

$$a_n = \frac{2}{L}\int_I f(x)\cos \tfrac{2\pi n}{L}x\ \mathrm{d}x \ \text{and}\ b_n = \frac{2}{L}\int_I f(x)\sin \tfrac{2\pi n}{L}x\ \mathrm{d}x, \qquad (14.31)$$

converges to f(x) at points x where f is continuous, and otherwise to the mean of the left and right limits (14.29); at both end-points a, b of the interval I, convergence is to $(1/2)[f(a^+) + f(b^-)]$. (This is consistent with extending f by periodicity, see Figure 14.16.) The series (14.30) is unique, given its convergence to $f(x)$ as described (a proof is given in Bracewell, 1986).

Example 14.26 Determine the Fourier series of the step function $f(x)$ on $[-\pi, \pi]$ given by $f(x) = -1$ if $x \le 0$ and $f(x) = 1$ if $x > 0$. Sketch the sum of the series over the interval $[-\pi, 5\pi]$, marking the values at discontinuites and end-points of $f(x)$. See Figure 14.16.

Notice that $L = 2\pi$, so $2\pi nx/L = nx$. Firstly, the symmetry of $f(x)$ gives $\pi a_0 = \int_I f(x)\mathrm{d}x = 0$.

$$\pi a_n = \int_{-\pi}^0 (-1)\cos nx\ \mathrm{d}x + \int_0^\pi \cos nx\ \mathrm{d}x = 0,\ \text{since}\ \sin(\pm n\pi) = 0\ (n \ge 1).$$

$$\pi b_n = \int_{-\pi}^0 (-1)\sin nx\ \mathrm{d}x + \int_0^\pi \sin nx\ \mathrm{d}x = \left[\frac{\cos nx}{n}\right]_{-\pi}^0 - \left[\frac{\cos nx}{n}\right]_0^\pi\ (n \ge 1)$$

$$= \frac{2 - 2(-1)^n}{n}\ \text{since}\ \cos(\pm n\pi) = (-1)^n\ \text{and}\ \cos(0) = 1$$

$$= 0\ \text{if}\ n\ \text{is even and}\ 4/n\ \text{if}\ n\ \text{is odd. Put}\ n = 2m - 1.$$

Hence the Fourier series of $f(x)$ is $S(x) = \frac{4}{\pi}\sum_{m=1}^{\infty}\frac{\sin(2m-1)x}{2m-1}$. Now see Figure 14.17. A useful source of many more examples is Murphy (1993). It is by no means obvious how successfully one can represent a step function (typified by Figure 14.16(a)) as a sum

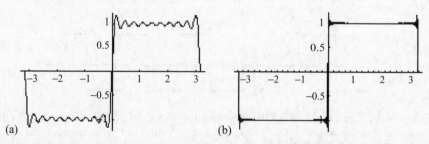

(a)   (b)

Figure 14.17 The Fourier series summed for the step function of Example 14.26: (a) sum of the first 10 terms, (b) sum of the first 100 terms.

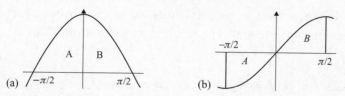

Figure 14.18 (a) Graph of the even function $\cos x$, where areas A and B are equal, (b) the odd function $\sin x$, with area $A = -(\text{area } B)$. This illustrates (14.33) with $L = \pi/2$.

of cosines, so let us see how close the fit is for, say, the first 10 and the first 100 terms. This is exemplified in Figure 14.17, and it is remarkable how well the series performs with just those 100 terms. The 10-term graph, (a), illustrates how convergence to the mean of left and right hand limits may proceed.

Even and odd functions An important simplification occurs in calculating (for example) the Fourier series of $f(x)$, if f is even or odd, as characterised below:

$$f(x) \text{ is } \begin{cases} \text{even}, & \text{if } f(-x) = f(x), \\ \text{odd}, & \text{if } f(-x) = -f(x). \end{cases} \tag{14.32}$$

This means that, for integrating over a symmetrical interval $[-L, L]$, the area B to the right of the vertical axis $x = 0$ is either doubled up or cancelled by a corresponding area A to the left, as in Figure 14.18. That is,

$$\int_{-L}^{L} f(x)\mathrm{d}x = \begin{cases} 2\int_0^L f(x)\mathrm{d}x, & \text{if } f \text{ is even}, \\ 0, & \text{if } f \text{ is odd}. \end{cases} \tag{14.33}$$

Example 14.27 (*Combining even and odd functions*) (1) If $g(x)$ is a product of functions, each even or odd, then, by counting minus signs, we see that $g(x)$ is even/odd according as its number of odd factors is even/odd. Thus, because $f(x)$ in Figure 14.16 is odd, so is $f(x)\cos nx$, giving $a_n = 0$ by (14.33), and hence a series of sine terms only. This does not, of course, apply to the constant term a_0, although this happens to be zero anyway.

(2) Similarly, an even function is a sum of cosines only.

(3) An easy example of a function that is neither even nor odd is $f(x) = \cos x + \sin x$. It also illustrates the general method of expressing $f = f_e + f_o$, the sum of even and odd parts given uniquely by $f_e(x) = (1/2)[f(x) + f(-x)]$, and $f_o = (1/2)[f(x) - f(-x)]$. The verification is left as an exercise (the argument is the same as for (7.16), where a matrix is expressed as the sum of a symmetric and a skew part).

Exercise Find the Fourier series of $f(x) = x^2$ on the interval $[-\pi, \pi]$.

Complex Fourier series

Can we apply the real Fourier series twice to obtain a corresponding complex series with sine and cosine terms compacted into the form e^{inx}? The answer is YES. For simplicity we'll take the finite interval as $[0, 2\pi]$; results are easily converted to $[0, L]$ by replacing x by $(2\pi/L)x$, and integrals are the same over any complete cycle of $\sin x$, such as $[-\pi, \pi]$.

An advantage of the complex series is its compactness; though the extra coefficients with negative subscripts are essential. The result is as follows (note the minus sign in the definition of c_n).

Theorem 14.28 *Let $f(x) = g(x) + ih(x)$, where g and h are piecewise continuous on the interval $[0, 2\pi]$. Then the Fourier series*

$$S(x) = \sum_{n=-\infty}^{\infty} c_n e^{inx}, \quad \text{where } c_n = \frac{1}{2\pi} \int_0^{2\pi} f(x) e^{-inx} dx, \quad (14.34)$$

converges to $f(x)$ at points x where f is continuous, and otherwise to the mean of the left and right limits; at both end-points $(a, b) = (0, 2\pi)$, convergence is to $(1/2)[f(a^+) + f(b^-)]$. The coefficients c_n are unique, given that $S(x)$ converges to $f(x)$ as described.

Proof We assume without loss of generality that f, g, h are continuous, and concentrate on the interval $[0, 2\pi]$. We show that if $f(x)$ has an expansion $\sum_n c_n e^{inx}$ then c_n has the form given in (14.34), and that, moreover, $S(x)$ equals the Fourier series for $g(x)$ plus i times that for $h(x)$. Thus the existence of the real series implies that of the complex, and the uniqueness of the complex series implies that of the real. For uniqueness we observe the *orthogonality relation*

$$\int_0^{2\pi} e^{inx} \cdot e^{-imx} dx = 2\pi \delta_{mn}. \quad (14.35)$$

Proof For $n = m$ the integrand becomes 1, so the integral equals 2π, otherwise we obtain

$$\int_0^{2\pi} e^{i(n-m)x} dx = \left[e^{i(n-m)x} / i(n - m) \right]_0^{2\pi} \quad \text{(by (14.24))} = 0,$$

since $e^{2\pi ki} = 1$ for any integer $k \, (= n - m)$. Now we can deduce the form of c_n as follows.

$$\int_0^{2\pi} f(x) e^{-imx} dx = \int_0^{2\pi} \left(\sum_{-\infty}^{\infty} c_n e^{inx} \right) e^{-imx} dx$$

$$= \sum_{n=-\infty}^{\infty} c_n \int_0^{2\pi} e^{inx} \cdot e^{-imx} dx \quad \text{interchanging limits}$$

$$= \sum_{n=-\infty}^{\infty} c_n (2\pi \delta_{mn}) \quad \text{by (14.35)}$$

$$= 2\pi c_m.$$

This establishes uniqueness of the coefficients c_m. For the *connection with real series* we split the complex sum into parts corresponding to positive and negative values of n, then apply the formulae $e^{inx} = \cos nx + i \sin nx$ and $e^{-inx} = \cos nx - i \sin nx$:

$$S(x) = c_0 + \sum_{n=1}^{\infty} c_n e^{inx} + \sum_{n=1}^{\infty} c_{-n} e^{-inx}$$

$$= c_0 + \sum_{n=1}^{\infty} (c_n + c_{-n}) \cos nx + \sum_{n=1}^{\infty} i(c_n - c_{-n}) \sin nx.$$

But

$$c_n + c_{-n} = \frac{1}{2\pi} \int_0^{2\pi} f(x)(e^{inx} + e^{-inx})dx = \frac{1}{2\pi} \int_0^{2\pi} (g(x) + ih(x)) \cdot 2\cos nx \, dx,$$

whereas $i(c_n - c_{-n}) = \frac{1}{2\pi} \int_0^{2\pi} (g(x) + ih(x)) \cdot 2\sin nx \, dx$. Considering (14.31) with $L = 2\pi$, this shows that $S(x)$ equals the sum of the series for $g(x)$ plus i times the series for $h(x)$, as asserted. That is, $S(x) = f(x)$, completing the proof of Theorem 14.28.

Remarks 14.29 Let us record in more detail the relationship between real and complex coefficients. Suppose that $f(x) = g(x) + ih(x)$, where g, h are real functions, and that f, g, h have respective Fourier coefficients $c_n, (a_n, b_n), (a_n', b_n')$. In this notation we have just shown that

$$c_n + c_{-n} = a_n + ia_n', \quad i(c_n - c_{-n}) = b_n + ib_n'. \tag{14.36}$$

Series for real functions Setting $a_n' = 0 = b_n'$ in (14.36) and rearranging, we obtain for real and complex series of a *real* function

$$\begin{cases} c_n = \frac{1}{2}(a_n - ib_n), \quad c_{-n} = \frac{1}{2}(a_n + ib_n), \\ a_n = c_n + c_{-n}, \quad b_n = i(c_n - c_{-n}). \end{cases} \tag{14.37}$$

Shortcuts (i) In particular, c_{-n} is the complex conjugate of c_n, and when these pairs are suitably combined we obtain for a real function the usual real series. (ii) Once a function is expressed as a sum of sines and cosines, with coefficients possibly complex, uniqueness of the complex series implies that we will obtain it correctly if we simply substitute

$$\cos nx = {}^1\!/{}_2(e^{inx} + e^{-inx}), \quad \sin nx = \frac{1}{2i}(e^{inx} - e^{-inx}).$$

Example 14.30 Determine the real and complex Fourier series of $f(x) = \sin x + \cos 3x$. *Real series* We simply observe that $f(x)$ is already expressed as a real Fourier series, and since such expression is unique there is nothing more to be done.
Complex series This must be $(1/2i)(e^{ix} - e^{-ix}) + (1/2)(e^{3ix} - e^{-3ix})$.

Exercise Find the complex series for $1 + 2\sin x \cos x + 2i\cos 5x$.

14.3.2 The DFT as approximation to the Fourier Transform

Suppose that $f(x)$ is zero outside the finite interval $I = [0, L]$ and we wish to approximate the Fourier transform

$$F(\omega) = \int_{-\infty}^{\infty} f(x)e^{-2\pi i\omega x}dx, \tag{14.38}$$

where we have replaced the earlier s by Greek ω in traditional fashion, to emphasise its later role as frequency. We approximate in one of the simplest ways, namely by writing $g(x) = f(x)e^{-2\pi i\omega x}$ and using the values $g(x_n)$ at equally spaced *grid points* x_n obtained by dividing I into N equal subintervals. That is, x_n and the grid width Δx are given by

$$\Delta x = L/N, \quad \text{and} \quad x_n = n\Delta_x \ (n = 0, 1, \ldots, N). \tag{14.39}$$

The following argument applies to the real and imaginary parts of $g(x)$ separately, and thence to $g(x)$ itself. One way to approximate the required area is to straighten the curved portion over each subinterval into a straight line segment and add up the trapezium-shaped areas T (this is known as the *Trapezoidal Rule*, see e.g. Swokowski, 2000). (See Figure 14.19.)

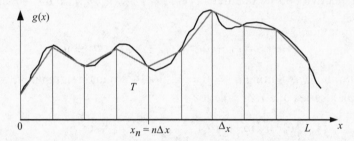

Figure 14.19 Area under a function $g(x)$, approximated by that under a sequence of straight line segments, namely the sum of areas of trapezia such as T.

Since the area of a trapezium equals the mean length of its parallel sides times the distance between them, this gives

$$F(\omega) \approx \tfrac{1}{2}\Delta_x \left[g(0) + g(L) + 2 \sum_{n=1}^{N-1} g(x_n) \right]. \tag{14.40}$$

Because the N-point DFT (14.1), by its definition, repeats at the Nth point, we should assume $g(L) = g(0)$, which simplifies (14.40) to

$$F(\omega) \cong \Delta_x \sum_{n=0}^{N-1} g(x_n) = \Delta_x \sum_{n=0}^{N-1} f(x_n)e^{-2\pi i\omega nL/N}, \text{ since } x_n = nL/N. \tag{14.41}$$

This is beginning to look like the DFT, except that it holds so far for all ω. Two equivalent considerations lead to the same choice of ω-values in their role as frequencies.

Reciprocity relations for the DFT The inverse of the DFT is unique. To make it operable here for values $\omega = \omega_k$ we require, according to (14.41) and (14.1), $2\pi i\omega_k nL/N = 2\pi ikn/N$, or $\omega_k = k/L$ ($k = 0, 1, \ldots, N-1$). Thus our grid spacing of $\Delta_x = L/N$ on the spatial axis implies a grid spacing on the frequency axis of

$$\Delta_\omega = 1/L, \quad \text{where } \omega_k = k\Delta_\omega. \tag{14.42}$$

See Figure 14.20.

Observe that the ω-grid spacing $\Delta_\omega = 1/L$ corresponds to a period L, the full extent of the spatial grid. Thus we could equivalently have begun with this maximum period as a hypothesis for the waves of (14.42) and inferred the correct ω_k for the DFT. Denoting

Figure 14.20 Spatial and frequency grid spacing for the DFT, with N subintervals.

the highest frequency N/L on the grid by Ω, we may now infer the important *reciprocity relations*

$$\Omega L = N, \tag{14.43}$$

$$\Delta_x \Delta_\omega = 1/N. \tag{14.44}$$

One interpretation of these relations is that, for given N, the spatial and frequency grid lengths vary inversely, as do their grid spacings. We have now derived the DFT as an approximation to the Fourier Transform. How good an approximation it is, and when it is exact, we will learn in the next section. The answer depends of course on the *sampling rate N*.

Exercise Deduce the reciprocity relations from the definitions of the Δs.

14.3.3 The DFT, Fourier series and sampling rate

Here is a result which will be fundamental to what follows.

Theorem 14.31 *Let the function* $f(x)$ *be zero outside of a finite interval I. Then the N-point DFT coefficients* $F_0, \ldots, F_{N-1}$ *are related to the complex Fourier series coefficients by*

$$\boxed{(1/N)F_k = c_k + \sum_{j=1}^{\infty} (c_{k+jN} + c_{k-jN}).} \tag{14.45}$$

It follows that if $c_s = 0$ *for* $|s| > \mu$, *where* $\mu \leq N/2$, *then the DFT and Fourier coefficients are identical (up to a constant multiple N).*

Proof For simplicity we take the finite interval as $[0, 2\pi]$. The case $[0, L]$ and translates thereof work the same way but look more complicated (see e.g. Briggs & Henson, 1995). Further, since we are dealing with Fourier series, convergence at the end-points is to their mean value, so we may without loss of generality take these values to be the same. Thus we divide the interval into N equal portions, set $x_n = 2\pi n/N$, and take $n = 0, 1, \ldots, N-1$ for the DFT. Let $w = e^{-2\pi i/N}$. Applying the Fourier series (14.34) to $f(x)$ at $x = x_n$, we may write

$$f_n = f(x_n) = \sum_{m=-\infty}^{\infty} c_m e^{imx_n} = \sum_{m=-\infty}^{\infty} c_m e^{im2\pi n/N} = \sum_{m=-\infty}^{\infty} c_m w^{-mn}. \tag{14.46}$$

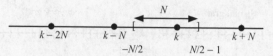

Figure 14.21 Position of integers $k \pm jN$ $(j \neq 0)$ relative to the interval $[-N/2, N/2 - 1]$.

On the other hand, applying the DFT to $f_0, \ldots, f_{N-1}$ yields

$$F_k = \sum_{n=0}^{N-1} f_n w^{kn} \quad \text{(by (14.8))} \quad = \sum_{n=0}^{N-1} w^{kn} \sum_{m=-\infty}^{\infty} c_m w^{-mn} \quad \text{(by (14.46))}$$

$$= \sum_{m=-\infty}^{\infty} c_m \sum_{n=0}^{N-1} w^{(k-m)n}, \quad \text{on interchanging limits.}$$

Now, the successive powers of w, as exhibited in Figure 14.2(b) at the start of this chapter, repeat with period N and no less. Therefore $w^{k-m} = 1$ if and only if k and m differ by an integral multiple of N, or $m = k \pm jN$ for some positive integer j. So by (14.6) with $\alpha = w^{k-m}$ the inner sum $\sum_n$ above is zero unless $m = k \pm jN$, when $w^{k-m} = 1$ and the sum becomes N. This establishes (14.45).

For the last part we take k in the symmetrical interval $-N/2, \ldots, 0, \ldots, N/2 - 1$. Then, for any k so placed, the integers $k - N, k - 2N, \ldots$ are to the left, outside the interval, and $k + N, k + 2N, \ldots$ are outside on the right, as depicted in Figure 14.21.

So if $c_s = 0$ for s outside this interval then (14.45) reduces to $(1/N)F_k = c_k$. But this condition on c_s is a consequence of the given one: $c_s = 0$ for $|s| > \mu$, where $\mu \leq N/2$.

The periodic band-limited case A real or complex function $f(x)$ is said to be *L-periodic* if $f(x)$ has period L, *band-limited* if its Fourier coefficients c_k are zero outside a finite range ('band') of k, and *piecewise monotone* on the finite interval I if the latter can be split into a finite number of subintervals, on each of which $f(x)$ is either non-increasing or non-decreasing.

Corollary 14.32 *(The Niquist sampling rate) Suppose the function $f(x)$ is zero outside a finite interval (or is L-periodic) and is band-limited to $|k| \leq k_{\max}$. Then the N-point DFT determines the function exactly if $N \geq 2k_{\max}$.*

Proof Theorem 14.31 applies with $\mu = k_{\max}$, for then $N \geq 2k_{\max}$ implies $\mu \leq N/2$.

Shannon (1949) proved a more general result, in which the hypothesis on Fourier coefficients becomes one on the Fourier Transform, and the corresponding *Niquist condition* is given in the notation of the reciprocity relations. Furthermore, his result gives the remarkable explicit formula below for reconstructing $f(x)$ using the *sinc* function in the form $\text{sinc}(x) = (\sin x)/x$.

Theorem 14.33 *(Shannon Sampling Theorem) Let f be a band-limited function whose Fourier Transform is zero outside of the interval $[-\Omega/2, \ \Omega/2]$. If Δ_x is chosen so that*

$\Delta_x \le 1/\Omega$, then f may be reconstructed exactly from its samples $f_n = f(x_n) = f(n\Delta_x)$ by

$$f(x) = \sum_{n=-\infty}^{\infty} f_n \mathrm{sinc}[\pi(x - x_n)/\Delta_x]. \qquad (14.47)$$

Aliasing The Shannon Theorem tells us that a band-limited function can be reconstructed by sampling provided we sample sufficiently often to 'resolve' its higher frequencies. If we do not, the higher frequencies will cause the introduction of lower frequencies which are not part of f, and which are therefore called *aliases* of these higher frequencies. We can see this already in (14.45). If there is no lower-frequency coefficient c_k, a higher frequency c_{k+N} will nevertheless make a contribution to a frequency k term F_k. This is illustrated in Figure 14.22, where the frequency -16 component of $f(t)$ cannot be resolved by the samples of less than the Niquist frequency of 2×16 points (though 28 points are better than 24) and is replaced by aliases at lower frequencies. The low-frequency component (frequency 1) is successfully reconstructed.

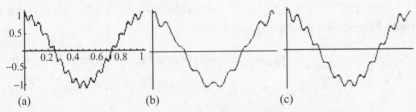

Figure 14.22 (Aliasing) (a) The original function $f(t) = \cos 2\pi t + (1/10)\cos 32\pi t$, (b) $f(t)$ reconstructed from a 24 point sample by (14.47). Aliasing has introduced gratuitous low-frequency components, (c) reconstruction from a 28 point sample-less aliasing.

Some 'real life' examples (i) Artifacts in a computer image caused by inadequate resolution (sampling rate). (ii) An effect on motion films, also called *strobing*: if the frame rate is too little then the wheels of a forward moving car (or waggon) can appear to rotate backwards. Of course, for every frame rate there is a speed for which the rotation will *not* be adequately captured by the camera. (iii) Similar effects may be obtained by not-rapid-enough periodic illumination of an otherwise darkened scene, which might include objects on a rotating turntable.

The periodic non-band-limited case We can bound the difference between F_k and c_k by using (14.45) and the following bound, of independent interest, on the Fourier coefficients.

Theorem 14.34 *Suppose that the pth derivative $f^{(p)}(x)$ is bounded and piecewise monotone on $[0, L]$, and that if $p \ge 1$ the first $p-1$ derivatives of f are L-periodic, and continuous on $[0, \ L]$. Then the Fourier and DFT coefficients of f satisfy, for* *constants C, D,*

$$|c_k| \leq C/|k|^{p+1} \quad (k \in Z), \tag{14.48}$$

$$|{}^1\!/_N F_k - c_k| \leq D/N^{p+1} \quad (|k| \leq N/2, p \geq 1). \tag{14.49}$$

We may take $C = (L/2\pi)^p \, \text{Max}_x |f^{(p)}(x)|$, *and* $D = 2^{p+1}\pi^2 C/3$.

Proof The first inequality We shall be content to prove that $|c_k| \leq C/|k|^p$ when $p \geq 1$. The improvement to index $p + 1$, and the special case $p = 0$, are found in e.g. Walker (1988). We integrate by parts p times as follows.

$$Lc_k = \int_0^L f(x)e^{-i2\pi kx/L}dx = \left[f(x)e^{-i2\pi kx/L}/(-i2\pi k/L) \right]_0^L$$

$$+ \frac{L}{i2\pi k} \int_0^L f'(x)e^{-i2\pi kx/L}dx \cdots = \left(\frac{L}{i2\pi k} \right)^p \int_0^L f^{(p)}(x)e^{-i2\pi kx/L}dx,$$

each successive constant term being zero because $e^{-i2\pi m} = 1$ for any integer m. The last *integral* is bounded in absolute value by LB, where B is the greatest absolute value of the integrand, $B = \text{Max}_x |f^{(p)}(x)|$ (this exists because $[0, L]$ is a closed bounded interval, see e.g. Hoggar, 1992). Hence $|c_k| \leq C/|k|^p$ with $C = B(L/2\pi)^p$, and we have dealt with (14.48). Proceeding to (14.49), we have

$$|(1/N)F_k - c_k| = \left| \sum_{j=1}^{\infty} (c_{k+jN} + c_{k-jN}) \right|, \text{ where } |c_m| \leq C/|m|^{p+1} \qquad \text{by (14.45)}$$

$$\leq \sum_{j=1}^{\infty} \{ C/|k + jN|^{p+1} + C/|k - jN|^{p+1} \} \qquad \text{by (14.48)}$$

$$= \frac{C}{N^{p+1}} \sum_{j=1}^{\infty} \{ 1/(j + k/N)^{p+1} + 1/(j - k/N)^{p+1} \}. \tag{**}$$

We were able to drop the modulus signs because $j - k/N$ is rendered positive by the (14.49) condition $|k| \leq N/2$, or $|k/N| \leq 1/2$. We see that the infinite sum is bounded by a quantity independent of N and k, as follows. Starting with $\pm k/N \geq -1/2$ (from $-1/2 \leq k/N \leq 1/2$), we have $j \pm k/N \geq j - 1/2 \geq j/2$ (since $j \geq 1$), whence

$$0 < 1/(j \pm k/N)^{p+1} \leq 2^{p+1}/j^{p+1} \leq 2^{p+1}/j^2 \quad (p \geq 1).$$

Now consider $\sum_j 1/j^2$. The *fact* that this sum converges is shown by an elementary test (see e.g. Ledermann & Vajda, 1982, or Swokowski, 2000, p. 566), and this is enough to establish the *existence* of the constant D. However, the value of the sum, $\pi^2/6$, may be computed in a standard way from a Fourier series expansion, as at the end of Example 14.35 below. Then our series (**) must converge to a sum bounded by $2^{p+1}\pi^2/3$, which is independent of N and k. This completes the proof, giving $|(1/N)F_k - c_k| \leq D/N^{p+1}$ with $D = 2^{p+1}\pi^2 C/3$ (for detailed rules on infinite sums, see the cited references).

Example 14.35 We consider bounds given by Theorem 14.34, starting with (1) Case $p = 0$ Here $f(x)$ is to be bounded and piecewise monotone, allowing jumps, so the step function of Figure 14.16 is an example. The first bound is $|c_k| \leq C/k$, which tells us that

c_k decreases at least as rapidly as the reciprocal $1/k$, as k increases through $1, 2, 3, \ldots$ What is the actuality? We found in Example 14.26 that $b_n = 0$ and $a_n = 4/\pi n$ for n odd (otherwise zero). Formulae (14.37) convert this to

$$c_k = (1/2)a_k = (2/\pi)/k, \quad \text{in agreement with the bound } C/k \ (k > 0).$$

(2) Case $p = 1$ Here we consider both the c_k themselves and how closely they are determined by the DFT. Now it is $f'(x)$ that must be bounded and monotonic, whilst $f(x)$ is L-periodic and continuous on $[0, L]$ (or any interval of width L). A useful example is $f(x) = x^2$ on $[-\pi, \ \pi]$, extended by periodicity. In Figure 14.23 we show $f(x)$ and its derivative over two periods. Note that $f'(x)$, though discontinuous, is nevertheless piecewise monotonic.

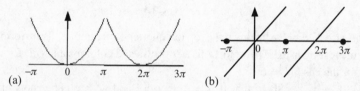

Figure 14.23 The graphs of (a) $f(x) = x^2$ and (b) $f'(x) = 2x$, both extended by periodicity from $[-\pi, \pi]$. The latter is piecewise monotonic, as required by Theorem 14.34.

Since $p + 1 = 2$, the *bounds* are $|c_k| = C/k^2$ and $|(1/N)F_k - c_k| \le D/k^2$. Let us determine C and D. Since $L/2\pi = 1$, we have $C = \text{Max}|2x| \ (-\pi \le x \le \pi) = 2\pi$, and $D = 4\pi^2 C/3 = 8\pi^3/3$. Turning now to the actual coefficients, note that the real Fourier series $f(x)$ is even, so $b_n = 0$ without further calculation, and we get (Theorem 14.25)

$$f(x) = \pi^2/3 + \sum_{n=1}^{\infty} \frac{4(-1)^n}{n^2} \cos nx, \tag{14.50a}$$

$$|c_k| \le 2\pi/k^2 \quad (\text{actual value } \pm 4/k^2), \quad \text{and} \quad |(1/N)F_k - c_k| \le (8\pi^3/3)/N^2, \tag{14.50b}$$

so, for instance, if $N = 256$ then the DFT coefficients determine the Fourier ones to within 0.001 approx. A further point of interest here is that (14.50) give us the sum S of reciprocal squares required in the proof of the inequality (14.49), for, setting $x = \pi$ in (14.50) and noting that $\cos n\pi = (-1)^n$, we obtain $\pi^2 = \pi^2/3 + 4S$, whence $S = \pi^2/6$ as quoted.

1. **Do the DFT coefficients define $f(x)$ completely?** YES, over any finite interval, provided $f(x)$ is band-limited and our sampling rate equals at least the Niquist rate (twice the maximum frequency, over the interval). See Corollary 14.32.
2. **How do the DFT and the Continuous Fourier Transform relate?** The DFT is essentially the Trapezoidal Rule approximation. See Section 14.3.2. The error is at worst of order Δ_x^2, but as little as zero under certain complicated conditions (Briggs & Henson, 1995).

3. **Any other connections?** The DFT solves the least squares curve fitting problem rather beautifully for a polynomial in $e^{(2\pi/L)ix}$ over an interval of width L, giving zero error (Briggs & Henson, 1995).

Some history of the FFT

We have noted the Fast Fourier Transform for its great improvement in speed as a way to calculate the DFT. Though Cooley and Tukey (1965) were not its first inventors, indeed the fundamental argument was known to Gauss, it was their landmark paper which introduced it for the first time to a wide readership and achieved general acceptance of its importance. See Heideman *et al.* (1985).

Exercises 14

1 √ (a) In the case $N = 4$, write down the top left quarter of the Fourier Transform matrix. Now deduce the rest by using Theorem 14.5 (i) for rows and columns and (iii) for rows only. (b) Repeat for the case $N = 6$.

2 √ (a) Let $w = e^{-2\pi i/N}$. Show that if $N = 6$ then w^2 and w^4 are cube roots of 1 other than 1 itself. Why does it follow that $1 + w^2 + w^4 = 0 = 1 + w^4 + w^8$? (b) Deduce that $[1 \ 0 \ 1 \ 0 \ 1 \ 0] \to [3 \ 0 \ 0 \ 3 \ 0 \ 0]$ under T (Theorem 14.5(v) may help). (c) Can you prove the general result for $N = 2M$, even?

3   Let $\{f_n\}$ be the sample values of $f(x) = (1/4)\sin 10\pi x + (1/2)\sin 40\pi x$ at 200 equally spaced points in the interval $[0, 1]$. Using the DFT, show f in both the spatial and the frequency domains (cf. Figure 14.3). Identify the peaks in the frequency domain with the components of f.

4 √ (a) Write down the 4-point DFT matrix and its inverse. (b) What are (i) the periods of $\sin 14t$ and $\cos 3x$, (ii) the frequencies of $\sin 2\pi Nx$, $\sin 8\pi x$ and $\sin 3\pi x$?

5 √ (a) Determine the convolution product $[1 \ 2 \ 3] * [1 \ 0 \ 2 \ 1]$ by polynomial multiplication. (b) Smooth the values $[1 \ 5 \ 2 \ -2 \ 4 \ 6]$ by the averaging effect of convolution with $[1/2 \ 1/2]$. Do this (i) by polynomial multiplication and (ii) by replacing old values with the appropriate linear combinations. (c) Verify the Convolution Theorem $T(f*g) = (Tf) \circ (Tg)$ in the case $f = [2 \ 1 \ 0]$, $g = [-1 \ 1 \ 0]$.

6 √ (a) Recover the DFT matrix T_4 from a 4-point butterfly diagram. (b) Implement the N-point DFT as simple matrix multiplication, and ALGO 14.2 for the FFT. Compare their times for $N = 2^n$, and $n = 3, 4, \ldots, 12$.

7 √ (Used in Example 14.21.) Let $I = \int_{-\infty}^{\infty} e^{-\pi(t+is)^2} dt$. Show that $dI/ds = 0$ and find I by setting $s = 0$.

8 √ (i) Show that the Fourier transform of df/dt is $2\pi is F(s)$. (You may assume that $|f(t)| \to 0$ as $t \to 0$.) (ii) Find the transform of $t^2 f(t)$, then that of $t^n f(t)$.

9 √ Let $b(t)$ be the unit box, $b(t) = 1$ for $0 < t < 1$, otherwise zero. (i) Calculate the transform $B(s)$. (ii) Use the Shift Theorem to show the transform of the centred unit box is sinc(s). (iii) What is the transform of the convolution product of n centred boxes?

10 √ Use the method of Example 14.24 to find the transform of $\sin(2\pi kt)$.

11 $\checkmark$ Let $f(x) = x$ $(-\pi < x < \pi)$. (i) Is this function even, odd, or neither? What kind of terms will the Fourier series $S(x)$ contain? (ii) Calculate $S(x)$, and sketch its graph from -3π to 3π. (iii) By setting $x = \pi/2$, find a formula for $1 + 1/3 + 1/5 + \cdots$.

12 $\checkmark$ Find the complex series for $1 + 2\sin x \cos x + 2i\cos 5x$.

13 $\checkmark$ Let $f(t) = \cos 2\pi t + (1/8)\cos 40\pi t$ on the interval $[0, 1]$. (i) What is the minimum sampling rate N for this function to be reconstructible? Perform reconstruction with (ii) $N/2$ samples, (iii) N samples.

15

Transforming images

Here we extend all things Fourier to two dimensions. Shortly we will be able to model many effects on an image, such as motion or focus blur, by the 2D version of *convolution*, which is handled especially simply by the Fourier Transform. This enables us to restore an image from many kinds of noise and other corruption. We begin Section 15.1 by showing how the Fourier Transform, and others, may be converted from a 1- to a 2-dimensional transform of a type called *separable*, reducing computation and adding simplicity. In the Fourier case we may apply the FFT in each dimension individually, and hence speed calculation still further.

In Section 15.1.3 we prove that certain changes in an image result in predictable changes in its transform. We include the effect of both rotation and projection, which are germane to computerised tomography in Chapter 18. In Section 15.1.4 we present consequences of the 2D Convolution Theorem for the Fourier Transform, and offer a polynomial-based proof that purports to show 'why' the result holds. Section 15.1.5 establishes connections between correlation and the Fourier Transform, for later use.

We begin Section 15.2 by considering the low-level operation of changing pixels solely on the basis of their individual values, then move on to the possibilites of 'filtering' by changing Fourier coefficients. Next we see how the same effect may be accomplished by convolving the original with a matrix of coefficients. We introduce filters that achieve edge-detection in an image.

Section 15.3 emphasises filters as a tool in reconstructing an image after a known type of distortion has occurred, such as by motion blur, inadequate camera lens or atmosphere effects. There is a huge variety of ideas here. Our selection includes the Wiener filter, based on probabilistic models of image and noise.

In Section 15.4 we focus on the use of transforms in compression, introducing the Discrete Cosine Transform, or DCT, which is a relative of the DFT. The DCT has advantages for natural images and is easily converted to two dimensions by the method of Section 15.1.1. Finally, we show how the DCT fits into the widely used JPEG compression method, indicating why, on theoretical grounds, it should be good for natural images.

$$\begin{pmatrix} 193 & 174 & 137 & 118 & 123 & 126 & 132 \\ 185 & 163 & 141 & 135 & 119 & 115 & 137 \\ 173 & 147 & 128 & 124 & 105 & 102 & 118 \\ 161 & 132 & 111 & 102 & 98 & 108 & 118 \\ 155 & 121 & 106 & 103 & 108 & 109 & 114 \\ 145 & 115 & 111 & 113 & 114 & 117 & 117 \\ 151 & 121 & 118 & 126 & 125 & 126 & 123 \end{pmatrix}$$

Figure 15.1

15.1 The Fourier Transform in two dimensions

15.1.1 Separable transforms in general

The object f to be transformed is now an array/matrix, say of grey values taken by a corresponding array of pixels in a digital image. These values are thought of as consisting of uniformly spaced samples from a continuous model of an original image. To make things more concrete, we show in Figure 15.1 an image of 109×128 pixels, and the submatrix of the first seven rows and columns of the array of its grey values. For simplicity, though, the theoretical discussion will be about square images.

But we have a problem. To apply a general linear transform to an $N \times N$ array or matrix, $f = [f_{mn}]_{0 \leq m,n \leq N-1}$, we must first rearrange the elements of f, say row by row, into a single vector f' of length N^2. Then a linear transform is given by $f' \to Kf'$, for some $N^2 \times N^2$ matrix K. So far so good, but K is very large, about one million square for images of size $N = 1024$, so this takes a great deal of computation. Given that multiplying a k-vector by a $k \times k$ matrix takes $k(2k - 1)$ arithmetic operations (Section 14.1.4), the requirement here is $N^2(2N^2 - 1)$, of order $O(N^4)$.

However, many transforms, including those in which we are most interested, can be put into effect by multiplying f on both sides by a matrix of the same size as itself. Thus our example of size one million reverts down to one thousand. The property is that of being *separable*, as we now describe.

The separable case A 2D transform on f is called *separable* if its effect may be obtained by applying a 1D transform $X \to MX$ to each column of f in turn, and then to each row of the resulting array. This, of course, gives a nice algorithm for performing the 2D transform by repeated use of a 1D routine (see Section 15.5.2 for the n-dimensional case). First we'll express the result in terms of M, where f has columns $D_0, \ldots, D_{N-1}$, and the 2D transform performs $f \to F$. Replacing each column D_i by MD_i as prescribed means $f \to [MD_0 \ldots MD_{N-1}]$, which equals Mf by (7.26). To transform the rows of this result we may transpose them to columns, pre-multiply by M, then transpose back: $Mf \to (Mf)^T \to M(Mf)^T \to MfM^T$. Thus we have the 2D transform–inverse pair

$$\boxed{\begin{aligned} F &= M f M^T, \\ f &= M^{-1} F (M^{-1})^T. \end{aligned}}$$

(15.1)

Table 15.1. *The number of arithmetic operations required by a 2D linear transform on an N × N array. The last row anticipates Theorem 15.6.*

transform type	number of operations	order
general	$N^2(2N^2 - 1)$	$O(N^4)$
separable	$2N^2(2N - 1)$	$O(N^3)$
Fourier, by the FFT	$3N^2 \log N$	$O(N^2 \log N)$
FFT on a separable array	$3N \log N + N^2$	$O(N^2)$

The formula for f is the result of simply multiplying each side of the DFT formula above it by M^{-1} on the left and by M^{-1} transposed on the right. It is not quite obvious in advance whether a different result is obtained if we transform the columns first, but the expression (15.1) makes clear that there is no difference, because of associativity of the matrix product, that is: $(Mf)M^T = M(fM^T)$. Now, considering computation, the number of arithmetic operations for multiplying two $N \times N$ matrices is $N^2(2N - 1)$, giving a total for the 2D transform (15.1) of $N^2(2N - 1)$. Thus a separable transform reduces a potential $O(N^4)$ operations to $O(N^3)$. This is a huge saving for large N.

Example 15.1 The 2D Discrete Fourier Transform (DFT) may be defined by (15.1) with $M = T$, the DFT matrix of Chapter 14, so it is indeed separable. The next section is devoted to some consequences. Here we note that because the DFT has a shortened method, the FFT, reducing N-vector times matrix to $(3/2)N \log N$ operations, we have the last reduction shown in Table 15.1.

Components and bases The idea of a basis for arrays of a given size has proved extremely fruitful, with the possibility of bases specially adapted to simplicity and economy of use (more on this later). We begin by supposing that M^{-1} has columns $C_0, \ldots, C_{N-1}$ and letting E_{jk} be the $N \times N$ matrix consisting of zeros *except for* 1 *in position* (j, k). Then we may write

$$
\begin{aligned}
f &= M^{-1} F(M^{-1})^T & \text{by (15.1)} \\
&= M^{-1}\left(\sum_{jk} F_{jk} E_{jk}\right)(M^{-1})^T & \text{since } F = \sum_{jk} F_{jk} E_{jk} \text{ by defn. of } E_{jk} \\
&= \sum_{jk} F_{jk} M^{-1} E_{jk} (M^{-1})^T & \text{by linearity} \\
&= \sum_{jk} F_{jk} C_j C_k^T & \text{by (7.32c) and } M^{-1} = [C_0, \ldots, C_{N-1}].
\end{aligned}
$$

That is,

$$
f = \sum_{jk} F_{jk} C_j C_k^T. \tag{15.2}
$$

This expresses an arbitrary array f as a linear combination of matrices $\{C_j C_k^T\}$. Moreover, these matrices form a basis for the $N \times N$ matrices (i.e. f may be *uniquely* so expressed), according to (7.10), because there are exactly the right number, N^2, of them.

Nature of the basis These matrices $\varepsilon_{jk} = C_j C_k^T$ are of a very special type; they are *rank 1 matrices*, meaning that each row is a multiple of one fixed nonzero row (see Section 8.2.2). For example, let $C_j = [2\ 3\ 0]$ and $C_k = [2\ 4\ 10]$. Then

$$\varepsilon_{jk} = \begin{bmatrix} 2 \\ 3 \\ 0 \end{bmatrix} [4\ \ 2\ \ 1] = \begin{bmatrix} 8 & 4 & 2 \\ 12 & 6 & 3 \\ 0 & 0 & 0 \end{bmatrix}.$$

We observe that the uth row of the product is the uth element of C_j times the row C_k^T. In fact, writing array positions in parenthesis, we have the equivalent expressions

$$\varepsilon_{jk} = C_j C_k^T, \quad \text{and } \varepsilon_{jk}(u, v) = C_j(u)C_k(v). \tag{15.3}$$

Inner products We want to see what happens to dot products and orthogonality when we pass from one to two dimensions of array. The dot/inner product of two equal-sized matrices A, B is defined to be their dot product as long vectors,

$$A \cdot B = \begin{cases} \Sigma_{j,k} a_{jk} b_{jk} & \text{(real case)}, \\ \Sigma_{j,k} a_{jk} \bar{b}_{jk} & \text{(complex case)}. \end{cases} \tag{15.4}$$

Notice that the complex case simply becomes the real definition if the numbers are real, when $\bar{b}_{ij} = b_{ij}$. Now we are ready to state the key results, of which only (15.5) remains to be proved.

Theorem 15.2 *Let* $M^{-1} = [C_0 \ldots C_{N-1}]$ *and* $\varepsilon_{jk} = C_j C_k^T$. *Then the 2D transform (15.1) defined by M sends an array f to its components* F_{jk} *w.r.t.* $\{\varepsilon_{jk}\}$ *as basis. Furthermore,*

$$\varepsilon_{jk} \cdot \varepsilon_{pq} = (C_j \cdot C_p)(C_k \cdot C_q). \tag{15.5}$$

Thus $\{\varepsilon_{jk}\}$ *is orthogonal/orthonormal according as the respective property holds for* $\{C_j\}$, *and if all* C_j *have length L then all* ε_{jk} *have length* L^2.

Proof
$$\begin{aligned}
\varepsilon_{jk} \cdot \varepsilon_{pq} &= \Sigma_{u,v}\, \varepsilon_{jk}(u, v)\bar{\varepsilon}_{pq}(u, v) & \text{by (15.4)} \\
&= \Sigma_{uv}\, C_j(u)C_k(v)\overline{C}_p(u)\overline{C}_q(v) & \text{by (15.3)} \\
&= \Sigma_u C_j(u)\overline{C}_p(u)\, \Sigma_v C_k(v)\overline{C}_q(v) & \text{by rearrangement} \\
&= (C_j \cdot C_p)(C_k \cdot C_q) & \text{by definition of } C_j \cdot C_k.
\end{aligned}$$

Exercise Deduce the last sentence of Theorem 15.2 from (15.5).

15.1.2 Constructing the 2D Fourier Transform

The DFT in two dimensions To convert the 1D Discrete Fourier Transform to a 2D version we simply follow the standard procedure we have just set up. That is, we substitute the Fourier matrix T for M in Equations (15.1). Since T is symmetric the result is as follows.

Theorem 15.3 *(Matrix formulation) The 2D Discrete Fourier Transform $f \to F$, between square arrays indexed by $0, 1, \ldots, N-1$, where $T = [w^{kn}]$ is the 1D transform matrix, with $w = \mathrm{e}^{-2\pi i/N}$, is given by*

$$
\begin{cases}
F = TfT, \\
f = T^{-1}FT^{-1} & \text{(DFT pair).}
\end{cases}
\tag{15.6}
$$

Now let us spell this out in terms of the elements of T. By the laws of matrix multiplication (see (7.17c)), the jkth element F_{jk} of F is given by

$$
\begin{aligned}
F_{jk} &= \sum_{m,n} (T)_{jm} f_{mn} (T)_{nk} \\
&= \sum_{m,n} w^{jm} f_{mn} w^{kn} \\
&= \sum_{m,n} f_{mn} w^{jm+kn}.
\end{aligned}
$$

Theorem 15.4 *(Equation formulation) The 2D Discrete Fourier Transform is given in terms of the elements of the 1D transform matrix $T = [w^{kn}]$ by*

$$
\begin{cases}
F_{jk} = \sum_{m,n=0}^{N-1} f_{mn} w^{jm+kn} \\
f_{mn} = \frac{1}{N^2} \sum_{j,k=0}^{N-1} F_{jk} w^{-(jm+kn)} & \text{(DFT pair).}
\end{cases}
\tag{15.7}
$$

Exercise (a) What is the image of an impulse at the origin, $f_{00} = 1$ and otherwise zero? (b) Derive the IDFT formula above from the formula $T^{-1} = \frac{1}{N^2}\overline{T}$.

Theorem 15.5 *(Basis formulation) With $T^{-1} = [C_0 \ldots C_{N-1}] = (1/N)[w^{-kn}]$, the 2D Discrete Fourier Transform sends an array f to its components F_{jk} w.r.t. an orthogonal basis $\{\varepsilon_{jk}\}$, where $\varepsilon_{jk} = C_j C_k^{\mathrm{T}}$ has length $1/N$. Moreover, in the present notation,*

$$
C_k(n) = (1/N)w^{-kn}, \quad \varepsilon_{jk}(u, v) = (1/N^2)w^{-ju-kv}.
\tag{15.8}
$$

Proof We apply Theorem 15.2. We saw earlier in the 1D case (14.9ff) that $\{C_j\}$ are orthogonal of length $1/\sqrt{N}$. Hence the $\{\varepsilon_{jk}\}$ are orthogonal of length $1/N$.

Example Note that an orthonormal basis in 2D is given by $\{N\varepsilon_{jk}\}$. Let us compute an example in the case $N = 4$.

$$
T = \begin{bmatrix} 1 & 1 & 1 & 1 \\ 1 & -i & -1 & i \\ 1 & -1 & 1 & -1 \\ 1 & i & -1 & -i \end{bmatrix}, \quad
T^{-1} = \frac{1}{4}\begin{bmatrix} 1 & 1 & 1 & 1 \\ 1 & i & -1 & -i \\ 1 & -1 & 1 & -1 \\ 1 & -i & -1 & i \end{bmatrix},
$$

$$
\varepsilon_{12} = C_1 C_2^{\mathrm{T}} = \frac{1}{16}\begin{bmatrix} 1 \\ i \\ -1 \\ -i \end{bmatrix}\begin{bmatrix} 1 & -1 & 1 & -1 \end{bmatrix} = \frac{1}{16}\begin{bmatrix} 1 & -1 & 1 & -1 \\ i & -i & i & -i \\ -1 & 1 & -1 & 1 \\ -i & i & -i & i \end{bmatrix}.
$$

Exercise Derive the (u, v) element of ε_{jk}.

The continuous case The 2D Fourier Transform, and in practice its discrete form the DFT, are of great value in both analysing and improving a digital image, as we shall indicate step by step. A most helpful simplifying feature of continuous as well as discrete Fourier Transforms is *separability*: a transform can be converted to higher dimensions by applying it one dimension at a time. Carrying out this idea for the 2-dimensional continuous case gives

$$F(u, v) = \int_{-\infty}^{\infty} \left(\int_{-\infty}^{\infty} f(x, y) e^{-2\pi i x u} dx \right) e^{-2\pi i y v} dy, \tag{15.9}$$

and hence the transform/inverse pair

$$\begin{cases} F(u, v) = \int_{-\infty}^{\infty} \int_{-\infty}^{\infty} f(x, y) e^{-2\pi i (xu+yv)} \, dx \, dy, \\ f(x, y) = \int_{-\infty}^{\infty} \int_{-\infty}^{\infty} F(u, v) e^{2\pi i (xu+yv)} \, du \, dv \quad \text{(Fourier pair).} \end{cases} \tag{15.10}$$

Also, by essentially the same argument as used in the 1D case, Example 14.23(i), we have

$$f(-x, -y) \to F(-u, -v) = \overline{F}(u, v). \tag{15.11}$$

Exhibiting the discrete transform

There are two important things to notice about the way the discrete transform is portrayed in Figure 15.2 and thereafter.

(1) It is the power spectrum that is shown That is, a point (j, k) of the array is assigned a grey value proportional to the squared amplitude of the complex number F_{jk}. Although this does not reveal the argument (phase angle) of F_{jk}, such a display turns out nevertheless to be extremely useful in practice.

(2) The origin is at the centre The 1-dimensional symmetry $F_{N-k} = \overline{F}_k$ of Theorem 14.5(v) leads in two dimensions to $F_{N-j, N-k} = \overline{F}_{jk}$. This means that with the origin in upper left hand position the low-frequency components would be distributed across the four corners, whereas with the origin centrally placed (say $-N/2 \le j, k < N/2$)

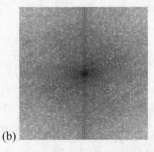

(a) (b)

Figure 15.2 (a) Jean Baptiste Joseph Fourier (1768–1830), and (b) the 2-dimensional Fourier Transform of his portrait. See the discussion in the text.

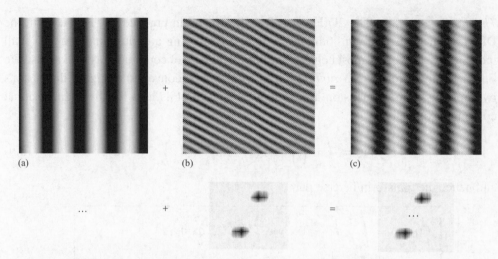

Figure 15.3 Three images (a), (b), (c) with periodicity, and their transforms shown below. Each frequency in the image transforms to a pair of dots (central symmetry), which coincide for the constant. Notice the additivity property: the sum of the first two images is the third, hence the same holds for their transforms.

the relation is equivalent by periodicity to $F_{-j,-k} = \overline{F}_{jk}$, made manifest now in the diagram by $|F_{-j,-k}| = |F_{jk}|$ (note: the amplitude of a complex number is unchanged by conjugation). This result is described as *central symmetry* (or 1/2 turn symmetry, or antipodality); it may be observed in Fourier's transformed image in Figure 15.2(b), and in Figures 15.2 and 15.4.

The effect of image periods Consider the periodic vertical bars and their transform in Figure 15.3(a). We have seen (Table 14.2) that a cosine function $\cos 2\pi wx$ transforms in one dimension to a pair of idealised spikes at frequencies $\pm w$, visible in their approximating DFT form. What can be expected in the 2-dimensional case if we have a cosine variation in one dimension only? An answer is provided by applying the continuous transform to $f(x, y) = \cos 2\pi wx$, conveniently done with the form (15.9).

$$
\begin{aligned}
F(u, v) &= \int_{-\infty}^{\infty} \left(\int_{-\infty}^{\infty} \cos(2\pi wx) e^{-2\pi ixu} \, dx \right) e^{-2\pi iyv} \, dy \\
&= \int_{-\infty}^{\infty} {}^{1}\!/_{2}[\delta(u+w) + \delta(u-w)] e^{-2\pi iyv} \, dy \qquad \text{by Examples 14.24} \\
&= {}^{1}\!/_{2}[\delta(u+w) + \delta(u-w)] \int_{-\infty}^{\infty} e^{-2\pi iyv} \, dy = \tfrac{1}{2}[\delta(u+w) + \delta(u-w)]\delta(v).
\end{aligned}
$$

Since $\delta(v) = 0$ for $v \neq 0$, the result is a pair of dots on the horizontal axis at coordinate positions $\pm w$. This is visible in Figure 15.3(a), with one central dot signifying a constant background (zero frequency) that happened to be included.

Rotation Consider Figure 15.3(b). This has bars, as does case (a), but the bars are closer, implying higher frequency, and furthermore slanted relative to the horizontal and vertical directions. We shall see (Corollary 15.8) that a rotation of the image causes an identical rotation of its transform, and therefore the effect of vertical bars in (a) implies the effect seen in (b), firstly in direction, and thence in the wider spacing of the (approximately) dots corresponding to frequency.

Additivity For Figure 15.3(c) we have added grey levels of the bars of (a) and (b) and, sure enough, the transform is the sum of their individual transforms. This is the *additivity property* of the transform, an easy consequence of the integral and matrix definitions. We survey basic properties in Table 15.2 at the end of this section.

Transforming separable arrays Sometimes an array is itself separable, the product of vectors, $f = gh^T$, where g, h are the column vectors with respective elements g_m and h_m, as exemplified below (the ε_{jk} of (15.3) are also examples). This simplifies computing the transform F which, by Theorem 15.6 below, is a separable array GH^T.

$$\begin{bmatrix} g_0h_0 & g_0h_1 & g_0h_2 \\ g_1h_0 & g_1h_1 & g_1h_2 \\ g_2h_0 & g_2h_1 & g_2h_2 \end{bmatrix} = \begin{bmatrix} g_0 \\ g_1 \\ g_2 \end{bmatrix} \begin{bmatrix} h_0 & h_1 & h_2 \end{bmatrix} \rightarrow \begin{bmatrix} G_0 \\ G_1 \\ G_2 \end{bmatrix} \begin{bmatrix} H_0 & H_1 & H_2 \end{bmatrix}$$

Complexity considerations (i) We require two applications of the FFT to determine G and H, then N^2 multiplications to construct GH^T. The total of $3N \log N + N^2$ was anticipated in Table 15.1. (ii) *We avoid Nth roots of unity with high N*, so as to preserve accuracy. Hence it is customary to divide a large image into 8×8 blocks. This gives the option of transforming each complete row or column of the image eight entries at a time by the 8-point 1-dimensionl FFT.

Theorem 15.6 (*Separable arrays*) *If the input is separable in the sense that*

$$f(x, y) = g(x)h(y) \quad (continuous\ case), \tag{15.12a}$$
$$f_{mn} = g_m h_n \quad (0 \leq m, n \leq N - 1), \tag{15.12b}$$

then the Fourier output factorises as respectively $F(u, v) = G(u)H(v)$, *and* $F_{jk} = G_j H_k$.

Proof For the discrete case, writing $f = gh^T$ gives $F = TfT^T$ (by (15.6)) $= Tgh^TT^T = (Tg)(Th)^T = GH^T$, a separable array, alternatively expressed as $F_{jk} = G_j H_k$. In the continuous case we have

$$F(u, v) = \int_{-\infty}^{\infty} \int_{-\infty}^{\infty} g(x)h(y)e^{-2\pi i(ux+vy)} \, dx \, dy$$

$$= \int_{-\infty}^{\infty} g(x)e^{-2\pi iux} \, dx \int_{-\infty}^{\infty} h(y)e^{-2\pi ivy} \, dy,$$

which equals $G(u)H(v)$ as required.

15.1.3 Rotation and projection theorems

Here we establish some powerful features of the Fourier Transform available only in two dimensions. Some can be proved with strict accuracy for the continuous case only, but tell us what to expect of the DFT in practice, provided sampling is done with reasonable detail. The cause of imprecision is that in general certain transforms such as rotation cannot be expressed exactly in integer coordinates. Our first result supplies the *similarity, rotation* and *shift* theorems which follow.

Theorem 15.7 *(Fourier Transform of generalised rotation) Let* $M = \text{Rows}[(a, b), (c, d)]$, *with determinant* $\Delta = ad - bc \neq 0$. *Then (i)* $f(ax + by, cx + dy) \rightarrow F(Au + Cv, Bu + Dv)/|\Delta|$, *where* $(A, C, B, D) = (d, -c, -b, a)/\Delta$, *the elements of* M^{-1}, *or (ii) in matrix terms*

$$f([x\ y]M) \rightarrow F([u\ v](M^{-1})^{\mathrm{T}})/|\Delta|.$$

Proof Write $f(ax + by, cx + dy) = g(x, y)$. Then we are to determine $G(u, v)$, where

$$G(u, v) = \int_{-\infty}^{\infty} \int_{-\infty}^{\infty} g(x, y)e^{-2\pi i(ux+vy)}\, \mathrm{d}x\, \mathrm{d}y.$$

For this, we make the change of variables $w = ax + by, z = cx + dy$. Then the infinite region of integration is unchanged. We must substitute for x, y in terms of w, z, and to this end we take

$$\begin{bmatrix} A & C \\ B & D \end{bmatrix} = \begin{bmatrix} a & c \\ b & d \end{bmatrix}^{-1} = \frac{1}{\Delta}\begin{bmatrix} d & -c \\ -b & a \end{bmatrix}.$$

Finally (Theorem 10.10), we have to multiply the integrand by the absolute value of the Jacobian determinant

$$J = \left|\frac{\partial(x, y)}{\partial(w, z)}\right| = \left|\frac{\partial(w, z)}{\partial(x, y)}\right|^{-1} = \begin{vmatrix} a & c \\ b & d \end{vmatrix}^{-1} = 1/\Delta.$$

Carrying out this prescription, we obtain

$$G(u, v) = \int_{-\infty}^{\infty} \int_{-\infty}^{\infty} |J| \cdot f(ax + by, cx + dy)e^{-2\pi i[(Aw+Bz)u+(Cw+Dz)v]}\, \mathrm{d}w\, \mathrm{d}z$$

$$= \int_{-\infty}^{\infty} \int_{-\infty}^{\infty} |J| \cdot f(w, z)e^{-2\pi i[(Au+Cv)w+(Bu+Dv)z]}\, \mathrm{d}w\, \mathrm{d}z$$

$$= F(Au + Cv, Bu + Dv)/|\Delta|, \text{ as required.}$$

Corollary 15.8 (i) *(Similarity Theorem)* $f(x/\alpha, y/\beta) \rightarrow |\alpha\beta| F(\alpha u, \beta v)$,

(ii) *(Rotation Theorem) If M is a rotation or reflection matrix, then*

$$\boxed{f([x\ y]M) \rightarrow F([u\ v]M),}$$

(iii) *(Shift Theorem)* $f(x - a, y - b) \rightarrow e^{-2\pi i(au+bv)} F(u, v)$.

Proof (i) In the notation of Theorem 15.7, $(A, C, B, D) = (1/\beta, 0, 0, 1/\alpha)\alpha\beta = (\alpha, 0, 0, \beta)$, whereas in (ii) we know from Section 7.4.1 that M is orthogonal: $(M^{-1})^T = M$ and $\det(M) = \pm 1$. In case (iii) we change variables by $w = x - a, z = y - b$, and the integral becomes

$$\int_{-\infty}^{\infty} \int_{-\infty}^{\infty} f(w, z)e^{-2\pi i[u(a+w)+v(z+b)]}dw\,dz$$

$$= e^{-2\pi i(ua+vb)} \int_{-\infty}^{\infty} \int_{-\infty}^{\infty} f(w, z)e^{-2\pi i[uw+vz]}dw\,dz.$$

Remarks 15.9 (1) According to the Shift Theorem, translating the image causes $F(u, v)$ to be multiplied by complex numbers $e^{i\theta}$ of unit modulus, leaving the displayed $|F(u, v)|$ unchanged (see the second column of Figure 15.4).

(2) By the Rotation Theorem, any rotation or reflection performed on the image is also performed on the DFT. The effect is visible in the, necessarily discrete, display, within the limits of accuracy (see the third and fourth columns of Figure 15.4). It follows that rotation or reflection symmetry in the original image is also present in the display.

(3) The Rotation Theorem is used in the theorem below, important for correcting lens blur in Section 15.3.3, and for tomography in Chapter 18, by extending from a single direction to all directions.

Theorem 15.10 (*Projection Theorem*) *The projection of $f(x, y)$ onto the x-axis,*

$$p(x) = \int_{-\infty}^{\infty} f(x, y)\,dy, \quad has\ 1D\ Fourier\ Transform\ equal\ to\ F(u, 0).$$

Hence, by the Rotation Theorem the projection of $f(x, y)$ onto a line at angle θ to the x-axis has 1D Fourier Transform equal to $F(u, v)$ evaluated along a line at angle θ to the u-axis

Proof The 1D Fourier Transform of $p(x)$ is by (14.25)

$$P(u) = \int_{-\infty}^{\infty} p(x)e^{-2\pi iux}\,dx = \int_{-\infty}^{\infty} \int_{-\infty}^{\infty} f(x, y)e^{-2\pi i(ux+0y)}dx\,dy = F(u, 0).$$

Example 15.11 (*Discrete Projection Theorem*) We show that the Projection Theorem has an exact discrete counterpart for the special case of projection onto one axis. A special case is given in Figure 15.5.

$$
\begin{aligned}
F_{jk} &= \sum_{m,n} f_{mn}w^{jm+kn} & &\text{the DFT in two dimensions, (15.7);} \\
F_{j0} &= \sum_{m,n} f_{mn}w^{jm} & &\text{restriction to the first dimension} \\
&= \sum_m \left(\sum_n f_{mn}\right)w^{jm} & &\text{on rearranging} \\
&= \sum_m p(m)w^{jm} & &\text{by definition of } p(m) \\
&= P(j) & &\text{the DFT of } p(m).
\end{aligned}
$$

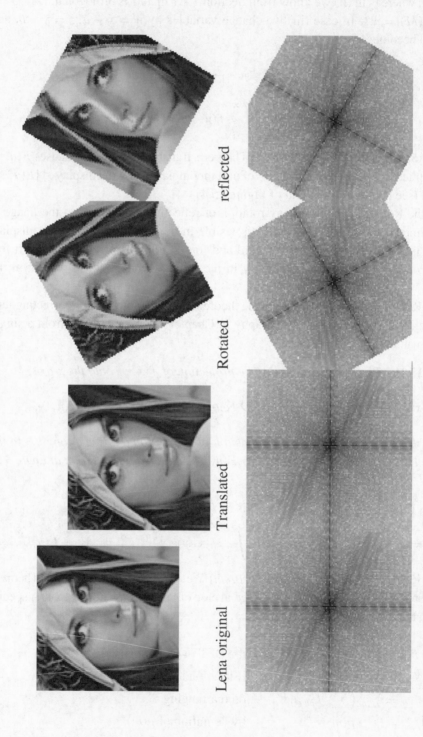

Figure 15.4 How the DFT is affected by indicated changes in the image (despite cropping, the full frames are easily inferred). Notice that the last image is a reflection.

Lena original   Translated   Rotated   reflected

$$[f_{mn}] = \begin{bmatrix} 1 & 3 & 2 & 6 \\ 2 & 0 & 5 & 9 \\ 0 & 7 & 3 & 8 \\ 6 & 4 & 8 & 5 \end{bmatrix}, \quad [p(m)] = [9 \ \ 14 \ \ 18 \ \ 28]$$

Figure 15.5 An array and its projection $p(m)$ onto the first axis/dimension.

Theorem 15.12 *(Fourier Transform of a Laplacian) Suppose that $f(x, y)$ and its first and second derivatives tend to zero as $|(x, y)|$ increases. Then $\nabla^2 f \to -4\pi^2(u^2 + v^2)F(u, v)$ under the Continuous Fourier Transform (this is first used in Example 15.18).*

Proof We recall that $\nabla^2 f = \partial^2 f/\partial x^2 + \partial^2 f/\partial y^2$. It suffices to show that $\partial^2 f/\partial x^2 \to -4\pi^2 u^2 F(u, v)$, and to note that a similar argument yields $\partial^2 f/\partial y^2 \to -4\pi^2 v^2 F(u, v)$. We have

$$\partial^2 f/\partial x^2 \to \int_{-\infty}^{\infty} \int_{-\infty}^{\infty} (\partial^2 f/\partial x^2) e^{-2\pi i(ux+vy)} \, dx \, dy = \int_{-\infty}^{\infty} I_x e^{-2\pi i vy} \, dy, \quad \text{where}$$

$$I_x = \int_{-\infty}^{\infty} (\partial^2 f/\partial x^2) e^{-2\pi i ux} \, dx \quad \text{(now integrate by parts)}$$

$$= \left[\frac{\partial f}{\partial x} e^{-2\pi i ux} \right]_{-\infty}^{\infty} - \int_{-\infty}^{\infty} \frac{\partial f}{\partial x} (-2\pi i u) e^{-2\pi i ux} \, dx$$

$$= \int_{-\infty}^{\infty} \frac{\partial f}{\partial x} (2\pi i u) e^{-2\pi i ux} \, dx$$

$$= \left[f(x, y)(2\pi i u) e^{-2\pi i ux} \right]_{-\infty}^{\infty} + \int_{-\infty}^{\infty} f(x, y)(2\pi i u)^2 e^{-2\pi i ux} \, dx$$

$$= -4\pi^2 u^2 \int_{-\infty}^{\infty} f(x, y) e^{-2\pi i ux} \, dx, \quad \text{hence finally}$$

$$\partial^2 f/\partial x^2 \to -4\pi^2 u^2 \int_{-\infty}^{\infty} \int_{-\infty}^{\infty} f(x, y) e^{-2\pi i ux} e^{-2\pi i vy} \, dx \, dy = -4\pi^2 u^2 F(u, v).$$

15.1.4 The discrete 2D Convolution Theorem

A huge number of operations on digital images (for example) amount to replacing each value in an array by a linear combination of its neighbours, suitably defined. Just as in the 1D case, this may be expressed as a convolution product, whose calculation is shortened by a convolution theorem relating the process to the Fourier Transform. As before, the way to make this work is to arrange that as we traverse a row within a neighbourhood, forming products, the column number increases in one array whilst decreasing in another, leaving the sum of column numbers constant, as in $g_{i3}h_{j2} + g_{i4}h_{j1} + g_{i5}h_{j0}$, in which the sum of second subscripts is 5. With this done similarly for row numbers, the result is once more to imitate polynomial multiplication, now in two variables. The earlier $h(x) = f(x)g(x)$ becomes:

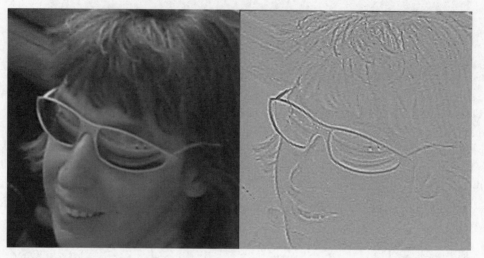

Figure 15.6 Image and its result after convolving with the edge-detecting Laplacian.

Definition 15.13 The polynomial corresponding to an array $f = [f_{ij}]$ is $f(x, y) = \Sigma_{i,j} f_{ij} x^i y^j$. The (discrete) *convolution product* $h = f{*}g$ of arrays f, g is the array h given by

$$h(x, y) = f(x, y)g(x, y). \tag{15.13a}$$

That is to say

$$h_{mn} = \sum_{\substack{p+s=m \\ q+t=n}} f_{pq} g_{st}, \tag{15.13b}$$

which is the coefficient of $x^m y^n$ in $f(x, y)g(x, y)$; or, equivalently,

$$h_{mn} = \sum_{p,q} f_{pq} g_{m-p, n-q}. \tag{15.13c}$$

The formulation (15.13a) shows that, just as in one dimension, convolution is associative, commutative, and distributive over addition (padding with zeros may be needed to ensure same-sized arrays for addition). In applications generally, we view a small array g, called the *kernel*, as transforming a much larger array f by the process of convolution with g, *and* we want the result to be the same size as the original f, with f_{mn} replaced by a linear combination of its original neighbours.

We may think of placing the central element of the matrix of g over the array, multiplying each array element by the matrix element above it, then adding the results. If the kernel is a square matrix of size $k = 2r + 1$, we then shift the subscripts so that g_{00} is the central element and take $-r \leq p, q \leq r$ in (15.13c).

Example 15.14 (*2D Laplacian edge-detection*) see Figure 15.6. We have already illustrated the 1D case, in which convolution with the vector $[1 \quad -2 \quad 1]$ replaces an array value by an approximation to the second derivative of the sampled function

(Example 14.11). A sufficiently small second derivative is taken as marking a maximal rate of change, and hence a boundary point. Applying this idea in two dimensions, we take edge pixels to occur at small values of the Laplacian $\nabla^2 f = \partial^2 f/\partial x^2 + \partial^2 f/\partial y^2$, now approximated by applying the formula of Example 14.11 in each dimension to give

$$\nabla^2 f_{mn} = (f_{m,n-1} - 2f_{m,n} + f_{m,n+1}) + (f_{m-1,n} - 2f_{m,n} + f_{m+1,n}). \qquad (15.14)$$

The result in convolution terms $g * f$ is, according to (15.13), an array larger than f. Since here we only want to exchange old values for new, we must drop terms corresponding to subscripts outside the range of f. On the other hand, Formula (15.14) with subscripts mn in a border row or column of f refers to subscripts outside the range of f. Here we supply the missing values via an *all-round border of zeros*, as illustrated below. For g of size $k = 2r + 1$ the border should be of width r, and then the new array is the same size as the old. In the present case g has size 3 and the border has width 1 all round. We may think of placing the central element of matrix g over each element of f in turn, to perform the calculation.

$$\begin{pmatrix} 0 & 1 & 0 \\ 1 & -4 & 1 \\ 0 & 1 & 0 \end{pmatrix} * \begin{pmatrix} 0 & 0 & 0 & 0 & 0 & 0 \\ 0 & 6 & 8 & 10 & 12 & 0 \\ 0 & 7 & 9 & 11 & 23 & 0 \\ 0 & 8 & 10 & 22 & 14 & 0 \\ 0 & 9 & 21 & 13 & 15 & 0 \\ 0 & 0 & 0 & 0 & 0 & 0 \end{pmatrix} = \begin{pmatrix} -9 & -7 & -9 & -15 \\ -5 & 0 & 20 & -55 \\ -6 & 20 & -40 & 4 \\ -7 & -52 & 6 & -33 \end{pmatrix}$$

$$\begin{array}{ccc} \text{(Laplacian)} & & \\ g & f & g * f \end{array}$$

Notice that, to achieve the given rules (15.13), we must first rotate g by $180°$, but, as is often the case, this leaves the matrix unchanged. A more sophisticated development is carried out, in Example 15.30, and the border issue is further discussed more generally below.

Border disputes Usually, of course, the boundary values are few in number compared with those calculated 'correctly'. For example, f might be 256×256 and g is commonly 3×3. If we can tolerate the error, perhaps by ensuring that nothing important is situated within half the width/height of g from the boundary, well and good. If not, there are several options.

(1) Extend the image by repeating border rows and columns enough times (we have just handled one 3×3 case of g, in Example 15.14).
(2) Allow the image to wrap around on itself, to supply the extra rows and columns. This simulates the image being periodic.
(3) Set the affected border and near-border output values to zero, or to some other constant that is acceptable.
(4) Eliminate the affected pixels in the output image and accept a slightly reduced size.

Separable kernels If a kernel g is separable, as defined in (15.12), then convolution by g can be achieved as a result of convolutions *in each dimension separately*. We recall that to say that g is *separable* means that g factors into a simple but unusual looking matrix product $g = ab^T$, where a, b are column vectors, such as

$$g = ab^T = \begin{bmatrix} 1 \\ 0 \\ 3 \end{bmatrix} \begin{bmatrix} 2 & 4 & 7 \end{bmatrix} = \begin{bmatrix} 2 & 4 & 7 \\ 0 & 0 & 0 \\ 6 & 12 & 21 \end{bmatrix}. \tag{15.15}$$

Thus g consists of repetitions of the row vector, with the ith copy multiplied by the ith element of the column. This situation is easily recognised for a small matrix. To spell out the consequences, let $a = [a_i]$, $b = [b_j]$, so that by definition $g_{ij} = a_i b_j$ and

$$g(x, y) = \Sigma_{i,j} g_{ij} x^i y^j = \Sigma_{i,j} a_i b_j x^i y^j = \Sigma_i a_i x^i \Sigma_j b_j y^j = a(x)b(y). \tag{15.16}$$

Thus $f(x, y)g(x, y) = [f(x, y)a(x)]b(y) = f(x, y)b(y)]a(y)$, which is to say that convolution by g is achievable as convolution by a and convolution by b, in either order. Notice that if f is $N \times N$ the number of multiplications is reduced from $k^2 N^2$ to $2kN^2$, a reduction by one third in the simplest case $k = 3$. An example follows.

Exercise Verify the reduction in calculation for a separable convolution, given above.

Example 15.15 (*Smoothing*) A simple way of smoothing a sequence of function values in 1D is to replace each value by the average of itself and two immediate neighbours, which is equivalent to convolution by $(1/3)[1 \quad 1 \quad 1]$. In one extension to 2D an average is taken over f_{mn} and its eight immediate neighbours, but in this case the convolution matrix is separable as

$$\frac{1}{9} \begin{bmatrix} 1 & 1 & 1 \\ 1 & 1 & 1 \\ 1 & 1 & 1 \end{bmatrix} = \frac{1}{9} \begin{bmatrix} 1 \\ 1 \\ 1 \end{bmatrix} \begin{bmatrix} 1 & 1 & 1 \end{bmatrix} = \frac{1}{3} \begin{bmatrix} 1 \\ 1 \\ 1 \end{bmatrix} \frac{1}{3}[1 \quad 1 \quad 1].$$

This can be accomplished by separate 1D convolutions, as illustrated in Figure 15.7.

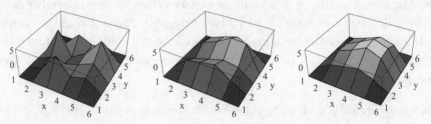

Figure 15.7 The separable convolution of Example 15.15. Array values are represented by height of the surface, and the arows indicate the successive smoothing directions.

Convolution and the DFT Just as was done in one dimension, we wish to apply the same sized DFT to f, g, and f^*g for the purpose of linking convolution and Fourier

Transform, for later use. The polynomial viewpoint tells us to what size f and g must be extended by zeros to achieve this link. We simply apply the 1D rule in both directions. Since we are keeping arrays square anyway, the new size, N, is

$$N = \text{size of } f + \text{ size of } g - 1. \tag{15.17}$$

Theorem 15.16 *(Convolution Theorem for the 2-dimensional DFT) Under the Discrete Fourier Transform in two dimensions, convolution becomes pointwise product:*

$$\boxed{f^*g \rightarrow \text{FoG.}} \tag{15.18}$$

Proof Rather than generalise the matrix proof of the 1-dimensional case, we use a more bare-handed approach which brings out the remarkable consequences of the property of $w = e^{-2\pi i/N}$ that $w^{r+s} = w^r \cdot w^s$. Here N is to be the size of arrays f, g and f^*g. Writing $f^*g = h$, we must show that $H_{jk} = F_{jk}G_{jk}$ ($0 \le j, k \le N - 1$). Recalling the formula TfT of (15.6) for the 2D transform, where $T = [w^{kn}]$ is the matrix of the N-point DFT in one dimension, we have

$$H_{jk} = \sum_{m,n} w^{jm} h_{m,n} w^{kn} \qquad \text{by (15.7)}$$

$$= \sum_{m,n,p,q} w^{jm} (f_{p,q} g_{m-p,n-q}) w^{kn} \quad \text{by (15.13c).}$$

Now we substitute $\lambda = m - p$ and $\mu = n - q$, and hence may sum over permissible λ, μ instead of m, n, eliminating the latter by $m = \lambda + p, n = \mu + q$. Then the powers of w split into $jm = jp + j\lambda$ and $kn = k\mu + kq$. Distributing these four appropriately gives

$$H_{jk} = \sum_{\lambda,\mu,p,q} (w^{jp} f_{p,q} w^{kq})(w^{j\lambda} g_{\lambda,\mu} w^{k\mu}) = \sum_{p,q} w^{jp} f_{p,q} w^{kq} \sum_{\lambda,\mu} w^{j\lambda} g_{\lambda,\mu} w^{k\mu}$$
$$= F_{jk} G_{jk}.$$

A polynomial proof The following proof, using the definition of convolution in terms of polynomials in two variables, may add insight into 'why' the Convolution Theorem holds. We parallel the polynomial proof of Theorem 14.12 in one dimension, and everything falls into place. By Definition 15.13, the convolution $h = f^*g$ of arrays is given by $h(x, y) = f(x, y)g(x, y)$, where $f(x, y)$ is the polynomial $\sum f_{mn}x^m y^n$, and similarly for g and h. The critical connection,

$$F_{jk} = f(w^j, w^k), \tag{15.19}$$

holds because $F_{jk} = \sum_{mn} w^{jm+kn} f_{mn} = \sum_{mn} f_{mn}(w^j)^m(w^k)^n$. But the polynomial identity $h(x, y) = f(x, y)g(x, y)$ has as a special case $h(w^j, w^k) = f(w^j, w^k)g(w^j, w^k)$ which, by (15.19) applied also to G and H, gives the Convolution Theorem $H_{jk} = F_{jk}G_{jk}$ ($0 \le j, k \le N - 1$).

The continuous 2D Convolution Theorem Besides the discrete version, we will have much use for the continuous convolution f^*g of functions f and g in two dimensions. It is defined analogously to that in one dimension, by

$$f^*g = \int_{-\infty}^{\infty} \int_{-\infty}^{\infty} f(s, t)g(x - s, y - t)ds\, dt. \tag{15.20}$$

Theorem 15.17 *(Convolution Theorem) In two dimensions the continuous Fourier transform converts convolution to pointwise product:* $f^*g \rightarrow F o G$.

Proof We let $f^*g = h$ and prove that $H(u, v) = F(u, v)G(u, v)$. Starting with the definition,

$$H(u, v) = \int_{-\infty}^{\infty} \int_{-\infty}^{\infty} h(x, y)e^{-i(ux+vy)}\, dx\, dy$$

$$= \int_{-\infty}^{\infty} \int_{-\infty}^{\infty} \int_{-\infty}^{\infty} \int_{-\infty}^{\infty} f(s, t)g(x - s, y - t)e^{-i(ux+vy)}dsdt\, dxdy$$

by (15.20).

We change the integration variables x, y to $p = x - s, q = y - t$, so that $dxdy$ becomes $dp\, dq, ux = up + us$ and $vy = vq + vt$, giving

$$H(u, v) = \int_{-\infty}^{\infty} \int_{-\infty}^{\infty} f(s, t)e^{-i(us+vt)}ds\, dt \int_{-\infty}^{\infty} \int_{-\infty}^{\infty} g(p, q)e^{-i(up+vq)}\, dp\, dq$$

$$= F(u, v)G(u, v) \quad \text{by definition of } F, G.$$

Example 15.18 With what function $g(x, y)$ should one convolve a function $f(x, y)$ so as to produce the Laplacian $\nabla^2 f$? We require $\nabla^2 f = g^*f$. Let us apply the Fourier Transform:

$$\nabla^2 f \rightarrow -4\pi^2(u^2 + v^2)F(u, v) \quad \text{by Theorem 15.12,}$$
$$g^*f \rightarrow G(u, v)F(u, v) \quad \quad \text{by Theorem 15.17.}$$

Therefore $G(u, v) = -4\pi^2(u^2 + v^2)$, and applying the inverse transform to it yields $g(x, y)$.

15.1.5 Fourier Transforms and the statistics of an image

In Section 15.3 we shall wish to explore the possibility of reconstructing a degraded image by convolving with some array (called a kernel), based upon a statistical analysis of the properties of this image, and general knowledge of its type. Here we lay some foundations. We suppose the image is of a certain type (X-ray image, traffic, face, natural scene, ...), and seek common characteristics in terms of correlation between values at different pixel positions.

$(s, t) = (2, 1)$ 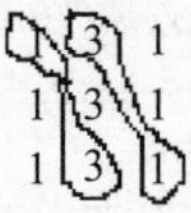 $(s, t) = (-1, 1)$

s, t	$9\,C_{ff}(s, t)$	s, t	$9\,C_{ff}(s, t)$	s, t	$9\,C_{ff}(s, t)$	s, t	$9\,C_{ff}(s, t)$
0, 0	$6 \times 1 + 3 \times 9 = 33$	1, 0	$4 \times 1 + 2 \times 4 = 12$	2, 0	$2 \times 1 + 9 = 11$	−1, 1	$4 \times 3 = 12$
0, 1	$6 \times 3 = 18$	1, 1	$4 \times 3 = 12$	2, 1	$2 \times 3 = 6$	−1, 2	$2 \times 1 = 2$
0, 2	$3 \times 1 = 3$	1, 2	$2 \times 1 = 2$	2, 2	$1 \times 1 = 1$	−2, 1	$2 \times 3 = 6$
						−2, 2	$1 \times 1 = 1$

Figure 15.8 Pairs with the same relative position (s, t) in an array, and a complete table.

Discrete correlation For this purpose we take each value f_{mn} to be a random variable and describe the array $f = [f_{mn}]$ as a *Markov Random Field* (these were studied in Chapter 11). The correlations are determined, at least approximately, by a sample of images in the class specified. However, a standard simplifying assumption, which is often vindicated by good results in image reconstruction, is that the random field is *ergodic*. That is, the correlation statistics of the whole class are sufficiently well approximated by those of an individual image. We assume ergodicity for the rest of the present section. This means we take the correlation between f_{mn} and $f_{m+s,n+t}$ to be the mean product of pixel values with the same relative positions (s, t). Let E stand for expected value. We thus define the *auto-correlation function* C_{ff} by

$$C_{ff}(s, t) = E[f_{mn} f_{m+s,n+t}] = (1/N^2) \sum_{m,n} f_{mn} f_{m+s,n+t}. \qquad (15.21)$$

Example 15.19 We compute the correlation function of the array $\begin{bmatrix} 1 & 3 & 1 \\ 1 & 3 & 1 \\ 1 & 3 & 1 \end{bmatrix}$ in Figure 15.8.

Continuous correlation We now proceed to the continuous case, thought of as underlying the discrete. Further, we widen the discussion to correlation between different arrays/functions, by defining the *cross-correlation* $R_{fg}(x, y)$ between random fields f and g, by

Definition 15.20

$$R_{fg}(x, y) = \int_{-\infty}^{\infty} \int_{-\infty}^{\infty} f(s, t) g(s + x, t + y) \mathrm{d}s\, \mathrm{d}t.$$

In terms of 2-dimensional coordinates $r = (x, y)$ and $s = (s, t)$, the ergodic hypothesis for this case is the second equality below (integrals are understood to be over the whole plane).

$$R_{fg}(r) = E[f(s)g(s + r)] = \int f(s)g(s + r)\mathrm{d}s. \qquad (15.22)$$

Table 15.2. *Some properties of the continuous 2D Fourier Transform.*

spatial domain	frequency domain	remarks
$g(x, y) + h(x, y)$	$G(u, v) + H(u, v)$	additivity
$g(x)h(y)$	$G(u)H(v)$	separable product
$f(x/\alpha, y/\beta)$	$\lvert\alpha\beta\rvert F(\alpha u, \beta v)$	Similarity Theorem
$f(x - a, y - b)$	$e^{-2\pi i(au+bv)} F(u, v)$	Shift Theorem
$f(x, y)$ rotated by θ)	$F(u, v)$ rotated by θ)	Rotation Theorem
$f(x, y)^* g(x, y)$	$F(u, v)G(u, v)$	Convolution Theorem
$\nabla^2 f = \partial^2 f/\partial x^2 + \partial^2 f/\partial y^2$	$-4\pi^2(u^2 + v^2)F(u, v)$	Laplacian
$g(-x, -y)$	$G(-u, -v) = \overline{G}(u, v)$	preserves even/oddness
R_{fg}	$S_{fg} = \overline{F}(u, v)G(u, v)$	cross-correlation
R_{ff}	$S_{ff} = \lvert F(u, v)\rvert^2$	auto-correlation

As a special case, R_{ff} is the *auto-correlation* of f. We can now prove two celebrated results pointing to future development of the Wiener filter (Section 15.3.4). Since R_{fg} already starts with a capital letter we will denote its Fourier transform by S_{fg}. Note that in this context a complex conjugate will be indicated by an overbar.

Theorem 15.21 *The continuous Fourier transform maps correlations as follows:*

$$
\begin{cases}
S_{fg} = \overline{F}(u, v)G(u, v) = \overline{S}_{gf} & \text{(the Correlation Theorem)}, \\
S_{ff} = \lvert F(u, v)\rvert^2 & \text{(the Wiener–Kinchine Theorem)}.
\end{cases}
\tag{15.23}
$$

Proof By an essentially identical argument to that used in one dimension (Example 14.23), we may express R_{fg} as a convolution and then the result is immediate by the Convolution Theorem. We have

$$
R_{fg} = f(-\mathbf{r})^* g(\mathbf{r}),
\tag{15.24}
$$

where we have suppressed an argument τ of R_{fg} for simplicity, the proof being

$$
f(-\mathbf{r})^* g(\mathbf{r}) = \int f(-\mathbf{r})g(\tau - \mathbf{r})\mathrm{d}\mathbf{r}
$$

$$
= \int f(s)g(s + \tau)\mathrm{d}s \text{ (putting } s = -\mathbf{r}) = R_{fg}(\tau).
$$

By the Convolution Theorem applied to (15.24), and using (15.11), we have $R_{fg} \rightarrow \overline{F}(u, v)G(u, v)$, and in particular $R_{ff} \rightarrow \overline{F}(u, v)F(u, v) = \lvert F(u, v)\rvert^2$.

Exercise Deduce the rest of (15.23) from its first equality.

15.2 Filters

We have laid the ground work for the general idea of a filter, which uses the powerful properties of the Fourier Transform and convolution, both to enhance and to transform digital images in other desirable ways. The first step is a short discussion of what may be done on a more elementary level before this power is brought to bear.

15.2.1 Greyscale transforms

We consider digital images in which each pixel is allocated a greyscale value, normally in the range $0, 1, \ldots, 255$, corresponding to an 8-bit word, or *byte*. This, of course, represents similar discussions for values that have other colour significance, such as red, green, blue. In so far as the images are for the direct benefit of humans, the following observed facts are influential (see e.g. Bruce, Green and Georgeson, 1996).

1. Brightness discrimination is poor if illumination is lacking.
2. Perceived brightness is not absolute, but depends on contrast with the background.
3. For a given background, perceived brightness varies as the logarithm of actual intensity.
4. The eye can distinguish up to about 40 grey levels.
5. If the number of grey levels is less than about 24, the eye may see contours where a smooth transition is being modelled.

For example, a radiograph may contain all the information an observer requires, but his/her eye does not perceive this because the image is poorly developed. Or perhaps a photograph was taken with poor illumination, so that boundaries, objects and distinctions may exist unperceived in the image, or may require inordinate effort and strain to see. For such reasons, we may employ a technique of changing each grey level p consistently to a suitably chosen new one q.

This method is illustrated by the three images in Figure 15.9. The first does indeed enshrine a picture, but the variation in brightness is almost invisible to the naked eye. However, after the brightness is increased (by a mapping of the form $p \to p + b$), to yield image (b), something is certainly visible, if rather vague. What it needs next is an increase in *contrast*, $p \to cp$, over some range. This is provided in image (c), now more clearly a view of foliage.

We would really like to automate this process, and a tool to aid both eye and automation is an image's *histogram*, namely a graph of the number (frequency) n_p of pixels with value p. Equivalently, we may plot the *relative* frequency $f_p = n_p/N^2$, a change of vertical scale in the graph, where the image is $N \times N$ and so has N^2 pixels in total. This is done in Figure 15.10 for each image in Figure 15.9.

(a)   (b)   (c)

Figure 15.9 Successive versions of an image after greyscale transformations.

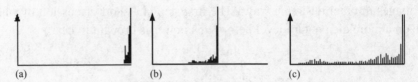

Figure 15.10 Histograms of the images of Figure 15.9. Largest/darkest values are to the right of the scale. Thus (a) is very dark with tiny contrast, (b) is brighter with only slightly more contrast, whilst (c) has reasonable contrast for the eye to see.

Histogram equalisation What we have used so far is a mapping $p \to q$ which divides the range of p into intervals, and over each interval applies a transformation of the form $p \to b + cp$, whose graph is a straight line of gradient c, the *contrast factor*. If, for example, we wished to stretch the p interval from 70–140 to 50–200, the graph of q against p could be that shown in Figure 15.11.

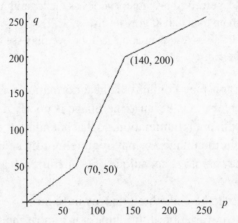

Figure 15.11 A function $p \to q$ expanding the greyscale interval 70–140 to 50–200. This is allowed for by a reduction in contrast for the intervals before and after, as may be seen from the gradients there, of value less than 1.

Exercise What is the middle contrast ratio in Figure 15.11?

Our ideal at this point is *histogram equalisation*, a greyscale transformation causing all pixel values to appear with the same frequency. This can be achieved exactly in the ideal case of pixel values varying continuously, and then quantisation to integer values gives the result approximately, but usually to good effect.

Suppose for simplicity that the pixel values lie in the interval [0, 1]. As the number of discrete values $p = p_i$ taken by p is allowed to increase, the graph of relative frequencies f_i approaches a probability density function $f(p)$ on [0, 1], which we may assume to be positive (see remarks following (9.27)). If we apply to this the transformation $q = F(p)$ (the *cdf* of p, see (9.29)) then the *new pdf* is

$$
\begin{aligned}
g(q) &= f(p)/|\mathrm{d}F/\mathrm{d}p| \quad && \text{(substituted in terms of } q \text{) by (9.32)} \\
     &= f(p)/|f(p)| \quad && \text{by Theorem 9.44, since } F \text{ is differentiable} \\
     &= 1 \quad && \text{where } |f(p)| = f(p) \text{ because } f(p) > 0.
\end{aligned}
$$

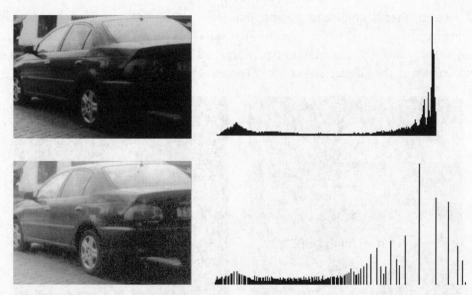

Figure 15.12 Car and its histogram of grey values before and after histogram equalisation. The first car may look better, but the second brings out some new details in the darker areas, including part of the rear number plate.

This is the desired constant value, and equals 1 because the interval width is 1 (Example 9.42). For the discrete counterpart we replace probability by relative frequency to obtain $p \to \sum_{r \leq p} f_r$ for the cdf function. To revert to values of p lying in $\{0, 1, \ldots, p_{max}\}$, we scale up the sum by p_{max} and round the result to the nearest integer. The rule becomes

$$p \to p_{max} \sum_{r \leq p} f_r \text{ (rounded)} = (p_{max}/N^2) \sum_{r \leq p} n_r \text{ (rounded)}. \qquad (15.25)$$

This is the automation we sought. Figure 15.12 shows the result of histogram equalisation on a car which is partly shrouded in darkness, with the histogram before and after the change. Notice that, although the histogram is by no means perfectly horizontal, a definite improvement in clarity is obtained around the dark wheels.

The median filter Here we discuss the removal of image degradation due to random pixel values being changed by a large amount, known as *impulse* noise, or *shot* noise (cf. Table 11.13). The median filter determines a new pixel value from a specified neighbourhood of that pixel, but not by convolution. Instead, the values at the pixel and its neighbours are put in order, with repetitions where these occur, and the *median*, or value midway through the list, is selected. Thus in the 3×3 neighbourhood below the new value is the fifth in the list, namely the integer 6.

5	6	7
4	40	5
6	7	5

4 5 5 5 6 6 7 7 40

↑

Median

The median filter is nonlinear, yet simple to apply. Notice that an averaging process would give undue weight to the value 40. An example is shown in Figure 15.13. It is true though that, generally, convolution-type filters are preferred because of their intimate connection with the Fourier Transform (Theorem 15.16).

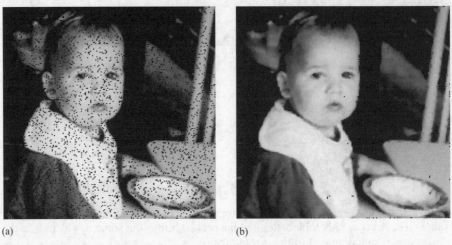

(a)   (b)

Figure 15.13 (a) Image with shot noise: each pixel has probability $1/10$ of being corrupted into black, (b) result after applying median filter with 3×3 neighbourhoods. A further application removes the remaining visible black spots, but leaves a slight blur.

15.2.2 Highpass and lowpass filters

The idea of changing an image f by modifying, or *filtering*, its frequency components, (15.7) or (15.10), is a natural extension from the corresponding process in one dimension, which was introduced in Section 14.1.2. The DFT case may be diagrammed as

$$f \xrightarrow{\text{DFT}} F \xrightarrow{\text{Filter}} F' \xrightarrow{\text{IDFT}} f'. \qquad (15.26)$$

It is often helpful to think of the filter process $F \to F'$ (F' not the derivative) as multiplying F by a *transfer function H*. That is, $F' = F \circ H$, or, in components, the alternative forms

$$F'_{jk} = F_{jk}H_{jk} \text{ (discrete)}, \qquad F'(u, v) = F(u, v)H(u, v) \text{ (continuous)}. \qquad (15.27)$$

A *highpass* filter passes on higher-frequency components at the expense of lower ones and so enhances finer details of an image. It is said to be *ideal* (idealised) if it operates a simple cutoff value k_0. That is, $H(u, v) = 1$, causing no change, except for

$$H(u, v) = 0 \quad \text{if } |u| < k_0 \text{ and } |v| < k_0 \quad \text{(box filter)}, \qquad (15.28a)$$
$$H(u, v) = 0 \quad \text{if } \sqrt{(u^2 + v^2)} < k_0 \qquad \text{(disk filter)}. \qquad (15.28b)$$

Lowpass filters similarly pass on low frequencies, so in terms of Figure 15.14 we would have $H = 0$ *outside* the shaded areas. The problem with an ideal, box-type filter is that,

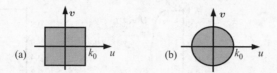

Figure 15.14 Ideal highpass filters, the transfer function being $H(u, v) = 0$ inside the shaded area, and 1 elsewhere. (a) Box filter, (b) disk filter.

besides performing its filtering task, it causes *ringing*, the multiple duplication of edges. We illustrate ringing with Figure 15.15, in which a deliberately simple image is used so as to make the effect stand out.

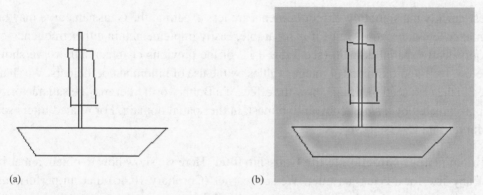

Figure 15.15 Illustration of ringing: (a) simple image f, (b) the result f' of applying to f an ideal highpass filter with cutoff $k_0 = 13$. The original edges are now accompanied by ghostly duplicates.

The cause and cure of ringing The Convolution Theorem (Theorem 15.17) tells us that by multiplying F by H and inverting we get the result $f*h$ of convolving f with the inverse h of H. The problem is that the sharp edges of H give rise to significant frequency components in h (the IDFT is similar to the DFT in this respect, because $T^{-1} = 1/N)\overline{T}$). This edge effect is illustrated in Figure 15.6 of the previous chapter. It is a special case of aliasing, for which see Theorem 14.33.

Each such component produces its own copy of an edge in f (by linearity), hence the ringing effect as seen in Figure 15.15. A cure is to mitigate the sharp cutoff possessed by H into a more gentle 'roll-off', and one way to do so is to use a *Butterworth filter* of order $n \geq 1$, defined in terms of $r = \sqrt{(u^2 + v^2)}$ by

$$H(u, v) = \begin{cases} 1/[1 + (r/k_0)^{2n}] & \text{(lowpass)}, \\ 1/[1 + (k_0/r)^{2n}] & \text{(highpass)}. \end{cases} \qquad (15.29)$$

The usefulness of this filter is illustrated in Figure 15.20 of Section 15.2.3, following a discussion of its implementation.

Butterworth versus Gaussian As we see in Figure 15.16, a suitable choice of Butterworth filter leaves a range of low frequencies relatively unaltered and cuts off the

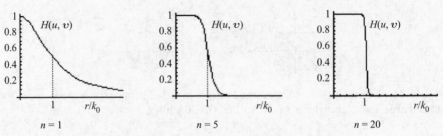

Figure 15.16 Butterworth lowpass filter for various orders n, where $r = \sqrt{(u^2 + v^2)}$. At $n = 1$ the cutoff is gradual. By $n = 20$ the filter is close to the ideal lowpass filter with a sharp cutoff at $r = k_0$ (where $r/k_0 = 1$).

rest quickly but smoothly. If requirements are less exacting, the Gaussian curve may be an excellent alternative, since it is separable, easily implemented in either frequency or equivalently spatial domain (see Table 14.2 of the previous chapter) and, as we show below, well-approximated at integer values by the use of binomial coefficients. We shall see in the next section, 15.2.3, how the effect of a Butterworth filter may be satisfactorily approximated by a small convolution mask in the spatial domain. For related filters see Marven and Ewers (1996).

Binomial approximation to the Gaussian filter Here we show how to obtain a matrix of any size for a Gaussian filter. We saw earlier (Corollary 10.46) that, in performing calculations with the binomial distribution involving many trials, results of acceptable accuracy could be obtained by computing areas under the standard normal (Gaussian) distribution. Now we need the return compliment. Over the range of integer values k for which we require to evaluate the *Gaussian function* $f(k)$, we may obtain a remarkably close approximation from the binomial coefficients themselves. If f has mean $n/2$ (easily changed) and variance $n/4$, then

$$f(k) \cong 2^{-n} \binom{n}{k} \quad (k = 0, 1, \ldots, n). \tag{15.30}$$

To see this we recall from Section 10.3.3 the binomial random variable $X \sim B(n, p)$, the number of successes in n independent trials, each with probability p of success. Here $P(X = k)$ equals approximately the area under the Gaussian $f(x) = (1/\sigma\sqrt{2\pi})\exp[-(x - \mu)^2/2\sigma^2]$ between $x = k - 1/2$ and $x = k + 1/2$, where $\mu = np$ and $\sigma^2 = np(1 - p)$. Considering Figure 15.17(a), this area is approximately that of the rectangle of width 1 and height $f(k)$, namely $f(k)$ *itself.*

The binomial formula (9.41), with coefficients written $_nC_k$, gives $f(k) = {}_nC_k p^k(1 - p)^{n-k}$. Setting $p = 1/2$ we obtain (15.30), which is the most accurate version (Remark 10.48), and usually yields sufficient cases of σ as n varies; Table 15.3 lists such cases. If desired, we can vary $\sigma^2 = np(1 - p)$ continuously downwards from its maximum of $n/4$, which occurs with $p = 1/2$. Figure 15.17 (b) and (c) illustrate the surprising accuracy of (15.30) in the cases $n = 4$ and 6. We take n even to obtain an odd number

Table 15.3. *Some parameters for the binomial approximation to the Gaussian mask.*

n	$\sigma = (1/2)\sqrt{n}$	mask/matrix size	1D coefficients ($\times 2^n$)
2	0.7	3×3	1, 2, 1
4	1.0	5×5	1, 4, 6, 4, 1
6	1.2	7×7	1, 6, 15, 20, 15, 6, 1
8	1.4	9×9	1, 8, 28, 56, 70, 56, 28, 8, 1

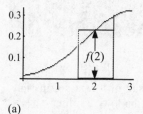 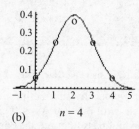 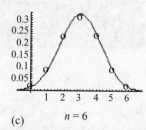

(a)   (b) $n = 4$ (c) $n = 6$

Figure 15.17 (a) Area under a Gaussian between $k - 1/2$ and $k + 1/2$ approximated by a rectangle; (b) and (c) represent consequent binomial approximations 'o' to the Gaussian.

of coefficients, hence a central member. The coefficients, by construction, add up to $2^{-n}(1+1)^n = 1$, and so *leave a region of constant intensity unchanged*.

Exercise Why (above) is a region of constant intensity unchanged?

Example 15.22 (*Convolution masks for Gaussian smoothing*) Since the 2D Gaussian is separable because of $e^{x^2+y^2} = e^{x^2} \cdot e^{y^2}$, we can obtain suitable matrices by the separable method of (15.15) and Table 15.3, as follows.

$$n = 2: \qquad \frac{1}{4}\begin{bmatrix} 1 \\ 2 \\ 1 \end{bmatrix} \frac{1}{4}\begin{bmatrix} 1 & 2 & 1 \end{bmatrix} = \frac{1}{16}\begin{bmatrix} 1 & 2 & 1 \\ 2 & 4 & 2 \\ 1 & 2 & 1 \end{bmatrix}, \qquad (15.31)$$

$$n = 4: \qquad \frac{1}{16}\begin{bmatrix} 1 \\ 4 \\ 6 \\ 4 \\ 1 \end{bmatrix} \frac{1}{16}\begin{bmatrix} 1 & 4 & 6 & 4 & 1 \end{bmatrix} = \frac{1}{256}\begin{bmatrix} 1 & 4 & 6 & 4 & 1 \\ 4 & 16 & 24 & 16 & 4 \\ 6 & 24 & 36 & 24 & 6 \\ 4 & 16 & 24 & 16 & 4 \\ 1 & 4 & 6 & 4 & 1 \end{bmatrix}. \qquad (15.32)$$

Here is a key observation, which relates blurring (lowpass filtration), to edge enhacement (highpass filtration). See also Figure 15.18.

A highpass filter may be achieved by subtracting from the
original image the result of applying a lowpass filter (and
vice versa).

Original   Gaussian blur (lowpass)   Highpass filter

Figure 15.18 A highpass filter created by subtracting the result of lowpass Gaussian
blur (approximated by binomials with $n = 6$). As is typical, the lowpass filter causes
edges to be less sharp, whilst the highpass filter retains edges but loses some distinctions
of shading.

15.2.3 Small convolution approximations to large filters

Suppose we have a filter $F \to F'$, with transfer function H. That is, $F'(u, v) = H(u, v)F(u, v)$. Then the Convolution Theorem tells us that $f' = h*f$, the convolution of f by kernel h. In general the exact h will be $N \times N$ and complex, comparing very unfavourably in this respect with the small and real convolution masks of (15.31) and (15.32) for the Gaussian. However, we will see how to approximate the effect of H by the best possible convolution mask $h = \hat{h}$, of a given size $r < N$. We'll see that a frequently found condition on H (being 'antipodal') ensures that h is real. In a mild abuse of notation we will normally drop the subscript and write $\hat{h}$ for both the size r mask and its extension by zeros to size N, retaining the r when emphasis is required.

Symmetry The antipodal property we want to define for h is intimitely related to other symmetry properties useful for reducing calculation and storage requirements. All are easy properties of both Gaussian and Butterworth filters, and we describe them in turn.

Definition 15.23 Let M be a square matrix of *odd* size $N - 1$ with rows $R_1, \ldots, R_{N-1}$ and columns $C_1, \ldots, C_{N-1}$. We consider symmetry operations on M. (i) Suppose we perform the row interchanges $R_k \leftrightarrow R_{N-k}$ for $1 \leq k \leq N - 1$. We may describe this as a reflection operation in a horizontal mirror at row $N/2$. In the 3×3 matrix of (15.33) it sends $R_1 \leftrightarrow R_3$, the mirror R_2 being unchanged by $R_2 \leftrightarrow R_2$. If this leaves all matrix elements unchanged we shall say M has a *horizontal mirror*. A similar definition holds for columns and a vertical mirror. The matrices of (15.31) and (15.32) have both horizontal and vertical mirror symmetry. Those of (15.33) below have neither.

(ii) The result of reflection in a horizontal and a vertical mirror (in either order) is that each element m_{kj} is sent to its antipodal counterpart $m_{N-k,N-j}$ $(1 \leq k, j \leq N - 1)$, and M to its *antipodal image*. We say M is *antipodal* if this image is M itself. This differs from *symmetric*, where $m_{kj} = m_{jk}$, and we compare these two symmetry properties below. The definitions apply formally unchanged when M has even order with rows $R_0, \ldots, R_{N-1}$, the extra row and column being numbered zero (more general antipodality is considered in Section 17.3.2).

$$\text{Symmetric:} \begin{bmatrix} 1 & 2 & 3 \\ 2 & 5 & 4 \\ 3 & 4 & 0 \end{bmatrix}, \text{ Antipodal:} \begin{bmatrix} 0 & 0 & 0 & 0 \\ 0 & 1 & 2 & 3 \\ 0 & 4 & 5 & 4 \\ 0 & 3 & 2 & 1 \end{bmatrix}. \tag{15.33}$$

If rows and columns are numbered relative to the *centre* $(N/2, N/2)$ the antipodal pairs become $m_{-k,-j} = m_{k,j}$. In any case the centre in each matrix above is the unique element 5.

Theorem 15.24 *The following hold, and also with the roles of f and F reversed, for the N-point DFT. (i) If f is symmetric then so is F, and similarly for (ii) the mirror and (iii) the antipodal property. (iv) F is real if and only if the antipodal image of f is its conjugate $\bar{f}$.*

Proof For a short proof we note that the row operations $R_k \leftrightarrow R_{N-k}$ $(1 \leq k \leq N - 1)$ on an $N \times N$ matrix M are equivalent, by Theorem 8.17, to forming the product PM, where P is the matrix which results from performing these operations on the identity matrix I_N. This is illustrated below in the case $N = 4$, for a simple choice of M.

$$\begin{array}{cccc}
I & P & M & PM \\
\begin{bmatrix} 1 & 0 & 0 & 0 \\ 0 & 1 & 0 & 0 \\ 0 & 0 & 1 & 0 \\ 0 & 0 & 0 & 1 \end{bmatrix}, & \begin{bmatrix} 1 & 0 & 0 & 0 \\ 0 & 0 & 0 & 1 \\ 0 & 0 & 1 & 0 \\ 0 & 1 & 0 & 0 \end{bmatrix}, & \begin{bmatrix} 0 & 0 & 0 & 0 \\ 1 & 1 & 1 & 1 \\ 2 & 2 & 2 & 2 \\ 3 & 3 & 3 & 3 \end{bmatrix}, & \begin{bmatrix} 0 & 0 & 0 & 0 \\ 3 & 3 & 3 & 3 \\ 2 & 2 & 2 & 2 \\ 1 & 1 & 1 & 1 \end{bmatrix}.
\end{array}$$

By Examples 8.21, P is symmetric as above, and performing the operations of P twice takes us back to the original M, so $P^2 = I$. Gathering some crucial properties of P we state:

$$P^{-1} = P = P^{\mathrm{T}}, \tag{15.34a}$$

$$PT = \overline{T} = TP. \tag{15.34b}$$

It remains to prove (15.34b). Since $R_0 = [1\ 1 \ldots 1] = \overline{R}_0$ in the Fourier matrix T, the first equality is equivalent to the relation $R_{N-k} = \overline{R}_k$ $(1 \leq k = N - 1)$ of Theorem 14.5. The second is obtained by transposing the first, upon observing that $T, \overline{T}$ and P are symmetric.

Using P The horizontal mirror property of (ii) becomes $PF = F$ if and only if $Pf = f$ (the vertical is an exercise). The antipodal image of a matrix M is PMP, because column operations $C_k \leftrightarrow C_{N-k}$ $(1 \le k \le N-1)$ are obtained by post-multiplying by $P^{\mathrm{T}}(= P)$ (see above Theorem 8.20), and of course a complex matrix is real if and only if it equals its complex conjugate. Now the proof reduces to showing

$$\text{(i)} f^{\mathrm{T}} \to F^{\mathrm{T}}, \quad \text{(ii)} Pf \to \mathrm{PF}, \quad \text{(iii)} PfP \to PFP, \quad \text{(iv)} P\bar{f}P \to \overline{F}, \qquad (15.35)$$

which follow from (15.34). This achieves the result because, for example, $f \to F$ and $f^{\mathrm{T}} \to F^{\mathrm{T}}$ carry the implication $f = f^{\mathrm{T}}$ if and only if $F = F^{\mathrm{T}}$. In (iv) $PfP = \bar{f} \Leftrightarrow P\bar{f}P = f \Leftrightarrow \overline{F} = f$.

Exercise Fill in the details of (15.35). See Exercise 15.10.

The convolution mask *We find an $r \times r$ matrix to best approximate the effect of a transfer function H on the N-point DFT.* One standard approach is to write an $N \times N$ array as a vector of length N^2, use $N^2 \times N^2$ matrices (see Gonzalez and Woods, 1993), and invoke the extremal properties of a pseudo-inverse matrix (see Remarks 8.57). In fact, it is possible to phrase the problem so as to keep within matrices of size N. However, a yet simpler way, and one which makes the solution clear by orthogonality, is to employ the standard basis $\{E_{jk}\}$ for $N \times N$ arrays where, we recall, E_{jk} has a 1 in position j, k and 0 elsewhere. This gives the general result below, which we then specialise to the most-used case.

Theorem 15.25 (*Approximating a convolution mask*) *Let T send $h \to H$ and $\hat{h} \to \hat{H}$. If $\hat{h}$ is fixed at certain entries, then $\|H - \hat{H}\|$ is minimised as $\hat{h}$ varies, by the rule: $\hat{h}_{jk} = h_{jk}$ except where otherwise constrained.*

Proof We determine $\|H - \hat{H}\|$ in terms of h and $\hat{h}$. Recalling the notation of Theorem 15.5, we write as before $T^{-1} = [C_0 \dots C_{N-1}] = (1/N)\overline{T}$, noting the implication that column j of T is $N\overline{C}_j$, and express the effect of T upon E_{jk} in terms of our earlier basis elements $\varepsilon_{jk} = C_j C_k^{\mathrm{T}}$.

$$\begin{aligned} E_{jk} \to TE_{jk}T &= (\text{column } j \text{ of } T)(\text{column } k \text{ of } T)^{\mathrm{T}} \quad \text{by (7.32c)} \\ &= N\overline{C}_j N\overline{C}_k^{T} = N^2 \bar{\varepsilon}_{jk}. \end{aligned}$$

Now it is easy to determine $\|H - \hat{H}\|$. We have

$$h = \Sigma_{jk} h_{jk} E_{jk} \to \Sigma_{jk} h_{jk} N^2 \bar{\varepsilon}_{jk} = H, \qquad (15.36)$$

$$\hat{h} = \Sigma_{jk} \hat{h}_{jk} E_{jk} \to \Sigma_{jk} \hat{h}_{jk} N^2 \bar{\varepsilon}_{jk} = \hat{H}, \qquad (15.37)$$

and so $H - \hat{H} = \Sigma(h_{jk} - \hat{h}_{jk})N^2 \bar{\varepsilon}_{jk}$. Crucially, by Theorem 15.5, $\{\varepsilon_{jk}\}$ are orthogonal of equal length and therefore so are $\{\bar{\varepsilon}_{jk}\}$. Thus

$$\|H - \hat{H}\|^2 = \Sigma_{jk} |h_{jk} - h_{jk}|^2 N^4 \|\bar{\varepsilon}_{jk}\|^2, \qquad (15.38)$$

which is minimised when we take $\hat{h} = h$ except at those entries where the former is fixed.

Remarks 15.26 The optimum $\hat{h}$ of Theorem 15.25 is the array we would obtain by computing h as $T^{-1}HT^{-1}$, then deleting all those rows and columns which are to be absent in $\hat{h}$. This is a remarkable property of the DFT, and holds true whatever row/column numbers are allowed by $\hat{h}$. (In fact, they need not be the first r, nor need they even be contiguous.) Having noted this, we may achieve the same result by reducing T^{-1} to a matrix S_r of only r columns, corresponding to the desired r rows/columns of the approximation:

$$\hat{h} = S_r^T H S_r. \tag{15.39}$$

This follows from the routine observation that the rows of $h = T^{-1}HT^{-1}$ are determined by the rows of the first factor and the columns by the last. Thus, (row k of h) = (row k of $T^{-1})HT^{-1} = C_k^T HT^{-1}$, so we reduce to the desired rows by taking $S_r^T HT^{-1}$. Considering the columns similarly reduces the latter to (15.39).

Example 15.27 (*A cure for under-sampling*) Let us approximate the Butterworth filter of order 1 with $N = 128$ and cutoff $k_0 = 20$, by convolution masks of various sizes. As illustrated in Figure 15.19, the 7×7 mask contains the 5×5 which in turn contains the 3×3 mask.

$$\hat{h}_7 = \begin{pmatrix} 0.18 & 0.37 & 0.64 & 0.87 & 0.64 & 0.37 & 0.18 \\ 0.37 & 0.89 & 1.7 & 2. & 1.7 & 0.89 & 0.37 \\ 0.64 & 1.7 & 5.1 & 9.3 & 5.1 & 1.7 & 0.64 \\ 0.87 & 2. & 9.3 & 26. & 9.3 & 2. & 0.87 \\ 0.64 & 1.7 & 5.1 & 9.3 & 5.1 & 1.7 & 0.64 \\ 0.37 & 0.89 & 1.7 & 2. & 1.7 & 0.89 & 0.37 \\ 0.18 & 0.37 & 0.64 & 0.87 & 0.64 & 0.37 & 0.18 \end{pmatrix}$$

Figure 15.19 Approximate convolution mask for a Butterworth filter, illustrating that the 7×7 contains the 5×5, which contains the 3×3 version. Each matrix is symmetric, antipodal, and has horizontal and vertical mirror symmetry, as predicted by Theorem 15.24.

These containments are, of course, implied by Theorem 15.25; changing the size does not alter previously computed elements. Further on, in Figure 15.20, we show comparative results of the various sized masks. First some practicalities. To function as a mask, $\hat{h}$ must be numbered from its centre, which simply means appropriate cyclic array rotations.

Calculating H and h The matrix H in both Gaussian and Butterworth cases can be expressed in terms of the distance r from the zero frequencies. In effect, we first translate this zero to the centre, so that $r = \sqrt{(u^2 + v^2)}$, where $u = j - N/2$, $v = k - N/2$. In Figure 15.20 we apply this matrix to compare the results of the Butterworth filter with sizes 3, 5 and 7, smoothing an under-sampled image which has the usual zigzag edges. ALGO 15.1 below is one way to incorporate the rotations in computing h.

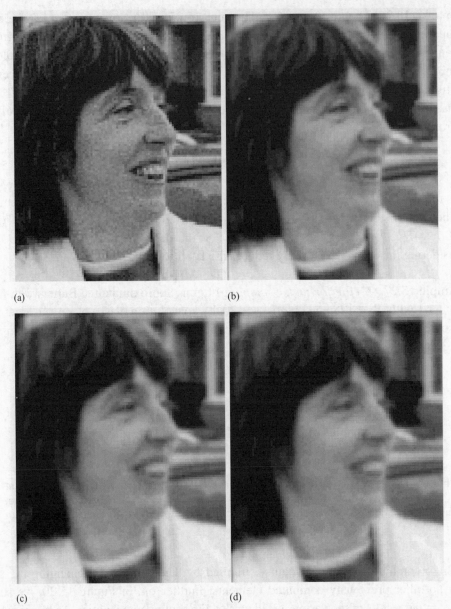

(a) (b)

(c) (d)

Figure 15.20 (a) 128×128 image (slightly cropped), undersampled, and therefore containing zigzag edges and other signs of 'pixillation', (b), (c), (d) smoothing with Butterworth filter of order 1 and cutoff 20, using respective sizes 3, 5, 7 as recorded in Example 15.27. The smoothing even by size 3 gives a dramatic improvement in quality at the expense of a slight blur. Perhaps only the mouth benefits by going up to size 7.

ALGO 15.1 Butterworth filter $H_{N \times N}$ of order d and cutoff k_0, and its approximating convolution mask h of size $2k + 1$.

Function *but(i, j)*:
$$r = \sqrt{[(i - N/2)^2 + (j - N/2)^2]}$$
$$but = 1/[1 + (r/k_0)^{2d}]$$
H = array *but* $(i - 1, j - 1), 1 \le i, j \le N$
Rotate H backwards $N/2$ rows and columns (centre to top left)
$h = $ InverseFourier $[H]$
Rotate h forwards k rows and columns
Return $\hat{h}$ as the first $2k + 1$ rows/columns

(Note: we may replace '*but*' by more general $H(r)$.)

Symmetry One result of the Butterworth dependence on r rather than separate coordinates is that H is not only antipodal but symmetric, and has both horizontal and vertical mirror symmetry. The reason is that, in terms of u and v, these symmetries involve only an interchange of u and v or a sign change of one or both, and r is unaffected by these. By Theorem 15.24, the same properties hold for $\hat{h}_r$ of whatever size. The symmetries are visible in the matrix of Figure 15.19 above. They generate the dihedral group D_8 (see Section 2.4), consisting of reflections in four equally spaced mirrors at $45°$, and multiples of a quarter turn.

This means we could get by with calculating less than a quarter of the elements of $\hat{h}$ and filling in the rest by symmetry (again, see Figure 15.19). Finally, we emphasise that, in spite of the non-real nature of the DFT, the elements of h and its approximations are real. Indeed, a finer analysis shows that they are positive for h of size less than about $N/8$, as we find in Figure 15.19.

Complexity The dot product of two m-vectors takes $2m - 1$ arithmetic operations, so (15.39) takes $2r(2N - 1)$, where r is typically between 3 and at most 9. This improves on the method in which arrays are written out row by row as long vectors, which requires $O(N^4)$ operations.

Power and cutoff Though we use cutoff 20 and it seems that the power in higher-frequency radii is negligible, this is not so; in fact, by removing these higher frequencies (smoothly) we achieve a significant improvement over the original jaggy and mottled appearance. See Table 15.4.

Table 15.4. *Power in various frequency bands for original in Figure 15.20.*

radius	0–10	10–20	20–30	30–40	40–50	50–60
power	109.866	0.7120	0.210	0.090	0.047	0.030

15.2.4 Edge-detection filters

Here we consider *edge-detection* as distinct from enhancement, meaning that we process an image so that what remains is an automated clear delineation of the edges, at the expense of all else. This is an important early step towards object recognition (Chapter 18), by providing a basis for segmenting the image into constituent parts. The methods we describe in this section are designed to cope with a certain amount of noise, unlike the pure Laplacian of Figure 15.6, which is very noise-sensitive. However, the Laplacian will shortly re-enter as part of the *zero-crossing* method of Marr and Hildreth (1980), Marr (1982). Meanwhile, we note the general schema, with two parts:

(a) smooth in one direction – to mitigate the effect of noise;
(b) take as edge pixels those whose value is changing most rapidly.

Typically, we smooth in one direction only, say horizontally, then estimate the gradient at right angles to this, as a difference between values. This may be repeated for several directions, then the maximum modulus or the sum of moduli of gradients is taken as edge indicator.

Example 15.28 *The Sobel edge-detector* Here we use the horizontal, vertical and one direction between, with smoothing by the 1D Gaussian. The masks are as follows.

$$h_1 = \begin{bmatrix} -1 \\ 0 \\ 1 \end{bmatrix} \begin{bmatrix} 1 & 2 & 1 \end{bmatrix} = \begin{bmatrix} -1 & -2 & -1 \\ 0 & 0 & 0 \\ 1 & 2 & 1 \end{bmatrix} \quad (\partial_1 f = h_1{}^* f)$$

$$h_2 = \begin{bmatrix} 1 \\ 2 \\ 1 \end{bmatrix} \begin{bmatrix} -1 & 0 & 1 \end{bmatrix} = \begin{bmatrix} -1 & 0 & 1 \\ -2 & 0 & 2 \\ -1 & 0 & 1 \end{bmatrix} \quad (\partial_2 f = h_2{}^* f)$$

$$h_3 = \begin{bmatrix} 0 & 1 & 2 \\ -1 & 0 & 1 \\ -2 & -1 & 0 \end{bmatrix} \quad (\partial_3 f = h_3{}^* f)$$

The mask h_3 is obtained by cycling the non-central elements of h_2 one place anti-clockwise. The criterion for an edge pixel is that $|\partial_1 f| + |\partial_2 f| + |\partial_3 f|$ exceed a threshold. Alternatively, we simply plot this value, as is done in Figure 15.23.

Example 15.29 *The Prewitt edge-detector* This time the smoothing is by simple average. The method is sometimes called the *compass operator*, for eight directions are explored, with masks all generated from h_1 shown below by repeated cycling of the non-centre elements. Now the the greatest of the eight absolute values is compared with a threshold. This method also gives a notional direction for the edge at right angles to the direction

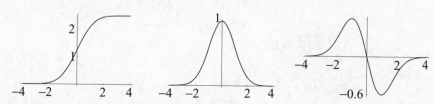

Figure 15.21 A function $f(x)$ and its first and second derivatives, indicating how the position of greatest slope at an edge leads to a zero crossing of the second derivative (i.e. a place where this derivative equals zero and so crosses the horizontal axis).

of greatest change.

$$h_1 = \begin{bmatrix} -1 \\ 0 \\ 1 \end{bmatrix} \begin{bmatrix} 1 & 1 & 1 \end{bmatrix} = \begin{bmatrix} -1 & -1 & -1 \\ 0 & 0 & 0 \\ 1 & 1 & 1 \end{bmatrix},$$

$$h_2 = \begin{bmatrix} -1 & -1 & 0 \\ -1 & 0 & 1 \\ 0 & 1 & 1 \end{bmatrix} \dots, h_8 = \begin{bmatrix} 0 & -1 & -1 \\ 1 & 0 & -1 \\ 1 & 1 & 0 \end{bmatrix}.$$

Example 15.30 *The zero-crossing edge-detector* Marr and Hildreth (1980), Marr (1982) based this approach on belief about how the human eye processes edges. The graphs in Figure 15.21 illustrate in one dimension how a maximum gradient corresponding to an edge implies a zero of the second derivative of pixel values at the edge position.

This time both smoothing and gradient check are performed in two dimensions. We smooth by the 2D Gaussian $g(r)$, then apply the Laplacian and determine the 'zero crossings' (or the pixels at which the Laplacian is below a threshold in absolute value). Thus, if h is a convolution mask for the Laplacian we compute $f \to h^*(g^* f)$, which equals $(h^*g)^* f$. But h^*g is a discrete version of $\nabla^2 g$, which we can calculate analytically. First of all we establish the useful formula for *any* suitably differentiable function $g(r)$:

$$\nabla^2 g(r) = g''(r) + g'(r)/r. \tag{15.40}$$

To see this we differentiate $r^2 = x^2 + y^2$ with respect to x to obtain $2r \partial r/\partial x = 2x$, whence $\partial r/\partial x = x/r$, and so

$$\begin{aligned}
\partial g(r)/\partial x &= \partial g/\partial r \cdot \partial r/\partial x = x[g'(r)/r], \\
\partial^2 g(r)/\partial x^2 &= g'(r)/r + x(\partial/\partial x)[g'(r)/r] && \text{by the Product Rule} \\
&= g'(r)/r + (x^2/r)\partial/\partial r[g'(r)/r] && \text{since } \partial r/\partial x = x/r \\
&= g'(r)/r + (x^2/r)[rg''(r) - g'(r)]/r^2 && \text{by the Quotient Rule.}
\end{aligned}$$

Similarly for $\partial^2 g(r)/\partial y^2$ and, adding the two parts and simplifying by $x^2 + y^2 = r^2$, we obtain (15.40). Specialising to the Gaussian $g(r) = \gamma \exp[-r^2/2\sigma^2](\gamma = 1/\sigma\sqrt{(2\pi)})$, we have the relation $g'(r) = -rg(r)/\sigma^2$ and, differentiating again with respect to r:

$$g''(r) = (r^2 - \sigma^2)g(r)/\sigma^4. \tag{15.41}$$

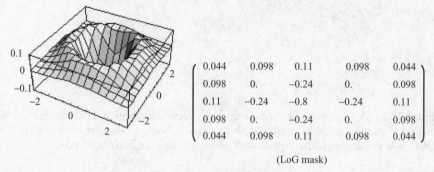

$$
\begin{pmatrix}
0.044 & 0.098 & 0.11 & 0.098 & 0.044 \\
0.098 & 0. & -0.24 & 0. & 0.098 \\
0.11 & -0.24 & -0.8 & -0.24 & 0.11 \\
0.098 & 0. & -0.24 & 0. & 0.098 \\
0.044 & 0.098 & 0.11 & 0.098 & 0.044
\end{pmatrix}
$$

(LoG mask)

Figure 15.22 (a) The Laplacian of Gaussian function ($\sigma = 1$) as a surface, and (b) the 5×5 convolution mask obtained by evaluating the function over $x, y = -2, \ldots, 2$. Note the D_8 symmetries (see Section 2.4), including horizontal, vertical and diagonal reflections.

Warning: this expression is sometimes mistakenly identified with the Laplacian, but according to (15.40) we have yet to add in the term $g'(r)/r$. When this is done, we have

$$
\nabla^2 g(r) = \frac{r^2 - 2\sigma^2}{\sigma^4} g(r). \tag{15.42}
$$

Firstly, here is a rough tryout of the LoG method (o stands for 'of') on the 54×61 image (a) below, consisting of two connected regions, differently shaded. Employing ALGO 15.1 with $H(r)$ from (15.42), we denote the image array by f, take $\sigma = 2$ in (15.42), and exhibit black those pixels satisfying the edge criterion $|(\text{LoG})^* f| < 45$.

This results in (b), which does distinguish the edges from the shading and white surround.

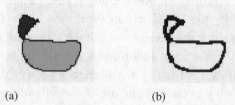

(a)   (b)

Remark Marr and Hildreth (1980) noted the difference of two Gaussians (DoG) function of Wilson and Bergen (1979) as a good approximation to their LoG operator over a certain range of σ ratios σ_1/σ_2. Indeed, LoG and DoG are proportionate as $\sigma_1/\sigma_2 \to 1$, but of course the limiting case is of no practical help. Marr and Hildreth showed that a good compromise is $\sigma_1/\sigma_2 = 1.6$, based on an engineering-type tradeoff between filter bandwith and sensitivity. For further developments see Castleman (1996).

Example 15.31 We compare the edge-detection properties of the Sobel, Prewitt and zero-crossing methods. The Prewitt and Sobel results for the present example, the windmill of Figure 15.23, are very hard to distinguish, and we give only the Sobel. The superiority of the Marr–Hildreth method comes out, for example, in its detection of edges in the lower left windmill vane, compared with a blur in the Sobel case.

An encyclopaedic study of *applications* is found in Russ (1995), whilst Baldock and Graham (2000) stress biomedical applications such as chromosomes. Seul, O'Gorman

Figure 15.23 An original windmill photo digitised at 327×233, followed by the result of the Sobel method, then the Marr–Hildreth Laplacian-of-Gaussian (LoG) method. The detail is superior in the LoG case.

and Sammon (2000) focus on practical issues in general. For a survey of methods and approaches to edge-detection, see Davies (1997).

15.3 Deconvolution and image restoration

In Chapter 11 we studied some probabilistic approaches to image restoration, assuming the presence of additive noise. Here we introduce firstly the method of *restoration by deconvolution* in the context of image blurring by motion, camera lens imperfection or atmospheric disturbance; this method is noise-sensitive. We then derive the all-purpose Wiener filter, based on probabilistic models of the image and its distortion, and allowing for *additive noise as well as blur*. We begin with the idea of expressing the image distortion as the convolution of the original with some mask.

15.3.1 Motion blur

The card number is		The card number is
7539813584763 98		7539813584763 98

(a) The original	(b) clarity lost (motion blur)	(c) clarity regained

Figure 15.24 (b) The original image is blurred due to motion during exposure to the camera, but restored in (c) by methods described below. Notice that the blur disguises both the card number and the identity of the child.

Let us suppose that a camera records light for a short time T during which the image moves a short distance, but that the shutter opens and closes sufficiently fast that no account need be taken of this transition. An important assumption that helps us to analyse the situation is that the object under observation is rigid, so that, if t denotes time from the start, every image point follows the same path $(a(t), b(t))$, $0 \le t \le T$. Consider first a continuous model, where $f(x, y)$ represents true image values and $g(x, y)$ the values as recorded.

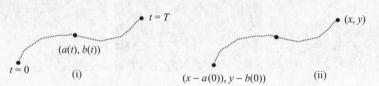

Figure 15.25 (i) The motion of every point, (ii) the path whose points contribute to $g(x, y)$.

By considering Figure 15.25, we conclude that $g(x, y)$ is given by a time average of f over the path that leads to (x, y). For the time that the camera would have spent collecting photons from a given small region R around (x, y) is, by virtue of the motion, expended across all parts that finally line up under R. The recorded image is therefore

$$g(x, y) = \frac{1}{T} \int_0^T f(x - a(t), \, y - b(t)) \, dt, \text{ with transform}$$

$$G(u, v) = \int_0^\infty \int_0^\infty g(x, y) \, e^{-2\pi i(ux+vy)} \, dx \, dy$$

$$= \frac{1}{T} \int_0^\infty \int_0^\infty \left[\int_0^T f(x - a(t), \, y - b(t)) dt \right] e^{-2\pi i(ux+vy)} \, dx \, dy$$

$$= \frac{1}{T} \int_0^T \left[\int_0^\infty \int_0^\infty f(x - a(t), \, y - b(t)) \, e^{-2\pi i(ux+vy)} \, dx \, dy \right] dt$$

$$= \frac{1}{T} \int_0^T F(u, v) \, e^{-2\pi i(ua(t)+vb(t))'} dt \quad \text{by the Shift Theorem, Table 15.2}$$

$$= F(u, v) H(u, v), \text{ since } F \text{ is independent of } t, \text{ where}$$

$$H(u, v) = \frac{1}{T} \int_0^T e^{-2\pi i(ua(t)+vb(t))'} dt. \tag{15.43}$$

Thus, provided the integration in (15.43) may be performed, we have discovered a transfer function H for the effect of motion, and we may recover $F(u, v) = G(u, v)/H(u, v)$ (unless H has a zero in the region of interest), and hence $f(x, y)$ from the Inverse Fourier Transform. Let us proceed with the case of uniform motion in the x-direction, say $a(t) = \alpha t/T$, and $b(t) = 0$. We have then

$$H(u, v) = \frac{1}{T} \int_0^T e^{-2\pi iuat/T} dt = \frac{1}{T} \left[e^{-2\pi iuat/T}/(-2\pi iua/T) \right]_0^T, \quad \text{by (14.24)}$$

$$= (1/2\pi iu\alpha)[1 - e^{-2\pi iu\alpha}]$$

$$= (1/2\pi iu\alpha)[e^{\pi iu\alpha} - e^{-\pi iu\alpha}] e^{-\pi iu\alpha}$$

$$= (1/\pi u\alpha) \sin \pi u\alpha \, e^{-\pi iu\alpha} \quad \text{since } e^{i\theta} - e^{-i\theta} = 2i \sin \theta, \quad \text{hence the}$$

Theorem 15.32 *Suppose image blur is caused by uniform motion through a distance α in the x-direction during exposure time. Then, writing* $\operatorname{sinc} x = (1/x) \sin x$, *we have a transfer function*

$$H(u, v) = \operatorname{sinc}(\pi u\alpha) e^{-i\pi u\alpha}. \tag{15.44}$$

Exercise Show that $H(-u, -v) = \overline{H}(u, v)$ in (15.44). It follows that $g = f*h$, where h is real although H is not (see Theorem 15.24).

Deducing the motion from the image If no zero of $H(u, v)$ exists within the range of interest, we may obtain the original image f as the inverse transform of $F(u, v) = G(u, v)/H(u, v)$. On the other hand we can, in one fell swoop, discover whether such zeros exist, and, if they do, deduce the motion distance from the spacing between lines in the transform G consequent upon these zeros. This facilitates solving the problem in the discrete version towards which we almost inevitably turn. Let us now consider this case.

The discrete case Suppose that a camera produces an $N \times N$ pixel array $f_{m,n}$ from the scene, that the uniformly covered horizontal distance is $d + 1$ pixel units, and that the area recorded is white up to the dth pixel horizontally, $n = 0, 1, \ldots, d - 1$. Then, for each m, the averaging process due to motion implies a new pixel value

$$g_{m,n} = (f_{m,n} + f_{m,n-1} + \cdots + f_{m,n-d})/(d + 1). \tag{15.45}$$

Example 15.33 To illustrate what happens in detail we take a 1×7 pixel strip, with an illumination scale ranging from $f = 0$ as black to $f = 1$ as white. Note that the *appearance* according to Equation (15.45) is the same whatever (uniformly related) scale we use, such as grey levels 0 to 255, or percentage illumination. The result is shown in Figure 15.26.

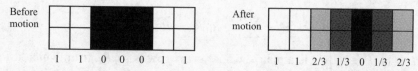

Figure 15.26 Light values captured by a camera when the scene is stationary, and when it moves uniformly three pixels to the right ($d = 2$). Here 0 is black and 1 is white.

Blurring and back We recapitulate that motion is to be $d + 1$ units in a horizontal direction. Suppose the image array of values has columns $C_0, \ldots, C_{N-1}$. If it is desired to simulate blur for aesthetic or other reasons, this can be done in place on the image itself by working from right to left (ALGO 15.2). The inverse operation exists and can be formulated so as to likewise replace the columns one by one, but this time working from left to right (ALGO 15.3). The algorithms are given below; they were applied in Figure 15.24 with $d = 12$.

ALGO 15.2 Blur the array	*ALGO 15.3 Deblur the array*
$[C_0, \ldots, C_{N-1}]$	$[B_0, \ldots, B_{N-1}]$
For $i = N - 1$ down to d	For $i = d$ to $N - 1$
$B_i = (C_i + C_{i-1} + \cdots + C_{i-d})/(d+1)$	$C_i = (d+1)B_i - B_{i-1} \cdots - B_{i-d}$

How ALGO 15.3 works The blurred and original arrays are by definition related by $B_i = (C_i + C_{i-1} + \cdots + C_{i-d})/(d+1)$, which rearranges as $C_i = (d+1)B_i - C_{i-1} - \cdots - C_{i-d}$. But this is the actual calculation performed by ALGO 15.2 in working from left to right, for $B_{i-1}, \ldots, B_{i-d}$ have been overwritten by the re-calculated $C_{i-1}, \ldots, C_{i-d}$.

The DFT estimation of blur Suppose we do not know the extent d of the blur. We aim to deduce the value of d from the DFT of the image $F \circ H$, specifically the positions of its zeros, where H is a discrete version of the transfer function (15.44). We shall see that the zeros of H occur very distinctly, in equally spaced vertical lines, and so the zero positions of $F \circ H$ will normally reveal this spacing. Notice first that the discrete blur operation (15.45) is equivalent to applying to f the following $1 \times (d+1)$ convolution mask h, based on $d + 1$ ones followed by d zeros:

$$h = (1 \quad 1 \ldots 1 \quad 0 \ldots 0)/(d+1).$$

We may say $g = f*h$, the result of convolving f with a vector h representing the motion that caused the blur. Since the zero positions of the inverse transform H are unaltered by nonzero scalings, including those generated by shifts (see Table 15.2), we may recast h as an $N \times N$ array whose nonzero elements are ones at positions $00, 01, \ldots, 0d$. To aid in determining H we use the $N \times N$ basis matrices E_{st} consisting of zeros except for '1' at position (s, t); then $(d+1)h = E_{00} + E_{01} + \cdots + E_{0d}$. This helps because (see (7.32c)) the DFT, with rows $R_0, \ldots, R_{N-1}$, sends E_{st} to (column s of T)^{T}(row t of T) $= R_s^{\mathrm{T}} R_t$, and so

$$(d+1)H = \sum\nolimits_{t=0}^{d} R_0^{\mathrm{T}} R_t = R_0^{\mathrm{T}} \sum\nolimits_{t=0}^{d} R_t.$$

Since $R_0 = [11 \ldots 1]$, this is a matrix whose *every* row is $\sum R_t$, from which it follows that the zeros of H indeed occur in complete columns. Continuing, we note that the case $k = 0$ of H_{jk} is special: $(d+1)H_j0 = \sum_t R_t(0)$ $(0 \le t \le d) = \sum_t 1 = d + 1$. But for

$0 < k \le N - 1$, with $w = e^{-2\pi i/N}$,

$$(d + 1)H_{jk} = \sum_{t=0}^{d} R_t(k) = \sum_{t=0}^{d} w^{tk}$$
$$= \sum_{t=0}^{d} (w^k)^t = [1 - (w^k)^{d+1}]/(1 - w^k),$$

where the last equality is from the summation formula $1 + r + \cdots + r^d = (1 - r^{d+1})/(1 - r)$, with $r = w^k \ne 1$. To simplify the expression for H_{jk} we observe that

$$1 - e^{-2i\alpha} = e^{-i\alpha}(e^{i\alpha} - e^{-i\alpha}) = e^{-i\alpha}2i \sin \alpha,$$

whence $(d + 1)H_{jk} = \dfrac{1 - e^{-2\pi ik(d+1)/N}}{1 - e^{-2\pi ik/N}} = \dfrac{e^{-\pi ik(d+1)/N}}{e^{-\pi ik/N}} \cdot \dfrac{\sin(\pi k(d + 1)/N)}{\sin(\pi k/N)}$, and finally

$$H_{jk} = \begin{cases} \dfrac{\sin(\pi k(d + 1)/N)}{(d + 1)\sin(\pi k/N)} \, e^{-\pi ikd/N}, & \text{if } 1 \le k \le N - 1, \\ 1, & \text{if } k = 0. \end{cases} \tag{15.46}$$

The denominator of H_{jk} ($k > 0$) is never zero, because $0 < \pi k/N < \pi$. The numerator is zero when $k(d + 1)/N$ is an integer; that is, when N divides $k(d + 1)$. If $K = N/(d + 1)$ is an integer, the least such k equals K and this is the spacing distance between the lines of zeros. If not, this situation obtains approximately, and we have an estimate $d + 1 = N/K$ from the lines of small grey level spaced approximately K apart.

Example 15.34 Figure 15.27 shows the DFT of the blurred image of Figure 15.24(b). The distance between the uniformly spaced vertical lines is 10 pixels, implying motion of $d + 1 = 128/10 = 12.8$ units, a reasonable approximation to the actual 13.

Continuous versus discrete The expressions (15.44) and (15.46) for H have some similarity, except that the discrete version has a period N. This is typical; the DFT, by its very definition, produces an expression *as if* the original function were periodic. Later we will use the discrete formula (15.46) to construct an example for the Wiener filter.

Figure 15.27 The DFT of the blurred image of Figure 15.24(b).

15.3.2 Gaussian optics – the thin lens

An image focussed through the usual spherical-faced lens is subject to some degree of blur, in spite of otherwise excellent focussing by the user. Our purpose in this section is to express the blur as a convolution of a perfect original, and thence to eliminate it. An excellent starting point is the first approximation, Gaussian optics, in which precise focus is possible. We begin with the exact laws. When a ray of light crosses a plane boundary between two media, it is refracted (deviated) towards or away from the surface normal at the crossing point in accordance with Snell's Law, (15.47) below, as shown in Figure 15.28. To medium i we attribute *refractive index* μ_i, defined as the ratio of light speed in that medium to light speed *in vacuo*.

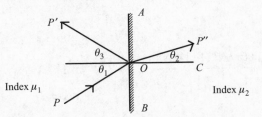

Figure 15.28 A ray PO incident at the media boundary gives rise to a reflected ray OP' and a refracted ray OP''. Implicitly $0 \leq \theta_1, \theta_2, \theta_3 \leq \pi/2$.

Theorem 15.35 *Referring to Figure 15.28, a reflected ray OP' and refracted ray OP'' both lie in the plane formed by the incident ray PO and surface normal OC. The Law of Reflection states further that $\theta_3 = \theta_1$, whilst the direction of the refracted ray is given by Snell's Law:*

$$\boxed{\mu_1 \sin \theta_1 = \mu_2 \sin \theta_2.} \tag{15.47}$$

Remarks 15.36 (*First implications of Snell's Law*)

(1) *Rays are reversible* That is, if $P''O$ is incident then OP is the refracted continuation.
(2) *A normal ray crosses the boundary with no change of direction* ($\theta_1 = 0$ implies $\theta_2 = 0$).
(3) *On entering a denser medium a ray swings towards the normal* ($\mu_1 < \mu_2$ implies $\theta_1 > \theta_2$).
(4) *As θ_1 increases, so does θ_2.* If the first medium is denser ($\mu_1 > \mu_2$), this increase continues until the ray skims the boundary ($\theta_2 = \pi/2$). After this critical value of θ_1, Snell's Law requires the impossible $\sin \theta_2 > 1$, and so we have only a reflected ray OP'. This *total internal reflection* enables optical fibres to channel light (see e.g. Born and Wolf, 1999).

Refraction at a spherical boundary In Figure 15.29, we represent the two cases we must investigate to obtain results for a lens. Here QRS is the path of a ray journeying from a medium of refractive index μ to one of index μ', the boundary being spherical with centre O, and concave towards the ray in (a) but convex in (b). The refracted ray RS, extended backwards, meets the *axis* in Q'. In case (a) we take $\mu > \mu'$, so by Remark 15.36(3) the ray is refracted *away* from the normal. In case (b) this is reversed. The result in both cases is that Q' is to the left of Q, as shown.

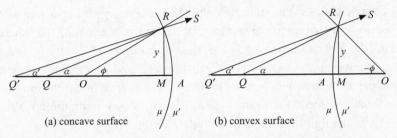

Figure 15.29 A ray QR is incident on the spherical boundary between two media, where relative to QR the boundary is (a) concave (and $\mu > \mu'$), and (b) convex (and $\mu < \mu'$).

Let α and α' be the *angles of divergence* of the rays, namely the angles RQA and $RQ'A$. To obtain the same formulae for both concave and convex cases we define the signed distances

$$r = AO, \; u = AQ, \; v = AQ', \tag{15.48}$$

and denote angle ROA by ϕ in (a) but by its negative $-\phi$ in (b) because rotation from OA to OR is in opposite directions in the two cases. We let $y = MR$, as shown.

The first-order approximation This means taking the labelled angles so small that, in the formulae $\cos\theta = 1 - \theta^2/2 + \cdots$ and $\sin\theta = \theta - \theta^3/6 + \cdots$, terms of degree higher than 1 may be neglected. Thus $\sin\theta = \theta$ and $\cos\theta = 1$, and we shall show that there follow

$$\alpha = -y/u, \; \alpha' = -y/v, \; \phi = -y/r. \tag{15.49}$$

Proof (i) AM is negligible, for $AM = AO - MO = RO - RO\cos\phi = 0$, (ii) $|QR| = |QR|\cos\alpha = |QM| = |QA|$, so that $\alpha = \sin\alpha = y/|QR| = y/|QA| = y/(-u)$, and similarly $\alpha' = y/(-v)$, (iii) for ϕ we have in case (a) that $\sin\phi = y/|OR| = y/|OA| = y/(-r)$, and in case (b) that $\sin\phi = -\sin(-\phi) = -y/|OR| = -y/|AO| = -y/r$, as before.

Applying Snell's Law Considering Figure 15.29, we have for the incidence–refraction pair $(\theta, \theta') = (\phi - \alpha, \phi - \alpha')$ in case (a) and its negative in case (b), and so we may in either case write Snell's Law as $\mu\sin(\phi - \alpha) = \mu'\sin(\phi - \alpha')$. Moreover, should Q and Q' lie on the opposite side of O to that portrayed then (θ, θ') has the opposite sign to that given here, so our result is the same again; they cannot themselves lie on opposite sides of O (by inspection of Figure 15.28). Now we use the assumed equality of an angle and its sine to express Snell's Law in the form

$$\mu(\phi - \alpha) = \mu'(\phi - \alpha'), \quad \text{or} \quad \mu'\alpha' - \mu\alpha = (\mu' - \mu)\phi,$$

whence, on substituting from (15.49) and dividing through by y,

$$\boxed{\frac{\mu'}{v} - \frac{\mu}{u} = \frac{\mu' - \mu}{r}.} \tag{15.50}$$

The thin convex lens A *lens* may be defined as a portion of a transparent refractive medium bounded by two spherical surfaces. Its *axis* is the line joining the sphere centres, and this cuts the lens at vertices A, A' as shown in Figure 15.30, where we represent a lens of refractive index μ convex towards the surrounding medium of air on either side. Following the sign convention in (15.48) we will say the first (leftmost) surface has radius $r > 0$ and the second has radius $s < 0$. The *thin lens* assumption is then that the thickness AA' is negligible (compared with the radii).

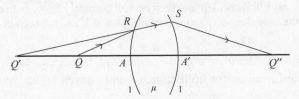

Figure 15.30 Passage of a light ray $QRSQ''$ through a thin convex lens.

Suppose a ray from Q on the axis is refracted on entering and leaving the lens, then meets the axis again at Q''. We seek a formula connecting the signed quantities $u = AQ$ and $v = AQ''$, using the intermediate $w = AQ'$. In this notation, and neglecting AA', we apply (15.50) to case (b) of Figure 15.29, and then to case (a), yielding

$$\mu/w - 1/u = (\mu - 1)/r \text{ and } 1/v - \mu/w = (1 - \mu)/s,$$

whence, on adding,

$$\boxed{\frac{1}{v} - \frac{1}{u} = (\mu - 1)\left(\frac{1}{r} - \frac{1}{s}\right) = \frac{1}{f},} \qquad (15.51)$$

say, where f, for reasons shortly to appear, is called the *focal length* of the lens. Notice that the position of Q'' therefore depends only on that of Q and not on the (small) angle α at which the ray leaves the axis. We say that Q is *focussed* at its *conjugate* Q''; the lens will focus the points of a small object placed at Q as points of an image at Q''. An important investigative tool in this regard is the behaviour of rays parallel to the axis. The effect of such a ray is obtained by letting $u \to -\infty$, when (15.51) gives a position F_2, say, for Q'', whilst $v \to \infty$ gives the position F_1 for Q such that a ray emerges parallel to the axis. The result from (15.51) is

$$\boxed{AF_1 = -f, \ AF_2 = f.} \qquad (15.52)$$

F_1, F_2 are called the *principal foci*, and are shown in Figure 15.31. Their equidistance from the lens is surprising because the curvatures of the lens faces may differ. They support an extremely useful formula of Isaac Newton, for estimating the relative positions of object and image:

$$\boxed{F_1Q \cdot F_2Q'' = -f^2.} \qquad (15.53)$$

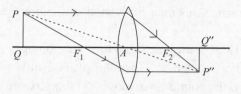

Figure 15.31 Constructing the image $Q'P''$ of an object QP.

Proof $F_1Q \cdot F_2Q'' = (AQ - AF_1)(AQ'' - AF_2) = (u + f)(v - f)$ by (15.51)

$$= uf \cdot vf(1/f + 1/u)(1/f - 1/v)$$

$$= uvf^2(1/v)(-1/u) = -f^2.$$

Finding the image Since the product in (15.53) is always negative, F_1Q and F_2Q'' have opposite signs, hence Q and Q'' are either both outside the interval $[F_1, F_2]$ or both within it. Further, as Q moves to the left, away from F_1, its conjugate Q'' must approach F_2, so that a ray parallel to the axis is refracted through the principal focus on the far side of the lens.

Now let QP be a small object represented by a straight line at right angles to the axis at Q. The paths of the arrowed rays leaving P in Figure 15.31 are determined by the principal foci and intersect at the image P'' of P. The fact that this is vertically below the image Q'' of Q is verified by the ray from P through the lens centre A, which for geometrical reasons passes through P'' also (an exercise). The *magnification M* obtained is considered negative because OP is inverted. It is (considering similar triangles PQA and $P''Q''A$)

$$\boxed{M = \frac{QP}{Q''P''} = \frac{v}{u} \, (< 0).} \tag{15.54}$$

Example 15.37 An object is placed on the axis of a thin lens of radii $r = 10, s = -12$, nearest the face of radius r, at a distance of 15 units from it. Given that the lens has refractive index 1.5, and that the refractive index of air may be assumed to be unity, determine (i) the focal length of the lens, (ii) the position of the image and (iii) the magnification.

Solution (i) According to (15.51), we have $1/f = (\mu - 1)(1/r - 1/s) = (1/2)(1/10 + 1/12) = 11/120$, whence $f = 10.9$ approx. (ii) Setting $u = -15$ and using $1/v - 1/u = 1/f$ from (15.51), we obtain $1/v = -1/15 + 11/120 = 1/40$, hence the image is 40 units to the right of the lens. (iii) The magnification is $v/u = -40/15 = -2.67$ approx.

15.3.3 Lens blur and atmospheric blur

Lens blur

The next step in accuracy is to allow that rays from one object/source point, rather than focus at a single point, may produce more generally a small spot of light of varying intensity in the image plane. This intensity variation is called the *point spread function*, or psf.

In terms of Figure 15.31 with z as signed distance along the axis, the spot area is increased if the light is collected in a parallel plane a little away from the *in-focus* position $z = v$. Again, if the point source moves off the z-axis to a point $P(x_0, y_0)$ in the object plane $z = u$, then the spot moves to P'' in the image plane $z = v$, namely

$$P''(Mx_0, My_0), \qquad \text{where } M = v/u. \tag{15.55}$$

Blur by convolution Two frequently reasonable assumptions lead us to model blur as the convolution of a *psf for the lens* with the original image. (i) *Linearity* Increasing the intensity of the point source causes a proportionate intensity increase in the spot, and the result of two point sources is the sum of their separate effects. (ii) *Shift invariance* For source points P close to the axis, the psf varies so little with P that we may treat it as invariant.

Finding the psf   (*The thin line method*) We give one approach which uses the Fourier Transform of the psf, called the *Optical Transfer Function*, or OTF. Denoting the latter by $H(u, v)$, we suppose an initial (continuous) image $f(x, y)$ becomes $g(x, y)$ under lens blur, where, in the usual notation,

$$G(u, v) = H(u, v)F(u, v). \tag{15.56}$$

Here the image is to be a thin line along the y-axis, represented as the product of an impulse $\delta(x)$ with the constant function 1 on the y-coordinate. Then $f(x, y)$ is the separable function

$$f(x, y) = \delta(x) \cdot 1_y. \tag{15.57}$$

The hope is that knowledge of $G(u, v)$ for this case alone will yield $H(u, v)$ in general. Now, the transform of the separable function (15.57) is the product of the 1D transforms of $\delta(x)$ and 1_y which, by Table 14.2 of Section 14.2, are 1_u and $\delta(v)$. Applying this to (15.56) gives $G(u, v) = H(u, v)1_u\delta(v)$, whence, with $v = 0$,

$$G(u, 0) = H(u, 0). \tag{15.58}$$

Since we may assume circular symmetry of the psf, a property possessed by the lens itself, the same holds for its transform $H(u, v)$, by the Rotation Theorem (Corollary 15.8). With this observation and Equation (15.58) we have

$$H(u, v) = H(r, 0), (r = \sqrt{(u^2 + v^2)}), = G(r, 0), \tag{15.59}$$

and consequently H may be determined from the measured transform of the image of a thin line. (This could actually be taken in any direction, according to the Rotation Theorem.)

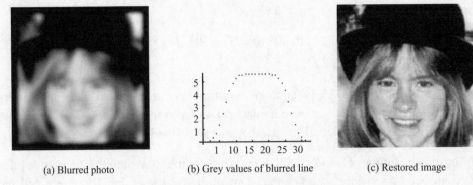

(a) Blurred photo   (b) Grey values of blurred line   (c) Restored image

Figure 15.32 Eliminating lens blur.

Example 15.38 Given a digital photo subject to lens blur, and a photo of a thin line under the same conditions, we eliminate blur as illustrated in the progression from (a) to (c) in Figure 15.32 and explained below.

Notice that, because we are working with a finite approximation, we cannot use (15.59) as it stands, but must construct a discrete version. Our assumptions are:

1. the psf of the camera lens has radial symmetry,
2. this psf is separable (not essential),
3. the original subject was surrounded by a region of white.

For greatest accuracy we want to ensure the Convolution Theorem holds exactly, no terms being neglected (this entails Assumption 3). To keep a precise hold on the calculation, we refer back to the polynomial definition of convolution, firstly in one dimension; thus, let $f = [f_0 f_1 \ldots]$, write $f(x) = \sum f_i x^i$, and similarly for vectors g, h. Then, we recall, the convolution product $g = h^* f$ is defined by the polynomial multiplication $g(x) = h(x)f(x)$. That is, $g = [g_i]$ if $g(x) = \sum g_i x^i$.

Now extend the vectors f, g, h by zeros to any length N which exceeds the degree of g, and the Convolution Theorem (14.15) gives $G_k = H_k F_k$ $(0 \le k \le N - 1)$.

Using the blurred line Suppose that in one dimension the psi has the effect of convolution with the kernel $a = [a_0 \ a_1 \ldots a_d]$, where radial symmetry implies $a_i = a_{d-i}$ $(0 \le i \le d)$. If this converts a line with constant pixel values 1 into one with values $b = [b_0 \ b_1 \ldots]$, then

$$
\begin{cases} b_0 = a_0, \\ b_1 = a_0 + a_1, \\ \ldots \\ b_d = a_0 + a_1 + \cdots + a_d, \end{cases}
\quad \text{whence} \quad
\begin{cases} a_0 = b_0, \\ a_1 = b_1 - b_0, \\ \ldots \\ a_d = b_d - b_{d-1}, \end{cases}
\quad \text{or } a = b - [0 \ b_0 \cdots b_{d-1}].
$$

$$(15.59')$$

The values b_i obtained in the present case are represented by heights in Figure 15.32(b). After applying (15.59'), the 1D kernel is seen to be the row vector, to three significant figures:

$$a = [0.0276 \ 0.0825 \ 0.203 \ 0.408 \ 0.671 \ 0.905 \ 1.000 \ 0.905 \ 0.671 \ 0.408$$
$$0.203 \ 0.0835 \ 0.0276].$$

Note that only the first $d + 1 = 14$ values of the blurred line are required in the calculation. By radial symmetry this defines the complete psi, though we use the simplifying second assumption listed, that it is actually separable, and so defined by the 13×13 matrix $a^{\mathrm{T}}a$.

Deblurring the image The polynomial argument for the Convolution Theorem applies equally in two dimensions (see (15.19)). Our blurred 2-dimensional image g and the kernel h are square, of respective sizes 128 and 13, corresponding to polynomial degrees 127 and 12, so we take the least possible value $N = 140$ for applying the DFT in each dimension. Denoting the original image by f, we have $g = h * f$, and hence by the 2D Convolution Theorem, (15.18),

$$G_{jk} = H_{jk}F_{jk} \ (0 \le j, k \le N - 1).$$

Provided that, as in this example, all H_{jk} are nonzero, we may divide to get $F_{jk} = G_{jk}/H_{jk}$, and then the inverse DFT converts F to the original f. The result is seen in Figure 15.32(c); it may be compared to the accurate but slightly cropped version at the start of the current chapter (Figure 15.1; the integer grey values shown there are recovered exactly). We conclude with a method of dealing with undesired zeros of the array H.

Dealing with zeros of H It is easy to construct an example in which $H_{jk} = 0$ occurs. Suppose we approximate the Gaussian kernel by $h = a^{\mathrm{T}}a$, where the vector a consists of the binomial coefficients in $(1 + x)^4/16$. In polynomial notation, $h(x, y) = (1 + x)^4(1 + y)^4/256$ and $H_{jk} = (1 + w^j)^4(1 + w^k)^4/256$, where $w = e^{-2\pi i/N}$ (see (15.19)). Looking for zeros, we observe that $1 + w^k = 0 \Leftrightarrow w^k = -1 \Leftrightarrow e^{-2k\pi i/N} = -1 \Leftrightarrow 2k/N$ is an odd integer $\Leftrightarrow 2k/N = 1$ (since $0 \le k \le N - 1$) $\Leftrightarrow k = N/2$.

Thus no problem arises if N is odd but, in the likely case that N is even, we may prevent zeros occurring by increasing N (as discussed above) to the next odd number. For general $h(x, y)$ we may try out varying values of N, and the deblurred image, cropped to its original size, will be the same for every N such that all H_{jk} are nonzero.

Lenses in general For more on the general properties of lenses, see e.g. Castleman (1996).

Atmospheric blur

When a distant object is focussed, turbulence in Earth's atmosphere may have a noticeably degrading effect on the image obtained. We outline the ingenious argument of Hufnagel and Stanley (1964) leading to their compact expression (15.65) below, for an OTF, which enables at least partial image restoration. Figure 15.33 indicates the geometry, with x, y, z coordinates.

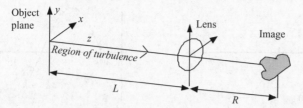

Figure 15.33 Configuration for image focus after turbulence.

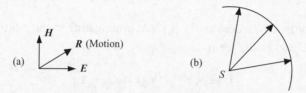

Figure 15.34 (a) Right-handed triad formed by the fields E, H and their mutual direction of propagation, (b) advancing wavefront of such triples from a source S.

The wave theory of light It was the Scottish physicist James Clerk Maxwell who first identified light as a form of electromagnetic radiation. In this parlance, a light ray in direction R corresponds to a sinusoidal (wavelike) variation in electric field E and magnetic field H, always at right angles to one another, propagating in the direction R perpendicular to the plane of E and H. This is indicated in Figure 15.34. In a uniform unimpeding situation a point source results in an infinity of rays covering all directions, corresponding to a sphere ('wavefront') of disturbance expanding at the speed of light. The eye experiences a colour determined by the wavelength $\lambda = 2\pi/f$, where f is the common frequency of E and H.

The behaviour of light is governed by *Maxwell's Equations*, shown in Table 15.5. Assuming a lossless medium, each component $V = V(x, y, z, t)$ of E or of H must satisfy the differential equation

$$\nabla^2 V = (n/c)^2 \partial^2 V/\partial t^2, \tag{15.60}$$

where the refractive index n is non-constant, but assumed not to vary appreciably over

---

Table 15.5. *Maxwell's equations for the propagation of light (no charge/flux).*

$$\nabla \times E = -\mu \partial H/\partial t, \nabla \cdot \varepsilon E = 0,$$
$$\nabla \times H = -\mu \partial E/\partial t, \nabla \cdot \mu H = 0.$$

μ(permeability) $= \mu_0$ in vacuo and most applications;
ε(permittivity) $= \varepsilon_0$ in vacuo, where $\sqrt{(\varepsilon/\varepsilon_0)} = n$, the refractive index;
$\times$ is the vector cross product (see Section 7.3.1);
$\nabla = i\partial/\partial x + j\partial/\partial y + k\partial/\partial z,$ (i, j, k are unit axis vectors, Section 7.1.2).

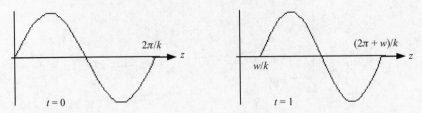

Figure 15.35 Graph of $\sin(kz - wt)$ against z at times $t = 0$ and $t = 1$. The wave advances at the speed of light.

distances of the order of a wavelength. A wave propagating in the z-direction is given by a solution (see below) of the form

$$V = Ae^{i(kz-wt)} \quad (k/w = n/c). \tag{15.61}$$

Why V is complex The solution, literally, is the real part of V. For example, if $A = a + ib$, the actual solution is $a\cos(kz - wt) - b\sin(kz - wt)$, but we add the imaginary part of $Ae^{i(kz-wt)}$ so as to form this exponential, because of the resulting gains in conciseness and ease of calculation. We may immediately illustrate this by the process of verifying (15.61) as a solution of (15.60) in the case A is constant. We have, using (14.24) to differentiate:

$$\partial V/\partial t = A(-iw)e^{i(kz-wt)} = (-iw)V, \text{ whence } \partial^2 V/\partial t^2 = -w^2 V,$$

whereas $\nabla^2 V = \partial^2 V/\partial z^2 = (ik)^2 V = -k^2 V = (n^2/c^2)\partial^2 V/\partial t^2$, as required.

Why V is a moving wave Consider, for example, the graph of $\sin(kz - wt)$ against z, as t varies. Figure 15.35 shows the result for $t = 0$ and $t = 1$, making clear that, as t increments, the sine wave simply moves to the right. In unit time it moves a distance w/k, which by (15.61) equals c/n, the *speed of light in a medium of refractive index n*.

Solving the impossible equation The particular form of (15.61) we require must take into account what goes on between the distant object and the lens; there is not only refraction but *diffraction*, the change in progress of light when its wavefront is restricted, and *scintillation*, the gratuitous sparkling effect that turbulence can engender (see e.g. Born & Wolf, 1999). Thus we must allow in (15.61) a non-constant $A = A(\mathbf{r}, t) = A(x, y, z, t)$, which leads to

$$\nabla^2 A + 2ik\, \partial A/\partial t + 2k^2 N A = 0, \tag{15.62}$$

where $N = N(\mathbf{r}, t)$ is a normalised form of the refractive index. Hufnagel remarks that no general analytic solution is known, but, assuming the result to be a photographic image, we are effectively averaging over exposure time, and therefore we may reasonably seek a solution expressible in terms of time averages $\langle \ldots \rangle$. This turns out to be tractible, and the solution with boundary condition $A \equiv 1$ at $z = 0$ (see Figure 15.33) is shown to be

Table 15.6. *Details of the 'structure constant'* C_N *(cgs units).*

$$C_N = 10^{-6}(\rho/\rho_0)C_\theta(z), \qquad \rho/\rho_0 = \text{pressure relative to that at ground level}$$
$$C_\theta = \alpha\varepsilon^{1/3}\gamma/\beta(>0) \qquad \theta = \text{temperature in degrees Kelvin}$$

ε	= energy/unit mass dissipated by viscous friction
β	= mean shear rate of wind
γ	= mean vertical temperature gradient
α	= constant determined by experiment

expressible as

$$H(u, v) = \exp[-(k^2/2)\langle S^2\rangle], \quad \text{where } S = \int_0^L [N(u, z) - N(v, z)]\mathrm{d}z, \qquad (15.63)$$

and $k = 2\pi/\lambda$ when the wavelength λ is in cgs units (centimetre–gram–second). The first equality, for its validity, requires $S(u, v)$ to be normal, with mean 0, which it arguably *is* by the Central Limit Theorem (as a sum of many random effects, see Section 10.3.3), and that radial symmetry holds. On the other hand, we have not assumed that diffraction and scintillation are absent, but rather eliminated them by the averaging process. By further physical considerations the authors simplify the integration in (15.63) to

$$\langle S^2\rangle = 2.9p^{5/3}\int_0^L C_N^2(z)\mathrm{d}z, \quad \text{where } p = \sqrt{(u^2 + v^2)}, \qquad (15.64)$$

and where the scientific details of the function C_N are those given in Table 15.6.

Example 15.39 (1) For a path through the whole atmosphere at angle α to the vertical,

$$\langle S^2\rangle = 2.9p^{5/3}\sec\alpha\int_0^\infty C_N^2\mathrm{d}h = (1.7 \times 10^{-10}\sec\alpha)p^{5/3}.$$

(2) For a horizontal path at altitude h, we have $C_N = \text{constant}$, and $\langle S^2\rangle = 2.9p^{5/3}LC_N^2$.

Example (Djurle and Bäck, 1961) Distance $L = 7$ miles $= 1.1 \times 10^6$ cm, height $h = 5 \times 10^3$ cm, wavelength $\lambda = 0.55$ microns, we have $k = 2\pi/\lambda = 1.1 \times 10^{-5}$ cm^{-1}, and

$$H(u, v) = \exp\left[-5.4(u^2 + v^2)^{5/6}\right].$$

Conclusion A useful way to determine the Optical Transfer Function $H(u, v)$ due to atmospheric turbulence, for a given image, is to start with the constant d below for a similarly obtained image, and to vary it until acceptable blur reduction is achieved (some other forms of blur may of course need to be reduced also, as discussed in earlier sections):

$$H(u, v) = \mathrm{e}^{-d(u^2+v^2)^{5/6}}, \quad \text{atmospheric blur.} \qquad (15.65)$$

15.3.4 Random fields and the Wiener filter

Here for the first time in this deconvolution section we introduce noise of unknown source. Suppose firstly that the colour values $J_0(\boldsymbol{r})$ at points $\boldsymbol{r} = (x, y)$ of an image suffer a blur or other degradation which can be expressed as a convolution of J_0 with some function $S(\boldsymbol{r})$, together with an independent additive error $N(\boldsymbol{r})$ (spatial noise) which accounts for such things as experimental error, background radiation, or granularity in photographic emulsion. That is, we may express the *observed* colour value $J(\boldsymbol{r})$ as

$$J(\boldsymbol{r}) = \int S(\boldsymbol{r}')J_0(\boldsymbol{r} - \boldsymbol{r}')\mathrm{d}\boldsymbol{r}' + N(\boldsymbol{r}), \tag{15.66}$$

where with suitable definitions the integral may be taken formally over the whole plane. Since $N(\boldsymbol{r})$ is unknown, Equation (15.66) cannot be solved directly for the desired original $J_0(\boldsymbol{r})$. Instead, we take J_0 and N to be independent random fields, N of zero mean, and estimate J_0 by a simple convolution

$$\hat{J}_0(\boldsymbol{r}) = \int M(\boldsymbol{r}')J(\boldsymbol{r} - \boldsymbol{r}')\mathrm{d}\boldsymbol{r}', \tag{15.67}$$

with M chosen to minimise the expected squared difference

$$e = E[(\hat{J}_0(\boldsymbol{r}) - J_0(\boldsymbol{r}))^2]. \tag{15.68}$$

A matrix approach

The analysis is here carried out in a matrix version for the discrete case as an approximation to the continuous, following the outline of Helstrom (1967), but with the addition of detailed proofs. Let J, J_0 and $\hat{J}_0$ represent vectors of image pixel values taken in the same order over a rectangular grid. Suppose the integrals in (15.66) and (15.67) are approximated by suitable quadrature formulae (such as Simpson's Rule). Then the two equations take the form

$$J = SJ_0 + N, \text{ and } \hat{J}_0 = MJ \tag{15.69}$$

(J_0 is the original, J is observed, S applies Simpson's Rule, and N is noise), where S and M are matrices, and we wish to choose M to minimise the expected sum of squared errors between the original J_0 and our estimate $\hat{J}_0$. In terms of a difference vector $D = \hat{J}_0 - J_0$, this quantity may be written $E[\|D\|^2]$. The independent noise vector N is assumed to have zero mean. Some preliminaries follow.

Given a matrix V of random variables, we consider its expected value $E[V]$, in which each entry v_{ij} is replaced by the expected value $E[v_{ij}]$. Here we let $\mathrm{Cov}(X)$ stand for $E[XX^{\mathrm{T}}]$, where X is a random column vector with mean not necessarily the zero vector. Let A, B be constant matrices and Y a random vector independent of X, with zero mean. Thus $E[X_iY_j] = E[X_i]E[Y_j] = 0$. Then by a small extension of Theorem 10.56 (see

Exercise 15.17):

$$E[AVB] = AE[V]B, \tag{15.70a}$$

$$\mathrm{Cov}[AX] = A\mathrm{Cov}[X]A^{\mathrm{T}}, \tag{15.70b}$$

$$\mathrm{Cov}[AX + BY] = \mathrm{Cov}[AX] + \mathrm{Cov}[BY]. \tag{15.70c}$$

Our first task is to express the minimisation in terms of covariance, aided by the matrix trace function $\mathrm{Tr}(P) = \sum_i p_{ii}$, the sum of diagonal elements. The connection is given by $\mathrm{Tr}\,(DD^{\mathrm{T}}) = \sum_i \sum_k d_{ik}d_{ik} = \|D\|^2$. We are thus to minimise

$$E[\|D\|^2] = E[\mathrm{Tr}(DD^{\mathrm{T}})] = \mathrm{Tr}\,E[DD^{\mathrm{T}}] \quad (\text{since trace is linear}) = \mathrm{Tr}[\mathrm{Cov}(D)],$$

by definition of Cov. To allow extra flexibility in the way particular differences influence the conclusion (e.g. to allow for some characteristic of the human visual system), we insert a positive definite matrix G and then minimise more generally

$$\mathrm{Tr}\,G\mathrm{Cov}(D). \tag{15.71}$$

Notice that, since G may be factorised in the form $H^{\mathrm{T}}H$ (Theorem 8.39), the expression (15.71) is equivalent to replacing each factor D by its own weighted form HD, because

$$\mathrm{Tr}\,G\mathrm{Cov}(D) = \mathrm{Tr}\,H^{\mathrm{T}}HE[DD^{\mathrm{T}}] = \mathrm{Tr}\,E[H^{\mathrm{T}}HDD^{\mathrm{T}}] \text{ by (15.70a)} = \mathrm{Tr}\,E[HDD^{\mathrm{T}}H^{\mathrm{T}}],$$

(since $\mathrm{Tr}(PQ) = \mathrm{Tr}(QP)$), which equals $\mathrm{Tr}\,\mathrm{Cov}(HD)$ by definition of Cov. Of course $G = I$ weights errors at all points equally, but, surprisingly, it turns out that the optimal M does not depend on the precise choice of G. We derive a necessary result on differentiation, then the main result.

Lemma 15.40 *For a function f of a matrix M, let $\partial f/\partial M$ denote the matrix $[\partial/\partial m_{ij}]$. Then, provided the implied derivatives and products exist for matrices M, A, B,*

$$\partial/\partial M\,\mathrm{Tr}(AMB) \quad = A^{\mathrm{T}}B^{\mathrm{T}},$$
$$\partial/\partial M\,\mathrm{Tr}(AMBM^{\mathrm{T}}) = A^{\mathrm{T}}MB^{\mathrm{T}} + AMB.$$

Proof $\partial/\partial m_{pq}\mathrm{Tr}(AMB) = \partial/\partial m_{pq}\sum_i \sum_{r,s} a_{ir}m_{rs}b_{si} = \sum_i a_{ip}b_{qi} = (A^{\mathrm{T}}B^{\mathrm{T}})_{pq}$, whilst

$$\partial/\partial m_{pq}\,\mathrm{Tr}(AMBM^{\mathrm{T}}) = \partial/\partial m_{pq}\sum_i \sum_{r,s,t} a_{ir}m_{rs}b_{st}m_{it}$$
$$= \sum_i \sum_{r,s,t}(a_{ir}m_{rs}b_{st}\partial m_{it}/\partial m_{pq} + a_{ir}(\partial m_{rs}/\partial m_{pq})b_{st}m_{it})$$
$$= \sum_{i,t} a_{ip}b_{qt}m_{it} + \sum_{r,s} a_{pr}b_{sq}m_{rs} \quad (p,q = r,s \text{ or } i,t)$$
$$= (A^{\mathrm{T}}MB^{\mathrm{T}} + AMB)_{p,q}.$$

Theorem 15.41 *With $\hat{J}_0$ as given in (15.69) and weighting matrix G of (15.71), let $\phi_n = \mathrm{Cov}(N)$ and $\phi_0 = \mathrm{Cov}(J_0)$. Then the minimising matrix M and minimised expected squared error $E[\|D\|^2]$, are given by*

$$M = \phi_0 S^{\mathrm{T}}(S\phi_0 S^{\mathrm{T}} + \phi_n)^{-1} \quad and \quad E[\|D\|^2] = \mathrm{Tr}\,G(\phi_0 - MS\phi_0) \tag{15.72}$$

Proof We are to minimise Tr $GCov(D)$

$$
\begin{aligned}
&= \text{Tr } GCov[(MS - I)J_0 + MN] && \text{by (15.69)} \\
&= \text{Tr } G[\text{Cov}((MS - I)J_0) + \text{Cov}(MN)] && \text{by (15.70c)} \\
&= \text{Tr } G[(MS - I)\phi_0(MS - I)^{\text{T}} + M\phi_n M^{\text{T}}] && \text{by (15.70b)} \\
&= \text{Tr } G[(MS)\phi_0(MS)^{\text{T}} - MS\phi_0 - (MS\phi_0)^{\text{T}} + \phi_0 + M\phi_n M^{\text{T}}].
\end{aligned}
$$

The derivatives of the various terms are given by Lemma 15.40, using the trace properties $\text{Tr}(AB) = \text{Tr}(BA) = \text{Tr}(BA)^{\text{T}}$ and the symmetry of G, ϕ_0 and ϕ_n. The result is

$$
\begin{aligned}
\partial/\partial M \text{ Tr } G \text{ Cov}(D) = 0 &\Leftrightarrow 2GM(S\phi_0 S^{\text{T}}) - 2G\phi_0 S^{\text{T}} + 2GM\phi_n = 0 \\
&\Leftrightarrow M(S\phi_0 S^{\text{T}}) - \phi_0 S^{\text{T}} + M\phi_n = 0 \quad \text{since } G \text{ is invertible} \\
&\Leftrightarrow M(S\phi_0 S^{\text{T}} + \phi_n) = \phi_0 S^{\text{T}}.
\end{aligned}
$$

This gives the expression for M. Multiplying by M^{T} on the right, we rewrite it in the form $(MS - I)\phi_0(MS)^{\text{T}} + M\phi_n M^{\text{T}} = 0$ and substitute in the third expression for Tr G Cov(D), converting the latter into Tr $G(I - MS)\,\phi_0$, the formula of (15.72) for $E[\|D\|^2]$.

Remarks At this point we need estimates for Cov(N) and Cov(J_0). These may be hard to come by with confidence. The situation is much improved by the Wiener filter, which we now introduce.

The Wiener filter

In the present approach we go as far as possible with the continuous model, and only discretise at the last possible moment. The Continuous Fourier Transform plays a crucial role, starting with Theorem 15.21 from the introductory Section 15.1.5.

Notation Changing slightly the notation of (15.66) and (15.67), we shall say that a random field $f(r)$ suffers distortion into random field $g(r)$ by convolution with field $h(r)$ and added random noise $n(r)$. The estimate $\hat{f}$ of the original f is to be convolution with a fixed function $m(r)$, chosen to minimise the *expected squared difference e*. Thus we write:

$$
g(r) = \int h(r - r')f(r')\mathrm{d}r' + n(r), \tag{15.73}
$$

$$
\hat{f}(r) = \int m(r - r')g(r')\mathrm{d}r', \tag{15.74}
$$

$$
e = E[(f(r) - \hat{f}(r))^2]. \tag{15.75}
$$

Method We find $\hat{f}$ by determining its Fourier Transform $\hat{F}$ as follows. Equation (15.74) states that $\hat{f} = m * g$, so, by the Convolution Theorem (Theorem 15.17),

$$
\hat{F}(v, v) = M(u, v)G(u, v). \tag{15.76}
$$

We are given the *measured g*, hence its transform G. Our goal is now to obtain a usable expression for $M(u, v)$, so that we may determine $\hat{F}$ from (15.76). We prove the key result below, then the ancillary results required for its application. Finally, we bring them together to deduce Wiener's formula.

Theorem 15.42 *The function $m(\mathbf{r})$ minimises the squared error e if it satisfies*

$$E[f(\mathbf{r})g(s)] = E[(g)(s)\int m(\mathbf{r}-\mathbf{r}')g(\mathbf{r})'\mathrm{d}\mathbf{r}'] \tag{15.77}$$

Proof We need only prove that, given (15.77), the error e' due to an arbitrary choice m' in place of m satisfies $e' \geq e$. Before taking expected values, we do some rearranging with arguments temporarily suppressed.

$$\left(f - \int m'g\mathrm{d}\mathbf{r}'\right)^2 = \left\{f - \int mg\mathrm{d}\mathbf{r}' + \int(m-m')\mathrm{d}\mathbf{r}'\right\}^2$$

$$= \left\{f - \int mg\mathrm{d}\mathbf{r}'\right\}^2 + \left\{\int(m-m')g\mathrm{d}\mathbf{r}'\right\}^2$$

$$+ 2\left\{f - \int mg\mathrm{d}\mathbf{r}'\right\} \times \left\{\int(m-m')g\mathrm{d}\mathbf{r}'\right\}.$$

Taking expected values, and noting that the square middle term must be non-negative, we have in succession, as shortly explained below,

$$e' \geq e + 2E\left[\left\{f - \int mg\mathrm{d}\mathbf{r}'\right\}\left\{\int(m(\mathbf{r}-s)-m'(\mathbf{r}-s))g(s)\mathrm{d}s\right\}\right],$$

$$= e + 2E\left[\int\left(f - \int mg\mathrm{d}\mathbf{r}'\right)(m(\mathbf{r}-s)-m'(\mathbf{r}-s))g(s)\mathrm{d}s\right],$$

$$= e + 2\int(m(\mathbf{r}-s)-m'(\mathbf{r}-s))E\left[g(s)\left(f - \int mg\mathrm{d}\mathbf{r}'\right)\right]\mathrm{d}s.$$

where we have substituted s for $\mathbf{r}'$ in the second integral of the first line. This implies the next line since $(f - \int mg\mathrm{d}\mathbf{r}')$ does not involve s. The third line follows because E and integration may be interchanged and $m-m'$ is fixed, not probabilistic. But the expected value is zero by (15.77), so we have $e' \geq e$ and the proof is complete.

Theorem 15.43 *In the usual notation, let S_{fg} and S_{gg} be the respective Fourier Transforms of the cross- and auto-correlation functions R_{fg} and R_{gg}. Then the Fourier Transform of m is given by*

$$\boxed{M(u, v) = S_{gf}(u, v)/S_{gg}(u, v).} \tag{15.78}$$

Proof From the definition (15.22) we have, with $\tau = \mathbf{r} - s$,

$$R_{gf}(\tau) = E[g(s)f(\mathbf{r})] = E\left[g(s)\int m(\mathbf{r}-\mathbf{r}')g(\mathbf{r}')\mathrm{d}\mathbf{r}'\right] \quad \text{by (15.77)}$$

$$= E\int m(\mathbf{r}-\mathbf{r}')g(\mathbf{r}')g(s)\mathrm{d}\mathbf{r}' \quad \text{since } s \text{ is independent of } \mathbf{r}'$$

$$= \int m(\mathbf{r}-\mathbf{r}')E[g(\mathbf{r}')g(s)]\mathrm{d}\mathbf{r}' \quad \text{switching } E \text{ and integration}$$

$$= \int m(\mathbf{r}-\mathbf{r}')R_{gg}(\mathbf{r}'-s)\mathrm{d}\mathbf{r}' \quad \text{by (15.22) (definition of } R_{gg}).$$

$$= \int m(t)R_{gg}(\tau-t)\mathrm{d}t \quad \text{where } t = \mathbf{r} - \mathbf{r}', \text{ and } \tau = \mathbf{r} - s.$$

This equals $m^* R_{gg}(\tau)$, whence, by the Convolution Theorem, $S_{gf}(u, v) = M(u, v)S_{gg}(u, v)$, and the proof is complete.

Remark We have not yet arrived, for in order to use (15.78), which depends crucially on its numerator, we must determine correlations between g and the original image f. But f is unknown. Eventually we will have to guess *something*, and the analysis which follows shows us that the ratio S_{nn}/S_{gg} is the thing to go for, by converting (15.78) into the more amenable form (15.80) of Theorem 15.45 below. Most of the work is done in the following lemma.

Lemma 15.44 *In the notation of (15.73), and with the zero mean assumption that f and n are uncorrelated, and at least one has zero mean, there holds*

$$S_{gg}(u, v) = S_{ff}(u, v)|H(u, v)|^2 + S_{nn}(u, v). \tag{15.79}$$

Proof We prove in succession three equalities, of which substituting the last two in the first results in (15.79):

(i) $S_{gg}(u, v) = \overline{H}(u, v) \, S_{fg}(u, v) + S_{ng}(u, v)$,
(ii) $S_{fg}(u, v) = H(u, v)S_{ff}(u, v)$,
(iii) $S_{ng}(u, v) = S_{nn}(u, v)$.

(i) We multiply (15.73) by $g(\boldsymbol{r} + \boldsymbol{s})$ and take expected values: $R_{gg}(\boldsymbol{s}) = E[g(\boldsymbol{r})g(\boldsymbol{r} + \boldsymbol{s})]$

$$= E\left[g(\boldsymbol{r} + \boldsymbol{s}) \int h(\boldsymbol{r} - \boldsymbol{r}')f(\boldsymbol{r}')\mathrm{d}\boldsymbol{r}'\right] + E[n(\boldsymbol{r})g(\boldsymbol{r} + \boldsymbol{s})]$$

$$= \int h(\boldsymbol{r} - \boldsymbol{r}')E[f(\boldsymbol{r}')g(\boldsymbol{r} + \boldsymbol{s})]\mathrm{d}\boldsymbol{r}' + R_{ng}(\boldsymbol{s})$$

$$= \int h(\boldsymbol{r} - \boldsymbol{r}')R_{fg}(\boldsymbol{r} + \boldsymbol{s} - \boldsymbol{r}')\mathrm{d}\boldsymbol{r}' + R_{ng}(\boldsymbol{s})$$

$$= \int h(-\alpha)R_{fg}(\boldsymbol{s} - \alpha)\mathrm{d}\alpha + R_{ng}(\boldsymbol{s}) \qquad (\alpha = \boldsymbol{r}' - \boldsymbol{r}).$$

This says that $R_{gg} = h(-\boldsymbol{t})^* R_{fg}(\boldsymbol{t}) + R_{ng}$, which the Convolution Theorem converts to (i).

(ii) Multiplying (15.73) by $f(\boldsymbol{r} - \boldsymbol{s})$ and taking expected values we obtain an equality in which the last term is $E[f(\boldsymbol{r} - \boldsymbol{s})n(\boldsymbol{r})] = E[f(\boldsymbol{r} - \boldsymbol{s})] \, E[n(\boldsymbol{r})] = 0$ by the zero mean assumption. Thus

$$R_{fg}(\boldsymbol{s}) = E\left[f(\boldsymbol{r} - \boldsymbol{s}) \int h(\boldsymbol{r} - \boldsymbol{r}')f(\boldsymbol{r}')\mathrm{d}\boldsymbol{r}'\right]$$

$$= \int h(\boldsymbol{r} - \boldsymbol{r}')E[f(\boldsymbol{r} - \boldsymbol{s})f(\boldsymbol{r}')]\mathrm{d}\boldsymbol{r}'$$

$$= \int h(\boldsymbol{r} - \boldsymbol{r}')R_{ff}(\boldsymbol{r}' - \boldsymbol{r} + \boldsymbol{s})\mathrm{d}\boldsymbol{r}'$$

$$= \int h(\alpha)R_{ff}(\boldsymbol{s} - \alpha)\mathrm{d}\boldsymbol{r}' \qquad (\alpha = \boldsymbol{r} - \boldsymbol{r}').$$

Thus $R_{fg} = h^* R_{ff}$ and the Convolution Theorem gives Equation (ii).

(iii) Finally, multiplying (15.73) by $n(r - s)$ and taking expected values gives

$$R_{ng}(s) = \int h(r - r')E[f(r')n(r - s)]dr' + R_{nn}(s).$$

But the expected value is zero by the zero mean assumption so, taking transforms, we arrive at (iii). Using (ii) and (iii) to substitute for $S_{fg}(u, v)$ and $S_{ng}(u, v)$ in (i) we obtain (15.79).

Theorem 15.45 *(The Wiener filter) We assume that the original field f and added noise are uncorrelated and at least one has zero mean. Then the transfer function $M(u, v)$, relating f to the estimate with least expected error, is given by*

$$M(u, v) = \frac{\overline{H}(u, v)}{|H(u, v)|^2 + S_{nn}(u, v)/S_{ff}(u, v)}. \tag{15.80}$$

Proof Starting from the basic equation $M(u, v) = S_{gf}/S_{gg}(u, v)$ of (15.78), we observe that the denominator is supplied in suitable form by (15.79) and that for the numerator we have $S_{gf}(u, v) = \overline{S}_{fg}(u, v)$ (by (15.23)) $= \overline{H}(u, v)S_{ff}(u, v)$ by (ii) of the proof of (15.79). Substituting (after which we divide through by $S_{ff}(u, v)$),

$$M(u, v) = \frac{\overline{H}(u, v)S_{ff}(u, v)}{S_{ff}(u, v)|H(u, v)|^2 + S_{nn}(u, v)}.$$

Remarks 15.46 (1) In the absence of noise, (15.80) reduces to simple deconvolution $M = 1/H$. In its *presence* there is no difficulty at points with $H(u, v) = 0$.

(2) If $H(u, v) \neq 0$, we can represent $M(u, v)$ (see below) as the usual non-noise part $1/H$ times a correction factor which is a real number, lying between 0 and 1, and which equals 1 in the absence of noise:

$$M(u, v) = \frac{1}{H(u, v)} \times \frac{|H(u, v)|^2}{|H(u, v)|^2 + S_{nn}/S_{ff}}. \tag{15.81}$$

(3) In the absence of information about S_{nn} and S_{ff}, the Wiener filter is often used successfully by a trial of several constant values of the ratio S_{nn}/S_{ff}, as indicated earlier. We demonstrate for the case of motion blur plus noise in the next example.

Example 15.47 In Figure 15.36 we show firstly an original image and its motion-blurred version which was successfully restored by an operation of deconvolution based on knowledge of the motion. In (c) we have added something on top of the blur, namely Gaussian noise with $\sigma = 10$. The next image, (d), illustrates the devastating effect noise may have on a deconvolution method which is otherwise perfectly accurate.

In (e) we make a first attempt at restoration using the Wiener filter, estimating the variable quantity S_{nn}/S_{ff} by the constant function with value 0.3. The result is far superior to simple deconvolution (d), but only a marginal improvement over (c). However, since the noise looks much less after Wiener, it is interesting to see if this helps deconvolution

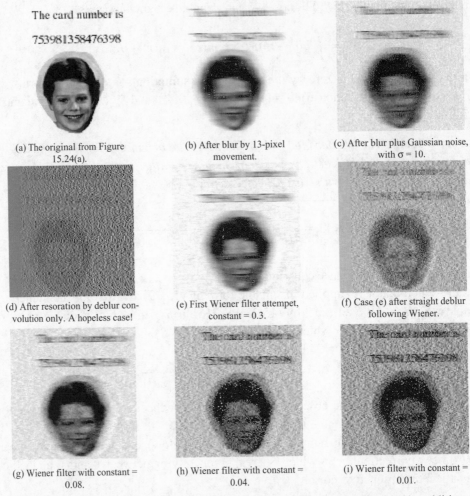

(a) The original from Figure 15.24(a).

(b) After blur by 13-pixel movement.

(c) After blur plus Gaussian noise, with σ = 10.

(d) After resoration by deblur convolution only. A hopeless case!

(e) First Wiener filter attempet, constant = 0.3.

(f) Case (e) after straight deblur following Wiener.

(g) Wiener filter with constant = 0.08.

(h) Wiener filter with constant = 0.04.

(i) Wiener filter with constant = 0.01.

Figure 15.36 The original blurred image of Figure 15.24 is further degraded by additive Gaussian noise with sigma = 10. Reconstruction by simple deblur now fails completely. The Wiener filter surmounts the noise to a considerable degree, rendering the numbers approx. 90% readable. See further comments below.

to succeed. It does help, as shown in (f), but the result is not an improvement on the noisy version (c) we began with. Here, as elsewhere, the Wiener filter gives an excellent chance of improvement through a small amount of trial and error used to determine a constant value for S_{nn}/S_{ff}.

References Castleman (1996), Petrou and Bosdogianni (2000).

The final improvement Our assessment of improvement depends what is wanted from the image. One criterion is 'What is most pleasing to the eye?' But let us focus on three others: (1) can we read the card number? (2) is the noise diminished? (3) is the face more recognisable?

If the card number is the main issue, the Wiener version of Figure 15.36 is probably best, with about 90% readability, a large improvement on the noisy blurred version. On the other hand, (h) is almost as readable yet with less noise. Yet, taking criterion (3) into account, (i) may be best overall because the boy's smile is beginning to reappear.

15.4 Compression

As observed earlier, one way to reduce storage requirements is simply to neglect the highest-frequency components of the DFT. This can be effective if, as is often the case, the neglected components are very small. In this section we present firstly the more general *pyramid method* of Burt and Adelson (1983), which does not make this high-frequency assumption. Secondly, in Sections 15.4.2–3, we lead up to the well-tried JPEG image compression, beginning with the Discrete Cosine Transform (DCT) which, though deterministic, is a good approximation to the statistically based K–L transform of Chapter 10.

15.4.1 Pyramids, sub-band coding and entropy

We will presently justify *pyramid* as a term for the coming method, noting at this stage that it combines the ideas both of *predictive* and of *sub-band* coding. In the former, a next section of data is predicted from that already encountered, by some fixed process known to the decoder (see e.g. Section 12.6). We then store the difference between prediction and reality. The more accurate our prediction, the fewer bits are required to store this difference. In the present case, prediction is based on sub-band encoding, in which a signal f, be it audio, image or other, is split into a sum $\sum f_i$ in such a way that each f_i has non-neglectable Fourier components only in a predetermined subrange, or *sub-band*, of that occupied by the original (see Section 15.2.2). The splitting is done by a collection or *bank* of filters, realised as convolution kernels. Then each f_i is encoded by a method that takes advantage of its particular frequency range.

Pyramid encoding Suppose we wish to encode an image array g_0 in compressed form. The method uses a Gaussian-like kernel, which we shall describe, to obtain a lowpass version w^*g_0. Because of the decreased range of frequencies, we should not lose much if we downsample w^*g_0 by throwing away alternate pixel values, to form a roughly half-sized array

$$g_1 = \text{REDUCE}(g_0).$$

Obviously this requires about a quarter the storage space of g_0. However, the prediction we actually subtract is a conversion $\text{EXPAND}(g_1)$ of g_1 back to the original size by interpolating for the missing values, as in (15.83) below. We store the difference

$$L_0 = g_0 - \text{EXPAND}(g_1).$$

Figure 15.37 A Gaussian pyramid formed by g_0 and its successors.

Figure 15.38 The Laplacian pyramid of differences $L_k = g_k - \text{EXPAND}(g_{k+1})$. This sequence is the encoded version of the original: $(L_4, L_3, L_2, L_1, L_0)$.

Since the pixel array values of the residue L_0 are, we assume, small, they may be stored with fewer bits than those of g_0. Given g_1, the original may be reconstructed as

$$g_0 = L_0 + \text{EXPAND}(g_1).$$

What do we do with g_1? The answer is, of course, that we repeat the process so as to reduce storage for g_1, then for its successor and so on, until we reach a satisfactorily simple g_N, having stored differences $L_0, L_1, \ldots, L_N$. Since each g_k is by construction half the size of its predecessor, the sequence may be described as *pyramidal* (see Figure 15.37), and is termed a *Gaussian pyramid* because of the approximately Gaussian kernel used. The saved sequence $\{L_i\}$ is termed a *Laplacian* pyramid (see Figure 15.38) because each member may be thought of as the difference between two Gaussians (an approximation to the Laplacian due to Marr and Hildreth, 1980, see remark preceding Example 15.31). There follow an example of the first pyramid and a pseudocode description of the encoding and decoding methods.

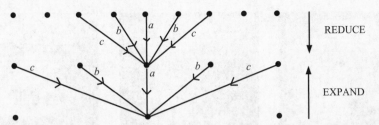

Figure 15.39 A 1-dimensional version of the Gaussian pyramid. The value of each node in a given level is the weighted average, with coefficients $u = (c, b, a, b, c)$, of five nodes in the level above.

ALGO 15.4 Pyramid encoding of image g_0	*ALGO 15.5 Pyramid decoding of*
For $k = 0$ to $N - 1$ do	$L_0, \ldots, L_N$
$\quad g_{k+1} = \text{REDUCE}(g_k)$	$h_N = L_N$
$\quad L_k = g_k - \text{EXPAND}(g_{k+1})$	For $k = N-1$ down to 0 do
$\quad$ Store L_k, delete g_k	Return h_0.
Store $L_N = g_N$	$\quad h_k = L_k + \text{EXPAND}(h_{k+1})$

Definitions 15.48 (i) *The kernel w* There is no loss in taking this as separable, $w(m, n) = u(m)u(n)$, and letting u be a symmetric 5-vector, say $u = (c, b, a, b, c)$. Thus w has size 5×5. Two further useful properties we opt to require are

Normalisation: $\sum u(m) = 1 (m = -2, \ldots, 2)$, and
Equal contribution: all nodes at a given level g_k contribute the same weight $1/4$ to nodes at the next g_{k+1}. According to Figure 15.39 this implies $a + 2c = 2b$, which, with normalisation $a + 2b + 2c = 1$, gives the general form $b = 1/4, c = 1/4 - a/2$, with a as a parameter.

(ii) REDUCE sends g_k to g_{k+1} by convolving with w, then deleting alternate sample points, i.e.

$$g_{k+1}(i, j) = \sum_{m,n=-2}^{2} w(m, n)g_k(2i + m, 2j + n). \tag{15.82}$$

(iii) EXPAND converts an array $h_{(M+1)\times(N+1)}$ to an array $k_{(2M+1)\times(2N+1)}$ by

$$k(i, j) = \sum_{m,n=-2}^{3} w(m, n)h\left(\frac{i - m}{2}, \frac{j - n}{2}\right) \quad (i - m \text{ and } j - n \text{ even}). \tag{15.83}$$

Notice that this is the same as inserting a zero between every horizontally or vertically adjacent pair of an array then convolving the result with w.

Decoding and progressive transmission A nice feature of the pyramid method of encoding and decoding is that it lends itself well to *progressive transmission*, in which

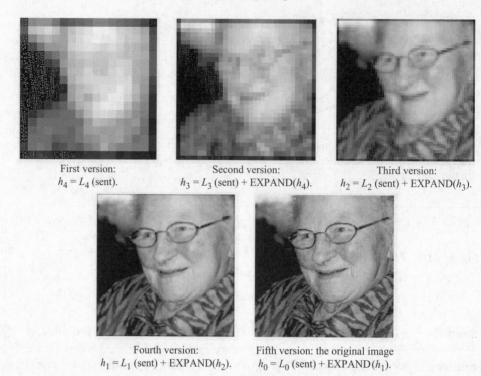

First version:
$h_4 = L_4$ (sent).

Second version:
$h_3 = L_3$ (sent) + EXPAND(h_4).

Third version:
$h_2 = L_2$ (sent) + EXPAND(h_3).

Fourth version:
$h_1 = L_1$ (sent) + EXPAND(h_2).

Fifth version: the original image
$h_0 = L_0$ (sent) + EXPAND(h_1).

Figure 15.40 Successively more accurate images obtained by progressive transmission using the Laplacian pyramid method. All images are kept at the same size, as they would be when viewed on the computer screen.

the recipient of an image is sent first a rather coarse electronic version L_N, followed by successive additions $L_{N-1}, \ldots, L_0$ which render the image more and more faithful to the original. The advantage of this is that the user need only accept sufficient transmission to obtain a version of the image adequate for his/her purposes. We show in Figure 15.40 the successively more accurate versions of the image we have been exemplifying.

Quantisation A key to compression is that, although we begin with one array and end by storing several, namely the L_i, these finally occupy considerably less memory space because (i) each L_i has $1/4$ the number of elements of its predecessor, and (ii) these difference arrays, if we have predicted well, will have a very small range of values only, and so may be stored using few bits. In other words we are going to *quantise* these values to pre-selected possibilities, or *quantisation levels*. In a uniform quantisation we simply divide all values by an integer, most conveniently a power of 2, and round each value to the nearest integer.

An important point for viewing purposes is that the human eye is more sensitive to errors at high frequencies, and so we should preferably allow more quantisation levels for an L_i with larger i, where high frequencies are more prevalent. Further details, including a reduction from eight bits per pixel overall to 1.58, are given in Burt and Adelson (1983).

Table 15.7. *Entropies of the various portions of the pyramid process, with probabilites estimated from histogram frequencies.*

original	level 1	level 2	level 3	level 4
4.73	5.69	5.47	5.63	5.74

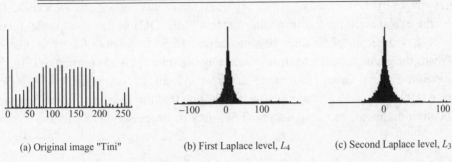

(a) Original image "Tini" (b) First Laplace level, L_4 (c) Second Laplace level, L_3

Figure 15.41 Histograms of original Tini and first two Laplace levels.

Entropy Our technique of subtracting predicted values can be expected to remove correlation between pixels and hence reduce entropy. The maximum entropy occurs, according to Theorem 12.6, when all 256 pixel values i are equally likely and so have probability $p(i) = 1/256$. The entropy of this distribution is then

$$H = -\sum_{i=0}^{235} p(i) \log_2 p(i) = -256(1/256)(-8) = 8. \tag{15.84}$$

The entropy of our untouched example is 4.73. We give some details related to this for various Laplacian levels L_i. Selected histograms appear in Figure 15.41, and entropies in Table 15.7.

Conclusion The frequencies are closely grouped around the zero grey level, as desired, and as we should expect. However, the entropies appear to increase rather than decrease. This is reasonably attributed to the effect of outliers – artifact grey levels with very low frequency, caused by noise, and not representative of the class of images which we are implicitly considering. In fact, the method works well as a compression technique. A detailed information-theoretic study of pyramid structures is caried out by Rao and Pearlman (1991). Including the original paper, general references are as given below.

References

Burt and Adelson (1983),
Castleman (1996),
Gonzalez & Woods (1993),
Marr and Hildreth (1980),
Strang and Nguyen (1997),
Watt and Policarpo (1998).

15.4.2 The Discrete Cosine Transform

The N-point Discrete Cosine Transform, or DCT, is related to the $2N$-point Discrete Fourier Transform, from which it may be computed (Remarks 15.52 below). Although it has the pleasant feature of being real, the DCT does not have all the properties of the DFT; however, it does have the advantage of superior results for the compression of natural images by the method of neglecting least important coefficients. We shall see that part of the explanation for the surprising success of the DCT is its 'asymptotic' relation to the K–L Transform of Chapter 10 (see Section 15.5.1). We note finally at this point that it was the foundational transform chosen by the international committee JPEG (the Joint Picture Experts Group) in seeking an agreed system for compression; a reference is Wallace (1991). By way of introduction, let us state that the Discrete Cosine Transform is by definition linear, and so (Theorem 7.56) may be expressed via a suitable matrix M as

$$f \to F, \quad \text{where } F = Mf, \tag{15.85}$$

with f written as a column vector with components f_0 to f_{N-1}, and similarly for F. We saw in (14.9) how choosing M is equivalent to choosing a basis $\{\phi_k\} = \{\phi_0, \ldots, \phi_{N-1}\}$ for the space of N-vectors, and expressing f in terms of that basis: $f = \sum_k F_k \phi_k$. In fact the ϕ_k are the columns of M^{-1} and the DCT is the special case in which ϕ_k is the vector whose nth component is

$$\phi_k(n) = \begin{cases} \sqrt{\dfrac{2}{N}} \cos \dfrac{(2n+1)k\pi}{2N}, & \text{for } n = 1, 2, \ldots, N-1, \\[2mm] \sqrt{\dfrac{1}{N}}, & \text{for } n = 0. \end{cases} \tag{15.86}$$

Here, as sometimes elsewhere, we write the discrete component number n in the form of a variable to avoid having too many subscripts at once, especially in the 2-dimensional case to follow. A crucial fact about the ϕ_k that simplifies calculation is that they are mutually orthogonal unit vectors, in other parlance an *orthonormal set*. That is, the dot product, or inner product, of any pair,

$$\phi_j \cdot \phi_k = \sum_{n=0}^{N-1} \phi_j(n)\phi_k(n), \tag{15.87}$$

is equal to 1 if $j = k$ and otherwise zero, or in shorthand notation (cf. (7.9))

$$\phi_j \cdot \phi_k = \delta_{jk}. \tag{15.88}$$

Theorem 15.49 *The set $\{\phi_k\}$ forms an orthonormal basis (ONB) for the space of real N-vectors.*

Proof We derive the orthonormality property, which implies (by Theorem 7.14) that $\{\phi_k\}$ forms a basis. Firstly, consider the special cases involving $n = 0$, for which we set $\alpha =$

$e^{k\pi i/2N}$ so that α^{2n+1} has real part $\cos((2n+1)k\pi/2N)$. Then $\phi_0 \cdot \phi_0 = (1/N)\sum 1 = (1/N)N = 1$, as required, whilst $\phi_0 \cdot \phi_k$ $(k \geq 1)$ is the real part

$$\text{Re} \sum_{n=0}^{N-1} \frac{\sqrt{2}}{N}\alpha^{2n+1} = \text{Re} \frac{\sqrt{2}}{N}\alpha \sum_{n=0}^{N-1}(\alpha^2)^n,$$

which is zero by (14.6), since $(\alpha^2)^N = 1$ but $\alpha^2 \neq 1$. Finally, for $j, k = 1, \ldots, N-1$ we have

$$\phi_j \cdot \phi_k = \frac{2}{N}\sum_{n=0}^{N-1} \cos\frac{(2n+1)j\pi}{2N}\cos\frac{(2n+1)k\pi}{2N} \qquad \text{by definition}$$

$$= \frac{1}{N}\sum_{n=0}^{N-1}\left[\cos\frac{(2n+1)(j+k)\pi}{2N} + \cos\frac{(2n+1)(j-k)\pi}{2N}\right] \qquad \text{by formula}$$

$$= \frac{1}{N}\text{Re}\sum_{n=0}^{N-1}[\beta^{2n+1} + \gamma^{2n+1}], \quad \text{where } \beta = e^{((j+k)/2N)\pi i}, \gamma = e^{((j-k)/2N)\pi i}.$$

Consider $z = \sum \beta^{2n+1} = \beta\sum(\beta^2)^n = \beta(1 - \beta^{2N})/(1 - \beta^2) = (1 - \beta^{2N})/(\beta^{-1} - \beta)$. Since $\beta^{2N} = \pm 1$ is real and $\overline{\beta} = \beta^{-1}$, the conjugate of z is $(1 - \beta^{2N})/(\beta - \beta^{-1}) = -z$, and so z has real part zero. The same argument holds for $\sum \gamma^{2n+1}$ unless $j = k$, when $\gamma = e^0 = 1$ and $\sum \gamma^{2n+1} = N$. Thus we have shown that $\phi_j \cdot \phi_k = \delta_{jk}$ as required.

Orthogonal matrices The orthonormality of $\{\phi_k\}$ derived above shows (by Section 7.2.4) that the matrix of columns $[\phi_k \cdots \phi_{N-1}]$ is orthogonal, so its transpose acts as inverse. Thus the matrices M and M^{-1} below are orthogonal, where ϕ_k is given by (15.86).

$$M = [\phi_0 \cdots \phi_{N-1}]^{\text{T}}, \quad M^{-1} = [\phi_0 \cdots \phi_{N-1}]. \tag{15.89}$$

The lines of Table 15.8 are immediate from (15.89). The extension to two dimensions is derived similarly to that of the Discrete Fourier Transform, by applying the 1D transform independently in the two directions of the array (see Section 15.1.1). The formula $f = M^{\text{T}}FM$ holds because $M^{-1} = M^{\text{T}}$. In fact line (iii) gives a secure base for spelling out its more barehanded versions, as we now do in Table 15.8.

Table 15.8. *Three aspects of the Discrete Cosine Transform $f \to F$, as defined by the orthogonal matrix M given in (15.89).*

(i) matrix view	$F = Mf$	hence $F_k = \phi_k \cdot f = \sum_n \phi_k(n)f_n$
(ii) basis view	$f = M^{-1}F$	which equals $\sum_k F_k\phi_k$
(iii) 2D extension	$F = MfM^{\text{T}}$	hence $f = M^{\text{T}}FM$ $\quad$ (f, F now $N \times N$)

Unpacking in terms of M To keep things as unified as possible we write M_{jk} for the j, k element of M, and M_{jk}^{T} ($= m_{kj}$) for that of the transpose, then apply the usual formula (7.17b) for the product of three matrices. Secondly, we put this in terms of the basis vectors $\{\phi_k\}$ by substituting $M_{jm} = \phi_j(m)$. All variables run from 0 to $N - 1$.

$$F_{jk} = \sum_{m,n} M_{jm} f_{mn} M_{nk}^{\mathrm{T}}, \quad \text{and} \quad f_{mn} = \sum_{jk} M_{mj}^{\mathrm{T}} F_{jk} M_{kn}. \tag{15.90}$$

$$F_{jk} = \sum_{m,n} [\phi_j(m)\phi_k(n)] f_{mn}, \quad \text{and} \quad f_{mn} = \sum_{j,k} [\phi_j(m)\phi_k(n)] F_{jk}. \tag{15.91}$$

The DCT barehanded Here we express the 2D Discrete Cosine Transform in terms of its constituent cosines. We first simplify summation by writing $d(k) = \sqrt{(2/N)}$ for $k = 1$, $2, \ldots, N - 1$ and $d(0) = \sqrt{(1/N)}$, so that for all k, $\phi_k(n) = d(k) \cos[(2n + 1)k\pi/2N]$. The result is the pair

$$F_{jk} = \sum_{m,n=0}^{N-1} \left[d(j)d(k) \cos \frac{(2m + 1)j\pi}{2N} \cos \frac{(2n + 1)k\pi}{2N} \right] f_{mn}, \tag{15.92}$$

$$f_{mn} = \sum_{j,k=0}^{N-1} \left[d(j)d(k) \cos \frac{(2m + 1)j\pi}{2N} \cos \frac{(2n + 1)k\pi}{2N} \right] F_{jk}. \tag{15.93}$$

Remark 15.50 (*The 2D basis*) The differently summed but identical expressions in (15.91) point to a basis $\{\sigma_{jk}\}$ for the space of $N \times N$ matrices such as f and F. The basis matrix with index jk has m, n element

$$\sigma_{jk}(m, n) = \phi_j(m)\phi_k(n). \tag{15.94}$$

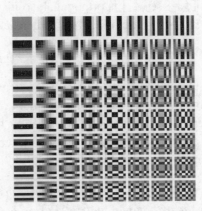

Figure 15.42 The 64 basis matrices for the 2-dimensional DCT in the case $N = 8$.

This choice was established in Section 15.1.1 for the complex case (which includes the real) in which we laid down how to convert an arbitrary invertible linear transform in 1D into a separable one in 2D (σ_{jk} was ε_{jk} and ϕ_k was C_k there). We already know from Theorem 15.2 that, because $\{\phi_k\}$ is an orthonormal basis, so is $\{\sigma_{jk}\}$. For this, the inner (dot) product of two matrices is the sum of products of corresponding elements, one from each matrix (i.e. their dot product when written out as long vectors). Figure 15.42 illustrates this basis in the normally used case $N = 8$. There are 64 basis arrays σ_{jk}, each being an 8×8 matrix of grey values.

Example 15.51 (*Image compression*) In Figure 15.43 we show a 272 × 168 image and its 2D transform (15.92). For this, the image is divided into successive 8 × 8 pixel squares, each transformed by the DCT with $N = 8$.

| Groningen tower | DC Transform | 25/64 coefficients | 9/64 coefficients | 1/64 coefficients |

Figure 15.43 Groningen tower, its Discrete Cosine Transform, and reconstructions.

Implementation issues Because the DCT is separable, we can achieve the result speedily and conveniently (see Table 15.1, line 2) by applying the 1D transform to the rows, then to the columns, of the image array. For this purpose a row or column is partitioned into 8-vectors and the 8 × 8 DCT matrix M applied to these in turn. At the end, each 8 × 8 subimage f has had both rows and columns transformed by $f \to MfM^T$, as required.

To test out compression by the DCT, we keep, say, the first t elements of a transformed 8-vector and set the rest to zero, so that, for each 8 × 8 square, only a $t \times t$ submatrix containing t^2 out of 64 coefficients is retained. Inverting the result in cases $t = 5, 3$ and 1, we obtain the last three images of Figure 15.43 as approximations to the original. Thus we can reduce the storage requirements for such an image without serious loss, and things only really break down at the reduction to 1/64 of the coefficients (at this stage each 8 × 8 portion is the mean grey shade of its original). In the next section we will see how compression may be taken considerably further.

Remarks 15.52 (1) (*The DCT from the 2N-point Fourier Transform*) There are various ways to compute the N-point DCT from the $2N$-point DFT, partly depending on which definitions of the transforms are adopted (see Section 14.1.5 for some choices). Suppose we want the DCT of vector $g = [g_0, \ldots, g_{N-1}]$. Let $f \to F$ denote the $2N$-point DFT, where $f = [f_n] = [0 \quad g_0 \quad 0 \quad g_1 \ldots 0 \quad g_{N-1}]$, each g_i padded on the left by a single zero. Then we claim that the DCT G of g is given by appropriately scaling the real part of F_k,

$$G_k = d(k) \, \mathrm{Re} F_k \qquad (k = 0, 1, \ldots, N - 1), \tag{15.95}$$

where $d(k) = \sqrt{(2/N)}$ for $i \le k \le N - 1$ and $d(0) = \sqrt{(1/N)}$.

Table 15.9. *The four steps of JPEG.*

1. Divide the image into 8×8 pixel blocks and apply the DCT to each
2. Quantise the DCT coefficients
3. Re-order the coefficients by the zigzag method
4. Apply Huffman (or arithmetic) encoding

Proof With $w = e^{-2\pi i/2N}$, the $2N$-point Fourier Transform is

$$F_k = \sum_{r=0}^{2N-1} f_r w^{rk} \quad \text{(now let } r = 2n \text{ or } 2n + 1, \text{ where } n = 0, \dots, N - 1)$$

$$= \sum_{n=0}^{N-1} f_{2n} w^{2nk} + \sum_{n=0}^{N-1} f_{2n+1} w^{(2n+1)k}$$

$$= \sum_{n=0}^{N-1} g_n w^{(2n+1)k} \quad \text{since } f_{2n} = 0 \text{ and } f_{2n+1} = g_n,$$

which has real part $\sum g_n \cos((2n + 1)k\pi/2N)$, as required. The $d(k)$ come from (15.86).

(2) (*Why the DCT is so good*) There are reasons why the DCT is especially good for compressing highly correlated images such as natural ones. Briefly, as correlation increases, the DCT basis becomes closer to that of the K–L Transform of Chapter 10, which has significant optimality properties. As mentioned earlier, we cover the theory in Section 15.5.1.

(3) (*Benefits of an ONB*) We claim that, as a consequence of our orthonormal basis $\{\sigma_{jk}\}$, the squared error obtained by omitting certain basis elements equals the sum of squares of neglected coefficients. To see this, let $f = \sum F_{jk}\sigma_{jk}$ for a certain 8×8 patch of an image, and let f become $\hat{f}$ when we negect certain coefficients. Then the resulting squared error is $\|f - \hat{f}\|^2 = (f - \hat{f}) \cdot (f - \hat{f}) = (\sum' F_{jk}\sigma_{jk}) \cdot (\sum' F_{pq}\sigma_{pq})$, where $\sum'$ denotes summation over the neglected terms. But, because of the orthogonality property that $\sigma_{jk} \cdot \sigma_{pq} = 0$ unless $(j, k) = (p, q)$, this sum simplifies to $\sum' F_{jk}^2 \sigma_{jk} \cdot \sigma_{jk}$, which equals $\sum' F_{jk}^2$, the sum of squares of neglected coefficients.

15.4.3 JPEG and beyond

History In 1987 a working party was set up, drawn from experts worldwide, with the objective of developing an internationally agreed system of image compression. After a great deal of research and testing, the result was published in 1991 (see e.g. Wallace, 1991) and thence referred to as JPEG, for Joint Picture Experts Group. Since then it has been widely used, not least as a standard method for picture transmission over the Internet. JPEG includes a system for lossless compression, but we shall concentrate on the mostly used 'lossy' system designed to give results acceptably accurate to the human eye whilst providing many-to-one compression. The system, based largely on the DCT, is summarised in Table 15.9 with details following.

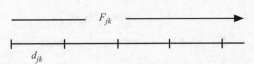

Figure 15.44 Quantising the coefficient F_{jk} by step size d_{jk}. Here F_{jk} is quantised to the integer $q_{jk} = 4$.

Some details

1. *DCT versus JPEG* Though the DCT is the first part of JPEG, the succeeding stages of Table 15.9 ensure that JPEG achieves considerably greater compression, for a given quality, than the DCT alone.
2. *Quantisation* Each block of DCT coefficients is quantised according to the same 8×8 table of *step sizes* d_{jk}, supplied either in the implementation or by a user. This means that a coefficient F_{jk} becomes an integer q_{jk}, equal to the rounded number of steps covered in F_{jk}. That is,

$$q_{jk} = \text{Round}(F_{jk}/d_{jk}).   \tag{15.96}$$

Thus, as portrayed in Figure 15.44, the coefficient is subject to an error of at most $\pm d_{jk}/2$ on inversion, when it is re-calculated as q_{jk} times d_{jk}. In practice this is the largest source of error. However, its effect is minimised by the d_{jk} being chosen with a view to greater accuracy in those coefficients found by experiment to be the more significant for image viewing (see e.g. Watt & Policarpo, 1998).

3. *Re-ordering* If the coefficients were ordered row by row in the usual manner, then the last of one row and first of the next would be contiguous in the ordering but over eight pixel widths apart in the image. To improve on this, a zigzag path is taken (Figure 15.45) so that contiguous coefficients in the ordering refer to pixels that are adjacent, either vertically, horizontally or diagonally.
4. *Entropy encoding* As a final but critical step the coefficients are converted to symbol sequences and encoded according to the entropy methods of Chapter 12. That is, most usually, by the Huffman encoding scheme, but permissibly by arithmetic encoding, which, though more complicated, is slightly closer to the entropy lower bound.

$$
\begin{bmatrix}
0 & 1 & 5 & 6 & 14 & 15 & & \\
2 & 4 & 7 & 13 & 16 & & & \\
3 & 8 & 12 & 17 & & & & \\
9 & 11 & 18 & & & & & \\
10 & 19 & & & & & & 54 \\
20 & & & & & & 55 & 60 \\
& & & & & 56 & 59 & 61 \\
& & & & 57 & 58 & 62 & 63
\end{bmatrix}
$$

Figure 15.45 The zigzag method of ordering an 8×8 array.

15.5 Appendix

15.5.1 The DCT and the K–L transform

The DCT was introduced by Ahmed, Natarajan and Rao (1974) as a transform whose performance compared favourably with the K–L Transform, in spite of the fact that the coefficients in the latter are not fixed, but rather optimised by taking into account statistical features.

The result in the K–L case (Section 10.4.4) is that the original pixel variables, constituting a vector $X = [X_0, \ldots, X_{N-1}]^T$, are transformed into *independent* variables $Y = [Y_0, \ldots, Y_{N-1}]^T$ with variance in decreasing order: $V(Y_0) \geq V(Y_1) \geq \cdots \geq V(Y_{N-1})$. The K–L transform is given by $Y = MX$, which projects X onto an ONB (orthonormal basis) formed by the rows of M, themselves eigenvectors of the covariance matrix C of $X_0, \ldots, X_{N-1}$. That is, the element of C are expected values $c_{ij} = E[X_i X_j]$. For simplicity we are taking the X_i to have zero mean and unit variance, but they are not assumed to be Gaussian.

Thus the DCT would give the same transform if its own corresponding orthonormal basis vectors coincided with the above-mentioned eigenvectors of C. Ahmed *et al.* exhibited their closeness for a useful special case in which $N = 8$. Our task is to show that, under the assumptions of Table 15.10, theory predicts they must always be close.

Table 15.10. *Assumptions which imply that the DCT approximates the KLT.*

A $X_0, X_1, X_2, \ldots$ form a first order Markov chain (Section 11.4.1): the conditional dependence of X_i given the preceding variables reduces to dependence only upon X_{i-1} ($i \geq 1$).

B The chain is stationary: individual X_i are identically distributed, on some range S, and the joint pdf of (X_i, X_{i+1}) is the same for all valid i.

C The inter-pixel correlation $\rho = E[X_0 X_1]$ is close to its maximum of 1 (see Section 10.4.1).

The form of the correlation matrix We need certain consequences of Assumption B. As an exercise let us deduce that, as we might expect, the correlation between any two adjacent pixels is the same. We have $E[X_i X_{i+1}] = \sum x_i x_{i+1}\, p(x_i, x_{i+1})\, (x_i, x_{i+1} \in S)$, which is the same for each i because p remains the same and the pair (x_i, x_{i+1}) runs through the same values. We may now write

$$E[X_i X_{i+1}] = \rho. \tag{15.97}$$

Theorem 15.53 *We have $E[X_k X_{k+n}] = \rho^n$ for all valid k and n.*

Proof The proof does not depend on k, so for simplicity we write it out for the case $k = 0$. Proceeding by induction on n, we note that the result is true for $n = 1$ by (15.97), and assume it inductively for some fixed $n \geq 0$. That is,

$$E[X_0 X_n] = \rho^n \ (n \text{ fixed}). \tag{15.98}$$

Define a new variable $e = X_{i+1} - \rho X_i$, which is independent of i by Assumption B, and which rearranges as $X_{i+1} = \rho X_i + e$. We claim that

$$E[eX_0] = 0. \tag{15.99}$$

For, $\rho = E[X_0 X_1] = E[X_0(\rho X_0 + e)] = E[\rho X_0^2 + eX_0] = \rho E[X_0^2] + E[eX_0]$, which equals $\rho + E[eX_0]$ by the assumption $E[X_0] = 0$, $V(X_0) = 1$ (why?). Subtracting ρ, we obtain $E[eX_0] = 0$, and may complete the inductive step by arguing that

$$\begin{aligned} E[X_0 X_{n+1}] &= E[X_0(\rho X_n + e)] = E[\rho X_0 X_n + eX_0)] \\ &= \rho E[X_0 X_n] + E[eX_0] \\ &= \rho^{n+1} \quad \text{by (15.99) and the inductive hypothesis } E[X_0 X_n] = \rho^n. \end{aligned}$$

Thus for $i \leq j$ we have $c_{ij} = E[X_i X_j]$ (by definition) $= \rho^{j-i}$, otherwise $c_{ij} = E[X_j X_i] = \rho^{i-j}$. The two cases may be combined into

$$c_{ij} = \rho^{|j-i|}. \tag{15.100}$$

In particular, c_{ij} is constant along any diagonal $j = i +$ constant, the defining property of a *Toeplitz matrix* (ours is a special case). Recalling that $E[X_i X_i] = V(X_i) = 1$ by hypothesis, we use (15.100) to write C in the form

$$C = \text{Rows}[S^i(1 \; \rho \; \rho^2 \ldots \rho^{n-1})], \tag{15.101}$$

That is, row i of C is the ith backward shift of $[1 \; \rho \; \rho^2 \cdots \rho^{n-1}]$, for $0 \leq i \leq N - 1$.

The eigenvalues of C Following Grenander and Szegö (1958) we perform row and column operations on the matrix $C - \lambda I$ in the eigenvalue (or *characteristic*) equation $|C - \lambda I| = 0$, yielding a recurrence relation for the determinant, and in due course expressions for the eigenvalues and vectors of C. For size $n + 1$ let us write the determinant in the form

$$\Delta_n(\lambda) = \begin{vmatrix} 1 - \lambda & r & r^2 & \cdots \\ r & 1 - \lambda & r & \cdots \\ r^2 & r & 1 - \lambda & \cdots \\ \cdots & \cdots & \cdots & \cdots \end{vmatrix} \quad (n \geq 2), \tag{15.102}$$

where λ denotes an eigenvalue to be found and we have replaced ρ by r for ease of vision. Now we perform the row and column operations $R_1 \to R_1 - rR_2$ and $C_1 \to C_1 - rC_2$ in (15.102), expand the result by its first row, then expand subdeterminants using Rules 7.28, to obtain the relation for $n \geq 2$,

$$\Delta_n(\lambda) = [1 - \lambda - r(1 + \lambda)]\Delta_{n-1}(\lambda) - r^2 \lambda^2 \Delta_{n-2}(\lambda). \tag{15.103}$$

It is useful to make this hold for $n \geq 1$, as we may by defining $\Delta_{-1} = 1$, and $\Delta_0 = 1 - \lambda$. Then (15.103) gives Δ_1 correctly as $(1 - \lambda)^2 - r^2$. The first trick is to express an eigenvalue λ in terms of a new variable, x, via the trigonometric function $\cos x$, by setting

$$\lambda = \frac{1 - r^2}{1 + r^2 - 2r \cos x}.$$ (15.104)

The second trick, a more standard one, is to seek a solution to (15.103) of the form $\Delta_n = z^n$. Substituting this, and observing that $1 - \lambda - r(1 + \lambda) = -2\lambda r \cos x$, gives a quadratic equation $z^2 + (2\lambda r \cos x)z + r^2\lambda^2 = 0$, with solutions $z = -\lambda r e^{\pm ix}$. The general solution may therefore be written $\lambda r(A e^{ix} + B e^{-ix})$, with A, B determined from the cases $n = -1$ and $n = 0$. Some tricky manipulation results in Table 15.11, after which (cf. Clarke, 1981) we show that the eigenvectors approach the basis vectors (15.86) of the DCT as $\rho \to 1$.

Table 15.11. *Eigenvalues, and the corresponding eigenvectors forming the orthonormal basis for the K–L (Karhunen–Loève) transform on variables $X_0, \ldots, X_{N-1}$, in the case that the correlation matrix C is given by $c_{ij} = \rho^{|j-i|}$ with $\rho = E[X_i X_{i+1}]$ being independent of i.*

Eigenvalues $\lambda_n = \dfrac{1 - \rho^2}{1 + \rho^2 - 2\rho \cos w_n}$,	where $w_n \in [0, \pi)$ are the solutions of
$\tan N w_n = \dfrac{-(1 - \rho^2) \sin w_n}{(1 + \rho^2) \cos w_n - 2\rho}$,	for $n = 0, 1, \ldots, N - 1$. (*)

$$\text{Eigenvectors } K_n = \left[\left(\frac{2}{N + \lambda_n} \right)^{1/2} \sin \left\{ w_n \left(t - \frac{N-1}{2} \right) + \frac{(n+1)\pi}{2} \right\} \right]_{0 \le t \le N-1}$$

Theorem 15.54 *In the limit as $\rho \to 1$ there are n solutions $w = w_n$ in the half-open interval $[0, \pi)$, and they are given by $w_n = n\pi/N$ for $0 \le n \le N - 1$. The eigenvalues (λ_n) are $(N, 0, \ldots, 0)$.*

Proof To ensure that the denominator in (*) of Table 15.11 is nonzero, first consider solutions w in the open interval $(0, \pi)$, for which $|\cos w| < 1$. Now, since $(1 + \rho^2) - 2\rho = (1 - \rho)^2$, we can get $1 + \rho^2$ arbitrarily close to 2ρ by taking ρ sufficiently close to 1 and hence ensure that the denominator is indeed nonzero. Letting $\rho \to 1$ we obtain $\tan Nw = 0$, with solutions $Nw = n\pi$ ($n \in \mathbf{Z}$). The solutions w lying in $(0, \pi)$ are $w_n = n\pi/N$ ($1 \le n \le N - 1$).

Secondly, we must investigate $w = 0$ as a possible solution. To let $\rho \to 1$ in this case we start with w small but nonzero and use the small-angle approximations $\tan Nw = Nw$, $\cos w = 1 - w^2/2$ in (*). We obtain the expression for Nw shown in (15.105) below, which tends to 0 as $\rho \to 1$, giving the solution $w = 0 = 0\pi/N$ and completing the proof for the w_n:

$$Nw = \frac{-(1 - \rho^2)w}{(1 + \rho^2)(1 - w^2/2) - 2\rho} = \frac{-(1 - \rho^2)w}{(1 - \rho)^2 - (1 + \rho^2)w^2/2}.$$ (15.105)

Eigenvalues Consider the formula for λ_n in Table 15.11. For $n > 0$ we have as before $|\cos w| < 1$ and, similarly to the case of (*), we ensure a nonzero denominator by taking ρ close enough to 1. Hence, in the limit, $\lambda_n = 0$. For $n = 0$ we must again start with w small but nonzero. Rearranging (15.105),

$$w^2 = (2/(1 + \rho^2))[(1 - \rho)^2 + (1 - \rho^2)/N]. \tag{15.106}$$

To let $\rho \to 1$ we take $\sigma = 1 - \rho$, then it suffices to expand w^2 up to the linear term in σ. The first factor in (15.106) becomes $2(2 - 2\sigma + \sigma^2)^{-1} = (1 - \sigma + \sigma^2/2)^{-1} = 1 + \sigma$. Substituting this gives $w^2 = (1 + \sigma)(\sigma^2 + (2\sigma - \sigma^2)/N) = 2\sigma/N = 2(1 - \rho)/N$. Replacing $\cos w$ by the small-angle formula $1 - w^2/2$ therefore gives the last expression below for λ which trivially tends to N as $\rho \to 1$, completing the proof:

$$\frac{1 - \rho^2}{1 + \rho^2 - 2\rho(1 - w^2/2)} = \frac{1 - \rho^2}{(1 - \rho)^2 + \rho w^2} = \frac{1 - \rho^2}{(1 - \rho)^2 + \rho \cdot 2(1 - \rho)/N}$$
$$= \frac{1 + \rho}{1 - \rho + 2\rho/N}.$$

The basis vectors With w_n and λ_n as determined, the formulae of Table 15.11 for the KLT eigenvectors yield

$$K_0(t) = \left(\frac{2}{N + N}\right)^{1/2} \sin(\pi/2) = \sqrt{\frac{1}{n}} = \phi_0(t),$$

$$K_n(t) = \left(\frac{2}{N}\right)^{1/2} \sin\left\{\frac{n\pi}{N}\left(t - \frac{N - 1}{2}\right) + \frac{(n + 1)\pi}{2}\right\} \quad (\text{next we use } \sin(\theta + \pi/2) = \cos\theta)$$

$$= \sqrt{\frac{2}{N}} \cos\left\{\frac{n\pi(2t + 1 - N)}{2N} + \frac{n\pi}{2}\right\} = \sqrt{\frac{2}{N}} \cos\frac{n\pi(2t + 1)}{2N} = \phi_n(t),$$

which is exactly the DCT basis. Therefore the transforms coincide, under the assumptions given in Table 15.10, and hence are close in practice.

15.5.2 The Fourier Transform in n dimensions

The Fourier Transform is *separable*, which means that an n-dimensional transform is implemented by applying the 1D version to each dimension separately. How this is done for the Fourier and other separable transforms, we have already seen in two dimensions at the start of this chapter, both in the discrete and continuous cases. For the present extension let us take coordinates $x = (x_1, \ldots, x_n)$ and $u = (u_1, \ldots, u_n)$. Following the prescription for moving up a dimension in the continuous case gives

$$F(u_1, \ldots, u_n) = \int_{-\infty}^{\infty} \left(\int_{x_1 \ldots x_{n-1}} f(x_1, \ldots, x_n)\, e^{-2\pi i(x_1 u_1 + \cdots + x_{n-1} u_{n-1})} dx_1 \ldots dx_{n-1} \right) e^{-2\pi i x_n u_n} dx_n. \tag{15.107}$$

In fact, writing $x_1u_1 + \cdots + x_nu_n = \mathbf{x} \cdot \mathbf{u}$ we may express the transform–inverse pair compactly as

$$F(\mathbf{u}) = \int_{\mathbb{R}^n} f(\mathbf{x}) e^{-2\pi \mathbf{x} \cdot \mathbf{u}} d\mathbf{x},$$
$$f(\mathbf{x}) = \int_{\mathbb{R}^n} F(\mathbf{u}) e^{2\pi \mathbf{x} \cdot \mathbf{u}} d\mathbf{u}. \tag{15.108}$$

The discrete case For simplicity we keep to the same coordinate notation and assume each x_i or u_j takes the same values $0, 1, \ldots, N - 1$. Then performing summation instead of integration and taking $w = e^{-2\pi i/N}$ we have

$$F(\mathbf{u}) = \sum_{\mathbf{x}} f(\mathbf{x}) w^{\mathbf{x} \cdot \mathbf{u}},$$
$$f(\mathbf{x}) = \sum_{\mathbf{u}} F(\mathbf{u}) w^{-\mathbf{x} \cdot \mathbf{u}}. \tag{15.109}$$

This may be achieved dimension by dimension, through the 1D routine, in which we multiply vectors by a matrix (or apply the FFT). For instance the nth dimension requires us to make the replacement

$$f_k \equiv f(x_1, \ldots x_{n-1}, k) \to \sum_{x_n} f(x_1, \ldots x_{n-1}, x_n) w^{kx_n} \quad (0 \le k \le N - 1). \tag{15.110}$$

or in vector terms $[f_k]_{0 \le k \le N-1} \to T[f_k]_{0 \le k \le N-1}$.

ALGO 15.6 The DFT for an n-dimensional array $f(x_1, \ldots, x_n)$

If $n = 1$ Return Tf, else set $F = f$
For $k = 1$ to n do
    For all $x_1, \ldots, x_{n-1}$ do {Fourier transform of vector}
      $[F(x_1, \ldots, x_{n-1}, k)]_{0 \le k \le N-1} = T[F(x_1, \ldots, x_{n-1}, k)]_{0 \le k \le N-1}$
    Forward-rotate coordinates of F
Return F
[For the inverse DFT, replace T by T^{-1}]

In Mathematica

```
dft[f_] := Module[{n, d, i, k, cycle, F = f},
    n = TensorRank[f]; d = Dimensions[f][[1]];
    cycle = RotateRight[Range[n]];
    If[n < 2, Return[Fourier[f]]];
    For[k = 1, k ≤ n, k++,
        F = Flatten[F, n - 2];
        Do[F[[i]] = Fourier[F[[i]]], {i, Length[F]}];
        Do[F = Partition[F, {d}], {n - 2}];
        F = Transpose[F, cycle]; ];
    Return[F]; ];
```

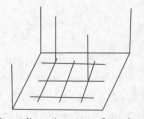
Every dimension to transformed.

Example 15.55 This very simple example in dimension $n = 3$ with $N = 2$ illustrates what is going on. Our function will be $f(x, y, z) = 4x + 2y + z + 1$. All numbers are

Table 15.12. *The values $f(x, y, z)$ and how they change under Fourier transform with respect to each coordinate z, y, x in turn.*

x, y, z	$f(x, y, z)$	Fourier w.r.t. z	Fourier w.r.t. y	Fourier w.r.t. x
000	1	3	10	36
001	2	-1	-2	-4
010	3	7	-4	-8
011	4	-1	0	0
100	5	11	26	-16
101	6	-1	-2	0
110	7	15	-4	0
111	8	-1	0	0

Table 15.13. *An overview. Brief definitions and results for the n-dimensional analogues of four key results of the Fourier transform. In (ii) we may take $\textbf{x}$, $\textbf{u}$ as columns, replacing $\textbf{x}M$ by $M\textbf{x}$ and $\textbf{u}(M^{-1})^T$ by $(M^{-1})^T\textbf{u}$. The discrete case of (iv) is found on the last line.*

title	definitions	result
(i) shift		$f(\textbf{x} - \textbf{a}) \rightarrow e^{-2\pi i \textbf{a} \cdot \textbf{u}} F(\textbf{u})$
(ii) 'rotation'	$D = |\text{Det}(M_{n \times n})| \neq 0$	$f(\textbf{x}M) \rightarrow F(\textbf{u}(M^{-1})^T/D$
(iii) projection	$p(x_1, \ldots, x_{n-1}) =$	$p(x_1, \ldots, x_{n-1}) \rightarrow$
	$\int f(x_1, \ldots, x_n) dx_n$	$F(u_1, \ldots, u_{n-1}, 0)$
(iv) convolution	$(f^*g)(\textbf{x}) = \int f(\textbf{t})g(\textbf{x} - \textbf{t})d\textbf{t}$	
	$h = f^*g$ if $h(\textbf{x}) = f(\textbf{x})g(\textbf{x})$	$f^*g \rightarrow FoG$

real, for the 2-point Fourier matrix is Rows($[1 \ 1], [1 \ -1]$). Table 15.12 shows how the values of f change when we transform with respect to z, y, x, in that order, as in ALGO 15.6.

For example, in the z column, $[f(0, 0, k)]_{0 \leq k \leq 1} = [1 \ 2] \rightarrow [3 \ -1]$. After completing this column we transform e.g. $[f(1, k, 0)]_{0 \leq k \leq 1} = [11 \ 15] \rightarrow [26 \ -4]$ and, when this column is complete, we perform e.g. $[f(k, 1, 1)]_{0 \leq k \leq 1} = [0 \ 0] \rightarrow [0 \ 0]$.

Main results for the n-dimensional Fourier Transform
Proofs of main results

(i) *Shift Theorem* $f(\textbf{x} - \textbf{a}) \rightarrow \int f(\textbf{x} - \textbf{a})e^{-2\pi i(\textbf{x} \cdot \textbf{u})}d\textbf{x}$ (put $\textbf{y} = \textbf{x} - \textbf{a}) = \int f(\textbf{y})$
$e^{-2\pi i(\textbf{y} + \textbf{a}) \cdot \textbf{u}}d\textbf{y} = e^{-2\pi i(\textbf{a} \cdot \textbf{u})} \int f(\textbf{y})e^{-2\pi i(\textbf{y} \cdot \textbf{u})}d\textbf{y} = e^{-2\pi i(\textbf{a} \cdot \textbf{u})} F(\textbf{u})$.

(ii) *'Rotation' Theorem* Beyond two dimensions it is easier to work with complete matrices rather than resorting to their elements. We write

$$f(\textbf{x}M) = g(\textbf{x}) \rightarrow G(\textbf{u}) = \int g(\textbf{x})e^{-2\pi i(\textbf{x} \cdot \textbf{u})}d\textbf{x}.$$

We change variables in the integral by $w = xM$, or $x = wM^{-1}$. Theorem 10.10 tells us how to do this. The Jacobian is $J = [\partial x/\partial w] = \mathrm{Det}(M)^{-1}$, which is constant, whence

$$G(u) = \int |J| f(w) e^{-2\pi i (wM^{-1} \cdot u)} dw.$$

Now we reconstruct the dot product to isolate w, by expressing it as a matrix product (here u is a row): $wM^{-1} \cdot u = wM^{-1}u^{\mathrm{T}} = w \cdot v$, where $v = u(M^{-1})^{\mathrm{T}}$. Then, with $|J| = 1/D$,

$$G(u) = \int |J| f(w) e^{-2\pi i (w \cdot v)} dw = F(v)/D, \text{ as required.}$$

(iii) *Projection*

$$p(x_1, \ldots, x_{n-1}) = \int f(x) dx_n \to \int \left(\int f(x) dx_n \right) e^{-2\pi i (x_1 u_1 + \cdots + x_{n-1} u_{n-1})} dx_1 \cdots dx_{n-1}$$

$$= \int f(x) e^{-2\pi i x \cdot (u_1, \ldots, u_{n-1}, 0)} dx = F(u_1, \ldots, u_{n-1}, 0).$$

(iv) *Continuous convolution*

$$(f^*g)(x) = \int f(x - t) g(t) dt \to \int \left(\int f(x - t) g(t) dt \right) e^{-2\pi i (x \cdot u)} dx$$

$$= \int \left(\int f(x - t) e^{-2\pi i (x \cdot u)} dx \right) g(t) dt$$

$$= \int e^{-2\pi i (t \cdot u)} F(u) g(t) dt \text{ (Shift Theorem)}$$

$$= F(u) \int g(t)^{-2\pi i (t \cdot u)} dt = F(u) G(u).$$

Proof (iv) (Discrete) We write f and F with discrete subscripts $f_{ij\ldots k}$ and $F_{rs\ldots t}$ and identify f with the polynomial $f(z_1, \ldots, z_n) = \sum_{i,j,\ldots,k} f_{ij\ldots k} z_1{}^i z_2{}^j \cdots z_n{}^k$. Then firstly (15.109) becomes the alternative,

$$F_{rs\ldots t} = \sum_{i,j,\ldots,k} f_{ij\ldots k} w^{ri + sj + \cdots + tk}, \qquad (15.111)$$

and, secondly, the index law, $w^{ri + sj + \cdots + tk} = (w^r)^i (w^s)^j \cdots (w^t)^k$, converts (15.111) into the equality

$$F_{rs\ldots t} = f(w^r, w^s, \ldots, w^t). \qquad (15.112)$$

Now the n-dimensional Convolution Theorem drops out: $f^*g = h \Rightarrow f(z)g(z) = h(z) \Rightarrow f(w^r, w^s, \ldots, w^t) g(w^r, w^s, \ldots, w^t) = h(w^r, w^s, \ldots, w^t)$ (all $r, s, \ldots, t$) $\Rightarrow F_{rs\ldots t} G_{rs\ldots t} = H_{rs\ldots t}$ and $FoG = H$.

Finally, we specialise to the version of the Projection Theorem required for some of the more developed forms of tomography (see the end of Section 18.4).

Example 15.56 *The 3D Projection Theorem* Let $p(x, y) = \int f(x, y, z)dz$ (projection onto the *xy*-plane). Then $p(x, y) \rightarrow F(u, v, 0)$.

Exercises 15

1 √ (i) Show that $\phi(f) = MfN$, a matrix product, is a linear transformation. (ii) Let M and N be invertible. Show that $\phi(f) = 0$ implies $f = 0$. (iii) Given $F = MfM^T$ (M invertible), express f in terms of F. (iv) Derive the alternative expression $\text{Tr}(AB^T)$ for the dot product (A, B) of real matrices. (v) Let $A = u^T u$, where u is a unit row vector. Simplify A^2.

2 √ (i) Use Formula (15.7) to determine the Discrete Fourier Transform of an impulse at the origin: $f_{mn} = 0$ except when $m = n = 0$. (ii) What is F, when f is a general impulse: $f_{mn} = 0$ except when $(m, n) = (\mu, \lambda)$? Express this as a (rank 1) matrix $u^T v$, where u, v are row vectors.

3 √ (*Using separability*) (i) Find the 2D Discrete Fourier Transform of the separable array $f = \text{Rows}[(1, 1, 1), (2, 2, 2), (3, 3, 3)]$, using $w^3 = 1$ and $1 + w + w^2 = 0$ to simplify the calculation. (ii) Repeat for $f = \text{Rows}[(1, 2, 3), (0, 0, 0), (1, 2, 3)]$.

4 Implement the DFT and test Theorem 15.7 in the manner of Figure 15.4.

5 √ (i) Show that discrete convolution with the Laplacian (15.14) gives zero if taken over a region of pixel values which change linearly. (ii) A 4×4 pixel array has constant value 1. What values does the Laplacian give (a) on pixels at the edge of the array (with all-round border of zeros appended), (b) on the 'interior'? What are the values if the original constant is changed to 100?

6 Convolve an image array with the discrete Laplacian. How well does it bring out the boundaries (see Figure 15.6).

7 √ (i) Find the discrete auto-correlation function of the array $\text{Rows}[(1, 2, 1), (0, 1, 2), (2, 0, 1)]$. (ii) Find the (continuous) Fourier Transform S_{ff} of the autocorrelation R_{ff}, when $f(x, y) = \exp[-\pi(x^2 + y^2)]$. (iii) Find S_{fg} if $g(x, y) = \cos 2\pi k(x + y)$. (Hint: split the cosine.)

8 (i) Experiment with brightness and contrast on several images, making some features invisible to the naked eye, and restoring them by another change of brightness and/or contrast. (ii) Perform histogram equalisation on a deserving candidates obtained in part (i). Add small spots to an image and then attempt to remove them by median filtering, in the manner of Figure 15.13.

9 √ (i) Show that the Butterworth transfer function $H(r)$ passes through the point $(k_0, 1/2)$ for all $n \geq 1$, and that the gradient is most negative when r equals a value which approaches k_0 as n increases. (ii) Why does convolution with the binomial approximation to the Gaussian filter leave an area of constant intensity fixed? (iii) Write down the matrix in the case $n = 3$. Determine the variance.

10 √ (a) Derive (15.35) from (15.34). (b) Prove Theorem 15.24 (ii) for a vertical mirror. (c) How many symmetry properties from Theorem 15.24 hold for the mask shown in Figure 15.22?

11 Repeat Figure 15.20 for another image.

12 (a) Implement ALGO 15.1 to obtain a 7×7 version of the LoG convolution mask. Check that Figure 15.22 is a submatrix (to within limits of accuracy). (b) Apply $3 \times 3, 5 \times 5$ and 7×7 versions to a simple multi-shaded image to detect edges. Did the 7×7 version perform noticeably the best?

13 (a) Write down all eight Prewitt masks as laid down in Example 15.29. (b) For a chosen image, compare the edge-detection capabilities of LoG, Sobel and Prewitt.

14 √ (a) Show that if $H(u, v) = \text{sinc}(\pi u\alpha)e^{-i\pi u\alpha}$ then $H(-u, -v)$ is the complex conjugate of $H(u, v)$. (ii) Use ALGO 15.2 to blur an image, then ALGO 15.3 to bring it back. (c) Examine the DFT of the blurred image in (b) to predict what the blur distance must have been (see Figure 15.27).

15 √ A small object is placed on the axis of a thin lens of radii $r = 12$ and $s = -16$, nearest the face of radius 12, at a distance of 16 units. The lens has refractive index $\mu = 1.6$. Assuming the surrounding medium is gaseous, of refractive index 1.0, determine (i) the focal length f of the lens, (ii) the position of the image, and (iii) the magnification achieved. Verify Newton's formula (15.53).

16 Start with a digital photo subject to lens blur and a photo of a thin line under the same conditions (or simulate this by applying a Gaussian blur to a digital image). (i) Measure the vector b of grey values for the blur of a thin line, as in Figure 15.32(b). (ii) Compute the kernel vector a by (15.59'). (iii) Determine the transfer function $H(u, v)$ by (15.59) (u, v are discrete for this). (iv) Calculate the DFT of the true image by $F(u, v) = G(u, v)/H(u, v)$, and recover the original by $F \to f$.

17 √ Derive the formulae of (15.70).

18 Add blur and noise to a digital image that includes portrayal of significant numbers. Try to regain legibility by experimenting with a range of fixed values of S_{nn}/S_{ff} for the Wiener filter.

19 Implement ALGOs 15.4 and 15.5, and produce Guassian and Laplacian pyramids for a digital image. What compression can you achieve?

20 (a) Partition a digital image into 8×8 blocks and apply the DCT to each. Reprint the image with successively fewer coefficients retained before inversion (see Figure 15.43). (b) Repeat with 4×4 blocks. Does this give any advantage?

21 Implement the N-point DCT via the $2N$-point DFT (Remarks 15.52), and check that it gives the correct matrix in two dimensions for $N = 8$.

22 (The n-dimensional Fourier Transform) (a) Repeat Example 15.55 with (i) $f(x, y, z) = 8 - 4x - 2y - z$ and (ii) $f = 1$, by hand and/or computer. Can you explain the relation between the three answers? (b) Write out a proof of the 3-dimensional Projection Theorem. (c) Check that the n-dimensional 'Rotation' Theorem with vectors treated as columns gives the stated result for this case.

16

Scaling

Both wavelets and fractals (even just fractal dimension) have seen an explosion of applications in recent years. This text will point mainly to the vision side, but at the end of this chapter we give references that indicate something of the range. The story begins with Section 16.1 which is about fractals; this points to the value of the scaling theme, thereafter explored through wavelets and multiresolution. The present chapter concentrates on wavelets with the most structure: the Haar and Daubechies types. In the next this is relaxed for application to B-splines, then to surface wavelets.

16.1 Nature, fractals and compression

The potential to compress an image has to do with its degree of redundancy, and so comes broadly under image analysis. Here, more specifically, we are interested in the redundancy that may come from self-similarity of different parts of the image, rather than from more general correlation. This idea arose essentially from Mandelbrot's observations about the nature of natural images. For example, one part may be approximately congruent to another at a different scale, as in Figure 16.1. The basic way to turn this into a method of compression goes back to Barnsley and Sloan (1988) and is the subject of Section 16.1.3. For subsequent exploitation see Section 16.1.4 plus Barnsley (1992), Barnsley and Hurd (1994), Peitgen *et al.* (1992), Fisher (1995) and Lu (1997).

16.1.1 The fractal nature of Nature

Natural scenes, including the human face, possess plenty of correlation, as revealed by Principal Component Analysis (Section 10.4.4) and its approximate relative the Discrete Cosine Transform (Section 15.4.2). Though correlation is expressed in numbers, much visual similarity is observable to the human eye. Perhaps the most easily seen similarities occur in objects with repeated branching. Examples are actual trees, river courses seen by satellite, and then lungs, blood vessels and the like. However, this property, of appearance at one scale being repeated at many others, occurs widely in non-branching situations too, such as clouds, coastlines, and mountains.

(a) This geological structure could be small, but it's part of the Svoge anticline in Bulgaria, with true scale indicated by the shadowy humans at bottom left.

(b) Clouds. Are we in an airliner about to enter, or viewing from several miles below?

Figure 16.1 Some natural scenes, illustrating similarity across a range of scales.

Here is a test. If this similarity holds, there should be many situations where it is impossible without further clues to have a reliable sense of distance. This is certainly borne out by human mis-estimation of how far away mountains, clouds and distant coastlines are. One symptom of the scale phenomenon is seen in Figure 16.1(a), where, in accordance with custom, a familiar object is included to give the scale. A small superimposed human figure would give a quite different impression!

Example 16.1 (*Modelling*) In respect of modelling Nature it was Mandelbrot's (1983) observation that many objects, hitherto considered as mathematical monsters to be avoided, had far greater potential than the usual lines, planes and spheres to represent natural things such as we have discussed. For example, he proposed the model of a snowflake consisting of three pieces of the *Koch curve*, Figure 16.2, now often called the *snowflake curve*.

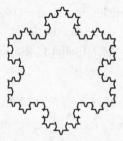

Figure 16.2 Snowflake represented by three pieces of the Koch curve fitting round a triangle (third stage of the construction in Figure 16.3).

We may say the curve consists of four copies of itself, scaled to 1/3 size, rotated and placed in positions *AB*, *BC*, *CD*, *DE* as indicated in Figure 16.3, where we show a recipe for constructing the curve, Mandelbrot's Initiator–Generator Method.

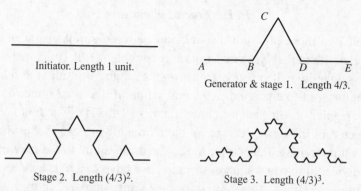

Figure 16.3 Three stages of the Koch curve. At each, we replace every line segment by a suitably scaled copy of the generator.

Obviously, for any given illustration the process must stop at some finite stage, but abstractly the Koch curve is the result of continuing ad infinitum. The property of having detail at *every* scale is implied by the fact that each 1/3 sized part is a copy of the whole and therefore so is each of its own parts, and so on. Mandelbrot gave the name *fractal* to such sets, from the Latin *fractus*, meaning broken. He provided a precise technical definition (see Section 16.1.3) and later (Feder, 1989) a rough but inclusive one:

A fractal is a shape made up of parts similar to the whole in some way. (16.1)

The complete (ad infinitum) Koch curve was considered a 'monster' on two accounts. (1) It has infinite length, for in passing from one stage to the next we increase the length by a factor 4/3, and (2) *non-smoothness*: a unique tangent does not exist at corner points B, C, D, and the proportion of such points tends to 1 as the construction stages proceed.

On the other hand, in practical situations we actually use not this monster, but its *approximation* up to some scale. One consequence of adopting (16.1) is that by interpreting *similar* in a non-technical sense we can apply the word fractal to such as both the Koch curve and its practical approximations. The same holds for the fern in Figure 16.11 of Section 16.1.3.

Artificial images of Nature Fractal ideas were used to computer-generate images of natural scenes which were both realistic and strikingly attractive. Early examples were the mountain, lake and valley combinations of Voss (1988), and the planet Genesis in *The Wrath of Khan*. The planet's fractal-based construction was undetected, and by that token a complete success. The cases cited used an extension of the Brownian motion model, in which fractal dimension (see the next section) appears as a parameter. A useful exposition of this is given by Feder (1989), along with applications to physics. Further visual examples are included in Peitgen and Saupe (1988) and of course in the text of the originator, Mandelbrot (1983).

16.1.2 Fractal dimension

Now we consider more precisely the relation between similar parts of an object at different scales. Remarkably, there is often a consistency of structure which enables us to define a quantity called *fractal dimension*, applying over all or at least a range of scales. It can be seen to emerge as a generalisation of the usual dimensions 1, 2, 3 as follows. If a regular object such as a line, square or cube is divided into N equal parts, then as N increases there is a decrease in the ratio r of part size to the whole. But how exactly does this decrease depend on N and the dimension? In the case of a square of side 1 unit divided into equal squares of ratio r we have $Nr^2 = 1$, hence $r = (1/N)^{1/2}$. Table 16.1 illustrates that r is given in respective dimensions 1, 2, 3 by

$$r = \frac{1}{N^{1/1}}, \frac{1}{N^{1/2}}, \frac{1}{N^{1/3}}. \tag{16.2}$$

Table 16.1. *Scaling properties in dimensions 1, 2 and 3,
corresponding to (16.2).*

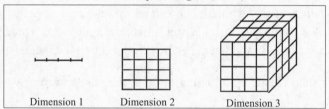

Dimension 1   Dimension 2   Dimension 3

The snowflake curve again Does a similar formula hold for a more general object divisible into N reduced copies of itself? A candidate is the snowflake curve where, at the kth stage, we have divided the original into 4^k copies, each of size $(1/3)^k$. So for each k there hold $N = 4^k$ and $1/r = 3^k$. The key idea here is to take logs, resulting in

$$\log_4 N = k = \log_3(1/r) = D \log_4(1/r) \text{ (change of base)},$$

where $D = \log_3 4$ according to the formula $\log_a x = (\log_a b)(\log_b x)$ of (12.8). Thus $N = (1/r)^D$ or, on rearranging,

$$r = \frac{1}{N^{1/D}}. \tag{16.3}$$

The significant thing here is that the non-integer quantity $D = 1.26$ fulfils the same role as dimension in Table 16.1. How far can we *usefully* take this? Let us consider something not quite so regular.

Coastlines and frontiers Here is the connection with our previous comments. The fact is that the measured length of a coastline or land frontier (henceforth referred to collectively as *borders*) depends on the size of your ruler units. This is aptly illustrated by the different lengths of their common frontier given by Belgium and The Netherlands,

Figure 16.4 Borders.

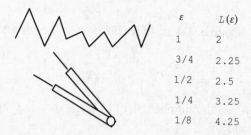

ε	$L(\varepsilon)$
1	2
3/4	2.25
1/2	2.5
1/4	3.25
1/8	4.25

Figure 16.5 Measuring $L(\varepsilon)$ for dividers set at width ε. The zigzag's actual length is about 4.85 units of the exhibited dividers.

respectively 449 and 380 km (Mandelbrot, 1983); see Figure 16.4. The reason is that, as the measurement unit, which we shall call ε, becomes smaller, we pick out greater detail. For a coastline this might be bays and inlets, then subinlets and the shape of jutting cliffs. Figure 16.5 shows the effect of measuring a zigzag line with dividers set at various widths. The reader may like to try out this exercise on other shapes, and indeed on a coastline as presented in an atlas.

We see that, as ε becomes smaller, the measured distance $L(\varepsilon)$ approaches the sum of the lengths of the component line segments. How does $L(\varepsilon)$ vary with ε for borders the world over? Is there a common theme or structure? The answer is found in the graphs of Figure 16.6 by L. F. Richardson (1961), page 609, who in his day could give no theoretical interpretation for these experimental results. The point to observe is that, within certain limits,

> the graph of $\log_{10}(L)$ against $\log_{10}(\varepsilon)$ is a straight line. (16.4)

The slope of this line characterises in some way the border it refers to. We will see that the straight line property is explicable on the hypothesis that over a fair range of scales the details of a border look much the same, though they are different details, of a different size. This has led to a concept of *dimension D*, calculated from the graph slope, and not necessarily a whole number. First, we must reformulate Richardson's results of Figure 16.6.

The straight line graph implies a linear relation

$$\log_{10} L = a + b \log_{10} \varepsilon \quad (b < 0),$$ (16.5)

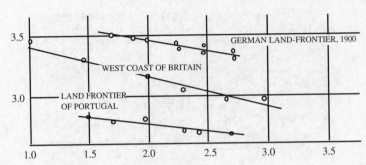

Figure 16.6 Part of Richardson's data on coastline and frontier lengths: $\log_{10}$(length) against $\log_{10}(\varepsilon)$. (Distances are in kilometres.)

in which the slope b is negative. Taking 10 to the power of each side, we obtain $L = A\varepsilon^b$ with $A = 10^a$, or

$$L = A\varepsilon^{1-D}, \quad \text{where } D = 1 - b. \tag{16.6}$$

But, since L equals ε times the number $N(\varepsilon)$ of steps of size ε used to measure L, we have $A\varepsilon^{1-D} = \varepsilon N(\varepsilon)$ and so

$$N(\varepsilon) \propto 1/\varepsilon^D, \tag{16.7}$$

where $\propto$ denotes proportional to. This rearranges also to

$$\varepsilon \propto 1/N^{1/D}, \tag{16.8}$$

which is essentially the same relation as (16.3). Thus we are led to interpret D as a dimension, reasonably called *fractal dimension*. We may think of it as pointing to a set's intricacy. The Richardson graphs provide a measure of the ruggedness of coastlines and borders that does not depend on one specific unit of measurement. For abstract fractals the dimension may apply over arbitrarily small scales, whilst for practical situations it is profitable to consider a convenient range of scales. In fact, the idea of fractal dimension has proved surprisingly fruitful for studying relationships between more general variables in science and engineering, so that conferences are held with the title of, for example, *Fractals in the Sciences* (e.g. Peitgen *et al.*, 1999). One nice example is that the power of a battery may be expressed in terms of the fractal dimension of an electrode surface (Avnir & Pfeifer, 1983). Many applications are detailed by Kaye (1989) in a volume of over 400 pages. Some further useful references are given at the end of this section.

Some practicalities In investigating the existence and value of a fractal-type power law between physical quantities it is useful to bear in mind the following.

(1) It is usually more convenient to plot $\log N$ (or an analogue) rather than $\log L$. How does this affect the graph? Setting $L = N\varepsilon$ and $D = 1 - b$ in the original (16.5) we obtain

$$\boxed{\log_{10} N = a - D \log_{10} \varepsilon.} \tag{16.9}$$

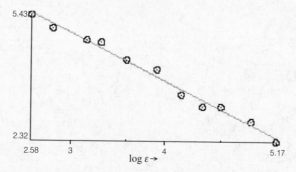

Figure 16.7 Richardson graph for the Belgian–Dutch border, with logs to base 2. The graph's slope is -1.19 (approx.), implying dimension $D = 1.19$.

Thus, provided we are justified in assuming the plotted points represent a straight line graph, *fractal dimension is given by the negative slope*. The 'best straight line' formula is (11.17).

(2) *We may use any fixed base of logarithms* Noting (Remark 12.2) the base change formula $(\log_d 10)(\log_{10} x) = \log_d x$, we multiply (16.9) through by $\log_d 10$ to obtain $\log_d N = (a \log_a 10) - D \log_d \varepsilon$. Thus, changing the base of logarithms leaves the graph's slope, and hence the measured value of fractal dimension, unchanged. See Figure 16.7.

(3) *We may use any fixed measurement unit* If the measurement unit is changed then (16.9) applies with ε multiplied by some constant α, allowing us to write $\log N = a - D \log(\alpha \varepsilon) = a - D(\log \alpha + \log \varepsilon) = (a - D \log \alpha) - D \log \varepsilon$, with slope unchanged at $(-D)$.

(4) *We may use the box counting method* (see e.g. Feder, 1989 or Falconer, 1997): we plot $\log N$ against $\log \varepsilon$ still, but now ε is the linear size of a mesh laid over a digitised image, and N is the number of mesh squares that intersect the object under consideration. In Figure 16.8 we show the build-up of 6-pixel sized squares in such a mesh, where they cut the Icelandic coastline.

Further applications of fractal dimension Some general references are Kaye (1989), Peitgen, Henriques and Penedo (1991), Mandelbrot (1983) and Schroeder (1991). There follows a selection for particular fields.

Astronomy:	Beer and Roy (1990),
Bio/medical:	West and Goldberger (1987),
Cartography:	Brivio and Marini (1993)
Chemistry:	Feder (1989), Avnir and Pfeifer (1983),
Engineering:	*New Scientist*, 9 June, 1990,
Geography:	Burrough (1981),
Geology:	Turcotte (1992),
Music:	Voss (1988),
Physics:	Petronero and Posati (1986).

Example 16.2 This is an investigation as to whether the trabecular (fissured) bone in the leg of a horse exhibits a fractal dimension (see Hoggar *et al.*, 1998, and Martinelli, 1999). We plot $\log_2 N$ against $\log_2 \varepsilon$, where ε is the linear size of a mesh laid over a

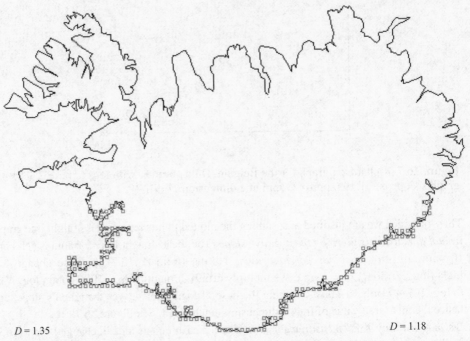

$D = 1.35$ $D = 1.18$

Figure 16.8 The coastline of Iceland, with sample mesh boxes which intersect it. By performing box counting calculations on different regions separately, we find that the West coast has a fractal dimension of 1.35, which is greater than that of the East at 1.18. This puts a numerical value on the apparent greater ruggedness of the West.

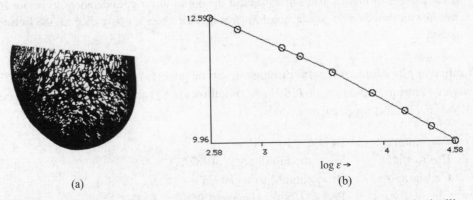

(a)   (b)

Figure 16.9 (a) Cross-section of trabecular bone from horse ankle (source: Martinelli, 1999), (b) Richardson-type graph of $\log N$, for investigating the existence and numerical value of fractal dimension.

digitised image of the relevant bone cross-section of a recently deceased horse, and N is the number of mesh boxes that intersect a part of the bone. With the image scanned at 800 dpi, measurements were expressed in pixels, with integer box sizes from 6 to 24. The result (Figure 16.9) models two fractal dimensions, each operative over a specific range of scales, namely 1.16 for the smaller and 1.45 for the larger scales.

16.1.3 Iterated Function Systems

The Koch snowflake curve, we noted, consists of four copies of itself which have been transformed in the sense of being scaled down by a factor 1/3. Of course, some rotation and translation were also necessary to put these pieces together. Reflection could also be usefully employed, to give a more symmetrical procedure with the same outcome. A remarkably wide range of images will emerge (a first example is Figure 16.11) if we allow also non-uniform scaling and shear, as illustrated in Figure 16.10 and explained thereafter.

(a) Original Lena. (b) The result of non-uniform scaling by 4/5 horizontally and 6/5 vertically. (c) Effect of horizontal shear with parameter 1/3.

Figure 16.10 Non-uniform scaling (b) and shear (c) applied to image (a).

A *shear* is performed relative to some straight line as axis, and according to a parameter α. In more detail, a general point P at signed distance d from the axis is moved a signed distance αd parallel to this axis. In Figure 16.10 the axis of shear is the x-axis, the distance of a point from this axis is of course its y-coordinate, and the parameter is 1/3. Thus $(x, y) \to (x + \alpha y, y)$ with $\alpha = 1/3$. More generally, all our permitted transforms may be represented in the matrix form

$$\begin{bmatrix} x \\ y \end{bmatrix} \to \begin{bmatrix} a & b \\ c & d \end{bmatrix} \begin{bmatrix} x \\ y \end{bmatrix} + \begin{bmatrix} e \\ f \end{bmatrix}, \tag{16.10}$$

collectively referred to as *affine*. We shall say (16.10) has *code* (a, b, c, d, e, f). Thus the transformations of Figure 16.10 are the special cases

$$\begin{bmatrix} x \\ y \end{bmatrix} \to \begin{bmatrix} 4/5 & 0 \\ 0 & 6/5 \end{bmatrix} \begin{bmatrix} x \\ y \end{bmatrix}, \quad \text{and} \quad \begin{bmatrix} x \\ y \end{bmatrix} \to \begin{bmatrix} 1 & 1/3 \\ 0 & 1 \end{bmatrix} \begin{bmatrix} x \\ y \end{bmatrix}, \tag{16.11}$$

with respective codes (4/5, 0, 0, 6/5, 0, 0) and (1, 1/3, 0, 1, 0, 0). These two transformations may be performed relative to arbitrary axes by judicious composition with isometries – *rotation, reflection* or *translation* (see e.g. Hoggar, 1992).

Example 16.3 (*The fern*) Figure 16.11 shows a version of the surprisingly lifelike fern from Barnsley (1992). It consists of four transformed copies of itself. Starting from the bottom, the stem is the result of squeezing and shortening the whole, whilst the lower two branches are obtained by non-uniform scaling down, rotating and translating into position. The rest, lying above the darkened branches, is the result of a contraction

Table 16.2. *IFS codes for the fern of Figure 16.11.*

	a	b	c	d	e	f
w_1	68	4	−1	71	40	3
w_2	20	51	−19	9	36	128
w_3	3	−51	24	21	212	63
w_4	1	0	0	42	139	92

Note: Entries to be divided by 100. For y-axis drawn downwards, change the sign of b, c and f.

towards the top, with a slight shear. Such observations lead to the main topic of the present section, below.

Figure 16.11 Fern represented as a union of transformed copies of itself: the lower stem and three differently shaded areas. The codes are given in Table 16.2.

Iterated Function Systems Let us regard an image X as a subset of the plane, and suppose it consists of N reduced copies of itself, transformed by affine maps $w_1, \ldots, w_N$ into their appropriate shapes and positions. That is,

$$X = w_1(X) \cup w_2(X) \cup \cdots \cup w_N(X). \tag{16.12}$$

If each w_i is *contractive*, reducing distances to not more than some multiple $r < 1$ of their original, or

$$|w(x) - w(y)| \le r|x - y|, \tag{16.13}$$

then we call $\{w_1, \ldots, w_N\}$ an *Iterated Function System (IFS)* for X. The great significance of this idea is that X can be reconstructed from the IFS alone, starting from an arbitrary compact set, according to the following result of Hutchinson (1981). Note that *compact* means bounded and closed, a property possessed by our image-representing sets by virtue

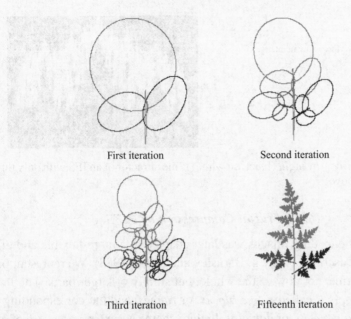

First iteration   Second iteration

Third iteration   Fifteenth iteration

Figure 16.12 The fern of Figure 16.11 reconstructed from its IFS maps (Table 16.2) by
(16.15), starting from a large circle.

of their finiteness. Now, starting with any compact set E, the IFS defines a new set

$$W(E) = w_1(E) \cup w_2(E) \cup \cdots \cup w_N(E), \qquad (16.14)$$

put together from component parts in the same way as X. Indeed, if $E = X$, this simply
gives us X back again. The remarkable result of Hutchinson says that, however different
E is from X, the successive new sets $W^n(E)$ become arbitrarily close to X itself, or

$$W^n(E) \to X, \quad \text{as} \quad n \to \infty. \qquad (16.15)$$

For a detailed proof see e.g. Hoggar (1992). It was an observation of Barnsley (1988)
that to record only the coefficients $a, \ldots, e$ for each transformation of an IFS would
take much less memory space than recording the pixel values, and would thus provide a
method of compression.

Example 16.4 (*The fern continued*) Let us test out in Figure 16.12 the IFS method
(16.15) for recovering the original fern image of Figure 16.11. Notice that we made
things rather hard for the IFS by starting with such a large and wrongly shaped object,
the circle. Nevertheless, Hutchinson's Theorem produced the correct final result after a
small number of iterations. Figure 16.13 is an accidental example that points to artistic
use (this direction is further explored on page 354 in Hoggar, 1992).

Project Determine affine maps $\{w_1, \ldots, w_4\}$ for an IFS to generate the snowflake curve
of Figure 16.3. Now recover the curve by computer iteration.

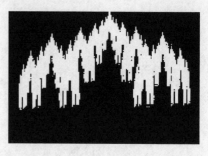

IFS codes for Moscow by night.

50	0	0	75	65	0
33	1	0	77	139	20
35	−1	0	77	29	22

Figure 16.13 *Moscow by night* (black on white) is the attractor of an IFS with only three maps, as listed above.

16.1.4 Fractal Compression by PIFS

The IFS method for encoding images was later adapted to a more flexible and efficient scheme, now to be described (see e.g. Barnsley and Sloan, 1988). We represent parts of an image as transforms, not now of the whole, but simply of larger parts. The image is partitioned into subsets R called *range blocks*, or *ranges*, and the corresponding larger sets D are their *domain blocks*, or *domains*. In this scheme we extend $a, \ldots, f$ of our IFS code (16.10) by new parameters s, t, in order to handle a greyscale value $g(x, y)$ at each pixel (x, y). The original (16.10) is extended to include a linear greyscale transformation $g \to sg + t$, resulting in (16.16) below. In this sense s plays the role of a *contrast* factor and t that of an increase in *brightness* (see Section 15.2.1).

$$w: \begin{bmatrix} x \\ y \\ g \end{bmatrix} \to \begin{bmatrix} a & b & 0 \\ c & d & 0 \\ 0 & 0 & s \end{bmatrix} \begin{bmatrix} x \\ y \\ g \end{bmatrix} + \begin{bmatrix} e \\ f \\ t \end{bmatrix}, \tag{16.16}$$

Reserving w for the extended use above, it is useful to retain a notation for the effect on points (x, y):

$$v(x, y) = (ax + by + e, cx + dy + f). \tag{16.17}$$

Let us take greyscale as a height function and model an image as a surface $z = g(x, y)$ over the plane region occupied by the image, where we know g at discrete pixel coordinates. Then the map w of (16.16) sends the portion of the surface lying above D to a surface $w(g)$ lying above R, with height $h = sg(x, y) + t$ at the point $v(x, y)$, as we illustrate in Figure 16.14.

Distinguishing the ranges and their associated domains and parameters by subscripts $i = 1, \ldots, N$, we define the *collage map* W by

$$W(g) = w_1(g) \cup \cdots \cup w_N(g). \tag{16.18}$$

Thus $W(g)$ is a surface over the image region, and hence is a new greyscale version of the image. We call $\{w_1, \ldots, w_N\}$, with its associated domain and range blocks, a *partitioned IFS*, or *PIFS* for the image. The idea is that if $W(h) = h$, at least up to an acceptable approximation, then under mild conditions shortly discussed under 'Some theory', the

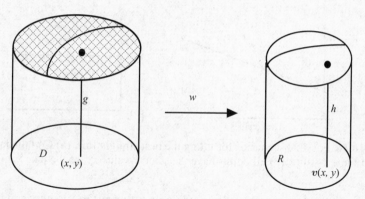

Figure 16.14 The greyscale surface g above domain D defines a surface h above R whose height at $v(x, y)$ is a linear function of g, namely $sg(x, y) + t$.

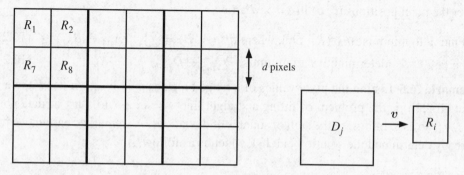

Figure 16.15 Each domain D_j is a 2×2 array of range blocks which is transformed to some range block R_i.

true greyscale h is recovered from any initial scale g by

$$\text{if } W(h) = h \text{ then } W^n(g) \to h. \tag{16.19}$$

First implementation It is helpful first to explore one simple implementation, illustrating how s and t are chosen. There are to be no rotations, reflections or shear; only scaling and translation, so $b = c = 0$ in (16.17). The image is partitioned into equal square range blocks of size $d \times d$, say, and each candidate domain consists of a 2×2 *array of range blocks*, such as that shown in Figure 16.15. The domains also partition the image.

Now we number the domains, say row by row from $j = 1$ to M. Restricting domain-to-range transformations to *scaling by 1/2, then translation into position*, we may specify a transform w of type (16.16) in the form

$$(j, t, s) = (\text{domain no, offset, scale}), \tag{16.20}$$

where D_j is the domain whose $2d \times 2d$ grey values transform as nearly as possible into the $d \times d$ values of range block R. Some details remain to be specified. Firstly, we are involved in mapping 2×2 arrays of pixels to single pixels, so one possibility is to down-sample, taking the top left of the four pixel values, before applying $g \to sg + t$.

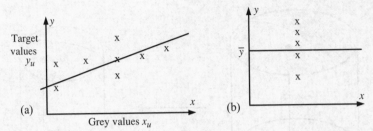

Figure 16.16 Possible scenarios for fitting the best straight line. (a) Certain data points have the same x-value, (b) all points have the same x-value x_u, so we take $x_u \to \bar{y}$.

However, a method that better utilises available information and hence may give better results is to reduce the four to their average. Suppose this converts D_j to $\bar{D}_j$. The code (16.20) for a range block R is determined in two stages, where summation takes place over the pixel positions (p, q) in a $d \times d$ array.

Find j to minimise $dist(R, \bar{D}_j)$, where $dist(A, B) = \sum_{p,q}(A_{pq} - B_{pq})^2$,   (16.21a)

determine s, t to minimise $\sum_{p,q}[s(\bar{D}_j)_{pq} + t - R_{pq}]^2$.   (16.21b)

Remark 16.5 Listing the pixel values of a range block as $u = 1, \ldots, n \, (= d^2)$, we see that (16.21b) is the problem of fitting a straight line $y = sx + t$ to a list of data points (x_u, y_u) so as to minimise the sum of squares of deviations. As remarked earlier, we have already determined the solution (11.17), which is as follows.

Letting

$$\bar{x} = (1/n)\sum_u x_u, \qquad \bar{y} = (1/n)\sum_u y_u,$$
$$S_{xy} = \sum_u x_u y_u - n\bar{x}\,\bar{y}, \qquad S_{xx} = \sum_u x_u^2 - n\bar{x}^2,$$

we set

$$s = S_{xy}/S_{xx}, \quad t = \bar{y} - s\bar{x}.$$ (16.22)

Two comments are in order. Firstly, the grey values x_u need not be distinct, so there may be clusters of data points in the same vertical line, as depicted in Figure 16.16. However, this does not invalidate (16.22). Secondly, because $S_{xx} = \sum_u(x_u - \bar{x})^2$ this quantity can be zero, but only if all x_u are the same. In this case we get the scenario depicted in Figure 16.16(b), and it is appropriate to take $s = 0$ and $t = \bar{y}$.

Example 16.6 We encode the image (a) ('Elleke') of Figure 16.17. For iteration/decoding, the initial image was that shown at (b), quite unlike the original. Notice that, even after only one iteration, the coded image is emerging; still more so with the smaller range block size $d = 4$. Of course, halving the range size quadruples the number of ranges and hence also the space used for encoding.

Example 16.7 (*Encoding the ranges for Elleke*) For the purpose of illustration it is convenient to take range blocks of size $d = 16$ pixels. The (square) image for encoding has size 128, so there are 8^2 such ranges, and 4^2 domains of size $2d = 32$. Part of the

Table 16.3. *PIFS codes for the first few ranges in Example 16.7, Figure 16.17.*

range	domain	offset	scale	range	domain	offset	scale
1	3	218	−0.007	9	10	−6	0.857
2	3	220	−0.034	10	10	−6	1.098
3	2	56	0.461	11	6	123	0.123
4	13	51	0.625	12	6	123	0.160
5	3	−3	0.863	13	3	4	0.889
6	3	215	0.050	14	3	215	0.046
7	3	230	−0.010	15	4	49	0.772
8	3	220	0.033	16	10	8	1.054

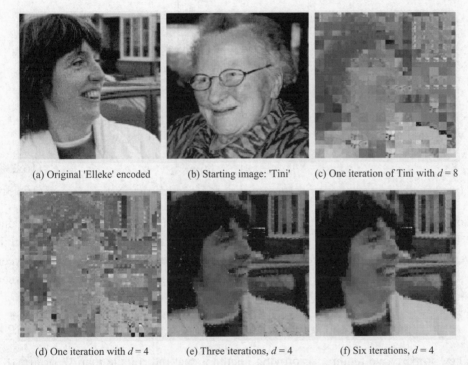

(a) Original 'Elleke' encoded   (b) Starting image: 'Tini'   (c) One iteration of Tini with $d = 8$

(d) One iteration with $d = 4$ (e) Three iterations, $d = 4$ (f) Six iterations, $d = 4$

Figure 16.17 (a) Image to be encoded, (b) initial image for iterated decoding, (c) result after single iteration step with 8×8 range block, (d) result after re-encoding with $d = 4$ and performing a single iteration.

code is shown in Table 16.3, with range numbers added. The original first row contained a header in the present implementation, in which the blocks are numbered row by row upwards relative to the displayed images. Figure 16.18 illustrates the code $(13, 51, 0.625)$ for range number 4.

Some theory of PIFSs Notice that in defining a PIFS we did not require that the plane transform parts $v(x, y)$, defined in (16.17), should be contractive. Indeed, because each w maps a vertical line of points over (x, y) to a vertical line over $v(x, y)$ (see Figure 16.14),

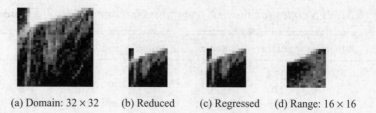

(a) Domain: 32×32 (b) Reduced   (c) Regressed   (d) Range: 16×16

Figure 16.18 Case of 16×16 sized range blocks. The range (d) is from Elleke's collar, and the best domain, (a), found for it is top left in the image (edge of hair).

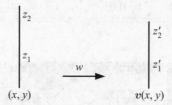

Figure 16.19 The map w brings points together in a vertical line.

it is enough that w be *z-contractive* (for details see Fisher, 1995). That is, if $w(x, y, z_1) = (x', y', z_1')$ and $w(x, y, z_2) = (x', y', z_2')$, then, as depicted in Figure 16.19,

$$|z_1' - z_2'| \leq r|z_1 - z_2|, \text{ or} \tag{16.23a}$$

$$|f(v(x, y)) - g(v(x, y))| \leq r|f(x, y) - g(x, y)|, \tag{16.23b}$$

for some r with $0 \leq r < 1$. For example, the *scale* column of Table 16.3 contains a value of r for each case of w implied. Inspection shows that two values slightly exceed 1; however, in practice this suffices for our purposes. We define the *distance d* between greyscale surfaces f, g over the *image area, I*, to be the greatest vertical spacing between them:

$$d(f, g) = \text{Max}_I |f(x, y) - g(x, y)|. \tag{16.24}$$

The key property we require for proving results is that the collage map W of (16.18), converting a surface f to a new surface $W(f)$ over the image area, is *contractive* in that, for any surfaces f, g over I,

$$d(W(f), W(g)) \leq \alpha d(f, g) \tag{16.25}$$

for some fixed α in the interval $0 \leq \alpha < 1$. Both here and in (16.23) the least parameter (r or α) for which the inequality holds is called the *contractivity or contraction ratio*. For an individual transformation by a matrix M this is the greatest eigenvalue of $M^T M$; see (8.35). Here is the theorem that says the PIFS method must decode to the exact original if we have the w_i exactly right – we'll deal with the approximation issue after that.

Theorem 16.8 *Let W be the collage map of a PIFS whose maps w_i are z-contractive with ratios r_i. Then W is contractive with ratio at most $\alpha = \text{Max}_i(r_i)$. Consequently, there is a unique surface $\mathcal{A}$ left unchanged by W and, for any initial surface g,*

$$W^n(g) \to \mathcal{A}. \tag{16.26}$$

Proof We observe that the height of $W(f)$ at (x, y) is denoted by $W(f)(x, y)$, and that the range R_i has domain D_i. Some D_i may coincide (cf. Table 16.3), but this is not a problem. As usual, I denotes the image region in the (x, y)-plane. We have

$$
\begin{aligned}
d(w(f), W(g)) &= \underset{(x,y)\in I}{\text{Max}} |W(f)(x, y) - W(g)(x, y)| \\
&= \underset{i}{\text{Max}} \underset{(x,y)\in R_i}{\text{Max}} |W(f)(x, y) - W(g)(x, y)| && \text{since } I = \cup_i R_i \\
&= \underset{i}{\text{Max}} \underset{(x,y)\in D_i}{\text{Max}} |f(v_i(x, y)) - g(v_i(x, y))| && \text{since } R_i = v_i(D_i) \\
&\leq \underset{i}{\text{Max}} \underset{(x,y)\in D_i}{\text{Max}} r_i|f(x, y) - g(x, y)| && \text{by (16.23b)} \\
&\leq \underset{i}{\text{Max}} \underset{(x,y)\in D_i}{\text{Max}} \alpha|f(x, y) - g(x, y)| && \text{since } \alpha = \underset{i}{\text{Max}}(r_i) \\
&= \alpha \underset{i}{\text{Max}} \underset{(x,y)\in D_i}{\text{Max}} |f(x, y) - g(x, y)| && \text{since } \alpha \text{ is constant} \\
&= \alpha \underset{(x,y)\in \cup_i D_i}{\text{Max}} |f(x, y) - g(x, y)| \\
&\leq \alpha \underset{(x,y)\in I}{\text{Max}} |f(x, y) - g(x, y)| && \text{since } \cup_i D_i \subseteq I \\
&= \alpha d(f, g) && \text{by definition of } d(f, g).
\end{aligned}
$$

The argument from here on is identical to that which derives (16.26) for the IFS case from the Banach Fixed Point Theorem. The topological details are omitted because they would take us too far afield, but they are developed in full in Hoggar (1992). However, we will prove the important Corollary 16.10.

Remarks 16.9 (i) The surface $\mathcal{A}$ in Theorem 16.8 is called the *attractor* of the PIFS, because $W^n(g) \to \mathcal{A}$. (ii) In practice, although we would like to find a PIFS for our target surface h, our best efforts produce an IFS for which $\mathcal{A}$ is only an approximation to h. Can we be sure that getting $W(h)$ close enough to h will ensure that $\mathcal{A}$ is close enough to the desired h? The following corollary answers in the affirmative.

Corollary 16.10 *(The Collage Theorem) With the hypotheses of Theorem 16.8, we have that if a surface g satisfies $d(g, W(g)) \leq \varepsilon$ then*

$$d(\mathcal{A}, g) \leq \frac{\varepsilon}{1 - \alpha}. \tag{16.27}$$

Proof We need the fact that d satisfies the distance axioms derived in Table 16.4. For brevity, write $g_n = W^n(g)$. This entails $g_0 = g$ and $d(g_n, g_{n+1}) = d(W(g_{n-1}), W(g_n)) \leq$

$\alpha d(g_{n-1}, g_n)$ (by Theorem 16.8) $\leq \alpha^2 d(g_{n-2}, g_{n-1})$, and so on. Therefore,

$$d(g_0, g_n) \leq d(g_0, g_1) + d(g_1, g_2) + \cdots + d(g_{n-1}, g_n) \qquad \text{see Table 16.4(iii)}$$

$$\leq d(g_0, g_1) + \alpha d(g_0, g_1) + \cdots + \alpha^{n-1} d(g_0, g_1) \quad \text{as observed}$$

$$= d(g_0, g_1)(1 + \alpha + \cdots + \alpha^{n-1})$$

$$= d(g_0, g_1)(1 - \alpha^n)/(1 - \alpha) \qquad\qquad \text{by the sum of a G.P.}$$

$$\leq \varepsilon(1 - \alpha^n)/(1 - \alpha) \qquad\qquad\qquad \text{since } d(g_0, g_1)$$

$$= d(g, W(g)) \leq \varepsilon.$$

Now let $n \to \infty$, so that $g_n = W^n(g_0) \to \mathcal{A}$ by (16.26) and also $\alpha^n \to 0$. This yields $d(g_0, \mathcal{A}) \leq \varepsilon/(1 - \alpha)$, as required.

Table 16.4. *The Distance Axioms for d(f, g).*

> (i) $d(f, g) \geq 0$ always, and $d(f, g) = 0$ implies $f = g$.
> (ii) $d(f, g) = d(g, f)$.
> (iii) $d(f, h) \leq d(f, g) + d(g, h)$ (The Triangle Inequality).
>
> *Proof* We apply the definition of d to the following respective observations for
>   any point x:
> (i) $0 \leq |f(x) - g(x)|$,   (ii) $|f(x) - g(x)| = |g(x) - f(x)|$,
> (iii) $|f(x) - h(x)| = |[f(x) - g(x)] + [g(x) - h(x)]|$
> $$\leq |f(x) - g(x)| + |g(x) - h(x)|.$$

Notice that our theory of PIFS allowed for a wider class of plane transformations than were included in Example 16.6, notably rotation and reflection, indeed anything *affine*, as defined by (16.17). We now consider such further options, of which some go beyond the partition restriction (though remaining within the IFS framework). Our motivations are accuracy and speed.

Sources of more accurate domains

 (i) *Bigger images* The small, 128-square images in Figure 16.17 illustrate a shortage of domains. As a general principle, larger images offer more scope for the across-scale similarity we need for accurately matching domain to range.

(ii) *Overlapping domains* So far our domains have exactly tiled the image. Another possibility is to double the number of domains in each direction by starting a new domain at each range position. This improves fitting, at a cost of two more bits to record the domain number for each range.

(iii) *Using symmetries of the square* Each original domain can provide up to eight possible fits with a range if we compose the original w_i with a symmetry of the square, that is, an isometry that sends the square onto itself. These are the multiples of a 1/4 turn about the square's centre, and (see Figure 16.20) reflections in its four axes of symmetry. Together they are called the *dihedral group* D_8 (see Section 2.4). We give the formulae required for implementation in Table 16.5.

Table 16.5. *The symmetries of a $d \times d$ square in terms of centre Cartesian coordinates (x, y) and row, column numbers (r, c), where $1 \leq r, c \leq d$. The reflection $R_{y=0}$ in the x-axis changes the sign of y but converts r to $\bar{r}$, where $\bar{r} = d + 1 - r$.*

symmetry	1/4 turn	1/2 turn	3/4 turn	$R_{y=0}$	$R_{y=x}$	$R_{x=0}$	$R_{y=-x}$
$(x, y) \rightarrow$	$(-y, x)$	$(-x, -y)$	$(y, -x)$	$(x, -y)$	(y, x)	$(-x, y)$	$(-y, -x)$
$(r, c) \rightarrow$	$(c, \bar{r})$	$(\bar{r}, \bar{c})$	$(\bar{c}, r)$	$(\bar{r}, c)$	(c, r)	$(r, \bar{c})$	$(\bar{c}, \bar{r})$

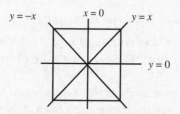

Figure 16.20 The axes of symmetry of a square centred at the origin. Other symmetries are given by multiples of a quarter turn.

Domain pools for speed

The idea of a *domain pool*, or library of available domains, is that they be classified according to a pre-determined system, before range-by-range encoding starts. Then each range in turn is classified and compared only with domains in the same class. This can greatly cut down the search for best domain. Early pioneers of this approach were Jacquin (1989), who classified domains as, for example, *flat*, *edge* or *texture*, and Jacobs *et al.* (1990) (see also Fisher, 1995).

An easily described method used by the latter is to compare the four quadrants of a square for (a) *mean brightness* and (b) *variance* (estimated as standard deviation) of brightness. If the quadrants comprise four levels then these can appear in $4 \times 3 \times 2 \times 1 = 24$ orders. However, each order is converted into eight others (including itself) by the rotations and reflections comprising D_8, as we described in (iii) above. This reduces the classification to the three classes represented in Figure 16.21. The possible permutations of brightness *variance* then raise this to $3 \times 24 = 72$ classes.

Exercise Find another representative for class (a) of Figure 16.21.

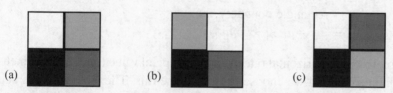

Figure 16.21 Representatives of the three classes of domain determined by mean brightness of each quadrant. None can be changed into another by an element of D_8, the group of symmetries of the square (1/4 turns and reflections).

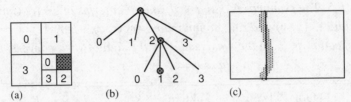

Figure 16.22 (a) A square twice subdivided, (b) corresponding part of the quadtree in which the top node represents the outer square, (c) HV partitioning of a rectangle close to an edge region (see (ii) HV partitioning).

Subdividing the ranges

We note two main methods for subdividing a range if closeness of fit to a domain cannot be obtained within some threshold. Further details are given in Fisher (1995).

(i) *Quadtree partitioning* We recursively divide as follows: if the rms difference between the current square and every candidate domain exceeds a chosen threshold, then subdivide the square into its quadrants. The subdivisions are recorded in a tree in which every node represents a square portion of the image and, if subdivision is made, has four subnodes corresponding to the quadrants numbered 0, 1, 2, 3 in, say, clockwise order (see Figure 16.22).

 We start with a tree of fixed depth, so that the image is already subdivided into equal squares, the image itself being represented by the root, and place some limit on the depth of subdivision. The domain pool has a judicious choice of domains of varying sizes, and a candidate domain is always twice the size of the range.

(ii) *HV partitioning* This is a way of subdividing ranges which adapts more flexibly, and hence more effectively, than the quadtree method. This flexibility is found in the method being:

 (a) not restricted to squares – rectangles are allowed,
 (b) not restricted to division into equal quadrants.

Positively, a rectangle is split by a horizontal or vertical line corresponding to the most edge-like part of the rectangular pixel array, with a bias towards the centre. The following search for a best vertical line (Figure 16.22(c)) is repeated analogously for the horizontal, then the better of the two is taken. With rectangle columns numbered from 0 to $W - 1$ we compute

$$c_j = \text{the mean pixel value in column } j,$$
$$bias(j) = \text{Min}(j, W - j - 1)/(W - 1), \text{ normalised distance to the}$$
$$\text{rectangle boundary,}$$
$$v_j = |c_j - c_{j+1}| \times bias(j).$$

Then v_j represents a horizontal rate of change of pixel value times a bias which increases towards the centre, and we choose j to maximise this. Thus, other things being equal, we prefer to divide at the centre, but the system responds to evidence of edges nearer the rectangle boundary too. A domain pool of rectangles is chosen, and a range may be fitted by a domain of two or three times the size independently in either direction. A classification scheme similar to Figure 16.21 is incorporated, with symmetries of the square reduced to those of a rectangle (identity, 1/2 turn, horizontal and vertical reflections), hence yielding six classes rather than three.

Further developments

(i) *Archetypes* (Boss and Jacobs, 1991) One seeks the member of a set best able to cover the rest. This ties in with *vector quantization*, as we shall see under 'Artificial Neural Networks' in Chapter 18.

(ii) *Orthonormal bases* (Vines and Hayes, 1994) Here we represent a pixel array as a long vector and a PIFS code becomes a matrix of corresponding size. Range blocks are coded by projection onto an orthonormal basis constructed by the Gram–Schmidt method (see Definition 7.17 and Section 7.4.3). The number of basis vectors required is minimised, reducing dimensionality of the procedure and leading to improved compression and decoding speed.

(iii) *Non-deterministic finite automata* This approach of Culik and Kari (1993) is integrated by them with a wavelet approach, to produce results better than those obtained by either method separately (wavelets are introduced in the next section).

(iv) *Fractal compression for images with texture*, see Obrador *et al.* (1995).

Comparison with JPEG

We compare Fractal Image Compression, or FIC, with the JPEG system based on the Discrete Cosine Transform, or DCT, details of the latter system being covered in Chapter 15. The general criteria will be speed, quality and compression ratio. For a wider ranging comparison, see Anson (1993).

(1) *Speed* Whereas JPEG encodes and decodes in similar times, the FIC is asymmetrical in this respect. One example generated the following times, in seconds.

	JPEG	FIC
Encode	41	480
Decode	41	7

Since then times have much decreased, but the situation so far is that FIC comes into its own when used for image databases, where encoding time is less important than decoding. An oft cited example is the 10000 FIC images of Microsoft's Encarta multimedia encyclopaedia. We come next to some benefits of FIC – why should it be used anyway?

(2) *Zooming* Displaying a JPEG image at higher resolution than its original encoding causes artifacts to appear. This is not generally true for FIC; where detail is absent due to scaling it fills in with a result more acceptable to the human eye (to double the resolution we double the plane translation parts of the PIFS codes). Thus FIC may be used for a wider range of scales without the necessity for re-scanning at higher resolutions.

(3) *Edge reproduction* Compression via JPEG/DCT means assuming that higher frequencies are less important. This unsharpens edges, sometimes creating a ripple effect. Not being subject to this limitation, FIC is better at handling edges.

(4) *Compression* A photographic quality image can be compressed by JPEG in the ratio 20–25 to 1 without degradation observable by the human eye, whereas FIC is able to achieve up to 100 : 1 where there is a large affine redundancy it can take advantage of. Furthermore, degradation and breakdown, when they occur, will generally continue to present a more natural appearance with FIC than with JPEG.

Postscript Though fractal encoding is slower than could be desired, much progress in both encoding and decoding speeds continues to be made, such as is reported in the papers of 'Further developments' above. We mention too the interesting work of McGregor *et al.* (1996).

16.2 Wavelets

Wavelets relate both to the previous section in using the idea of varied scale and to the previous chapter, Fourier Transforms, in the provision of a basis for the transform which is at once an insight-provider and a practical tool. Wavelets provide a basis which picks out information, not at varying freqencies but at different scales. To give a broad hint of this, let V^j be a space of functions which provide detail up to a resolution of 2^{-j} units, where $V^0 \subseteq V^1 \subseteq V^2 \subseteq \cdots$. We envisage expressing an image function to best approximation as a linear combination of basis functions of V^j.

This means that better resolution is obtained as we proceed from using V^j to using V^{j+1}. The step is accomplished through basis functions additional to those of V^j, called wavelets: $\psi_0^j, \psi_1^j, \ldots$; the function is corrected by multiples of these. Furthermore, and a reason wavelet families can be hard to discover, these *level j* wavelets may be obtained for each j from a *mother wavelet* ψ by scaling and translation,

$$\psi_i{}^j(x) = \psi(2^j x - i).$$

In a similar manner, the basis functions for V^j must be derivable from a so-called *scaling function* ϕ (sometimes called a father wavelet). The sequence of V^j is said to provide a *multiresolution* approach.

A few types of wavelet were in use long before the name for them arose naturally in 1975 work on seismic waves (see e.g. Hubbard, 1996). The functions of Gabor (1946) are amongst the first, and we shall discuss them in their place. Those due to Haar (1955) may be regarded as the simplest case in several families known; in particular the wavelet family introduced by Daubechies which has proved so effective in applications (see Section 16.3). We begin with the Haar case and apply it to the compression of images.

16.2.1 The Haar approach

Like the N-point DFT and DCT of Chapter 15, the Haar transform is linear, $f \to Mf$, where M is a matrix whose rows form an orthogonal basis of N-space. However, compared with the frequency tuning supplied by the former transforms, the Haar version captures fine geometrical detail, down to a level governed by the value of N. The scale changes are *octaves*, or multiples of 2. Further, for each scale there is a basis vector element corresponding to every possible position.

Consider a 1D image of N pixels over the half-open interval $[0, 1) = \{x : 0 \le x < 1\}$. Let us regard the profile of pixel values $[a_0 \ldots a_{N-1}]$ as a piecewise constant function on $[0, 1)$, in which each constant a_i is the function's value over a subinterval of width $1/N$.

Our transform is built from repetitions of the case $N = 2$, in which a key observation is that $[a_0 a_1]$ can be recovered from its *mean* $m = (1/2)(a_0 + a_1)$, and *half-difference*, or *detail coefficient* $d = (1/2)(a_0 - a_1)$, as

$$[a_0 \quad a_1] = [m + d \quad m - d] = m \times [1 \quad 1] + d \times [1 \quad -1]. \tag{16.28}$$

At every level we replace successive pairs like a_0, a_1 by their mean m together with a detail coefficient d specifying how far a_0 and a_1 differ from their mean. For reconstruction, the pair m, d reverts to $m + d, m - d$.

Example 16.11 Case $N = 4$. Here is the result for pixel values $[10 \quad 6 \quad 1 \quad 3]$, with *means* shown in the first vertical list and detail coefficients in the second.

10	6	1	3	(Detail coefficients)	
	8		2	2	−1
		5		3	

For the first scaling level we replace 10, 6 by mean 8 and detail coefficient 2; similarly 1, 3 becomes 2 with coefficient −1. At the last level, the pair 8, 2 becomes mean 5 and detail coefficient 3. Reconstruction begins with overall mean 5 converted by coefficient 3 to 8, 2 through the formulation $m, d \to m + d, m - d$. Then coefficients 2, −1 are used similarly to convert respectively 8 to 10, 6 and 2 to 1, 3. Now we express the process in terms of basis vectors, resulting in the build-up of Table 16.6.

Exercise Transform and then reconstruct the 1D image [9 6 5 3] similarly to Example 16.11.

Deriving basis functions

To recapitulate, we are looking for a basis which will define the Haar Transform. Returning to (16.28), we may write $[a_0 \quad a_1] = m\phi(x) + d\psi(x)$, where ϕ is a unit box function and ψ a *split box*, defined to be zero except for

$$\phi(x) = 1, \quad \text{if} \quad 0 \le x < 1,$$
$$\psi(x) = \begin{cases} 1, & \text{if} \quad 0 \le x < 1/2, \\ -1, & \text{if} \quad 1/2 \le x < 1. \end{cases} \tag{16.29}$$

We move from one scale level to the next by the halving process of (16.28). At level j the unit interval is divided into 2^j subintervals of width $(1/2)^j = 2^{-j}$, so we need versions of ϕ and ψ scaled horizontally to take their nonzero values on precisely such intervals, and also translated so as to be nonzero on the ith interval for suitable i. These 2^{-j}-sized boxes and split boxes are illustrated in Figure 16.23 and formally defined as follows:

$$\boxed{\begin{aligned} \phi_i^j(x) &= \phi(2^j x - i), \\ \psi_i^j(x) &= \psi(2^j x - i), \end{aligned} \quad (0 \le i < 2j).} \tag{16.30}$$

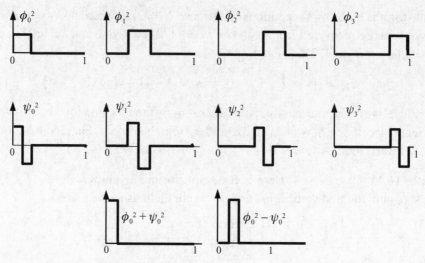

Figure 16.23 Box and split box functions (wavelets) in the case $j = 2$. The first row form a basis for the space V^2. Comparing a box with its split version in row 2 we see that $\phi_i^2 \pm \psi_i^2$ give half-width boxes as in row 3. Hence the first two rows together span V^3.

These are correct, because, for example, $\phi_i^j(x) = 1 \Leftrightarrow 0 \leq 2^j x - i < 1 \Leftrightarrow i \leq 2^j x < (i+1) \Leftrightarrow i \cdot 2^{-j} \leq x < (i+1) \cdot 2^{-j}$, that is, x lies in the ith subinterval of width 2^{-j}; and simply splits this interval into a positive and a negative half. Those derived from ψ are now known as *wavelets* of ψ.

16.2.2 The box basis and multiresolution

For $N = 2^j$ the function/pixel profile $[a_0 \ldots a_{N-1}]$ takes value a_i on the ith subinterval and so it equals a unique linear combination of boxes $\sum_i a_i \phi_i^j$. That is to say $\{\phi_i^j\}_{0 \leq i < 2^j}$ form a basis of the space V^j of such functions, the *box basis*. In fact, the case $j = 2$ (subinterval width $1/4$) is the first row of Figure 16.23.

Further, V^j *is contained in* V^{j+1} because a function constant on the ith subinterval is constant on its two half-width subintervals. We thus have the sequence

$$V^0 \subseteq V^1 \subseteq V^2 \subseteq \cdots, \tag{16.31}$$

which is called a *multiresolution*, because as j increases the relevant subintervals become smaller and so we can better approximate a function on $[0, 1)$ by one in V^j. An example is given in Table 16.6, further ahead. We need to extend slightly the idea of an inner product of N-vectors to that of two functions f, g on $[0, 1)$, namely

$$\langle f, g \rangle = \int_0^1 f(x)g(x)dx, \tag{16.32}$$

provided they are square-integrable, that is $\langle f, f \rangle$ is a well-defined non-negative number so that we can write $\|f\| = \langle f, f \rangle^{1/2}$ just as for ordinary vectors. (More generally, we integrate over a common interval of definition of f and g.) Now, if $i \neq k$ then the box functions ϕ_i^j and ϕ_k^j are never nonzero simultaneously (Figure 16.23), so they are *orthogonal*, or in symbols $\langle \phi_i{}^j, \phi_k{}^j \rangle = 0$. But if $i = k$ they are both 1 precisely on the ith subinterval, hence

$$\langle \phi_i^j, \phi_i^j \rangle = \text{area of } (2^{-j} \times 1) \text{ box} = 2^{-j}. \tag{16.33}$$

Thus $\{\phi_i^j\}_{0 \leq i < 2^j}$ is an orthogonal basis of V^j. Indeed, $\{2^{j/2}\phi_i^j\}$ is an ONB, or orthonormal basis, with members not only orthogonal but of unit length.

The next level

As noted after (16.29), Equation (16.28) indicates the way to move from one level of detail V^j to the next by using split-box functions ψ_i^j. As may be seen from Figure 16.23, for example, $\phi_i^2 + \psi_i^2 = 2\phi_{2i}^3$ and $\phi_i^2 - \psi_i^2 = 2\phi_{2i+1}^3$. The same diagram at half the scale size shows that functions ϕ_i^4 may be determined from $\phi_i^3 \pm \psi_i^3$, the previous superscripts being increased by 1. We need the following auxiliary result.

Theorem 16.12 (a) ψ_i^j and ψ_p^k are orthogonal unless they are identical, when $\|\psi_i^j\|^2 = 2^{-j}$. (b) For fixed j, every ψ_i^j is orthogonal to the elements of V^{j+1}.

Proof (a) If $j = k$ but $i \neq p$ the two functions are never nonzero simultaneously, so their inner product (16.32) is zero. If $j < k$ and the functions are nonzero on a common interval then the kth takes values ± 1 where the other is constant, hence the integral consists of two areas of opposite sign summing to zero (Figure 16.24). Also, $\langle \psi_i^j, \psi_i^j \rangle = $ area of a $(2^{-j} \times 1)$ box $= 2^{-j}$. Part (b) is similar since we only need to show that ψ_i^j is orthogonal to our box basis functions for V^j.

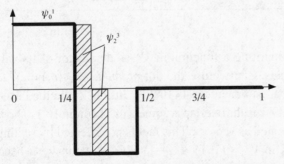

Figure 16.24 The inner product (16.32) of split boxes from different scales is zero because, where they are both nonzero, one is constant and the other is $+1$ and -1 over equal intervals. Here both are nonzero on $[2/8, 3/8]$, and the product is $(1)(1/16) + (-1)(1/16) = 0$.

Corollary 16.13 *Let W^j be the space spanned by $\{\psi_i{}^j\}_{0 \le i < 2^j}$. Then these functions are an orthogonal basis of W^j, and*

$$V^j \oplus W^j = V^{j+1}. \tag{16.34a}$$

The equality says that every function in V^{j+1} is a unique sum $f + g$ of functions f in V^j and g in W^j. Theorem 16.12(b) reveals that f, g are orthogonal. It follows by applying this equality with $j = 0, 1, 2, \ldots$ that

$$V^j = V^0 \oplus W^0 \oplus W^1 \oplus \cdots \oplus W^{j-1}, \tag{16.34b}$$

and an ONB for V^j is given by ϕ_0^0 and $\{2^{k/2}\psi_i^k\}$ for $0 \le k < j, 0 \le i < 2^k$.

Example 16.14 With the data of Example 16.11 we build up the function [10 6 1 3] through the increasing resolutions V^j, by adding on the computed components of the wavelet (split box) basis functions ψ_i^j. The stages are shown in Table 16.6. They illustrate $V^2 = V^0 \oplus W^0 \oplus W^1$ and $f = 5\phi_0^0 + 3\psi_0^0 + 2\psi_0^1 - \psi_1^1$.

Table 16.6. *Adding on wavelet components up to the maximum resolution, in Example 16.14.*

summand		result	resolution
$5 \times$		$=$	in V^0
$+3\times$		$=$	in V^1
$+2 \times$			in V^2
$-1 \times$		$=$	

As vectors We are writing a function in V^k as the vector of its values on successive 2^{-k} wide subintervals. Can we use the dot product $(a_i) \cdot (b_i) = \sum a_i b_i$ instead of the all-encompassing but harder integral (16.32)? Inside V^k lie the basis functions ϕ_0^0 and $\{2^{k/2}\psi_i^k\}$ ($j \le k - 1$), and the overlap argument of Theorem 16.12 shows that they remain orthogonal when treated as vectors. This fact is not affected by scaling; for example the dot product $\phi_0^0 \cdot \psi_0^0$ in V^1 is $(1, 1) \cdot (1, -1) = 0$, whilst in V^2 it becomes $(1, 1, 1, 1) \cdot (1, 1, -1, -1)$, which is again zero.

Length The unit interval $[0, 1)$ is divided into 2^k equal parts, so for $j \le k$ the function vectors ϕ_i^j and ψ_i^j have absolute value 1 over an interval of width 2^{-j}, covering

$2^{-j}/2^{-k} = 2^{k-j}$ coordinate positions. Therefore, to maintain unit length they should be normalised by a factor $2^{(j-k)/2}$. The ONB in case $k = 3$ is listed in Figure 16.25.

$$
\begin{aligned}
\phi_0^0 &= (1 \quad 1 \quad 1 \quad 1 \quad 1 \quad 1 \quad 1 \quad +1)/\sqrt{8} \\
\psi_0^0 &= (1 \quad 1 \quad 1 \quad 1 \quad -1 \quad -1 \quad -1 \quad -1)/\sqrt{8} \\
\psi_0^1 &= (1 \quad 1 \quad -1 \quad -1 \quad 0 \quad 0 \quad 0 \quad 0)/\sqrt{4} \\
\psi_1^1 &= (0 \quad 0 \quad 0 \quad 0 \quad 1 \quad 1 \quad -1 \quad -1)/\sqrt{4} \\
\psi_0^2 &= (1 \quad -1 \quad 0 \quad 0 \quad 0 \quad 0 \quad 0 \quad 0)/\sqrt{2} \\
\psi_1^2 &= (0 \quad 0 \quad 1 \quad -1 \quad 0 \quad 0 \quad 0 \quad 0)/\sqrt{2} \\
\psi_2^2 &= (0 \quad 0 \quad 0 \quad 0 \quad 1 \quad -1 \quad 0 \quad 0)/\sqrt{2} \\
\psi_3^2 &= (0 \quad 0 \quad 0 \quad 0 \quad 0 \quad 0 \quad 1 \quad -1)/\sqrt{2}
\end{aligned}
$$

Figure 16.25 The Haar ONB in the case $k = 3$.

16.2.3 The 2D Haar Transform

We recall (Section 15.1.1) the schema for a 1D transform $f \to Mf$, where $M^{-1} = [C_0 \dots C_{N-1}]$, which equals M^T when, as here, the columns C_r form an ONB. Thus M consists of the ONB written as rows $R_i = C_i^T$. The related cases are:

> *One dimension* (f is a vector): $f \to Mf$, the coefficients w.r.t. orthonormal basis $\{C_r\}$.
> *Two dimensions* (f is a matrix): $f \to Mf M^T$, coefficients w.r.t. orthonormal basis $\{C_r C_s^T\}$.

Let $N = 2^k$ and write our basis vectors as N-vectors. We have just listed the case $k = 3$ in Figure 16.25. The consequent 2D version $\{C_r C_s^T\}_{0 \le r,s \le 7}$ is depicted in Figure 16.26.

Orthogonality, coefficient ordering and error (see also under DCT) Here we have linearly ordered the whole 2D array of Haar coefficients and deleted the smallest in absolute value up to various chosen levels, resulting in Figure 16.27. Table 16.7 recalls the theory and ALGO 16.1 implements it for the present purpose.

Table 16.7. *Approximation using an orthonormal basis (ONB).*

Let $e_1, \dots, e_n$ be an ONB and let $f = c_1 e_1 + \cdots + c_n e_n$, with $c_1^2 \le c_2^2 \le \cdots \le c_n^2$. If we drop the first t coefficients, to approximate f by g, the squared error is

$$
\|f - g\|^2 = (f - g) \cdot (f - g) = \left(\sum_{i=1}^t c_i e_i \right) \cdot \left(\sum_{j=1}^t c_j e_j \right)
$$
$$
= \sum_{i,j} c_i c_j e_i \cdot e_j \quad = \sum_{i,j} c_i c_j \delta_{ij} \text{ (ON basis)} = \sum_{i=1}^t c_i^2.
$$

$$
\% \text{ error} = 100 \sqrt{\frac{c_1^2 + \cdots + c_t^2}{c_1^2 + \cdots + c_n^2}}, \quad \% \text{ coefficients used} = 100(n - t)/t.
$$

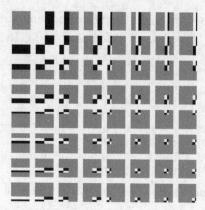

Figure 16.26 Representation of the 8×8 Haar basis, with $1 =$ white, $0 =$ grey, and $-1 =$ black, except in the top left basis element, with the constant 1 shown as grey. We may compare the corresponding diagram for the DCT in Figure 15.42 of the previous chapter.

Original 'Jo'.	1% error, using	5% error, using	10% error, using
(128×128)	55% of coefficients.	12% of coefficients.	3% of coefficients.

Figure 16.27 Compression of this 128×128 image down to 12% of coefficients gives no discernible deterioration. The percentage and sum of squares error are measured as in Table 16.7. Thus, for example, there are 128^2 coefficients to start with.

ALGO 16.1 To approximate f using the transform $f \to M \cdot f \cdot M^{\mathrm{T}}$ with given % error, where M has columns $C_1, \ldots, C_w$.

Function $B_{ij}(p)$ (pth 2D basis element)
$\quad i = 1 + \mathrm{Floor}[(p-1)/w]; \quad j = 1 + (p-1)\mathrm{Mod}\, w$
RETURN $C_i C_j{}^{\mathrm{T}}$

HaarComp(F, percentErr)
$\quad$ For $i, j = 1$ to w do $p = (i-1)w + j; \quad d_p = F_{ij}$ (F becomes w^2-vector $[d_p]$)
$\quad$ Order the pairs (d_p^2, d_p) in ascending order of d_p^2 (new array 'pairs')
$\quad$ $err = 0; \quad threshold = (\sum_p d_p^2)(percentErr/100)^2$
$\quad$ While $err + pairs(1, 1) \leq threshold$ do $err = err + pairs(1, 1)$; delete $pairs(1)$
$\quad$ $f = f - f; \quad nCoeffs = Length\,(pairs)$
$\quad$ For $n = 1$ to $nCoeffs$ do (reconstruct approx. f)
$\quad\quad$ $p = pairs(n, 2); f = f + d_p{}^* B_{ij}(p)$
$\quad$ PRINT(% coefficients used, $100^* nCoeffs/w^2$); RETURN f.

Four wavelet features of Haar

1. $V^0 \subseteq V^1 \subseteq V^2 \subseteq \cdots$ (multiresolution),
2. $V^j \oplus W^j = V^{j+1}$ (W^j = further details).

There are functions ϕ, ψ such that

3. $\{\phi(2^j x - i)\}_{0 \le i < 2^j}$ is a basis of V^j (ϕ = scaling function),
4. $\{\psi(2^j x - i)\}_{0 \le i < 2^j}$ is a basis of W^j (ψ = mother wavelet).

Four properties not possessed by all wavelets, and hard to achieve simultaneously, are that the bases of V^j and W_j be orthogonal, and that ϕ and ψ have *compact support*. The last phrase, for a function f, means that f is zero outside of some finite closed interval $[a, b]$. The least such interval is the actual *support*. Thus the box wavelet ϕ had compact support $[0, 1]$. We shall see how other wavelets fare.

16.3 The Discrete Wavelet Transform

Our second main study leads up to the wavelets discovered by Daubechies (1988, 1992) which have proved to be so successful as the FBI's chosen method of compression for fingerprint data (Brislawn, 1995).

Earlier, in Section 16.2, we performed the Discrete Wavelet Transform, or DWT, in the Haar case, by the standard method of generating an explicit orthonormal basis and projecting coordinate vectors onto it. With basis vectors as rows of a matrix M (which is therefore an orthogonal matrix), the transform becomes $x \to Mx$, with 2D form $g \to MgM^T$ for an array g. We pause here to establish the more general framework of filter banks which do not require orthogonality; it is foundational, a source of insights and techniques in this and the following chapter.

16.3.1 Filter banks for multiresolution

At this point we presuppose only a multiresolution sequence $\{V^j\}$ with complementary wavelet spaces $\{W^j\}$. That is, denoting the dimensions by v_j and w_j, we are given

$$V^0 \subseteq V^1 \subseteq V^2 \subseteq \cdots, \text{ where } V^k \oplus W^k = V^{k+1} \text{ for } k = 0, 1, 2, \ldots, \quad (16.35a)$$

$$v_k = \dim V^k, \quad w_k = \dim W^k \quad \text{(hence } v_k + w_k = v_{k+1}\text{).} \quad (16.35b)$$

To proceed further some choice of bases must be made, but there are no requirements of orthogonality, or the existence of a mother or father wavelet. Thus the $\oplus$ sign here means simply that W^k is a subspace of V_{k+1}, and every element of V_{k+1} is a unique sum $f + g$ of an element f in V^k and an element g in W^k. The first step is to combine the basis elements $\phi_i^j(x)$ of V^j and $\psi_i^j(x)$ of W^j into row vectors:

$$\Phi^j(x) = \begin{bmatrix} \phi_0^j(x) & \phi_1^j(x) & \ldots \end{bmatrix}, \quad (16.36)$$

$$\Psi^j(x) = \begin{bmatrix} \psi_0^j(x) & \psi_1^j(x) & \ldots \end{bmatrix}. \quad (16.37)$$

This notation enables us to express the element of V^j with coordinates $c^j = \begin{bmatrix} c_0^j & c_1^j & \ldots \end{bmatrix}^T$, in the form of a matrix product $\Phi^j(x)c^j$. And similarly for the element of W^j with coordinate vector d^j. In more detail,

$$\sum_i c_i^j \phi_i^j(x) = \Phi^j(x) \cdot c^j \quad \text{(element of } V^j\text{)}, \tag{16.38}$$

$$\sum_i d_i^j \psi_i^j(x) = \Psi^j(x) \cdot d^j \quad \text{(element of } W^j\text{)}. \tag{16.39}$$

On the other hand, $V^{j-1} \subseteq V^j$ from (16.35) implies that every generator of V^{j-1} is a linear combination of those of V^j, say $\phi_i^{j-1}(x) = \sum_k p_{ki} \phi_k^j(x)$ for scalars p_{ki} which together form the elements of a matrix P^j. Similarly $W^{j-1} \subseteq V^j$ implies a coefficient matrix Q^j. Thus in matrix notation

$$\Phi^{j-1}(x) = \Phi^j(x)P^j, \tag{16.40a}$$

$$\Psi^{j-1}(x) = \Phi^j(x)Q^j. \tag{16.40b}$$

The filter bank Figure 16.28 portrays the *filter bank* arising from the multiresolution (16.35) with which we began. It consists of the matrices P^j, Q^j, and the *coordinate vectors* c^j, d^j together with matrices A^j, B^j shortly to be determined, which convert between c^j, d^j as shown. The A, B matrices are designated *analysis matrices*, because they are used to decompose c^j into constituent parts, whilst the P, Q are called *synthesis matrices* since they may be used to reconstitute c^j. The needed formulae are derived in Theorem 16.16, after an example of the P, Q calculation.

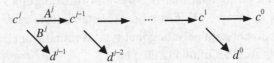

Figure 16.28 Filter bank for a multiresolution. From this we write down the Discrete Wavelet Transform as Equation (16.41). According to (16.35), the vector c^j and its transform have the same number of coordinates. We reverse direction by $c^j = P^j c^{j-1} + Q^j d^{j-1}$.

$$\text{The Discrete Wavelet Transform is } c^j \rightarrow (c^0, d^0, d^1, \ldots, d^{j-1}). \tag{16.41}$$

Example 16.15 We determine P^2 and Q^2 of (16.40) for the Haar wavelets of the previous section. Here $\phi_i^j(x)$ is the box function with value 1 on the interval $2^{-j}[i, i+1)$, so we can read off the required relationships from Figure 16.29.

The notation is $\Phi^1(x) = [\phi_0^1(x) \quad \phi_1^1(x)]$, and $\Phi^2(x) = [\phi_0^2(x) \quad \phi_1^2(x) \quad \phi_2^2(x) \quad \phi_3^2(x)]$, and the figure reveals that $\phi_0^1(x) = \phi_0^2(x) + \phi_1^2(x)$ and $\phi_1^1(x) = \phi_2^2(x) + \phi_3^2(x)$. Expressing this in the form $\Phi^{j-1}(x) = \Phi^j(x)P^j$,

$$[\phi_0^1(x) \quad \phi_1^1(x)] = [\phi_0^2(x) \quad \phi_1^2(x) \quad \phi_2^2(x) \quad \phi_3^2(x)] \begin{bmatrix} 1 & 0 \\ 1 & 0 \\ 0 & 1 \\ 0 & 1 \end{bmatrix} \ (= P^2). \tag{16.42}$$

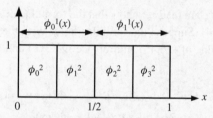

Figure 16.29 Relation between box functions at levels 1 and 2. The diagram indicates where each function takes the value 1 (elsewhere it is zero).

Notice that, on the right hand side of the equality, the columns of this matrix product correspond to the *columns* of the *second* matrix, P^2. It is well to be aware of this fact about matrix products!

The split box function $\psi_i^1(x)$ may be found from the box $\phi_i^1(x)$ by reversing the sign in its right half. Thus, considering Figure 16.29, $\psi_0^1(x) = \phi_0^2(x) - \phi_1^2(x)$ and $\psi_1^1(x) = \phi_2^2(x) - \phi_3^2(x)$. In the notation $\Psi^1(x) = \Phi^2(x)Q^2$, this becomes

$$\begin{bmatrix} \psi_0^1(x) & \psi_1^1(x) \end{bmatrix} = \begin{bmatrix} \phi_0^2(x) & \phi_1^2(x) & \phi_2^2(x) & \phi_3^2(x) \end{bmatrix} \begin{bmatrix} 1 & 0 \\ -1 & 0 \\ 0 & 1 \\ 0 & -1 \end{bmatrix} \quad (= Q^2). \quad (16.43)$$

The filter bank relations The filter bank diagram asserts that we may obtain c^{j-1} and d^{j-1} from c^j by multiplying by respective matrices A^j and B^j, and that we may go in the reverse direction using P^j and Q^j. We now show how this can be arranged.

Theorem 16.16 *(Filter Bank Theorem) The filter matrices A^j and B^j may be defined, and c^j recovered from c^{j-1} and d^{j-1}, by the following relations:*

$$\begin{bmatrix} A^j \\ B^j \end{bmatrix} = \begin{bmatrix} P^j \mid Q^j \end{bmatrix}^{-1}, \quad \text{and hence } c^j = P^j c^{j-1} + Q^j d^{j-1}. \quad (16.44)$$

Proof

(i) *Inverses* Let us establish that $[P^j|Q^j]$ is necessarily invertible. By (16.35b) it is square, so it suffices to show that no nonzero linear combination of the columns of P^j and Q^j can be zero (see Rules 7.28). But by (16.40) such a combination gives $v + w = 0$, where v is in V^{j-1} and w is in W^{j-1}. Then $V^j = V^{j-1} \oplus W^{j-1}$ from (16.35) implies the unique solution $v = w = 0$, so the columns are independent and the matrix is invertible (see Rules 7.28).

(ii) *A uniqueness property* Recall that a coefficient vector c^j defines an element $\Phi^j(x)c^j$ in V^j. But the connection $V^j = V^{j-1} \oplus W^{j-1}$ renders this as a unique sum of an 'averaging' component $\Phi^{j-1}(x)c^{j-1}$ in V^{j-1} plus a 'detail' component $\Psi^{j-1}(x)d^{j-1}$ in W^{j-1}. That is,

$$\Phi^{j-1}(x)c^{j-1} + \Psi^{j-1}(x)d^{j-1} = \Phi^j(x)c^j. \quad (16.45)$$

(iii) With this preparation we are ready to show that the formulae $c^{j-1} = A^j c^j$ and $d^{j-1} = B^j c^j$ are equivalent to (16.44). Suppose the formulae hold. With them we substitute for c^{-1} and d^{j-1} in the left hand side of (16.45) and replace $\Phi^{j-1}(x)$ and $\Psi^{j-1}(x)$ using (16.44). The result is

$$\Phi^j(x)P^j A^j c^j + \Phi^j(x)Q^j B^j c^j = \Phi^j(x)c^j, \text{ or, factorising,}$$
$$\Phi^j(x)(P^j A^j + Q^j B^j)c^j = \Phi^j(x)c^j.$$

Since this is to hold for *all* c^j, we may drop the factor c^j and then, because $\Phi^j(x)$ is a basis,

$$P^j A^j + Q^j B^j = I, \text{ that is } [P^j \,|\, Q^j]\begin{bmatrix} A^j \\ B^j \end{bmatrix} = I. \tag{16.46}$$

Thus the two partitioned matrices are inverses, as in (16.44). Now suppose *conversely* that (16.46) holds. Multiply on the left by $\Phi^j(x)$ and on the right by c^j, and substitute for $\Phi^j(x)P^j$ and $\Phi^j(x)Q^j$ by (16.40) to obtain

$$\Phi^{j-1}(x)(A^j c^j) + \Psi^{j-1}(x)(B^j c^j) = \Phi^j(x)c^j.$$

By the uniqueness of c^{j-1} and d^{j-1} in (16.45), the last equation shows that $A^j c^j = c^{j-1}$ and $B^j c^j \doteq d^{j-1}$, as required. Thus the equivalence is established. Finally, multiply (16.46) on the right by c^j, then replace $A^j c^j$ by c^{j-1} and $B^j c^j$ by d^{j-1} to get $P^j c^{j-1} + Q^j d^{j-1} = c^j$. This completes the proof of Theorem 16.16.

Example 16.17 (*A^2 and B^2 for Haar wavelets*) Example 16.15 supplies P^2 and Q^2 for the Haar case. By Theorem 16.16,

$$\begin{bmatrix} A^2 \\ B^2 \end{bmatrix} = [P^2 \,|\, Q^2]^{-1} = \begin{bmatrix} 1 & 0 & 1 & 0 \\ 1 & 0 & -1 & 0 \\ 0 & 1 & 0 & 1 \\ 0 & 1 & 0 & -1 \end{bmatrix}^{-1}.$$

We could determine the inverse by Cramer's Rule or by row operations (ALGO 8.2), but here it is easily observed that the rows of the matrix $D = [P^2 | Q^2]$ are orthogonal, with common squared length 2. This says that $DD^T = 2I$ and so $D^{-1} = (1/2)D^T$ (see (7.20)). Thus

$$A^2 = \tfrac{1}{2}\begin{bmatrix} 1 & 1 & 0 & 0 \\ 0 & 0 & 1 & 1 \end{bmatrix}, \quad B^2 = \tfrac{1}{2}\begin{bmatrix} 1 & -1 & 0 & 0 \\ 0 & 0 & 1 & -1 \end{bmatrix}, \quad \text{e.g. in Figure 16.28:}$$

$$c^2 = \begin{bmatrix} 1 \\ 2 \\ 3 \\ 4 \end{bmatrix} \begin{array}{l} \xrightarrow{A^2} c^1 = \tfrac{1}{2}\begin{bmatrix} 3 \\ 7 \end{bmatrix} \in V^1, \\[2ex] \xrightarrow{B^2} d^1 = \tfrac{1}{2}\begin{bmatrix} -1 \\ -1 \end{bmatrix} \in W^1. \end{array}$$

Recovery $c^2 = P^2 c^1 + Q^2 d^1$

$$= \begin{bmatrix} 1 & 0 \\ 1 & 0 \\ 0 & 1 \\ 0 & 1 \end{bmatrix} \tfrac{1}{2} \begin{bmatrix} 3 \\ 7 \end{bmatrix} + \begin{bmatrix} 1 & 0 \\ -1 & 0 \\ 0 & 1 \\ 0 & -1 \end{bmatrix} \tfrac{1}{2} \begin{bmatrix} -1 \\ -1 \end{bmatrix}$$

$$= \tfrac{1}{2} \begin{bmatrix} 3 \\ 3 \\ 7 \\ 7 \end{bmatrix} + \tfrac{1}{2} \begin{bmatrix} -1 \\ 1 \\ -1 \\ 1 \end{bmatrix} = \tfrac{1}{2} \begin{bmatrix} 2 \\ 4 \\ 6 \\ 8 \end{bmatrix} = \begin{bmatrix} 1 \\ 2 \\ 3 \\ 4 \end{bmatrix}.$$

The transform (DWT) and its inverse Here are recursive algorithms to calculate the Discrete Wavelet Transform in one dimension, the standard extension to two dimensions (Section 15.1.1), and their inverse transforms. They are based on Table 16.8.

ALGO 16.2. The Discrete Wavelet Transform (DWT)

The recursive routine *dwt(c)* converts the global variable *trans*, initialised empty, to the DWT of *c*. Assumes the matrices A^j and B^j are available.

> *dwt(c)*:
> $j = \log_2 \text{Length}(c)$
> If $j \geq 2$ then extend *trans* by $B^j \cdot c$ and call *dwt*($A^j \cdot c$)
>   else RETURN *trans* extended by $A^1 \cdot c$, $B^1 \cdot c$

> *inverse_dwt(y)*;
> $k = \log_2 \text{Length}[y]$
> function $d[j]$ = elements $2^j + 1$ to 2^{j+1} of y
> function $c[j] = P^j \cdot c[j-1] + Q^j \cdot d[j-1]$ $(j \geq 2)$
> function $c[1] = P^1 \cdot y[1] + Q^1 \cdot y[2]$
> RETURN $c[k]$

2D version: assume array *pic* has rows R_1 to R_K and columns C_1 to C_L. For the inverse, *replace dwt by inverse_dwt*.

> *DWT(pic)*;
> For $i = 1$ to K do $R_i = dwt(R_i)$;
> For $j = 1$ to L do $C_j = dwt(C_j)$;
> RETURN matrix $[C_1 \ldots C_L]$.

Remarks 16.18 We are about to move to our strongest case of multiresolution, orthogonal wavelets. They are a powerful tool, but applications to B-splines and surfaces are powerful in other ways and require varying sets of additional assumptions to the minimalist (16.35). These will be presented in the next chapter.

Table 16.8. *Summary of steps leading to a filter bank, Figure 16.28.*

item	comment
$V^0 \subseteq V^1 \subseteq V^2 \subseteq \cdots$	we start with this nesting of spaces, a multiresolution
$V^j = V^{j-1} \oplus W^{j-1}$	W^{j-1} is called a *complement* of V^{j-1} in V^j
V^j has basis $\Phi^j(x)$	$= \left[\phi_i^j(x) \right], 0 \leq i < v_j$
c^j defines element $\Phi^j(x)c^j$	$= \sum_i c_i^j \phi_i^j(x)$
$\Phi^{j-1}(x) = \Phi^j(x)P^j$	refining relations (defines P^j)
W^{j-1} has basis $\Psi^{j-1}(x)$	
d^{j-1} defines an element $\Psi^{j-1}(x)d^{j-1}$	
$\Psi^{j-1}(x) = \Phi^j(x)Q^j$	
$c^{j-1} = A^j c^j$ and $d^{j-1} = B^j c^j$	analysis filters A^j, B^j
$c^j = P^j c^{j-1} + Q^j d^{j-1}$ (recovery of c^j)	synthesis filters P^j, Q^j

16.3.2 Orthogonal wavelets

So far in Section 16.3 our discussion has been based on the minimal assumptions used for multiresolutions: the existence of the increasing sequence of spaces $\{V_j\}$ and the definition of W^j as some complement of V^j in V^{j+1} with the ramifications outlined in Table 16.8. We now add the three orthogonality possibilities, i.e. that

> V_j and W_j are orthogonal, and their bases are orthonormal.

We throw in what is generally assumed for wavelets, and nearly true for the end-point corrected subdivision wavelets of Chapter 17, namely that the basis functions $\phi_i^j(x)$ may be obtained by *scaling and translation from a single function* $\phi(x)$, and similarly for the $\psi_i^j(x)$. We recall the nomenclature of ϕ as scaling function, sometimes father wavelet, and ψ as mother wavelet. A formal definition follows.

Definition 16.19 We say wavelets derived from a multiresolution are *orthogonal* if, in the notation of Table 16.8, W^j is the *orthogonal* complement to V^j (see also Definition 7.19ff), and there are functions $\phi(x)$ and $\psi(x)$ such that, for each valid j,

$$\Phi^j(x) = \left\{ \phi_i^j(x) \right\} \quad \text{is orthonormal and } \phi_i^j(x) = \phi(2^j x - i), \qquad (16.47)$$

$$\Psi^j(x) = \left\{ \psi_i^j(x) \right\} \quad \text{is orthonormal and } \psi_i^j(x) = \psi(2^j x - i). \qquad (16.48)$$

Gram matrices The lemma below will be extremely useful. Let F be a row vector of functions $f_1, \ldots, f_p$ and let G be a row vector of functions $g_1, \ldots, g_q$. Then $\langle F, G \rangle$ denotes the matrix with $\langle f_r, g_s \rangle$ in the (r, s) place. This $p \times q$ *matrix of inner products* is also known as the *Gram matrix* of F and G. We need to know what happens when the entries of F and G are replaced by linear combinations of their originals. Here is the answer.

Lemma 16.20 *In the notation above, let P, Q be real matrices for which the products FP and GQ exist. Then*

$$\langle FP, GQ \rangle = P^{\mathrm{T}} \langle F, G \rangle Q. \tag{16.49}$$

Proof Let $(C)_{uv}$ be the (u, v) entry of a matrix C, and $(X)_u$ the uth entry of a vector X. Then we must show that the two sides of Equation (16.49) have equal (u, v) entries for arbitrary permissible u, v. This is achieved as follows.

$$
\begin{aligned}
(\langle FP, GQ \rangle)_{uv} &= \langle (FP)_u, (GQ)_v \rangle & \text{by definition of} \langle, \rangle \\
&= \langle \textstyle\sum_r f_r (P)_{ru}, \sum_s g_s (Q)_{sv} \rangle & \text{matrix multiplication} \\
&= \textstyle\sum_{r,s} (P)_{ru} (Q)_{sv} \langle f_r, g_s \rangle & \text{by linearity} \\
&= \textstyle\sum_{r,s} (P^{\mathrm{T}})_{ur} (\langle F, G \rangle)_{rs} (Q)_{sv} & \text{by definition of } P^{\mathrm{T}} \text{ and } \langle, \rangle \\
&= (P^{\mathrm{T}} \langle F, G \rangle Q)_{uv} & \text{by (7.17b).}
\end{aligned}
$$

Sometimes it is convenient to work with bases that are only orthogonal and to insert scaling factors at a later stage. We allow for this in the following formulation of first implications of orthogonality for wavelets (we do not yet use the existence of the father or mother wavelet).

Theorem 16.21 *Assume the spaces V^j and W^j are orthogonal to each other. Write P for P^j and Q for Q^j. If the bases of V^j and W^j are both orthonormal then $[P|Q]$ is an orthogonal matrix, i.e. $A^j = P^{\mathrm{T}}$, $B^j = Q^{\mathrm{T}}$, and $P^{\mathrm{T}} Q = 0$ ($= Q^{\mathrm{T}} P$). If the bases are orthogonal with respective constant squared lengths λ_j and μ_j, then*

$$P^{\mathrm{T}} P = (\lambda_{j-1}/\lambda_j) I, \quad \text{and} \quad Q^{\mathrm{T}} Q = (\mu_{j-1}/\mu_j) I, \tag{16.50}$$

$$A^j = (\lambda_j/\lambda_{j-1}) P^{\mathrm{T}}, \quad \text{and} \quad B^j = (\lambda_j/\mu_{j-1}) Q^{\mathrm{T}}. \tag{16.51}$$

Proof We are given that $\langle \Phi^j, \Phi^j \rangle = \lambda_j I$, $\langle \Psi^j, \Psi^j \rangle = \mu_j I$, and $\langle \Phi^j, \Psi^j \rangle = 0$. Invoking (16.40) to express Ψ^{j-1} and Φ^{j-1} in terms of Φ^j, we have the respective consequences:

$$
\begin{aligned}
\lambda_{j-1} I &= \langle \Phi^{j-1}, \Phi^{j-1} \rangle = P^{\mathrm{T}} \langle \Phi^j, \Phi^j \rangle P \quad \text{(see Lemma 16.20)} = \lambda_j P^{\mathrm{T}} P, \\
\mu_{j-1} I &= \langle \Psi^{j-1}, \Psi^{j-1} \rangle = Q^{\mathrm{T}} \langle \Phi^j, \Phi^j \rangle Q \quad \text{(see Lemma 16.20)} = \lambda_j Q^{\mathrm{T}} Q, \\
0 &= \langle \Phi^{j-1}, \Psi^{j-1} \rangle = P^{\mathrm{T}} \langle \Phi^j, \Phi^j \rangle Q \quad \text{(see Lemma 16.20)} = \lambda_j P^{\mathrm{T}} Q.
\end{aligned}
$$

The first two yield (16.50); the three together imply the block matrix product

$$
\begin{bmatrix} (\lambda_j/\lambda_{j-1}) P^{\mathrm{T}} \\ (\lambda_j/\mu_{j-1}) Q^{\mathrm{T}} \end{bmatrix} [P|Q] = \begin{bmatrix} I & 0 \\ 0 & I \end{bmatrix}. \quad \text{But } [P|Q]^{-1} = \begin{bmatrix} A^j \\ B^j \end{bmatrix} \text{ (Table 16.8),}
$$

and so we have (16.51). Then setting $\lambda_j = \mu_j = 1$ gives orthogonality of the matrix $[P|Q]$.

Implications of father and mother wavelets For fixed j the basis functions $\phi_i^j(x) = \phi(2^j x - i)$ are shifted copies. That is, the columns of P^j are shifts of each other. More formally, let P^j have (i, k) element $p(j, i, k)$. Then the relation $\Phi^{j-1}(x) = \Phi^j(x)P^j$ of (16.40) becomes

$$\phi_k^{j-1}(x) = \sum_i p(j, i, k)\phi_i^j(x), \qquad (16.52a)$$

and to determine the implications for P^j we observe that

$$
\begin{aligned}
\phi_{k+1}^{j-1}(x) &= \phi_k^{j-1}(x - 1) & \text{by (16.47)} \\
&= \sum_i p(j, i, k)\phi_i^j(x - 1) & \text{by (16.52)} \\
&= \sum_i p(j, i, k)\phi_{i+1}^j(x) & \text{by (16.47)} \\
&= \sum_i p(j, i - 1, k)\phi_i^j(x) & \text{by relabelling.}
\end{aligned}
$$

Comparing with (16.52a) shows that $p(j, i, k + 1) = p(j, i - 1, k)$, that is, the $(k + 1)$st column of P^j is the kth shifted down one place. Similar considerations apply to Q^j, A^j and B^j; this is visible in the Haar case, Example 16.17, and still more significantly in Examples 16.22 below.

> The columns of P^j are rotations of the first. Similarly
> for the columns of Q^j and rows of A^j, B^j

$$(16.52b)$$

(when father and mother wavelet exist).

16.3.3 Daubechies wavelets

Up till the mid 1980s it was widely believed that orthogonal wavelets with compact support were restricted to the ubiquitous Haar wavelets (see end of Section 16.2). Daubechies (1988) changed all that with her discovery of a whole family whose simplest case is the Haar. For every positive integer N there is a scaling function $\phi = \phi_N$, with support $[0, 2N - 1]$, and related mother wavelet ψ defined via ϕ. These arise from a sequence $h_0, \ldots, h_{2N-1}$ with remarkable properties, constructed by Daubechies (see Theorem 16.25).

Since our primary objective in this section is to try out the Daubechies wavelets as a compression tool, we will begin by highlighting their matrices which enable us to use the DWT without knowing bases. Property (16.52b) allows the following concise definition.

Matrix A^j The first row of A^j is $[h_0 \quad h_1 \quad \ldots \quad h_{2N-1} \quad 0 \quad 0 \quad \ldots \quad 0]$, of length 2^j, and successive rows are obtained by cycling forward two places. Thus orthonormality of the rows of A^j says

$$\sum_n h_{n-2k}h_{n-2i} = \delta_{ki}. \qquad (16.53)$$

Matrix B^j This matrix is formed similarly to A^j, from $[g_0\, g_1 \ldots g_{2N-1}\, 0\, 0 \ldots 0]$ of length 2^j, where

$$g_n = (-1)^n h_{2N-1-n}. \qquad (16.54)$$

Thus we also know the transposes P^j, Q^j and can perform the appropriate DWT and its inverse in one or more dimensions by ALGO 16.2. (Further, we can use P^j and Q^j to generate the wavelet basis curves by recursive subdivision, a theme of Chapter 17.)

Examples 16.22 (*The simplest Daubechies wavelets*)
(1) $N = 1$ (*Haar wavelets*) Here ϕ_N is the unit box, $h_0 = h_1 = 1/\sqrt{2}$, and Equation (16.54) gives $g_0 = h_1$, $g_1 = -h_0$. Thus

$$A^2 = \begin{bmatrix} h_0 & h_1 & 0 & 0 \\ 0 & 0 & h_0 & h_1 \end{bmatrix} = \frac{1}{\sqrt{2}} \begin{bmatrix} 1 & 1 & 0 & 0 \\ 0 & 0 & 1 & 1 \end{bmatrix}, \text{ and}$$

$$B^2 = \begin{bmatrix} g_0 & g_1 & 0 & 0 \\ 0 & 0 & g_0 & g_1 \end{bmatrix} = \frac{1}{\sqrt{2}} \begin{bmatrix} 1 & -1 & 0 & 0 \\ 0 & 0 & 1 & -1 \end{bmatrix}.$$

(2) $N = 2$ We are given $(h_0, \dots, h_3) = (1/4\sqrt{2})(1 + \sqrt{3}, 3 + \sqrt{3}, 3 - \sqrt{3}, 1 - \sqrt{3})$, and (16.54) supplies $(g_0, \dots, g_3) = (h_3, -h_2, h_1, -h_0)$. Noting that P_2 and Q_2 are the respective transposes of A^2 and B^2, we have, for example,

$$A^2 = \begin{bmatrix} h_0 & h_1 & h_2 & h_3 \\ h_2 & h_3 & h_0 & h_1 \end{bmatrix} \text{ and } A^3 = \begin{bmatrix} h_0 & h_1 & h_2 & h_3 & & \\ & & h_0 & h_1 & h_2 & h_3 \\ & & & & h_0 & h_1 & h_2 & h_3 \\ h_2 & h_3 & & & & & h_0 & h_1 \end{bmatrix},$$

$$B^2 = \begin{bmatrix} h_3 & -h_2 & h_1 & -h_0 \\ h_1 & -h_0 & h_3 & -h_2 \end{bmatrix} \text{ and } B^3 = \begin{bmatrix} h_3 & -h_2 & h_1 & -h_0 & & \\ & & h_3 & -h_2 & h_1 & -h_0 \\ & & & & h_3 & -h_2 & h_1 & -h_0 \\ h_1 & -h_0 & & & & & h_3 & -h_2 \end{bmatrix}.$$

(3) $N = 3$ This is the last case for which solutions for g, h can be given explicitly. However, it requires multiple square roots, and so we shall be content to record the 9-digit decimal forms: $h = \{0.332\ 670\ 552, 0.806\ 891\ 509, 0.459\ 877\ 502, -0.135\ 011\ 020, -0.085\ 441\ 274, 0.035\ 226\ 292\}$.

Theorem 16.23 *The Daubechies relations (16.53), (16.54) imply that the rows of B^j are orthonormal, and orthogonal to those of A^j. Thus $[A^j/B^j]$ and $[P|Q]$ are orthogonal matrices.*

Proof (i) The inner products of rows of B^j are the same sums as those of A^j (hence orthonormality) because a double shift cancels the effect of the factor $(-1)^n$, and the subscript change $n \to 1 - n$ shifts, then reverses the direction of, the row elements. (ii) More explicitly here, orthogonality of the rows of A^j to those of B^j means that $\sum_n h_{n-2k} g_{n-2i} = 0$ (all k, i). By cyclic shifting of subscripts we simplify this for convenience to $\sum_n h_n g_{n-2i} = 0$, that is, to $\sum_n (-1)^n h_n h_{2i+1-n} = 0$. But these terms cancel in pairs:

$$(-1)^n h_n h_{2i+1-n} + (-1)^{2i+1-n} h_{2i+1-n} h_n = 0.$$

Example 16.24 Let us compare the potential of the Daubechies wavelets in cases $N = 1$ (Haar) and $N = 2, 3$. At 10% error the Haar version starts to break up (see the earlier Figure 16.27), so we shall apply all three at this level. Though subjectively the comparison is not clearcut, the pixillation does decrease as N increases. The results are shown in Figure 16.30.

Original 'Jo'.	$N = 1$: 10% error, using	$N = 2$: 10% error using	$N = 3$: 10% error using
(128×128)	3% of coefficients.	2.01% of coefficients.	2.25% of coefficients.

Figure 16.30 The first three Daubechies wavelets compared at 10% error for picture quality and for percentage of coefficients retained at this level. Case $N = 1$, Haar, reproduced from Figure 16.27.

Some theory We can only give here a small flavour of this ground-breaking work, since a great many technical details are involved. However, here is the Fundamental Theorem from Daubechies (1988, 1992), in which are found exact details on the required speed of convergence. The notation $\hat{\phi}$ is used for the Fourier Transform of ϕ.

Theorem 16.25 *Let $\{h_n\}$ be a sequence satisfying (i) $|h_n|$ does not increase too fast with n, and moreover $\sum_n h_n = \sqrt{2}$, (ii) $\sum_n h_{n-2k}h_{n-2i} = \delta k_i$ (orthogonality). Define*

$$H(x) = (1/\sqrt{2}) \sum_n h_n e^{-inx}, \tag{16.55}$$

and suppose that for some positive integer N there is a factorisation

$$H(x) = [(1 + e^{-ix})/2]^N \sum_n f_n e^{-inx} \tag{16.56}$$

where $|f_n|$ does not increase too fast with n (this condition involves N). Define

$$\begin{cases} g_n &= (-1)^n h_{1-n}, \\ \hat{\phi}(x) &= \prod_{j=1}^{\infty} H(2^{-j}x), \\ \psi(x) &= \sqrt{2} \sum_n g_n \phi(2x - n). \end{cases} \tag{16.57}$$

Then ϕ is a scaling function (father wavelet) and ψ is the corresponding mother wavelet. These wavelets are orthogonal.

Examples 16.26 (1) *The case $N = 1$* This is easily obtained by taking $h_0 = h_1 = 1/\sqrt{2}$, and hence $H(x) = [(1 + e^{-ix})/2]^1$. Then $\hat{\phi}(x) = \prod_{j=1}^{\infty} H(2^{-j}x) = (1 - e^{-ix})/ix$ (see Daubechies, 1992). We can identify this expression from Table 14.2 of Chapter 14, lines 1, 4, 5, which reveal that ϕ is a certain box function (see Exercise 16.12).

(2) *The case* $N = 2$ With the given values of $h_0, \ldots, h_3$, and setting $z = e^{-ix}$ and $r = \sqrt{3}$ to simplify notation, we may write $H = (1/4)[(1+r)+(3+r)z+(3-r)z^2+(1-r)z^3]$. This is to be divisible by $(1/4)(1+z)^2$. Performing the calculation, we find that exact division is indeed possible, and the quotient is $(1+r)+(1-r)z$.

Exercise Perform the Fourier calculation of (1), and the division in (2) above.

16.3.4 Fingerprints

Figure 16.31 Part of a sample fingerprint

On each human finger and thumb is a system of *ridges*, unique for each individual, indeed for each finger. It is laid down early, and remains constant except for increase in size before adulthood. This remarkable pattern, or *fingerprint*, such as in Figure 16.31, exhibits about 150 features recognizable to a human expert, though it is considered that a subset of 10–12 features suffices to establish legally a person's identity. A desciption of how to compare prints, such as may be found on the FBI's website www.LANL.gov, is extremely detailed, but we indicate in Figure 16.32 the three key types: loops, arches and whorls, from which further subdivisions are made.

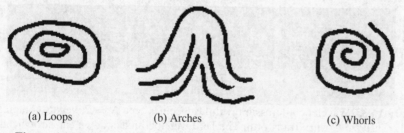

(a) Loops (b) Arches (c) Whorls

Figure 16.32 The highest level features formed from fingerprint ridges.

Problems of space and speed The issue is well illustrated by statistics of the United States FBI. Each day about 5000 fingerprints arrive to be stored and 35 000 to be compared with the data held, of the order of 300 million prints. Until the start of digitisation all data was held on cards, with some degree of categorisation so that the final expert check was not too laborious for a given case. However, the sheer numbers demand more economical storage and a way to drastically shorten the turnaround time for an identification request. Faster transmission is highly desirable too (see Chapter 13 for the issue of error-free transmission). A huge step towards solving these problems is digital compression.

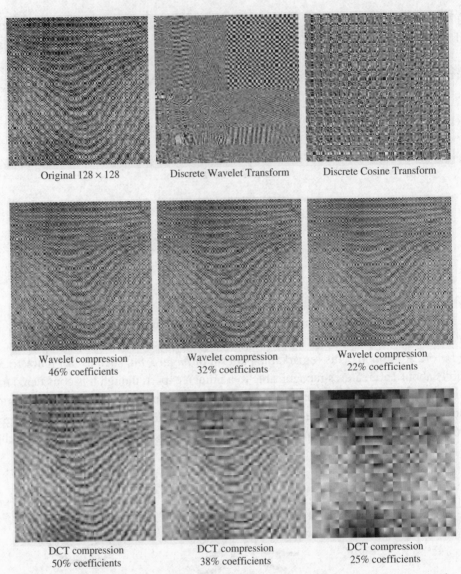

Figure 16.33 Wavelet compression with Daubechies type $N = 2$, versus compression by the Discrete Cosine Transform. The DCT version breaks down catastrophically by reduction to 25% of coefficients, whilst the wavelet is slightly blurred but nevertheless decipherable.

Enter wavelets Given that fingerprints are to be scanned, the resolution was fixed at 500 ppi (pixels per inch), and compression methods were explored for reduction of around 15:1. The anticipated best method was JPEG, based on the DCT, the Discrete Fourier Transform (see Chapter 15). However, it was found that at such ratios the DCT, unlike wavelets, did not preserve ridges with sufficient accuracy. An example is given in Figure 16.33. Typically, a wavelet-compressed fingerprint became only gradually more blurred with over-compression. A partial explanation is that the 8×8 JPEG tiles are too closely related to the natural frequency of ridges at 500 dpi. Thus the wavelet method was preferred.

Some implementation details As in JPEG, the wavelet coefficients are passed through a further stage, of entropy compression as symbol sequences. Huffman encoding (see Chapter 12) was chosen for this because, although arithmetic encoding is theoretically superior, it requires more computation and in this case gave no gain in compression. It should be mentioned that just before this stage the coefficients are quantised according to an empirical formula developed at the FBI (see e.g. Brislawn, 1995). Also, although *vector* quantisation (Chapter 18) is theoretically superior to *scalar* (one value at a time) the latter was in this case equally good and so was chosen. The result was termed WSQ, for Wavelet Scalar Quantisation.

Finally, the FBI system would accept some variety of wavelet formulation from out-side, with co-transmission of wavelet filter coefficients, quantisation parameters, and Huffman information.

16.4 Wavelet relatives

16.4.1 Discrete versus continuous wavelets

We introduce briefly the Continuous Wavelet Transform, or CWT. It arguably precedes the discrete transform in the logical order of things. In any case, some contexts call for an initial continuous model, even if it is to be later approximated by a discrete one. Indeed, it is an extremely useful property of wavelets that the correspondence between continuous and discrete filter banks is even closer than in the Fourier case. See, for example, Strang and Nguyen (1997). As preparation we suppose, given a real function $g(x)$ such that the following integral C_g exists:

$$C_g = \int_{-\infty}^{\infty} |u|^{-1} |G(u)|^2 du < \infty, \tag{16.58}$$

where $G(u)$ is the Fourier Transform of $g(x)$ (see Chapter 14). This implies in particular that the integrand doesn't 'blow up' at $x = 0$, so $G(0) = 0$, which says (by definition of $G(0)$) that the mean of $g(x)$ exists and is zero, $\int g(x)dx = 0$. Therefore $g(x)$ has a sign change, and tends to zero as $|x| \to \infty$. Terming g a *basic wavelet*, we define a family of wavelets $g_{a,b}(x)$ given by

$$g_{a,b}(x) = |a|^{-1/2} g\left(\frac{x-b}{a}\right) \tag{16.59}$$

where the parameters $a \neq 0$ and b are *continuous*, i.e. lie on the real line **R**. Then the corrresponding *Continuous Wavelet Transform* (CWT) and its inverse, established by Grossman and Morlet (1984), are given by the pair

$$\begin{cases} F(a,b) = \int_{-\infty}^{\infty} f(x)g_{a,b}(x)dx, \\ f(x) = C_g^{-1} \int_{-\infty}^{\infty} \int_{-\infty}^{\infty} a^{-2} F(a,b)g_{a,b}(x)da\, db. \end{cases} \tag{16.60}$$

Dyadic Wavelet Transform It turns out that, under conditions which are not unduly demanding, we can still recover $f(x)$ after throwing away the transform for 'almost all' values of a. The values we retain are those of the *dyadic* form 2^j for j in the set $Z = \{\ldots, -2, -1, 0, 1, 2, \ldots\}$. To arrive at this conclusion we first express the CWT as a convolution so as to bring to bear the Fourier Transform as a tool. Consider a function $\psi(x)$, which we'll think of as a potential basic wavelet though all we ask at first is that it have zero mean. We define the *dilation of ψ by scaling factor s* to be

$$\psi_s(x) = (1/s)\psi(x/s). \tag{16.61}$$

The initial factor $1/s$ simplifies taking the Fourier Transform $\hat{\psi}_s$ of ψ_s (the Fourier 'hat' is convenient for Greek letters). For we have, by the Similarity Theorem (Table 14.2) applied to (16.61),

$$\hat{\psi}_s(w) = s^{-1} \cdot s\hat{\psi}(sw) = \hat{\psi}(sw). \tag{16.62}$$

This supports the following reformulation of the CWT. The *Wavelet Transform of $f(x)$ at scale s and position x is*

$$\boxed{W_s f(x) = (f^*\psi_s)(x).} \tag{16.63}$$

This unpacks as $\int f(y)(1/s)\psi((x - y)/s)dy$, so we have simply inserted an extra factor and changed the sign of the argument of ψ. The *Dyadic Wavelet Transform* (DWT) of f *defined by* ψ is the sequence of functions $\{W_{2^j} f(x)\}_{j\in Z}$. We'll see that *inversion is possible*, that is, f may be recovered from this sequence, provided certain bounds exist on the Fourier Transform of ψ. Specifically, there are constants $A, B > 0$ such that the *dyadic condition* holds:

$$A \le \sum_j |\hat{\psi}(2^j w)|^2 \le B. \tag{16.64}$$

To prove this, we first observe that W_2^j and its Fourier Transform $\hat{W}$ obey

$$W_{2^j} f(x) = (f^*\psi_{2^j})(x), \tag{16.65}$$
$$\hat{W} f_{2^j}(x) = \hat{f}(w)\hat{\psi}(2^j w), \tag{16.66}$$

where the first equality is the case $s = 2$ of (16.63), and the second follows by the Convolution Theorem and (16.62). We have

Theorem 16.27 *Let $\psi(x)$ satisfy the dyadic condition (16.64). Let $\chi(s)$ be any function satisfying $\hat{\chi}(2^j w) = \hat{\psi}(-2^j w)/\Sigma_j|\hat{\psi}(2^j w)|^2$. Then the Dyadic Wavelet Transform of f (w.r.t ψ) is stable and invertible:*

$$A\|f\|^2 \le \sum_j \|W_{2^j} f\|^2 \le B\|f\|^2, \tag{16.67}$$

$$f(x) = \sum_j W_{2^j} f(x)^* \chi_{2^j}(-x). \tag{16.68}$$

Proof of (16.68) Since the Fourier Transform of a function $g(-x)$ is the complex conjugate of $\hat{g}(w)$, the right hand side of (16.68) has Fourier Transform

$$\sum_j \hat{f}(w)\hat{\psi}(2^j w)\overline{\hat{\psi}(2^j w)} / (\sum_j |\hat{\psi}(2^j w)|^2) = \hat{f}(w) \sum_j |\hat{\psi}(2^j w)|^2 / (\sum_j |\hat{\psi}(2^j w)|^2)$$

$$= \hat{f}(w), \quad \text{proving (16.68)}$$

16.4.2 The Gabor Transform

Interestingly, Gabor (1946) discovered his transform as the solution to an optimisation problem in the theory of communication, not long before the appearance of Shannon's (1948) Information Theory.

To describe the transform we need to go back to the wavelet-related idea of a window, introduced to mitigate the problem of the Continuous Fourier Transform's infinite support by restricting calculation to a chosen region (the window). As noted by Strang and Nguyen (1997), wavelets come from a mother wavelet by translation and *scaling*, whereas windows come from a single window function $g(t)$ by translation and *modulation*:

$$g_{mn}(t) = e^{im\Omega t} g(t - nT). \tag{16.69}$$

Thus unit increase in n gives translation by T, but the same change in m increases frequency by Ω, the modulation effect. The Gabor window is created by a Gaussian

$$g(t) = g(0)\exp[-t^2/2\sigma^2]. \tag{16.70}$$

Applying the Gabor Transform to a signal means projecting it onto the $\{g_{mn}\}$ as basis functions. Each g_{mn} has its own window and so abstracts information in a certain region. But this is a region encapsulating both space (or time) and frequency, because of the choice of modulation rather than scaling. The specific choice of g is Gabor's unique solution for minimising (in a technical sense defined by him) the combined error. According to Daugman (1985) this is similar to the operation of the human visual cortex, and so the Gabor filter is a good candidate for studying the former.

A disadvantage is that the Gabor basis is not orthogonal, so projection onto this basis does not have the simplicity of orthogonal wavelets, for example. However, some methods for doing so are surveyed in Ibrahim and Azimi-Sadjadi (1996). Finally, the transform is not invertible, which perhaps explains why it appears to have been overtaken by wavelets. However, the Gabor coefficients continue to provide insight in their many applications.

16.4.3 Canny edge-detection

We make a useful comparison with the Marr–Hildreth edge-detector (Section 15.2.4), where, for each pixel, Gaussian smoothing is followed by the Laplacian. The argument is that edge pixels are those at which the magnitude of the intensity gradient is a local maximum, hence the second derivative is zero. The Laplacian supplies the greatest second derivative over all directions, so where it is zero we have a gradient maximum. The two processes are combined into a single Laplacian of Gaussian operator LoG.

Canny (1986) sought to improve on this. His initial point of departure was to use the first derivative of the Gaussian as an operator *DG* and determine its greatest value, rather than proceeding to the second derivative. This is slightly more accurate than LoG; however, it was actually arrived at by mathematical analysis as a close approximation to the optimal operator for the criteria

1. *low error rate*: no spurious edges but none missed,
2. *good localisation*: the detector points to the centre of the edge.

This means employing a threshold above which *DG* is to lie for an edge pixel, which admits the possibility of *streaking*, in which part of a contour fails to clear the hurdle, and so is lost. Canny's solution is *hysteresis* – if some pixels pass, then nearby ones are reconsidered with a lower threshold. Alongside this, the effect of noise is deduced and reduced through a Wiener filter (15.3.4).

Scaling We now have probabilistic information about the noise which enables the detector to output the probability of error should we designate a pixel as edge (by a Bayesian method, Section 11.2). This is where Canny introduces scaling. There is a discrete choice of operator widths σ, and one chooses the least (if any) for which we are below the new threshold. This choice is seen to improve performance in 1 and 2 above. It should be mentioned that Canny has refinements not given here.

Conclusions The result is generally considered to be amongst the best. The main drawback is a high computational cost compared with other edge-detectors, though as computer power increases this may become less significant. Clearly, the greater the importance of accuracy, the more attractive Canny's method is. Amongst such applications is probably scene analysis (see Section 13.4), but in the next section we follow Mallat's wavelet version and a medical application.

16.4.4 Wavelets in edge-detection

Mallat and Zhong (1992) incorporate the basic edge-detectors of Marr, Hildreth and Canny into a wavelet scheme which both offers simplifications and leads to further developments such as the medical image technique of Example 16.28 below. They use the previously introduced dyadic scales $s = 2^j$ $(j = 0, \pm 1, \ldots)$. We recall that the dyadic wavelet transform (DWT) at scale *s* defined by $\psi(x)$ is given by

$$W_s f(x) = (f^* \psi_s)(x), \quad \text{where } \psi_s(x) = (1/s)\psi(x/s). \tag{16.71}$$

For present purposes we choose $\psi(x)$ to be the first or second derivative of a smoothing function $\theta(x)$, which must satisfy $\int \theta(x)\mathrm{d}x = 1$ and $\theta(x) \to 0$ as $x \to \pm\infty$ (here assumed to be Gaussian). Denoting the respective transforms by W^a and W^b, we will

show that

$$W_s^a f(x) = s\frac{d}{dx}(f * \theta_s)(x),$$

$$W_s^b f(x) = s^2\frac{d^2}{dx^2}(f * \theta_s)(x),$$ (16.72)

which has the desirable effect of smoothing at scale s then differentiating, and hence providing the output for the respective detectors on a multiscale basis (so far in dimension 1). To prove this we observe that by definition $(\theta')_s(x) = (1/s)\theta'(x/s)$, whereas $(\theta_s)'(x) = \frac{d}{dx}[\frac{1}{s}\theta(x/s)] = \frac{1}{s^2}\theta'(\frac{x}{s})$. Thus $W_s^a f(x) = f*(\theta')_s = sf*(\theta_s)' = s\frac{d}{dx}(f*\theta_s)$, where Theorem 10.21 supplies the last equality, and similarly for W^b.

The extension to 2D. Define the gradient $\nabla f(x, y)$ of a function $f(x, y)$ to be the vector in the direction of greatest rate of increase of f, and length equal to that increase, at the point (x, y). Then $\nabla f(x, y)$ is at right angles to the lines of constant f, as portrayed in Figure 16.34(a), and is independent of the choice of origin and axis directions. We'll prove that, whatever the choice of axes, ∇f equals the vector $(\partial f/\partial x, \partial f/\partial y)$, and show how to obtain the derivative of f in any direction via ∇f.

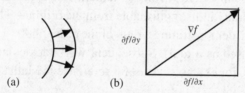

Figure 16.34 (a) The gradient of $f(x, y)$ is perpendicular to lines $f = $ constant, (b) $\nabla f = (\partial f/\partial x, \partial f/\partial y)$.

Without loss of generality we determine ∇f at the *origin*. Differentiating f along a ray $t(\cos\theta, \sin\theta)$, we have $\partial f/\partial t = \partial f/\partial x \ dx/dt + \partial f/\partial y \ dy/dt = (\partial f/\partial x, \partial f/\partial y) \cdot (\cos\theta, \sin\theta) = |(\partial f/\partial x, \partial f/\partial y)| \cdot 1 \cdot \cos\lambda$, where λ is the angle between vectors $(\partial f/\partial x, \partial f/\partial y)$ and $(\cos\theta, \sin\theta)$. Hence the greatest value of $\partial f/\partial t$ occurs when $\cos\lambda = 1, \lambda = 0$, giving

$$\nabla f = (\partial f/\partial x, \partial f/\partial y), \quad \text{and } \partial f/\partial t = \boldsymbol{n} \cdot \nabla f,$$ (16.73)

the latter for differentiating along a ray pointing in the direction of unit vector $\boldsymbol{n}$. The smoothing function now has the form $\theta(x, y)$ with scaled version $\theta_s(x, y) = (1/s^2)\theta(x/s, y/s)$. Using partial differentiation we can apply (16.72) in the x- and y-directions separately to get the first equality below for the components of a 2D wavelet $W = (W^x, W^y)$ (see Exercise 16.14). The second equality is (16.73).

$$\begin{bmatrix} W_s^x \\ W_s^y \end{bmatrix} = s\begin{bmatrix} \frac{\partial}{\partial x}(f * \theta_s)(x, y) \\ \frac{\partial}{\partial y}(f * \theta_s)(x, y) \end{bmatrix} = s\nabla(f * \theta_s)(x, y).$$ (16.74)

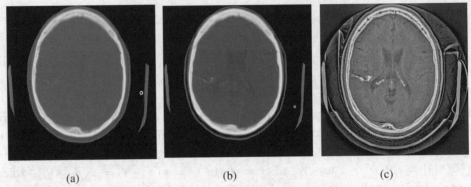

(a)   (b)   (c)

Figure 16.35 (a) X-ray computerised tomography image of human head, 256×256 Pixels. (b) Contrast enhancement by simple stretch of intensity gradient magnitudes. (c) Result with stretch factor $\propto$ 1/(gradient magnitude). (Images by Lu, Healy and Weaver, 1994.)

Thus Canny detection is equivalent to locating the maxima of a wavelet transform modulus. Mallat and Zhong (1992) show that, using multiscale information in this form, the whole dyadic wavelet transform can be recovered from its value at edge pixels, with sufficient accuracy that the inverted wavelet (Theorem 16.27) presents an image which, to the human eye, is generally indistinguishable from the original. They adapt their method for image compression, demonstrating a ratio of the order of 30 : 1 (in all this, the Fourier Transform is widely used as a tool). Subsequent work tackles noise reduction and the special case of texture, for example. A useful reference is Mallat (1999).

Example 16.28 (*Medical imaging*) Lu, Healy and Weaver (1994) consider the problem of low contrast in medical images such as computed tomography, magnetic resonance, and ultrasound (see Section 18.4). The standard solutions of linear change of grey intensity and even histogram equalisation (see Section 15.2.1) have drawbacks. For example, they may magnify noise, or be hard to automate satisfactorily.

Lu *et al.* have had considerable success in reducing such problems by their method based on the Mallat–Zhong theory, in which contrast is enhanced automatically by scaling the multiscale gradient maxima from (16.74), then applying the reconstruction algorithm. The method enables extra features such as selectively enhancing objects of a chosen size. Important examples are shown in Figures 16.35 and 16.36.

Some application areas of wavelets

Astronomy and the Hubble telescope problem: Jaffard *et al.* (2001),
Contrast enhancement: Lu *et al.* (1994),
Curves and surfaces: Lounsbery *et al.* (1997),
Denoising a signal, music and speech: Hubbard (1996),
Edge-detection: Mallat and Zhong (1992),
Fingerprint storage and look-up for FBI: Brislawn (1995),

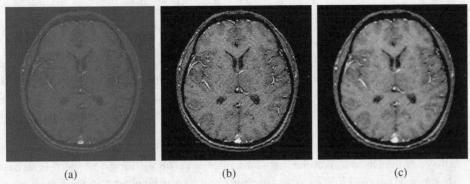

(a)   (b)   (c)

Figure 16.36 (a) MR (magnetic resonance) image of human head, 256×256 pixels, (b) contrast enhancement by simple stretch of intensity gradient magnitudes, (c) result with smaller stretch at fine scales to reduce effect of noise. (Images by Lu, Healy and Weaver, 1994.)

Image compression: Mallat (1999),

Remote sensing and registration (Fitting together partial images, however acquired.):
   Starck *et al.* (2000), Djamdji *et al.* (1993a,b),

Seismic waves: Koornwinder (1993),

Turbulence: Jaffard *et al.* (2001),

Video compression: Strang and Nguyen (1997).

Exercises 16

1   Program Mandelbrot's Initiator–Generator construction for the snowflake curve of Figure 16.3.

2   Plot a Richardson graph (see Figure 16.6) for the Sweden–Norway border using dividers, with map blow-up if necessary.

3 √   Write down the matrix A for which $f : x \to Ax$ gives a shear in the x-direction of two units per unit height. Find geometrically the image under f of a triangle with vertices $(0, 0)$, $(-1, 0)$, $(0, 1)$ and check that your matrix gives the same result.

4 √   Determine affine maps $\{w_1, \ldots, w_4\}$ for an IFS whose attractor is the snowflake curve of Figure 16.3, with ends $(0, 0)$ and $(1, 0)$. (Complex numbers may help.) Now recover the curve by computer iteration.

5   Implement Fractal Compression via (16.20–22). Select two unlike same-sized images; compress one, then decompress using the second image for starting set, as exemplified in Figure 16.17.

6 √   (*Haar wavelets*) Similarly to Example 16.11, transform and then reconstruct the 1D image values, (i) [9   6   5   3], and (ii) [6   8   13   7   4   8].

7 √   Illustrate $V^2 = V^0 \oplus W^0 \oplus W^1$ by decomposing the function on the interval $[0, 1]$ represented by [3 1 6 10] (see Example 16.4). Can you express this composition geometrically (see Table 16.6)?

8 √ Write out the vector orthonormal basis of V^2. Find the component of the vector $f = (10, 6, 1, 3)$ of Example 16.14 with respect to each basis vector, by the ususal dot product. Why does this NOT contradict the expression for f in that example?

9 √ (a) Write down the matrix $M = \text{Rows}(R_0, \ldots, R_3)$ for the 1D transform based on the Haar ONB for V^2. (b) What are the 2D generators g_{ij} in terms of the R_k? (c) Compute the generators g_{12} and g_{23} and verify that they are orthogonal, of unit length. (d) Prove that $\{g_{ij}\}$ must form an ONB, based on properties of $R_0, \ldots, R_3$. Evaluate the inner product of $2g_{12} + g_{23}$ and $g_{24} - 2g_{23}$.

10 √ (a) Draw the diagram for a filter bank in the case $j = 2$ (see Figure 16.28). Determine as a 4-vector the Discrete Wavelet Transform of $c^2 = [1\ 2\ 3\ 4]^T$ for the unscaled Haar bases (begun in Example 16.17). (b) Verify your result by working back up the filter bank via $c^k = P^k c^{k-1} + Q^k d^{k-1}$ (ALGO 16.2 does this for *inverse-dwt*). (c) Implement ALGO 16.2 and test it with the data of parts (a) and (b).

11 √ (a) Given $P_{p \times r}$ and $Q_{q \times s}$, what are the dimensions of the matrices involved in $\langle FP, GQ \rangle$ of (16.49)? (b) In the notation of Theorem 16.21, what are λ_j for the inner product (16.32) on Haar basis functions (16.30)? Expressing split boxes in terms of boxes, and using linearity of inner products, deduce $\mu_j = \lambda_j$ (argued geometrically in the text). What relationships result from Theorem 16.21? (c) Repeat for the Haar basis functions as unscaled vectors in V^k for fixed $k > j$ (see after Example 16.14), and deduce that the relationships are unchanged.

12 √ (a) Use Table 14.2, lines 1, 4, 5 to show that if the Fourier transform $\hat{\phi}$ is $(1 - e^{-is})/is$ then ϕ is a certain box of size 2π (see Examples 16.26). (b) Verify the quotient in Example 16.26 (2).

13 Use ALGO 16.2 to compare Haar and more general Daubechies wavelets, as in Figure 16.30.

14 √ Define the 2D wavelet $W_s = (W_s^x, W_s^y)$ by $W_s^z f = f^* \psi_s^z$ ($z = x$ or y), where $\psi^z = \partial\phi/\partial z$, the derivative of the standard 2D Gaussian. Verify that $W_s f = s\nabla(f^*\psi_s)$ in the case $f(x, y) = xy$.

Part VI

See, edit, reconstruct

17

B-spline wavelets

The B-spline has long been important in computer graphics for representing curves and surfaces, but it was recently realised that the recursive subdivision method of construction could be used to formulate B-splines in wavelet terms; this led to excellent new applications (see Stollnitz *et al.*, 1996) in which curves and surfaces could be analysed or modified at any chosen scale, from local to global. In addition to proving results, we provide some exemplification of these things.

By introducing an equivalent definition of B-splines as an *m*-fold convolution of boxes we bring out an intimate connection with the Fourier transform. This in turn provides an alternative derivation of such formulae as the Cox–de Boor relations.

The last two sections are designated as appendices, optional follow-up to the main treatment. In Section 17.4 we derive wavelet-identifying formulae that hold for arbitrary size of control polygon, whilst Section 17.5 addresses mathematical aspects of the natural generalisation from curve to surface wavelets achievable by the subdivision system of Loop (1987). Multiresolution and editing examples are exhibited.

17.1 Splines from boxes

We begin with Bézier splines, to give background and to introduce some of the ideas behind splines, including that of convexity in Section 17.1.2. Moving on to the even more useful B-splines in Section 17.1.3, we present their definition as a convolution of box functions, excellent for the coming wavelet formulation. We have, of course, considered box functions in the context of Haar wavelets (Section 16.2), and convolution in connection with the Fourier Transform (Chapter 14). This relationship makes it easy to apply the transform to B-splines (Section 17.1.4), and gives a convenient way to derive the Cox–de Boor relations of Section 17.1.5; these then confirm that the convolution definition has returned the usual B-splines (see e.g. Farin, 2002). Finally, in Section 17.1.6, we derive features of the *cubic* B-splines which are useful in applications. This case is the one in which we shall be most interested.

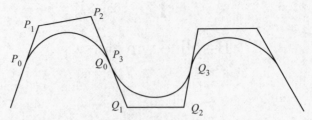

Figure 17.1 Splicing three 4-knot Bézier curves so as to keep first-order continuity (i.e. fixed tangent direction) at the joins. Note that P_3 and Q_0 label the same point. A similar result is achieved by a single B-spline in Figure 17.11.

17.1.1 The Bézier background

One way to design or to approximate a curve is to form a *spline*. That is, a sequence of curves agreeing at their end-points, with parallel tangents there (see Figure 17.1). It was for car-body design that Paul Bézier (1966, 1972) introduced to Renault the splines bearing his name, in which each contributing curve is a polynomial of some degree n defined by $n + 1$ *control points* (or *knots*) $P_0, \ldots, P_n$. These points are in general 3-dimensional, but here we focus on the plane. The Bézier curve $P(t)$ is given by

$$P(t) = \sum_{i=0}^{n} \binom{n}{i} t^i (1 - t)^{n-i} P_i \quad (0 \le t \le 1), \tag{17.1}$$

where we identify a point P_i with its coordinates/position vector so that we may form this linear combination. The coefficients are *Bernstein polynomials*,

$$B_{n,i}(t) = \binom{n}{i} t^i (1 - t)^{n-i}. \tag{17.2}$$

Example 17.1 (*Cubic Bézier splines*) In the case $n = 3$ (four knots) let us highlight the binomial coefficients by writing them explicitly as 1 3 3 1, in

$$P(t) = \mathbf{1}(1 - t)^3 P_0 + \mathbf{3}(1 - t)^2 t P_1 + \mathbf{3}(1 - t)t^2 P_2 + \mathbf{1}t^3 P_3. \tag{17.3}$$

Considering tangents in Figure 17.1, differentiation gives $P'(0) = 3(P_1 - P_0)$, and $P'(1) = 3(P_3 - P_2)$, so the Bézier curve is *tangent at its end-points* to respective line segments $P_0 P_1$ and $P_2 P_3$. Further, as we shall soon see, the Bézier curve lies within its *defining polygon* $P_0 P_1 P_2 P_3$. These two properties make for a judicious splicing together of cubic Bézier pieces to design a longer curve (again, see Figure 17.1). Our next task is to establish the polygon property but to note some limitations, before introducing the more powerful B-splines. For this we need the idea of a convex set.

17.1.2 Convexity properties

Definition 17.2 A set S is *convex* if, when points A, B are in S, so is the whole line segment AB. Figure 17.2 gives examples of convex and non-convex sets. The third is not convex because it contains the points A and B but not the complete segment AB.

convex

convex

non-convex

Figure 17.2 Some convex and non-convex sets.

We have the following formula, giving the points of a segment AB in terms of position vectors:

$$AB = \{sA + tB: \quad s, t \geq 0, \quad s + t = 1\}, \tag{17.4}$$

for with s, t so restricted, $sA + tB$ is, by (1.3) of Chapter 1, the point on AB dividing AB in the ratio $t : s$ (with A, B as respective special cases $t = 0$ and $s = 0$). This simple idea motivates the definition of the *convex hull* of a set of points $A_1, \ldots, A_n$ as the set of all *convex linear combinations*:

$$s_1 A_1 + \cdots + s_n A_n; \quad \text{all } s_i \geq 0 \text{ and } \sum_i s_i = 1. \tag{17.5}$$

For example, the convex hull of A, B is the segment AB, and that of three points A, B, C is the filled-in triangle ABC, whereas the second case in Figure 17.2 is its own convex hull. This follows from the theorem below, which gives us a good handle on convex sets. One convex combination is the centre of gravity, $(A + B + C)/3$.

Theorem 17.3 *The convex hull of points $A_1, \ldots, A_n$, B consists of the line segments AB, where A is in the convex hull of $A_1, \ldots, A_n$. In particular, a convex hull is itself convex.*

Proof Let A be in the convex hull of the A_i and let P lie on AB. Then in vector terms

$$\begin{aligned} P &= rA + tB & (r, t \geq 0, r + t = 1) \\ &= r \sum s_i A_i + tB & (\text{all } s_i \geq 0 \text{ and } \sum s_i = 1). \end{aligned}$$

This is a linear combination of $A_1, \ldots, A_n$, B, and, moreover, it lies in their convex hull because all the coefficients are non-negative, with sum $\sum (r s_i) + t = r(\sum s_i) + t = r + t = 1$. Conversely, let P be in the convex hull of $A_1, \ldots, A_n$, B (where we omit the trivial case $t = 1$),

$$P = \sum_i m_i A_i + tB \quad (m_i, t \geq 0, \text{ and } m_1 + \cdots + m_n + t = 1).$$

Then we may write $P = (1 - t) \sum_i (m_i/(1 - t)) A_i + tB$, where $\sum_i (m_i/(1 - t)) A_i$ is in the convex hull of $A_1 \ldots A_n$ alone since it has coefficient sum $\sum_i (m_i/(1 - t)) = (\sum_i m_i)/(1 - t) = (1 - t)/(1 - t) = 1$. See Figure 17.3.

Remarks 17.4 (i) (*Barycentric coordinates*) Triangle ABC consists of the points

$$P = rA + sB + tC, \quad \text{with } r, s, t \geq 0 \text{ and } r + s + t = 1.$$

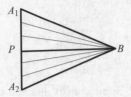

Figure 17.3 By Theorem 17.3, the convex hull of $\{A_1, A_2, B\}$ is filled in by line segments PB, where P lies on A_1A_2. Thus the convex hull is the filled-in triangle A_1A_2B.

Figure 17.4 An affine transformation sends convex sets to convex sets, illustrated here by rectangle, triangle, and circle. The effect on Bézier curves is illustrated in Figure 17.5.

In fact, r, s, t are unique (unless ABC degenerates into a straight line, Exercise 17.2), and so may be used as alternative coordinates for P. They are called barycentric coordinates, important in Section 17.5.3.

(ii) A set need not be closed to be convex, though ours will be. Convex hulls are closed because their defining equations (17.5) don't involve strict inequalities (Hoggar, 1992).

(iii) As noted earlier, each of the three Bézier curves in Figure 17.1 lies within the convex polygon formed by its control points. This is the *convexity property* of Bézier curves, which we will now prove.

Corollary 17.5 *A Bézier curve lies within the convex hull of its control points.*

Proof A point $P(t)$ on a general Bézier curve with control points $A_1, \ldots, A_n$ is given by the formula (17.1). Clearly, the coefficients (17.2) are non-negative, so it remains to show their sum is 1. But for any value of t these coefficients are precisely the summands in the binomial expansion of $(t + (1 - t))^n = 1^n$, which equals 1 as required.

The result of affine transformations Later we will be particularly concerned with what happens to splines under scaling; for example, does the scaled control polygon control the scaled curve? The answer is fortunately YES, for this and for more generally rotation, reflection and shear, summed up in the name *affine* (see Section 16.1.3, especially Figure 16.10). The following result shows that both control and convexity are preserved.

Theorem 17.6 *Let f be an affine transformation, $f(P) = MP + c$, where M is a matrix and c is a vector. Then (i) f sends lines to lines, and convex sets to convex sets; indeed, if points A, B, P are collinear and sent by f to A', B', P', then P' divides $A'B'$ in the same ratio as P divides AB; (ii) if $P(t)$ is the Bézier curve with control points $\{P_i\}$ then $f(P(t))$ is the Bézier curve with control points $\{f(P_i)\}$. See Figures 17.4 and 17.5.*

Proof One formula handles all cases. Let $P_0, \ldots, P_n$ be points, and let $s_0, \ldots, s_n$ be constants with $\sum s_i = 1$. We do not assume the s_i are non-negative, but it nevertheless follows that

$$f\left(\sum s_i P_i\right) = \sum s_i f(P_i). \tag{17.6}$$

This is because, starting from the right, we have $\sum s_i(MP_i + c) = \sum s_i M P_i + (\sum s_i)c = M \sum s_i P_i + c = f(\sum s_i P_i)$. Note the use of $\sum s_i = 1$. For (i) we take $n = 1$ and $P_0 P_1 = AB$, and recall from (1.3) of Chapter 1 that *any* point P on the line through A, B has the form $sA + tB$ with $s + t = 1$ (s or t is negative outside the segment AB). Equation (17.6) says that P is sent by f to $sA' + tB'$, which establishes both the ratio property and the fact that f sends lines to lines. Specialising to the case $s_i \geq 0$, we have that f sends a line segment AB to a line segment $A'B'$, and hence convex sets to convex sets. For (ii) we simply put $s_i = B_{n,i}(t)$ in (17.6).

Example 17.7 We design a simple car outline by splicing together two Bézier curves, of respectively four and nine knots. The second curve has repeated, or double, knots, so as to enhance the radiator part by pulling the curve towards those knots. Here are the control polygons, with coordinates relative to the axes in Figure 17.5.

First control polygon: $(0, 0), (2, 8), (16, 8), (16.5, 6)$.
Second control polygon: $(16.5, 6), (17, 4), (20, 4), (23, 4), (23, 4), (23, 2), (23, 0), (23, 0), (0, 0)$.

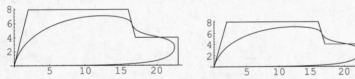

Figure 17.5 Our first 'car outline' consists of Bézier control polygons meeting at the windscreen. The second, sleeker model, is obtained from the first by a vertical uniform contraction. Since scaling is affine, the second model is similarly formed of Bézier curves (Theorem 17.6). Later, a single B-spline will suffice, see e.g. Figures 17.14 and 17.15.

Bézier limitations In spite of having some excellent properties, the Bézier curves carry two inconvenient limitations in practical use. Firstly, if we attempt to exercise greater flexibility by adding control points, we thereby increase its degree as a polynomial, so that small changes can have large unsought-for consequences. Secondly, we cannot change small parts of a curve in isolation. This is because, considering the Bézier formula, each basis function (17.2) contributes throughout the whole domain $[0, 1]$ of $P(t)$ (see Figure 17.6). Thus we generalise next to B-splines, which have the advantages of Bézier splines but overcome their limitations.

Note De Casteljau at Citroën developed a similar theory no later than Bézier himself, and gave the following geometrical construction for the point $r(t)$, $0 \leq t \leq 1$, on the Bézier curve with control points $P_0 P_1 P_2 P_3$: let v_i be the point on $P_i P_{i+1}$ dividing it as $t : 1$ and let w_i do the same for the v_i. Then $r(t)$ does the same for the w_i. Equivalence with

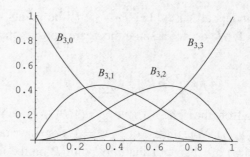

Figure 17.6 The Bernstein basis for Bézier curves. Notice that each basis function contributes over the whole interval (though some become very small near the end-points).

the algebraic definition (17.3) is derived in e.g. Hoggar (1992), and most texts involving such splines.

17.1.3 B-splines by convolution

We define *spline functions* $\phi_k(t)$, which are piecewise polynomial on the interval $[0, k + 1]$. This means that on each unit subinterval $[i, i + 1]$ $(0 \le i \le k)$ the function $\phi_k(t)$ equals some polynomial $p_i(t)$. Apart from this, $\phi_k(t)$ is zero. The first few cases are illustrated in Figure 17.7, where it is apparent that the polynomial pieces fit together smoothly. In fact (Theorem 17.8) the polynomials agree as closely as possible without being identical.

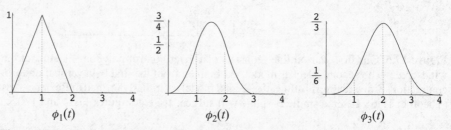

Figure 17.7 The B-spline functions $\phi_k(t)$ for $k = 1, 2, 3$. Dotted lines show ϕ_k composed of $k + 1$ polynomial pieces of unit width, which fit together smoothly; it is zero outside the open interval $(0, k + 1)$.

It might be thought that the $\phi_k(t)$ are very complicated to handle. But this is not the case, for after some initial results the individual polynomials fade from sight; we are using relationships that do not reference them. Why should this be so? One answer is that a polynomial-free definition can be given.

Our choice, via the continuous convolution product, has two additional benefits. Firstly, it provides an effortless link to the Fourier Transform (see Table 17.1), demonstrating an intrinsic connection, and offering a further polynomial-free approach to results and calculation. Secondly, and perhaps most importantly, it leads in a natural way to a key result (Theorem 17.21) connecting splines with recursive subdivision.

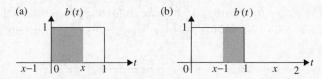

Figure 17.8 Calculating $\phi_1(x)$ as $b(t)^*b(t)$, which equals by (17.8) the area of the shaded portion in each case: (a) $0 \le x \le 1$, and (b) $1 \le x \le 2$. The result is given below.

Starting with $\phi_0 = b(t)$, the *box function* equal to 1 on the interval [0, 1], and otherwise zero, we define

$$\phi_k = b^*\phi_{k-1} = b^*b^* \cdots {}^*b \quad (k+1 \text{ factors}, \ k \ge 1). \tag{17.7}$$

Later we will see how these convolutions of boxes generalise the Haar box functions of Section 16.2. Here we note in passing that ϕ_k approaches the normal distribution curve as k increases, because ϕ_k is the pdf of the sum of many independent variables, each with pdf the box function (see Section 10.2.2). Meanwhile we must derive some first properties.

We begin by calculating the first few functions directly from the definition. See Figure 17.8. Taking x as the new variable, applying the first equality of (17.7), and setting $u = x - t$, we may write

$$\phi_k(x) = \int_{-\infty}^{\infty} b(t)\phi_{k-1}(x-t)\mathrm{d}t = \int_0^1 \phi_{k-1}(x-t)\mathrm{d}t = \int_{x-1}^x \phi_{k-1}(u)\mathrm{d}u. \tag{17.8}$$

Sample polynomials Here we apply (17.8) directly. The first line shows how to obtain formula (17.9) below.

$$0 \le x \le 1: \phi_1(x) = \int_0^x 1 \cdot \mathrm{d}u = x, \text{ whence } \phi_2(x) = \int_0^x \phi_1(u)\mathrm{d}u = x^2/2,$$

$$1 \le x \le 2: \phi_1(x) = \int_{x-1}^1 1 \cdot \mathrm{d}u \text{ (since } \phi_0(u) = 0 \text{ for } u > 1) = 2 - x, \text{ whence}$$

$$\phi_2(x) = \int_{x-1}^1 \phi_1(u)\mathrm{d}u + \int_1^x \phi_1(u)\mathrm{d}u = \int_{x-1}^1 u\mathrm{d}u + \int_1^x (2-u)\mathrm{d}u$$

$$= -(2x^2 - 6x + 3)/2,$$

$$2 \le x \le 3: \phi_2(x) = \int_{x-1}^2 \phi_1(u)\mathrm{d}u = \int_{x-1}^2 (2-u)\mathrm{d}u = (x-3)^2/2,$$

$$\phi_k(x) = x^k/k! \quad \text{for } 0 \le x \le 1. \tag{17.9}$$

The calculation above shows how, because $b(t)$ is zero outside the unit interval [0, 1], ϕ_k becomes a different polynomial on successive intervals $[i, i+1]$. The next result shows that the polynomial pieces agree smoothly, and suggests the general shape depicted in Figure 17.7.

Theorem 17.8 *The spline function $\phi_k(x)$ has the following properties: (i) it is symmetric on the interval $(0, k + 1)$ and zero outside it; (ii) it possesses derivatives up to order $k - 1$, where (for all x)*

$$\phi_k'(x) = \phi_{k-1}(x) - \phi_{k-1}(x - 1)\ (k \geq 2);\qquad(17.10)$$

(iii) $\phi_k(x)$ has a unique maximum, on its line of symmetry $x = (k + 1)/2$; to the left it is strictly increasing, and to the right decreasing $(0 < x < k + 1)$.

Proof (i) *Symmetry* A curve $y = f(x)$ is symmetric, with $x = a$ as line of symmetry, if $f(2a - x) = f(x)$. Clearly, the box function is symmetric, $b(1 - x) = b(x)$, so suppose inductively that ϕ_{k-1} is symmetric, which means $\phi_{k-1}(k - x) = \phi_{k-1}(x)$. Then, by (17.8),

$$\phi_k(x) = \int_{x-1}^{x} \phi_{k-1}(u)\mathrm{d}u = \int_{x-1}^{x} \phi_{k-1}(k - u)\mathrm{d}u = \int_{k-x}^{k-x+1} \phi_{k-1}(y)\mathrm{d}y\ (y = k - u),$$

which equals $\phi_k(k + 1 - x)$, again by (17.8). That is, ϕ_k is symmetric. We consider only *the case $x \leq 0$*, then symmetry covers $x \geq k + 1$. Firstly, $\phi_1(x) = 0$ by (17.8) because $b(u) = 0$ on $[x - 1, x]$ except in the case $u = x = 0$, a single point, which does not affect the integral. Similarly, (17.8) now shows inductively that $\phi_k(x) = 0$ for $k \geq 1$.

(ii) *Derivatives* Suppose that ϕ_{k-1} is continuous (everywhere). Then its integral from 0 to x exists as a function $F(x)$, say. By (17.8), $\phi_k(x) = F(x) - F(x - 1)$, whence ϕ_k is differentiable with $\phi_k'(x) = F'(x) - F'(x - 1)$. But this equals the the right hand side of (17.10) as required, since $F'(t) = \phi_{k-1}(t)$ (by the Fundamental Theorem of Calculus). Substituting the continuous function ϕ_1 in the right hand side of (17.10), we see that ϕ_2 has continuous first derivative. Then repeated differentation of (17.10) shows that ϕ_k has derivatives up to order $k - 1$.

(iii) *Maximum* We proceed by induction on $k \geq 1$. The result is true for $k = 1$ because $\phi_1(x) = x$ for $0 \leq x \leq 1$, and is symmetric about $x = 1$ (see Figure 17.7). Assume the result holds for some $k \geq 1$; we must deduce its truth for ϕ_{k+1}. By symmetry, it suffices to show that $\phi_{k+1}'(x) > 0$ for $0 < x < (k + 2)/2$, or equivalently, by (17.10), that $\phi_k(x - 1) < \phi_k(x)$ there. But the inductive hypothesis gives $\phi_k(x - 1) < \phi_k(x)$ provided $0 < x < (k + 1)/2$, the region of increase of ϕ_k, so it remains to establish the inequality over the remaining range $(k + 1)/2 \leq x < (k + 2)/2$ for ϕ_{k+1}. We invoke symmetry: $\phi_k(x) = \phi_k(k + 1 - x)$; to apply this we observe that $x - 1 < k + 1 - x \Leftrightarrow 2x < k + 2 \Leftrightarrow x < (k + 2)/2$. Since the latter inequality does hold, we have

$$\phi_k(x - 1) < \phi_k(k + 1 - x) = \phi_k(x),$$

so $\phi_{k+1}'(x) < 0$ by (17.10), and the inductive step is complete.

Example 17.9 (*Explicit continuity checks*) In calculational terms, (17.9) gives the $(k - 1)$st derivative as x, which is trivially zero at $x = 0$. Thus, by symmetry, there is a zero of order $k - 1$ at each end-point of the interval $[0, k + 1]$. This is also predicted by Theorem 17.8 as follows: since ϕ_k is identically zero outside the interval $[0, k + 1]$, so is its $(k-1)$st derivative, and hence by continuity this derivative is zero at the end-points $0, k+1$. This explains ϕ_3's faster approach to zero than ϕ_2, in Figure 17.7.

We check that the derivative ϕ_2' is continuous, as asserted by Theorem 17.8. A glance at Figure 17.7 reminds us that, assuming symmetry, we need only check the point $x = 1$. Let $f(a-)$ and $f(a+)$ stand for the limits as x approaches a through values respectively less/greater than a. From the sample polynomials below Figure 17.8,

$$\phi_2'(1-) = \mathop{\mathrm{Lim}}_{x \to 1} \frac{\mathrm{d}}{\mathrm{d}x}(x^2/2) = \mathop{\mathrm{Lim}}_{x \to 1} x = 1, \text{ and}$$

$$\phi_2'(1+) = \mathop{\mathrm{Lim}}_{x \to 1} \frac{\mathrm{d}}{\mathrm{d}x}(-2x^2 + 6x - 3)/2 = \mathop{\mathrm{Lim}}_{x \to 1}(3 - 2x) = 1.$$

Exercise Check by calculation, as above, that ϕ_2' is continuous at $x = 2$.

17.1.4 The Fourier Transform

Our definition of ϕ_k as the convolution of $k+1$ copies of the box function $b(t)$ is ideal for deriving certain kinds of relations between the splines, because of the Convolution Theorem and the fact that the Fourier Transform of $b(t)$ is straightforward (Exercise 14.9). The theory of the (continuous) Fourier Transform may be reviewed from Section 14.2.

What we need is summarised in Table 17.1. We'll use it here to derive the well-known relations discovered independently by Cox (1972) and de Boor (1972). Historically, these relations have provided a recursive method for computer calculation of ϕ_k at given points using only the operations of addition (allowing for spill), and a shift to divide by 2. They are themselves a possible starting point for a derivation of B-splines (Farin, 2002).

Table 17.1. *The Continuous Fourier Transforms of certain functions (cf. Table 14.2 of Section 14.2.2). Here $b(t)$ is the unit box at the origin, with value 1 on $0 \le x \le 1$ (sometimes $0 < x < 1$, the transform being the same).*

function	transform	function	transform
(i) $b(t)$	$B(s) = (1 - e^{-2\pi i s})/2\pi i s$	(iv) $f(t-a)$	$e^{-2\pi i a s} F(s)$
(ii) $f(t)^*g(t)$	$F(s)G(s)$	(v) $tf(t)$	$(i/2\pi)F'(s)$
(iii) $\phi_k(t)$	$B(s)^{k+1}$	(vi) $f'(t)$	$2\pi i s F(s)$

We verify the transform of $\phi_k(t)$. The transform of $b(t)$ is by definition (see (14.25))

$$B(s) = \int_{-\infty}^{\infty} b(t)e^{-2\pi i s t}\,\mathrm{d}t = \int_0^1 e^{-2\pi i s t}\,\mathrm{d}t = \left[e^{-2\pi i s t}/(-2\pi i s)\right]_0^1$$

$$= (1 - e^{-2\pi i s})/2\pi i s,$$

as asserted. Now the Convolution Theorem, represented by entry (ii) of Table 17.1, gives the transform of the $(k+1)$-fold convolution product ϕ_k as a table entry $B(s)^{k+1}$. We are ready for a first application of the Fourier Transform to splines, to give a 'polynomial-free' proof of the *Cox-de Boor relations* (this needs no consideration of intervals). In the present notation they assert that, starting from $\phi_0(t) = b(t)$:

$$\phi_k(t) = \frac{t}{k}\phi_{k-1}(t) + \frac{k+1-t}{k}\phi_{k-1}(t-1) \quad (k \geq 1). \tag{17.11}$$

Proof A useful point to note here is that the derivative of $sB(s)$ simplifies to $\mathrm{e}^{-2\pi\mathrm{i}s}$, whence

$$sB'(s) + B(s) = \mathrm{e}^{-2\pi\mathrm{i}s}. \tag{17.12}$$

The right hand side of (17.11) simplifies by the derivative formula (17.10) (see the exercise below) to $1/k$ times $t\phi_k'(t) + (k+1)\phi_{k-1}(t-1)$, so we must show that the latter transforms to $kB(s)^{k+1}$. According to Table 17.1 the transform is

$$\frac{\mathrm{i}}{2\pi}\frac{\mathrm{d}}{\mathrm{d}s}[2\pi\mathrm{i}sB(s)^{k+1}] + (k+1)\mathrm{e}^{-2\pi\mathrm{i}s}B(s)^k$$

$$= -[s(k+1)B(s)^kB'(s) + B(s)^{k+1}] + (k+1)\mathrm{e}^{-2\pi\mathrm{i}s}B(s)^k$$

$$= B(s)^k[(k+1)(\mathrm{e}^{-2\pi\mathrm{i}s} - sB'(s)) - B(s)],$$

which simplifies to $kB(s)^{k+1}$ as required, on substituting (17.12). This completes the proof.

Exercise Prove (17.10) by Fourier Transforms.

Convexity We now prove a result that will imply a much more powerful convexity property for B-splines than for Bézier (except when the two coincide as a very special case).

Theorem 17.10 *The sum $S_k(t) = \phi_k(t) + \phi_k(t-1) + \cdots + \phi_k(t-k)$ is equal to 1 when t lies in the interval $[k, k+1]$.*

Proof Proofs can be given using (17.11) or the Fourier Transform, but we offer a proof that aims at exposing the 'real' reason why the result holds, based on the probability origins of convolution. We have by (17.8):

$$S_k(t) = \sum_{j=0}^{k}\int_{t-j-1}^{t-j}\phi_{k-1}(u)\mathrm{d}u = \int_{t-k-1}^{t}\phi_{k-1}(u)\mathrm{d}u, \tag{17.13}$$

since the areas summed are, in reverse order, contiguous. But because $\phi_{k-1}(x)$ is zero outside the interval $[0, k]$, and we are considering $k \leq t \leq k+1$ (or equivalently $t \geq k$ and $t - k - 1 \leq 0$), the integral (17.13) is simply the area under the curve $\phi_{k-1}(x)$ illustrated in Figure 17.9.

This area is 1 for a very simple reason. Because $b(t) \geq 0$ and the area under its graph is unity, $b(t)$ is a pdf, or probability density function. Therefore $\phi_{k-1}(t)$, as the convolution

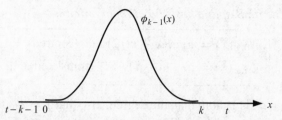

Figure 17.9 The graph of a probability density function, or pdf. Under such a curve the area is always unity (see Section 9.3.2).

product of copies of $b(t)$, is also a pdf (see Section 10.2.2), and hence has sub-curve area 1 as asserted.

Table 17.2. *How convolution is affected by translation, scaling and addition (Chapter 10, Theorem 10.21).*

convolution $f(t)^*g(t)$	result $h(x)$
(i) $f(t+a)^*g(t)$	$h(t+a)$
(ii) $f(t/d)^*g(t/d)$	$d \times h(x/d)$
(iii) $(\lambda + \mu)^*\sigma$	$\lambda^*\sigma + \mu^*\sigma$

17.1.5 Basis functions: Cox–de Boor relations

We obtain a B-spline basis function $N_{i,m}(x)$ by first centring ϕ_{m-1} about the origin, a left translation of $m/2$ units, then translating right by i units. This is seen in Figure 17.10, whose graphs are, as prescribed, translated copies of those belonging to Figure 17.7. To shift a function $f(x)$ by α units to the left, we replace x by $x + \alpha$ in the argument. Table 17.2(i) shows that, if we centre the box function by replacing t by $t + 1/2$, then ϕ_k in (17.7) is shifted $1/2$ unit more than ϕ_{k-1}, as it should be, so (17.7) defines centred ϕ_k if it starts with centred boxes. Formal B-spline definitions follow.

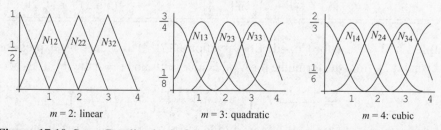

Figure 17.10 Some B-spline basis functions $N_{i,m}(t)$ in the cases $m = 2, 3$ and 4. We will normally use the cubic case, $m = 4$. Note that the line of symmetry is $x = i$ and that $N_{i,4}(x)$ is positive only for x less than $m/2$ units either side of this line, otherwise zero.

Definition 17.11 The *ith B-spline basis function of order* $m \geq 2$ $(0 \leq i \leq m)$ is given by

$$N_{0,m}(x) = \phi_{m-1}(x + m/2) \qquad \text{(centred)}, \qquad (17.14)$$

$$N_{i,m}(x) = N_{0,m}(x - i) \qquad \text{(translated)}. \qquad (17.15)$$

Notice that the order, m, is 1 more than the degree; also that $x = i$ *is the line of symmetry of* $N_{i,m}$ and contains its maximum. We now deduce three useful consequences of the definition of $N_{i,m}$, namely:

$$N_{i+1,m}(x) = N_{i,m}(x - 1), \qquad (17.16)$$

$$N_{i,m}(x) = 0 \text{ if } x \leq i - m/2 \text{ or } x \geq i + m/2, \qquad (17.17)$$

$$\text{i.e. } |x - i| \geq m/2,$$

and the *Cox–de Boor relations*

$$N_{i,m}(x) = \frac{m - 2x}{2(m - 1)} N_{i,m-1}\left(x - \tfrac{1}{2}\right) + \frac{m + 2x}{2(m - 1)} N_{i,m-1}\left(x + \tfrac{1}{2}\right). \qquad (17.18)$$

Proof For (17.16) we observe that both sides of the equation are by definition equal to $N_{0,m}(x - i - 1)$. In the case of (17.17) we argue that $N_{i,m}(x) = N_{0,m}(x - i) = \phi_{m-1}(x + m/2 - i)$, which by Theorem 17.8 is zero *except* between end-points: $0 < x + m/2 - i) < m$, that is except for $i - m/2 < x < i + m/2$. Thus we have (17.17). The updated Cox–de Boor relations (17.18) in terms of $N_{i,m}$ may be obtained by centring the ϕ_k of (17.11) and substituting in terms of $N_{0,m}$. Then the case $i = 0$ implies that of general $i = 0, 1, 2, \ldots$, by (17.15).

Table 17.3 shows some explicitly calculated B-spline basis functions.

Table 17.3. *Low-degree B-spline basis functions. We extend results to the case $x < 0$ by symmetry: $N_{0,m}(-x) = N_{0,m}(x)$, and to the case $i > 0$ by translation, (17.15).*

$N_{0,2}(x)$	$N_{0,3}(x)$	$N_{0,4}(x)$
$1 - x$ on $[0, 1]$	$\frac{3}{4} - x^2$ on $\left[0, \tfrac{1}{2}\right]$	$\frac{1}{6}(3x^3 - 6x^2 + 4)$ on $[0, 1]$
	$\frac{1}{2}\left(x - \tfrac{3}{2}\right)^2$ on $\left[\tfrac{1}{2}, \tfrac{3}{2}\right]$	$\frac{1}{6}(2 - x)^3$ on $[1, 2]$

Example 17.12 We use the Cox–de Boor relations (17.18) to deduce the expression for $N_{0,4}(x)$ on $[1, 2]$, from the formulae for $N_{0,3}$. With $i = 0$ and $m = 4$ the relations become

$$N_{0,4}(x) = \frac{4 - 2x}{2 \cdot 3} N_{0,3}\left(x - \frac{1}{2}\right) + \frac{4 + 2x}{2 \cdot 3} N_{0,3}\left(x + \frac{1}{2}\right).$$

Given that x lies in $[1, 2]$, we have $x - 1/2$ in $[1/2, 3/2]$, and $x + 1/2$ in the interval $[3/2, 5/2]$. Also, $N_{0,3}$ is zero in the latter interval. Therefore

$$N_{0,4}(x) = \frac{4 - 2x}{2 \cdot 3} \cdot \frac{(x - 2)^2}{2} + 0 = \frac{1}{6}(2 - x)^3.$$

B-splines Now we are ready to define a B-spline curve with control points $P_0, \ldots, P_n$. It is a parametric curve in the same dimension as the points P_i, here taken in the plane. The curve is traced out as the parameter t *increases from 0 to n*. We derive two fundamental properties, then concentrate on the cubic case, our main theme.

Definition 17.13 *The B-spline of order m (degree m − 1) and control points $P_0, \ldots, P_n$ is the function*

$$B_m(t) = \sum_{i=0}^{n} N_{i,m}(t)\, P_i \quad (0 \le t \le n). \tag{17.19}$$

Theorem 17.14 (a) *(Affine invariance) If f is an affine transformation then $f(B_m(t))$ is the B-spline with control points $f(P_i)$.* (b) *(Strong convexity) $B_m(t)$ lies in the convex hull of m successive control points. They are symmetrically numbered relative to the pair P_r, P_{r+1} if t is in $[r, r + 1]$ (m even), and relative to P_r if t is in $[r − 1/2, r + 1/2]$ (m odd).*

Proof (a) Similarly to the case of Bézier splines, we apply Equation (17.6) with $s_i = N_{i,m}(t)$. For (b) we start with the convexity relations of Theorem 17.10, setting $t = x + m/2 − i$ and $k = m − 1$, to obtain, by definition of $N_{i,m}$,

$$N_{i,m}(x) + N_{i+1,m}(x) + \cdots + N_{i+m-1,m}(x) = 1 \quad (x \text{ in } [i + m/2 − 1, i + m/2]). \tag{17.20}$$

For this range of x we have $B(x) = \sum_j N_{j,m}(x)\, P_j$ $(i \le j \le i + m − 1)$. Other terms are zero by (17.17) because $j \le i − 1$ implies $x \ge i + m/2 − 1 \ge j + m/2$, and because $j \ge i + m$ implies $x \le i + m/2 \le j − m + m/2 = j − m/2$. Here the coefficient sum is unity by (17.20), and hence $B(x)$ lies in the convex hull of the m points $P_i, \ldots, P_{i+m-1}$. The proof is completed by expressing the cases of m even/odd as

$m = 2s$: x in $[i + s − 1, i + s]$,

    $B(x)$ in convex hull of $P_i \ldots P_{i+s-1} P_{i+s} \ldots P_{i+2s-1}$ (put $r = i + s − 1$),

$m = 2s + 1$: x in $[i + s − 1/2, i + s + 1/2]$,

    $B(x)$ in convex hull of $P_i \ldots P_{i+s} \ldots P_{i+2s}$ (put $r = i + s$).

Example 17.15 (i) *The case $m = 3$.* Here $B(x)$ lies in the convex hull of $P_3 P_4 P_5$ if x lies in the range $3.5 \le x \le 4.5$.

(ii) *The cubic case, $m = 4$.* Now $B(x)$ is in the convex hull of $P_2 P_3 P_4 P_5$ if $3 \le x \le 4$. Notice that $B(3)$ lies in the intersection of the convex hulls of $P_1 P_2 P_3 P_4$ and $P_2 P_3 P_4 P_5$ (why?). Hence in Figure 17.11 it lies on the segment $P_2 P_3 P_4$.

17.1.6 Cubic B-splines

Remarks 17.16 (a) *(Zeros)* Recalling that the absolute value $|t − i|$ is the distance of t from i, we have from (17.17) that cubic B-splines satisfy

$$N_{i,4}(t) = 0 \text{ if and only if } |t − i| \ge 2. \tag{17.21}$$

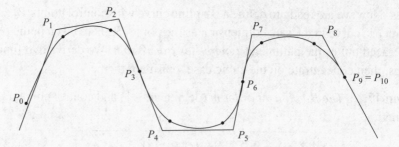

Figure 17.11 Single cubic B-spline curve, using the control points previously distributed between three Bézier curves in Figure 17.1. Successive dark dots denote curve points $B(i)$.

(b) (*Near-zeros*) When t is two units from i, the function has a zero of order 3. This may be proved by setting $x = 2$ in the expression of Table 17.3 for $N_{0,4}$, and illustrated by $N_{2,4}$ and $N_{3,4}$ in Figure 17.10. Thus, for t slightly closer than two units to i, we may expect $N_{i,4}(t)$ to be negligibly different from zero. Here are some useful values.

distance of t from i	0	0.5	1	1.5	1.8	1.9	2
$N_{i,4}(t)$		2/3	23/48	1/6	1/48	$\leq 10^{-3}$	$\leq 2 \cdot 10^{-4}$	0

$$(17.22)$$

(c) (*Derivatives*) $N'_{0,4}(\pm 1) = \mp 1/2$, otherwise $N'_{0,4}$ (integer) $= 0$.

Proof $N'_{0,4}(1) = [d/dt(2-t)^3/6]_{t=1}$ (Table 17.3) $= -3/6 = -1/2$, so by symmetry $N'_{0,4}(-1) = 1/2$. Also $N'_{0,4}(0) = 0$ by symmetry, and the remaining integers j satisfy $|j - i| \geq 2$ as in case (a).

Exercise Verify the above values of $N_{i,4}(t)$ (it suffices to take $i = 0$).

(d) (*Sketching*) Figure 17.12 illustrates two properties of a cubic B-spline which may facilitate sketching, given the control polygon $P_0 \ldots P_n$.

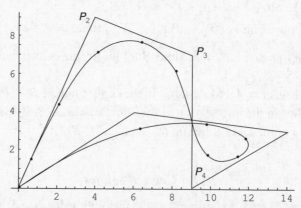

Figure 17.12 Cubic B-spline with points highlighted at parameter increments of 1/2. The control points are $(0, 0)$, $(0, 0)$, $(4, 9)$, $(9, 7)$, $(9, 0)$, $(14, 3)$, $(6, 4)$, $(0, 0)$, $(0, 0)$. The double points ensure tangency at the end-points of the curve, see Remarks 17.17(e).

(i) $B(i + 1/2)$ is close to the midpoint of $P_i P_{i+1}$, and
(ii) $B(i)$ is 1/3 of the way from P_i to the midpoint of $P_{i-1} P_{i+1}$.

These apply, of course, whilst the cited subscripts are within range. Explicit formulae are (i) $B(i + \frac{1}{2}) = \frac{23}{24} \times \frac{1}{2}(P_i + P_{i+1}) + \frac{1}{24} \times \frac{1}{2}(P_{i-1} + P_{i+2})$, (ii) $B(i) = \frac{2}{3}P_i + \frac{1}{3} \times \frac{1}{2}(P_{i-1} + P_{i+1})$. We derive formula (ii), leaving (i) for Exercise 17.9. By (17.21) there are only the following nonzero terms when, as here, i is an integer:

$$B(i) = N_{i-1,4}(i)P_{i-1} + N_{i,4}(i)P_i + N_{i+1,4}(i)P_{i+1}$$
$$= (1/6)P_{i-1} + (2/3)P_i + (1/6)P_{i+1},$$

by (17.22). Notice that (i) says $B(i + 1/2)$ is 1/24 of the way along the join of the midpoint of $P_i P_{i+1}$ to the midpoint of $P_{i-1} P_{i+2}$.

Using collinear and double control points

Remarks 17.17 (*Collinear control points and convexity*) Suppose a cubic B-spline has four successive control points *PQRS* in a *straight line*. Then, by convexity, Theorem 17.14(b), part of the curve lies along the segment *QR*. Moreover, if we allow *P* to approach *Q* and/or *S* to approach *R*, and to form double points, then we obtain the useful special cases below. Detailed calculation shows that in these cases not quite all of *QR* is included in the curve. However, by the list in (17.22), the departure may be so small as to be invisible in practice. Here, a control point is represented by a small circle, which is filled in if the point is double.

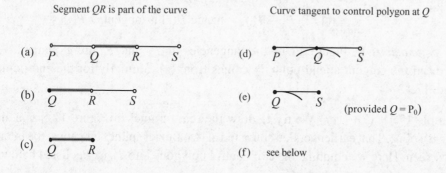

Segment *QR* is part of the curve   Curve tangent to control polygon at *Q*

(a) $P \quad Q \quad R \quad S$ (d) $P \quad Q \quad S$

(b) $Q \quad R \quad S$ (e) $Q \quad S$ (provided $Q = P_0$)

(c) $Q \quad R$ (f) see below

Case (f): *three point* $P_{i-1} P_i P_{i+1}$, *collinear and equally spaced* The curve satisfies $B(i) = P_i$ and is tangent to the control polygon there ($i = 1$ below).

Discussion and Proof of (f) The following serves to establish (f) for *any* three successive control points that are collinear and equally spaced. Consider a control polygon $P_0 P_1 \ldots P_n$ for a cubic B-spline curve $B(t)$, in which the first three points are collinear, equally spaced, as represented in Figure 17.13. Because $N_{i,4}(t) = 0$ for $|t - i| \geq 2$ (see (17.21)), we have for $t \leq 2$,

$$B(t) = N_{0,4}(t)P_0 + N_{1,4}(t)P_1 + N_{2,4}(t)P_2 + N_{3,4}(t)P_3 \ (+ \text{ no more terms}).$$

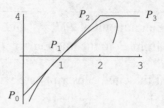

Figure 17.13 Cubic B-spline curve for control polygon $P_0 P_1 P_2 P_3$ with three points collinear. The curve is *tangent to the polygon at* P_1, and this remains true if the polygon is extended to $P_4 P_5 \ldots P_n$ because $N_{i,4}(t) = 0$ for $t \leq i - 2$ and $t \geq i + 2$.

Let us establish whether $B(0) = P_0$. We have $B(0) = N_{0,4}(0)P_0 + N_{1,4}(0)P_1 = (2/3)P_0 + (1/6)P_1$, which is not even on the *line* through P_0, P_1 because $2/3 + 1/6 \neq 1$ (see (17.4)). The non-coincidence is well brought out in Figure 17.13, but what happens at P_1? We have

$$
\begin{aligned}
B(1) &= N_{0,4}(1)P_0 + N_{1,4}(1)P_1 + N_{2,4}(1)P_2 & \text{by (17.21)} \\
&= (1/6)P_0 + (2/3)P_1 + (1/6)P_2 & \text{by (17.22)} \\
&= P_1, \text{ because } P_0 + P_2 = 2P_1.
\end{aligned}
$$

This is a promising start. One approach to the tangency is to consider the interval $1 \leq t \leq 1.1$, where the table of (17.21) tells us that P_3 contributes at most $2 \cdot 10^{-4} P_3$, and so near to P_1 the curve will appear to coincide with the polygon, as illustrated in Figure 17.13. In fact we have, in terms of derivatives,

$$
\begin{aligned}
B'(1) &= N'_{0,4}(1)P_0 + N'_{1,4}(1)P_1 + N'_{2,4}(1)P_2 \\
&= (-1/2)P_0 + 0P_1 + (1/2)P_2 \\
&= (1/2)(P_2 - P_0), \quad \text{hence } B(t) \text{ is tangent at } P_1.
\end{aligned}
$$

First conclusions In Figure 17.11 the tangencies at P_3 and P_6 are explained by (f) above and the tangent at end-point P_9 comes from (e). Similarly for the end-points in Figure 17.12.

Example 17.18 (*The car*) We try to draw the 'car outline' of Figure 17.5 as a single cubic B-spline. That earlier version consisted of two Bézier splines tangent at the intended windscreen. Here we combine the two control polygons into P_0 to P_{12} listed below:

$$(0, 0), (2, 8), (16, 8), (16.5, 6), (16.5, 6), (17, 4), (20, 4), (23, 4), (23, 4),$$
$$(23, 2), (23, 0), (23, 0), (0, 0).$$

The points are shown in Figure 17.14(i), with repeats filled-in. The resulting B-spline curve (ii) is nevertheless closer to the designer's very conservative intentions in respect of (a) a straighter windscreen, (b) rectangular front and (c) straight underside. These were aimed for by use of the repeated points. This measure of success derives from Theorem 17.14(b), and is obtained by exploiting the configurations in Remarks 17.17. See also Figure 17.15.

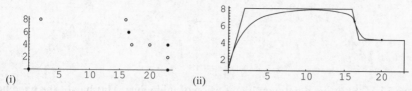

Figure 17.14 (i) Control points, with repeats shown filled, (ii) the car outline $B(t)$ as a single B-spline, within its control polygon. Note that the car is a parametric curve, traced out as t increases from 0 to 12.

Exercise Use Remarks 17.17 to explain the tangents and straight line portions of Figure 17.14. Can any points be omitted?

Figure 17.15 The previous car made more curvaceous by addition of further control points. The final list is shown below.
(0, 0), (0, 0), (2, 8), (16, 8), (16.5, 6), (16.5, 6), (17, 4), (20, 4), (22.6, 4), (23, 3.6), (23, 2), (23, 0), (23, 0), (20, 0), (20, 0), (18, −2), (16, 0), (16, 0), (7, 0), (7, 0), (5, −2), (3, 0), (3, 0), (0, 0), (0, 0).

17.2 The step to subdivision

17.2.1 A fundamental theorem

Here we consider B-splines $\sum_i N_{i,m}(t)P_i$ which are *uniform* in the sense that successive control points $P_0, \ldots, P_n$ have x-coordinates incremented by a fixed *mesh width d*, say $x(P_k) = kd$.

Scaling To prove the Fundamental Theorem 17.21 on generating B-splines by recursive subdivision, we need to know what happens with $N_{i,m}$ when unit 1 is scaled to unit d. To find out, we replace x by x/d in the above definition (similarly in Table 17.3), and add an extra argument d. Thus, beginning with the centred unit box $b(d, x)$, we may define

$$N_{0,1}(d, x) = b(d, x) = \begin{cases} 1 & \text{if } x \in [-\frac{d}{2}, \frac{d}{2}], \\ 0, & \text{otherwise,} \end{cases} \tag{17.23}$$

and, taking into account Table 17.2(ii) for convolution, this results in

$$N_{i+1,m}(d, x) = N_{i,m}(d, x - d) \ (m \geq 1), \tag{17.24}$$

$$d \times N_{i,m}(d, x) = b(d, t)^* N_{i,m-1}(d, t), \tag{17.25}$$

$$N_{i,m}(d, x) = 0 \text{ if } \begin{cases} x \leq i - md/2 \text{ or } x \geq i + md/2, \\ \text{i.e. } |x - i| \geq md/2. \end{cases} \tag{17.26}$$

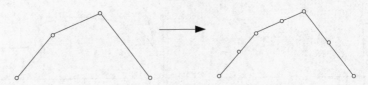

Figure 17.16 Splitting a polygon by insertion of midpoints. This halves the fixed horizontal distance between successive vertices.

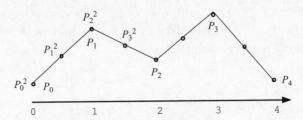

Figure 17.17 Split polygon with first few new vertices labelled. The defined linear B-spline coincides with the polygon before, and hence also after, the split (Theorem 17.19).

Exercise Write down an expression for $N_{0,4}(x, d)$ valid for $0 \le x \le d$ (see Table 17.3).

Splitting The first step in recursive subdivision is called *splitting*, which means refinement of a polygon by inserting the midpoint of each edge, as in Figure 17.16. Thus a polygon $P_0 \dots P_n$ with $n + 1$ vertices becomes a polygon of $n + 1 + n = 2n + 1$ vertices, which we'll denote by $P_0^2 P_1^2 \dots P_{2n}^2$. The new vertices are given in terms of the old by $P_{2i}^2 = P_i$ and $P_{2i+1}^2 = \frac{1}{2}(P_i + P_{i+1})$. We are about to show formally that a *linear* B-spline $B_2(t)$ is unaffected by splitting. That is, the two expressions below are equal:

$$B_2(t) = \sum_{i=0}^{n} N_{i,2}(1, t) P_i \quad \text{(original)}, \tag{17.27}$$

$$B_2(t) = \sum_{j=0}^{2n} N_{j,2}\left(\tfrac{1}{2}, t\right) P_j^2 \quad \text{(after split)}. \tag{17.28}$$

Theorem 17.19 *(Linear B-splines, $m = 2$) A linear B-spline coincides with its control polygon. Hence splitting leaves the B-spline unchanged. See Figure 17.17.*

Proof We prove the result for the case $d = 1$ and then it will follow for general $d > 0$ because scaling converts one case to the other (Theorem 17.14). Thus we begin with the formula (17.27) for the B-spline $B_2(t)$ and show that it coincides with its own control polygon $P_0 \dots P_n$.

Let the parameter t lie in the interval $[i, i + 1]$. Then $B_2(t)$ lies in the convex hull of P_i and P_{i+1} (Theorem 17.14 with $m = 2$), which is the line segment $P_i P_{i+1}$. It remains to prove that $B_2(t) = P_i$ for $0 \le i \le n$. But (17.17) gives $N_{j,2}(i) = 0$ for $|j - i| \ge 1$, that is for $j \ne i$, and we know that $N_{i,2}(i) = 1$ (see e.g. Figure 17.10) so, omitting terms that are zero, $B_2(i) = N_{i,2}(i) P_i = P_i$. This completes the proof.

Subdivision A subdivision step consists of splitting followed by an averaging step, in which a new polygon is formed whose vertices are weighted averages of the old. Our

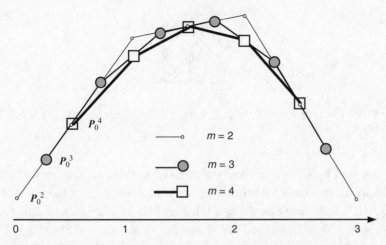

Figure 17.18 The result of splitting followed by two simple averaging steps. Note how the initial point moves 1/4 unit horizontally on each averaging.

averaging step will consist of $m - 2$ repeats of what is naturally termed a *simple* averaging step, in which a new polygon is formed by averaging successive vertex pairs of the old. Thus the sequence $\{P_i\}$ becomes $\{(P_i + P_{i+1})/2\}$ and the number of vertices is reduced by 1. In summary

$$\text{Subdivision step} = \text{split} + \text{average, where}$$
$$\text{Average} = m - 2 \text{ simple averages in succession.}$$

We have denoted the original control polygon by $P_0 \ldots P_n$ and the result of a splitting step by $P_0^2 P_1^2 \ldots P_{2n}^2$. The resulting polygon after the first simple average will be labelled $P_0^3 P_1^3 \ldots P_{2n-1}^3$ ($m = 3$), the next $P_0^4 P_1^4 \ldots P_{2n-2}^4$ ($m = 4$), and so on. This is illustrated in Figure 17.18, where for simplicity we take $d = 1$. To revert to general d, soon to be needed, we just multiply horizontal distances by d.

Remark 17.20 With unit mesh $d = 1$, each simple averaging step does the following:

(i) reduces the number of control points by 1,
(ii) retains the mesh width $1/2$,
(iii) starts the new polygon $1/4$ unit to the right of the previous polygon, by (ii),
(iv) cuts corners.

Theorem 17.21 (*Fundamental Theorem, Lane and Riesenfeld, 1980*) *Let $P_0 \ldots P_n$ be the control polygon of a uniform B-spline of order $m \geq 2$. Then, after subdivision consisting of splitting once, then $m - 2$ simple averaging steps, the new polygon $P_0^m P_1^m \ldots P_{2n-(m-2)}^m$ defines a B-spline which agrees with the original over the reduced range $e \leq x \leq n - e$, where $e = (m - 2)/2$. That is, if we define*

$$\begin{cases} P_{2i}^2 = P_i, \\ P_{2i+1}^2 = \frac{1}{2}(P_i + P_{i+1}) \end{cases} \quad \text{and } P_i^{k+1} = \frac{1}{2}(P_i^k + P_{i+1}^k) \, (k \geq 2), \quad (17.29)$$

then
$$\sum_{i=0}^{n} N_{i,m}(1, x) P_i = \sum_{i=0}^{2n-m+2} N_{i,m}\left(\tfrac{1}{2}, x - e/2\right) P_i^m. \quad (17.30)$$

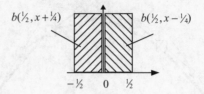

Figure 17.19 Illustration of $b(1, x)$ as the sum of $1/2$-width boxes, $b(1, x) = b(1/2, x + 1/4) + b(1/2, x - 1/4)$.

Proof We proceed by induction from the already established case $m = 2$ of Theorem 17.19. To apply the inductive hypothesis, i.e. the truth of the present theorem for B-splines of order $m - 1$, we observe that the box function $b(1, x)$ is the sum of half-width boxes centred at $x = \pm 1/4$, as illustrated in Figure 17.19. Note that the shift of $1/4$ to the left for a half-width box originally centred at $x = 0$ is achieved by replacing x by $x + 1/4$. For the rightwards shift, x becomes $x - 1/4$. This gives the hatched boxes of the figure.

Now we are ready for the inductive step from $m - 1$ to m, brought about naturally by the convolution definition of B-splines.

$$\sum_{i=0}^{n} N_{i,m}(1, x) P_i = \sum_{i=0}^{n} b(1, x)^* N_{i,m-1}(1, x) P_i \qquad \text{by (17.25)}$$

$$= b(1, x) * \sum_{i=0}^{n} N_{i,m-1}(1, x) P_i \qquad \text{(* is distributive)}$$

$$= b(1, x) * \sum_{i=0}^{2n-m+3} N_{i,m-1}\left(\tfrac{1}{2}, y\right) P_i^{m-1}$$
$$\text{(inductive hypothesis)}$$

$$\text{where } y = x - e/2, e = (m - 3)/2, e \leq x \leq n - e,$$

$$= \sum_{i=0}^{2n-m+3} b(1, x)^* N_{i,m-1}\left(\tfrac{1}{2}, y\right) P_i^{m-1} \qquad \text{(* is distributive)}$$

$$= \sum_{i=0}^{2n-m+3} b\left(\tfrac{1}{2}, x - \tfrac{1}{4}\right) * N_{i,m-1}\left(\tfrac{1}{2}, y\right) P_i^{m-1} + \sum_{i=0}^{2n-m+3} b\left(\tfrac{1}{2}, x + \tfrac{1}{4}\right) *$$
$$N_{i,m-1}\left(\tfrac{1}{2}, y\right) P_i^{m-1}, \qquad \text{on splitting } b(1, x) \text{ as in Figure 17.19}$$

$$= \tfrac{1}{2}\sum_{i=0}^{2n-m+3} N_{i,m}\left(\tfrac{1}{2}, y - \tfrac{1}{4}\right) P_i^{m-1} + \tfrac{1}{2}\sum_{i=0}^{2n-m+3} N_{i,m}\left(\tfrac{1}{2}, y + \tfrac{1}{4}\right) P_i^{m-1}$$
$$\text{by (17.25),}$$

with $d = 1/2$ and the translation rule of Table 17.2(i). Now we can drop a term from each sum (last of the first, first of the second), as follows. We know from (17.26) that $N_{0,m}(1/2, t) = 0$ if $t \geq m/4$ or $t \leq -m/4$, and so may argue using (17.24) that, since $y - 1/4 = x + 1/2 - m/4$,

$$N_{2n-m+3,m}\left(\frac{1}{2}, y - \frac{1}{4}\right) = N_{0,m}\left(\frac{1}{2}, x - n - 1 + \frac{m}{4}\right) = 0 \quad \text{if } x \leq n - \frac{m - 2}{2},$$

$$N_{0,m}\left(\frac{1}{2}, y + \frac{1}{4}\right) = N_{0,m}\left(\frac{1}{2}, x + 1 - \frac{m}{4}\right) = 0 \qquad \text{if } x \geq \frac{m - 2}{2}.$$

This reduces the sums to

$$\frac{1}{2} \sum_{i=0}^{2n-m+2} N_{i,m} \left(\frac{1}{2}, y - \frac{1}{4}\right) P_i^{m-1} + \frac{1}{2} \sum_{i=1}^{2n-m+3} N_{i,m} \left(\frac{1}{2}, y + \frac{1}{4}\right) P_i^{m-1}$$

$$= \frac{1}{2} \sum_{i=0}^{2n-m+2} N_{i,m} \left(\frac{1}{2}, y - \frac{1}{4}\right) P_i^{m-1} + \frac{1}{2} \sum_{i=0}^{2n-m+2} N_{i+1,m} \left(\frac{1}{2}, y + \frac{1}{4}\right) P_{i+1}^{m-1}$$

after replacing i by $i + 1$ in the second sum

$$= \frac{1}{2} \sum_{i=0}^{2n-m+2} N_{i,m} \left(\frac{1}{2}, y - \frac{1}{4}\right) P_i^{m-1} + \frac{1}{2} \sum_{i=0}^{2n-m+2} N_{i,m} \left(\frac{1}{2}, y - \frac{1}{4}\right) P_{i+1}^{m-1}$$

by (17.24)

$$= \sum_{i=0}^{2n-m+2} N_{i,m} \left(\frac{1}{2}, y - \frac{1}{4}\right) P_i^m \quad \text{by (17.29)},$$

which is the result for B-splines of order m. This completes the proof by induction on m.

17.2.2 B-splines by subdivision

Binomials It turns out that the averaging part of the subdivision step is given by *binomial coefficients*. In the cubic case $m = 4$, for example, we have after the two simple averagings:

$$P_i^4 = \frac{1}{4} \left[1 \cdot P_i^2 + 2 \cdot P_{i+1}^2 + 1 \cdot P_{i+2}^2\right].$$

The binomial coefficients 1 2 1 are no accident because, apart from factors 1/2, we are performing the calculation of Pascal's triangle for multiplying by $1 + x$, when we take P_i^{k+1} as the sum of the two elements above it in level k. Thus, after doing this three times we have multiplied by $(1 + x)^3$, and so taken a linear combination of the starting layer with coefficients 1 3 3 1 (and divided by 2^3). If we perform $m - 2$ averagings the coefficients are those in the expansion of $[(1 + x)/2]^{m-2}$ and then, by Theorem 9.12 of Chapter 9, the general formula is

$$P_i^m = (1/2^{m-2}) \sum_{k=0}^{m-2} \binom{m-2}{k} P_{i+k}^2. \tag{17.31}$$

Equivalently, we may say that simple averaging is, by its definition, convolving the sequence of heights of the control points with the sequence $\{1/2, 1/2\}$, and the same conclusion follows (cf. our use of continuous convolution to prove Theorem 17.21).

Exercise Use Pascal's triangle to determine coefficients for the averaging step in the case $m = 7$.

Recursive subdivision We have defined a single subdivision step for the control polygon of a B-spline to be splitting followed by $m - 2$ simple averagings, where m is the order of the spline. The Fundamental Theorem of the previous section shows that the result is the control polygon of a B-spline that agrees with the original over a reduced domain of definition which excludes an interval of width $(m - 2)/2$ from each end.

Recursive subdivision is a sequence of subdivision steps, each performed on the result of the previous step. After performing k iterations of subdivision, we arrive at a control polygon $P_0^{m,k} P_1^{m,k} \dots P_{r_k}^{m,k}$, which we shall refer to as the *kth (subdivision) iterate*, where the last subscript r_k tends to infinity with k. By Remarks 17.20(iii) we have, after the first iteration, $x(P_0^{m,1}) = (m - 2)/4$. For the next iteration the mesh starts at $d = 1/2$, so the initial polygon point moves on half as far, i. e. by $(m - 2)/8$. After k iterations the total comes to

$$x\left(P_0^{m,k}\right) = \frac{m - 2}{4} \left(1 + \frac{1}{2} + \frac{1}{2^2} + \dots + \frac{1}{2^{k-1}}\right)$$

$$\to \frac{m - 2}{4} \cdot \frac{1}{1 - 1/2} = \frac{m - 2}{2}, \text{ as } k \to \infty.$$

Thus the limit curve covers exactly the interval $e \le x \le n - e$, over which it equals (by Theorem 17.21) the specified B-spline.

Theorem 17.22 *(Convergence) In the notation above, the kth iterate of the control polygon approaches the B-spline it defines, as $k \to \infty$. In symbols, if $e = (m - 2)/2$, then*

$$P_0^{m,k} P_1^{m,k} \dots P_{r_k}^{m,k} \to \{B_m(x - e) \colon e \le x \le n - e\}. \tag{17.32}$$

Proof Considering any stage k of subdivision, let P be a point on the B-spline curve itself. Then by strong concavity, Theorem 17.14, this point lies in the convex hull of m successive points of the latest control polygon. Therefore, if the diameter, or greatest distance between points of such hulls, tends to zero as k increases, it will follow that the polygons approximate the curve with arbitrary precision as $k \to \infty$. Thus it suffices to show that for any finite permissible i and $i + s$ (say $s \le m$) we have

$$\left|P_{i+s}^{m,k} - P_i^{m,k}\right| \to 0, \text{ as } k \to \infty, \tag{17.33}$$

where $|A - B|$ equals the length $|AB|$ of a line segment. But by the triangle inequality

$$\left|P_{i+s}^{m,k} - P_i^{m,k}\right| \le \left|P_{i+s}^{m,k} - P_{i+s-1}^{m,k}\right| + \left|P_{i+s-1}^{m,k} - P_{i+s-2}^{m,k}\right|$$
$$+ \dots + \left|P_{i+1}^{m,k} - P_i^{m,k}\right|,$$

so we need only prove (17.33) for an arbitrary pair of adjacent points, the case $s = 1$. Now let $\delta = \text{Max}_i |P_{i+1} - P_i|$, and consider the first subdivision. We first insert the splitting midpoints, reducing the maximum edge length to $\delta/2$. Successive simple averaging cannot increase the maximum, as Figure 17.20 confirms.

In either case, $|PQ| = (1/2)|AC| \le (1/2)\{|AB| + |BC|\} \le \text{Max}\{|AB|, |BC|\} \le \delta/2$. It follows that, after k subdivisions,

$$\left|P_{i+1}^{m,k} - P_i^{m,k}\right| \le \delta/2^k \to 0, \text{ as } k \to \infty. \tag{17.34}$$

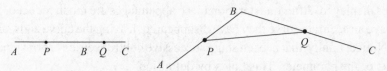

Figure 17.20 The two cases of simple average performed *after* splitting. Here P bisects AB and Q bisects BC, where $|AB|, |BC| \leq \delta/2$.

This completes the proof. Before illustrating this result we prepare for a little more control of the curve.

End-correcting cubic B-splines In the cubic case, $m = 4$, the subdivision method of Theorem 17.21 provides a B-spline that starts at $x = (m-2)/2 = 1$, losing one control point, with symmetrical loss of a single point on the right. We can retain the original end-points and cause the B-spline to be tangent there, as follows.

Construction 17.23 (*End-point tangency*) On the left we simply add a 'virtual' control point P_{-1} that satisfies $P_{-1}P_0 = P_0P_1$ as vectors. Then the B-spline is tangent at P_0 to P_0P_1, where the subdivision-constructed version begins. This is Figure 17.13 with $P_0P_1P_2$ relabelled $P_{-1}P_0P_1$. The right hand end of the polygon is modified similarly.

$$\overline{P_{-1} \quad P_0 \quad P_1}$$

Example 17.24 Figure 17.21 is our first example of a cubic B-spline by recursive subdivision, validated by Theorems 17.21 and 17.22, with the end-correction proposed in Construction 17.23. Original polygon heights $1, 0, 4, 2, 4$ become $2, 1, 0, 4, 2, 4, 6$ with the addition of the new end-points P_{-1}, P_6. Notice that as few as six iterations suffice to produce a convincing curve.

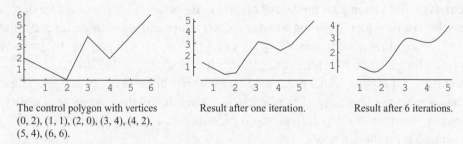

The control polygon with vertices $(0, 2), (1, 1), (2, 0), (3, 4), (4, 2), (5, 4), (6, 6)$.

Result after one iteration.

Result after 6 iterations.

Figure 17.21 From control polygon to recursive B-spline curve, tangent at end-points.

Parametric and crossing curves Suppose we wish to model a curve with multiple y-values for given x. Then we treat it as a parametric curve. This means applying the previous uniform spline function methods to x and y coordinates separately. Thus to each value of the uniformly increasing parameter t we allocate a pair (x, y), and are back to the situation where the control polygon may cross itself.

Example 17.25 We model a simplified face, using the end correction as described above. The control polygon is shown in Figure 17.22(a) at reduced scale to accommodate the extra edges displayed. After one iteration these appendages are much reduced, and by the time we have an accurate curve they have disappeared, leaving the curve ends tangentially directed. Notice, finally, that at each stage successive control vertices correspond to equal increments of the parameter. This holds by definition.

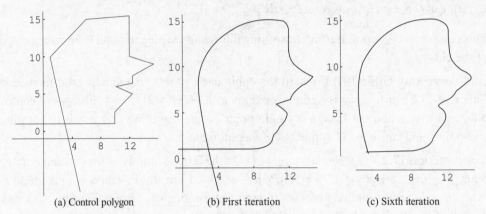

(a) Control polygon   (b) First iteration   (c) Sixth iteration

Figure 17.22 Parametric B-spline for 'face'. The end-correction points are intrusive in the control polygon but disappear after six iterations. Later we see how to avoid them altogether (see e.g. Figure 17.29). The original vertices were (3, 1), (10, 1), (10, 2.5), (12.5, 5), (10, 6), (12.5, 6.5), (12.5, 7.5), (15.5, 9), (12, 10), (12, 13), (12, 15.5), (6, 15), (1, 10), (3, 1).

Exercise Write down the extra control points of Figure 17.22.

17.2.3 Subdivision and basis functions

Recursive subdivision Our method of obtaining B-splines is but one example of recursive subdivision, which we'll outline in its wider sense and show to be equivalent to a nested system of function spaces $V^0 \subseteq V^1 \subseteq V^2 \subseteq \cdots$. This will prepare the ground for a wavelet formulation. The idea is to create a function $f(x)$ as the limit of successive refinements $f^j(x)$ of an initial function $f^0(x)$ which is linear between integer values of x (thus piecewise linear). On each refinement the mesh, i.e. the interval of linearity, is halved by insertion of midpoints, so the vertices at which $f^j(x)$ is to be calculated are (the so-called *dyadic integers*):

$$x = i/2^j \tag{17.35}$$

for fixed j. A convenient way to incorporate together the splitting and averaging steps that convert level $j - 1$ into level j is to write

$$f^j \left(\frac{i}{2^j} \right) = \sum_k r_k f^{j-1} \left(\frac{i+k}{2^j} \right), \tag{17.36}$$

where for each i we allow k to vary. A key observation is that $\frac{i+k}{2^j} = \frac{1}{2^{j-1}} \cdot \frac{i+k}{2}$. This means that, because the last factor $(i + k)/2$ is alternately an integer and a half-integer as k

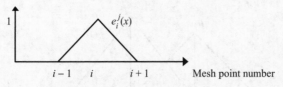

Figure 17.23 A hat function $e_i^j(x)$.

increases, the expression $(i + k)/2^j$ alternates between a vertex from the previous level and the midpoint between two such vertices. The sequence of coefficients $r = (r_k) = (\ldots, r_{-1}, r_0, r_1, \ldots)$ is called the *averaging mask* (the same idea is used for discrete convolution). The subdivision system is called *stationary* if, as is normally assumed, r does not vary with level, and *uniform* if r remains constant as we vary i for a given level.

Example 17.26 (*B-splines by Theorem 17.21*) (i) The choice $r = (r_0, r_1) = (1/2)(1, 1)$ is our B-spline construction: splitting, then a simple average, giving when iterated a quadratic B-spline. This is *Chaikin's Algorithm*, and originally due to him (Chaikin, 1974).

(ii) The choice $r = (r_{-1}, r_0, r_1) = (1/4)(1, 2, 1)$ is a B-spline of order 4, or cubic B-spline.

(iii) Setting $r = (r_{-1}, r_0, r_1, r_2) = (1/8)(1, 3, 3, 1)$ yields the B-spline of order 5 (degree 4).

Subdivision and hat functions Let the function values at level j form a vector f^j with ith entry f_i^j. One basis for the vectors f^j consists of vectors $e_i^j = [0 \ \ldots \ 0 \ 1 \ 0 \ \ldots \ 0]$ of appropriate length, and all zeros except for 1 in position i. Thus we may write

$$f^j = \sum_i f_i^j e_i^j. \tag{17.37}$$

We write either $f^j(x)$ or 'the function f^j' for the piecewise linear function which interpolates linearly between the values forming the vector f^j. The function $e_i^j(x)$ shown in Figure 17.23 is called a *hat function* because of its shape. Notice that we need the consistency assertion of Theorem 17.27 below.

Theorem 17.27 *Consistency holds: given* $f^j = \sum_i f_i^j e_i^j$, *we have*

$$f^j(x) = \sum_i f_i^j e_i^j(x). \tag{17.38}$$

Proof It suffices to check the second equality on the overlap of two hat functions. We may take this overlap to be the interval $[0, 1]$, for translation and scaling do the rest. Consider Figure 17.24. The sum of the hat functions at t in $[0, 1]$ is $(1 - t)y_1 + ty_2$. But this is the required interpolation between P_1 and P_2.

Basis functions As a special case of a control polygon, $e_i^j(x)$ has a limit under subdivision; it depends on i and j, say

$$\boxed{e_i^j(x) \to \phi_i^j(x).} \tag{17.39}$$

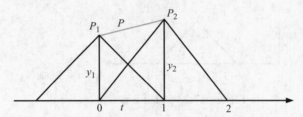

Figure 17.24 Adding hat functions on their overlap.

We'll soon see that the $\phi_i^j(x)$ are the basis functions we require. First observe that $f^j(x)$, being a stage on the way to $f(x)$, tends to the same limit $f(x)$ under subdivision, for every starting stage j. Therefore we have, by equating limits of the two sides in (17.38), and replacing j by $j-1$, that

$$f(x) = \sum_i f_i^j \phi_i^j(x) = \sum_i f_i^{j-1} \phi_i^{j-1}(x). \tag{17.40}$$

Example 17.28 We illustrate in Figure 17.25 the convergence $e_i^j(x) \to \phi_i^j(x)$ in the cases of the cubic B-spline, with averaging mask $(1, 2, 1)/4$ and of the Daubechies fractal basis function with mask $(1 + \sqrt{3}, 1 - \sqrt{3})/2$. In both cases six iterations are ample, but we show the original followed by the results of one, two and three iterations for the purpose of comparison. The 6-iteration version of the Daubechies case will be found shortly in Figure 17.26.

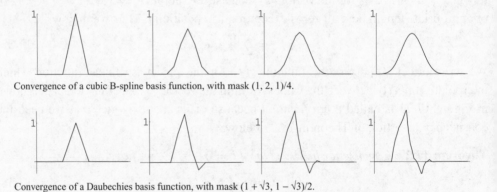

Convergence of a cubic B-spline basis function, with mask $(1, 2, 1)/4$.

Convergence of a Daubechies basis function, with mask $(1 + \sqrt{3}, 1 - \sqrt{3})/2$.

Figure 17.25 Convergence of a hat function to a basis function for cubic B-splines and to a fractal basis function of Daubechies, under their respective averaging masks. In each case, the original is followed by three iterations of subdivision.

Identifying the functions We now have two sets of functions for the B-spline case, the ϕ_i^j and the Ns. To see that they coincide, recall from (17.19) the definition $B_m(t) = \sum_s N_{s,m}(t)P_s$. If we choose the vertices P_i to be those of $e_i^j(x)$ as a control polygon, then (17.19) reduces to $B_m(t) = N_{i,m}(t)$. But by Theorems 17.21 and 17.22 this is also the result obtained by recursive subdivision.

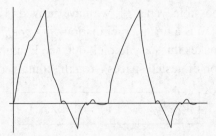

Figure 17.26 Daubechies' fractal basis functions $\phi_2^3(x)$ and $\phi_5^3(x)$ generated by recursive subdivision (17.36), with uniform averaging mask $(r_0, r_1) = (1 + \sqrt{3}, 1 - \sqrt{3})/2$.

Independence Let's get a small but important detail out of the way. How do we know the spanning functions $\phi_0^j(x)$, $\phi_1^j(x)$, ... (j fixed) are linearly independent and hence can be *basis functions*? It suffices to show that we cannot have f_i^j not all zero but yet have $\sum_i f_i^j \phi_i^j(x) = 0$. But if we *did*, our subdivision scheme would convert the nonzero vector f^j into the zero function, which is impossible by hypothesis, and clearly so for the averaging schemes we consider.

Exercise How do we know the first case in Figure 17.25 does not extend further along the x-axis?

17.2.4 Nested spaces

Having shown how a convergent subdivision process provides the functions $\phi_i^j(x)$, we assemble all $\phi_i^j(x)$ for fixed j into a row vector $[\phi_i^j(x)]$ and denote the space they span by V^j. Thus we write

$$\Phi^j(x) = \left[\phi_0^j(x) \quad \phi_1^j(x) \ldots\right], \tag{17.41}$$

$$V^j = \text{span } \Phi^j, \text{ of dimension } v_j. \tag{17.42}$$

For example, a control polygon $P_0 \ldots P_n$ gives $\Phi^0(x) = [\phi_0^0(x) \, \phi_1^0(x) \ldots \phi_n^0(x)]$, spanning the space V^0, of dimension $v_0 = n + 1$. Now we show that V^{j-1} is contained in V^j (all j) by using the subdivision process to express each generator $\phi_i^{j-1}(x)$ of the first space V^{j-1} as a linear combination from the second. This is Equation (17.44) below. We shall deduce it from (17.43). Firstly, according to (17.36), each entry of f^j is linear in those of the previous level, so there is some matrix P^j for which the first equation below holds:

$$
\boxed{
\begin{array}{lll}
f^j = P^j f^{j-1} & \text{(subdivision),} & (17.43) \\
\Phi^{j-1}(x) = \Phi^j(x)P^j & \text{(refining relations),} & (17.44)
\end{array}
}
$$

where the f^j are expressed as columns. To infer (17.44) we observe that the equality of sums in (17.40) may be written in matrix form $\Phi^j(x)f^j = \Phi^{j-1}(x)f^{j-1}$, giving

$$\Phi^{j-1}(x)f^{j-1} = \Phi^j(x)f^j = \Phi^j(x)P^j f^{j-1} \quad \text{(by (17.43)).}$$

Since this holds for all possible j and f^j, we have proved (17.44). Notice that it tells us in particular that $\phi_i^{j-1}(x)$ is a linear combination with *coefficients in column i* of P^j. For the matrix rule that makes this easy to pick out, see Example 7.22(4). We have now the wavelet-ready situation of nested spaces ('rough' contained in 'refined'):

$$V^{j-1} \subseteq V^j \quad (j = 1, 2, \ldots). \tag{17.45}$$

Corollary 17.29 *Any convergent subdivision system defines a sequence of nested spaces, and conversely any nested system of spaces can be defined by a subdivision system.*

The uniform case A key observation is that, with the averaging mask uniform, successive $\phi_i^j(x)$ at the same level will be shifted copies of each other, say $\phi_i^j(x) = \phi_0^j(x - i \cdot 2^{-j})$. This applies to the B-splines considered so far, and was illustrated in Figure 17.10. A further example comes from the uniform mask for the Daubechies case, illustrated in Figure 17.26.

Furthermore (assuming stationarity, which will hold in all our cases), each time we move to a new level, the basis functions keep the same shape but are shrunk by a factor 2. Taking these two facts together, there is a *scaling function*/father wavelet $\phi(x)$ from which all the basis functions may be derived by scaling and translation:

$$\phi_i^j(x) = \phi(2^j x - i) \quad \text{(uniform stationary case)}.$$

Example 17.30 (P^j *for cubic B-splines*) Determine P^1 for cubic B-splines with (i) three control points, (ii) five control points.

Solution The midpoint insertions of the splitting step convert $N (= n + 1)$ points at one level to $2N - 1$ at the next. The new points may be expressed in terms of the old by a matrix S^j sending variables $y_0, y_1, \ldots$ to $z_0, z_1, \ldots$, say. Its rows are shifted copies of the first two because of repeating the same linear combination with shifted subscripts. Similarly, averaging may be performed by a matrix R^j, sending $z_0, z_1, \ldots$ to $w_0, w_1, \ldots$ with each row a shifted copy of the mask $(1, 2, 1)/4$. This converts $2N - 1$ points to $2N - 3$, so the complete subdivision step is accomplished by the matrix $P^j = R^j S^j$, of dimensions $2N - 3 \times N$, highlighted below. Hence in the case $N = 3$, for example, we finish with a 3×3 matrix. The calculations are as follows.

(i) *The case of $N = 3$ control points*

$$S^1 \text{ split} \begin{bmatrix} z_0 \\ z_1 \\ z_2 \\ z_3 \\ z_4 \end{bmatrix} = \begin{bmatrix} y_0 \\ (y_0 + y_1)/2 \\ y_1 \\ (y_1 + y_2)/2 \\ y_2 \end{bmatrix} = \begin{bmatrix} 1 & & \\ \frac{1}{2} & \frac{1}{2} & \\ & 1 & \\ & \frac{1}{2} & \frac{1}{2} \\ & & 1 \end{bmatrix} \begin{bmatrix} y_0 \\ y_1 \\ y_2 \end{bmatrix},$$

$$
R^1 \text{ average} \begin{bmatrix} w_0 \\ w_1 \\ w_2 \end{bmatrix} = \begin{bmatrix} \frac{1}{4}(z_0 + 2z_1 + 2z_2) \\ \frac{1}{4}(z_1 + 2z_2 + 2z_3) \\ \frac{1}{4}(z_2 + 2z_3 + 2z_4) \end{bmatrix} = \frac{1}{4} \begin{bmatrix} 1 & 2 & 1 & & \\ & 1 & 2 & 1 & \\ & & 1 & 2 & 1 \end{bmatrix} \begin{bmatrix} z_0 \\ z_1 \\ z_2 \\ z_3 \\ z_4 \end{bmatrix},
$$

$$
\text{Subdivision: } P^1 = R^1 S^1 = \frac{1}{4} \begin{bmatrix} 1 & 2 & 1 & \\ & 1 & 2 & 1 \\ & & 1 & 2 & 1 \end{bmatrix} \times \frac{1}{2} \begin{bmatrix} 2 & \\ 1 & 1 \\ & 2 \\ & 1 & 1 \\ & & 2 \end{bmatrix} = \frac{1}{8} \begin{bmatrix} 4 & 4 & 0 \\ 1 & 6 & 1 \\ 0 & 4 & 4 \end{bmatrix}.
$$

(ii) *The case of $N = 5$ control points*

$$
P^1 = R^1 S^1 = \frac{1}{4} \begin{bmatrix} 1 & 2 & 1 & & & & & \\ & 1 & 2 & 1 & & & & \\ & & 1 & 2 & 1 & & & \\ & & & 1 & 2 & 1 & & \\ & & & & 1 & 2 & 1 & \\ & & & & & 1 & 2 & 1 \\ & & & & & & 1 & 2 & 1 \end{bmatrix} \frac{1}{2} \begin{bmatrix} 2 & & & & \\ 1 & 1 & & & \\ & 2 & & & \\ & 1 & 1 & & \\ & & 2 & & \\ & & 1 & 1 & \\ & & & 2 & \\ & & & 1 & 1 \\ & & & & 2 \end{bmatrix}
$$

$$
= \frac{1}{8} \begin{bmatrix} 4 & 4 & & & \\ 1 & 6 & 1 & & \\ & 4 & 4 & & \\ & 1 & 6 & 1 & \\ & & 4 & 4 & \\ & & 1 & 6 & 1 \\ & & & 4 & 4 \end{bmatrix}_{7 \times 5}.
$$

Clearly something pretty symmetrical is going on here and we might hope that some simple formula applies. Notice that the columns of P^1 are the binomial coefficients in $(1 + x)^4$, with cutoff at top and bottom. We tie all this together through *banded matrices* in Section 17.4 (see Equation (17.67)). Here is a reminder of some matrix dimensions.

$$
P^j_{(2N-3) \times N} = R^j_{(2N-3) \times (2N-1)} \, S^j_{(2N-1) \times N} \quad \text{(uniform case).}
$$

Exercise Find P^1 for a 4-point control polygon.

17.2.5 An end-correction for tangency

In this section we pursue the end-corrected (hence non-uniform) cubic B-splines which will be used in applications. We recall Construction 17.23 in which, to ensure a cubic

B-spline is tangent at an end-point P_0, we extend the control polygon by a virtual point P_{-1} such that P_0 is the midpoint of $P_{-1}P_1$.

Can we replace such virtual points by a modification of the averaging mask? The key observation is that the mask $(1, 2, 1)/4$ leaves unchanged any vertex which is midway between its two neighbours in the polygon. For, if Q_i is the midpoint of $Q_{i-1}Q_{i+1}$, then the mask performs

$$Q_i \to (Q_{i-1} + 2Q_i + Q_{i+1})/4 = (Q_{i-1} + Q_{i+1} + 2Q_i)/4$$
$$= (2Q_i + 2Q_i)/4 = Q_i.$$

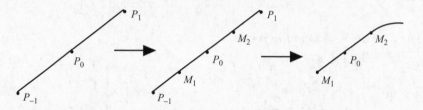

Figure 17.27 Splitting, then averaging, steps as they affect the first few polygon points. Notice P_0 is unchanged and finishes as it began, midway between its current neighbours.

Thus the first subdivision step, as represented in Figure 17.27, results in no change to the position of P_0, which, moreover, acquires a new virtual point M_1. The next subdivision repeats this process except that of course the mesh halves each time. Therefore the same limit is achieved very simply, without points, by changing the mask r to a not-quite-uniform one.

> The mask: $r = (1)$ at end-points, otherwise $r = (1, 2, 1)/4$.   (17.46)

Example 17.31 For the end-corrected cubic B-spline we have, in the case of $N = 3$ polygon vertices (and similarly for higher levels),

$$P^1 = R^1 S^1 = \frac{1}{4} \begin{bmatrix} 4 & & \\ 1 & 2 & 1 \\ & 1 & 2 & 1 \\ & & 1 & 2 & 1 \\ & & & & 4 \end{bmatrix} \frac{1}{2} \begin{bmatrix} 2 & 0 & 0 \\ 1 & 1 & 0 \\ 0 & 2 & 0 \\ 0 & 1 & 1 \\ 0 & 0 & 2 \end{bmatrix} = \frac{1}{8} \begin{bmatrix} 8 & 0 & 0 \\ 4 & 4 & 0 \\ 1 & 6 & 1 \\ 0 & 4 & 4 \\ 0 & 0 & 8 \end{bmatrix}.$$

Remarks 17.32 In terms of the matrix P^j, the difference between (17.46) and the uniform case considered earlier is the appending of an extra row $[8 \ 0 \ \dots \ 0]/8$ at the start and $[0 \dots 0 \ 8]/8$ at the end. This means that N points at one level become $2N - 1$ at the next, rather than $2N - 3$.

The form of P^j means that we have rediscovered a scheme due to Hoppe *et al.* (1994). The symmetry of the mask (17.46) ensures that not only S^j but also R^j is antipodal, and hence also their product P^j (see Exercise 17.15 and Section 17.3.2). As before, here is a reminder of the relevant matrix dimensions.

$$P^j_{(2N-1) \times N} = R^j_{(2N-1) \times (2N-1)} \ S^j_{(2N-1) \times N} \quad \text{(end-corrected)}.$$

Exercise Compute P^2 for the example above.

Example 17.33 Corresponding to a control polygon with $N = 3$ vertices we determine the basis functions ϕ_i^1 and ϕ_i^2 for an end-corrected cubic B-spline, and plot them in Figure 17.28, where they may be compared. In the first case of j we start from each hat function vector $(1, 0, 0, 0, 0), \ldots, (0, 0, 0, 0, 1)$ in turn, and apply the subdivision step given by the mask (17.46) and implemented in ALGO 17.1 (this is more economical than matrix multiplication, though we shall need P^j later). In the second case, $j = 2$, the hat functions have $2 \times 5 - 1 = 9$ entries.

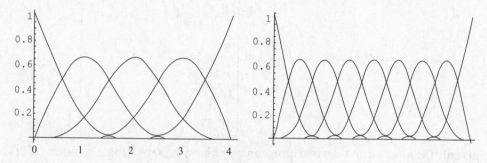

Figure 17.28 (a) The end-corrected cubic B-spline basis functions (17.41) at level 1 and at level 2 by ALGO 17.1. Notice that the first and last functions in each case differ most noticeably from the rest because of the non-uniform end-correction. We may compare the uniform basis functions of Figure 17.10.

Example 17.34 (*The face revisited*) In Figure 17.29, the same stages as Figure 17.22 are used to create the B-spline face, but using the *non-uniform mask* (17.46) instead of extra points. Thus the extraneous lines and partial curves disappear.

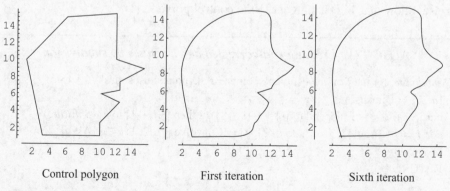

Control polygon   First iteration   Sixth iteration

Figure 17.29 The face from Figure 17.22, now by non-uniform subdivision (17.46).

An explicit basis The chosen edge-correction simply extends the original control polygon $P_0 P_1 \ldots P_n$ by a dependent point P_{-1}, positioned so that P_0 is the mean of P_{-1} and P_1, or equivalently $P_{-1} = 2P_0 - P_1$, and similarly for P_{n+1} after P_n. Subject to this, the resulting B-spline curve is in the usual notation, where $N_i(t) = N_{i,4}(t)$,

$$
\begin{aligned}
B(t) &= N_0(t)P_{-1} + N_1(t)P_0 + N_2(t)P_1 + N_3(t)P_2 + \cdots \qquad (1 \le t \le n+1) \\
&= N_0(t)[2P_0 - P_1] + N_1(t)P_0 + N_2(t)P_1 + N_3(t)P_2 + \cdots \\
&= [N_1(t) + 2N_0(t)]P_0 + [N_2(t) - N_0(t)]P_1 + N_3(t)P_2 + \cdots,
\end{aligned}
$$

so the basis has changed by

$$
[N_0 \quad N_1 \quad N_2 \quad \cdots] \to [N_1 + 2N_0 \quad N_2 - N_0 \quad N_3 \cdots]
$$

$$
= [N_0 \quad N_1 \quad \cdots \quad N_{n+2}]
\begin{bmatrix}
2 & -1 & \cdots & & 0 & 0 \\
1 & & & & & \\
 & 1 & & & & \\
 & & 0 & & & \\
 & & & \ddots & & \\
 & & & & 1 & \\
 & & & & & 1 \\
0 & 0 & \cdots & & -1 & 2
\end{bmatrix}.
\qquad (17.47)
$$

Thus only the first two and last two basis functions have departed from uniformity. This is visible in Figure 17.28 at the two different scales employed. Note that we make use of N_0 to N_{n+2}, and that when drawing the curve we restrict the parameter t to $1 \le t \le n+1$. For further reassurance let us check tangency at the end-points. Recalling that, for example, $N_0(1) = 1/6$, $N_0'(1) = -1/2$ (Remarks 17.16), we find that $B(t)$ is indeed tangent to the control polygon at P_0, because

$$
\begin{aligned}
B(1) &= [N_1(1) + 2N_0(1)]P_0 + [N_2(1) - N_0(1)]P_1 \\
&= (2/3 + 2/6)P_0 + (1/6 - 1/6)P_1 = P_0, \\
B'(1) &= [N_1'(1) + 2N_0'(1)]P_0 + [N_2'(1) - N_0'(1)]P_1 = P_1 - P_0.
\end{aligned}
$$

Exercise Show that $B(t)$ is tangent to the control polygon at P_n.

ALGO 17.1 Creating end-corrected cubic splines by subdivision

(a) *Subdivide*: for list f of values, plane points, or 3D points; uses mask (17.46).
$\{d, k\} = \text{Dimensions}[f]$; $g = f[1]$;
For $i = 1$ to $d - 1$, append $(f[i] + f[i+1])/2$ then $f[i+1]$ to g; (*Splitting*)
For $j = 1$ to k, $g[\{2, 3, \ldots, 2d - 2\}, j] = \text{Convolve}\,[\{1, 2, 1\}/4, g\,[\text{All}, j]]$
(*Averaging*)
RETURN [g].

(b) *Basis function* ϕ_i^j; heights at level J
$g = \text{Row } i$ of a size v_j identity matrix
Do $g = \text{subdivide }[g]$ $J - j$ times
RETURN[g].

(c) *Cubic spline*: level J approximation
Do $f = \text{subdivide }[f]$ J times
RETURN [f].

17.3 The wavelet formulation

Reviewing progress so far, we have a multiresolution system $V^0 \subseteq V^1 \subseteq V^2 \subseteq \cdots$ for cubic B-splines, in which subdivision down to level j gives an approximation lying in V^j. We distinguish two cases, the *uniform* one with which we began, and the *non-uniform* adaption (Section 17.2) designed to produce tangency at the control polygon end-points. Non-uniformity refers to not *all* the basis functions at the same level being translates of each other, though most are in this case (see e.g. Figure 17.28).

We are ready to introduce a wavelet system assisting us to move between levels, and giving the potential to manipulate the curve at any chosen scale independently of others.

17.3.1 Semi-orthogonal wavelets

Manipulating a B-spline curve at any scale lies in our ability to construct a filter bank, as described in the previous chapter at Section 16.3.1. Table 17.4 shows the present position.

Table 17.4. *For achieving a B-spline filter bank, what we have is summarised in line (i) and what we further require appears in line (ii).*

	space and basis	matrix relation
(i)	$\Phi^j = [\phi_0{}^j \ \phi_1{}^j \ \ldots]$ is basis of $V^j \subseteq V^{j+1}$	$\Phi^{j-1} = \Phi^j P^j$
(ii)	$\Psi^j = [\psi_0{}^j \ \psi_1{}^j \ \ldots]$ is basis of W^j and $V^j \oplus W^j = V^{j+1}$	$\Psi^{j-1} = \Phi^j Q^j$

To achieve line (ii) of the table we begin with the wavelet spaces W^j. The minimal requirement is that W^j be *complementary* to V^j in the larger space V^{j+1}, meaning that each f in V^{j+1} is a unique sum $g + h$, where g is taken from V^j and h from W^j. This is the assertion $V^j \oplus W^j = V^{j+1}$. As we observed earlier, there are many choices for W^j, analogously to choosing the y-axis in *any* direction not parallel to the x-axis. Our actual selection corresponds to making the y-axis perpendicular to the x-axis. That is, of all possible complements of V^j in V^{j+1}, we let W^j be the unique *orthogonal* one,

$$W^j = \{h \in V^{j+1}: \langle g, h \rangle = 0 \text{ for all } g \text{ in } V^j\}. \tag{17.48}$$

This makes W^j the most efficient way to 'upgrade' an element of V^j to one in V^{j+1} (perpendicular to the 'old' vector). For a proof that W^j is actually complementary to V^j, see Definition 7.19ff. Now, Equation (17.48) defines W^j, but leaves open the precise form of wavelets, i.e. the basis fuctions $\psi_i{}^j$ which, whatever the choice, we bring together as a row vector, writing

$$\begin{cases} \Psi^j(x) = \begin{bmatrix} \psi_0^j(x) & \psi_1^j(x) & \ldots \end{bmatrix}, \\ W^j = \text{span } \Psi^j(x), \text{ of dimension } w_j = v_{j+1} - v_j. \end{cases} \tag{17.49}$$

Since the basis functions of W^{j-1} lie within V^j, they are linear combinations of its basis and may be expressed in terms thereof by some matrix Q^j, giving the first equation below. The second is the earlier noted (17.44), expressing the basis of V^{j-1} in terms of that of V^j, and is paired here for convenience of reference.

$$\Psi^{j-1}(x) = \Phi^j(x)Q^j, \tag{17.50a}$$

$$\Phi^{j-1}(x) = \Phi^j(x)P^j. \tag{17.50b}$$

These equations are crucial for our next task, which is to express (17.48) as an equation for Q^j. The wavelets we find are called *semi-orthogonal* because, out of three orthogonality properties (Section 16.3.2) that may hold, namely that V^j is orthogonal to W^j and both have orthonormal bases, it is practicable to insist upon the first, (17.48), but no more.

The equation $MQ = 0$ To get an explicit equation for Q^j we recall the following from (16.49) of the previous chapter. Let $F = [f_1 \dots f_p]$ and $H = [h_1 \dots h_q]$ be row vectors of functions. Then their *Gram matrix* $G = \langle F, H \rangle$ is the $p \times q$ matrix of their inner products, with (k, i) entry $\langle f_k, h_i \rangle$, and we have

$$\langle FP, HQ \rangle = P^{\mathrm{T}} \langle F, H \rangle Q, \tag{17.51}$$

where P, Q are real matrices for which the products FP and HQ exist. Now the semi-orthogonal property may be written in terms of bases as $\langle \Phi^{j-1}, \Psi^{j-1} \rangle = 0$. The idea is then to express the two bases in terms of one by Equations (17.50), obtaining $\langle \Phi^j P^j, \Phi^j Q^j \rangle = 0$. By (17.51) this is the same as

$$MQ^j = 0, \quad \text{where } M = (P^j)^T \langle \Phi^j, \Phi^j \rangle. \tag{17.52}$$

Thus Q^j is formed from vectors in the (column) null-space of M. Indeed, its columns are to be a basis thereof according to the dimension information assembled for reference in Table 17.5. Note that the matrices P^j, Q^j, and the partition $[P^j | Q^j]$ each have independent

Table 17.5. *Dimensions of some matrices involved in computing spline wavelets, where $v_j = \mathrm{Dim}\, V^j = $ number of vertices in jth subdivision, which equals $2v_{j-1} - 3$ in the uniform case and $2v_{j-1} - 1$ in the non-uniform.*

matrix	dimensions (general j)
P^j	$v_j \times v_{j-1}$
$G^j = \langle \Phi^j, \Phi^j \rangle$	$v_j \times v_j$
M	$v_{j-1} \times v_j$
Q^j	$v_j \times w_{j-1}$

columns (see Theorem 16.16). We derive some useful implementation details before exemplifying the result.

Exercise Why are the columns of Q^j a basis for the null-space of M (see Exercise 17.17)?

Finding G and M To determine the equation for matrix M we must first compute the *Gram matrix* $G^j = \langle \Phi^j, \Phi^j \rangle$. But what should be the inner product? Importantly, the formula (17.51) expressing M in terms of G holds independently of this choice, and in the present context it works well to standardise on the integral definition of Chapter 16,

$$\langle f, g \rangle = \int_{-\infty}^{\infty} f(x)g(x)\mathrm{d}x.$$

We begin with the uniform case, from which the non-uniform edge-corrected case follows by (17.47) with the aid of Formula (17.51). The basis functions at level 0 are $N_i(x) = N_{i,4}(x)$.

Theorem 17.35 (*Uniform cubic B-splines*) *The inner products at level j are a constant multiple of those at level 0. There are four nonzero distinct inner products at a given level:*

$$\langle \phi_i^j, \phi_k^j \rangle = 2^{-j}\langle N_i, N_k \rangle = 2^{-j}c_{|i-k|}, \qquad (17.53)$$

$$where \; [c_0 \; c_1 \; c_2 \; \ldots] = [2416 \; 1191 \; 120 \; 1 \; 0 \ldots 0]/140. \qquad (17.54)$$

Proof (i) Because the averaging mask is not only stationary but uniform, $\phi_i^j(x) = N_0(2^j x - i)$, and so with the substitution $t = 2^j x$ we obtain

$$\langle \phi_i^j, \phi_k^j \rangle = \int_{-\infty}^{\infty} N_0(2^j x - i)N_0(2^j x - k)\mathrm{d}x = 2^{-j}\int_{-\infty}^{\infty} N_0(t - i)N_0(t - k)\mathrm{d}t$$

$$= 2^{-j}\langle N_i, N_k \rangle.$$

On the other hand,

$$\langle N_k, N_i \rangle = \int_{-\infty}^{\infty} N_0(x - k)N_0(x - i)\mathrm{d}x = \int_{-\infty}^{\infty} N_0(t)N_0(t - (i - k))\mathrm{d}t$$

$$= \langle N_0, N_{i-k} \rangle,$$

but, since i and k may be interchanged in $\langle N_i, N_k \rangle$, the result depends only on $|i - k|$, and so may be written in the form $c_{|i-k|}$. Finally, $c_s = 0$ for $s \geq 4$ because then N_0 and N_s are not zero simultaneously, so the calculation simplifies to four inner products, determined by simple integration, and involving only the polynomials of Table 17.3.

Example 17.36 (*The uniform B-spline case with $v_{j-1} = 4$*) After using Theorem 17.35 to give the appropriate 5×5 Gram matrix G we compute $M = P^{\mathrm{T}}G$ (the bold entries are explained below).

$$
\frac{1}{8}
\begin{pmatrix}
4 & 1 & 0 & 0 & 0 \\
4 & 6 & 4 & 1 & 0 \\
0 & 1 & 4 & 6 & 4 \\
0 & 0 & 0 & 1 & 4
\end{pmatrix}
\frac{1}{140}
\begin{pmatrix}
2416 & 1191 & 120 & 1 & 0 \\
1191 & 2416 & 1191 & 120 & 1 \\
120 & 1191 & 2416 & 1191 & 120 \\
1 & 120 & 1191 & 2416 & 1191 \\
0 & 1 & 120 & 1191 & 2416
\end{pmatrix}
$$

$$
= \frac{1}{1120}
\begin{pmatrix}
10855 & \mathbf{7180} & 1671 & 124 & 1 \\
17291 & 24144 & 18481 & 7904 & 1677 \\
1677 & 7904 & 18481 & 24144 & 17291 \\
1 & 124 & 1671 & \mathbf{7180} & 10855
\end{pmatrix}.
$$

17.3.2 Finding Q with symmetry

Symmetry Notice that the matrix M in Example 17.36 above is not symmetric but it is *antipodal*. That is, every element equals its antipodes, obtained by reflection through the centre of the array. For example, the bold antipodal pair in M takes the (numerator) value 7180, another pair is 7904. The property is also known as *central symmetry*; or as $1/2$ *turn symmetry* because the matrix remains unchanged under a $1/2$ turn. We'll show that M is always antipodal and use this fact to shorten and simplify the calculation of Q.

If we let $\alpha(A)$ denote the result of replacing every element of A by its antipodes, then $\alpha(A) = A$ is equivalent to A being antipodal. As hinted, we may think of α as $1/2$ turn about the array centre. For a row or column vector this simply reverses the order of elements, whilst a more general matrix has both rows and columns reversed.

Example 17.37 (i) $\alpha[1\ 2\ 3] = [3\ 2\ 1]$,

(ii) $\alpha \begin{bmatrix} 0 & 1 & 2 & 3 \\ 6 & 5 & 4 & 0 \end{bmatrix} = \begin{bmatrix} 0 & 4 & 5 & 6 \\ 3 & 2 & 1 & 0 \end{bmatrix}$ (think of a $1/2$ turn),

(iii) $\alpha : \begin{bmatrix} 1 & 2 \\ 3 & 4 \end{bmatrix} \rightarrow \begin{bmatrix} 3 & 4 \\ 2 & 1 \end{bmatrix} \rightarrow \begin{bmatrix} 4 & 3 \\ 1 & 2 \end{bmatrix}$ (switch rows, then columns),

(iv) $\alpha \begin{bmatrix} 0 & 1 & 2 & 3 \\ 3 & 2 & 1 & 0 \end{bmatrix} = \begin{bmatrix} 0 & 1 & 2 & 3 \\ 3 & 2 & 1 & 0 \end{bmatrix}$ (antipodal case),

(v) $\alpha \begin{bmatrix} 1 & 0 \\ 0 & 1 \end{bmatrix} = \begin{bmatrix} 1 & 0 \\ 0 & 1 \end{bmatrix}$, and in general $\alpha(I_n) = I_n$.

$\alpha(A)$ *as a matrix product* We know from Section 8.2.1 that, if A is an $r \times s$ matrix and if P_n denotes the result of reversing the order of rows in the identity matrix I_n, then $\alpha(A)$ may be obtained by multiplying A on the left by P_r and on the right by P_s^T. Here is an example. Notice that, in terms of rows R_i, the effect is: $P_3 \cdot \text{Rows}(R_1, R_2, R_3) = \text{Rows}(R_3, R_2, R_1)$.

$$P_3 A P_2^T = \begin{bmatrix} 0 & 0 & 1 \\ 0 & 1 & 0 \\ 1 & 0 & 0 \end{bmatrix} \begin{bmatrix} a & d \\ b & e \\ c & f \end{bmatrix} \begin{bmatrix} 0 & 1 \\ 1 & 0 \end{bmatrix} = \begin{bmatrix} c & f \\ b & e \\ a & d \end{bmatrix} \begin{bmatrix} 0 & 1 \\ 1 & 0 \end{bmatrix}$$

$$= \begin{bmatrix} f & c \\ e & b \\ d & a \end{bmatrix} = \alpha(A).$$

Further, since P_n is restricted to *permutations* of rows it is orthogonal, as observed in Example 8.21(iii). In summary, we have

$$\alpha(A) = P_r A P_s^T, \quad \text{and} \quad P_n^{-1} = P_n^T. \tag{17.54}$$

Theorem 17.38 *(i) A matrix product AB satisfies $\alpha(AB) = \alpha(A)\alpha(B)$, (ii) the property of being antipodal is preserved under taking products, inverses, and transposes, (iii) if the vector w is a solution of $Ax = 0$ then so is $\alpha(w)$.*

Proof (i) Let A be $r \times s$ and B be $s \times t$. Applying (17.54) we have $\alpha(A)\alpha(B) = P_r A P_s^T \cdot P_s B P_t^T = P_r A B P_t^T = \alpha(AB)$.

(ii) If A, B are antipodal then $\alpha(AB) = \alpha(A)\alpha(B) = AB$, so AB is antipodal. Now let the invertible matrix A be antipodal. Then $I = \alpha(A \cdot A^{-1}) = \alpha(A) \cdot \alpha(A^{-1}) = A \cdot \alpha(A^{-1})$, implying that $\alpha(A^{-1}) = A^{-1}$, whence A^{-1} is antipodal. The result for A^T is left as an exercise.

(iii) Let $Aw = 0$. Then $\alpha(A)\alpha(w) = 0$ by part (i), so if A is antipodal we have $A \cdot \alpha(w) = 0$. that is, $\alpha(w)$ is also a solution of $Ax = 0$.

Corollary 17.39 *(Antipodal masks) Suppose $\alpha(ith \ mask \ from \ last) = ith \ mask$, for all valid i, and level j of a subdivision scheme. Then, in wavelet notation, the matrices P^j and M^j are antipodal and there is an antipodal solution for Q^j.*

Proof (i) The argument is helpfully illustrated in Example 17.36. We have $P^j = R^j S^j$, where matrix S^j is defined by the insertion of midpoints and is clearly antipodal (a useful exercise), whilst R^j is antipodal because of the antipodally related masks. By Theorem 17.38 the product P^j and its transpose are antipodal.

(ii) *Antipodal solution* Suppose the level j basis functions are labelled $\phi_1, \ldots, \phi_{N-1}$ By the mask hypothesis the graph of ϕ_{N-i} is the reflection of that of ϕ_i in a vertical axis through the centre of the interval $[1, N]$. Therefore integration gives $\langle \phi_i, \phi_k \rangle = \langle \phi_{N-i}, \phi_{N-k} \rangle$, which means that $\langle \Phi^j, \Phi^j \rangle$ is antipodal, and hence by Theorem 17.38 that $M = (P^j)^T \langle \Phi^j, \Phi^j \rangle$ is antipodal also. Finally, by the last part of Theorem 17.38, the solutions of $Mx = 0$ occur in antipodal pairs, and so can be assembled into an antipodal solution for the matrix Q^j.

Solving for Q

Remarks 17.40 Let M be $s \times t$ and have independent rows. (i) We seek $t - s$ independent solutions of $Mx = 0$, to form the columns of Q (see Corollary 8.24). In our case $t - s$ is even, and our strategy is to look first for $(t - s)/2$ solutions, each having its first nonzero entry one further on than the previous solution vector. Theorem 17.38 shows their antipodes are also solutions, so we complete Q by appending the present matrix of solutions after a half turn.

(ii) Let M have columns C_1 to C_t. Then, because these are s-vectors, any set of $s + 1$ columns, $M_c = [C_c \ldots C_{c+s}]$, is linearly dependent; equivalently there is some nonzero column vector z with $M_c z = 0$ (Theorem 7.7 shows how to find z). Suitably padding z with zeros fore and aft gives a solution $x = z$ of $Mx = 0$, with its first nonzero entry at some position c', possibly greater than c, and we look next at columns c' to $c' + s$. The following Mathematica implementation (ALGO 17.2) allows $t - s$ odd as well as even, the last but one line creating the appropriate antipodal images. *If M has exact rational entries, so has the solution Q.*

(iii) This strategy in principle could fail, either in finding $(t - s)/2$ solutions in the echelon form demanded, or by the complete set admitting dependence. However, neither problem occurred in the B-spline context. Should failure occur, we can always fall back upon a standard package and proceed without the convenience of antipodality.

Exercise Use (17.54) to show that if A is antipodal then so is its transpose.

ALGO 17.2 Find an antipodal solution Q to MQ = 0 (Mathematica)

```
find Q[M_] := Module[{s, t, j, c, Q, y, a1, a2, Q2, sol, cols},
   { s, t } = Dimensions[M]; a2 = Ceiling[(t − s)/2];
   Q = { }; c = 1;
   Do[sol = {};
      For[j = 1, (j ≤ s) & & (sol == {}), j++,
         cols = Take[M, All, {c, c + j}];
         sol = NullSpace[cols];]; (End For)
      y = Join[Table[0, {c − 1}], sol[[1]]]; y = PadRight[y, t];
      Q = Append[Q, y];
      While[y[[c]] == 0, c = c + 1]; c = c + 1, a2]; (End Do)
   Q2 = Take[Q, t − s − a2];
   Q2 = Reverse[Transpose[Reverse[Transpose[Q2]]]];
   Return[Transpose[Join[Q, Q2]]];        ];
```

Example 17.41 (*Uniform cubic splines*) Starting with $v_0 = 5$, we use ALGO 17.2 to solve for Q^1 and hence determine a basis of W^0 in the form $\Psi^0 = \Phi^1 Q^1$. The general case may be found in Section 17.4 (Appendix). We refer to Table 17.5 of Section 17.3.1 for dimensions, and for matrix sizes. Thus $v_1 = 2v_0 - 3 = 7$ and $w_0 = v_1 - v_0 = 2$;

consequently $MQ = 0$ has just two independent solutions and there are two wavelet basis functions. The matrices P^T and M are 5×7, and so Q is 7×2. See Figure 17.30.

$$M = P^T G = \frac{1}{1120} \begin{bmatrix} 10855 & 7180 & 1671 & 124 & 1 & 0 & 0 \\ 17291 & 24144 & 18481 & 7904 & 1677 & 124 & 1 \\ 1677 & 7904 & 18482 & 24264 & 18482 & 7904 & 1677 \\ 1 & 124 & 1677 & 7904 & 18481 & 24144 & 17291 \\ 0 & 0 & 1 & 124 & 1671 & 7180 & 10855 \end{bmatrix}$$

$$Q = \begin{bmatrix} -7.18 & 0. \\ 14.69 & 1. \\ -17.41 & -5.22 \\ 12.62 & 12.62 \\ -5.22 & -17.41 \\ 1. & 4.69 \\ 0. & -7.18 \end{bmatrix}$$

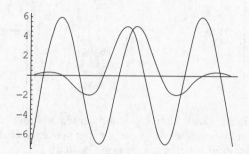

Figure 17.30 The solution of $MQ = 0$, and consequent wavelet basis $\Phi^1 Q^1$ of W_0, in the case $v_0 = 5$ (uniform). The solution for Q is shown to two decimal places.

Example 17.42 (1) *Non-uniform cubic B-spline* Here we calculate for the end-corrected case. We take $v_0 = 5$ again, but this time $v_1 = 2v_0 - 1 = 9$ (Table 17.5), and $w_0 = v_1 - v_0 = 4$, so there are four wavelets. Let us review the relevant matrix dimensions from Table 17.5:

$$(P^T)_{5\times 9} \, G_{9\times 9} \, Q_{9\times 4}. \tag{17.55}$$

The Gram matrix G is 9×9 but because this is the non-uniform case we must convert it from the uniform Gram matrix G_{11} of size 11 by taking

$$G = E^T G_{11} E \tag{17.56}$$

(see (17.47) and (17.51)), where $E_{11\times 9}$ is the identity matrix I_9 with a row $[2 - 1 \ 0 \dots 0]$ prefixed and the reverse of this row appended. Figure 17.31 gives the result, using ALGO 17.2 to find Q.

(2) *An aide-mémoire* In the next section it will be very important that the block matrix $[P^j | Q^j]$ is square, in fact invertible. The following easily remembered picture shows how the respective dimensions ensure squareness.

$$[P^j | Q^j] = v_j \quad \boxed{\begin{array}{c|c} P^j & Q^j \end{array}} \quad (w_{j-1} = v_j - v_{j-1})$$

$$v_{j-1} \qquad w_{j-1}$$

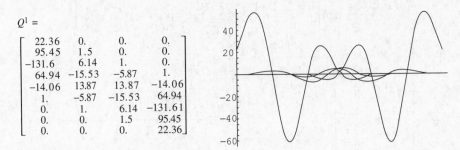

$$M = P^{\mathrm{T}}G = \frac{1}{1120} \begin{bmatrix} 116506 & -17178 & 8152 & 1679 & 124 & 1 & 0 & 0 & 0 \\ -17632 & 25989 & 24140 & 18481 & 7904 & 1677 & 124 & 1 & 0 \\ 126 & 1676 & 7904 & 18482 & 24264 & 18482 & 7904 & 1676 & 126 \\ 0 & 1 & 124 & 1677 & 7904 & 18481 & 24140 & 25989 & -17632 \\ 0 & 0 & 0 & 1 & 124 & 1679 & 10855 & -17178 & 116565 \end{bmatrix}$$

$$Q^1 = \begin{bmatrix} 22.36 & 0. & 0. & 0. \\ 95.45 & 1.5 & 0. & 0. \\ -131.6 & 6.14 & 1. & 0. \\ 64.94 & -15.53 & -5.87 & 1. \\ -14.06 & 13.87 & 13.87 & -14.06 \\ 1. & -5.87 & -15.53 & 64.94 \\ 0. & 1. & 6.14 & -131.61 \\ 0. & 0. & 1.5 & 95.45 \\ 0. & 0. & 0. & 22.36 \end{bmatrix}$$

Figure 17.31 Matrix Q^1, and consequent four basis wavelets for W^0. Notice that the last two columns of Q^1 are the first two reversed, because we have, as we may, taken an antipodal solution for Q^1 (see Corollary 17.38).

17.3.3 The filter bank and curve editing

The filter bank The idea of a filter bank was first introduced in Section 16.3.1. We now have in place the components of a wavelet filter bank for B-splines. This will enable us, as discussed, to edit B-spline curves at any chosen scales independently. In the present notation a *filter bank* is a collection of pairs of linear transforms defined by *filter matrices* $A^j: V^j \to V^{j-1}$ and $B^j: V^j \to W^{j-1}$, providing conversion across levels of detail. They fit together in Figure 17.32, and invert the action of P^j and Q^j, as recalled in Equations (17.57) to (17.59) below.

Notation review c^j is a column vector whose length is the dimension v_j of V^j. The elements y of c_j may be extended to coordinate pairs (x, y). In either case the basis function $\phi_i^j(t)$ is the limit of the hat function e_i^j as subdivision is repeated with mask (17.46). In calculation we stop at some level J judged sufficiently accurate, and represent ϕ_i^j as the column vector of values at mesh points. We assemble the columns ϕ_i^j for fixed

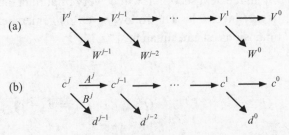

Figure 17.32 Representations of a filter bank: (a) how the filter bank relates the spaces $\{V^j\}$ and $\{W^j\}$, (b) transforming explicit vectors c^j. We recover c^j from the filtered values c^{j-1} and d^{j-1} by Equation (17.59): $c^j = P^j c^{j-1} + Q^j d^{j-1}$.

Table 17.6. *Summary of relations leading to a filter bank. The lines specific to the case of B-splines (i.e. specifying semi-orthogonality), are lines 2 and 6.*

item	comment
$V^0 \subseteq V^1 \subseteq V^2 \subseteq \cdots$	we start with this nest of spaces (multiresolution)
$V^j = V^{j-1} \oplus W^{j-1}$	$W^{j-1} = \{v \in V^j : \langle v, x \rangle = 0 \text{ for all } x \in V^{j-1}\}$
V^j has basis $\Phi^j(x)$	$= [\phi_i^j(x)], 1 \le i \le v_j$ or $0 \le i \le v_j - 1$
c^j defines element $\Phi^j(x)c^j$	$= \Sigma_i c_i^j \phi_i^j(x)$
$\Phi^{j-1}(x) = \Phi^j(x)P^j$	refining relations (defines P_j)
$\Psi^{j-1}(x) = \Phi^j(x)Q^j$	$\langle V^{j-1}, W^{j-1} \rangle = 0$ defines Q^j, whence $\Psi^{j-1}(x)$
W^{j-1} has basis $\Psi^{j-1}(x)$	
d^{j-1} defines an element $\Psi^{j-1}(x)d^{j-1}$	
$c^{j-1} = A^j c^j$ and $d^{j-1} = B^j c^j$	analysis filters A^j, B^j
$c^j = P^j c^{j-1} + Q^j d^{j-1}$ (recovery of c^j)	synthesis filters P^j, Q^j

j into a matrix Φ^j which replaces $\Phi^j(t)$. Thus the matrix product $\Phi^j \cdot c^j$ is correctly a linear combination (or pair of linear combinations) of these columns. To recapitulate:

> Φ^i is obtained by recursive subdivision.

P^j is the subdivision matrix and determines Q^j by the semi-orthogonal wavelet condition that spaces V^j and W^j be orthogonal. Then we can use the following three standard formulae, established earlier (Section 16.3.1) for filter banks in general. One may say that A and B are called *analysis* matrices or filters because they take things apart; P and Q are *synthesis* filters because they put parts together. A fuller résumé is given in Table 17.6.

$$\begin{bmatrix} A^j \\ B^j \end{bmatrix} = [P^j | Q^j]^{-1}, \tag{17.57}$$

> $c^{j-1} = A^j c^j$, and $d^{j-1} = B^j c^j$ (analysis), $\qquad$ (17.58)
> $c^j = P^j c^{j-1} + Q^j d^{j-1}$ (synthesis). $\qquad$ (17.59)

Which B-spline? We standardise henceforth on the slightly non-uniform cubic B-spline of Section 17.2.5, referred to as end-corrected, and designed to be tangent to the control polygon at its end-points. In this case we noted that $v_{j+1} = 2v_j - 1$. This implies that, if $v_j = 2^j + 1$ for any given level j, then the same formula holds for every level. That is the option we take for simplicity:

$$v_j = 2^j + 1 \ (v_j = \text{Dim } V^j). \tag{17.60}$$

Curve editing at different scales

We shall be concerned with plane parametric curves (and surfaces in Section 17.5), but firstly we suppose we are given a curve $y = f(x)$ *specified up to level L*. That is, $f(x)$ may be written as a linear combination of level L basis functions

$$f(x) = \sum_i c_i^L \phi_i^L(x) \ (= \Phi^L(x) \cdot c^L). \tag{17.61}$$

The actual control points are then $(i \cdot 2^{-L}, c_i^L)$, where the heights c_i^L form the components of a vector c^L whose length is v_L, the dimension of V^L. The problem is to modify the curve (17.61) (and its parametric relatives) at one level, whilst leaving it intact in other respects. In particular, how may we edit the *overall sweep* but keep the *local character*/fine detail, or change the local character whilst preserving the overall sweep?

(a) Changing the sweep We derive the necessary formula and apply it to a 2D animation. The formula and proof apply equally whether the rows of c^j are single scalars, or coordinate pairs/triples.

Theorem 17.43 *The overall change Δc^L in the curve height (17.61) due to a change Δc^k at level k is given by*

$$\Delta c^L = P^L P^{L-1} \cdots P^{k+1}(\Delta c^k). \tag{17.62}$$

Proof In this calculation the ds will cancel each other, as indicated in the formula asserted. We have, from level k up to level $k + 1$ in the filter bank of Figure 17.32,

$$\begin{aligned} \Delta c^{k+1} &= \text{new } c^{k+1} - \text{old } c^{k+1} \qquad \text{by definition} \\ &= [P^{k+1}(c^k + \Delta c^k) + Q^{k+1}d^k] - [P^{k+1}c^k + Q^{k+1}d^k] \quad \text{by (17.59)} \\ &= P^{k+1}(\Delta c^k). \end{aligned}$$

Repeating this argument for levels above the $(k + 1)$st, we arrive at the relation (17.62).

Example 17.44 (*Animation 'Nessie arises'*) We use Theorem 17.43 to change the overall sweep of an originally supine 'Nessie' (component vector c^5, Figure 17.33) to the raised position of the template in Figure 17.34, whose component vector is $\Delta c^2 = [0, 2, 0, 6, 4]$. To do so we first compute the effect of Δc^2 on c^5, namely $\Delta c^5 = P^5 P^4 P^3 \Delta c^2$. Let Φ^j

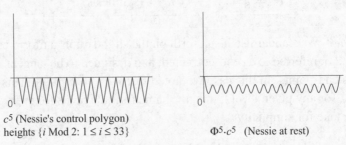

c^5 (Nessie's control polygon)
heights $\{i \text{ Mod } 2: 1 \le i \le 33\}$

$\Phi^5 . c^5$ (Nessie at rest)

Figure 17.33 Inventing Nessie.

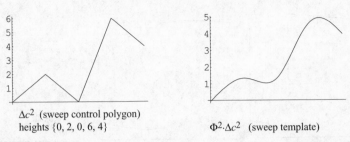

Δc^2 (sweep control polygon)
heights $\{0, 2, 0, 6, 4\}$ $\Phi^2 \cdot \Delta c^2$ (sweep template)

Figure 17.34 Preparing Nessie animation, from polygons to B-spline versions.

stand for the approximation of the basis functions in $\Phi^j(x)$ by subdivision up to level 8. Then the successive frames of the animation are the curves $ness(t) = \Phi^5 \cdot (c^5 + t\Delta c^5)$, say for $t = 0, \dots, 1$. See Figure 17.35.

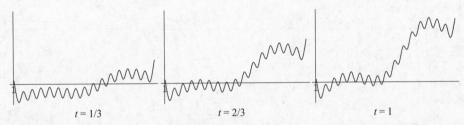

$t = 1/3$ $t = 2/3$ $t = 1$

Figure 17.35 Stages in Nessie animation: the curve $ness\ (t) = \Phi^5 \cdot (c^5 + t\Delta c^5)$.

(b) Smoothing a curve Here we use the filter bank matrices $A^j : c^j \to c^{j-1}$ to smooth over several levels in succession: $c^8 \to c^7 \to \cdots \to c^2 \to c^1$ (see Figure 17.37). To determine A^j we use ALGO 17.2 to solve the equation $MQ^j = 0$ of (17.52) and then invert $[P^j | Q^j]$ as recalled in (17.57). (This will be done for all cases simultaneously in Section 17.4.)

Example 17.45 First we make a wobbly figure 2 on which to experiment, then we perform the smoothing. The 2 will be specified in *parametric form* by a control polygon c^8. Thus c^8 lists control points rather than just their heights, and now our curves can curl back upon themselves as required. We recall that Rows $[u, v, \dots]$ is a matrix with rows as listed, and define

two $a^3 =$ Rows $[(2, 14), (14, 15), (14, 17), (3, 1), (1.5, 1.5), (4, 5), (9, 2),$
                     $(12, 0.8), (18, 2)]$,
wobble $a^8 = \{(t, 10 \cos[\pi t/4]) : t = 1, 2, 3 \dots, 257\}$, ∿∿∿∿∿∿∿∿∿∿∿∿∿∿∿∿∿∿∿∿∿
wobbly two $c^8 = a^8 + P^8 \cdot P^7 \cdot P^6 \cdot P^5 \cdot P4 \cdot a^3\ (8^5/1000)$.

We obtain smoother versions of the wobbly figure of Figure 17.36, represented in *parametric form* by c^8. We follow a path through the filter bank diagram by first computing the analysis filters $A^8, A^7, \dots, A^3$. The result is shown in Figure 17.37.

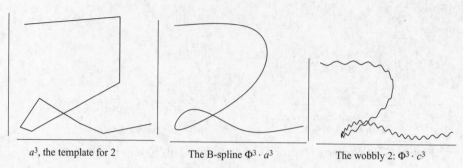

a^3, the template for 2   The B-spline $\Phi^3 \cdot a^3$ The wobbly 2: $\Phi^3 \cdot c^3$

Figure 17.36 Creating the wobbly 2.

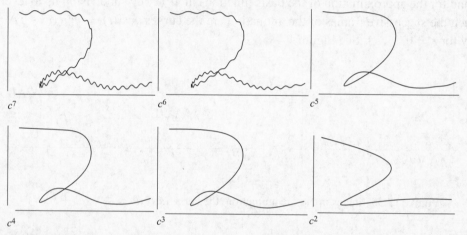

c^7 c^6 c^5

c^4 c^3 c^2

Figure 17.37 Using the filter bank to smooth a wobbly 2 through levels c^8 down to c^2.

It is hard to distinguish between c^8 and c^7, but by c^6 there are clear signs of smoothing. From c^6 to c^5 there is a sudden shakeout of wrinkles, with slight improvement by c^4. A Niquist view (see Section 14.3.3) is that c^5 has only 33 components, so it cannot sustain the vibration frequency offered by the wobble at level 8. The image remains visually constant down to c^3, by which time the best possible job is done because at the next level, c^2, the '2' looks significantly different though still recognisable. By the last level (not shown) its identity has gone, leaving only a curved line.

(c) Changing the character at different scales We explore changing the character of various facial features, using a small library of 'characters' adaptable to different scales. The features will be simultaneously displayed B-splines of the end-corrected type upon which we have standardised. Likewise, all basis functions will be subdivided down to level 8.

Example 17.46 (*The face*) Below are the control polygons for the unchanged face, where Rows $[u, v, \ldots]$ is a matrix with rows as listed. We keep symmetry, taking the second eye and brow to be the reflections of the first in the y-axis. A polygon *pol* with $2^j + 1$

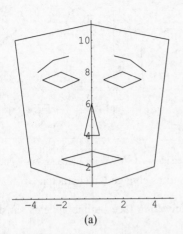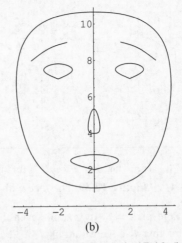

(a)   (b)

Figure 17.38 (a) Control polygons for the face and features of Example 17.46, (b) the B-spline version that results.

vertices contributes as feature the B-spline $\Phi^j \cdot pol$.

$face$ = Rows[(0, 1), (1, 1), (4, 2), (5, 10), (0, 11), (−5, 10), (−4, 2), (−1, 1), (0, 1)],
$mouth$ = Rows[(0, 2), (2, 2.5), (0, 3), (−2, 2.5), (0, 2)],
$eye1$ = Rows[(−2, 7), (−0.8, 7.5), (−2, 8), (−3.2, 7.5), (−2, 7)],
$nose$ = Rows[(0, 4), (1/2, 4), (0, 6), (−1/2, 4), (0, 4)],
$brow1$ = Rows[(−3, 8), (−2, 8.75), (−1, 9)].

In Figure 17.38 we show firstly the control polygons great and small that define the initial face outline and features, and secondly the face as an amalgam of the specified B-spline components.

The library Each item except curls is a sequence of $257 = 2^8 + 1$ plane points. A subsequence of n copies of the origin $(0, 0)$ is denoted by $\mathbf{0}^n$. These enable us to line up effects on the face outline at the desired positions.

$$curls = \left\{ \tfrac{1}{2}(2 - t/16 + \cos(\pi t/4), \sin(\pi t/4)) \right\}_{1 \le t \le 64},$$
$$hair = \mathbf{0}^{96}, \ curls, \ \mathbf{0}^{97},$$
$$lash = \left\{ (t/512, \tfrac{1}{10} \cos(\pi t/d)) \right\}_{1 \le t \le 257} \quad \text{with } d = 4,$$
$$lightlash = lash \text{ with } d = 8,$$
$$beard = \tfrac{1}{4} \ curls, \ \mathbf{0}^{129}, \tfrac{1}{4} \ curls$$

Armed with these items we produce the three variations shown in Figure 17.39, by changing the character at scales appropriate to the various cases.

Conclusions

1. We have changed the character of the original face of Figure 17.38(b) in regard to hair, brows (twice) and beard; the respective scales were $j = 4, 1$ and 7.
2. A contribution $\Phi^j \cdot pol$, whatever the scale, is a B-spline approximated as a polygon on $v_8 = 257$ vertices. This is consequent upon the choice of representing Φ^j by approximation

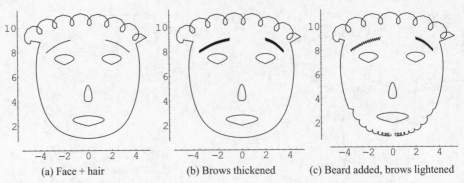

(a) Face + hair   (b) Brows thickened   (c) Beard added, brows lightened

Figure 17.39 The face with some features changed in character.

down to level $L = 8$. In practice even the relatively long face outline appears satisfactorily smooth; otherwise we would try $L = 9$, and so on.

3. Clearly, much more could be done with this example. For instance, we could easily extend the library by a design for teeth. On the other hand, the character of hair, brows and beard can be modified further by changing parameters such as magnitude and frequency (already done with the brows). To assist the reader, we confirm some details in Table 17.7.

Table 17.7. *The B-spline components in Example 17.46. The symbol Pjk denotes the matrix product $P^j P^{j-1} \cdots P^k$ generated by the application of (17.62).*

Figure	Components
original face, 17.38(b)	$\Phi^3 \cdot face$, $\Phi^2 \cdot mouth$, $\Phi^2 \cdot eye1$, $\Phi^2 \cdot eye2$, $\Phi^2 \cdot nose$, $\Phi^1 \cdot brow1$, $\Phi^1 \cdot brow2$
change of hair, 17.39(a)	$\Phi^3 \cdot face \to \Phi^8 \cdot (hair + P84 \cdot face)$
change of brow, 17.39(b)	$\Phi^1 \cdot brow\alpha \to \Phi^8 \cdot (lash + P82 \cdot brow\alpha)$ $(\alpha = 1, 2)$
change of brow/beard, 17.39(c)	$lash \to lightlash$, $\Phi^8 \cdot (hair + P84 \cdot face) \to$ $\Phi^8 \cdot (hair + beard + P84 \cdot face)$

Note: *hair* is obtained by changing the character of the face outline in an appropriate region of the parameter.

17.4 Appendix: band matrices for finding Q, A and B

We have shown how to compute transform matrices P, Q, A, B at each level j for a B-spline wavelet filter bank, and applied them to a class of problems. A key tool was recursive subdivision (see Section 17.2.2). We found Q by solving $MX = 0$ (see (17.52)) where M is the product of the refining/subdivision matrix P^j, transposed, and a matrix G of inner products of basis functions.

Our objective now is a solution valid simultaneously for all values of j. The first thing to note is that the matrix M is *banded*, that is, its nonzero entries are confined to a band around the main diagonal. But there is more to it than this (besides antipodality); we will succeed by reducing almost all matrix products we encounter to the same calculation as multiplying two polynomials (this is Theorem 17.51). Then the simple observation that a polynomial product of the form $g(x)g(-x)$ has no odd powers leads to an almost complete solution of $MX = 0$ in Section 17.4.2. This is applied to uniform and non-uniform B-splines in Section 17.4.3, and we conclude with the problem of inverting $[P|Q]$ once we have got it.

17.4.1 Band matrices and polynomials

In this section we define and gather needed results, about polynomials and the related matrices we'll work with. In a general polynomial $f(x)$ the coefficient of x^i will be denoted by f_i. Then in a polynomial product $h(x) = f(x)g(x)$ the term $h_i x^i$ equals the sum of all products $(f_j x^j)(g_k x^k)$ with total degree $j + k$ equal to i. For example, if, as we typically suppose, f, g have respective degrees r, s then $h_0 = f_0 g_0, h_1 = f_0 g_1 + f_1 g_0, \ldots, h_{r+s} = f_r g_s$. For the connection with matrices we may visualise these products by writing the *reversed* coefficients of $g(x)$ below those of $f(x)$, with an overlap:

$$f_0 \ldots f_i \ldots f_r$$
$$g_s \ldots g_i \ldots g_0$$

$$\text{implying } h_i = f_0 g_i + f_1 g_{i-1} + \cdots + f_i g_0. \tag{17.63}$$

These expressions will shortly reappear as elements in matrix products, providing a usable connection in our special case. Firstly we need the following observation. It relates to polynomials such as $1 + 3x + 3x^2 + x^3$ which are symmetrical (antipodal), but it is not restricted to binomial powers and Pascal's Triangle (for these see Section 9.1.4).

Lemma 17.47 *(a) If polynomials $f(x)$ and $g(x)$ are symmetrical then so is their product $f(x)g(x)$, (b) for any polynomial $f(x)$, the product $f(x)f(-x)$ has no odd powers.*

Proof (a) Let $f(x), g(x)$ have respective degrees r, s and product $h(x)$. Define the *reciprocal* $f_*(x) = x^r f(1/x)$. This is f with the order of coefficients reversed, so 'f is symmetrical' means $f = f_*$. Considering products,

$$(fg) * (x) = x^{r+s} f(1/x)g(1/x) = x^r f(1/x) x^s g(1/x) = f_*(x)g_*(x). \tag{17.63b}$$

Hence $f_* = f$ and $g_* = g$ together imply $(fg)_* = fg$, as required. For (b) we write $a(x) = f(x)f(-x) = a_0 + a_1 x + \cdots$ Then $a(-x) = f(-x)f(x) = a(x)$, and equating coefficients of x^{2i+1} in the equation $a(-x) = a(x)$ gives $(-1)^{2i+1} a_{2i+1} = a_{2i+1}$, whence $a_{2i+1} = 0$.

Examples 17.48 (a) The product of symmetrical polynomials $(1 + 7x + x^2)(1 + 2x + 2x^2 + x^3) = 1 + 9x + 17x^2 + 17x^3 + 9x^4 + x^5$ is symmetrical. (b) Let $h(x) = (1 + x)^{10}$. Then $h(x)h(-x) = (1 + x)^{10}(1 - x)^{10} = [(1 + x)(1 - x)]^{10} = (1 - x^2)^{10}$, with no odd powers. Less easily predictable is the disappearance of the odd terms in $(1 + 2x - 5x^2 + x^3)(1 - 2x - 5x^2 - x^3) = (1 - 14x^2 + 2x^4 - x^6)$.

Why band matrices?

Definition 17.49 A matrix G *is banded with polynomial* $g(x) = g_0 + g_1 x + g_2 x^2 + \cdots + g_n x^n$ *and shift* d if the first row of G is the sequence $g_0 g_1 g_2 \ldots g_n$ followed by zeros and each row is the previous one shifted d places to the right. For example, the matrix below is banded with polynomial $1 + 2x + 5x^2 + x^3$ and shift 2. As usual a blank entry denotes zero.

$$\begin{bmatrix} 1 & 2 & 5 & 1 & & & \\ & & 1 & 2 & 5 & 1 & \\ & & & & 1 & 2 & 5 & 1 \end{bmatrix}$$

A look at this matrix helps us to see that, given n and d, the dimensions of $G_{r \times c}$ are not independent, in fact

$$c = n + 1 + (r - 1)d. \tag{17.64}$$

Now consider the matrix equation below, in which G is banded with shift 1.

$$[f_0 \ldots f_r \; 0 \ldots 0] \begin{bmatrix} g_0 & g_1 & & g_s & & \\ 0 & g_0 & & g_{s-1} & g_s & \\ & \ddots & & & \ddots & \\ & & g_0 & g_1 & & g_s \end{bmatrix}_{m \times n} = [h_0 \ldots h_{r+s} \; 0 \ldots 0].$$
$$\qquad 1 \times m \qquad\qquad\qquad\qquad\qquad\qquad\qquad\qquad\qquad 1 \times n \tag{17.65}$$

The definition of matrix multiplication tells us that $h_i = [f_0 \ldots f_r \; 0 \ldots 0]$ [ith column of G]. For example $h_0 = f_0 g_0$, $h_1 = f_0 g_1 + f_1 g_0, \ldots, h_{r+s} = f_r g_s$, whilst for general i:

$$h_i = \sum_k f_k g_{i-k} \text{ (note: the subscripts add up to } i)$$
$$= \text{coefficient of } x^i \text{ in } h(x) = f(x) g(x), \quad \text{by (17.63a)}$$

Thus in (17.65) *we are performing polynomial multiplication in matrix form*. The next observation is that, if vector f is shifted d places, the corresponding polynomial is $x^d f(x)$. But $x^d f(x) \times g(x) = x^d h(x)$, so the vector h is shifted d places too. Applying this row by row with $d = 2$ gives the example below, and general d gives Theorem 17.51 following it.

Exercise A band matrix G has polynomial $(1 + x)^3$, shift 2, and 4 rows. Compute the number of columns by (17.63) then verify by writing out the matrix.

Example 17.50 Here we use the important fact that row i of a matrix product $H = FG$ equals (row i of F) $\cdot G$, to deduce that since F below has shift 2, so does H (the notation is carried over from (17.65)).

$$\begin{bmatrix} f_0 & f_1 & \cdots & f_{r-1} & f_r & 0 & 0 & 0 & 0 \\ 0 & 0 & f_0 & f_1 & & \cdots & f_{r-1} & f_r & 0 & 0 \\ 0 & 0 & 0 & 0 & f_0 & f_1 & \cdots & & f_{r-1} & f_r \end{bmatrix} \begin{bmatrix} \\ G \\ \\ \end{bmatrix} = \begin{bmatrix} h_0 & \ldots & h_{r+s} & 0 & 0 & 0 & 0 \\ 0 & 0 & h_0 & \ldots & h_{r+s} & 0 & 0 \\ 0 & 0 & 0 & 0 & h_0 & \ldots & h_{r+s} \end{bmatrix}.$$

Theorem 17.51 *(Band multiplication) Let F, G be banded with respective polynomials f, g but shifts d and 1. Then FG (if it exists) is banded with shift d and polynomial $f(x)g(x)$.*

Example 17.52 (i) (d = 1) We take $f(x) = (1 + x)^2$ and $g(x) = (1 + x)^3$. Then Theorem 17.51 tells us that, since $f(x)g(x) = (1 + x)^5 = 1 + 5x + 10x^2 + 10x^3 + 5x + 1$,

$$
\begin{bmatrix} 1 & 2 & 1 & & \\ & 1 & 2 & 1 & \\ & & 1 & 2 & 1 \end{bmatrix}
\begin{bmatrix} 1 & 3 & 3 & 1 & & & & \\ & 1 & 3 & 3 & 1 & & & \\ & & 1 & 3 & 3 & 1 & & \\ & & & 1 & 3 & 3 & 1 & \\ & & & & 1 & 3 & 3 & 1 \end{bmatrix}
=
\begin{bmatrix} 1 & 5 & 10 & 10 & 5 & 1 & & \\ & 1 & 5 & 10 & 10 & 5 & 1 & \\ & & 1 & 5 & 10 & 10 & 5 & 1 \end{bmatrix}.
$$

$$3 \times 5 \qquad\qquad 5 \times 8 \qquad\qquad\qquad 3 \times 8$$

Notice that the nonzero coefficient sequences were all symmetrical, as predicted by Lemma 17.47(a). (ii) (d = 2) Now consider the following product, for which a shortcut is clearly desirable.

$$
\begin{bmatrix} 1 & 2 & 3 & 4 & & \\ & 1 & 2 & 3 & 4 & \\ & & 1 & 2 & 3 & 4 \end{bmatrix}
\begin{bmatrix} 1 & -2 & 3 & -4 & & & & & & & \\ & 1 & -2 & 3 & -4 & & & & & & \\ & & 1 & -2 & 3 & -4 & & & & & \\ & & & 1 & -2 & 3 & -4 & & & & \\ & & & & 1 & -2 & 3 & -4 & & & \\ & & & & & 1 & -2 & 3 & -4 & & \\ & & & & & & 1 & -2 & 3 & -4 & \\ & & & & & & & 1 & -2 & 3 & -4 \end{bmatrix}.
$$

We try for a band matrix solution. The first matrix F is banded with polynomial $f(x) = 1 + 2x + 3x^2 + 4x^3$ and shift 2, whilst the second, G, is banded with polynomial $f(-x)$ and shift 1. By Theorem 17.51 the result is banded with polynomial $h(x) = f(x)f(-x)$ and shift 2. Further, Lemma 17.47 tells us that $h(x)$ has only even powers, which means that in multiplication we need not even calculate the coefficents of odd powers. In fact such a product may be evaluated as the difference of two squares, $h(x) = (1 + 3x^2)^2 - (2x + 4x^3)^2 = 1 + 2x^2 - 7x^4 - 16x^6$. Thus the first row of $H_{3 \times 11}$ is $[1 \ 0 \ 2 \ 0 \ -7 \ 0 \ -16 \ 0 \ldots 0]$.

Products of truncations

We shall need products of polynomial band matrices which are *truncated* in the sense of the first and last few columns being removed. The first case we deal with has been settled by other means, but now we give it a new perspective before proceeding further. A small version suffices, in which the transposed refining matrix P^T is a product $M_1 M_2$, say (transposing Example 17.30),

$$8P^{\mathrm{T}} = \begin{bmatrix} 2 & 1 & & \\ & 1 & 2 & 1 & \\ & & 1 & 2 \end{bmatrix}_{3\times 5} \begin{bmatrix} 1 & & \\ 2 & 1 & \\ 1 & 2 & 1 \\ & 1 & 2 \\ & & 1 \end{bmatrix}_{5\times 3} = \begin{bmatrix} 4 & 1 & 0 \\ 4 & 6 & 4 \\ 0 & 1 & 4 \end{bmatrix}_{3\times 3}.$$

The entries obviously have something to do with the coefficients in the expansions of $(1+x)^2$ and $(1+x)^4$. In fact the left hand matrices are distinct trunctations of band matrices with polynomial $(1+x)^2$, the first band matrix having shift $d = 2$. The question is whether the product could have been abstracted from a band matrix with polynomial $(1+x)^4$ and $d = 2$. The answer is YES because there are enough zeros around. Consider the product with truncated parts restored, but judiciously partitioned:

$$\begin{bmatrix} 1 & 2 & 1 & & \\ & 1 & 2 & 1 & \\ & & 1 & 2 & 1 \end{bmatrix}_{3\times 7} \begin{bmatrix} 1 & 2 & 1 & & & \\ & 1 & 2 & 1 & & \\ & & 1 & 2 & 1 & \\ & & & 1 & 2 & 1 \\ & & & & 1 & 2 & 1 \\ & & & & & 1 & 2 & 1 \\ & & & & & & 1 & 2 & 1 \end{bmatrix}_{7\times 9} = \begin{bmatrix} 1 & 4 & 6 & 4 & 1 & & \\ & 1 & 4 & 6 & 4 & 1 & \\ & & 1 & 4 & 6 & 4 & 1 \end{bmatrix}_{3\times 9}.$$

This has the partitioned form

$$\left[L_1 \mid M_1 \mid N_1 \right]_{1\times 3} \begin{bmatrix} x & 0 & x \\ x & M_2 & x \\ x & 0 & x \end{bmatrix}_{3\times 3} = \left[x \mid M_1 M_2 \mid x \right]_{1\times 3}, \qquad (17.66)$$

which shows that to find the product of such truncated matrices we may simply multiply the corresponding polynomials to find the product of the non-truncated (enlarged) versions and take $M_1 M_2$ as the middle columns of the resulting band matrix, as in (17.65), where 'middle' refers to the column positions taken by M_2 within its enlargement. In particular,

> (*Uniform B-splines*) P^{T} is obtained by deleting the first three and last three columns of the band matrix with polynomial $(1+x)^4/8$, shift 2, and given number of rows. $\qquad (17.67)$

17.4.2 Solving the matrix equation $FX = 0$

We'll see that determining Q from the equation $MQ = 0$ of (17.52) can be done in two parts, corresponding to (i) an end-point correction involving the first three or four columns of Q, and (ii) the rest. Although part (ii) can involve an arbitrary number of vertices, there is at least one very simple solution, given by the result now stated.

Theorem 17.53 *Let $F_{a\times b}$ be a band matrix with polynomial $f(x)$ and shift 2. Suppose $a < b$ and that f_0 and f_n are nonzero. Then a set of $(b - a)$ distinct solutions of the equation $FX = 0$ is given by the alternate interior columns of the b-rowed band matrix with polynomial $f(-x)$ and shift 1. That is*

$$[-f_1 \ f_0 \ 0 \ldots 0], [-f_3 \ f_2 - f_1 \ f_0 \ 0 \ldots 0], \ldots, [0 \ldots 0 \pm f_n \ \mp f_{n-1}].$$

Exercise Verify that the alternate interior columns are as stated.

Proof of theorem Consider the product $FG = H$, where $g(x) = h(-x)$. All rows and columns are to be numbered starting from zero. We are given the shifts $d = 2$ for $F, d = 1$ for G, and hence $d = 2$ for H. Also, and crucially, $h_s = 0$ when s is odd, by Lemma 17.47(b). Therefore we may write

$$F \cdot (\text{column } 2i + 1 \text{ of } G) = \text{column } 2i + 1 \text{ of } H = \begin{bmatrix} h_{2i+1} \\ h_{2i-1} \\ h_{2i-3} \\ \cdots \end{bmatrix} = \begin{bmatrix} 0 \\ 0 \\ 0 \\ \cdots \end{bmatrix}.$$

Thus the odd-numbered columns of G (i.e. the alternate interior ones) *are* solutions of $FX = 0$. They are distinct because f_0 and f_n are nonzero. Let G be $b \times c$. It remains to verify that the number $(c - 1)/2$ of odd columns is equal to $b - a$. But since F is $a \times b$ with shift 2 we have from formula (17.64) that $b = n + 1 + 2(a - 1) = n + 2a - 1$ and, since G is $b \times c$, that $c = (n + 1) + 1(b - 1) = n + b$. Eliminating, we obtain $b - a = (c - 1)/2$, as required.

Example 17.54 Solve the equation $FX = 0$, where $F = \begin{bmatrix} 1 & 2 & 3 & & & & \\ & 1 & 2 & 3 & & & \\ & & 1 & 2 & 3 & & \end{bmatrix}_{3\times 7}$.

Solution The matrix G of Theorem 17.53, with polynomial $g(x) = f(-x)$, and the corresponding matrix S of columns that are solutions of $FX = 0$, are given by

$$G = \begin{bmatrix} 1 & -2 & 3 & & & & \\ & 1 & -2 & 3 & & & \\ & & 1 & -2 & 3 & & \\ & & & 1 & -2 & 3 & \\ & & & & 1 & -2 & 3 \\ & & & & & 1 & -2 & 3 \\ & & & & & & 1 & -2 & 3 \end{bmatrix}, S = \begin{bmatrix} -2 & & & \\ 1 & 3 & & \\ -2 & & & \\ 1 & 3 & & \\ -2 & & & \\ & 1 & 3 \\ & -2 \end{bmatrix}.$$

Since the rows of $F_{a\times b}$ are linearly independent, the number of independent solutions to be found is $b - a = 7 - 3 = 4$ (see Examples 8.25(iv)). If the four solutions we already have are independent, then the task is complete. But independence is established by the observation that there are four rows in S which may be combined to form -2 times the identity I_4, so we are done.

Remarks 17.55 (i) Although the four solutions in the example above turned out to be independent, this is not guaranteed by Theorem 17.53. In fact, a counter-example is given by $F_{3 \times 8}$ based on $f(x) = p + qx + px^2 + qx^3$. The five solution vectors we obtain are *not* independent. However, the cases we want in practice do have independence, and Theorem 17.53 presents the correct number of solutions.

(ii) According to Corollary 8.24, the number of independent solutions equals the *nullity* of F, that is $b - r(F)$, where $r(F)$ may be defined as the number of nonzero rows in any echelon form of F. However, the d-fold shift ensures that F is already in echelon form, so, in the present polynomial banded case, the number of independent solutions of $FX = 0$ is simply $b - a$.

Exercise Find a nonzero linear combination of the solutions in Remark 17.55(i) which equals the zero vector.

17.4.3 Application to cubic B-splines

We aim to compute in general the matrix $Q = Q^j$ expressing a wavelet basis in terms of the cubic spline basis, which at level $j = 0$ is $\{N_i \equiv N_{i,4}(x) \equiv N_{0,4}(x - i)\}$. The semi-orthogonality condition has identified the columns of Q as a maximal sized set of independent solutions of the matrix equation $(P^T G)X = 0$, where G is the matrix of inner products of the N_i (see (17.53)).

Application 1: uniform splines

We begin with the solutions of $FX = 0$ offered by Theorem 17.53, then extend slightly to get a complete set for Q. Let us look at the forms of P^T and G.

The matrix P^T Prompted by (17.67) we set $p(x) = (1 + x)^4/8$ so that we may write the antipodal P^T, with $L \,(= v_{j-1})$ rows, in the form

$$P^T = \begin{bmatrix} p_3 & p_4 & & & & & & \\ p_1 & p_2 & p_3 & p_4 & & & & \\ 0 & p_0 & p_1 & p_2 & p_3 & p_4 & & \\ 0 & 0 & 0 & p_0 & p_1 & p_2 & p_3 & p_4 & \cdots \\ \cdots & \cdots & \cdots & \cdots & \cdots & \cdots & \cdots & \cdots & \cdots \end{bmatrix}_{L \times 2L-3} \tag{17.68}$$

The matrix G According to (17.53) the Gram matrix G at level j has (i, k) element $2^{-j} c_{|i-k|}$, where $[c_0 c_1 c_2 \ldots] = \frac{1}{140}[2416\ 1191\ 120\ 1\ 0 \ldots 0]$, involving only four distinct nonzero values. The symmetry between i and k means that the rows after the first three are successive shifts of the 7-vector $[c_3 c_2 c_1 c_0 c_1 c_2 c_3]$.

We relabel this as a vector $g = [g_0 \ldots g_6] = \frac{1}{140}[1\ 120\ 1191\ 2416\ 1191\ 120\ 1]$, so that the *middle rows* (all but the first and last three) of G constitute a band matrix with polynomial $g(x)$ and shift 1. Finally, since the solution of $(P^T G)X = 0$ does not depend on the constant factor 2^{-j}, we omit this and write

$$
G = \begin{bmatrix}
g_3 & g_4 & g_5 & g_6 & & & \\
g_2 & g_3 & g_4 & g_5 & g_6 & & \\
g_1 & g_2 & g_3 & g_4 & g_5 & g_6 & \\
\hline
g_0 & g_1 & g_2 & g_3 & g_4 & g_5 & g_6 \\
& g_0 & g_1 & g_2 & g_3 & g_4 & g_5 & g_6 \\
& & & & & & & & \\
\end{bmatrix}
$$
$$(2L-3)\times(2L-3).$$

(17.69)

Most of $P^\mathrm{T} G$ is accounted for by the argument that the middle $L - 6$ rows of $P^\mathrm{T} G$ equal the middle $L - 6$ rows of P^T, times G, namely a banded matrix with polynomial $h(x) = p(x)g(x)$, where, dropping constant multipliers, the coefficients in $h(x)$ form the vector

$$h = [1\ \ 124\ \ 1677\ \ 7904\ \ 18482\ \ 24624\ \ 18482\ \ 7904\ \ 1677\ \ 124\ \ 1]. \qquad (17.70)$$

Considering now the first three rows of P^T, we can use (17.63) to identify all elements of the corresponding rows of H (a case of matrix M in (17.52)) with entries taken from the vector h, except for the elements a_i, b_j:

$$
H = \begin{bmatrix}
a_0 & a_1 & a_2 & h_9 & h_{10} & & & & & & \\
b_1 & b_2 & b_3 & h_7 & h_8 & h_9 & h_{10} & & & & \\
h_2 & h_3 & h_4 & h_5 & h_6 & h_7 & h_8 & h_9 & h_{10} & & \\
\hline
h_0 & h_1 & h_2 & h_3 & h_4 & h_5 & h_6 & h_7 & h_8 & h_9 & h_{10} \\
0 & 0 & h_0 & h_1 & h_2 & h_3 & h_4 & h_5 & h_6 & h_7 & h_8 & h_9 & h_{10} \\
\hdashline
& & & h_0 & h_1 & h_2 & h_3 & h_4 & h_5 & h_6 & h_7 & h_8 & h_9 & h_{10} \\
& & & & h_0 & h_1 & h_2 & h_3 & h_4 & h_5 & h_6 & h_7 & h_8 & h_9 & h_{10} \\
\hline
\end{bmatrix}
$$

(antipodal images of first 3 rows)

$$\Big\updownarrow \text{ the } L-6 \text{ middle rows.}$$

Observe that P^T, G and hence H, are antipodal by Theorem 17.38. This entails $h(x)$ being symmetric, which it is because $p(x)$ and $g(x)$ are symmetric (Lemma 17.47). Notice that both P^T and H are $L \times (2L - 3)$ for some L. Therefore by Remark 17.55(ii) we must find $(2L - 3) - L = L - 3$ independent solutions to $HX = 0$.

The $L - 9$ middle solutions Recall that $HX = 0$ is equivalent to X satisfying $R_i X = 0$ for each row R_i of H. The matrix μ of middle rows of H has rank $(2L - 3) - (L - 6) = L + 3$, and Theorem 17.53 gives us that many solutions from $h(-x)$, of which the *first six* are

$$[-h_1\ h_0\ 0\ldots0],\ [-h_3\ h_2\ -h_1\ h_0\ 0\ \ldots\ 0],\ \ldots,\ [0\ h_{10}\ -h_9\ \cdots\ -h_1\ h_0\ 0\ \ldots\ 0].$$

This shows that *all but* the first six and last six solutions have a minimum of three leading and three trailing zeros and hence satisfy $HX = 0$ in spite of any nonzero elements in the first three and last three columns of H. Thus far we have a total of $L + 3 - 12 = L - 9$ solutions, so there are six more to find.

The six end solutions We shall seek three solutions with respectively 0, 1, 2 leading zeros and as many trailing zeros as possible. Their antipodal images provide the remaining three. Now, because of shifting in the middle rows, the first eight columns of H have only zeros after the seventh row, giving eight vectors of length 7 which must therefore be linearly dependent (Theorem 7.7), say $u_1 C_1 + \cdots + u_8 C_8 = 0$. Thus $X_1 = [u_1 \ldots u_8 \ 0 \ldots 0]^T$ satisfies $HX = 0$. Similarly, we guarantee to find $X_2 = [0 \ v_2 \cdots v_9 \ 0 \cdots 0]$ and $X_3 = [0 \ 0 \ w_3 \ldots w_{10} \ 0 \ldots \ 0]$ as solutions, by considering respectively eight and nine rows. ALGO 17.2 will find solutions in this form. Rewriting the columns of Q as rows for compactness, we obtain

u_1	u_2	u_3	$\ldots$	u_6	-124	1	0	0	0	0	0	0	$\ldots$
0	v_1	v_2	$\ldots$	v_5	v_6	v_7	-124	1	0	0	0	0	$\ldots$
0	0	w_1	$\ldots$	w_4	w_5	w_6	w_7	w_8	-124	1	0	0	$\ldots$

band matrix with polynomial $x^3 h(-x)$ and shift 2
antipodal image of the first three rows

where u, v, w are perturbations of the last few coefficients in $h(x)$, varying more as we move leftwards. For comparison, here are the entries of u rounded to integers, compared with h; precise rational or accurate decimal answers are of course produced by ALGO 17.2, depending on the type of arithmetic used.

u		-10641	21776	-25835	18822	-7999	1677	-124	1
h	$\ldots$	-7904	18482	-24264	18482	-7904	1677	-124	1

Scaling Although our solution is independent of scale, it may be useful to scale Q^j by a factor such as 2^{-j}.

Application 2: end-corrected cubic B-splines

We seek the solution of $(P^T G)X = 0$ with P^T and G as adapted from the uniform case, for edge-correction. We saw in Remarks 17.32 that P acquires an additional row $[1 \ 0 \ \ldots \ 0]$ at the start and $[0 \ \ldots \ 0 \ 1]$ at the end. These become columns in the $L \times (2L - 1)$ matrix P^T. Both P and P^T are still antipodal.

As previewed in Example 17.42, the new Gram matrix is $E^T GE$, where G is the uniform case of size $2L + 1$ and E is the identity matrix I_{2L-1} preceded by $[2 \ -1 \ 0 \ \ldots \ 0]$ and followed by its reverse.

u_1	u_2	u_3	u_4	u_5	u_6	-124	1	0	0	0	0	0	0	0 ...
0	v_1	v_2	v_3	v_4	v_5	v_6	v_7	-124	1	0	0	0	0	0 ...
0	0	w_1	w_2	w_3	w_4	w_5	w_6	w_7	w_8	-124	1	0	0	0 ...
0	0	0	z_1	z_2	z_3	z_4	z_5	z_7	z_7	z_8	z_9	-124	1	0 ...

band matrix with polynomial $x^3 h(-x)$ and shift 2

antipodal image of the first four rows

Figure 17.40 The matrix Q^T, with first four rows non-standard.

The only change in the form of G is to the submatrix formed by the first three rows and columns (and its antipodal image). Pre-multiplying by P^T to get the new version, say $M = P^T G$, we obtain a matrix which differs from the uniform version H above only in replacement of the top left 3×3 submatrix with one of dimensions 3×4, the extra column being part of one at the start of M.

The extra column means that we have to begin our standard solutions one double shift further on and so we use ALGO 17.2 to find four special solutions rather than three. As observed, this is a small price to pay when the solutions run to many more. The matrix Q^T in Figure 17.40 shows how to specify a solution of any size, taking into account that it is antipodal.

As in the uniform case, the special solutions found by *find Q* (ALGO 17.2) have last two entries $-124, 1$, and as a whole they are recognizably perturbations of the last few coefficients in $h(x)$. Here, finally, is ALGO 17.3 to output the solution for arbitrary j.

ALGO 17.3 Find Q at arbitrary level j for non-uniform
B-splines (Mathematica)

```
width = 2^j + 1;
If[j ≤ 4, Return[findQ(j)]]; (ALGO 17.2)
z = {0, 0, 1, −124, 1677, −7904, 18482, −24264, 18482, −7904, 1677, −124, 1};
z = PadRight[z, width];
H = Transpose[findQ [(j = 4 )]]; (Solve MX = 0 in small case only)
H2 = PadLeft[Take[H, −4], {4, width } ];
H = PadRight[Take[H, 4], {4, width } ];
Do[z = RotateRight[z, 2]; H = Append[H, z], {2^(j − 1) − 8} ];
H = Join[H, H2];
Return[Transpose[H]]; ];
```

Figure 17.41 shows the wavelet basis in the case $j = 3$.

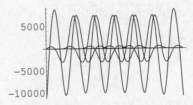

Figure 17.41 End-corrected wavelet basis in the end-corrected case. Note the degree of homogeneity away from the first and last.

Application 3: inverting $[P|Q]$ to obtain A, B

1. *Rescaling Q* If the determinant of $[P|Q] = [P^j|Q^j]$ is out of range for successful inversion, this may be remedied by rescaling Q to λQ, where λ is some positive number. The result is that A is unaffected but B is scaled by λ^{-1}, because

$$[P|Q]\begin{bmatrix} A \\ B \end{bmatrix} = I \Leftrightarrow PA + QB = I \Leftrightarrow PA + (\lambda Q)(\lambda^{-1}B) = I. \qquad (17.72)$$

2. *Interleaving* The matrix $[P|Q]$ is sparse in the sense that its nonzero elements are restricted to a relatively narrow band around the main diagonal. However, this band becomes narrower still if the columns of P and Q are interleaved. On a modest 500 MHz computer running Mathematica the inversion time for $[P|Q]$ of size 1025 was reduced from 164 to 29 seconds, a factor of about 5.5. A routine supplied with the actual band dimensions after interleaving, and using triangular decomposition, would probably be fastest (see e.g. Golub & van Loan, 1996).

3. *Getting the true inverse* We began with a modified $[P|Q]$; how do we get the inverse we actually want? The answer is to de-interleave the rows, as the following argument shows. Let $[P|Q]$ have size $2d + 1$ and let S be the result of interleaving the rows of the identity matrix I_{2d+1}, then

   we interleave the columns, obtaining $[P|Q]S^T$ \qquad (see above Theorem 8.20)

   we invert the result, obtaining \qquad $(S^T)^{-1}[P|Q]^{-1}$

   which we should pre-multiply by S^T. But, since S performs permutation only, we have from Example 8.21(iii) that $S^T = S^{-1}$. Thus we should de-interleave the rows.

ALGO 17.4 Interleaving routines (Mathematica)

Interleave rows of pq ('ILrows')
```
d = (Length[pq] − 1)/2;
m = Table[0, {2d + 1}, {2d + 1}];
m[[Range[1, 2d + 1, 2] ]] = Take[pq, d + 1];
m[[Range[2, 2d, 2] ]] = Take[pq, −d];
Return[m];
```

De-interleave rows of pq
```
d = (Length[pq] − 1)/2;
A = Take[pq, {1, 2d + 1, 2}];
B = Take[pq, {2, 2d, 2}];
Return[Join[A, B]];
```
Interleave columns of pq ('ILcolsL')
```
Transpose[ILrows[Transpose[pq]]];
```

Further developments For analysis of subdivision via eigenvalues and -vectors see Farin (2002). For using connections between B-splines and Bézier polynomials to convert scanned data to polynomials, see Stollnitz *et al.* (1996).

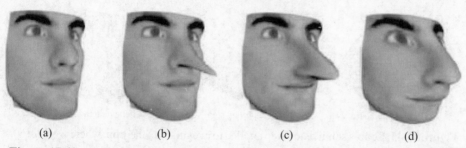

(a)   (b)   (c)   (d)

Figure 17.42 (a) Original face as bicubic tensor-product B-spline surface, (b), (c), (d): face changed at respectively narrow, intermediate, and broad scale. (Images by Stollnitz *et al.*, 1996.)

17.5 Appendix: surface wavelets

How should the subdivision method for B-splines be generalised to two dimensions for multiresolution? A natural first approach is to consider how a 1D transform is extended to 2D (see Section 15.1.1) and look for an analogy in the spline context. This suggests we start with two spline bases $\{N_{j,m}(s)\}_{0 \leq j \leq M}$ and $\{N_{k,m}(t)\}_{0 \leq k \leq N}$, and form a 2D basis consisting of all products $N_{j,m}(s)N_{k,m}(t)$. Then a set of control points $\{P_{jk}\}$ in 3-space defines a surface whose point with parameters s, t is.

$$P(s, t) = \sum_{j,k} N_{j,m}(s)N_{k,m}(t)P_{jk}. \tag{17.73}$$

Such *tensor product surfaces* are a well-established technique (Farin, 2002), and multiresolution may be performed through, for example, the hierarchical B-splines of Forsey and Bartels (1988). In fact, though, subdivision applied to surfaces was pioneered as early as 1978 by Doo and Sabin and by Catmull and Clark.

The first wavelet approach to multiresolution of surfaces with arbitrary topology was that of Lounsbery (1994) and Hoppe *et al.* (1994), using the triangular face subdivision system of Loop (1987). Their work led not only to applications in multiresolution and compression but to editing at different scales, image look-up, scan conversion and more (Stollnitz *et al.* 1996). We introduce some of the mathematics, and then note later contributions by Bertram *et al.* (2004).

17.5.1 Loop subdivision

We start with a triangulated surface which has *subdivision connectivity*: that is, it may be obtained from a simpler *control polyhedron* by successive subdivisions of the type proposed. Eck *et al.* (1995) provide an algorithm to ensure this. We reinterpret, for such a surface, the steps formerly carried out in creating a B-spline from its control polygon. As before, a single iteration of subdivision consists formally of

Splitting step: insert the midpoint of every edge,
Averaging step: replace every vertex by a linear combination.

Control polyhedron, M_0 After splitting step, $M_0{}^1$ After averaging step, M^1

Figure 17.43 Loop's subdivision step applied to a regular octahedron, where $w \to \rho(w)$. For the *M*-notation, see the text.

The splitting step For the B-spine splitting we had to specify which vertex pairs formed an edge after the midpoint insertion; the implied rule was that an edge *AB* with midpoint *M* is replaced by edges *AM, MB*. Here, rather than new edges, we must specify the new triangles: in fact, they form a natural division of each original triangle into four half-sized copies, as indicated in Figure 17.43.

The averaging step Each vertex is replaced by a linear combination of itself and its neighbours (the vertices joined to it by an edge). The process is described as an *averaging* scheme because the coefficients are chosen so as to sum to unity. In Loop's system, the simplest to yield a smooth surface, a vertex w_0 with n neighbours $w_1, \ldots, w_n$, *after the* splitting step, undergoes

$$w_0 \to \frac{w_1 + w_2 + \cdots + w_n + \alpha(n)w_0}{n + \alpha(n)}, \tag{17.74}$$

where $\alpha(n) = n(1 - \beta)/\beta$, and $\beta = \beta(n) = \frac{5}{4} - \left(3 + 2\cos\frac{2\pi}{n}\right)^2/32$. $\tag{17.75}$

Most coefficients that occur in practice may be read from Table 17.8.

Table 17.8. *Some coefficients in Loop's averaging formula, for central vertex with n neighbours.*

n	2	3	4	5	6
$\alpha(n)$	$-14/39$	$-1/3$	$4/31$	$(3 + 16\sqrt{5})/41 \approx 0.946$	2
$1/(n + \alpha(n))$	$39/64$	$3/8$	$31/128$	0.168	$1/8$

Getting the base mesh Before we can consider multiresolution of a surface, which we'll assume is subdivided into a mesh in some way (see e.g. Turk and Levoy, 1994 or Kobbelt *et al.*, 1999), it must be approximated to required accuracy by a surface obtainable specifically by Loop subdivision, from some *base mesh* (control polyhedron) *M*. The property of being so obtainable from *M* is called Loop *subdivision connectivity* to *M*.

Determining a suitable approximating surface is highly non-trivial. In their ingenious method Eck *et al.* (1995) invoke properties of harmonic maps going back to Eels and

Figure 17.44 Approximating a triangulated figure for Loop subdivision (Eck *et al.*, 1995).

Lemaire (1988). They aggregate mesh pieces into Voronoi regions (Section 11.2.2), then take the dual (Section 6.3.1) triangulation. The process is partially illustrated in Figure 17.44.

17.5.2 Parameters and basis functions

Let us denote the control polyhedron by M_0, a topological space provided with a list of points called *vertices* and a list of the vertex triples that constitute its *triangles*, the latter implying which point pairs are to be *edges*. After j subdivision steps we obtain a polyhedron M^j with 4^j times as many triangular faces as M_0. To tie in subdivision with wavelets, we must next parametrise M^j.

We need an analogue to the parameter t of B-splines. In that case t lies in some interval $[a, b]$, topologically equivalent to the B-spline curve. We see that t *could* be taken on the control polygon itself, and this points the way to the step from curves to surfaces.

Suppose the subdivisions starting from M_0 are performed without the averaging step. The result M_0^j has the same point set as M_0 but acquires a list of vertices and triangles in exact correspondence with those of M^j. This provides a natural parametrisation,

$$\sigma = \sigma^j \colon M_0^j \to M^j, \tag{17.76}$$

where, if u_i is a typical vertex of M_0^j and v_i is the corresponding vertex of M^j, we define σ by $\sigma(u_i) = v_i$ on vertices and by linearity over the triangles of M_0^j. Thus σ is piecewise linear on M_0. Figure 17.43 provides an illustration in the case $j = 1$.

Hat functions To proceed by analogy with B-spline wavelets we shall require basis functions mapping M_0 into the real numbers: for each vertex u of M_0^j, we define firstly the *hat function* $e_u : M_0 \to \mathbf{R}$ to be the unique *piecewise linear* function on M_0 which sends u to 1, sends all other vertices to 0, and is linear on triangles. If u lies in a flat part of M_0 we may conveniently represent $e_u(x)$ as a height. Thus e_u is represented as a pyramid

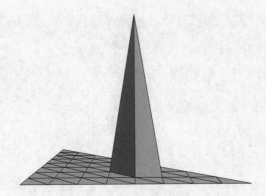

Figure 17.45 Hat function for surface wavelets.

with base polygon $u_1 \ldots u_n$ formed from the neighbours of u in M_0^j. This is illustrated in Figure 17.45.

Barycentric coordinates Consider the triangle with vertices u, v, w. We saw in Section 17.1.2 that every point of this triangle may be written $ru + sv + tw$ for unique non-negative numbers r, s, t satisfying $r + s + t = 1$, called its *barycentric coordinates*. Further, if θ is an affine transformation (linear, possibly combined with translation), then θ preserves barycentric coordinates:

$$\theta(ru + sv + tw) = r\theta(u) + s\theta(v) + t\theta(w). \tag{17.77}$$

This is one reason why barycentric coordinates are so useful, and the following theorem shows how they fit in well with hat functions.

Theorem 17.56 *A piecewise linear function* $\rho: M_0^j \to M^j$ *is a linear combination of hat functions, as follows. If* $\rho(u_i) = v_i$, *where* u_i *is the ith vertex of* M_0^j *with hat function* e_i, *then*

$$\rho(x) = \sum_i v_i e_i(x). \tag{17.78}$$

Proof It suffices to check the equality over an arbitrary triangle Δ of M_0^j, with vertices u_1, u_2, u_3 say. Let x be a point of Δ with barycentric coordinates r_1, r_2, r_3. Notice that, using (17.77) with $\theta = e_1$, we have $e_1(x) = e_1(r_1u_1 + r_2u_2 + r_3u_3) = r_1e_1(u_1) + r_2e_2(u_2) + r_3e_3(u_3) = r_1$, since $e_i(u_k) = \delta_{ik}$, and similarly

$$e_i(x) = r_i \ (i = 1, 2, 3). \tag{17.79}$$

Now, considering the sum in (17.78), the only e_i that are nonzero anywhere on Δ are e_1, e_2, e_3 themselves, so the sum evaluates at x to

$$v_1e_1(x) + v_2e_2(x) + v_3e_3(x) = r_1v_1 + r_2v_2 + r_3v_3 \quad \text{by(17.79)}$$
$$= \sum_i r_i \rho(u_i)$$
$$= \rho(x), \ \text{by(17.77) with } \theta = \rho.$$

Basis functions If the vertices in M^j are $v_i^j (i = 1, 2, \ldots)$, then by Theorem 17.56 we may write the parametrisation of M^j as

$$\sigma^j(x) = \sum_i v_i^j e_i^j(x), \tag{17.80}$$

where $e_i^j(x)$ is the hat function of the ith vertex at level j. To see what happens as further subdivisions are performed, we consider a matrix equivalent to (17.80), in which a piecewise function on M_0^j is specified by a column vector listing its values at the vertices of M_0^j. Thus $e_i^j(x)$ becomes a column vector $e_i^j = [0 \ \ldots \ 0 \ 1 \ 0 \ \ldots \ 0]^T$ with 1 in position i, and we may write

$$\sigma^j = \sum_i e_i^j v_i^j. \tag{17.81}$$

Since the passage from the jth to the $(j+1)$st subdivision is linear, it is given by some *subdivision matrix* P^{j+1}. That is,

$$\sigma^{j+1} = P^{j+1} \sum_i e_i^j v_i^j = \sum_i \left(P^{j+1} e_i^j \right) v_i^j, \tag{17.82}$$

whence $\sigma^{j+2} = \sum_i (P^{j+2} P^{j+1} e_i^j) v_i^j$, and so on. The limit of $\ldots P^{j+2} P^{j+1} e_i^j$ as more subdivisions are performed is $\phi_i^j(x)$, the *ith basis function at level j*. Thus, taking limits in (17.82),

$$\boxed{\sigma(x) = \sum_i \phi_i^j(x) v_i^j.} \tag{17.83}$$

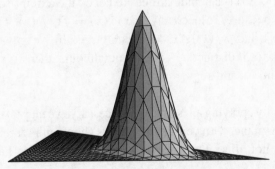

Figure 17.46 An approximation to $\phi_i^3(x)$, starting from the hat function of Figure 17.45.

The $\phi_i^j(x)$, exemplified in Figure 17.46, play a role similar to those used earlier for B-splines. At a given level, these functions have approximately the same shape, and when we go up one level the shape is maintained but the scale decreases by a factor 4. For fixed j the $\phi_i^j(x)$ are linearly independent and so form a basis of the space V^j spanned by them; we list these basis elements as a *row vector* $\Phi^j(x)$. Formally,

$$\Phi^j(x) = \left[\phi_1^j(x) \ \phi_2^j(x) \ldots \right],$$
$$V^j = \text{span} \ \Phi^j(x), \ v_j = \dim V^j,$$
$$\Phi^{j-1}(x) = \Phi^j(x) P^j, \tag{17.84}$$

and we are part-way to recreating the filter bank of Figure 17.32 for surface wavelets. Our next task is to establish an inner product.

17.5.3 The inner product

To define wavelets we need an inner product $\langle \,, \rangle$ on the spaces V^j. Suppose that our greatest refinement is level J; then all V^j lie within V^J and we need only define $\langle \,, \rangle$ on V^J. Let τ, with area $|\tau|$, be a typical triangle in the Jth splitting M_0^J and let f, g be real functions on the space M_0. Then we define their *inner product* $\langle f, g \rangle$ to be the sum over all such triangles:

$$\langle f, g \rangle = \sum \tfrac{1}{|\tau|} \int_\tau f(x)g(x)\mathrm{d}x. \tag{17.85}$$

Theorem 17.57 *(a) The inner product $\langle \,, \rangle$ satisfies the axioms of (7.8). That is, for f, g, h in V^J and real λ we have (i) $\langle g, f \rangle = \langle f, g \rangle$, (ii) $\langle f, g + h \rangle = \langle f, g \rangle + \langle f, h \rangle$, (iii) $\langle \lambda f, g \rangle = \lambda \langle f, g \rangle$.*
(b) Let u, v be vertices of M_0^J. Then

$$\langle e_u, e_v \rangle = \begin{cases} \tfrac{1}{12} \times \textit{no. of triangles with edge } uv, \textit{ if } v \neq u, \\ \tfrac{1}{6} \times \textit{no. of triangles with vertex } u, \textit{ if } v = u. \end{cases} \tag{17.86}$$

Proof (a) Because (17.85) is a sum it suffices to check the axioms for an arbitrary term, and there they hold because, respectively, $g(x)f(x) = f(x)g(x)$, $f(x)(g(x) + h(x)) = f(x)g(x) + f(x)h(x)$, and $(\lambda f(x))g(x) = \lambda(f(x)g(x))$. (b) We only need to consider the two cases in (17.86), for if distinct u, v are not neighbours, then $e_u(x)e_v(x) = 0$ for all x by definition of e_u and e_v, and so $\langle e_u, e_v \rangle = 0$.

Now observe that, by applying an isometry if necessary, we may take a typical triangle τ of M_0^J to lie in the xy-plane, with vertices u, v, w, as shown in Figure 17.47. This change of coordinates does not affect the integral because the Jacobian has absolute value 1 (Theorem 10.10).

Let $P(x, y)$ have barycentric coordinates r, s, t. Since $r = 1 - s - t$, a point of τ is uniquely determined by the pair (s, t). Also, the condition $r \geq 0$ is equivalent to $s + t \leq 1$, so τ consists of points with $s, t \geq 0, s + t \leq 1$. To change coordinates in the

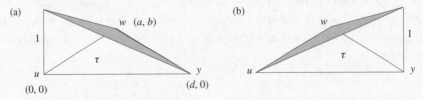

Figure 17.47 Shaded heights of (a) $e_u(x)$ and (b) $e_v(x)$ over the triangle τ.

integral from (x, y) to (s, t), note

$$(x, y) = ru + sv + tw = (sd + ta, tb), \quad \text{and hence} \quad \frac{\partial(x, y)}{\partial(s, t)} = \begin{vmatrix} d & a \\ 0 & b \end{vmatrix} = bd = 2|\tau|,$$

whence $\dfrac{1}{|\tau|} \displaystyle\int_\tau F \mathrm{d}x \mathrm{d}y = \dfrac{1}{|\tau|} \int_\tau F \times \left| \dfrac{\partial(x, y)}{\partial(s, t)} \right| \mathrm{d}s \mathrm{d}t = 2 \int_0^1 \mathrm{d}t \int_{s=0}^{1-t} F \mathrm{d}s.$ (17.87)

It suffices to show that the contribution of τ is $1/12$ or $1/6$, as indicated. The heights of e_u, e_v fall off linearly from 1, their graphs over τ being represented by the shaded surfaces in Figure 17.47. A point x of τ with barycentric coordinates r, s, t satisfies $e_u(x)e_v(x) = rs = (1 - s - t)s$. Hence, according to (17.87) integration over τ makes a contribution to $\langle e_u, e_v \rangle$ of

$$2 \int_0^1 \mathrm{d}t \int_{s=0}^{1-t} (1 - s - t)s \mathrm{d}s = \tfrac{1}{3} \int_0^1 (1 - t)^3 \mathrm{d}t = \tfrac{1}{12}$$

and to $\langle e_u, e_u \rangle$ of $2 \displaystyle\int_0^1 \mathrm{d}t \int_{s=0}^{1-t} (1 - s - t)^2 \mathrm{d}s = \tfrac{2}{3} \int_0^1 (1 - t)^3 \mathrm{d}t = \tfrac{1}{6}$ as required.

ALGO 17.5 The matrix $G = G^J$ of inner products on V^J

$G = 0 \, (v_J \times v_J)$
$A = \text{Rows}[(2, \quad 1, \quad 1), (1, \quad 2, \quad 1), (1, \quad 1, \quad 2)]$
For each triangle $\{a, b, c\}$ of M_0^J, increment
  $G[\{a, b, c\}, \{a, b, c\}]$ by A (*)
Return $G/12$

(*) Increment g_{aa}, g_{bb}, g_{cc} by 2 and g_{ab} etc. by 1.

G^j, *in general* Having determined G^J, we can work down step by step for $G^{J-1}, G^{J-2}, \ldots$ using a relation (Exercise 17.27) which holds as before because $\langle , \rangle$ obeys the axioms, namely for an inner product (Theorem 17.57)

$$G^{j-1} = (P^j)^{\mathrm{T}} G^j P^j. \quad (17.88)$$

17.5.4 Building orthogonality

We aim to convert 'coarse' functions at level $j - 1$ to more refined versions at level j by adding on a 'difference'. Now that we have inner products we can use orthogonality to make this efficient. That is, we can get good improvement for small differences because they point close to the optimum direction (which is at right angles to the coarse version).

More specifically, we convert the coarse functions in V^{j-1} to the more refined ones of V^j by adding functions from a space W^{j-1}, whose members are called *wavelets*. The minimum requirement is

$$V^{j-1} \oplus W^{j-1} = V^j, \quad (17.89)$$

meaning (as before) that every f in V^j is a unique sum of members g in V^{j-1} and h in W^{j-1}. Then W^{j-1} is described as a complement (or complementary subspace) of V^{j-1} in V^j. For B-spline curves we were able to take W^{j-1} as the unique *orthogonal* complement (every such pair g, h orthogonal), but in the case of surfaces there are too many constraints for this. Fortunately, in practical terms we are able to get satisfactorily close, by three stages:

1. use easily chosen 'lazy' wavelets – no attempt at orthogonality;
2. modify these towards orthogonality ('lifting');
3. introduce biorthogonal bases (see shortly).

Lazy wavelets Let us exhibit the two kinds of basis functions corresponding to old versus new points by writing $\Phi^j(x) = [\phi_1^j \ldots \phi_\alpha^j \, \phi_{\alpha+1}^j \ldots \phi_\beta^j]$, where $\alpha = v_{j-1}$ and $\beta = v_j$. The functions numbered from $\alpha + 1$ to β correspond to the midpoints inserted in converting M^{j-1} to M^j. We make these our lazy wavelets, and take W^{j-1} as the space they span, defining

$$\begin{cases} \Psi_{lz}^{j-1}(x) = \left[\psi_1^{j-1} \, \psi_2^{j-1} \, \ldots \right], \psi_m^{j-1} = \phi_{m+v_{j-1}}^j, \\ W^{j-1} \quad = \operatorname{span} \Psi_{lz}^{j-1}(x), \\ w_{j-1} \quad = \operatorname{Dim} W^{j-1} = v_j - v_{j-1}. \end{cases} \tag{17.90}$$

Lifting We improve each lazy wavelet ψ_m^{j-1} in the direction of orthogonality to the members of V^{j-1}, by subtracting a linear combination of generators of V^{j-1} which are associated with certain vertices in M^{j-1}. These vertices are to form a *k-disk* neighbourhood of m, which we'll now describe. Let m be the (index of) the midpoint of the edge with indices $\{p, q\}$. The *distance* between two vertices in M^{j-1} is defined as the least number of edges in any path between them. For any integer $k \geq 0$, the *k-disk at m*, denoted by KD_m, consists of the points whose distance from the nearer of p or q does not exceed k.

This is illustrated in Figure 17.48. The pseudoinverse (Remarks 8.57) yields the coefficients which cause the sum of squares of inner products $\langle \Phi^{j-1}, \Psi^{j-1} \rangle$, ideally zero, to be at least minimised. In the matrix the lazy part is $\Psi^{j-1} = \Phi^j Q^j$, where Q^j has

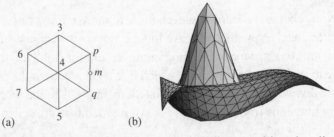

Figure 17.48 (a) Vertices are referred to by their indices (positions in a list). At m we have the 0-disk $\{p, q\}$, the 1-disk $\{p, q, 3, 4, 5\}$, and the 2-disk $\{p, q, 3, 4, 5, 6, 7\}$. (b) A lifted wavelet in the case $J = 5$, $K = 2$.

the form $[0|I]^T$ so that computing A, B as before is particularly simple. Lifting adds certain linear combinations from $\Phi^{j-1} = \Phi^j P^j$, expressible by a matrix T^j and giving $\Psi^{j-1} = \Phi^j(Q^j - P^j T^j)$.

This preserves the simplicity because (see Exercise 17.27)

$$[P|Q]^{-1} = \begin{bmatrix} A \\ B \end{bmatrix} \text{ implies } [P\,|(Q - PT)]^{-1} = \begin{bmatrix} A + TB \\ B \end{bmatrix}. \tag{17.91}$$

Biorthogonal bases Recall that, if $U = \{u_1, \ldots, u_n\}$ is an ONB for a space S and $w = \sum_i x_i u_i$ is a vector in S, then the components x_i are given by the easy formula $x_i = \langle w, u_i \rangle$. For a general basis U this does not hold; however, if we find the *dual basis* $V = \{v_1, \ldots, v_n\}$, defined by

$$\boxed{\begin{aligned} \langle U, V \rangle &= I, \\ \text{then } x_i &= \langle w, v_i \rangle. \end{aligned}}$$

$$\langle U, V \rangle = I, \tag{17.92}$$

$$\text{then } x_i = \langle w, v_i \rangle. \tag{17.93}$$

The defining equation (17.92) says that any given v_i satisfies $\langle u_i, v_i \rangle = 1$ but is at right angles to the rest of U. Since v_i is thus orthogonal to an $n - 1$ dimensional subspace of S, which defines it up to multiplication by a scalar, the condition $\langle u_i, v_i \rangle = 1$ ensures uniqeness. We call U the *primal* basis; however, the symmetry $\langle V, U \rangle = \langle U, V \rangle$ means that if V is the dual of U then U is the dual of V, so one may say U, V are *biorthogonal duals*. To prove (17.93) we start from the right: $\langle w, v_i \rangle = \langle \sum_r x_r u_r, v_i \rangle = \sum_r x_r \langle u_r, v_i \rangle = \sum_r x_r \delta_{ri} = x_i$.

Example 17.58 Figure 17.49 depicts a basis u_1, u_2, u_3 of 3-space, in which u_1, u_2 are at 120° but u_3 is a vector of length 2 perpendicular to both. We make some deductions about the dual basis v_1, v_2, v_3.

(i) By the duality condition (17.92), v_1, v_2 are perpendicular to v_3, which puts them in the plane of u_1 and u_2.

(ii) v_3 is easily computed (in terms of u_3). By (17.92) it is perpendicular to u_1, u_2 and so is parallel to u_3. Thus $v_3 = \alpha u_3$ for some scalar α, and $\langle u_i, v_i \rangle = 1$ implies $1 = \langle u_3, \alpha u_3 \rangle = \alpha \langle u_3, u_3 \rangle = 4\alpha$, giving $\alpha = 1/4$ and $v_3 = (1/4)u_3$.

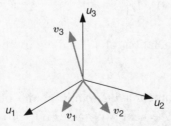

Figure 17.49 A basis u_1, u_2, u_3 for 3-space, and the dual basis.

Theorem 17.59 *(i) The dual of an orthonormal basis is itself, (ii) if U, V are dual bases then* $\langle V, V \rangle = (\langle U, U \rangle)^{-1}$.

Proof (i) Orthonormality of U is equivalent to $\langle U, U \rangle = I$. But this means that $V = U$ is the unique solution of $\langle U, V \rangle = I$. (ii) Let $e_1, \ldots, e_n$ be an orthonormal basis for S, and let the components of u_i, v_i with respect to this basis form the ith columns of matrices $L = [L_{ri}]$ and $M = [M_{si}]$. That is, $u_i = \sum_r L_{ri} e_r$ and $v_i = \sum_s L_{si} e_s$. Then

$$\langle u_i, u_k \rangle = \sum_{r,s} L_{ri} L_{sk} \langle e_r, e_s \rangle = \sum_r L_{ri} L_{rk} = (L^{\mathrm{T}} L)_{ik}.$$

That is, $\langle U, U \rangle = L^{\mathrm{T}} L$; similarly $\langle V, V \rangle = M^{\mathrm{T}} M$, and further we have $I = \langle U, V \rangle = L^{\mathrm{T}} M$. But the last says that, since L^{T}, M are square, they are inverse matrices, so we can reverse their order and take transposes to get $M L^{\mathrm{T}} = I = L M^{\mathrm{T}}$. Finally, these equalities give $\langle U, U \rangle \langle V, V \rangle = L^{\mathrm{T}} L M^{\mathrm{T}} M = L^{\mathrm{T}} \cdot I \cdot M = I$. This suffices to establish that the square matrices $\langle U, U \rangle$ and $\langle V, V \rangle$ are inverse, and the proof is complete.

Example 17.60 (a) Find the dual basis V of $U = \{(1, 1), (1, 2)\}$. (b) Use this to find the components with respect to U of the vector $x = (3, 5)$, and check their correctness.

Solution (a) $v_1 \cdot u_2 = 0$ says v_1 may be written $\alpha(2, -1)$. Then $v_1 \cdot u_1 = 1$ requires $\alpha = 1$. Similarly, $v_2 \cdot u_1 = 0$ gives $v_2 = \beta(1, -1)$ and $v_2 \cdot u_2 = 0$ yields $\beta = -1$. Thus $V = \{(2, -1), (-1, 1)\}$.
   (b) $x = x_1 u_1 + x_2 u_2$, where (17.93) predicts $x_1 = x \cdot v_1 = (3, 5) \cdot (2, -1) = 1$ and $x_2 = (3, 5) \cdot (-1, 1) = 2$. We have found $x = 1(1, 1) + 2(1, 2)$, which is clearly correct.

Example 17.61 In an implementation of Example 17.58, write $c = \cos(2\pi/3)$, $s = \sin(2\pi/3)$, and take $U = \{(1, 0, 0), (c, s, 0), (0, 0, 1)\}$. We compute that $V = \{(s, -c, 0)/s, (0, 1, 0)/s, (0, 0, 1)\}$ (Figure 17.47 facilitates this), whence, in illustration of Theorem 17.79,

$$\langle U, U \rangle = \begin{bmatrix} 1 & c & 0 \\ c & 1 & 0 \\ 0 & 0 & 1 \end{bmatrix}, \langle V, V \rangle = (1/s^2) \begin{bmatrix} 1 & -c & 0 \\ -c & 1 & 0 \\ 0 & 0 & 1 \end{bmatrix}.$$

Exercise Perform the computation of V and verify that the matrices above are inverses.

   Now we have the ingredients for a *filter bank*, multiresolution, and editing of wavelet surfaces at different scales. The next two figures ((17.50) and (17.51)) illustrate these capabilities in turn.

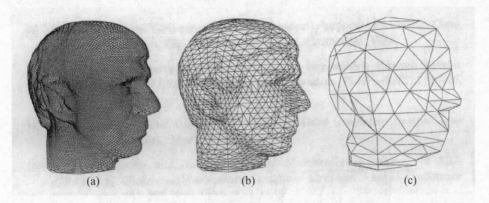

Figure 17.50 (a) Head approximated by Loop subdivision, (b) intermediate resolution, (c) coarse resolution. (Stollnitz *et al.*, 1996.)

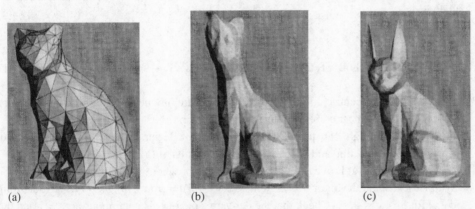

Figure 17.51 (a) Medium resolution cat, (b) surface edited at a coarse level, (c) surface edited at a finer level. (Eck *et al.*, 1995.)

Further work

Bertram *et al.* (2000) returned to the idea of tensor products (17.73) for surface wavelets, offering the necessary algorithm for converting any polyhedral surface into a square mesh to start with. A key objective of theirs was to handle extremely complex surfaces required in scientific visualisation such as computational physics and medical imaging. Thus it was especially important to avoid the need for working with matrices which are global to the surface, linked simultaneously to a huge range of variables.

Subsequently to the work of Lounsbery and others it was realised that their lifting operations fitted in a framework of Sweldens (1996) for biorthogonal wavelets. Bertram *et al.* (2000, 2004) developed bicubic and more general subdivision surfaces in which computation with large matrices was replaced by a sequence of simple lifting operations of the typical form $v = \alpha u + w$, each having an equally simply written inverse. Figure 17.52 was obtained by Bertram (2004) by applying local lifting with Loop subdivision.

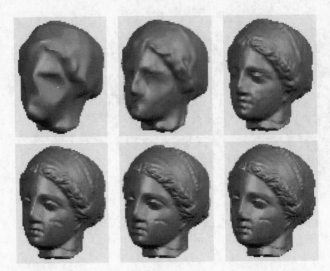

Figure 17.52 Progressive transmission of Venus data (Bertram, 2004), using Loop subdivision.

Exercises 17

1√ Find the convex hull of the points $A(-1, 1)$, $B(-1, -1)$, $C(0, 0)$, $D(1, 1)$, $E(1, -1)$, $F(3/2, 0)$.

2√ Prove that (i) barycentric coordinates in a triangle are unique, (ii) a convex linear combination of convex linear combinations is convex linear.

3   (a) Design a rough car profile by splicing two Bézier curves. (b) Implement de Casteljau's construction and check it against the results of (a).

4√ (See Figure 17.7.) (a) Prove from the polynomial expressions of Figure 17.8 ff that $\phi_2(x)$ is symmetrical about the line $x = 3/2$, that is, $\phi_2(3 - x) = \phi_2(x)$. (b) Use (17.9) to determine $\phi_3(x)$ for $3 \le x \le 4$. (c) Check that the derivative of $\phi_2(x)$ is continuous at $x = 1$ and that it satisfies (17.10) there.

5√ (Section 17.1.4) (a) Differentiate $s B(s)$. (b) Prove the formula $\phi_k'(x) = \phi_{k-1}(x) - \phi_{k-1}(x - 1)$ by Fourier Transforms.

6   Starting from the box ϕ_0, use (17.11) and computer generation to graph in succession $\phi_1(x)$, $\phi_2(x)$ and $\phi_3(x)$.

7√ (a) Use Table 17.3 to find polynomial expressions for (i) $N_{1,4}(x)$ on $[2, 3]$, (ii) $N_{0,4}(x)$ on $[-2, 0]$. (b) Use the Cox–de Boor relations in the form (17.18) to reproduce (by computer generation) the graphs of Figure 17.10, starting from the centred box.

8   Graph the cubic B-spline based on the second control polygon of Example 17.7. Check the strong convexity prediction of Theorem 17.14.

9√ (a) Verify the near-zeros of (17.22) via $N_{0,4}(t)$. (b) Derive formula (i) of Remark 17.16(d). (c) Using (i) and (ii) of that remark, draw a prospective control polygon and sketch the path of its B-spline.

10 (a) Use Remarks 17.17 to explain the tangents and straight line portions of the car in Figure 17.14. (b) Design and implement a car profile similar to that of Figure 17.15.

11√ (Section 17.2.1) Write down expressions for $N_{0,4}(x, d)$ on $[0, d]$ and $[d, 2d]$ (see Table 17.3).

12.√ (B-splines by subdivision, Section 17.2.2) (a) Use Pascal's triangle to detemine coefficients for subdivision in the case $m = 8$. (b) Write down the two extra control points required in Figure 17.22 and hence implement subdivision for cubic B-splines with this control polygon. After how many subdivision iterations is the curve smooth to the eye?

13.√ (Uniform B-splines) What are the subdivision masks required to obtain basis functions $\phi_i^j(x)$ for (a) quadratic B-splines, (b) quartic B-splines? How will the graph change as j varies? As i varies? Perform six iterations for (a), (b), starting from suitable hat functions $e_i^j(x)$, with $i = 0$ and 1.

14.√ Determine $P^1 = R^1 S^1$ for uniform cubic B-splines with four control points (see Example 17.30).

15.√ (End-corrected B-splines, Section 17.2.5) (a) A matrix $A_{m \times n}$ with rows numbered 1 to $m - 1$ and columns 1 to $n - 1$ for convenience is *antipodal* if each element a_{ij} equals its *antipodal image* $a_{m-i,n-j}$. Show that if $B_{n \times p}$ is also antipodal then so is AB (see Section 17.3.2 for another approach). (b) Compute $P^2 = R^2 S^2$ for Example 17.31, exhibiting enough of each matrix that antipodality defines the rest, and stating the dimensions.

16.√ (a) Show that an end-corrected cubic B-spline with control points P_0 to P_n is tangent to the control polygon at P_n (similar to P_0, handled at the end of Section 17.2.5). (b) Use ALGO 17.1 to plot the basis functions at levels 3 and 4. Verify by eye that only the first two and last two depart from being uniform. (c) Construct a control polygon with a view to the corresponding cubic B-spline forming the semblance of a face. Now apply ALGO 17.1. If necessary, modify your polygon and repeat the recursive subdivision.

17.√ (Section 17.3.1) (a) Given that Φ^j is LI (linearly independent), prove that $G = \langle \Phi^j, \Phi^j \rangle$ is invertible. (b) Show that the space of solutions of $Mx = 0$ has dimension w_{j-1}, where $M = (P^j)^T G$.

18. Use computer algebra and exact integration of polynomials to verify the four inner products in (17.53b) (the original calculation was performed by Mathematica).

19.√ (Section 17.3.2) Show that, if a matrix $A_{r \times s}$ is antipodal, so is its transpose.

20.√ (Exercise/project) (a) For Example 17.41 with v_0 changed to 6, note the levels and dimensions of the relevant matrices P^T, G, M and Q. Write or print them out, using (17.53b) and ALGO 17.2. (b) Now compute and graph the wavelet basis functions of W^0 determined by Q.

21. (Exercise/project) (a) Considering the end-corrected B-spline of Example 17.42 with the same value $v_0 = 5$, verify the levels and dimensions of the relevant matrices P, G, M, Q. Determine G as specified and verify M, and then Q according to ALGO 17.2. (b) Graph the non-uniform wavelet basis functions of W^0.

22. (Exercise/project) Rerun Example 17.44 with different sweep polygon heights.

23. (Exercise/project) Revisit Example 17.45 with your own template for '2'. Repeat for another symbol.

24. (Exercise/project) (a) Repeat Example 17.46. (b) Modify hair, brows and beard, in turn. (c) Add teeth to the library, then to the face.

25.√ (Section 17.4.1) (a) A band matrix F has polynomial $f(x) = (1 + x)^3$, shift 2 and five rows. Compute the number of columns by (17.64), then verify this by writing out the matrix. (b) The product $H = FG$ exists, where G is banded with polynomial $g(x) = (1 + x)^2$ and shift 1. Determine H. (c) The 6-rowed matrix F is banded with polynomial $1 - 2x + 3x^2 + x^3$

and shift 2, whilst G is banded with polynomial $1 + 2x + 3x^2 - x^3$. The product FG exists; find it.

26.✓ (Section 17.4.2) (a) Solve the equation $FX = 0$, where F is the band matrix with first row $[1\ 0\ 2\ 4\ 0\ 0\ 0\ 0]$ and shift 2. (b) Find a nonzero linear combination of the solutions in Remark 17.55(i) which equals the zero vector.

27.✓ (Section 17.5.3) (a) Determine the matrix G^0 of inner products when M_0 consists of triangles $\{1, 2, 3\}, \{1, 2, 4\}$. (b) Derive the relation $G^{j-1} = (P^j)^{\mathrm{T}} G^j P^j$. (c) Derive the relation (17.91).

28.✓ (a) Find the components of $x = (2, 3)$ with respect to the basis $U = \{(1, 0), (1, 2)\}$ in the plane, by first finding the dual basis V. Check your conclusion and verify that $\langle U, U \rangle = \langle V, V \rangle^{-1}$. (b) Find the components of $y = (1, 0, -3)$ with respect to the basis U of Example 17.61, and verify your conclusion. (c) Find the dual basis of $U = \{(1, 2, 2)/3, (2, 1, -2)/3, (2, -2, 1)/3\}$. (N.B. Theorem 17.59(i).)

18

Further methods

An artificial neural network, or just net, may be thought of firstly in pattern recognition terms, say converting an input vector of pixel values to a character they purport to represent. More generally, a permissible input vector is mapped to the correct output, by a process in some way analogous to the neural operation of the brain (Figure 18.1). In Section 18.1 we work our way up from Rosenblatt's Perceptron, with its rigorously proven limitations, to *multilayer nets* which in principle can mimic any input–output function. The idea is that a net will generalise from suitable input–output examples by setting free parameters called *weights*.

In Section 18.2 the nets are mainly *self-organising*, in that they construct their own categories of classification. We include learning vector quantisation and the topologically based Kohonen method. Related nets give an alternative view of Principal Component Analysis. In Section 18.3 Shannon's extension of entropy to the continuous case opens up the criterion of Linsker (1988) that neural network weights should be chosen to maximise mutual information between input and output. We include a 3D image processing example due to Becker and Hinton (1992). Then the further Shannon theory of rate distortion is applied to vector quantization and the LBG quantiser.

In Section 18.4 we begin with the Hough Transform and its widening possibilities for finding arbitrary shapes in an image. We end with the related idea of *tomography*, rebuilding an image from projections. This proves a fascinating application of the Fourier Transform in two and even in three dimensions, for which the way was prepared in Chapter 15.

18.1 Neural networks

The human visual system is to this day shrouded in a great deal of mystery. For example, how are objects recognised and internally processed so effectively? Though much progress has been made (Bruce *et al.*, 1996), simulating the process by computer lags far behind the human brain. And this, in spite of the hints picked up by intensive study of the neural networks embodied in both human and animal brains.

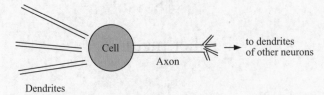

Figure 18.1 Notional diagram of a neuron, with synaptic gap between dendron and cell.

Nevertheless, as discussed in Davies (1997), neural networks are now established as a standard tool in computer vision.

In the biological case, as portrayed in Figure 18.1, electrical signals arrive at a *neuron cell* via connecting tissue called *dendrites*, the signals are modified in regions called *synaptic gaps*, and the result charges up the cell. When charge reaches a certain threshold, a signal is conducted by the cell's axon to the dendrites of other cells to which it is thus connected, then the cell's potential drops back, and the process restarts in response to new signals.

After noting an early attempt at neural simulation in Section 18.1.1, we consider some basic vision tasks achievable by Rosenblatt's single-celled perceptron in Section 18.1.2. His learning algorithm is proved in Section 18.1.3, and some limitations established. However, we show in Section 18.1.4 how the limitations of the single cell or layer thereof may be overcome by recourse to several layers of cells, once the *back propagation* learning algorithm is available. In all these cases, learning is of the *supervised* type, in which desired outcomes are specified in advance.

In Section 18.1.5 we see how net output for classification problems can be designed as a probability, and finally, in Section 18.1.6, how distributing data into an ensemble of nets gives special benefits. We conclude with examples from cancer screening and from remote sensing.

18.1.1 In the beginning McCulloch–Pitts

Although the idea of interconnected neuron cells communicating with each other was known earlier, the first abstract calculational model was proposed by McCulloch and Pitts (1943). This used the relatively new discovery that incoming signals could be inhibitory, preventing the discharge of a cell. We simplify their scheme to two kinds of computing units, in which input and output signals take the values 0 and 1 only. They are represented in Figure 18.2.

The cell 'fires' in the sense that the output z is 1, if and only if the total input attains the value shown mid-cell, as follows. Case (a) has the effect of an OR function because $x + y \geq 1$ holds when either x or y or both take value 1. In case (b) the inputs y_i are made to be inhibitory by having their sign reversed before adding their effect, and then the threshold requirement

$$(x_1 + \cdots + x_n) + (y_1 + \cdots + y_m) \geq n \qquad (18.1)$$

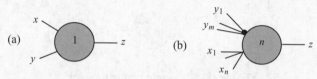

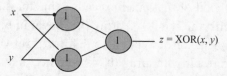

Figure 18.2 McCulloch–Pitts units. (a) Simple OR unit: outputs 1 if $x + y \geq 1$, that is x, y or both are 1. (b) General AND unit. A dark circle denotes sign reversal, hence output z is 1 if and only if all x_i are 1 and all y_j are 0.

Figure 18.3 McCulloch–Pitts units implementing the XOR function.

allows output 1 if all x_i are 1 and all y_i are 0, but for no other combination of values. In fact, every logical function $f(x, \ldots, z)$ is a multiple OR of such functions, and so can be implemented by a circuit of McCulloch–Pitts units. We illustrate in Figure 18.3 with the XOR function $f(x, y) = 1$ on (1, 0) and (0, 1), otherwise $f(x, y) = 0$. The top left cell outputs 1 if $x = 0$, $y = 1$, whilst that below gives 1 if $x = 1$, $y = 0$.

Exercise Draw a McCulloch–Pitts circuit for $f(x, y, z) = 1$ when exactly one of x, y, z is 1.

18.1.2 Rosenblatt's Perceptron

Although any function can be approximated with arbitrary precision by a McCulloch–Pitts network, the topology quickly becomes very complex. In the same vein, *adapting* a network is liable to be a cumbersome process. With the aim of improving on this situation and having in mind the application to object recognition, Rosenblatt (1958, 1962) introduced his *perceptron* cell, in which the topology was very simple, but there were free parameters called *weights* which could be changed as an adaption or even learning process.

In a single perceptron cell, input values $x_1, \ldots, x_n$ arrive at the cell along connecting lines, or *edges* in graphical terminology. As indicated in Figure 18.4, we associate with the ith edge a real number w_i, the ith *weight*, which modifies the effect of input x_i in the *threshold criterion*

$$w_1 x_1 + w_2 x_2 + \cdots + w_n x_n \geq \theta, \quad \text{or} \quad \boldsymbol{w} \cdot \boldsymbol{x} \geq \theta, \tag{18.2}$$

where $\boldsymbol{x} = (x_1, \ldots, x_n)$ and $\boldsymbol{w} = (w_1, \ldots, w_n)$ are called respectively the *input vector* and *weight vector*, and θ is the *threshold*.

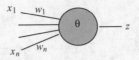

Figure 18.4 A single perceptron cell.

The perceptron as edge-detector In the pixel array of an image, one type of criterion for a pixel to belong to an edge is that a certain linear combination (or *convolution*) of values over a neighbourhood of that pixel exceeds some threshold. This is exactly the test a perceptron will perform. The 3×3 array (b) shown in Figure 18.5 approximates the Marr–Hildreth edge-detector of Section 15.2.4, for pixel values ranging from 0 as white to 1 as black. The result with array (b) as weights, and threshold 4, is shown in Figure 18.5(c). Notice that the image edges are successfully abstracted, in spite of two different shades of grey filling.

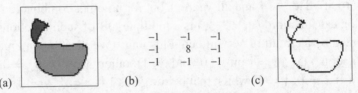

(a)   (b)   (c)

Figure 18.5 (a) Greyscale version of image, (b) perceptron weights corresponding to pixels in a neighbourhood, (c) edge pixels isolated by perceptron with threshold 4.

Parallel processing Although the calculation above can be carried out in serial fashion, pixel by pixel, parallel processing of all pixels at once is obviously possible if a separate perceptron is available for each pixel, as is not unusual in biological systems.

The perceptron as letter-detector With its threshold system, a single perceptron can detect the presence of a letter, say 'T', in a small matrix of pixels, each of which provides an input variable. An example is the 5×5 case below, in which the weights $+1$ delineate the letter itself. Thus a perfect T has vector $x = (1, 1, 1, 1, 1, 0, 0, 1, 0, 0, \ldots)$ and the weight vector is set at $w = (1, 1, 1, 1, 1, -1, -1, 1, -1, -1, \ldots)$. The first issue is sensitivity to noise. Each pixel flip from black (1) to white (0) or vice versa reduces $w \cdot x$ by 1 (why?). Figure 18.6 illustrates that we can recover from 2 or 3 noisy pixels by *setting the threshold at* 6. This is fine provided the perceptron does not have to cope with

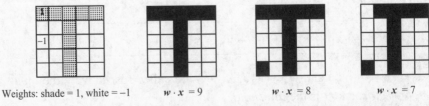

Weights: shade = 1, white = −1 $w \cdot x = 9$ $w \cdot x = 8$ $w \cdot x = 7$

Figure 18.6 Pattern of weights and value of $w \cdot x$ in 'T' and two noisy versions.

a translated or rotated version. However, we shall shortly introduce multi-layer networks, which can handle such variations.

Exercise What happens to $w \cdot x$ in Figure 18.6 if the 'T' is moved a pixel to the left?

The perceptron as linear separator Since a perceptron fires, or outputs 1, in response to input x satisfying $w \cdot x \geq \theta$ and outputs 0 if $w \cdot x < \theta$, it has separated points into opposite sides of the hyperplane $w \cdot x = \theta$. We say opposite because, given a finite set of points so separated, we can reduce θ by a sufficiently small amount that any points formerly on the hyperplane are now on the positive side. Indeed, we'll normally choose θ to avoid equality (we discussed such divisions earlier, in Section 11.2.2). The situation is perhaps easiest to see for points in the plane case $n = 2$, for which $w \cdot x = \theta$ is a straight line. Two examples follow.

Considering logical functions of two variables, can we find a perceptron to implement the AND function? That is, to place a line between the point $(1, 1)$ and the set of points $\{(1, 0), (0, 1), (0, 0)\}$? Two possibilities are illustrated in Figure 18.7. The first line $L_1: x + y = 3/2$ is the case $w = (1, 1)$ and $\theta = 3/2$.

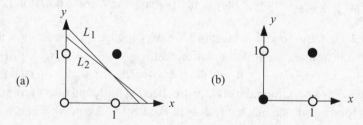

Figure 18.7 (a) Implementing the AND function by $L_1: x + y = 3/2$, that is $w = (1, 1)$, $\theta = 3/2$. An alternative is $L_2: x/5 + y/7 = 4$. (b) Implementing the XOR function means separating the dark points from the light, a task that looks impossible, and is proved so below.

Theorem 18.1 *A single perceptron cell cannot implement the XOR function.*

Proof Suppose for a contradiction that $f(x_1, x_2)$ is the XOR function and there are weights w_1, w_2 and a threshold θ such that $w \cdot x \geq \theta \Leftrightarrow f(x_1, x_2) = 1$. Then we have the following table.

x_1	x_2	f	implications
0	0	0	$w_1 \cdot 0 + w_2 \cdot 0 < \theta$
0	1	1	$w_1 \cdot 0 + w_2 \cdot 1 \geq \theta$
1	0	1	$w_1 \cdot 1 + w_2 \cdot 0 \geq \theta$
1	1	0	$w_1 \cdot 1 + w_2 \cdot 1 < \theta$

Adding the first and last lines gives $w_1 + w_2 < 2\theta$, but adding the middle two gives the contradiction $w_1 + w_2 \geq 2$.

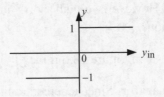

Figure 18.8 Activation function f for a perceptron cell, where $y_{in} = w \cdot x$. Here $f(z) = -1, 0$ or 1 according as $z < 0$, $z = 0$ or $z > 0$; also known as $\text{sgn}(z)$.

18.1.3 The Perceptron Learning Algorithm

So far we have exemplified setting the perceptron weights for edge-detection with $n = 9$ and letter recognition with $n = 25$ in Figure 18.4. More generally, we would like the cell itself to learn to recognise variants of the same letter (for example) in agreement with our human opinion. For this it requires a set of training vectors, some designated as legitimate variants, some alien. A reasonable spread of cases is required, to give the best chance of *generalising*, that is of correctly identifying future input after training is complete. We shall shortly introduce Rosenblatt's learning algorithm, ALGO 18.1, which finds the desired weights povided only that they actually exist. First, some notation is useful.

Notation 18.2 (i) *Absorbing the threshold* We may reduce all cases to $\theta = 0$ by incorporating an extra weight, via the observation that $w_1 x_1 + \cdots + w_n x_n \geq \theta$ if and only if $w_1 x_1 + \cdots + w_n x_n + (-\theta) \cdot 1 \geq 0$, and similarly for the strict and reversed inequalities. Thus we take $-\theta$ as an additional weight w_0, called the *bias*, and insert an extra but fixed input $x_0 = 1$ (portrayed as a black circle as in Figure 18.12 below). Then with x and w so extended the threshold condition becomes $w \cdot x \geq 0$.

(ii) *The excitation function* Another simplifying notational device is to arrange for the perceptron to output $+1$ for x with $w \cdot x > 0$, and -1 in response to $w \cdot x < 0$. The undesirable $w \cdot x = 0$ is to result in output zero. We call $w \cdot x$ the *activation* of the cell, by analogy with the biological neuron cell's build-up of charge, and the function converting this to the perceptron cell's response is termed the *activation function*, say $f(z)$. Thus the function presented here is a step function with discontinuity at zero, as portrayed in Figure 18.8. The learning algorithm ALGO 18.1 results. The remarkable fact is that it works.

ALGO 18.1 (Perceptron learning) For training pairs x_i, t_i $(1 \leq i \leq L)$.

      Initialise w, say $w = \mathbf{0}$.
      REPEAT (cycle)
        For each training pair x, t do
          $y = f(w \cdot x)$
          If $y \neq t$ then $w = w + tx$
      UNTIL no weight change occurs during cycle.

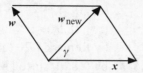

Figure 18.9 *Updating the weights.* When $w \cdot x \leq 0$, which means w, x are at angle $\geq \pi/2$, the update is $w_{\text{new}} = w + x$. The angle is reduced to γ as illustrated. However, convergence of the process must be established by logical proof.

Theorem 18.3 *(Convergence of perceptron learning, Rosenblatt, 1962) Suppose a perceptron has training vectors x_i, with target inputs $t_i = \pm 1$ $(1 \leq i \leq L)$. Then ALGO 18.1 terminates after a finite number of cycles provided there exists a solution. That is, if there exists a weight vector w^* for which*

$$w^* \cdot x_i > 0 \quad \text{if} \quad t_i = 1, \quad \text{and} \quad w^* \cdot x_i < 0 \quad \text{if} \quad t_i = -1. \tag{18.3}$$

Proof The two conditions of (18.3) combine into the single condition $w^* \cdot (t_i x_i) > 0$, rendering the problem as: find w^* such that $w^* \cdot x > 0$ for each training vector x. In other terms the angle between w^* and x is to be acute. A further simplification is that, since the sign of $w^* \cdot x$ is unaffected by multiplying w^* by a positive constant, we may take $\|w^*\| = 1$. We define

$$\delta = \text{Min}\{w^* \cdot x_i\}, \quad \text{and} \quad M = \text{Max}\|x_i\|^2. \tag{18.4}$$

Following Minsky and Papert (1988) we assume for simplicity that the initial weight vector is zero, $w(0) = \mathbf{0}$. As the training vectors are tested in succession, a weight update occurs whenever a training vector x_i is found for which the latest (rth) update, which we'll term $\mathbf{w}(r)$, satisfies $\mathbf{w}(r) \cdot x_i \leq 0$. See Figure 18.9. Then, given the existence of w^*, we get one of two key inequalites by $w^* \cdot w(r+1) = w^* \cdot [w(r) + x_i] = w^* \cdot w(r) + w^* \cdot x_i \geq w^* \cdot w(r) + \delta$, by (18.4), whence

$$\boxed{w^* \cdot w(n) \geq n\delta \quad \text{after } n \text{ updates.}} \tag{18.5}$$

If we can find a fixed upper bound on n, we will have shown that the algorithm halts. Consider the standard argument $\|a + b\|^2 = (a + b) \cdot (a + b) = a \cdot a + b \cdot b + 2a \cdot b = \|a\|^2 + \|b\|^2 + 2a \cdot b$. This supplies the inequality in

$$\|w(r+1)\|^2 = \|w(r) + x_i\|^2 = \|w(r)\|^2 + \|x_i\|^2 + 2w(r) \cdot x_i$$
$$\leq \|w(r)\|^2 + M \quad \text{by (18.4), since } w(r) \cdot x_i \leq 0,$$

hence

$$\boxed{\|w(n)\|^2 \leq nM \quad \text{after } n \text{ updates.}} \tag{18.6}$$

Finally

$$n\delta \le w^* \cdot w(n) \qquad \text{(by (18.5))}$$
$$\le \|w^*\| \|w(n)\| \qquad \text{by Remark 7.20 } (\cos\theta \le 1)$$
$$\le \sqrt{(nM)} \qquad \text{by (18.6), since } \|w^*\| = 1.$$

Squaring, then dividing both sides by n, yields $n \le M/\delta^2$. Thus, after at most this number of updates no further change is called for, and the algorithm halts.

Remark If the initial weight vector $w(0)$, is not zero, the above arguments adapt slightly to give (Exercise 18.4)

$$[w(0) \cdot w^* + n\delta]^2 \le \|w(0)\|^2 + nM.$$

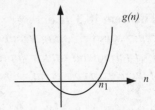

That is, a certain quadratic $g(n) = \delta^2 n^2 + \alpha n + \beta$, with positive leading coefficient δ^2, is non-positive for all permissible n. Thus n is bounded by an axis crossing n_1, as shown in Figure 18.10.

Figure 18.10

Example 18.4a Here is a simple example with four training vectors, $(1, 1, 1), (1, 0, 1), (1, 1, 0), (0, 1, 1)$ and respective targets $1, -1, -1, -1$. In accordance with Notation 18.2, the training vectors are given an extra coordinate $x_0 = 1$, and the weight vector has a bias component w_0 which is determined along with the other components during the iteration of ALGO 18.1. Equilibrium was reached after 25 cycles, with $w = (-8, 3, 4, 2)$. Thus the separating plane is $3x + 4y + 2z = 8$. This is depicted between separated points, in Figure 18.11, accompanied by some intermediate results.

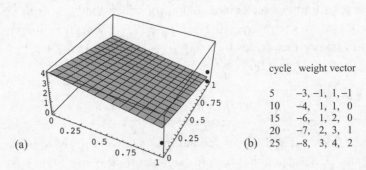

cycle	weight vector
5	$-3, -1, 1, -1$
10	$-4, 1, 1, 0$
15	$-6, 1, 2, 0$
20	$-7, 2, 3, 1$
25	$-8, 3, 4, 2$

(a)   (b)

Figure 18.11 (Example 18.4) (a) Separating plane $3x + 4y + 2z = 8$ determined by the Perceptron Learning Algorithm, (b) the weight vector after every fifth cycle, the last being being constant.

The single-layer perceptron net

Example 18.4b In a *single-layer perceptron net*, a sequence, or *layer*, of perceptrons receives the same inputs, but each is trained separately to a different outcome by ALGO 18.1. In the present example the input values x_1 to x_{63} are the values in a 9×7

pixel array representing one of the letters ABCDEJK. The configuration is indicated in Figure 18.12, where the bias unit with fixed input $x_0 = 1$ is represented by a black circle.

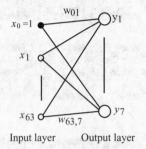

Figure 18.12 Configuration of the single-layer perceptron net in Example 18.4b.

The data of Figure 18.13 (adapted from Fausett, 1994) was used to train each perceptron to recognise a single one of the seven letters and reject the rest, the corresponding outputs being 1 and -1.

After training, the net was fed in turn each of the 21 noisy versions shown in Figure 18.14.

Results Of the 21 letters tested, 14 gave exactly the corect response, with one output being $+1$ and the rest -1. Of the rest, four letters were identified as themselves or one other; that is, there were two outputs $+1$ and five -1s (further details in Porn-charoensin, 2002). This can be improved by inserting another layer, as we see in the next section.

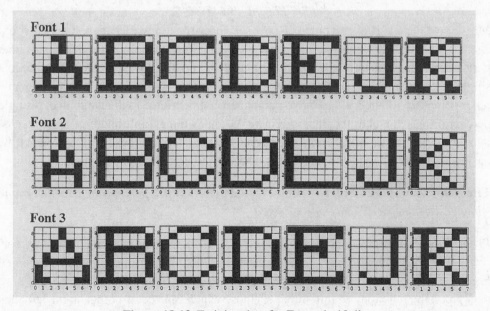

Figure 18.13 Training data for Example 18.4b.

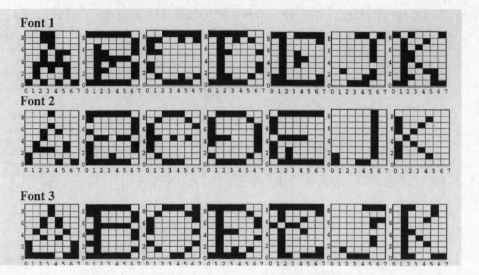

Figure 18.14 Noisy test data for Example 18.4b.

The Pocket Algorithm If no separating plane exists, the Perceptron Learning Algorithm continues until terminated by a limit on its number of cycles. A useful all-round solution is to modify the original so as to retain ('pocket') a copy of the weight vector which so far has correctly classified the most training vectors, and a note of how many. This is due to Gallant (1990), who showed that, in spite of occasional loss of a potentially good solution, the probability of *minimal mis-classification* is arbitrarily close to 1 after sufficiently many cycles.

Limitations of the perceptron

Minsky and Papert (1969) set out to discover and prove rigorously what a perceptron could and could not do. They considered a general scenario in which information from different parts of an image was processed by functions ψ_i in any fixed way and sent as input to a single perceptron. The key point is that, although the functions may use thresholds or any other computing device, all adaptive parameters are restricted to the weights of a single perceptron which makes the final judgment. Of many remarkable and ingenious results, one concerned the *diameter-limited* perceptron, indicated in Figure 18.15, in which ψ_i has no access to the whole image, but is restricted to its own 'receptive field'.

Theorem 18.5 *(Minsky and Papert) No diameter-limited perceptron can determine whether a geometrical figure is connected.*

Proof Suppose on the contrary that a certain diameter-limited perceptron can correctly classify geometric figures as connected or not. Then, for a suitable version of Figures 18.16 (A)–(D) below, no receptor field contains points from both ends, so we may group the functions ψ_i into three: (1) those which can access points on the left ends of the figures, (2) those which can access the right and (3) the rest. With $\sum$ subscript

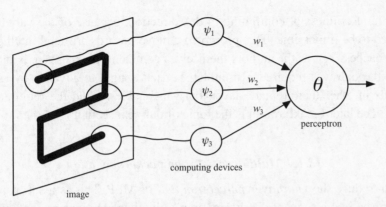

Figure 18.15 General perceptron system considered by Minsky and Papert. Adaptive parameters are restricted to the weights w_i of the single perceptron and its threshold θ.

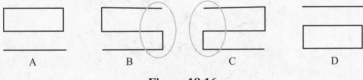

Figure 18.16

indicating group number, the perceptron computes

$$I = \sum_1 w_i x_i + \sum_2 w_i x_i + \sum_3 w_i x_i, \tag{18.7}$$

and we may assume without loss of generality that $I(X) > 0$ when a figure X is connected, and otherwise $I(X) < 0$. In particular, $I_A = I(A) < 0$ because figure A is not connected.

(i) In a transition from figure (A) to the connected figure (B), only $\sum_2$ changes, say by Δ_2, resulting in $I_A + \Delta_2 > 0$.
(ii) Passing from (A) to the connected figure (C), only $\sum_1$ changes, say by Δ_1, resulting in $I_A + \Delta_1 > 0$.
(iii) In passing from (A) to (D), $\sum_1$ is the same as for (C), and $\sum_2$ the same as for (B), so the change is $\Delta_1 + \Delta_2$, resulting in $I_A + \Delta_1 + \Delta_2 < 0$ because (D) is *not* connected. But (i) and (ii) together give $2I_A + \Delta_1 + \Delta_2 > 0$, so we must have $I_A > 0$. This contradiction proves the theorem.

Remarks (1) The edge-detecting potential of a perceptron was illustrated in Figure 18.5, where we imply the presence of a *bank* of perceptrons, one for each pixel. These perceptrons, having fixed weights, could therefore be used as the functions ψ_i in Figure 18.15. However, according to Theorem 18.5, this information is not sufficient for a perceptron to determine in general whether a figure is connected. Interestingly, though, as shown by Minsky and Papert (1988), a perceptron *can* perform the desired task if equipped with a knowledge of the number of holes in a geometrical figure.

(2) Nevertheless, after much work had been expended in exploring the pattern recognition properties of a perceptron, the 1969 book of Minsky and Papert seemed to throw

doubt on the usefulness of continuing in this direction, because of the variety of tasks they proved to be impossible. This prompted a move towards artificial intelligence and other approaches. Yet, as the authors themselves comment, the message is rather that a new breakthrough was required. Rosenblatt himself sought to advance by assembling perceptrons in other than a single layer, but was unable to find the required learning algorithm. The later breakthrough is the topic of our next section.

18.1.4 Multilayer nets and backpropagation

First we introduce the *multilayer perceptron net*, or MLP. This is a set of perceptron cells organised into a sequence of layers, in which all connections are one-way (called *forward*) from a perceptron to every cell in the next layer. A first illustration appears in Figure 18.17.

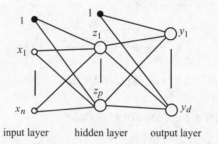

Figure 18.17 Two-layer perceptron net. The units shown as black circles supply fixed input 1 for treating threshold as a weight, as described in Notation 18.2.

A circle labelled y_i represents a cell Y_i with output y_i, and similarly for z_i. The x_i circles represent input points rather than actual cells. In each layer of weights the zeroth input is fixed at 1, as prescribed in Notation 18.2, so that we may reduce the thresholds to 0 by introducing an extra weight (the *bias*). In a general multilayer net, the *number of layers* means the number of perceptron layers, or equivalently the number of layers of weights. Thus Figure 18.17 represents a 2-layer net and requires a new algorithm for determining weights.

Example 18.6 A 2-layer MLP realising the XOR function is adapted from the McCulloch–Pitts solution of Figure 18.3, with excitation function $f(x) = 1$ if $x > 1/2$, otherwise $f(x) = 0$. Since a threshold is used, no bias is required. The resulting diagram is given in Figure 18.18. In the accompanying table, subscript 'in' signifies input.

x_1	x_2	$z_{1,in}$	$z_{2,in}$	z_1	z_2	y
0	0	0	0	0	0	0
0	1	-1	1	0	1	1
1	0	1	-1	1	0	1
1	1	0	0	0	0	0

Figure 18.18 MLP for Example 18.6.

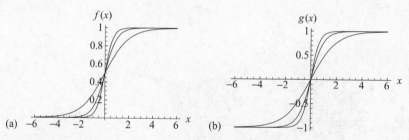

Figure 18.19 Sigmoid curves: (a) the binary sigmoid $f(x) = 1/(1 + e^{-\sigma x})$ with $\sigma = 1, 2, 3$, (b) the corresponding bipolar sigmoid $g(x) = 2f(x) - 1 = \tanh(\sigma x/2)$.

The now well-known *backpropagation* method for training an MLP was discovered independently by several workers (see e.g. Rumelhart, Hinton and Williams, 1986). It requires the activation function to be differentiable so that a method called *gradient descent* (see later) can be incorporated.

Thus the sharp jump at the origin in Figure 18.8 should be commuted to a smooth transition, resulting in a sigmoid-type function. This is a curve $f(z)$ with the general S-shape of those in Figure 18.19. More specifically, the gradient is everywhere positive, the graph is symmetric under a $1/2$ turn, and there are values $a < b$ to which $f(z)$ tends as z tends to infinity in either direction. The standard *binary sigmoid* with range $(0, 1)$, and its derivative, may be written

$$f(x) = 1/(1 + e^{-\sigma x}), \qquad f'(x) = \sigma f(x)[1 - f(x)]. \tag{18.8}$$

Thus the slope at any point increases with σ, as illustrated in Figure 18.19, and furthermore, by considering $f(x)$ for negative, zero and positive x, we see that as σ tends to 0 the family approaches the earlier discontinuous activation function of Figure 18.8, which we have therefore succeeded in 'smoothing out'.

Finally, we convert the range $(0, 1)$ to $(-1, 1)$ by a stretch and translation $y \to 2y - 1$, obtaining the *bipolar sigmoid* $g(x) = 2f(x) - 1 = (1 - e^{-\sigma x})/(1 + e^{-\sigma x}) = \tanh(\sigma x/2)$.

Discovering the backpropagation method

Imitating the simple perceptron algorithm, we would like to cycle repeatedly through the training vectors, adjusting the weights after each vector (x_i) has propagated forward to produce output (y_k), until no (or minimal) further adjustment is required. As before, t_k denotes the target value of y_k. Thus the weights will be adjusted on the basis of minimising the squared error:

$$E = (1/2) \sum_k (t_k - y_k)^2 \quad \text{(to be minimised).} \tag{18.9}$$

We can proceed by considering gradients, because the activation functions are differentiable and E is a differentiable function of all the weights, say $w_1, \ldots, w_N$, and so

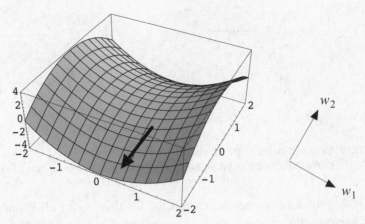

Figure 18.20 Surface $E(w_1, w_2) = w_1^2 - w_2^2$. An arrow shows the direction of steepest descent at a point $P(1/2, -1, E)$, in agreement with $\nabla E = 2(w_1, -w_2)$ and Theorem 18.7.

we can aim for a minimum of E by determining the direction of steepest descent of E in $(w_1, \ldots, w_N)$-space. This is the *method of steepest descent* applied to our case. It is illustrated in Figure 18.20 for $N = 2$.

Theorem 18.7 *The greatest rate of increase of a differentiable function $E(w_1, \ldots, w_N)$ occurs in the direction of the gradient $\nabla E = (\partial E/\partial w_1, \ldots, \partial E/\partial w_N)$. Hence the greatest rate of decrease is in the direction $-\nabla E$.*

Proof We require the instantaneous rate of change of E as we move from a given point P in the direction of a unit vector $\boldsymbol{u}$. That is, the rate of change of E as we move along a ray $\boldsymbol{w}(s) = P + s\boldsymbol{u}$, evaluated at $s = 0$. Here $\boldsymbol{w} = (w_1, \ldots, w_N)$, where each w_i is a function of the parameter s. See Figure 18.21. Then

$$\frac{dE}{ds} = \frac{\partial E}{\partial w_1}\frac{dw_1}{ds} + \cdots + \frac{\partial E}{\partial w_N}\frac{dw_N}{ds} \qquad \text{by the Chain Rule}$$

$$= (\nabla E) \cdot \left(\frac{dw_1}{ds}, \ldots, \frac{dw_n}{ds}\right) \qquad \text{by definition of } \nabla E$$

$$= (\nabla E) \cdot \boldsymbol{u} \qquad \text{since } dw_i/ds = u_i.$$

As $\boldsymbol{u}$ varies, this has greatest value when $\boldsymbol{u}$ is in the direction of ∇E, since the lengths of ∇E and $\boldsymbol{u}$ are fixed.

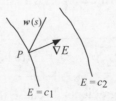

Figure 18.21 Proof of Theorem 18.7.

Conclusion To move the overall weight vector w closer to a minimum of E we should increment by a suitably chosen negative multiple of ∇E, say $\Delta w = -\gamma \nabla E$. Thus, keeping the same *learning constant* $\gamma > 0$ throughout, we increment a general weight α, *in whatever layer it may be*, by the quantity $\Delta \alpha = -\gamma \partial E / \partial \alpha$. Differentiating (18.9), we may write

$$\Delta \alpha = \gamma \sum_k (t_k - y_k) \partial y_k / \partial \alpha \quad \text{(weight update)}. \tag{18.10}$$

The problem now is to *determine $\partial y / \partial \alpha$ for any output y and weight α.* We'll take it that all excitation functions are the same, denoted by f; the notation will show where any variants should be inserted if they exist. As a general notation, c_{in} denotes the input into a cell C, with output $f(c_{\text{in}})$. First we note two very simple but valuable relations obtained by differentiation, based on a weight w on the connection from cell t to cell u of Figure 18.22. This result does not depend on the number of other cells in the same layer as T or U.

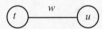

Figure 18.22

$$\partial u / \partial w = t f'(u_{\text{in}}), \tag{18.11a}$$
$$\partial u / \partial t = w f'(u_{\text{in}}). \tag{18.11b}$$

Proof We have $u = f(u_{\text{in}})$ and $u_{\text{in}} = tw + $ (terms independent of w and t). Differentiating, $\partial u / \partial w = f'(u_{\text{in}}) \partial u_{\text{in}} / \partial w = t f'(u_{\text{in}})$, whereas $\partial u / \partial t = f'(u_{\text{in}}) \partial u_{\text{in}} / \partial t = w f'(u_{\text{in}})$.

Notation 18.8 In Figure 18.23, z_j is the output of the jth cell in one layer and y_k is the kth output in the next. The connection weights w_{jk} between these cells form a *weight matrix* $[w_{jk}]$ whose kth column w_k lists the connection weights to cell Y_k. The outputs z_j form a vector z, and similarly for other layers.

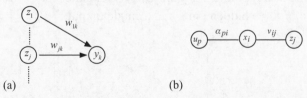

(a)   (b)

Figure 18.23 (a) Here Z is the last layer before output, (b) any successive layers U, X, Z.

Theorem 18.9 *(Backpropagation) Suppose a training vector for an MLP gives outputs y_k corresponding to target vectors t_k. Then the gradient descent formula (18.10) implies that weights may be updated in reverse order of layers. Expressed in Notation 18.8 we have*

(i) (output layer) $\Delta\mathbf{w}_k = A_k z$,   where $A_k = \gamma(t_k - y_k)f'(y_{k-\text{in}})$,
(ii) (working back) if $\Delta\mathbf{v}_j = N_j \mathbf{x}$ then $\Delta\boldsymbol{\alpha}_i = P_i \mathbf{u}$, where $P_i = f'(x_{i-\text{in}})\sum_j v_{ij} N_j$.

Proof (i) Consider Figure 18.23(a). In this case the sum in (18.10) reduces to a single element and we have $\Delta w_{jk} = \gamma(t_k - y_k)\partial y_k/\partial w_{jk} = \gamma(t_k - y_k)f'(y_{k-\text{in}})z_j$, by (18.11a) with $t = x_i$ and $u = y_k$. This is the equality of jth elements in (i), and hence establishes that result. For the next part we move to Figure 18.23(b).

(ii) $\Delta v_{ij} = \sum_k \gamma(t_k - y_k)\partial y_k/\partial v_{ij}$ by (18.10)

$= \sum_k \gamma(t_k - y_k)\partial y_k/\partial z_j \times \partial z_j/\partial v_{ij}$ by the Chain Rule

$= \left[\sum_k \gamma(t_k - y_k)\partial y_k/\partial z_j f'(z_{j-\text{in}})\right] \times x_i$ by (18.11a) with $t = x_i, u = z_j$.

This has the form $N_j x_i$, with N_j independent of i, so Δv_j can indeed be expressed as $N_j \mathbf{x}$. Continuing, we derive an expression for the previous layer of weights and relate it to what we have just found. We have

$\Delta\alpha_{pi} = \sum_k \gamma(t_k - y_k)\partial y_k/\alpha_{pi}$ by (18.10)

$= \sum_k \gamma(t_k - y_k)\partial y_k/\partial x_i \times \partial x_i/\partial\alpha_{pi}$ by the Chain Rule

$= \sum_k \gamma(t_k - y_k) \sum_j \partial y_k/\partial z_j$ by the Chain rule

$\times \partial z_j/\partial x_i f'(x_{i-\text{in}})u_p$ and (18.11a)

$= \sum_k \gamma(t_k - y_k) \sum_j \partial y_k/\partial z_j$

$\times f'(z_{j-\text{in}})v_{ij} f'(x_{i-\text{in}})u_p$ by (18.11b)

$= f'(x_{i-\text{in}}) \sum_j v_{ij} N_j u_p$ by definition of N_j, which completes the proof.

Example 18.10 For now we'll set the learning constant γ at 1. Before doing anything big let us investigate convergence when weights are found for the XOR function. This will bring out some useful pointers. Figure 18.24 shows the result of trying for the XOR function with two or three hidden units and a single output.

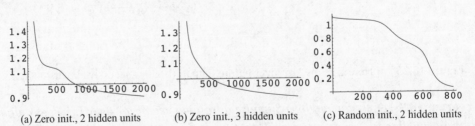

(a) Zero init., 2 hidden units   (b) Zero init., 3 hidden units   (c) Random init., 2 hidden units

Figure 18.24 Error against number of cycles in backpropagation training for the XOR function, with one hidden layer. Weights are initialised at zero in cases (a) and (b). However, (c), with initial weights randomised between $\pm 1/2$, is dramatically better.

Here are the approximate weight matrices for the two weight layers obtained in case (c) of Figure 18.24, with third row corresponding to bias/threshold. The net was trained to produce outputs 0, 1, 1, 0 in response to the input vectors (0, 0), (0, 1), (1, 0), (1, 1), with total square error < 0.05.

$$V = \begin{pmatrix} -3.285\,79 & -5.468\,73 \\ -3.266\,25 & -5.541\,2 \\ 4.697\,38 & 1.838\,69 \end{pmatrix}, \quad W = \begin{pmatrix} 6.189\,47 \\ -6.771\,58 \\ -2.675 \end{pmatrix} \quad \begin{array}{l} \text{output } 0.1, 0.9, 0.9, 0.1 \\ \text{target } \;\; 0, 1, 1, 0. \end{array}$$

Thus the rounded output gives the desired targets. For further improvements in initialisation, see Fausett (1994). It is widely reported that bipolars ± 1 with tanh sigmoid yield noticeably faster convergence than binaries, although the two choices are mathematically equivalent. An explanation suggested by Rojas (1996) is that two vectors with entries ± 1 have greater likelihood of being orthogonal than two with entries 0, 1.

ALGO 18.2 *(Backpropagation) For 2-layer MPL with input units X_i, hidden units Z_j, output units Y_k, and weight matrices $[v_{ij}]$, $[w_{jk}]$.*

Initialise weights. Set activation function f, learning rate γ, and *max-Error*.
REPEAT (cycle)
  Set *etotal* $= 0$;
  For each training pair x, t do
              (*Feed forward*)
    $z_0 = x_0 = 1$ (for bias)
    For $j = 1$ to *jmax* do $z_{j-\text{in}} = v_j \cdot x$; $z_j = f(z_{j-\text{in}})$;
    For $k = 1$ to *kmax* do $y_{k-\text{in}} = w_k \cdot z$; $y_k = f(y_{k-\text{in}})$;
    etotal $= $ *etotal* $+ \|t - y\|2$;
              (*Propagate back*)
    For $k = 1$ to *kmax* do $A_k = \gamma(t_k - y_k)f'(y_{k-\text{in}})$;
    For $j = 1$ to *jmax* do $B_j = f'(z_{j-\text{in}})\sum_k w_{jk}A_k$;
              (*Update weights*)
    For $k = 1$ to *kmax* do $w_k = w_k + A_k z$;
    For $j = 1$ to *jmax* do $v_j = v_j + B_j x$;
  UNTIL *etotal* $<$ *maxError*.

The examples we are about to discuss in some detail happen to be medical ones, so let us first note two other types of application. (1) *Denoising* Networks with backpropagation are compared with other methods of reducing noise in Davies (1997). (2) *Pattern recognition* One useful example is the recognition of handwritten characters, such as in Mayraz and Hinton (2002). See Section 18.1.5 for further background.

Example 18.11 (*Testing the human eye*) A basic objective is to automate eye testing for a very large list of potential eye defects, so that a sufficiently large section of the population can be tested as appropriate, in spite of a relatively small resource of human

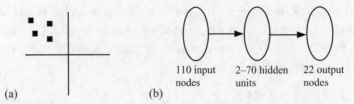

Figure 18.25 (a) Sample points in the eye's visual field at which a small flash may be undetected, indicating one catgegory of defect, (b) 2-level net used for classification.

experts. Our first of two examples concerns visual field defects of the eye, of which 22 types are categorised according to positions on a grid at which a person fails to detect a small flash (Figure 18.25).

Keating *et al.* (1993) convert results at 110 grid positions into an input vector for a 2-layer neural network with output layer of 22 units, each trained to target value 1 for a particular defect. The authors experiment with a single hidden layer of between 2 and 70 units; best performance was obtained with 30–40 units, there being even a slight deterioration thereafter for the chosen number of 15 000 iterations of the training set.

Training/results A set of 490 input vectors was split into 440 training vectors (an equal number of each defect), and 50 reserved for testing the net's generalisation. Out of the 22 output values, in the interval [0, 1], the value nearest to 1 was taken as the net's diagnosis of defect. After training, the net's first choices were 98.2% correct. The test inputs were only slightly less ably diagnosed, at 96% (many more details appear in the cited paper).

Second example: screening of diabetic patients A person with diabetes has enhanced risk of retinal defect and in a worst case, of eventual blindness. It is estimated that the latter risk is halved by regular checks.

As noted, clinicians are too few, and so research proceeds for a method of automating the procedure with suficient credibility to be relied upon by an expert. This time (Gardner *et al.*, 1996) data comes from 700×700 digital images of the retina. The question here is, can a neural net identify two retinal conditions typical of diabetes: *haemorrhage*, or leakage from blood vessels, which appears in the form of a flame, blot or dots, and *exudates* (exuded matter, appearing as flaky, or discrete yellow)? See Figure 18.26.

Input Starting from 147 diabetic and 32 normal images the authors generate a total of 200 diabetic and 101 normal inputs, available as either 30×30 or 20×20 squares of pixels. In preparation for training these were classified by human expert into one of:

1. *normal*, and without blood vessels,
2. *vessels*: normal but with blood vessels,
3. *exudate*: the square contains exudated material,
4. *haemorrhage*: the square contains leaked haemorrhage.

Training/results Amongst other projects the net was trained three times, for distinguishing between normal and cases 2, 3, 4 above. As in the first example, the authors experimented

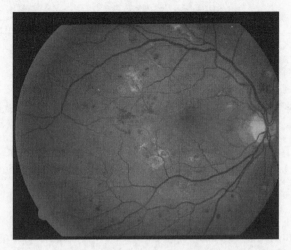

Figure 18.26 Digital photograph of human retina showing blood vessels, haemorrhage, and exudates (light in the greyscale image). Courtesy of David Keating, Tennant Institute, Glasgow, UK.

to find the most efficient number of hidden units. This increased dramatically for the haemorrhage case, which also required the larger 30×30 square (deemed unnecessary in the other cases). Some results are summarised in Table 18.1. The overall conclusion is that nets are a promising adjunct to the clinical process but that more work needs to be done.

Table 18.1. *Results for neural network identification of diabetic eye symptoms.*

compared	hidden units	size of square	iterations	% correct
vessels	80	20	120 000	93.7
exudates	80	20	300 000	94.1
haemorrhage	300	30	380 000	89.6

18.1.5 Classification: can outputs be probabilities?

In using a net for classification, the idea is that each input vector belongs to one of certain predetermined classes. Each class is to be associated with a particular output unit, which is given a training target of 1 for input in its own class and (we assume for now) zero otherwise. After training, however, unless there is a fixed threshold applied, say converting output exceeding 0.8 into 1, we get a result lying anywhere in the interval [0, 1]. Is it possible this can be interpreted as a probability? We'll consider first a particular case, then a general one.

Figure 18.27 Single-layer net for allocating input into two classes.

Example 18.12 Consider a single-layer net with input vector x and two outputs, corresponding to classes C_1 and C_2. The sigmoid is to be binary, $f(x) = 1/(1 + e^{-x})$. See Figure 18.27.

We address the problem: choose weights so that, for input x, the kth output is the probability $p(C_k|x)$ that x lies in class C_k. Shortly we'll come up against the need for an expression for the distribution of x given its class, but first let us see what Bayes' Theorem can do to help. We have

$$p(C_1|x) = \frac{p(x|C_1)p(C_1)}{p(x|C_1)p(C_1) + p(x|C_2)p(C_2)}$$

$$= [1 + p(x|C_2)p(C_2)/p(x|C_1)p(C_1)]^{-1}, \quad \text{or}$$

$$p(C_1|x) = [1 + e^{-\alpha}]^{-1}, \quad \text{where} \quad \alpha = \ln \frac{p(x|C_1)p(C_1)}{p(x|C_2)p(C_2)}. \tag{18.12}$$

This works because of the properties $\exp[\ln z] = z$ and $-\ln z = \ln(1/z)$. Suppose that $p(x|C_k)$ follows a normal distribution (multivariate since x is a vector) with vector means μ_1, μ_2 for the respective clases, but having equal correlation matrices of common inverse $Q\ (= Q^T)$. That is (see Equation (10.54)), for some normalisation constant γ,

$$p(x|C_k) = \gamma \exp[-^1/_2(x - \mu_k)Q(x - \mu_k)^T]. \tag{18.13}$$

Can we substitute this in (18.12) and finish by writing α in the form $w \cdot x + w_0$ for some weight vector w? We have

$$\alpha = \ln \frac{\gamma \exp[-\frac{1}{2}(x - \mu_1)Q(x - \mu_1)^T] \, p(C_1)}{\gamma \exp[-\frac{1}{2}(x - \mu_2)Q(x - \mu_2)^T] \, p(C_2)}$$

$$= \ln \exp\{-\tfrac{1}{2}\big(xQx^T - \mu_1 Qx^T - xQ\mu_1^T + \mu_1 Q\mu_1^T\big)$$

$$\qquad + \tfrac{1}{2}\big(xQx^T - \mu_2 Qx^T - xQ\mu_2^T + \mu_2 Q\mu_2^T\big)\} + \ln[p(C_1)/p(C_2)]$$

$$= (\mu_1 - \mu_2)Qx^T + \tfrac{1}{2}\big(\mu_2 Q\mu_2^T - \mu_1 Q\mu_1^T\big) + \ln[p(C_1)/p(C_2)],$$

since $\ln \exp z = z$ and because $xQ\mu_k^T$, as a 1×1 matrix, equals its own transpose $\mu_k Qx^T$. Thus $\alpha = w \cdot x + w_0$, with $w = (\mu_1 - \mu_2)Q$, and w_0 is given by the terms independent of x.

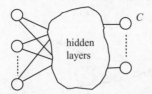

Figure 18.28 General multilayer net, with focus on a single output class C.

The general case More general distributions and more layers are allowed in Bishop (1995), but here we follow an approach due to Rojas (1996). Thus we allow a multilinear net with no specific model of distribution. Any number of outputs/classes may be taken; we simply focus on an arbitrary choice of one, say C. See Figure 18.28. The first observation is that the trained net defines a function $v \to y(v)$ from input space to output at C, which we require to lie in the interval [0, 1] after the action of some differentiable sigmoid.

Suppose input space may be divided into volumes V centred at (or at least containing) points v, with V so small that we may take the probability of x being in class C to be the same for all x in V. Then we may define

$$p(v) = p(C|x \in V(v)). \tag{18.14}$$

If x is in class C the output target is 1 so the error is $1 - y(v)$. If not, the error is $y(v)$ since the output should be 0. The total expected squared error at C is obtained by summing the contributions due to all small volumes V, namely

$$E_C = \sum_V \{p(v)[1 - y(v)]^2 + [1 - p(v)]y(v)^2\}. \tag{18.15}$$

We assume ('plasticity') that $y \to y(v)$ can be computed independently for each small volume V. As a consequence E_C can be minimised by minimising each term of (18.15) separately. Thus, after perfect training the derivative of each term with respect to y is zero, on each small volume V, or

$$2p(v)[1 - y(v)](-1) + 2[1 - p(v)]y(v) = 0,$$

which simplifies to $y(v) = p(v)$. That is, *the output may be treated as a probability.* Finally, this gives

$$E_C = \sum_V p(v)(1 - p(v)) \quad \text{(variance)}.$$

Remark 18.13 In the discussion above, the output lying in, say, $[-1, 1]$ is not really a restriction, for we can convert it to [0, 1] by a simple transformation $y \to 2y - 1$. Thus we could calculate internally in terms of bipolar sigmoids if desired.

Overtraining Figure 18.29 illustrates the result of too rigorous a training. At the point marked STOP, the error in output is still decreasing as more training cycles are completed but the error in a separate test set has started to increase. This means that training

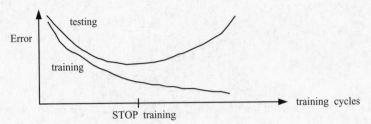

Figure 18.29 Comparative error in output for training vectors and a test set, as the number of training cycles increases (see text).

has begun to build in peculiarities of the training vectors which we do not wish to require of subsequent data. A suitable time to stop training in this case is the point indicated.

18.1.6 Getting the right minimum (ensembles)

A committee solution Continuing the theme above, it is possible for nets with the same topology (structure of connections), trained on different though representative sets of data, to differ too much in their subsequent performance. This form of instability may be attributed to finding a local rather than a global minimum of squared error. A widely used method of improving this situation is to distribute the available training vectors between several training schedules and average the results of the nets. Let us see how much, and under what assumptions, this can help.

For simplicity we consider the case of a single output, aiming to approximate a true but unknown function $\phi(x)$ of the input. Figure 18.30 represents a division of training vectors between a *committee*, or *ensemble*, of nets, with output functions $y_i(x)$ after training. However, in the following discussion we assume only that the nets have been trained *somehow*, and may vary in the size and number of hidden layers. In any case, the ith net has error a function of x,

$$\varepsilon_i(x) = y_i(x) - \phi(x) \quad (1 \leq i \leq N). \tag{18.16}$$

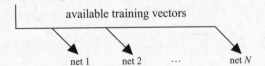

Figure 18.30 Dividing the available training input between an ensemble, or commitee, of nets, with a view to optimal use of information.

The general committee Let us consider a general linear combination of the nets' outputs, $y(x) = \sum_i w_i y_i(x)$, subject to $\sum_i w_i = 1$, of which an important special case is the average, given by $w_i = 1/N$. To find an expression for the expected squared error $\mathcal{E}_{\text{gencom}}$

of the committee, we begin with the error itself, thus:

$$y(x) - \phi(x) = \left[\sum w_i y_i(x)\right] - \phi(x) = \sum [w_i y_i(x) - w_i \phi(x)] \text{ (since } \sum_i w_i = 1)$$
$$= \sum w_i \varepsilon_i(x),$$

$$\boxed{\mathcal{E}_{\text{gencom}} = E\left[\{\sum w_i \varepsilon_i(x)\}^2\right].} \tag{18.17}$$

The averaging committee Let $\mathcal{E}_{\text{avecom}}$ be the expected squared error of the averaging committee, the case $w_i = 1/N$. To get a bound for this, consider the result of averaging the errors of the nets taken individually,

$$\boxed{\mathcal{E}_{\text{ave}} = E\left[(1/N)\sum \varepsilon_i(x)^2\right].} \tag{18.18}$$

The conclusion that follows from this is most striking if we suppose that the signed errors ε_i not only have mean zero, but are uncorrelated. That is, $E[\varepsilon_j \varepsilon_k] = 0$ for $j \neq k$. Then the only terms remaining in (18.17) after we set $w_i = 1/N$ are $\mathcal{E}_{\text{avecom}} = E\left[\sum (1/N^2)\varepsilon_i(x)^2\right]$. Comparing this with (18.18) yields

$$\boxed{\mathcal{E}_{\text{avecom}} = \frac{1}{N}\mathcal{E}_{\text{ave}},} \tag{18.19}$$

a most welcome improvement. Of course, the $\varepsilon_i(x)$ could happen to be highly correlated, leaving (18.19) very far from true; however, there is no risk of disaster in proceeding with the averaging committee, for it remains true that

$$\mathcal{E}_{\text{avecom}} \leq \mathcal{E}_{\text{ave}}, \tag{18.20}$$

as may be seen by setting $w_i = 1/N$ in the inequality $(\sum w_i \varepsilon_i)^2 \leq (\sum w_i^2)(\sum \varepsilon_i^2)$ (see Remark 7.20), then taking expected values. Thus in practice a very useful improvement may well be obtained in this way, even with as few as $N = 2$ or 3 nets. But is there anything we can do to *ensure* improvement over $\mathcal{E}_{\text{ave}}$? After all, some nets of the ensemble may deserve to make a more highly weighted contribution than others. We'll next discuss how such weighting might be determined.

Optimum committees To progress we need an estimate of $E[\varepsilon_j \varepsilon_k]$, obtained by taking a finite sample, which here means a sequence of training vectors and their target outputs, say (x_m, t_m) for $1 \leq m \leq M$. The sample error row vector for the ith net may be written

$$e_i = (y_i(x_m) - t_m)_{1 \leq m \leq M}. \tag{18.21}$$

Since the sample size is M, the standard estimate (11.11) for $E[\varepsilon_j \varepsilon_k]$ is $\frac{1}{M-1} e_j e_k^{\text{T}}$ (with extra terms if the errors are not zero-mean). This is by definition the (j, k) element of the correlation matrix S which, we'll need to assume, has an inverse Q. From (18.17) we may write

$$\mathcal{E}_{\text{gencom}} = E\left[\left(\sum w_i \varepsilon_i\right)^2\right] = E\left[\sum w_j w_k \varepsilon_j \varepsilon_k\right] (1 \le j, k \le N)$$
$$= \sum w_j w_k E[\varepsilon_j \varepsilon_k],$$

which is now estimated as $\sum w_j w_k S_{jk}$, or in vector form wSw^{T}, where $w = (w_1, \dots, w_N)$. If we also write j for the all-ones vector $[1\ 1 \dots 1]$, the objective is to choose w so as to:

$$\text{minimise } wSw^{\mathrm{T}}, \text{ subject to } jw^{\mathrm{T}} = 1, \tag{18.22}$$

where S is given and w varies. According to the Lagrange Multiplier method (see e.g. Bishop, 1995) we may achieve this by intoducing an extra variable λ and finding the stationary value of the function $F = w\,Sw^{\mathrm{T}} + \lambda(jw^{\mathrm{T}} - 1)$. We have, by Remarks 8.57,

$$(\partial F/\partial w_1, \dots, \partial F/\partial w_N) = 2wS + \lambda j = 0, \tag{18.23}$$
$$\partial F/\partial \lambda = jw^{\mathrm{T}} - 1 = 0. \tag{18.24}$$

Equation (18.23) gives $wS = (-\lambda/2)j$ and since S has an inverse Q we have $w = (-\lambda/2)jQ$. Substituting this in (18.24) to *determine* λ gives $1 = jw^{\mathrm{T}} = (-\lambda/2)jQj^{\mathrm{T}}$, in which Q is symmetric ($Q^{\mathrm{T}} = Q$) because S is symmetric. Hence, finally, the easily remembered formula for the optimum combination to be used for the committee,

$$\boxed{w = \frac{jQ}{jQj^{\mathrm{T}}},} \tag{18.25}$$

where the denominator is a '1×1' matrix and therefore a scalar. (It is positive because S, and therefore Q, is positive definite: see e.g. Corollary 8.35 and Theorem 10.54.) For a survey of ensemble methods, see Sharkey (1999). Notice finally that our arguments did not depend on the input–output conversions being performed specifically by nets; this fact will be useful in Example 18.16 shortly.

Remark (*Global minima in the linear case*) If all excitation functions are the identity or at least linear, the input–output mapping is linear. For this case Baldi and Hornik (1999) have completely classified the landscape of local and global minima that can occur.

Example 18.14 *Screening for cancer*

Screening against breast cancer means examining a photograph of the area at risk (see Figure 18.31), for microcalcification of tissue, a pointer to the possibility of cancer (easily cured with early diagnosis). The second step is a judgement as to whether changed tissue is benign or malignant. An excellent example of work towards the automation of step 1, with its drawbacks of smallness and low contrast, is Papadopoulos *et al.* (2002), here cited for its use of networks in combination. This use takes place after preparatory steps which include a reduction of input variables from 22 to 9 through a Principal Components Analysis (see Section 10.4.4) which shows that these nine variables contribute 97% of

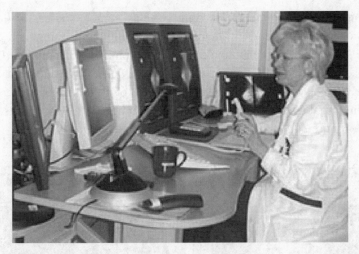

Figure 18.31 X-ray photographs of suspect mammary tissue. Source: Hans Killgren Consulting, Sweden.

the variance. Experimentation leads to a choice of net with two hidden layers (3-layer) as depicted in Figure 18.32.

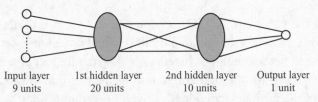

| Input layer | 1st hidden layer | 2nd hidden layer | Output layer |
| 9 units | 20 units | 10 units | 1 unit |

Figure 18.32 Neural net used in cancer research.

After training and averaging over two nets, the authors find that their system identifies more than 90% of cases of microcalcification, over a large number of samples.

Example 18.15 (*Medical decision support*) By contrast with the previous example, Cunningham *et al.* (2000) used an ensemble of ten neural nets in their work on predicting the success or failure of in vitro fertilisation, or IVF. The selected features to be used for prediction were converted into 53 input variables. A single hidden layer was implemented. Data samples comprised 290 successful and 1065 unsuccessful cases.

The nets were seen to overfit after about 250 training cycles. Amongst the results were that accuracy across individual nets varied from 46 to 68% so that a lucky strike would give a false implication of 68% correctness. What of the ensemble? This more accurate calculation stabilised results at a realistic 59%.

Example 18.16 (*Remote sensing*) At one time remote sensing, e.g. by satellite, was considered a military method only, but in recent decades it has broadened out massively. Often satellite data is the only information available for large tracts of the ocean, mountains and tropical forests. Civilian applications include identifying mineral and oil reserves, monitoring crops, locust breeding grounds, remote sources of flooding, pollution, weather forecasting and invaluable developments in mapping land cover, urban or otherwise. The general problem under consideration here (Giacinto *et al.*, 2000) was to allocate each pixel of a remotely sensed image to one of a given list of classes. The specific case is an agricultural area near the village of Feltwell, England, divided into small irregularly shaped fields with five classes: sugar beet, potatoes, carrots, stubble and bare soil. See Figure 18.33.

 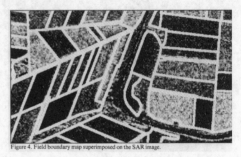

Figure 3. Part of a SAR image taken on 30th June. Area covered is 2.5 km x 1.5 km. Figure 4. Field boundary map superimposed on the SAR image.

Figure 18.33 Remote sensing of patchwork of crops near Feltwell, UK (1984). (a) Part of radar image, (b) the same with field boundary subsequently superimposed.

The thrust of the paper is this: 90% accuracy here, by a neural net or otherwise, is known to require a great deal of preliminary design and processing, so suppose instead we combine several net and non-net functions $x \to y(x)$ into an ensemble of five. We aim for a variety noted for the non-correlation of their errors. We may expect to improve over any of the methods individually, given Equations (18.19) and (18.25) for, as noted at the derivation of these equations, it is not necessary for the functions all to be nets.

Some details The remote-sensing equipment provided six optical and nine radar-type measurements, a total of 15 input values per pixel. Some 10 000 pixels were split between training and testing (further database details are in Serpico and Roli, 1995). The desired accuracy was achieved.

From theory to practice Although artificial neural networks, or ANNs, have demonstrated much potential, their application thus far in clinical medicine is sparse, especially considering the amount of related research to be found. The problem is tackled head-on and frankly in a special issue of *Cancer* (Vol. 91 (2001), 1589–1697), from which some of the following observations are taken. In mind are automated assistance in diagnosis, decision-making, treatment and prognosis.

Problem 1: getting the data is hard A vast reservoir of data exists, scattered, worldwide and variously recorded. The difficulty is to agree on a uniform system and computerise it. By the appearance of this text, a multi-billion-dollar operation may be far advanced (Levine, 2001).

Problem 2: finding out what to do is hard Firstly, the information a clinician needs may be found only in engineering journals (some exceptions are *Artificial Intelligence in Medicine*, and *Computers in Medicine and Biology*). Secondly, 'The challenge to those who advocate neural networks is to make the system transparent, so that it overtly will generate the variables that the oncologist requires in decision-making' (Yarbro, 2001). This could mean that, after training, a net might be converted to one from which rules comprehensible to a human user can be extracted. Promising results in this direction have been obtained by Hayashi *et al.* (2000). A text on general visual inspection by ANNs is Rosandich (1997).

18.2 Self-organising nets

Why *self-organising*? It may be that we cannot apply supervised learning (the output for every traing vector being specified) because the desired outputs are simply not known in advance. In that case there are techniques, mostly biologically inspired, to discover much of the deep structure of the data itself. This may reveal, for example, significant feature vectors which could be used in classification (cf. Section 11.2.2). A useful example to think of is the determination of principal components, Section 18.2.1, for which self-organised, or *unsupervised*, learning provides an alternative to conventional methods (cf. Section 10.4.4).

Again, there is a wealth of classification methods, each best in its own domain, but unsupervised learning gives the opportunity to construct a net which optimises itself for particular applications *as their sample data is encountered*. More generally, we may use one part of a net hierarchy to design other parts (see especially Behnke, 2003, for this).

Within the unsupervised/self-organised theme there is a broad division of learning methods into reinforcement versus competitive types. These are introduced in respective Sections 18.2.1 and 18.2.2, and followed in 18.2.3 by Kohonen's two special types of competitive net.

18.2.1 Hebbian reinforcement learning and PCA

One of the earliest learning paradigms was enunciated by Hebb (1949) in a book entitled *The Organization of Behaviour*. Biologically, it says 'when an axon of cell *A* is near enough to excite a cell *B* and repeatedly... takes part in firing it... *A*'s efficiency as one of the cells firing *B* is increased'. This is generally described as *reinforcement learning*; one simple artificial analogy is as follows.

For the *i*th cell input x_i $(1 \leq i \leq n)$ feeding into a cell with output $y = w \cdot x$, as portrayed in Figure 18.34, we take the weight update Δw_i to be

$$\Delta w_i = \alpha y x_i, \tag{18.26}$$

or, in vector notation,

$$\Delta w = \alpha y x, \tag{18.27}$$

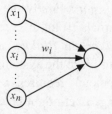

Figure 18.34 Part of a network with one layer of weights.

where α is called the *learning constant*, and is there to help ensure the changes in w_i are not too abrupt. Note that this learning is *unsupervised*, for no 'correct' output is prescribed corresponding to the training vectors.

Principal Component Analysis Oja (1982), starting from Equation (18.27), devised an algorithm for computing the principal components of a set of data vectors $x_1, x_2, \ldots, x_N$, in which activation, as before, leaves the input $w \cdot x$ to cell Y unchanged (so $y = w \cdot x$), and a dampening term proportional to y^2 is subtracted. That is,

$$\Delta w = \alpha(yx - y^2 w), \quad \text{where} \quad y = w \cdot x. \tag{18.28}$$

The extra term was cleverly devised so that the size of w does not increase without limit; in fact w approaches a unit vector as iteration proceeds. The proof of convergence to (approximately) the principal component is too specialised to give here, but may be found in Oja's original paper or in Haykin (1994).

We recall that principal components can be used, for example, to facilitate data compression, to reduce the dimension of a set of data, or to supply feature vectors. The *first principal component* of a set of vectors $x_1, x_2, \ldots, x_N$ in n-space is an n-vector w with direction such as to minimise the sum of squared errors resulting if every x_i were replaced by its projection onto w. In the plane this gives the direction of the best straight line through a scattering of data points.

The *second principal component* of $x_1, x_2, \ldots, x_N$ is the first principal component of the residuals obtained by subtracting their projections onto w, and so on recursively for the third and later components. Thus any method which gives the first component leads to the rest. We showed in Section 10.4.4 that these components are a set of eigenvectors for the correlation matrix of $x_1, x_2, \ldots, x_N$.

Example 18.17 Let us compare results with the earlier Example 10.69: coordinates (x_1, x_2) for a rough car outline. The points after subtraction of the mean were

x_1	-5.80	-0.79	2.03	3.44	4.15	-3.01
x_2	0.12	-1.86	-0.66	-1.08	0.65	2.83

The first principal component was computed to be a unit vector $R_1 = (0.988, -0.155)$. In applying Oja's method, an *epoch* will denote a sequence of updates (18.28), one from each of the six data vectors. The first thing we expect to notice is how the choice of

Table 18.2. *Computing the first principal component by Oja's neural net method.*

	no. of epochs	vector		no. of epochs	vector
$\alpha = 0.1$	10	$(0.992, -0.138)$	$\alpha = 0.01$	150	$(0.989, -0.145)$
	20	$(0.989, -0.158)$		200	$(0.989, -0.151)$
	30	$(0.988, -0.161)$		250	$(0.988, -0.154)$
$\alpha = 0.02$	150	$(0.988, -0.155)$		300	$(0.988, -0.155)$
	200	$(0.988, -0.156)$			

learning constant α affects the speed of convergence and the accuracy of the final result. Table 18.2 gives some specimen cases, in each of which there is no change after the last stage shown.

Remarks 18.18 (1) We see in Table 18.2 that as α decreases the final result becomes more accurate, though it may take longer to reach. On the other hand, if α is increased to too large a value, no amount of iteration will restore accuracy.

(2) For general-dimensional cases, rather than computing principal components one at a time we can introduce further cells and make each yield a different component, by passing information between them in one direction only – to cells earmarked for lower components. This is the method of Sanger (1989). Notice that although the neurons are converging at the same time, the second is unlikely to converge correctly until the first is well on the way, and so on. In spite of this, the time required for training is less than if the net were trained one weight vector at a time (see e.g. Haykin, 1994).

(3) PCA may also be approached through nets with supervised learning, by taking output to be the same as input (see e.g. Davies, 1997). A detailed analysis of this case appears in Baldi and Hornik (1989). For PCA and neural nets in general, see Diamantaras and Kung (1996).

Other Hebbian examples

(1) Object recognition strategies: Draper and Baek (2000).
(2) Finding significant components of a visual scene: Edelman *et al.* (2002).
(3) Hierarchical neural networks for image interpretation: Behnke (2003).

18.2.2 Competitive learning

In the previous section we considered unsupervised learning *by reinforcement*. Now we look at the *competitive* kind. We have, as before, a set of n nodes for n-vector input, and a single layer of weights. The number of output units is specified in advance, and the result of training is that, when a vector x is input, a responding '1' is output only by the *winning* cell, that is the one with greatest excitation $w_m \cdot x$. All other cells output zero. The weight vector w_m is then considered a representative or exemplar for this

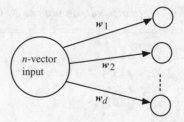

Figure 18.35 Cell connections for competitive learning, where w_i is the weight vector to the *i*th output node.

mth *category* or *class* of input. Standard applications include pattern recognition and compression. See Figure 18.35.

Notice that greatest excitation corresponds to least distance, provided all input vectors are normalised to some fixed length a and all weights are kept at the same length b, for then the squared distance between w and x is $(w - x) \cdot (w - x) = w \cdot w - 2w \cdot x + x \cdot x = a + b - 2w \cdot x$.

The basic training scheme is that, with input and weight vectors normalised to unit length, an input vector x causes update only to the weight vector w_m nearest to it. This scheme is for obvious reasons designated *winner takes all*. A simple form of update is $\Delta w_m = x$, but a more sophisticated one, with greater flexibility, is

$$\Delta w_m = \alpha(x - w_m), \tag{18.29}$$

where as usual α is a learning constant in the range $0 < \alpha < 1$. It is understood that after a weight vector is updated it is renormalised to unit length. The usual procedure is to decrease α gradually as learning proceeds, either by a fixed amount or by a fixed ratio, so that progressively finer adjustments are made.

The k-means algorithm Though not originally in neural network terms (MacQueen, 1967), this method arrives at an updating scheme which is effectively a subcase of (18.29). It has the convenience of allowing the input vectors and their representatives to vary in length, and, in keeping with this, the 'winner' is based on least distance rather than greatest inner product. Specifically, a training vector x is allocated to the class of the nearest repesentative w_m, which is then reset as the *mean* of its enlarged class (hence the title k-means).

To derive the update formula, suppose that the class size is $n - 1$ before updating. Then the sum of its members is $(n - 1)w_m$ and the new representative may therefore be written as $[(n - 1)w_m + x]/n$. The increment Δw_m is this last expression minus w_m, and simplifies to

$$\boxed{\Delta w_m = (1/n)(x - w_m) \\ (k\text{-means}),} \tag{18.30}$$

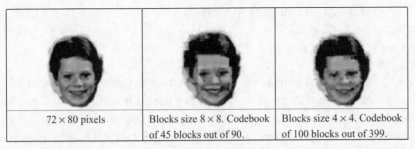

| 72 × 80 pixels | Blocks size 8 × 8. Codebook of 45 blocks out of 90. | Blocks size 4 × 4. Codebook of 100 blocks out of 399. |

Figure 18.36 The *k*-means algorithm applied to a small face. By using a smaller block size in the third case we double the compression with little loss in quality overall.

which is (18.29) with α replaced by $1/n$, the latter quantity conveniently decreasing each time w_m is updated. It is worth noting that the choice of mean as class representative minimises the sum of squared deviations of class members from itself (Exercise 18.10). Let us record a simple procedure for applying the *k*-means technique, in ALGO 18.3.

ALGO 18.3 (k-means algorithm)

Choose *k* initial representatives $w_1, \ldots, w_k$
REPEAT (epoch)
   For each training vector x
      allocate x to the class with representative w_m nearest to x
      reset w_m as the mean of its class, using Equation (18.30)
UNTIL all changes are zero (or below some defined threshold).

Exercise Derive (18.30) from the paragraph above it.

Example 18.19 We experiment with two faces, the first with white background (Figure 18.36), and the second with a street background (Figure 18.37). In the first instance, each image is divided into 8×8 pixel blocks, whose values are written as 64-vectors, and used for training (in principle the system should be trained on many photos repesenting the

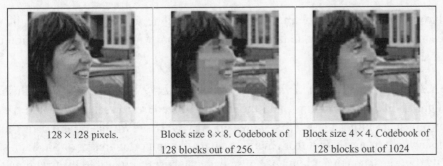

| 128 × 128 pixels. | Block size 8 × 8. Codebook of 128 blocks out of 256. | Block size 4 × 4. Codebook of 128 blocks out of 1024 |

Figure 18.37 The *k*-means algorithm applied to a larger face. This time the 4×4 blocks give quadrupled compression (altogether 8:1) with little if any loss, between the second and third cases.

type to be compressed). The intial representatives were chosen randomly from amongst the training vectors. The results are shown in Figures 18.36 and 18.37. Stability was attained after at most eight epochs.

Remarks 18.20 Although k-means compression does not have the power of some, such as PCA, or fractal or wavelet compression, it is a useful benchmark, and an illustration of the widely used idea of grouping vectors into *clusters*. In such a method the cluster representatives are said to form a *codebook*, or *look-up table*. It is also, importantly, an example of *vector quantisation*, a topic to be revisited later in this chapter under the heading of Information Theory.

Further examples

(1) Self-organizing receptor fields (simulating cells of the visual cortex): Fukushima (1999).
(2) Recognising partly occluded patterns, especially the human face and its various components: Fukushima (2000).
(3) Extracting faces from a scene, recognising and tracking: Walder and Lovell (2003).

18.2.3 Kohonen nets and LVQ

Our main purpose in this section is to introduce *Kohonen nets*, whose speciality is to organise data into a space of chosen (lower) dimension and topological type. Learning here is described as *unsupervised* because the output resulting from a training vector is not specified in advance. We pair Kohonen nets with his related but contrasting *Learning Vector Quantisation*, or LVQ, in which supervision *is* applied (see Figure 18.38). The link is that in both cases the learning is competitive. See e.g. Kohonen (1982, 1988, 2001).

The training proceeds in one of two directions, depending on whether we wish primarily to

(A) quantise each member of a class by its exemplar, or
(B) represent the data in a lower-dimensional form.

Similarly to k-means, it is helpful and commonly done to consider the exemplars as entries in a *codebook* or look-up table, in which one may find the quantised version/class of a given vector.

Case A. Learning Vector Quantisation Also known as *LVQ*, this simpler case is illustrated in Figure 18.38 (after training), and the update procedure for each presented training vector, given its target class T, is shown in ALGO 18.4. We have here a method of quantising vectors as distinct from merely scalars. An important result of Shannon states roughly (but see later) that a sequence of scalars can best be quantised by arranging them as a set of n-vectors ($n \geq 2$). The title 'learning' reflects the fact that the net learns from the training vectors how the exemplars should be chosen. After the net has been trained by suitably representative data, every input vector is assigned to the class of its nearest representative.

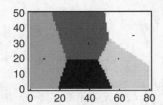

Figure 18.38 Plane input vectors into classes by exemplars (shown bold), as a result of Learning Vector Quantisation. Notice the boundaries bisect the joins of the exemplars at right angles. We have seen this situation before in Bayesian classification, Section 11.2.2.

Case B. The Kohonen net This is really an ingenious unsupervised relative of (A) inspired by the mystery of the brain's representation of our 3-dimensional world in lesser dimensions (the *cerebral cortex*, see e.g. Rojas, 1996), in which exemplars are constrained to form a lower-dimensional structure. This constraint is applied by updating not only an exemplar but its *neighbourhood N_i* of exemplars. How they enshrine the dimension is illustrated by some low dimensional cases as follows. We list the nodes 1 to d on a lattice of the desired dimension: along an axis for dimension 1 and as an array for dimension 2. We define the *neighbourhood of radius r* for node i by:

$$N_i = N_i(r) = \{k \colon 1 \le k \le d, \partial(i, k) \le r\}, \qquad (18.31)$$

where the distance $\partial(i, k)$ is $|i - k|$ in one dimension. Figure 18.39 illustrates how the neigbourhoods can be defined so as to produce either an open curve or a closed one (the two are of course toplogically different).

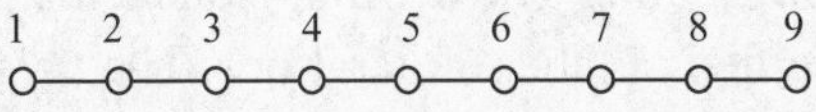

$$
\begin{array}{ccccccccc}
1 & 2 & 3 & 4 & 5 & 6 & 7 & 8 & 9 \\
\circ\!\!-\!\!\!&\!\!\circ\!\!-\!\!\!&\!\!\circ\!\!-\!\!\!&\!\!\circ\!\!-\!\!\!&\!\!\circ\!\!-\!\!\!&\!\!\circ\!\!-\!\!\!&\!\!\circ\!\!-\!\!\!&\!\!\circ\!\!-\!\!\!&\!\!\circ
\end{array}
$$

$N_i = \{i - 1, i, i + 1\}$ if $2 \le i \le 8$, in both cases.

Figure 18.39 Neighbourhoods for constraining the exemplars into a curve which is (a) *open*, with $N_1 = \{1, 2\}$ and $N_9 = \{8, 9\}$ or (b) *closed*, with $N_1 = \{9, 1, 2\}$ and $N_9 = \{8, 9, 1\}$.

Two-dimensional neighbourhoods Figure 18.40 illustrates how two different but standard definitions of distance in two dimensions give rise by Equation (18.31) to different shapes of neighbourhood, namely a circle and a square. Hexagonal neighbourhoods are sometimes used also – see e.g. Fausett (1994).

Initialisation and parameter setting The initial exemplars are usually a subset of the training vectors, or perhaps chosen randomly. As seen in ALGO 18.4, a learning parameter α is used which, along with the neighbourhood radius, must be reduced as iteration proceeds, according to some plan or *schedule*. Commonly α is either reduced or scaled

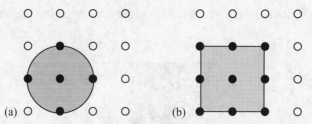

Figure 18.40 Two-dimensional neighbourhoods of radius 1 defined by two cases of distance $\partial = \partial((x, y), (a, b))$. (a) Euclidean: $\partial = \sqrt{[(x - a)^2 + (y - b)^2]}$, (b) $\partial = \text{Max}\{|x - a|, |y - b|\}$.

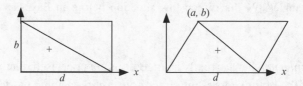

Figure 18.41 A random point '+' of the 1/2 rectangle shears to the random point '+' of a general triangle.

down by a fixed constant on each iteration. These two scheduling methods are called respectively *arithmetic* and *geometric*. A third is to take $\alpha = 1/t$, where t is the number of the current iteration. Satisfactory results may require a little experimentation.

Iteration may be performed by random selection from the training set, or by repeatedly cycling through this set. There is so far no general convergence theorem, though partial results are known (see e.g. Kohonen, 2001).

Example 18.21 We attempt to convert the 2D area of an equilateral triangle into a 1D open line. The result is that the line moves towards a space-filling curve, as illustrated in Figure 18.42. Here are some details. The learning constant γ is reduced geometrically from 1 to 0.01 over the specified number of iterations. The *neighbours* of the winner are those immediately before and after it in the list (except that end points have only one such neighbour). They are updated with reduced learning constant $\gamma/2$.

Simulation We require a sequence of random points, uniformly distributed over whatever triangle is chosen. Figure 18.41 depicts a suitable procedure for an arbitrary triangle. We choose random points uniformly over a rectangle, take those which fall into the lower triangular half, and map them by a shear onto the chosen triangle. Since the shear is area-preserving, we retain a uniform choice. The procedure is formalised in (18.32).

$x = y = \infty$
While $x/d + y/b > 1$ do $(x, y) = (\text{Random in } [0, d], \ \text{Random in } [0, b])$ (18.32)
Return $(x + (a/b)y, y)$.

Figure 18.42 shows this method in use for training Kohonen weight vectors.

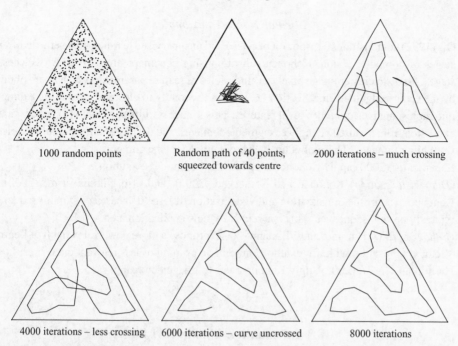

1000 random points

Random path of 40 points, squeezed towards centre

2000 iterations – much crossing

4000 iterations – less crossing   6000 iterations – curve uncrossed   8000 iterations

Figure 18.42 Stages in Kohonen training of 40 weight vectors along a path. Training vectors are random points of an *equilateral* triangle, the learning constant reduced geometrically over 10 000 iterations. Kohonen (1982, 2001) obtains a Peano curve this way.

Remarks 18.22 We have cited Kohonen's original version of LVQ. Subsequent developments are discussed in Ripley (1996). In the topographic case the radius may be reduced with time and, within this, α may be reduced for points away from the centre. Here are the two algorithms under the heading ALGO 18.4.

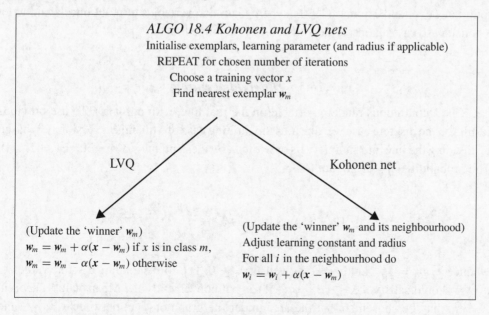

ALGO 18.4 Kohonen and LVQ nets
Initialise exemplars, learning parameter (and radius if applicable)
REPEAT for chosen number of iterations
Choose a training vector x
Find nearest exemplar w_m

LVQ

Kohonen net

(Update the 'winner' w_m)
$w_m = w_m + \alpha(x - w_m)$ if x is in class m,
$w_m = w_m - \alpha(x - w_m)$ otherwise

(Update the 'winner' w_m and its neighbourhood)
Adjust learning constant and radius
For all i in the neighbourhood do
$w_i = w_i + \alpha(x - w_m)$

Further Kohonen examples

(1) Oja (1992) demonstrates how both supervised and unsupervised learning are useful at different stages of computer vision. Kohonen self-organising nets/maps are used at two successive stages: firstly to cluster image pixels around triples of feature parameters (such as are obtained by the Canny edge-detector, Section 16.4.3), and secondly to cluster the resulting exemplars into representatives of higher-level features. This is successfully applied to (a) texture feature extraction from textured but not yet segmented images, and (b) global curve feature extraction from binary images. These of course have potential for data compression.

(2) Lamar *et al.* (2000) apply Kohonen maps to hand gesture recognition.

(3) (*Data visualisation*) Kohonen and Somervuo (2002), and also Nikkilä *et al.* (2002) use Kohonen nets for the organization and visualisation of large databases of symbol sequences, typically protein sequences. This is a relatively new application area.

(4) (*Enhanced LVQ*) Hammer and Villmann (2002) propose a more powerful version of Learning Vector Quantisation with, for example, automatic pruning of less relevant data.

(5) Haritopoulos *et al.* (2002) apply Kohonen nets to image denoising.

18.3 Information Theory revisited

We have reviewed a number of algorithms for artificial neural networks, but so far Information Theory has played no part. Yet it is natural to ask if *maximising information* between input and output variables could either imply previous methods or create new and better ones.

This approach was pioneered by Linsker (1988, 1992, 1993, 1997), and we provide an introduction to the results. To do so we must extend our earlier study of entropy and mutual information from the discrete to the continuous case. There are several ways to derive the result of this extension (see e.g. Kolmogorov, 1956 b). We adapt the method found in Cover and Thomas (1991), where Gaussian variables turn out once again to be a benchmark case against which others may be judged.

18.3.1 Differential entropy

Let X be a continuous random variable on the real line, with pdf $f(x)$. To use previous results on the discrete case we take X as the limiting case of a quantised version X^Δ, based on dividing the line into subintervals of width Δ by mesh points $n\Delta$ ($n = 0, \pm 1, \pm 2, \ldots$). The probabilities p_n of X^Δ are to be

$$p_n = P(n\Delta \leq X \leq (n+1)\Delta) = \int_{n\Delta}^{(n+1)\Delta} f(x)\mathrm{d}x, \qquad (18.33)$$

whence $\sum p_n = \int_{\mathbf{R}} f(x)\mathrm{d}x = 1$, as well as $p_n \geq 0$. The corresponding discrete values x_n of X^Δ should satisfy $n\Delta \leq x_n \leq (n+1)\Delta$, but conveniently the Mean Value Theorem says x_n may be chosen so that the area under the graph of $f(x)$ between $x = n\Delta$ and

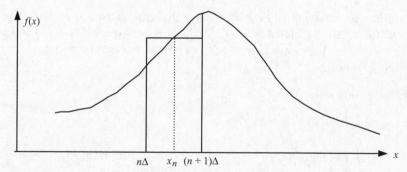

Figure 18.43 The pdf of a continuous random variable X, with x_n chosen so that the area $P(n\Delta \leq X \leq (n+1)\Delta)$ equals that of the rectangle shown, of height $f(x_n)$.

$(n+1)\Delta$ equals the rectangular area $\Delta f(x_n)$ in Figure 18.43. That is,

$$p_n = \Delta \times f(x_n). \tag{18.34}$$

With the aid of (18.34) we find that, although entropy for continuous variables is undefined, mutual information comes through unscathed. First let us apply the definition of discrete entropy (see (12.7)) to our approximation X^Δ and see what happens as $\Delta \to 0$. We have

$$
\begin{aligned}
H(X^\Delta) &= -\sum_n p_n \log p_n \\
&= -\sum_n p_n \log[\Delta f(x_n)] && \text{by (18.34)} \\
&= -\sum_n p_n [\log \Delta + \log f(x_n)] && \text{by } \log(ab) = \log(a) + \log(b) \\
&= -\log \Delta \sum_n p_n - \sum_n \Delta f(x_n) \log f(x_n) && \text{by (18.34)} \\
&= -\log \Delta - \sum_n [f(x_n) \log f(x_n)]\Delta && \text{since } \sum_n p_n = 1.
\end{aligned}
$$

As $\Delta \to 0$, the first term tends to infinity, and we'll come back to that. The second term approaches what is called the *differential entropy*, $h(X) = -\int f(x) \log(f(x)) dx$ (assuming the integral exists). This does not measure information directly, but suppose Z is another continuous real variable with pdf $g(x)$ and quantization Z^Δ. Then because the terms $\log \Delta$ cancel in the subtraction we may write

$$H(X^\Delta) - H(Z^\Delta) = -\sum_n [f(x_n) \log f(x_n)]\Delta + \sum_n [g(x_n) \log(g(x_n))]\Delta$$

$$\to h(X) - h(Z).$$

But, since mutual information is a difference between entropies, it too tends to a finite limit as $\Delta \to 0$, and many arguments used for mutual information in the discrete case carry over to the continuous, with summation replaced by integration. The appropriate definitions are gathered in Table 18.3.

Example 18.23 $I(X;Y) = E \log 1/p(x) + E \log 1/p(y) - E \log 1/p(x,y) = h(X) + h(Y) - h(X,Y)$. The reader may like to show similarly that $I(X;Y) = h(X) - h(X|Y)$ (Exercise 18.12).

Theorem 18.24 *Let* $X_1, \ldots, X_n$ *be independent continuous random variables; then* $h(X_1, \ldots, X_n) = h(X_1) + h(X_2) + \cdots + h(X_n)$.

Proof It suffices to handle the case $n = 2$, since this can be used as an inductive step to reach any n. Taking the variables as X, Y, let their respective pdfs be $f(x)$ and $g(y)$. As independent variables they have a joint pdf $p(x, y) = f(x)g(y)$, so that, with integrals over the whole real line,

$$
\begin{aligned}
h(X, Y) &= -E \log p(x, y) \\
&= -\iint p(x, y) \log p(x, y) \mathrm{d}x \mathrm{d}y \\
&= -\iint f(x)g(y)[\log f(x) + \log g(y)]\mathrm{d}x\mathrm{d}y \quad \text{using } \log(ab) = \log a + \log b \\
&= -\iint g(y)[f(x) \log f(x)]\mathrm{d}x \, \mathrm{d}y - \iint f(x)[g(y) \log g(y)]\mathrm{d}x \, \mathrm{d}y \\
&= -\int f(x) \log f(x)\mathrm{d}x - \int g(y) \log g(y)\mathrm{d}y, \quad \text{since } \int f(x)\mathrm{l}\mathrm{d}x = 1 \\
&= \int g(y)\mathrm{d}y = h(X) + h(Y).
\end{aligned}
$$

Table 18.3. *Definitions and relations for differential entropy. The various pdfs are all denoted by p, with arguments removing any ambiguity. The last line defines the mutual information of X and Y in the present, continuous case. The use of expected value E allows convenient comparison of the four entities defined.*

name	definition	other expressions
differential entropy of X	$h(X) = E \log 1/p(x)$	$-\int p(x) \log p(x)\mathrm{d}x$
joint differential entropy of X and Y	$h(X, Y) = E \log 1/p(x, y)$	$-\iint p(x, y) \log p(x, y)\mathrm{d}x\mathrm{d}y$
differential entropy of X given Y	$h(X\mid Y) = E \log 1/p(x\mid y)$	$h(X, Y) - h(Y)$
mutual information of X and Y	$I(X; Y) = E \log[p(x, y)/ \\ p(x)p(y)]$	$h(X) + h(Y) - h(X, Y) \\ = h(Y) - h(Y\mid X)$

Gaussian random vectors It will be extremely useful to have an explicit formula for the differential entropy of Gaussian variables (also called *normal*). We have already derived the necessary properties (Section 10.4.3). A continuous n-dimensional random vector $X = (X_1, \ldots, X_n)$ is defined to be *Gaussian* if, for some positive definite $n \times n$ matrix Q and n-vector μ, it has a pdf

$$
f(x) = (2\pi)^{-n/2}|Q|^{1/2} \exp[-\tfrac{1}{2}(x - \mu)Q(x - \mu)^{\mathrm{T}}]. \tag{18.35}
$$

Remarks 18.25 It follows that each X_i is Gaussian with mean μ_i, where $\mu = (\mu_1, \ldots, \mu_n)$, and variance σ_i^2 given by the ith diagonal element of $\mathrm{Cov}(X)$. Further, Q is the inverse covariance matrix, $Q = \mathrm{Cov}(X)^{-1}$. Note that the X_i need not be independent, but if they are then $\mathrm{Cov}(X)_{ij} = E[(X_i - \mu_i)(X_j - \mu_j)]$ (by definition) $= 0$ for

$i \neq j$. Finally, we recall the useful formula in which y is an n-vector and Q_{ij} is the (i, j) entry of Q:

$$y Q y^{\mathrm{T}} = \sum_{i,j} Q_{ij} \, y_i y_j. \tag{18.36}$$

Examples 18.26 (1) *Case n = 1* Here $X = X_1$, $\mu = \mu_1$, $\sigma = \sigma_1$ and the 1×1 matrix Q is the scalar $\mathrm{Cov}(X)^{-1} = 1/E[(X - \mu)^2] = 1/\sigma^2$. We recover the familiar form

$$f(x) = (2\pi\sigma^2)^{-1/2} \exp[-(x - \mu)^2/2\sigma^2]. \tag{18.37}$$

(2) *Case n = 2*. Let $Q = \begin{bmatrix} 1 & -1 \\ -1 & 2 \end{bmatrix}$, $\mu = (0, 0)$. Determine the variances and the pdf.

Solution We have $|Q| = 1$ so (18.36) gives $f(x_1, x_2) = (2\pi)^{-1} \exp[-\frac{1}{2}(x_1^2 - 2x_1x_2 + x_2^2)]$. Secondly, $\mathrm{Cov}(X) = Q^{-1} = \mathrm{Rows}[(2, 1), (1, 1)]$, whence $\sigma_1^2 = 2$ and $\sigma_2^2 = 1$.

Theorem 18.27 *An n-dimensional Gaussian variable* $X = (X_1, \ldots, X_n)$ *has differential entropy*

$$\boxed{h(X) = \tfrac{n}{2}[1 + \log(2\pi|Q|^{-1/n})] \,]or, \text{ to base } e, \tfrac{n}{2}\ln(2\pi e|Q|^{-1/n}).} \tag{18.38}$$

Proof We use (18.35) to write the pdf as $\gamma \exp[-\frac{1}{2}(x - \mu)Q(x - \mu)^{\mathrm{T}}]$ with $\gamma = (2\pi)^{-n/2}|Q|^{1/2}$. Then

$$h(X) = -\int f(x) \log f(x) dx$$

$$= -\int f(x) \log \gamma \, dx + \tfrac{1}{2} \int f(x)(x - \mu)Q(x - \mu)^{\mathrm{T}} dx$$

$$= -\log \gamma + \tfrac{1}{2} \int f(x) \sum_{ij} Q_{ij}(x - \mu)_i (x - \mu)_j \, dx \quad \text{by (18.36)}$$

$$= -\log \gamma + \tfrac{1}{2} \sum_{ij} Q_{ij} \int f(x)(x - \mu)_i (x - \mu)_j \, dx$$

$$= -\log \gamma + \tfrac{1}{2} \sum_{ij} Q_{ij} E[(x - \mu)_i (x - \mu)_j] \quad \text{by definition of expectation } E$$

$$= -\log \gamma + \tfrac{1}{2} \sum_{ij} Q_{ij}(Q^{-1})_{ji} \qquad \text{since } \mathrm{Cov}(X) = Q^{-1}$$

$$= -\log \gamma + \tfrac{1}{2} \sum_i \sum_j Q_{ij}(Q^{-1})_{ji}$$

$$= -\log \gamma + \tfrac{1}{2} \sum_i (QQ^{-1})_{ii} = -\log \gamma + \frac{n}{2} \quad (\text{since } QQ^{-1} = I).$$

Finally, $-\log \gamma = (n/2)\log(2\pi) - (1/2)\log|Q| = (n/2)\log(2\pi|Q|^{-1/n})$. This gives the first expression of (18.38) for $h(X)$, and the second follows because $1 = \log_e e$.

Corollary 18.28 *Let* $X = (X_1, \ldots, X_n)$, *where* $X_1, \ldots, X_n$ *are independent and* X_i *is Gaussian with mean* μ_i *and variance* σ_i^2 $(1 \leq i \leq n)$. *Then to base* e

$$\boxed{h(X) = \tfrac{n}{2} \ln 2\pi e \big(\sigma_1^2 \cdots \sigma_n^2\big)^{1/n}; \quad \textit{for one variable: } \tfrac{1}{2} \ln(2\pi e \sigma^2).}$$ (18.39)

Proof Since the X_i are independent, $E[(x - \mu)_i (x - \mu)_j] = 0$ for $i \neq j$ so $\mathrm{Cov}(X) = \mathrm{diag}(\sigma_1^2, \ldots, \sigma_n^2)$ and $|Q| = (\sigma_1^2 \cdots \sigma_n^2)^{-1}$. Substituting in (18.38) gives the simpler (18.39).

Exercise When is the differential entropy of a Gaussian random *vector* positive?

Exercise Deduce (18.39) from the case $n = 1$. (Hint: use Theorem 18.24.)

Continuous random vectors Now for the result that tells us the sense in which Gaussians are a unique extremal case, with which others may be compared.

Theorem 18.29 *Let* $X = (X_1, \ldots, X_n)$ *be an n-dimensional continuous random variable, in which the components* X_i *need not be independent, but the variance of* X_i *is given to be* σ_i^2. *Then,*

$$\boxed{h(X) \leq \tfrac{n}{2} \ln 2\pi e \big(\sigma_1^2 \cdots \sigma_n^2\big)^{1/n},}$$ (18.40)

with equality if and only if the X_i *are independent Gaussians.*

Proof Let the pdf of X be $p(x)$. Then X_i has a pdf $p_i(x_i)$, the marginal pdf, obtained by integrating $p(x)$ over all the component variables except x_i itself (see Section 10.1.1), and, consequently,

$$\int p(x)(x_i - \mu_i)^2 \mathrm{d}x = \int p_i(x_i)(x_i - \mu_i)^2 \mathrm{d}x_i = \sigma_i^2.$$ (18.41)

Now let $Y = (Y_1, \ldots, Y_n)$, where the Y_i are independent Gaussian variables with joint pdf $g(y) = \Pi_i g_i(y_i)$. Let Y_i have the same parameters as X_i, so $g_i(y_i) = (2\pi \sigma_i^2)^{-1/2} \exp[-(y_i - \mu_i)^2 / 2\sigma_i^2]$. The main proof proceeds by an ingenious combination of $p(x)$ and $g(x)$. We note firstly that

$$-\int p(x) \log g(x) \mathrm{d}x = -\int p(x) \sum_i \log g_i(x_i) \mathrm{d}x \quad \text{(logs to base e)}$$

$$= \sum_i \int p(x) \tfrac{1}{2} \big[\log 2\pi \sigma_i^2 + (x_i - \mu_i)^2 / \sigma_i^2 \big] \mathrm{d}x$$

$$= \tfrac{1}{2} \sum_i \big(\log 2\pi \sigma_i^2 + 1 \big) \qquad \text{by (18.41)}$$

$$= \tfrac{n}{2} \log 2\pi e \big(\sigma_1^2 \cdots \sigma_n^2\big)^{1/n} \qquad \text{(Exercise 18.12)}$$

$$= h(Y) = -\int g(y) \log g(y) \mathrm{d}y, \quad \text{by (18.39)}.$$

Therefore $h(X) - h(Y) = -\displaystyle\int p(x)\log p(x)\mathrm{d}x + \int p(x)\log g(x)\mathrm{d}x$

$$= \int p(x)\log \frac{g(x)}{p(x)}\,\mathrm{d}x = E\log[g(x)/p(x)]$$

$$\leq \log \int p(x)\frac{g(x)}{p(x)}\,\mathrm{d}x \quad \text{by Jensen's Inequality, (9.51)}$$

$$= \log \int g(x)\mathrm{d}x = \log(1) = 0,$$

with (by Jensen's result) equality if and only if $g(x)/p(x) = 1$ almost everywhere, and so the proof is complete since isolated function values do not affect the value of an integral.

Example 18.30 (*Example 18.26 revisited*) Let us test out the upper bound (18.40) on Gaussian differential entropy. Consider the case $n = 2$ with $\mathrm{Cov}(X) = Q^{-1} =$ Rows$[(2, 1), (1, 1)]$. From this we read off the values $\sigma_1^2 = 2, \sigma_2^2 = 1$, and so the *upper bound* for such an example is

$$h(X) \leq \ln 2\pi \mathrm{e}\bigl(\sigma_1^2\sigma_2^2\bigr)^{1/2} = \ln(2\pi\mathrm{e}\sqrt{2}).$$

The entropy in this specific case of Q is, by (18.38),

$$h(X) = \ln\bigl(2\pi\mathrm{e}|Q|^{-1/2}\bigr) = \ln(2\pi\mathrm{e}),$$

which is strictly less than the upper bound, as predicted by the non-independence of the components of X (the off-diagonal elements of $\mathrm{Cov}(X)$ being nonzero).

18.3.2 Mutual information and neural nets

Now we are ready to explore Linsker's (1988) principle of maximum information for nets, or *Infomax*. The application will be to self-organising nets with a single layer of weights, with the question: how should the net adapt in the presence of various kinds of noise? The examples are due to Linsker, and conclude with one that preserves topology in the sense of Kohonen. To incorporate noise the following lemma is useful. It is questionably obvious to intuition, so the agreement with theory is reassuring.

Lemma 18.31 *Suppose that the continuous random variables Y, U, Z satisfy $Y = U + Z$, where U and Z are independent. Then $h(Y|U) = h(Z)$.*

Proof Being independent, (U, Z) have a joint pdf $p(u)g(z)$, where p, g are respective pdfs of U and Z. The substitution $z = y - u$, or equivalently the change of variables $u, y \to u, z\ (= y - u)$ has Jacobian 1 (see Theorem 10.10), so we may say that U, Y

have joint pdf $f(u, y)$, with

$$f(u, y) = p(u)g(z), \quad \text{and} \quad p(y|u) = f(u, y)/p(u) = g(z). \tag{18.42}$$

Hence
$$\begin{aligned}
h(Y|U) &= -\iint f(u, y) \log p(y|u) \mathrm{d}u \, \mathrm{d}y \\
&= -\iint p(u)g(z) \log g(z) \mathrm{d}u \, \mathrm{d}z, \quad \text{on substituting} \\
&\qquad\qquad\qquad\qquad\qquad\qquad\qquad z = y - u, \text{ by (18.42)} \\
&= -\int g(z) \log g(z) \mathrm{d}z \qquad\qquad \text{since } \int p(u) \mathrm{d}u = 1 \\
&= h(Z).
\end{aligned}$$

Example 18.32 (*Processing noise, single neuron*) Consider a single neuron with input vector X, output Y (a single scalar), weight vector w, and additive noise $\mathcal{N}$ on the output. Our model is $Y = w \cdot X + \mathcal{N}$, where

$$Y \text{ is } N(\mu, \sigma^2), \quad \mathcal{N} \text{ is } N(0, \sigma_0^2), \quad \text{and } X, \ \mathcal{N} \text{ are independent.}$$

We wish to maximise the mutual information between input and output, namely

$$\begin{aligned}
I(X; Y) &= h(Y) - h(Y|X) \quad \text{(see Table 18.3)} \\
&= h(Y) - H(\mathcal{N}) \quad \text{by Lemma 18.31 with } U = w \cdot X \text{ and } Z = \mathcal{N} \\
&= \tfrac{1}{2} \ln(2\pi e \sigma^2) - \tfrac{1}{2} \ln(2\pi e \sigma_0^2) \quad \text{by (18.39)} \\
&= \ln(\sigma/\sigma_0) \text{ (a version of the signal to noise ratio, or } SNR\text{).}
\end{aligned}$$

Conclusion: we should aim for greatest output variance.

Example 18.33 (*Processing noise, two neurons*)

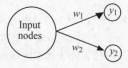

Figure 18.44 Single-layer net with two neurons.

Now we extend the number of neurons to two, as portrayed in Figure 18.44, with input X, output pair $Y = (Y_1, Y_2)$, weight vectors w_1, w_2, and noise vector $\mathcal{N} = (\mathcal{N}_1, \mathcal{N}_2)$. The noise is additive as before, that is $Y_1 = w_1 \cdot X + \mathcal{N}_1$, $Y_2 = w_2 \cdot X + \mathcal{N}_2$; in fact we take

$$Y = U + \mathcal{N}, \text{ where } U_i = w_i \cdot X_i \text{ is in } N(0, \sigma_i^2), \tag{18.43}$$
$$\mathcal{N}_i \text{ and } X_j \text{ are independent for all } i, j, \tag{18.44}$$
$$\mathcal{N}_1, \mathcal{N}_2 \sim N(0, \sigma_0^2), \text{ and are independent.} \tag{18.45}$$

Mutual information Writing $R = \text{Cov}(Y)\ (= Q^{-1})$, the covariance matrix, we may use the results of the previous section to compute $I(X; Y)$ (see also basic results of Section 10.2.3). Thus:

$$
\begin{aligned}
I(X; Y) &= h(Y) - h(\mathcal{N}) \qquad \text{by Lemma 18.31} \\
&= \log\left(2\pi e |R|^{1/2}\right) - \log\left(2\pi e (\sigma_0^2 \cdot \sigma_0^2)^{1/2}\right) \quad \text{by (18.38), (18.39)} \\
&= \log\left(|R|^{1/2}/\sigma_0^2\right).
\end{aligned}
$$

The covariance matrix We take the noise variances σ_0^2 as fixed and so maximising $I(X; Y)$ means maximising $|R|$; it will turn out there are two cases of interest. Note that we assume noise is independent of the U_i (as well as zero mean), hence zero covariances $E[U_i \mathcal{N}_j]$. Write $R = [R_{ij}]$, then

$$
\begin{aligned}
R_{ii} &= V[Y_i] = V[U_i + \mathcal{N}_i] = V[U_i] + V[\mathcal{N}_i] \quad \text{(by independence)} = \sigma_i^2 + \sigma_0^2, \\
R_{12} = R_{21} &= E[(U_1 + \mathcal{N}_1)(U_2 + \mathcal{N}_2)] \qquad \text{since } U_i, \mathcal{N}_i \text{ have zero means} \\
&= E[U_1 U_2 + U_1 \mathcal{N}_2 + U_2 \mathcal{N}_1 + \mathcal{N}_1 \mathcal{N}_2] \\
&= E[U_1 U_2] \quad \text{by (18.44) and (18.45)} \\
&= \sigma_1 \sigma_2 \sigma_{12}, \text{ if } \rho_{12} \text{ is the correlation coefficient (Section 10.4)} \\
&\qquad \text{of } U_1, U_2.
\end{aligned}
$$

Finally, $|R| = R_{11} R_{22} - R_{12}^2 = \sigma_0^4 + \sigma_0^2(\sigma_1^2 + \sigma_2^2) + \sigma_1^2 \sigma_2^2 (1 - \rho_{12}^2)$. With σ_0 fixed, the mutual input–output information will be greatest when $|R|$ is greatest, and we want to know what properties of σ_1 and σ_2 will achieve this. There are two cases, between which a tradeoff must be made.

Case 1: large noise variance With σ_0 large the third term of $|R|$ is neglible compared with the other two, and the first is fixed, so we should maximise the overall output variance $\sigma_1^2 + \sigma_2^2$ (measured in the absence of noise). We may characterise this as REDUNDANCY, as opposed to the next case, where the best policy is diversity.

Case 2: small noise variance When σ_0 is small, it is the third term of $|R|$ which dominates, and this time the system performs best if σ_1^2 and σ_2^2 are individually large (for instance it is no good here having a large sum if one of them is zero). That is, we need DIVERSITY.

Example 18.34 (*Image processing*) Suppose we are given adjacent but non-overlapping pixel patches of an image. They might appear as in Figure 18.45.

Figure 18.45 Adjacent patches of an image have something in common due to their shared history, and mutual information is one approach to making use of this fact.

We don't know what the picture values should be but we do know that different parts have common cause(s), such as

> lighting,
> orientation,
> reflective properties,
> slightly different version, e.g. due to motion;

therefore we expect, not equality between patches, but some form of coherence. We cannot expect that patches have minimal squared difference, but we may hypothesise that they have *shared information*. The method of Becker and Hinton (1992) proceeds via a net with one hidden layer, globally represented in Figure 18.46, in which a patch labelled A sends input to a module and thence to an output Y_a. It is argued that we should maximize, over all possible weight connection vectors, the information which the mean of Y_a and Y_b conveys about the common underlying signal X. That is, maximize $I[(Y_a + Y_b)/2; X]$, based on model (18.46) and Formula (18.47) below.

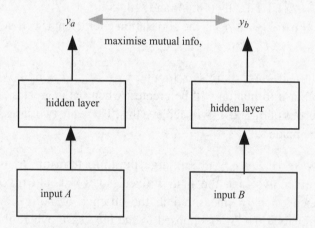

Figure 18.46 Overall plan for two patches of an image.

We assume that the modules of Figure 18.46 receive input produced by a common Gaussian signal X that is corrupted by independent Gaussian noise additions $\mathcal{N}_a, \mathcal{N}_b$. That is,

$$Y_a = X + \mathcal{N}_a, \quad \text{and} \quad Y_b = X + \mathcal{N}_b. \tag{18.46}$$

Lemma 18.35 *(Becker, 1992) With the model (18.46), and assuming all variables to be Gaussian, the mutual information $I(Y_a; Y_b)$ is given by*

$$I(Y_a; Y_b) = \tfrac{1}{2} \log \frac{V(Y_a + Y_b)}{V(Y_a - Y_b)}. \tag{18.47}$$

Proof We may write $Y = (Y_a + Y_b)/2 = (\mathcal{N}_a + \mathcal{N}_b)/2 + X$. Now, a linear combination of Gaussian variables is Gaussian (see Example 10.41), and this applies in particular to

Y, $(Y_a \pm Y_b)/2$, and $(\mathcal{N}_a \pm \mathcal{N}_b)/2$, so we may argue as follows.

$$
\begin{aligned}
I(Y; S) &= h(Y) - h(Y|X) && \text{see Table 18.3} \\
&= h(Y) - h[(\mathcal{N}_a + \mathcal{N}_b)/2] && \text{by Lemma 18.31} \\
&= (1/2)\log 2\pi e V(Y) - (1/2)\log 2\pi e V[(\mathcal{N}_a + \mathcal{N}_b)/2] && \text{by (18.39)} \\
&= (1/2)\log\{V[(Y_a + Y_b)/2]/V[(\mathcal{N}_a + \mathcal{N}_b)/2]\} && \log a - \log b = \log(a/b) \\
&= (1/2)\log[V(Y_a + Y_b)/V(\mathcal{N}_a + \mathcal{N}_b)] && V(rZ) = r^2 V(Z) \\
&= (1/2)\log[V(Y_a + Y_b)/V(\mathcal{N}_a - \mathcal{N}_b)] && \mathcal{N}_a, \mathcal{N}_b \text{ independent} \\
&= (1/2)\log[V(Y_a + Y_b)/V(Y_a - Y_b)] && \mathcal{N}_a - \mathcal{N}_b = Y_a - Y_b.
\end{aligned}
$$

Becker and Hinton (1992) construct a net which, given examples from a random-dot stereogram, can learn features such as depth and surface curvature. This work is further extended in Becker and Hinton (1993). For more details, see these cited papers.

Remarks 18.36 (1) *Edge and motion detection* Tang (1991) obtains an exact analytic solution to a class of network information minimisation problems, and applies it to edge-detection and motion detection.

(2) *The Gaussian assumption* Linsker (1993) shows that it is justified to assume that the input is Gaussian, in the sense that the correct maximum will be obtained for given means and variances, provided the input–output relation is *linear*, i.e. no sigmoid or other nonlinear function is employed. This reference is also a source for the relevance of mutual information to multiresolution, wavelets and pyramid encoding.

(3) *Information and texture* Mumford *et al.* (1997) propose a *Minimax Entropy Principle* applied to texture, which leads to a new Markov Random Field model of texture.

18.3.3 A general learning rule

We have tackled the special case of two output nodes in Example 18.33, but *Infomax*, Linsker's principle of maximising the input–output mutual information $I(X; Y)$, can do more. In fact it leads to a weight updating analogous to the backpropagation algorithm of supervised learning, provided we can find a way to perform gradient ascent of $I(X; Y)$. That is, if we can find an expression for the derivative of $I(X; Y)$ with respect to the weights; for then we know the update directions which will increase mutual information. Following Linsker (1992), we'll denote the matrix of weights by C, and so take, with X, Y, N as column vectors,

$$
Y = CX + \mathcal{N}, \tag{18.48}
$$

where $\mathcal{N}$ is an additive noise vector with zero mean. Then, as in Example 18.33,

$$
I(X; Y) = h(Y) - h(Y|X) = h(Y) - h(\mathcal{N}). \tag{18.49}
$$

We assume, though, that the noise is independent of the weights, so for the purpose of differentiation we may focus on $h(Y)$ alone. *Let w be any weight c_{ni},* and denote differentiation with respect to w by a superscript dash (prime). Then $I'(X; Y) = h'(Y)$.

Further, writing $R = \text{Cov}(Y)$, the covariance matrix of Y, we have by Equation (18.38) that $h(Y)$ equals a constant plus $(1/2) \ln |R|$. In summary, therefore,

$$I'(X; Y) = \frac{\partial}{\partial w} \frac{1}{2} \ln |R|. \tag{18.50}$$

Construction 18.37 *Functions of matrices* To tackle (18.50) we must extend the matrix background of Chapter 8. For $A = [a_{ij}]$ we let $A' = \partial A/\partial w = [a'_{ij}]$, the matrix of derivatives (when these exist). The *product rule* $(AB)' = A'B + AB'$ holds because $(AB)'$ has (i, j) entry $(\sum a_{is}b_{sj})' = \sum a'_{is}b_{sj} + \sum a'_{is}b_{sj}$. For present purposes we may take A to be a real symmetric $n \times n$ matrix, giving the benefit (Theorem 8.30) that A is closely related to the diagonal matrix $D = \text{diag}(\lambda_1, \ldots, \lambda_n) = \text{diag}[\lambda_j]$ of its eigenvalues λ_j, which are necessarily real. Specifically, there is an invertible matrix P such that

$$A = PDP^{-1} = P \cdot \text{diag}[\lambda_j] \cdot P^{-1}, \tag{18.51}$$

and, conversely, if A may be so represented then the λ_j are the eigenvalues of A. This is very powerful because it shows that many results about numbers hold for complete matrices, via 'cancellation' of P and P^{-1}. Note firstly that we may form powers A^k and hence polynomials $f(A)$. For example, $A^2 = PDP^{-1} \cdot PDP^{-1} = PD^2P^{-1} = P \cdot \text{diag}[\lambda_j^2] \cdot P^{-1}$, and more generally

$$f(A) = P \cdot f(D) \cdot P^{-1} = P \cdot \text{diag}[f(\lambda_j)] \cdot P^{-1}, \tag{18.52}$$

$$A' = PD'P^{-1} = P \cdot \text{diag}[\lambda'_j] \cdot P^{-1}. \tag{18.53}$$

$$A^{-1} = P \cdot \text{diag}[\lambda_j^{-1}] \cdot P^{-1}. \tag{18.54}$$

Exercise Verify (18.54) by checking that $A \cdot A^{-1} = I$.

Because any two diagonal matrices D_1 and D_2 *commute* ($D_1 \cdot D_2 = D_2 \cdot D_1$), the same holds for any two plynomials in A, which in turn commute with A' and A^{-1}, as seen through the examples above. Observe that exponentials e^A are well-defined because (18.52) shows that if $p_k(x) \to p(x)$ then $p_k(A) \to p(A)$, and we may take for $p_k(x)$ the sum of the first k terms in the series expansion of e^x.

Similarly for $\ln A$, provided A is positive definite so that the λ_j are positive (see Corollary 8.35) and their logarithms exist; that is, $\ln A = P \, \text{diag}[\ln \lambda_j] P^{-1}$. Now we can state two results that take us on from (18.50).

Lemma 18.38 *If A is positive definite then $\partial/\partial w \ln |A| = \text{Tr}(A^{-1}A')$.*

Proof We note that the determinant of a matrix equals the product of its eigenvalues λ_j and the trace of A equals their sum (Lemma 8.5). According to (18.51) the eigenvalues of $\ln A$ are the values $\ln(\lambda_j)$. Thus $\ln |A| = \ln \Pi \lambda_j = \sum \ln(\lambda_j) = \text{Tr} \ln(A)$, and it remains to observe that

$$\partial/\partial w \ln A = P \cdot \text{diag}[\partial/\partial w \ln(\lambda_j)] \cdot P^{-1} = P \cdot \text{diag}[\lambda_j^{-1}\lambda'_j] \cdot P^{-1} = A^{-1}A'.$$

Lemma 18.39 *Let* $\langle Z \rangle = (1/N) \sum Z_i$, *the estimated expected value of Z over N samples Z_i. Then $R' = (CLC^T)'$, where, averaging over a given set of N training column vectors, we take*

$$L = \text{Cov}(X) = \langle XX^T \rangle, \quad and \quad R = \text{Cov}(Y) = \langle YY^T \rangle. \qquad (18.55)$$

Proof If M, P are fixed matrices for which MZP exists, then $\langle MZP \rangle = (1/N) \sum MZ_i P = M[(1/N) \sum Z_i] P = M \langle Z \rangle P$. Thus with $Y = CX + \mathcal{N}$, and the additive noise $\mathcal{N}$ independent of X and C, the term $\text{Cov}(\mathcal{N})$ drops out when we differentiate the final equality below:

$$
\begin{aligned}
R = \langle YY^T \rangle &= \langle (CX + \mathcal{N})(CX + \mathcal{N})^T \rangle \\
&= C \langle XX^T \rangle C^T + C \langle X\mathcal{N}^T \rangle + \langle \mathcal{N}X^T \rangle C^T + \langle \mathcal{N}\mathcal{N}^T \rangle, \\
&= CLC^T + \text{Cov}(\mathcal{N}), \quad \text{by definition of } L.
\end{aligned}
$$

Remarks 18.40 It is necessary to make the reasonable assumption that training vectors are chosen so that, as a set of n-vectors, they span the whole space $\mathbf{R}^n$. It follows that the covariance matrix R is positive definite (see Exercise 18.14) and therefore, as remarked earlier, $\ln R$ is well-defined. The following theorem provides a basis for gradient ascent of $I(X; Y)$ by giving its derivatives in terms of the weight matrix C.

Theorem 18.41 $\partial I / \partial c_{ni} = (R^{-1}CL)_{ni}$ *for each entry c_{ni} of C, that is*

$$\partial I / \partial C = R^{-1}CL.$$

Proof Putting together the various pieces, we may argue as follows, starting from (18.50).

$$
\begin{aligned}
\partial I / \partial w = \partial / \partial w \tfrac{1}{2} \text{Tr}(R^{-1}R') & \quad \text{by Lemma 18.38} \\
= \tfrac{1}{2} \text{Tr} R^{-1}[CLC'^T + C'LC^T] & \quad \text{by Lemma 18.39 and the Product Rule} \\
= \text{Tr } R^{-1}CLC'^T & \quad \text{since both terms contribute the same} \\
= \sum_{m,p} (R^{-1}CL)_{mp} \partial c_{mp} / \partial c_{ni} & \quad \text{Tr } AB^T = \sum a_{mp} b_{mp} \\
= (R^{-1}CL)_{ni} & \quad \text{the only nonzero term.}
\end{aligned}
$$

Making the learning rule local We're now in a position to perform gradient ascent by the updating rule

$$\Delta c_{ni} = \gamma (R^{-1}CL)_{ni}, \qquad (18.56)$$

but there is a problem: the factor R^{-1} makes the update depend in a complicated way upon values at all nodes, and so this rule cannot be described as *local*. The ingenious approach of Linsker (1992) uses the fact that we don't actually need R^{-1} on its own, for

$$(R^{-1}CL)_{ni} = \langle R^{-1}CXX^T \rangle_{ni} = \langle R^{-1}Y \cdot X^T \rangle_{ni} = \langle (R^{-1}Y)_n (X)_i \rangle.$$

The aim becomes to estimate the product $R^{-1}Y$ by an updating process. For this we begin with a matrix $F = I - \alpha R$, with $0 < \alpha < 1$ chosen to aid/ensure convergence of the sequence $\{y_t\}$ defined by

$$y_0 = Y, \quad y_{t+1} = Y + F y_t \quad (t = 0, 1, 2, \ldots). \tag{18.57}$$

This works because if $y_t \to y_\infty$ then $y_\infty = Y + (I - \alpha R)y_\infty$, from which $R^{-1}Y = \alpha y_\infty$. On the other hand, we need the matrix $R = \langle YY^T \rangle$ for F in order to calculate y_∞. An estimate $\hat{R}$ is updated by each new training vector (the same idea was used for k-means at (18.30)), as prescribed in step 2 of the algorithm below.

ALGO 18.5 Weight matrix for maximum mutual information

Initialise C and $\hat{R}$ to zero; set α, γ and an integer t
Repeat for $M = 1, 2, 3, \ldots$
    1. Choose a training vector X and determine the output Y
    2. Perform update $\Delta\hat{R} = \frac{1}{M}(YY^T - \hat{R})$
    3. Estimate y_∞ as y_t, using (18.57)
    4. Compare y_{t+1} and repeat step 3 with new α if necessary
    5. Perform update $\Delta C = \gamma\alpha(y_\infty X^T)$
Until changes are within tolerance.

Locality This learning scheme is indeed local in that $\Delta\hat{R}_{mn}$ uses information only at positions m and n of Y and at (m, n) in $\hat{R}$; further, Δc_{ni} uses only $(y_\infty)_n$ and $(X)_i$.

Further developments (i) *More noise* The model so far allowed additive noise after application of the weight matrix, implying that, to know Y, we must be able to measure the output. Continuing this point, Linsker extends his method to include input noise also: $X = S + N$, where S is the original input signal and N is noise. This is done by first allowing the net to learn R with noise only, as input; then in a second phase it learns R with signal plus input noise. Details are found in Linsker (1992).

(ii) *Nonlinear activation* Bell and Sejnowski (1995) study the case in which nonlinear activation functions such as sigmoids are used, obtaining a learning method which incorporates the derivatives of these functions. They show that, in this case, one can obtain output variables that are statistically independent: $p(x, y) = p(x)p(y)$. This situation is called *independent component anaysis*, or ICA, as distinct from PCA, where the components are just uncorrelated. However, the results depend on taking no account of noise.

(iii) Linsker (1997) showed how his earlier learning algorithm can incorporate the results of Bell and Sejnowski so as to remove both their restriction on noise and his restriction to Gaussian input and linearity, whilst still keep learning fully local.

(iv) *Kohonen learning* A useful introduction to *Infomax* learning in the case of Kohonen's topographic map approach is given by Haykin (1994). A powerful learning algorithm was developed recently by van Hulle (2002).

18.3.4 Shannon's Rate Distortion Theory

Information Theory has something to say about quantisation. Importantly, it predicts that, if we have a set of symbols to quantise, it is better to quantise them together in blocks rather than separately, for this will result in better compression for the same permitted error.

We begin with the idea of a *source sequence* $U = (U_1, \ldots, U_k)$ of *independent* variables U_i, with common pdf, whose values are symbols from the *source alphabet* $\mathcal{A}_U$. The sequence is processed through some channel and becomes $V = (V_1, \ldots, V_k)$, where each V_i takes values in the *destination alphabet* $\mathcal{A}_V$ (which usually contains $\mathcal{A}_U$). The source (and entropy) will be *discrete*, that is the alphabets will be finite, until we consider the Gaussian source. We emphasise that, until other possibilities are explicitly considered, the source will be *memoryless*, another way of saying the U_i are independent.

An error or *distortion* $d(u_i, v_i)$ is considered to occur when u_i is reproduced by the channel as v_i. The distortion between sequences u and v is then simply defined as

$$d(u, v) = \sum_i d(u_i, v_i) \quad (1 \le i \le k). \tag{18.58}$$

Example 18.42 $(k = 2)$ $\mathcal{A}_U = \mathcal{A}_V = \{0, 1, 2, \ldots, 9\}$ with $d(u_i, v_i) = |u_i - v_i|$. Taking $u = (1, 2)$ and $v = (4, 7)$ gives $d(u, v) = |1 - 4| + |2 - 7| = 3 + 5 = 8$.

Assumptions 18.43 The case $\mathcal{A}_U = \mathcal{A}_V$ above is fairly typical. We don't need $\mathcal{A}_V$ to be completely general and it will be enough to assume two things:

(i) for each u in $\mathcal{A}_U$ there is some $v = v_u$ with $d(u, v_u) = 0$,
(ii) for each v in $\mathcal{A}_V$ there is at most one u with $d(u, v) = 0$.

Equivalently, in the *distortion matrix* $[d(u, v)]$, with rows u and columns v, each row has at least one zero, and each column at *most* one. This is certainly true for the *Hamming distance* $d(u, v) = 0$ if $u = v$, otherwise $d(u, v) = 1$. For example, in the case $\mathcal{A}_U = \mathcal{A}_V$ and $U = (U_1, U_2, U_3)$ the distortion matrix is

$$[d(u, v)] = \begin{bmatrix} 0 & 1 & 1 \\ 1 & 0 & 1 \\ 1 & 1 & 0 \end{bmatrix}.$$

Definitions 18.44 We define the *rate distortion function* $R(D)$, which we'll see represents the number of binary bits need to represent a source symbol if distortion D is acceptable. It is a minimum of mutual information which exists similarly to (13.20), as follows:

$$R_k(D) = \text{Min}\{I(U; V) \colon E[d] \le kD\}, \tag{18.59a}$$

$$R(D) = \text{Min}_k(1/k)R_k(D) \quad \text{(mean per symbol)}. \tag{18.59b}$$

Formula (18.59b) converts a mean distortion over k symbols to a per-symbol distortion. In fact it may be shown that $R(D) = R_1(D)$ (we omit the technical proof of this fact). That is

$$\boxed{R(D) = \text{Min}\{I(U; V) \colon E[d] \le D\} \quad (k = 1).} \tag{18.60}$$

Test channels It should be explained that the minimum of $I(U; V)$ is taken over all *test channels*, that is choices of $\{p(v|u)\}$, with the *source statistics* $p(u)$ fixed, and subject to the constraint $E[d] \le D$. We express this constraint in terms of $p(v|u)$ by noting that u, v have a joint pdf $p(u, v) = p(u)p(v|u)$, whence

$$E[d] = \sum_{u,v} p(u)p(v|u)d(u, v). \tag{18.61}$$

The compression interpretation of $R(D)$ Suppose that $U = (U_1, \ldots, U_k)$ can be represented by n bits $X = (X_1, \ldots, X_n)$ from which V can be recovered with distortion limited by $E[d] \le kD$. Considering the diagram $U \to X \to V$ with logs to base 2, we have by Corollary 13.19, Theorem 13.3 and Theorem 13.21 in succession, that

$$n \ge H(X) \ge I(X; V) \ge I(U; V),$$

which is at least $kR(D)$ by (18.59b). Thus $n/k \ge R(D)$, meaning at least $R(D)$ *bits per symbol* are needed.

Some properties of $R(D)$ This function is hard to compute exactly except in a few special cases such as the Gaussian (Theorem 18.48 below). However, the problem was considered solved with the advent of an effective numerical algorithm due to Blahut (1972) (see also Gray, 1990). The graph of $R(D)$ has a fairly simple general appearance. We show that, as in Figure 18.47,

$R(D)$ is non-decreasing between two values $D_{\min}$ and $D_{\max}$,
undefined to the left, and zero to the right of these.

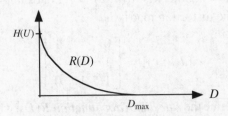

Figure 18.47 Typical graph of $R(D)$, the rate distortion function. Its general shape is derived in the text.

Working with single (rather than k) symbols we may consider $u \in \mathcal{A}_U$.

(a) $D_{\min} = 0$. Since $D < 0$ is impossible (D is a distortion) we show that $R(0)$ exists, i.e. that there exists a test channel for which $E[d] = 0$. Define $p(v|u) = 1$ if $v = v_u$ (see Assumptions 18.43), otherwise zero. Then $E[d] = \sum_{u,v} p(u)p(v|u)d(u, v) = \sum_u p(u)d(u, v_u) = 0$.

(b) $R(D)$ *is non-increasing* Let $0 \le D_1 < D_2$. Then $E[d] \le D_1$ implies $E[d] \le D_2$, hence the set inclusion $\{I(U; V): E[d] \le D_1\} \subseteq \{I(U; V): E[d] \le D_2\}$. But enlarging a set cannot increase its minimum, so $R(D_2) \le R(D_1)$. That is, $R(D)$ is non-increasing.

(c) $R(D) = 0$ for $D \geq D_{\max}$, where we define

$$D_{\max} = \text{Min}_v \sum_u p(u)d(u, v) = \sum_u p(u)d(u, v_0), \text{ say.} \qquad (18.62)$$

Proof Referring to (18.59) we see that $R(D_{\max}) = 0$ follows if we produce a test channel with $I(U; V) = 0$ and $E[d] = D_{\max}$. For this channel we ensure $I(U; V) = 0$ by a deterministic choice: $p(v|u) = 1$ if v is the symbol v_0 of (18.62), otherwise $p(v|u) = 0$ (see Exercise 13.5). This gives $E[d] = \sum_{u,v} p(u)p(v|u)d(u, v) = \sum_u p(u)d(u, v_0) = D_{\max}$ as required. Thus $R(D_{\max}) = 0$. It remains to remark that, since $R(D)$ is non-increasing, it stays zero for $D > D_{\max}$. Now we note a useful equality for $R(0)$, proved below and indicated earlier, in Figure 18.47:

$$R(0) = H(U). \qquad (18.63)$$

To see this, recall that $R(0) = \text{Min}\{I(U; V): E[d] = 0\}$ and let (U, V) be a test channel achieving this minimum. We need $H(U|V)$, which is defined by $\{p(u|v)\}$. For this we note firstly that if the channel sends u to v then $p(v|u)$ is nonzero and the zero sum $0 = E[d] = \sum p(u)p(v|u)d(u, v)$ implies that $d(u, v)$ is zero. Hence, given v, there is by Assumption 18.43(ii) at most one candidate u for $u \to v$.

Thus the 'reverse channel' (V, U) has the special property that $p(u|v)$ is always 0 or 1, and so $H(U|V) = -\sum p(v)p(u|v) \ln p(u|v)$, which is zero since $1 \cdot \ln(1)$ and $0 \cdot \ln(0)$ are both zero. Finally, $R(0) = I(U; V) = H(U) - H(U|V) = H(U)$.

Calculating *R(D)* As exemplified above, a standard method we will use to determine $R(D)$ is to bound it below on general grounds, say $R(D) \geq B$, then to show this bound is tight by exhibiting a special channel with $I(U, V) = B$, implying $R(D) \leq B$. We start with an inequality that relates $H(X|Y)$ to the probability P_e of error if we guess that $X = Y$.

Theorem 18.45 *(Fano's Inequality) Let X, Y be random variables taking the same r values. Writing $P_e = P(X \neq Y)$, we have*

$$H(X|Y) \leq H(P_e) + P_e \log(r - 1). \qquad (18.64)$$

Proof Let Z be another discrete random variable, and define the function $G(z) = \sum_{x,y} p(y)p(z|x, y)$. We claim that $H(X|Y) \leq H(Z) + E[\log G]$, for

$$H(X|Y) = E[\log 1/p(x|y)] \qquad \text{see Section 13.1.2}$$
$$= \sum_{x,y,z} p(x, y, z) \log 1/p(x|y) \qquad \text{since } p(x, y) = \sum_z p(x, y, z)$$
$$= \sum_z p(z) \sum_{x,y} [p(x, y, z)/p(z)] \log 1/p(x|y)$$
$$\leq \sum_z p(z) \log\{\sum_{x,y} [p(x, y, z)/p(z)] \, 1/p(x|y)\} \qquad \text{by Jensen's Inequality}$$
$$\qquad (9.54), \text{ since } p(x, y, z)/p(z)] \text{ sums over } x, y \text{ to } 1,$$
$$= \sum_z p(z) \log 1/p(z) + \sum_z p(z) \log \sum_{x,y} p(x, y, z)/p(x|y).$$

But the $\sum_{x,y}$ term equals $G(z)$ because $p(x, y, z) = p(x, y)p(z|x, y) = p(y)p(x|y)p(z|x, y)$, giving the claimed inequality. For Fano's Inequality (unpublished, 1952) we define $Z = 0$ if $X = Y$ and $Z = 1$ if $X \neq Y$. Writing $\sum_{x,y} = \sum_{x=y} + \sum_{x \neq y}$ we find that $G(0) = 1$ and $G(1) = r - 1$. Thus $E[\log G] = P(Z = 0)\log(1) + P(Z = 1)\log(r - 1) = P_e \log(r - 1)$, completing the proof.

Exercise With $G(z)$ as above, verify that $G(0) = 1$.

Example 18.46 Determine $R(D)$ for the binary symmetric source ($\mathcal{A}_U = \mathcal{A}_V = \{0, 1\}$), with Hamming distance, and source statistics $\{p, q\}$ ($p \leq q$).

Solution We showed that $D_{\min} = 0$, and (18.62) gives $D_{\max} = \text{Min}\{p \cdot 0 + q \cdot 1, p \cdot 1 + q \cdot 0\} = p$, so we now let $0 < D < p$. Notice that, for any (U, V) channel with Hamming distance,

$$E[d] = P(U = 0, V = 1) \cdot 1 + P(U = 1, V = 0) \cdot 1 = P(U \neq V). \tag{18.65}$$

For a lower bound on $R(D)$, let channel (U, V) achieve $R(D)$, so that $D = E[d] = P_e$, by (18.65), where we set $(X, Y) = (U, V)$ in Fano's Inequality to obtain $H(U|V) \leq H(P_e) + P_e \log(1) = H(D)$, whence $R(D) = I(U; V) = H(U) - H(U|V) \geq H(U) - H(D)$.

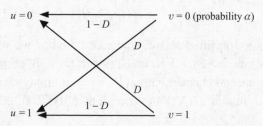

Figure 18.48 'Backwards' test channel for Example 18.46, defined by $p(u|v) = D$ if $v \neq u$ and $P(V = 0) = \alpha$.

To prove that our inequality is actually an equality we need a special test channel with $E[d] = D$ and $I(U; V) = H(U) - H(D)$. It suffices to insist, as in Figure 18.48, that $p(u|v) = D$ if $u \neq v$ (Exercise 18.15). This can be realised provided the implied value α of $P(V = 0)$ lies in the open interval $(0, 1)$; the implied $\{p(v|u)\}$ is automatically a genuine pdf because $\sum_v p(v|u) = \sum_v p(u, v)/p(u) = p(u)/p(u) = 1$. To compute α we observe that $p = P(U = 0)$, so

$$p = P(U = 0|V = 0)P(V = 0) + P(U = 0|V = 1)P(V = 1)$$
$$= (1 - D)\alpha + D(1 - \alpha),$$

whence $\alpha = (p - D)/(1 - 2D)$. With $0 < D < p \leq 1/2$, we have $0 < p - D < 1 - 2D$, so $0 < \alpha < 1$ as required. Thus we have shown $R(D) = H(U) - H(D)$ for the binary symmetric channel.

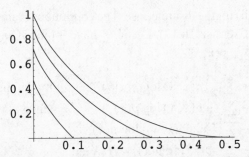

Figure 18.49 Graph of $R(D) = H(p) - H(D)$ for the binary symmetric source with statistics $\{p, q\}$, and $p = 0.1, 0.2, 0.3, 0.5$.

Graphs We can conveniently graph some possibilities, because $H(U) = H(p)$ (see (12.9)), and so $R(D) = H(p) - H(D)$. This is shown in Figure 18.49 for various values of p.

18.3.5 Source coding and the Gaussian source

The definition of rate distortion $R(D)$, being based on mutual information, carries over with $I(X; Y)$ to the continuous case. Now we are ready to consider a source which is *Gaussian $N(0, \sigma^2)$, with squared error distortion*. That is, the source emits independent symbols $U_1, U_2, \ldots$, where U_i is $N(0, \sigma^2)$, converted by a channel to V_i, say, and with distortion measured for single symbols by $d(u, v) = (u - v)^2$. To determine the rate distortion function, which in this case can be done explicitly, we consider three assertions of which the last two are intuitively expected.

Theorem 18.47 *Differential entropy satisfies (i) $h(aX) = h(X) + \log |a|$ provided a is a nonzero constant, (ii) $h(X|Y) \leq h(X)$ (conditioning cannot increase entropy), and (iii) $h(X \pm Y|Y) = h(X|Y)$. Properties (ii) and (iii) also hold for discrete entropy.*

Proof (i) Let X have pdf $f(x)$. Then the pdf of $Y = aX$ is $f_Y(y) = |a|^{-1} f(y/a)$ by (9.33). Thus

$$h(Y) = -\int f_Y(y) \log f_Y(y) \mathrm{d}y \qquad \text{by definition, Table 18.3}$$

$$= -\int |a|^{-1} f(y/a) \log(|a|^{-1} f(y/a)) \mathrm{d}y \qquad \text{now substitute } y = ax$$

$$= -\int f(x) \log(|a|^{-1} f(x)) \mathrm{d}x \qquad \text{whether } |a| = -a \text{ or } a$$

$$= \int f(x) \log |a| \mathrm{d}x - \int f(x) \log f(x) \mathrm{d}x$$

$$= \log |a| + h(X).$$

(ii) We prove (ii) and (iii) for the discrete case. The continuous is analogous, with integrals in place of sums (see Exercise 18.17). Let X, Y have joint pdf $p(x, y)$; then X has the marginal pdf $p(x) = \sum_y p(x, y)$.

$$
\begin{aligned}
H(X|Y) &= -\sum_{x,y} p(x, y) \log p(x|y) && \text{by definition} \\
&\leq -\sum_{x,y} p(x, y) \log p(x) && \text{since } p(x|y) \leq p(x) \\
&= -\sum_x [\sum_y p(x, y)] \log p(x) \\
&= -\sum_x p(x) \log p(x) = H(X).
\end{aligned}
$$

(iii) We let $Z = X + Y$ and show that $H(Z|Y) = H(X|Y)$ (the case $Z = X - Y$ is similar). We write $p(y) = P(Y = y)$ and $p(x|y) = P(X = x|Y = y)$. Then $P(Z = z|Y = y) = P(X = z - y|Y = y) = p(z - y|y)$. Hence, using the substitution $x = z - y$ to transform the summation,

$$
\begin{aligned}
H(Z|Y) &= -\sum_{z,y} p(y) p(z - y|y) \log p(z - y|y) \\
&= -\sum_{x,y} p(y) p(x|y) \log p(x|y) = H(X|Y).
\end{aligned}
$$

Theorem 18.48 *The rate distortion function for a Gaussian $N(0, \sigma^2)$ source with squared error distortion is zero for $D > \sigma^2$, otherwise*

$$
\boxed{R(D) = \tfrac{1}{2} \log(\sigma^2/D), \quad for\, 0 < D \leq \sigma^2.}
\tag{18.66}
$$

Proof Let U be the proposed Gaussian source. (a) Let (U, V) be a test channel achieving $I(U; V) = R(D)$, where $0 < D \leq \sigma^2$. Then, writing $\tau^2 = \mathrm{Var}[U - V]$,

$$
\begin{aligned}
R(D) = I(U; V) &= h(U) - h(U|V) && \text{by Table 18.3} \\
&= h(U) - h(U - V|V) && \text{by Theorem 18.47 (iii)} \\
&\geq h(U) - h(U - V) && \text{by Theorem 18.47 (ii)} \\
&\geq h(U) - h(W), \quad \text{where } W \sim N(0, \tau^2) && \text{by (18.40),} \\
&\geq h(U) - h(Z), \quad \text{where } Z \sim N(0, D) && \text{by (18.39),} \\
&\quad \text{since } \tau^2 = E[(U - V)^2] - (E[U - V])^2 \\
&\quad \leq E[d] \leq D \\
&= \tfrac{1}{2} \log 2\pi e \sigma^2 - \tfrac{1}{2} \log 2\pi e D && \text{by (18.39)} \\
&= \tfrac{1}{2} \log(\sigma^2/D).
\end{aligned}
$$

(b) We have proved that $R(D) \geq \tfrac{1}{2} \log(\sigma^2/D)$. Now we need an explicit test channel with $I(U; V) = \tfrac{1}{2} \log(\sigma^2/D)$, which will imply the reverse inequality $R(D) \leq \tfrac{1}{2} \log(\sigma^2/D)$ and so establish the desired *equality*. We define the required channel (U, V) by defining a joint pdf for its 'reverse' (V, U). This is done implicitly by defining $U = V + Z$, where

$Z \sim N(0, D)$ is independent of V. Then $E[d] = E[(U - V)^2] = E[Z^2] = D$, and

$$
\begin{aligned}
I(U; V) &= h(U) - h(U|V) \\
&= h(U) - h(V + Z|V) \\
&= h(U) - h(Z) \text{ by Lemma 18.31, } V \text{ and } Z \text{ being independent} \\
&= \tfrac{1}{2} \log 2\pi e \sigma^2 - \tfrac{1}{2} \log 2\pi e D \text{ by Formula (18.39)} \\
&= \tfrac{1}{2} \log(\sigma^2/D).
\end{aligned}
$$

(c) *The case $D \geq \sigma^2$* We know that $R(D) \geq 0$ so it remains to exhibit a test channel with $I(U; V) = 0$ (implying $R(D) \leq 0$). We do so by taking $V = 0$. Then $E[d] = E[(U - V)^2] = E[U^2] = \sigma^2 \leq D$, as required, and, since in this case $h(U|V) = h(V)$ (see Exercise 18.16),

$$
I(U; V) = h(U) - h(U|V) = h(U) - h(U) = 0.
$$

Example 18.49 Let us rearrange $R = \tfrac{1}{2} \log(\sigma^2/D)$ to get $D = \sigma^2 2^{-2R}$. This says that with one bit per symbol the expected distortion is $\sigma^2 2^{-2} = \sigma^2/4$, whilst two bits per symbol improve this to distortion only $\sigma^2/16$. In fact, *each further bit of description divides the expected distortion by a factor of* 4.

The Source Coding Theorem

Now suppose a channel converts a source k-vector u to its *nearest neighbour* $f(u)$ in a list $C = \{v_1, v_2, \ldots, v_M\}$, called a *source code*, or *codebook*, where each v_i is a k-vector over $\mathcal{A}_V$. This is of course *vector quantisation*, or VQ. How should we evaluate the merit of C? A clever code causes little distortion in spite of having few codewords, say $M \leq 2^n$ with small n. Then the codewords may be indexed by n-bit words and the rate is n/k. More precisely, we define the *rate of C* to be

$$
\boxed{R = (\log_2 M)/k.} \tag{18.67}
$$

Thus a code quantises well if it keeps the rate down, for a given distortion. With this in mind we'll say the code C is *D-admissible* if the expected distortion for a single symbol u in $\mathcal{A}_U$ (the case $k = 1$) satisfies

$$
\boxed{E[d(u, f(u))] \leq D.} \tag{18.68}
$$

We are ready to state the remarkable *Source Coding Theorem* of Shannon, which we shall do in the form offered by Berger (1971) (see Section 13 for *channel* coding). It states in effect that there is a limit to the efficacy of quantisation, determined by the statistics of the source, but that this limit may be approached arbitrarily closely by encoding the data in sufficiently large blocks at a time.

Theorem 18.50 *(Source Coding/VQ) Given $\varepsilon > 0$ and $D \geq 0$, then provided k is sufficiently large there is a $(D + \varepsilon)$-admissible code of length k, with rate $R < R(D) + \varepsilon$. Conversely, no D-admissible code has a rate less than $R(D)$.*

Gaussians again

The form of $R(D)$ for a Gaussian $N(0, \sigma^2)$ source leads to a helpful geometrical viewpoint. Recall that it is the expected value or average of distortion that is to be considered. Bearing this in mind, we may say that the codewords $\{v_1, v_2, \ldots, v_M\}$ must be arranged in space so that no k-vector can be further than squared distance kD from its quantising codeword. That is, each k-vector must lie in a sphere of radius $\sqrt{(kD)}$ centred at that codeword.

Since this applies to every k-vector these spheres must together cover the region of $\mathbf{R}^k$ occupied by the k-vectors. But this is limited by the fact that the expected squared length of a k-vector is $kE[U_i^2] = k\sigma^2$, so they occupy a sphere of radius $\sqrt{(k\sigma^2)}$ centred at the origin, as suggested in Figure 18.50. Thus the number M of small spheres/codewords is at least the ratio of sphere volumes, and a lower bound for M is (cf. Theorem 18.50)

Figure 18.50 The M codeword-centred spheres of radius $\sqrt{(kD)}$ lie within a larger sphere of radius $\sqrt{(k\sigma^2)}$.

$$\left(\frac{\text{big radius}}{\text{small radius}}\right)^k = \left(\frac{\sqrt{k\sigma^2}}{\sqrt{kD}}\right)^k = \left(\frac{\sigma^2}{D}\right)^{k/2}.$$

How does this compare with the Source Coding Theorem, which says we get arbitrarily close to a code with $R = R(D)$? With M denoting the number of codewords, we have from (18.67) and (18.66) that $(\log_2 M)/k = R = (1/2)\log_2(\sigma^2/D)$, hence (Exercise 18.16)

$$M = 2^{kR} \qquad \text{(any source), and} \qquad (18.69a)$$

$$M = \left(\frac{\sigma^2}{D}\right)^{k/2} \qquad \text{(Gaussian source),} \qquad (18.69b)$$

which meet our geometrically obtained lower bound. Thus we have sketched a proof of the Source Coding Theorem for a Gaussian source (in general see Cover and Thomas (1991)).

Example 18.51 *Codes in the plane, $k = 2$* The arrangement for equal overlapping disks that just cover a plane region (Kershner, 1939) is shown in Figure 18.51(a). With each codeword x being at the centre of a disk, the *Voronoi region of x*, or set of points nearer to x than to any other centre, forms a regular hexagon, as illustrated in Figure 18.51(b). A point on the boundary of two Voronoi regions is thus equidistant from two codewords, and may be quantised to either. Similarly in higher dimensions than 2.

The hexagon centres form a *lattice*, meaning that they consist of all integral linear combinations $ma + nb$ of two independent vectors, say $a = (1, 0)$ and $b = (1, \sqrt{3})/2$. For general k the problem is naturally more complicated, but best solutions are known in many dimensions, typically equipped with an especially simple algorithm for determining

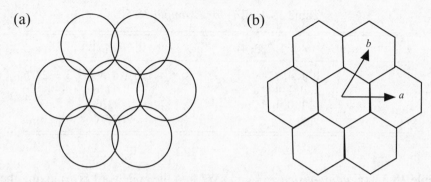

Figure 18.51 (a) The best covering of the plane by equal disks, (b) the corresponding tiling of the plane by regular hexagons. Their centres form the plane lattice consisting of all integral linear combinations $ma + nb$ as described in the text.

the nearest lattice point/codeword to an arbitrary point. Such quantisers, sending each point to its nearest lattice point, are called *lattice quantisers*. An excellent reference for all this is Conway and Sloane (1988). But see also Gray (1990).

18.3.6 The LBG quantiser

The rate distortion function $R(D)$ depends on the distribution $p(u)$ of the input vectors. Can one produce a VQ algorithm which is guided explicitly by this distribution so as to keep distortion low? Following Linde, Buzo and Gray (1980) we show that alternating between the two steps below produces a non-increasing sequence of expected distortions $E[d]$. This forms the basis of their *LBG quantiser*, expressed as ALGO 18.6.

Step A. Given a set of codewords, find the partition into nearest neighbour subsets (the Voronoi regions of the codewords).

Step B. Given a partition $\{S_1, \ldots, S_M\}$ of k-space, find codewords $\hat{x}(S_i)$ to minimise the expected distortion over each S_i.

Consider first the feasibility of Step B. In the case of uniformly distributed u and distortion $d(u, x) = (u - x)^2$, the codewords should be simply the centres of gravity. But this is by no means always the requirement. Here are two simple examples with non-uniform pdfs to illustrate both the discrete and continuous cases of $p(u)$.

Example 18.52 (*Discrete case, $k = 1$*) Let $S_i = \{1, 2, 3, 4\}$ with corresponding probabilities $p(u) = 1/6, 1/6, 1/3, 1/3$. Table 18.4 shows $E[d]$ for each choice of codeword $x = x_i$.

The expected distortion is least when $x = 3$, that is $\hat{x}(S_i) = 3$. Notice for later that the same conclusion will follow (to a good approximation) if we estimate the probabilities from a sufficiently large sample of values of u. In this context these samples are referred to as training vectors.

Table 18.4. $E[d]$ *for Example 18.52.*

x	$d(u, x)$ $(u = 1, 2, 3, 4)$	$E[d]$
1	0, 1, 4, 9	$0/6 + 1/6 + 4/3 + 9/3 = 27/6$
2	1, 0, 1, 4	$11/6$
3	4, 1, 0, 1	$7/6$
4	9, 4, 1, 0	$15/6$

Example 18.53 (*Continuous case, $k = 1$*) We find the codeword $\hat{x}(S_i)$ giving the least mean distortion in a continuous non-uniform case. Let S_i be the interval $[0, 1]$, with pdf $p(u) = \gamma e^{-2u}$ for some constant γ (its value does not affect the outcome). We have, for a codeword with coordinate x,

$$E[(u - x)^2] = \int_0^1 (u - x)^2 p(u) \mathrm{d}u = \gamma \int_0^1 (u - x)^2 e^{-2u} \mathrm{d}u,$$

which has the form $f(x) = ax^2 + bx + c$, after integration by parts. Because $a > 0$ the minimum occurs when $\mathrm{d}f/\mathrm{d}x = 0$, i.e. when $x = -b/2a = (e^2 - 3)/(2(e^2 - 1))$. Thus $\hat{x}(S_i) = 0.34$ approx., which is *not* the midpoint of the interval $[0, 1]$ as it would be in the uniform case.

Notation 18.54 We suppose the values of u lie in a set S partitioned into M subsets $S_1, \ldots, S_M$ and that in each S_i a codeword x_i has been chosen. Let E_i denote expected value when u is restricted to S_i. We show that, with every u in S_i quantised to $q(u) = x_i$ $(1 \leq i \leq M)$, the overall mean distortion is

$$E[d] = \sum_{i=1}^M E_i[d(u, x_i)] P(U \in S_i). \tag{18.70}$$

Proof Consider the discrete case of $p(u)$ (the continuous is similar). Let $f(u)$ be the function on S defined by $f(u) = d(u, x_i)$ if $x \in S_i$. Then the overall expected distortion is $\sum_u f(u) p(u)$ which splits into sums over the S_i separately as

$$\sum_i \sum_{S_i} f(u) p(u) = \sum_i \sum_{S_i} f(u) P(U = u | U \in S_i) P(U \in S_i)$$
$$= \sum_i E_i[f(u)] P(U \in S_i).$$

Theorem 18.55 *The mean distortion $E[d]$ is not increased by Steps A or B.*

Proof for Step A: improving the partition We exchange the existing partition for the Voronoi one. Before, each u was quantised to some codeword, now it is sent to the nearest one. Hence the mean distortion cannot increase. *Step B: improving the codewords*. We are given a partition $\{S_i\}$ and codewords x_i. In each S_i we exchange x_i for the distortion-minimising $\hat{x}(S_i)$. Thus, by definition, $E_i[d(u, \hat{x}(S_i))] \leq E_i[d(u, x_i)]$, and so by (18.70) the overall mean distortion $E[d]$ does not increase.

ALGO 18.6 LBG Quantiser based on a distribution, or on training vectors

Initialisation Set the value of M, codewords $x_1, \ldots, x_M$, a *distortion threshold* $\varepsilon \geq 0$, and a maximum number MAX of iterations. Set $m = 0$ and $D_0 = \infty$.

REPEAT ($m = 1, 2, 3, \ldots$)
   Change the current partition to Voronoi (Step A)
   Compute the mean distortion $D_m = E[d]$ by (18.70) or (18.71)
   If $(D_{m-1} - D_m)/D_m \leq \varepsilon$ then return current codewords
     else replace current codewords by $\{\hat{x}(S_i)\}$ (Step B)
UNTIL return has occurred or $m = MAX$.

Remarks 18.56 (1) (*Using training vectors*) Suppose we are to simulate the distribution of u by N training vectors. Then, unlike in the k-means method, Steps A and B straightforwardly involve all N vectors at every iteration, as does the mean distortion,

$$E[d] = \tfrac{1}{N} \sum_{i=1}^{M} \sum_{u \in S_i} d(u, x_i). \tag{18.71}$$

(2) According to Theorem 18.55 we have in ALGO 18.6 that $D_0 \geq D_1 \geq D_2 \geq \cdots \geq 0$, whence (see e.g. Hoggar, 1992) D_m must converge to some limit D_∞. If this limit is reached, successive iterations produce no change, indeed a finite number of iterations suffice in the discrete case (Gray, Kieffer and Linde, 1980, page 188).

(3) The algorithm is valid for a wide range of pdfs and measures of distortion, an important advance on previous results. For more on this, see Linde, Buzo and Gray (1980). The case $k = 1$ is due to Lloyd (1957).

Example 18.57 (*The case $k = 2$, $M = 3$, $N = 55$*) For a simple example we set $k = 2$ so that both our 55 training vectors and the progressing codewords, three in number, may be illustrated in the plane. This is seen in Figure 18.52, where points quantised to the ith codeword are allocated the ith shading, for $i = 1, 2, 3$. Codewords are marked by a circle for clarity, their cluster of data points being obvious. The rate is

$$R = (\log_2 M)/k = 0.79 \text{ bits/symbol},$$

and only ten iterations are required to achieve a constant mean distortion of 3.46. The final codewords are $(2.33, 4.67)$, $(2.73, 8.86)$, $(6.94, 9.72)$.

Example 18.58 *The case $M = 2^k$ codewords ($k = 1, \ldots, 6$), with $N = 100\,000$ samples* This example investigates, for constant rate $R = 1$, the reduction in distortion as k increases from the scalar case $k = 1$ to a vector quantiser of block size $k = 6$. A Gaussian-generated sample of $100\,000$ was used (see Section 11.3.5 for how to do this). The number M of codewords to be used was determined by $1 = R = (\log_2 M)/k$, implying $M = 2^k$.

Results (after Linde, Buzo and Gray, 1980) are indicated in Figure 18.53. Notice that the lower bound distortion of Shannon's Theorem is only predicted to be approachable for arbitrary large k.

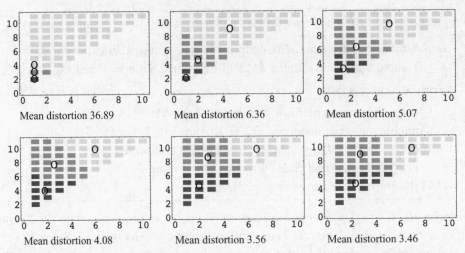

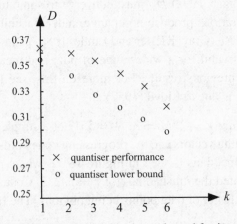

Figure 18.52 Movement of the three codewords 'O' towards their distortion-minimising positions, the start and then every second iteration. Rectangles represent the fixed training vectors; those quantised to the same codeword are shaded similarly, so that their requantisation may be easily observed as iteration proceeds.

Figure 18.53 Quantiser distortion and its lower bound for increasing block size.

Fortunately a lower bound for *finite k* was discovered by Yamada, Tazaki and Gray (1980, page 12 with $r = 2$), which may be written in the form

$$D^{(k)}(R) = D(R) \cdot \left\{ \frac{e}{1 + k/2} \Gamma(1 + k/2)^{2/k} \right\}. \tag{18.72}$$

For $\Gamma(z)$ see Section 9.3.6. Comparison with this bound is made in Figure 18.53: block length $k = 6$ gives a result within 6% of that optimal figure.

Example 18.59 *Comparison with k-means (see Section 18.2.2)* We refer to Figure 18.54 for this case, in which LBG required only three iterations to achieve its minimum squared distortion of 1614, in the case $\varepsilon = 0.1$. The distortion was reduced successively by taking

Original image   *k*-means method
128 × 128 pixels   Distortion 2034

LBG method ($\varepsilon = 0.1$)   LBG method ($\varepsilon = 0.01$)   LBG method ($\varepsilon = 0.001$)
Distortion 1614   Distortion 1549   Distortion 1494

Figure 18.54 LBG and *k*-means quantisation compared for an image of 128 × 128 pixels. As anticipated, the LBG algorithm achieves significantly smaller distortion. Surprisingly, the human visual system appears to prefer the *k*-means result (see discussion in the text). The first two images are reproduced from Figure 18.37. The original image is split into 1024 blocks of size 4 × 4, which are quantised to 128 codewords. Blocks are expressed as vectors of length $k = 16$.

$\varepsilon = 0.01$ and 0.001. The result in the latter case is perhaps acceptable visually, and yet the human visual system seems to prefer the more distorted *k*-means version. This raises the issue of how we ought to measure distortion in the case of natural images. A difficult question and the subject of much research. We give some indication of progress in the sequel.

Examples and developments

Some issues that emerge are: should one use a lattice quantiser, the LBG algorithm or Bayesian theory with prior knowledge of images; how can we define distortion so as to agree more closely with human visual perception of an image; what weight should we give to different kinds of visual information so that our system will best recognise human faces, medical clues, military vehicles etc? We cite below a selection of both books and papers which address these questions.

Advances in VQ – books and papers

Vector Quantization and Signal Compression (Gersho and Gray, 1992).
Information Theory: 50 years of Discovery (Verdú and McLaughlin, 2000).

(1) (*Lattices*) Lattice quantisers applied to non-Gaussian sources such as DCT coefficients of an image (see Section 15.4.2). Distortion results are good (Sayood, Gibson and Rost, 1984).

(2) (*Lattices*) Lattice quantisers are applied to wavelet coefficients of images. Low distortion results (da Silva, Sampson and Ghanbari, 1996).

(3) (*Complexity*) The authors use a sequence of codebooks in such a way that, following probabilistic considerations, they reduce calculational complexity and retain low distortion. Test images are natural scenes (Kossentini, Chung and Smith, 1996).

(4) (*Bayesian risk*) The authors observe that VQ can be viewed as a form of classification, since it assigns a single codeword to a group of input pixels. They use this idea to explore simultaneous compression and classification, applying the method of Bayesian risk (see Section 11.2). Their application is to CT lung images (Perlmutter *et al.*, 1996).

(5) (*VQ for medical images*) By using histograms based on a suitable number of medical examples, the authors obtain statistics for the DCT coefficients of such images. The results may be regarded as Laplacian (see Section 9.4.4) and deviations therefrom. Based on this they construct a VQ algorithm which gives good results for their application of interest, namely sections of the human heart (Mohsenian, Shahri and Nasrabadi, 1996).

VQ and human vision – books and papers

Digital Images and Human Vision (Watson, 1993)
Handbook of Medical Image Processing (Bankman, 2000)

(1) Extending LBG with free parameters that may be determined by subjective image quality (Wegmann and Zetzsche, 1996).

(2) Distortion measure for images using hypothesis testing techniques, with application to identifying signs of breast cancer (García *et al.*, 2003).

(3) Using rate distortion theory to quantify accuracy of an estimated object orientation as a function of codebook size (Dong and Carin, 2003).

(4) Quantising colour and spatial information simultaneously for face and object recognition, with distortion measured by Mahalanobis distance (see Section 12.8.2) (Walder and Lovell, 2003).

VQ and memory If we abandon the memoryless assumption for sources, a finer analysis can provide greater compression. Some approaches are: Wyner and Ziv (1971), stationary sources with memory; Davisson and Pursley (1975), direct proof of coding theorem; Lee and Laroia (2000), using Viterbi codebook; and Lu and Pearlman (2004, to appear), very fast algorithm.

18.4 Tomography

Suppose we want information about the internal structure of an object which we wish to avoid damaging, such as a human brain, or which we cannot reach, such as a distant black hole. Then a suitable probe is required, and Deans (1993) lists ten that have been used, including X-rays, gamma rays, the electron microscope, sound waves (e.g. ultrasound scanners), nuclear magnetic resonance (or NMR) and the radio waves of astronomy.

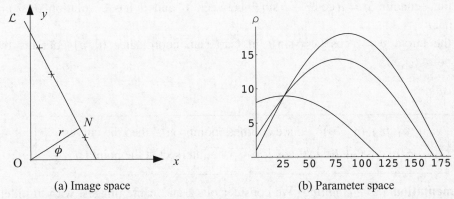

(a) Image space   (b) Parameter space

Figure 18.55 Three collinear points + in (x, y)-space (a) yield three intersecting curves in (θ, ρ)-space (b). They meet at approximately $\theta = 27°$, $\rho = 9$, in agreement with the line's equation $x/10 + y/20 = 1$.

Within all this, *tomography*, from Greek *tomos*, or slice, means to produce an image of a plane section of an object. In Computerised Tomography (CT), Computer Assisted Tomography (CAT) or Computerised Axial Tomography (also CAT) the desired image is reconstructed by a computer calculation from information generated by probes. More precisely how this is done, based on the famous transform of Radon (see Deans, 1993), will be described in Section 18.4.2. We begin with what was shown by Deans (1981) to be a special case, the remarkably useful transform of Hough (1962).

18.4.1 The Hough Transform

In its basic form the Hough Transform detected straight lines in images, originally particle tracks in a bubble chamber, but it can be generalised to detect almost any bounded plane object, as we shall see. Some sample applications are industrial: auto-inspection of biscuits, cakes etc., machine parts (Davies, 1997) and medical: vertebrae in X-ray images (Tezmol *et al.*, 2002).

Theory We construct a transform in which collinear points are sent to a single point. This begins with the observation that, as illustrated in Figure 18.55(a), an arbitrary line $\mathcal{L}$ in the (x, y)-plane has an equation in the form

$$\mathcal{L}: x \cos \phi + y \sin \phi = r \ (r \geq 0, 0 \leq \phi < 2\pi),\qquad(18.73)$$

where r is the distance $|ON|$ from the origin to $\mathcal{L}$, and ϕ is the angle between ON and the positive x-axis. Thus r and ϕ are determined uniquely from the line.

Exercise Verify that $(\theta, \rho) = (27, 9)$ correctly identifies the line in Figure 18.55.

We now argue as follows: $\mathcal{L}$ contains the point (a, b)

⇔ the equation $\rho = a\cos\theta + b\sin\theta$ between ρ and θ has a solution $(\theta, \rho) = (\phi, r)$

⇔ the curve $\rho = a\cos\theta + b\sin\theta$ in Cartesian coordinates (θ, ρ) contains the point (ϕ, r).

Conclusion

> if $(a_1, b_1), (a_2, b_2), \ldots$ are collinear points on $\mathcal{L}$ then the curves
> $\rho = a_i\cos\theta + b_i\sin\theta$ in (θ, ρ)-space intersect at the point (ϕ, ρ).

Implementation (*Vote counting*) We consider black and white images, with lit pixels as black. The (θ, ρ)-space is also called *parameter space* or Hough space. Suppose for each black pixel with coordinates (a, b) we plot in parameter space the curve $\rho = a\cos\theta + b\sin\theta$. Then the image with shot noise in Figure 18.56(a) results in Figure 18.56(b), in which a straight line (18.73) yields many curves through the corresponding point (ϕ, r). More precisely, since the line is drawn on a grid and therefore approximately, and because the values of θ and ρ are quantised, we get instead a small cloud of points with multiple hits. Each hit is termed a *vote*. Thus vote counting yields approximately the parameters ϕ, r of a line in the image. Figure 18.56(c) illustrates the small cloud of points forming predictably a 'butterfly' shape which facilitates a more accurate estimation of the values of ϕ, r.

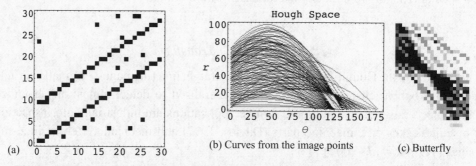

(a)   (b) Curves from the image points   (c) Butterfly

Figure 18.56 (a) Image of two lines plus shot noise, (b) the curves generated by black pixels of the image, each point shaded according to the number of curves passing through it, (c) the butterfly effect around a point corresponding to the pixels of an image line.

Unless lines are very short the Hough Transform picks them out even in the presence of other figures, such as circles, and much noise. This property of *robustness* is very advantageous, and carries over to the more general version we now describe.

The Generalised Hough Transform (GHT) For a time it was thought that the Hough Transform was no longer a research topic, until the realisation came that it was not just a trick that worked for one case but that its vote counting principle could be widely applied. For this, we consider images with continuously varying (though to be quantised) colour intensity. As exemplified in Figure 18.57, we compute for each edge pixel P a normal

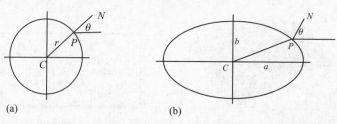

Figure 18.57 Two figures identified by vote-counting to determine their centres: (a) circle with given radius r, (b) ellipse with given parameters a, b. We take $c = P \pm (a\cos\phi, b\sin\theta)$, where $\tan\phi = (b/a)\tan\theta$ (Exercise 18.21).

direction PN and hence an estimated position of the object's centre C or other chosen reference point. This may be done analytically (by formula) or by a look-up table. Then vote counting over the edge pixels gives the position of C.

We use the Sobel matrices of Chapter 15, Example 15.28 to estimate the intensity gradients g_x, g_y at a point P, set $g = \sqrt{(g_x^2 + g_y^2)}$, and conclude that P *belongs to an edge* if g exceeds some threshold H. Then the normal vector PN at P makes an angle θ with the positive x-axis, where

$$(\cos\theta, \sin\theta) = (g_x, g_y)/g. \tag{18.74}$$

Remarks 18.60 (1) (*Sense of the normal*) In the absence of information as to which sense of the calculated normal is required we may simply allow both, and vote counting picks out the true centre with the others as noise.

(2) (*Orientation*) If we are only detecting the centre then the parameter space can be a copy of the image space. If, however, say in the case of an ellipse, we want to detect both centre and orientation, this may be handled by an extra parameter taking values $0, 1, \ldots, 359$, i.e. the parameter space goes up a dimension. But this entails an exponential increase in the number of points for computation, a highly undesirable situation.

An alternative solution is to keep the 2D parameter space but insert a centre for every possible orientation, at every edge point. Certainly in the case of an ellipse, as the analysis of Davies (1997) shows, the combined true centre and true orientation retain the popular vote and are clearly identified.

(3) (*Size*) We may replace orientation by size in the discussion above, but if we want to detect ellipses (say) of any *orientation and size* then the parameter space must be 3-dimensional.

(4) (*Probability*) A probabilistic analysis of the Hough Transform is carried out by Stephens (1991), whilst the *Randomised Hough Transform* (RHT) of Xu and Oja (1993) reduces computation by a probabilistic sampling of the data.

Excellent general references are Leavers (1992) and Davies (1997).

Example 18.61 Finding a circular cell of radius 28.5 units in a figure of dimensions 83×167. In this case we dispensed with the threshold H for gradient g and computed

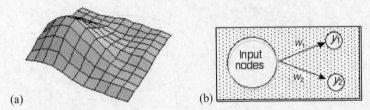

(a)   (b)

Figure 18.58 Finding the cell, given its radius 28.5. The image is 83×167 pixels. (a) Vote counting totals near the maximum, (b) the computed circle overlaid on the original image.

candidate centres from every point that yielded a nonzero gradient. Then an averaging step was performed in which each pixel was allocated the votes of the 3×3 block centred upon it. This yielded a unique maximum of 61, as indicated in Figure 18.58. Some nearby points had vote totals close to this, as may be expected, but the computed centre is fairly close to the true.

18.4.2 Tomography and the Radon Transform

In the medical and other spheres we need to know internal properties of a 3D object, say a heart or brain, whose interior we cannot directly access, or do not wish to disturb by doing so. A common approach is to build up a 3D picture from cross-sections, thus reducing the problem to inference about a thin slice – the literal meaning of tomography, as noted earlier. One solution is radiology, in which X-rays are projected through the slice in a series of straight lines (Figure 18.59), and the loss in power (*attenuation*) measured for each ray by exterior sensors. Will some mathematical theory enable us to infer a density distribution across the slice? The answer for this and many other forms of tomography begins with the observation that, for each ray, we are measuring the value of *density integrated along the ray's straight line path*. In the case of radiology this may be seen as follows.

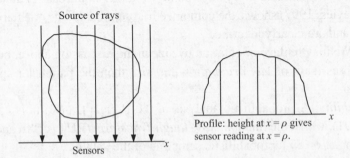

Figure 18.59 We represent one group of parallel rays sent through a slice, and the corresponding measurements. This is repeated for a series of equally spaced directions.

According to physical theory, if a ray of intensity I_0 travels a distance x through a homogeneous medium of *attenuation coefficient u*, the intensity drops to

$$I = I_0 e^{-ux}. \tag{18.75}$$

Thus if it traverses successive paths of lengths x_i through media of coefficients u_i, the emerging ray has intensity

$$I = I_0 e^{-u_1 x} e^{-u_2 x} \cdots e^{-u_n x} = I_0 e^{-\sum u_i x_i}.$$

If u varies continuously, modelled by letting n tend to infinity, then the sum becomes by definition an integral,

$$I = I_0 e^{-\int_L u(x) dx},$$

where L denotes the straight line path through the medium. Taking the logarithm to base e, of both sides, we obtain

$$\log I = \log I_0 + \log e^{-\int u(x) dx} = \log I_0 - \int u(x) dx, \text{ or}$$

$$\int u(x) dx = \log(I_0/I), \tag{18.76}$$

which is what we can measure by recording both I_0 and its attenuated version I by means of suitably placed sensors.

We wish to determine the values of a plane density function $f(x, y)$, given the integrals of f along certain lines L in the plane. Such an integral is also termed the *projection of f along L*. How many projections suffice to fix the 2-dimensional function f? In the continuous case, where (x, y) are real numbers, the answer is an infinity, and the Inverse Radon Transform converts these projections to the 2D function $f(x, y)$ (see Deans, 1993, Appendix A).

18.4.3 The Fourier method of reconstruction

Paradoxically, perhaps, it is by first investigating the continuous case that we are led to an appropriate discrete approximation through a projection property of the Fourier Transform. An especially simple discrete version was established in Example 15.11 for projection along lines parallel to the y-axis, where we found in that special case that an exact result holds. Of course, we cannot expect precision when non-rational sines and cosines are introduced as a consequence of arbitrary directions, but the continuous is the place to start. We may think of an arbitrary line L for projection as the result of rotating an arbitrary vertical line $x = \rho$ about the origin, through some angle ϕ, as depicted in Figure 18.60.

We now need the value of $f(x, y)$ at the arbitrary point P, with signed coordinate η measured along L from O' as indicated. But this point, given its position on L, is the

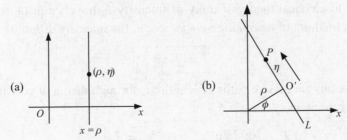

Figure 18.60 *Arbitrary line L obtained by rotating the line $x = \rho$ about O through angle ϕ.*

rotated image of (ρ, η), and so can be expressed by a matrix product $[\rho\ \eta]R$, where R is the rotation matrix given in (7.39),

$$R = \begin{bmatrix} \cos\phi & \sin\phi \\ -\sin\phi & \cos\phi \end{bmatrix}. \tag{18.77}$$

In these terms the *projection of f along L* is by definition

$$p_\phi(\rho) = \int_{-\infty}^{\infty} f([\rho\ \eta]R)\mathrm{d}\eta, \tag{18.78}$$

which, for given ϕ, is a function of ρ, with 1D Fourier Transform

$$\begin{aligned} P_\phi(u) &= \int_{-\infty}^{\infty} p_\phi(\rho)\mathrm{e}^{-2\pi iu\rho}\mathrm{d}\rho && \text{by (14.25)} \\ &= \int_{-\infty}^{\infty}\left(\int_{-\infty}^{\infty} f([\rho\ \eta]R)\mathrm{d}\eta\right)\mathrm{e}^{-2\pi iu\rho}\mathrm{d}\rho, && \text{by substituting (18.78)} \\ &= \int_{-\infty}^{\infty}\int_{-\infty}^{\infty} g(\rho, \eta)\mathrm{e}^{-2\pi i(\rho u + 0v)}\mathrm{d}\rho\,\mathrm{d}\eta, && \text{writing } g(\rho, \eta) = f([\rho\ \eta]R) \\ &= G(u, 0), \end{aligned}$$

where G is the Fourier Transform (15.10) of g. But g is obtained from f by rotating the coordinate pair $[\rho\ \eta]$, so by the Rotation Theorem (Corollary 15.8) we may write in turn

$$G(u, 0) = F([u\ 0]R) = F(u\cos\phi,\ u\sin\phi), \quad \text{by Formula (18.77)}.$$

We state our conclusion formally, then see how it may be used in practice.

Theorem 18.62 *(General projection property of the Fourier Transform) Let $p_\phi(\rho)$ be the projection of $f(x, y)$ along the line (ρ, ϕ): $x\cos\phi + y\sin\phi = \rho$ (see Figure 18.60(b)). If the 1D Fourier Transform of p_ϕ is $P_\phi(u)$, then the 2D Fourier Transform F of f satisfies*

$$F(u\cos\phi, u\sin\phi) = P_\phi(u) \quad (u \neq 0). \tag{18.79}$$

Approximation In principle the original function may be recovered as the inverse 2D Fourier Transform of F, where F is given by (18.79) (we'll see how to take care of the origin). The only obstacle to a discrete version is that F is thus specified at points given by polar coordinates, and we must in some way interpolate these values onto a uniform rectangular grid. We shall shortly adopt a simple bilinear approach.

Consider an image of $N \times N$ pixels, $N = 2n$, occupying an origin-centred square bounded by the four lines $x = \pm 1$ and $y = \pm 1$. We suppose a scale has been chosen so that the *grey values* $f(x, y)$ are zero outside and on the unit circle $x^2 + y^2 = 1$. Also, $f(x, y)$ is constant over each pixel, but nevertheless the integral of $f(x, y)$ along a *projection line* (ρ, ϕ) increases continuously as the line is traversed. The mesh/pixel width is $\Delta m = 1/n$, and a pixel with lower left coordinates $(i, j)\Delta m$ is labelled (i, j). An example is Figure 18.61(a).

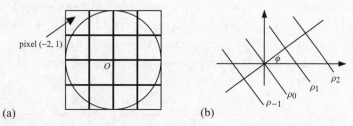

Figure 18.61 (a) In the simple case $n = 2$, the pixel $(-2, 1)$ must have value 0 since it lies partly outside the unit circle, (b) projection lines (ρ_r, ϕ) for $r = -1, 0, 1, 2$.

We divide the ranges $[-1, \ 1]$ of ρ and $[0, \pi]$ of ϕ into $N = 2n$ equal parts, with increments and discrete values therefore given by

$$\Delta \rho = \Delta m = 1/n, \quad \rho_r = r \Delta \rho, \quad -n \leq r \leq n, \tag{18.80a}$$

$$\Delta \phi = \pi / 2n, \quad \phi_s = s \Delta \rho, \quad 0 \leq s \leq n. \tag{18.80b}$$

Now we are ready to invoke the Projection Theorem. For every fixed ϕ_s we have the following equality of $2n$-vectors:

$$F(\rho_r \cos \phi_s, \ \rho_r \sin \phi_s)_{-n \leq r \leq n-1} = P_{\phi_s}(\rho_r)_{-n \leq r \leq n-1} \qquad \text{by (18.79)}$$
$$= \Delta \rho \times \text{DFT of } p_{\phi_s}(\rho_r)_{-n \leq r \leq n-1} \text{ (approx),}$$

where the DFT approximation to the Continuous Fourier Transform comes from the Trapezium Rule for integration, which holds in this finite form because $p_\phi(\rho)$ is zero for ρ outside the finite interval $[-1, \ 1]$ and at its end-points (see Section 14.3.2).

Computing the projections Let the constant grey value on pixel (i, j) be denoted by f_{ij}. If a line (ρ, ϕ) crosses the pixel, entering at P_0 and leaving at P_1, the contribution to projection along this line is $|P_0 P_1| f_{ij}$, as in Figure 18.62. Should the line lie along the common boundary of adjacent pixels, a decision is required. We could use the mean grey value of the two pixels, but this would model two pixels of equal value, a potential blurring effect. It seems preferable to adopt a consistent choice of one pixel or the other as contributor, and Figure 18.62 indicates that we choose the pixel to the right of a vertical line and that above a horizontal one, i.e. we take the greater i or j where there is a choice.

Further methods

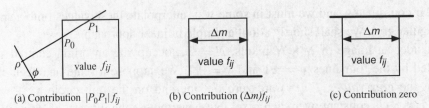

(a) Contribution $|P_0 P_1| f_{ij}$ (b) Contribution $(\Delta m) f_{ij}$ (c) Contribution zero

Figure 18.62 How the pixel at position (i, j) with grey value f_{ij} contributes to projection along the line (ρ, ϕ), if (a) the line enters at P_0 and exits at P_1, (b), (c) it lies along an edge.

Calculating the projection can become complicated. Here is a simple algorithm for determining the intercept of the line (ρ_r, ϕ_s) on the pixel (i, j), applicable to all cases. It is based on the formula $(1 - t)A + tB$ for the points of the extended line through A, B, in which $0 \leq t \leq 1$ identifies those points on the segment AB itself (see Section 17.1.2 and/or (1.3) of Chapter 1).

ALGO 18.7 Intercept of line (ρ_r, ϕ_s) on pixel (i, j)

Input r, s, n, i, j and set *meets* = {} (this is to be P_0, P_1)
$v = (\cos(s\pi/2n), \sin(s\pi/2n))$
verts = {$(i, j), (i, j + 1), (i + 1, j + 1), (i + 1, j)$} (cyclic order of vertices)
REPEAT four times
    {A, B} = first two vertices
    $t = (r - A \cdot v)/((B - A) \cdot v)$
    If $0 \leq t \leq 1$ then append $(tB + (1 - t)A)/n$ to *meets*
    Cycle *verts* one place to left
meets = Union(*meets*) (removes any duplicates)
If $|meets| < 2$ OR both *meets* have $y = (j + 1)/n$ OR both have $x = (i + 1)/n$,
then return zero (see Figure 18.62(c)),
else set {$P_0 P_1$} = *meets* and return $\sqrt{[(P_0 - P_1) \cdot (P_0 - P_1)]}$

Exercise Derive the expression for t in ALGO 18.7 (Exercise 18.22).

Interpolating for $F(x, y)$ We must handle the fact that the sequences $f_{-n}, \ldots, f_{n-1}$ to which we are to apply the DF do not have their origin at the start, the required position for our standard version $F_k = \sum_{r=0}^{N-1} f_r w^{rk}$ ($w = e^{2\pi i/N}$, $N = 2n$). Instead we should take $F_k = \sum_{r=-n}^{n-1} f_r w^{rk}$. But this is easily achieved: cycle f back n places, apply the standard DFT, then cycle forward n places. A similar remark applies to the inverse DFT, and in two dimensions we simply apply the cycle to both dimensions (see Section 15.1.2)

Thus we compute the values of $F(x, y)$ at the points with polar coordinates (ρ_r, ϕ_s) for $-n \leq \rho \leq n - 1, 0 \leq s \leq n - 1$. These points, all circle–radius intersections, are illustrated in Figure 18.63(a) for the case $n = 4$. The intersections needed for interpolation but not explicitly accounted for have $F = 0$, arising from the arrangement that

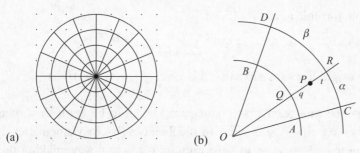

(a)   (b)

Figure 18.63 (a) The case $n = 4$: the radius–circle intersections at which $F(x, y)$ is known, and the rectangular grid points for which it must be interpolated (or is known to be zero). (b) Sandwiching a grid point P between concentric circles $\rho = \rho_r, \rho_{r+1}$, and between successive radius vectors OC, OD at angles ϕ_s, ϕ_{s+1} to the x-axis.

nonzero-valued pixels are restricted to the interior of the unit circle (the largest circle in Figure 18.63(a)). This excludes the origin, a special case dealt with in Remarks 18.63 below. Referring to Figure 18.63, let f_X denote the value of f at a point X. Then linear interpolation along QR specifies that

$$\frac{f_R - f_P}{f_P - f_Q} = \frac{t}{q} \quad \text{or, on rearranging,} \quad f_P = \frac{q f_R + t f_Q}{q + r},$$

where q denotes the length of QP and t the length of PR. Similarly, linear interpolation along the arcs AQB and CRD gives

$$f_Q = \frac{\alpha f_B + \beta f_A}{\alpha + \beta} \quad \text{and} \quad f_R = \frac{\alpha f_D + \beta f_C}{\alpha + \beta}.$$

Substituting these in the expression for f_P completes our bilinear interpolation formula (notice that $\alpha + \beta = \Delta\phi$ and $q + t = \Delta\rho$):

$$f_P = \frac{q(\alpha f_D + \beta f_C) + t(\alpha f_B + \beta f_A)}{(\alpha + \beta)(q + t)}. \tag{18.81}$$

Remarks 18.63 (*What to do at the origin*) The central value seems to present a problem for F since each of the $2n$ directions in which we computed a 1-dimensional DFT offers its own value for $F_{0,0}$. We could in hope take their average, but the following arguments show that any value will do for our purposes, so it may as well be zero.

(1) The origin is not used in the interpolation process for any other grid point P, because OP is longer than $\Delta\rho$ (see Exercise 18.22) and so P lies between two circles away from the origin as in Figure 18.63(b) above.

(2) Adding a constant δ to $F_{0,0}$ has the effect of adding the same constant δ/N^2 to every value $f(x, y)$, on applying the (2D) inverse DFT to $F(x, y)$. This is sometimes referred to as *impulse becomes constant under the DFT*. To prove it, since the DFT is linear, we need only show that if F_{ij} is zero except for $F_{0,0} = 1$ then $f_{ij} = 1/N^2$ for all

i, j. A suitable formula to use is (15.7):

$$f_{ij} = (1/N^2) \sum_{m,p} F_{mp} w^{-(mi+pj)}. \tag{18.82}$$

Provided the origin has subscripts 0, 0 this gives $f_{ij} = (1/N^2)F_{0,0}w^{-(0i+0j)} = 1/N^2$ as required.

(3) Finally, the true outer pixel values are known to be zero, so if their calculated mean value is γ we simply subtract γ from all values (but in Mathematica, for example, the values are translated so as to have minimum zero anyway, making this correction unnecessary).

Example 18.64 (*Pre-interpolation*) Consider the case $n = 4$ with just one nonzero pixel value, 100, at the origin. Write down the projections $p_\phi(\rho_r)$ for $s = 2$ and apply the DFT.

Solution We are to take $\phi = s\Delta\phi = 2(\pi/8)$. As seen in the partial diagram (Figure 18.64), $p_\phi(\rho_r)$ is nonzero only when $r = 1$. By elementary geometry, the required intercept for a unit square would be $2(\sqrt{2} - 1)$, so here it is $2(\sqrt{2} - 1)/4 = 0.207$. Thus $p_\phi(\rho_r)_{-4 \le r \le 3} = (0, 0, 0, 0, 0, 20.7, 0, 0)$. For the DFT we have the situation $f = (0, \dots, 0, 1, 0, \dots, 0)$ ($f_1 = 1$), whence

$F_k = \sum_r f_r w^{rk}$ ($w = e^{-\pi i/4}$) $= f_1 w^k$, and in this case

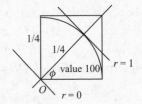

Figure 18.64 Solution of Example 18.64.

$$P_\phi = 20.7(w^{-4}, w^{-3}, \dots, w^0, \dots, w^3). \tag{18.83}$$

By plotting these powers around a circle (see e.g. Figure 14.2 of Chapter 14) we can easily write each in the form $(\pm 1 \pm i)/\sqrt{2}$. Note the simplification $w^4 = w^{-4} = -1$.

Example 18.65 It is time for a reconstruction trial. We begin with the simple square of Figure 18.65, all pixel boundaries shown.

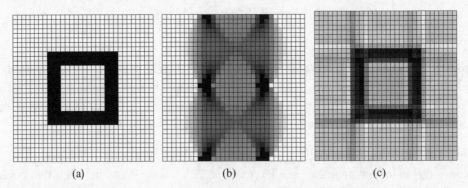

(a)   (b)   (c)

Figure 18.65 (a) Original 32×32 pixel image, (b) projection profiles $p_\phi(\rho_r)$, represented as rows of grey values, (c) the reconstructed image.

Example 18.66 Figure 18.66 is a more seriously sized case at 64×64 pixels, a not-too-well contrasted heart-type image.

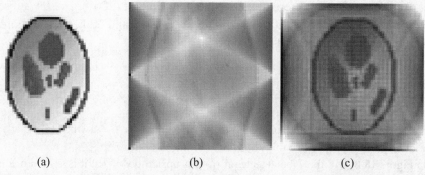

| (a) | (b) | (c) |

Figure 18.66 (a) Original 64 × 64 pixel image, (b) projection profiles represented as rows of grey values, (c) the reconstructed image.

18.4.4 Further developments

Gridding We have presented the basic Fourier Transform approach to reconstructing an image from its projections. It works because of the Fourier Projection Property (18.79). It is fast because of its implementation by the FFT (Fast Fourier Transform, Section 14.1.4). A drawback is the need for interpolation from (ρ, ϕ) to (x, y) coordinates, which reduces accuracy compared with some competing methods (see e.g. Deans, 1993).

However, this problem was solved by O'Sullivan (1985), who used the Fourier Convolution Property to replace interpolation by the more general *gridding*, in which the original greyscale function is considered to be convolved with a sinc function (see Figure 14.13) and resampled at the grid points. The values obtained are not necessarily good interpolants, but the Fourier-inverted result *is* accurate provided the region of interest lies in a rectangle whose width and height are half those of the original image.

Gridding became a standard method. Amongst further developments, Jackson *et al.* (1991) compared use of the sinc funtion with other candidates such as Gaussians, and found that improvements were possible in some circumstances. A detailed analysis by Sedarat and Nishimura (2000) showed that it could be improved by introducing and optimising certain extra parameters.

Probabilistic approaches The approach via probability is well illustrated in a recent paper of Denisova (2004), who remarks that statistical reconstructed methods are becoming standard in tomography. The general approach is the MAP, or maximum a posteriori algorithm (see Section 11.4.6), using a Markov Random Field to model the (in this case) emitted photons. As with Sedarat and Nishimura, the optimisation of parameters is an objective. In an earlier paper, Ding and Liu (1996) use the MAP approach to focus on edges in the image. We are well-prepared for the probabilistic theory since Chapter 11.

Higher dimensions Certain forms of tomography lend themselves to a 3D approach, as distinct from building up slices. Examples are Positron Emission Tomography (PET) and Nuclear Magnetic Resonance (NMR). The analogue of the Projection Theorem in one higher dimension is used and, after a version of gridding, we apply the 3-dimensional

Fourier Transform. Useful references are Matej and Lewitt (2001), and the subsequent development by Matej *et al.* (2004). The 3D Transform and Projection Theorem are covered in Chapter 15, Section 15.5.2.

Exercises 18

1 √ Draw McCulloch–Pitts networks for $f(x, y, z)$ in the cases $f = 1$ when (a) exactly one of x, y, z is 1, (b) exactly two of x, y, z are 1, (c) all three are 1.

2 √ In Figure 18.6, will the T be detected if (a) it is upside-down, (b) it is shifted one pixel to the left (in a suitably enlarged array), (c) its three extremities are lost?

3 √ Can the plane sets $S = \{(1, 2.5), (3, 4.5)\}$, $T = \{(2, 4.1), (4, 6.3)\}$ be linearly separated (draw lines through the points of S and of T)? If so, find a separating line and write down the weights and threshold of a corresponding perceptron cell.

4 √ (Convergence of perceptron learning) In the proof of Theorem 18.3, what do (18.5) and (18.6) become if we do not assume $w(0) = 0$? Combine them to get the inequality noted after the main proof.

5 √ (a) Perform two cycles of the Perceptron Learning Algorithm (ALGO 18.1) for input vectors $(x_1, x_2) = (1, 0), (0, 1), (0, 0), (1, 1)$ with respective targets $1, 1, 1, -1$. (b) Implement ALGO 18.1 to add in $x_0 = 1$ for input vectors, run (a), check your calculation, and show the final result in the (x, y)-plane.

6 (Section 18.1.4) Implement ALGO 18.2 for backpropagation and hence obtain a 2-layer perceptron net which reproduces the XOR function (cf Example 18.10).

7 √ (Section 18.1.5) Check the details for arriving at an expression for α in Example 18.12.

8 √ (Section 18.1.6.) (a) Deduce the expression $\mathcal{E}_{\text{avecom}} = (1/N^2) \sum E[\varepsilon_i(x)^2]$ in the case of uncorrelated errors. (b) Show that in the correlated case we still have $\mathcal{E}_{\text{avecom}} = \mathcal{E}_{\text{ave}}$, as stated in (18.20).

9 Compute the PCA vectors for the car of Example 18.17, using the algorithm of Equation (18.28), with learning parameter 0.2, 0.15, 0.1, 0.05, 0.01, 0.001. Compare the results for speed and accuracy.

10 √ (a) Show that for fixed points $a_1, \ldots, a_N$ in n-space the sum of squared deviations from a point x is least when x is the mean, $(1/N) \sum a_i$. (b) Derive the k-means update formula (18.30) from the paragraph preceding it. (c) Apply the k-means algorithm, ALGO 18.3, to a small face using 8×8 versus 4×4 blocks in the manner of Figures 18.36 and 18.37.

11 (a) Use Equation (18.32) to generate 1000 points of the right-angled triangle with vertices $(0, 0), (1, 0), (0, 1)$. (b) Apply the Kohonen method of Figure 18.42 to generate a preliminary stage of a space-filling curve in your triangle.

12 √ (Section 18.3.1) (a) Prove from the definitions that $I(X; Y) = h(X) - h(X|Y) = h(Y) - h(Y|X)$. (b) Prove that $\frac{1}{2} \sum_i (\log 2\pi\sigma_i^2 + 1) = \frac{n}{2} \log 2\pi e(\sigma_1^2 \cdots \sigma_n^2)^{1/n}$ (used in the proof of Theorem 18.29).

13 √ (Section 18.3.1) (a) For what values of $|Q|$ is the differential entropy of a Gaussian random vector positive? (b) Deduce (18.39) from the case $n = 1$ (hint: Theorem 18.24).

14 √ (Section 18.3.3) Let A be a real symmetric matrix with eigenvalues λ_j. (a) Show that $A^{-1} = P \operatorname{diag}[\lambda_j^{-1}] P^{-1}$ for some matrix P. (b) Show that A^2 commutes with its derivative

with respect to any variable. (c) Show that if a set of training vectors X of length n span real n-space then $R = \langle X X^T \rangle$ is positive definite.

15 $\sqrt{}$ (a) (Proof of Fano's Inequality) Show that $G(0) = 1$ and $G(1) = r - 1$ for the function $G(z) = \sum_{x,y} p(y) p(z|x, y)$, where X, Y take the same r values and $Z = 0$ if $X = Y$, otherwise $Z = 1$. (b) (Example 18.46) A channel (U, V) satisfies $p(u|v) = D$ if $u \neq v$, where $0 \leq D \leq 1$. Show that $H(U|V) = H(D)$.

16 $\sqrt{}$ (a) Let U be in $N(0, s^2)$ and define a channel (U, V) by $V = 0$. Show that $h(U|V) = h(U)$. (b) Deduce (18.69) from (18.66) and (18.67).

17 $\sqrt{}$ Prove that (a) $h(X|\alpha Y) = |\alpha| h(X|Y)$, and (b) $h(X + Y|Y) = h(X|Y)$, then deduce (c) $h(X - Y|Y) = h(X|Y)$.

18 $\sqrt{}$ (a) Find the position x of a codeword to minimise its sum of squared distances from points $x_1, \ldots, x_M$ in n-space (take any valid shortcuts). (b) Find the position of a codeword to minimise expected squared distance from points u in $[a, b]$ uniformly distributed. (c) Repeat for the interval $[0, 1]$ and $p(u)$ proportional to e^{-u}.

19 Implement ALGO 18.6, then compare LBG and k-means results for the face of Exercise 18.10.

20 $\sqrt{}$ (a) Verify that the curve intersection $\theta = 27°$, $\rho = 9$ in Figure 18.55(b) correctly identifies the line $x/10 + y/20 = 1$. (b) Take three points on the line $x/8 + y/5 = 1$ and show that the common point of the three corresponding curves identifies the line.

21 $\sqrt{}$ An ellipse with centre (p, q) has a parametric form $(p, q) + (a \cos \phi, b \sin \phi)$ $(0 \leq \phi \leq 2\pi)$ (circle squeezed by factor b/a in y-direction). Verify this and use it to derive the formula for the centre given at Figure 18.57.

22 $\sqrt{}$ (a) (Section 18.4.2) Why does the bilinear interpolation in Figure 18.63 not involve the origin? (b) Derive the expression for the parameter t in ALGO 18.7.

References

Aggarval, J. K. and Cai, Q. (1999), Human motion analysis, a review, *Computer Vision and Image Understanding* **73**, 428–440.

Ahmed, N., Natarajan, T. and Rao, K. R. (1974), Discrete Cosine Transform, *IEEE Trans. on Computers* **23**, 90–93.

Anson, L. A. (1993) Fractal Image Compression, *Byte Magazine*, October 1993.

Avnir, D. and Pfeifer, P. (1983), Fractal dimension in chemistry, *Nouv. J. Chim.* **7**, 71–72.

Baldi, P. and Hornik, K. (1999), Neural networks and principal component analysis: learning from examples without local minima, *Neural Networks* **2**, 53–58.

Baldock, R. and Graham, J. (2000), *Image Processing and Analysis, a Practical Approach*, Oxford University Press.

Bankman, I. N., ed. (2000), *Handbook of Medical Image Processing*, Academic Press.

Barnsley, M. F. (1992) *Fractals Everywhere*, 2nd edn., Academic Press.

Barnsley, M. F. and Hurd, L. P. (1994), *Fractal Image Compression*, A. K. Peters.

Barnsley, M. F. and Sloan, A. D. (1988), A better way to compress images, *Byte Magazine*, January 1988.

Barron, A., Rissanen, J. and Yu, B. (1998), The minimum description length principle in coding and modelling, *IEEE Trans. on Information Theory*, **44**, 2743–2760.

Becker, S. (1992), An Information-Theoretic Unsupervised Learning Algorithm for Neural Networks, Ph.D. Thesis, University of Toronto, Department of Computer Science.

Becker, S. and Hinton, G. E. (1992), A self-organizing neural network that discovers surfaces in random-dot stereograms, *Nature* (London) **355**, 161–163.

(1993), Learning mixture models of spatial coherence, *Neural Computation* **5**, 267–277.

Beer, P. and Roy, A. E. (eds.) (1990), *Fractals in Astronomy*. Special issue of *Vistas in Astronomy*, Vol. **33** Part 3/4.

Behnke, S. (2003), *Hierarchical Neural Networks for Image Interpretation*, Springer Lecture Notes in Computer Science, 2766.

Bell, A. J. and Sejnowski, T. J. (1995), An information-maximization approach to blind separation and blind deconvolution, *Neural Computation* **7**, 1129–1159.

Berger, T. (1971), *Rate Distortion Theory*, Prentice-Hall.

Berlekamp, E. (1974), *Key Papers in the Development of Coding Theory*, IEEE Press.

Berrou, C. and Glavieux, A. (1996), Near optimum error correcting coding and decoding: turbo-codes. *IEEE Trans. on Communications* **44**, 1261–1271.

Berrou, C., Glavieux, A. and Thitimajshima, P. (1993), Near Shannon limit error-correcting coding and decoding: turbo-codes. In *Proceedings of the IEEE International Conference on Communications*.

Bertram, M. (2004), Biorthogonal loop-subdivision wavelets. *Computing* **72**, 29–39.

Bertram, M., Duchaineau, M. A., Hamann, B. and Joy, K. I. (2000), Bicubic subdivision-surface wavelets for large-scale isosurface representation and visualization, *IEEE Proc. Visualization 2000*, 389–396, 579.

(2004), Generalized B-spline subdivision-surface wavelets for geometry compression. *IEEE Trans. on Visualization and Computer Graphics* **10**, 326–338.

Besag, J. (1974), Spatial interaction and the statistical analysis of lattice systems, *J. R. Statist. Soc.* B **32**, 192–236.

(1986), On the statistical analysis of dirty pictures, *J. R. Statist. Soc.* B **48**, 259–302.

(2000), *Markov Chain Monte Carlo for Statistical Inference*, Working Paper No. 9, Centre for Statistics and Social Sciences, University of Washington, USA.

Bézier, P. (1966) Définition numérique des courbes et surfaces I, *Automatisme*, **XI**, 625–632 (also **XII** (1967), 17–21).

(1972) *Numerical Control: Mathematics and Applications*, Wiley. Translated from original French text by A. R. Forrest.

Birkhoff, G. and MacLane, S. (1963) *A Survey of Modern Algebra*, 3rd edn. Macmillan.

Bishop, C. M. (1995), *Neural Networks for Pattern Recognition*, Oxford University Press.

Blahut, R. E. (1972), Computation of channel capacity and rate distortion functions, *IEEE Trans. on Information Theory*, **IT-18**, 460–473.

(1987), *Principles and Practice of Information Theory*, Addison-Wesley.

Born, M. and Wolf, E. (1999), *Principles of Optics* (7th edn.), Cambridge University Press.

Bose, R. C. and Ray-Chaudhuri, D. K. (1960), On a class of error correcting binary group codes, *Information & Control* **3**, 68–79.

Boss, R. D. and Jacobs, E. W. (1991) *Studies of Iterated Transform Image Compression, and Its Application to Colour and DTED*, Technical Report 1468, Naval Ocean Systems Center, San Diego, CA.

Bracewell, R. N. (1986), *The Fourier Transform and Its Applications*, McGraw-Hill.

Briggs, W. L. and Henson, Van E. (1995), *The DFT: An Owner's Manual for the Discrete Fourier Transform*, SIAM.

Brigham, E. O. (1988), *The Fast Fourier Transform and Its Applications*, Prentice-Hall.

Brislawn, C. M. (1995) Fingerprints go digital, *Notices of the AMS* **42**, 1278–1283.

Brivio, P. A. and Marini, D. (1993) A fractal method for digital elevation model construction and its application to a mountain region, *Computer Graphics Forum* **12**, 297–309.

Bruce, V., Green, P. R. and Georgeson, M. A. (1996), *Visual Perception*, Psychology Press.

Burrough, P. A. (1981), Fractal dimension of landscapes and other environmental data, *Nature* (London), **294**, 204–242.

Burt, P. J. and Adelson, E. H. (1983), The Laplacian pyramid as a compact image code, *IEEE Trans. Comm.* **31**, 532–540.

Canny, J. (1986), A computational approach to edge-detection. *IEEE Trans. on Pattern Analysis and Machine Intelligence* **PAMI-8**, 679–698.

Capocelli, R. M., Giancarlo, R. and Taneja, I. J. (1986), Bounds on the redundancy of Huffman codes, *IEEE Trans. on Information Theory*, **IT-32**, 854–857.

Castleman, K. R. (1996), *Digital Image Processing*, Prentice-Hall.

Catmull, E. and Clark, J. (1978) Recursively generated B-spline surfaces on arbitrary topological meshes. *Computer-Aided Design* **10**(6), 350–355.

Chaikin, G. M. (1974) An algorithm for high speed curve generation, *Computer Graphics & Image Processing* **3**(4), 346–349.

Chaitin, G. J. (1966), On the length of programs for computing finite binary sequences, *J. ACM* **13**, 547–569.

(1975), A theory of program size formally identical to information theory, *J. ACM* **22**, 329–340.

Clarke, R. J. (1981), On the relation between the Karhunen–Loève and cosine transforms, *IEE Proceedings Part F: Commun. Radar, Signal Processing* **128**, 359–360.

Conway, J. H. and Sloane, N. J. A. (1988), *Sphere Packings, Lattices, and Groups*, Springer-Verlag.

Cooley, J. W. and Tukey, J. W. (1965), An algorithm for the machine calculation of complex Fourier series. *Math. of Comp.* **19**, 297–301.

Cootes, T. F., Taylor, C. J., Cooper, D. H. and Graham, J. (1995), Active shape models – their training and application, *Computer Vision and Image Understanding* **61**, 38–59.

Cover, T. M. and Thomas, J. S. (1991), *Elements of Information Theory*, Wiley Interscience.

Cox, M. G. (1972) The numerical evaluation of B-splines. *J. Inst. Maths. Applics.* **10**, 134–149.

Coxeter, H. S. M. (1973) *Regular Polytopes*. 2nd edn. Collier-Macmillan, New York, 1963; 3rd edn., Dover, New York, 1973.

(1974) *Regular Complex Polytopes*. Cambridge University Press.

(1987) (Co-editor) M. C. Escher: Art and Science. *Proceedings of the International Congress on M. C. Escher, Rome, 1985*. 2nd edn. Elsevier Science Publishing.

Critchlow, K. (1976) *Islamic Patterns. An Analytical and Cosmological Approach*. Schocken Books, Thames & Hudson.

Culik, K. and Kari, J. (1993), Image compression using weighted finite automata. *Computers and Graphics* **17**, 305–313.

Cunningham, P., Carney, J. and Jacob, S. (2000), Stability problems with artificial neural networks and the ensemble solution, *Artificial Intelligence in Medicine* **20**, 217–225.

da Silva, A. B., Sampson, D. G. and Ghanbari, M. (1996), A successive approximation vector quantizer for wavelet transform image coding, *IEEE Trans. on Image Processing* **5**, 299–310.

Darrel, T. and Pentland, A. (1995), Cooperative robust estimation using layers of support, *IEEE Trans. Pattern Analysis and Machine Intelligence* **17**, 474–487.

Daubechies, I. (1988) Orthonormal bases of compactly supported wavelets, *Comm. Pure and Applied Math.* **41**, 909–996.

(1992) *Ten Lectures on Wavelets*, SIAM.

Daugman, J. (1985), Uncertainty relation for resolution in space, spatial frequency, and orientation optimised by two-dimensional visual cortex filters, *J. Opt. Soc. Amer.* **2**, 1160–1169.

Davies, E. R. (1997), *Machine Vision: Theory, Algorithms, Practicalities*. Academic Press.

Davies, R. H., Coores, T. F., Twining, C. J. and Taylor, C. J. (2001), An information theoretic approach to statistical shape modelling. *Proc. British Machine Vision Conference 2001*. BMVA.

Davisson, L. D. and Pursley, M. B. (1975), A direct proof of the coding theorem for discrete sources with memory, *IEEE Trans. on Information theory*, **IT-21**, 310–317.

de Boor, C. (1972) On calculating with B-splines, *J. Approx. Theory* **6** (1), 50–62.

Deans, S. R. (1981), Hough Transform from the Radon Transform, *IEEE Trans. on Pattern Analysis and Imaging*, **PAMI-3**, 185–188.

Deans, S. R. (1993), *The Radon Transform and Some of Its Applications*, Krieger.

Denison, D. G. T., Mallick, B. K. and Smith, A. F. M. (1998), Automatic Bayesian curve fitting, *J. R. Statist. Soc.* **60**, 333–350.

Denisova, N. V. (2004), Bayesian reconstruction in SPECT with entropy prior and iterative statistical regularization, *IEEE Trans. on Nuclear Science* **51**, 136–141.

Devaney, B. (1989) *The Harmony Guide to Colourful Machine Knitting*. Lyric Books, Hodder & Stoughton.

Diamantaris, K. I. and Kung, S. Y. (1996), *Principal Component Neural Networks*, Wiley-Intersience.

Ding, W. and Liu, B. (1996), Tomographic image sequence reconstruction by edge-preserving interslice MAP methods, *IEEE Trans. Image Processing* **5**, 178–183.

Djamdji, A., Bijaoui, A. and Manière, R. (1993a), Geometrical registration of images: the multiscale approach, *Photogramm. Eng. & Remote Sensing* **59**, 645–653.

(1993b), Geometrical registration of remotely sensed images with the use of the wavelet transform, *SPIE Int. Symposium on Optical Engineering and Phototonics, Orlando*, Vol. 1938, 412–422.

Djurle, E. & Bäck, A. (1961), Some measurements of the effect of air turbulence on photographic images, *J. Opt. Soc. of Amer.* **51**, 1029–1030.

Dobkin, D. P. (1988) Computational geometry – then and now. In *Theoretical Foundations of Computer-Graphics and CAD*, NATO ASI series F40 (R. A. Earnshaw, Ed.). Springer-Verlag.

Dong, Y. and Carin, L. (2003), Rate-distortion analysis of discrete-HMM pose estimation via multiaspect scattering data, *IEEE Trans. on Pattern Analysis and Machine Intelligence* **25**, 872–883.

Doo, D. W. H. and Sabin, M. (1978) Behaviour of recursive division surfaces near extraordinary points, *Computer-Aided Design* **10**(6), 356–360.

Draper, B. A. and Baek, K. (2000), Unsupervised learning of biologically plausible object recognition strategies, *Springer Lecture Notes in Computer Science* **1811**, 238–247.

Dryden, I. L. and Mardia, K. V. (1998), *Statistical Shape Analysis*, John Wiley.

Eck, M., DeRose, T., Duchamp, T., Hoppe, H., Lounsbery, J. M. and Stuetzle, W. (1995), Multiresolution analysis of arbitrary meshes. *Proceedings of SIGGRAPH '95*, 173–182. ACM Press.

Edelman, S., Intrator, N. and Jacobson, J. S. (2002), Unsupervised learning of visual structure, Springer *Lecture Notes in Computer Science* **2525**, 629–642.

Edmonds, J. and Karp, R. M. (1972), Theoretical improvements in algorithmic efficiency for network flows, *J. ACM* **19**, 248–264.

Eels, J. and Lemaire, L. (1988), Another report on harmonic maps. *Bull. London Math. Soc.* **20**, 385–524.

Elias, P. (1955), Coding for noisy channels, *IRE Convention Record* **4**, 37–47.

Escher, M. C. (1989) *Escher on Escher – Exploring the Infinite*, Meulenhoff International, Harry N. Abrams Inc.

Even, S. (1973), *Algorithmic Combinatorics*, Macmillan.

Falconer, K. J. (1997), *Techniques in Fractal Geometry*, Wiley.

Farin, G. (2002) (5th edn.) *Curves and Surfaces for CAGD*. Academic Press.

Fausett, L. (1994), *Fundamentals of Neural Networks*, Prentice-Hall.

Feder, J. (1989), *Fractals*, Plenum Press.

Feller, W. (1968), *An Introduction to Probability Theory and Its Applications*, Vol. II, John Wiley.

Ferrari, P. A., Frigessi, A. and Gonsaga de Sa, P. (1995), Fast approximate maximum a posteriori restoration of multicolour images, *J. R. Statist. Soc.* B **57**, 485–500.

Field, R. (1988) *Geometric Patterns from Roman Mosaics*. Tarquin Publications.

Fisher, Y. (1995), ed., *Fractal Image Compression*, Springer-Verlag.

Ford, L. R. and Fulkerson, D. R. (1962), *Flows in Networks*, Princeton University Press.

Forsey, D. and Bartels, R. (1988), Tensor products and hierarchical fitting, in *Curves and Surfaces in Computer Vision and Graphics II*, Proc. SPIE, Vol. 1610, pp. 88–96.

Freeman, W. T., Pasztor, E. C. and Thouis, R. J. (2002), Example based super-resolution. *IEEE Computer Graphics and Applications* **22**, 56–65.

Frey, B. J. (1998) *Graphical Models for Machine Learning and Computation*. MIT Press.

Frey, B. J. and MacKay, D. J. C. (1998), A revolution: belief propagation in graphs with cycles. *Advances in Neural Information Processing Systems* **10**. MIT Press.

Fua, P. and Hanson, A. J. (1991), An optimisation framework for feature extraction, *Machine Vision Applications* **4**, 59–87.

Fukushima, K. (1999), Self-organization of shift-invariant receptive fields, *Neural Networks* **12**, 791–801.

(2000), *Active and Adaptive Vision: Neural Network Models*, Springer Lecture Notes in Computer Science **1811**, 623–634.

Gabor, D. (1946), Theory of Communications, *J. IEE*, **93**, 429–457.

Gallager, R. G. (1963), *Low Density Parity Check Codes*, Monograph, MIT Press.

(1978) Variations on a theme by Huffman, *IEEE Trans. on Information Theory*, **24**, 668–674.

Gallant, S. I. (1990), Perceptron-based learning algorithms, *IEEE Trans. on Neural Networks*, **1**, 179–191.

García, J. A., Fdez-Valdivia, J., Fdez-Vidal, X. R. and Rodriguez-Sánchez, R. (2003), On the concept of best achievable compression ratio for lossy image coding, *Pattern Recognition* **36**, 2377–2394.

Gardner, G. G., Keating, D., Williamson, T. H. and Elliot, A. T. (1996), Automatic detection of diabetic retinopathy using an artificial neural network: a screening tool. *British J. Ophthalmology* **30**, 940–944.

Gelman, A. (1996), Inference and monitoring convergence, in *Markov Chain Monte Carlo in Practice* (Gilks, W. R., Richardson, S. and Spiegelhalter, D. J., eds.) Chapman & Hall.

Geman, D. and Geman, S. (1984), Stochastic relaxation, Gibbs distributions, and the Bayesian restoration of images, *IEEE Trans. on Pattern Analysis and Machine Intelligence* **6**, 721–741.

Gersho, A. and Gray, R. M. (1992), *Vector Quantization and Signal Compression*, Kluwer.

Giacinto, G., Roli, F. and Bruzzone, L. (2000), Combination of neural and statistical algorithms for supervised classification of remote-sensing images, *Pattern Recognition Letters* **21**, 385–397.

Gilks, W. R., Richardson, S. and Spiegelhalter, D. J. (1997), *Markov Chain Monte Carlo in Practice*, Chapman & Hall.

Golub, G. H. and van Loan, C. F. (1996), *Matrix Computations*, Johns Hopkins University Press.

Gonzalez, R. C. and Woods, R. E. (1993), *Digital Image Processing*, Addison-Wesley.

Gray, R. M. (1990) *Source Coding Theory*, Kluwer.

Gray, R. M., Kieffer, J. C. and Linde, Y. (1980), Locally optimal block quantizer design, *Information & Control* **45**, 178–198.

Green, P. J. (1995), Reversible jump Markov chain Monte Carlo computation and Bayesian model determination, *Biometrika* **82**, 711–732.

(1996), MCMC in image analysis, in *Markov Chain Monte Carlo in Practice*, (Gilks, W. R., Richardson, S. and Spiegelhalter, D. J., eds.) Chapman & Hall.

Grenander, U. and Szegö, G. (1958), *Toeplitz Forms and Their Applications*, University of California Press.

Grieg, D. M., Porteous, B. T. and Seheult, A. H. (1989), Exact maximum a posteriori estimation for binary images, *J. R. Statist. Soc.* B **51**, 271–279.

Grossman, A. and Morlet, J. (1984), Decomposition of Hardy functions into square-integrable wavelets of constant shape, *SIAM J. Appl. Math.* **15**, 723–736.

Grünbaum, B. and Shephard, G. C. (1987) *Tilings and Patterns*. Freeman.

Haar, A. (1955) Zur Theorie der orthogonalen Funktionen-System, Inaugural Dissertation, *Math. Annalen* **5**, 17–31

Häggström, O. (2002), *Finite Markov Chains and Algorithmic Applications*, Cambridge University Press.

Hammer, B. and Villmann, T. (2002), Generalised relevance learning vector quantization, *Neural Networks* **15**, 1059–1068.

Hammersley, J. M. and Handscomb, D. C. (1964), *Monte Carlo Methods*, Chapman & Hall.

Hamming, R. V. (1950), Error detecting and error-correcting codes, *Bell Sys. Tech. J.* **29**, 147–160.

Hansen, M. and Yu, B. (2000), Wavelet thresholding via MDL for natural images, *IEEE Trans. on Information Theory* **46**, 1778–1788.

Haritopoulos, M., Yin, H. and Allinson, N. M. (2002), Image denoising using SOM-based nonlinear independent component analysis, *Neural Networks* **15**, 1085–1098.

Hartley, R. V. L. (1928), Transmission of information, *Bell Sys. Tech. Journal* **7**, 617.

Hastings, W. K. (1970) Monte Carlo sampling methods using Markov chains, and their applications, *Biometrika* **57**, 97–109.

Hayashi, Y., Setiono, R. and Yoshida, K. (2000), A comparison between two neural network rule extraction techniques for the diagnosis of hepatobiliary disorders, *Artificial Intelligence in Medicine* **20**, 205–216.

Haykin, S. (1994), *Neural Networks: a Comprehensive Foundation*, Macmillan.

Hebb, D. (1949), *The Organization of Behaviour*, Wiley.

Heckbert, P. S. (1989) *Fundamentals of Texture Mapping and Image Warping*. Rept. UCB/CSD 89/516. Computer Science Division, University of California, Berkeley.

Heegard, C. and Wicker, S. B. (1998), *Turbo Coding*, Kluwer International Series in Engineering and Computer Science, vol. **476**.

Heideman, M., Johnson, D. and Burrus, C. (1985), Gauss and the history of the fast Fourier transform. *Arch. Hist. Exact Sciences* **34**, 265–277.

Helstrom, C. W. (1967), Image restoration by the method of least squares, *J. Opt. Soc. Amer.* **57**, 297–303.

Hennie, F. C. and Stearns, R. E. (1966), Two-tape simulation of multitape turing machines, *J. ACM* **13**, 533–546.

Hocquenghem, P. A. (1959), Codes correcteurs d'erreurs, *Chiffres* **2**, 147–156.

Hoggar, S. G. (1992), *Mathematics for Computer Graphics*, Cambridge University Press.

Hoggar, S. G., Martinelli, M. J. and Bennett, D. (1998), Fractal dimension and equine bone, *Proceedings of 16th Eurographics UK Conference*, 191–198.

Hoppe, H., DeRose, T., Duchamp, T., Halstead, M., Jin, H., McDonald, J., Schweizer, J. and Stuetzle, W. (1994), Piecewise smooth surface reconstruction, *Proceedings of SIGGRAPH 94*, 295–302, ACM Press.

Hotelling, H. (1933), Analysis of a complex of statistical variables into principal components, *J. Educ. Psychol.* **24**, 417–441, 498–520.

Hough, P. (1962), *Method and Means for Recognizing Complex Patterns*, US Patent 3069654. United States Patent Office.

Hubbard, B. B. (1996), *The World According to Wavelets*, A. K. Peters.

Huffman, D. A. (1952), A method for the construction of minimum redundancy codes, *Proc. IRE* **40**(9), 1098–1101.

Hufnagel, R. E. and Stanley, N. R. (1964), Modulation transfer function associated with image transmission through turbulent media, *J. Optical Soc. of America* **54**, 52–62.

Hutchinson, J. E. (1981), Fractals and self similarity. *Indiana University Mathematics J.* **30**, 713–747.

Ibrahim, A. and Azimi-Sadjadi, M. R. (1996), A fast learning algorithm for Gabor transformation. *IEEE Trans. on Image Processing* **5**, 171–175.

Jackson, J. E. (1991), *A User's Guide to Principal Components*. Wiley.

Jackson, J. I., Meyer, C. H., Nishimura, D. G., and Macovski, A. (1991), Selection of a convolution function for Fourier inversion using gridding, *IEEE Trans. on Medical Imaging* **10**, 473–478.

Jacobs, E. W., Boss, R. D. and Fisher, Y. (1990), Fractal-Based Compression II. Technical report 1362. Naval Ocean Systems Centre, San Diego, CA, June 1990.

Jacquin, A. (1989), *A Fractal Theory of Iterated Markov Operators with Applications to Digital Image Coding*, Ph.D. Thesis, Georgia Institute of Technology.

Jaffard, S., Meyer, I. and Ryan, R. D. (2001), *Wavelets: Tools for Science and Technology*, SIAM.

Jaynes, C., Riseman, E. and Hanson, A. (2003), Recognition and reconstruction of buildings from multiple aerial images, *Computer Vision & Image Understanding* **90**, 68–98.

Jaynes, E. T. (1982), On the rationale of maximum entropy methods, *Proc. IEEE* **70**, 939–952.

Jepson, A. and Mann, R. (1999). Qualitative probabilities for image interpretation. *Proc. IEEE ICCV*.

838   *References*

Johnson, V. E. (1994), A model for segmentation and analysis of noisy images, *J. Amer. Stat. Assoc.* **89**, 230–241.

Jollife, I. T. (1986), *Principal Component Analysis*, Springer-Verlag.

Justesen, J. (1972), A class of constructive asymptotically good algebraic codes, *IEEE Trans. on Info. Theory*, **IT-18**, 652–656.

Kabashima, Y. and Saad, D. (1998), Belief propagation vs. TAP for decoding corrupted messages, *Europhys. Lett.* **44**, 668.

  (2004), Statistical mechanics of low density parity check codes. *J. Phys.* A **37**, R1.

Kalos, M. H. and Whitlock, P. A. (1986), *Monte Carlo Methods*, Vol. I, Wiley.

Kaye, B. H. (1989), *A Random Walk through Fractal Dimensions*, VCH Publishers.

Keating, D., Mutlukan, E., Evans, A., McGarvie, J. and Damato, B. (1993), A backpropagation network for the classification of visual field data. *Phys. Med. Biol.* **38**, 1263–1270.

Kershner, R. (1939), The number of circles covering a set, *Amer. J. Math.* **61**, 665–671.

Kinderman, R. and Snell, J. L. (1980), *Markov Random Fields and Their Applications*, AMS.

Kittler, J. and Föglein, J. (1984), Contractual decision rules for objects in lattice configurations. *Proc. 7th Int. Conf. on Pattern Recognition*, Montreal 1984, 270–272.

Knuth, D. (1981), *Seminumerical Algorithms*, Addison-Wesley.

Kobbelt, L. P., Vorsatz, J., Labsik, U. and Seidel, H.-P. (1999), A shrink wrapping approach to remeshing polygonal surfaces, *Computer Graphics* **18**, *Proceedings of Eurographics '99*, Blackwell Publishers, 119–129.

Kohonen, T. (1982), Self-Organizing formation of topologically correct feature maps, *Biological Cybernetics* **43**, 59–69.

  (1988), Learning vector quantisation, *Neural Networks* **1** (Supplement 1), 303.

  (2001), *Self-Organizing Maps*, 3rd edn., Springer.

Kohonen, T. and Somervuo, P. (2002), How to make large self-organizing maps for nonvectorial data, *Neural Networks* **15**, 945–952.

Kolmogorov, A. N. (1956a), *Foundations of Probability*, Chelsea Publishing Company.

  (1956b), On the Shannon theory of information transmission in the case of continuous signals, *IRE Transactions on Information Theory* **IT-2**, 102–108.

  (1965), Three approaches to the quantitative definition of information, *Problems of Information & Transmission* **1**, 4–7.

  (1968), Logical basis for information theory and probability theory, *IEEE Trans. on Information Theory*, **14**, 662–664.

Koornwinder, T. H. (ed.) (1993) *Wavelets: an Elementary Treatment of Theory and Applications*, World Scientific.

Kossentini, F., Chung, W. C. and Smith, M. J. T. (1996), Conditional entropy-constrained residual VQ with application to image coding, *IEEE Trans. on Image Processing* **5**, 311–320.

Kotz, S. and Johnson, N. L. (1985), *Encyclopedia of Statistical Sciences*, Vol. 5, Wiley.

Lamar, M. V., Bhuiyan, M. S. and Iwata, A. (2000), *T-CombNET – a Neural Network Dedicated to Hand Gesture Recognition*, Springer Lecture Notes in Computer Science **1811**, 613–622.

Lane, J. M. and Riesenfeld, R. F. (1980) A theoretical development for the computer generation and display of piecewise polynomial surfaces, *IEEE Trans. on Pattern Analysis and Machine Intelligence* **2**, 35–46.

Leavers, V. (1992), *Shape Detection in Computer Vision Using the Hough Transform*, Springer-Verlag.

Leclerc, Y. G. (1989), Constructing simple stable descriptions for image partitioning, *J. Computer Vision* **3**, 73–102.

Ledermann, W. and Vajda, S. (1982), *Handbook of Applicable Mathematics IV: Analysis*. Wiley.

Lee, C.-C. and Laroia, R. (2000), Trellis-based scalar vector quantization of sources with memory, *IEEE Trans. on Information Theory*, **IT-46**, 153–170.

Leherte, L., Glasgow, J., Baxter, K., Steeg, E. and Fortier, S. (1997), Analysis of 3-D protein images, *J. AI Research* **7**, 125–159.

Leonard, T. and Hsu, J. S. J. (1999), *Bayesian Methods*, Cambridge University Press.

Levine, R. F. (2001), Clinical problems, computational solutions, *Cancer* **91** (2001), 1595–1602.

Levinson, S. E. and Shepp, L., eds. (1991) *Image Models and Their Speech Model Cousins*, IMA Vol. 80 on Mathematics and Its Applications, Springer.

Levitt, T. S., Hedgcock, M. W. Jr., Dye, J. W., Johnston, S. E., Shadle, V. M. and Vosky, D. (1993), Bayesian inference for model-based segmentation of computed radiographs of the hand, *Artificial Intelligence in Medicine* **5**, 365–387.

Lidl, R. and Niederreiter, H. (1986), *Introduction to Finite Fields and Their Applications*, Cambridge University Press.

Lin, S. and Costello, D. J. (1983), *Error Control Coding*, Prentice-Hall.

Linde, Y., Buzo, A. and Gray, R. M. (1980), An algorithm for vector quantizer design, *IEEE Trans. on Communications*, **Com-28**, 84–95.

Lindeberg, T. and Li, M.-X. (1997), Segmentation and classification of edges using minimum description length approximation and complementary junction clues, *Computer Vision & Image Understanding* **67**, 88–98.

Linsker, R. (1988), Self-organization in a perceptual network, *Computer* **21**, 105–117.

(1992), Local synaptic learning rules suffice to maximize mutual information in a linear network, *Neural Computation* **4**, 691–702.

(1993), Deriving receptive fields using an optimum encoding criterion. In *Advances in Neural Information Processing Systems* **5** (Cowan, J. D., Hanson, S. J. and Giles, C. L., eds.), 953–960, Morgan Kaufmann.

(1997), A local learning rule that enables information maximisation for arbitrary input distributions, *Neural Computation* **9**, 1661–1665.

Lipschutz, S. (1981), *Probability*, Schaum's Outline Series, McGraw-Hill.

Lloyd, E. (1984a), *Handbook of Applicable Mathematics II: Probability*, Wiley.

(1984b), *Handbook of Applicable Mathematics VI: Statistics*, *Part A*, Wiley.

(1984c), *Handbook of Applicable Mathematics VI: Statistics*, *Part B*, Wiley.

Lloyd, S. P. (1957), *Least Squares Quantization in PCMs*, Bell Telephone Laboratories Paper, Murray Hill, NJ.

Lockwood, E. H. and Macmillan, R. H. (1978), *Geometric Symmetry*, Cambridge University Press.

Loop, C. T. (1987) *Smooth Subdivision Surfaces Based on Triangles*. Master's thesis, Department of Mathematics, University of Utah.

Lounsbery, J. M. (1994), *Multiresolution Analysis for Surfaces of Arbitrary Topological Type*. Ph.D. thesis, University of Washington.

Lounsbery, J. M., DeRose, T. D. and Warren, J. (1997) Multiresolution analysis for surfaces of arbitrary topological type, *ACM Trans. on Graphics* **16**(1), 34–73.

Lovasz, L. (1979), On the Shannon capacity of a graph, *IEEE Trans. on Information Theory*, **IT-25**, 1–7.

Lu, J., Healy, D. M. and Weaver, J. B. (1994), Contrast enhancement of medical images using multiscale edge representation, *Optical Engineering* **33**, 2151–2161.

Lu, L. and Pearlman, W. A. (2005), Conditional entropy-constrained tree-structured vector quantization with applications to sources with memory, *IEEE Trans. on Information Theory*, to appear.

Lu, N. (1997), *Fractal Imaging*, Academic Press.

MacGillavry, C. H. (1976), *Symmetry Aspects of M. C. Escher's Periodic Drawings*, 2nd edn., International Union of Crystallography, Bohn, Scheltema & Holkema.

MacKay, D. J. C. and Neal, R. M. (1997), Near Shannon performance of low density parity check codes. *Electronics Letters* **33**, 457–458.

MacQueen, J. (1967), Some methods for classification and analysis of multivariate observations. In *Proceedings of the 5th Berkeley Symposium on Mathematical Statistics and Probability*, Vol. **I**, 281–297. University of California Press.

Mallat, S. G. (1999), *A Wavelet Tour of Signal Processing*, Academic Press.

Mallat, S. G. and Zhong, S. (1992), Wavelet transform maxima and multiscale edges. In *Wavelets and their Applications*, (Ruskai, M. B., Beylkin, G. M., Coifman, R., Daubechies, I., Mallat, S., Meyer, Y. and Raphael, L., eds.), 67–109. Jones & Bartlett.

Manber, U. (1989), *Introduction to Algorithms*, Addison-Wesley.

Mandelbrot, B. (1983), *The Fractal Geometry of Nature*. Freeman.

Mann, W. B. and Binford, T. O. (1992), An example of 3D interpretation of images using Bayesian networks, *Proc. DARPA Image Understanding Workshop*, 193–801.

Marr, D. (1982), *Vision*, Freeman.

Marr, D. and Hildreth, E.(1980), Theory of edge-detection, *Proc. R. Soc. London*, B **207**, 187–217.

Martinelli, M. J. (1999), *Morphometric Analyses of Bone and Cartilage of the Equine Metacarpophalangeal Joint*, Ph.D. Thesis, Faculty of Veterinary Medicine, University of Glasgow.

Marven, C. and Ewers, G. (1996), *A Simple Approach to Digital Signal Processing*, Wiley.

Matej, S. and Lewitt, R. M. (2001), 3D-FRP: direct Fourier reconstruction with Fourier reprojection for fully 3-D PET, *IEEE Trans. on Nuclear Science* **48**, 1378–1385.

Matej, S., Fessler, J. A. and Kazantsev, I. G. (2004), Iterative tomographic image reconstruction using Fourier-based forward and back-projectors, *IEEE Trans. on Medical Imaging* **23**, 401–412.

Maxwell, E. A. (1962), *An Analytical Calculus*, Vol. IV, Cambridge University Press.

Maybank, S. J. and Fraile, R. (2000), Minimum description length method for facet matching, *International J. Pattern Recognition & Artificial Intelligence*, **14**, 919–927.

Mayraz, G. and Hinton, G. E. (2002), Recognizing hand written digits by using hierarchical products of experts. *IEEE Trans. on Pattern Analysis and Machine Intelligence* **24**, 189–197.

McColl, J. H. (1997), *Probability*, Edward Arnold.

McCulloch, W. S. and Pitts, W. (1943), A logical calculus of the ideas immanent in nervous activity, *Bull. of Math. Biophysics* **5**, 115–133.

McEliece, R. J. (1983) *The Theory of Information and Coding* (Encyclopedia of Mathematics Vol. 3), Addison-Wesley.

McEleice, R. J. and Yaldireiu, M. (2003), Belief propogation on partially ordered sets. In *Mathematical Systems Theory in Biology, Communications, Computing and Finance*, (Gillian, D. S. and Rosenthal, J., eds.), IMA vol. 134, Springer.

McGregor, D. R., Fryer, R. J., Cockshott, P. and Murray, P. (1996), Fast fractal compression, *Dr Dobb's J.* **21**, no. 243, January 1996.

McGregor, J. and Watt, A. (1984) *The Art of Microcomputer Graphics*. Addison-Wesley.

Metropolis, N., Rosenbluth, A. W., Rosenbluth, M. N., Teller, A. H. and Teller, E. (1953), Equations of state calculations by fast computing machines, *J. Chem. Phys.* **21**, 1087–1092.

Meyer, P. L. (1970), *Introductory Probability and Statistical Applications*, Addison-Wesley.

Minsky, M. L. and Papert, S. A. (1969, expanded edn. 1988), *Perceptrons*, MIT Press.

Mohsenian, X., Shahri, H. and Nasrabadi, N. M. (1996), Scalar–vector quantization of medical images, *IEEE Trans. on Image Processing* **5**, 387–392.

Montesinos, J. M. (1987) *Classical Tessellations and Three-Manifolds*. Springer-Verlag.

Moore, D. J. (2003) *Calculus: a First Course*. Moodiesburn Publishers.

Mumford, D., Zhu, S.-C. and Wu, Y. (1997), Minmax entropy principle and its application to texture modeling, *Neural Computation* **9**, 1627–1650.

Murphy, I. S. (1993), *Advanced Calculus*, Arklay Publishers.

Murray, J. D. and van Ruyper, W. (1996), *Graphics File Formats*, O'Reilly Associates.

Nikkilä, J., Toronen, P., Kaski, S., Venna, J., Castren, E. and Wong, G. (2002), Analysis and visualization of gene expression data using self-organizing maps, *Neural Networks* **15**, 953–966.

Niquist, H. (1924), Certain factors affecting telegraph speed, *Bell Systems Technical Journal* **3**, p. 324.

Niven, I. and Zuckerman, H. S. (1980), *An Introduction to the Theory of Numbers*. (4th edn.) Wiley.

Obrador, P., Caso, G. and Jay Kuo, C.-C. (1995) A fractal-based method for textured image compression, *SPIE* **2418**, 36–47.

Oja, E. (1982), A simplified neuron model as a principal component analyser, *Int. J. of Neural Systems* **1**, 61–68.

(1992), Self-organising maps and computer vision, in *Neural Networks for Perception* (H. Wechslar, ed.), Vol. 1, 368–385. Academic Press.

Oliver, J. (1979), *Polysymmetrics*, Tarquin Publications.

O'Sullivan, J. D. (1985), A fast sinc function gridding algorithm for Fourier inversion in computer tomography, *IEEE Trans. on Medical Imaging* **MI-4**, 200–207.

Papadopoulos, A., Fotiadis, D. I. and Likas, A. (2002), An automatic microcalcification detection system based on a hybrid neural network classifier, *Artificial Intelligence in Medicine* **25**, 149–167.

Park, S. and Aggraval, J. K. (2003), Recognition of two-person interactions using a hierarchical Bayesian network. *ACM SIGMM International Workshop on Video Surveillance*, 65–76. ACM Press.

Patterson, J. W., Hoggar, S. G. and Logie, J. L. (1991) Inverse displacement mapping. *Computer Graphics Forum* **10** (1991), 129–139.

Pearl, J. (1997), *Probabilistic Reasoning in Intelligent Systems*, Morgan Kaufman.

Pearson, K. (1900), On a criterion that a system of deviations from the probable in the case of a correlated system of variables is such that it can be reasonably supposed to have arisen in random sampling, *Phil. Mag.* **50**, 157.

(1901), On lines and planes of closest fit to systems of points in space, *Phil. Mag.* **(6) 2**, 559–572.

Peitgen, H.-O. and Saupe, D. (eds.) (1988), *The Science of Fractal Images*, Springer-Verlag.

Peitgen, H.-O., Henriques, J. M. and Penedo, L. F. (eds.) (1991), *Fractals in the Fundamental and Applied Sciences* (Proc. 1st IFIP Conference), North-Holland.

Peitgen, H.-O., Jürgens, H. and Saupe, D. (1992), *Chaos and Fractals*, Springer-Verlag.

Penrose, J. (1999), *The Emperor's New Mind*, Oxford Paperbacks, Oxford University Press.

Pentland, A. (1989), Part segmentation for object recognition, *Neural Computation* **1**, 82–91.

Perlmutter, K. O., Perlmutter, S. M., Gray, R. M., Olshen, R. A. and Oehler K. L. (1996), Bayes risk weighted vector quantization with posterior estimation for image compression and classification, *IEEE Trans. on Image Processing* **5**, 347–360.

Petronero, L. and Posati, E. (eds.) (1986), *Fractals in Physics*, Elsevier.

Petrou, M. and Bosdogianni, P. (2000), *Image Processing – the Fundamentals*, Wiley.

Phillips, F. C. (1971), *Introduction to Crystallography*, Oliver & Boyd.

Porncharoensin, H. (2002), LVQ and Kohonen nets as human, for comparing ASM generated faces, M.Sc. Thesis, Department of Mathematics, University of Glasgow.

Pretzel, O. (1992), *Error-Correcting Codes and Finite Fields*, Oxford University Press.

Propp, J. G. and Wilson, B. M. (1996), Exact sampling with coupled Markov chains and applications to statistical mechanics, *Random Structures & Algorithms* **9**, 223–252.

Rao, R. P. and Pearlman, W. A. (1991), On entropy of pyramid structures, *IEEE Trans. on Information Theory* **37**, 407–413.

Rao, T. R. N. and Fujiwara, E. (1989), *Error-Control Coding for Computer Systems*. Prentice-Hall.

Reed, I. S. and Solomon, G. (1960), Polynomial codes over certain finite fields, *J. Soc. Indus. Appl. Maths.* **8**, 300–304.

Richardson, L. F. (1961) The problem of contiguity: an appendix of statistics of deadly quarrels. *General Systems Yearbook* **6**, 139–187. Reprinted in: *Collected Papers of Lewis Fry Richardson* (I. Sutherland, ed.) (1993), Vol. 2, Cambridge University Press.

Ripley, B. D. (1987), *Stochastic Simulation*, Wiley.

(1996), *Pattern Recognition and Neural Networks*, Cambridge University Press.

Rissanen, J. (1978), Modelling by shortest data description, *Automatica* **14**, 465–471.

(1983), A universal prior for integers and estimation by minimum description length, *Ann. Stat.* **11**, 416–431.

(2000), MDL denoising, *IEEE Trans. on Information Theory* **46**, 2537–2543.

Robert, C. P. and Casella, G. (1999), *Monte Carlo Statistical Methods*, Springer.

Roberts, G. O. (1996), Markov chain concepts related to sampling algorithms, in *Markov Chain Monte Carlo in Practice* (Gilks, W. R., Richardson, S. and Spiegelhalter, D. J., eds.), Chapman & Hall.

Rojas, R. (1996), *Neural Networks*, Springer.

Rosandich, R. G. (1997), *Intelligent Visual Inspection*, Chapman & Hall.

Rosenblatt, F. (1958), The perceptron, a probabilistic model for information storage and organization, *Psychological Review* **65**, 386–408.

(1962), *Principles of Neurodynamics*, Spartan Press.

Rossi, M., Vicenzi, R. and Zorzi, M. (2004), Accurate analysis of TCP on channels with memory and finite round-trip delay, *IEEE Trans. on Wireless Communications* **3**, 627–640.

Rubinstein, R. Y. (1981), *Simulation and the Monte Carlo Method*, Wiley.

Rumelhart, D. E., Hinton, G. E. and Williams, R. J. (1986), Learning representations by back-propagating errors. *Nature* **323**, 533–536.

Rusmeviechientong, P. and Van Roy, B. (2001), An analysis of belief propagation on the turbo decoding graph with gaussian densities, *IEEE Trans. on Information Theory*, **47**, 745–765.

Russ, J. (1995), *The Image Processing Handbook*, CRC Press.

Sanger, T. D. (1989), Optimal unsupervised learning in a single-layer feedforward neural network, *Neural Networks* **2**, 459–473.

Sayood, K., Gibson, J. D. and Rost, M. C. (1984), An algorithm for uniform vector quantizer design, *IEEE Trans. on Information Theory*, **IT-30**, 805–815.

Schalkoff, R. (1992) *Pattern Recognition*, John Wiley.

Schattschneider, D. and Walker, W. (1982) *M. C. Escher Kaleidocycles*. Tarquin Publications.

Schroeder, M. R. (1991) *Fractals, Chaos, Power Laws*, Freeman.

Schwarzenberger, R. L. E. (1980) *N-Dimensional Crystallography*, Research Notes in Mathematics, Pitman.

Serpico, S. B. and Roli, F. (1995), Classification of multi-sensor remote-sensing images by structured neural networks, *IEEE Trans. on Geoscience and Remote Sensing* **33**, 562–578.

Sedarat, H. and Nishimura, D. G. (2000), On the optimality of the gridding construction algorithm, *IEEE Trans. on Medical Imaging* **19**, 306–317.

Seul, M., O'Gorman, L. and Sammon, M. J. (2000), *Practical Algorithms for Image Analysis*, Cambridge University Press.

Shannon, C. E. (1948) A mathematical theory of communication, *Bell Systems Tech. J.* **27**, 379–423 and 623–656.

(1949), Communication in the presence of noise, *Proc. IRE* **37**, 10–21.

(1956), The zero-error capacity of a noisy channel, *IRE Trans. on Information Theory*, **IT-2**, 8–19.

Sharkey, A. J. C. (ed.) (1999), *Combining Artificial Neural Networks*, Springer.

Slepian, D. (1974) *Key Papers in the Development of Information Theory*, IEEE Press.

Sloane, N. J. A. and MacWilliams, F. J. (1977), *The Theory of Error-Correcting Codes*, North-Holland.

Sloane, N. J. A. and Wyner, A. D., eds. (1993), *Collected Papers of Claude Elwood Shannon*, IEEE Press.

Smith, P., Drummond, T. and Cipolla, R. (2000), Segmentation of multiple motions by edge tracking between two frames, *Proc. Brit. Machine Vision. Conf. 2000*, 342–351.

Sneddon, I. N. (1961), *Special Functions of Mathematical Physics and Chemistry*, Longman.

Solomonov, R. J. (1964), A formal theory of inductive inference, *Inform. & Control* **7**, 1–22, 224–254.

Souafi-Bensafi, S., Parizeau, M., LeBourgeois, F. and Emptoz, H. (2002), Bayesian networks classifiers applied to documents, *Proc. 16th International Conference on Pattern Recognition*, 483–486.

Sourlas, N. (1989), Citebase – the statistical mechanics of turbocodes, *Nature* **339**, 693–694.

Spiegel, M. R. and Wrede, R. C. (2002), Calculus, Schaum's Outline Series, McGraw-Hill.

Spiegel, M. R., Schiller, J. J. and Srinivasan, R. A. (2000), *Probability and Statistics*, Schaum's Outline Series, McGraw-Hill.

Spiegelhalter, D. J., Best, N. G., Gilks, W. R. and Inskip, H. (1996), Hepatitis B: a case study in MCMC methods, in Gilks, W. R., Richardson, S. and Spiegelhalter, D. J., *Markov Chain Monte Carlo in Practice*, Chapman & Hall.

Starck, J.-L., Murtagh, F. and Bijaoui, A. (2000) *Image Processing and Data Analysis: the Multiscale Approach*. Cambridge University Press.

Stephens, R. S. (1991), Probabilistic approach to the Hough transform, *Image Vision Comput.* **9**, 66–71.

Stollnitz, E. J., DeRose, A. D. and Salesin, D. H. (1996), *Wavelets for Computer Graphics*, Morgan Kaufmann.

Strang, G. and Nguyen, T. (1997), *Wavelets and Filter Banks*, Wellesley-Cambridge Press.

Sugiyama, Y., Kasahara, M., Hirasawa, S. and Namekawa, T. (1975), A method for solving key equation for decoding Goppa codes, *Inform. & Control* **27**, 87–99.

Sweldens, W. (1996), The lifting scheme: a custom-design construction of biorthogonal wavelets, *Applied and Computational Harmonic Analysis* **3**, 186–200.

Swokowski, E. W. (2000), *Calculus*, Brooks Cole.

Takeshita, O. Y. and Costello, D. J. (2000), New deterministic interleaver designs for turbo codes, *IEEE Trans. Info. Theory*, **46**, 1988–2006.

Tang, D. S. (1991), Information theory and early information processing. In *Self-organization, Emerging Properties, and Learning* (A. Babloyantz ed.), 113–125. NATO ASI series B: Physics Vol. **260**. Plenum Press.

Tezmol, A., Sari-Sarraf, H., Mitra, S., Long, R. and Gururajan, A. (2002), Customized Hough transform for robust segmentation of cervical vertebrae from X-ray images, *Proc. 5th IEEE Southwest Symposium on Image Analysis and Interpretation*, IEEE Computer Society.

Thodberg, H. H. and Olafsdottir, H. (2003), Adding curvature to minimum description length models. *Proc. British Machine Vision Conference 2003*. BMVA.

Tierney, L. (1994), Markov chains for exploring posterior distributions, *Ann. Statist.* **22**, 1701–1762.

(1996), Introduction to general state-space Markov chain theory, in Gilks, W. R., Richardson, S. and Spiegelhalter, D. J. (1997), *Markov Chain Monte Carlo in Practice*, Chapman & Hall.

Turcotte, D. L. (1992), *Fractals and Chaos in Geology and Geophysics*, Cambridge University Press.

Turing, A. M. (1936), On computable numbers with an application to the Entscheidungsproblem, *Proc. London Math. Soc.* (2) **42**, 230–265.

Turk, G. and Levoy, M. (1994), Zippered polygon meshes from range images. *Proceedings of SIGGRAPH '94*, 311–318. ACM Press.

Ulichney, R. (1987) *Digital Halftoning*. MIT Press.

Van Hulle, M. M. (2002), Kernel-based topographic map formation achieved with an information-theoretic approach, *Neural Networks* **15**, 1029–1039.

Van Loan, C. (1992), *Computational Framework for the Fast Fourier Transform*, SIAM.

Verdú, S. and McLaughlin, S. W. (eds.) (2000), *Information Theory: 50 Years of Discovery*, IEEE Press.

Vines, G. and Hayes, M. H. (1994) IFS image coding using an orthonormal basis. *ISCAS 1994*, 621–624.

Vitanyi, P. M. B. and Li, M. (2000), Minimum description length, induction, Bayesianism, and Kolmogorov complexity, *IEEE Trans. Information Theory*, **46**, 446–464.

Voss, R. F. (1988) Fractals in nature: from characterisation to simulation. In *The Science of Fractal Images*. (Peitgen, H.-O. and Saupe, D., eds.), Springer-Verlag.

Vranic, D. V. and Saupe, D. (2001a), 3D shape descriptor based on 3D Fourier-transform, in *Proc. EURASIP Conference on Digital Signal Processing for Multimedia Communications and Services* (ECMCS 2001) (K. Fazekas, ed.), Budapest, Hungary, 2001, 271–274.

(2001b) A feature vector approach for retrival of 3D objects in the context of MPEG-7, in *Proceedings of the International Conference on Augmented Virtual Environments and Three-dimensional Imaging* (ICAV3D 2001) (V. Giagourta and M. G. Strinzis, eds.), Mykonos, Greece, 2001 pp. 37–40.

Walder, C. J. and Lovell, B. C. (2003), Face and object recognition using colour vector quantisation, In *Proc. of Workshop on Signal Processing and its Applications*, (V. Chandra, ed.), Brisbane, Australia, 2002.

Walker, J. S. (1988), *Fourier Analysis*, Oxford University Press.

Wallace, C. S. and Boulton, D. M. (1968), An information measure for classification, *Computer J.* **11**, 185–195.

Wallace, G. (1991), The JPEG still picture compression standard, *Comm. ACM* **34**, No 4, 31–44.

Watson, B, ed. (1993), *Digital Images and Human Vision*, MIT Press.

Watt, A. and Policarpo, F. (1998), *The Computer Image*, Addison-Wesley.

Wegmann, B. and Zetzsche, C. (1996), Feature-specific vector quantization of images, *IEEE Trans. on Image Processing* **5**, 274–288.

Welch, T. A. (1984), A technique for high performance data compression, *IEEE Computer* **17**, 8–20.

Welsh, D. J. A. (1988), *Codes and Cryptography*, Oxford University Press.

West, B. J. and Goldberger, A. L. (1987), Physiology in Fractal Dimensions, *Amer. Sci.* **75**, 354–365.

Wilson, H. R. and Bergen, J. R. (1979), A four mechanism model for spatial vision. *Vision Research* **19**, 19–32.

Winkler, G. (1991), *Image Analysis, Random Fields and Dynamic Monte Carlo Methods*, Springer-Verlag.

Witten, I. H., Moffatt, A. and Bell, T. C. (1994), *Managing Megabytes*, Van Nostrand Reinhold.

Wyner, A. and Ziv, J. (1971) Bounds on the rate distortion function for stationary sources with memory, *IEEE Trans. on Information Theory*, **IT-17**, 508–513.

Xu, L. and Oja, E. (1993), Randomized Hough Transform (RHT): basic mechanisms, algorithms, and computational complexities, *Computer Vision and Image Understanding* **57**, 131–154.

Yamada, Y., Tazaki, S. and Gray, R. M. (1980), Asymptotic performance of block quantizers with a difference distortion measure, *IEEE Trans. on Information Theory* **IT-26**, 6–14.

Yarbro, J. W. (2001), Introductory remarks to the conference on prognostic factors and staging in cancer management, *Cancer* **91**, 1593–1594.

Zemel, R. S. and Hinton, G. E. (1995), Learning population codes by minimising description length, *Neural Computation* **7**, 549–564.

Ziv, J. and Lempel, A. (1977) A universal algorithm for sequential data compression, *IEEE Trans. on Information Theory*, **IT-23**, 337–343.

(1978) Compression of individual sequences via variable rate coding, *IEEE Trans. on Information Theory*, **IT-24**, 530–536.

Index